P9-CCS-131

America

The Essential Learning Edition

Second Edition

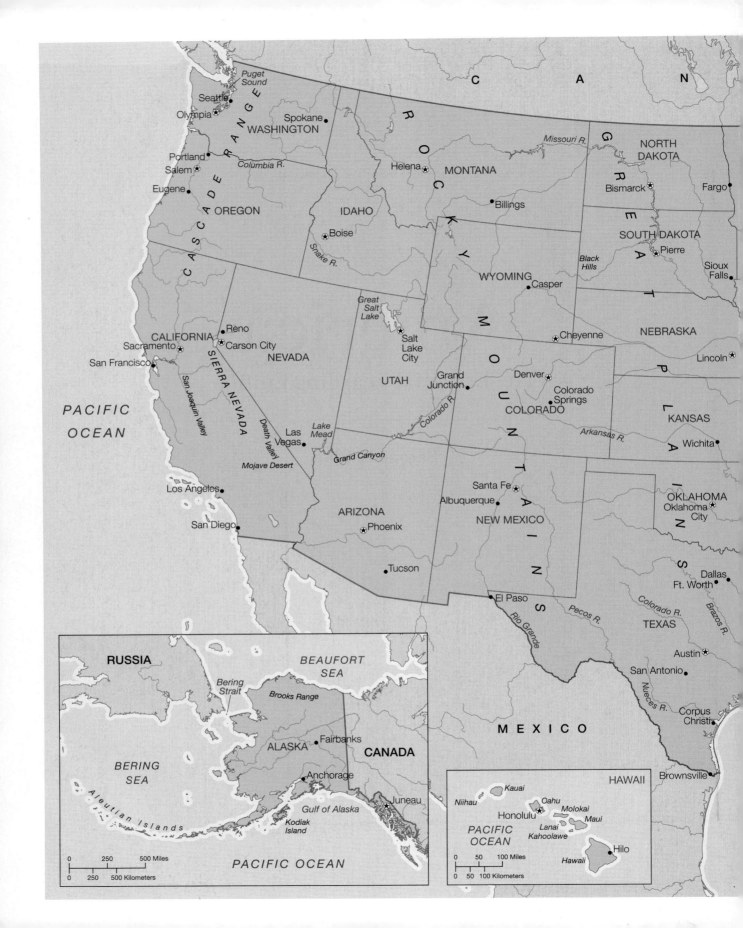

PACIFIC OCEAN

Puget Sound

Seattle
Olympia ★

Spokane

WASHINGTON

CASCADE RANGE

Portland
Salem ★
Eugene

Columbia R.

OREGON

IDAHO

Boise

Snake R.

Helena ★

MONTANA

Billings

ROCKY

Missouri R.

NORTH
DAKOTA

Bismarck ★

Fargo

GREAT

SOUTH DAKOTA

Pierre ★

Black
Hills

Sioux
Falls

Reno
CALIFORNIA
Sacramento ★
San Francisco

Carson City

NEVADA

SIERRA NEVADA

San Joaquin Valley

Death Valley

Las
Vegas

Mojave Desert

Great
Salt
Lake

Salt
Lake
City

UTAH

Lake
Mead

Grand
Junction

WYOMING

Casper

Cheyenne

Denver ★

Colorado
Springs

COLORADO

NEBRASKA

Lincoln

KANSAS

Wichita

Colorado R.

Grand Canyon

Arkansas R.

PLA

Los Angeles

San Diego

ARIZONA

Phoenix

Santa Fe ★
Albuquerque

NEW MEXICO

El Paso

Tucson

MOUNTAINS

Rio Grande

Pecos R.

OKLAHOMA
Oklahoma
City ★

Dallas
Ft. Worth

Colorado R.

Brazos R.

I N S

TEXAS

Austin ★

San Antonio

Nueces R.

Corpus
Christi

M E X I C O

Brownsville

**PACIFIC
OCEAN**

C   A   N   A   D   A   N

RUSSIA

Bering
Strait

BEAUFORT
SEA

Brooks Range

BERING
SEA

ALASKA

Fairbanks

CANADA

Anchorage

Gulf of Alaska

Kodiak
Island

Juneau

Aleutian Islands

| 0 | 250 | 500 Miles |
| 0 | 250 | 500 Kilometers |

PACIFIC OCEAN

HAWAII

Niihau

Kauai

Oahu

Honolulu ★

Molokai

Maui

PACIFIC
OCEAN

Lanai
Kahoolawe

Hawaii

Hilo

| 0 | 50 | 100 Miles |
| 0 | 50 | 100 Kilometers |

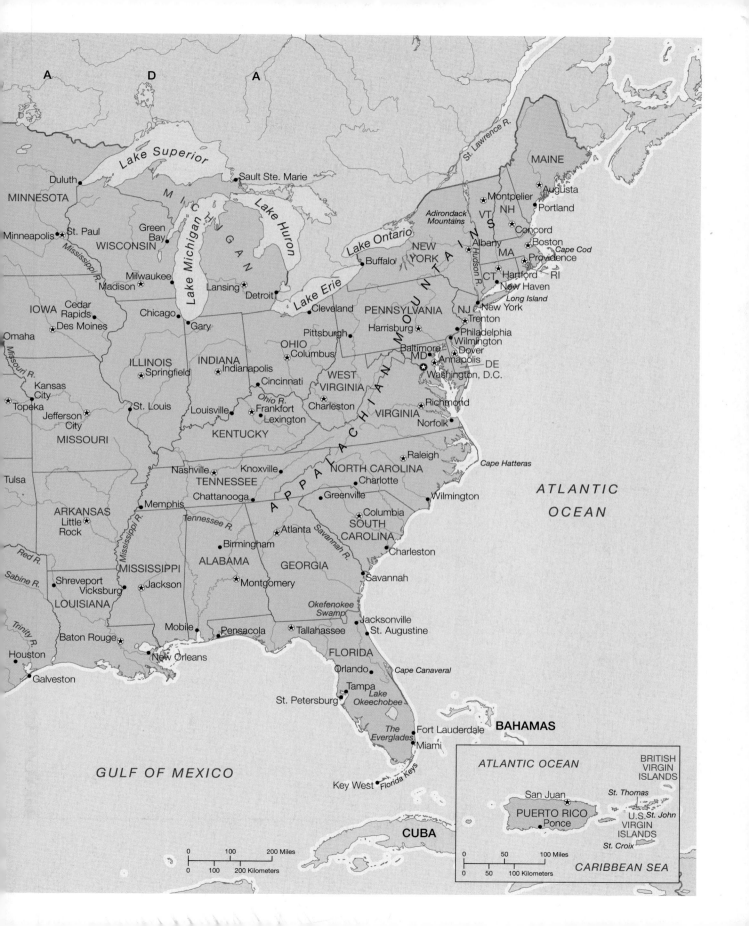

America
The Essential Learning Edition

VOLUME ONE

DAVID EMORY SHI

Second Edition

W. W. Norton & Company, Inc.
New York • London

W. W. Norton & Company has been independent since its founding in 1923, when William Warder Norton and Mary D. Herter Norton first published lectures delivered at the People's Institute, the adult education division of New York City's Cooper Union. The firm soon expanded its program beyond the Institute, publishing books by celebrated academics from America and abroad. By midcentury, the two major pillars of Norton's publishing program—trade books and college texts—were firmly established. In the 1950s, the Norton family transferred control of the company to its employees, and today—with a staff of four hundred and a comparable number of trade, college, and professional titles published each year—W. W. Norton & Company stands as the largest and oldest publishing house owned wholly by its employees.

Copyright © 2018 by W. W. Norton & Company, Inc.
All rights reserved
Printed in the United States of America

Editor: Jon Durbin
Project Editor: Melissa Atkin
Editorial Assistant: Kelly Rafey, Lily Gellman
Marketing Manager, History: Sarah England Bartley
Manuscript Editor: Jude Grant
Managing Editor, College: Marian Johnson
Managing Editor, College Digital Media: Kim Yi
Production Manager: Andy Ensor, Elizabeth Marotta
Media Editor: Laura Wilk
Media Project Editor: Rachel Mayer
Media Associate Editor: Sarah Rose Aquilina
Associate Design Director: Hope Miller Goodell
Photo Editor: Stephanie Romeo
Permissions Manager: Megan Schindel
Permissions Specialist: Bethany Salminen
Composition: Graphic World
Manufacturing: LSC Communications—Kendallville

A catalogue record for the full edition is available from the Library of Congress.

This edition:
ISBN 978-0-393-61660-6 (pbk.)

W. W. Norton & Company, Inc., 500 Fifth Avenue, New York, NY 10110-0017
wwnorton.com
W. W. Norton & Company Ltd., 15 Carlisle Street, London W1D 3BS

3 4 5 6 7 8 9 0

For George Tindall, teacher, scholar, writer—gentleman

About the Author

DAVID EMORY SHI is professor of history and the president emeritus of Furman University in Greenville, South Carolina, an institution he led from 1994 to 2010. An Atlanta native, he earned degrees in history from Furman University and the University of Virginia before starting his academic career at Davidson College, where he won the Outstanding Teacher Award and chaired the history department. He is the author of several books on American cultural history, including the award-winning *The Simple Life: Plain Living and High Thinking in American Culture* and *Facing Facts: Realism in American Thought and Culture, 1850–1920*. More recently, he published a collection of speeches, newspaper columns, and essays titled *The Belltower and Beyond* and co-edited with Holly Mayer a book of primary sources called *For the Record: Documents in American History*. He lives in Brevard, North Carolina.

Contents in Brief

PART ONE   An Old "New" World   3

CHAPTER 1   The Collision of Cultures in the 16th Century   7

CHAPTER 2   England and Its American Colonies, 1607–1732   43

CHAPTER 3   Colonial Ways of Life, 1607–1750   83

CHAPTER 4   From Colonies to States, 1607–1776   109

PART TWO   Building a Nation   153

CHAPTER 5   The American Revolution, 1776–1783   157

CHAPTER 6   Creating a "More Perfect Union," 1783–1800   191

CHAPTER 7   The Early Republic, 1800–1815   229

PART THREE   An Expanding Nation   269

CHAPTER 8   The Emergence of a Market Economy, 1815–1850   273

CHAPTER 9   Nationalism and Sectionalism, 1815–1828   299

CHAPTER 10   The Jacksonian Era, 1828–1840   325

CHAPTER 11   The South and Slavery, 1800–1860   355

CHAPTER 12   Religion, Romanticism, and Reform, 1800–1860   387

PART FOUR   A House Divided and Rebuilt   427

CHAPTER 13   Western Expansion and Southern Secession, 1830–1861   431

CHAPTER 14   The War of the Union, 1861–1865   481

CHAPTER 15   Reconstruction, 1865–1877   533

Contents

List of Maps   xvi

List of THINKING LIKE A HISTORIAN *features*   xviii

List of WHAT'S IT ALL ABOUT? *features*   xx

Preface   xxi

Acknowledgments   xxviii

PART ONE | An Old "New" World   3

CHAPTER 1 The Collision of Cultures in the 16th Century   7

Early Cultures in the Americas   9

The Expansion of Europe   17

The Spanish Empire   27

The Columbian Exchange   30

Spanish Exploration in North America   31

REVIEWING THE CORE OBJECTIVES   40

CHAPTER 2 England and Its American Colonies, 1607–1732   43

The English Background   44

Settling the American Colonies   48

Native Peoples and English Settlers   67

Slavery and Servitude in the Colonies   75

Thriving Colonies   79

REVIEWING THE CORE OBJECTIVES   80

CHAPTER 3 **Colonial Ways of Life, 1607–1750**   83

The Shape of Early America   84
"Women's Work" in the Colonies   85
Society and Economy in the Colonies   87
Race-Based Slavery in the Colonies   95
First Stirrings of a Common Colonial Culture   97
REVIEWING THE CORE OBJECTIVES   106

CHAPTER 4 **From Colonies to States, 1607–1776**   109

Troubled Neighbors   110
Warfare in the Colonies   117
Tightening Control over the Colonies   125
The Crisis Grows   132
REVIEWING THE CORE OBJECTIVES   146

THINKING LIKE A HISTORIAN: Debating the Origins of the
American Revolution   148

PART TWO | Building a Nation   153

CHAPTER 5 **The American Revolution, 1776–1783**   157

Mobilizing for War   158
Setbacks for the British (1777)   166
American Society at War   178
War as an Engine of Change   180
Equality and Its Limits   184
REVIEWING THE CORE OBJECTIVES   188

CHAPTER 6 **Creating a "More Perfect Union,"
1783–1800**   191

The Confederation Government   192
Creating the Constitution   198
The Fight for Ratification   204
The Federalist Era   209
Foreign and Domestic Crises   215
REVIEWING THE CORE OBJECTIVES   226

CHAPTER 7 The Early Republic, 1800–1815   229

Jeffersonian Republicanism   230

War in the Mediterranean and Europe   242

The War of 1812   247

The Aftermath of the War   257

REVIEWING THE CORE OBJECTIVES   262

THINKING LIKE A HISTORIAN: Debating Thomas Jefferson and Slavery   264

PART THREE | An Expanding Nation   269

CHAPTER 8 The Emergence of a Market Economy, 1815–1850   273

The Market Revolution   274

Industrial Development   280

Immigration   288

Organized Labor and New Professions   291

REVIEWING THE CORE OBJECTIVES   296

CHAPTER 9 Nationalism and Sectionalism, 1815–1828   299

A New Nationalism   300

Debates over the American System   305

"Era of Good Feelings"   306

Nationalist Diplomacy   310

The Rise of Andrew Jackson   314

REVIEWING THE CORE OBJECTIVES   322

CHAPTER 10 The Jacksonian Era, 1828–1840   325

Jacksonian Democracy   327

Nullification   333

Jackson's Indian Policy   338

Political Battles   342

Jackson's Legacy   350

REVIEWING THE CORE OBJECTIVES   352

CHAPTER 11 **The South and Slavery, 1800–1860**   355

The Distinctiveness of the Old South   356
The Cotton Kingdom   359
Whites in the Old South   364
Black Society in the South   368
Forging a Slave Community   375

REVIEWING THE CORE OBJECTIVES   384

CHAPTER 12 **Religion, Romanticism, and Reform, 1800–1860**   387

Religion   388
Romanticism in America   397
The Reform Impulse   402
The Anti-Slavery Movement   411

REVIEWING THE CORE OBJECTIVES   420

THINKING LIKE A HISTORIAN: Debating Separate Spheres   422

PART FOUR | A House Divided and Rebuilt   427

CHAPTER 13 **Western Expansion and Southern Secession, 1830–1861**   431

Moving West   432
The Mexican-American War   447
Slavery in the Territories   450
The Emergence of the Republican Party   462
The Response in the South   474

REVIEWING THE CORE OBJECTIVES   478

CHAPTER 14 The War of the Union, 1861–1865   481

Mobilizing Forces in the North and South   482

Emancipation   499

The War behind the Lines   508

The Faltering Confederacy   513

A Transforming War   527

REVIEWING THE CORE OBJECTIVES   530

CHAPTER 15 Reconstruction, 1865–1877   533

The War's Aftermath in the South   534

The Battle over Political Reconstruction   535

Reconstruction in Practice   546

The Grant Years and Northern Disillusionment   555

Reconstruction's Significance   563

REVIEWING THE CORE OBJECTIVES   564

THINKING LIKE A HISTORIAN: Debating
Reconstruction   566

Glossary   G-1

Appendix   A-1

The Declaration of Independence   A-1

Articles of Confederation   A-5

The Constitution of The United States   A-11

Amendments to the Constitution   A-20

Presidential Elections   A-30

Admission of States   A-36

Population of The United States   A-37

Immigration to The United States, Fiscal Years 1820–2015   A-38

Immigration by Region and Selected Country of Last Residence,
Fiscal Years 1820–2015   A-40

Presidents, Vice Presidents, and Secretaries of State   A-49

Further Readings   R-1

Credits   C-1

Index   I-1

Maps

CHAPTER 1

The First Migration   8
Pre-Columbian Indian Civilizations in Middle and South America   12
Pre-Columbian Indian Civilizations in North America   15
Columbus's Voyages   20
Spanish Explorations of the Mainland   32
English, French, and Dutch Explorations   36

CHAPTER 2

Land Grants to the Virginia Company   50
Early Virginia and Maryland   52
Early New England Settlements   55
Early Settlements in the South   60
The Middle Colonies   64
European Settlements and Indian Tribes in Early America   69
The African Slave Trade, 1500–1800   76

CHAPTER 3

Atlantic Trade Routes   92
Major Immigrant Groups in Colonial America   94

CHAPTER 4

The French in North America   111
Major Campaigns of the French and Indian War   118
North America, 1713   123
North America, 1763   124
Lexington and Concord, April 19, 1775   139

CHAPTER 5

Major Campaigns in New York and New Jersey, 1776–1777   165
Major Campaigns in New York and Pennsylvania, 1777   169
Western Campaigns, 1776–1779   172
Major Campaigns in the South, 1778–1781   175
Yorktown, 1781   176
North America, 1783   177

CHAPTER 6

Western Land Cessions, 1781–1802   194
The Old Northwest, 1785   195
The Vote on the Constitution, 1787–1790   207
Treaty of Greenville, 1795   218
Pinckney's Treaty, 1795   220
The Election of 1800   225

CHAPTER 7

Explorations of the Louisiana Purchase, 1804-1807   240
Major Northern Campaigns of the War of 1812   253
Major Southern Campaigns of the War of 1812   255

CHAPTER 8

Transportation West, about 1840   275
The Growth of Railroads, 1850 and 1860   277
The Growth of Industry in the 1840s   286
The Growth of Cities, 1820 and 1860   287
Population Density, 1820 and 1860   288

CHAPTER 9

The National Road, 1811–1838   302
The Missouri Compromise, 1820   309
Boundary Treaties, 1818–1819   311
The Election of 1828   320

CHAPTER 10

Indian Removal, 1820–1840   340

CHAPTER 11

Cotton Production, 1821   362
Population Growth and Cotton Production, 1821–1859   363
The Slave Population, 1820 and 1860   381

CHAPTER 12

Mormon Trek, 1830–1851   396

CHAPTER 13

Wagon Trails West   433
The Oregon Dispute, 1818–1846   446
The Compromise of 1850   458
The Kansas-Nebraska Act, 1854   464
The Election of 1856   466
The Election of 1860   473

CHAPTER 14

Secession, 1860–1861   483
Campaigns in the West, February–April   494
The Peninsular Campaign, 1862   497
Campaigns in Virginia and Maryland, 1862   505
Campaigns in the East, 1863   517
Grant in Virginia, 1864–1865   521
Sherman's Campaigns, 1864–1865   525

CHAPTER 15

Reconstruction, 1865–1877   554
The Election of 1876   562

Thinking Like A Historian

PART ONE

Debating the Origins of the American Revolution   148

Secondary Sources

- Bernard Bailyn, *The Ideological Origins of the American Revolution* (1992)
- Gary Nash, "Social Change and the Growth of Prerevolutionary Urban Radicalism" (1976)

Primary Sources

- John Dickinson, "Letter from a Farmer in Pennsylvania" (1767)
- Governor Francis Bernard, "Letter to the Lords of Trade" (1765)

PART TWO

Debating Thomas Jefferson and Slavery   264

Secondary Sources

- Douglas L. Wilson, "Thomas Jefferson and the Character Issue" (1992)
- Paul Finkelman, "Jefferson and Slavery" (1993)

Primary Sources

- Thomas Jefferson, a draft section omitted from the *Declaration of Independence* (1776)
- Thomas Jefferson, *Notes on the State of Virginia* (1787)
- Thomas Jefferson, Letter to M. Warville (1788)
- Thomas Jefferson, Letter to John Holmes (1820)

PART THREE

Debating Separate Spheres   422

Secondary Sources

- Catherine Clinton, "The Ties that Bind" (1984)
- Nancy A. Hewitt, "Beyond the Search for Sisterhood: American Women's History in the 1980s" (1985)

Primary Sources

- Lucretia Mott, *Discourse on Women* (1849)
- Sojourner Truth, "And Ar'n't I a Woman?" (1851)
- Harriett H. Robinson, *Loom and Spindle or Life among the Early Mill Girls* (1898)

PART FOUR

Debating Reconstruction   566

Secondary Sources

- William Dunning, from *Reconstruction, Political and Economic, 1865–1877* (1907)
- Eric Foner, from *The Story of American Freedom* (1998)

Primary Sources

- Union Army General Carl Schurz, from *Report on the Condition of the South* (1865)
- Mississippi Vagrant Law (1865)
- Civil Rights Act of 1866
- Radical Republican Thaddeus Stevens, from "The Advantages of Negro Suffrage" (1867)

What's It All About?
(In the Norton Coursepack)

CHAPTER 1   The Columbian Exchange and the Spanish Empire in North America

CHAPTER 2   Different Beginnings, Common Trends: The English Colonies in North America, 1600–1700

CHAPTER 3   Comparing the Three English Colonial Regions

CHAPTER 4   The Road to the American Revolution

CHAPTER 5   From Subjects to Citizens

CHAPTER 6   Federalists versus Republicans

CHAPTER 7   Managing Foreign Policy in the Early Republic

CHAPTER 8   Technological Innovation and a National Marketplace

CHAPTER 9   Sectional Conflict and Economic Policies

CHAPTER 10   Creating a Two-Party System: Democrats versus Whigs

CHAPTER 11   Cotton and the Transformation of the South

CHAPTER 12   Abolitionism

CHAPTER 13   Slavery, Territorial Expansion, and Secession

CHAPTER 14   Why Was the North Victorious in the Civil War?

CHAPTER 15   From Slave to Citizen

Preface

This second edition of *The Essential Learning Edition* continues to nurture *America*'s long-established focus on history as a storytelling art. It features colorful characters and anecdotes informed by balanced analysis and social texture, all guided by the unfolding of key events and imperfect but often fascinating human actors with an emphasis on the culture of everyday life. *The Essential Learning Edition* continues to provide a unique package of features to introduce students to the methods and tools used by historians to study, revise, and debate efforts to explain and interpret the past.

As always, the first step in my preparing a new edition is to learn from students and professors what can be improved, polished, added or deleted. The results of dozens of survey instruments provided a strong consensus: students want an inexpensive, visually interesting textbook written in lively prose that focuses on the essential elements of American history while telling the dramatic stories about the ways that individuals responded to and shaped events. Too many textbooks overwhelm them, students responded, either by flooding them with too much information or by taking too much for granted in terms of the knowledge that students bring to the introductory course. Students stressed that textbooks need to help them more readily identify the most important developments or issues to focus on (and remember) as they read.

To address these student concerns, I have continued to provide contextual explanations for events or developments that too often are taken for granted by authors. For example, this edition includes more material about the Native American experience, the nature and significance of the Protestant Reformation, the texture of daily life, the impact of the cotton culture on the global economy, and the march of capitalism.

When asked what they most wanted in an introductory text, instructors said much the same as their students, but they also asked for a textbook that introduced students to the nature of historical research, analysis, and debate. Many professors also mentioned the growing importance to them and their institutions of *assessing* the success of their students in meeting the learning goals established by their department. Accordingly, I have aligned *The Essential Learning Edition* with specific learning outcomes for the introductory American history survey course approved by various state and national organizations, including the American Historical Association. These learning outcomes also extend to the accompanying media package, enabling instructors to track students' progress towards mastery of these important learning goals.

These and other suggestions from students and professors have shaped this new version of *The Essential Learning Edition*. Each of the 30 chapters begins with a handful of **Core Objectives**, carefully designed to help students understand—and remember—the major developments and issues in each period. To make it easier for students to grasp the major developments, every chapter aligns the narrative with the learning objectives. Each Core Objective is highlighted at the beginning of each major section in the chapter for which it is relevant. **Core Objective flags** appear in the page margins to reinforce key topics in the narrative that are essential to understanding the broader Core Objectives. **Key terms**, chosen to reinforce the major concepts, are bolded in the text and defined in the margin, helping reinforce their significance. At the end of each chapter, review features continue to reiterate and review the Core Objectives, including pithy chapter summaries, lists of key terms, and chapter chronologies.

This book continues to be distinctive for its creative efforts to make every component—maps, images, etc.— a learning opportunity and teaching point. Maps, for example, include lists of questions to help students interpret the data embedded in them.

Interactive maps are but just one example of the innovative elements in this book designed to deepen student learning and get them more *engaged* in the learning dynamic. Chapters in *The Essential Learning Edition* also include a **What It's All About** feature, which visually summarizes in a graphical format major issues. These are now available exclusively in the Norton Coursepack for instructors to use in ways that are best suited for their courses. Some examples include:

- Chapter 3: Comparative examination of how different regions of the English colonies were settled and developed.
- Chapter 9: Analyzes sectional conflicts and the role the economic policies of Henry Clay and Andrew Jackson played in those conflicts.
- Chapter 12: Abolitionist versus pro-slavery arguments on slavery.
- Chapter 15: Tracing the legal and legislative road from slavery to freedom for African Americans in the former Confederate States.
- Chapter 23: The First New Deal compared to the Second New Deal.

Another unique new feature, called **Thinking Like a Historian,** helps students better understand—and apply—the research techniques and interpretive skills used by historians. Through carefully selected examples, the Thinking Like a Historian segments highlight the foundational role of primary and secondary sources as the building blocks of history and illustrates the ways in which historians have differed in their interpretations of the past. There is one Thinking Like a Historian feature for each of the seven major periods of American history; each feature takes on a major interpretive issue in that era. In Part I of the activity, students first read excerpts from two original secondary sources that offer competing interpretive views framing that period. In Part II, students then read some of the original primary sources that those same historians used to develop their arguments. Finally, students must answer a series of questions that guide their reading and analysis of the sources.

As always, this new edition also includes new content. As I created this new edition of *The Essential Learning Edition*, I have complemented the political narrative by incorporating more social and cultural history into the text. Key new discussions include:

- Chapter 1: Enriched coverage of pre-Columbian peoples, especially the Maya, Mexica (Aztecs), and Algonquians—and European explorations in North America. Additional material about the Renaissance and Reformation, especially Martin Luther and the Anglican Reformation.
- Chapter 2: Additional material on the social structure of European societies during the Age of Discovery, the crucially important and highly profitable Caribbean colonies, especially Barbados, and the process of enslaving Africans and shipping them to the Americas.
- Chapter 3: The everyday life of women and the role of women in evangelical revivals; enhanced treatment of Great Awakening; and, additional details on infant mortality and family dynamics in the colonial period.
- Chapter 4: New insights into the growing resistance to British authority in the colonies leading up to 1775.
- Chapter 5: Enriched treatment of Revolutionary War battles, the everyday life of soldiers, and the role of women revolutionaries and those who served as "camp followers" in support of the Continental armies.
- Chapter 6: Additional insights into Shays's Rebellion and the early stages of American capitalism.
- Chapter 7: Enhanced profile of Thomas Jefferson and his contradictory stance on slavery and women.
- Chapter 8: More information about the development of the cotton gin and its impact on the national economy. Added insights into the development of the textile mill system in New England and the daily life of Irish immigrants in seaboard cities as well as women in early labor unions.
- Chapter 10: A more robust portrait of Andrew Jackson and his distinctive life and personality as well as the Peggy Eaton Affair.
- Chapter 11: Delves more deeply into the economic significance and everyday dynamics of slavery and the culture of slave communities. More coverage of the "slave trail" from the Upper South to the Gulf coast states and of the nature of slave auctions. New details on the lives of plantation mistresses, their duties, double-standards, and systemic sexism they endured
- Chapter 12: Enriched treatment of the abolitionist movement and utopianism, especially the Shakers and the Oneida Community.

- Chapter 13: Additional color and texture about life on the Overland trails, Sutter's Fort, and the mining communities associated with the California Gold Rush. Also more in-depth treatment of the Fugitive Slave Act.
- Chapter 14: Enhanced attention to the everyday experience of Civil War soldiers—why they fought, what they ate, camp life, the horrors of battle and their sense of manly duty.
- Chapter 16: Deepened the discussion of the impact of the railroad boom on the Gilded Age economy and everyday life.
- Chapter 17: Reorganized the section on Native Americans in the West, including new sections on the Sand Creek Massacre, and Grant's Indian Policy, and expanded coverage on Custer, the Great Sioux War, and the Battle of the Little Big Horn. Added a profile of Ida Wells—African American woman who led the crusade against racial lynchings.
- Chapter 18: New section added that better frames the discussion of political life during the Gilded Age, including the balance between the two major parties, the surprising level of public participation in everyday politics, and the relationships between business & politics and industry & agriculture.
- Chapter 19: Details added about Theodore Roosevelt and the Rough Riders during the Cuba campaign.
- Chapter 20: Added a portrait of Walter Rauschenbusch and his role in promoting the social gospel.
- Chapter 21: More material about the everyday experience of soldiers in the Great War, especially the nature of trench warfare in the Western Front and the role of shellshock.
- Chapter 22: An enriched profile of Al Capone and more detailed treatment of the famous Democratic Convention of 1924.
- Chapter 23: A more textured account of the human effects of the Great Depression on the American people.
- Chapter 27: Enhanced treatment of John F. Kennedy, Lyndon B. Johnson, and Martin Luther King Jr., and a profile of civil rights leader Medgar Evers.
- Chapter 30: New coverage of the Obama administration, the ongoing wars in Iraq and Afghanistan, the rise of voter populism, the surprising victory of Donald Trump in the 2016 election, and his tempestuous first year as president.

In sum, *The Essential Learning Edition* includes the most dramatic changes ever made in a resilient book that has been in print for more than thirty years.

Media Tools for Students and Instructors

America: The Essential Learning Edition, Second Edition, is supported by a robust collection of digital resources to support the core objectives and historical developments discussed in each chapter, while also building students' history "skills."

INQUIZITIVE

Norton InQuizitive uses interactive questions and guided feedback to motivate students to read and understand the key concepts, events, and historical developments. A variety of question types featuring images, maps, and sources prompt critical and analytical thinking on each of the chapter's Core Objectives. In a case study with *The Essential Learning Edition*, First Edition, 80% of history students said they think InQuizitive helped them learn the material from the textbook, 88% of students said they prefer InQuizitive to previous standard multiple-choice quizzes, and 92% of students would recommend that the instructor continue using InQuizitive.

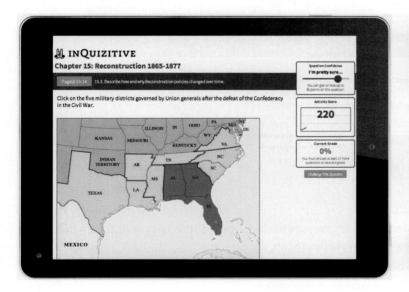

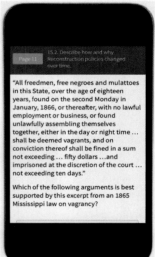

New! History Skills Tutorials

With the Second Edition we've expanded our digital resources to include a new series of tutorials to build students' critical analysis skills. The History Skills Tutorials combine video and interactive assessments to teach students how to analyze documents, images, and maps. By utilizing a three-step process, students learn a framework for analysis through videos featuring

David Shi, and then are challenged to apply what they have learned through a series of interactive assessments. The History Skills Tutorials can be assigned at the beginning of the semester to prepare students for analysis of the sources in the textbook and beyond, or integrated as remediation tools throughout the semester.

Student Site

This free site offers students access to additional resources to support student learning. Features include NEW! Chapter overview videos that prepare students for the reading by highlighting key events and themes that emerge in the chapter. In addition, there is a comprehensive collection of author videos exploring the core objectives from each chapter. Interactive iMaps, as well as an online reader featuring additional primary source documents, provide students with even more opportunities to engage with primary sources.

W. W. Norton & Company, Inc.
INDEPENDENT PUBLISHERS SINCE 1923

Colorblind Mode: ON | OFF
W. W. NORTON HOME | HELP | CREDITS

America
The Essential Learning Edition

DAVID SHI · GEORGE TINDALL

OFFICE HOUR VIDEOS   ONLINE READER   IMAPS

Preview Site

ⓘ This site will launch in **July, 2015**. Please visit the **demo chapter 15** on *Reconstruction 1865-1877*.

Office Hour Videos

New Office Hour videos feature author David Shi discussing American History topics important for each chapter.

Purchase: Hardcover | eBook

SHARE

INQUIZITIVE
If your instructor assigns homework in InQuizitive, log in here.

NORTON EBOOK
The ebook version of this book offers the full content of the print version at half the price.

PART I: A NOT-SO-"NEW" WORLD

Chapter 1: The Collision of Cultures in the Sixteenth Century	∨
Chapter 2: England and its American Colonies 1607-1732	∨
Chapter 3: Colonial Ways of Life 1607-1750	∨
Chapter 4: From Colonies to States 1600-1776	∨

PART II: BUILDING A NATION

Chapter 5: The Revolution 1776-1783	∨
Chapter 6: Creating a "More Perfect Union" 1783-1800	∨
Chapter 7: The Early Republic 1800-1815	∨

Norton Ebooks

Norton Ebooks give students and instructors an enhanced reading experience at a fraction of the cost of a print textbook. Students are able to have an active reading experience and can take notes, bookmark, search, highlight, and even read offline. As an instructor, you can even add your own notes for students to see as they read the text. Norton ebooks can be viewed on—and synced between—all computers and mobile devices.

Norton Coursepacks

Easily add high-quality Norton digital media to your online, hybrid, or lecture course—all at no cost. Norton Coursepacks work within your existing learning management system; there's no new system to learn, and access is free and easy. Content is customizable and includes

- **Primary-Source Exercises** prompt students to compare documents and images with multiple-choice and short-answer questions for analysis.
- **Guided Reading Exercises** walk students through a three-step critical reading process: noting the important main points, summarizing in your own words, and answering short-answer questions to confirm understanding.
- **What's It All About** visually summarizes in a graphical format major issues. This feature from the First Edition has been fully revised for the Second Edition and can now be assigned directly to students through the Coursepack.
- **Online Reader** features additional primary-source documents and images that go beyond what is in textbooks.
- **Chapter Review Quizzes** include multiple-choice, chronological matching, and true/false questions.
- **Author Videos,** including the NEW! Chapter Overview videos, illuminate key events, developments, and concepts in each chapter by bringing the narrative to life with additional context and anecdotes.
- **iMaps** are interactive versions of maps from the text that allow students to practice their map-reading skills, with map worksheets for self-testing and labeling exercises.
- And all of the **Student Site** resources.

Classroom Presentation Tools

- **Lecture PowerPoints** (Bettye Hutchins, Vernon College) and **Art PowerPoints** feature photographs and maps from the book, retouched for in-class presentation.
- The **Norton American History Digital Archive** includes over 1,700 images, audio and video files that are arranged chronologically and by theme.

Instructor's Manual (Chad Garick, Jones County Junior College; Kenneth Howell, Blinn College)

The Instructor's Manual for *The Essential Learning Edition* has everything instructors need to prepare lectures and classroom activities: chapter summaries, suggestions for teaching Core Objectives, as well as lecture ideas, classroom activities, and lists of recommended books, films, and websites.

Test Bank (Thomas Born, Blinn College; Linda Coslett, Chattanooga State Community College)

The Test Bank features multiple-choice, true/false, and essay questions aligned with the chapter's Core Objectives and classified according to level of difficulty, and Bloom's Taxonomy, offering multiple avenues for content and skill assessment. All Norton test banks are available with ExamView Test Generator software, allowing instructors to easily create, administer, and manage assessments.

Acknowledgments

The quality and range of reviews on this project were truly exceptional. The book and its accompanying media components benefited from the insights of numerous instructors.

Milan Andrejevich, Ivy Tech College–South Bend
Carol A. Bielke, San Antonio Independent School District
April Birchfield, Asheville-Buncombe Technical Community College
Howard Bodner, Houston Community College
Matt Brent, Rappahannock Community College
Sharon J. Burnham, John Tyler Community College
Michael Collins, Texas State University
Scott Cook, Motlow State Community College
Carrie Coston, Blinn College
Nicholas P. Cox, Houston Community College
Carl E. Creasman Jr., Valencia College
Stephen K. Davis, Texas State University
Frank De La O, Midland College
Jim Dudlo, Brookhaven College
Robert Glen Findley, Odessa College
Brandon Franke, Blinn College
Chad Garick, Jones County Junior College
Mark S. Goldman, Tallahassee Community College
Devethia Guillory, Lone Star College–North Harris
Justin Hoggard, Three Rivers College
Andrew G. Hollinger, Tarrant County College

David P. Hopkins Jr., Midland College

Justin Horton, Thomas Nelson Community College

Theresa R. Jach, Houston Community College

Robert Jason Kelly, Holmes Community College

Nina McCune, Baton Rouge Community College

Richard Randall Moore, Metropolitan Community College–Longview

Ken S. Mueller, Ivy Tech College–Lafayette

Lise Namikas, Colorado State University–Global

Brice E. Olivier, Temple College

Candice Pulkowski, The Art Institutes

Carey Roberts, Liberty University

John Schmitz, Northern Virginia Community College–Annandale

Greg Shealy, University of Wisconsin–Madison

Thomas Summerhill, Michigan State University

Scott M. Williams, Weatherford College

Laura Matysek Wood, Tarrant County College Northwest

Crystal R.M. Wright, North Central Texas College

Once again, I thank my friends and colleagues at W. W. Norton for their consummate professionalism and good cheer, especially Jon Durbin, Laura Wilk, Sarah England, Melissa Atkin, Julie Sindel, Roy McClymont, Jonathan Mason, Kelly Rafey, Lily Gellman, Marian Johnson, Kim Yi, Rachel Mayer, Stephanie Romeo, Sarah Rose Aquilina, Hope Miller Goodell, Debra Morton-Hoyt, Andy Ensor, Liz Marotta, and Jude Grant.

Finally, I have dedicated this new version of *America* to George Brown Tindall, who died in 2006 at the age of eighty-five. When George and I first met in Manhattan in 1984 to discuss collaborating on this textbook project, we discovered that we shared an alma mater (Furman University), a passion for classroom teaching and student advising, and a commitment to exposing students to the color and drama of the past through lively narrative prose. George once told me that he taught not because his students needed him but because he needed them. Education was his calling; history was his passion. That so many of his former students became his closest friends testifies to his distinctive success as a professor.

A free-thinking, plain-speaking man, George was truly one of the nation's most distinguished historians. And, for over twenty years, he was my partner, mentor, and friend, but more than that, he was an inspiration. His love for language and for learning exercised a seductive charm on me. How bracing it was to be in the company of a gentleman for whom scholarship was a heroic enterprise. How refreshing it was to know someone for whom a perpetual bow-tie bespoke gentility and grace rather than pomposity. How beneficial it was to be challenged to become a better writer, a clearer thinker, and a more tenacious defender of one's own values and conclusions.

George Tindall remains a continuing influence on me. While few of his words and phrases remain in this latest edition, his robust spirit, pristine integrity, and refreshing humor live on—as they should.

America

The Essential Learning Edition

An Old "New" World

History is filled with ironies. Luck and accidents — the unexpected happenings of life — often shape events more than intentions. Long before Christopher Columbus lucked upon the Caribbean Sea in an effort to find a westward passage to the Indies (east Asia), the indigenous peoples he mislabeled "Indians" had occupied and transformed the lands of the Western Hemisphere (also called the Americas—North, Central, and South).

The "New World" he encountered was *new* only to the Europeans who began exploring, conquering, and exploiting the region at the end of the fifteenth century. By 1492, when Columbus began his famous voyage west from Spain, there were millions of Native Americans living in the Western Hemisphere. Over thousands of years, they had developed diverse and often highly sophisticated societies, some rooted in agriculture and others focused on trade or conquest.

The Native American peoples were decimated and transformed by the arrival of Europeans and Africans. Very different societies collided, each having its own distinct heritage and worldview. Indians were exploited, infected, enslaved, displaced, and exterminated.

Yet the conventional story of tragic conquest oversimplifies the complex process by which Indians, Europeans, and Africans interacted in the Western Hemisphere. The Native Americans were more than passive victims of

European power; they were also trading partners and both allies and rivals of the transatlantic newcomers. The indigenous peoples became neighbors and advisers, converts and spouses. As such, they participated jointly in the creation of the new society known as America.

The Europeans who risked their lives to settle in the Western Hemisphere were a diverse lot. Young and old, men and women, they came from Spain, Portugal, France, the British Isles, the Netherlands (Holland), Scandinavia, Italy, and the German states. (Germany would not become a united nation until 1871.)

A variety of motives inspired them to undertake the dangerous transatlantic voyage. Some were adventurers and fortune seekers eager to gain glory and find gold and silver. Others were passionate Christians eager to create kingdoms of God in the New World. Still others were prisoners, debtors, servants, landless peasants, and political or religious exiles. Many were simply seeking a piece of land, higher wages, and greater economic opportunity. A settler in Pennsylvania noted that "poor people (both men and women) of all kinds can here get three times the wages for their labor than they can in England."

Yet such wages never attracted enough workers to keep up with the rapidly expanding colonial economies, so the Europeans early in the seventeenth century turned to Africa for their labor needs. European nations—especially Portugal and Spain—had been transporting captive Africans to the Western Hemisphere, from Chile to Canada, throughout the sixteenth century. Thereafter, the English and Dutch joined the effort to use enslaved Africans for the hardest labor in the colonies. Few Europeans during the colonial era saw the contradiction between the promise of freedom in America for themselves and the expanding institution of race-based slavery.

The intermingling of people, cultures, and ecosystems from the continents of Africa, Europe, and the Western Hemisphere gave colonial American society its distinctive vitality and variety. The shared quest for a better life gave America much of its drama—and conflict.

During the seventeenth and eighteenth centuries, fierce rivalries among the Spanish, French, English, and Dutch triggered costly wars fought in Europe and around the world. European monarchs struggled to manage often-unruly colonies, which, they discovered, played crucial roles in their frequent European wars.

Many of the colonists had brought with them to America a feisty independence, which led them to resent government interference in their affairs. A British official in North Carolina reported that the settlers were "without any Law or Order. Impudence is so very high, as to be past bearing."

The colonists and their British rulers maintained an uneasy partnership throughout the seventeenth century. But as the royal authorities tightened their control during the mid–eighteenth century, they met resistance from colonists, which exploded into revolution.

DE SOTO AND THE INCAS This 1596 color engraving shows Spanish conquistador Hernando de Soto's first encounter with King Atahualpa of the Inca Empire. Although artist Theodor de Bry never set foot in North America, his engravings reflect Spanish perceptions of Native Americans in the sixteenth century.

The Collision of Cultures

IN THE 16TH CENTURY

Debate still rages about when and how the first humans arrived in North America. Until recently, archaeologists had assumed that ancient peoples from northeast Asia, some 12,000 to 45,000 years ago, were the first arrivals in the Western Hemisphere. Those Asian wanderers ("nomads") who hunted the massive woolly mammoths and other big game animals had journeyed over a thousand miles across "Beringia," a wide, grassy plain connecting Siberia with Alaska, when global sea levels were much lower than today.

Archaeologists call these first peoples Paleo-Indians (Old or Ancient Indians). Over thousands of years, as the climate warmed and the glaciers melted, a steady stream of small groups fanned out southward on foot or in small boats across the entire Western Hemisphere, from the Arctic Circle in the north to the southern tip of South America. They lived in mobile huts with wooden frames covered by animal skins or grasses ("thatch"). Paleo-Indians were skilled "hunter-gatherers" (as well as stone toolmakers and warriors) whose weapons were clubs, knives, and spears. Their food consisted of large mammals and edible wild plants, berries, and seeds.

Recent archaeological discoveries in Oregon, Pennsylvania, Virginia, and Chile suggest that prehistoric humans may have arrived on boats from

CORE OBJECTIVES InQUIZITIVE

1. Explain why there were so many diverse human societies in the Americas before Europeans arrived.

2. Summarize the major developments in Europe that enabled the Age of Exploration.

3. Describe how the Spanish were able to conquer and colonize the Americas.

4. Assess the impact of the Columbian Exchange between the "Old" and "New" Worlds.

5. Analyze the legacy of the Spanish form of colonization on North American history.

THE FIRST MIGRATION

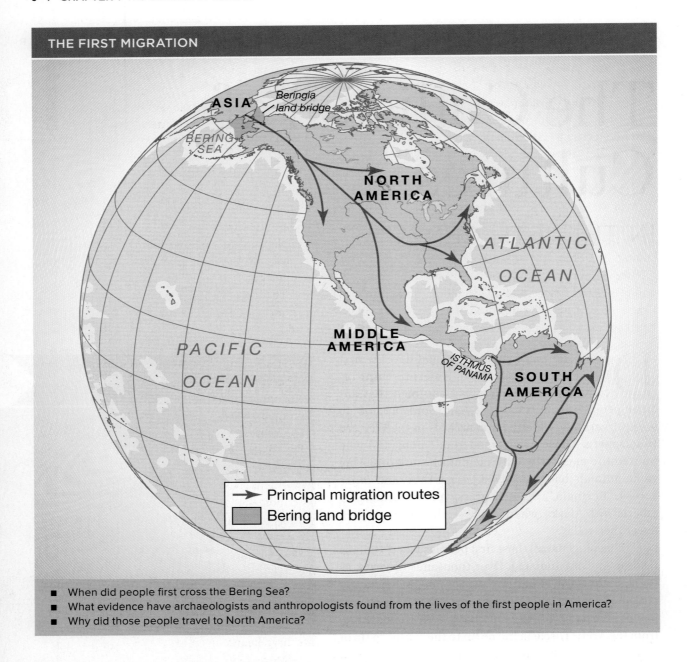

- When did people first cross the Bering Sea?
- What evidence have archaeologists and anthropologists found from the lives of the first people in America?
- Why did those people travel to North America?

various parts of Asia—and some may even have crossed the Atlantic Ocean from southwestern Europe. Regardless of when ancient people first set foot on the North American continent, the region eventually became a crossroads for various peoples from around the globe: Europeans, Africans, Asians, and others—all of whom brought with them distinctive backgrounds, cultures, technologies, and motivations that, taken together, helped form the American mosaic.

Early Cultures in the Americas

CORE **OBJECTIVE**
1. Explain why there were so many diverse human societies in the Americas before Europeans arrived.

For at least 20,000 years before the arrival of Europeans, Native Americans had occupied the vastness of North America undisturbed by outside invaders. By the time Christopher Columbus happened upon the Western Hemisphere, the hundreds of Indian societies living in North America may have numbered over 10 million people. They lived in a diverse array of communities in which more than 300 languages were spoken.

Archaeologists have labeled the earliest arrivals in North America the *Clovis* peoples, named after a site in New Mexico where ancient hunters around 9500 B.C.E. (before the Common Era) killed tusked woolly mammoths (fourteen feet tall) using distinctive "Clovis" stone spear points that made hunting large mammals much more efficient. Clovis people lived in small bands of five to ten families. Over many centuries, as the post–Ice Age climate warmed, sea levels rose, growing seasons lengthened, and snowfall and rainfall lessened, leading many lakes to dry up into deserts. The largest mammals—mammoths, mastodons, giant bison, single-hump camels, huge beavers—eventually died out. Hunters then began stalking smaller, yet more abundant mammals: deer, antelope, elk, moose, and caribou.

As the climate grew hotter and drier through global warming, grasslands gave way to forests, which provided plants and small animals for human consumption. The ancient Indians adapted to the diverse new environments—coastal forests, grassy plains, southwestern deserts, eastern woodlands—by developing new ways to survive and flourish. Some continued to hunt large mammals, while others fished and trapped small animals; some gathered wild plants and herbs and collected acorns and seeds, while others farmed. Many did some of each. Contrary to the romantic myth of early Indian civilizations living in perfect harmony with nature and one another, indigenous peoples often engaged in warfare and exploited the environment by burning large wooded areas in order to plant fields. They also developed their own nature-centered religions, mastered the use of fire, and improved technology such as spear points, basketry, and pottery.

Global warming and climatic and environmental diversity

By about 5000 B.C.E., people living in Mexico began adapting to the warmer climate by transforming themselves into farming societies. They became expert at growing the plant foods that would become the primary crops of the hemisphere: chiefly **maize (corn)** to be ground into flour, beans, and squash but also chili peppers, avocados, and pumpkins. More food spurred population growth, the construction of cities, and new industries. Agricultural societies grew larger and more complex, with their own distinctive social, economic, and political institutions.

Agricultural revolution

maize (corn) The primary grain crop in Mesoamerica, yielding small kernels often ground into cornmeal. Easy to grow in a broad range of conditions, it enabled a global population explosion after being brought to Europe, Africa, and Asia.

The Mayas, Incas, and Mexica

Around 1500 B.C.E., farming towns first appeared in Mexico, enabling people to live in one place rather than move with the seasons. The more settled life in turn provided time for the cultivation of religion, art and crafts, science,

MAYAN SOCIETY A fresco depicting a dressing ceremony of a high priest. He stands in the center garbed in a jaguar skin and embroidered bell, surrounded by his less elaborately clad attendants. **What does this image reveal about the social hierarchy of Mayan society?**

governmental administration—and frequent warfare. Agriculture supported the development of densely populated cities complete with gigantic pyramids, temples, and palaces in Middle America (*Mesoamerica*, what is now Mexico and Central America).

The Mayas, who dominated Central America for more than 600 years, also developed a rich written language and elaborate works of art. They used sophisticated mathematics and astronomy to create a yearly calendar more accurate than the one the Europeans were using at the time of Columbus. Mayan civilization was highly developed, featuring sprawling cities, hierarchical government, terraced farms, spectacular pyramids, and a cohesive ideology.

In about 900 B.C.E. the complex Mayan culture collapsed. Why it disappeared remains a mystery, but a major factor was ecological. The Mayas overexploited the rain forest, upon whose fragile ecosystem they depended. As an archaeologist has explained, "Too many farmers grew too many crops on too much of the landscape." Widespread deforestation led to hillside erosion and a catastrophic loss of nutrient-rich farmland.

Overpopulation added to the strain on Mayan society, prompting civil wars. Mayan war parties destroyed each other's cities and took prisoners to be sacrificed to the gods in theatrical rituals. Whatever the reasons for the weakening of Mayan society, it succumbed to the Toltecs, a warlike people who conquered most of the region in the tenth century. Around 1200 B.C.E., however, the Toltecs mysteriously withdrew after a series of droughts, fires, and invasions.

Farther south, as many as 12 million people speaking at least twenty different languages made up the sprawling Inca Empire. By the fifteenth century, the Incas' vast realm stretched some 2,500 miles along the Andes Mountains in the western part of South America, transforming their mountainous empire into a flowering civilization with fertile farms fed by irrigation systems, enduring stone buildings, and interconnected networks of paved roads.

> **Vast empires and monumental cities**

During the late thirteenth century, the **Mexica** (Me-SHEE-ka)—whom Europeans later called Aztecs ("People from Aztlán," the place they claimed as their homeland)—began drifting southward to the central highlands of Mexico. Displaying tireless energy and shocking ruthlessness, they eventually took control of the entire region, where they built in the fourteenth century the spectacular city of Tenochtitlán on an island in Lake Tetzcoco, the site of present-day Mexico City.

Tenochtitlán would become the largest city in the Western Hemisphere by the end of the fifteenth century. It served as the capital of a sophisticated **Aztec Empire** ruled by a semidivine emperor and divided into two social classes: the nobility/priesthood (about 5 percent of the population) and the commoners—merchants, craftsmen, farmers, and slaves.

Warfare was a sacred ritual for the Mexica. Gradually, they expanded their control over neighboring societies in central Mexico, forcing them to pay tribute in goods and services each year and developing a thriving trade in gold, silver, copper, and pearls as well as agricultural products. Towering stone temples, broad paved avenues, thriving markets, and some 70,000 adobe huts dominated the capital city of Tenochtitlán.

> **Religion, war, tribute, and trade**

Like most agricultural peoples, the Mexica were intensely spiritual. Their religious beliefs focused on the interconnection between nature and human life and the sacredness of natural elements—the sun, moon, stars, rain, mountains, rivers, and animals. Mexica believed that the gods had sacrificed themselves at the beginning of creation to benefit humankind. To repay their debt to the gods and to ensure good harvests and victory in battle, the Mexica, like most Mesoamericans, regularly offered ritual sacrifices of live people—captive warriors, slaves, women, and children. In elaborate weekly ceremonies, priests used stone knives to cut out the beating hearts of victims. To the Mexica, human blood and hearts provided the sun god with the vital energy to enable fertile crops. The constant need for

Mexica Otherwise known as Aztecs, a Mesoamerican people of northern Mexico who founded the vast Aztec Empire in the fourteenth century, later conquered by the Spanish under Hernán Cortés in 1521.

Aztec Empire Established in the fourteenth century under the imperialistic Mexica, or Aztecs, in the valley of Mexico.

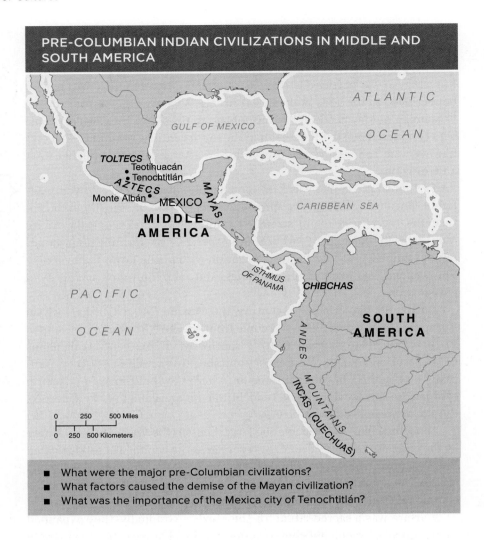

■ What were the major pre-Columbian civilizations?
■ What factors caused the demise of the Mayan civilization?
■ What was the importance of the Mexica city of Tenochtitlán?

more human sacrifices fed the Mexica's relentless warfare against other
indigenous groups. A Mexica song celebrated their warrior code: "Proud of
itself / is the city of Mexico-Tenochtitlán / Here no one fears to die in war.
/ This is our glory."

North American Civilizations before 1500

Diverse regional societies

North of Mexico, numerous indigenous civilizations existed in the present-
day United States. They shared several fundamental spiritual myths and social beliefs, especially concerning the sacredness of nature, the necessity of
communal living, and respect for elders, but the different societies developed in different ways at different times and in different places. In North
America alone, there were probably 10 million Native Americans organized
into 240 different societies speaking many different languages when the
Europeans arrived.

Native Americans had well-defined social roles. Men were hunters and warriors, while women tended children, made clothes, blankets, jewelry, and pottery. Women also dried animal skins, wove baskets, and gathered, grew, and cooked food. Extended family groups often lived together in a lodge or tipi (a Sioux word meaning "dwelling").

The dry Southwest (what is now Arizona, New Mexico, Nevada, and Utah) hosted corn-growing societies, elements of which exist today and heirs to which (the Hopis, Zunis, and others) still live in the multistory cliffside villages (called *pueblos* by the Spanish) erected by their distant ancestors. About 500 C.E., the Hohokam people from present-day Mexico migrated to southern and central Arizona, where they constructed hundreds of miles of irrigation canals to water their crops. They also crafted decorative pottery and turquoise jewelry, and they constructed temple mounds (earthen pyramids used for sacred ceremonies).

CLIFF DWELLINGS Ruins of Anasazi cliff dwellings in Mesa Verde National Park, Colorado. **Why might the Southwestern societies have built their villages deep into cliff faces?**

The most widespread and best known of the Southwest pueblo cultures were the Anasazi (Ancient Ones). In ancient times they developed extensive settlements in the "Four Corners" region where the modern-day states of Arizona, New Mexico, Colorado, and Utah meet. Anasazi society was remarkable for *not* having a rigid class structure. The religious leaders and warriors worked much as the rest of the people did. And the Anasazi engaged in warfare only as a means of self-defense. (*Hopi* means "Peaceful People.")

Southwest pueblo cultures

Along the heavily forested northwest Pacific coast, where shellfish, salmon, seals, whales, deer, and edible wild plants were abundant, there was little need for farming. In fact, many of the Pacific Northwest peoples needed to work only two days to provide enough food for a week.

Such social density enabled the Pacific peoples to develop intricate religious rituals and sophisticated woodworking skills, aspects of which were embodied in the carved totem poles they created and erected. For shelter, they built large, earthen-floored, cedar-plank houses up to 100 feet long, where whole bands of families lived together. Socially, the Indian bands along the Northwest Pacific coast were hierarchical, divided into slaves, commoners, and chiefs. Seashells were used as money. An abundance of food, a mild climate, and a prosperous trading network made the Pacific coast the most densely populated of all the regions in North America.

The peoples living on the Great Plains (Plains Indians), a vast, flat land of cold winters and hot summers west of the Mississippi River, and in the Great Basin (present-day Utah and Nevada) included the Arapaho, Blackfeet,

GREAT SERPENT MOUND At over 1,300 feet in length and three feet high, this snake-shaped burial mound in Adams County, Ohio, is the largest of its kind in the world.

Cheyenne, Comanche, Crow, Apache, and Sioux. They were nomadic hunter-gatherers, following on foot enormous herds of bison across a sea of grassland, collecting seeds, nuts, roots, and berries as they roamed.

Eastern "mound builders"

East of the Great Plains, in the vast woodlands from the Mississippi River to the Atlantic Ocean that would eventually become the American South and Midwest, several "mound-building" cultures flourished as predominantly agricultural societies growing corn, beans, and squash. First the Adena and later the Hopewell peoples (both names derive from archaeological sites) developed thriving communities along rivers in the Ohio Valley between 800 B.C.E. and 400 C.E. The Adena-Hopewell cultures focused on agriculture, including tobacco. They left behind enormous earthworks and 200 elaborate **burial mounds** shaped like great snakes, birds, and other animals, several of which were nearly a quarter mile long.

burial mounds A funereal tradition, practiced in the Mississippi and Ohio Valleys by the Adena-Hopewell cultures, of erecting massive mounds of earth over graves, often shaped in the designs of serpents and other animals.

By the sixth century, however, the Hopewell culture disappeared, giving way to a new phase of Native American development east of the Mississippi River, the Mississippian culture, which flourished from 800 to 1500 C.E. The Mississippians, centered in the southern Mississippi Valley, were also mound-building and corn-growing peoples who built substantial towns around central plazas and temples.

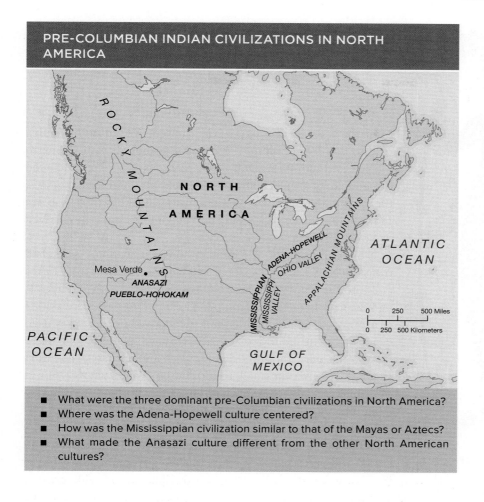

PRE-COLUMBIAN INDIAN CIVILIZATIONS IN NORTH AMERICA

ROCKY MOUNTAINS

NORTH AMERICA

ATLANTIC OCEAN

Mesa Verde •
ANASAZI
PUEBLO-HOHOKAM

MISSISSIPPIAN
MISSISSIPPI VALLEY
OHIO VALLEY
ADENA-HOPEWELL
APPALACHIAN MOUNTAINS

PACIFIC OCEAN

GULF OF MEXICO

0   250   500 Miles
0   250   500 Kilometers

- What were the three dominant pre-Columbian civilizations in North America?
- Where was the Adena-Hopewell culture centered?
- How was the Mississippian civilization similar to that of the Mayas or Aztecs?
- What made the Anasazi culture different from the other North American cultures?

The largest of these advanced regional centers, called *chiefdoms*, was **Cahokia** (1050–1250 C.E.), in southwest Illinois, just a few miles across the Mississippi River from what is now St. Louis, Missouri. There the Mississippians constructed an enormous, intricately planned farming settlement with pole-and-thatch houses, temples (where humans were sacrificed to the gods), monumental public buildings, spacious ceremonial plazas, and over a hundred flat-topped earthen pyramids with thatch-roofed temples on top. Cahokia hosted 15,000 people on some 3,200 acres, making it the largest city north of Mexico.

Yet Cahokia mysteriously vanished after 1400. What caused its collapse remains a mystery, but the most likely reason was environmental. The overcutting of trees to make fortress walls may have set in motion ecological changes that doomed the community when a massive earthquake struck around 1200 C.E. The loss of trees led to widespread flooding and the erosion of topsoil, which finally forced people to look for better lands for corn

Cahokia The largest chiefdom of the Mississippian Indian culture located in present-day Illinois and the site of a sophisticated farming settlement that supported up to 15,000 inhabitants.

ALGONQUIAN CHIEF IN WAR PAINT This sketch from the notebook of English settler John White depicts a Native American chief.

Eastern Woodland peoples Various Native American peoples, particularly the Algonquian, Iroquoian, and Muskogean regional groups, who once dominated the Atlantic seaboard from Maine to Louisiana.

growing elsewhere. As Cahokia disappeared, however, its former residents carried with them its cultural traditions, thereby spreading its advanced ways of life to other areas across the Midwest and into what is now the American South.

Eastern Woodland Peoples and European Contact

After the collapse of Cahokia, the **Eastern Woodland peoples** rose to dominance along the Atlantic seaboard from Maine to Florida and along the Gulf coast to Louisiana. They included three regional groups distinguished by their different languages: the Algonquian, the Iroquoian, and the Muskogean. These are the societies the English would first encounter when they arrived in North America.

The hundreds of Algonquian-speaking peoples stretched from the New England seaboard to lands along the Great Lakes and into the Upper Midwest and south to New Jersey, Virginia, and the Carolinas. The Algonquians along the coast were skilled at fishing; the inland Algonquians excelled at hunting. They used canoes made of hollowed-out tree trunks ("dugouts") or made from birch bark to travel down rivers and across lakes. Most Algonquians lived in small, round shelters called *wigwams* or in multifamily "longhouses." Their villages typically ranged in size from 500 to 2,000 inhabitants, but they often moved their villages with the seasons.

The Algonquians foraged for wild food (nuts, berries, and fruits) and practiced agriculture to some extent, regularly burning dense forests to improve soil fertility and provide grazing room for deer. To prepare their vegetable gardens, women broke up the ground with hoes tipped with clamshells or the shoulder blades from deer. In the spring, they planted corn, beans, and squash in mounds. As the cornstalks rose, the tendrils from the climbing bean plants wrapped around them for support. Once the crops ripened, women made *succotash*, a nutritious meal combining corn, beans, and squash.

West and south of the Algonquians were the Iroquoian-speaking peoples (including the Seneca, Onondaga, Mohawk, Oneida, and Cayuga nations, as well as the Cherokee and Tuscarora to the south), whose lands spread from upstate New York southward through Pennsylvania and into the upland regions of the Carolinas and Georgia. The Iroquois built no great mounds or pyramids. They were farmers who lived together in extended family groups ("clans"), sharing bark-covered longhouses in towns of 3,000 or more people. The most important crops were corn and squash, both of which figure prominently in Iroquois mythology.

Unlike the patriarchal Algonquian culture in which men were dominant, in Iroquoian society women held the key leadership roles (hence such cultures are called matriarchal). As an Iroquois elder explained, "In our society, women are the center of all things. Nature, we believe, has given women the ability to create; therefore, it is only natural that women be in positions of power to protect this function." Men and women were not treated as equals, however. Rather, the two genders operated in two separate social domains. No woman could be a chief; no man could head a clan. Women selected the chiefs, controlled the distribution of property, and planted as well as harvested the crops. After marriage, the man moved in with the wife's family.

War between rival groups of Native Americans, especially the Algonquians and Iroquois, was commonplace, usually as a means of settling feuds or gaining slaves. Success in fighting was a warrior's highest honor. As a Cherokee explained in the eighteenth century, "We cannot live without war. Should we make peace with the Tuscaroras, we must immediately look out for some other nation with whom we can engage in our beloved occupation."

> Warfare and rivalries

The third major Native American group in the Eastern Woodland included the southern peoples along the Gulf coast who spoke the Muskogean language: the Creek, Choctaw, Chickasaw, Seminole, Natchez, Apalachee, and Timucua. Like the Iroquois, these Muskogean-speaking peoples were often matrilineal societies, meaning that ancestry was traced only through the mother's line, but they had a more rigid class structure. The Muskogeans lived in towns arranged around a central plaza. In the Lower South (the current states of South Carolina, Georgia, Florida, Mississippi, and Alabama) many of their thatch-roofed houses had no walls because of the heat.

Over thousands of years, the indigenous North Americans had displayed remarkable resilience, adapting to the uncertainties of frequent warfare, changing climate, and varying environments. They would display similar resilience in the face of the challenges created by the arrival of Europeans. In the process of adapting their heritage and ways of life to unwanted new realities, the Native Americans played a significant role in shaping America.

The Expansion of Europe

> CORE **OBJECTIVE**
> **2.** Summarize the major developments in Europe that enabled the Age of Exploration.

The European exploration of the Western Hemisphere resulted from several key developments in the "Old World" during the fifteenth century. Dramatic intellectual changes and scientific discoveries affected religion, warfare, family life, and the economy. In addition, the resurgence of the old vices—greed, conquest, exploitation, oppression, racism, and slavery—would help fuel European expansion abroad.

By the end of the fifteenth century, medieval feudalism's static agrarian social system, whereby peasant serfs worked for local nobles in order to live on and farm the land, had largely died out. People were no longer forced to remain in the same locality and keep the same social status in which they were born. A new "middle class" of profit-hungry bankers, merchants, and investors emerged, men who were committed to a more dynamic commercial economy driven by innovations in banking, currency, accounting, and insurance.

> Rise of a middle class

Powerful new nations

The growing trade-based economy in Europe freed monarchs from their dependence on feudal nobles, enabling the monarchs to unify the scattered cities ruled by princes (principalities) into larger kingdoms with stronger, more centralized governments. The rise of towns, cities, and a merchant class provided monarchs with new tax revenues, and lesser agrarian-based nobles were displaced by the emergence of powerful new commercial *nations* governed by these centralized monarchical bureaucracies with the power to collect taxes.

The Renaissance

At the same time, the rediscovery of ancient Greek and Roman texts during the fourteenth and fifteenth centuries spurred the *Renaissance* (rebirth), an intellectual revolution that transformed the arts as well as traditional attitudes toward religion and science. The Renaissance began in Italy and spread across western Europe, bringing with it a more *secular* outlook that took greater interest in humanity than in religion.

Renaissance thinkers embraced intellectual curiosity and scientific inquiry. Educated people throughout Europe began to challenge medieval beliefs as well as the absolute authority of rulers and priests. They discussed controversial new ideas about politics, religion, and science; engaged in scientific research; and unleashed their artistic creativity—all in an effort to deepen their understanding of the natural world and human life, what colleges now call the humanities.

Innovations in shipbuilding, navigation, and weaponry lead to global revolution in maritime trade

This "rebirth" of learning began a long process of demystifying the biblical-centered view of the world by using scientific research to identify the natural laws that governed the universe. The Renaissance also involved the practical application of new ideas that enabled the Age of Exploration. New knowledge and new technologies made possible the construction of stronger, larger sailing ships armed with cannons and capable of oceanic voyages. The development of more-accurate magnetic compasses, maps, and navigational instruments enabled sailors to determine their location by reference to the sun or stars. The fifteenth and sixteenth centuries also witnessed the invention of gunpowder, cannons, and firearms—and the printing press.

The Rise of Global Trade

By the end of the fifteenth century, trade between western European nations and the Middle East and Asia became more important than ever. The Portuguese, blessed with expert sailors and fast new three-masted ships with multiple sails called *caravels*, launched the Age of Exploration during the fifteenth century. At the behest of Prince Henry the Navigator, a visionary ruler, Portuguese ships explored the Azores and the Canary Islands in the Atlantic. They also roamed far down the west coast of Africa in search of coveted grains, gold, ivory, spices (cinnamon, cloves, nutmeg, and ginger), and slaves. By the end of the fifteenth century, these profit-seeking mariners continued all the way around Africa in search of the fabled Indies (India and Southeast Asia), as well as China and Japan, rich with spices, silk cloth, and other exotic trade goods.

By 1500 C.E., four powerful nations had emerged in western Europe: England, France, Portugal, and Spain. The marriage of King Ferdinand of Aragon and Queen Isabella of Castile in 1469 resulted in the unification of their homelands into a single nation, Spain. Both Spanish monarchs were aggressive Christian expansionists. By 1492, they had forcibly expelled all Jews who did not convert to Christianity and were making plans for exploring west across the Atlantic Ocean.

The Voyages of Columbus

These were the circumstances that led Christopher Columbus's efforts to find a faster route to Japan and China by exploring west across the Atlantic. Born in Genoa, Italy, in 1451, the son of a weaver, Columbus took to the sea at an early age, teaching himself geography, navigation, and Latin. By the 1480s, he was eager to spread Christianity across the globe. The tall, blue-eyed Columbus initially asked Portugal to finance his explorations, but he was rebuffed. The dogged Columbus eventually persuaded Ferdinand and Isabella to finance his voyage. The legend that the queen had to sell the crown jewels to finance the voyage is as false as the fable that Columbus set out to prove the earth was round rather than flat. Most educated Europeans at the time knew that the earth was round.

On August 3, 1492, Columbus and ninety men and boys from eight different nations, set sail on three tiny ships, the *Santa María*, the *Pinta*, and the *Niña*. From Palos, Spain, they sailed first to Lisbon, Portugal, and then headed west. For weeks they journeyed across the open sea, hoping to sight land at any moment, only to be disappointed. By early October, the worried sailors grew rebellious at the "madness" of sailing blindly and threatened to take over the ships and turn back. Columbus was forced to promise that they would turn back if land were not sighted within three days.

Then, at dawn on October 12, a sailor stationed at the masthead yelled, *"Tierra! Tierra!"* ("Land! Land!"). He had spied "a white stretch of land" on an island in the Bahamas east of Florida that Columbus named San Salvador (Blessed Savior). Columbus mistakenly concluded that they must be near the Indies, so he called the island people *"Indios."* He reported that they went without clothes, painted their faces, wore necklaces, were "very timid" and "affectionate," had no "weapons," and would make "good subjects." At every encounter with these people, known as Tainos or Arawaks, he used sign language to ask if they had any gold. If they did, the Spaniards seized it; if they did not, the Europeans forced them to search for it.

After leaving San Salvador, Columbus continued to search for a passage to the Indies through the Bahamas and westward to Cuba, which he thought was part of Asia. There Columbus went ashore, sword in one hand, cross in the other, exclaiming that this was the "most beautiful land human

CHRISTOPHER COLUMBUS
A prominent and momentous explorer, Columbus reached the island of San Salvador in 1492, though he was under the impression he had landed by the Indies. Columbus made several trips back and forth across the Atlantic in the decade that followed, motivated by a combination of missionary zeal and the desire for the glory and riches that would come with the discovery of a new trade route to Asia.

Lust for gold

COLUMBUS'S VOYAGES

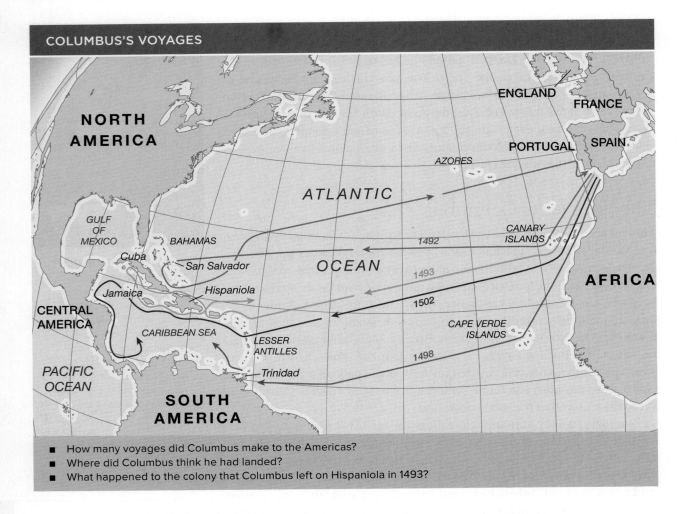

- How many voyages did Columbus make to the Americas?
- Where did Columbus think he had landed?
- What happened to the colony that Columbus left on Hispaniola in 1493?

eyes have ever beheld." He then sailed eastward to the island he named Hispaniola (later divided into Haiti and the Dominican Republic). There he met indigenous people who wore gold jewelry and introduced him to smoking tobacco.

At the end of 1492, Columbus, still convinced he had reached an outer island of Japan, sailed back to Spain after leaving about forty men on Hispaniola and capturing ten Arawaks to present as gifts to the king and queen. Upon reaching Spain, Columbus received a hero's welcome as he described a fascinating new world he had discovered, one alive with wonder, danger, and riches. "In thirty-three days," he reported, "I reached the *Indies*." Thanks to the newly invented printing press, news of his westward voyage spread rapidly across Europe. The Spanish monarchs, Ferdinand and Isabella, told Columbus to prepare for a second voyage, instructing him to "treat the Indians very well and lovingly and abstain from doing them any injury." Columbus and his men would repeatedly defy this order.

The Spanish monarchs wanted to strengthen their legal claim to the New World in case rival Portugal decided to send ships across the Atlantic. With the help of the Catholic pope (a Spaniard), rivals Spain and Portugal signed the Treaty of Tordesillas (1494), dividing the non-Christian world, with most of the New World given to Spain and with Africa and what would become Brazil granted to Portugal. In practice, this meant that while Spain developed its American empire in the sixteenth century, Portugal provided it with most of its enslaved African laborers.

Treaty of Tordesillas (1494)

Flush with the fame resulting from his first voyage, Columbus returned across the Atlantic in 1493 with seventeen ships, 1,400 men, and a few women. Also on board were Catholic priests and monks eager to convert the Indians to Christianity. Upon reaching the Caribbean, Columbus discovered that the men he had left behind on Hispaniola had lost their senses, raping women, robbing villages, and, as Columbus's son later added, "committing a thousand excesses for which they were mortally hated by the Indians."

Even more ghastly, however, was a hidden killer on board the Spanish ships. The Europeans carried with them a range of infectious diseases—smallpox, measles, mumps, typhus—that were unknown in the Americas and proved disastrous for the indigenous peoples, for they had no natural immunities to them. As many as 90 percent of the Native Americans were eventually killed by European-borne diseases. Proportionally, it was the worst human death toll in history.

Columbus would make two more voyages to the Caribbean, each time sending back to Spain hundreds of enslaved Indians. To the end of his life, he insisted that his ships had discovered the outlying parts of Asia, not a new continent. By one of history's greatest ironies, this led Europeans to name the New World not for Columbus but for another Italian sailor-explorer, Amerigo Vespucci, a talented merchant turned explorer. In 1499, with the support of Portugal's monarchy, Vespucci sailed west across the Atlantic, navigating by his knowledge of the sun and stars. He landed at Brazil and then sailed along 3,000 miles of the South American coastline in hopes of finding Asia. In the end, Vespucci reported that South America was so large that it must be a *new* continent he called the "New World," rather than Asia, as Columbus still believed. In 1507, a German mapmaker paid tribute to Vespucci's navigational skills by labeling the New World using the feminine variant of the explorer's first name: America.

Vespucci's New World continent

Professional Explorers

News of the remarkable voyages of Columbus and Vespucci stimulated many other expeditions to the Western Hemisphere. Over the next two centuries, Spain, Portugal, France, Britain, the Netherlands, and Russia would dispatch ships and claim territory in the Americas by "right of discovery."

The first explorer to sight the North American continent was John Cabot, an Italian sponsored by King Henry VII of England. Cabot's landfall

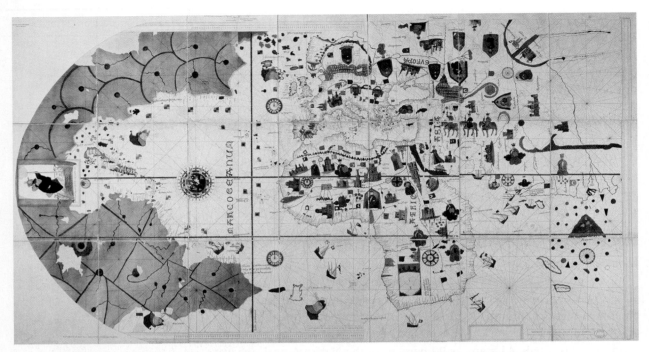

THE OLD AND NEW WORLDS The *mappa mundi*, or "map of the world," was drawn by Juan de la Cosa in 1500 and is the first known European map to include the "New World." An explorer himself, de la Cosa made many trips across the Atlantic, some of them in the company of Columbus and Vespucci. **According to this map, what misconceptions did European explorers have about the world's geography?**

in 1497 at what the king called "the new founde lande," in present-day Canada, gave England the basis for a later claim to *all* North America.

The English were then unaware that Norsemen ("Vikings") from Scandinavia had in fact been the first Europeans to "discover" and colonize areas of North America. As early as the tenth century, Norsemen had explored Greenland, a vast island off the northeast coast of North America, and established settlements there that lasted for almost 500 years.

The Spanish were determined to keep the English and any other Europeans out of the New World they claimed for themselves. In 1505, a Spanish ship unloaded pigs and goats in Puerto Rico, intending them to grow and multiply in anticipation of settling a colony there. It would be the first European settlement on what would much later become a territory of the United States of America.

Religious Conflict in Europe

At the same time that the European explorers were crossing the Atlantic, powerful religious conflicts were tearing Europe apart in ways that would greatly influence settlement in the New World. The Protestant Reformation became one of the most powerful forces reshaping Europe—and its colonies.

When Columbus sailed west in 1492, Roman Catholicism had long been the unifying force of Europe. All of Europe acknowledged the thousand-year-old supremacy of the Roman Catholic Church and its pope in Rome. The brutal efforts of the Spanish to convert Indians to **Roman Catholicism** illustrated the murderous intensity with which Europeans embraced religious life in the sixteenth century. Spiritual concerns inspired, comforted, and united people. People believed in heaven and hell, devils and witches, demons and angels, magic and miracles. And Christians were willing to kill and die for their beliefs.

Yet the enforced unity of Catholic Europe began to crack on October 31, 1517, when Martin Luther (1483–1546), an obscure thirty-three-year-old German monk who taught at the University of Wittenberg, nailed ninety-five "theses" to the door of All Saints' Church. His purpose was to generate a debate about the "corrupt" Catholic Church. Little did he know that his rebellious ideas would launch one of history's fiercest spiritual dramas, the **Protestant Reformation**, or that his ideas would change the course of history.

Luther was a profound and combative spiritual thinker, a true spiritual revolutionary who fractured Christianity by undermining the authority of the Catholic Church. He called the pope "the greatest thief and robber that has appeared or can appear on earth." Luther especially criticized the widespread sale of *indulgences* (whereby priests would forgive sins in exchange for money). For centuries, the Catholic Church had used the revenue from indulgences to raise armies and build cathedrals. Luther condemned indulgences as a crass form of thievery. God alone, through the grace and sheer mercy of Christ, he insisted, offered people salvation; people could not earn everlasting life through *good works,* nor could they buy it with money. As Luther exclaimed, "By faith alone are you saved!"

Through this simple but revolutionary doctrine, Luther sought to revitalize Christianity's original faith and spirituality. The common people, he insisted, represented a "priesthood of all believers." Because God was responsible for the salvation of each believer, priests, bishops, and the huge Catholic bureaucracy were no longer necessary. Luther's insistence on what he called "personal thinking" over the authority of priests and bishops became the Reformation's great contribution to the evolution of the Christian faith.

Luther democratized Christianity by urging believers to learn to read and write so that they could read the Bible for themselves rather than blindly follow the dictates of Catholic priests and the distant pope in Rome. To enable Christians to be their own "priests," Luther produced the first Bible in a German translation.

MARTIN LUTHER A theologian and critic of the Catholic Church, Luther is best remembered for his ninety-five "theses," an incendiary document that served as a catalyst for the Protestant Revolution.

Roman Catholicism The Christian faith and religious practices of the Roman Catholic Church, which exerted great political, economic, and social influence on much of western Europe and, through the Spanish and Portuguese Empires, on the Americas.

Protestant Reformation Sixteenth-century religious movement initiated by Martin Luther, a German monk whose public criticism of corruption in the Roman Catholic Church and whose teaching that Christians can communicate directly with God gained a wide following.

Pope Leo X and other horrified Catholic officials lashed out at Luther's "dangerous doctrines," calling him a "wild boar" and "a leper with a brain of brass and a nose of iron." Luther fought back with equal fury, declaring that he was "born to war." In 1520, he charged in an open letter to the pope that the Catholic Church, "once the holiest of all, had become the most licentious den of thieves, the most shameless of brothels, the kingdom of sin, death, and hell." Luther refused to abide by any papal decrees, declaring that he was bound only by his conscience. "I will recant nothing!" The "die is cast!" Luther stressed, "and I will have no reconciliation with the Pope for all eternity."

> **Protestant Reformation**

When the pope expelled Luther from the Catholic Church in 1521 and the Holy Roman emperor sentenced him to death, civil war erupted throughout the German principalities (the various German-speaking regions did not become a united nation until 1871). A powerful German prince protected Luther from the church's wrath.

> **Wars and upheavals**

What had begun as a religious movement now became a political reformation spanning the entire continent of Europe. Luther was no longer simply an outspoken priest; he was a spiritual revolutionary, a folk hero, and a political prophet, encouraging German princes and dukes to separate themselves from the Italian papacy. A settlement between warring Lutherans and Catholics did not come until 1555, when each prince was allowed by the Treaty of Augsburg to determine the religion of his subjects.

Soon after Martin Luther began his revolt against the shortcomings of Catholicism, Swiss Protestants also challenged papal authority. In Geneva, the movement looked to John Calvin (1509–1564), a brilliant French scholar who had fled to that city and brought it under the sway of his powerful beliefs. In his great theological work, *The Institutes of the Christian Religion* (1536), Calvin set forth a stern doctrine. All people, he taught, were damned by Adam's original sin, but the sacrifice of Christ on the cross made possible the redemption of those whom God had "elected" and thus had predestined to salvation from the beginning of time.

Intoxicated by godliness and driven by a reforming spirit, Calvin set about transforming Geneva into a strictly regulated godly city. He insisted upon strict morality and hard work, values that especially suited the rising middle class. Moreover, he taught that God valued every form of work, however menial it might be. Calvin also permitted lay members a share in the governance of the church through a body of elders and ministers called the presbytery. At the same time, however, Calvin ruled Geneva like a tyrant, demanding absolute obedience. He ordered fifty-eight people put to death and banished many more.

Calvinism spread like wildfire across France, Scotland, and the Netherlands and even penetrated Lutheran Germany. It formed the basis for the German Reformed Church, the Dutch Reformed Church, the Presbyterians in Scotland, some of the Puritans in England (and eventually America), and the Huguenots in France.

Through these and other groups, John Calvin exerted a greater effect upon religious belief and practice in the English colonies than did any other leader of the Reformation. His insistence on the freedom of individual believers, as well as his recognition that monarchs and political officials were sinful like everyone else, helped contribute to the evolving ideas in Europe of representative democracy and the importance of separating church power from state (governmental) power, ideas that crossed the Atlantic and formed the foundation of American religious and political life.

The Catholic Church resisted the emergence of new "protestant" faiths by launching a "Counter-Reformation" that reaffirmed basic Catholic beliefs while addressing some of the concerns about priestly abuses raised by Luther, Calvin, and others. In Spain, the monarchy created an "Inquisition" to root out protestants and heretics. In 1534, a Spanish soldier named Ignatius de Loyola organized the Society of Jesus, a militant new monastic order created to revitalize Catholicism around the world. Its members, the black-robed Jesuits, fanned out across Europe and the Americas as courageous Catholic missionaries and teachers.

Catholic Counter-Reformation

Despite such Catholic efforts to blunt the appeal of Protestantism, the Reformation succeeded in permanently fragmenting Christianity. It spread rapidly across northern Europe during the sixteenth century. Most of Germany, along with Scandinavia, became Lutheran, often calling themselves the "Protesting Estates," from which derived the label "Protestants." The Reformation thus became in part a theological dispute, in part a political movement, and in part a *catalyst* for social change, civil strife, and imperial warfare.

Throughout the sixteenth and seventeenth centuries, Catholics and Protestants persecuted, imprisoned, tortured, and killed each other in large numbers in Europe—and in the Americas. Protestants also warred against rival Protestants. Every major international conflict became, to some extent, a religious holy war between Catholic and Protestant nations. Equally important, the Protestant worldview, with its emphasis on the freedom of the individual conscience and personal Bible reading, would play a major role in the colonization of America and the development of the American character.

The Reformation in England

In England, the Reformation followed a unique course. The Church of England, or the Anglican Church, emerged through a gradual process of integrating Calvinism with English Catholicism. In early modern England, the church and government were united and mutually supportive. The monarchy required people to attend religious services and to pay taxes to support the church. English rulers also supervised the church officials and often instructed religious leaders to preach sermons in support of particular government policies. As one English king explained, "People are governed by the pulpit more than the sword in time of peace."

Purely political reasons initially led to the rejection of papal authority in England. Henry VIII, who ruled between 1509 and 1547, won from the pope the title Defender of the Faith for refuting Martin Luther's rebellious ideas. Henry's marriage to Catherine of Aragon, his brother's widow, had produced no male heir, however, and for him to marry again required that he convince the pope to annul, or cancel, his marriage. Catherine, however, was the aunt of Charles V, king of Spain and ruler of the Holy Roman Empire, whose support was vital to the Catholic Church. The pope refused to grant an annulment. In a fit of rage, Henry severed England's nearly 900-year-old connection with the Catholic Church. He then named a new archbishop of Canterbury, who granted the annulment, thus freeing Henry to marry his mistress, Anne Boleyn.

In one of history's greatest ironies, Anne Boleyn gave birth not to the male heir that Henry demanded but to a daughter named Elizabeth (1533–1603). The disappointed king took vengeance on his wife, accusing her of adultery, ordering her beheaded, and declaring the infant princess Elizabeth a bastard.

Yet the unwanted Elizabeth, tutored by distinguished scholars, grew up to be quick-witted and nimble, cunning and courageous, a woman so strong,

QUEEN ELIZABETH The *Armada Portrait*, painted in 1588 by George Gower, portrays Queen Elizabeth at the height of her reign. A scene in the background features England's victory over the attacking Spanish fleet, the Armada, while in the foreground Elizabeth's right hand rests on a globe, signifying the English expansion into the New World.

a ruler so skillful, a monarch so charismatic, that she united a small, fragmented, and poor island society into a nation of global ambition. After the bloody reigns of her Protestant half brother, Edward VI, and her zealously Catholic half sister, Mary I, she ascended to the throne in 1558, at the age of twenty-five.

Over the next forty-five years, Elizabeth proved to be the greatest female ruler in history. Her long reign was punctuated by political turmoil, religious strife, economic crises, menacing threats, and foreign wars. Yet Queen Elizabeth, an unmarried Protestant in a still Catholic- and male-dominated Europe, a monarch who escaped numerous assassination attempts and persecuted as well as executed Catholics, ruled confidently over England's golden age. She once told Parliament to remember her as "a Queen, having reigned, lived, and died a virgin." To the end, she was married only to England. "We all loved her," wrote her godson, "for she said she loved us."

The Spanish Empire

During the sixteenth century, Catholic Spaniards used a mixture of courage, cruelty, piety, and greed to create the world's most powerful empire. At its height, it encompassed much of Europe, most of the Americas, parts of Africa, and various trading outposts in Asia. But it was the gold and silver looted from the Americas that fueled the engine of Spain's "Golden Empire." By plundering, conquering, and colonizing the Americas and enslaving the indigenous peoples, the Spanish planted Christianity in the Western Hemisphere and gained the resources to rule the world.

> CORE **OBJECTIVE**
> **3.** Describe how the Spanish were able to conquer and colonize the Americas.

The Caribbean Sea served as the gateway through which Spanish power entered the Americas. After establishing colonies on Hispaniola, including Santo Domingo, which became the capital of the West Indies, the Spanish proceeded eastward to Puerto Rico (1508) and westward to Cuba (1511–1514). Their motives, as one soldier explained, were "to serve God and the king, and also to get rich."

> Spanish foothold in the Caribbean

Many of the Europeans in the first wave of settlement in the New World died of malnutrition or disease. But the Native Americans suffered far more casualties, for they were ill equipped to resist the European invaders. Disunity everywhere—civil disorder, rebellion, and tribal warfare—left them vulnerable to division and foreign conquest. Attacks by well-armed soldiers and deadly germs from Europe overwhelmed entire indigenous societies.

A Clash of Cultures

The often-violent encounter between Spaniards and Native Americans involved more than a clash between different cultures. It also involved contrasting forms of technological development. The Indians of Mexico used wooden canoes for water transportation, while the Europeans crossed the seas in

> Lethal weapons and warhorses

much larger, heavily armed sailing vessels. The Spanish ships carried not only human cargo but also warhorses and fighting dogs, long steel swords, crossbows, firearms, explosives, and armor. The wood-tipped arrows and tomahawks used by Native Americans were no match. "The most essential thing in new lands is horses," reported one Spanish soldier. "They instill the greatest fear in the enemy and make the Indians respect the leaders of the army."

Cortés's Conquest

Rivals collaborate against the Mexica

The most dramatic European conquest of a major Indian civilization on the North American mainland occurred in Mexico. On February 18, 1519, Hernán Cortés, driven by audacious dreams of gold and glory, set sail for Mexico from Cuba. He had grown weary of seeking a fortune in Cuba, explaining that "I came here to get rich, not to till the soil like a peasant." His fleet of eleven ships carried nearly 600 soldiers and sailors. Also on board were 200 indigenous Cubans, sixteen warhorses, greyhound fighting dogs, and cannons. After the Spanish landed on the coast of the Gulf of Mexico, Cortés, greatly benefiting from the services of an Indian woman, Doña Marina, as an interpreter (she would later bear Cortés a son), convinced the local Totomacs to join his assault against the Mexica, their hated rivals. To prevent any of his soldiers, called **conquistadores** (conquerors), from deserting, Cortés had the ships scuttled, sparing one vessel to carry the expected gold back to Spain.

With his small army and Indian allies, Cortés brashly set out to conquer the sprawling Mexica (Aztec) Empire, which extended from central Mexico to what is today Guatemala. The nearly 200-mile trek of Cortés's army through the mountains to the magnificent Mexica capital of Tenochtitlán took nearly three months.

Spanish Invaders

As the Spanish invaders marched across Mexico, they heard fabulous accounts of the splendor and riches of Tenochtitlán. With more than 200,000 inhabitants, it was the largest city in the Americas and much larger than most European cities. Cortés wrote the Spanish king that the imperial palace was "so marvelous that there is nothing like it in Spain." The market square, he added, was larger than those in any European city. Every day, 60,000 people gathered there to buy food and other items. Graced by wide canals, stunning gardens, and formidable stone streets, houses, and pyramids, the lake-encircled capital seemed unconquerable, but Cortés made the most of his assets. Through a combination of threats and deceptions, Cortés and his Indian allies entered Tenochtitlán peacefully and captured the emperor, Montezuma II. Cortés explained to the Aztec ruler why the invasion was necessary: "We Spaniards have a disease of the heart that only gold can cure."

After taking the Mexicas' gold and silver, the Spanish forced them to mine more of the precious metals. Then, in the spring of 1520, disgruntled Mexica

conquistadores Spanish term for "conquerors," applied to Spanish and Portuguese soldiers who conquered lands held by indigenous peoples in central and southern America as well as the current states of Texas, New Mexico, Arizona, and California.

CORTÉS IN MEXICO A page from the *Lienzo de Tlaxcala*, a historical narrative from the sixteenth century. The scene, in which Cortés is shown seated on a throne, depicts the arrival of the Spanish in Tlaxcala.

decided that Montezuma was a traitor. They rebelled, stoned him to death, and attacked the Spaniards. Forced to retreat to the mainland, the Spaniards lost about a third of their men. Their 20,000 Indian allies remained loyal, however, and Cortés regrouped his forces. For months, sporadic fighting continued. In 1521, having been reinforced with more soldiers from Cuba and thousands more Native Americans eager to defeat the despised Mexica, he surrounded the imperial city for eighty-five days, cutting off its access to water and food and allowing a smallpox epidemic to devastate the inhabitants.

For three months, the Mexica bravely defended their capital. Then the siege came to a bloody end. The ravages of smallpox and starvation, as well as the support of 75,000 anti-Mexica Indian allies, help explain how such a small force of determined Spaniards was able to vanquish a proud nation of nearly 1 million people. After 15,000 Mexica were slaughtered, the others surrendered. A merciless Cortés ordered the leaders hanged and the priests devoured by dogs. In two years, Cortés and his disciplined army had conquered a fabled empire that had taken centuries to develop.

Cortés's conquest of Mexico established the model for waves of plundering conquistadores to follow. Within twenty years, Spain had established a vast empire in Mexico and the Caribbean, which Cortés called "New Spain," based on a pattern of ruthless violence and enslavement of the indigenous peoples followed by oppressive rule over them—just as the Mexica had done in forming their own empire.

In 1531, another Spaniard, Francisco Pizarro, led a band of soldiers down the Pacific coast of Central and South America from Panama toward Peru, where they brutally subdued the Inca Empire. From Peru, Spain extended its control southward through Chile by about 1553 and north, to present-day Colombia, by 1538.

> Cortés conquers the Mexica, and Pizarro invades the Inca

Spanish America

The crusading conquistadores transferred to Hispanic America a socioeconomic system known as the ***encomienda***, whereby favored officers were transformed into privileged landowners who controlled Indian villages. As *encomenderos*, they protected the villages in exchange for the Indians' providing them with goods and labor. Hispanic America therefore developed a society of extremes: wealthy conquistadores, *encomenderos,* and priests at one end of the spectrum and Indians held in poverty at the other end.

CORE **OBJECTIVE**

4. Assess the impact of the Columbian Exchange on the "Old" and "New" Worlds.

The Columbian Exchange

The first European contacts with the Native Americans of the Western Hemisphere unleashed an unprecedented and unintended **Columbian Exchange**, now sometimes called the Great Biological Exchange—a worldwide transfer of plants, animals, and diseases that ultimately worked in favor of the Europeans at the expense of the indigenous peoples.

If anything, the plants, animals, insects, and microbes of the two worlds were more different from each other than were the peoples and their ways of life. Europeans had never seen creatures such as iguanas, bison, cougars, armadillos, opossums, sloths, and hummingbirds. Turkeys, guinea pigs, llamas, and alpacas were also new to Europeans. Nor did the Native Americans know of horses, cattle, pigs, sheep, goats, chickens, and rats, which soon arrived from Europe in abundance.

The exchange of plant life between the Americas and Europe/Africa transformed the diets of both hemispheres. Before Columbus's voyage, three foods were unknown in Europe: maize (corn), potatoes (sweet and white), and many kinds of beans (snap, kidney, lima, and others). The white potato, although commonly called Irish, originated in South America. Explorers brought it back to Europe, where it thrived. The "Irish potato" was eventually transported to North America by Scots-Irish immigrants during the early eighteenth century. Other Western Hemisphere food plants included peanuts, squash, peppers, tomatoes, pumpkins, pineapples, sassafras, papayas, guavas, avocados, cacao (the source of chocolate), and chicle (for chewing gum). Europeans in turn introduced rice, wheat, barley, oats, wine grapes,

encomienda A land-grant system under which Spanish army officers (*conquistadores*) were awarded large parcels of land taken from Native Americans.

Columbian Exchange The transfer of biological and social elements, such as plants, animals, people, diseases, and cultural practices, among Europe, the Americas, and Africa in the wake of Christopher Columbus's voyages to the New World.

melons, coffee, olives, bananas, "Kentucky" bluegrass, daisies, and dandelions to the Americas.

The beauty of the biological exchange was that the food plants were more complementary than competitive. Corn, it turned out, could flourish almost anywhere in the world. The nutritious food crops exported from the Americas, especially the potato, helped nourish a worldwide population explosion probably greater than any since the invention of agriculture. The new food crops spurred a dramatic increase in the European population that in turn provided the restless, adventurous young people who would colonize the New World.

By far, however, the most significant aspect of the biological exchange was the transmission of **infectious diseases**. During the three centuries after Columbus's first voyage, Europeans and Africans brought with them deadly diseases that Native Americans had never encountered: smallpox, typhus, malaria, mumps, chickenpox, and measles. The results were catastrophic. Far more people—tens of millions—died from smallpox than from combat. By 1568, just seventy-five years after Columbus's first voyage, infectious diseases had killed 80–90 percent of the Indian population—the greatest loss of human life in history.

SMALLPOX The infectious diseases colonists carried with them to the New World decimated the Native American population. In this illustration, Aztec victims of the 1538 smallpox epidemic are covered in shrouds (center) as two others lie dying (at right).

Spanish Exploration in North America

> CORE **OBJECTIVE**
> **5.** Analyze the legacy of Spanish colonization on North American history.

Throughout the sixteenth century, no European power other than Spain held more than a brief foothold in the Americas. Spain had the advantage not only of having arrived first but also of having stumbled onto those regions that would produce the quickest profits. While France and England were preoccupied with political disputes and religious conflict, Catholic Spain had forged an authoritarian national and religious unity that enabled it to dominate Europe as well as the New World. The treasures seized from Mexico and Peru added to Spain's power, but the single-minded focus on gold and silver also tempted the Spanish government to live beyond its means. Between 1557 and 1662, the kings of Spain were forced to declare bankruptcy ten times.

For most of the colonial period, much of what is now the United States, from the Southwest across the continent to Florida, an area larger than western Europe, was claimed by Spain, and Spanish culture etched a lasting imprint upon America's future ways of life. Spain's crusade to spread Hispanic power, culture, and Catholicism across the Americas lasted more than three centuries. New Spain was centered in Mexico, but its frontier outposts in

infectious diseases Also called contagious diseases, illnesses that can pass from one person to another by way of invasive biological organisms able to reproduce in the bodily tissues of their hosts. Europeans unwittingly brought many such diseases to the Americas, devastating the Native American peoples.

SPANISH EXPLORATIONS OF THE MAINLAND

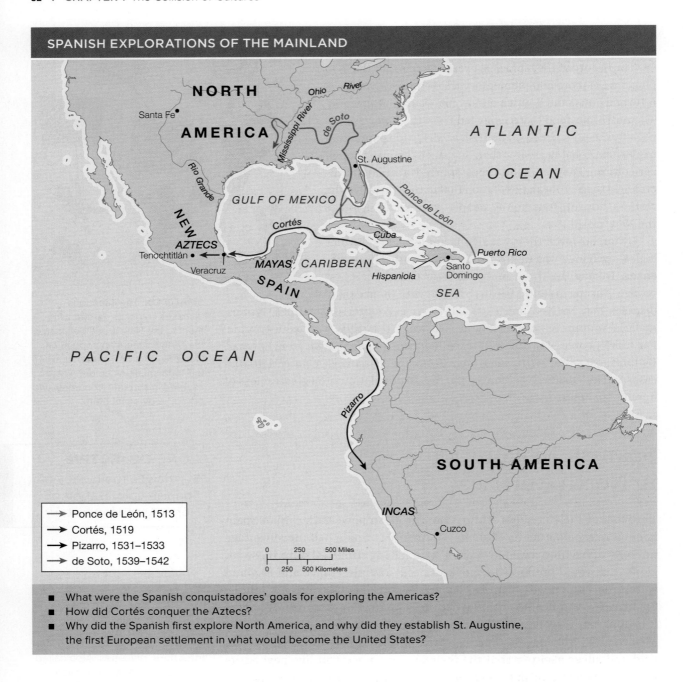

Ponce de León, 1513
Cortés, 1519
Pizarro, 1531–1533
de Soto, 1539–1542

0   250   500 Miles
0   250   500 Kilometers

■ What were the Spanish conquistadores' goals for exploring the Americas?
■ How did Cortés conquer the Aztecs?
■ Why did the Spanish first explore North America, and why did they establish St. Augustine, the first European settlement in what would become the United States?

North America extended from California to Virginia and from Florida to Alaska. Hispanic place-names—San Francisco, Santa Barbara, Los Angeles, San Diego, Santa Fe, San Antonio, Pensacola, and St. Augustine—survive to this day, as do Hispanic influences in art, architecture, literature, music, law, and food.

In 1513, Juan Ponce de León, then governor of Puerto Rico, made the earliest known European exploration of Florida, hoping to find gold and

> Three centuries of Spanish domination and Hispanic influence

Indian slaves. Meanwhile, Spanish explorers sailed along the Gulf of Mexico coast from Florida to Mexico, scouted the Atlantic coast all the way to Canada, and established a short-lived colony on the Carolina coast.

In 1539, Hernando de Soto and 600 conquistadores landed on Florida's west coast, traveled north as far as western North Carolina, and then moved westward across Tennessee, Georgia, Alabama, and the Mississippi River. Along the way, they encountered many large Indian towns and vast cornfields. After crossing the Mississippi, they went up the Arkansas River, looting and destroying Indian villages along the way, leaving behind shattered lives and burnt communities. In the spring of 1542, de Soto died near Natchez, Mississippi; the next year, the survivors among his party floated down the Mississippi River, and 311 of the original adventurers made their way to Spanish Mexico.

The Spanish established provinces in North America not so much as commercial enterprises but as defensive buffers protecting their more profitable empires in Mexico and South America. In 1565, Pedro Menendez de Aviles, a Spanish smuggler, led a ragtag group of 1,500 soldiers and colonists in founding an outpost on the Florida coast, St. Augustine, which became the first permanent European settlement in the present-day United States. It included a fort, church, hospital, fish market, and over a hundred shops and houses—all built decades before the first English settlements at Jamestown and Plymouth. While other early American outposts failed, St. Augustine, the only Hispanic settlement in Florida until Pensacola was founded in 1698, survived as a defensive base perched on the southern edge of a continent.

The Spanish Southwest

The Spanish eventually established other permanent settlements in what are now New Mexico, Texas, and California. Missionaries built Catholic missions, where they imposed Christianity on the Indians and treated them like slaves. After about ten years, a mission would be secularized: its lands would be divided among the converted Indians, the mission chapel would become a parish church, and the inhabitants would be given full Spanish citizenship—including the privilege of paying taxes. The soldiers who were sent to protect the missions were housed in *presidios*, or forts.

The land that would later be called **New Mexico** was a center of Catholic missionary activity in the American Southwest. In 1598, Juan de Oñate, the rich son of a Spanish mining family in Mexico, received a land grant for the territory north of Mexico above the Rio Grande. He then recruited soldiers and hundreds of Mexican Indians and *mestizos* (the offspring of Spanish fathers and Indian mothers), including women, children, and priests. The caravan of colonists, including animals and carts carrying supplies, began moving north from the mountains above Mexico City. After walking over 800 miles in seven months, they established the colony of New Mexico near present-day Santa Fe ("Holy Faith" in Spanish), and sent

New Mexico A region in the American Southwest, originally established by the Spanish, who settled there in the sixteenth century, founded Catholic missions, and exploited the region's indigenous peoples.

CULTURAL CONFLICT This Peruvian illustration, from a 1612–1615 manuscript by Felipe Guamán Poma de Ayala, shows a Dominican Catholic friar forcing an indigenous woman to weave. **What does this image show about the Spanish missionary's treatment of the indigenous peoples?**

out expeditions to search for gold and silver. Oñate told the local Indians, called Pueblos, that they now belonged to Spain, but he promised that the Spaniards would bring them peace, justice, prosperity, and protection. If they embraced Christianity, Oñate added, the Indians would receive "an eternal life of great bliss" instead of "cruel and everlasting torment."

Some Indians welcomed the Spanish missionaries as "powerful witches" capable of easing their burdens. Others tried to use the European invaders as allies against rival Indian groups. Still others saw no alternative but to submit. The Indians living in Spanish New Mexico were required to pay tribute to their *encomenderos* and perform personal tasks for them, including sexual favors.

Before the end of New Mexico's first year as a colony, in December 1598, the Pueblos revolted, killing several soldiers. During three days of relentless fighting, vengeful Spanish soldiers killed 500 Pueblo men and 300 women and children. Survivors were enslaved. To discourage rebelliousness, Oñate ordered that all Pueblo men over the age of twenty-five have one foot cut off. Children were taken from their parents into a Catholic mission, where, Oñate pledged, they would "attain the knowledge of God and the salvation of their souls."

Spanish New Mexico expanded very slowly. The hoped-for deposits of gold and silver were never found, and a lack of rain for farming blunted the interest of potential colonists. In 1608, the government decided to turn New Mexico into a royal province. The following year it dispatched a royal governor, and in 1610, as the first English settlers were struggling to survive at Jamestown, in Virginia, the Spanish moved the province's capital to Santa Fe, the first permanent seat of government in the present-day United States. By 1630, there were fifty Catholic churches and monasteries in New Mexico, as well as some 3,000 Spaniards.

Roman Catholic missionaries in New Mexico claimed that 86,000 Pueblos had been converted to Christianity during the seventeenth century. In fact, however, few of the coerced conversions were genuine. Resentment among the Pueblos against Spanish Catholic authority increased with time.

Catholicism in New Spain and the Pueblo Revolt (1680)

"The heathen," reported a Spanish soldier, "have conceived a mortal hatred for our holy faith and enmity [hatred] for the Spanish nation."

In 1680, a powerful Indian leader named Popé organized what is called the Pueblo Revolt, a massive rebellion against the Spanish. The Pueblo rebels burned Catholic churches; tortured, mutilated, and executed priests; destroyed all relics of Christianity, and banned the Spanish language. More than 400 Spaniards were killed out of a population of 2,500. Terrified survivors fled down the Rio Grande to El Paso. Popé then established Santa Fe as the capital of his confederacy.

The Pueblo Revolt of 1680 was the greatest defeat that Indians ever inflicted on European efforts to conquer the New World. It took fourteen years and four military campaigns for the Spanish to reestablish control over New Mexico.

Horses and the Great Plains

Another major consequence of the Pueblo Revolt was the opportunity it gave Indians to take hundreds of Spanish horses (Spanish authorities had made it illegal for Indians to own horses). The Pueblos in turn established a thriving horse trade with Navajos, Apaches, Comanches, and others who became expert and ferocious horseback warriors. By 1690, horses were in Texas, and they soon spread across the Great Plains, the vast, rolling grasslands extending from the Missouri Valley in the east to the base of the Rocky Mountains in the west.

Prior to the arrival of horses, Native Americans hunted on foot and used dogs as their beasts of burden. Dogs are carnivores, however, and it was always difficult to find enough meat to feed them. The introduction of the **horse** changed everything, though, providing the Plains Indians with a new source of mobility and power. Horses are grazing animals, and the vast grasslands of the Great Plains offered plenty of forage. Horses could also haul up to seven times as much weight as dogs, and their speed and endurance made the indigenous people much more effective hunters and warriors. They relieved women of many burdensome duties and allowed warriors to make crushing raids against other tribes. Horses grew so valuable that they became a form of Indian currency and a sign of wealth and prestige.

| Horses and bison |

French and Dutch Exploration of America

Catholic Spain's conquests in the Western Hemisphere spurred Portugal, France, England, and the Netherlands (Holland) to begin their own exploration and exploitation of the New World. The French were the first to pose a serious threat to New Spain. Spanish treasure ships sailing home from Mexico, Peru, and the Caribbean islands offered tempting targets for French privateers (privately owned warships) and pirates. The French also began looking for a passage to Asia through the Americas. In 1524, the French king sent the Italian Giovanni da Verrazano westward across the Atlantic. Upon sighting land (probably at Cape Fear, North Carolina), Verrazano ranged

| Spanish rivals for New World wealth |

horse The Spanish introduced horses to the Americas, eventually transforming many Native American cultures.

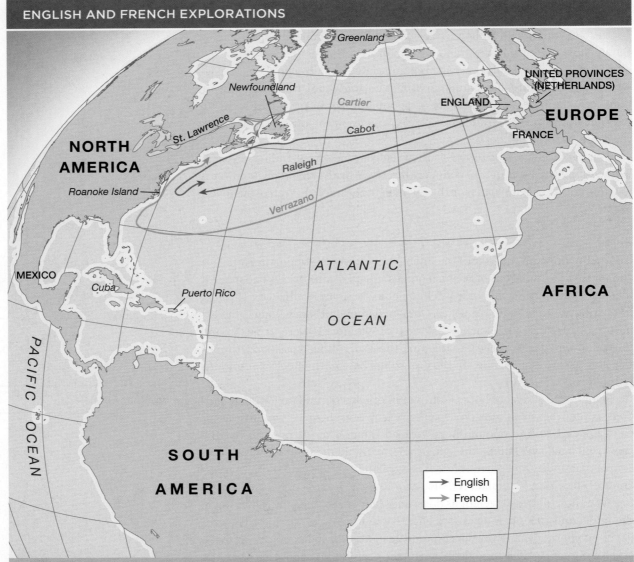

ENGLISH AND FRENCH EXPLORATIONS

- Who were the first European explorers to rival Spanish dominance in the New World, and why did they cross the Atlantic?
- Why was the defeat of the Spanish Armada important to the history of English exploration? What was the significance of Raleigh's voyages?

along the coast as far north as Maine. On a second voyage, in 1528, he was killed in the West Indies by Carib Indians.

Unlike the Verrazano voyages, those of Jacques Cartier, beginning in the next decade, led to the first French effort at colonization in North America. During three voyages, Cartier explored the Gulf of St. Lawrence and ventured up the St. Lawrence River, now the boundary between Canada and

New York. Twice he got as far as present-day Montreal, and twice he wintered at the site of Quebec, near which a short-lived French colony appeared in 1541–1542. From that time forward, however, French kings lost interest in Canada for over a half century.

Greater threats to Spanish power arose from the Dutch and the English. The United Provinces of the Netherlands, which had passed by inheritance to the Spanish king but had become largely Protestant, rebelled against Spanish Catholic rule in 1567. A long, bloody struggle for independence ensued in which Protestant England aided the Dutch.

Almost from the beginning of the Protestant Dutch revolt against Catholic Spain, the Dutch plundered Spanish treasure ships in the Atlantic and carried on illegal trade with Spain's colonies. While England's Queen Elizabeth, a Protestant, steered a tortuous course to avoid open war with Spain, she secretly encouraged both Dutch and English privateers ("sea dogs") to attack Spanish ships and their colonies in the Americas.

The Defeat of the Armada

The English raids on Spanish shipping continued for twenty years before open war erupted between the two nations. Determined to conquer England, Philip II, the king of Catholic Spain who was Queen Elizabeth's brother-in-law and fiercest opponent, assembled in 1588 the massive **Spanish Armada**: 132 warships, 8,000 sailors, and 18,000 soldiers—the greatest invasion fleet in history to that point. On May 28, 1588, the Armada sailed north, determined to conquer the English and restore them to Catholicism. As the battle unfolded, the larger Spanish warships could not compete with the speed and agility of the smaller English ships. The English chased the Armada through the English Channel before a terrible storm swept the Spanish fleet into the North Sea, destroying dozens of the world's finest warships. The shipwrecked soldiers or sailors who made it to shore were executed on the spot. England's stunning defeat of Catholic Spain's fearsome Armada strengthened the Protestant cause across Europe.

> The English defeat the Spanish Armada (1588).

The great naval victory was the climactic event of Queen Elizabeth's long reign. England at the end of the sixteenth century was surging with new power and optimism, filled with a youthful zest for exploring new worlds. The defeat of the Spanish Armada marked the beginning of England's global naval supremacy and cleared the way for English colonization of America. English colonists could now make their way to North America without fear of Spanish interference.

English Exploration of America

English efforts to colonize America began a few years before the great battle with the Spanish Armada. In 1584, Queen Elizabeth asked Sir Walter Raleigh, a favorite of the queen, to organize a colonizing mission. Raleigh's expedition discovered the Outer Banks of North Carolina and landed at Roanoke Island. Raleigh named the area Virginia, in honor of childless Queen Elizabeth,

Spanish Armada A massive Spanish fleet of 130 warships that was defeated at Plymouth in 1588 by the English navy during the reign of Queen Elizabeth I.

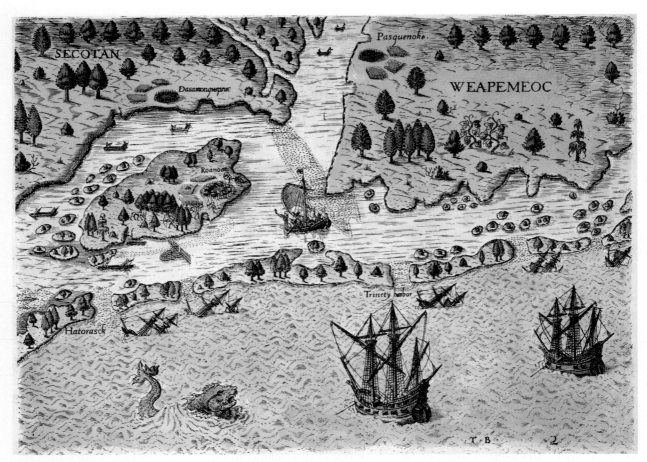

THE ENGLISH IN VIRGINIA This map depicts the arrival of English explorers on the Outer Banks. Roanoke Island and its colony are on the left.

the "Virgin Queen," who herself chose the name. After several false starts, Raleigh in 1587 sponsored another expedition of about a hundred colonists, including 26 women and children, led by Governor John White. White spent a month on Roanoke Island and then returned to England for supplies, leaving behind his daughter, Eleanor, and his granddaughter, Virginia Dare, the first English child born in the New World. White's journey back to Virginia was delayed because of the naval war with Spain. When he finally returned to America in 1590, he discovered that the Roanoke outpost had been abandoned and looted.

The lost Roanoke colony

No trace of the "lost colonists" was ever found. Indians may have killed them, or hostile Spaniards—who had certainly planned to attack—may have done the job. The most recent evidence indicates that the "Lost Colony" suffered from a horrible drought that prevented them from growing enough food to survive. While some of the colonists may have gone south, the main group of them appears to have gone north, to the southern shores of Chesapeake Bay, where they lived for some years until they were killed by local Indians.

There was not a single English colonist in North America when the great Queen Elizabeth died in 1603. The Spanish controlled the only colonial outposts on the continent. That would soon change, however. Inspired by the success of the Spanish in exploiting the Americas, and emboldened by their defeat of the Spanish Armada in 1588, the English—as well as the French and the Dutch—would soon develop American colonial empires of their own, quite different from that of the Spanish.

New Spain at Its Height

During the sixteenth century, Spanish America (called New Spain) gradually developed into a settled society. From the outset, the Spanish behaved more like occupying rulers than permanent settlers, carefully regulating every detail of colonial administration and life. They were less interested in creating self-sustaining colonial communities than they were devoted to taking gold and silver and to enslaving the indigenous peoples and converting them to Christianity. Between 1545 and 1660, the Spanish forced Native Americans and Africans to mine 7 million pounds of silver in the New World, twice as much silver as existed in all of Europe in 1492.

The legacy of New Spain is, therefore, decidedly mixed. While connecting the cultures of Europe and the Americas, the Spanish explorers, conquistadores, and priests imposed on the Indians the Catholic faith as well as a cruel system of economic exploitation and dependence. That system created terrible disparities in wealth, education, and opportunity that would trigger repeated revolts and political instability. Bartolomé de Las Casas, a courageous Spanish priest in Mexico who tirelessly called for humane treatment of the Indians, concluded, "The Spaniards have shown not the slightest consideration for these people, treating them (and I speak from first-hand experience, having been there from the outset) . . . as piles of dung in the middle of the road. They have had as little concern for their souls as for their bodies."

New Spain's legacy

Reviewing the
CORE OBJECTIVES | INQUIZITIVE

■ **Native American Societies**
Asian hunter-gatherers came across the Bering Strait by foot and settled the length and breadth of the Americas, forming groups with diverse cultures, languages, and customs. Global warming enabled an agricultural revolution, particularly the growing of *maize*, that allowed former hunter-gatherer peoples like the *Mexica* to settle and build empires in the *Aztec Empire*. Some North American peoples developed an elaborate continental trading network and impressive cities like *Cahokia*. The *Eastern Woodland peoples* included both patriarchal and matriarchal societies as well as extensive language-based alliances. The Algonquian, Iroquoian, and Muskogean were among the major Indian nations. Warfare was an important cultural component, leading to shifting rivalries and alliances among indigenous communities and with European settlers.

■ **Age of Exploration** By the 1490s, Europeans were experiencing a renewed curiosity about the world. Warfare, plagues, and famine undermined the old agricultural feudal system in Europe, and in its place arose a middle class that monarchs could tax. Powerful new nations replaced the landed estates and cities ruled by princes. A revival of interest in antiquity led to the development of modern science and the creation of better maps and navigation techniques, as well as new weapons and ships. Navies became the critical component of global trade and world power. When the Spanish began to colonize the New World, the conversion of Indians to *Roman Catholicism* was important, but the search for gold and silver was primary. The national rivalries sparked by the *Protestant Reformation* in Europe shaped the course of conquest in the Americas.

■ **Conquering and Colonizing the Americas** Spanish *conquistadores* such as Hernán Cortés used their advantages in military technology, including steel, gunpowder, and domesticated animals such as *horses*, in order to conquer the powerful Aztec and Inca Empires. European diseases, first introduced by Columbus's voyages, did even more to ensure Spanish victories. The Spanish *encomienda* system demanded goods and labor from the indigenous peoples. As the Indian population declined, the Portuguese and Spanish began to import enslaved Africans into the Americas.

■ **Columbian Exchange** Contact between the Old World and the New resulted in a great biological exchange, sometimes called the *Columbian Exchange*. Crops such as *maize*, beans, and potatoes became staples in the Old World. Native Americans incorporated into their culture such Eurasian animals as the *horse* and pig. But the invaders also carried *infectious diseases* that set off pandemics of smallpox, plague, and other illnesses to which Indians had no immunity. The Americas were depopulated and cultures destroyed.

Spanish Legacy Spain left a lasting legacy in the borderlands from California to Florida. Spanish horses eventually transformed Indian life on the plains. Catholic missionaries contributed to the destruction of the old ways of life by exterminating "heathen" beliefs in the Southwest, a practice that led to open rebellion in *New Mexico* in 1598 and 1680. Spain's rival European nation-states began competing for gold and glory in the New World. England's defeat of the *Spanish Armada* cleared the path for English dominance in North America.

KEY TERMS

maize (corn)   *p. 9*

Mexica   *p. 11*

Aztec Empire   *p. 11*

burial mounds   *p. 14*

Cahokia   *p. 15*

Eastern Woodlands peoples   *p. 16*

Roman Catholicism   *p. 23*

Protestant Reformation   *p. 23*

conquistadores   *p. 28*

encomienda   *p. 30*

Columbian Exchange   *p. 30*

infectious diseases   *p. 31*

New Mexico   *p. 33*

horse   *p. 35*

Spanish Armada   *p. 37*

CHRONOLOGY

by 22,000 B.C.E.	Humans have migrated to the Americas
5000 B.C.E.	The agricultural revolution begins in Mexico
1050–1250 C.E.	The city of Cahokia flourishes in North America
1325	The Mexica (Aztec) Empire is established in Central Mexico
1492	Columbus leads first voyage of discovery in the Americas
1503	Spaniards bring the first enslaved Africans to the Americas
1517	Martin Luther launches the Protestant Reformation
1519	Cortés begins the Spanish conquest of Mexico
1531	Pizarro subdues the Inca Empire in South America for Spain
1565	Spaniards build settlement at St. Augustine, the first permanent European outpost in the present-day United States
1584–1587	Raleigh's Roanoke Island venture
1588	The English navy defeats the Spanish Armada.
1680	Pueblo Revolt

ᕫINQUIZITIVE

Go to InQuizitive to see what you've learned—and learn what you've missed—with personalized feedback along the way.

OLD VIRGINIA As one of the earliest explorers and settlers of the Jamestown colony, John Smith put his intimate knowledge of the region to use by creating this seventeenth-century map of Virginia. In the upper right-hand corner is a Susquehannock, whom Smith called a "G[i]ant-like people."

England and Its American Colonies

1607–1732

The England that Queen Elizabeth governed at the beginning of the seventeenth century was a unique blend of elements. The Church of England mixed Protestant theology with Catholic rituals to produce the Anglican form of worship. England was also distinctive in that its monarchs shared considerable power with Parliament, the legislature, unlike the absolute monarchs of France and Spain.

The English settlers who poured into coastal America and the Caribbean during the seventeenth century found not a "virgin land" of uninhabited wilderness but a developed region populated by Native Americans. As was true in New Spain and New France, European diseases such as smallpox overwhelmed the Indians. Epidemics wiped out whole societies, leaving Indian villages in the coastal areas "a widowed land." Governor William Bradford, the leader of the Plymouth colony in Massachusetts, reported that the Indians "fell sick of the smallpox, and died most miserably . . . like rotten sheep."

Native Americans dealt with Europeans in different ways. Many resisted, others retreated, and still others developed thriving trade relationships with the newcomers. In some areas, land-hungry colonists quickly displaced or decimated the Indians. In others, Indians found ways to live in cooperation with English settlers—if the Native Americans were willing to adopt the English way of life.

CORE OBJECTIVES INQUIZITIVE

1. Identify the economic, political, and religious motivations for the establishment of England's diverse American colonies.

2. Describe the political, economic, social, and religious characteristics of English colonies in the Chesapeake region, New England, the Carolinas, and the middle colonies prior to 1700.

3. Analyze the ways by which English colonists and Native Americans adapted to each other's presence.

4. Analyze the role of indentured servants and the development of slavery in colonial America.

5. Explain how the English colonies became the most populous, prosperous, and powerful region in North America by 1700.

After creating the Virginia and Maryland colonies in the Chesapeake Bay region and the New England colonies during the first half of the seventeenth century, the English would go on to conquer Dutch-controlled New Netherland, settle Carolina, and eventually fill out the rest of the thirteen original American mainland colonies. In the middle Atlantic region between New England and Maryland, four new colonies taken from the Dutch emerged: New York, New Jersey, Pennsylvania, and Delaware.

The diverse English colonies had one thing in common: to one extent or another, they all took part in the enslavement of other peoples, either Native Americans or Africans and sometimes both. Slavery, a dreadful practice throughout the world in the seventeenth and eighteenth centuries, enriched a few, corrupted many, and compromised the American dream of equal opportunity for all.

The English Background

People and Profits

The English colonies in the Americas were different in important ways from the Spanish colonies. Spanish settlements were royal expeditions; most of the wealth they seized in the Americas became the property of the monarchs who funded the conquistadores. In contrast, English colonization in the Americas was led by two different groups that sometimes overlapped: those seeking freedom from religious persecution in England, both Protestants and Catholics, and those seeking land and profits.

English colonies were thus private business ventures or religious experiments rather than government enterprises. And they were expensive. Few individuals were wealthy enough to finance a colony over a long period. Those interested in colonization thus decided to band together and share the financial risks of starting colonies in the "American wilderness." Investors purchased shares of stock in the planned colony to form **joint-stock companies**. That way, large amounts of money could be raised, and if a colony failed, no single investor would suffer the whole loss. If a colony succeeded, the profits would be shared among the investors in the joint-stock companies. The joint-stock companies represented the most important organizational innovation of the Age of Exploration, and they provided the first instruments of English colonization in America.

The English settlements in America were more compact than those in New Spain, adjoining one another in concentrated geographical areas. England's American empire, therefore, did not focus on conquering sprawling Native American empires as Spain had done in Mexico and Peru. The native peoples along the Atlantic coast of America were less numerous, more scattered, and less wealthy than the Mexica and the Incas. Unlike the male-dominated French and Spanish colonies, where fur traders and

---

CORE **OBJECTIVE**

1. Identify the economic, political, and religious motivations for the establishment of England's diverse American colonies.

Joint-stock companies

joint-stock companies
Businesses owned by investors, who purchase shares of stock and share the profits and losses.

Spanish conquistadores often lived among the Indians and intermarried, most English settlers viewed the Indians as an impediment to be removed as they created family-based agricultural and trading communities. By 1750, English colonists (male and female) outnumbered the French in North America (mostly male) nearly 20 to 1—1.3 million to 70,000—whereas in what became Texas, New Mexico, Arizona, Florida, and California, there were only 20,000 Spaniards.

The English government had two primary goals for the American colonies: (1) to provide the mother country with valuable raw materials such as timber for shipbuilding, tobacco for smoking, and fur pelts for hats and coats and (2) to develop a thriving consumer market in America for English manufactured goods and luxury items. To populate their new colonies, the English encouraged social rebels (including convicts), religious dissenters, and the homeless and landless to migrate to America, thereby reducing social and economic tensions at home.

> Provide raw materials and develop consumer markets

By far, the best way to entice people to become settlers in America was to offer them land and the promise of a better way of life: what came to be called the American dream. Land, plentiful and cheap, was English America's miraculous treasure—once it was taken from the Native Americans.

> Massive immigration

Political Traditions

English colonists brought to America their own political institutions and social folkways. Over the centuries, the island nation of England had developed political practices and principles quite different from those on the continent of Europe. Traditional European societies were tightly controlled hierarchies. People knew their place in the social order: commoners bowed to priests, priests bowed to bishops, peasants pledged their loyalty to landowners, and nobles knelt before the monarchs, who claimed God had given them absolute power to rule over their domain.

Since the thirteenth century, however, the English monarchs had *shared* power with the nobility and a lesser aristocracy called the *gentry*. Their

> Parliament, civil rights, and liberties

CHEROKEE CHIEFS A print depicting seven Cherokee chiefs who had been taken from Carolina to England in 1730.

representatives formed the national legislature known as the **Parliament**, made up of the hereditary and appointed members of the House of Lords and the elected members of the House of Commons. The most important power allocated to Parliament was the authority to impose taxes. By controlling government tax revenue, the legislature exercised great leverage over the monarchy.

England's parliamentary monarchy was unique in sixteenth-century Europe in its recognition of civil liberties going back to the Magna Carta (Great Charter) of 1215, a statement of basic rights that rebellious nobles had forced the king to approve. The Magna Carta established the foundational principle that everyone was equal before the law. No person—not even a king or a queen—was above the law.

Religious Conflict and War

When Queen Elizabeth, who never married, died in 1603 without a child of her own to inherit the throne, James VI of Scotland, her distant cousin, became King James I of England. While Elizabeth had ruled through constitutional authority, James defied Parliament by claiming to govern by "divine right," by which monarchs answered only to God.

A divided Church of England

King James I confronted a divided Church of England, with the reform-minded **Puritans** in one camp, and the Anglican establishment, headed by the archbishop and bishops, in the other. In seventeenth-century England, those who criticized the official Anglican Church were called *Dissenters*. The Puritans were theologically conservative dissenters who believed that the Church of England needed further "purifying." They demanded that all "papist" (Roman Catholic) rituals be eliminated. No use of holy water. No organ music. No elegant priestly robes ("vestments"). No jeweled gold crosses or wedding rings. No kneeling for communion. No tyrannical bishops and archbishops. They even sought to ban the use of the term *priest*.

Religious persecution

The Puritans wanted to simplify religion to its most basic elements: people worshipping God in plain, self-governing congregations without the formal trappings of Catholic and Anglican ceremonies. They had hoped the new king would support their efforts to "purify" the Church of England. But James I, born of Catholic parents who baptized him in the Catholic faith, embraced the Anglican church to avoid a civil war and sought to banish the "bothersome" Puritans from England.

Some of the Puritans eventually decided that the Church of England should not be fixed but abandoned, so they created their own congregations separate from the Anglican churches, thus earning the name *Separatists*. Such rebelliousness infuriated the leaders of the Church of England, who required people by law to attend Anglican church services.

During the late sixteenth century, the Separatists (also called *Nonconformists*) were "hunted & persecuted on every side." English authorities imprisoned and hanged Separatist leaders. In 1604, King James I vowed to "make them conform or I will hurry them out of the land or do worse." Many

Parliament Legislature of Great Britain, composed of the House of Commons, whose members are elected, and the House of Lords, whose members are either hereditary or appointed.

Puritans English religious dissenters who sought to "purify" the Church of England of its Catholic practices.

Separatists left England to escape persecution, and some, who would eventually be known as Pilgrims, decided to sail for America.

James's son, Charles I, succeeded his father as king in 1625 and proved to be an even more stubborn defender of absolute royal power. He took the shocking step of disbanding Parliament from 1629 to 1640, he raised taxes without consulting Parliament, and he stepped up the persecution of Puritans. Some fled to Europe; others went to islands in the West Indies. Most of them, however, went to America.

The monarchy went too far, however, when it tried to impose Anglican forms of worship on Presbyterian Scots. In 1638, Scotland rose in revolt against English tyranny, and in 1640 King Charles, desperate for money to fund his Royalist army and save his skin, revived Parliament, ordering its members to raise taxes for the defense of his kingdom against the Scots. Parliament refused, going so far as to condemn to death the king's chief minister. Militant Puritans took the lead in Parliament, insisting that all bishops in the Church of England be eliminated.

EXECUTION OF CHARLES I
Flemish artist John Weesop witnessed the king's execution and painted this gruesome scene from memory. He was so disgusted by "a country where they cut off their king's head" that he refused to visit England again.

In 1642, when the king tried to arrest five members of Parliament, a bloody civil war erupted between Royalists and Parliamentarians. In 1646, parliamentary forces captured King Charles and convicted him of high treason, labeling him a "tyrant, traitor, murderer, and public enemy." He was beheaded in 1649.

Oliver Cromwell, the skilled Puritan commander of the parliamentary army, operated like a military dictator. He extended religious toleration to all except Roman Catholics and Anglicans, but his dictatorship fed growing resentment, prompting many Royalists, called *Cavaliers*, to flee by sailing to Virginia. After Cromwell's death in 1658, the army allowed new elections for Parliament and in 1660 supported the Restoration of the monarchy under young Charles II, son of the executed king.

Unlike his father, King Charles II agreed to rule jointly with Parliament. His younger brother, the Duke of York (who became James II upon succeeding to the throne in 1685), was less flexible. He openly embraced Catholicism, had political opponents murdered or imprisoned, defied Parliament, and appointed Roman Catholics to key positions.

The English people tolerated James II's rule only for as long as they expected one of his Protestant daughters, Mary or Anne, to succeed him. In 1688, however, the birth of a royal son who would be reared in the Roman Catholic faith brought matters to a crisis. Determined to avoid a Catholic monarch, political, religious, and military leaders invited the king's Protestant daughter, Mary Stuart, and her Protestant husband, the ruling Dutch prince William III of Orange, to displace King James II and assume the English throne as joint monarchs.

When William landed in England with a Dutch army, his father-in-law, King James II, not wanting to lose his head, fled to France. Amid this dramatic transfer of power, which soon became known as the "Glorious Revolution," Parliament reasserted its right to counterbalance the authority of the monarchy. Kings and queens could no longer suspend Parliament, create armies, or impose taxes without Parliament's consent. The monarchy would henceforth derive its power not from God but from the people through their representatives in Parliament.

CORE **OBJECTIVE**

2. Describe the political, economic, social, and religious characteristics of English colonies in the Chesapeake region, New England, the Carolinas, and the middle colonies prior to 1700.

Settling the American Colonies

During these tumultuous years in English political and social history, all of England's North American colonies except Georgia were founded. The first waves of colonists were energetic, courageous, and often ruthless people willing to risk their lives in hopes of improving them. Many of those who were jobless and landless in England would find their way to America, already in the early seventeenth century viewed as a land of opportunity. Yet what many of them discovered instead was disease, drought, starvation, warfare, and death.

The Chesapeake Region

In 1606, King James I chartered a joint-stock enterprise called the Virginia Company, owned by merchant investors seeking to profit from the gold and silver they hoped would be found. He also ordered the Virginia Company to bring the "Christian religion" to the Indians, who "live in darkness and miserable ignorance of the true knowledge and worship of God." As was true of many colonial ventures, however, such missionary activities were quickly dropped in favor of making money. No one foresaw what the first permanent English colony in America would actually become: a place to grow tobacco.

Jamestown

A fragile Jamestown

In 1607, the Virginia Company sent to America three ships carrying about a hundred men and boys, many of them from prominent English families. In May, after five storm-tossed months at sea, they reached Chesapeake Bay. They ventured up a river with a northwest bend—in the hope of finding a passage to Asia—and settled about forty miles inland, to avoid Spanish raiders. They called the river the James, in honor of the king, and named their first settlement James Fort, later renamed Jamestown.

On a marshy peninsula fed by salty water and swarming with mosquitoes, the sea-weary colonists built a fort, huts, and a church. They struggled to find enough to eat, for most of the colonists were either townsmen unfamiliar with farming or "gentleman" adventurers who despised manual labor. Of the original settlers, only thirty-eight survived the first nine months.

Fortunately for the Virginia colonists, they found an effective leader in Captain John Smith, a twenty-seven-year-old international mercenary (a soldier for hire). With the colonists on the verge of starvation, Smith, brave, ruthless, and ambitious, imposed strict military discipline and forced all to work if they wanted to eat. When no gold or silver was discovered, the Virginia Company shifted its focus to the sale of land, which would rise in value as the colony grew in population. The company recruited more settlers, including a few courageous women, by promising that Virginia would "make them rich."

Hundreds of new settlers nearly overwhelmed the struggling colony. During the winter of 1609–1610, the food supply again ran out, forcing desperate settlers to eat their horses, cats, and dogs, then rats and mice. One hungry man killed, salted, and ate his pregnant wife. Horrified by such murderous cannibalism, his fellow colonists tortured and executed him.

Over the next several years, the Jamestown colony limped along until it gradually found a profitable crop: **tobacco**. The plant had been grown on Caribbean islands for years, and smoking had become a popular habit in Europe. In 1612, Englishman John Rolfe began growing Virginia tobacco for export to England, and Virginia's tobacco production soared during the seventeenth century.

In 1618, Sir Edwin Sandys, a prominent member of Parliament, became head of the Virginia Company and launched a new **headright** (land grant) policy: any Englishman who bought a share in the company and could pay for passage to Virginia could have fifty acres upon arrival and fifty more for any servants he brought along. The following year, the company promised that the settlers would have all the "rights of Englishmen," including a legislature elected by the people, arguing that "every man will more willingly obey laws to which he has yielded his consent." This was a crucial development, for the English had long enjoyed the broadest civil liberties and the least intrusive government in Europe. Now the colonists in Virginia were to enjoy the same rights. On July 30, 1619, the first General Assembly of Virginia met in the

VIRGINIA COMPANY This pamphlet was printed in London in 1609 in an effort to promote immigration to Virginia. What does this advertisement promise its potential settlers, and how does that promise conflict with the reality that greeted them?

tobacco A "cash crop" grown in the Caribbean as well as the Virginia and Maryland colonies, made increasingly profitable by the rapidly growing popularity of smoking in Europe after the voyages of Columbus.

headright A land-grant policy that promised fifty acres to any colonist who could afford passage to Virginia and fifty more for any accompanying servants. The headright policy was eventually expanded to include any colonists—and was also adopted in other colonies.

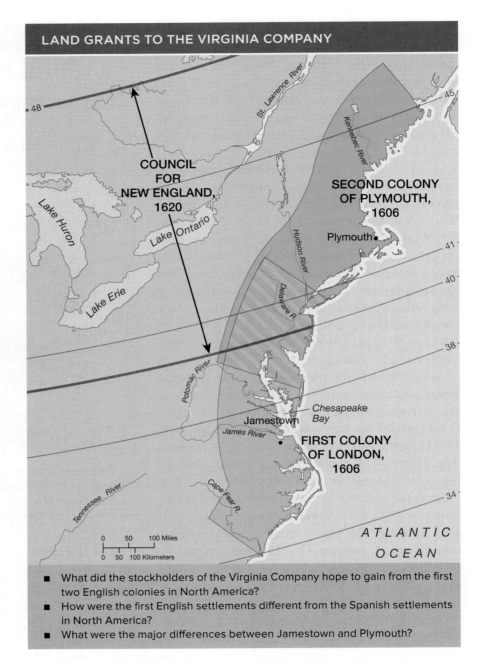

LAND GRANTS TO THE VIRGINIA COMPANY

- What did the stockholders of the Virginia Company hope to gain from the first two English colonies in North America?
- How were the first English settlements different from the Spanish settlements in North America?
- What were the major differences between Jamestown and Plymouth?

Jamestown church, "sweating & stewing, and battling flies and mosquitoes," as it assumed responsibility for governing on behalf of the residents.

The year 1619 was eventful in other respects. The settlement had outgrown James Fort and was formally renamed Jamestown. Also in that year, a ship with ninety young women aboard arrived in Jamestown. Men rushed to claim them as wives by providing 125 pounds of tobacco to cover the cost of their trip.

A third significant development occurred in 1619 when an English ship called the *White Lion* stopped at Point Comfort, Virginia, near Jamestown, and unloaded "20 Negars," the first Africans known to have reached English America. The "Negars," from the Portuguese colony of Angola in West Africa, had been loaded on a Portuguese vessel and shipped to Mexico, where English privateers intercepted them and took their human cargo. The *White Lion* headed for Virginia, where the Africans were sold into slavery. They were the first of some 450,000 people who would be shipped from Africa to America and sold as slaves. Overall, Europeans would transport 12.5 million enslaved Africans to the Western Hemisphere, 15 percent of whom died in passage. Over 90 percent of the captive Africans were sent to the Caribbean "sugar" islands, where the heat, humidity, and awful working conditions brought early death to many of them.

The first enslaved Africans

By 1624, some 14,000 English men, women, and children had migrated to Jamestown since 1607, but most of them had died; the population in 1624 was still only 1,132. In that year, an English court dissolved the struggling Virginia Company, and "weak and miserable" Virginia became a royal colony. No longer would the settlers be mere laborers toiling for a distant joint-stock company; they were now free to own private property and start business enterprises. But their governors would thereafter be appointed by the king. Sir William Berkeley, who arrived as Virginia's royal governor in 1642, presided over the colony's rapid growth for most of the next thirty-five years. Tobacco prices surged, and the wealthiest planters began to dominate the social and political life in the colony.

Maryland

In 1634, ten years after Virginia became a royal colony, a neighboring settlement appeared on the northern shore of Chesapeake Bay. Named Maryland in honor of English queen Henrietta Maria, its 12 million acres were granted to Sir George Calvert, Lord Baltimore, by King Charles I. Maryland became the first *proprietary* colony—that is, it was owned by an individual, not by a joint-stock company.

Maryland: The first proprietary colony and a refuge for English Catholics

Calvert died before the Maryland colony could be established, so it fell to his son, Cecilius Calvert, the second Lord Baltimore, to establish the colony. Like his father, he wanted Maryland to be a refuge for English Catholics, a persecuted minority in Anglican England. Yet he also wanted his new colony to be profitable and to avoid antagonizing Protestants, so he instructed his brother, Leonard, the colony's first proprietary governor, to ensure that the Catholic colonists worship in private and remain "silent upon all occasions of discourse concerning matters of religion."

In 1634, the Calverts planted the first settlement in coastal Maryland at St. Marys, near the mouth of the Potomac River. They sought to learn from the mistakes made at Jamestown. To do so, they recruited a more committed group of colonists—families intending to stay in the colony rather than single men seeking quick profits. In addition, the Calverts did not want Maryland to be a colony of scattered farms and settlements like Virginia or to

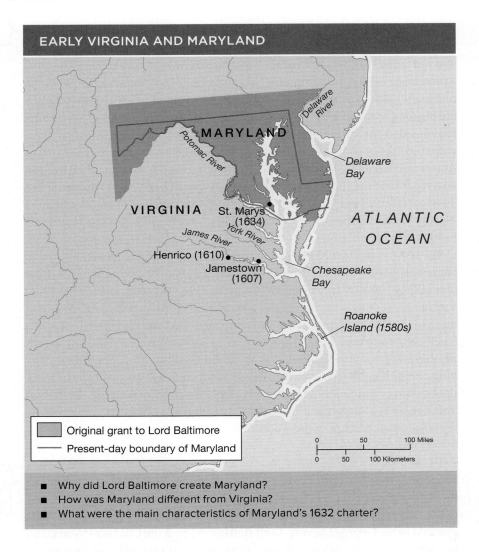

EARLY VIRGINIA AND MARYLAND

■ Why did Lord Baltimore create Maryland?
■ How was Maryland different from Virginia?
■ What were the main characteristics of Maryland's 1632 charter?

become dependent solely on tobacco. They wanted instead to create fortified towns, carefully designed to promote social interaction. The Calverts also wanted to avoid the extremes of wealth and poverty that had developed in Virginia by ensuring that the government would "do justice to every man" regardless of their economic or social status.

The charter from the king gave the Calverts power to make laws with the consent of the freemen (that is, all property holders). Yet they could not attract enough Roman Catholics to develop a self-sustaining economy. The majority of the servants who came to the colony were Protestants, both Anglicans and Puritans. To recruit servants and settlers, the Calverts had to offer them small farms, most of which grew tobacco. Unlike Virginia, which struggled for its first twenty years, Maryland succeeded more quickly because of its focus on growing tobacco from the start. And its long coastline along the Chesapeake Bay gave planters easy access to shipping.

Despite the Calverts' caution "concerning matters of religion," squabbles over religion impeded Maryland's early development. When Oliver Cromwell and the Puritans took control in England after the English Civil War, Cecilius Calvert feared he might lose the colony. To avoid such a catastrophe, he wrote the Toleration Act (1649), which welcomed all Christians regardless of their denomination or beliefs (it also promised to execute anyone who denied the divinity of Jesus).

Toleration Act (1649)

The Maryland legislature passed the Toleration Act in the hope that it would protect the Catholic minority in Maryland. But it did not work. Protestants in Maryland seized control of the government and rescinded the Toleration Act in 1654. The once-persecuted Puritans had become persecutors themselves, at one point driving Calvert out of his own colony. Were it not for the colony's success in growing tobacco, Maryland may well have disintegrated. In 1692, following the Glorious Revolution in England, Catholicism was banned in Maryland. Only after the American Revolution would Marylanders again be guaranteed religious freedom.

New England

Very different English settlements were emerging north of the Chesapeake Bay colonies. Unlike the Jamestown settlers, the New England colonists were often middle-class families that could pay their own way across the Atlantic. There were relatively few indentured servants and no elite plantation owners. Most male settlers were small farmers, merchants, seamen, or fishermen. New England also attracted more women than did the southern colonies as whole communities relocated from England to New England.

CROSSING THE ATLANTIC
This sixteenth-century woodcut depicts sailors on an oceangoing vessel using the stars to chart their course, the same method English colonists used to navigate across the Atlantic.

Although its soil was not as fertile as that of the Chesapeake region and its growing season was much shorter, New England was a healthier place to live. Because of its colder climate, settlers avoided the infectious diseases like malaria that ravaged the southern colonies and killed so many during the first waves of settlement.

During the seventeenth century, only 21,000 colonists arrived in New England, compared with the 120,000 who went to the Chesapeake Bay colonies. By 1700, however, New England's thriving white population exceeded that of Maryland and Virginia. Over several generations, New Englanders had larger families and relatively fewer diseases than their southern counterparts.

Plymouth

The first permanent English settlement in New England was established by a group of pious farm families who were forced to leave England because of their refusal to worship in Anglican churches. (Accordingly, in their own time they were known as Separatists; only much later would this particular group of Separatists be remembered as "the Pilgrims.") They first moved to Holland, only to worry that their children were becoming Dutch.

The Pilgrims at Plymouth and the Mayflower Compact (1620)

So in September 1620, about a hundred women, men, and children crammed aboard the *Mayflower*, a vessel only 100 feet long, and headed across the Atlantic bound for the Virginia colony, where they had obtained permission to settle. It was hurricane season, however, and storms blew the ship off course to Cape Cod, just south of what became Boston, Massachusetts. Since they were outside the jurisdiction of any organized government, the forty-one Separatists on board the *Mayflower* signed the **Mayflower Compact**, a formal agreement by the congregation to abide by the laws made by leaders of their own choosing.

The colonists settled in a deserted Indian village and named their colony Plymouth, after the English port from which they had embarked. They, too, experienced a "starving time" as had the early Jamestown colonists. During their first winter, half the Pilgrims died, including thirteen of the eighteen married women. Only the discovery of stored Indian corn buried underground enabled the colony to survive.

Unlike the Jamestown colonists, the Separatists at Plymouth were motivated primarily by religious ideals. The Pilgrims wanted to create a model Christian society in accordance with God's commandments. This meant "purifying" their church of all Catholic and Anglican rituals and enacting a code of laws and a government structure based upon biblical principles. Such a holy settlement, they hoped, would provide a living example of righteousness for a wicked England to imitate.

Mayflower Compact (1620) A formal agreement signed by the Separatist colonists aboard the *Mayflower* to abide by laws made by leaders of their own choosing.

Throughout its existence, until it was absorbed into Massachusetts Bay Colony in 1691, the Plymouth colony governed itself on the basis of the Mayflower Compact, which was a covenant (that is, a group contract) to form a church. Thus the civil government grew out of the church government, and the members of each were identical. The signers of the Mayflower Compact at first met as the General Court, which chose the governor and

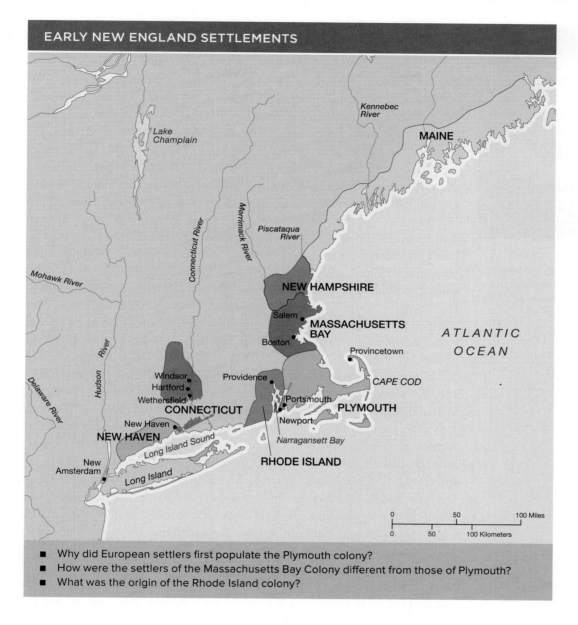

EARLY NEW ENGLAND SETTLEMENTS

- Why did European settlers first populate the Plymouth colony?
- How were the settlers of the Massachusetts Bay Colony different from those of Plymouth?
- What was the origin of the Rhode Island colony?

his assistants (or council). Others were later admitted as members, or "freemen," but only church members were eligible. Eventually, as the colony grew, the General Court became a legislative body of elected representatives from the various towns.

Massachusetts Bay

The Plymouth colony's population never rose above 7,000, and ten years later it would be overshadowed by its much larger neighbor, the **Massachusetts Bay Colony**. That colony, too, was intended to be a holy commonwealth for Puritans, some of whom migrated to America in search of a life blessed with riches while most of them sought a life rich in religion.

Massachusetts Bay Colony
English colony founded by Puritans in 1630 as a haven for persecuted Congregationalists.

JOHN WINTHROP The first governor of the Massachusetts Bay Colony, Winthrop envisioned a community that would be "a city upon a hill."

Puritan New England

The Massachusetts Bay Puritans, however, were different from the Pilgrims. They were nonseparating Congregationalists who wanted to purify the Church of England from within. They were called *Congregationalists* because their churches were governed by their congregations rather than by an Anglican bishop in distant England. Like the Pilgrims, their self-governing churches elected their own ministers and limited church membership to "visible saints"—those who could demonstrate that they had received the gift of God's grace.

In 1629, the same year that King Charles I shut down Parliament, the monarchy gave a royal charter to a joint-stock company called the Massachusetts Bay Company. It consisted of a group of Puritans led by John Winthrop, a prosperous lawyer with intense religious convictions. Winthrop wanted the colony to be a haven for persecuted Puritans and a model Christian community—"a city upon the hill," as Winthrop declared, borrowing the phrase from Jesus's Sermon on the Mount. To that end, he shrewdly took advantage of an oversight in the company charter: it did not require that the joint-stock company maintain its home office in England. Winthrop's group took its royal charter with them, thereby transferring government authority from London to Massachusetts, where they hoped to govern themselves.

It is hard to exaggerate the crucial role Winthrop played in establishing the Massachusetts Bay Colony, centered on Boston. He was a strong leader, a virtual dictator who prized stability and order and hated the idea of democracy—the people ruling themselves. Like most Puritan leaders, Winthrop never embraced religious toleration, political freedom, social equality, or cultural diversity. He believed that the role of government should be to enforce religious beliefs and ensure social stability. Ironically, the same Puritans who had fled persecution in England did not hesitate to persecute people of other religious views in New England. Catholics, Anglicans, Quakers, and Baptists had no rights in Puritan New England; they were punished, imprisoned, banished, or even executed.

The transfer of the Massachusetts Bay Colony's royal charter, whereby an English trading company evolved into a provincial government, was a unique venture in colonization. Unlike "Old" England, New England had no powerful lords or bishops, kings or queens. The Massachusetts General Court, wherein power rested under the royal charter, consisted of all the shareholders, called freemen.

At first, the freemen had no power except to choose "assistants," who in turn chose the governor and deputy governor. In 1634, however, the freemen turned themselves into the General Court, with two or three deputies to represent each town. A final stage in the democratization of the government came in 1644, when the General Court organized itself like the Parliament with a House of Assistants, corresponding roughly to the House of Lords, and a House of Deputies, corresponding to the House of Commons. All decisions had to be ratified by a majority in each house.

Thus, over a period of fourteen years, the joint-stock Massachusetts Bay Company evolved into the governing body of a holy commonwealth in which freemen were given increasing power. Puritans had fled not only religious persecution but also political repression, and they ensured that their liberties in New England were spelled out and protected. Over time, membership in a Puritan church replaced the purchase of stock as the means of becoming a freeman, or voter, in Massachusetts Bay.

> Rights and representation in New England

Rhode Island

More by accident than design, the Massachusetts Bay Colony became the staging area for other New England colonies created by people dissatisfied with Puritan control. Young Roger Williams (1603–1683), who had arrived from England in 1631, was among the first to cause problems, precisely because he was the purest of Puritans—a Separatist. He criticized Puritans for not completely cutting their ties to the "whorish" Church of England. Where John Winthrop cherished strict governmental and clerical authority, Williams stubbornly championed individual liberty and criticized the way the Indians were being shoved aside. The combative Williams posed a radical question: If one's salvation depends solely upon God's grace, why bother to have churches at all? Why not give individuals the right to worship God in their own way?

> Rhode Island challenges Puritan control

In Williams's view, true *puritanism* required complete separation of church and government and freedom from all coercion in matters of faith. "Forced worship," he declared, "stinks in God's nostrils." According to Williams, governments should be impartial regarding religions.

> Separation of church and state

Such radical views led the General Court to banish Williams to England. Williams, however, slipped away during a raging blizzard and found shelter among the Narragansett Indians. In 1636, he bought land from the Indians and established the town of Providence at the head of Narragansett Bay, the first permanent settlement in Rhode Island and the first in America to allow complete freedom of religion.

From the beginning, Rhode Island was the most democratic of the colonies, governed by the heads of households rather than by church members. Newcomers could be admitted to full citizenship by a majority vote, and the colony welcomed all who fled religious persecution in Massachusetts Bay. For their part, the Massachusetts Puritans came to view Rhode Island as a refuge for rogues. A Dutch visitor reported that Rhode Island was "the sewer of New England. All the cranks of New England retire there." Thus the colony of Rhode Island and Providence Plantations, the smallest in America, began as a sanctuary for those who insisted that governments had no right to impose religious beliefs.

Roger Williams was only one of several prominent Puritans who clashed with Governor John Winthrop's stern, unyielding governance of the Bay Colony. Another, Anne Hutchinson, quarreled with Puritan leaders for different reasons. The strong-willed, intelligent wife of a prominent merchant,

ROGER WILLIAMS An outspoken Separatist, Williams challenged Winthrop's strict authority and treatment of the Native Americans.

THE TRIAL OF ANNE HUTCHINSON In this nineteenth-century wood engraving, Anne Hutchinson stands her ground against charges of heresy from the all-male leaders of Puritan Boston.

Hutchinson raised thirteen children and hosted meetings in her Boston home to discuss sermons. Soon, however, the discussions turned into large gatherings (of both men and women) at which Hutchinson shared her strong feelings about religious matters. According to one participant, she "preaches better Gospel than any of your black coats [male ministers]." Blessed with vast biblical knowledge and a quick wit, Hutchinson claimed to know which of her neighbors had truly been saved and which were damned, including ministers.

A pregnant Hutchinson was hauled before the all-male General Court in 1637 for trying to "undermine the Kingdom of Christ." For two days she sparred on equal terms with the Puritan leaders. Her ability to cite chapter-and-verse biblical defenses of her actions led an exasperated Governor Winthrop to explode: "We are your judges, and not you ours. . . . We do not mean to discourse [debate] with those of your sex." He told Hutchinson that she had "stepped out of your place" as a woman in a man's world. As the trial continued, Hutchinson was eventually lured into convicting herself by claiming direct revelations from God—blasphemy in the eyes of Puritans.

In 1638, the General Court banished Hutchinson as a "leper" not fit for "our society." She initially settled with her family and about sixty followers on an island in Rhode Island's Narragansett Bay. The hard journey took its toll, however. Hutchinson grew sick, and her baby was stillborn, leading her critics in Massachusetts Bay to claim that the "monstrous birth" was God's way of punishing her.

Hutchinson's spirits never recovered. After her husband's death, in 1642, she moved just north of New Amsterdam (New York City), which was then under Dutch control. The following year, she and six of her children were massacred by Indians. Her fate, wrote a spiteful John Winthrop, was "a special manifestation of divine justice."

Connecticut, New Hampshire, and Maine

New England expands

Connecticut had a more conventional beginning than Rhode Island. In 1636, the Reverend Thomas Hooker led three church congregations from Massachusetts Bay to the Connecticut Valley, where they organized the self-governing colony of Connecticut. In 1639, the Connecticut General Court adopted the Fundamental Orders, a series of laws that provided for a "Christian Commonwealth" like that of Massachusetts, except that voting was not limited to church members. The Connecticut constitution specified that the Congregational churches would be the colony's official religion. The governor was commanded to rule according to "the word of God."

To the north of Massachusetts, most of what are now the states of New Hampshire and Maine was granted in 1622 to Sir Ferdinando Gorges and Captain John Mason. In 1629, Mason and Gorges divided their territory, with Mason taking the southern part, which he named the Province of New Hampshire, and Gorges taking the northern part, which became the Province of Maine. During the early 1640s, Massachusetts took over New Hampshire and in the 1650s extended its authority to the scattered settlements in Maine. This led to lawsuits, and in 1678 English judges decided against Massachusetts in both cases. In 1679, New Hampshire became a royal colony, but Massachusetts continued to control Maine. A new Massachusetts charter in 1691 finally incorporated Maine into Massachusetts.

The Carolinas

From the start, the Carolina colony consisted of two widely separated areas of settlement that eventually became two different **Carolina colonies**. The northernmost part, long called Albemarle, had been settled in the 1650s by colonists who had drifted southward from Virginia. For a half century, Albemarle remained a remote scattering of farms along the shores of Albemarle Sound.

The eight nobles, called lords proprietors, to whom the king had given Carolina neglected Albemarle and instead focused on more-promising sites to the south. They recruited experienced English planters from the Caribbean island of Barbados to bring to southern Carolina the profitable West Indian sugar-plantation system based on the hard labor of enslaved Africans.

The Barbados island colony was dominated by a few wealthy planters who exercised powerful influence in the mother country. The renowned philosopher John Locke reported that the Barbadian English planters "endeavored to rule all." They also worked their slaves to death; the mortality rate for slaves in Barbados was twice that in Virginia—forcing English planters on the island to buy huge numbers of slaves each year as replacements. By 1670, however, all available land on Barbados had been claimed, and the sons and grandsons of the planter elite were forced to look elsewhere to find estates of their own. Many of them seized the chance to settle Carolina and bring the Barbadian plantation system to the new colony.

The first English colonists arrived in southern Carolina in 1669 at Charles Town (later named Charleston). Over the next twenty years, half the southern Carolina colonists came from Barbados and other English island colonies in the Caribbean. Most of them brought African slaves with them, putting them to work clearing land, cutting wood, planting gardens, and herding cattle. In a reference to Barbados and the other Caribbean colonies, John Yeamans, an Englishman in Carolina, explained in 1666 that "these settlements have been made and upheld by Negroes and without constant supplies of them cannot subsist."

Slavery in the Carolinas

Carolina colonies English proprietary colonies composing North and South Carolina, whose semitropical climate made them profitable centers of rice, timber, and tar production.

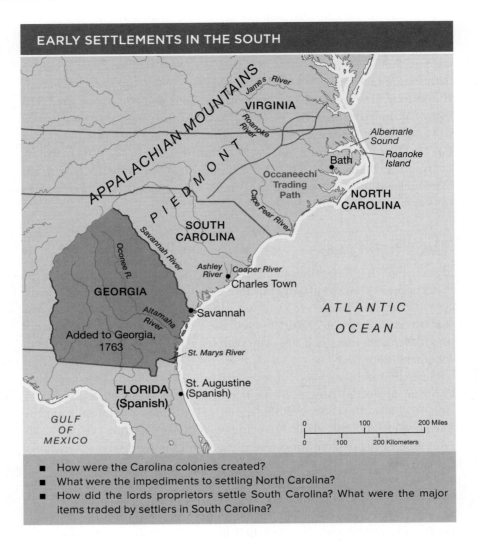

EARLY SETTLEMENTS IN THE SOUTH

- How were the Carolina colonies created?
- What were the impediments to settling North Carolina?
- How did the lords proprietors settle South Carolina? What were the major items traded by settlers in South Carolina?

Religious tolerance

The government of Carolina rested upon one of the most curious documents of colonial history, the Fundamental Constitutions of Carolina, drawn up by one of the eight proprietors, Lord Anthony Ashley Cooper, with the help of his secretary, John Locke. Its provisions for a formal titled nobility had little effect in the colony except to encourage a practice of awarding large land grants to prominent Englishmen. From the beginning, however, smaller headrights were given to every immigrant who could pay for passage across the Atlantic.

The Fundamental Constitutions granted religious toleration as a means of encouraging immigration, which gave Carolina a greater degree of religious freedom (extending to Jews and "heathens") than England or any other colony except Rhode Island. After rebelling against the lords proprietors, South Carolina became a royal colony in 1719. North Carolina remained under proprietary rule for ten more years, until it, too, became a royal colony.

Rice became as much the dominant commercial crop in coastal South Carolina as tobacco was in Virginia and Maryland. Planters discovered that the translucent grain was perfectly suited to the growing conditions in the semitropical coastal areas known as the low country. Because rice, like sugarcane and tobacco, was labor-intensive, planters used enslaved Africans to work their rice plantations in the Carolinas. Both Carolinas also had huge forests of yellow pine trees, which provided lumber for shipbuilding. The resin from trees could be boiled to make tar, which was needed to waterproof the seams of wooden ships (which is why North Carolinians came to be called Tar Heels).

The Middle Colonies and Georgia

The area between New England and the Chesapeake—Maryland and Virginia—included colonies in New York, New Jersey, Delaware, and Pennsylvania. By 1670, the mostly Protestant Dutch had the largest merchant fleet in the world and the highest standard of living. They controlled northern European commerce and had become one of the most diverse and tolerant societies in Europe—and England's most ferocious competitor in international commerce.

New Netherland Becomes New York

In London, King Charles II decided to pluck out that old thorn in the side of the English colonies in America: **New Netherland**. The Dutch colony was older than New England. The Dutch East India Company (organized in 1602) had hired an English sea captain, Henry Hudson, to explore America in hopes of finding a northwest passage to the spice-rich Indies. Sailing along the coast of North America in 1609, Hudson discovered Delaware Bay and then sailed up the river eventually named for him in what is now New York State.

> The Dutch in North America

Like Virginia and Massachusetts, New Netherland was created as a profit-making enterprise. And like the French in Canada, the Dutch were primarily interested in the fur trade with Indians. In 1610, they established fur-trading posts on Manhattan Island and upriver at Fort Orange (later called Albany).

> Profits and pluralism

In 1626, the Dutch governor purchased Manhattan (an Indian word meaning "island of many hills") from the Indians for 60 gilders, or about $1,000 in current values. The Dutch then built a fort at the lower end of the island. The village of New Amsterdam (eventually New York City), which grew up around the fort, became the capital of New Netherland. Unlike their Puritan counterparts in Massachusetts Bay, the Dutch in New Amsterdam were preoccupied more with profits and freedoms than with religion and restrictions. They promoted free enterprise as well as ethnic and religious pluralism. (They also coined the word *Yankee* to describe New England farmers who harassed them.)

New Netherland Dutch colony conquered by the English in 1667, out of which four new colonies were created—New York, New Jersey, Pennsylvania, and Delaware.

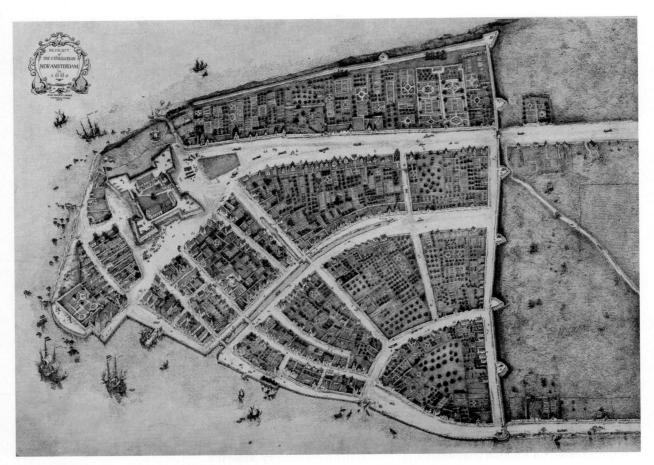

CASTELLO PLAN OF NEW AMSTERDAM A map of New Amsterdam in 1660, shortly before the English took the colony from the Dutch and christened it New York City.

Dutch settlements gradually emerged wherever fur pelts might be found. In 1638, a Swedish trading company established Fort Christina at the site of present-day Wilmington, Delaware, and scattered settlements up and down the Delaware River. The Dutch in 1655 took control of New Sweden. The chief contribution of the short-lived New Sweden to American culture was the idea of the log cabin, which the Swedes and a few Finnish settlers had brought from the woods of Scandinavia to Delaware.

The Dutch governors of New Netherland were mostly stubborn autocrats, either corrupt or inept, and especially clumsy at Indian relations. They depended upon a small army for defense, and the colonists, many of whom were not Dutch, were hardly devoted to the government. New Amsterdam was one of the most ethnically diverse colonial cities—as is New York City today. Its residents included not only the Dutch but also Swedes, Norwegians, Spaniards, Jews, free and enslaved blacks, English, Germans, and

Finns. In 1664, the diverse colonists showed almost total indifference when Governor Peter Stuyvesant called them to arms against a threatening English fleet. Stuyvesant blustered and stomped about on his wooden leg but finally surrendered the colony to the English without firing a shot.

The English conquest of New Netherland had been hatched by the Duke of York, who would become King James II. Upon the capture of New Amsterdam, his brother, King Charles II, granted the entire Dutch region to him, and the English promptly renamed both New Netherland and the city of New Amsterdam as New York, in honor of James, and they renamed Fort Orange, farther up the Hudson River, as Albany.

JEWISH CEMETERY
A seventeenth-century Jewish cemetery in New York City shows the legacy of religious diversity in New Amsterdam, enduring even as the city developed around it.

In September 1654, ten years before the English took control of New Netherland, a French ship arrived in New Amsterdam harbor. On board were twenty-three Sephardim, Jews of Spanish Portuguese descent. Penniless and weary, they had come seeking refuge from Portuguese-controlled Brazil. They were the first Jewish settlers to arrive in North America.

The Dutch officials embraced the homeless Jews, explaining that they wanted to "allow everyone to have his own belief, as long as he behaves quietly and legally, gives no offense to his neighbor, and does not oppose the government." But it would not be until the late seventeenth century that Jews could worship in public. Such restrictions help explain why the American Jewish community grew so slowly. In 1773, over 100 years after the first Jewish refugees arrived in New Amsterdam, Jews represented only one tenth of 1 percent of the entire colonial population. Not until the nineteenth century would the American Jewish community experience dramatic growth.

| The first Jewish settlers |

New Jersey

Shortly after the conquest of New Netherland, James Stuart, the Duke of York, granted the lands between the Hudson and Delaware Rivers to Sir George Carteret and Lord John Berkeley (brother of Virginia's governor) and named the territory for Carteret's native Jersey, an island in the English Channel. In 1676, by mutual agreement, New Jersey was divided into East and West Jersey, with Carteret taking the east, Berkeley the west. But neither Jersey colony prospered, so in 1702, East and West Jersey were united as the single royal colony of New Jersey.

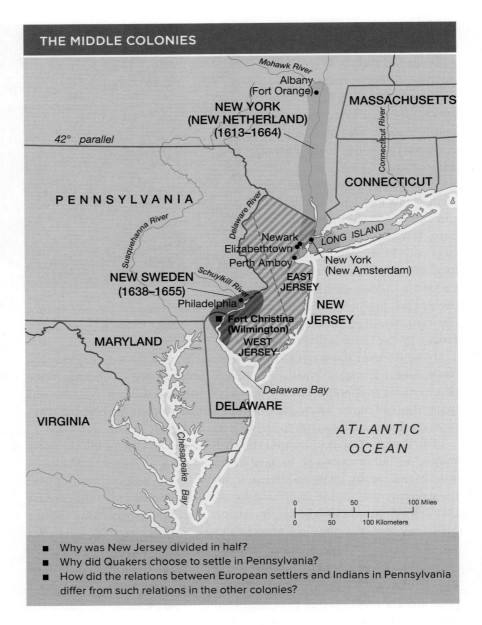

THE MIDDLE COLONIES

- Why was New Jersey divided in half?
- Why did Quakers choose to settle in Pennsylvania?
- How did the relations between European settlers and Indians in Pennsylvania differ from such relations in the other colonies?

Pennsylvania

The Quaker sect, as the Religious Society of Friends was called in ridicule (because they were supposed to "tremble at the word of the Lord"), became the most influential of many intense religious groups that emerged from the turbulence of the English Civil War. Founded in England in 1647 by George Fox, a saintly roving preacher, the Quakers, like the Puritans, rejected the formalism of the Anglican Church. But they did more. The Quakers rebelled against *all* forms of political and religious authority, including salaried ministers, military service, and paying taxes. Quakers insisted that everyone, not just a select few, could experience a personal revelation from God, what they called the "Inner Light." Quakers discarded all formal religious rituals, and even a formal ministry, and embraced a fierce pacifism. Some Quakers went barefoot, others wore rags, and a few went naked to demonstrate their "primitive" commitment to Christ. Quakers demanded complete religious freedom for everyone and promoted equality of the sexes, including the full participation of women in religious affairs.

Quakers suffered intense persecution. New England Puritans banned them, tortured them, and executed them. Often, the Quakers seemed to invite such abuse. In 1663, for example, Lydia Wardell, a Quaker in Newbury, Massachusetts, grew so upset with the law requiring everyone to attend Puritan religious services that she arrived at the church naked to dramatize her protest. Puritan authorities ordered her "to be severely whipped," after which she and her husband moved to New Jersey.

The settling of English Quakers in West Jersey encouraged other Friends to migrate, especially to the Delaware River side of the colony, where William Penn's Quaker commonwealth, the colony of Pennsylvania, soon arose. Penn, the son of Admiral Sir William Penn, had become a Quaker while a student at Oxford University. Upon his father's death, he inherited a substantial estate, including a huge tract of land in America. The land was named, at the king's insistence, for Penn's father—Pennsylvania (literally, "Penn's Woods"). Unlike John Winthrop in Massachusetts, Penn encouraged people of different religions to settle in his new colony. By the end of 1681, a town was emerging at the junction of the Schuylkill and Delaware Rivers. Penn called it Philadelphia (meaning "City of Brotherly Love").

> Quaker-controlled Pennsylvania

The colony's government, which rested on three Frames of Government drafted by Penn, resembled that of other proprietary colonies except that the freemen (taxpayers and property owners) elected the council members as well as the assembly. The governor had no veto, although Penn, as proprietor, did. Penn hoped to show that a government could operate in accordance with Quaker principles, that it could maintain peace and order, and that religion could flourish without government support and with absolute freedom of conscience concerning religious matters.

Over time, however, the Quakers struggled to forge a harmonious colony. In Pennsylvania's first ten years, it went through six governors. A disappointed Penn wrote from London: "Pray stop those scurvy quarrels that break out to the disgrace of the province."

Delaware

In 1682, the Duke of York also granted Penn the area of Delaware, another part of the former Dutch territory (which had been New Sweden before being acquired by the Dutch in 1655). At first, Delaware—taking its name from the Delaware River, which had been named to honor Thomas West, Baron De La Warr (1577–1618), Virginia's first colonial governor—became part of Pennsylvania, but after 1704 it was granted the right to choose its own legislative assembly. From then until the American Revolution, Delaware had a separate assembly but shared Pennsylvania's governor.

Georgia

The last of the English colonies, Georgia, was established a half century after Pennsylvania. During the seventeenth century, settlers pushed southward into the borderlands between Carolina and Spanish Florida. They brought with them enslaved Africans and a desire to win the Indian trade from the Spanish. Each side used guns, gifts, and rum to court the Indians, and the Indians in turn played off the English against the Spanish.

> Georgia established for the "worthy poor"

In 1732, King George II gave the land between the Savannah and Altamaha Rivers to twenty-one trustees appointed to govern the Province of Georgia, named in honor of the king. In two respects, Georgia was unique

SAVANNAH, GEORGIA The earliest known view of Savannah, Georgia (1734). The town's layout was carefully planned.

among the colonies: it was to provide a military buffer against Spanish Florida and also to serve as a social experiment bringing together settlers from different countries and religions, many of them refugees, debtors, or members of the "worthy poor." General James E. Oglethorpe, a prominent member of Parliament, was appointed to head the colony.

In 1733, a band of about 120 colonists founded Savannah on the Atlantic coast near the mouth of the Savannah River. Carefully laid out by Oglethorpe, the old town, with its geometric pattern of crisscrossing roads graced by numerous parks, remains a wonderful example of city planning. Protestant refugees from Austria began to arrive in 1734, followed by Germans and German-speaking Moravians and Swiss, who for a time made the colony more German than English. The addition of Welsh, Highland Scots, Sephardic Jews, and others gave the early colony a diverse character like that of Charleston, South Carolina.

As a buffer against Spanish Florida, the Georgia colony succeeded, but as a social experiment creating a "common man's utopia," it failed. Initially, landholdings were limited to 500 acres in order to promote economic equality. Rum was banned, and the importation of slaves was forbidden. The idealistic rules soon collapsed, however, as the colony struggled to become self-sufficient. The regulations against rum and slavery were widely disregarded and finally abandoned. By 1759, all restrictions on landholding had been removed.

In 1754, Georgia became a royal colony. It developed slowly over the next decade but grew rapidly in population and wealth after 1763. Georgians exported rice, lumber, beef, and pork, and they carried on a lively trade with the islands in the West Indies. Almost unintentionally, the colony had become an economic success and a slave-centered society.

Native Peoples and English Settlers

> CORE **OBJECTIVE**
> **3.** Analyze the ways by which English colonists and Native Americans adapted to each other's presence.

The process of creating English colonies in America did not occur in a vacuum: Native Americans played a crucial role in their development. Most English colonists adopted a different strategy for dealing with the Indians than the French and the Dutch. Merchants from France and the Netherlands focused on exploiting the profitable fur trade. The thriving commerce in animal skins—especially beaver, otter, and deer—helped spur exploration of the vast American continent. It also enriched and devastated the lives of Indians. To get fur pelts from the Indians, the French and Dutch built trading outposts in upper New York and along the Great Lakes, where they established friendly relations with the Hurons, Algonquians, and other Indians in the region, who greatly outnumbered them. The Hurons and Algonquians also sought French support in their ongoing wars with the mighty Iroquois Nations. In contrast to the French experience in Canada, the English colonists were more interested in pursuing their "God-given" right to hunt and farm on Indian lands and to fish in Indian waters.

Food and Land

The English settled along the Atlantic seaboard, where Indian populations were much smaller than those in Mexico or on the islands in the Caribbean. Moreover, the indigenous peoples of North America were fragmented, often fighting among themselves over disputed land. There was no powerful Aztec or Inca Empire to conquer and exploit. In most cases, the English colonists established their own separate communities near Indian villages.

POCAHONTAS After being captured by the English settlers, Pocahontas converted to Christianity and adopted the name "Lady Rebecca." She is shown here, in an illustration from 1616, in European dress.

The Jamestown settlers, for example, had come to America expecting to find gold, friendly Indians, and easy living. Most did not know how to exploit the area's abundant game and fish. When some of the starving Jamestown residents tried to steal food from nearby Indian villages, the Indians ambushed and killed them. John Ratcliffe, the initial leader, was captured and skinned alive by women using oyster shells, then burned. Only the effective leadership of John Smith and timely trade with the Indians, who taught the ill-prepared colonists to grow corn, enabled a remnant of the original colonists to survive.

The short, stocky Smith, a seasoned soldier for hire, had himself been wounded in another battle and narrowly escaped execution when a lively, young Indian princess known as Pocahontas (Playful One) convinced the warriors to exchange the Englishman for muskets, hatchets, beads, and trinkets. Thereafter, the Native Americans around Jamestown fluctuated between exchanging goods with the English and trying to kill them.

By 1616, the discovery that tobacco flourished in Virginia intensified the settlers' lust for more land. English tobacco planters especially coveted the fields already cultivated by Indians because they had been cleared and were ready to be planted. In 1622, the Indians tried to repel the land-grabbing English. Captain Smith reported that the "wild, naked natives" attacked twenty-eight farms and plantations along the James River, "not sparing either age or sex, man, woman, or childe" and killing a fourth of the settlers. Houses were burned, crops destroyed, equipment wrecked, and animals killed or scattered. The English retaliated by decimating the Indians of Virginia. Smith said the colonists were determined to "force the Savages to leave their Country."

Battles over Indian lands

The indigenous peoples of the Chesapeake region were dominated by the **Powhatan Confederacy**. Powhatan was the name for the supreme chief of several hundred villages (of about a hundred people each) organized into thirty chiefdoms in eastern Virginia. At the time, the Powhatan Confederacy may have been the most powerful group of Indians along the Atlantic coast. Largely an agricultural society focused on raising corn, the Powhatans lived in oval-shaped houses framed with bent saplings and covered with bark or mats.

Powhatan Confederacy
An alliance of several powerful Algonquian tribes under the leadership of Chief Powhatan, organized into thirty chiefdoms along much of the Atlantic coast in the late sixteenth and early seventeenth centuries.

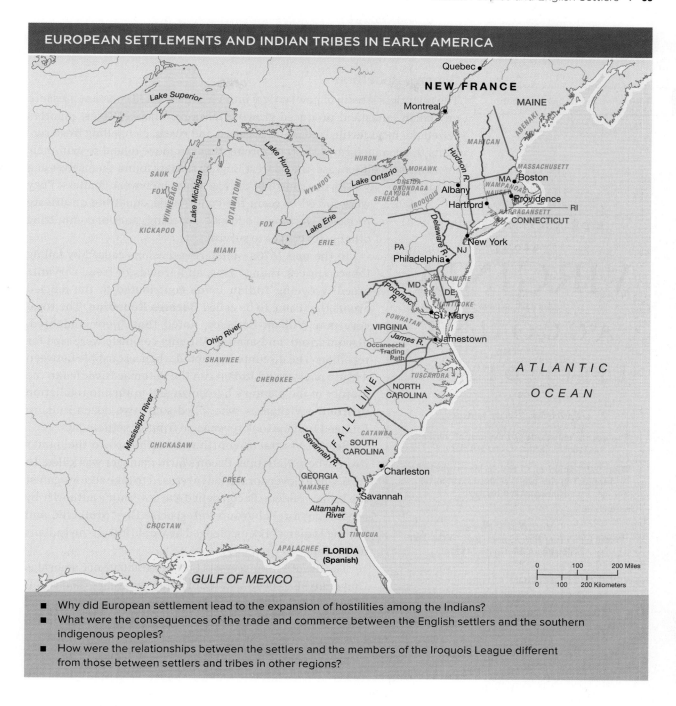

EUROPEAN SETTLEMENTS AND INDIAN TRIBES IN EARLY AMERICA

- Why did European settlement lead to the expansion of hostilities among the Indians?
- What were the consequences of the trade and commerce between the English settlers and the southern indigenous peoples?
- How were the relationships between the settlers and the members of the Iroquois League different from those between settlers and tribes in other regions?

Chief Powhatan (his proper name was Wahunsenacawh) lived in a huge lodge on the York River, not far from Jamestown, where he was protected by forty bodyguards and a hundred wives who bore him scores of children. Powhatan forced the rival peoples he had conquered to give him most of their corn. He also traded with the English colonists, exchanging corn and hides for hatchets, swords, and muskets. But he realized too late that the newcomers wanted more than corn; they planned to seize his lands and en-slave his people.

Bacon's Rebellion

Intensified conflict with Indians

The relentless stream of new settlers into Virginia exerted constant pressure on Indian lands and produced growing tensions. The wealthiest planters seized the most fertile land along the coast and rivers, compelling freed servants to become farmworkers or forcing them to move inland to gain their own farms. In either case, the poorest English settlers found themselves at a disadvantage. By 1676, one fourth of the free white men were landless. They were forced to roam the countryside, squatting on private property, working at odd jobs, poaching game, or committing other petty crimes to survive.

In the mid-1670s, simmering tensions caused by falling tobacco prices, rising taxes, and crowds of freed servants greedily eyeing Indian lands contributed to the tangled events that came to be called **Bacon's Rebellion**. The royal governor, William Berkeley, noted that "poor, indebted, discontented, and armed" Virginia colonists were ripe for rebellion. The discontent erupted when a squabble between a white planter and Indians on the Potomac River led to the murder of the planter's herdsman and in turn to retaliation by frontier vigilantes, who killed some two dozen Indians. Enraged Indians took revenge on frontier settlements.

Scattered attacks continued southward to the James River, where Nathaniel Bacon's farm manager was killed. In 1676, when Governor Berkeley refused to take action against the Indian raiders, Bacon defied the governor's authority by organizing a rebel group to terrorize the "protected and darling Indians." Bacon pledged he would kill all the Indians in Virginia.

STRANGE NEWS

FROM

VIRGINIA;

Being a full and true

ACCOUNT

OF THE

LIFE and DEATH

OF

Nathanael Bacon Esquire,

Who was the only Cause and Original of all the late Troubles in that COUNTRY.

With a full Relation of all the Accidents which have happened in the late War there between the Christians and Indians.

LONDON,
Printed for *William Harris,* next door to the Turn-Stile without *Moor-gate.* 1677.

NEWS OF THE REBELLION A pamphlet printed in London provided details about Bacon's Rebellion.

The twenty-nine-year-old Bacon, a graduate of Cambridge University, had been in Virginia only two years. The rebellion he led quickly became a battle of landless servants, small farmers, and even slaves against Virginia's wealthiest planters and political leaders. Bacon, however, was also the spoiled son of a rich family with a talent for trouble. His ruthless assaults against peaceful Indians and his greed for power and land sparked his conflict with the governing authorities and the planter elite.

Bacon's Rebellion (1676)
Unsuccessful revolt led by planter Nathaniel Bacon against Virginia governor William Berkeley's administration, which, Bacon charged, had failed to protect settlers from Indian raids.

For his part, Governor Berkeley opposed Bacon's plan to destroy the Indians, not because he liked Native Americans but because he didn't want to disrupt the profitable deerskin trade with the Indians. Bacon, whose ragtag "army" now numbered in the hundreds, issued a "Declaration of the People of Virginia" accusing Berkeley of corruption and attempted to take the governor into custody. Berkeley's forces resisted—feebly—and Bacon's men burned Jamestown in frustration. Bacon, however, fell ill and died a month later. With Bacon dead, his rebellion gradually disintegrated. Governor Berkeley had twenty-three of the rebels hanged. For such severity, the king denounced Berkeley as a "fool" and recalled him to England, where he died within a year.

Native Americans and Christianity

In the spring of 1621, the Pilgrims in Plymouth were struggling with hunger and disease, just as the Jamestown settlers had before them. And as was true in Virginia, Indians were crucial to their survival. Nevertheless, once they were established, the New England Puritans aggressively tried to convert Native Americans to Christianity and "civilized" living. They insisted that Indians abandon their religions and languages, their clothes, long hair, names, and villages, forcing them to move to what were called "praying towns" to separate them from their "heathen" brethren.

Religious conversion and land confiscation

One reason that Roger Williams of Rhode Island was considered so dangerous by the Puritan leaders was his insistence that all faiths—including those of the Indians—should be treated equally. He labeled efforts by governments to impose Puritanism on everyone "soul rape."

The relations between the Indians and the Quakers in Pennsylvania were friendly from the beginning, in part because of William Penn's careful policy of purchasing land titles from the Native Americans rather than simply seizing their lands. Penn, like Roger Williams, also took the trouble to learn the

ALGONQUIAN CEREMONY
As with most Native Americans, the Algonquians' religious beliefs were shaped by their dependence on nature for survival, as illustrated in this celebration of the harvest.

local Indian language, something few colonists ever attempted. For some fifty years, the Pennsylvania settlers and the neighboring Indian peoples lived in peace.

The Pequot War

Generally, Indians in the English colonies who fought to keep their lands were forced out. New England Puritans, like the colonists in Virginia, viewed Indians as demonic savages, "barbarous creatures," "merciless and cruel heathens." As one colonist asserted, Indians had no place in a "new England."

In 1636, settlers in Massachusetts accused a Pequot of murdering a colonist; they took revenge by setting fire to a Pequot village. As the Indians fled the flames, the Puritans killed them—men, women, and children. The militia commander declared that God had guided his actions "to smite our Enemies . . . and give us their land for an Inheritance."

> **The Pequot Nation destroyed**

Sassacus, the Pequot chief, organized the survivors and counterattacked. During the ensuing Pequot War of 1636–1637, the colonists and their Narragansett allies killed hundreds of Pequots in their village near West Mystic, in the Connecticut Valley. Under the terms of the Treaty of Hartford (1638), the Pequot Nation was dissolved. Only a few colonists regretted the massacre. Roger Williams warned that the lust for land would become "as great a God with us English as Gold was a God with the Spanish."

King Philip's War

> **Bloody war between Puritans and Wampanoags**

After the Pequot War, relations between colonists and Indians improved somewhat, but the era of peaceful coexistence came to a bloody end during the last quarter of the seventeenth century. Native American leaders, especially the chief of the Wampanoags, Metacomet (known to the colonists as King Philip), resented the English efforts to convert Indians to Christianity. In the fall of 1674, John Sassamon, a Christian Indian who had graduated from Harvard College, warned the English that the Wampanoags were preparing for war. A few months later, Sassamon was found dead in a frozen pond. Colonial authorities convicted three Wampanoags of murder and hanged them. Enraged Wampanoag warriors then burned Puritan farms on June 20, 1675. Three days later, an Englishman shot a Wampanoag, and the Wampanoags retaliated by ambushing and beheading a group of Puritans.

King Philip's War (1675–1678) A war in New England resulting from the escalation of tensions between Native Americans and English settlers; the defeat of the Native Americans led to broadened freedoms for the settlers and their dispossessing the region's Native Americans of most of their land.

The gruesome violence soon spun out of control in what came to be called **King Philip's War**, or Metacomet's War. The brutal fighting killed more people and caused more destruction in New England in proportion to the population than any American conflict since. Vengeful bands of warriors destroyed fifty English towns while killing and mutilating hundreds of men, women, and children. Rival Indians fought on both sides.

Within a year, the colonists launched a surprise attack that killed 300 Narragansett warriors and 400 women and children. The Narragansetts retaliated by destroying Providence, Rhode Island. They then threatened Boston itself, prompting a prominent minister to call this "the saddest time with New England that was ever known." The situation grew so desperate that the colonies passed America's first conscription laws, drafting into the militia all males between the ages of sixteen and sixty.

In the end, 5 percent of the male English population died during the war. The Wampanoags and their allies suffered even higher casualties as well as shortages of food and ammunition. Some surrendered, many succumbed to disease, and others fled westward. Those who remained were forced to move to villages supervised by English officials. Metacomet initially escaped, only to be hunted down and killed. The victorious colonists marched his severed head to Plymouth, where it was displayed atop a pole for twenty years, a grisly reminder of the English determination to ensure their dominance over Native Americans, once and for all.

Enslaving Indians in Carolina

Unlike the New England experience, English colonists in Carolina developed a flourishing trade with Indians. By 1690, traders from Charles Town had made their way up the Savannah River to arrange deals with the Cherokees, Creeks, and Chickasaws. Between 1699 and 1715, Carolina exported to England an average of 54,000 deerskins per year, where the valuable hides were transformed into leather gloves, belts, hats, work aprons, and book bindings. The growing trade in deerskins entwined Indians in a dependent relationship with Europeans that would prove disastrous to their traditional way of life. Beyond seizing and enslaving Indians, English traders began providing them with goods, firearms, and rum as payment for their capturing rivals to be sold as slaves.

The eight English proprietors of Carolina, meanwhile, wanted the colony to focus on producing the most profitable crops. Doing so required laborers. Some Carolina planters had brought enslaved Africans and white servants with them from the English-controlled islands in the West Indies, but slaves and servants were expensive to purchase and support.

The profitability of captive Indian workers, on the other hand, prompted a frenzy of slaving activity among English settlers. As many as 50,000 Indians, most of them women and children, were sold as slaves in Charles Town between 1670 and 1715. Thousands more captured Indians were sold to "slavers" who took them to islands in the West Indies through New England ports. The growing trade in enslaved Indians triggered bitter struggles between rival nations, ignited unprecedented colonial warfare, and generated massive internal migrations across the southern colonies.

KING PHILIP'S WAR A 1772 engraving by Paul Revere depicts Metacomet (King Philip), leader of the Wampanoags. **How does this representation of King Philip compare with John White's sketch of a Native American chief on p. 16?**

Native American slave traders

The Iroquois League

One of the most significant effects of European settlement in North America during the seventeenth century was the intensification of warfare among Indians. The same combination of forces that wiped out the Indian populations of New England and Carolina affected the indigenous peoples around New York City and the lower Hudson Valley. The inability of various Indian groups to unite against the Europeans, as well as their vulnerability to infectious diseases, doomed them to conquest and exploitation.

Iroquois relations with French and English

In the interior of New York, however, a different situation arose. There, sometime before 1600, the Iroquois Nations had forged an alliance so strong that the outnumbered Dutch and, later, English traders were forced to work with them to acquire beaver pelts. By the early seventeenth century, some fifty sachems (chiefs) governed the 12,000 members of the **Iroquois League**, known to its members as the *Haudenosaunee*. Its capital was Onondaga, a bustling town a few miles south of what later became Syracuse, New York.

The League was governed by a remarkable constitution, called the Great Law of Peace, which had three main principles: peace, equity, and justice. Each person was to be a shareholder in the wealth or poverty of the nation. The constitution established a Great Council of fifty male *royaneh* (religious-political leaders), each representing one of the female-led clans of the Iroquois Nations. The Great Law of Peace gave essential power to the people. It insisted that every time the *royaneh* dealt with "an especially important matter or a great emergency," they had to "submit the matter to the decision of their people," both men and women, for their consent.

WAMPUM BELT Woven to certify treaties or record transactions, the white squares on this belt likely denote nations and alliances, while the purple often conveys apprehension.

Iroquois League An alliance of the Iroquois Nations, originally formed sometime between 1450 and 1600, that used their combined strength to pressure Europeans to work with them in the fur trade and to wage war across what is today eastern North America.

The search for furs and captives led Iroquois war parties to range widely across what is today eastern North America. They gained control over a huge area from the St. Lawrence River south to Tennessee and from Maine west to Michigan. For more than twenty years, warfare raged across the Great Lakes region between the Iroquois (supported by Dutch and English fur traders) and the Algonquians and Hurons (and their French allies). In the 1690s, the French and their Indian allies destroyed Iroquois crops and villages, infected them with smallpox and other diseases, and reduced the male population by more than a third. Facing extermination, the Iroquois made peace with the French in 1701. During the first half of the eighteenth century, they stayed out of the struggle between the two rival European powers, which enabled them to play the English off against the French while creating a thriving fur trade for themselves.

Slavery and Servitude in the Colonies

CORE **OBJECTIVE**
4. Analyze the role of indentured servants and the development of slavery in colonial America.

Indentured Servitude

During the seventeenth century, the English colonies, especially Virginia and Maryland along the Chesapeake Bay, grew so fast that they needed more workers than there were settlers. As early as 1619, the connection between growing tobacco and the need for more laborers was clear. If "all our riches for the present do consist in Tobacco," explained a Jamestown planter, then it followed that "our principal wealth . . . consisteth in servants." The colonies needed what another planter called "lusty laboring men . . . capable of hard labor, and that can bear and undergo heat and cold."

To solve the labor shortage, the planters at first recruited **indentured servants** from England, Ireland, Scotland, and continental Europe. The term derived from the *indenture*, or contract, which enabled a person to pay for passage to America by promising to work for a fixed number of years (usually between three and seven). As tobacco production soared during the seventeenth century, indentured servants did most of the work. Of the 500,000 English immigrants to America from 1610 to 1775, some 350,000 came as indentured servants. Not all the servants went voluntarily. Many homeless children in London were "kid-napped" and sold into servitude in America. In addition, Parliament in 1717 declared that convicts could avoid prison or the hangman by relocating to the colonies.

Once in the colonies, servants were provided food and a bed, but life was harsh and their rights were limited. As a Pennsylvania judge explained in 1793, indentured servants occupied "a middle rank between slaves and free men." They could own property but could not engage in trade. Marriage required the master's permission. Masters could whip servants and extend their length of service as punishment for bad behavior. Once the indenture ended, the servant could claim the "freedom dues" set by custom and law: a little money, a few tools, some clothing and food, and occasionally small tracts of land. Indeed, some former servants did very well for themselves. In 1629, seven members of the Virginia legislature were former indentured servants.

Indentured servitude solves labor shortage.

INDENTURED SERVANTS An advertisement from the *Virginia Gazette*, October 4, 1779, publicizing the upcoming sale of indentured servants. **What does this advertisement indicate about the people who entered into indentured servitude?**

Slavery in North America

In 1700, there were enslaved Africans in every one of the American colonies, and they made up 11 percent of the total population (slaves would constitute more than 20 percent by 1770). But slavery in English North America differed greatly from region to region. Africans were a tiny minority in New

indentured servants Settlers who signed on for a temporary period of servitude to a master in exchange for passage to the New World.

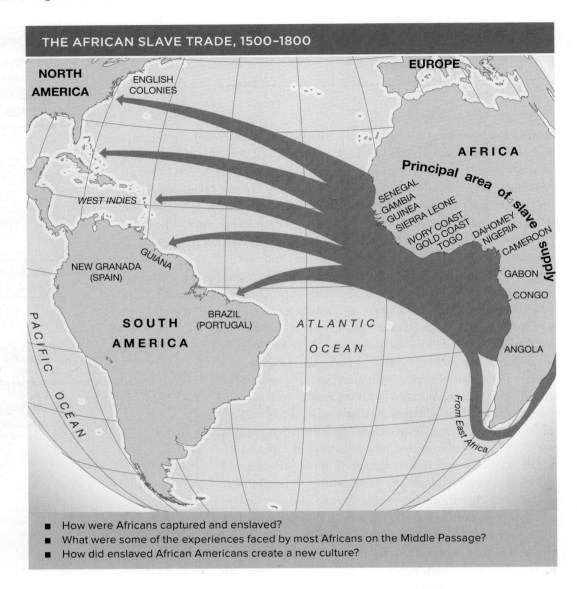

THE AFRICAN SLAVE TRADE, 1500–1800

NORTH AMERICA

ENGLISH COLONIES

EUROPE

AFRICA

Principal area of slave supply

SENEGAL
GAMBIA
GUINEA
SIERRA LEONE
IVORY COAST
GOLD COAST
TOGO
DAHOMEY
NIGERIA
CAMEROON
GABON
CONGO
ANGOLA

WEST INDIES

NEW GRANADA (SPAIN)

GUIANA

BRAZIL (PORTUGAL)

SOUTH AMERICA

ATLANTIC OCEAN

PACIFIC OCEAN

From East Africa

- How were Africans captured and enslaved?
- What were some of the experiences faced by most Africans on the Middle Passage?
- How did enslaved African Americans create a new culture?

England (about 2 percent). Slavery was much more common in the Chesapeake colonies and the Carolinas, where large plantations dominated. By 1730, the enslaved black population in Virginia and Maryland had become the first in the Western Hemisphere to achieve a self-sustaining rate of population growth. By 1750, about 80 percent of the slaves in the Chesapeake region, for example, had been born there.

Growth of slavery in the colonies

African Roots

The transport of African captives, mostly young, across the Atlantic to the Americas was the largest forced migration in world history. More than 10 million people eventually made the terrifying journey, the vast majority of whom were taken to Brazil or the Caribbean sugar islands.

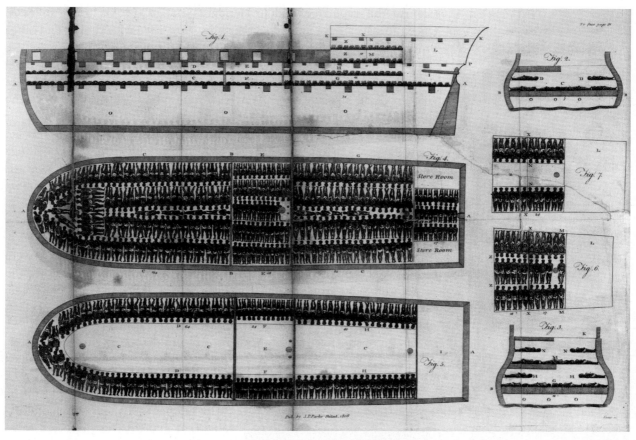

SLAVE SHIP One in six Africans died from the brutal and cramped conditions while crossing the Atlantic in ships like this one, from an American diagram ca. 1808.

Enslaved Africans came from quite different places in Africa, spoke as many as fifty different languages, and worshipped many different gods. Some had lived in large kingdoms and others in dispersed villages. In their homelands, Africans had preyed upon other Africans for centuries. Warfare was constant, as rival tribes conquered, kidnapped, enslaved, and sold one another.

During the seventeenth and eighteenth centuries, African slave traders brought captives to dozens of "slave forts" along the West African coast, where they were sold to Europeans. Once purchased, the millions of people destined for slavery in the Western Hemisphere were branded with a company mark, chained, and loaded onto slave ships. They were packed as tightly as livestock in the constant darkness below deck. They then were subjected to a brutal four-week to six-month transatlantic voyage, known as the **Middle Passage** because it served as the middle leg of the so-called triangular trade.

On the first leg, European ships carried rum, clothing, household goods, and guns to Africa which they exchanged for slaves. The slaves then were

Middle Passage The hellish and often deadly middle leg of the transatlantic "triangular trade" in which European ships carried manufactured goods to Africa, then transported enslaved Africans to the Americas and the Caribbean, and finally conveyed American agricultural products back to Europe.

taken on the second (or "middle") leg of the triangular trade to the Americas. Once the slaves were unloaded, the ships were filled with timber and other products for the return voyage to English and European ports.

The Middle Passage was horrific. One in six African captives died along the way. Almost one in every ten of these floating prisons experienced a revolt during the crossing. Some captives committed suicide by jumping off the ships. Yet many of the whites engaged in slave trafficking considered their work highly respectable. "What a glorious and advantageous trade this is," wrote James Houston, who worked for a slave-trading firm. "It is the hinge on which all the trade of this globe moves." Almost half the 12.5 million enslaved Africans were taken to Brazil. Jamaica received over a million, almost twice as many as were sent to America.

> **High profits and widespread racism**

The rapid growth of slavery in the Western Hemisphere was driven by high profits and justified by a widespread racism that viewed Africans as beasts of burden rather than human beings. Once in America, Africans were treated as property ("chattel"), herded in chains to public slave auctions, and sold to the highest bidder. Their owners required them to cook and clean; care for the owner's babies and children; dig ditches; drain swamps; clear, plant, and tend fields; and feed livestock.

> **Slave resistance**

On large southern plantations that grew tobacco, sugarcane, or rice, groups of slaves were organized into work gangs supervised by black "drivers" and white overseers. The slaves were often quartered in barracks, fed like livestock, and issued ill-fitting work clothes and shoes so uncomfortable that many slaves preferred to go barefoot.

Enslaved Africans, however, found ingenious ways to resist being "mastered." Some rebelled against their captors by resisting work orders, sabotaging crops, stealing tools, faking illness or injury, or running away. If caught, runaways faced certain punishment—whipping, branding, and even the severing of an Achilles tendon. Runaways also faced uncertain freedom. Where would runaway blacks run *to* in a society ruled by whites and governed by racism?

AFRICAN HERITAGE IN THE SOUTH The survival of African culture among enslaved Americans is evident in this late-eighteenth-century painting of a South Carolina plantation. The musical instruments and pottery are of African (probably Yoruban) origin.

Slave Culture

In the process of being forced into lives of bondage in a new world, Africans from diverse homelands forged a new identity as African Americans. At the same time, they wove into American culture many strands of their African heritage, including new words that entered the language, such as *tabby*, *tote*, *goober*, *yam*, and *banana*, as well as the names of the Coosaw, Pee Dee, and Wando Rivers in South Carolina. More significant are African influences upon American music, folklore, and religious practices. Slaves often used songs, stories, and religious preachings to circulate coded messages expressing their distaste for masters or overseers. The fundamental theme of slave religion, adapted from the Christianity that was forced upon them, was deliverance: God would eventually free African Americans and open the gates to heaven's promised land.

> African and American cultural exchange

Thriving Colonies

By the early eighteenth century, England's American colonies had outstripped those of both the French and the Spanish as tensions among the three major European powers grew. English America, both the mainland colonies and those in the Caribbean, had become the most populous, prosperous, and powerful of the European empires. American colonists were better fed, clothed, and housed than their counterparts in Europe, where a majority of the people lived in landless poverty.

> CORE **OBJECTIVE**
> **5.** Explain how the English colonies became the most populous, prosperous, and powerful region in North America by 1700.

The English colonists enjoyed crucial advantages over their European rivals. The tightly controlled colonial empires created by the monarchs of Spain and France stifled innovation. By contrast, the English organized colonies as profit-making enterprises with a minimum of royal control. Where New Spain was dominated by wealthy men who controlled vast estates and often intended to return to Spain, many English colonists ventured to America because, for them, life in England had grown intolerable. The leaders of the Dutch and non-Puritan English colonies, unlike the Spanish and French, welcomed people from a variety of nationalities and religions who came in search of a new life. Perhaps most important, the English colonies enjoyed a greater degree of self-government, which made them more dynamic and innovative than their French and Spanish counterparts.

> Organized for profit and self-governing, with widespread land ownership

Throughout the seventeenth century, geography reinforced England's emphasis on concentrated settlements. No one great river offered a highway to the interior. The farthest westward expansion of English settlement stopped at the eastern slopes of the Appalachian Mountains. To the east of the mainland colonies lay the wide expanse of the Atlantic Ocean, which served as a highway for the transport of people, ideas, commerce, and ways of life from Europe to America. But the Atlantic also provided a barrier separating old ideas from new, allowing the English colonies to evolve in new ways in a "new world"—while developing new ideas about economic freedom and political liberties that would flower later in the eighteenth century.

Reviewing the
CORE OBJECTIVES |

■ **English Background** England's colonization of North America differed from that of its European rivals and reflected its unique traditions and developments in the seventeenth century. While chartered by the Crown, English colonization was funded by *joint-stock companies* or groups of proprietors eager for profits from the colonies. Their colonial organization and governments reflected the governmental model of a two-house *Parliament* and long-held English views on civil liberties and representative institutions. The colonization of the eastern seaboard of North America occurred at a time of religious and political turmoil in England, strongly affecting colonial culture and development.

■ **English Settlers and Colonization** The early years of Jamestown and Plymouth were grim. The Virginia Company used the *headright* system of granting fifty acres to any Englishmen who bought passage and fifty more for each servant he brought along. The *tobacco* economy flourished, but this success also initiated a slave-based economy in the South. Sugar, and later rice, plantations developed in the proprietary *Carolina colonies*, which operated with minimal royal intrusion. Family farms and a mixed economy characterized the middle and New England colonies. Religion was the primary motivation for the founding of several colonies. *Puritans* drafted the *Mayflower Compact* and founded *Massachusetts Bay Colony* as a

Christian commonwealth outside the structure of the English government and the Anglican Church. Rhode Island was established by Roger Williams, a religious dissenter from Massachusetts. Maryland was founded as a refuge for English Catholics. William Penn, a Quaker, founded *Pennsylvania* and invited Europe's persecuted religious sects to his colony. The Dutch, with their policy of toleration, allowed members of all faiths to settle in *New Netherland*, but commercial rivalry between the Dutch and the English led to war, during which the Dutch colony of *New Netherland* surrendered to the English in 1664.

■ **Indian Relations** Settler-Indian relations were complex. Trade with the *Powhatan Confederacy* in Virginia enabled Jamestown to survive its early years, but brutal armed conflicts such as *Bacon's Rebellion* occurred as settlers invaded Indian lands. Puritans retaliated harshly against Indian resistance in the Pequot War of 1636–1637 and in *King Philip's War* from 1675 to 1676. Among the chief colonial leaders, only Roger Williams and William Penn treated Indians as equals. The powerful *Iroquois League* played the European powers against each other to control territories from Tennessee into Canada.

■ **Indentured Servants and Slaves** The colonies increasingly relied on *indentured servants* for their labor supply, but by the end of the seventeenth century, enslaved Africans had replaced indentured servants as the primary form of labor to produce tobacco in the Chesapeake. The demand for slaves in the sugar plantations of the West Indies drove European slave traders to organize the transport of Africans via the dreaded *Middle Passage* across the Atlantic. With the supply of slaves seemingly inexhaustible, the Carolinas soon adopted African slavery to cultivate rice. African cultures fused with others in the Americas to create a native-born African American culture.

■ **Thriving English Colonies** By 1700, England had become a great trading empire. English America was the most populous and prosperous region of North America. Minimal royal interference in the proprietary for-profit colonies and widespread landownership encouraged settlers to put down roots for a sustainable future. Religious diversity attracted a variety of investors. By relying increasingly on slave labor, the southern colonies provided England with tobacco and other plantation crops.

KEY TERMS

joint-stock companies, *p. 44*

Parliament, *p. 46*

Puritans, *p. 46*

tobacco, *p. 49*

headright, *p. 49*

Mayflower Compact (1620), *p. 54*

Massachusetts Bay Colony, *p. 55*

Carolina colonies, *p. 59*

New Netherland, *p. 61*

Powhatan Confederacy, *p. 68*

Bacon's Rebellion (1676), *p. 70*

King Philip's War (1675–1678), *p. 72*

Iroquois League, *p. 74*

indentured servants, *p. 75*

Middle Passage, *p. 77*

CHRONOLOGY

1603	James I takes the throne of England
1607	The Virginia Company establishes Jamestown, the first permanent English colony
1612	John Rolfe begins growing tobacco for export
1619	The first Africans arrive in English America
1620	Plymouth Colony is founded by Pilgrims who agree to the Mayflower Compact
1622	War between Indians and colonists begins
1630	Massachusetts Bay Colony is founded
1634	The settlement of Maryland begins
1636–1637	Pequot War in New England
1642–1651	English Civil War (Puritans vs. Royalists)
1649	Toleration Act in Maryland
1660	Restoration of English monarchy
1669	Charles Town is founded in the Carolina colony
1675–1676	King Philip's War in New England
1676	Bacon's Rebellion erupts in Virginia
1681	Pennsylvania is established
1733	Georgia is founded

INQUIZITIVE

Go to InQuizitive to see what you've learned—and learn what you've missed—with personalized feedback along the way.

THE ARTISANS OF BOSTON (1766) While fishing, shipbuilding, and maritime trade dominated New England economies, many young men entered apprenticeships under master craftsmen in the hopes of becoming blacksmiths, carpenters, gunsmiths, printers, candlemakers, leather tanners, and more.

Colonial Ways of Life

1607–1750

The process of carving a new civilization out of an abundant New World involved often-violent encounters among European, African, and Indian cultures. War, duplicity, conquest, displacement, and enslavement were the tragic results. On another level, however, the process of transforming the American continent was a story of blending and accommodation, of diverse peoples and resilient cultures engaged in the everyday tasks of building homes, planting crops, trading goods, raising families, enforcing laws, and worshipping their gods.

Those who colonized America during the seventeenth and eighteenth centuries were part of a massive social migration occurring throughout Europe and Africa. Everywhere, it seemed, people were in motion— moving from farms to villages, from villages to cities, and from homelands to colonies.

Most of the English and Europeans who migrated to America were responding to powerful social and economic forces. Rapid population growth and the rise of commercial agriculture squeezed poor farmworkers off the land and into cities, where they struggled to survive. That most Europeans in the seventeenth and eighteenth centuries were desperately poor helps explain why so many were willing to risk their lives by journeying to the American colonies. Others sought political security or religious freedom. A tragic exception was the Africans, who were captured and transported to new lands against their will.

CORE OBJECTIVES INQUIZITIVE

1. Explain the major factors that contributed to the demographic changes that took place in the English colonies during the eighteenth century.

2. Describe women's various roles in the English colonies.

3. Compare the societies and economies of the southern, New England, and middle colonies.

4. Describe the creation of race-based slavery during the seventeenth century and its impact on the social and economic development of colonial America.

5. Analyze the impact of the Enlightenment and Great Awakening on the colonies.

Those who initially settled in colonial America were mostly young (more than half were under twenty-five), male, and poor, and almost half were indentured servants or slaves. During the eighteenth century, England would transport some 50,000 convicts to the North American colonies to relieve overcrowded jails and provide needed workers. Once in America, many of the newcomers kept moving within and across colonies in search of better lands or new business opportunities. This extraordinary mosaic of adventurous people created America's enduring institutions and values as well as its distinctive spirit and restless energy.

CORE **OBJECTIVE**

1. Explain the major factors that contributed to the demographic changes that took place in the English colonies during the eighteenth century.

The Shape of Early America

Population Growth

Life in early America was hard and often short. Many in the first wave of colonists died of disease, starvation, or in warfare with Native Americans. The average **death rate** in the first years of settlement was 50 percent. Once colonial life became more settled and secure, however, the colonies grew rapidly. On average, the population doubled every twenty-five years during the colonial period. By 1750, the number of colonists had passed 1 million; by 1775, it approached 2.5 million. By comparison, the combined population of England, Scotland, and Ireland in 1750 was 6.5 million.

Philadelphia's Benjamin Franklin, a keen observer of social changes in the new colonies, said that the extraordinary population growth resulted from two facts: land in America was plentiful and cheap, and laborers were scarce and expensive. The opposite conditions prevailed in Europe. There the "enclosure movement" had led nobles—who had traditionally opened their estates to all farmers for common purposes, such as grazing animals—to fence their lands and focus on large-scale commercial ("cash") crops and herds, such as sheep. Many landless farmers were thus displaced, creating widespread unemployment, homelessness, and starvation. As a result, America's plentiful lands lured people eager to have their own farms. Once in the colonies, the settlers tended to have large families, in part because farm children could lend a hand in the fields.

Plentiful land, scarce labor, and better living conditions

Birth and Death Rates

Colonists tended to marry and start families at an earlier age than Europeans. In England, the average age at marriage for women was twenty-six; in America, it dropped to twenty. Men in the colonies also married at a younger age. The **birth rate** rose accordingly, since women who married younger had time for about two additional pregnancies during their childbearing years. On average, a married woman had a child every two to three years before menopause, making for large families. Benjamin Franklin, for example, had sixteen brothers and sisters.

Rapid population growth

death rate Proportion of deaths per 1,000 of the total population; also called *mortality rate*.

birth rate Proportion of births per 1,000 of the total population.

Birthing children, however, was also dangerous, since most babies were delivered at home in often unsanitary conditions and harsh weather. Miscarriages were common. Between 25 and 50 percent of women died during birthing or soon thereafter, and almost a quarter of all babies died as infants, especially during the early stages of a colonial settlement. Each year, more deaths occurred among young children than any other age group.

Equally responsible for the fast-growing colonial population was a much lower death rate than that in Europe. By the middle of the seventeenth century, infants had a better chance of reaching maturity in New England than in England, and adults lived longer in the colonies. Lower mortality rates in the colonies resulted from several factors. Since fertile land was plentiful, famine seldom occurred after the early years of colonization, and although the winters were more severe than in England, firewood was abundant. Being younger—the average age in 1790 was sixteen—Americans were less susceptible to disease than were Europeans. That they were more scattered than in Europe also meant they were less exposed to infectious diseases. That began to change as colonial cities grew larger and more densely populated. By the mid–eighteenth century, the colonies experienced levels of disease much like those in the cities of Europe.

COLONIAL FARM This plan of a newly cleared American farm shows how trees were cut down with axes and the stumps left to rot.

Women in the Colonies

CORE **OBJECTIVE**
2. Describe women's various roles in the English colonies.

In contrast to the colonies of New Spain and New France, English America had far more women, which largely explains the difference in population growth rates among the European empires competing in the Americas. Higher numbers of women did not mean greater equality, however. Most European colonists brought to America deeply rooted convictions about the inferiority of women. As a New England minister stressed, "The woman is a weak creature not endowed with [the] strength and constancy of mind [of men]."

Women, as had been true for centuries, were expected to focus their time and talents on the "domestic sphere." They were to obey and serve their husbands, nurture their children, and maintain their households. Governor John Winthrop spoke for most men when he insisted that a "true wife" would find contentment only "in subjection to her husband's authority." The wife's role, said another Puritan, was "to guide the house etc. and not guide the husband."

THE FIRST, SECOND, AND LAST SCENE OF MORTALITY (CA. 1776) Prudence Punderston's needlework shows the domestic path, from cradle to coffin, followed by most colonial women.

Women in most colonies could not vote, hold office, attend schools or colleges, bring lawsuits, sign contracts, or become ministers. Divorces were usually granted only for desertion or "cruel and barbarous treatment," and no matter who was named the "guilty party," the father received custody of the children. A Pennsylvania court did see fit to send a man to prison for throwing a loaf of hard bread at his wife, "which occasioned her Death in a short Time."

Virtually every member of a household, regardless of age or gender, worked, and no one was expected to work harder than women. As John Cotton, a Boston minister, admitted in 1699, "Women are creatures without which there is no Comfortable living for a man."

women's work Traditional term referring to routine tasks in the house, garden, and fields performed by women; eventually expanded in the colonies to include medicine, shopkeeping, upholstering, and the operation of inns and taverns.

During the eighteenth century, **women's work** typically centered on activities in the house, garden, and fields. Yet the scarcity of workers in the colonies created new opportunities for women outside the home or farm. In towns, women commonly served as tavern hostesses and shopkeepers and occasionally also worked as doctors, printers, upholsterers, painters, and silversmiths. Other women operated laundries or bakeries. Technically, any money earned by a married woman was the property of her husband.

Farm women usually rose and prepared breakfast by sunrise and went to bed soon after dark. They were responsible for building the fire and hauling water from a well or creek. They fed and watered the livestock, woke the children, churned butter, tended the garden, prepared lunch (the main meal of the day), played with the children, worked the garden again, prepared dinner, milked the cows, got the children ready for bed, and cleaned the kitchen before retiring. Women also combed, spun, spooled, wove, and bleached wool for clothing; knitted linen and cotton; hemmed sheets; pieced quilts; made candles and soap; chopped wood; hauled water; mopped floors; and washed clothes.

On occasion, circumstances forced women to exercise leadership outside the domestic sphere. One such woman was South Carolinian Elizabeth Lucas Pinckney (1722–1793). Born in the West Indies, raised on the island of Antigua, and educated in England, "Eliza" moved with her family to Charleston, South Carolina, at age fifteen, when her father, George Lucas, inherited three plantations. After her father, a British army officer, was called back to Antigua, fifteen-year-old Eliza cared for her ailing mother and younger sister while managing three plantations worked by enslaved Africans. She decided to grow a West Indian plant called *indigo*, which provided a much-coveted blue dye for coloring fabric. Indigo made her family a fortune, as it did for many other plantation owners on the Carolina coast.

Society and Economy in the Colonies

CORE **OBJECTIVE**
3. Compare the societies and economies of the southern, New England, and middle colonies.

In the early eighteenth century, England and Scotland merged. The Act of Union in 1707 announced a new name for the joint monarchies: Great Britain. The British American colonies were part of a complex North Atlantic commercial network, trading sugar, wheat, tobacco, rum, rice, and many other commodities as well as African and Indian slaves, with Great Britain and its highly profitable island colonies in the West Indies such as Bermuda, Barbados, and Jamaica. In addition, American merchants also traded ("smuggled") with Spain, France, Portugal, Holland, and their colonies, which were often at war with Britain and therefore officially off limits to Americans. Out of necessity, the colonists were dependent on Britain and Europe for manufactured goods and luxury items such as wine, glass, and jewelry.

Finding laborers for a rapidly expanding economy

The colonies were blessed with abundant natural resources, but they struggled to find enough laborers for their rapidly expanding economy. The primary solution to the shortage of workers in the colonies was called indentured servitude. This practice, whereby servants agreed to work three to seven years in exchange for their "master" paying for their travel to America, accounted for probably half the white settlers (mostly from England, Ireland, Scotland, or Germany) in all the colonies outside New England. These unfree workers brought their own folkways to the regions where they lived, creating a diverse ethnic mix, especially in the southern and middle colonies. During the late seventeenth and eighteenth centuries, however, the southern colonies turned from using indentured servants to purchasing Indians or Africans as lifelong slaves to satisfy the growing demand for agricultural workers on vast tobacco and rice plantations.

The Southern Colonies

> Rising inequality and a slave-based economy in the South

As the southern colonies matured, inequalities of wealth became more visible and social life grew more divided by marked differences in clothing, housing, wealth, and status. The use of enslaved Indians and Africans to grow tobacco, sugarcane, rice, and indigo created enormous wealth for a few large landowners ("planters") and their families. Socially, the planters and merchants increasingly became a class apart. They dominated the colonial legislatures, bought luxury goods from London and Paris, and built brick mansions with formal gardens like those in England—all the while looking down upon their social "inferiors," both whites and blacks as well as Native Americans.

VIRGINIA PLANTATION WHARF Southern colonial plantations were often constructed along rivers, with easy access to oceangoing vessels, as shown on this 1730 tobacco label. **How does this illustration represent the rigid class system of the southern colonies?**

Warm weather and plentiful rainfall enabled the southern colonies to grow the **staple crops** (most profitable) valued by the mother country: tobacco, rice, sugarcane, and indigo. In the Chesapeake region of the Upper South, Virginia, as King Charles I put it, was "founded upon smoke." Tobacco production soared during the seventeenth century. "In Virginia and Maryland," wrote a royal official in 1629, "tobacco . . . is our All, and indeed leaves no room for anything else."

The same was true for rice cultivation along the South Carolina coast. Over time, the rice planters became the wealthiest group in the British colonies, forcing their slaves to "work for hours in mud and water." Using only hand tools, Africans transformed the landscape of coastal South Carolina and, eventually, Georgia, removing trees from swamps and wetlands infested with snakes, alligators, and mosquitos. They then created a system of floodgates to allow workers to drain or flood the rice fields as needed.

As plantations grew in size, the demand for enslaved laborers, first male Indians and later Africans, rose dramatically. Almost 90 percent of the Africans transported to the American mainland went to the southern colonies. South Carolina had a black majority throughout the eighteenth century. As one visitor observed, "Carolina looks more like a negro country than like a country settled by white people."

staple crops Profitable market crops, such as cotton, tobacco, and rice, that predominate in a given region.

New England

There was remarkable diversity among the American colonies during the seventeenth century and after. Few New England colonists, for example, owned huge tracts of land, as was common in Carolina, Virginia, Maryland, and Dutch New Netherland. In New England, settlers, often already gathered into a church congregation, would ask the general court for a township and then divide its acreage in roughly equal parcels: those who invested more or had larger families or greater status might receive more land. Over time, as the population grew, the land was divided into separate farms more distant from the original village.

> New England townships

Religion

Whenever New England towns were founded, the first public structure built was usually a church. The Puritans believed that God had created a *covenant*, or contract, in which people formed a congregation for worship. This led to the idea of people joining together to form governing bodies, too, but "democracy" was not part of Puritan political thought. Puritan leaders sought to do the will of God, not to follow the will of the people, and the ultimate source of authority in Puritan New England was not majority rule but the Bible as interpreted by ministers and magistrates (political leaders). By law, every town had to collect taxes to support a church. And every resident—whether a church member or not—was required to attend midweek and Sunday religious services. The average New Englander heard 7,000 sermons in a lifetime.

> Church and state

Over time, Puritan New England experienced a gradual erosion of religious commitment. More and more children and grandchildren of the original "visible saints" could not give the required testimony of spiritual conversion. Another blow to Puritan ideals came with the Massachusetts royal charter of 1691, which required toleration of religious dissenters (such as Quakers) and based the right to vote in public elections on property ownership rather than church membership.

The strains accompanying Massachusetts's transition from Puritan utopia to royal colony reached a tragic climax in the witchcraft hysteria at Salem Village (now the town of Danvers) in 1692–1693. Belief in witchcraft was widespread throughout Europe and the colonies in the seventeenth century. Prior to the dramatic witch hunt in Salem, almost 300 New Englanders (mostly middle-aged women) had been accused of practicing witchcraft, and more than 30 had been hanged.

HOUSING IN COLONIAL NEW ENGLAND This frame house, built in the 1670s, belonged to Rebecca Nurse, one of the women hanged as a witch in Salem Village in 1692.

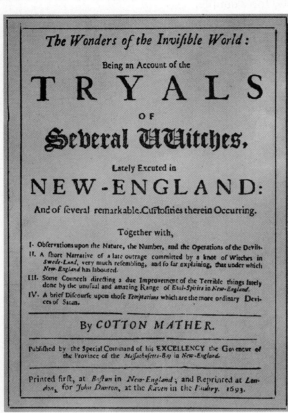

THE WONDERS OF THE INVISIBLE WORLD Title page of the 1693 London edition of Cotton Mather's account of the Salem witchcraft cases. Mather, a prominent Boston minister, warned his congregation that the devil's legions were assaulting New England.

The Salem episode was unique in its scope and intensity, however. During the winter of 1692, several adolescent girls became fascinated with the fortune-telling and voodoo practiced by Tituba, a West Indian slave. The entranced girls began to behave oddly—shouting, barking, crawling, and twitching for no apparent reason. When asked who was tormenting them, the girls claimed that three women—Tituba, Sarah Good, and Sarah Osborne—were Satan's servants. Authorities then arrested the three accused women. They were tried and two were hanged.

Within a few months, the village jail was filled with townspeople—men, women, and children—all accused of practicing witchcraft. As the accusations multiplied, leaders of the Massachusetts Bay Colony began to worry that the witch hunts were out of control. The governor finally intervened when his own wife was accused of serving the devil. He disbanded the special court in Salem and ordered the remaining suspects released. Nineteen people had been hanged—all justified by the biblical verse that tells believers not to "suffer a witch to live." More than 100 others had been jailed. A year after it had begun, the witchcraft frenzy was finally over.

What explains Salem's hysteria? It may have represented nothing more than theatrical adolescents trying to enliven the dreary routine of everyday life. Some historians have stressed that most of the accused witches were women, many of whom had in some way defied the traditional roles assigned to females. Still another interpretation suggests that the witchcraft accusations may have reflected the hysteria caused by frequent Indian attacks occurring just north of Salem, along New England's northern frontier. Whatever its actual causes, the witchcraft controversy reflected the peculiar social tensions of Salem Village. Nothing quite like it occurred anywhere else in the colonies.

Economy

Not all New England towns were founded as religious communities. In coastal towns, residents were often more devoted to catching fish and engaging in trade or operating taverns than worship. After a Puritan minister delivered his first sermon to a congregation in the port of Marblehead, a crusty fisherman scolded him for being so spiritual: "You think you are preaching to the people of the Bay. Our main end is to catch fish."

Cod, a tasty fish that can weigh hundreds of pounds, had been a regular element of the European diet for centuries, and the waters off the New

England coast had the heaviest concentrations of cod in the world. Whales, too, were numerous in New England waters and supplied oil for lighting and lubrication. The waters off New England supplied plenty of cod for export to Europe, with lesser grades of fish going to the West Indies as food for slaves. The fishing and whaling activities spurred shipbuilding, which in turn facilitated a profitable trade with Europe and other colonies.

The system of trade in New England and the middle colonies differed from that in the South in two respects: the lack of staple crops—tobacco, rice, and indigo—to exchange for English goods was a relative disadvantage, but New England's shipbuilding, fishing, and maritime trading were profitable enterprises.

The New England colonies eventually specialized in shipping goods to foreign markets through what came to be called the **triangular trade**. Merchants shipped rum to the west coast of Africa, where they exchanged it for slaves; ships then took the enslaved Africans to be sold in the West Indies; they then returned home with various Caribbean commodities, including molasses, from which they manufactured more rum. In another version of the trading triangle, they shipped products such as meat and fish to the West Indies, where they acquired sugar and molasses, which they transported to England and then returned to America with manufactured goods and luxury items from Britain and Europe.

PROFITABLE FISHERIES Fishing for, curing, and drying cod in Newfoundland in the early 1700s. The rich fishing grounds of the North Atlantic provided New Englanders with a prosperous industry for centuries. **Who provided the labor for northern fisheries?**

"Triangular" trade networks

The Middle Colonies

Both geographically and culturally, the middle colonies (New York, Pennsylvania, New Jersey, Delaware, and Maryland) stood between New England and the South, including aspects of both regions. As such, they more completely reflected the diversity of colonial life and more fully foreshadowed the pluralism of America.

The primary crops in the middle colonies were those of New England—wheat, barley, oats, and livestock—but more plentiful, owing to more fertile soil and a longer growing season. The middle colonies harvested crop surpluses for export to the slave-based plantations of the South and the West Indies. Three great rivers—the Hudson, the Delaware, and the Susquehanna—and their tributaries gave the middle colonies access to the backcountry of Pennsylvania and New York, which opened up a rich fur trade with Native Americans. As a consequence, the region's bustling trade, centered in New York City, Philadelphia, and Baltimore, rivaled that of New England.

triangular trade A network of trade in which exports from one region were sold to a second region; the second sent its exports to a third region that exported its own goods back to the first country or colony.

ATLANTIC TRADE ROUTES

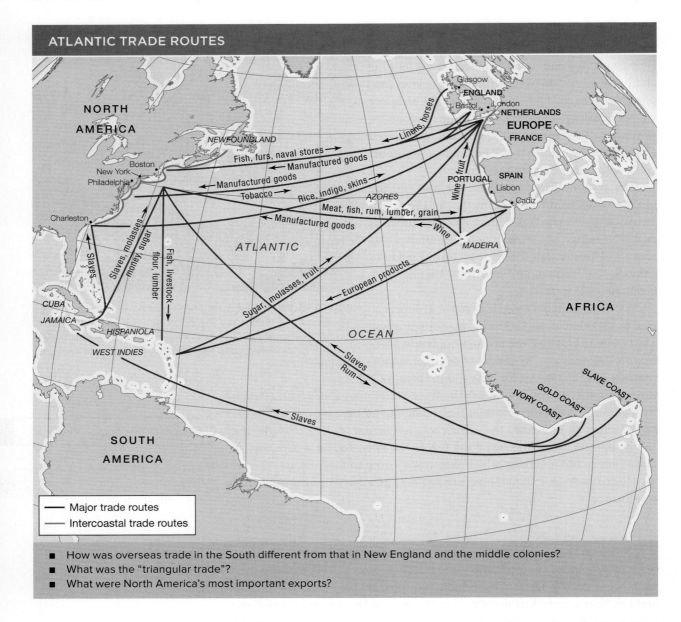

- How was overseas trade in the South different from that in New England and the middle colonies?
- What was the "triangular trade"?
- What were North America's most important exports?

Ethnic diversity in the middle colonies

In the makeup of their population, the middle colonies differed from both New England's Puritan settlements and the biracial plantation colonies to the south. In New York and New Jersey, for instance, Dutch culture and language lingered. Along the Delaware River near Philadelphia, the first settlers—a small number of Swedes and Finns—were overwhelmed by an influx of English and Welsh Quakers, followed in turn by other European ethnic groups of Germans, Irish, and Scots-Irish. By the mid-eighteenth century, the middle colonies were the fastest-growing region in North America.

The Germans came to America (primarily Pennsylvania) mainly from the Rhineland region of Europe devastated by brutal religious wars that pitted Protestants against Catholics. William Penn's re-cruiting brochures in German translation circulated throughout central Europe, and his promise of religious freedom in Pennsylvania appealed to many persecuted sects, especially the Mennonites, German Baptists whose beliefs resembled those of the Quakers.

In 1683, a group of Mennonites founded German-town, near Philadelphia. They were the first among a surge of German migration in the eighteenth century, a large proportion of whom paid their way to America as indentured servants, or "redemptioners," as they were commonly called. The waves of German immigrants during the eighteenth century alarmed many British col-onists. Benjamin Franklin worried that the Germans "will soon . . . outnumber us."

Throughout the eighteenth century, the feisty Scots-Irish moved still farther out into the Pennsylva-nia backcountry. ("Scotch-Irish" is the more common but inaccurate name for the Scots-Irish, a mostly Pres-byterian population transplanted from Scotland to northern Ireland by the English government a century earlier in order to give Catholic Ireland a more Protes-tant tone.) There were so many Scots-Irish streaming into Pennsylvania during the eighteenth century that the colony could not contain them all, so they kept moving southwest into the fertile valleys in central Virginia and western Carolina.

WILLIAM PENN In this eighteenth-century engraving, William Penn welcomes a German immigrant to Philadelphia. **What factors in Europe brought so many Germans to Pennsylvania in the eighteenth century?**

Tradition of social tolerance

The Scots-Irish and the Germans became the largest non-English ethnic groups in the colonies. Other ethnic minorities also enriched the population in the middle colonies: Huguenots (French Protestants whose religious freedom had been revoked in 1685, forcing many to leave France), Irish, Welsh, Swiss, and Jews. New York had inherited from the Dutch a tradition of ethnic and religious tolerance, which had given the colony a diverse pop-ulation before the English conquest: French-speaking Walloons (a Celtic people from southern Belgium), French, Germans, Danes, Portuguese, Spaniards, Italians, Bohemians, Poles, and others, including some New England Puritans.

The eighteenth century saw soaring population growth in British North America, during which the colonies grew even more diverse. In 1790, the white population was 61 percent English; 14 percent Scottish and Scots-Irish; 9 percent German; 5 percent Dutch, French, and Swedish; 4 percent Irish; and 7 percent "unidentifiable," a category that included people of mixed origins as well as "free blacks." If one adds to the 3,172,444 whites in the 1790 census the 756,770 nonwhites, without even considering the almost 100,000 Native Americans who went uncounted, only about half the nation's inhabitants, and perhaps fewer, could trace their origins to England.

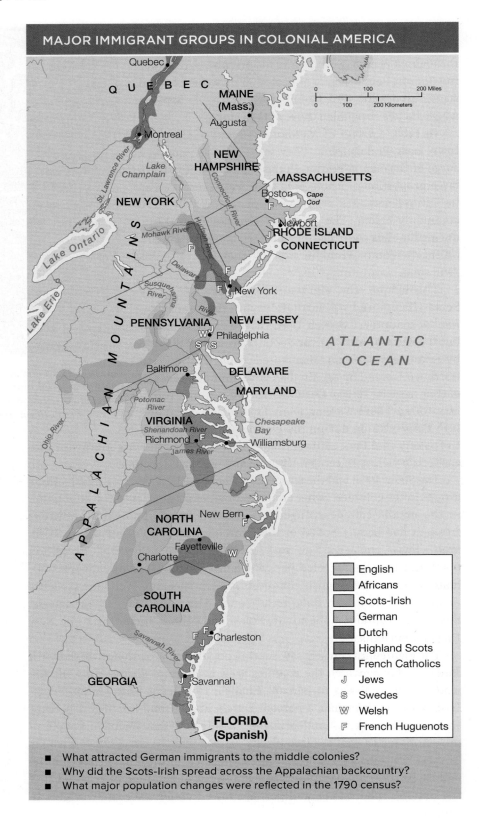

MAJOR IMMIGRANT GROUPS IN COLONIAL AMERICA

Legend:
- English
- Africans
- Scots-Irish
- German
- Dutch
- Highland Scots
- French Catholics
- J Jews
- S Swedes
- W Welsh
- F French Huguenots

- What attracted German immigrants to the middle colonies?
- Why did the Scots-Irish spread across the Appalachian backcountry?
- What major population changes were reflected in the 1790 census?

Race-Based Slavery in the Colonies

CORE **OBJECTIVE**

4. Describe the creation of race-based slavery during the seventeenth century and its impact on the social and economic development of colonial America.

By the eighteenth century, the economy in the southern colonies had become utterly dependent on enslaved workers, either Indians or Africans. The profound economic, political, and cultural effects of African slavery in the Americas would be felt far into the future. Most Europeans during the colonial period viewed **race-based slavery** as a normal aspect of everyday life in an imperfect world; few considered it a moral issue. They instead believed that God determined one's "station in life." Slavery was thus considered a "personal misfortune" dictated by God rather than a social evil. It was not until the late eighteenth century that large numbers of white Europeans and Americans began to raise ethical questions about slavery.

African Slavery in North America

African slave-trading networks

The continent of Africa during the sixteenth and seventeenth centuries experienced almost constant civil wars among competing groups and kingdoms. Africans kidnapped and sold each other into slavery in large numbers. Slave-trading networks crisscrossed the African continent. Some came from lands as remote from each other as Angola and Senegal, thousands of miles distant, and they spoke many different languages. Most of the enslaved were young—twice as many men as women—between the ages of fifteen and thirty.

Virginia and Maryland plantation owners favored slaves from West Africa, where the cultivation of yams (sweet potatoes) was similar to the cultivation of tobacco. Fulani from West and Central Africa were prized as cattle herdsmen. South Carolina rice planters preferred slaves from Africa's "Rice Coast," especially Gambia, where rice cultivation was commonplace. Owners of slaves from the lowlands of Africa used their talents as boatmen in the coastal waterways. In a new colonial society, many slaves became skilled workers: blacksmiths, carpenters, coopers (barrel makers), bricklayers, and the like. Many enslaved women worked as household servants and midwives, helping to deliver babies.

Colonial Race Relations

Enslaved workers were eventually used in virtually every activity within the expanding colonial economy. To be sure, the vast majority were agricultural workers, often performing strenuous labor from dawn to dusk in oppressive heat and humidity. Jedidiah Morse, a prominent minister in Charleston, South Carolina, admitted in the late eighteenth century that "no white man, to speak generally, ever thinks of settling a farm, and improving it for himself, without negroes." In 1750, the vast majority of slaves in the American colonies were in Virginia and Maryland, numbering about 150,000, compared with 60,000 in South Carolina and Georgia, and only 33,000 in all the northern colonies.

race-based slavery Institution that uses racial characteristics and myths to justify enslaving a people by force.

SLAVERY IN NEW AMSTERDAM (1642) African slaves had become a mainstay of the economy so early on in American history that they appear hefting tobacco in this rare early engraving of the Dutch colony, New Amsterdam, later known as New York City.

Most slaves in the northern colonies lived in towns or cities, which gave them more opportunities to circulate within the larger society than their southern counterparts living on large plantations distant from town. By 1740, New York City was second only to Charleston in the percentage of slaves in colonial cities. Most of the enslaved blacks in New York City came from the Caribbean sugar islands rather than directly from Africa.

As the number of slaves increased in the congested city, racial tensions mounted and occasionally exploded. In 1712, several dozen slaves revolted; they started fires and then used swords, axes, and guns to kill whites who rushed to fight the fires. Called out to restore order, the militia captured twenty-seven slaves. Six committed suicide, and the rest were executed; some were burned alive.

New York officials thereafter passed a series of laws—called a "black code"—strictly regulating the lives of slaves. Any slave caught with a weapon, for example, would be whipped, and owners could punish their slaves as they saw fit as long as they did not kill them. New York and other states modeled their **slave codes** after those in South Carolina—which had been written in 1691 and allowed whites to abuse blacks, both verbally and physically. In 1680, the Virginia legislature had ordered thirty lashes with a whip "if any negro or other slave shall presume to lift up a hand in opposition against any Christian." Even the enlightened Thomas Jefferson, who owned almost three hundred slaves, ordered that runaways be "severely flogged."

At its most basic level, slavery is a system in which the powerless are brutalized by the powerful. Slaves who ran away in colonial America faced ghastly punishments when caught; many were hanged or burned at the stake. Antonio, a West African man shipped as a slave to New Amsterdam and then to Maryland during the first half of the seventeenth century, worked in the tobacco fields alongside indentured servants and enslaved Native Americans. Antonio tried to escape several times. After his last attempt, in 1656, his owner, a young Dutch planter named Syman Overzee, recaptured Antonio (a "dangerous Rogue"), whipped his "bare back" with branches from a pear tree, poured hot grease into his wounds, and then tied him to a ladder where he slowly died. Overzee was charged with murder—and acquitted.

In a few cases, as had happened in New York City, slaves organized armed rebellions, stealing weapons, burning and looting plantations, and

slave codes Ordinances passed by a colony or state to regulate the behavior of slaves, often including severe punishments for infractions.

occasionally killing their masters. In 1739, some twenty slaves attacked a store in Stono, South Carolina, south of Charleston. They killed the owner, seized weapons, and headed toward freedom in Spanish-controlled Florida, gathering more recruits along the way. Within a few days, the slaves participating in the **Stono Rebellion** had killed twenty-five whites, whereupon the militia caught up with them. Most of the rebels were killed, and in the weeks that followed, some sixty more were captured by enraged planters who "cut off their heads and set them up at every Mile Post."

> Stono Rebellion

Slavery in the Western Hemisphere was a rapidly growing phenomenon by the time of the American Revolution. It was driven by high profits and justified by a pervasive racism. Although race-based slavery entailed the dehumanization of an entire class of human beings, white Europeans believed they were justified in doing so because of the supposed "backwardness" of Africans and Indians. Not even the American Revolution's ideals of freedom and equality (for whites) would change that attitude.

First Stirrings of a Common Colonial Culture

> **CORE OBJECTIVE**
> **5.** Analyze the impact of the Enlightenment and the Great Awakening on the colonies.

By the middle of the eighteenth century, the thirteen colonies were rapidly growing and maturing. Schools and colleges were springing up, and the standard of living was rising as well. More and more colonists were able to read about the latest ideas circulating in London and Paris while purchasing the latest consumer goods from Europe.

During the eighteenth century, prosperous Americans became addicted to buying the latest "baubles" from Britain. The rage for British luxury goods, especially jewelry, fine clothing, and beaver hats, heightened social inequality, particularly in the cities. Many ministers complained that wealthy Americans were so preoccupied with buying luxury goods from London that they were ignoring their religious commitment to Christian ideals. In 1714, a Bostonian regretted the "great extravagance that people are fallen into, far beyond their circumstances, in their purchases, buildings, families, expenses, apparel—generally in their whole way of living."

English merchants required Americans to buy their goods only with *specie* (gold or silver coins). This left little "hard money" in the colonies themselves. American merchants tried various ways to get around the shortage of specie. Some engaged in *barter*, using commodities such as tobacco or rice as currency in exchange for manufactured goods and luxury items from England. The issue of money—what kind and how much—would become one of the major subjects of dispute between the colonies and Britain leading to the Revolution.

> Commerce and culture

Stono Rebellion (1739) A slave uprising in South Carolina that was brutally quashed, leading to executions as well as a severe tightening of the slave codes.

Colonial Cities

An urban elite and city problems >

Throughout the seventeenth and eighteenth centuries, the American colonies were mostly populated by farmers or farmworkers. But a handful of cities blossomed into dynamic urban centers of political and social life. Economic opportunity drove most city dwellers. In New York City, for example, a visitor said the "art of getting money" dominated everything the residents did.

Colonial cities hugged the coastline or, like Philadelphia, sprang up on rivers large enough to handle oceangoing vessels. Never comprising more than 10 percent of the colonial population, the large coastal cities had a disproportionate influence on commerce, politics, society, and culture. By the end of the colonial period, Philadelphia, with some 30,000 people, was the largest city in the colonies, and New York City, with about 25,000, ranked second. Boston numbered 16,000; Charleston, South Carolina, 12,000; and Newport, Rhode Island, 11,000.

The urban social elite was dominated by wealthy merchants and property owners served by a middle class of shop owners, innkeepers, and skilled craftsmen. Almost two thirds of the urban male workers were artisans, people who made their living at handicrafts. These skilled workers included carpenters and coopers, shoemakers and tailors, silversmiths and blacksmiths, sailmakers, stonemasons, weavers, and potters. At the bottom of the social order were sailors, manual laborers, servants, and slaves.

THE RAPALJE CHILDREN (1768)
John Durand painted the children of a wealthy Brooklyn merchant wearing clothing typical of upper-crust urban society.

Colonial cities were busy, crowded, and dangerous. The use of open fireplaces for heating led to frequent fires, which in turn led to the development of fire companies. Rising crime and violence required increased policing of neighborhoods by sheriffs and local militias. Colonists also were concerned about the poor and homeless. The number of Boston's poor receiving assistance from colonial authorities rose from 500 in 1700 to 4,000 in 1736; in New York City, the number rose from 250 in 1698 to 5,000 in the 1770s. In colonial America, those designated "helpless" among the destitute poor, especially the disabled, elderly, widows, and orphans, were often provided money, food, clothing, and firewood by the county, town, or city. In some towns, "poorhouses" were built to house the homeless poor and provide them with jobs.

The Urban Web

Travel and taverns: The circulation of new ideas >

The first American roads were Indian trails that were widened with frequent travel, then made into dirt-packed roads. Overland travel was initially by horse or by foot. The first public stagecoach line opened in 1732. Taverns and inns (also called pubs or public houses) were important in the colonial era, since travel at night was treacherous. (During this period, it was said that

TAVERN CULTURE A tobacconist's business card from 1770 captures men talking in a Philadelphia tavern while they drink ale and smoke pipes.

when the Spanish settled an area, they would first build a church; the Dutch, in their settlements, would first erect a fort; and the English, in theirs, would first construct a tavern.) By the end of the seventeenth century, there were more taverns in America than any other business. Colonial taverns and inns were places to eat, drink, relax, read a newspaper, play cards, gossip about people or politics, learn news from travelers, or conduct business.

The Enlightenment in America

The most significant of the new European ideas circulating in eighteenth-century America grew out of a burst of innovative intellectual activity known as the **Enlightenment**. The Enlightenment celebrated freedom of thought, rational inquiry, critical thinking, scientific research, political liberty, and individual freedom. Enlightened people were those who sought the truth, wherever it might lead, rather than remain content with dogmas passed down through the ages or taken from the Bible. Curious, well-educated, and well-read people were no longer willing simply to accept biblical explanations of the universe as sufficient and complete. Immanuel Kant, the eighteenth-century German philosopher, summed up the Enlightenment point of view this way: "Dare to know! Have the courage to use your own understanding." He and others used the power of reason to analyze the

Enlightenment A revolution in thought begun in Europe in the seventeenth century that emphasized reason and science over the authority and myths of traditional religion.

workings of nature. To do so, they employed new tools like microscopes and telescopes to engage in close observation, scientific experimentation, and precise mathematical calculation.

The scientific revolution

The Enlightenment, often called the Age of Reason, greatly accelerated the rate of intellectual change. It was triggered by a scientific revolution in the early sixteenth century, in which the ancient Christian view that the God-created earth was at the center of the universe, the sun revolving around it, was overthrown by the controversial heliocentric (sun-centered) solar system described by Nicolaus Copernicus, a Polish astronomer who was also a Catholic priest. In 1533, he asserted that the earth and other planets orbit the sun. Catholic officials scorned Copernicus's theory before it was later confirmed by other scientists.

The climax to the initial scientific revolution came in 1687, when Englishman Isaac Newton (1642–1727), the inventor of calculus and the reflecting telescope, announced his controversial theory of the earth's gravitational pull. Like Copernicus, Newton challenged biblical notions of the world's workings by depicting a mechanistic universe moving in accordance with natural laws and held together by universal gravitation that could be grasped by human reason and explained by mathematics. He implied that natural laws rather than God's actions govern all things, from the orbits of the planets to the science of human relations: politics, economics, and society.

Deism

Some enlightened people, called Deists, carried Newton's scientific outlook to its logical conclusion, claiming that God created the world and designed its "natural laws," and these laws, not God directly, governed the operation of the universe. In other words, **Deism** maintained that God planned the universe and set it in motion but no longer interacted directly with the earth and its people. So the rational God of the Deists was nothing like the intervening God of the Christian tradition, to whom believers prayed for daily guidance and direct support.

Evil in the world, according to the Deists, resulted not from humanity's inherent *sinfulness* as outlined in the Bible but from human *ignorance* of the rational laws of nature. Therefore the best way to improve both society and human nature, according to Deists such as Thomas Jefferson and Benjamin Franklin, was by cultivating Reason, which was the highest Virtue (Enlightenment thinkers often capitalized both words). By doing so, by using education, reason, and scientific analysis, societies were bound to improve their knowledge as well as their quality of life. A naive optimism about human progress was thus one of the most important beliefs of the Enlightenment.

Equally important was the enlightened notion of political freedom. Both Jefferson and Franklin were intrigued by the English political philosopher John Locke (1632–1704), who maintained that "natural law" called for a government resting on the consent of the governed and respecting the "natural rights" of all. It was not far from such an idea to finding justification for revolution against tyrannical monarchies, like those governing Great Britain and France.

Deism Enlightenment thought applied to religion, emphasizing reason, morality, and natural law rather than scriptural authority or an ever-present god intervening in the daily life of humans.

The Age of Reason in America

Benjamin Franklin epitomized the Enlightenment in the eyes of both Americans and Europeans. Born in Boston in 1706, a descendant of Puritans, Franklin left home at the age of seventeen, bound for Philadelphia. There, before he was twenty-four, he bought a print shop where he edited the *Pennsylvania Gazette,* one of the leading newspapers in the colonies. When he was twenty-six, he published *Poor Richard's Almanack,* a collection of weather forecasts, puzzles, household tips, and witty sayings about success and happiness. Before he retired from business at the age of forty-two, Franklin had founded a public library, started a fire company, helped create the academy that became the University of Pennsylvania, and organized a debating club that grew into the American Philosophical Society.

Benjamin Franklin was devoted to scientific investigation. Skeptical and curious, pragmatic and irreverent, he was an inventive genius. His wide-ranging scientific experiments ranged across the fields of medicine, meteorology, geology, astronomy, and physics, among others. He developed the Franklin stove, the lightning rod, bifocal spectacles, and a glass harmonica.

BENJAMIN FRANKLIN
A champion of reason, Franklin was an inventor, philosopher, entrepreneur, and statesman.

Franklin's love of science and reason clashed with prevailing Christian beliefs. Although raised as a Presbyterian, he became a Deist who prized science and reason over orthodox religion. He questioned the divinity of Jesus and the assumption that the Bible was truly the word of God. Like the European Deists, Franklin came to believe that God had created a universe directed by natural laws, laws that curious people could discover through the use of reason and the scientific method. For Franklin and others in the eighteenth century, to be "enlightened" meant developing the confidence and capacity to think for oneself, to think critically rather than simply accepting what tradition or ministers dictated as truth.

The Great Awakening

The growing popularity of Enlightenment rationalism posed a direct threat to traditional religious life in Europe and America. But religious faith has always shown remarkable resilience in the face of challenging new ideas. This was certainly true in the early eighteenth century, when the American colonies experienced a widespread revival of spiritual zeal designed to restore the primacy of emotion in the religious realm.

Religious response to the
Enlightenment

Between 1700 and 1750, when the controversial ideas of the Enlightenment were circulating among the best-educated colonists, hundreds of new Christian congregations were founded. Most Americans (85 percent) lived in colonies with an "established" church, meaning that the colonial government officially endorsed—and collected taxes to support—a single official denomination. The Church of England, also known as Anglicanism, was the established church in Virginia, Maryland, Delaware, and the Carolinas. Puritan Congregationalism was the official faith in New England. In New York, Anglicanism vied with the Dutch Reformed Church for control. Pennsylvania had no single state-supported church, but Quakers dominated the legislative assembly. New Jersey and Rhode Island had no official denomination and hosted numerous Christian splinter groups.

Most colonies organized religious life on the basis of well-regulated local parishes, which defined their theological boundaries and defended them against people who did not hold to the same faith. In colonies with official religions, people of other faiths could not preach without the permission of the local parish. Then, in the 1730s and 1740s, the parish system was thrown into turmoil by the arrival of outspoken traveling evangelists, called *itinerants*, who claimed that most of the local parish ministers were incompetent. In their emotionally charged sermons, the itinerants, several of whom were white women and African Americans, insisted that Christians must be "reborn" in their convictions and behavior.

Traveling evangelists and intense
revivals

During the early 1730s, a widespread sense of religious decline and the need for "rebirth" helped spark a series of emotional revivals known as the **Great Awakening**. The revivals began in the southern colonies and quickly spread up the Atlantic coast to New England. Whole towns were swept up in the ecstasy of renewed spiritual passion. Unlike the Enlightenment, which affected primarily the intellectual elite, the evangelical energies unleashed by the Great Awakening appealed mostly to the masses. As a skeptical Benjamin Franklin observed of the Awakening, "Never did the people show so great a willingness to attend sermons. Religion is become the subject of most conversation." The Awakening was the first popular movement before the American Revolution that affected all thirteen colonies, and as such, it helped create ties across the colonies that would later help coordinate revolutionary activities against the British government.

Jonathan Edwards In 1734–1735, a remarkable spiritual transformation occurred in the congregation of Jonathan Edwards, a prominent Congregationalist minister in the western Massachusetts town of Northampton. One of America's most brilliant philosophers and theologians, Edwards had entered Yale College in 1716, at age thirteen, and graduated at the top of his class four years later. In 1727, Edwards was named minister of the Congregational church in Northampton. He was shocked at the town's lack of religious conviction. Edwards claimed that the young people of Northampton were

Great Awakening Emotional religious revival movement that swept the thirteen colonies from the 1730s through the 1740s.

preoccupied with sinful pleasures; they indulged in "lewd practices" that "corrupted others." Moreover, Christians had become obsessed with making and spending money. He also warned that the rebellious new ideas associated with the Enlightenment were eroding the importance of religious life. Edwards attacked Deists for believing that "God has given mankind no other light to walk by but their own reason."

To counteract the secularizing forces of the Enlightenment, Edwards resolved to restore the emotional side of religion. "Our people," he said, "do not so much need to have their heads stored [with new scientific knowledge] as to have their hearts touched [with spiritual intensity]." His own vivid descriptions of the sufferings of hell and the delights of heaven helped rekindle spiritual intensity among his congregants. By 1735, Edwards could report that "the town seemed to be full of the presence of God; it never was so full of love, nor of joy." To judge the power of the religious awakening, he thought, one need only observe that "it was no longer the Tavern" that drew local crowds "but the Minister's House."

JONATHAN EDWARDS One of the foremost preachers of the Great Awakening, Edwards was known for his incendiary rhetoric that provoked spiritual guilt and fear of the afterlife in his followers.

Radical Evangelists While Jonathan Edwards was promoting a revival of religious emotion in Puritan New England, William Tennent, an Irish-born Presbyterian revivalist, was stirring souls in Pennsylvania. He and his sons charged that many of the local ministers were "cold and sapless," afraid to "thrust the nail of terror into sleeping souls." Tennent's oldest son, Gilbert, defended their aggressive (and often illegal) tactics by explaining that he and other traveling evangelists invaded parishes only when the local minister showed no interest in the "Getting of Grace and Growing in it."

The Tennents caused great anxiety because they preached to those at the bottom of the social scale—farmers, laborers, sailors, and servants. By promoting a passionate piety, urging people to renounce their conventional ministers, and attacking the luxurious excesses of the wealthiest and most powerful colonists, the radical evangelists disrupted the social order in the colonies. Worried members of the colonial elite charged that the revivalists were spreading "anarchy, levelling, and dissolution."

Women and Revivals The Great Awakening's most controversial element was the emergence of women who defied the biblical injunction against speaking in religious services. Scores of women served as lay exhorters, including Sarah Haggar Osborne, a Rhode Island schoolteacher who organized prayer meetings that eventually included men and women, black and white. When told to stop, she refused to "shut [her] mouth and doors and creep into obscurity." Similarly, in western Massachusetts, Bathsheba Kingsley stole her husband's horse to spread the gospel among her rural neighbors because she had received "immediate revelations from heaven." When her husband tried to intervene, she pummeled him with "hard words and blows," praying loudly that he "go quick to hell." Jonathan Edwards

GEORGE WHITEFIELD PREACHING Another influential figure of the Great Awakening was George Whitefield, an Anglican preacher who made several trips to America to spread his religious sentiments. This painting by Englishman John Collet does not depict the massive crowds Whitefield was known to attract, but it does represent their diversity of age, sex, and class. **Why did the message of the Great Awakening appeal to such a wide range of people?**

denounced Kingsley as a "brawling woman" who should "keep chiefly at home." For all the turbulence created by the revivals, churches remained male bastions of political authority.

Peak of the Great Awakening

Jonathan Edwards: "Sinners in the Hands of an Angry God"

The Great Awakening reached its peak in 1741 when Jonathan Edwards delivered his most famous sermon, "Sinners in the Hands of an Angry God." It was designed in part to frighten people into seeking salvation. Edwards reminded his Massachusetts congregation that hell is real and that God "holds you over the pit of hell, much as one holds a spider, or some loathsome insect, over the fire, abhors you, and is dreadfully provoked. He looks upon you as worthy of nothing else, but to be cast into the fire." When Edwards finished, he had to wait several minutes for the agitated congregants to quiet down before he led them in a closing hymn.

The Great Awakening made religion intensely personal by creating both a deep sense of spiritual guilt and a yearning for redemption. Yet while the Great Awakening saved souls, it also undermined many of the established churches by emphasizing that individuals, regardless of wealth or social status, could receive God's grace without the guidance of their local ministers.

It also gave people more religious choices. During the Great Awakening, the major denominations fractured: Presbyterians divided into "Old Side" critics of revivalism and "New Side" supporters; Congregationalists into "Old Light" and "New Light" factions. Jonathan Edwards regretted the emergence of warring factions. We are "like two armies," he said, "separated and drawn up in battle array, ready to fight one another." New England's religious life would never be the same.

The Heart versus the Head

Like a ferocious fire that burned intensely before dying out, the Great Awakening subsided by 1750. The emotional Awakening, like its counterpart, the rational Enlightenment, influenced the American Revolution and set in motion powerful currents that still flow in American life.

Ministers could no longer control the direction of religious life, as more and more people took charge of their own spirituality and new denominations sprouted like mushrooms. The Awakening implanted in American culture the evangelical impulse and the emotional appeal of revivalism, weakened the status of the old-fashioned clergy and state-supported churches, and encouraged believers to exercise their own judgment. By encouraging the proliferation of denominations, it heightened the need for toleration of dissent.

In some respects, however, the Awakening and the Enlightenment, one stressing the urgings of the spirit and the other celebrating the cold logic of reason, led by different roads to similar ends. Both movements cut across the mainland colonies and thereby helped bind them together. Both emphasized the power and right of individual decision-making, and both aroused hopes that America would become the promised land in which people might attain the perfection of piety or reason, if not both.

By urging believers to exercise their own spiritual judgment, revivals weakened the authority of the established churches and their ministers, just as colonial resentment of British economic regulations would later weaken the colonists' loyalty to the king. As such, the Great Awakening and the Enlightenment helped nurture an American commitment to individual freedom and resistance to authority that would play a key role in the rebellion against British "tyranny" in 1776.

Reviewing the
CORE OBJECTIVES |

- **Colonial Demographics** Cheap land lured most poor immigrants to America, and the initial shortage of women eventually gave way to a more equal gender ratio and a tendency to marry earlier than in Europe, leading to higher *birth rates* and larger families. People also lived longer on average in the colonies than in Europe. The lower *death rates* led to rapid population growth in the colonies.

- **Women in the Colonies** English colonists brought their traditional beliefs and prejudices with them to America, including convictions about the inferiority of women. Colonial women remained largely confined to *women's work* in the house, yard, and field. Over time, though, necessity created new opportunities for women outside their traditional roles.

- **Colonial Differences** A thriving colonial trading economy sent raw materials such as fish, timber, and furs to England in return for manufactured goods. The expanding economy created new wealth and a rise in the consumption of European goods, and it fostered the expansion of slavery. Agriculture diversified: tobacco was the *staple crop* in Virginia, rice in the Carolinas. Plantation agriculture based on slavery became entrenched in the South. New England's prosperous shipping industry created a profitable *triangular trade* among Africa, America, and England. By 1790, German, Scots-Irish, Welsh, and Irish immigrants and other European ethnic groups had settled in the middle colonies, along with members of religious groups such as Quakers, Jews, Huguenots, and Mennonites.

- **Race-Based Slavery** Deep-rooted color prejudice led to *race-based slavery*. Africans were considered "heathens" whose supposed inferiority entitled white Americans to use them for slaves. Diverse Africans brought skills from Africa to build America's economy. The use of African slaves was concentrated in the South, where landowners used them to produce lucrative *staple crops*, such as tobacco, rice, and indigo, but slaves lived in cities, too, especially New York. As the population of slaves increased, race relations grew more tense, and *slave codes* were created to regulate the movement and activities of enslaved people. Sporadic slave uprisings, such as the *Stono Rebellion*, occurred in both the North and South.

- **The Enlightenment and the Great Awakening** Printing presses, higher education, and city life created a flow of new ideas that circulated via long-distance travel, tavern life, the postal service, books, and newspapers. The attitudes of the *Enlightenment* were transported along international trade routes. Sir Isaac Newton's scientific discoveries culminated in the belief that reason could improve society. Benjamin Franklin, who believed that people could shape their own destinies, became the face of the Enlightenment in America.

Deism expressed the religious views of the Age of Reason. By contrast, during the 1730s, a revival of faith, the *Great Awakening*, swept through the colonies. New congregations formed as evangelists insisted that Christians be "reborn." Individualism, not orthodoxy, was stressed in this first popular religious movement in America's history.

KEY TERMS

death rate *p. 84*

birth rate *p. 84*

women's work *p. 86*

staple crops *p. 88*

triangular trade *p. 91*

race-based slavery *p. 95*

slave codes *p. 96*

Stono Rebellion (1739)
  p. 97

Enlightenment *p. 99*

Deism *p. 100*

Great Awakening *p. 102*

CHRONOLOGY

1683	German Mennonites arrive in Pennsylvania
1687	Sir Isaac Newton publishes his theory of universal gravitation
1691	South Carolina passes first slave codes; other states follow
1692–1693	Salem witch trials
1712	Slave revolt in New York City; New York passes stricter laws governing slaves
1730s–1740s	The Great Awakening
1739	Stono Rebellion
1750	Colonial population passes 1 million
1775	Colonial population passes 2.5 million

INQUIZITIVE

Go to InQuizitive to see what you've learned—and learn what you've missed—with personalized feedback along the way.

BOSTON TEA PARTY In one of the most famous insurrections that contributed to the colonists' anti-British fervor, a swarm of Patriots disguised as Native Americans seized three British ships and dumped more than 300 chests of East India Company tea into the Boston harbor.

From Colonies to States

1607–1776

Four great naval European powers—Spain, France, England, and the Netherlands (Holland)—created colonies in North America during the sixteenth and seventeenth centuries as part of their larger fight for global supremacy. Throughout the eighteenth century, wars raged across Europe, mostly pitting the Catholic nations of France and Spain against Protestant Great Britain and the Netherlands. The conflicts increasingly spread to the Americas, and by the middle of the eighteenth century, North America had become a primary battleground, involving both colonists and Native Americans allied with different European powers.

Spain's sparsely populated settlements in the borderlands north of Mexico were small and weak compared to those in the British colonies. The Spanish had failed to create colonies with robust economies. Instead, Spain emphasized the conversion of native peoples to Catholicism, prohibited manufacturing within its colonies, strictly limited trade with the Native Americans, and searched—in vain—for gold.

The French and British colonies developed a thriving trade with Native Americans at the same time that the fierce rivalry between Great Britain and France gradually shifted the balance of power in Europe. By the end of the eighteenth century, Spain and the Netherlands would be in decline, leaving France and Great Britain to fight for global supremacy. The nearly constant warfare led Great Britain to tighten its control

CORE OBJECTIVES INQUIZITIVE

1. Compare how the British and French Empires administered their colonies before 1763.

2. Analyze how the French and Indian War changed relations among the European powers in North America.

3. Describe how after the French and Indian War the British tightened their control over the colonies, and then summarize the colonial responses.

4. Explain the underlying factors amid the events in the 1770s that led the colonies to declare their independence from Britain.

over the American colonies to raise the funds needed to combat France and Spain. Tensions over the British effort to preserve its empire at the expense of American freedoms would lead first to rebellion and eventually to revolution.

CORE **OBJECTIVE**

1. Compare how the British and French Empires administered their colonies before 1763.

Troubled Neighbors

The French established colonies in North America at the same time as the English. Their bitter rivalry fed France's desire to challenge the English presence in the Americas by establishing Catholic settlements in the Caribbean, Canada, and the region west of the Appalachian Mountains. Yet France never invested the people or resources in North America that the English did. During the 1660s, the population of New France was less than that of the tiny English colony of Rhode Island. By the mid-eighteenth century, the residents of New France numbered less than five percent of British Americans.

New France

The actual settlement of New France began in 1605, when the enterprising soldier-explorer Samuel de Champlain, the "Father of New France," founded Port-Royal in Acadia, along the Canadian Atlantic coast. Then, three years later, Champlain established a settlement at Quebec, to the west, along the St. Lawrence River (*Quebec* is an Algonquian word meaning "where the river narrows"). Champlain was the first European to explore and map the Great Lakes.

French fur-trading companies, religious restrictions, and limited immigration

Until his death in 1635, Champlain governed New France on behalf of trading companies exploiting the fur trade with the Indians and fishing off the Atlantic coast. The trading companies sponsored Champlain's voyages in hopes of creating a prosperous commercial colony. In 1627, however, the French government ordered that only Catholics could live in New France. This restriction stunted its growth—as did the harsh winter climate. As a consequence, the number of French who colonized Canada was *much* smaller than the number of British, Dutch, and Spanish colonists in other North American colonies. From the start, France spent far more money maintaining its North American colony than it gained from the furs and fish sent to France for sale.

Coureurs des bois

Champlain knew that the French could survive only by befriending the native peoples. To that end, he dispatched young trappers and traders to live with the indigenous peoples; learn their languages, customs, and ways of war; marry Indian women; and serve as ambassadors of New France. Many of these hardy woodsmen were *coureurs des bois* (runners of the woods), who pushed into the forested regions around the Great Lakes and developed a flourishing fur trade with the Indians.

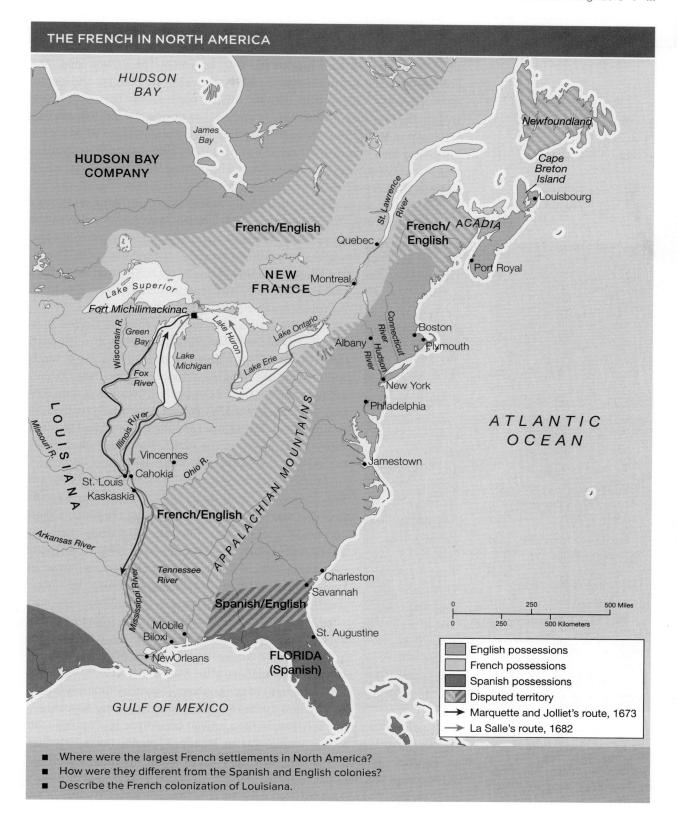

THE FRENCH IN NORTH AMERICA

HUDSON BAY

James Bay

HUDSON BAY COMPANY

Newfoundland

Cape Breton Island

· Louisbourg

French/English

ACADIA

St. Lawrence River

French/ English

Quebec ·

NEW FRANCE

· Montreal

Port Royal ·

Lake Superior

Fort Michilimackinac

Wisconsin R.

Green Bay

Lake Huron

Lake Ontario

Connecticut River

Boston

Fox River

Lake Michigan

Lake Erie

Albany

Hudson River

Plymouth

Illinois River

New York

Philadelphia

LOUISIANA

Missouri R.

Vincennes

Cahokia

Ohio R.

St. Louis

Kaskaskia

Jamestown

ATLANTIC OCEAN

APPALACHIAN MOUNTAINS

French/English

Arkansas River

Tennessee River

Charleston

Savannah

Spanish/English

Mobile

Biloxi

· New Orleans

FLORIDA (Spanish)

St. Augustine

GULF OF MEXICO

| 0 | 250 | 500 Miles |
| 0 | 250 | 500 Kilometers |

- English possessions
- French possessions
- Spanish possessions
- Disputed territory
→ Marquette and Jolliet's route, 1673
→ La Salle's route, 1682

■ Where were the largest French settlements in North America?
■ How were they different from the Spanish and English colonies?
■ Describe the French colonization of Louisiana.

In 1663, French king Louis XIV changed struggling New France into a royal colony led by a governor-general who modeled his rule after that of the absolute monarchy. New France was fully subject to the French king. The French colonists had no political rights or elected legislature, and public meetings could not be held without official permission. To solidify New France, the king dispatched soldiers and settlers during the 1660s, including shiploads of young women, known as the King's Daughters, to be wives for the mostly male colonists. Louis XIV also awarded large grants of land, called *seigneuries*, to lure aristocratic settlers. The poorest farmers usually rented land from the *seigneur*.

Yet none of these efforts transformed New France from being essentially a fur trading outpost. Only about 40,000 French immigrants came to the Western Hemisphere during the seventeenth and eighteenth centuries, even though the population of France was three times that of Spain. By 1750, when the British colonists in North America numbered about 1.5 million, the total French population was 70,000.

From their Canadian outposts along the Great Lakes, French explorers in the early 1670s moved southward down the Mississippi River to the Gulf of Mexico. Louis Jolliet, a fur trader born in Quebec, teamed with Father Jacques Marquette, a Jesuit priest fluent in Indian languages, to explore the Wisconsin River south to the Mississippi River. Traveling in canoes, they paddled south to within 400 miles of the Gulf of Mexico, where they turned back for fear of encountering Spanish soldiers.

Other French explorers followed. In 1682, René-Robert Cavelier, sieur de La Salle, organized an expedition that started in Montreal, crossed the Great Lakes, and made it all the way down the Mississippi River to the Gulf of Mexico, the first European to do so. La Salle, who learned seven different Indian languages, hoped to create a string of fur trading posts along the entire length of the river. Near what is today Venice, Mississippi, he buried an engraved plate and erected a cross, claiming for France the vast Ohio and Mississippi Valleys—all the way to the Rocky Mountains. He named the region Louisiana, after King Louis XIV.

JESUITS IN NEW FRANCE Founded in 1539, the Jesuits sought to convert Indians to Catholicism, in part to make them more reliable trading and military partners.

Settlement of the Louisiana territory finally began in 1699, when the French established a colony near Biloxi, Mississippi. The main settlement then moved to Mobile Bay on the Gulf coast and, in 1710, to the present site of Mobile, Alabama. For nearly fifty years, the driving force in Louisiana was Jean-Baptiste Le Moyne, sieur de Bienville. Sometimes called the Father of Louisiana, he served periodically as governor, and in 1718 he founded New Orleans, which shortly thereafter became the capital of the sprawling Louisiana colony encompassing much of the interior of the entire North American continent. That same year, the Spanish, concerned about the French presence in Louisiana, founded San Antonio in the Texas province of New Spain. They built a Catholic mission (later called the "Alamo") and then a fort (*presidio*) to convert the indigenous people and to fend off any efforts by the French to expand into Texas.

Two centuries later, the American historian Francis Parkman explained that "France in America had two heads, one amid the snows of Canada, the other amid the [sugar] canebrakes of Louisiana." Although having far fewer colonists than British America, New France had one important advantage over its rival: access to the great inland rivers that led to the heartland of the continent and the valuable pelts of fur-bearing animals: beaver, otter, and mink.

Because of geography as well as deliberate policy, however, New France remained during the eighteenth century a vast region traversed by a mobile population of traders, trappers, missionaries, and mainly Indians. By building closer bonds and encroaching far less upon Native American lands, the French won Native American allies against the more numerous British Americans. For well over a century, in fact, Native Americans would determine the military balance of power within North America.

Native American allies

The British System

The diverse British colonies in North America were quite different from those of New France. Colonial governments were typically headed by a royal governor or proprietor who could appoint and remove officials, command the militia, and grant pardons to people convicted of crimes. However, the American colonists enjoyed some rights and powers absent in Britain—as well as in New France. The British colonies in America, unlike the Spanish, French, or Dutch colonies, had *elected* legislative assemblies. The representatives in the "lower" houses in each colony were chosen by popular vote, but only adult males owning a specified amount of property could vote. But because property holding was widespread in America, a greater proportion of the male population could vote in the colonies than anywhere else in the world. Women, Native Americans, and African Americans were excluded from the political process.

Elected legislative assemblies

The most important political trend in eighteenth-century America was the growing power of the colonial legislatures. Like Parliament, the assemblies controlled the budget, and they could pass laws and regulations. Most of the colonial assemblies also influenced the royal governors by setting their salaries. Throughout the eighteenth century, the assemblies expanded their power and influence relative to the royal governors. Unlike the situation in New France, where the governor-general exercised absolute power and there were no legislative assemblies, self-government in British America became first a habit, then a cherished "right."

Mercantilism

Throughout much of the seventeenth and eighteenth centuries, British officials exercised what one politician called a **salutary neglect** by not strictly enforcing the laws regulating the American colonies, especially those involving trade restrictions. Smuggling was commonplace, a way to escape paying taxes on goods imported from other countries.

The perpetual struggle between Parliament and the British kings made it difficult to develop either consistent colonial policies around the world or to create effective means of enforcing such policies. The English Civil War (1642–1646) sharply reduced the flow of money and people from England to America and created great confusion regarding England's colonial policies. It also forced English Americans to take sides in the conflict between Royalists and Puritans.

The 1651 victory of Oliver Cromwell's Puritan army over the monarchy had direct effects in the colonies. As England's new ruler, Cromwell embraced **mercantilism**, a political and economic policy adopted by most European monarchs during the seventeenth century. In a mercantile system, the government controlled all economic activities in an effort to strengthen national power. Key industries were regulated, taxed, or "subsidized" (supported by payments from the government). People with specialized skills or knowledge of new industrial technologies, such as textile machinery, were not allowed to leave the country.

Mercantilism also supported the creation of global empires. Colonies, it was assumed, enriched nations in several ways: (1) by providing silver and gold as well as the raw materials (furs, fish, grains, timber, sugar, tobacco, indigo, tar, etc.) needed to supply food, build ships, and produce goods; (2) by creating a captive market of colonial consumers who would be forced to buy goods created in the home country; (3) by relieving social tensions and political unrest in the home country, because colonies could provide a new home for the growing numbers of poor, unemployed, and imprisoned; and, (4) by not producing goods that would compete with those produced in the "home country."

Navigation Acts

Such mercantilist assumptions prompted Oliver Cromwell to adopt the first in a series of **Navigation Acts** intended to increase England's control over its colonial economies. The Navigation Act of 1651 required that all goods going to and from the colonies be carried *only* in English-owned ships built in England. The law intended to hurt the Dutch, who had developed a flourishing business shipping goods between America and Europe. Dutch shippers charged much less to transport goods than did the English, and they actively encouraged smuggling in the American colonies as a means of defying the Navigation Acts. By 1652, England and the Netherlands were at war, the first of three naval conflicts that erupted between the two Protestant rivals.

From salutary neglect to mercantilism

salutary neglect Informal British policy during the first half of the eighteenth century that allowed the American colonies freedom to pursue their economic and political interests in exchange for colonial obedience.

mercantilism Policy of England and other imperial powers of regulating colonial economies to benefit the mother country.

Navigation Acts (1650–1775) Restrictions passed by Parliament to control colonial trade and bolster the mercantile system.

BOSTON FROM THE SOUTHEAST This view of eighteenth-century Boston shows the importance of shipping and its regulation in the colonies, especially in Massachusetts Bay.

After the English monarchy returned to power in 1660, the new royalist Parliament passed the Navigation Act of 1660, which specified that certain colonial products such as tobacco were to be shipped *only* to England or other English colonies. The Navigation Act of 1663, called the Staples Act, required that *all* shipments of goods from Europe to America must first stop in England to be offloaded and taxed before being sent on to the colonies.

In 1664, an English fleet of warships conquered New Netherland, removing the Dutch rival from North America. Over time, the Navigation Acts worked as planned: by 1700, the English had surpassed the Dutch as the world's leading maritime power. What the English government did not predict or fully understand was that its mercantile system would arouse growing bitterness in the colonies.

> Navigation Acts target Dutch

Resentment in the Colonies

Colonial merchants and shippers resented and resisted the Navigation Acts. New England, which shipped 90 percent of all American exports, was particularly hard hit. In 1678, a defiant Massachusetts legislature declared that the Navigation Acts had no legal standing in the colony. Six years later, in 1684, King Charles II tried to teach the rebellious colonists a lesson by revoking the royal charter for Massachusetts.

The following year, in 1685, King Charles II died and his brother, King James II, succeeded him. The new king reorganized all the New England

> Dominion of New England

colonies into a single royal supercolony called the Dominion of New England. In 1686, the newly appointed royal governor, Sir Edmund Andros, arrived in Boston to take control of the Dominion. Andros stripped New Englanders of their civil rights and imposed new taxes as well as the Anglican religion, ignored the authority of town governments, strictly enforced the Navigation Acts, and punished American smugglers who tried to avoid regulation altogether.

The Glorious Revolution

In 1688, the Dominion of New England added the former Dutch provinces of New York, East Jersey, and West Jersey to its control, just a few months before the **Glorious Revolution** erupted in England in December. It was "Glorious" because, unlike the English Civil War, it took place with little bloodshed. After James II fled to France, the king's Protestant daughter Mary and her Protestant husband William III (the ruling Dutch prince) assumed the English throne.

William III and Mary II would rule as constitutional monarchs, their powers limited by the Parliament and English common law. The new monarchs issued a religious Toleration Act and a Bill of Rights to ensure that there never again would be an absolute monarchy in England.

In 1689, Bostonians staged their own "glorious" revolution. A group of merchants, ministers, and militiamen (citizen-soldiers) arrested Governor Andros and his aides and removed Massachusetts Bay Colony from the new Dominion of New England. Within a few weeks, the other colonies that had been absorbed into the Dominion also restored their independence.

William and Mary allowed all the New England colonies to regain their former status except Massachusetts Bay and Plymouth, which after some delay were united under a new charter in 1691 as the royal colony of Massachusetts Bay. However, William and Mary were also determined to crack down on American smuggling and rebelliousness. To that end, they appointed new royal governors in Massachusetts, New York, and Maryland. In Massachusetts, the new governor was given authority to veto acts of the colonial assembly, and he removed the Puritans' religious qualification for voting.

The Glorious Revolution had significant long-term effects on American history. The removal of King James II revealed that a hated monarch could be deposed. In addition, the long-standing geographical designation "Great Britain" for the island shared by England, Scotland, and Wales would soon be revived as the official name of the nation.

A powerful justification for revolution appeared in 1690 when the English philosopher John Locke published his *Two Treatises on Government*, which had an enormous impact on political thought in the colonies. Locke rejected the traditional "divine" right of monarchs to govern with absolute power. He also insisted that people are endowed with **natural rights** to life, liberty, and property. After all, as Locke noted, it was the need to protect

JOHN LOCKE An English philosopher and strong believer in natural rights, Locke's writings rationalized revolutionary movements to overthrow unsatisfactory governments.

Glorious Revolution (1688) Successful coup, instigated by a group of English aristocrats, that overthrew King James II and instated William of Orange and Mary, his English wife, to the English throne.

natural rights An individual's basic rights (life, liberty, and property) that should not be violated by any government or community.

those "natural" rights that led people to establish governments in the first place. When rulers failed to protect the property and lives of their subjects, Locke argued, the people had the right—in extreme cases—to overthrow the monarch and change the government.

Natural rights vs. royal absolutism

Warfare in the Colonies

CORE **OBJECTIVE**
2. Analyze how the French and Indian War changed relations among the European powers in North America.

The Glorious Revolution of 1688 transformed relations among the great powers of Europe. William and Mary were passionate foes of Catholic France's Louis XIV. William organized an alliance of European nations against the French in a transatlantic war known in the American colonies as King William's War (1689–1697). It was the first of four major wars fought in Europe and the colonies over the next seventy-four years. In each case, Britain and its European allies fought against Catholic France or Spain and their allies. By the end of the eighteenth century, the struggle between the British and the French would shift the balance of power among the great nations of Europe.

The French and Indian War

The most significant conflict between Britain and France in North America was the French and Indian War (1754–1763). Unlike the three previous wars between Britain and France and their allies, it ended with a decisive British victory. Sparked by competing claims over the Indian lands in the vast Ohio Valley, the "most fertile country of America," the stakes were high. Both the British and the French governments believed that whichever nation controlled the "Ohio Country" would come to control the entire continent because of the strategic importance of the Ohio and Mississippi Rivers.

To defend their interests in the Ohio Valley, the French pushed south from Canada and built forts in upstate New York and western Pennsylvania. When the Virginia governor learned of the French forts, he sent a twenty-one-year-old Virginia militia officer, Major George Washington, to warn the French to leave the area.

With an experienced guide and a few others, Washington made his way on foot and by horseback, canoe, and raft over 450 miles to Fort Le Boeuf (just south of Lake Erie, in northwest Pennsylvania) in late 1753. He demanded that the French withdraw from the Ohio Country; the French captain refused. A frustrated George Washington returned to Virginia through the deepening snow.

A few months later, in the spring of 1754, George Washington, now a lieutenant colonel, went back to the Ohio Country. This time he led 150 volunteers and Indian allies to build a fort where the Allegheny, Monongahela, and Ohio Rivers converged (where the city of Pittsburgh later developed). The so-called Forks of the Ohio was the strategic gateway to the vast western

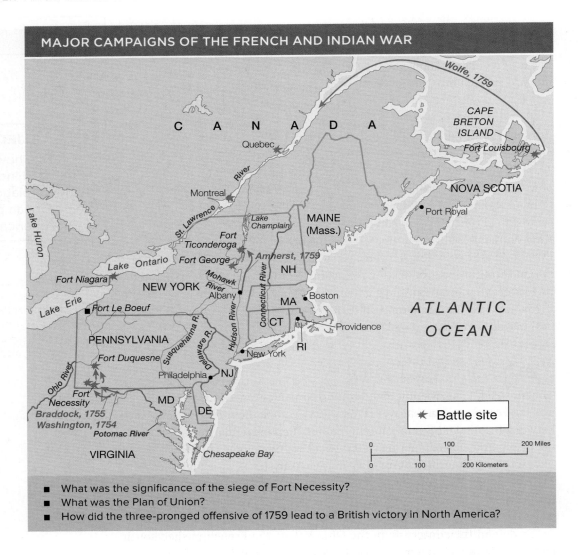

MAJOR CAMPAIGNS OF THE FRENCH AND INDIAN WAR

- What was the significance of the siege of Fort Necessity?
- What was the Plan of Union?
- How did the three-pronged offensive of 1759 lead to a British victory in North America?

territory west of the Appalachian Mountains, and both sides were determined to control it.

After two months of difficult travel through densely forested, hilly terrain, Washington learned that French soldiers had beaten him to the site and built Fort Duquesne. Washington and his men made camp about forty miles from the fort. The next day, the Virginians ambushed a French scouting party, killing ten French soldiers—the first fatalities in what would become the French and Indian War, a global conflict that would become a financial and imperial disaster for the French.

George Washington and his troops, reinforced by more Virginians and British soldiers dispatched from South Carolina, hastily constructed a crude circular fort, called Fort Necessity, which a large force of French soldiers surrounded and attacked a month later, on July 3, 1754. After the daylong

Battle of Great Meadows, Washington surrendered, having seen a third of his 300 men killed or wounded. France was now in undisputed control of the Ohio Country.

George Washington's expedition had triggered a series of events that would ignite a massive world war. As a British politician exclaimed, "The volley fired by a young Virginian in the backwoods of America set the world on fire."

Albany Plan

British officials in America, worried about war with the French and their Indian allies, hastily organized a meeting of delegates from the northern colonies as far south as Maryland. Twenty-one representatives from seven colonies gathered in Albany, in upstate New York. It was the first time that a large group of colonial delegates had met to take joint action.

THE FIRST AMERICAN POLITICAL CARTOON First appearing on May 9, 1754 in the *Pennsylvania Gazette*, this widely circulated political cartoon by Benjamin Franklin urged the colonies to unite against the French. Twenty years later, when the French became an ally of the colonies and the British became the primary threat to American liberty, this cartoon was revived with new meaning.

At the urging of Pennsylvania's Benjamin Franklin, the Albany Congress (June 19–July 11, 1754) approved the **Albany Plan of Union**. It called for eleven colonies to band together, headed by a president appointed by the king. Each colonial assembly would send two to seven delegates to a "grand council," which would have legislative powers. The Union would have jurisdiction over Indian affairs.

The Albany Plan of Union was too radical for the time, however. The colonial legislatures, eager to maintain their powers, and British officials, who wanted simply a military alliance against Indian attacks, rejected it. Benjamin Franklin later maintained that the 1754 Plan of Union, had it been approved, may have postponed or eliminated the eventual need for a full-scale colonial revolution. Franklin's proposal, however, did have a lasting significance in that it would be the model for the form of governance (Articles of Confederation) created by the new American nation in 1777.

War in North America

With the failure of the Albany Plan, the British government decided to force a showdown with the "presumptuous" French in North America. In June 1755, a British fleet captured the French forts protecting Acadia, a colony of New France along the Atlantic coast of Canada. The British then expelled 11,500 of the Catholic French residents, called Acadians. They were crammed onto ships and scattered throughout the British colonies, from Maine to Georgia. Hundreds uprooted by the "Great Expulsion" eventually found their way to French Louisiana, where they became known as Cajuns (the name derived from *Acadians*).

Albany Plan of Union (1754) A failed proposal by the seven northern colonies in anticipation of the French and Indian War, urging the unification of the colonies under one Crown-appointed president.

FROM LA ROQUE'S
ENCYCLOPÉDIE DES VOYAGES
An Iroquois warrior in an
eighteenth-century French
engraving. **How does La Roque's
representation of this Iroquois
warrior differ from how Braddock
viewed the Native Americans?**

**French and Indian War (Seven
Years' War) (1756–1763)**
The last and most important
of four colonial wars between
England and France for control
of North America east of the
Mississippi River.

Braddock's Defeat In 1755, the British government sent a thousand soldiers to Virginia to force the French out of the Ohio Country. The British commander-in-chief in America, General Edward Braddock, was a stubborn, overconfident officer who refused to recruit Indian allies. Braddock viewed Indians with open contempt, telling those willing to fight with him that he would not reward them for doing so: "No savage should inherit the land." His dismissal of the Indians and his ignorance of unconventional warfare in American forests would prove fatal. Neither he nor his Irish troops had any experience fighting in the wilderness.

With the addition of some American militiamen, including George Washington as a volunteer officer, Braddock's force hacked a 125-mile-long road west through the rugged Allegheny Mountains toward Fort Duquesne. The British were on the verge of success when, on July 9, 1755, six miles from Fort Duquesne, they were ambushed by French soldiers, Canadian militiamen, and Indians. Attacked on three sides, the British troops suffered horrific losses. General Braddock was mortally wounded and would die three days later. Twenty-three-year-old George Washington, his coat riddled by four bullets, helped lead a hasty retreat.

What came to be called the Battle of Monongahela was one of the worst British defeats in history. The French and Indians had killed sixty-three of eighty-six British officers, 914 out of 1,373 soldiers, and captured the British cannons, supplies, and secret papers. Indians burned alive twelve of the wounded British soldiers left behind on the battlefield. A devastated George Washington wrote his brother that the British army had "been scandalously beaten by a trifling body of men." The vaunted redcoats "broke & run as sheep before hounds," but the Virginians "behaved like Men and died like Soldiers."

A World War

Braddock's stunning defeat sent shock waves through the colonies. Inspired by the news, Indians allied with the French attacked Americans living on isolated farms throughout western Pennsylvania, Maryland, and Virginia.

Not until May 1756, however, did Britain and France formally declare war. The **French and Indian War**, as it was known in North America, became the world's first truly global conflict. Known as the Seven Years' War in Europe, it became a clash between the Protestant and Catholic nations, a conflict eventually fought on four continents and three oceans around the globe. In the end, it would redraw the political map of the world—including North America.

France, a nation governed by an inept king, Louis XV, entered the war without excitement, fought with little distinction, and emerged battered, humiliated, and bankrupt. When the war began, the British had a smaller army than the French but three times as many warships. By the end of the war, the French had lost nearly a hundred warships, and the British had captured more than 64,000 French sailors.

> The French and Indian War becomes the Seven Years' War

In 1759, the French and Indian War reached its climax with a series of British triumphs on land and at sea. The most decisive British victory was at Quebec, the capital of French Canada. Thereafter, the war in North America dragged on until 1763. In the South, fighting flared up between the Carolina settlers and the Cherokee Nation. A force of British regulars and colonial militia broke Cherokee resistance in 1761.

Meanwhile, the much larger Seven Years' War played out around the globe. Most of the fighting was in Europe, where Great Britain's allies, especially Prussia, and the nations allied with France and Spain, primarily Austria, Sweden, and Russia, ravaged each other. Hundreds of towns and cities were plundered and over a million people killed.

A New British King

On October 25, 1760, while the war still raged on, King George II arose at 6 A.M., drank his morning chocolate milk, and suddenly died on his toilet after rupturing an artery. His death shocked the nation and brought an untested new king to the throne.

The new twenty-two-year-old king, George III, was inexperienced and had been despised by his grandfather, George II. Although initially shy and insecure, the boyish king turned into a strong-willed leader. He oversaw the military defeat of France and Spain, which made Great Britain the ruler of an enormous world empire. Within three years of George III's ascension to the throne, Britain became the largest, richest, and most powerful empire in the world.

GEORGE III In 1760 the young George III became King of Great Britain, and soon he governed the most powerful empire in the world.

The Treaty of Paris (1763)

More territory was transferred from the vanquished to the victors after the French and Indian War than any other war before or since. In the **Treaty of Paris**, signed in February 1763, victorious Britain took ownership of several profitable French "sugar island" colonies in the West Indies, most of the French colonies in India, and France's North American possessions east of the Mississippi River: Canada and what was then called Spanish Florida (including much of present-day Alabama and Mississippi). As compensation, the treaty gave Spain control over the vast Louisiana Territory, including New Orleans and all French land west of the Mississippi River.

> The British gain most of North America; the Spanish gain the Louisiana Territory

Treaty of Paris (1763)
Settlement between Great Britain and France that ended the French and Indian War.

British Americans were delighted with the outcome of the war. As a New England minister declared, Great Britain had reached the "summit of earthly grandeur and glory." The British now controlled most of the continent of North America. In compensation for its loss of Florida in the Treaty of Paris, Spain received from France the vast Louisiana Territory (including New Orleans and all French land west of the Mississippi River). The loss of Louisiana left France with no territory on the continent. British power reigned supreme over North America east of the Mississippi River.

Britain's spectacular military success also created massive challenges, however. The British victory was costly; Britain's national debt doubled during the war. Moreover, the cost of maintaining the North American empire, including the permanent stationing of thousands of British soldiers in the colonies, was staggering. And the victory meant that Britain now had to manage a *half-billion* acres of new colonial territory in North America. In assuming control of a vastly larger North American empire, the British would soon find themselves at war with their own colonies.

Managing a New Empire

Colonists taxed to pay staggering British war debts

No sooner was the Treaty of Paris signed than young King George III and his cabinet began strictly enforcing economic regulations on the colonies as a means of reducing the crushing national debt caused by the war. During and after the war, the British government increased taxes to fund the military expenses. In 1763, the average Englishman paid twenty-six times as much in taxes each year as the average American colonist paid. With that in mind, British leaders thought it only fair that the Americans should pay more of the expenses for administering and defending the colonies.

Many Americans disagreed, however, arguing that the various Navigation Acts restricting their economic activities were already a form of tax on their liberties. The tension between the British need for greater revenue from the colonies and the Americans' defense of their rights and liberties set in motion a chain of events that would lead to revolution and independence. "It is truly a miserable thing," said a Connecticut minister in December 1763, "that we no sooner leave fighting our neighbors, the French, but we must fall to quarreling among ourselves."

Pontiac's Rebellion

No sooner had the war with France ended than colonists began squabbling over Indian-owned lands west of the Appalachian Mountains that the French had ceded to the British in the Treaty of Paris. Native American leaders, none of whom were allowed to participate in the negotiations leading to the Treaty of Paris in 1763, were shocked to learn that the French had "given" their ancestral lands to the British. Ohio Indians complained to a British army officer that "as soon as you conquered the French, you did not care how you treated us." One chieftain claimed that the British now treated them "like slaves."

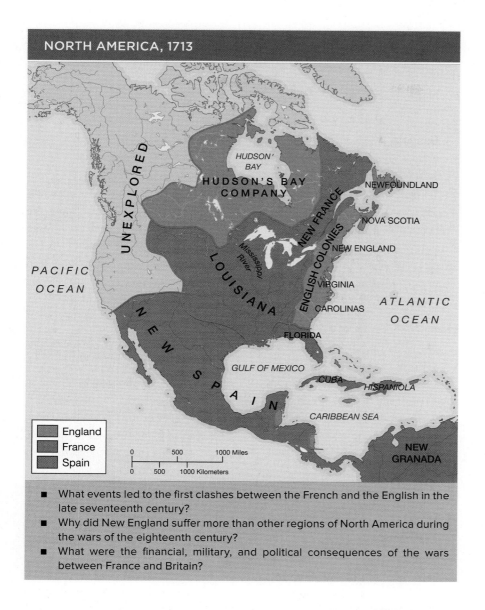

NORTH AMERICA, 1713

England
France
Spain

- What events led to the first clashes between the French and the English in the late seventeenth century?
- Why did New England suffer more than other regions of North America during the wars of the eighteenth century?
- What were the financial, military, and political consequences of the wars between France and Britain?

In a desperate effort to recover their lands, Indians fought back in the spring of 1763, capturing most of the British forts around the Great Lakes and in the Ohio Valley. They also raided colonial settlements in Pennsylvania, Maryland, and Virginia, destroying hundreds of farm cabins and killing or capturing several thousand people.

The widespread Indian attacks in the spring and summer of 1763 came to be called **Pontiac's Rebellion** because of the prominent role played by the inspiring Ottawa chief. Embarrassed by their losses, British officials eventually negotiated an agreement with the Indians that allowed British troops to reoccupy the frontier forts in exchange for a renewal of the fur trade. Still, as

Pontiac's Rebellion (1763)
A series of Native American attacks on British forts and settlements after France ceded to the British its territory east of the Mississippi River, as part of the Treaty of Paris without consulting France's Native American allies.

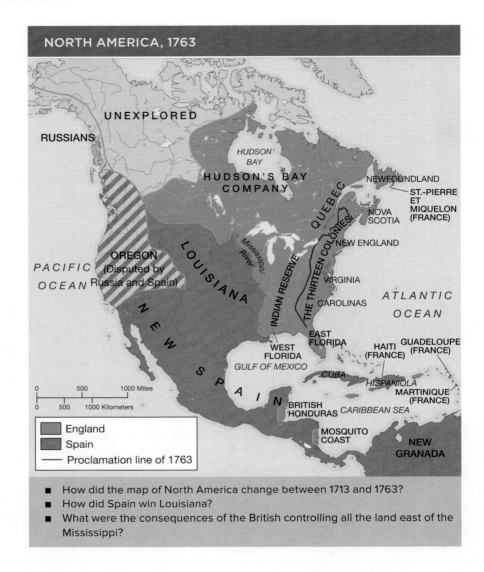

NORTH AMERICA, 1763

■ How did the map of North America change between 1713 and 1763?
■ How did Spain win Louisiana?
■ What were the consequences of the British controlling all the land east of the Mississippi?

Chief Pontiac stressed, the Indians steadfastly denied British claims to their territory under the terms of the Treaty of Paris. He told a British official that the "French never conquered us, neither did they purchase a foot of our Country, nor have they a right to give it to you."

The Proclamation Line

Royal Proclamation of 1763 Proclamation drawing a boundary along the Appalachian Mountains from Canada to Georgia in order to minimize occurrences of settler–Native American violence; colonists were forbidden to go west of the line.

To help keep peace with the Indians, King George III issued the **Royal Proclamation of 1763**, which drew an imaginary "proclamation line" along the crest of the Appalachian Mountains from Canada to Georgia. The proclamation prohibited white settlers ("our loving subjects") from going west of the line so that the Indians would not be "molested or disturbed" on their ancestral lands.

For the first time, royal officials has curtailed American territorial expansion. The British government sent 10,000 soldiers to enforce the new boundary line separating Indians and whites and to ensure that the former French colonists in Canada did not cause trouble. Yet the proclamation line was impossible to enforce. Land-hungry settlers continued to push across the Appalachian ridges into Indian country. By 1767, an Indian chief was complaining that whites were "making more encroachments on their Country than ever they had before."

Tightening Control over the Colonies

CORE **OBJECTIVE**

3. Describe how after the French and Indian War the British tightened their control over the colonies, and then summarize the colonial responses.

The Royal Proclamation of 1763 was the first of several efforts by the British government after the French and Indian War to increase its control over the colonies. Little did the king and royal officials know that their efforts would spark a revolution.

Grenville's Colonial Policy

Just as the Proclamation of 1763 was being drafted, a new British government led by George Grenville began to grapple with the huge debts accumulated during the war along with the added expenses of maintaining British troops in America. Grenville insisted that the Americans, whom he called the "least taxed people in the world," pay for the British soldiers defending them. Grenville also targeted the large number of American merchants who engaged in smuggling to avoid paying taxes on imported goods.

British warships target American smugglers

After the war, Americans went on a buying binge, eager to purchase the latest fashionable items from Britain and France, and they preferred buying from smugglers—it was cheaper. So Grenville ordered colonial officials to tighten the enforcement of the Navigation Acts, and he dispatched warships to capture American smugglers.

New taxes and regulations

The Sugar Act (1764)

Grenville's effort to enforce the various Navigation Acts posed a serious threat to New England's prosperity. Making rum out of molasses, a sweet syrup made from sugarcane, had become quite profitable, especially if the molasses could be smuggled in from Caribbean islands still controlled by the French. To generate more money from the colonies, Grenville put through the American Revenue Act of 1764, commonly known as the Sugar Act, which cut the tax on molasses in half. Doing so, he believed, would reduce the temptation to smuggle French molasses or to bribe royal customs officers. The Sugar Act, however, also added new duties (taxes) on other goods (sugar, wines, coffee, spices) imported into America. The new revenues generated by the Sugar Act,

"THE GREAT FINANCIER" A British cartoon from 1765 depicts the struggling British economy. Grenville stands in the center holding up a scale to measure British "Debts" and "Savings," the debts far outweighing the savings. On the left a Native American woman wearing a yoke represents America, burdened by taxes without representation. **Why was Britain in such financial straits in the early 1760s and how did Grenville attempt to pay off Britain's debts?**

Grenville estimated, would help pay for "the necessary expenses of defending, protecting, and securing, the said colonies."

With the Sugar Act, Parliament, for the first time, adopted a policy designed to raise *revenues* from the colonies and not merely to *regulate* trade with other nations. Colonists claimed that the Sugar Act taxed them without their consent, since they had no elected representatives in Parliament. British officials argued, however, that Parliament's power was absolute and indivisible. If the Americans accepted parliamentary authority in *any* area, they had to accept its authority in *every* area, including taxation.

The Currency Act (1764)

Americans equally hated another of Grenville's new regulatory measures, the Currency Act of 1764. It prohibited the colonies from printing more paper money and stipulated that all payments for British goods must be in gold or silver coins or a commodity like tobacco. This caused the value of existing paper money to plummet and dried up much of American commerce. As a Philadelphia newspaper noted, "The Times are Dreadful, Dismal, Doleful, Dolorous, and DOLLAR-LESS."

The Quartering Act (1765)

Then, in 1765, Grenville persuaded Parliament to pass the Quartering Act as part of his new system of colonial regulations. The Quartering Act required the colonies to feed and house British troops. Such a step seemed perfectly appropriate to Grenville, since he and many others in Britain believed that the Americans should contribute to the expense of defending the colonies. In the view of many Americans, however, the Quartering Act was yet another form of tax as well as another form of repression. Many Americans saw no need for so many British soldiers in colonial cities. If the British were there to defend against Indians, why were they in cities rather than along the frontier? Some colonists decided that the Quartering Act was actually an effort to use British soldiers to bully the Americans.

The Stamp Act (1765)

Britain's prime minister, George Grenville, aggravated the controversy with the colonists by pushing through an even more controversial measure to raise money in America: a stamp tax. On February 13, 1765, Parliament

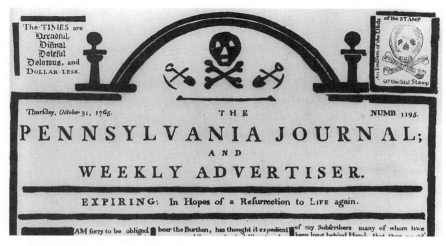

OPPOSITION TO THE STAMP ACT On October 31, 1765, The *Pennsylvania Journal* printed a skull and crossbones on its masthead in protest of the Stamp Act, which was to take effect the next day. **Why was the Stamp Act met with such opposition by the colonists?**

passed the **Stamp Act**, which required colonists to purchase stamped paper for virtually every possible use: newspapers, pamphlets, bonds, leases, deeds, licenses, insurance policies, college diplomas, even playing cards. The requirement was to go into effect November 1, nine months later. The Stamp Act was especially important because it affected all the colonists, not just New England merchants and shippers, and it was the first effort by Parliament to place a direct—or "internal"—tax specifically on American goods and services rather than an "external" tax on imports and exports. Not a single colony supported the new measure.

The Whig Point of View

Grenville's colonial policies outraged many Americans, especially those in the largest cities. Unwittingly, the prime minister had stirred up a storm of protest and set in motion a violent debate about the proper relationship between Great Britain and her American colonies. Slowly, more and more colonists began developing what could be called an American rather than a British point of view. It was not based on a common ancestry, a shared religion, or even a common culture. Rather, the American perspective involved defending certain essential principles and practices: self-government, equality of economic opportunity, religious freedom, and territorial expansion.

Now, all those deeply embedded values seemed threatened by Parliament's determined efforts to tighten control over its colonies after 1763. In the late eighteenth century, the Americans who opposed British policies

Stamp Act (1765) Act of Parliament requiring that all printed materials in the American colonies use paper with an official tax stamp in order to pay for British military protection of the colonies.

began to call themselves Patriots or *Whigs,* a name earlier applied to British critics of royal power, and to label the king and his "corrupt" government ministers and Parliamentary supporters as *Tories,* a word meaning friends of the king.

In 1764 and 1765, Whigs decided that Grenville was violating their rights in several ways. A professional army was usually a weapon used by tyrants, and now, with the French defeated and Canada solidly under British control, thousands of British soldiers remained in the colonies. Were the troops there to protect the colonists or to scare them into obedience?

Virtual representation

Whigs also argued that British citizens had the right to be taxed only by their elected representatives in Parliament, but Americans had no such representatives. British leaders replied that the colonists enjoyed **virtual representation** by all the members of Parliament acting in the national interest.

William Pitt, a staunch supporter of American rights in Parliament, dismissed Grenville's concept of "virtual representation" as "the most contemptible idea that ever entered into the head of a man." Many others, in both Britain and America, agreed. Sir Francis Bernard, the royal governor of Massachusetts, correctly predicted that the new stamp tax "would cause a great Alarm & meet much Opposition" in the colonies.

Protests in the Colonies

The Stamp Act aroused fierce resentment and resistance. A New Yorker wrote that "this single stroke has lost Great Britain the affection of all her colonies." In a flood of pamphlets, speeches, resolutions, and street protests, critics repeated a slogan familiar to all Americans: "No taxation without representation [in Parliament]."

Stamp Act Resolutions

Through the spring and summer of 1765, this simmering resentment boiled over at meetings, parades, bonfires, and other demonstrations. The protesters, calling themselves **Sons of Liberty**, emerged in every colony, often meeting beneath "liberty trees"—in Boston a great elm and in Charleston, South Carolina, a live oak. In New York City, the Sons of Liberty erected "liberty poles" as symbols of their resistance (British soldiers would tear them down almost as soon as they were put up). In Virginia, Patrick Henry convinced the assembly to pass the "Stamp Act Resolutions," which asserted yet again that the colonists could not be taxed without first being consulted by the British government or represented in the British Parliament by their own elected representatives.

In mid-August 1765, nearly three months before the Stamp Act was to take effect, a mob of angry Bostonians plundered the homes of the royal lieutenant governor and the royal official in charge of enforcing the stamp tax. Thoroughly shaken, the Boston stamp agent resigned, and stamp agents throughout the colonies were hounded out of office. By November 1, its effective starting date, the Stamp Act was dead.

virtual representation The idea that the American colonies, although they had no actual representative in Parliament, were "virtually" represented by all members of Parliament.

Sons of Liberty First organized by Samuel Adams in the 1770s, groups of colonists dedicated to militant resistance against British control of the colonies.

THE LIBERTY TREE At this mid-August meeting of the Sons of Liberty, the angry colonists hanged effigies of two tax collectors from the branches of a Liberty Tree.

The Nonimportation Movement

Americans opposed to the Stamp Act knew that the most powerful form of leverage they had against the British was economic. To demonstrate their resolve and to put pressure on British merchants to ask Parliament to change its American policies, colonists by the thousands signed nonimportation and nonconsumption agreements, promising not to import or buy a long list of goods produced in Britain. "Save your money and save your country!" boycotters in Boston shouted in 1767. Patriots must buy only American-made goods.

These boycotts of imported British products were an especially effective tactic because American consumers had become a major boon to the British economy during the eighteenth century, going ever more deeply into debt to buy the latest in British fashion and conveniences. Now this profitable trade was at risk, and many London merchants sided with the Americans against the proposed Stamp Act, fearful of losing their profitable business with their overseas customers.

The nonimportation movements of the 1760s and 1770s united Whigs from different communities and different colonies. It also enabled women to play a significant public role resisting Britain's new colonial policies. Calling themselves **Daughters of Liberty**, many colonial women stopped buying imported British clothes and made their own. The Daughters of Liberty also participated in public "spinning circles" or "spinning bees," whereby groups of women would gather to spin yarn, linen, or wool into threads and then weave into fabric for clothes, known as "homespun." While weaving they

Daughters of Liberty Colonial women who protested the British government's tax policies by boycotting British products, such as clothing, and who wove their own fabric, or "homespun."

would socialize and discuss politics. In 1769, the *Boston Evening Post* reported that the "industry and frugality of American ladies" were "enabling the political salvation of the whole continent."

Boycotts of British goods

Patriots saw the bold, innovative effort to boycott British products not only as a new form of political protest but also as a way to restore their own virtue. A Rhode Islander declared that a primary cause of America's problems was the "luxury and extravagance" brought on by their freewheeling purchases of British goods. The nonimportation movement would help Americans restore their "frugality, industry, and simplicity of manners." Plain living soon became a sign of American patriotism. A Boston minister claimed that those who could not do without British luxury goods and be satisfied with "plainness and simplicity" did not deserve to be American citizens.

Colonial Unity

Virginia Resolves

The grassroots boycotts worked; imports of British goods fell by 40 percent. At the same time, the Virginia House of Burgesses struck the first official blow against the Stamp Act with the Virginia Resolves (1765), a series of resolutions inspired by the fiery young Patrick Henry. Virginians, Henry declared, were entitled to all the rights of Englishmen, who could be taxed only by their own elected representatives. Newspapers spread the Virginia Resolves throughout the colonies, and other colonial assemblies hastened to follow Virginia's example.

"No taxation without representation!" became the rallying cry for American Whigs opposed to the Stamp Tax. New York Patriots argued that if Britain "would strip us of all the advantages derived to us from the English constitution, why should we desire to continue our connection [with the mother country]? We might as well belong to France, or any other power."

The Stamp Act Congress and the Declaration of Rights and Grievances

In 1765, the Massachusetts House of Representatives invited the other colonial assemblies to send delegates to meet in New York to discuss their opposition to the Stamp Act. Nine responded, and from October 7 to October 25, 1765, the so-called Stamp Act Congress formulated a protest to Parliament called the Declaration of the Rights and Grievances of the Colonies. The delegates insisted that they would accept no taxes being "imposed on them" without "their own consent, given personally, or by their representatives." Parliament, in other words, had no right to tax people who were unrepresented in that body. In response, Grenville denounced his colonial critics as "ungrateful" for the many benefits provided them by the British government.

Repeal of the Stamp Act

The storm over the Stamp Act had scarcely erupted before Prime Minister Grenville was out of office. He had lost the confidence of the king, who replaced him with Lord Rockingham in July 1765. The growing violence in America and the success of the nonimportation movement convinced Rockingham that the Stamp Act was a mistake. In February 1766, a

OR THE FUNERAL OF MISS AME.-STAMP

REPEAL OF THE STAMP ACT
This 1766 cartoon shows Grenville carrying the dead Stamp Act in its coffin. In the background, trade with America starts up again.

humiliated Parliament repealed the Stamp Act. To save face, it also passed the Declaratory Act, which asserted the power of Parliament to govern the colonies "in all cases whatsoever." The repeal of the Stamp Act set off excited demonstrations throughout the colonies. Perhaps the worst was over, they hoped.

The Townshend Acts Fan the Flames

In July 1766, King George III replaced Lord Rockingham with William Pitt, a former prime minister who had exercised heroic leadership during the French and Indian War. For a time in 1767, the guiding force in the Pitt ministry was the witty but reckless Charles Townshend, the treasury chief whose "abilities were superior to those of all men," said a colleague, "and his judgment [common sense] below that of any man."

In 1767, Townshend, determined like his predecessors to extract more revenue from the colonies in order to pay for the costs of governing and defending them, pushed his ill-fated plan through Parliament; a few months later he died at age forty-two, leaving behind a bitter legacy: the **Townshend Acts**.

More taxes under Townshend

The Revenue Act of 1767, which taxed colonial imports of glass, lead, paint, paper, and tea, was the most hated of the new colonial laws. It posed an even more severe threat than Grenville's taxes had done, for Townshend planned to use the new tax revenues to pay the salaries of the royal governors in the colonies. Until that point, colonial assemblies had paid the salaries, thus giving them some leverage over the governors. John Adams observed that Townshend's plan would make the royal governors "independent of the people" and disrupt "the balance of power which is essential to all free governments."

Townshend Acts (1767) Parliamentary measures to extract more revenue from the colonies; the Revenue Act of 1767, which taxed tea, paper, and other colonial imports, was one of the most notorious of these policies.

CORE OBJECTIVE

4. Explain the underlying factors amid the events in the 1770s that led the colonies to declare their independence from Britain.

The Crisis Grows

American Patriots

The Townshend Acts, passed against the objections of William Pitt, who later resigned in protest, surprised and angered the colonists. As American rage bubbled over, loyalty to Britain waned. Firebrand Samuel Adams of Boston emerged as one of the most radical rebels. He decided that a determined group of Patriots could generate a mass protest movement against the British. "It does not take a majority to prevail," Adams insisted, "but rather an irate, tireless minority, keen on setting brushfires for freedom in the minds of men."

Early in 1768, Adams and the Boston attorney James Otis convinced the Massachusetts Assembly to circulate a letter they had written to the other colonies. The letter's tone was polite and logical: it restated the illegality of taxation without colonial representation in Parliament and invited the support of other colonies. British officials ordered the Massachusetts Assembly to withdraw the Adams-Otis letter. The assembly refused, and the king ordered the assembly dissolved.

SAMUEL ADAMS Adams was a fiery organizer of the Sons of Liberty.

In response to an appeal by the royal governor of Massachusetts, 4,000 British troops were sent to Boston in October 1768 to maintain social order. **Loyalists**, as the American Tories who supported the king and Parliament were often called, welcomed the soldiers; **Patriots**, the increasingly popular name for those rebelling against British authority, viewed the British troops as an occupation force intended to crush dissent. Meanwhile, in London the king appointed a new chief minister, Frederick, Lord North, in January 1770.

The Boston Massacre (1770)

British troops and the Boston Massacre

Massachusetts had long been the center of resistance to British authority. In Boston, the presence of thousands of British soldiers had become a constant source of irritation. Crowds frequently heckled the soldiers, many of whom earned the abuse by harassing and intimidating Americans.

On the evening of March 5, 1770, two dozen Boston rowdies—teens, Irishmen, blacks, and sailors—began taunting Hugh White, a British soldier guarding the Custom House. Someone rang the town fire bell, drawing a larger crowd to the scene as the taunting continued: "Kill him, kill him, knock him down. Fire, damn you, fire, you dare not fire!"

A squad of soldiers arrived to help White, but the surly crowd surrounded them. When someone threw a club that knocked a soldier down, he arose and fired his musket. Others joined in. When the smoke cleared, five people lay dead or dying, and eight more were wounded. The first one killed, or so the story goes, was African American Crispus Attucks, a former slave who worked at the docks.

Loyalists Colonists who remained loyal to Britain before and during the Revolutionary War.

Patriots Colonists who rebelled against British authority before and during the Revolutionary War.

THE BLOODY MASSACRE Paul Revere created this engraving of the Boston Massacre about three weeks after the event, and it was one of the most effective pieces of political propaganda of the revolutionary period. It inaccurately depicts an organized and merciless row of British soldiers shooting down an unarmed cluster of colonists, richly-dressed and putting themselves in the line of fire as they carry their wounded compatriots to safety. **What would a more accurate representation of the Boston Massacre show?**

The so-called **Boston Massacre** sent shock waves throughout the colonies and all the way to London. Thousands of Bostonians attended the funerals for the deceased. At the same time, the impact of a revived colonial boycott of British imported goods persuaded Lord North to modify the Townshend Acts. Late in April 1770, Parliament repealed all the Townshend duties except for the tea tax. Colonial discontent diminished for two years thereafter. The redcoats left Boston, but they remained stationed nearby in Canada, and the British navy still patrolled the New England coast chasing smugglers.

Boston Massacre (1770)
Violent confrontation between British soldiers and a Boston mob on March 5, 1770, in which five colonists were killed.

The *Gaspée* Incident (1772)

The *Gaspée* incident

In June 1772, a naval incident further eroded the colonies' fragile relationship with the mother country. Near Warwick, Rhode Island, the HMS *Gaspée*, a British warship, ran aground while chasing suspected smugglers, and its hungry crew went ashore and seized local sheep, hogs, and chickens. An angry crowd from the town then boarded the ship, shot the captain, removed the crew, and set fire to the vessel.

The *Gaspée* incident symbolized the intensity of anti-British feelings among growing numbers of Americans. When the British tried to take the suspects to London for trial, Patriots organized in protest. Thomas Jefferson said that it was the threat of transporting Americans for trials in Britain that reignited anti-British activities in Virginia.

In response to the *Gaspée* incident, Samuel Adams in Boston organized the **Committee of Correspondence**, which issued a statement of American rights and grievances and invited other towns to do the same. Similar committees sprang up across Massachusetts and in other colonies, forming a network of rebellion. A Massachusetts Loyalist called the committees "the foulest, subtlest, and most venomous serpent ever issued from the egg of sedition." The crisis was escalating. "The flame is kindled and like lightning it catches from soul to soul," reported Abigail Adams, the high-spirited and politically astute wife of future president John Adams.

The Boston Tea Party (1773)

Boston Tea Party

The new British prime minister, Lord North, soon provided the colonists with the spark to ignite colonial resentment. In 1773, he tried to bail out the struggling East India Company, which had in its British warehouses some 17 million pounds of tea that it desperately needed to sell before it rotted. Parliament passed the Tea Act of 1773 to allow the company to send its tea directly to America without paying any taxes. British tea merchants could thereby undercut the prices charged by their American competitors, most of whom were smugglers who bought tea from the Dutch. At the same time, King George III told Lord North to "compel obedience" in the colonies.

In Massachusetts, the Committees of Correspondence, backed by Boston merchants, alerted colonists that the British government was trying to purchase colonial submission with cheap tea. The reduction in the price of tea was a clever trick to make them accept taxation without consent. In Boston, enraged Patriots decided that their passion for liberty outweighed their love for tea. On December 16, 1773, scores of Patriots disguised as Indians boarded three British ships in Boston harbor and dumped overboard 342 chests filled with forty-six tons of East India Company tea.

The **Boston Tea Party** pushed British officials to the breaking point. The destruction of so much valuable tea convinced the king and his advisers that a forceful response was required. "The colonists must either submit or triumph," George III wrote to Lord North, who decided to make an example of

Committee of Correspondence Group organized by Samuel Adams to address American grievances, assert American rights, and form a network of rebellion.

Boston Tea Party (1773) Demonstration against the Tea Act of 1773 in which the Sons of Liberty, dressed as Indians, dumped hundreds of chests of British-owned tea into Boston Harbor.

THE ABLE DOCTOR, OR AMERICA SWALLOWING THE BITTER DRAUGHT This 1774 engraving shows Lord North, the Boston Port Act, in his pocket, pouring tea down America's throat and America spitting it back.

Boston to the rest of the colonies. "We are now to establish our authority [over the colonies]," North said, "or give it up entirely." In the end, his reassertion of royal control helped make a revolution that would cost Britain far more than three shiploads of tea.

The Coercive Acts

In 1774, Lord North convinced Parliament to punish rebellious Boston by enacting a cluster of harsh laws, called the **Coercive Acts** (referred to by Americans as the "Intolerable" Acts). The Boston Port Act closed the harbor until the city paid for the lost tea. A new Quartering Act ordered colonists to provide lodging for British soldiers. In May, Lieutenant-General Thomas Gage, commander-in-chief of British forces in North America, was named governor of Massachusetts and assumed command of the British soldiers in Boston.

The Intolerable Acts shocked colonists. No one had expected such a severe reaction to the Boston Tea Party. Colonists rallied to help Boston, raising money, sending supplies, and boycotting as well as burning British tea. In Williamsburg, when the Virginia Assembly met in May, a young member of the Committee of Correspondence, Thomas Jefferson, suggested that June 1, the effective date of the Boston Port Act, become an official day of fasting and prayer in Virginia.

The royal governor responded by dissolving the Virginia Assembly, whose members then retired to the Raleigh Tavern where they decided to form a Continental Congress to represent all the colonies more effectively in

Coercive Acts (1774) Four parliamentary measures that required the colonies to pay for the Boston Tea Party's damages: closed the port of Boston, imposed a military government, disallowed colonial trials of British soldiers, and forced the quartering of troops in private homes.

the confrontation with Great Britain. As Samuel Savage, a Connecticut Patriot wrote in May 1774, the conflict had come down to a single question: "Whether we shall or shall not be governed by the British Parliament."

The First Continental Congress

The First Continental Congress

On September 5, 1774, the fifty-five delegates making up the First Continental Congress assembled in Philadelphia. Never before had all the colonies met to coordinate resistance to British policies. Over seven weeks, the Congress endorsed the Suffolk Resolves, which urged Massachusetts to resist British tyranny with force. The Congress then adopted a Declaration of American Rights, which proclaimed once again the rights of Americans as British citizens and denied Parliament's authority to regulate internal colonial affairs. "We demand no new rights," said the Congress. "We ask only for peace, liberty, and security."

Finally, the Congress adopted the Continental Association of 1774, which recommended that every colony organize committees to enforce a new and complete boycott of all imported British goods, a dramatic step that would be followed by a refusal to send American goods to Britain. The association was designed to show that Patriots could deny themselves what Samuel Adams called the "Baubles of Britain" in order to demonstrate their commitment to colonial liberties and constitutional rights.

The county and city committees forming the Continental Association became the organizational network for the resistance movement. Seven thousand men across the colonies served on the local committees, and many more women put the boycotts into practice. The committees required colonists to sign an oath refusing to purchase British goods. In East Haddam, Connecticut, Patriots tarred, feathered, and rubbed pig dung on a Loyalist opposed to the boycott. Such violent incidents led Loyalists to claim that it was better to be a slave to the king than to a Patriot mob.

Thousands of ordinary men and women participated in the boycott of British goods, and their sacrifices on behalf of colonial liberties provided the momentum leading to revolution. For all the attention given to colonial leaders such as Samuel Adams and Thomas Jefferson, it was common people who enforced the boycott, volunteered in Patriot militia units, attended town meetings, and exerted pressure on royal officials in the colonies. As the people of Pittsfield, Massachusetts, declared in a petition, "We have always believed that the people are the fountain of power."

Last-Minute Compromise

In London, King George fumed. He wrote Lord North that "blows must decide" whether the Americans "are to be subject to this country or independent." In early 1775, Parliament declared that Massachusetts was officially "in rebellion" and prohibited the New England colonies from trading with any nation outside the British Empire. On February 27, 1775, Lord North issued the Conciliatory Propositions, which offered to resolve the festering dispute by eliminating all taxes on any colony that voluntarily paid both its share for military defense and the salaries of the royal governors. In other words, North was asking the colonies to tax themselves. By the time the Conciliatory Propositions arrived in America, shooting had already started.

Bold Talk of War

While most of the Patriots believed that Britain would back down in the face of united colonial resistance, in Virginia Patrick Henry dramatically declared that war was unavoidable. He urged Americans to prepare for combat. Henry, a farmer, deer hunter, and storekeeper turned lawyer, told Virginia's Revolutionary Convention on March 20, 1775, that the colonies "have done everything that could be done to avert the storm which is now coming on," but their efforts had been met only by "violence and insult" from the British authorities. War was "inevitable. And let it come!" Freedom, the defiant Henry shouted, could be bought only with blood: "We must fight!" If forced to choose, he shouted, "Give me liberty"—then paused dramatically, clenched his fist as if it held a dagger, and plunged it into his chest—"or give me death." The delegates were initially stunned to silence. Then a few Loyalists shouted, "Treason!" But many more stood and applauded.

As Patrick Henry had predicted, events during 1775 quickly moved toward armed conflict. By mid-1775, the king and Parliament had effectively lost control of their colonies; they could neither persuade nor force the Patriots to accept new regulations and revenue measures. In Boston, General Gage warned his British superiors that armed conflict with the Americans would unleash the "horrors of civil war." Lord Sandwich, the head of the British navy, was not worried by the idea of warfare. He dismissed the rebels as "raw, undisciplined, cowardly men."

Lexington and Concord

On April 14, 1775, the British army in Boston received secret orders to stop the "open rebellion" in Massachusetts. General Gage had decided to arrest rebel leaders such as Samuel Adams and seize the American militia's gunpowder stored at Concord, sixteen miles northwest of Boston. After dark on April 18, some 700 redcoats secretly boarded barge boats in Boston and crossed the Charles River after midnight. Then, chilled and wet in their bright-scarlet uniforms, they set out westward on foot to Lexington. When Patriots learned of the plan, Paul Revere and William Dawes mounted their horses for their famous "midnight ride" to warn the rebel leaders that the British were coming. Each village had drummers assigned to beat an alarm while others rang church bells. Startled in their sleep, the militiamen grabbed their muskets and powder horns and rushed out the door, telling their families to hide.

In the gray dawn light of April 19, the British advance guard of 238 redcoats found Captain John Parker, a veteran of the French and Indian War and

PATRICK HENRY OF VIRGINIA Henry was a longtime advocate of colonial rights, fighting for the Stamp Tax Resolutions to be passed in Virginia in 1765. A decade later, in a speech to Virginia's Revolutionary Convention, he made the famous declaration, "Give me liberty, or give me death!"

Shots fired at Lexington and Concord

father of seven, organizing about eighty "Minutemen" (Patriot militia who could assemble at a "minute's" notice), lined up on the Lexington town square, while about a hundred fascinated villagers watched. Parker and his men, many of them father-and-son teams, intended only a silent protest. Parker ordered them to "stand your ground; don't fire unless fired upon, but if they mean to have a war, let it begin here." Major John Pitcairn of the Royal Marines, however, was spoiling for a fight. He haughtily rode onto the Lexington Green, swinging his sword and yelling, "Disperse, you damned rebels! You dogs, run!"

The outnumbered militiamen had already begun backing away in the confusion when someone, perhaps an onlooker, fired a shot. The British soldiers, without orders, began wildly shooting at the Minutemen, then charged them with bayonets, leaving eight dead and ten wounded. Jonathan Harrington, a militiaman who was shot in the back, managed to crawl across the green, only to die on his doorstep.

The British officers brought their men under control and led them seven miles to Concord, announcing their arrival with fifes and drums. In Concord, they searched buildings for hidden military supplies, destroying what they found. While marching out of the town, they encountered American riflemen at the North Bridge. Shots were fired, and a dozen or so British soldiers

THE BATTLE OF LEXINGTON (1775) Amos Doolittle's impression of the Battle of Lexington as combat begins between the Royal Marines and the Minutemen.

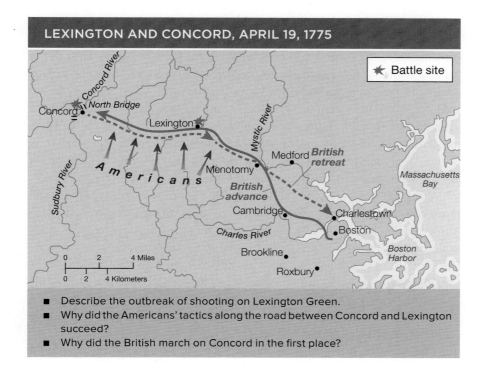

LEXINGTON AND CONCORD, APRIL 19, 1775

★ Battle site

- Describe the outbreak of shooting on Lexington Green.
- Why did the Americans' tactics along the road between Concord and Lexington succeed?
- Why did the British march on Concord in the first place?

were killed or wounded. More important, the short skirmish and ringing church bells alerted hundreds, then thousands, of rebel farmers, ministers, craftsmen, and merchants from nearby communities to grab their muskets.

By noon, the British began a ragged retreat back to Lexington. Less than a mile out of Concord, they suffered the first of many ambushes. The narrow road back to Boston turned into a gauntlet of death as hundreds of rebel marksmen fired on the British troops from behind stone walls, trees, barns, and houses. "It was a day full of horror," one of the soldiers recalled. "The Patriots seemed maddened." By nightfall, the redcoat survivors were safely back in Boston, having suffered three times as many dead and wounded as the Americans. A British general reported to London that the feisty Americans had earned his respect: "Whoever looks upon them as an irregular mob will find himself much mistaken."

Outright Rebellion

The colonial resistance movement had grown into an outright rebellion, but few Patriots in 1775 were yet calling for American independence. They still considered themselves British subjects whose rights had been repeatedly violated by an arrogant king and a misguided Parliament. When the Second Continental Congress convened at Philadelphia on May 10, 1775, the delegates gathered under a British flag. Most Americans in 1775 still wanted Parliament to restore their rights so that they could go back to being loyal British colonists.

Meanwhile, the British army in Boston was encircled and under siege by American militia units and small groups of musket-toting men who had raced from across New England to join in the rebellion. They were still farmers, not trained soldiers, and the uprising was not yet an army; it lacked an organized command structure and effective support system. The Patriots also lacked training, discipline, cannons, muskets, bullets, gunpowder, and blankets. They did not even have a name for their ragtag army. But they did have a growing sense of confidence and resolve. As a Massachusetts Patriot warned in urging Americans to join the revolt, "Our all is at stake. Death and devastation are the instant consequences of delay. Every moment is infinitely precious."

With each passing day in the spring of 1775, war fever infected more and more colonists. "Oh that I were a soldier!" John Adams wrote to his wife, Abigail, from Philadelphia. "I will be. I am reading military books. Everybody must, and will, and shall be a soldier." On the very day that Congress met, the British Fort Ticonderoga, on Lake Champlain in upstate New York near the Canadian border, fell to a Patriot force of "Green Mountain Boys" led by Ethan Allen of Vermont and Massachusetts volunteers under Benedict Arnold. Two days later, the Patriots captured a smaller British fort at Crown Point, north of Ticonderoga.

The Spreading Conflict

On June 15, 1775, the Second Continental Congress unanimously selected forty-three-year-old George Washington to lead a new national professional army. Washington's service in the French and Indian War had made him one of the few experienced American officers. And he *looked* like a leader. Tall and strong, he was a superb horseman and fearless fighter. Washington humbly accepted the new responsibility but refused to be paid. To have refused the request to command the Revolutionary forces, he explained to his wife, "would have reflected dishonor upon myself" and "given pain to my friends."

The Battle of Bunker Hill

On Saturday, June 17, the very day that the Congress named George Washington commander in chief, Patriot militiamen engaged British forces in their first major clash, the Battle of Bunker Hill outside of Boston (adjoining Breed's Hill was the battle's actual location).

The first major battle: Bunker Hill

At the order of General William Howe, the British commander, 2,400 British troops dressed in beautiful yet impractical uniforms advanced up the hill in tight formation through waist-high grass and across pasture fences as Americans watched from behind their earthworks. The militiamen, mostly farmers, waited until the redcoats had come within thirty paces, then loosed a volley that shattered the front British ranks. The British re-formed their lines and attacked again, but the Patriot riflemen forced them to retreat a second time.

All of General Howe's aides had been killed or wounded. Major Pitcairn, the British officer who had led the assault on the Lexington militiamen, was fatally wounded. He fell into the arms of his son, who carried him to the shore, placed him on a boat, kissed him farewell, and returned to the battle. During the third British assault, the colonials, out of gunpowder and musket balls, retreated in panic and confusion. "I jumped over the walls," Peter Brown remembered, "and ran for about half a mile while [musket] balls flew like hailstones and cannons roared like thunder."

The British took the high ground but were too tired to pursue the rebels. Victory came at a high price. The British suffered 1,054 casualties, over twice the American losses. "A dearly bought victory," reported British general Henry Clinton, noting that "another such would have ruined us." Rhode Island's Nathaniel Greene, an American officer destined for greatness, wished the Patriots could sell the British "another hill at the same price." The two armies, American and British, settled in for a nine-month stalemate around Boston, each hoping for a negotiated end to the crisis.

"Open and Avowed Enemies"

Three weeks after the Battle of Bunker Hill, on July 6–8, 1775, the Continental Congress sent the king the Olive Branch Petition, urging him to negotiate with his angry colonies. When the Olive Branch Petition reached London, however, King George refused even to look at it. On August 22, he declared the American rebels "open and avowed enemies."

> Olive Branch Petition rejected

Independence

The Revolutionary War was well under way in January 1776 when Thomas Paine, a recent English immigrant to America, provided the Patriot cause with a stirring pamphlet titled **Common Sense**. Until it appeared, most colonists had directed their grievances at the British Parliament; only a few colonists then considered independence an option. Paine, however, directly attacked the British monarchy. The "common sense" of the matter, he stressed, was that King George III had caused the rebellion. Americans, Paine urged, should abandon the British monarchy and declare their independence: "The blood of the slain, the weeping voice of nature cries, 'tis time to part." Only by declaring independence, Paine predicted, could the colonists gain the crucial support of France and Spain: "The cause of America is in great measure the cause of all mankind." Paine added that the "sun had never shone on a cause of greater worth."

Within three months, more than 150,000 copies of Paine's stirring pamphlet were circulating throughout the colonies, an enormous number for the time. "*Common Sense* is working a powerful change in the minds of men," George Washington reported. Paine's *Common Sense* inspired the colonial population from Massachusetts to Georgia, helping to convince British subjects still loyal to the king to embrace the radical notion of independence.

Common Sense (1776) Popular pamphlet written by Thomas Paine attacking British principles of hereditary rule and monarchical government and advocating a declaration of American independence.

THE COMING REVOLUTION The Continental Congress votes for independence, July 2, 1776.

The momentum for independence was building. In Congress, the Pennsylvanian John Dickinson, perhaps the most underrated of the "Founding Fathers," urged delay. On June 1, he warned that independence was a dangerous step since America had no national government or European allies. But his was a lone voice of caution.

In June 1776, one by one, the colonies authorized their delegates in the Continental Congress to take the final step. On June 7, Richard Henry Lee of Virginia moved "that these United Colonies are, and of right ought to be, free and independent states." Lee's resolution passed on July 2, a date that "will be the most memorable epoch in the history of America," John Adams wrote to his wife, Abigail. The more memorable date, however, became July 4, 1776, when the Congress formally adopted the **Declaration of Independence**.

Jefferson's Declaration

Declaration of Independence (1776) Formal statement, principally drafted by Thomas Jefferson and adopted by the Second Continental Congress on July 4, 1776, that officially announced the thirteen colonies' break with Great Britain.

In June 1776, thirty-three-year-old Thomas Jefferson wrote a first draft of a statement of independence that was submitted to the Congress. Others then edited and polished Jefferson's document. The resulting Declaration of Independence was crucially important not simply because it marked the creation of a new nation but because of the ideals it expressed. It asserted that "all men are created equal" in having the right to maintain governments of

DECLARATION OF INDEPENDENCE The Declaration in its most frequently reproduced form, an 1823 engraving by William J. Stone.

their own choosing. Governments, in Jefferson's words, derive "their just Powers from the consent of the people," who are entitled to "alter or abolish" those governments when they deny citizens their "unalienable rights" to "life, Liberty, and the pursuit of Happiness." Because King George was trying to impose "an absolute Tyranny over these States," the "Representatives of the United States of America" therefore declared the thirteen "United Colonies" to be "Free and Independent States."

News of the Declaration of Independence so excited New Yorkers that they toppled a statue of King George and had it melted down to make 42,000 bullets for the war. General George Washington ordered the Declaration read to every unit in the Continental army. Benjamin Franklin

PHILLIS WHEATLEY A portrait of America's first African American poet.

acknowledged how high the stakes were: "Well, Gentlemen," he told the Congress, "we must now hang together, or we shall most assuredly hang separately."

The Contradictions of Slavery

George Washington had declared that Boston's fight against British tyranny "now is and ever will be considered as the cause of America." The alternative, Washington warned, was to become "tame and abject slaves, as the blacks we rule over with such arbitrary sway [absolute power]." Washington and other American slaveholders, such as Thomas Jefferson and James Madison, were in part so resistant to "British tyranny" because they witnessed every day what actual slavery was like— for the African Americans under their control.

Jefferson acknowledged their moral hypocrisy. "Southerners," he wrote to a French friend, are "jealous of their own liberties but trampling on those of others." The contradiction between American slaveholders demanding liberty for themselves from British oppression was not lost on other observers at the time, either. Phillis Wheatley, the first African American writer to see her poetry published in America, highlighted the "absurdity" of white colonists claiming their freedom while continuing to exercise "oppressive power" over enslaved Africans.

"We Always Had Governed Ourselves"

There were many causes of the Revolution: the clumsy British efforts to tighten their regulation of colonial trade, the restrictions on colonists eager to acquire western lands, the growing tax burden, the mounting debts to British merchants, the lack of American representation in Parliament, and the role of revolutionary agitators such as Samuel Adams and Patrick Henry in stirring up anti-British feelings.

Each of those factors (and others) helped ignite the Revolutionary War. Yet colonists sought liberty from British tyranny for reasons that were not always selfless or noble. The Boston merchant John Hancock embraced the Patriot cause in part because he was the region's foremost smuggler. Paying more British taxes would have cost him a fortune. Likewise, South Carolina's Henry Laurens and Virginia's Landon Carter, wealthy planters, worried that the British might abolish slavery.

The difficult decision to declare independence from Great Britain was not simply about "taxation without representation." A larger issue had emerged by 1776. Many Americans had become determined to develop their own society in the ways they wished. Yes, most American Patriots still spoke the same language and worshipped the same God as the British, but they no longer thought the same way about things that mattered. Rebellious Americans wanted to trade freely with the world and to expand what Jefferson called their "empire of liberty" westward, across the Appalachians.

Perhaps the last word on the complex causes of the Revolution should belong to Levi Preston, a Minuteman from Danvers, Massachusetts. Asked late in life about the British efforts to impose new taxes and regulations on the colonists, Preston responded by asking his young interviewer, "What were they? Oppressions? I didn't feel them." He was then asked, "What, were you not oppressed by the Stamp Act?" Preston replied that he "never saw one of those stamps. . . . I am certain I never paid a penny for one of them." What about the tax on tea? "Tea-tax! I never drank a drop of the stuff; the boys threw it all overboard." His interviewer finally asked why he decided to fight for independence. "Young man," Preston explained, "what we meant in going for those Redcoats was this: we always had governed ourselves, and we always meant to. They didn't mean we should."

Reviewing the
CORE OBJECTIVES |

■ **British and French Colonies** New France followed the model of absolute power in governing its far-flung trading outposts. Few French colonists settled in the vast geography of Canada and the Louisiana territory, but friendships with Native Americans and a profitable fur trade kept the balance of power in North America. On the other hand, the British policy of *salutary neglect* allowed the British colonies a large degree of self-government, until the British government's decision to enforce more rigidly its policy of *mercantilism*, as seen in such measures as the *Navigation Acts*, became a means for Britain to enrich its global empire. The *Glorious Revolution* in Great Britain inspired new political philosophies that challenged the divine right of kings with the *natural rights* of free men.

■ **The French and Indian War** Four European wars affected America between 1689 and 1763 as the British and French, joined by their allies, fought each other throughout the world. Worried colonies created the *Albany Plan of Union*, which was ultimately rejected but formed an early blueprint for an independent American government. The *Seven Years' War* (1754–1763), known as the *French and Indian War* in the American colonies, was the first world war, eventually won by the British. In the *Treaty of Paris* in 1763, France lost all its North American possessions, Britain gained Canada and Florida, and Spain acquired the vast Louisiana territory. With the war's end, Native Americans fought to regain control of their land in *Pontiac's Rebellion*. Great Britain negotiated peace in the *Royal Proclamation of 1763*, but land-hungry settlers ignored the Proclamation Line.

■ **British Colonial Policy** After the French and Indian War, the British government was saddled with an enormous national debt. To reduce that burden, George Grenville's colonial policy imposed various taxes to compel colonists to pay for their own defense. Colonists resisted, claiming that they could not be taxed by Parliament because they were not represented in Parliament. Colonial reaction to the *Stamp Act* of 1765 was the first sign of real trouble for British authorities. Conflicts between Whigs and Tories intensified when the *Townshend Acts* imposed additional taxes. The *Sons of Liberty* and the *Daughters of Liberty* mobilized resistance with successful boycotts of British goods, helping convince Parliament to repeal the Stamp Act.

■ **Road to the American Revolution** But the crisis worsened. Spontaneous resistance led to the *Boston Massacre*; organized protesters later staged the *Boston Tea Party*. The British response, called the *Coercive Acts*, sparked further violence between *Patriots* and *Loyalists*. The First Continental Congress formed *Committees of Correspondence* to organize and spread resistance. Thomas Paine's pamphlet *Common Sense* helped kindle revolutionary fervor as well as plant the seed of independence, and conflicts over trade regulations, taxes, and expansion now erupted into war. In the heat of battle, compromise became less likely, and finally impossible, and the Continental Congress delivered its *Declaration of Independence.*

KEY TERMS

salutary neglect *p. 114*

mercantilism *p. 114*

Navigation Acts (1650–1775) *p. 114*

Glorious Revolution (1688) *p. 116*

natural rights *p. 116*

Albany Plan of Union (1754) *p. 119*

French and Indian War (Seven Years' War) (1754–1763) *p. 120*

Treaty of Paris (1763) *p. 121*

Pontiac's Rebellion (1763) *p. 123*

Royal Proclamation of 1763 *p. 124*

Stamp Act (1765) *p. 127*

virtual representation *p. 128*

Sons of Liberty *p. 128*

Daughters of Liberty *p. 129*

Townshend Acts (1767) *p. 131*

Loyalists *p. 132*

Patriots *p. 132*

Boston Massacre (1770) *p. 133*

Committee of Correspondence *p. 134*

Boston Tea Party (1773) *p. 134*

Coercive Acts (1774) *p. 135*

Common Sense (1776) *p. 141*

Declaration of Independence (1776) *p. 142*

CHRONOLOGY

1651	First Navigation Act passed by Parliament
1688–1689	Glorious Revolution
1754	Albany Plan of Union
1756–1763	Seven Years' War (French and Indian War)
1763	Treaty of Paris ends Seven Years' War
	Pontiac's Rebellion begins
	Royal Proclamation Act
1764–1765	Sugar Act and Stamp Act
1765	Stamp Act Congress
1766	Repeal of the Stamp Act
1767	Townshend Acts
1770	Boston Massacre
1773	Tea Act and Boston Tea Party
1774	Coercive Acts
	First meeting of Continental Congress
1775	Military conflict at Lexington and Concord
	The Continental Congress creates an army
1776	Thomas Paine publishes *Common Sense*
	The Continental Congress declares independence

INQUIZITIVE

Go to InQuizitive to see what you've learned— and learn what you've missed—with personalized feedback along the way.

DEBATING the Origins of the American Revolution

History is more than just the memorization of *what* happened. It also involves interpreting *why* the past unfolded as it did. In seeking to understand *why*, historians often find themselves disagreeing. This happens for many reasons. Historians themselves are influenced by their own outlook and the society they live in. Historians can revise their thinking in light of fresh information from newly discovered *primary sources*. They can also interpret previously examined sources in new ways by applying new methodologies and theories. The study of how interpretations of history have changed is called *historiography*. It is the history of the field of history! For Part 1, "An Old 'New' World," the case study of the origins of the American Revolution demonstrates how historians can disagree because they use different types of sources. Thus it is an excellent topic for sharpening your historiographical skills.

For this exercise you have two tasks:

PART 1: Compare the two secondary sources on the American Revolution.

PART 2: Using primary sources, evaluate the arguments of the two secondary sources.

PART I Comparing and Contrasting Secondary Sources

Below are excerpts from two prominent historians of the American Revolution who are at odds over its origins. The first piece comes from Bernard Bailyn of Harvard University, who has explored how *ideology* shaped the American Revolution—the system of ideas, ideals, and beliefs that undergird political and economic theory and practice. Bailyn focuses on the way that ideas from the English Whigs, who argued that the English constitution limited the power of the king (see page 000), influenced American Revolutionaries. The author of the second excerpt, Gary Nash of the University of California, Los Angeles, has studied the role that common people, as well as the economic forces that affected their lives, played in the American Revolution. Nash seeks to uncover not just the Whig ideology that is the focus of Bailyn's work but also the ideas and forces that motivated people to participate in this great struggle. While Bailyn and Nash agree on much, their work illustrates how different methodologies lead to different historical interpretations. On the one hand, Bailyn looks at the ideas and writings of the Revolutionary elite— their ideas and arguments—to explain what people actually did. On the other hand, Nash examines the actions and economic circumstances of Revolutionaries who

produced no written records in order to understand their motivations. So while Bailyn seeks to understand the causes of the Revolution through the writing of the colonial elite, Nash looks at the actions of common people to understand why they participated in this struggle.

Compare the views of these two historians by answering the following questions. Be sure to find specific examples in the text to support your answers.

■ What is the topic of each excerpt?

■ Are there any similarities between these two excerpts?

■ According to each author, what role did ideology play in the origins of the American Revolution?

■ According to each author, what role did economics and material conditions play in the origins of the Revolution?

■ What type of primary sources does each author mention?

■ What might account for the differences (if any) in interpretation between the authors?

Secondary Source 1

Bernard Bailyn, *The Ideological Origins of the American Revolution* (1992)

Study of the pamphlets [thin booklets] confirmed my rather old-fashioned view that the American Revolution was above all else an ideological, constitutional, political struggle and not primarily a controversy between social groups undertaken to force changes in the organization of the society or the economy. It confirmed too my belief that intellectual developments in the decade before Independence led to a radical idealization and conceptualization of the previous century and a half of American experience, and that it was this intimate relationship between Revolutionary thought and the circumstances of life in eighteenth-century America that endowed the Revolution with its peculiar force and made it so profoundly a transforming event. But if the pamphlets confirmed this belief, they filled it with unexpected details and gave it new meaning.

. . . . I began to see a new meaning in phrases that I, like most historians, had readily dismissed as mere rhetoric and propaganda: "slavery," "corruption," "conspiracy." These inflammatory words were used so forcefully by writers of so great a variety of social statuses, political positions, and religious persuasions; they fitted so logically into the pattern of radical and opposition thought; and they reflected so clearly the realities of life in an age in which monarchical autocracy flourished, in which the stability and freedom of England's "mixed" constitution was a recent and remarkable achievement, and in which the fear of conspiracy against constituted authority was built into the very structure of politics, that I began to suspect that they meant something very real to both the writers and their readers: that there were real fears, real anxieties, a sense of real danger behind these phrases, and not merely the desire to influence by rhetoric and propaganda the inert minds of an otherwise passive populace. The more I read, the less useful, it seemed to me, was the whole idea of propaganda in its modern meaning when applied to the writings of the American Revolution. . . . In the end I was convinced that the fear of a comprehensive conspiracy against liberty throughout the English speaking world—a conspiracy believed to have been nourished in corruption, and of which, it was felt, oppression in America was only the most immediately visible part—lay at the heart of the Revolutionary movement.

Source: Bailyn, Bernard. *The Ideological Origins of the American Revolution.* Cambridge, Mass.: Belknap Press of Harvard University Press, 1992. xx–xxiii.

Secondary Source 2

Gary Nash, "Social Change and the Growth of Prerevolutionary Urban Radicalism" (1976)

One of the purposes of this essay is to challenge these widely accepted notions that the "predicament of poverty" was unknown in colonial America, that the conditions of everyday life among "the inarticulate" had not changed in ways that led toward a revolutionary predisposition, and that "social discontent," "economic disturbances," and "social strains" can generally be ignored in searching for the roots of the Revolution. I do not suggest that we replace an ideological construction with a mechanistic economic interpretation, but argue that a popular ideology, affected by rapidly changing economic conditions in American cities, dynamically interacted with the more abstract Whig ideology borrowed from England. These two ideologies had their primary appeal within different parts of the social structure, were derived from different sensibilities concerning social equity, and thus had somewhat different goals. The Whig ideology, about which we know a great deal through recent studies, was drawn from English sources, had its main appeal within upper levels of colonial society, was limited to a defense of constitutional rights and political liberties, and had little to say about changing social and economic conditions in America or the need for change in the future. The popular ideology, about which we know very little, also had deep roots in English culture, but it resonated most strongly within the middle and lower strata of society and went far beyond constitutional rights to a discussion of the proper distribution of wealth and power in the social system. It was this popular ideology that undergirded the politicization of the artisan and laboring classes in the cities and justified the dynamic role they assumed in the urban political process in the closing decades of the colonial period.

To understand how this popular ideology swelled into revolutionary commitment within the middle and lower ranks of colonial society, we must first comprehend how the material conditions of life were changing for city dwellers during the colonial period and how people at different levels of society were affected by these alterations. We cannot fathom this process by consulting the writings of merchants, lawyers, and upper-class politicians, because their business and political correspondence and the tracts they wrote tell us almost nothing about those below them in the social hierarchy. But buried in more obscure documents are glimpses of the lives of both ordinary and important people—shoemakers and tailors as well as lawyers and merchants. The story of changing conditions and how life in New York, Philadelphia, and Boston was experienced can be discerned, not with perfect clarity but in general form, from tax, poor relief, and probate records.

The crescendo of urban protest and extralegal activity in the prerevolutionary decades cannot be separated from the condition of people's lives. . . . The willingness of broad segments of urban society to participate in attacks on narrowly concentrated wealth and power—both at the polls where the poor and propertyless were excluded, and in the streets where everyone, including women, apprentices, indentured servants, and slaves, could engage in action—should remind us that a rising tide of class antagonism and political consciousness, paralleling important economic changes, was a distinguishing feature of the cities at the end of the colonial period. It is this organic link between the circumstances of people's lives and their political thought and action that has been overlooked by historians who concentrate on Whig ideology, which had its strongest appeal among the educated and well-to-do.

Source: Nash, Gary. "Social Change and the Growth of Prerevolutionary Urban Radicalism." *The American Revolution: Explorations in the History of American Radicalism*, edited by Alfred F. Young, 6–7. DeKalb: Northern Illinois University Press, 1976.

PART II Using Primary Sources to Evaluate Secondary Sources

When historians are faced with competing interpretations of the past, they often look at *primary* source material as part of the process of evaluating the different arguments. Below is a selection of primary source materials relating to the origins of the American Revolution.

The first document is an excerpt from a series of letters by Pennsylvania Quaker John Dickinson that he published anonymously under the pen name "A Farmer." Dickinson wrote the first letter in 1767, following Parliament's suspension of the New York Assembly for failure to comply with the Quartering Act of 1765, which required the colonies to provide British troops with food and shelter.

The second document is an excerpt from a letter sent by Massachusetts Bay governor Francis Bernard to British officials in London following the Stamp Act Riots in Boston during August of 1765. The riots began on August 13 with an attack upon the house of Andrew Oliver, who was responsible for the collection of the tax. This act of destruction was widely celebrated by Samuel Adams and other Sons of Liberty. A few days later a mob ransacked and looted the house of the lieutenant-governor, Thomas Hutchinson. This mob acted without the support of Adams or other elite leaders.

Carefully read the primary sources and answer the following questions. Decide which of the primary source documents support or refute Bailyn's and Nash's arguments about this period. You may find that the documents do both but for different parts of each historian's interpretation. Be sure to identify which specific components of each historian's argument the documents support or refute.

■ Which of the two historians' *arguments* is best supported by the *primary source* documents? If you find that both arguments are well supported by the evidence, why do you think the two historians had such different interpretations about the period?

■ Based on your comparison of the two historians' arguments and your analysis of the primary sources, what have you learned about historiography and the ways historians interpret the past?

Primary Source 1

John Dickinson, "Letter from a Farmer in Pennsylvania" (1767)

My dear COUNTRYMEN,

I am a FARMER settled after a variety of fortunes, near the banks of the river *Delaware* in the province of *Pennsylvania*. . . . Being master of my time, I spend a good deal of it in a library. . . . I believe I have acquired a greater share of knowledge in history, and the laws and constitution of my country, than is generally attained by men of my class. . . . From my infancy I was taught to love humanity and liberty. Inquiry and experience have since confirmed my reverence for the lessons then given me, by convincing me more fully of their truth and excellence. . . . With a good deal of surprise I have observed, that little notice has been taken of an act of Parliament, as injurious in its principle to the liberties of these colonies, as the STAMP ACT was: I mean the act for suspending the legislation of New-York. . . . It [the Act] is a parliamentary assertion of the *supreme authority* of *the British legislature* over these colonies in *the part of taxation*; and is intended to COMPEL *New-York* into a submission to that authority. It seems therefore to me as much a violation of the liberty of the people of that province, and consequently of all these colonies, as if the parliament had sent a number of regiments to be quartered upon them till they should comply. For it is evident, that the suspension is meant as a compulsion; and the *method* of compelling is totally indifferent. It is indeed probable that the sight of red coats, and the beating of drums would have been most alarming, because people are generally more influenced by their eyes and ears than by their reason: But whoever seriously considers the matter, must perceive, that a dreadful stroke is aimed at the liberty of these colonies: For the cause of *one* is the cause of *all*. If the parliament may lawfully deprive *New-York* of any of its rights, it may deprive any, or all the other colonies of their rights; and nothing can possibly so much encourage such attempts, as a mutual inattention to the interests of each other. *To divide, and thus to destroy*, is the first political maxim in attacking those who are powerful by their union. He certainly is not a wise man, who folds his arms and reposes himself at home, viewing with unconcern the flames that have invaded his neighbour's house, without any endeavors to extinguish them.

Source: Dickinson, John. "Letters from a Farmer." *Letters from a Farmer in Pennsylvania, to the Inhabitants of the British Colonies.* Edited by R. T. H. Halsey, 6–12. New York: The Outlook Company, 1903.

Primary Source 2

Governor Francis Bernard, "Letter to the Lords of Trade" (1765)

The disorders of the town having been carried to much greater lengths than what I have informed your lordships of. After the demolition of Mr. Oliver's house was found so practicable and easy, and that the government was obliged to look on, without being able to take any one step to prevent it, and the principal people of the town publicly avowed and justified the act; the mob, both great and small, became highly elated, and all kinds of ill-humours were set on foot; everything that, for years past, had been the cause of any unpopular discontent, was revived; and private resentments against persons in office worked themselves in, and endeavoured to exert themselves under the mask of the public cause. . . . Towards evening, some boys began to light a bonfire before the town-house, which is an usual signal for a mob. Before it was quite dark, a great company of people gathered together, crying 'Liberty and Property;' which is their usual notice of their intention to plunder and pull down a house.

. . .

The lieutenant-governor [Thomas Hutchinson] . . . was at supper with his family when he received advice that the mob was coming to him. . . . As soon as the mob had got into the house, with a most irresistible fury, they immediately looked about for him, to murder him, and even made diligent enquiry whither he was gone. They went to work with a rage scarce to be exemplified by the most savage people. Every thing moveable was destroyed in the most minute manner, except such things of value as were worth carrying off. . . . It was now becoming a war of plunder, of general leveling, and taking away the distinction of rich and poor: so that those gentlemen, who had promoted and approved the cruel treatment of Mr. Oliver, became now as fearful for themselves as the most loyal person in the town could be. When first the town took this new turn, I was in hopes that they would have disavowed all the riotous proceedings; that of the first night, as well as the last. But it is no such thing; great pains are taken to separate the two riots: what was done against Mr. Oliver is still approved of, as a necessary declaration of their resolution not to submit to the Stamp Act.

Source: Bernard, Francis. "Extract from a Letter to the Lords of Trade, dated August 31, 1765." *The Parliamentary History of England, from the Earliest Period to the Year 1803. From which Last-Mentioned Epoch It Is Continued Downwards in the Work Entitled, "The Parliamentary Debates."* Vol. 16, A. D. 1765–1771. London: Printed by T. C. Hansard, Peterborough-Court, Fleet-Street: for Longman, Hurst, Rees, Orme, & Brown; J. Richardson; Black, Parry, & Co.; J. Hatchard; J. Ridgway; E. Jeffery; J. Booker; J. Rodwell; Cardock & Joy; R. H. Evans; E. Budd; J. Booth; and T. C. Hansard, 1813. 129–131.

BURNING of the FRIGATE PHILADELPHIA in the HARBOUR of TRIPOLI. 16 Feb 1804.

INHABITANTS OF AMERICA,

PART

2

Building a Nation

It was one thing for Patriot leaders to declare American independence and quite another to win it on the battlefield. The Revolution was thus a work in progress, and the outcome was uncertain. The odds greatly favored the British; fewer than half the colonists were Patriots who *actively* supported the Revolution, and many others—the Loyalists—fought against it. Still others sought most of all to stay alive, often by changing sides "with the circumstances of every day," as Thomas Paine groaned. Most Americans were initially worried and confused by the course of events, suspicious of both sides, and hesitant to embrace an uncertain cause. Some wanted to stay out of the conflict. The political stability of the new nation was uncertain, and General George Washington, the ambitious tobacco planter turned Patriot commander, found himself facing the world's greatest military power with a poorly supplied, often unpaid, and inexperienced army.

Yet against all odds the Revolutionaries would persevere and prevail. Washington and his lieutenants grew skilled at holding the fractious revolutionary forces together and taking advantage of geography. They knew the American landscape much better than the British did. Even more important was the decision by the French to join the war against Britain. The Franco-American military alliance, ably negotiated in 1778 by Benjamin Franklin, was the decisive event in the war. In 1783, after eight years of sporadic fighting and heavy human and financial losses, the British gave up the fight and surrendered their American colonies.

While fighting the British, the Patriots also had to create new governments for themselves. Diverse colonies suddenly became coequal states. The deeply ingrained resentment of British imperial rule led the Americans to give more power to the individual states than to the new national government. As Thomas Jefferson declared, "Virginia is my country."

Such powerful local ties help explain why the Articles of Confederation, the original American constitution organizing the thirteen states into a revolutionary nation, provided only minimal national authority when it was ratified in 1781. Final power to make and execute laws remained with the states.

After the Revolutionary War, the flimsy political bonds authorized by the Articles of Confederation could not meet the needs of the new nation. This realization led to the calling of the Constitutional Convention in 1787. The process of drafting and approving the new constitution prompted a heated debate about the respective powers granted to the states and the national government, a debate that became the central theme of American political thought ever since.

The Revolution also unleashed social forces that would help reshape American culture. What would be the role of women, African Americans, and Native Americans in the new nation? How would the diverse regions of the new United States develop different economies? Who would control access to the vast Native American lands to the west of the original thirteen states? At the same time, how would the upstart United States of America relate to the other nations of the world?

These questions gave birth to the first national political parties in the United States. During the 1790s, the Federalist party, led by George Washington and Alexander Hamilton, and the first Republican party, led by Thomas Jefferson and James Madison, furiously debated the political and economic future of the new nation.

With Jefferson's election as president in 1800, the Republicans gained the upper hand in national politics and would remain dominant for the next quarter century. In the process, they presided over a maturing republic that aggressively expanded westward at the expense of the Native Americans, embraced industrial development, engaged in a second war with Great Britain, and witnessed growing tensions between North and South over slavery.

THE DEATH OF GENERAL MERCER AT THE BATTLE OF PRINCETON (ca. 1789–1831) Soon after the American victory in Trenton, New Jersey, George Washington (center, on horseback) and his men had another unexpected win at the Battle of Princeton. One of the casualties, however, was Washington's close friend, General Hugh Mercer (bottom), who became a rallying symbol for the revolution.

The American Revolution

1776–1783

F ew foreign observers thought the untested American revolutionaries could win a war against the world's richest and most powerful empire—and, indeed, the Americans did lose most of the battles in the Revolutionary War. In the end, however, they outlasted the British, eventually forcing them to grant independence to the upstart United States of America. This stunning result reflected the tenacity of the Patriots as well as the difficulties the British faced in fighting a prolonged war thousands of miles from home.

What began as a war for independence became both a civil war between Americans (Patriots versus Loyalists), joined by their Indian allies, and a world war involving numerous "allied" European nations. The crucial development during the war was the ability of the United States to forge military alliances with France, Spain, and the Netherlands, all of which were eager to humble Great Britain and seize its colonies around the world. Those nations provided the American revolutionaries desperately needed money, supplies, soldiers, and warships. Ninety percent of the gunpowder used by American soldiers came from Europe.

Wars, of course, affect civilians as well as combatants. The War of Independence unleashed unexpected social and political changes, as the chaos of war enabled "common people" to take a more active

CORE OBJECTIVES INQUIZITIVE

1. Explain the challenges faced by both British and American military leaders in fighting the Revolutionary War.

2. Identify key turning points in the Revolutionary War, and explain how they changed the direction of the war.

3. Describe the ways in which the American Revolution was also a civil war.

4. Examine how the Revolutionary War was an "engine" for political and social change.

5. Compare the impact of the Revolutionary War on African Americans, women, and Native Americans.

role in governments at all levels, local, state, and national. After all, as the Declaration of Independence asserted, governments derive "their just powers from the consent of the governed." The "common people" readily took advantage of the new opportunities provided by republicanism to participate in the political process. In Virginia, for example, voters in 1776 elected a new state legislature that, as an observer noted, "was composed of men not quite so well dressed, nor so politely educated, nor so highly born" as had been the case in the past.

CORE **OBJECTIVE**

1. Explain the challenges faced by both British and American military leaders in fighting the Revolutionary War.

Mobilizing for War

British Military Power

The British Empire sent some 35,000 soldiers and half its huge navy across the Atlantic to put down the American rebellion. The British also hired foreign soldiers (mercenaries). Almost 30,000 professional German soldiers served in the British armies in America. Most of them were from the German state of Hesse-Cassel—Americans called them *Hessians*. The British also recruited American Loyalists, Native Americans, and African Americans to fight on their behalf, but there were never as many enlisting as British leaders had hoped. Further, it was a formidable challenge for the British to keep their large army in America supplied. They initially assumed that there would be enough food for their troops and forage for their horses in America. In fact, however, most of the supplies would have to come from Britain. It took two to three months for ships to make the 3,000-mile Atlantic crossing, depending upon the weather, and the war in America soon became terribly expensive, both in dollars and lives.

American challenges: Massive British forces

The British government under Lord North led Great Britain into a far-away war without a clear strategy for waging it. Initially, the British focused on blockading New England's seaports in order to strangle American trade and eventually force the rebels to surrender. When that failed, the British military leaders sought to destroy George Washington's Continental army in New York. Despite their initial success in driving the Americans out of the city, the British generals failed to pursue the retreating Continental army. The British next tried to drive a wedge between New England and New York, splitting the colonies in two. That, too, would fail, leading to the final British strategy: moving its main army into the southern colonies in hopes of rallying Loyalists in that region to beat back the Revolutionaries.

Although victorious in most conventional battles against the Americans, the British never devised an overall strategy capable of defeating the Patriot cause. Ultimately, the Americans—fighting in their homeland for their independence and generously aided by the French—were able to outlast the British in a war of endurance.

The Continental Army

While the Patriots had the advantage of fighting on their home ground—the American commanders knew the terrain and the people—they also had to create an army and navy from scratch and with little money. Recruiting, supplying, equipping, training, and paying soldiers and sailors were monumental challenges for the new nation. At the start of the fighting, there were no uniforms, and American weapons were "as various as their costumes."

The Patriot soldiers that encircled the British in Boston in 1775 were poorly trained and lightly armed volunteers who had enlisted for only six months. Unlike the professional soldiers in the British army, these part-time **citizen-soldiers** were mostly poor farmers or recent immigrants who had been indentured servants. They often came and went as they pleased and drank liquor freely. The states rarely provided their requested share of the war's expenses, and the Continental Congress reluctantly had to allow the Patriot armies to take supplies—grain and livestock—directly from farmers in return for promises of future payment.

Before the war for independence, militiamen (citizen-soldiers) were primarily a home guard—civilians called out from their farms and shops on short notice to defend their local communities. To repel an attack, the militiamen somehow mustered themselves; once the danger was past, they disappeared, for there were chores to do at home. Many of the local militiamen were unreliable and ungovernable. They were, reported General Washington, "nasty, dirty, and disobedient." They "come in, you cannot tell how, go, you cannot tell when, and act you cannot tell where, consume your provisions, exhaust your stores [supplies], and leave you at last at a critical moment."

Washington knew that the Patriots could not win against veteran British and German soldiers using only militiamen. They needed a professional army of their own, with full-time soldiers enlisted from all thirteen colonies. As he organized such an army, General Washington noticed that the men from different colonies were developing a national (or "continental") viewpoint, in which they thought of themselves as fighting for a new *nation*, not just protecting their particular communities like militiamen. Washington thus decided to call it the *Continental army*.

What the Continental army needed most were capable officers, intensive training, strict discipline, and multiyear enlistment contracts. Washington and his officers soon began whipping the Continental army into shape. Recruits who violated army rules were jailed, flogged, or sent packing. Some deserters were hanged as an example to others.

George Washington at Princeton Commissioned for Independence Hall in Philadelphia, this 1779 painting by Charles Willson Peale portrays Washington as the hero of the Battle of Princeton.

> American challenges: Finance and supply for the military, citizen-soldiers

citizen-soldiers Part-time non-professional soldiers, mostly poor farmers or recent immigrants who had been indentured servants, who played an important role in the Revolutionary War.

American and British challenges: Recruiting Native Americans

Native Americans and the Revolution

Both the British and Americans recruited Indian allies to "take up the hatchet" and fight with them, but the British were far more successful, because they promised to protect Indian lands and provided more gifts. The peoples making up the Iroquois League split their allegiances, with most Mohawks, Onondagas, Cayugas, and Senecas, led by Mohawk Joseph Brant and Seneca Old Smoke, joining the British, and most Oneidas and Tuscaroras supporting the Patriots. The Cherokees also joined the British in hopes of driving out Americans who had taken their lands. Most Indians in New England tried to remain neutral or sided with the Patriots. The Stockbridge Indians in Massachusetts, mostly Mahicans, formed a company of Minutemen who fought alongside Patriot units. They pledged that "wherever your armies go, there we will go; you shall always find us by your side; and if providence calls us to sacrifice our lives in the field of battle, we will fall where you fall, and lay our bones by yours. Nor shall peace ever be made between our nation and the Red-Coats until our brothers—the white people—lead the way."

Disaster in Canada

In July 1775, the Continental Congress authorized an ill-fated attack against Quebec, Canada, in the vain hope of convincing the French inhabitants in Canada to support the revolutionary cause. The American forces arrived outside Quebec in September, exhausted and hungry. A silent killer then ambushed them: smallpox.

As the deadly virus raced through the American camp, General Richard Montgomery faced a brutal dilemma. Most of his soldiers had signed up for short tours of duty, and many of them were scheduled for discharge at the end of the year. He could not afford to wait until spring for the small-pox to subside. Seeing little choice but to fight, Montgomery ordered a desperate attack on the British forces at Quebec during a blizzard, on December 31, 1775.

The New Year's Eve assault was a disaster. Montgomery was killed early in the battle. Over 400 Americans were taken prisoner. The rest of the Pa-triot force retreated to its camp outside the walled city as the smallpox virus spread throughout the American army. As fresh troops arrived, they, too, fell victim to the disease. The British, sensing the weakness of the Americans, attacked and sent the ragtag Patriots on a frantic retreat up the St. Lawrence River and eventually back to New York and New England.

The failed Canadian campaign was the first military setback for the Rev-olutionaries. It would not be the last. By the summer of 1776, Americans knew that their quest for independence would be neither short nor easy, for King George III and the British government were determined to crush the revolt and restore their empire. To do so, they were willing to gather the most powerful fighting force in the world.

Washington's Narrow Escape

On July 2, 1776, the day the Continental Congress voted for independence, British redcoats landed on undefended Staten Island, across New York City's harbor from Manhattan. They were the first wave in a determined effort to smash the American Revolution by conquering New York and thereby splitting New England from the rest of the rebellious states. A divided rebellion would almost surely collapse, the British reasoned. That New York had more Loyalists than in all New England reinforced the focus on that key state.

During the summer of 1776, a massive British fleet of 427 warships carrying 32,000 British and German troops, 1,200 Loyalists, and 10,000 sailors began landing on Long Island near New York City. It was the largest seaborne military expedition in history. "I could not believe my eyes," recalled a Pennsylvania militiaman. "I declare that I thought all London was afloat."

Meanwhile, Washington could gather only about 19,000 raw militiamen and recruits in the new Continental army. It was too small a force to defend New York, but the Continental Congress wanted to keep the city in Patriot hands—at all costs. Although a veteran of frontier fighting, Washington had never commanded a large force. As he confessed to the Continental Congress, he had no "experience to move [armies] on a large scale" and had only "limited . . . knowledge . . . in military matters." In August 1776, he was still learning the art of generalship, and the British invasion of New York taught him some costly and painful lessons.

Short of weapons and greatly outnumbered, the American army entrenched on Long Island waited anxiously for the British to attack. General Washington walked back and forth with two loaded pistols, warning the soldiers that he would shoot anyone who turned tail and ran. He assured them that he would "fight as long as I have a leg or an arm."

Many Americans lost arms and legs as the Battle of Long Island and White Plains unfolded. The American soldiers had never seen war like this. A Marylander reported that a British cannon ball careened through the American lines. It "first took the head off . . . a stout heavy man; then took off Chilson's arm, which was amputated. . . . It then struck Sergeant Garret . . . on the hip. . . . What a sight that was to see . . . men with legs and arms and packs all in a heap." As Washington watched the slaughter, he groaned: "Good God! What brave fellows I must lose this day!"

Had the British moved more quickly, they could have trapped Washington's entire army as it fled. The British commander, however, ordered his men to halt and rest. "The Troops had for that day done handsomely enough," he said. The following morning rain drenched the tired and disheartened Americans, who had no tents. The rain was a blessing, however, for when it finally ended two days later, the Americans used the fog and mist to organize a miraculous escape, ferrying 9,500 soldiers in small boats across the East River to Manhattan. For two weeks, the shocked British commanders did nothing. Then, on September 15, they crossed the river and attacked. Again,

Lord Stirling at the Battle of Long Island The Battle of Long Island was a devastating loss for Washington, his troops, and American morale. In this dramatic painting by Alonzo Chappel, Washington's troops attack the British to enable the retreat of other units to Manhattan.

the outmatched Americans were forced to retreat northward. They crossed the Hudson River, fled into New Jersey and then over the Delaware River into eastern Pennsylvania.

Washington said those were the worst days of his life, for escaping was not winning. By December 1776, the American Revolution was at risk of disintegrating. British armies controlled large sections of New Jersey, New York, and Rhode Island. And the American army was fast vanishing. Of the 30,000 soldiers who had mobilized during the summer, fewer than 3,000 remained under George Washington's command, and they were ragged and worried after six months of punishing losses. A British officer reported that many of the "rebels" were "without shoes or stockings, and several were observed to have only linen drawers . . . without any proper shirt. They must

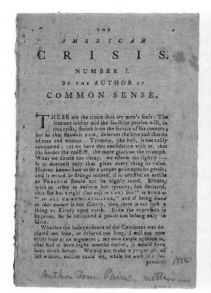 

THOMAS PAINE'S *The American Crisis* Thomas Paine's inspiring pamphlet was originally published anonymously "by the author of the Common Sense," because the British viewed its content as evidence of treason. **What was the immediate impact of Paine's** *The American Crisis***?**

suffer extremely." Washington described his unprofessional soldiers as being "comers and goers." Thousands of militiamen had simply gone home to sit out the winter or tend to their farms. Unless a new army could be raised quickly, Washington warned, "I think the game is pretty near up." His own morale, he said, was sustained only by the "justice of our cause."

Yet willpower and determination in battle can at times overcome long odds. Help for the Americans emerged from an unexpected source: Englishman Thomas Paine. Having opened the eventful year of 1776 with his inspiring pamphlet *Common Sense*, Paine confronted the "black times of '76" by composing *The American Crisis*, in which he wrote these stirring lines:

> These are the times that try men's souls: The summer soldier and the sunshine patriot will, in this crisis, shrink from the service of his country; but he that stands it NOW deserves the love and thanks of man and woman. Tyranny, like Hell, is not easily conquered. Yet we have this consolation with us, that the harder the conflict, the more glorious the triumph.

Paine's rousing pamphlet boosted Patriot spirits. Soon the Continental Congress's decision to offer fresh army recruits cash, land, clothing, and blankets would provide further support for what Paine's pamphlet inspired.

Washington also had learned some hard lessons in leadership. The feisty frontier militiamen he had relied upon to bolster the Continental army came and went as they pleased, in part because they resented and resisted traditional forms of military discipline. Washington acknowledged that "a people unused to restraint must be led; they will not be driven."

The American commander's genius was to learn from his mistakes and to use resilience and flexibility as weapons. With soldiers deserting every day, Washington modified his conventional top-down approach in favor of more democratic opportunities for soldiers to tell him their concerns and offer suggestions. What he heard led him to change his strategy. The British would not be defeated in large battles. He needed to use his limited forces in surprise attacks, hit-and-run campaigns that would enable him to confuse the British and preserve his struggling army. Unknowingly, the British fell blindly into his trap.

In December 1776, General William Howe, commander in chief of the British forces in North America, settled down to wait out the winter in New York City. (Eighteenth-century armies rarely fought during the winter months.) By not pursuing the Americans into Pennsylvania, Howe had lost a great opportunity to end the Revolution. In coming months, he would continue to miss chances to destroy the struggling Continental army, leading one American general to conclude that the passive Howe "shut his eyes, fought his battles, drank his bottle and had his little whore" (twenty-five-year-old Elizabeth Lloyd Loring, the beautiful wife of a prominent American Loyalist: "a brilliant, unprincipled" and "flashing blonde woman" whose husband tolerated her adultery because Howe awarded him a lucrative job supervising the handling of American prisoners of war).

A Desperate Gamble

George Washington, however, was not ready to hibernate for the winter. He decided that the revolutionary cause desperately needed "some stroke" of good news after the devastating defeats around New York City. So he hatched a plan to surprise the cocky British forces before more of his soldiers decided to return home. On Christmas Day 1776, Washington secretly led some 2,400 men, packed into forty-foot-long boats, from Pennsylvania across the icy, swollen Delaware River into New Jersey. It was a risky endeavor, made even riskier by the awful weather and the rough river currents.

Just as the Americans were crossing the river, a ferocious winter storm nearly defeated them. Twice they were forced to turn back, but the third time they made it to the New Jersey shore. It had taken nine hours to get all the men and equipment across the river, and the howling winds, sleet, and blinding snow slowed their progress as they marched inland in the darkness.

Near dawn at Trenton, the tired but determined Americans surprised 1,500 sleeping Hessians. It was a total rout; only 500 Hessians escaped. Just two of Washington's men were killed and four wounded, one of whom was James Monroe, the future president. After the Battle of Trenton, Washington hurried his men and their German captives back across the river, urging the Americans to treat the prisoners "with humanity, and let them have no reason to complain of our copying the brutal example of the British army."

Four days later, the Americans again crossed the now-frozen Delaware River, won another battle at Trenton, and then headed north to attack British forces around Princeton before taking shelter in winter quarters at

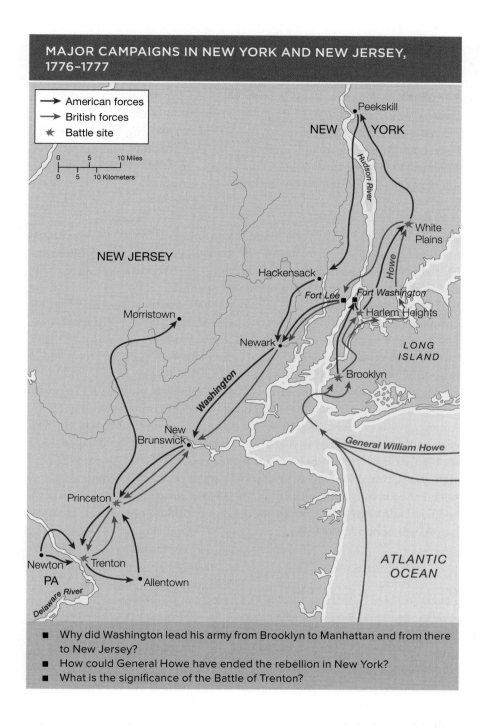

MAJOR CAMPAIGNS IN NEW YORK AND NEW JERSEY, 1776–1777

→ American forces
→ British forces
✳ Battle site

0   5   10 Miles
0   5   10 Kilometers

Peekskill

NEW YORK

Hudson River

White Plains

NEW JERSEY

Hackensack

Fort Lee

Fort Washington

Howe

Harlem Heights

LONG ISLAND

Morristown

Newark

Washington

Brooklyn

New Brunswick

General William Howe

Princeton

ATLANTIC OCEAN

Newton

Trenton

PA

Allentown

Delaware River

- Why did Washington lead his army from Brooklyn to Manhattan and from there to New Jersey?
- How could General Howe have ended the rebellion in New York?
- What is the significance of the Battle of Trenton?

Morristown, in the hills of northern New Jersey. A British officer grumbled that the Americans had "become a formidable enemy." As Washington had hoped, the surprising American victories at Princeton and Trenton saved the cause of independence. A fresh wave of Patriots signed up to serve in Washington's army. And the American commander regained the confidence of his men. They had seen his boldness, calmness, and courage under fire.

Winter in Morristown

American challenges:
Demoralized troops

During the winter at Morristown in early 1777, George Washington's army nearly disintegrated amid brutal weather, inadequate food, and widespread disease. One soldier recalled that "we were absolutely, literally starved. . . . I saw several of the men roast their old shoes and eat them."

With the spring thaw, however, recruits began arriving to claim the $20 in cash and 100 acres of land offered by the Continental Congress to those who would enlist for three years. With a new army of 9,000 troops, Washington began planning his strategy for 1777.

A Strategy of Evasion

British challenges: American evasion and selective confrontation; high supply costs

General Howe, the British commander, continued to think in conventional military terms, hoping to maneuver the struggling American army into fighting a single decisive battle that the superior British forces would surely win, thereby ending the war in one glorious engagement.

George Washington refused to take the bait, however. He knew that his outmanned army could not defeat the British in a large traditional battle. The only way to beat them, he decided, was to evade the main British army, carefully select when and where to attack when opportunities arose, and in the end, wear down the British will to carry on a long war.

The Americans did not have to win large battles; they simply had to avoid losing the war. Britain, on the other hand, could win only by destroying the American will to resist. Victory would come to the side that fought the longest, and with each passing year it became more difficult—and expensive— for the British to supply its large army and navy in America. During the next eight years, the Americans would follow a strategy of evasion punctuated by selective confrontations. Over time, the British government and the British people would tire of the human and financial expense of conducting a prolonged war across the Atlantic.

CORE **OBJECTIVE**
2. Identify key turning points in the Revolutionary War, and explain how they changed the direction of the war.

Setbacks for the British (1777)

In 1777, the British devised a fresh plan to defeat the "American rebellion." It centered on a three-pronged assault on the crucial state of New York. By gaining control of New York, the British would cut off New England from the rest of the colonies. The plan called for a British army, based in Canada and led by General John Burgoyne, to advance southward from Quebec via Lake Champlain to the Hudson River, while another British force moved eastward from Oswego, in western New York. Howe, meanwhile, would lead a third British army up the Hudson River from New York City.

As often happens with such complicated war plans, however, the British failed in their execution. At the last minute, Howe changed his mind and decided to load his army on ships and sail south to attack the Patriot capital,

Philadelphia. By doing so, Howe left Burgoyne's army in upstate New York at the mercy of gathering American forces.

To meet the British threat in Pennsylvania, General Washington withdrew most of his men from New Jersey to protect Philadelphia. On September 11, 1777, at Brandywine Creek, the British overpowered the Americans and then occupied Philadelphia, the largest and wealthiest American city. The members of the Continental Congress fled the city. Washington and his army had to withdraw to winter quarters twenty miles away at Valley Forge, while Howe and his men remained in the relative comfort of Philadelphia.

The Campaign of 1777

Meanwhile, an overconfident General Burgoyne (nicknamed "General Swagger") led his army (including 225 women and 500 children) southward from Canada through dense forests and across rivers and creeks, eventually reaching Lake Champlain in June 1777. The army then pushed south toward the Hudson River, struggling to cross the wooded, marshy terrain in upstate New York. Eventually, they ran short of food and provisions, leaving them no choice but to push forward in a desperate attempt to reach Albany. Growing numbers of Patriot soldiers slowed their advance in September, however.

GENERAL JOHN BURGOYNE After three weeks of fighting, Burgoyne, commander of Britain's northern forces, surrendered to the Americans at Saratoga on October 17, 1777.

The American army commander in New York facing Burgoyne's redcoats was General Horatio Gates. As Patriot militiamen converged from across central New York, Burgoyne pulled his forces back to the village of Saratoga (now called Schuylerville), where the reinforced American army surrounded the outnumbered British.

In the ensuing three-week-long **Battles of Saratoga**, the British twice tried—and failed—to break through the encircling Americans. Then on October 17, 1777, Burgoyne surrendered his outnumbered army. "The fortunes of war," he told General Gates, "have made me your prisoner." Burgoyne also turned over 5,800 troops, 7,000 muskets, and forty-two cannons to Gates. King George was devastated by the news, falling "into agonies on hearing the account" of Burgoyne's devastating surrender. The Saratoga campaign was the greatest loss that the British had ever suffered, and they would never recover from it.

> Battles of Saratoga (1777)

Alliance with France

The surprising American victory at Saratoga was a strategic turning point because it convinced the French, who had lost four wars to the British in the previous eighty years, to sign two crucial treaties in early 1778 that

Battles of Saratoga (1777) Decisive defeat of almost 6,000 British troops under General John Burgoyne in several battles near Saratoga, New York, in October 1777; the American victory helped convince France to enter the war on the side of the Patriots.

created an American **alliance with France**. Under the Treaty of Amity and Commerce, France officially recognized the new United States and offered trade concessions, including important privileges to American shipping. Next, under the Treaty of Alliance, both parties agreed that (1) if France entered the war, both countries would fight until American independence was won, (2) neither would conclude a "truce or peace" with Great Britain without "the formal consent of the other," and (3) each would guarantee the other's possessions in America "from the present time and forever against all other powers."

France further bound itself to seek neither Canada nor other British possessions on the mainland of North America. In the end, it was the French intervention that determined the outcome of the war. By June 1778, British vessels had fired on French ships, and the two nations were at war once again. The Americans would also form alliances with the Spanish (1779) and the Dutch (1781), but neither of those allies provided as much support as the French.

The French alliance turned the tide for the American revolutionaries. After the British defeat at Saratoga and the news of the French alliance with the United States, the British Parliament tried to end the war by granting all the demands that the American rebels had made in 1776, before they had declared independence. The Continental Congress, however, would not negotiate until Britain recognized American independence and withdrew its forces. King George refused.

Valley Forge and Stalemate

> Winter of 1777–1778 at Valley Forge

For George Washington's army at **Valley Forge**, near Philadelphia, the winter of 1777–1778 was a time of intense suffering. The 12,000 Patriots, including some precocious twelve-year-old soldiers accompanied by their mothers, endured unrelenting cold, hunger, and disease. Many soldiers lacked shoes and blankets, all were miserably hungry, and their 900 makeshift log-and-mud huts offered little protection from the howling winds and bitter cold. Bare feet froze in the cold, turned black, and were amputated. "Why are we sent here to starve and freeze?" wrote a suffering Connecticut Patriot. "Poor food . . . hard logging . . . cold weather . . . it snows. . . . I'm sick. . . . I can't endure it. . . . Lord, Lord, Lord."

By February, 7,000 troops were too ill for duty. More than 2,500 soldiers died at Valley Forge; another 1,000 deserted. Fifty officers resigned on one December day. Several hundred more left before winter's end. Washington sent urgent messages to the Congress, warning that if fresh food and supplies were not provided, the army would be forced "to starve, dissolve, or disperse."

Fortunately for the revolutionaries, their plodding nemesis, General Howe, again remained content to ride out the winter amid the comforts of Philadelphia, not the least of which was his charming evening companion,

alliance with France Critical diplomatic, military, and economic alliance between France and the newly independent United States, codified by the Treaty of Amity and Commerce and the Treaty of Alliance (1778).

Valley Forge (1777–1778) American military encampment near Philadelphia, where more than 3,500 soldiers deserted or died from cold and hunger in the winter.

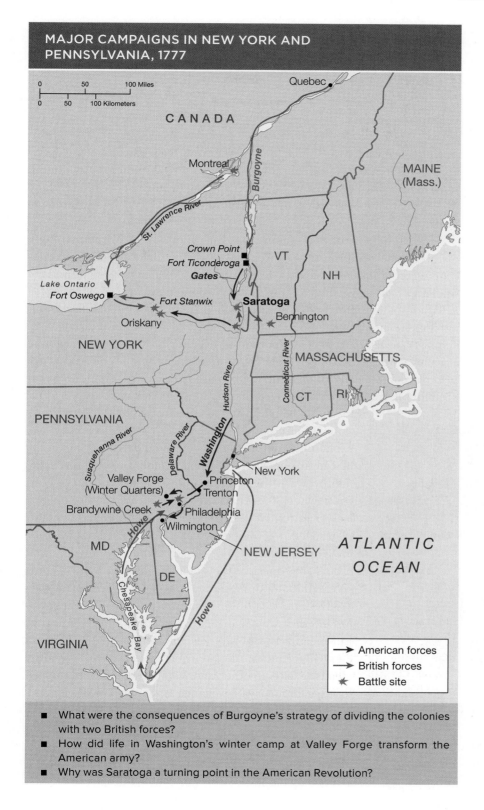

MAJOR CAMPAIGNS IN NEW YORK AND PENNSYLVANIA, 1777

0   50   100 Miles
0   50   100 Kilometers

Quebec

CANADA

Montreal

Burgoyne

St. Lawrence River

MAINE
(Mass.)

Crown Point
Fort Ticonderoga
Gates
VT
NH

Lake Ontario
Fort Oswego
Fort Stanwix
Saratoga
Bennington
Oriskany

NEW YORK

Hudson River
Connecticut River

MASSACHUSETTS

CT   RI

PENNSYLVANIA

Susquehanna River
Delaware River
Washington

New York

Valley Forge
(Winter Quarters)
Princeton
Trenton
Brandywine Creek
Philadelphia
Wilmington

Howe

MD

DE

NEW JERSEY

ATLANTIC
OCEAN

Chesapeake Bay

Howe

VIRGINIA

→ American forces
→ British forces
✳ Battle site

- What were the consequences of Burgoyne's strategy of dividing the colonies with two British forces?
- How did life in Washington's winter camp at Valley Forge transform the American army?
- Why was Saratoga a turning point in the American Revolution?

Mrs. Loring, who continued to travel with him. Their cozy relationship prompted a Patriot to pen a bawdy song:

Sir William, he, snug as a flea
Lay all this while a snoring;
Nor dream'd of harm as he lay warm
In bed with Mrs. Loring.

Yet there was little singing among the Americans encamped at Valley Forge. Desperate to find relief for his long-suffering soldiers, Washington sent men across New Jersey, Delaware, and the Eastern Shore of Maryland to confiscate horses, cattle, and hogs in exchange for "receipts" promising future payment.

By March 1778, the once-gaunt troops at Valley Forge saw their strength restored. Their improved health enabled Washington to begin a rigorous training program, designed to bring unity and discipline to his ragtag array of soldiers. To do so, Washington turned to an energetic, heavyset, short-legged Prussian soldier of fortune, Friedrich Wilhelm, baron von Steuben, who volunteered without rank or pay. Soon after his arrival at Valley Forge on February 23, 1778, he reported being shocked at the "horrible conditions" he found at Valley Forge, with some of the men "literally naked" in the cold.

An accomplished drill master, Steuben used an interpreter and frequent profanity as he stomped and raged instructions to the haggard Americans, teaching them how to march, shoot, and attack in formation. He also educated the Americans in basic hygiene, explaining that field kitchens and latrines should be placed at opposite ends of the camp and requiring the men to wash their hands and faces at least once a day. Once, when Steuben had grown frustrated at the soldiers' lack of attentiveness, he screamed for his translator: "These fellows won't do what I tell them. Come swear for me!" In Europe, he complained, soldiers blindly followed orders; in America, they demanded to know *why* they should do something.

Steuben was one of many foreign volunteers who joined the American army at Valley Forge. Another European was a twenty-year-old red-haired French soldier, Gilbert du Motier, Marquis de Lafayette. A wealthy idealist excited by the American cause, Lafayette agreed to serve for no pay in exchange for being named a general. General Washington was initially skeptical of the young French aristocrat, but Lafayette soon became the commander in chief's most trusted aide, a courageous soldier and able diplomat. He wrote to friends in France that George Washington was destined for greatness. He would be "revered throughout the centuries by all who love humanity and liberty."

BARON VON STEUBEN George Washington leads Baron von Steuben on a tour through Valley Forge, where he would embark on a rigorous training program to bring the American soldiers up to caliber. **What conditions did Steuben find when he arrived at Valley Forge?**

The Continental army's morale rose when the Congress promised extra pay and bonuses after the war. The good news from France about the formal military alliance also helped raise the Patriots' spirits. In the spring of 1778, British forces withdrew from Pennsylvania to New York City, with the American army in hot pursuit. From that time on, the major campaigns and battles in the North settled into a long stalemate.

War in the West

The one significant American military success of 1778 occurred in the West. The Revolution had created two wars. In addition to the main conflict between British and American armies in the east, a frontier guerrilla war pitted Indians and Loyalists against isolated Patriot settlers living along the northern and western frontiers. In the Ohio Valley as well as western New York and Pennsylvania, the British urged frontier Loyalists and their Indian allies to raid farm settlements and offered to pay bounties for American scalps.

> Terror tactics in Indian country

To end the English-led attacks, early in 1778 young George Rogers Clark took 175 Patriot frontiersmen on flatboats down the Ohio River. On the evening of July 4, the Americans captured English-controlled Kaskaskia (in present-day Illinois). Then, without bloodshed, Clark took Cahokia (in present-day Illinois across the Mississippi River from St. Louis) and Vincennes (in present-day Indiana).

After the British retook Vincennes, Clark marched his men (almost half of them French volunteers) through icy rivers and flooded prairies, sometimes in water neck deep, and prepared to attack the astonished British garrison. Clark's men, all hardened woodsmen, captured five Indians carrying American scalps. Clark ordered his men to kill the Indians in sight of the fort. After watching the terrible executions, the British surrendered.

While Clark's Rangers were in the Indiana territory, a much larger American military expedition moved through western Pennsylvania to attack Iroquois strongholds in western New York, where Loyalists ("Tories") and their Indian allies had been terrorizing frontier settlements throughout the summer of 1778. Led by Mohawk chief Joseph Brant, the Iroquois had killed hundreds of militiamen along the Pennsylvania frontier. In response, George Washington sent 4,000 men under General John Sullivan to crush "the hostile tribes" and "the most mischievous of the Tories." At Newtown, New York, on August 29, 1779, Sullivan's soldiers burned about forty Seneca and Cayuga villages, together with their orchards and food supplies, leaving many of the Indians homeless and without enough food to survive. The campaign broke the power of the

JOSEPH BRANT This 1786 portrait of Thayendanegea (Joseph Brant) by Gilbert Stuart features the Mohawk leader who fought against the Americans in the Revolution.

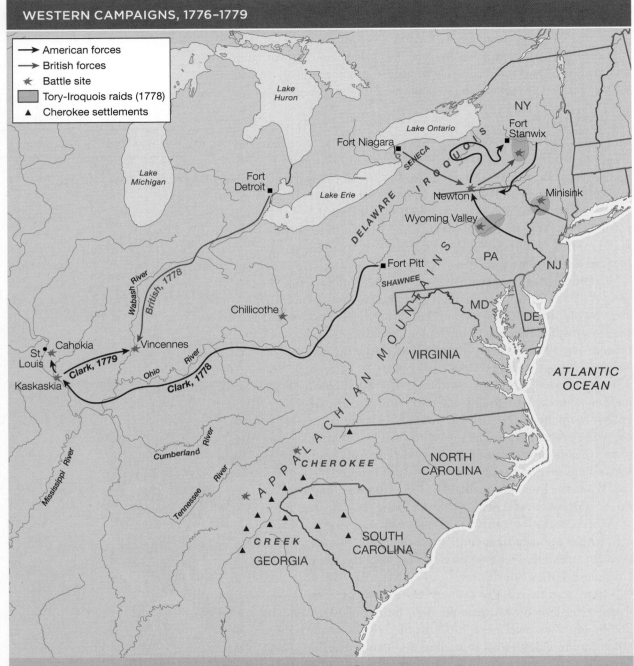

WESTERN CAMPAIGNS, 1776–1779

→ American forces
→ British forces
★ Battle site
▮ Tory-Iroquois raids (1778)
▲ Cherokee settlements

Lake Huron

Lake Ontario

Lake Michigan

Lake Erie

NY

Fort Niagara

SENECA

Fort Stanwix

Fort Detroit

DELAWARE

IROQUOIS

Newton

Minisink

Wyoming Valley

Wabash River

British, 1778

Fort Pitt

SHAWNEE

PA

NJ

Chillicothe

MD

DE

St. Louis

Cahokia

Vincennes

Clark, 1779

Ohio River

Clark, 1778

VIRGINIA

ATLANTIC OCEAN

Kaskaskia

Mississippi River

Cumberland River

Tennessee River

APPALACHIAN MOUNTAINS

CHEROKEE

NORTH CAROLINA

CREEK

SOUTH CAROLINA

GEORGIA

- How did George Rogers Clark secure Cahokia and Vincennes?
- Why did the American army destroy Iroquois villages in 1779?
- Why were the skirmishes between Indians and settlers on the western frontier significant for the future of the trans-Appalachian frontier?

Iroquois Confederacy for all time, but sporadic fighting continued until the end of the war.

In the Kentucky territory, Daniel Boone and his small band of settlers repeatedly clashed with the Shawnees and their British and Loyalist allies. In 1778, Boone and some thirty men, aided by their wives and children, held off an assault by more than 400 Indians at Boonesborough. Later, Boone himself was twice shot and twice captured. Indians killed two of his sons, a brother, and two brothers-in-law. His daughter was captured, and another brother was wounded four times.

In early 1776, a delegation of northern Indians—Shawnees, Delawares, and Mohawks—had talked the Cherokees into striking at frontier settlements in Virginia and the Carolinas. Swift retaliation had followed as Carolina militiamen led by Andrew Pickens burned dozens of Cherokee villages just east of the Blue Ridge Mountains, destroying their corn, orchards, and livestock. By weakening the major Native American nations along the frontier, the American Revolution cleared the way for white settlers to seize Indian lands after the war.

The War Moves South

In late 1778, the new commander of British forces in America, General Sir Henry Clinton, sent 3,000 redcoats, Hessians, and Loyalists to take the port city of Savannah, on the southeast Georgia coast, and roll northeast toward Charleston, South Carolina. While doing so, he enlisted support from local Loyalists and the Cherokees, led by Chief Dragging Canoe, who promised to leave the ground "dark and bloody."

Initially, Clinton's southern strategy worked. Within twenty months, the British and their allies had defeated three American armies; seized the strategic port cities of Savannah and Charleston; occupied Georgia and much of South Carolina; and killed, wounded, or captured some 7,000 American soldiers. The success of the "southern campaign" led a British official to predict a "speedy and happy termination of the American war."

But his optimistic prediction fell victim to three developments: (1) the Loyalist strength in the South was less than estimated, (2) the British effort to unleash Indian attacks convinced many undecided backcountry settlers to join the Patriot side, and (3) some British and Loyalist soldiers behaved so harshly that they drove other Loyalists to switch to the rebel side.

War in the Carolinas The Carolina campaign took a major turn when British forces, led brilliantly by Generals Clinton and Charles Cornwallis, bottled up an American army in Charleston. On May 12, 1780, the American general surrendered Charleston and its 5,500 defenders, the single greatest Patriot loss of the war.

General Cornwallis, in charge of the British troops in the South, defeated a much larger American force at Camden, South Carolina. Cornwallis had Georgia and most of South Carolina under British control by 1780. Much of the fighting in the Carolinas was a civil war pitting Americans against Americans, Patriots fighting Loyalists, and both sides looted farms and plantations and tortured, scalped, and executed prisoners.

The Battle of King's Mountain Cornwallis's two most ruthless cavalry officers, Sir Banastre Tarleton and Major Patrick Ferguson, who were in charge of training Loyalist militiamen, eventually overreached themselves. In a war without mercy, the British officers let their men burn Patriot farms, liberate slaves, and destroy livestock.

Major Ferguson sealed his doom when he threatened to march over the Blue Ridge Mountains, hang the mostly Scots-Irish Presbyterian frontier Patriot leaders ("backwater barbarians"), and destroy their farms. Instead, the feisty "overmountain men" from southwestern Virginia and western North and South Carolina (including "Tennesseans") went hunting for Ferguson and his army of Carolina Loyalists.

On October 7, 1780, the two sides clashed near King's Mountain, a heavily wooded ridge along the North Carolina border with South Carolina. There, in a ferocious hour-long battle, Patriot sharpshooters devastated the Loyalist troops. Major Ferguson, the only British soldier in the battle, had boasted beforehand that "all the rebels in hell could not push him off" King's Mountain. His body was riddled with seven bullet holes. Seven hundred Loyalists were captured, twenty-five of whom were later hanged. "The division among the people is much greater than I imagined," an American officer wrote to one of General Washington's aides. The Patriots and Loyalists, he said, "persecute each other with . . . savage fury."

As with so many confrontations during the war in the South, the Battle of King's Mountain was like an extended family feud. Seventy-four sets of brothers fought on both sides, and twenty-nine sets of fathers and sons. After the battle, Patriot captain James Withrow refused to help his Loyalist brother-in-law, who had been badly wounded. "Look to your friends for help," he said, leaving him to die on the battlefield. When Withrow's wife learned how her husband had treated her brother, she asked for a separation.

Five brothers in the Goforth family from Rutherford County, North Carolina, fought at King's Mountain; three were Loyalists, and two were Patriots. Only one of them survived. The Battle of King's Mountain was a crucial American victory, for it undermined the British strategy in the South. By proving that the British and their Loyalist supporters could be beaten, the Battle of King's Mountain inspired farmers to join Patriot units under colorful leaders such as Francis Marion, "the Swamp Fox," and Thomas Sumter, "the Carolina Gamecock."

The Tide Turns in the South In late 1780, the Continental Congress chose a new commander for the American army in the South: General Nathanael Greene, "the fighting Quaker" of Rhode Island. He was George Washington's ablest general—and well suited to the drawn-out war against the British forces. From Charlotte, North Carolina, where Greene arrived

The Battle of King's Mountain (1780)

NATHANAEL GREENE One of Washington's best generals, Greene led the Americans to victory at the battle at Cowpens.

in December 1780, he moved his army eastward while sending General Daniel Morgan, one of the heroes of the Battles of Saratoga, with about 700 riflemen on a sweep to the west of Cornwallis's headquarters at Winnsboro, South Carolina.

On January 17, 1781, Morgan's force took up positions near Cowpens, an area of cattle pastures in northern South Carolina, where they lured Tarleton's army into an elaborate trap. Tarleton rushed his men forward, only to be ambushed by Morgan's cavalry. More than 100 British soldiers were killed and 700 taken prisoner. Cowpens was the most complete tactical victory for the American side in the Revolution (Morgan called it a "devil of a whipping") and was one of the few times that Americans won a battle in which the two sides were evenly matched. When British general Cornwallis learned of the American victory, he snapped his sword in two, saying that the news "broke [his] heart."

> American victory at Cowpens

General Greene then lured Cornwallis's starving army north, attacking the redcoats at Guilford Courthouse (near what became Greensboro, North Carolina) on March 15, 1781. The Americans lost the battle but inflicted such heavy losses that Cornwallis left behind his wounded and marched his men off toward Wilmington, on the North Carolina coast, to rest and take on supplies from British ships. The British commander reported that the Americans had "fought like demons."

Greene then resolved to go back into South Carolina in the hope of drawing Cornwallis after him or forcing the British to give up the state. Greene joined forces with local guerrilla bands led by Francis Marion and Thomas Sumter. Together they worked to win the war by using hit-and-run tactics that prolonged the fighting.

A War of Endurance

The Revolutionary War had become a contest of endurance, and the Americans held the advantage in time, men, and supplies. They knew they could outlast the British as long as they avoided a catastrophic defeat in any single battle. "We fight, get beat, rise, and fight again," General Greene said.

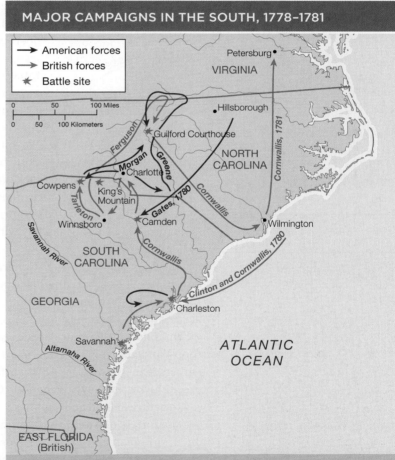

MAJOR CAMPAIGNS IN THE SOUTH, 1778–1781

→ American forces
→ British forces
✶ Battle site

- Why did the British suddenly shift their military campaign to the South in 1778?
- Why were the battles at Savannah and Charleston major victories for the British?
- How did Nathanael Greene undermine British control of the Carolinas?

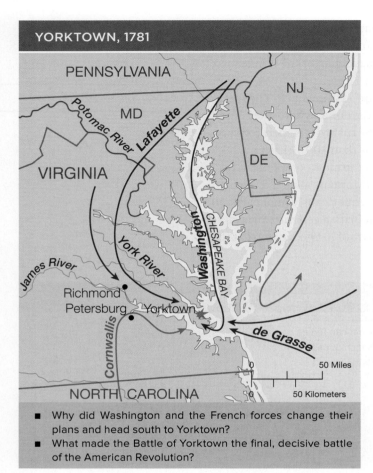

YORKTOWN, 1781

PENNSYLVANIA

NJ

Potomac River

MD

Lafayette

DE

VIRGINIA

Washington

CHESAPEAKE BAY

York River

James River

Richmond

Petersburg

Yorktown

Cornwallis

de Grasse

NORTH CAROLINA

0   50 Miles

0   50 Kilometers

- Why did Washington and the French forces change their plans and head south to Yorktown?
- What made the Battle of Yorktown the final, decisive battle of the American Revolution?

Yorktown: French forces tip the balance, and British surrender

Battle of Yorktown (1781) Last major battle of the Revolutionary War; General Cornwallis, along with over 7,000 British troops, surrendered to George Washington at Yorktown, Virginia, on October 17, 1781.

By September 1781, the Americans had narrowed British control in the South to Charleston and Savannah, although local Patriots and Loyalists would continue to battle each other for more than a year in the backcountry, where there was "nothing but murder and devastation in every quarter," Greene said.

Meanwhile, General Cornwallis had pushed his British army northward from Wilmington. Before the Carolinas could be subdued, he decided, Virginia must be eliminated as a source of American reinforcements and supplies.

Yorktown

Cornwallis picked Yorktown, Virginia, a small tobacco port between the York and James Rivers on the Chesapeake Bay, as his base of operations. He was not worried about an American attack, since General Washington's main force remained in New York, and the British navy controlled American waters.

Washington, however, surprised the British. As Cornwallis's army moved into Virginia, Washington persuaded the commander of the French army in Rhode Island to join in an attack on the British army in New York. The two armies linked up in July, but before they could strike, word came that Admiral François-Joseph-Paul de Grasse was headed for the Chesapeake Bay with his large French fleet and some 3,000 soldiers.

The unexpected news led General Washington to change his strategy. He immediately began moving his army south toward Yorktown. At the same time, French ships slipped out of the British blockade at Newport, Rhode Island, and also headed south.

On August 30, Admiral de Grasse's fleet reached Yorktown, and French troops landed to join the Americans confronting Cornwallis's army. On September 6, the day after a British fleet appeared, de Grasse attacked and forced the British navy to abandon Cornwallis's army, leaving them with no way to get fresh food and supplies.

The **Battle of Yorktown** commenced on September 28, 1781. The combined American and French troops soon closed off Cornwallis's last route of escape and began bombarding the besieged British troops with artillery, sending some 3,600 shells raining down on the French lines. "Against so powerful an attack," Cornwallis admitted, "we cannot hope to make a very long resistance."

And they didn't. On October 17, 1781, a glum Cornwallis surrendered. Two days later, the British force of more than 7,000 marched out with the British band playing a sad song that proved especially apt for the occasion. It included the words: "If summer were spring and the other way round / Then all the world would be upside down." The world had indeed been turned upside down by the unexpected American victory in its Revolutionary War. It would not be the last time that upstart America would surprise people around the world.

The Treaty of Paris (1783)

Any lingering British hopes of victory vanished at Yorktown. In London, the news of Cornwallis's surrender led Lord North to exclaim: "Oh God, it is all over." On February 27, 1782, Parliament voted to end the war, and on March 20 Lord North resigned.

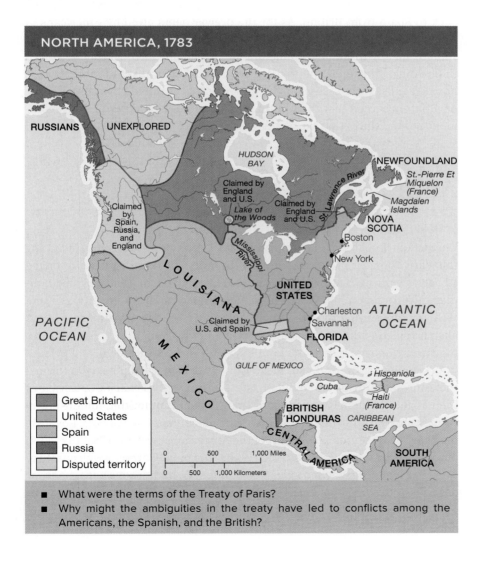

NORTH AMERICA, 1783

- What were the terms of the Treaty of Paris?
- Why might the ambiguities in the treaty have led to conflicts among the Americans, the Spanish, and the British?

Upon learning of the British decision to negotiate, the Continental Congress named a group of prominent Americans to go to Paris to discuss terms with the British. The commissioners included John Adams, who was then representing the United States in the Netherlands; John Jay, minister (ambassador) to Spain; and Benjamin Franklin, already in France. The negotiations with the British dragged on for months until, on September 3, 1783, the Treaty of Paris was signed. Its provisions were quite favorable to the United States—Franklin, Jay, and Adams had done very well. Great Britain recognized the independence of the thirteen former colonies and—surprisingly—agreed that the Mississippi River was America's western boundary, thereby more than doubling the territory of the new nation. Native American leaders were given no role in the negotiations, and Indians were by far the biggest losers in the final treaty.

The treaty's unclear references to America's northern and southern borders would be a source of dispute for years. Florida, as it turned out, passed back to Spain from Britain. As for the prewar debts owed by Americans to British merchants, the U.S. negotiators promised that British merchants should "meet with no legal impediment" in seeking to collect money owed them. And on the tender point of the thousands of Loyalist Americans whose homes, lands, and possessions had been seized by state governments, the negotiators agreed that the Continental Congress would "earnestly recommend" to the states that the confiscated property be restored.

CORE **OBJECTIVE**

3. Describe the ways in which the American Revolution was also a civil war.

American Society at War

Choosing Sides

The Revolution was as much a brutal civil war among Americans (including the Native American peoples allied with both sides) as it was a prolonged struggle against Great Britain. The necessity of choosing sides divided families and friends, towns and cities. Benjamin Franklin's illegitimate son, William, for example, was the royal governor of New Jersey. An ardent Loyalist, he sided with Great Britain during the Revolution, and his Patriot father later removed him from his will.

Colonists divided

The colonists were divided into three groups: (1) Patriots, who formed the Continental army and fought in state militias; (2) Loyalists, or Tories, as the Patriots mockingly called them; and (3) a less committed middle group swayed mostly by the better organized and more energetic Patriots. Loyalists may have represented 20 percent of the American population, but the Patriots were probably the largest of the three groups. Some Americans (like Benedict Arnold) switched sides during the war, and there were numerous deserters, spies, and traitors on both sides.

The Patriots, both moderates and radicals, supported the war for independence because they had finally decided that the only way to protect their

***Four Soldiers* (CA. 1781)** This illustration by a French lieutenant captures the varied appearances of Patriot forces in the war (left to right): a black soldier (freed for joining the First Rhode Island Regiment), a New England militiaman, a frontiersman, and a French soldier. **What does this illustration show about the Patriot forces?**

liberty was to separate themselves from British control and also from the British monarchy and aristocracy. Patriots also wanted to establish an American republic, a unique form of government in the late eighteenth century that would convert them from being *subjects* of a king to being *citizens* with the power to elect their own government and pursue their own economic interests. "We have it in our power," wrote Thomas Paine, "to begin the world over again. . . . The birthday of a new world is at hand."

The Loyalists, also called Tories, Royalists, or "King's Men," had no desire to "dissolve the political bands" with Britain, as the Declaration of Independence demanded. Instead, as some 700 of them in New York City said in a petition to British officials, they "steadily and uniformly opposed" this "most unnatural, unprovoked Rebellion." Where the Patriots rejected the monarchy, the Loyalists staunchly upheld royal authority and appreciated being defended by British soldiers. Loyalists believed that the British constitution was more likely to protect their rights and liberties than the American aristocrats parading as revolutionaries. They viewed the Revolution as an act of treason and were horrified by the idea of independence.

Loyalists were most numerous in the seaport cities, especially New York City and Philadelphia, as well as the Carolinas, but they came from all walks of life. Governors, judges, and other royal officials were almost all Loyalists; most Anglican ministers also preferred the mother country, as did many Anglican worshippers. In the backcountry of New York and across the Carolinas, many small farmers who had largely been unaffected by the controversies over British efforts to tighten colonial regulations rallied to the British side. More New York men joined Loyalist regiments than the Continental army. Many Loyalists calculated that the Revolution would fail or feared that it would result in mob rule. In few places, however, were there enough Loyalists to assume control without the support of British troops.

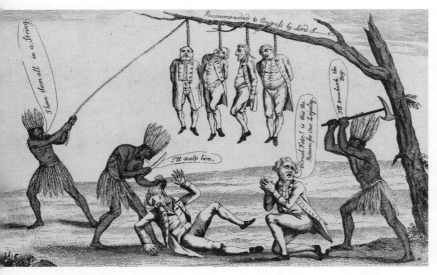

***The Fate of the Loyalists* (1783)** After the Revolution, many Loyalists fled to British colonies in the Caribbean and Canada. This British cartoon shows Patriots, depicted as "savages let[ting] loose," mercilessly hanging and scalping Loyalists.

The Loyalists Flee

The Loyalists suffered greatly for their stubborn support of King George and for their refusal to pledge allegiance to the new United States. During and after the Revolution, their homes, farms, and lands were confiscated, and many were assaulted and executed by Patriots (and vice versa). After the American victory at Yorktown, tens of thousands of panicked Loyalists headed to seaports to board British ships to flee the new United States. Thousands of African Americans, mostly runaway slaves, also flocked to New York City, Charleston, and Savannah, with many of their angry owners in hot pursuit.

Some 80,000 desperate refugees—white Loyalists, free blacks, slaves, and Indians who had allied with the British—scattered throughout the British Empire, transforming it in the process. The largest number of Loyalist exiles landed in Canada, including 3,500 former slaves who had been given their freedom in exchange for joining the British army.

The departure of so many Loyalists from America was one of the most important social consequences of the Revolution. Their confiscated homes, vast tracts of land, and vacated jobs created new social, economic, and political opportunities for Patriots.

CORE **OBJECTIVE**

4. Examine how the Revolutionary War was an "engine" for political and social change.

War as an Engine of Change

Like all major wars, the Revolution had unexpected effects on political, economic, and social life. It not only secured American independence and created a unique system of self-governance, but it also began a process of societal change that has remained a defining element in the American experiment in representative democracy. The turmoil of eight years of war upset traditional social relationships and affected the lives of people who had long been discriminated against—African Americans, women, and Native Americans. In important ways, then, the Revolution was much more than simply a war for independence. It was an engine for political experimentation and social change.

A Political Revolution

Debating the forms of government

The Americans had won their War of Independence. Had they experienced a political revolution as well? Years later, retired President John Adams insisted that the Revolution had begun long before the shooting started: "The

Revolution was in the minds and hearts of the people. . . . This radical change in the principles, opinions, sentiments, and affections of the people was the real American Revolution." Yet Adams's observation notwithstanding, the war itself ignited a prolonged debate about what forms of government would best serve the new American republic.

Republican Ideology

American revolutionaries embraced a **republican ideology** instead of the monarchical outlook that had long dominated Europe. The new American republic was not a democracy in the purest sense of the word. In ancient Greece, the Athenians practiced *direct democracy*, which meant that the citizens voted on all major decisions affecting their society, not unlike the town meetings in New England villages today. The new United States, rather, was technically a *representative democracy*, in which property-holding white men governed themselves through the concept of republicanism, whereby they elected representatives, or legislators, to make key decisions on their behalf. As Thomas Paine observed, representative democracy had many advantages over monarchies, one of which was greater transparency: "Whatever are its excellencies and defects, they are visible to all."

> Representative democracy and individuals' rights

To preserve the delicate balance between liberty and power in the new American republic, the Revolutionary leaders believed that their new governments must protect the rights of individuals and states from being violated by the national government. The war for independence thus sparked a wave of new **state constitutions** that remains unique in history. Not only was a new nation coming into being, but also new state-level governments were being created, all of which were designed to reflect the principles of the "republican ideology" limiting the powers of government so as to protect the people's rights.

State Governments

Most of the political experimentation between 1776 and 1787 occurred at the state level in the form of written constitutions in which the people granted limited authority to their governments. The first state constitutions created governments much like the colonial governments but with *elected* governors and senates instead of royally *appointed* governors and councils. Most of the constitutions also included a bill of rights that protected the time-honored rights of freedom of speech, trial by jury, freedom from self-incrimination, and the like. Most of them limited the powers of governors and strengthened the powers of the legislatures.

The Articles of Confederation

Once the American colonies had declared their independence in 1776, the Patriots needed to form a *national* government as well as thirteen *state* governments in the midst of the war. Before March 1781, the Continental Congress had exercised emergency powers without any legal or official authority. Plans for a permanent form of government emerged quickly, however. As

republican ideology Political belief in representative democracy in which citizens govern themselves by electing representatives, or legislators, to make key decisions on the citizens' behalf.

state constitutions Charters that define the relationship between the state government and local governments and individuals, also protecting their rights from violation by the national government.

early as July 1776, a committee appointed by the Continental Congress had produced a draft constitution called the *Articles of Confederation and Perpetual Union.* When the **Articles of Confederation** finally were ratified (approved by the states) five years later, in March 1781, they essentially legalized the way things had been operating since independence had been declared.

The Confederation government reflected the long-standing American fears of monarchy by not allowing for a president or chief executive. The Confederation Congress had full power over foreign affairs and over disputes between the states. Yet the Confederation Congress had no courts and no power to enforce its resolutions and ordinances. It also had no power to levy taxes and had to rely for its own budgetary needs on requisitions from the states, which state legislatures often ignored.

The states were in no mood to create a strong central government. The Confederation Congress, in fact, had less power than the colonists had once accepted in Parliament, since it could not regulate interstate and foreign commerce. For certain important acts, moreover, a "special majority" was required. Nine states had to approve measures dealing with war, treaties, coinage, finances, and the army and navy. Unanimous approval from the states was needed to levy tariffs (called "duties," or taxes) on imports. Amendments to the Articles also required unanimous ratification by the states. The Confederation had neither an executive nor a judicial branch; there was no administrative head of government (only the president of the Confederation Congress, chosen annually), and there were no federal courts.

For all its weaknesses, however, the Confederation government represented the most practical structure for the new nation. After all, the Revolution on the battlefields had yet to be won, and an America besieged by British armies and warships could not risk divisive debates over the distribution of power that other forms of government might have entailed. The new state governments were not willing in 1776 to create a strong national government that might threaten their liberties.

Expansion of Political Participation

Participation in the Revolutionary army or militia excited men who previously had taken little interest in politics. The new political opportunities afforded by the creation of state governments led more citizens to participate than ever before. The property qualifications for voting, which already admitted an overwhelming majority of white men, were lowered after 1776. As a group of farmers explained, "No man can be free and independent" unless he possesses "a voice . . . in the most important officers in the legislature." In Pennsylvania, Delaware, North Carolina, and Georgia, any male taxpayer could vote. In addition, farmers, tradesmen, and shopkeepers were soon elected to state legislatures. In general, a higher percentage of American males could vote in the late eighteenth and early nineteenth century than their counterparts in Great Britain.

Limited government and states' rights

Articles of Confederation
The first form of government for the United States, ratified by the original thirteen states in 1781; weak in central authority, it was replaced by the U.S. Constitution drafted in 1787.

A Social Revolution

The Revolutionary War helped excite a sense of common nationality. American nationalism embodied a stirring idea. This new nation, unlike the old-world nations of Europe, was not rooted in antiquity. Its people, except for the Native Americans, had not inhabited it over many centuries, nor did they all share the same ethnic background. "The American national consciousness," one observer wrote, "is not a voice crying out of the depth of the dark past, but is proudly a product of the enlightened present, setting its face resolutely toward the future."

Political revolutions often spark social revolutions. What did the Revolution mean to those workers, servants, farmers, and freed slaves who participated? Many hoped that the Revolution would remove, not reinforce, the elite's traditional political and social advantages. Many wealthy Patriots, on the other hand, would have been content to replace royal officials with the rich, the wellborn, and the able—and let it go at that. The poor did not overthrow the rich during the American Revolution, but the new republic's social fabric was visibly different after the war. The energy created by the concepts of liberty, equality, and democracy changed the dynamics of American social and political life in ways that people could not have imagined in 1776. The Philadelphia doctor and scientist Benjamin Rush recognized that unexpected changes were on the way: "The American war is over: but this is far from being the case with the American Revolution. On the contrary, but the first act of the great drama is closed."

Freedom of Religion

The Revolution also tested traditional religious loyalties and set in motion important changes in the relationship between church and government. Before the Revolution, Americans *tolerated* religious dissent; after the Revolution, Americans insisted on complete *freedom* of religion as embodied in the principle of separation of church and state.

The Anglican Church, established as the official religion in five colonies and parts of two others, was especially vulnerable to changes prompted by the war. Anglicans tended to be pro-British, and non-Anglicans, notably Baptists and Methodists, outnumbered Anglicans in all states except Virginia. All but Virginia eliminated tax support for the church before the fighting was over, and Virginia did so soon afterward. Although Anglicanism survived in the form of the new Episcopal Church, it never regained its pre-Revolutionary stature.

RELIGIOUS DEVELOPMENT The Congregational Church developed a national presence in the early nineteenth century. Lemuel Haynes, depicted here, was its first African American preacher. **What was the relationship between the American Revolution and religious freedom?**

Religious freedom

In 1776, the Virginia Declaration of Rights had guaranteed the free exercise of religion. In 1786 the **Virginia Statute of Religious Freedom** (written by Thomas Jefferson) declared that "no man shall be compelled to frequent or support any religious worship, place or ministry whatsoever" and "that all men shall be free to profess, and by argument to maintain, their opinions in matters of religion." These statutes, and the Revolutionary ideology that justified them, helped shape the course that religious life would take in the new United States: diverse and voluntary rather than monolithic and enforced by the government. Even religious life was revolutionized.

CORE **OBJECTIVE**

5. Compare the impact of the Revolutionary War on African Americans, women, and Native Americans.

Equality and Its Limits

The Paradox of Slavery

The sharpest irony of the American Revolution is that Britain offered enslaved blacks more opportunities for freedom than did the new United States. In November 1775, the British promised freedom to slaves and indentured servants who would fight for the Loyalist cause. Thousands of slaves took advantage of the offer. Harry Washington, for example, was born in Africa, became one of George Washington's slaves in 1763, escaped to join the British army, and served in the Revolutionary War as a corporal in one of the black regiments organized by the British army.

The British recruitment of slaves outraged George Washington, Thomas Jefferson, and other white plantation owners in Virginia, where 40 percent of the population was black. Twenty-three slaves escaped from Jefferson's Monticello plantation. The man who drafted the Declaration of Independence eventually reclaimed six of them, only to sell them for their "disloyalty" in seeking liberty for themselves.

British recruit and free slaves, while slavery is abolished in the North

In the end, however, the British policy of recruiting slaves into the military backfired. The "terrifying" prospect of British troops arming slaves persuaded many southerners to join the Patriot cause, and for many whites, especially in Virginia, the Revolution became primarily a war to defend slavery. Edward Rutledge of South Carolina said that the British decision to arm slaves did more to create "an eternal separation between Great Britain and the colonies than any other expedient." Slaves accused of disloyalty faced terrible punishment. In 1775, Thomas Jeremiah, a free black, was executed in Charleston, South Carolina, for telling slaves that British troops were coming "to help the poor Negroes."

In response to the British recruitment of enslaved African Americans, at the end of 1775 General Washington authorized the enlistment of free blacks—but not slaves—into the American army. Southerners, however, convinced the Continental Congress to instruct Washington in February 1776 to enlist no more African Americans, free or enslaved. But as the American war effort struggled, some states ignored southern wishes. Massachusetts organized two all-black army units, and Rhode Island organized one, which also included Indians. However, two states, South Carolina and Georgia, refused

Virginia Statute of Religious Freedom (1786) A Virginia law, drafted by Thomas Jefferson in 1777 and enacted in 1786, that guarantees freedom of, and from, religion.

to allow any blacks to serve in the Patriot forces. About 5,000 African Americans fought on the Patriot side, most of them free blacks from northern states.

The white Belknap family of Framingham, Massachusetts, freed their African American slave Peter Salem so that he might enlist in the Massachusetts militia. Salem was with the Minutemen at Concord in 1775 and also fought alongside other blacks at the Battles of Bunker Hill and Saratoga. Another former slave who fought at Bunker Hill, Salem Poor, was commended after the battle for being a "Brave & gallant Soldier" who "behaved like an experienced officer, as well as an excellent soldier."

In the end, the British army, which liberated 20,000 enslaved blacks during the war, was a far greater instrument of emancipation than the American forces. Most of the newly freed blacks found their way to Canada or to British colonies on Caribbean islands.

While thousands of free blacks and runaway slaves fought in the war, the vast majority of African Americans did not choose sides so much as they chose freedom. Several hundred thousand enslaved blacks, mostly in the southern states, took advantage of the disruptions caused by the war to seize their freedom. In the North, which had far fewer slaves than the South, the ideas of liberty and freedom that inspired the Patriots led most states to end slavery, either during the war or shortly afterward. In other words, the ideals of the Revolution provided the impulse to end slavery in the North, while at the same time many southerners were prompted to join the Revolution to keep the British from freeing their slaves. These paradoxical attitudes would continue to shape the political disputes of the young nation.

AFRICAN AMERICANS AT WAR Peter Salem, a former slave of a Massachusetts family freed so that he could join the American militia, is depicted here fighting in the Battle of Bunker Hill. **How did the British, the southerners, and the northerners differ in their approach to African Americans' involvement in the war?**

The Status of Women

The idea of liberty spawned by the Revolution applied to the status of women as much as to that of African Americans. The legal status of women in the colonies was governed by British common law, which essentially treated them like children, limiting their roles to child-rearing and maintaining the household. Women could not vote or hold office. Nor could they preach. Few had access to formal education. Boys were taught to read and write; girls were taught to read and sew. Most New England women in the eighteenth century could not write their own names. Until married, women were subject to their fathers. Once a woman married, she essentially became the property of her husband, and her goods became his. A married woman had no right to buy, sell, or manage property. Technically, any wages a wife earned belonged to the husband. Women could not sign contracts or sue others or testify in court. A husband could beat and even rape his wife without fearing legal action. Divorces were extremely difficult to obtain; wives were required to obey their husbands.

Yet the Revolution offered women new opportunities to broaden their social roles. Thousands of women, mostly wives, mothers, or sisters of soldiers, supported the armies in various ways. They handled supplies, served as messengers or spies, and worked as "camp followers," cooking, washing, sewing, and nursing the soldiers in exchange for daily rations. (Men, too, were camp followers, often serving as herdsmen, butchers, wagon drivers, clergymen, or "sutlers"—men who sold a variety of goods to soldiers.) Some officers paid women to be their personal servants, cooking, washing, and cleaning. Colonel Ebenezer Huntington, for example, sought "to hire some women to live in camp to do the washing for [him] self and some of the officers."

Often women had no choice but to follow their husbands in war because they had no place to live or food to eat. Some camp followers tended cattle, sheep, or hogs, and guarded supplies. Others sold various items. A few of the single women were prostitutes. In 1777, George Washington ordered that commanders take measures to "prevent an inundation of bad women [prostitutes] from Philadelphia." He also urged that soldiers fraternize only with "clean" women to prevent the spread of venereal diseases.

Wives who were camp followers sometimes brought along their children (often because they had no choice). General Washington would have preferred to ban women and children as camp followers. He once expressed frustration at "the multitude of women . . . especially those who are pregnant, or have children" clogging the movement of his army. He ordered his officers "to use every reasonable method in their power to get rid of all such as are not absolutely necessary." In the end, however, he was forced to accept the permanence of camp followers because he was afraid to lose "a number of men, who very probably would have followed their wives" home.

Women risked their lives in battle, tending the wounded or bringing water to the soldiers. On occasion, wives took the place of their soldier-husbands in battle. In 1777, some 400 armed women mobilized to defend Pittsfield, Vermont. The men of the town had gone off to fight when a band of Loyalists and Indians approached the village. In a daylong battle, the women held off the attackers until help arrived.

Several women disguised themselves and fought as ordinary soldiers. An exceptional case was Deborah Sampson, who joined a Massachusetts regiment as "Robert Shurtleff" and served from 1781 to 1783 by the "artful concealment" of her gender. Ann Bailey did the same. In 1777, eager to get the enlistment bonus payment, she cut her hair, dressed like a man, and used a husky voice to join the Patriot army in New York as "Samuel Gay." Bailey performed so well that she was promoted to corporal, only to be discovered as a woman, dismissed, jailed, and fined.

Little progress for women

Early in the Revolutionary struggle, Abigail Adams, one of the most learned, spirited, and independent women of the time, wrote to her husband, John: "In the new Code of Laws which I suppose it will be necessary for you to make, I desire you would remember the Ladies. . . . Do not put such unlimited power into the hands of the Husbands." Since men were

"Naturally Tyrannical," she wrote, "why then, not put it out of the power of the vicious and the Lawless to use us with cruelty and indignity with impunity." Otherwise, "if particular care and attention is not paid to the Ladies we are determined to foment a Rebellion, and will not hold ourselves bound by any Laws in which we have no voice, or Representation." Husband John responded that he could not help but "laugh" at her proposals. While surprised that women might be dissatisfied, he insisted on retaining the traditional privileges enjoyed by males: "Depend upon it, we know better than to repeal our Masculine systems." If women were to be granted equality, he warned, then "children and apprentices" and "Indians and Negroes" would also demand equal rights and freedoms.

Thomas Jefferson shared Adams's stance. In his view, there was no place in the new American republic for female political participation. When asked about women's voting rights, he replied that "the tender breasts of ladies were not formed for political convulsion." Improvements in the status of women would have to wait. New Yorker Margaret Livingston admitted as much in 1776 when she wrote her daughter that "our Sex are *doomed* to be obedient [to men] at every stage of life so that we shan't be great gainers by this contest [the Revolutionary War]."

ABIGAIL ADAMS A 1766 portrait of Abigail Adams, the wife of John Adams. Though an ardent Patriot, she and other women like her saw few changes in women's rights emerging in the new United States.

Native Americans and the Revolution

The war for American independence had lasting effects on the Indians in the southern backcountry and in the Old Northwest territory west of New York and Pennsylvania. Most Native Americans sought to remain neutral in the war, but both British and American agents urged the chiefs to fight on their side. The result was the disintegration of the alliance among the six nations making up the Iroquois League. Most Mohawks, for example, accepted British promises to protect them from encroachments by American settlers on their lands. The Oneidas, on the other hand, fought with the Patriots. Indians on both sides attacked villages, burned crops, and killed civilians.

The new American government assured its Indian allies that it would respect their lands and their rights. But the American people adopted a very different goal: they used the disruptions of war to destroy and displace many Native Americans. Once the war ended and independence was secured, there was no peace for the Indians. The new U.S. government turned its back on most of the pledges made to Native Americans. By the end of the eighteenth century, land-hungry whites were again pushing into Indian territories on the western frontier. Independence for Americans would bring growing exploitation of Native Americans.

> Displacement and destruction of Native Americans

Reviewing the
CORE OBJECTIVES | INQUIZITIVE

- **Military Challenges** In 1776, the British had the mightiest army and navy in the world. The Americans had to create an army—the Continental army—and sustain it. To defeat the British, George Washington realized that the Americans had to turn unreliable *citizen-soldiers* into a disciplined fighting force. He decided to wage a long, costly war, wagering that the British army was fighting thousands of miles from its home base and would eventually give up in order to cut its losses.

- **Turning Points** The French were likely allies for the colonies from the beginning of the conflict because they resented their losses to Britain in the Seven Years' War. After the British defeat at the *Battles of Saratoga*, the first major turning point, France agreed to fight with the colonies until independence was won. Washington was able to hold his ragged forces together despite daily desertions and two especially difficult winters in Morristown and *Valley Forge*, the second and third major turning points. The British lost support on the frontier and in their southern colonies when terrorist tactics backfired. The Battle of King's Mountain drove the British into retreat, and the *alliance with France* meant that French supplies and the French fleet would tip the balance and ensure the American victory at the *Battle of Yorktown*, the final turning point.

- **Civil War** The American Revolution was also a civil war, dividing families

and communities. There were at least 100,000 Loyalists in the colonies. They included royal officials, Anglican ministers, wealthy southern planters, and the elite in large seaport cities; they also included many humble people, especially recent immigrants. After the hostilities ended, many Loyalists, including slaves who had fled their plantations to support the British cause, left for Canada, the West Indies, or Great Britain.

- **A Political and Social Revolution** The American Revolution disrupted and transformed traditional social relationships. American revolutionaries embraced a *republican ideology* in contrast to a monarchy, and more white men gained the right to vote as property requirements were removed. But fears of a monarchy being reestablished led colonists to vest power in the states rather than a powerful national government under the *Articles of Confederation*. The states wrote new *state constitutions* that instituted more elected positions. The *Virginia Statute of Religious Freedom* led the way in guaranteeing the separation of church and state, and religious toleration was transformed into religious freedom for all, including Roman Catholics and Jews.

- **African Americans, Women, and Native Americans** Northern states began to free slaves after the Revolutionary War, but southern states refused to do so. Although many women had undertaken nontraditional roles during the war, afterward they remained largely confined to the domestic sphere, with no changes to their legal or political status. The Revolution had catastrophic effects on Native Americans, regardless of which side they had embraced during the war. During and after the Revolution, American settlers seized Native American land, often in violation of existing treaties.

KEY TERMS

citizen-soldiers *p. 159*

Battles of Saratoga (1777) *p. 167*

alliance with France *p. 168*

Valley Forge (1777–1778) *p. 168*

Battle of Yorktown (1781) *p. 176*

republican ideology *p. 181*

state constitutions *p. 181*

Articles of Confederation *p. 182*

Virginia Statute of Religious Freedom (1786) *p. 184*

CHRONOLOGY

1776 British forces seize New York City

General Washington's troops defeat British forces at the Battle of Trenton

States begin writing new constitutions

1777 American forces defeat British in a series of battles at Saratoga, New York

1778 Americans and French form a crucial military alliance

George Rogers Clark's militia defeats British troops in the Mississippi Valley

American forces defeat the Iroquois Confederacy at Newtown, New York

British seize Savannah and Charleston

1779 American forces defeat the Iroquois Confederacy at Newtown, New York.

1780 Patriots defeat Loyalists at the Battle of King's Mountain

1781 British invasion of southern colonies turned back at the Battles of Cowpens and Guilford Courthouse

American and French forces defeat British at Yorktown, Virginia

1783 Treaty of Paris is signed, formally ending Revolutionary War

1786 Virginia adopts the Statute of Religious Freedom

INQUIZITIVE

Go to InQuizitive to see what you've learned—and learn what you've missed—with personalized feedback along the way.

WASHINGTON AS A STATESMAN AT THE CONSTITUTIONAL CONVENTION (1856) This painting by Junius Brutus Stearns is one of the earliest depictions of the drafting of the Constitution, capturing the moment after convention members, including George Washington (right), decided to present the Constitution to the public.

Creating a "More Perfect Union"

1783–1800

The unlikely American victory in the Revolutionary War stunned the world, but the Patriots had little time to celebrate, for they faced the overwhelming task of creating the world's first large republic. Forging a new nation out of thirteen colonies posed huge challenges during and after the war. The period from the drafting of the Declaration of Independence in 1776, through the creation of the new national constitution in 1787, and ending with the election of Thomas Jefferson as president in 1800 was an especially turbulent time during which the new nation experienced growing political divisions, foreign troubles, and courageous statesmanship. In the end, the process of forming a new republic created powerful tensions that gave birth to the first national political parties and, to this day, continue to complicate the American experiment in federalism (the sharing of power among national, state, and local governments).

CORE OBJECTIVES INQUIZITIVE

1. Identify the strengths and weaknesses of the Articles of Confederation and explain how they prompted the creation of a new U.S. Constitution in 1787.

2. Describe the political innovations that the 1787 Constitutional Convention developed for the new nation.

3. Summarize the major debates surrounding the ratification of the Constitution and explain how they were resolved.

4. Compare the Federalists' vision for the United States with that of their Republican opponents during the 1790s.

5. Assess how attitudes toward Great Britain and France shaped American politics in the late eighteenth century.

CORE **OBJECTIVE**

1. Identify the strengths and weaknesses of the Articles of Confederation and explain how they prompted the creation of a new U.S. Constitution in 1787.

The Confederation Government

During the 1780s, the widespread distrust of centralized government power, originally directed at the British monarchy, now focused on the new American government created under the Articles of Confederation. The union of states formed in 1776 was a wartime alliance of necessity that, politically and economically, often functioned poorly. After the Revolutionary War ended in 1783, riots and rebellions protesting government policies erupted with growing frequency. The weaknesses of the Confederation government in dealing with such turmoil led political leaders to design a new national constitution and federal government in 1787, both of which proved to be more effective—and lasting—than the Confederation government.

A Loose Alliance of States

By design, the Articles of Confederation, drafted in 1776–1777 and approved by the states in 1781, had created not so much a united nation as a loose alliance ("confederation") of thirteen independent states. The first national government under the Articles of Confederation had only one component, a one-house (unicameral) congress. There was no president, no executive branch, no separate national judiciary (court system). State legislatures appointed the members of the Confederation Congress; each state, regardless of size or population, had one vote. This meant that Rhode Island, with 68,000 people, had the same power in Congress as Virginia, with over 747,000 inhabitants. Because revising the Articles of Confederation required a *unanimous* vote of both the Congress and the thirteen state legislatures, they were never amended.

> A deliberately weak central government

The Confederation Congress was weak by design so as not to violate the rights of the thirteen states. It had little authority or resources, leading George Washington to call it "a half-starved, limping government, always moving upon crutches and tottering at every step."

The Confederation Congress could neither regulate trade between the states or with other nations nor pay off the country's large war debts; it could approve treaties with other nations but had no power to enforce their terms; it could call for the raising of an army but could not force men to serve. The Congress had no power to enforce its own laws and ran up a budget deficit every year of its existence. When the states did not provide sufficient contributions to pay for the national government, the Confederation Congress resorted to printing paper money called Continentals, whose value plummeted as more were printed, leading to the joking phrase, "Not worth a Continental."

An Important Foundation

> Successes: Support of "republicanism" and negotiation of Treaty of Paris (1783)

Yet in spite of its limitations, the weak Confederation Congress somehow managed to survive the difficult war years and to lay important foundations for the new national government. The Articles of Confederation were crucially important in supporting the political concept of "republicanism," which meant that the American Republic would be governed not by monarchs or aristocrats but "by the authority of the people."

The Confederation government also concluded the Treaty of Paris with Great Britain in 1783, ending the Revolutionary War. Perhaps most important, the Confederation established the basic principles of land distribution and territorial government that would guide America's westward expansion for decades to come.

Land Policy

In ending the Revolutionary War, the Treaty of Paris doubled the size of the United States. Between 1784 and 1787, the Confederation Congress issued three major policies, called *ordinances*, providing for the orderly development of the vast territories west of the thirteen original states. These documents—among the most important in American history—created the procedures that the United States would follow in its eventual westward expansion all the way to the Pacific.

Thomas Jefferson drafted the Land Ordinance of 1784, which urged states to drop their competing claims to Indian-held territory west of the Appalachian Mountains, north of the Ohio River, and east of the Mississippi River. That way, the vast, unmapped area could be divided into as many as seventeen *new* states. When a western territory's population equaled that of the smallest existing state (Rhode Island), the territory would be eligible for statehood.

The next year, the Confederation Congress created the Land Ordinance of 1785, which outlined a plan of land surveys that would stamp a rectangular pattern on what was called the Northwest Territory (the sprawling area that would become the states of Ohio, Michigan, Indiana, Illinois, and Wisconsin). Wherever Indian lands were purchased—or taken—they were divided into six-mile-square townships laid out along a grid of lines running east-west and north-south. Each township was in turn divided into thirty-six sections one mile square (640 acres), with each section divided into four farms. The 640-acre sections of "public lands" were to be sold at auctions, the proceeds of which went into the national treasury.

The Northwest Ordinance (1787)

The third major land policy created by the Confederation Congress was the **Northwest Ordinance** of 1787. It outlined two key principles: that the new western territories could become states that would be treated as equals rather than as colonies and that slavery was banned from the western region (but slaves already there would remain slaves). The Northwest Ordinance

LAND ORDINANCE OF 1785
A map of the Northwest Territory of the United States as of 1785. The land was divided into a series of townships, which were split up into farms for auction.

Success: Creation of land ordinances

Northwest Ordinance (1787)
Land policy for new western territories in the Ohio Valley that established the terms and conditions for self-government and statehood while also banning slavery from the region.

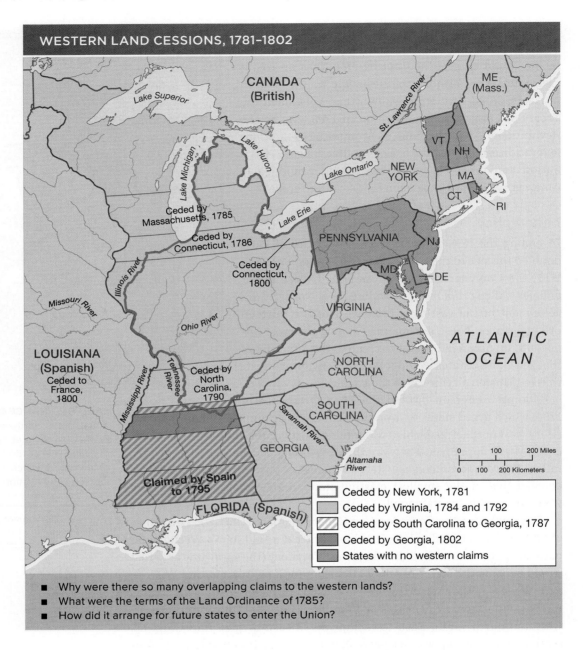

WESTERN LAND CESSIONS, 1781–1802

Ceded by New York, 1781
Ceded by Virginia, 1784 and 1792
Ceded by South Carolina to Georgia, 1787
Ceded by Georgia, 1802
States with no western claims

- Why were there so many overlapping claims to the western lands?
- What were the terms of the Land Ordinance of 1785?
- How did it arrange for future states to enter the Union?

also included a promise (which would be repeatedly broken) that Indian lands "shall never be taken from them without their consent."

The Northwest Ordinance specified that a new territory would become a state through a three-stage process. First, Congress would appoint a territorial governor and other officials to create a legal code, keep the peace, and administer justice. Second, when the territorial population of adult males reached 5,000, a legislature would be elected. Third, when a territory's population reached 60,000 "free inhabitants," it could create a state constitution and apply to Congress for statehood. In 1803, Ohio was the first territory to be granted statehood in this way.

Foreign Tensions

After the Revolutionary War, the Confederation government confronted issues with Great Britain and Spain that it was powerless to resolve. Both European nations kept trading posts and forts on American soil, in violation of the Treaty of Paris (1783). Another major irritant in U.S.-British relations was the seizure of Loyalist property (homes, farms, plantations, slaves, businesses, etc.) by Patriots during and after the war. The British government demanded that the United States pay the Loyalists for their losses.

With Spain, the chief issues were the disputed southern boundary of the United States along the Gulf of Mexico and the right of Americans to send boats or barges filled with their crops and products down the Mississippi River to the valuable Spanish-controlled port of New Orleans. In 1784, the Spanish governor in New Orleans closed the lower Mississippi River to Americans, thus cutting off settlers in Tennessee and Kentucky from world commerce.

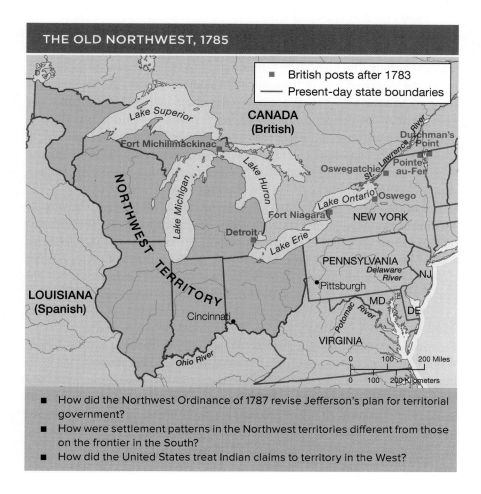

THE OLD NORTHWEST, 1785

■ British posts after 1783
— Present-day state boundaries

Lake Superior
CANADA (British)
Fort Michilimackinac
Dutchman's Point
Oswegatchie
Pointe au-Fer
Lake Huron
St. Lawrence River
Lake Michigan
Lake Ontario
Oswego
Fort Niagara
NEW YORK
Detroit
Lake Erie
NORTHWEST TERRITORY
PENNSYLVANIA
Delaware River
NJ
Pittsburgh
MD
DE
LOUISIANA (Spanish)
Cincinnati
Potomac River
VIRGINIA
Ohio River

0   100   200 Miles
0   100   200 Kilometers

■ How did the Northwest Ordinance of 1787 revise Jefferson's plan for territorial government?
■ How were settlement patterns in the Northwest territories different from those on the frontier in the South?
■ How did the United States treat Indian claims to territory in the West?

DOMESTIC INDUSTRY American craftsmen, such as these letterpress printers, favored tariffs on foreign goods that competed with their own products.

Trade and the Economy

Failure: Regulation of interstate commerce and foreign relations

The Confederation government also struggled to manage complex economic issues. Seven years of warfare against Great Britain had nearly bankrupted the new nation. The plantation economies of the southern states were hard hit by the escape of tens of thousands of enslaved workers during and after the war. And the national economy was devastated by the loss of its trading network with the British Empire, which before the Revolution was the primary source of American prosperity. The British decision after the war to close its Caribbean island colonies such as Bermuda, Jamaica, and Barbados to American trade eliminated what had been a thriving market for timber, wheat, and farm products.

In an effort to force the British government to end its restrictions on American commerce, some state governments imposed tariffs (taxes on imports) on British goods. The British responded by sending their goods to states whose tariffs were lower. As a result, states ended up competing against each other for foreign trade. By 1787, a clear need had emerged for the national government to regulate interstate trade and foreign relations.

Scarce Money

Failure: No national currency

Financial issues further threatened the stability of the new nation. There was no national currency and only a handful of banks. Farmers who had profited during the war now found themselves squeezed by lower crop prices and mounting debts and taxes. Creditors (people who loaned money to others) demanded that debtors (mostly farmers) pay back their loans or mortgages in gold or silver coins, which were always in short supply.

By 1785, demands that states print new paper currency to supplement scarce coins became the single most divisive issue in politics. Farmers saw adding paper currency as a simple way to raise prices for their crops and livestock and thereby help them pay their debts and taxes. In 1785–1786, seven states began issuing their own paper money to help farmers and to pay the cash bonuses promised to war veterans. The Rhode Island legislature issued so much paper money that creditors fled the state to avoid being paid in paper currency of such unstable value.

Shays's Rebellion (1786–1787)

In neighboring Massachusetts, however, the legislature took a different stance. Hard-pressed farmers in the western part of the state, many of them military veterans who had not received their promised pay during the war, urged the state to issue new paper money and demanded more time to pay the taxes owed on their lands. When the Massachusetts legislature ignored such demands, three rural counties erupted in revolt.

Led by thirty-nine-year-old Daniel Shays, who had served as a captain in the Revolutionary War, armed groups of angry farmers forced judges to stop farm foreclosures. Shays urged them on, yelling, "Close down the courts!" The state government responded by sending 4,400 militiamen armed with cannons to end the rebellion. They scattered Shays's debtor army with a single volley that left four farmers dead. The farmers ran for the hills; Shays fled to Vermont. The rebels nevertheless won a victory of sorts, as the state legislature decided to eliminate some of the taxes and fees on farmers.

The most important consequence of **Shays's Rebellion** was to spread panic among wealthy Americans. In Massachusetts, Abigail Adams dismissed Shays and his followers as "ignorant, restless desperadoes, without conscience or principles." In Virginia, George Washington was equally disturbed. "Good God!" he exclaimed. America needed a "government by which our lives, liberty, and properties will be secured." The rebellion in Massachusetts, he feared, might tempt other angry debtor groups around the country to violate the law and disturb the peace.

SHAYS'S REBELLION In this engraving, a line of militiamen fire at Shays and his followers while the surviving rebels turn and flee. Shays demanded a more flexible monetary policy and the right to postpone paying taxes until the postwar agricultural depression lifted. **Why, given the rebels' defeat in combat, might the state legislature have decided to grant some of their demands?**

Shays's Rebellion (1786–1787) Storming of the Massachusetts federal arsenal in 1787 by Daniel Shays and 1,200 armed farmers seeking debt relief from the state legislature through issuance of paper currency and lower taxes.

CORE **OBJECTIVE**

2. Describe the political innovations that the 1787 Constitutional Convention developed for the new nation.

Creating the Constitution

In the wake of Shays's Rebellion, many public officials agreed with Virginian James Madison that the "crisis is arrived"—it was time to empower the national government to bring order and stability to the new nation.

The Constitutional Convention (1787)

In 1787, the Confederation Congress called for a special convention to gather in Philadelphia's Old State House (now Independence Hall) for the "purpose of revising the Articles of Confederation." Twelve of the thirteen states eventually participated; tiny Rhode Island refused. Twenty-nine delegates began meeting on May 25, 1787 (altogether, fifty-five men served as delegates at one time or another). After four months of deliberations carried out in stifling heat behind closed windows and locked doors, thirty-nine delegates signed the new federal constitution on September 17, 1787. Only three refused to sign what has become the longest-functioning written constitution in the world.

The durability of the ideas and institutions contained in the Constitution reflects the abilities of the men who made it. The convention delegates were surprisingly young; their average age was forty-two, and the youngest was twenty-six. Most of the framers of the Constitution, later dubbed the "Founding Fathers," were members of the nation's political and economic

SIGNING THE CONSTITUTION Thomas Pritchard Rossiter's painting shows George Washington presiding over what Thomas Jefferson called "an assembly of demi-gods" in Philadelphia on September 17, 1787.

elite (Thomas Jefferson and John Adams did not participate because they were serving as diplomats in Europe). Twenty-six delegates were college graduates; two were college presidents. Thirty-four were lawyers. Nearly all were considered "gentlemen" or "natural aristocrats." Yet they were also practical men of experience, tested in the fires of the Revolutionary War. Twenty-two had served in the war (five were captured and imprisoned by the British), seven had been state governors, and eight had helped write their state constitutions. Most had been members of the Continental Congress, and eight had signed the Declaration of Independence. In the summer of 1787, they gathered in Philadelphia "to form a more perfect union," as the preamble to the new Constitution asserted.

Drafting the Constitution George Washington served as presiding officer of the Constitutional Convention but participated little in the debates. Most active in the debates was James Madison. He was the ablest political theorist in the group and the central figure at the convention. The thirty-six-year-old Madison, a Virginia attorney, had arrived in Philadelphia with trunks full of books about political theory and a head full of ideas about how to strengthen the Confederation. Barely five feet tall and weighing only 130 pounds (a colleague said he was "no bigger than half a piece of soap"), Madison had an agile mind, a huge appetite for learning, and a lifelong commitment to public service. He was determined to create a new constitution that would ensure the "supremacy of national authority." The logic of his arguments—and his willingness to support repeated compromises—proved decisive in shaping the new constitution. "Every person seems to acknowledge his greatness," one delegate said of Madison.

JAMES MADISON This 1783 miniature shows Madison at thirty-two years old, just four years before he would assume a major role in drafting the Constitution.

Most delegates agreed with Madison that their young nation needed a stronger national government and less powerful state governments. A New Hampshire delegate explained that he "saw no more reason to be afraid of the central [national] government than of the state governments."

Two basic and interrelated assumptions guided the Constitutional Convention: (1) that the national government must have direct authority over the citizenry rather than governing the people only through the state governments and (2) that the national government must derive its "sovereignty" (powers) directly from the people rather than from the state governments. The insistence on the authority of "the people" was the most important political innovation since the Declaration of Independence, for by declaring the Constitution to be the voice of "the people," the founders authorized the federal government to limit the powers of the individual states.

> Innovation: All authority derived from "the people"

Experience with the Articles of Confederation had persuaded the delegates that an effective national government needed new authority to collect taxes, borrow and issue money, regulate interstate commerce and international relations, fund an army and navy, and make laws binding upon individual citizens. Experience also suggested to them that the states must be stripped of certain powers: to print paper money, make treaties with other

> Innovation: Federalism

nations, wage war, and levy taxes on imported goods. This concept of dividing governmental authority between the national government and the states came to be called **federalism**, another major contribution of the new American republic to the rest of the world.

The Virginia and New Jersey Plans James Madison drafted the framework for the initial discussions at the Constitutional Convention. His proposals, called the Virginia Plan, started with a revolutionary suggestion: that the delegates scrap their original instructions to *revise* the Articles of Confederation and instead create an entirely *new* federal constitution.

Madison's Virginia Plan called for a new Congress divided into two houses: a lower House of Representatives and an upper house, to be called the Senate. States with larger populations, such as Virginia and Pennsylvania, would have more representatives in Congress than the smaller states.

Critics of the Virginia Plan submitted an alternative written by William Paterson of New Jersey. The New Jersey Plan sought to keep the existing structure of equal representation of the states in a unicameral (one-house) Congress but gave Congress the power to levy taxes and regulate commerce and the authority to name a chief executive as well as a supreme court.

Innovation: The Great Compromise

After intense debate over the two plans, the dispute was resolved by the Great Compromise (sometimes called the Connecticut Compromise), which used elements of both plans in creating a new legislative structure for the national government. The more populous states won apportionment (the number of delegates representing each state) by population in the proposed House of Representatives, while the delegates who sought to protect states' power won equality of representation in the Senate, where each state would have two members.

The Structure of the Federal Government

Innovation: Separation of powers

The delegates at the 1787 Constitutional Convention were preoccupied with *power*: who should have it and how it would be used. The new constitution created a "federal" structure in which each citizen is governed by both a state government and the national government. To prevent power from being abused, each branch of the new national government—executive, legislative, and judicial—was given a separate sphere of authority as well as the responsibility to counterbalance the other branches, a principle known as the **separation of powers**, to keep any one of the three branches of the government from growing too powerful.

federalism Concept of dividing governmental authority between the national government and the states.

separation of powers Strict division of the powers of government among three separate branches (executive, legislative, and judicial), which in turn check and balance each other.

Legislature (Congress) As a result of the Great Compromise, the delegates at the Constitutional Convention embedded the concept of a separation of powers in the new Congress, for it would have two "houses," each intended to counterbalance the other, with one (the House of Representatives) representing the voters at large and the other, the Senate, representing the state legislatures.

The "lower house" of Congress, the House of Representatives, was designed to be closer to the voters, who elected its members every two years. Under the Articles of Confederation, voters had not elected the members of Congress; instead, they had been chosen by state legislatures. James Madison argued that allowing individual citizens to elect at least one house of the new legislature was "essential to every plan of free government."

The "upper house," or Senate, would be a more elite group, elected for six-year terms, not by voters directly but by state legislatures. The Senate was to be a conservative force, using its power, when necessary, to overrule either the House of Representatives or the president. The more prestigious Senate, explained Madison, would help "protect the minority of the opulent against the majority."

Executive (President) The delegates at the Constitutional Convention struggled mightily over the design of a new executive branch of government. Most of them expected the Congress to be the dominant branch. By contrast, Alexander Hamilton, a delegate from New York who was a celebrated attorney and the former chief of staff for General George Washington during the Revolution, wanted the president to serve for life, but the delegates eventually decided that the president should stand for election every four years.

The president could veto acts of Congress, subject to being overridden by a two-thirds vote in each house. The president became the nation's chief diplomat as well as the commander in chief of the armed forces and was responsible for the execution of the laws.

But the powers of the new president were also to be limited in key areas. The chief executive could neither declare war nor make peace; only Congress could exercise those powers. Unlike the British monarch, moreover, the president could be sacked. The House of Representatives could impeach (put on trial) the chief executive and other civil officers on charges of treason, bribery, or "other high crimes and misdemeanors." An impeached president could be removed from office if two-thirds of the Senate voted for conviction.

To preserve the separation of the three branches, the president would be elected not by the Congress but by "electors" chosen by "the people" in local elections. The number of "electors" in each state would vary depending upon the combined number of congressional representatives and U.S. senators. This "Electoral College" was a compromise between those wanting the president elected by a vote in Congress and those preferring election by a popular vote of qualified citizens.

Judiciary (Court System) The third proposed branch of government, the judiciary, sparked surprisingly little debate. The Constitution called for a national supreme court headed by a chief justice. The role of the national judiciary was not to make laws (which was reserved to Congress) or execute or enforce the laws (which was reserved to the presidency) but to interpret the law as applied to specific cases and to ensure that every citizen received equal justice under the law. The U.S. Supreme Court had final authority in interpreting the U.S. Constitution as well as in adjudicating disputes arising from the various state constitutions. Furthermore, Article VI of the Constitution declared that the federal Constitution, federal laws, and treaties are "the supreme Law of the Land." That is, when federal laws and state laws conflicted, the federal law would triumph.

"We the People"

The men who drafted the new constitution claimed to be representing all the American people. The Constitution begins with the words "We the people." In fact, however, there were important groups of Americans left out of the Constitution's protections. Native Americans, for example, could not be citizens unless they paid taxes, which very few did. The Constitution declared that Native American "tribes" were not part of the United States but instead were separate "nations." Only the U.S. Congress, not the states or individuals, could negotiate treaties with the Indian nations. Not until 1924 would Native Americans qualify for American citizenship.

Dealing with Slavery Of all the issues that emerged during the Constitutional Convention, none was more explosive than the question of slavery. Many of the framers viewed slavery as an embarrassing contradiction to the principles of liberty and equality expressed in the Declaration of Independence and the new Constitution. A New Jersey delegate declared that slavery was "utterly inconsistent with the principles of Christianity and humanity."

By contrast, delegates from the southern states strenuously defended slavery. During the eighteenth century, the agricultural economies of Maryland, Virginia, the Carolinas, and Georgia had become dependent upon huge numbers of enslaved laborers, and delegates from those states were determined to protect the future of slavery. Caught in the middle were Virginia slaveholders like George Washington, Thomas Jefferson, and James Madison, who hated slavery but saw no way to eliminate it without civil war.

Madison told the Convention that the "distinction of color" had created "the most oppressive dominion ever exercised by man over man." Because the southern delegates would have walked out of the convention, the framers did not even consider abolishing slavery, nor did some of them view slaves as human beings with civil rights. Such moral blindness to basic human dignities reflected the prevailing attitudes among most whites at the time.

CHARLES CALVERT AND HIS SLAVE **(1761)** In military regalia, the five-year-old descendant of Lord Baltimore towers over his slave, dressed as a drummer boy.

But if the slaves were not to be freed or their rights to be acknowledged, how were they to be counted? Since the size of state delegations in the proposed House of Representatives would be based on population, southern delegates argued that slaves should be counted along with whites. Northerners said it made no sense to count slaves for purposes of political representation when slaves were not treated as people but as property.

The delegates finally agreed to a compromise proposed by James Wilson of Pennsylvania, whereby three-fifths of "all other persons" (that is, the enslaved) would be included in a state's population count as a basis for apportioning a state's congressional delegation.

By design, the original Constitution never mentions the word *slavery*. Instead it speaks of "free persons" and "all other persons" and of persons "held to service of labor." Under the 1787 Constitution, the national government had no authority to deal with slavery in the states. The success of southern delegates in getting slaves counted for purposes of calculating a state's representation in the House of Representatives and the Electoral College would give the southern states disproportionate power in the Congress by increasing the number of southern votes in the House of Representatives. This in turn increased southern influence in the Electoral College, since the number of each state's electors was to be the total of its senators and representatives. It was thus no accident that in the nation's first sixteen presidential elections, between 1788 and 1848, all but four chose a southern slaveholder.

> Limitation: Failure to deal with slavery

The Absence of Women in the Constitution While the delegates refused to liberate slaves, they similarly considered irrelevant any discussion of political rights for women. Yet not all women were willing to maintain their traditional subordinate role. During and after the Revolutionary War, there were many declarations of independence, many forms of resistance to old ways of doing things, indeed many personal "revolutions"—some successful, some not. Just as the Revolutionary War enabled many African Americans to seize their freedom, it led some brave women to demand political equality for themselves.

Eliza Yonge Wilkinson, born in 1757 to a wealthy plantation family living near Charleston, South Carolina, lost her husband early in the war. In June 1780, after Wilkinson was assaulted and robbed by "inhuman" British soldiers during their forty-day siege of Charleston, she became a fiery Patriot who "hated Tyranny in every shape." Wilkinson's "saucy" personality led her to be openly critical of the British during their eighteen-month occupation of the city. She assured a friend, "We may be *led*, but we never will be *driven*!" And she showed great courage and resilience in helping American prisoners of war while managing her family's plantations during the war.

> Limitation: No political rights for women

Such unconventional experiences led Wilkinson to expect greater freedom for women after the war. "The men say we have no business [with politics]," she wrote to a friend. "It is not our sphere! I won't have it thought that

anti-Federalists Opponents of the Constitution as an infringement on individual and states' rights, whose criticism led to the addition of a Bill of Rights to the document. Many anti-Federalists later joined Thomas Jefferson's Democratic-Republican party.

The Federalist Papers Collection of eighty-five essays, published widely in newspapers in 1787 and 1788, written by Alexander Hamilton, James Madison, and John Jay in support of adopting the proposed U.S. Constitution.

because we are the weaker sex as to bodily strength, my dear, we are capable of nothing more than minding the dairy, visiting the poultry-house, and all such domestic concerns." Wilkinson demanded more. "They won't even allow us the liberty of thought, and that is all I want."

With more and more women like Wilkinson calling themselves "perfect statesmen" and "great Politician[s]," Judith Sargent Murray, an essayist, playwright, and poet in Gloucester, Massachusetts, predicted the dawn of "a new era of female history" after the Revolution. She argued that the rights and liberties fought for by Patriots belonged not just to men but to women, too. In her essay "On the Equality of the Sexes," written in 1779 but not published until 1790, she, like Eliza Wilkinson, challenged the prevailing view that men had greater intellectual capacities than women. She insisted instead that whatever differences existed between the knowledge displayed by men and women resulted from prejudice and discrimination that prevented women from having access to formal education and worldly experience.

Like many other of the most radical voices of the Revolutionary era, Murray's support for gender equality was met largely by shock and disapproval among both men and women. At the Constitutional Convention in Philadelphia, there was never any formal discussion of women's rights, nor does the Constitution even include the word *women*. The Founding Fathers still defined politics and government as realms for men only. Writing from Paris, Thomas Jefferson expressed the hope that American "ladies" would be "contented to soothe and calm the minds of their husbands returning ruffled from political debate" rather than getting involved themselves. Neither Jefferson nor most Americans, he added, were "prepared" to support women holding elected office.

The Fight for Ratification

CORE **OBJECTIVE**
3. Summarize the major debates surrounding the ratification of the Constitution and explain how they were resolved.

The final draft of the Constitution was submitted to the states for approval (ratification) on September 28, 1787. For the first time in world history, the diverse peoples making up a large nation were able to discuss, debate, and decide by a peaceful vote how they would be governed. In the fierce ten-month-long debate, those supporting the new Constitution were called Federalists; their opponents became **anti-Federalists**. The two factions formed the seeds for America's enduring two-party political system.

A Fiery Debate

States' rights vs. expanding federal authority

Among the supreme legacies of the dramatic debate over the Constitution is *The Federalist Papers*, a collection of eighty-five essays published in 1787 and 1788. Written in support of the new Constitution by James Madison of Virginia and Alexander Hamilton and John Jay of New York, the essays defended the principle of a strong national government. In perhaps the most famous Federalist essay, No. 10, James Madison argued that the size and diversity of the expanding nation would make it impossible for any single faction to form a dangerous majority that could dominate the federal government. This contradicted the conventional wisdom of the time, which insisted that republics could survive only in small nations like Switzerland. Large republics, it was thought, would self-destruct as a result of warring factions. Not so, Madison insisted. Given a balanced federal government, a large republic could work better than a small one. "Extend the [geographic] sphere," he wrote, "and you take in a greater variety of parties and interests; you make it less probable that a majority of the whole will have a common motive to invade the rights of other citizens."

Anti-Federalists versus Federalists The anti-Federalists opposed the new Constitution by highlighting the dangers of placing more power in the hands of the central government. They predicted that the federal government would eventually grow corrupt and tyrannical. Mercy Otis Warren of Massachusetts, the most prominent woman in the new nation to write regular political commentary, warned that the proposed constitution would put "shackles on our own necks." She and other anti-Federalists emphasized the absence of a bill of rights to protect individuals and states from the growing power of the national government.

The Federalists, also called nationalists, had several advantages in the debate over the Constitution. First, they had a concrete proposal; their opponents had nothing to offer instead of the Constitution but criticism. Second, many of the Federalist leaders had been members of the Constitutional

FEDERALISTS VERSUS ANTI-FEDERALISTS This satirical engraving by Amos Doolittle portrays the conflicts that arose over the ratification of the Constitution. In the center, stuck in the mud, is a wagon that represents Connecticut, laden with debt. On either side, the Federalists (right) and anti-Federalists (left) engage in a tug-of-war, pulling Connecticut in opposite directions. The three merchant ships at the bottom are carrying goods from Connecticut to New York, and the phrase below criticizes the tariffs that states imposed on such interstate imports. **Who does Doolittle appear to agree with, the Federalists or the anti-Federalists?**

Convention who were familiar with the disputed issues in the document. Third, the Federalists were more unified, better organized, and better able to manage the national debate. By contrast, the anti-Federalist leaders—Virginians Patrick Henry, George Mason, Richard Henry Lee, and future president James Monroe; George Clinton of New York; Samuel Adams, Elbridge Gerry, and Mercy Otis Warren of Massachusetts; and Luther Martin and Samuel Chase of Maryland—were mostly older figures who never forged an effective opposition group. Regardless of the voices on each side, the tension between preserving states' rights and expanding federal authority at the center of the debate over ratification would not end in 1787; it became a defining dispute in American politics thereafter.

The States Decide The heated debate over ratification of the Constitution at times boiled over into violence. Riots erupted in several cities. Newspapers took sides, leading one New Englander to remark that the papers were being "read more than the Bible." Amid the intense feelings, ratification of the new Constitution gained momentum at the end of 1787. The state legislatures in Delaware, New Jersey, and Georgia voted unanimously in favor of ratification. Massachusetts, still sharply divided in the aftermath of Shays's Rebellion, was the first state legislature in which the outcome was close, approving the Constitution by a vote of 187 to 168.

On June 21, 1788, New Hampshire became the ninth state to ratify the Constitution, thereby meeting the minimum number of states needed for approval. But the new Constitution and the government it created could hardly succeed without the approval of Virginia, the largest, wealthiest, and most populous state, or New York, which had the third-highest population and occupied a key position geographically. Both states included strong opposition groups who were eventually won over by the same pledge as had been made in Massachusetts—the promise of adding a bill of rights to the Constitution to specify protections of individual rights.

Upon notification that New Hampshire had become the ninth state to ratify the Constitution, the Confederation Congress selected New York City as the temporary national capital and fixed the date for the first national elections in 1788–1789.

The Bill of Rights

The Constitution was adopted at last, but because of the spirited resistance it faced, in May 1789 James Madison proposed to the new Congress a cluster of constitutional amendments designed to protect individual rights. As Thomas Jefferson explained, a "bill of rights is what the people are entitled to against every government on earth, general or particular, and what no just government should refuse."

RATIFICATION OF THE CONSTITUTION

Order of Ratification	State	Date of Ratification
1	Delaware	December 7, 1787
2	Pennsylvania	December 12, 1787
3	New Jersey	December 18, 1787
4	Georgia	January 2, 1788
5	Connecticut	January 9, 1788
6	Massachusetts	February 6, 1788
7	Maryland	April 28, 1788
8	South Carolina	May 23, 1788
9	New Hampshire	June 21, 1788
10	Virginia	June 25, 1788
11	New York	July 26, 1788
12	North Carolina	November 21, 1789
13	Rhode Island	May 29, 1790

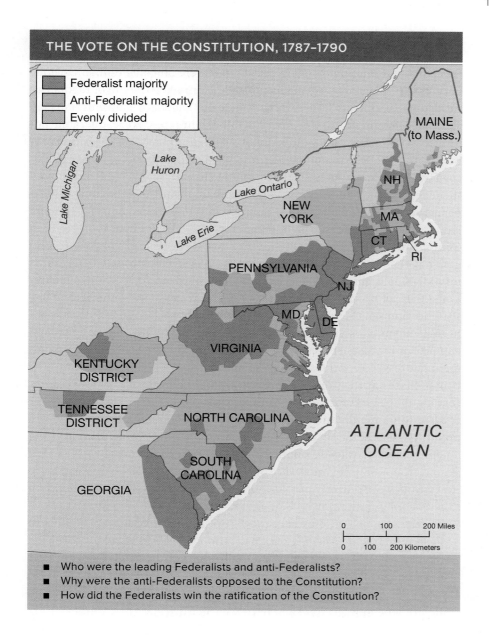

THE VOTE ON THE CONSTITUTION, 1787–1790

Federalist majority
Anti-Federalist majority
Evenly divided

MAINE (to Mass.)

Lake Michigan

Lake Huron

Lake Ontario

NEW YORK

NH

MA

Lake Erie

CT

RI

PENNSYLVANIA

NJ

MD

DE

VIRGINIA

KENTUCKY DISTRICT

TENNESSEE DISTRICT

NORTH CAROLINA

ATLANTIC OCEAN

SOUTH CAROLINA

GEORGIA

0   100   200 Miles
0   100   200 Kilometers

- Who were the leading Federalists and anti-Federalists?
- Why were the anti-Federalists opposed to the Constitution?
- How did the Federalists win the ratification of the Constitution?

After considerable discussion and debate, Congress approved twelve amendments in September 1789. By the end of 1791, the necessary three fourths of the states had approved *ten* of the twelve proposed amendments, now known as the **Bill of Rights**.

The First Amendment declared that "Congress shall make no law respecting an establishment of religion or prohibiting the free exercise thereof." This statement has since become one of the most controversial principles of American government. The men who drafted and amended the Constitution made no direct mention of God, for they were determined to protect freedom of religion from government interference and coercion.

> Protecting individual rights vs. the power of the state

Bill of Rights (1791) First ten amendments to the U.S. Constitution, adopted in 1791 to guarantee individual rights and to help secure ratification of the Constitution by the states.

In the late eighteenth century, the United States was virtually alone among nations in not declaring a single "established" religion funded by the government. France and Spain, for example, were officially Roman Catholic nations; Great Britain was Anglican. In addition, when the Bill of Rights was ratified, most states still used tax revenues to support a single established religion. Dissenters, the members of other churches, were tolerated but forced to pay taxes for the state-supported religion, and they were often prohibited from voting or holding political office.

The First Amendment changed that at the national level. It prohibited the federal government from endorsing or supporting any religion or interfering with the religious choices that people make. As Thomas Jefferson later explained, the First Amendment erected a "wall of separation between Church and State."

The other original amendments to the Constitution provided safeguards for individual rights of speech, assembly, and the press; the right to own firearms; the right to refuse to house soldiers; protection from unreasonable searches and seizures; the right to refuse to testify against oneself; the right to a speedy public trial, with an attorney present, before an impartial jury; and protection against "cruel and unusual" punishment. The Tenth Amendment addressed the widespread demand that "powers not delegated to the United States by the Constitution, nor prohibited by it to the States, are reserved to the States respectively, or to the people."

The ten amendments constituting the Bill of Rights were written in broad language that seemed to exclude no one, but in fact, the first ten amendments technically applied only to property-owning white males. Whole groups of Americans were officially left out of its protections. Native Americans were entirely outside the constitutional system, defined as an "alien people" in their own land.

Like the Constitution itself, the Bill of Rights gave no protections to enslaved Americans. Instead of constitutional rights, they were governed by state "slave codes" that regulated virtually every aspect of their lives. They had no access to the legal system: they could not go to court, make contracts, or own property. Similar restrictions applied to women, who could not vote in most state and national elections.

A Flexible Framework

"Our constitution is in actual operation," Benjamin Franklin wrote to a friend in 1789; "everything appears to promise that it will last; but in this world nothing is certain but death and taxes." George Washington was even more uncertain about the nation's future under the new plan of government. He predicted that the Constitution would not "last for more than twenty years."

The Constitution has lasted much longer, of course, and in the process it has provided a model of resilient republican government whose features have been repeatedly borrowed by other nations. The Constitution, in other words, was not *completed* in 1787 but instead it has remained a living experiment, just as the United States is a living experiment in republicanism. It was, however, flawed from the beginning, just as the nation was flawed, for by evading the issue of slavery, the framers of the Constitution unwittingly allowed growing tensions over the expansion of slavery to reach the point in 1861 where there could be no political solution—only civil war.

The Federalist Era

CORE **OBJECTIVE**

4. Compare the Federalists' vision for the United States with that of their Republican opponents during the 1790s.

It was one thing to ratify a new U.S. Constitution and quite another to make the new federal government run smoothly. During the 1790s, the debates between Federalists and anti-Federalists gave birth to the nation's first political parties: Federalists and Republicans (also called the Democratic Republicans or **Jeffersonian Republicans**). The two political parties came to represent two very different visions of America's future development. In 1790, the United States was predominantly a rural society; 80 percent of households were involved in agricultural production. The Republicans were mostly southerners like Thomas Jefferson and James Madison who wanted America to remain a nation of small farmers and few large cities.

The Federalists sharply disagreed. Led by Alexander Hamilton, they embraced urban and commercial growth. Hamilton became the champion of northern efforts to promote trade, banking, finance, and manufacturing as the most essential elements of America's future economy.

The Constitution provided a framework for nationhood but not a blueprint; it left unanswered many questions about the actual structure and conduct of the new government. As James Madison acknowledged, "We are in a wilderness without a single footstep to guide us."

On the whole, the Jeffersonian Republicans promoted a strict interpretation of the Constitution, while Federalists believed that the language of the Constitution should be interpreted broadly to enable the new federal government to take decisive action when necessary. One of George Washington's greatest challenges as the nation's first president was to bridge the growing divides between Federalists and Republicans, northerners and southerners, merchants and planters.

A New Government

On March 4, 1789, the new Congress convened its first meeting in New York City. In April, the presiding officer of the Senate certified that George Washington had been named the first president by the Electoral College; John Adams became vice president.

Washington was a reluctant first president, but he agreed to serve because he had been "summoned by [his] country." A self-made man who had lost his father at age eleven and had little formal education, he had never visited Europe. Vice President John Adams groused that Washington was "too illiterate, unlearned, unread for his station and reputation."

Jeffersonian Republicans Political party founded by Thomas Jefferson in opposition to the Federalist party led by Alexander Hamilton and John Adams; also known as the Democratic-Republican party.

WASHINGTON'S INAUGURATION An aggrandizing portrayal of Washington as he arrived at the Battery in New York, for his 1789 inauguration. **Note the presence of the Native Americans in the lower right and the foreign flags in the distance—in what ways does this painting exaggerate Washington's support and in what ways is it an accurate representation of the sentiment at the time?**

George Washington, however, had virtues that John Adams lacked. As a French diplomat commented after watching the inaugural ceremony, Washington "has the soul, look, and figure of a hero in action." He was a military hero who had married a wealthy young widow and become a prosperous planter. Washington brought to his new office a capacity for leadership that helped keep the young republic from disintegrating. Although capable of angry outbursts, Washington was remarkably self-disciplined; he possessed extraordinary stamina and patience, integrity and resolve, courage and resilience. Few doubted that he was the best person to lead the new nation.

Shaping a Federal Union

America's first president took charge of a tiny national government that faced massive challenges. (George Washington had a larger staff at his plantation in northern Virginia than he did as president.) During the summer of 1789, Congress created executive departments corresponding to those formed under the Confederation. To lead the Department of State, Washington named Thomas Jefferson, recently back from his diplomatic duties in France. To head the Department of the Treasury, Washington picked his brilliant thirty-four-year-old wartime aide, Alexander Hamilton, now a celebrated New York lawyer.

The Rise of American Capitalism

In 1776, the same year that Americans were declaring their independence from the British monarchy, Adam Smith, a Scottish philosopher, published a pathbreaking book titled *An Inquiry into the Nature and Causes of the Wealth of Nations*. It provided the first full description of a modern *capitalist* economy and its social benefits.

Like the American Revolution, *The Wealth of Nations* was a declaration of independence from Great Britain's mercantilist system. Under mercantilism, national governments had exercised tight controls over economic life in the contest for world power. In *The Wealth of Nations*, Smith argued for just the opposite. Instead of controlling economic activity, governments should allow energetic individuals and efficient businesses to compete freely for profits in the marketplace. Doing so, he promised, would provide the best path to individual success and national prosperity. The grinding poverty that had entrapped the masses of Europe for centuries would end to the extent that governments allowed for "free enterprise," by which individuals through their hard work and ingenuity could at last gain earthly happiness and prosperity.

ALEXANDER HAMILTON
A fervent Federalist and prolific contributor to *The Federalist Papers*, Hamilton served as George Washington's secretary of the Treasury from 1789 to 1795. Faced with the daunting challenge of repaying the national debt, Hamilton promoted an economic system that established federal taxes and a national bank.

Smith also explained that modern capitalism involved diverse national economies in which *all* the major sectors were flourishing—agriculture, trade, banking, finance, and manufacturing—because the dynamic engine of capitalism—competition—was allowed to work its magic. Under capitalism, Smith argued, ordinary people were increasingly given the freedom to unleash their entrepreneurial energies without government interference. By allowing investors to funnel cash into productive enterprises, jobs would be created, profits would soar, and national economic growth would occur naturally rather than through government manipulation.

Alexander Hamilton greatly admired *The Wealth of Nations* and embraced the idea of a diverse capitalist economy in which the engine of competition drove prosperity. America's first secretary of the Treasury was determined to use the energies of capitalism to transform a weak cluster of states into a global economic power comparable to Great Britain. He also recognized, however, that the fragile American republic's capitalist economy required *temporary* government assistance to enable it to compete with the much more advanced economies of Europe. In addition, the federal treasury was virtually empty. Something had to be done quickly to generate enough cash for the new federal government to operate. To that end, Hamilton submitted to Congress a series of brilliant reports between January 1790 and December 1791. **Alexander Hamilton's economic reforms** outlined his bold vision for the new nation's economic development.

Alexander Hamilton's economic reforms Various measures designed to strengthen the nation's capitalist economy and generate federal revenue through the promotion of new industries, the adoption of new tax policies, the payment of war debts, and the establishment of a national bank.

Paying Debts

The United States was born in debt. And it fell to Alexander Hamilton to figure out how the debts should be repaid. In the first of two "Reports on Public Credit" sent to Congress, Hamilton outlined how the new federal government should absorb the massive debt incurred during the War of Independence. Some argued that the debts should not be repaid. Hamilton countered that not paying war debts was unjust and dishonorable. Only by paying its debts in full could the new nation gain credibility among the leading nations of the world. He also explained that the state debts from the Revolution were a *national* responsibility because all Americans had benefited from the war for independence. A federal debt that absorbed the state debts, he claimed, would be a "national blessing," provide a "mechanism for national unity," and promote long-term prosperity.

James Madison led the opposition to Hamilton's "debt-funding" plan in Congress. Madison did not question whether the war-related debt should be paid; he was troubled, however, that far more debt was owed to northerners than to southerners.

The dispute over the debt issue ended in the summer of 1790 with a secret deal. In return for northern votes in favor of locating the permanent national capital on the Potomac River between Maryland and Virginia, Madison pledged to seek enough southern votes in Congress to pass Hamilton's debt-assumption plan.

The Compromise of 1790 worked as planned. The national capital would be moved from New York City to Philadelphia for ten years, after which it would be settled at a new federal city (soon to be called Washington) to be built on the Potomac River in the new federal District of Columbia.

Once implemented, Hamilton's debt-financing plan was an immediate success. By making the United States financially solvent, he set in motion the greatest economic success story in history.

Raising Federal Revenue

Governments have three basic ways to raise money to pay their bills: (1) they can impose taxes or fees on individuals, businesses, and specific products; (2) they can borrow money by selling interest-paying government bonds to investors; and (3) they can print currency. To raise urgently needed funds, Congress in 1789, at the urging of Washington and Hamilton, imposed a 5 percent tariff on a wide variety of imported items.

Hamilton's revenue plan: The first federal taxes

The creation of federal tariffs marked but the beginning of Hamilton's ambitious effort to put the new capitalist republic on sound financial footing. His next effort, in 1791, was to convince Congress to impose federal "excise" taxes on specific items: carriages, sugar, salt, and alcoholic beverages.

The new tax on whiskey outraged many frontier farmers because it taxed their most profitable commodity. During the eighteenth and early nineteenth centuries, nearly all Americans drank alcoholic beverages: beer, hard cider, ale, wine, rum, brandy, or whiskey. In the areas west of the Appalachian Mountains, the primary cash commodity was liquor distilled from grains (mostly corn and rye) or fruit (peaches and apples). It was far easier for western farmers to convert their crops to liquor and then take it across the mountains or down the Mississippi River than it was to transport the bulky grains or fruits. Unlike grain and fruit crops, distilled spirits could be easily stored, shipped, or sold—and at higher profits. A bushel of corn worth 25¢ could yield two and a half gallons of liquor, worth ten times as much.

A National Bank

After securing congressional approval for federal tariffs and excise taxes, Hamilton called for the establishment of a national bank modeled after the powerful Bank of England. Once again, Madison and Jefferson led the opposition, arguing that the Constitution said nothing about a national bank and therefore the government could not create one. Hamilton and his supporters countered that creating a bank was an "implied power" within the Constitution.

> Hamilton's national bank

Congress ended up agreeing with Hamilton, with virtually all northern congressmen voting for the new bank while most southerners opposed it. Still, the fundamental debate between Jefferson and Hamilton over how to interpret the Constitution has continued to this day: should government officials be allowed to stretch the original language of the Constitution to adjust to new realities?

Hamilton's proposed **Bank of the United States** (B.U.S.) would have three primary responsibilities: (1) to hold government funds and make transfers of monies to other nations; (2) to provide loans to the federal government and to other banks to promote economic development; and (3) to manage the nation's money supply by regulating the power of state-chartered banks to issue paper currency, or banknotes. The B.U.S. could issue banknotes as needed to address the chronic shortage of gold and silver coins.

THE BANK OF THE UNITED STATES Proposed by Alexander Hamilton, the Bank of the United States opened in 1791 in Philadelphia, the nation's temporary capital.

Encouraging Manufactures

In the "Report on Manufactures," the last of his major proposals to Congress, Hamilton called for the federal government to help launch new industries that would reduce America's dependence on manufactured goods imported from Europe. Industrialization, Hamilton believed, would accomplish several goals: diversify an American economy overly dependent on agriculture; improve productivity through greater use of machinery; encourage immigration to entice skilled workers from abroad; and create more opportunities for economic expansion.

> Hamilton's "Report on Manufactures"

Bank of the United States (1791) National bank responsible for holding and transferring federal government funds, making business loans, and issuing a national currency.

To encourage industrial development, Hamilton recommended that the federal government provide financial incentives to help people start new industries and spur inventors to create new technologies. He claimed that such government support was needed to enable new American companies to compete "on equal terms" with companies in the more advanced economies of Europe. Finally, Hamilton asked Congress to fund an improved transportation system across the young nation, including the development of roads, canals, and rivers for commercial traffic.

Few of Hamilton's proindustry proposals were enacted in the 1790s because of strong opposition among southerners. His ideas were not forgotten, however. They provided an arsenal of arguments for the advocates of manufacturing and transportation improvements in years to come.

Hamilton's Achievement

Largely owing to the skillful Hamilton, the Treasury Department during the early 1790s accumulated a surplus that enabled it to begin paying off the Revolutionary War debts, and foreign capitalists began to invest heavily in the growing American economy. A Boston merchant reported in late 1790 that the United States had never "had a brighter sunshine of prosperity. . . . Our agricultural interest smiles, our commerce is blessed, our manufactures flourish." Yet however beneficial Hamilton's policies were to the nation's long-term economic development, they continued to arouse fierce opposition among Republicans.

The Republican Alternative

By supporting industry and commerce as well as the expansion of federal authority at the expense of the states, Hamilton infuriated a growing number of people, especially in the agricultural South and along the western frontier. Because the southern states had virtually no manufacturing enterprises and much less varied commercial activity than New York and New England, Thomas Jefferson, James Madison, and other Republicans viewed Hamilton's economic policies as discriminating against them. The tax on whiskey, for example, infuriated farmers in western Pennsylvania.

The increasingly bitter disputes between Secretary of the Treasury Hamilton and Secretary of State Jefferson soon fractured President Washington's cabinet. Hamilton was an intense nationalist, but he very much admired the powerful British economy and its political system (a limited monarchy and a parliament governed by a constitution). The British government was, he observed, "the best model the world ever produced," and he wanted Great Britain to remain America's largest trading partner. He also championed a strong central government and a powerful national bank.

THOMAS JEFFERSON Jefferson, Hamilton's chief rival, fought against Hamilton's emphasis on industrial development. Jefferson pushed for an agrarian America instead, inspired in part by his love of French culture.

By contrast, Jefferson was anti-British and pro-French; he loved French culture, cuisine, and wine. Unlike Hamilton, the Virginian hated banks and big cities. His dream for America was to preserve a decentralized agrarian republic made up primarily of small farmers. "Those who labor in the earth," he wrote, "are the chosen people of God, if ever he had a chosen people, whose breasts He has made His peculiar deposit for genuine and substantial virtue." Jefferson feared that Hamilton's campaign for American industries would produce a growing class of landless factory workers dependent upon others for their livelihood and therefore subject to political manipulation and economic exploitation.

> Hamilton and Jefferson's conflicting visions

By mid-1792, Hamilton and Jefferson could no longer hide their hatred for each other. The two strongest members of the cabinet became mortal enemies—as well as the leaders of two emerging parties. Jefferson, twelve years older than Hamilton, told a friend that he and his rival fought daily in the cabinet like "two cocks" [roosters]. President Washington begged his chief officers to put an end to their "wounding suspicions and irritating charges." They did not. In September 1792, Jefferson told President Washington that "I was duped . . . by the Secretary of the Treasury, and made a fool for forwarding his [economic] schemes, not then sufficiently understood by me; and of all the errors of my political life, this has occasioned the deepest regret."

Foreign and Domestic Crises

> CORE **OBJECTIVE**
> **5.** Assess how attitudes toward Great Britain and France shaped American politics in the late eighteenth century.

In 1789, the same year that George Washington became president, frenzied violence erupted in France, as masses of enraged people, inspired in part by the example of the American Revolution, revolted against the monarchy and sent shock waves throughout Europe. By 1792, when Washington was unanimously reelected to serve a second term as president, the **French Revolution** was careening out of control. The radicals executed the king and queen as well as hundreds of aristocrats. On February 1, 1793, the revolutionary government declared war on archenemy Great Britain, along with the Netherlands and Spain. Thereafter, the most violent of the French revolutionaries—called *Jacobins*—used guillotines to execute thousands of political prisoners and Catholic priests.

Secretary of State Thomas Jefferson, the former U.S. ambassador to France, called for the United States to aid revolutionary France in its war against the European monarchies. "To back away from France," he claimed, "would be to undermine the cause of republicanism in America." President Washington (and Alexander Hamilton), however, wanted no part of the European conflict. On April 22, 1793, Washington announced that the United States would not take sides in the war. Instead of settling matters, however, Washington's neutrality proclamation brought to a boil the ugly feud between Hamilton and Jefferson. In 1793, Jefferson urged his friend James Madison to "take up [his] pen" and cut Hamilton "to pieces" in the newspapers.

> Neutrality proclamation

French Revolution Revolutionary movement beginning in 1789 that overthrew the monarchy and transformed France into an unstable republic before Napoleon Bonaparte assumed power in 1799.

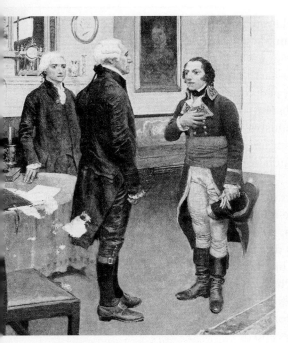

CITIZEN GENET The French ambassador, known as Citizen Genet, meets the disapproving George Washington after the French official had blatantly violated American neutrality laws.

Citizen Genet

While not wanting the United States to get involved in the European war, President Washington did accept Jefferson's argument that the United States should recognize the new French revolutionary government (becoming the first nation to do so). The French government then sent its first ambassador to the United States—the impulsive thirty-year-old Edmond-Charles-Édouard Genet.

Citizen Genet, as he quickly became known (a nod to newly egalitarian France), landed at Charleston, South Carolina, to a hero's welcome. He then openly violated America's neutrality by recruiting four American privateers (privately owned warships) to capture English and Spanish merchant vessels. He also conspired with frontiersmen and land speculators to organize an attack on Spanish Florida and Louisiana.

As Genet made his way to Philadelphia, then America's capital, he was greeted along the way by large crowds cheering the French Revolution. Once in Philadelphia, Genet continued his reckless efforts to draw America into war on the side of France. When he threatened to go around President Washington and appeal directly to the American people, even Jefferson disavowed "the French monkey." In August 1793, President Washington demanded that the French government replace Genet.

Americans Take Sides

French Revolution divides Federalists and Republicans

The war of the European monarchies against revolutionary France deeply divided public opinion in the United States. Republicans tended to support the French rebels; Federalists were more skeptical of their motives and methods and sided with the British in the growing war. Thomas Jefferson was so disgusted by President Washington's refusal to support the French Revolution and Alexander Hamilton's economic policies and political scheming that he resigned as secretary of state at the end of 1793, eager to be rid of the "hated occupation of politics." Vice President John Adams greeted the news of Jefferson's departure by saying "good riddance." George Washington felt the same way. He never forgave Jefferson and James Madison for organizing networks of Republicans across the nation to oppose the administration's policies. After accepting Jefferson's resignation, Washington never spoke to him again.

Jay's Treaty

President Washington's challenges in leading the new nation only increased with time. During 1794, tensions between the United States and Great Britain threatened to renew warfare between the old enemies. The Treaty of

Paris (1783) that ended the Revolutionary War had left the western and southern boundaries of the United States in dispute. In addition, in late 1793 British warships violated international law by seizing American ships that carried French goods or were sailing for French ports. By early 1794, several hundred American ships had been confiscated, and their crews were given the choice of joining the British navy or being imprisoned. At the same time, British troops in the Ohio Valley gave weapons to Indians, who in turn attacked American settlers.

Early in 1794, however, the British gave President Washington a timely opening. They stopped seizing American ships, and on April 16, 1794, Washington sent Chief Justice John Jay to London to settle the major issues between the two nations: getting the British out of frontier forts and fur-trading posts near the Canadian-American border (as had been called for by the Treaty of Paris in 1783), securing payment ("reparations") for the losses of American ship-owners and compensation for southern slaves carried away by British ships in 1783, and negotiating a new commercial treaty that would reopen American trade with the British West Indies.

JAY'S TREATY A firestorm of controversy greeted Jay's treaty in America. Opponents of the treaty rioted and burned Jay in effigy.

To win his objectives, Jay accepted the British argument that American products needed for the construction of French warships could not be shipped to French ports. Through Jay's negotiations, Britain also gained advantages in its trade with the United States and a promise that French privateers would not be outfitted in American ports. Finally, Jay conceded that the British need not compensate U.S. citizens for the enslaved African Americans who had escaped during the Revolutionary War and that the pre-Revolutionary American debts to British merchants would be paid by the U.S. government.

In return for these concessions, the chief justice won *three* important promises from the British: they would (1) evacuate their six forts in northwest America by 1796, (2) reimburse Americans for the seizures of ships and cargo in 1793–1794, and (3) grant American merchants the right to trade with the British West Indies.

Jay's Treaty with Great Britain (1794)

Jay's Treaty (1794)
Controversial agreement between Britain and the United States, negotiated by Chief Justice John Jay, that settled disputes over trade, prewar debts owed to British merchants, British-occupied forts in American territory, and the seizure of American ships and cargo.

But when the terms of **Jay's Treaty** were revealed, Americans were outraged that they favored Britain over France. The heated dispute over the treaty helped sharpen the differences between the Jeffersonian Republicans and the Federalists. Thomas Jefferson and the Republicans who supported France in its war with Britain were furious; they wanted no concessions to the hated British. Jefferson dismissed Jay's Treaty as an "infamous act."

The uproar over Jay's Treaty created the most serious crisis of George Washington's presidency. Some critics even called for his impeachment. Yet Washington, while admitting that the treaty was imperfect, concluded that it was the only way to avoid a war with Britain, a war that America was bound to lose (the U.S. Army then had only 672 men, and there was no navy). In the end, Jay's Treaty barely won the necessary two-thirds majority in the Senate. Most of those voting against the treaty were southerners.

Frontier Tensions

Meanwhile, new conflicts erupted in the Ohio Valley between American settlers and Native Americans. President Washington named Revolutionary War hero General "Mad" Anthony Wayne to lead a military expedition into the disputed region. In the fall of 1793, Wayne marched into the Northwest Territory's "Indian country" with some 2,600 men, built Fort Greenville in Ohio, and soon went on the offensive.

In August 1794, some 2,000 Shawnee, Ottawa, Chippewa, Delaware, and Potawatomi warriors, armed by the British and reinforced by Canadian militiamen, engaged Wayne's troops and Indian allies in the Battle of Fallen Timbers along the Michigan-Ohio border, near present-day Toledo, Ohio. The Americans decisively defeated the Indians, destroyed their crops and villages, and built a line of forts in northern Ohio and Indiana, one of which became the city of Fort Wayne, Indiana. The Indians finally agreed to the Treaty of Greenville, signed in August 1795, by which the United States bought most of the territory that would form the state of Ohio and the cities of Detroit and Chicago.

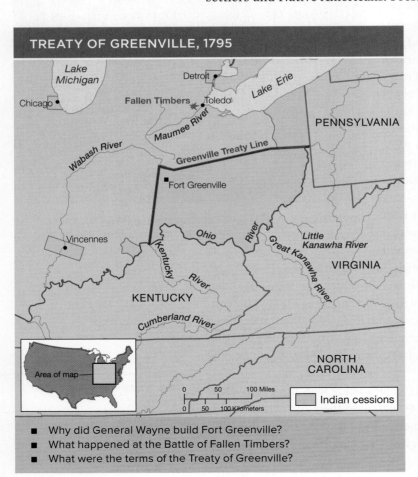

TREATY OF GREENVILLE, 1795

■ Why did General Wayne build Fort Greenville?
■ What happened at the Battle of Fallen Timbers?
■ What were the terms of the Treaty of Greenville?

The Whiskey Rebellion

Soon after the Battle of Fallen Timbers, the Washington administration displayed another show of strength in the sparsely populated hill country west of the Appalachian Mountains—this time against the so-called **Whiskey Rebellion**. Throughout the rural western region, from north Georgia up to western Pennsylvania, the whiskey tax of 1791 had ignited resistance. Some angry rebels, inspired by the example of the French Revolution, threatened to leave the Union.

In the summer of 1794, discontent exploded into open rebellion in western Pennsylvania. A mob of angry farmers burned the house of the federal tax collector. Other rebels threatened an assault on Pittsburgh. On August 7, 1794, President Washington issued a proclamation ordering the rebels home. When they failed to respond, he led 13,000 militiamen from four states to Pennsylvania to suppress the rebellion. Washington was the first—and last—president to lead troops into battle while in office.

The massive show of federal force worked: the whiskey rebels vanished into the hills. The new federal government had made its point and showed its strength, but many critics claimed it had become tyrannical. The government's use of so many soldiers led those who sympathized with the "whiskey rebels" to become Republicans, and Thomas Jefferson's party scored big gains in the next Pennsylvania elections.

WHISKEY REBELLION George Washington as commander in chief reviews the troops mobilized to quell the Whiskey Rebellion in 1794. **Why did Washington's controversial action against the rebels lead to a surge in Republican support at the polls?**

Pinckney's Treaty

While these turbulent events were unfolding in western Pennsylvania, the Spanish began negotiations over Louisiana and Florida, which they had gained from the British through provisions of the treaties that ended the American Revolution. U.S. negotiator Thomas Pinckney, the former governor of South Carolina, pulled off a diplomatic triumph in 1795 when he convinced the Spanish to accept a southern American boundary at the 31st parallel in west Florida, along the coast of the Gulf of Mexico. The Spanish also agreed to allow Americans to ship goods down the Mississippi River to Spanish-controlled New Orleans. Senate ratification of Pinckney's Treaty (also called the Treaty of San Lorenzo) came quickly, for westerners were eager to use the Mississippi River to transport their crops to market.

Whiskey Rebellion (1794) Violent protest by western Pennsylvania farmers against the federal excise tax on corn whiskey, put down by a federal army

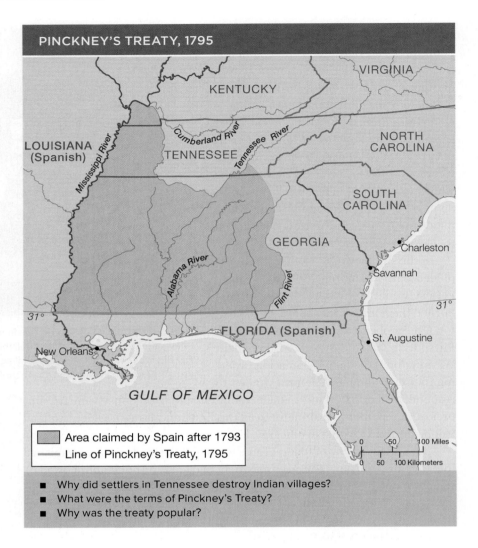

PINCKNEY'S TREATY, 1795

- Area claimed by Spain after 1793
- Line of Pinckney's Treaty, 1795

- Why did settlers in Tennessee destroy Indian villages?
- What were the terms of Pinckney's Treaty?
- Why was the treaty popular?

Settlement of New Lands and the Wilderness Road

The important treaties with Great Britain and Spain negotiated by John Jay and Thomas Pinckney spurred a new surge of Americans into the western territories. The lure of western lands led thousands of settlers to follow pathfinder Daniel Boone along the Wilderness Road he had helped cut into the territory known as Kentucky, from the Indian name Ken-Ta-Ke (Great Meadow).

In the late eighteenth century, the Indian-held lands in Kentucky were a farmer's dream and a hunter's paradise; the vast area boasted fertile soil and abundant forests filled with buffalo, deer, and wild turkeys. Over the years, Boone and other whites bought or stole most of the Indians' ancestral lands in Kentucky. Born on a small farm in 1734 in central Pennsylvania, Boone was a deadeye marksman by the age of twelve and would become a successful farmer and an accomplished woodsman. After hearing about the fertile territory over the mountains, Boone set out alone in 1769 to find a trail into Kentucky. Armed with a rifle, tomahawk, and hunting knife, he found what was called the Warriors' Path, a narrow trail that buffalo, deer, and Indians had worn along the steep ridges.

In 1773, Boone led the first group of settlers through the Appalachian Mountains at the Cumberland Gap. Two years later, he and thirty woodsmen used axes to widen the Warriors' Path into what became known as the Wilderness Road, a passage that more than 300,000 settlers would use over the next twenty-five years.

Washington's Farewell

By 1796, George Washington had decided that two terms as president were enough. Frustrated by heated partisan politics, he was eager to retire to Mount Vernon, his plantation in northern Virginia. He would leave behind a formidable record of presidential achievements: the organization of a national government, a prosperous economy, the recovery of territory from Britain and Spain, a stable northwestern frontier, and the admission of three new states: Vermont (1791), Kentucky (1792), and Tennessee (1796).

DANIEL BOONE ESCORTING SETTLERS THROUGH CUMBERLAND GAP In this 1851 painting by George Caleb Bingham, a Missouri artist known for his mythologizing portraits of frontier life, Daniel Boone leads a group of settlers westward through the Appalachian Mountains. **How does Bingham's portrayal of the settlers reveal his vision of westward expansion and the spirit of those who made the difficult journey?**

On September 17, 1796, Washington delivered a farewell address to the nation in which he stressed that the United States should avoid getting involved in Europe's quarrels and wars. It was, he said, "our true policy to steer clear of permanent alliances with any portion of the foreign world." The key word here is *permanent*. Washington agreed that "temporary alliances for extraordinary emergencies" might be needed. His warning against permanent foreign entanglements would serve as a fundamental principle in U.S. foreign policy until the early twentieth century.

The Election of 1796

With George Washington out of the race, the United States had its first contested election for president in 1796. The Federalist "caucus," a group of leading congressmen, chose Vice President John Adams as their presidential candidate. Thomas Pinckney of South Carolina, fresh from his

JOHN ADAMS Political philosopher and politician, Adams won the election of 1796 by a thin margin, becoming the second president of the United States. He was the first president to take up residence in the White House, in early 1801.

diplomatic triumph in Spain, also ran as a Federalist candidate (at this time there were no candidates for the vice presidency; whoever came in second, regardless of party affiliation, became the vice president).

As expected, the Republicans chose Thomas Jefferson. Aaron Burr, a brilliant young attorney and senator from New York, also ran as a Republican.

The campaign of 1796 was nasty. Republicans labeled Adams a monarchist because of his elitism (Adams wanted people to refer to the president of the United States as "His Highness"). The Federalists countered that Jefferson was a French-loving atheist eager for another war with Great Britain. They also charged that the philosophical Jefferson was not decisive enough to be president. The increasing strength of the Republicans, fueled by the smoldering resentment of Jay's Treaty as far too lenient with the British, nearly swept Jefferson into office. Instead, Adams became president and Jefferson became his opponent's vice president by winning 68 electoral votes to Adams's 71.

The Adams Administration

Vain and prickly, opinionated and stubborn, John Adams had crafted a distinguished career as a Massachusetts lawyer; as a leader in the Revolutionary movement; as the hardest-working member of the Continental Congress; as a talented diplomat in France, Holland, and Great Britain; and as George Washington's vice president. Adams lusted for the presidency, but he refused to compromise his principles to ensure his election. He was an independent thinker with a combative spirit and fiery temper who fought as often with his fellow Federalists as he did with his Republican opponents. Benjamin Franklin said Adams was "always an honest man, often a wise one, but sometimes . . . absolutely out of his senses."

Adams had many virtues, however. He was fiercely patriotic, intelligent, experienced, and conscientious. No one had served the new nation with as much dedication and energy. He had helped persuade the Continental Congress to declare independence in 1776 and had assisted Jefferson in drafting the Declaration of Independence. Adams had also helped negotiate the Treaty of Paris, which ended the Revolutionary War in 1783.

The Quasi-War with France

French retaliation against Jay's Treaty

As America's second president, Adams inherited a naval "quasi-war" with France, a by-product of revolutionary France's angry reaction to Jay's Treaty between the United States and Great Britain. When John Jay accepted the British insistence that food and military supplies being shipped from the United States to nations at war with Britain would be seized, the French announced that they would retaliate by confiscating American cargo headed for British ports. By the time of Adams's inauguration, in 1797, French naval vessels had plundered some 300 American ships and severed diplomatic relations with the United States.

President Adams immediately tried to restore good relations with France. In 1797, he sent three U.S. diplomats to Paris to negotiate a settle-

CONFLICT WITH FRANCE
A cartoon indicating the anti-French sentiment generated by the XYZ affair. In the background, a savage-looking figure bearing the French flag operates the guillotine, while on the left the three American negotiators reject the Paris Monster's demand for money.

ment of the dispute. When the Americans arrived in Paris, however, they were accosted by three French officials (labeled "X," "Y," and "Z" by Adams in his report to Congress), who announced that negotiations could begin only if the United States paid a bribe of $250,000.

Such bribes were common eighteenth-century diplomatic practice, but the answer from the humiliated American side was "no, no, not a sixpence." No sooner was the so-called XYZ affair reported in America, hostility toward France soared. Many Republicans—with the notable exception of Vice President Jefferson—joined the chorus crying for revenge. President Adams asked Congress to authorize the construction of more warships and the expansion of the army. By the end of 1798, an undeclared naval war, or quasi-war, with France had begun in the West Indies.

The XYZ affair

The success of the American navy in capturing nearly 100 French ships, combined with other French defeats around the world, now led the French government to ask for negotiations. In a treaty called the Convention of 1800, the Americans won the best terms they could from the French, including the end of the military alliance with the United States dating back to the Revolutionary War. The Senate quickly ratified the agreement, which became effective on December 21, 1801.

The Convention of 1800

The War at Home

The naval war with France sparked an intense debate between Federalists eager for war and the Republicans most sympathetic to France. Pro-French Thomas Jefferson told a French official that President Adams was "a vain, irritable, stubborn" man. In 1797, Vice President Jefferson secretly sponsored a vicious pamphlet that described Adams as a deranged monarchist intent upon naming himself king of the United States. Adams, who learned of his vice president's efforts to undermine his presidency, regretted losing

CONGRESSIONAL PUGILISTS
An infamous print of the fight between Roger Griswold and Matthew Lyon on the House Floor portrays the absurd degree of conflict between the Federalists and Republicans over the Sedition Acts. After a volley of verbal abuse, Lyon spat tobacco juice at Griswold, who retaliated by attacking Lyon with a wooden cane, who in turn took up a pair of fire tongs.

Jefferson as a friend but "felt obliged to look upon him as a man whose mind is warped by prejudice."

Jefferson and other Republicans were convinced that the real purpose of the French crisis was to provide Federalists with an excuse to quiet their American critics. The infamous **Alien and Sedition Acts of 1798** seemed to confirm the Republicans' suspicions. These vengeful acts, passed by the Federalists amid the surge of patriotic war fever, limited freedom of speech and the press as well as the liberty of "aliens" (immigrants who had not yet gained citizenship). John Adams's support for the Alien and Sedition Acts would prove to be the greatest mistake of his presidency.

Three of the four Alien and Sedition acts reflected hostility to French immigrants, many of whom had become militant Republicans in the United States. The Naturalization Act lengthened from five to fourteen years the residency requirement for U.S. citizenship. The Alien Act empowered the president to deport "dangerous" aliens, and the Alien Enemies Act authorized the president in wartime to expel or imprison enemy aliens at will. Finally, the Sedition Act outlawed writing, publishing, or speaking anything of "a false, scandalous and malicious" nature against the government or any of its officers.

In response, Thomas Jefferson and James Madison drafted the Kentucky and Virginia Resolutions, passed by the legislatures of both states in 1798. The resolutions denounced the Alien and Sedition Acts as "alarming infractions" of constitutional rights and argued that the states should "nullify" (reject and ignore) acts of Congress that violated the First Amendment's guarantee of free speech. George Washington told Patrick Henry in Virginia that Jefferson was threatening to "dissolve the union."

Alien and Sedition Acts of 1798 Four measures passed during the undeclared war with France that limited the freedoms of speech and press and restricted the liberty of immigrants.

Republican Victory in 1800

The furor over the Alien and Sedition Acts influenced the pivotal presidential election of 1800. The Federalists nominated John Adams for a second term over the objection of leading Federalists such as New York's Alexander Hamilton, who questioned Adams's fitness to be president, citing his "disgusting egotism." Thomas Jefferson and Aaron Burr, the Republican candidates, represented the alliance of the two most powerful states, Virginia and New York, where Burr was a prominent political figure.

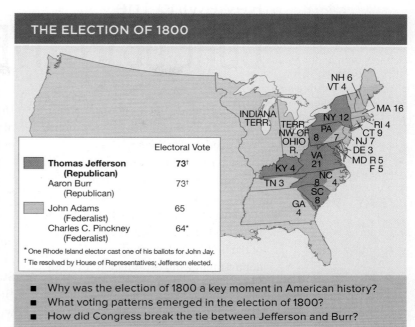

THE ELECTION OF 1800

	Electoral Vote
Thomas Jefferson (Republican)	73†
Aaron Burr (Republican)	73†
John Adams (Federalist)	65
Charles C. Pinckney (Federalist)	64*

* One Rhode Island elector cast one of his ballots for John Jay.

† Tie resolved by House of Representatives; Jefferson elected.

- Why was the election of 1800 a key moment in American history?
- What voting patterns emerged in the election of 1800?
- How did Congress break the tie between Jefferson and Burr?

The Federalists again attacked Jefferson for supporting the radical French Jacobin revolutionaries. His election, they claimed, would bring civil war and anarchy to America. Jefferson's supporters portrayed him as a passionate idealist and optimist who was the friend of farmers and the courageous champion of states' rights, limited government, and personal liberty.

In the **election of 1800**, Jefferson and Burr tied for the lead with 73 electoral votes each. Adams received only 65. The tie vote in the Electoral College for Jefferson and Burr sent the choice of the president to the House of Representatives (a constitutional defect corrected in 1804 by the Twelfth Amendment). It took thirty-six ballots for the House of Representatives to choose Thomas Jefferson as the new president, making Burr the vice president.

Before the Federalists turned over power to the Jeffersonian Republicans on March 4, 1801, Congress passed the Judiciary Act of 1801. It was intended to ensure Federalist control of the judicial system by creating sixteen federal circuit courts with a new judge for each. Before he left office, Adams appointed Federalist judges to all the new positions. The defeated Federalists, in the words of Jefferson, "had retired into the judiciary as a stronghold." They would never again exercise political power.

A bitter John Adams refused to attend Thomas Jefferson's inauguration in the new federal capital in Washington, D.C. Instead, unnoticed and unappreciated, the ex-president boarded a stagecoach for the 500-mile trip to his home in Massachusetts. He and Jefferson would not communicate for the next twelve years. As Adams returned to his Massachusetts farm with his wife, Abigail, he told his eldest son, John Quincy, who would later become the nation's sixth president, that anyone governing the new United States faced "a hard, laborious, and unhappy life."

election of 1800 Presidential election involving Thomas Jefferson and John Adams that resulted in the first Democratic-Republican victory after the Federalist administrations of George Washington and John Adams.

Reviewing the
CORE OBJECTIVES |

■ **Confederation Government**
Despite the weak form of government organized under the Articles of Confederation, the Confederation government managed to construct important alliances during the Revolutionary War, help win the War of Independence, and negotiate the Treaty of Paris (1783). It created executive departments and established through the *Northwest Ordinance* the process by which new western territories would be organized and governments formed before they applied for statehood. The Articles of Confederation, however, did not allow the national government to raise taxes to fund its debts. *Shays's Rebellion* made many Americans fear that such uprisings would eventually destroy the new republic unless the United States formed a stronger national government.

■ **Constitutional Convention** When delegates gathered at the convention in Philadelphia in 1787 to revise the existing government, they decided to scrap the Articles of Confederation and start over. An entirely new document emerged, which created a system called *federalism* in which a strong national government with clear *separation of powers* among executive, legislative, and judicial branches functioned alongside state governments. Arguments about how best to ensure that the rights of individual states were protected and also that "the people" were represented in the new Congress were resolved by establishing a Senate, with equal representation for each state, and a

House of Representatives, the number of whose delegates was determined by population counts.

■ **Ratification of the Constitution**
Ratification of the Constitution was hotly contested. *Anti-Federalists* such as Virginia's Patrick Henry opposed the new structure of government because it lacked a bill of rights. To sway New York State toward ratification, Alexander Hamilton, James Madison, and John Jay wrote *The Federalist Papers*. Ratification became possible only when Federalists promised to add a *Bill of Rights*.

■ **Federalists versus Republicans**
Strengthening the economy was the highest priority of the Washington administration. Alexander Hamilton and the Federalists wanted to create a diverse economy in which agriculture was balanced by trade, finance, and manufacturing. As part of *Alexander Hamilton's economic reforms*, he crafted a federal budget that funded the national debt through tariffs on imports and tax revenues, and he created a national bank, the first *Bank of the United States*. Thomas Jefferson and others, known as the *Jeffersonian Republicans*, worried that Hamilton's plans violated the Constitution and made the federal government too powerful. They envisioned a nation dominated by farmers and planters in which the rights of states would be protected against federal power.

■ **Trouble Abroad** With the outbreak of war throughout much of Europe during the *French Revolution*, George

Washington's policy of neutrality violated the terms of America's 1778 treaty with France. At the same time, Americans sharply criticized *Jay's Treaty* with the British for giving too much away. French warships began seizing British and American ships in an undeclared naval war. Federalists supported Washington's approach; Republicans were more supportive of France. During the presidency of John Adams, this undeclared naval war continued, which led to the controversial *Alien and Sedition Acts of 1798*.

KEY TERMS

Northwest Ordinance (1787) *p. 193*

Shays's Rebellion (1786–1787) *p. 197*

federalism *p. 200*

separation of powers *p. 200*

anti-Federalists *p. 204*

The Federalist Papers *p. 204*

Bill of Rights (1791) *p. 207*

Jeffersonian Republicans *p. 209*

Alexander Hamilton's economic reforms *p. 211*

Bank of the United States (1791) *p. 213*

French Revolution *p. 215*

Jay's Treaty (1794) *p. 218*

Whiskey Rebellion (1794) *p. 219*

Alien and Sedition Acts of 1798 *p. 224*

election of 1800 *p. 225*

CHRONOLOGY

1781	Articles of Confederation take effect
1783	Treaty of Paris ends the war for independence
1784–1785	Land Ordinances
1786–1787	Shays's Rebellion
1787	Northwest Ordinance
	The Constitutional Convention convenes in Philadelphia
1787–1788	*The Federalist Papers* are published
1789	President George Washington is inaugurated
1791	Bill of Rights is ratified
	Bank of the United States is created
1793	Washington issues a proclamation of neutrality
1794	Jay's Treaty is negotiated with England
	U.S. Army defeats Indians in the Battle of Fallen Timbers
	Whiskey Rebellion in Pennsylvania
1795	Treaty of Greenville
	Pinckney's Treaty is negotiated with Spain
1796	John Adams is elected president
1798–1800	Quasi-war with France
1798	Alien and Sedition Acts are passed
1800	Thomas Jefferson is elected president

🐰 INQUIZITIVE

Go to InQuizitive to see what you've learned—and learn what you've missed—with personalized feedback along the way.

WE OWE ALLEGIANCE TO NO CROWN (CA. 1814) The War of 1812 generated a renewed spirit of nationalism, inspiring Philadelphia sign painter John Archibald Woodside to create this patriotic painting.

The Early Republic

1800–1815

When President Thomas Jefferson took office in early 1801, the United States and its western territories reached from the Atlantic Ocean to the Mississippi River. The nation remained primarily rural and agricultural. Nine of ten Americans lived or worked on land, with most of them growing enough food and raising enough livestock to feed their families but rarely producing enough to sell outside the community, much less overseas.

That changed during the nineteenth century. With each passing year, more and more farmers began to produce surplus crops and livestock to sell in regional and world markets. Such commercial agriculture was especially evident in the South, where European demand for cotton caused prices to soar.

The growing market economy produced boom-and-bust cycles, but overall the years from 1790 to 1830 were prosperous, with enterprising Americans experiencing unprecedented opportunities for land ownership, economic gain, and geographic mobility. The American desire for profits was, according to Congressman Henry Clay, "a passion as unconquerable as any with which nature has endowed us. You may attempt to regulate [it]—[but] you cannot destroy it."

Everywhere people were on the move and on the make, leading one newspaper to claim that what made America different from other nations was "the almost universal ambition to get forward." Americans were preoccupied

CORE
OBJECTIVES InQUIZITIVE

1. Summarize the major domestic political developments that took place during Thomas Jefferson's administration.

2. Describe how foreign events affected the United States during the Jefferson and Madison administrations.

3. Explain the primary causes of the American decision to declare war on Great Britain in 1812.

4. Analyze the most significant outcomes of the War of 1812 on the United States.

with westward expansion, economic development, rapid population growth, and intense political activity. Retiring president John Adams observed, "There is no people on earth so ambitious as the people of America ... because the lowest can aspire as freely as the highest."

At the end of the Revolutionary War, George Washington predicted that Americans would move across the mountains into the Ohio Valley "faster than any other ever did, or any one would imagine." By 1840, more than 40 percent of the population lived west of the Appalachian Mountains in eight new states. "The woods are full of new settlers," marveled a traveler in upstate New York in 1805.

Thomas Jefferson described the United States in the early nineteenth century as an "empire of liberty" (for whites only) spreading westward. In 1800, people eager to own farms bought 67,000 acres of government-owned land; the next year they bought 498,000 acres. Native Americans fiercely resisted the invasion of their ancestral lands but ultimately succumbed to a federal government determined to relocate them or kill them.

Most whites, however, were less concerned about taking land owned by Indians and Hispanics than they were about seizing their own economic opportunities. Isaac Weld, a British visitor, remarked that the Americans at the beginning of the nineteenth century were a "restless people, always on the lookout for something better or more profitable." Restless mobility and impatient striving soon came to define the American way of life.

CORE **OBJECTIVE**

1. Summarize the major domestic political developments that took place during Thomas Jefferson's administration.

Jeffersonian Republicanism

The "People's President"

The 1800 presidential campaign between Federalists and Jeffersonian Republicans was so fiercely contested that some predicted civil war as the House of Representatives decided the outcome of the disputed election. On March 4, 1801, however, the fifty-seven-year-old Thomas Jefferson was inaugurated without incident, leading some people to call his election "the peaceful revolution," for it was the first democratic election in modern history that saw the peaceful transfer of power from one party to another.

Jefferson was the first president inaugurated in the new national capital named Washington, District of Columbia, sandwiched between the slave states of Virginia and Maryland. The new city, still raw and unfinished, was crisscrossed with muddy avenues connecting a few buildings clustered around two incomplete centers, Capitol Hill and the "President's House." Cows grazed along the Mall while pigs prowled the unpaved and unlit streets. Workers, many of them enslaved, had barely completed the Capitol and the "president's mansion" before Jefferson was sworn in.

During his inauguration, Jefferson emphasized his connection to the "plain and simple" ways of the "common" people. Instead of wearing a cere-

THE CAPITOL BUILDING This 1806 watercolor of the Capitol building was painted by Benjamin Henry Latrobe, its architect, and inscribed to Thomas Jefferson. A tall dome would be added later, after the building was damaged in the War of 1812.

monial sword and riding in an elegant horse-drawn carriage, as George Washington and John Adams had done at their inaugurations, Jefferson, a widower, left his boardinghouse on New Jersey Avenue and walked to the Capitol building, escorted by members of Congress and Virginia militiamen. He read his inaugural address in a "femininely soft," high-pitched voice, then took the presidential oath administered by Chief Justice John Marshall, his Virginia cousin, with whom he shared a cordial hatred.

Jefferson intended his deliberate display of **republican simplicity** to highlight the difference between the monarchical trappings of the Federalists and the down-to-earth simplicity and frugality of the Republicans. As president, he did not wear fancy clothes or host elegant parties. Jefferson often answered the door of the President's House himself, wearing a robe and slippers. A Frenchman reported that the president "greets guests in slovenly clothes and without the least formality."

In his eloquent inaugural address, the tall, thin Jefferson, his red hair streaked with gray, urged Americans to temper their political partisanship and work together. "We are all Republicans—we are all Federalists," he

republican simplicity Deliberate attitude of humility and frugality, as opposed to monarchical pomp and ceremony, adopted by Thomas Jefferson in his presidency.

declared, stressing that "every difference of opinion is not a difference of principle." He asked Americans to "unite with one heart and one mind."

It was a splendid message, but Jefferson's appeal for a united nation failed, in part because he himself retained his fierce partisanship and bitter anti-Federalist prejudices. In a letter to a British friend, Jefferson described his Federalist opponents as "insane" men: "Their leaders are a hospital of incurables." He still believed that many Federalists were madmen determined to destroy "the liberties of the people" and convert the republic into a monarchy (he called them "monocrats").

A More Democratic Culture

> Expanded political participation

Jefferson's inauguration ushered in a more democratic era. With each passing year, an increasing proportion of white males gained the right to vote as state after state eliminated requirements that only property owners could vote. In many northern states, the percentage of eligible voters increased from 20 percent to 80 percent by eliminating or reducing the property requirements. More and more commoners also entered politics. Men of humble origins, some of whom were uneducated and illiterate, began to displace the social and political elite in the state legislatures. And over half the members of the Republican-controlled Congress were newly elected.

Die-hard Federalists abhorred the "democratization" of politics. "We are sliding down into the mire of a democracy," moaned Fisher Ames of Massachusetts. When the "pot boils," another Federalist noted, the "scum will rise." Before long, John Adams grumbled, even the poorest men "will demand an equal voice with any other."

Adams and other Federalists prized the stability and predictability of government by elites over the chaos of mass democracy represented by Thomas Jefferson. Indeed, Jefferson represented the turbulence of the era, for he himself was a bundle of contradictions. He loathed political skullduggery yet was a master at it. He castigated the "evils" of slavery yet profited enormously from them. Jefferson wrote heatedly about the evils of racial mixing, yet he used a mulatto slave, Sally Hemings, as his concubine; she gave birth to six of his children, all of whose births Jefferson dutifully noted in his diary, along with the new horses he had acquired and the pigs he had killed. Hemings became for the widower Jefferson what one of his friends called his "substitute for a wife."

On one hand, Jefferson was a wealthy, slave-owning aristocratic planter with expensive tastes in food, wine, and furnishings. Charming and brilliant, he was an

AT LEISURE AT MONTICELLO A scene of Jefferson's Monticello estate, showing his descendants playing in the garden. Designed by Jefferson himself after the sixteenth-century Italian architect, Andrea Palladio, Monticello stands as a testament to Jefferson's classical tastes. **How did Jefferson's aristocratic lifestyle conflict with his persona as the "people's president"?**

inventive genius of staggering learning and exceptional abilities. No political leader, then or since, had such expansive and varied interests. As an architect, he designed the state capitol in Richmond, Virginia, as well as his thirty-three-room mountaintop mansion near Charlottesville called *Monticello* (Little Mountain). He also was expert at constitutional law, civil liberties, and political philosophy; religion and ethics; classical history; progressive education; natural science, paleontology, and mathematics; music and linguistics; and farming, gardening, cooking, and wine.

Yet while Jefferson lived the luxurious life of an enlightened slaveholding planter, he championed the "honest heart" of the common people. His faith in expanding the number of eligible voters and his determination to reduce the power of the national government opened a more democratic era in American life in which the founding generation of aristocratic "gentlemen" such as John Adams and George Washington were gradually displaced in positions of power by men from more common backgrounds.

For all his natural shyness and admitted weakness as a public speaker, Jefferson was the first president to pursue the role of party leader, openly cultivating congressional support at frequent dinner parties. In the new president's cabinet, the leading figures were Jefferson's best friend, neighbor, and political ally, Secretary of State James Madison, and Secretary of the Treasury Albert Gallatin, a Swiss-born Pennsylvania Republican whose financial skills had won him the respect of the Federalists.

In filling lesser offices, however, Jefferson often succumbed to pressure from the Republicans to remove Federalists, only to discover that there were few qualified candidates to replace some of them. When Gallatin asked if he might appoint able women to some posts, Jefferson revealed the limits of his liberalism: "The appointment of a woman to office is an innovation for which the public is not prepared, nor am I." In one area—the federal judiciary—the new president decided to remove most of the offices altogether, in part because the court system was the only branch of the government still controlled by Federalists.

Marbury v. Madison

In 1802, at Jefferson's urging, the Republican-controlled Congress repealed the Judiciary Act of 1801, which the Federalists had passed just before the transfer of power to the Jeffersonian Republicans on March 4, 1801. The Judiciary Act of 1801 ensured Federalist control of the judicial system by creating sixteen federal circuit courts and appointing—for life—a new Federalist judge for each. The controversy over Jefferson's rescinding the judgeships sparked the landmark case of ***Marbury v. Madison*** (1803), the first in which the U.S. Supreme Court declared a federal law unconstitutional.

The case involved the appointment of Maryland Federalist William Marbury as justice of the peace in the District of Columbia. Marbury's "midnight" letter of appointment, or commission, signed by President Adams just two days before he left office, was still undelivered when Madison took office

Marbury v. Madison (1803)

Marbury v. Madison **(1803)** First Supreme Court decision to declare a federal law—the Judiciary Act of 1789—unconstitutional.

as the new secretary of state. President Jefferson directed Madison to withhold it. Marbury then filed suit to force Madison to deliver his commission.

The Supreme Court's unanimous opinion in *Marbury v. Madison* (1803), written by Chief Justice John Marshall, a brilliant Virginia Federalist and fierce critic of Jefferson, who happened to be his cousin, held that Marbury deserved his commission but denied that the Court had jurisdiction in the case. The Federal Judiciary Act of 1789, which gave the Court authority in such proceedings, was unconstitutional, the Marshall court ruled, because the Constitution specified that the Court should have original jurisdiction only in cases involving foreign ambassadors or nations. The Court, therefore, could issue no order in the case. With one bold stroke, Marshall had reprimanded the Jeffersonian Republicans while avoiding an awkward confrontation with an administration that might have defied his order to give Marbury his judgeship. More important, with the *Marbury* ruling the Court declared a federal law invalid because it violated provisions of the Constitution.

Marshall stressed that the Supreme Court was empowered "to say what the law is." In other words, in crafting the *Marbury* decision, the Supreme Court granted itself a power not mentioned in the Constitution: the right of *judicial review*, or deciding whether acts of Congress were constitutional. So even though William Marbury never gained his judgeship, Marshall and the other justices established that the Supreme Court decided constitutional interpretations.

President Jefferson fumed over what he called Marshall's "irregular" ruling. Giving judges "the right to decide which laws are constitutional, and what not," he wrote Abigail Adams, "would make the judiciary a despotic branch."

Jefferson, however, would lose that argument. Although the Court did not declare another federal law unconstitutional for fifty-four years, it has since struck down more than 150 acts of Congress and more than 1,100 "unconstitutional" acts of state legislatures, all in an effort to protect individual liberties and civil rights.

Jefferson's Economic Policies

Although John Marshall got the better of Thomas Jefferson in court, the president's first term included a series of triumphs in domestic affairs. Jefferson did not set out to dismantle Alexander Hamilton's Federalist economic program, despite his harsh criticism of it. Instead, following the advice of Treasury secretary Gallatin, Jefferson, who like many other southern planters never understood the function of banks and hated them, learned to accept the national bank as essential to economic growth.

Jefferson did, however, reject Hamilton's insistence that a federal debt was a national "blessing" because it gave bankers and investors who bought government bonds a direct financial stake in the success of the new republic. Jefferson believed that a large federal debt resulting from the sale of bonds would bring high taxes and government corruption, so he set about paying down the debt by slashing the federal budget.

In his first message to Congress in 1801, Jefferson foreshadowed modern political conservatives by promising to reduce the size, expense, and power of the federal government ("too complicated, too expensive"), shrink the government bureaucracy, and restore the authority of the sovereign states. He fired all federal tax collectors and cut the military budget in half, saying, incorrectly, that the state militias provided the nation with adequate defense. Jefferson's was the first government in history that intentionally sought to reduce its scope and power.

Shrinking the government

Jefferson's goal of reducing the federal government pleased many voters, especially those living outside the large cities on the Atlantic seaboard. He once admitted that he had a peculiar affection for the "men from the Western side of the mountains."

To address the grievances of grain farmers and backwoods distillers, Jefferson repealed the federal whiskey tax that Alexander Hamilton had instituted in 1791. Fortunately for Jefferson, the economy was prosperous enough by then to enable the federal budget to absorb the loss of the whiskey tax revenue. Money from federal tariffs on imports rose, and the sale of government-owned western lands soared.

Western Expansion

Where Alexander Hamilton always faced east, looking to Great Britain for his model of national greatness, Thomas Jefferson looked to the west for his inspiration, across the mountains and even across the Mississippi River. Only by expanding westward across the continent, he believed, could America avoid the social turmoil and misery common in the overcrowded cities of Europe. Only by "enlarging the empire of liberty" could America remain a nation primarily of farmers.

To ensure continuing westward settlement, Jefferson and the Republicans strove to reduce the cost of federal lands, and appreciative settlers flocked to buy property in the western territories. Ohio's admission to the Union in 1803 increased the number of states to seventeen. Government land sales west of the Appalachian Mountains skyrocketed in the early nineteenth century as settlers shoved Indians aside and established homesteads. But Jefferson wanted much more western land, and in 1803 a stroke of good fortune enabled him to double the size of the new American nation.

The Louisiana Purchase

Jefferson's **Louisiana Purchase** (1803) was so vast that no one knew its precise boundaries. It included 875,000 square miles extending far beyond present-day Louisiana. It comprised the entire Mississippi Valley west of the great river to the Rocky Mountains. Six states in their entirety, and most or part of nine more, would be carved out of the Louisiana Purchase. How it happened was itself a grand story of coincidental timing, shrewd diplomacy, and colossal luck.

Louisiana Purchase (1803) President Thomas Jefferson's purchase of the Louisiana Territory from France for $15 million, doubling the size of U.S. territory.

THE CESSION OF NEW ORLEANS The United States purchased the Louisiana Territory from Napoléon in 1803, effectively doubling the nation's size. In this contemporary watercolor, the French flag is raised over the city of New Orleans one final time, soon to be replaced with the American flag. **Why was the city of New Orleans an important acquisition for the United States?**

In 1801, soon after Jefferson learned that Spain had transferred the Louisiana Territory to Napoleonic France, he sent Robert R. Livingston to Paris to acquire the area. Spain in control of the Mississippi River outlet was bad enough, but the power-hungry Napoléon Bonaparte in control of the territory on America's western border could only mean serious trouble for the United States. "The day that France takes possession of New Orleans," Jefferson wrote Livingston, "we must marry ourselves to the British fleet and nation"—an unhappy prospect for the French-loving Jefferson.

Early in 1803, Jefferson sent James Monroe, his trusted Virginia friend and neighbor, to assist Livingston in Paris. Their initial goal was simply to acquire the strategic port city of New Orleans, strategically situated along the banks of the Mississippi River near its outlet at the Gulf of Mexico. Over the years, New Orleans under Spanish and French rule had become a dynamic crossroads community where people of all races and classes intermingled, reinventing themselves as Americans while garnering huge profits from the vast amount of goods floating down the mighty Mississippi to be shipped from the city to markets around the globe. For years, Americans living in Tennessee and Kentucky had threatened to secede if the federal government did not ensure that they could send their crops and goods down the river to New Orleans.

So Jefferson desperately wanted to convince the French to sell New Orleans. They did not need much convincing. No sooner had James Monroe arrived in Paris to negotiate a deal than the French asked if the United States would buy not just New Orleans but *all* of France's immense Louisiana Territory. The Americans quickly snapped up the offer.

The unpredictable Napoléon was willing to sell the Louisiana Territory because his army in Saint-Domingue (Haiti) had been decimated by a massive slave revolt and an epidemic of yellow fever. After losing 57,000 French soldiers to disease and warfare, Napoléon decided to cut French losses in the Americas by selling the Louisiana Territory and thereby helping finance his ongoing war with Great Britain.

By the Treaty of Cession, dated April 30, 1803, the United States obtained the Louisiana Territory for the modest sum of $15 million. This surprising turn of events presented Jefferson with a "noble bargain"—as well as a constitutional dilemma. Nowhere did the Constitution mention the purchase of territory. Was such an action legal? Jefferson admitted that the Constitution did not authorize such a purchase of land, but his desire to expand the American republic trumped his legal concerns.

Acquiring the territory, the president explained, would serve "the immediate interests of our Western citizens" and promote "the peace and security of the nation in general" by removing French control and creating a protective buffer separating the United States from the rest of the world. Besides, Jefferson and his supporters argued, if the nation waited to pass a constitutional amendment to enable the acquisition, Napoléon might change his mind.

New England Federalists, however, were not convinced that the purchase was a good idea. They worried that the growing numbers of Americans moving west were driving up wages on the Atlantic coast by reducing the workforce and lowering the value of real estate in their region. They also feared that new western states would likely be settled by southern slaveholders who were Jeffersonian Republicans. So, in a political reversal that anticipated many more reversals on constitutional issues, Federalists found themselves arguing for strict construction of the Constitution in opposing the Louisiana Purchase. Jefferson and the Republicans brushed aside Federalist reservations; the opportunity to double the size of the United States outweighed any legal reservations.

On October 17, 1803, Jefferson called a special session of Congress, whereupon the Senate ratified the treaty purchase by an overwhelming vote of 26–6. On December 20, 1803, U.S. officials took formal possession of the sprawling Louisiana Territory. At first the Spanish kept West Florida, but in 1810 American settlers revolted against Spanish rule and proclaimed the Republic of West Florida, which was quickly annexed and occupied by the United States as far east as the Pearl River. In 1813, with Spain itself a battlefield for French and British forces, Americans took over the rest of West Florida, out of which the states of Mississippi and Alabama would emerge.

Legally, as the U.S. government has claimed ever since, all these areas were included in the Louisiana Purchase, the most significant event of

A MAP OF LEWIS AND CLARK'S JOURNEY In their journals, Lewis and Clark sketched detailed maps of previously unexplored regions, such as this one.

Lewis and Clark expedition (1804–1806) Led by Meriwether Lewis and William Clark, a mission to the Pacific coast commissioned for the purposes of scientific and geographical exploration.

Jefferson's presidency and one of the most important developments in American history. It spurred western exploration and expansion, and especially enticed cotton growers to settle in what was called the Old Southwest—Alabama, Mississippi, and Louisiana. Andrew Jackson, then a slaveholding planter in Tennessee, congratulated Jefferson on acquiring the Louisiana Territory: "Every face wears a smile, and every heart leaps with joy."

Lewis and Clark

To learn more about the Louisiana Territory's geography, plants, and animals, as well as its prospects for trade and agriculture, Jefferson asked Congress to fund a scientific expedition. The president then appointed two army officers, Virginians Meriwether Lewis and William Clark, to lead what came to be known as the **Lewis and Clark Expedition**. The 29-year-old Lewis was Jefferson's private secretary. The president admired him for his "boldness, enterprise, and discretion." Clark, it was said, was "a youth of solid and promising parts, and as brave as Caesar."

On a rainy May morning in 1804, Lewis and Clark's "Corps of Discovery," numbering nearly fifty men, set out from a small village near the former French town of St. Louis in several large canoes (called pirogues) and one large flat-bottomed keelboat filled with food, weapons, medicine, and gifts to share with Indians. They traveled up the treacherous Missouri River through some of the most rugged wilderness in North America.

Unsure of where they were going and what they might encounter, the explorers were eager to discover if the Missouri, the longest river in North America, made its way to the Pacific Ocean. Six months later, near the Mandan Sioux villages in what would become North Dakota, the Corps of Discovery built Fort Mandan and wintered in relative comfort, sending downriver a barge loaded with maps, soil samples, the skins and skeletons of weasels, wolves and antelope, and live prairie dogs and magpies, previously unknown in America.

In the spring of 1805, the Corps of Discovery added two guides: a French fur trader and his remarkable wife, a young Shoshone woman named Sacagawea. In appreciation for Lewis and Clark's help in delivering her baby, Sacagawea provided crucial assistance as a guide, translator, and negotiator as they explored the upper Missouri and encountered various Native Americans, most of whom were "hospitable, honest, and sincere people."

The Lewis and Clark expedition crossed the Rocky Mountains on foot and on horseback and used canoes to descend the Snake and Columbia Rivers to the Pacific Ocean, where they arrived in November 1805. Near the future site of Astoria, Oregon, at the mouth of the Columbia River, they built Fort Clatsop, where they spent a cold, rainy winter. The following spring they headed back, having been forced to eat their dogs and horses, and having weathered blizzards, broiling sun, fierce rapids, raging grizzly bears, numerous injuries and illnesses, and swarms of mosquitoes.

The expedition returned to St. Louis in 1806, having been gone nearly 28 months and covered some 8,000 miles. Lewis and Clark brought back extensive journals describing their experiences and observations while detailing some 180 plants and 125 animals. Their maps attracted traders and trappers to the region and led the United States to claim the Oregon Country by right of discovery and exploration.

Political Schemes

The Lewis and Clark Expedition and the Louisiana Purchase strengthened Jefferson's already solid support in the South and West. In New England, however, Federalists panicked because they assumed that new states carved out of the Louisiana Territory would be dominated by Republicans.

To protect their interests, Federalists hatched a complicated scheme to link New York politically to New England by trying to elect Vice President Aaron Burr, Jefferson's ambitious Republican rival, as governor of New York. The cunning Burr chose to drop his Republican affiliation and run for governor as an independent candidate.

Several leading Federalists opposed the scheme, however. Alexander Hamilton urged Federalists not to vote for the conniving Burr, calling him "a dangerous man, and one who ought not to be trusted with the reins of government." Burr ended up losing the New York election to the Republican candidate, who had been endorsed by Jefferson.

A furious Burr blamed Hamilton for his defeat and challenged him to a duel. At dawn on July 11, 1804, the two met near Weehawken, New Jersey. Hamilton, whose son had been killed in a duel at the same location, fired first but intentionally missed as a demonstration of his religious and moral principles. Burr showed no such scruples. He shot Hamilton in the hip; the bullet ripped through his liver and lodged in his spine. He died the next day. Burr, who was still the vice president, was charged with murder by New Jersey authorities. He fled to South Carolina, where his daughter lived.

In the meantime, the presidential campaign of 1804 began when a congressional caucus of Republicans renominated Jefferson and chose George Clinton of New York as the vice presidential candidate. By then, to avoid the problems associated with parties running multiple candidates for the presidency, Congress had passed, and the states would soon ratify, the Twelfth Amendment, stipulating that the national electors use separate ballots to vote for the president and vice president. The Federalist candidates, Charles C. Pinckney and Rufus King, never had a chance. Jefferson and Clinton won 162 of the 176 electoral votes.

SACAGAWEA Of the many memorials devoted to Sacagawea, this statue by artist Alice Cooper was unveiled at the 1905 Lewis and Clark Centennial Exposition in the presence of several more pioneering women, including feminist Susan B. Anthony.

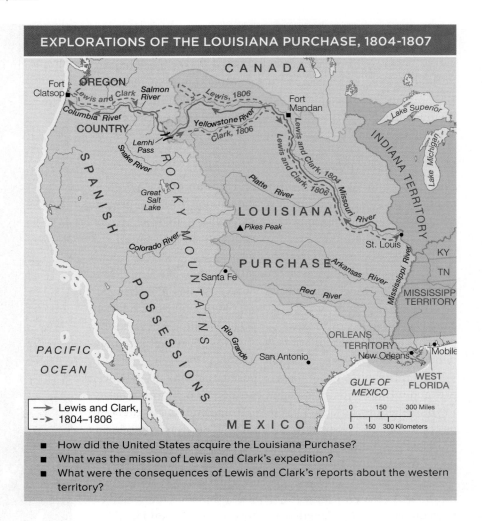

EXPLORATIONS OF THE LOUISIANA PURCHASE, 1804-1807

- How did the United States acquire the Louisiana Purchase?
- What was the mission of Lewis and Clark's expedition?
- What were the consequences of Lewis and Clark's reports about the western territory?

Divisions in the Republican Party

Freed from strong opposition—Federalists made up only a quarter of the new Congress—the dominant Republican majority began to fragment into warring factions. Fiery young Virginian John Randolph was initially a loyal Jeffersonian, but over time he emerged as the most colorful of the radically conservative "Old Republicans"—mostly southern agrarians who were more consistent than Jefferson in defending states' rights. Randolph, for example, detested Madison for his role in drafting and winning approval of the U.S. Constitution.

The imperious Randolph, another Jefferson cousin, stood out in the Senate. He often entered the chamber wearing a long white coat and white boots with spurs, carrying a horsewhip, and trailed by a hunting hound that would sleep under his desk. He lubricated his speeches with regular gulps of whiskey.

Randolph quickly became the wittiest insulter in the Congress, famously ordering opponents to sit down and shut up (he and Henry Clay would engage in a duel in 1826). He described himself as "an aristocrat. I love liberty. I hate equality." Randolph and other Old Republicans were best known for what they opposed: any compromise with the Federalists, any expansion of federal authority at the expense of states' rights or a strict interpretation of the Constitution, any new taxes or tariffs, and any change in the South's agrarian way of life rooted in slavery.

The Jeffersonian Republicans, on the other hand, were more moderate and pragmatic than Randolph and the Old Republicans. They were willing to compromise their states' rights principles to maintain federal tariffs on imports and tolerate a national bank, and to stretch the "implied powers" of the Constitution to accommodate the Louisiana Purchase. Such compromises, said Randolph, were catastrophic: "The old Republican party is already ruined, past redemption."

AARON BURR Burr graduated from what is now Princeton University at the age of sixteen, where he studied theology. After the United States gained its independence, Burr changed his focus to law, a profession he would return to after his failed conspiracy to take control of the Louisiana Territory ruined his hopes of government service.

The Burr Conspiracy

Meanwhile, Aaron Burr continued to plot and scheme. After the controversy over his duel with Alexander Hamilton subsided, he tried to carve out his own personal empire in the West. What came to be known as the Burr conspiracy was hatched when Burr and General James Wilkinson, an old friend then serving as senior general of the U.S. Army and secretly being paid by the Spanish for spying, plotted to use a well-armed force of volunteers to separate part of the Louisiana Territory from the Union and declare it an independent republic, with New Orleans as its capital and Burr as its ruler. Burr claimed that "the people of the western country were ready for revolt."

In late 1806, Burr floated down the Mississippi River with 100 volunteers, only to be arrested and transported to Richmond, Virginia, to face trial for treason before Chief Justice John Marshall. President Jefferson became personally involved, urging the court to convict Burr. In the end, however, Burr was acquitted for a lack of evidence. With further charges pending, he skipped bail and took refuge in France. He returned in 1812 and resumed practicing law in New York.

Slave Trade Legislation

President Jefferson had little time to fret over the escapades of Aaron Burr; other pressing issues demanded his attention. On December 2, 1806, in his annual message to Congress, Jefferson deplored the "violations of human rights" caused by the global trafficking in enslaved Africans. He reminded Congress that the Constitution allowed for the ending of the international slave trade on January 1, 1808. Congress agreed, and in 1807 the president signed a landmark bill that stopped the importation of enslaved Africans into the United States. At the time, South Carolina was the only state that still permitted the foreign slave trade. The new law ending the importation of slaves did nothing to stop the buying and selling of slaves within the

United States, however. In fact, the banning of slaves imported from Africa made enslaved Americans even more valuable, and the number of slave auctions actually increased as the southern cotton economy flourished.

War in the Mediterranean and Europe

The Barbary Pirates

Issues of foreign relations emerged early in Jefferson's first term, when events in the distant Mediterranean Sea gave him second thoughts about the need for American warships. On the Barbary Coast of North Africa, the Islamic rulers of Morocco, Algiers, Tunis, and Tripoli had specialized in piracy, preying upon European and American ships. After the Revolution, **Barbary pirates** continued to capture American vessels and enslave the crews. The U.S. government made ransom payments, first to Morocco in 1786, then to the others in the 1790s. In 1801, however, the pasha (ruler) of Tripoli upped

***BURNING OF THE FRIGATE*, PHILADELPHIA** Lieutenant Stephen Decatur set fire to the captured *Philadelphia* during the United States' standoff with Tripoli over the enslavement of American sailors.
Why was the United States at war with Tripoli?

his demands and declared war on the United States. Jefferson sent warships to blockade Tripoli. A naval war dragged on until 1805, punctuated in 1804 by the notable exploit of Lieutenant Stephen Decatur, who slipped into Tripoli Harbor by night and set fire to the frigate *Philadelphia*, which had been captured (along with its crew) after it ran aground. The pasha finally settled for a $60,000 ransom and released the *Philadelphia*'s crew, whom he had held hostage for more than a year. It was still ransom (called "tribute" in the nineteenth century), but far less than the $300,000 the pasha had initially demanded and much less than the cost of war.

Naval Harassment by Britain and France

In his first term, Jefferson had been able to avoid most foreign entanglements, particularly the new war in Europe pitting Napoleonic France against Great Britain. During his second term, however, the expanding European war (1803–1815) forced him to take action to protect America's economic interests. In May 1806, Britain's desperate war with France led it to declare a naval blockade of the entire European coast to prevent merchant ships from making port in France. Because the United States was officially "neutral" in the war, its ships were allowed by international law to carry cargo from the islands in the French and Spanish West Indies through the British blockade to French ports. The British quickly decided to end such commerce, however.

The tense situation posed a dilemma for American merchants. If they agreed to British demands to stop trading with the French, their Europe-bound cargoes would be subject to seizure by the French navy, and vice versa. French and British efforts to control trade across the Atlantic soon brought Americans into the war. Hundreds of American ships were intercepted by both warring nations and their cargoes seized.

For American seamen, the danger was heightened by the British practice of *impressment*, whereby British sailors forcibly boarded American ships and captured Americans they claimed were British citizens who had deserted the Royal Navy. American merchant ships paid seamen more than twice as much as did the Royal Navy, so thousands of British sailors had deserted the navy to work on American ships. Needing 12,000 new sailors each year to man its growing fleet of warships, the British wanted their deserters back, but they often did not bother to determine the citizenship of those they took off American vessels and impressed into service for the British navy. The British often impressed American citizens who had been born in Britain, claiming "once a British citizen, always a British citizen," even if the United States had granted citizenship.

To Americans, the British practice of impressment assaulted the honor and dignity of the newly independent nation. As Senator John Quincy Adams, the son of former president John Adams, groused, impressment was "kidnapping on the ocean." Between 1803 and 1811, some 6,200 American sailors were impressed into the British navy.

In early 1807, Napoléon responded to the British blockade of Europe by sending French warships to blockade the ports of Great Britain. The British

> "Impressment"

Barbary pirates North Africans who waged war (1801–1805) on the United States after Jefferson refused to pay tribute (a bribe) to protect American ships.

PREPARATION FOR WAR TO DEFEND COMMERCE
Shipbuilders, like those pictured here constructing the *Philadelphia*, played an important role in the war efforts against America's many rivals.

then announced that they would no longer allow any foreign ships to trade with the French islands in the Caribbean.

Again, the United States was caught in the crossfire between the two warring European powers. On June 22, 1807, the British warship HMS *Leopard* stopped a U.S. vessel, the *Chesapeake*, about eight miles off the Virginia coast. After the *Chesapeake*'s captain refused to allow the British to search his ship for British deserters, the *Leopard* opened fire, killing three Americans and wounding eighteen. The *Chesapeake* was forced to surrender. A British search party seized four men, one of whom was later hanged for desertion from the British navy.

The British attack on the *Chesapeake* was both an act of war and a national insult. "We have never, on any occasion, witnessed . . . such a thirst for revenge," the *Washington Federalist* reported. Public anger was so great that President Jefferson could have declared war on the spot.

In early July, Jefferson met with his cabinet before issuing a proclamation banning all British warships from American waters. He also called on state governors to mobilize their militia units. Like John Adams before him, however, Jefferson resisted war fever, in part because the United States was not prepared for a major war. Jefferson's caution outraged his critics. A politician eager for war called Jefferson a "dish of skim milk curdling at the head of our nation."

The Embargo Act (1807)

Eager to avoid a war with Britain, President Jefferson convinced Congress to cut off all American trade with Europe. As Jefferson said, his choices were "war, embargo, or nothing." The unprecedented **Embargo Act** (December 1807) stopped all American ships from leaving for foreign ports. Trade with foreign nations was banned. Jefferson and his secretary of state, James Madison, assumed that the loss of trade with America would quickly force the warring nations of Europe to quit violating American rights. Jefferson and Madison, however, would be proven wrong, as neither Britain nor France yielded.

With each passing month, the embargo devastated the American economy, especially in New England, where merchants howled because the embargo cut off their primary industry: oceangoing commerce. The value of American exports plummeted from $48 million in 1807 to $9 million a year later. Shipbuilding declined by two-thirds, and prices for farm crops were cut in half. New England's once-thriving port cities—Boston, Salem, and Providence—were like ghost towns. Thirty thousand unemployed American

Embargo Act (1807) A law promoted by President Thomas Jefferson prohibiting American ships from leaving for foreign ports, in order to safeguard them from British and French attacks. This ban on American exports proved disastrous to the U.S. economy.

sailors wandered the streets, drinking and cursing Jefferson's unpopular embargo.

Meanwhile, smuggling grew rampant, especially along the border with Canada. While American merchant ships sat idle, the British gained a near monopoly on trade with Canada and the islands in the West Indies. Americans in every region but especially New England grew furious at "Jefferson's embargo." A Bostonian wrote the president to report that he was "in a starving condition" and accused Jefferson of being "one of the greatest tyrants in the whole world." Another told the president that he had paid $400 to four friends "to shoot you if you don't take off the embargo."

OGRABME, OR, THE AMERICAN SNAPPING-TURTLE A merchant trying to trade with the British is held back by a so-called Ograbme (*embargo* spelled backward) in this political cartoon from 1807. **Why was Jefferson's Embargo Act so unpopular?**

The embargo turned American politics upside down. Jefferson, the nation's leading spokesman for *reducing* the power of the federal government, now found himself *expanding* federal power into every aspect of the nation's economic life. The tiny U.S. Navy was deployed to enforce the embargo. In effect, the United States blockaded its own harbors, cutting off the profitable trade with foreign nations in an effort to avoid war. New England Federalists, eager to renew trade with Europe, now argued that the federal government was violating states' rights.

The outrage over "Jefferson's embargo" demoralized the president and other Republicans and helped revive the Federalist party in New England, which charged that the president was trying to help the French by shutting off American trade with Great Britain. At the same time, farmers and planters in the South and West also suffered; they needed to sell their surplus grain, cotton, and tobacco in Europe.

A gloomy Jefferson finally accepted failure and repealed the ill-conceived embargo in 1809, shortly before he ended the "splendid misery" of his presidency and eagerly retired "to my family, my books, and my farms" in Virginia. No one, he said, could be more relieved "on shaking off the shackles of power."

Jefferson learned a hard lesson that many of his successors would also confront: a second presidential term is rarely as successful as the first. As Jefferson admitted, "No man will ever carry out of that office [the presidency] the reputation which carried him into it."

In the election of 1808, the presidency passed to another prominent Virginian, Jefferson's close friend and fellow Republican, Secretary of State James Madison. The Federalists, backing Charles C. Pinckney of South Carolina and Rufus King of New York, won only 47 electoral votes to Madison's 122.

ANTI-JEFFERSON SENTIMENT
This 1807 Federalist cartoon compares Washington (left, flanked by a British lion and American eagle) and Jefferson (right, with a snake and a lizard). Below Jefferson are volumes of French philosophy while Washington's volumes simply read: *Law, Order,* and *Religion.*

LOOK ON THIS PICTURE, AND ON THIS.

James Madison and the Drift to War

In his inaugural address, President Madison acknowledged that he inherited a situation "full of difficulties." He soon made them worse. Although Madison was a talented legislator and the "Father of the Constitution," he proved to be a poor chief executive, weak and indecisive. When members of Congress questioned several of his cabinet appointments, the president backed down and ended up naming second-rate men to key positions. In fact, Madison's sparkling wife, Dolley, was the only truly excellent member of his inner circle. Seventeen years younger than the president and twice his size, she was a superb First Lady who excelled at using the White House to entertain political leaders and foreign dignitaries. Journalists called her the "Queen of Washington City."

From the beginning, Madison's presidency was entangled in foreign affairs and crippled by his lack of executive experience. Madison and his advisers repeatedly overestimated the young republic's diplomatic leverage and military strength in shaping foreign policy. The result was humiliation.

Like Jefferson, Madison insisted on upholding the principle of freedom of the seas for the United States and other neutral nations, but he was unwilling to create a navy strong enough to enforce it. He continued the policy of "peaceable coercion," which was as ineffective for Madison as it had been for Jefferson. In place of the disastrous embargo, Madison convinced Congress to pass the Non-Intercourse Act (1809), which reopened trade with all countries *except* France and Great Britain and their colonies. It also authorized

Non-Intercourse Act (1809)

the president to reopen trade with France or Great Britain if either stopped violating American rights.

Madison's restrictions on American trade sparked an economic recession and brought no change in the British navy's misbehavior on the high seas. By 1811, the United States was again on the verge of war, with Americans divided again about whether Britain or France was more responsible for violating American shipping rights. When the British refused to give in, Madison reluctantly asked Congress to declare war on June 1, 1812. If the United States did not defend its rights as a neutral nation, the president explained, then Americans were "not independent people, but colonists and vassals."

On June 5, 1812, the House of Representatives voted for war, 79–49. Two weeks later, the Senate concurred by a narrower vote, 19–13. Every Federalist in Congress resisted what they called "Mr. Madison's War"; 80 percent of Republicans supported it. The southern and western states wanted war; the northeastern states, fearful of losing their essential maritime trade, opposed it.

America declares war on Great Britain (1812)

By declaring war, Republicans hoped to unite the nation, discredit the Federalists, and put an end to British-led Indian attacks along the Great Lakes and in the Ohio Valley. To generate popular support, Jefferson advised Madison that he needed, above all, "to stop Indian barbarities. The conquest of Canada will do this." Jefferson and others lusting for war were convinced that the French Canadians were eager to rise up against their British rulers. With their help, the Republicans assumed, Americans would easily conquer Britain's sprawling northern colony. It did not work out that way.

The War of 1812

In the **War of 1812** the United States found itself in yet another conflict with Great Britain, barely thirty years after the Revolutionary War had ended. It was the first time in American history that Congress formally used its war-making powers detailed in the Constitution. Great Britain did not want the war; it was preoccupied with defeating Napoléon in Europe. In fact, on June 16, 1812, the British government sought to avert war by deciding to quit interfering with American shipping. But President Madison and the Republicans were not satisfied; they said the war would proceed in order to put an end to the British practice of impressment as well as British-inspired Indian attacks. Why the United States chose to declare the war remains a puzzle still debated among historians.

CORE **OBJECTIVE**

3. Explain the primary causes of the American decision to declare war on Great Britain in 1812.

War of 1812 (1812–1815) Conflict fought in North America and at sea between Great Britain and the United States over American shipping rights and British-inspired Indian attacks on American settlements. Canadians and Native Americans also fought in the war on each side.

American Shipping Rights and Honor

The main cause of the war—the repeated British violations of American shipping rights and the humiliating practice of impressing sailors off American ships dominated President Madison's war message. Most of the votes for war came from congressmen representing rural regions from Pennsylvania

BRITISH IMPRESSMENT Three American sailors were forced to abandon their ship and join the British forces. This humiliating practice was common in the years before the War of 1812. **How did Congress use impressment as one of its justifications for the war?**

southward and westward, where farmers and planters grew surpluses for export to Europe. They had real economic interests that were being hurt by the raids on American merchant ships. However, the representatives from the New England states, which bore the brunt of British attacks on U.S. shipping, voted *against* the declaration of war, 20–12. As a New England minister roared, let the "southern *Heroes* fight their own battles."

One explanation for this seeming inconsistency is that many Americans in the South and West, especially Tennessee and Kentucky, voted for war because they believed America's honor was at stake. A proud Tennessean, Andrew Jackson, declared that he was eager to fight "for the re-establishment of our national character." When asked what the United States would "lose by maintaining the peace," Kentucky congressman Henry Clay, the new Speaker of the House, answered forcefully: "Commerce, character, [and] a nation's best treasure, honor!" In the popular phrase of the time, the war was needed to protect "Free Trade and Sailors' Rights!"

Native American Conflicts

The British-allied Indian attacks in Ohio Valley

Another factor leading to war was the growing number of British-allied Indian attacks in the Ohio Valley. During the early nineteenth century, land-hungry settlers and speculators kept moving into Indian lands. It was an old story, dating from the Jamestown settlement, but one that took a new turn with the rise of two brilliant Shawnee leaders, Tecumseh and his half brother, Tenskwatawa.

Tecumseh (Shooting Star) knew that the fate of the Indians depended on their being unified. His hope was to create a single nation powerful enough, with British assistance, to fend off further American expansion. Tenskwatawa (Open Door), a one-eyed recovering alcoholic with a fierce temper who was known as "the Prophet" and claimed to have been visited by the Great Spirit, gained a large following among Native Americans for his repeated prediction that the white Americans ("children of the devil") were on the verge of collapse. He demanded that the indigenous peoples abandon all things European: clothing, customs, Christianity, and especially liquor. If they did so, the Great Spirit would reward them by turning the whites' gunpowder to sand.

From his large village called Prophetstown on the Tippecanoe River in northern Indiana, Tecumseh, inspired by his brother's spiritual message, traveled in 1811 from Canada to the Gulf of Mexico to form alliances with other Native American nations (Shawnee and Creek; Cherokee and Mohegan; Miami, Delaware, and Kickapoo; Choctaw and Chickasaw; Chippewa and Ottawa) to defend their hunting grounds. "The whites have driven us from the sea to the lakes," he declared. "We can go no further." Tecumseh disavowed the many treaties whereby indigenous peoples had "sold" ancient Indian lands. "No tribe," he declared, "has the right to sell [land], even to each other, much less to strangers. . . . Sell a country!? Why not sell the air, the great sea, as well as the earth? Didn't the Great Spirit make them all for the use of his children?"

William Henry Harrison, governor of the Indiana Territory, learned of Tecumseh's bold plans, met with him twice, and described him as "one of those uncommon geniuses who spring up occasionally to produce revolutions and overturn the established order of things." Yet Harrison vowed to eliminate Tecumseh and his dream of a unified Indian nation.

In the fall of 1811, Harrison gathered 1,000 troops and advanced on Prophetstown, while Tecumseh was away. Tenskwatawa was lured into making a foolish attack on Harrison's encampment. The **Battle of Tippecanoe** was a disastrous defeat for the Native Americans. Harrison's troops burned the village and destroyed its supplies. **Tecumseh's Indian Confederacy** went up in smoke, and he fled to Canada.

TECUMSEH A leader of the Shawnee, Tecumseh tried to unite Native American nations in opposition to European culture and in defense of their ancestral lands; he was later killed in 1813 at the Battle of the Thames.

The Lust for Canada and Florida

Some Americans wanted war with Great Britain because they lusted to acquire Canada, not only as a means of expanding American territory and eliminating the British presence there but also as a way to gain a monopoly over the lucrative fur trade with the indigenous peoples ("First Nations") in Canada. That there were nearly 8 million Americans in 1812 and only 300,000 Canadians led many prowar Americans to believe that the conquest of Canada would be quick and easy. An ill-informed Jefferson had told Madison that the American "acquisition of Canada" was simply a "matter of marching" north with a military force.

The British were also vulnerable far to the south. East Florida, which the British had returned to Spain in 1783, posed a threat to the Americans because Spain was too weak (or simply unwilling) to prevent Indian attacks across the border with Georgia. In the absence of effective Spanish control of the border, British agents and traders remained in East Florida, smuggling goods and conspiring with Indians along the coast of the Gulf of Mexico. Spanish Florida had also long been a haven for runaway slaves from Georgia and South Carolina. Many Americans living along the Florida-Georgia border hoped that the

Battle of Tippecanoe (1811) Battle in northern Indiana between U.S. troops and Native American warriors led by prophet Tenskwatawa, the half-brother of Tecumseh.

Tecumseh's Indian Confederacy A group of Native American nations under leadership of Shawnees Tecumseh and Tenskwatawa; its mission of fighting off American expansion was thwarted at the Battle of Tippecanoe (1811), when the confederacy fell apart.

war against Great Britain would enable them to oust the British and Spain from Florida and make it an American territory.

War Fever

Defending America's "national honor"

Such concerns helped generate excited support for war against Great Britain. In the Congress that assembled in late 1811, new young representatives from southern and western districts shouted for war in defense of "national honor" and to rid the Northwest of the "Indian problem." Among the "war hawks" were Henry Clay of Kentucky and John C. Calhoun of South Carolina. After they entered the House, John Randolph of Virginia said, "We have heard but one word . . . one eternal monotonous tone—Canada! Canada! Canada!" Clay, the new Speaker of the House, was a tall, rawboned man who yearned for war. He was all "for resistance by the *sword*" and boasted that the Kentucky militia alone could conquer British Canada.

Clay's bravado inspired others. "I don't like Henry Clay," Calhoun said. "He is a bad man, an imposter, a creator of wicked schemes. I wouldn't speak to him, but, by God, I love him" for wanting war. When Calhoun heard about Madison's decision for war, he threw his arms around Clay's neck and led his colleagues in an Indian war dance.

In New England and much of New York, however, there was little enthusiasm for war. Another conflict with Great Britain threatened to cripple the region's dominant industry, shipping, since Great Britain remained the region's largest trading partner. Federalists not only criticized President Madison for declaring war; a few of them, both men and women, were charged with being British spies ("the blackest treason"—but technically not yet a crime for civilians to do so) while others were caught smuggling goods to the British. In 1814, the Massachusetts governor secretly asked the British what they would do if New England seceded from the United States. Republicans dismissed the anti-war Federalists as traitors. Former president Jefferson claimed that the "Republicans are the nation," implying that the Federalists were "Tories," British loyalists.

War Preparations

As it turned out, the war hawks would get neither Canada nor Florida because the United States was unprepared for war, both financially and militarily. The emphasis of Republican presidents Jefferson and Madison on small federal budgets and military cutbacks proved to be an ineffective way to win a war, and Madison, a small, soft-spoken man, lacked the military qualities needed to inspire national confidence and resolve. He was no George Washington.

Moreover, the national economy was weak. In 1811, despite pleas from the Treasury secretary, Congress had let the charter of the Bank of the United States expire. In addition, once war began, the mighty British navy blockaded American ports and cut off imports, a major source of national revenue. By March 1813, Albert Gallatin warned Madison that the U.S. Treasury had "hardly enough money to last till the end of the month." Furthermore, the demise of the Bank of the United States brought confusion to the nation's financial system. Loans were needed to cover the war's costs, and critics of the war were reluctant to lend money to the federal government.

The military situation was almost as bad. When the War of 1812 began, the U.S. Army numbered only 3,287 ill-trained and poorly equipped men, led by mostly incompetent officers. In January 1812, Congress authorized an army of 35,000 men, but a year later, just 18,500 had been recruited, many of them poor Irish immigrants who hated the English. President Madison refused to allow free blacks or slaves to serve in the army, so he had to plead with the state governors to provide militiamen, only to see the Federalist governors in anti-war New England refuse.

The British, on the other hand, had thousands of soldiers stationed in Canada and the West Indies. And, as was true during the Revolutionary War, the British, offering food, guns, and ammunition, recruited more Native American allies than did the Americans in 1812. In all, more than two dozen Indian nations participated in the war.

The U.S. Navy was in better shape than the army, with able officers and well-trained seamen, but it had only 16 warships, compared to Britain's 600. In the first year of the war, the navy produced the only U.S. victories, in isolated duels with British vessels. Courageous American seamen, however, could not stop the British from blockading the U.S. coast, except for New England, where the British hoped to strengthen antiwar sentiment. The lopsided military strength of the British led President Madison to mutter that the United States was in "an embarrassing situation."

A Continental War

The War of 1812 was really three wars fought on three separate fronts. One theater of conflict was the Chesapeake Bay along the coast of Maryland and Virginia, including Washington, D.C. The second was in the South, in Alabama, Mississippi, and Florida, culminating in the Battle of New Orleans in 1815. In that region, American forces led by General Andrew Jackson invaded lands owned by the Creeks and the Spanish. The third war might be more accurately called the Canadian-American War. It began in the region around Lakes Huron and Michigan. There the fighting raged back and forth along the ill-defined border between the United States and British Canada.

The War in the North

The only place where the United States could attack the British on land was Canada. There the war would essentially become a civil war, very much like the American Revolution. One side—Canadians, many of whom were former American Loyalists who had fled north in 1783—remained loyal to the British Empire, while the Americans and a few French Canadians sought to push Britain out of North America. Indians armed with British-supplied weapons dominated the heavily wooded area around the Great Lakes. Michigan's

U.S. NAVAL VICTORIES
In this cartoon, John Bull (the personification of England) is "stung to agony" by *Wasp* and *Hornet*, two American ships that clinched early victories in the War of 1812.

governor recognized that the British and their Indian allies were dependent upon each other: "The British cannot hold Upper Canada without the assistance of the Indians," but the "Indians cannot conduct a war without the assistance of a civilized nation [Great Britain]."

For the American assault on British Canada, President James Madison approved a three-pronged plan. It called for one U.S. army to move north through upstate New York, along Lake Champlain, to take Montreal, while another was to advance into Upper Canada by crossing the Niagara River between Lakes Ontario and Erie. The third attack would come from the west, with an American force moving east into Upper Canada from Detroit, Michigan.

The plan was to have all three attacks begin at the same time in order to force the British troops in Canada to split up. Like so many complex war plans, however, this one was a disaster, in large part because the Americans could barely field one army, much less three, and communications among the various commanders was spotty at best.

In July 1812, General William Hull, a Revolutionary War veteran and governor of the Michigan Territory, marched his disorganized and poorly supplied army across the Detroit River into Canada, announcing to the Canadians, most of them French, that he was there to free them from British "tyranny and oppression."

The American invaders, however, were soon pushed back to Detroit by a smaller number of British troops and their Indian allies. Sickly and distracted by too much whiskey, the timid Hull was tricked by the opposing British commander's threats to unleash thousands of Indian warriors led by Tecumseh. Fearing a massacre by "savages," Hull suddenly surrendered his entire force to the British bluff. His surrender shocked the nation. Madison and the Republicans felt humiliated; the American soldiers appeared to be cowards. In Kentucky a Republican said General Hull must be a "traitor" or "nearly an idiot" or "part of both."

The second prong of the American invasion plan, the assault on Montreal, never got off the ground. The third American attack began at dawn on October 13, 1812. U.S. troops led by General Stephen Van Rensselaer, New York's wealthiest landowner, rowed across the Niagara River from Lewiston, New York, to invade the Canadian village of Queenston but suffered a crushing defeat in the Battle of Queenston Heights. Some 925 American soldiers surrendered, and Van Rensselaer resigned his command in shame. The failures led many Americans to fear the war would be lost. In early 1813, a Kentuckian warned that any more military disasters would result in "disunion," and the "cause of Republicanism will be lost."

Thereafter, in the northern borderland between the United States and Canada, a powerful alliance of British troops, Canadian militiamen, and Indians repeatedly repelled U.S. invasion attempts. The bruised Americans then sought to gain naval control of the Great Lakes and other inland waterways along the Canadian border. If they could control Lake Erie, they could divide the British and their Indian allies.

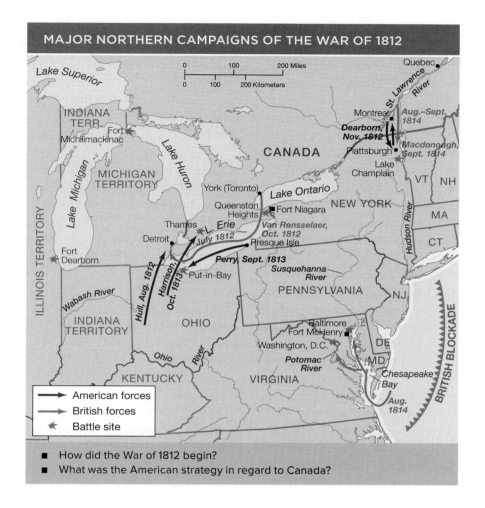

MAJOR NORTHERN CAMPAIGNS OF THE WAR OF 1812

- How did the War of 1812 begin?
- What was the American strategy in regard to Canada?

In 1813 at Presque Isle, Pennsylvania (near Erie), twenty-eight-year-old Oliver Hazard Perry supervised the construction of warships from timber cut in nearby forests. By the end of the summer, Commodore Perry set out in search of the British, finally finding them at Lake Erie's Put-in-Bay on September 10. After completing preparations for battle, Perry told his aide, "This is the most important day of my life."

Two British warships used their superior weapons to pound the *Lawrence*, Perry's flagship. After four hours of intense shelling, none of the *Lawrence*'s guns were working, and most of the crew were dead or wounded. Perry refused to quit, however. He switched to another vessel, kept fighting, and miraculously ended up forcing the surrender of the entire British squadron. Hatless and bloodied, Perry famously reported that "we have met the enemy and they are ours."

American naval control of Lake Erie forced the British to evacuate Upper Canada. They gave up Detroit and were then defeated at the Battle of the Thames in southern Canada on October 5, 1813. During the battle, the British fled, leaving Tecumseh and 500 warriors to face the wrath of the Americans. When Tecumseh was killed, the Indians retreated.

Perry's victory on Lake Erie and the army's defeat of Tecumseh and the British force enabled the Americans to recover control of Michigan and seize the Western District of Upper Canada. At last, the war on the western front had turned in favor of the Americans. Thereafter, the war in the north lapsed into a military stalemate along the Canadian border punctuated by occasional plunder and looting, with neither side able to dislodge the other.

The Creek War

In the South, too, the war flared up in 1813. The Creeks in Georgia and Alabama had split into two factions: the Upper Creeks (or Red Sticks), who opposed American expansion into their lands and sided with the British and Spanish during the War of 1812, and the Lower Creeks, who wanted to remain on good terms with the Americans. On August 30, Red Sticks, allied with the British, attacked Fort Mims, on the Alabama River thirty miles above the Gulf coast town of Mobile, killing 553 men, women, and children, butchering and scalping half of them.

The massacre outraged Americans. Thirsting for revenge, Andrew Jackson, commanding general of the Army of West Tennessee, recruited about 2,500 volunteers and headed south. Jackson was a natural warrior and a gifted commander. From a young age, he had embraced violence, gloried in it, and prospered by it. He had a volcanic temper and a ferocious will that inspired obedience and loyalty. He told all "brave Tennesseans" that their "frontier [was] threatened with invasion by the savage foe" and that the Indians were advancing "with scalping knives unsheathed, to butcher your wives, your children, and your helpless babes. Time is not to be lost."

Jackson's volunteers crushed the Red Sticks in Alabama. The decisive battle occurred on March 27, 1814, at Horseshoe Bend on the Tallapoosa River. Jackson's soldiers and their Cherokee and Creek allies surrounded a Red Stick fort, set fire to it, and shot the Indians as they tried to escape. Nine hundred of them were killed, including 300 who drowned in a desperate effort to cross the river. Jackson reported to his wife that the *"carnage was dreadful."* His men had "regained all the scalps taken from Fort Mims." Fewer than fifty of Jackson's soldiers were killed.

The Battle of Horseshoe Bend was the worst defeat ever inflicted upon Native Americans. With the Treaty of Fort Jackson, signed in August 1814, the devastated Red Stick Creeks were forced at gunpoint to give up two thirds of their land—some 23 million acres—including southwest Georgia and much of Alabama. Red Eagle, chief of the Red Sticks, told Jackson: "I am in your power. . . .My people are all gone. I can do no more but weep over the misfortunes of my nation." For his part, Jackson declared that "the power of the Creeks is I think forever broken." President Madison rewarded Jackson by naming him a major general in the regular army of the United States.

Soon after the Battle of Horseshoe Bend, events in Europe took a dramatic turn when the British, Spanish, and Portuguese armies repelled French emperor Napoléon's effort to conquer Spain and Portugal. Now free to deal with the United States, the British in the summer of 1814 sent 16,000 veteran

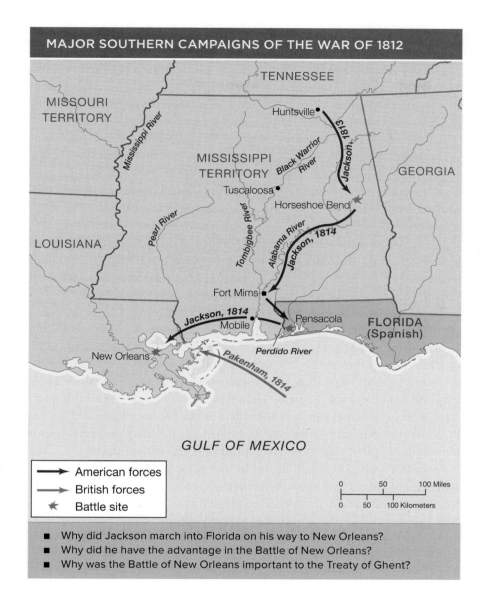

MAJOR SOUTHERN CAMPAIGNS OF THE WAR OF 1812

- Why did Jackson march into Florida on his way to New Orleans?
- Why did he have the advantage in the Battle of New Orleans?
- Why was the Battle of New Orleans important to the Treaty of Ghent?

soldiers from Europe to try again to invade America from Canada. The British navy extended their blockade to include the New England ports, and they bombarded coastal towns from Delaware to Florida. The final piece of the British plan was to seize New Orleans and sever American access to the Mississippi River, the economic lifeline of the western states.

Thomas Macdonough's Naval Victory

The main British military effort in the War of 1812 focused on launching a massive invasion of the United States from Canada. But the outnumbered American defenders at Plattsburgh, New York, along Lake Champlain, were saved by the superb ability of Commodore Thomas Macdonough, commander of the U.S. naval squadron. On September 11, 1814, the British soldiers attacked the Americans at Plattsburgh while their warships engaged Macdonough's navy in a battle that surprisingly ended with the entire British fleet either destroyed or captured. The Battle of Lake Champlain (also called the Battle of Plattsburgh) forced the British to abandon the northern campaign. The British forces retreated into Canada. When the British officers came aboard the American flagship to surrender, Macdonough said, "Gentlemen, return your swords to your scabbards; you are worthy of them."

Fighting in the Chesapeake

The American naval victory at Lake Champlain could not have been more timely. Just weeks before, U.S. forces had suffered the most humiliating experience of the war as British troops captured and burned Washington, D.C. In August 1814, 4,000 British soldiers landed at Benedict, Maryland, and headed briskly for the American capital, thirty-five miles away. Thousands of frightened Americans fled the city. President Madison frantically called out the militia, then courageously left the White House (Madison was the first president to call it that) to encourage the soldiers confronting the British army. His words had little effect: the Americans melted in the face of the British attack.

On August 24, 1814, the British marched unopposed into the American capital. British officers ate a meal in the White House that had been prepared for Madison and his wife, Dolley, who had fled the grounds just in time, after first saving a copy of the Declaration of Independence and George Washington's portrait. The vengeful British, aware that American troops had earlier burned the Canadian capital at York (Toronto), then torched the White House, the Capitol, the Library of Congress, and most other government buildings. A tornado the next day compounded the damage, but a violent thunderstorm dampened both the fires and the enthusiasm of the British forces, who headed north to assault Baltimore.

The destruction of Washington, D.C., infuriated Americans. A Baltimore newspaper reported that the "spirit of the nation is roused." That spirit of determination showed itself when fifty British warships sailed into Baltimore Harbor on September 13 while the British army assaulted the city on land. About a thousand Americans held Fort McHenry on an island in the harbor.

The British fleet unleashed a nightlong bombardment of the fort. Yet the Americans refused to surrender. Francis Scott Key, a Washington, D.C., lawyer and occasional poet, watched the siege from a British ship, having been sent to negotiate the release of a captured American. The sight of the American flag still flying over Fort McHenry at dawn meant that the city had survived the British onslaught. The scene inspired Key to scribble the verses of what came to be called "The Star-Spangled Banner," which began, "Oh, say can you see by the dawn's early light?" Later revised and set to the tune of an English drinking song, it eventually became America's national anthem. The inability of the British to conquer Fort McHenry led them to abandon the attack on Baltimore.

THE BURNING OF THE CAPITOL
This 1817 etching of the burnt Capitol shows shackled slaves (bottom right) and angels overhead. It appeared in a book arguing that the destruction of "the temple of freedom" was a sign that God disapproved of slavery.

The war in the Chesapeake, despite the destruction of Washington, D.C., was ultimately a British failure, since the invading army withdrew to its ships and left the region. Still, the British raids into Maryland and Virginia shocked Americans, especially slaveholders, because the presence of British troops encouraged thousands of slaves to run away and join the invaders. As had happened during the Revolutionary War, the British promised freedom to slaves who aided or fought with them, and almost 3,000 escaped to join British units before eventually being taken to Canada. One of them, Jeremiah West, wrote his former owner in Virginia in 1818: "Thank God I can enjoy all comforts under the flag of England and here I shall remain."

The Aftermath of the War

While the fighting raged in the United States, American diplomats had begun meetings in Ghent, near Brussels in present-day Belgium, to discuss ending the war. The negotiations were at a standstill when news arrived of the American victory at the Battle of Lake Champlain and the failure of the British invasion of Baltimore. The news led the British to grow more flexible, but negotiations dragged on throughout the fall. Finally, on Christmas Eve 1814, the diplomats reached an agreement to stop the fighting.

The Treaty of Ghent

The war-weary British decided to end the war in part because of military setbacks but also because London merchants were eager to renew the profitable trade with America. By the **Treaty of Ghent**, signed on December 24, 1814, the two sides agreed to end the war, return the prisoners, and restore

> CORE **OBJECTIVE**
> **5.** Analyze the most significant outcomes of the War of 1812 on the United States.

Treaty of Ghent (1814) Agreement between Great Britain and the United States that ended the War of 1812.

the previous boundaries. The British also pledged to stop supporting Indian attacks along the Great Lakes. What had begun as an American effort to protect its honor, end impressment, and invade and conquer Canada had turned into a second war of independence against the world's greatest empire. Although the Americans lost the war for Canada and saw their national capital captured and burned, they won the southern war to defeat the Indians and take their lands. More important, the treaty saved the fragile and splintered republic from possible civil war and financial ruin.

The Battle of New Orleans

Because it took six weeks for news of the Treaty of Ghent to reach the United States, fighting continued in America. Along the Gulf coast during December 1814, forty-seven-year-old General Andrew Jackson had, without authorization, invaded the Panhandle region of Spanish Florida and taken Pensacola, putting an end to British efforts to organize Indian attacks on American settlements in Georgia.

In mid-December, Jackson was in Louisiana, where he supervised efforts to defend New Orleans. A British fleet, with some 8,000 seasoned soldiers fresh from victory over Napoléon in Europe, took up positions just south of New Orleans, the second-busiest port in the United States (after New York City). The British hoped to capture New Orleans and thereby control the entire Mississippi Valley. New England Federalists, fed up with "Mr. Madison's War," predicted that New Orleans would be lost; some called for Madison's impeachment.

British general Sir Edward Pakenham's painfully careful approach—he waited weeks until he had cannons in place to support his soldiers—gave Jackson time to organize hundreds of slaves "loaned" by planters to erect American defenses around New Orleans. The Americans built up an almost invulnerable position, but Pakenham rashly ordered a frontal assault at dawn on January 8, 1815. His brave redcoats, including all-black units from the Caribbean islands, ran into a murderous hail of artillery shells and rifle fire. Before the British withdrew, nearly 2,000 had been wounded or killed, including Pakenham and two other generals. American casualties were minimal. A British officer wrote that there "never was a more complete failure." When the British finally boarded their ships to leave America, several hundred runaway slaves joined them.

Although the **Battle of New Orleans** occurred after the Treaty of Ghent had been signed in Europe, it was still a vitally important psychological victory, as the treaty had yet to be officially ratified by either the United States or Great Britain. Had the British won at New Orleans, they might have tried to revise the treaty in their favor. Jackson's lopsided victory ensured that both governments would act quickly to officially approve the treaty—and it made Jackson a hero. The general, wrote a southerner in April 1815, "is everywhere hailed as the savior of the country. . . . He has been feasted, caressed, & I may say idolized."

Battle of New Orleans (1815) Final major battle in the War of 1812, in which the Americans under General Andrew Jackson unexpectedly and decisively countered the British attempt to seize the port of New Orleans, Louisiana.

JACKSON'S ARMY DEFENDS NEW ORLEANS Unaware that the war was over, in January 1815 Andrew Jackson led his troops (many of them slaves) to a decisive victory over the British at New Orleans. **What was the diplomatic and symbolic importance of Jackson's victory?**

The Hartford Convention

Weeks before the Battle of New Orleans, many New Englanders, fed up with the war and the loss of revenue caused by the stoppage of British trade, tried to take matters into their own hands at a meeting in Hartford, Connecticut. The **Hartford Convention** was the climax of New England's disgust with "Mr. Madison's War." Both Massachusetts and Connecticut had refused to contribute soldiers to the war effort, and merchants had continued to sell supplies to British troops in Canada. In 1814, however, the British navy extended its blockade to New England, occupied Maine, and raided several coastal towns. Even Boston seemed threatened. Instead of rallying to the American flag, however, Federalists in the Massachusetts legislature voted in October 1814 to hold a convention of New England states to protest the war.

On December 15, 1814, the Hartford Convention assembled with delegates from Massachusetts, Rhode Island, Connecticut, Vermont, and New Hampshire. The convention proposed several constitutional amendments designed to limit Republican (and southern) influence: (1) abolishing the counting of slaves in determining a state's representation in Congress, (2) requiring a two-thirds supermajority rather than a simple majority vote to declare war or admit new states, (3) prohibiting trade embargoes lasting more than sixty days, (4) excluding foreign-born people from holding federal office, (5) limiting the president to one term, and (6) barring successive presidents from the same state (a provision clearly directed at Virginia).

Their call for a later convention in Boston carried the unmistakable threat of secession—the possibility of New England leaving the United States—if these demands were dismissed. Yet the threat quickly evaporated. In February 1815, when messengers from Hartford reached Washington,

Hartford Convention (1815) A series of secret meetings in December 1814 and January 1815 at which New England Federalists protested American involvement in the War of 1812 and discussed several constitutional amendments, including limiting each president to one term, designed to weaken the dominant Republican party.

D.C., they found the battered capital celebrating the good news from New Orleans. "Their position," according to a French diplomat, was "awkward, embarrassing, and lent itself to cruel ridicule." Ignored by Congress and the president, the Hartford delegates swiftly withdrew their recommendations. The incident proved fatal to the Federalist party, which never recovered from the shame of disloyalty stamped on it by the Hartford Convention.

The War's Legacies

There was no clear victor in the War of 1812, nor much clarification about the issues that ignited the war. The Treaty of Ghent ended the fighting but failed to address the reasons why President Madison had declared war in the first place: the disputes about maritime rights and the British practice of impressment.

"Second war of independence"

Yet that did not mean that the war was without consequences. For all the clumsiness with which it was fought, the war generated an intense patriotism across much of the nation and reaffirmed American independence. The young republic was at last secure from British or European threats. "By the war," said Secretary of State James Monroe, "we have acquired a character and a rank among the other nations, which we did not enjoy before." The nation grew more confident and more powerful by surviving a "second war of independence" against the greatest power on earth. America emerged from the fighting with new symbols of nationhood and a new gallery of heroes. The people, observed Treasury secretary Albert Gallatin, "are more American; they feel and act more as a nation; and I hope that the permanency of the Union is thereby better secured."

Economic independence

The war also propelled the United States toward economic independence, as the wartime interruption of trade with Europe encouraged the growth of America's own industrial sector. The British blockade of the American coast during the war created a shortage of cotton cloth in the United States, leading to the creation of the nation's first cotton-manufacturing industry, in Waltham, Massachusetts. By the end of the war, there were over a hundred cotton mills in New England and sixty-four more in Pennsylvania. "Our people have 'cotton mill fever,' as it is called," said Moses Brown of Rhode Island. "Every place [is] almost occupied with cotton mills."

After nearly forty years of independence, the new American republic was emerging as an agricultural, commercial, and industrial world power. "Never did a country occupy more lofty ground," said U.S. Supreme Court Justice Joseph Story in 1815. "We have stood the contest, single-handed, against the conqueror of Europe; and we are at peace, with all our blushing victories thick crowding on us."

Emergence as a world power

One of the strangest results of the War of 1812 and its aftermath was a reversal of attitudes toward government policy by the Republicans and the Federalists. The wartime experience taught James Madison and the Republicans some lessons in nationalism. First, the British invasion of

Washington, D.C., impressed upon Madison the necessity of a strong army and navy. Second, the lack of a national bank had greatly complicated the financing of the war; state banks were so unstable and in such turmoil that it was difficult for states and the federal government to raise the funds needed to support the war effort. In 1816, Madison, who had been formerly opposed to a national bank, changed his mind and created the Second Bank of the United States. Third, the rise of new industries during the war prompted business owners to call for increased tariffs on imports to protect the new American companies from unfair foreign competition. Madison went along, despite his criticism of tariffs in the 1790s.

While Madison reversed himself by embracing a more fervent nationalism and a broader interpretation of the Constitution, the Federalists similarly reversed themselves and took up Madison's and Jefferson's original emphasis on states' rights and strict construction of the Constitution as they tried to defend the special interests of their regional stronghold, New England. It was the first great reversal of partisan political roles in constitutional interpretation. It would not be the last.

> Reversal of political roles for Republicans and Federalists

While no borders changed because of the War of 1812, the end of the fighting proved devastating to all the eastern Indian nations, most of which had fought with the British. By agreeing to the Treaty of Ghent, the British essentially abandoned their Indian allies. None of their former lands were returned to them, and the British vacated their frontier forts that had long served as supply centers for the Indians. The Lakota chief Little Crow expressed the betrayal felt by all the British-allied Native Americans when he rejected the consolation gifts from the British commander: "After we have fought for you, endured many hardships, lost some of our people, and awakened the vengeance of our powerful neighbors, you make peace for yourselves. . . . You no longer need our service; you offer us these goods to pay us for [your] having deserted us. But no, we will not take them; we hold them and yourselves in equal contempt." In the years after the war, the United States negotiated over 200 treaties with native peoples that transferred Indian lands to America and created reservations west of the Mississippi River where the Indians were relocated.

As the Indians were pushed out, tens of thousands of Americans moved west into the Great Lakes region and southwest into Georgia, Alabama, and Mississippi after the war, occupying more territory in a single generation than had been settled in the 150 years of colonial history. With nearly an entire continent to explore and exploit, Americans streamed westward. Between 1800 and 1820, the trans-Appalachian population rose from 300,000 to 2 million. By 1840, more than 40 percent of Americans lived west of the Appalachians in eight new states. At the same time, the growing significance of slavery and its controversial extension into new western territories set in motion an explosive national debate that would test again the grand American experiment in republican government.

> Westward expansion

Reviewing the
CORE OBJECTIVES |

■ **Jefferson's Administration**
The Jeffersonian Republicans did not dismantle much of Hamilton's Federalist economic program, but they did repeal the whiskey tax, cut back on government expenditures, and promoted what was called *republican simplicity*—smaller government and plain living. While Republicans idealized the agricultural world that had existed prior to 1800, the first decades of the 1800s were a period of explosive economic and population growth in the United States, transforming the nation. Large-scale commercial agriculture and exports to Europe flourished; Americans moved west in huge numbers. The *Louisiana Purchase* dramatically expanded the boundaries of the United States. The *Lewis and Clark expedition* explored the new region and published reports that excited interest in the Far West. In *Marbury v. Madison* (1803), the Federalist chief justice of the Supreme Court, John Marshall, declared a federal act unconstitutional for the first time. With that decision, the Court assumed the right of judicial review over acts of Congress and established the constitutional supremacy of the federal government over state governments.

■ **War in Europe** Thomas Jefferson sent warships to subdue the *Barbary pirates* in North Africa and negotiated with the Spanish and French to ensure that the Mississippi River remained open to American commerce. Renewal of war between Britain and France in 1803 complicated matters for American commerce with Europe. Neither country wanted its enemy to purchase U.S. goods, so both blockaded each other's ports. In retaliation, Jefferson convinced Congress at the end of 1807 to pass the *Embargo Act*, which prohibited all foreign trade.

■ **War of 1812** Renewal of the European war in 1803 created naval conflicts with Britain and France. President James Madison ultimately declared war against Great Britain over the issue of neutral shipping rights and the fear that the British were inciting Native Americans to attack frontier settlements. Indian nations took sides in the war. Earlier, at the *Battle of Tippecanoe* (1811), U.S. troops had defeated elements of *Tecumseh's Indian Confederacy*, an alliance of Indian nations determined to protect their ancestral lands. Tecumseh led the Confederacy against the Americans during the War of 1812. At the Battle of the Thames (1813), Tecumseh was killed and the Confederacy disintegrated soon thereafter.

■ **Aftermath of the War of 1812**
The *Treaty of Ghent* (1814) ended the war by essentially declaring it a draw. A smashing American victory in January of 1815 at the *Battle of New Orleans* occurred before news of the peace treaty had reached the continent, but the lopsided American triumph helped ensure that the treaty would be ratified and enforced. One effect of the conflict was to establish the economic

independence of the United States, as goods previously purchased from Great Britain were now manufactured at home. During and after the war, Federalists and Republicans seemed to exchange roles: delegates from the waning Federalist party met at the *Hartford Convention* (1815) to defend states' rights and threaten secession, while Republicans now promoted nationalism and a broad interpretation of the Constitution.

KEY TERMS

republican simplicity *p. 231*

Marbury v. Madison (1803) *p. 233*

Louisiana Purchase (1803) *p. 235*

Lewis and Clark expedition (1804–1806) *p. 238*

Barbary pirates *p. 243*

Embargo Act (1807) *p. 244*

War of 1812 (1812–1815) *p. 247*

Battle of Tippecanoe (1811) *p. 249*

Tecumseh's Indian Confederacy *p. 249*

Treaty of Ghent (1814) *p. 257*

Battle of New Orleans (1815) *p. 258*

Hartford Convention (1815) *p. 259*

CHRONOLOGY

1801 Thomas Jefferson inaugurated as president in Washington, D.C.

Barbary pirates harass U.S. shipping and capture American sailors

The pasha of Tripoli declares war on the United States

1803 Supreme Court issues *Marbury v. Madison* decision

Louisiana Purchase

1804–1806 Lewis and Clark expedition

1804 Jefferson overwhelmingly reelected

1807 British interference with U.S. shipping increases

1808 International slave trade ended in the United States

1811 Defeat of Tecumseh's Indian Confederacy at the Battle of Tippecanoe

1812 Congress declares war on Britain

U.S. invasion of Canada

1813–1814 Creek War

1814 British capture and burn Washington, D.C.

Hartford Convention

1815 Battle of New Orleans

News of the Treaty of Ghent reaches the United States

INQUIZITIVE

Go to InQuizitive to see what you've learned—and learn what you've missed—with personalized feedback along the way.

DEBATING Thomas Jefferson and Slavery

One of the more difficult tasks that historians face is assessing the actions of historical figures within an ethical framework. Should people in the past be assessed by the standards of their time or by those of today? Should we hold celebrated historical figures to a higher ethical standard? For Part 2, *"Building a Nation,"* the complex relationship of Thomas Jefferson to slavery demonstrates how historians can disagree when they evaluate historic individuals from an ethical perspective.

This exercise involves two tasks:

PART 1: Compare the two secondary sources on Thomas Jefferson and slavery.
PART 2: Using primary sources, evaluate the arguments of the two secondary sources.

PART I Comparing and Contrasting Secondary Sources

Below are two secondary sources focused on the question of Jefferson and his relationship with slavery. The first is from Douglas L. Wilson, professor emeritus of English and codirector of the Lincoln Studies Center at Knox College; the second is written by Paul Finkelman, professor of law and public policy at the Albany Law School. In these selections, Wilson and Finkelman explore one of the great contradictions in early American history: that Thomas Jefferson, an outspoken critic of slavery, was himself a slave owner. Further complicating the matter was Jefferson's relationship with Sally Hemings, a slave with whom he had several children. Both passages grapple with the issue of *presentism*, the application of present-day ideas and beliefs onto the past.

Compare the views of these two scholars by answering the following questions. Be sure to find specific examples in the selections to support your answers.

- How does each author address the issue of presentism?

- What ethical standards do the authors use to evaluate Jefferson?

- What evidence do they offer when evaluating Jefferson?

- How does each author assess Jefferson's ethical standards?

- What ethical standard would you use?

Secondary Source 1

Douglas L. Wilson, "Thomas Jefferson and the Character Issue" (1992)

How could the man who wrote that "All men are created equal" own slaves? This, in essence, is the question most persistently asked of those who write about Thomas Jefferson, and by all indications it is the thing that contemporary Americans find most vexing about him. . . . The question carries a silent assumption that because he practiced slave holding, Jefferson must have somehow believed in it, and must therefore have been a hypocrite. My belief is that this way of asking the question . . . reflects the pervasive presentism of our time. Consider, for example, how different the question appears when inverted and framed in more historical terms: How did a man who was born into a slave holding society, whose family and admired friends owned slaves, who inherited a fortune that was dependent on slaves and slave labor, decide at an early age that slavery was morally wrong and forcefully declare that it ought to be abolished?

But when the question is explained in this way, another invariably follows: If Jefferson came to believe that holding slaves was wrong, why did he continue to hold them? ... Obstacles to emancipation in Jefferson's Virginia were formidable, and the risk was demonstrably great that emancipated slaves would enjoy little, if any, real freedom and would, unless they could pass as white, be more likely to come to grief in a hostile environment. In short, the master whose concern extended beyond his own morality to the well-being of his slaves was caught on the horns of a dilemma. Thus the question of why Jefferson didn't free his slaves only serves to illustrate how presentism involves us in mistaken assumptions about historical conditions— in this case that an eighteenth-century slave holder wanting to get out from under the moral stigma of slavery and improve the lot of his slaves had only to set them free.

Although we may find Jefferson guilty of failing to make adequate allowance for the conditions in which blacks were forced to live, Jefferson did not take the next step of concluding that blacks were fit only for slavery. This rationalization of slavery was indeed the common coin of slave holders and other whites who condoned or tolerated the "peculiar" institution, but it formed no part of Jefferson's thinking. In fact, he took the opposite position: that having imposed the depredations of slavery on blacks, white Americans should not only emancipate them but also educate and train them to be self-sufficient, provide them with necessary materials, and establish a colony in which they could live as free and independent people.

Source: Wilson, Douglas L. "Thomas Jefferson and the Character Issue." *Atlantic Monthly* November 1992, pp. 57–74.

Secondary Source 2
Paul Finkelman, "Jefferson and Slavery" (1993)

An understanding of Jefferson's relationship to slavery requires analysis of his statements on and beliefs about the institution and an account of his actions as a public leader and a private individual. Scrutinizing the contradictions between Jefferson's professions and his actions does not impose twentieth-century values on an eighteenth-century man. Because he was the author of the Declaration of Independence and a leader of the American Enlightenment, the test of Jefferson's position on slavery is not whether he was better than the worst of his generation, but whether he was the leader of the best; not whether he responded as a southerner and a planter, but whether he was able to transcend his economic interests and his sectional background to implement the ideals he articulated. Jefferson fails the test. When Jefferson wrote the Declaration, he owned over 175 slaves. While many of his contemporaries freed their slaves during and after the Revolution, Jefferson did not.

In the fifty years from 1776 until his death in 1826, a period of extraordinary public service, he did little to end slavery or to dissociate himself from his role as the master of Monticello. To the contrary, as he accumulated more slaves he worked assiduously to increase the productivity and the property values of his labor force. Nor did he encourage his countrymen to liberate their slaves, even when they sought his blessing. Even at his death Jefferson failed to fulfill the promise of his rhetoric. In his will he emancipated only five bondsmen, condemning nearly two hundred others to the auction block. . . .

. . . He knew slavery was wrong. It could not have been otherwise for an eighteenth-century natural law theorist. Many of his closest European and American friends and colleagues were leaders of the new abolition societies. Jefferson was part of a cosmopolitan "republic of letters" that was overwhelmingly hostile to slavery. But, for the most part, he suppressed his doubts, while doing virtually nothing to challenge the institution. On this issue Jefferson's genius failed him. As David Brion Davis observes, "Jefferson had only a theoretical interest in promoting the cause of abolition."

Jefferson could not live without slaves. They built his house, cooked his meals, and tilled his fields. In contrast to George Washington, Jefferson carelessly managed his lands and finances and lived beyond his means. Washington refused to traffic in slaves. Chronically in debt, Jefferson overcame his professed "scruples about selling negroes but for delinquency or on their own request," selling scores of slaves in order to make ends meet. Jefferson could not maintain his extravagant life style without his slaves and, to judge from his lifelong behavior, his grand style was far more important than the natural rights of his slaves. . . .

Throughout his life, as he condemned slavery, Jefferson implied that, however bad it was for slaves, the institution was somehow worse for whites. His concerns about the institution had more to do with its effect on whites and white society than on its true victims. . . . Jefferson's concerns were solely with the "morals and manners" of the master class. He was concerned that slavery leads to despotism by the masters; but he never expressed regret for the mistreatment of the slave. Similarly, throughout his life Jefferson expressed his fears of miscegenation and a weakening of white society through contact with blacks. He favored some form of colonization that would put blacks "beyond the reach of mixture."

Source: Finkelman, Paul. "Jefferson and Slavery: 'Treason against the Hopes of the World.'" In *Jeffersonian Legacies*, edited by Peter S. Onuf, 181–221. Charlottesville: University Press of Virginia, 1993.

PART II Using Primary Sources to Evaluate Secondary Sources

When historians are faced with competing interpretations of the past, they often look at primary source material as part of the process of evaluating the different arguments. Below are primary source materials relating to Thomas Jefferson's relationship with slavery. The first document is an excerpt from a draft of the Declaration of Independence largely written by Thomas Jefferson. This excerpt was removed from the final version of the declaration. The second document is a selection from Jefferson's 1785 book on the state of Virginia, relating to slaves and slavery. The third document is a letter Jefferson wrote while serving in Paris as the U.S. minister (ambassador) to France in 1788, and the fourth is a letter from April 1820 expressing his feelings regarding the Missouri Compromise, which admitted Missouri as a slave state and created a northern boundary for slavery in the western territories.

Carefully read the primary sources and answer the following questions. Decide which of the primary source documents support or refute Wilson's and Finkelman's arguments about Jefferson. You may find that some documents do both but for different parts of each historian's interpretation. Be sure to identify which specific components of each historian's argument the documents support or refute.

■ Which of the two historians' *arguments* is best supported by the *primary source* documents? If you find that both arguments are well supported by the evidence, why do you think the two historians had such different interpretations about Jefferson?

■ Based on the ethical standard you choose in Part I and these documents, how would *you* assess Jefferson's relationship with slavery? You may consider how Jefferson's views change over time.

■ What has using primary sources to evaluate the Wilson and Finkelman arguments taught you about making ethical assessments of historical figures?

Primary Source 1

Thomas Jefferson, *a draft section omitted from the Declaration of Independence (1776)*

He [King George III] has waged cruel war against human nature itself, violating its most sacred rights of life & liberty in the persons of a distant people [Africans] who never offended him, captivating & carrying them into slavery in another hemisphere, or to incur miserable death in their transportation thither. This piratical warfare, the opprobrium of infidel powers, is the warfare of the Christian king of Great Britain. Determined to keep open a market where men should be bought & sold, he has prostituted his negative for suppressing every legislative attempt to prohibit or to restrain this execrable [disgusting] commerce: and that this assemblage of horrors might want no fact of distinguished die, he is now exciting those very people to rise in arms among us, and to purchase that liberty of which he has deprived them, & murdering the people upon whom he also obtruded them; thus paying off former crimes committed against the liberties of one people, with crimes which he urges them to commit against the lives of another.

Source: Jefferson, Thomas. "Thomas Jefferson, June 1776, Rough Draft of the Declaration of Independence," 1776. *The Thomas Jefferson Papers Series 1. General Correspondence. 1651–1827.* American Memory, Library of Congress, Washington, D.C.

Primary Source 2

Thomas Jefferson, *Notes on the State of Virginia* (1787)

It will probably be asked, Why not retain and incorporate the Blacks into the State [after emancipation], and thus save the expense of supplying, by importation of white settlers, the vacancies they will leave? Deep-rooted prejudices entertained by the Whites; ten thousand recollections by the Blacks, of the injuries they have sustained; new provocations; the real distinctions which nature has made; and many other circumstances, will divide us into parties, and produce convulsions, which will probably never end but in the extermination of the one or the other race. To these objections, which are political, may be added others, which are physical and moral. . . . Comparing them by their faculties of memory, reason, and imagination, it appears to me, that in memory they are equal to the Whites; in reason much inferior, . . . and that in imagination they are dull, tasteless and anomalous. . . .

To our reproach it must be said, that though for a century and a half we have had under our eyes the races of Black and of Red men, they have never yet been viewed by us as subjects of natural history. I advance it therefore as a suspicion only, that the Blacks, whether originally a distinct race, or made distinct by time and circumstances, are inferior to the Whites in the endowments both of body and mind. It is not against experience to suppose, that different species of the same genus, or varieties of the same species, may possess different qualifications. Will not a lover of natural history then, one who views the gradations in all the races of animals with the eye of philosophy, excuse an effort to keep those in the department of man as distinct as nature has formed them? This unfortunate difference of colour, and perhaps of faculty, is a powerful obstacle to the emancipation of these people. Many of their advocates, while they wish to vindicate the liberty of human nature, are anxious also to preserve its dignity and beauty. Some of these, embarrassed by the question 'What further is to be done with them?' join themselves in opposition with those who are actuated by sordid avarice [greed] only. Among the Romans emancipation required but one effort. The slave, when made free, might mix with, without staining the blood of his master. But with us a second is necessary, unknown to history. When freed, he is to be removed beyond the reach of mixture. . . . There must, doubtless, be an unhappy influence on the manners of our people, produced by the existence of slavery among us. The whole commerce between master and slave is a perpetual exercise of the most boisterous passions, the most unremitting despotism on the one part, and degrading. . . . For if a slave can have a country in this world, it must be any other in preference to that in which he is born to live and labor for another.

Source: Jefferson, Thomas. "Laws, Query XIV." *Notes on the State of Virginia*. London: Printed for John Stockdale, Opposite Burlington-House, Piccadilly, 1787. 229–271.

Primary Source 3

Thomas Jefferson, Letter to M. Warville [a Frenchman] (February 11, 1788)

Sir,

I am very sensible of the honor you propose to me, of becoming a member of the society for the abolition of the slave-trade. You know that nobody wishes more ardently, to see an abolition, not only of the trade, but of the condition of slavery: and certainly nobody will be more willing to encounter every sacrifice for that object. But the influence and information of the friends to this proposition in France will be far above the need of my association. I am here as a public servant, and those whom I serve, having never yet been able to give their voice against the practice, it is decent for me to avoid too public a demonstration of my wishes to see it abolished. Without serving the cause here, it might render me less able to serve it beyond the water. I trust you will be sensible of the prudence of those motives, therefore, which govern my conduct on this occasion, and be assured of my wishes for the success of your undertaking, and the sentiments of esteem and respect, with which I have the honor to be, Sir, your most obedient, humble servant,

Th: Jefferson.

Source: Jefferson, Thomas. "Jean Plumard Brissot de Warville to Thomas Jefferson, February 11, 1788," 1788. *The Thomas Jefferson Papers*. Series 1: General Correspondence, 1651–1827. American Memory, Library of Congress, Washington, D.C.

Primary Source 4

Thomas Jefferson, Letter to John Holmes (April 22, 1820)

I thank you, dear Sir, for the copy you have been so kind as to send me of the letter to your constituents on the Missouri question [the admission of Missouri as slave state]. . . . The cession of that kind of property [slaves] (for so it is misnamed) . . . would not cost me a second thought, if, in that way, a general emancipation and expatriation could be effected: and, gradually, and with due sacrifices, I think it might be. But as it is, we have the wolf by the ears, and we can neither hold him, nor safely let him go. Justice is in one scale, and self-preservation in the other. Of one thing I am certain, that as the passage of slaves from one State to another, would not make a slave of a single human being who would not be so without it, so their diffusion over a greater surface would make them individually happier, and proportionally facilitate the accomplishment of their emancipation. . . .

Th: Jefferson.

Source: Jefferson, Thomas. "Thomas Jefferson to John Holmes, April 22, 1820," 1820. *The Thomas Jefferson Papers*, Series 1: General Correspondence, 1651–1827. American Memory, Library of Congress, Washington, D.C.

A CARD.

BLOUNT & DAWSON,
NERAL BROKERS

the Purchase and Sale of NEGROES and OTHER PROPERTY.

AVANNAH,   GEORGIA.

ken the Office and New Jail completed by Wm Wright. Esq., we are rd secure and good accommodations for all negroes left with us for Sale ping, would respectfully solicit a share of public patronage.

Two Doors East of J. Bryan & Co., opposite the State Bank.

LOUNT.   W. C. DAWSON.

g leased the above gentlemen my office and jail, would take pleasure in ding them to my patrons and the public generally.

WM. WRIGHT.

An Expanding Nation

During the nineteenth century, the United States experienced wrenching changes. With each passing decade, its predominantly agrarian society developed a more diverse economy, with factories and cities emerging alongside farms and towns. The pace of life quickened, and ambitions soared. Between 1790 and 1820, the nation grew rapidly; its boundaries expanded and its population—both white and black—skyrocketed, while the number of Native Americans continued its relative decline. By the early 1820s, the total number of enslaved Americans was more than two and a half times greater than in 1790, and the number of free blacks had doubled. The white population of the United States grew just as rapidly.

Accompanying the industrialization of the economy was relentless westward expansion. The great theme of nineteenth-century development was the migration of millions of people westward across the Allegheny and Appalachian Mountains into the Middle West. Waves of adventurous emigrants then crossed the Mississippi River and spread out across the Great Plains. By the 1840s, Americans had reached the Pacific Ocean, transported there by horses, wagons, canals, flatboats, steamboats, and, eventually, railroads and steamships.

While the feverish expansion into the West brought more conflict with Native Americans, Mexicans, the British, and the Spanish, most Americans believed it was their God-given destiny to spread across the continent—at whatever cost and at whomever's expense. In 1845, an editorial in the *United States Journal* claimed that "we, the American people, are the most independent, intelligent, moral, and happy people on the face of the earth." The constitutional republic governed by highly educated "natural aristocrats" such as Thomas Jefferson, James Madison, James Monroe, and John Quincy Adams gave way to the frontier democracy promoted by frontiersman Andrew Jackson. Americans began to demand government of, by, and for the people.

During the first half of the nineteenth century, two very different societies—North and South—developed in the United States. The North was the more dynamic and faster-growing region. It embraced the Industrial Revolution, large cities, foreign immigrants, and the ideal of "free labor." By contrast, the South remained rural, agricultural, and increasingly committed to enslaved labor as the backbone of its cotton-centered economy. Two great underlying fears worried southerners: the daily threat of slave uprisings and the growing possibility that a northern-controlled Congress might abolish slavery. The planter elite's aggressive efforts to preserve and expand slavery stifled reform impulses in the South and ignited a prolonged political controversy with the North that would eventually lead to civil war.

The so-called Jacksonian Era during the first half of the nineteenth century celebrated individual freedom and self-expression. Religious life, for example, experienced another wave of energetic revival centered on the power of individuals to embrace Christ and attain salvation on their own. Such an emphasis on individualism and freedom of expression shaped cultural life in general.

The Romantic movement, originating in Europe and then spreading to America, applied democratic ideals to virtually every field: philosophy,

religion, literature, and the fine arts. In New England, Ralph Waldo Emerson and Henry David Thoreau joined other "transcendentalists" in promoting a radical individualism. At the same time, activists of all types fanned out to reform and even "perfect" American society by creating public schools accessible to all children, working to abolish slavery, combating the consumption of alcohol, and striving to improve living conditions for the disabled, the insane, the poor, and the imprisoned.

LACKAWANNA VALLEY (1855) Often hailed as the father of American landscape painting, George Inness was commissioned by a railroad company to capture its trains coursing through the lush Lackawanna Valley in northeastern Pennsylvania. New inventions and rapid industrial growth would continue to change the American landscape.

The Emergence of a Market Economy

1815–1850

Amid the postwar celebrations in 1815, Americans set about transforming their victorious young nation. Soon after the war's end, prosperity returned as British and European markets again welcomed American ships and commerce. During the war, the loss of trade with Britain and Europe had forced the United States to develop more factories and mills of its own, spurring the development of the more diverse economy that Alexander Hamilton had championed in the 1790s.

Between 1815 and 1850, the United States became a transcontinental power, expanding all the way to the Pacific coast. Hundreds of thousands of land-hungry people streamed westward toward the Mississippi River and beyond. Between 1815 and 1821, six new states joined the Union (Alabama, Illinois, Indiana, Mississippi, Missouri, and Maine).

The lure of cheap land and plentiful jobs, as well as the promise of political and religious freedom, attracted millions of immigrants in the first half of the nineteenth century. This great wave of humanity was not always welcomed, however. Ethnic prejudices, anti-Catholicism, and language barriers made it difficult for many new immigrants, mostly from Ireland, Germany, and China, to adapt to American culture.

In the Midwest, large-scale commercial agriculture emerged as big farms grew corn and wheat and raised pigs and cattle to be sold in distant markets. In the South, cotton became so profitable that it increasingly dominated the

CORE OBJECTIVES INQUIZITIVE

1. Describe how changes in transportation and communications altered the economic landscape during the first half of the nineteenth century.

2. Explain the impact of the Industrial Revolution on the way people worked and lived.

3. Analyze how immigration altered the nation's population and shaped its politics.

4. Evaluate the impact of the expanding capitalist "market economy" on workers, professionals, and women.

region's economy, luring farmers and planters (wealthy farmers with hundreds or even thousands of acres worked by large numbers of slaves) into the new states of Alabama, Mississippi, Louisiana, and Arkansas. As the cotton culture expanded into new southern territories and states, it required growing numbers of enslaved workers, many of whom were sold and relocated from Virginia and the Carolinas.

Meanwhile, the Northeast experienced an industrial revolution that reshaped the region's economy as mills and factories began to dot the landscape and transform the nature of work; most of the early mill workers were young women from farms or abroad. In the North and Midwest, an urban middle class emerged as Americans left farms and moved to towns and cities, drawn primarily by jobs in new mills, factories, and banks.

By 1850, the United States boasted the world's fastest growing economy. Dramatic improvements in communication and transportation transformed the economy into an interconnected national marketplace. In the process, the nation began to divide into three powerful regional political blocs—North, South, and West—whose shifting alliances would shape political life until the Civil War.

CORE **OBJECTIVE**

1. Describe how changes in transportation and communications altered the economic landscape during the first half of the nineteenth century.

The Market Revolution

During the first half of the nineteenth century, a market revolution transformed the young American economy. In the eighteenth century, most Americans had been enmeshed in a local "household economy." That is, they produced enough food, livestock, and clothing for their own family's needs and perhaps a little more to barter (exchange) with their neighbors. During the nineteenth century, however, more and more farmers began producing surplus crops and livestock to sell, for cash, in more distant regional markets reached by rivers, canals, and roads. Such large-scale commercial agriculture, the first stage of a **market economy**, produced boom-and-bust cycles, but overall the standard of living rose and Americans experienced unprecedented opportunities for economic gain and geographic mobility.

Transportation

Until the nineteenth century, travel had been slow, tedious, and expensive. It took a stagecoach four days to travel from New York City to Boston. Because of long travel times, many farm products could be sold only locally before they spoiled.

That changed during the first half of the nineteenth century. An array of transportation innovations—larger horse-drawn wagons, called *Conestogas*; new roads; canals; steamboats; and the first railroads—knit together the expanding national market for goods and services and greatly accelerated the pace of life.

market economy Large-scale manufacturing and commercial agriculture that emerged in America during the first half of the nineteenth century, displacing much of the premarket subsistence and barter-based economy and producing boom-and-bust cycles while raising the American standard of living.

TRANSPORTATION WEST, ABOUT 1840

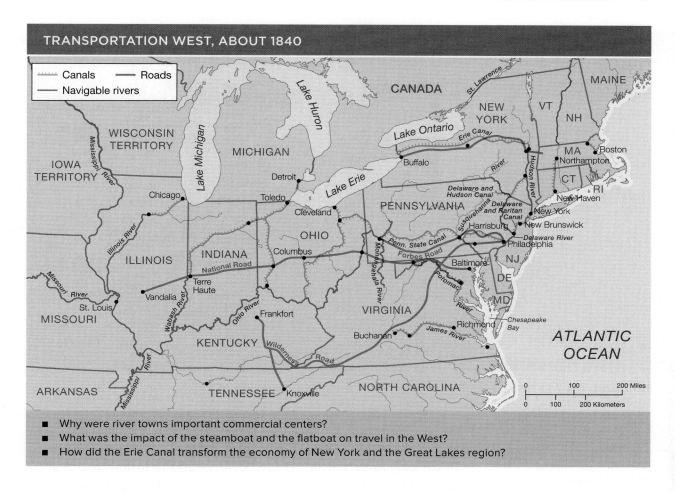

Legend:
- ⌇⌇⌇ Canals
- — Roads
- — Navigable rivers

- ■ Why were river towns important commercial centers?
- ■ What was the impact of the steamboat and the flatboat on travel in the West?
- ■ How did the Erie Canal transform the economy of New York and the Great Lakes region?

During the first quarter of the nineteenth century, stagecoaches increased their speed as the quality of roads improved. In addition, coach lines began using continual relays, or "stages," of fresh horses made available every forty or so miles. These "stagecoaches" made travel faster, less expensive, and more accessible to more people.

New Roads

As settlers moved west, people demanded better roads. In 1795, the Wilderness Road, along the walking trail first blazed by Daniel Boone twenty years earlier, opened to wagon and stagecoach traffic, thereby easing the over-the-mountains route from Virginia and North Carolina into Kentucky and Tennessee. To the northeast, a movement for graded and paved roads (using packed-down crushed stones) gathered momentum after the Philadelphia-Lancaster Turnpike was completed in 1794 (the term *turnpike* derives from a pole, or pike, at the tollgate, which was turned to admit the traffic in exchange for a small fee). By 1821, some 4,000 miles of turnpikes had been built.

Road transportation: Building turnpikes

TRAVELING THE WESTERN WATERS Three steamboats are docked at the levee at St. Paul, Minnesota, in 1859.

Water Transportation

Water transportation: Steamboats

By the early 1820s, the turnpike boom was giving way to dramatic advances in water transportation. River steamboats, flatboats, and canal barges carried people and goods far more cheaply than did horse-drawn wagons. The first steamboat appeared in 1807 when Robert Fulton and Robert R. Livingston steered the *Clermont* north up the Hudson River from New York City. Thereafter, the use of wood-fired **steamboats** spread rapidly to other eastern rivers and to the sprawling Ohio and Mississippi river systems, opening nearly half the continent to water traffic. By bringing two-way traffic to the Mississippi Valley, steamboats created a transcontinental market and an agricultural empire that produced much of the nation's timber, wheat, corn, cattle, and hogs. By 1836, there were 750 steamboats operating on American rivers, more than twice the number in Europe.

Canals also sped the market revolution. The historic **Erie Canal** in central New York enabled a truly national economy. After it opened in 1825, having taken eight years to build, the new canal drew eastward many of the midwestern crops and goods that earlier had been forced to make the long journey down the Ohio and Mississippi Rivers to the Gulf of Mexico. The Erie Canal had enormous economic and political consequences, tying together the regional economies of the Midwest and the East while further isolating the Deep South.

steamboats Ships and boats powered by wood-fired steam engines that made two-way traffic possible in eastern river systems, creating a transcontinental market and an agricultural empire.

Erie Canal (1817) Most important and profitable of the many barge canals built in the early nineteenth century, connecting the Great Lakes to the Hudson River and conveying so much cargo that it made New York City the nation's largest port.

THE GROWTH OF RAILROADS, 1850 AND 1860

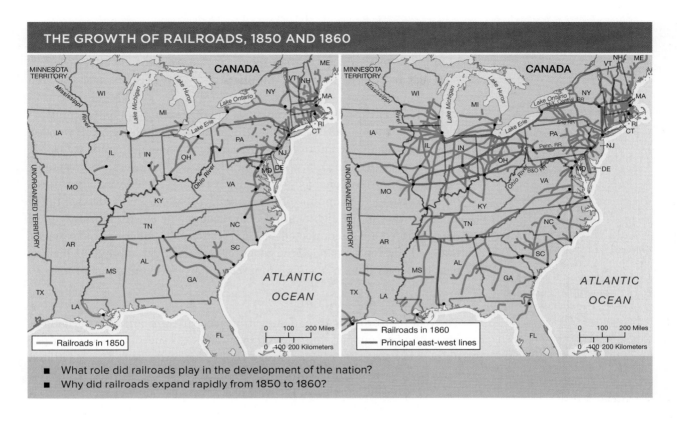

- What role did railroads play in the development of the nation?
- Why did railroads expand rapidly from 1850 to 1860?

Water transportation: Canal systems

The Erie Canal, forty feet wide and four feet deep, extended 364 miles across New York from Albany west to Buffalo. Built by tens of thousands of laborers, mostly German and Irish immigrants, the canal brought a "river of gold" to New York City in the form of an unending stream of goods going to and from the Midwest. The Erie Canal reduced travel time from New York City to Buffalo from twenty days to six, and the cost of moving a ton of freight plummeted from $100 to $5. Such dramatic improvements enabled New York City to rush past Boston, New Orleans, and Baltimore and become the nation's busiest port. The success of the New York canal system inspired the construction of more canals in other states. By 1837, there were 3,000 miles of canal waterways across the nation.

Railroads

Railroads connect the continent

The canal era was short-lived, however. During the second quarter of the nineteenth century, a more versatile and powerful form of transportation emerged: the railroad. In 1825, the year the Erie Canal was completed, the world's first steam-powered railway began operating in England. Soon thereafter, a railroad-building craze struck the United States. In 1830, the nation had only 23 miles of railroad track. Over the next twenty years, railroad coverage grew to 30,626 miles.

The railroad surpassed other forms of transportation because trains could carry more people and freight faster, farther, and cheaper. The ability of railroads to operate year-round also gave them a huge advantage over canals that froze over in winter and dirt roads that became rivers of mud during rainstorms.

Building **railroads** stimulated the national economy not only by improving transportation but also by creating a huge demand for iron, wooden crossties, bridges, locomotives, freight cars, and other equipment. Railroads also became the nation's largest corporations and employers. Perhaps most important, railroads enabled towns and cities not served by canals or turnpikes to compete economically. In other words, the railroads eventually changed what in the eighteenth century had been a cluster of mostly local markets into an interconnected national marketplace for goods and services. Railroads thereby expanded the geography of American capitalism, making possible larger industrial and commercial enterprises from coast to coast.

Ocean Transportation

The year 1845 brought a great innovation in ocean transport with the launching of the first clipper ship, the *Rainbow*. Built for speed, the sleek **clipper ships** were the nineteenth-century equivalent of the supersonic jetliner. They were twice as fast as the older merchant ships. Long and lean, with taller masts and more sails, they cut dashing figures during their brief but colorful career, which lasted less than two decades. It was the American

railroads Steam-powered vehicles that improved passenger transportation, quickened western settlement, and enabled commercial agriculture in the nineteenth century.

clipper ships Tall, slender ships favored over older merchant ships for their speed; ultimately gave way to steamships because clipper ships lacked cargo space.

BUILDING A CLIPPER SHIP This 1833 oil painting captures the Messrs. Smith & Co. Ship Yard in Manhattan, where shipbuilders are busy shaping timbers to construct a clipper ship.

thirst for Chinese tea that prompted the clipper boom. Asian tea leaves had to reach the market quickly after harvest, and the fast clipper ships made this possible. Even more important, the discovery of gold in California in 1848 lured thousands of prospectors and entrepreneurs from the Atlantic seaboard. The massive wave of would-be miners generated an urgent demand for goods on the West Coast, and the clippers met it. In 1854 the *Flying Cloud* took eighty-nine days and eight hours to travel from New York to San Francisco, less than half as long as the trip would have taken in a conventional ship. But clippers, while fast, lacked ample space for cargo or passengers. After the Civil War, the clipper ship would give way to the steamship.

> Ocean transportation: Clipper ships enable high-speed ocean travel

Communications

Innovations in transportation also helped spark improvements in communications, which knit the nation even closer together. At the beginning of the nineteenth century, it took days—often weeks—for news to travel along the Atlantic seaboard. For example, after George Washington died in 1798 in Virginia, the news of his death did not appear in New York City newspapers until a week later. By 1829, however, relay horse riders delivered President Andrew Jackson's inaugural address from Washington, D.C., to New York City in fewer than twenty hours.

Mail deliveries also improved. The number of U.S. post offices soared from 75 in 1790 to 28,498 in 1860. In addition, new steam-powered printing presses reduced the cost of newspapers from 6¢ to a penny each, enabling virtually everyone to benefit from the news contained in the "penny press."

The century's most important advance in communications occurred with the development of a national electromagnetic **telegraph system**, invented by Samuel F. B. Morse, a portrait painter turned inventor. In May 1844, Morse sent the first intercity telegraph message from Washington, D.C., to Baltimore, Maryland. It read: "What Hath God Wrought?"

By the end of the decade, most major cities benefited from telegraph lines. By enabling people to communicate faster and more easily across long distances, the telegraph system triggered many changes, not the least of which was helping railroad operators schedule trains more precisely and thus avoid collisions. A New Orleans newspaper claimed that with the invention of the telegraph "scarcely anything now will appear to be impossible."

The Role of Government

The transportation improvements were financed by both state governments and private investors. The national government did play a role, however, despite intense political debates over whether it was constitutional to use federal funds to finance such "internal improvements." The national government bought stock in turnpike and canal companies and, after the success of the Erie Canal, awarded land grants to several western states to support canal and railroad projects. By 1860, Congress had given railroad companies more than 20 million acres of federal lands.

> Government financing for internal improvements

telegraph system System of electronic communication invented by Samuel F. B. Morse that could transmit messages instantaneously across great distances.

CORE **OBJECTIVE**
2. Explain the impact of the Industrial Revolution on the way people worked and lived.

Industrial Development

The concentration of huge numbers of people in cities, coupled with the transportation and communication revolutions, greatly increased the number of potential customers for a given product. This in turn gave rise to *mass production*, whereby companies used new technologies (machine tools) to produce greater quantities of products, which could thereby be sold at lower prices while generating higher profits. The application of water-powered mills and coal-powered steam engines, as well as the development of new machinery to make manufacturing more efficient, sparked an industrial revolution in Europe and America from the mid–eighteenth century to the late nineteenth century.

The **Industrial Revolution**, centered on the invention of the steam engine, was the most important development in human history since the advent of agriculture. Prior to 1800, most products were made by hand by skilled artisans. That changed quickly with the development, first, of textile machinery, soon followed by a dazzling array of machinery invented to manufacture almost everything. As a consequence, factories, mills, and industrial plants emerged during the first half of the nineteenth century to replace many artisans and craftsmen making clothing, shoes, clocks and watches, furniture, firearms, and an array of other items. "It is an extraordinary era in which we live," reported Daniel Webster in 1847. "It is altogether new. The world has seen nothing like it before."

American Technology

During the nineteenth century, Americans became known around the world for their "practical" inventiveness. Between 1790 and 1811, the U.S. Patent Office approved an annual average of seventy-seven new patents certifying new inventions; by the 1850s, the Patent Office was approving more than 28,000 new inventions each year.

Many of the new inventions generated dramatic changes. In 1844, for example, Charles Goodyear patented a process for "vulcanizing" rubber, which made the product stronger, more elastic, waterproof, and winterproof. Vulcanized rubber was used for a variety of products, from shoes and boots to seals, gaskets, hoses, and eventually tires. In 1846, Elias Howe patented his design of the sewing machine, soon improved upon by Isaac Merritt Singer, who founded the Singer Sewing Machine Company, which first produced only industrial sewing machines for use in textile mills but eventually offered machines for home use.

The availability of sewing machines helped revolutionize "women's work." Sewing machines dramatically reduced the time for making clothes at home, thus freeing up more leisure time for many women.

Technological advances improved living conditions; houses could be larger, better heated, and better illuminated. The first sewer systems helped

American inventiveness: The sewing machine (1846)

Industrial Revolution Major shift in the nineteenth century from handmade manufacturing to mass production in mills and factories using water-, coal-, and steam-powered machinery.

clean up cities by ridding their streets of human and animal waste. Machine-made clothes using standardized forms fit better and were cheaper than those sewn by hand; machine-made newspapers and magazines were more abundant and affordable, as were clocks, watches, guns, and plows.

One invention launched an economic revolution. In 1792, Eli Whitney, a recent Yale graduate from New England, spent several months at Mulberry Grove plantation on the Georgia coast, where he "heard much said of the difficulty of ginning cotton"—that is, separating the fibers from the seeds. Cotton had been used for clothing and bedding from ancient times, but until the nineteenth century, cotton cloth was rare and expensive because it took so long to remove the seeds. One person working all day could separate barely one pound by hand.

At Mulberry Grove, Whitney learned that the person who could invent a "machine" to gin cotton would become wealthy overnight. That was incentive enough for him. Within a few weeks, Whitney had devised "an absurdly simple contrivance," using nails attached to a roller, to remove the seeds from cotton bolls.

Completed in 1793, Whitney's **cotton gin** (short for *engine*) proved to be fifty times more productive than a hand laborer. Almost overnight, the gin made the white fiber America's most profitable cash crop. In the process, it transformed southern agriculture, northern industry, race-based slavery, and national politics.

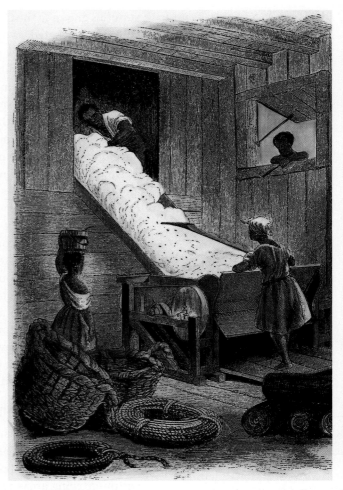

COTTON GIN Before Eli Whitney's cotton gin, it would have taken the four people in this engraving days to pick through the avalanche of cotton depicted here and separate the cotton seeds from the fibers. **How did the cotton gin affect the economy of the South and the nation more broadly?**

King Cotton

During the first half of the nineteenth century, southern-grown **cotton** became the dominant force driving both the national economy and the controversial efforts to expand slavery into the western territories. Cotton became so profitable that people called it "white gold"; it brought enormous wealth to southern planters and merchants as well as New England textile mill owners and New York shipowners and cotton traders.

By 1812, the widespread use of cotton gins had reduced the cost of producing cotton yarn by 90 percent. Suddenly cotton clothing was affordable and available to everyone. By the mid–nineteenth century, people worldwide were wearing more-comfortable and easier-to-clean cotton clothing. When British textile manufacturers chose the less brittle American cotton over the

cotton gin Hand-operated machine invented by Eli Whitney that quickly removed seeds from cotton bolls, enabling the mass production of cotton in nineteenth-century America.

cotton White fibers harvested from plants that made comfortable, easy-to-clean products, especially clothing; the most valuable cash crop driving the economy in nineteenth-century United States and Great Britain.

varieties grown in the Caribbean, Brazil, and India, the demand for southern cotton skyrocketed, as did its price. Cotton became America's largest export and the primary driver of the nation's extraordinary economic growth. By 1860, British textile mills were processing a billion pounds of cotton a year, 92 percent of which came from the American South.

The commercial growing of cotton for world markets spread plantation slavery across the South, especially the Carolinas, Georgia, Tennessee, Alabama, Mississippi, Louisiana, Arkansas, and Texas. It also spurred the development of textile mills in New England; expanded the shipping fleets of New York City; and made the ports of New Orleans, Mobile, Savannah, and Charleston sources of enormous profits for the regional and national economies.

Cotton growing first engulfed the Piedmont region of the Carolinas and Georgia, between the coast and the mountains. After the War of 1812, it migrated into the contested Indian lands to the west—Tennessee, Alabama, Florida, Mississippi, Louisiana, Arkansas, and Texas. New Orleans became a bustling port—and active slave market—because of the cotton grown throughout the region and shipped down the Mississippi River. From the mid-1830s to 1860, cotton accounted for more than half of American exports. The South harvested raw cotton, and northern buyers and shipowners carried it to New England, Great Britain, and France, where textile mills spun the fiber into thread and fabric.

The Expansion of Slavery

Cotton production expands slavery

Cotton is a labor-intensive crop, requiring 70 percent more labor than corn did. As a result, the price of slaves soared with the price of cotton, and many Virginia and Maryland planters sold their surplus slaves to work in the new cotton-growing areas in Georgia, Alabama, Mississippi, and Louisiana. Between 1790 and 1860, some 835,000 slaves were "sold south." Slaves became so valuable that stealing them became a common problem in the southern states, especially in Alabama and Mississippi.

Farming the Midwest

By 1860, more than half of Americans lived west of the Appalachian Mountains. The fertile farmlands in the Midwest—Ohio, Michigan, Indiana, Illinois, and Iowa—drew farmers from the rocky hillsides of New England and the exhausted soils of Virginia. By 1860, 30-40 percent of Americans born in New England had moved west. People traveled on foot, on horseback, and in jarring wagons, all in an effort to make a fresh start on their *own* land made available by the government.

A new national land law of 1820 reduced the price of federal land. Even that was not enough for westerners, however. They demanded "preemption," the right of squatters (people who simply built a cabin and started farming without actually purchasing government land) to purchase land at the minimum price, and "graduation," the progressive reduction of the price of land that did not sell immediately.

Congress eventually responded to the land mania with two bills. Under the Preemption Act of 1830, squatters could get 160 acres at the minimum price of $1.25 per acre. Under the Graduation Act of 1854, prices of unsold lands were to be lowered in stages over thirty years.

Technology also enabled greater agricultural productivity. The development of durable iron plows (rather than wooden plows) eased the backbreaking job of tilling the soil. In 1819, Jethro Wood of New York introduced an iron plow with separate parts that were easily replaced when needed. Further improvements would follow, including Vermonter John Deere's steel plow (1837), whose sharp edges could cut through the tough prairie grass in the Midwest and the Great Plains. By 1845, Massachusetts alone had seventy-three plants making more than 60,000 plows per year. Most were sold to western farmers, illustrating the emergence of a national marketplace for goods and services made possible by the transportation revolution.

> Growth of commercial agriculture: Steel plows (1837) and mechanical reapers (1831)

Other technological improvements quickened the growth of large-scale commercial agriculture. By the 1840s, new mechanical seeders had replaced the process of sowing seed by hand. Even more important, in 1831 twenty-two-year-old Virginian Cyrus Hall McCormick invented a mechanical reaper pulled by horses to harvest wheat, a development as significant to the agricultural economy of the Midwest, Old Northwest, and Great Plains as the cotton gin was to the South.

In 1847, the **McCormick reaper** began selling so fast that its inventor moved to Chicago and built a manufacturing plant. Within a few years, McCormick had sold thousands of the giant farm machines, transforming the scale of commercial agriculture. Using a handheld sickle, a farmer could harvest a half acre of wheat a day; with a McCormick reaper, two people could work twelve acres a day.

McCormick reaper Mechanical reaper invented by Cyrus Hall McCormick in 1831 that dramatically increased the production of wheat.

MCCORMICK'S REAPING MACHINE This illustration appeared in the catalog of the Great Exhibition, held at the Crystal Palace in London in 1851. The plow eased the transformation of rough plains into fertile farmland, and the reaping machine accelerated farm production.

Early Textile Manufacturers

While technological breakthroughs such as the cotton gin, mechanical harvester, and railroads had quickened agricultural development and enabled a national economy, other technologies altered the economic landscape even more profoundly by giving rise to the factory system.

Mills and factories were initially powered by water wheels and then by coal-fired steam engines. The shift from water power to steam as a source of energy is what quickened the growth rate of the textile industry (and industries of all types), initiating an industrial revolution destined to end Britain's domination of the world economy.

In 1800, the output of America's mills and factories amounted to only one sixth of Great Britain's production. The growth of American textile production was slow and faltering until Thomas Jefferson's embargo in 1807 stimulated the domestic production of cloth. By 1815, hundreds of textile mills in New England, New York, and Pennsylvania were producing thread, cloth, and clothing. By 1860, the output of America's factories would be a third and by 1880 two thirds that of the British industry.

After the War of 1812, British textile companies had flooded American markets with cheap cotton cloth in an effort to regain their customers. Such "dumping" nearly killed the infant American textile industry by lowering the prices of thread and cloth. A delegation of New England mill owners traveled to Washington, D.C., to demand a federal tariff on imported cloth to deter the British from selling their cloth in the United States for less than the prices charged by American manufacturers. The efforts of the American mill owners to gain political assistance created a culture of industrial lobbying for congressional tariff protection that continues to this day.

What the mill owners neglected to admit was that tariffs hurt American consumers by forcing them to pay higher prices. Over time, as Scotsman Adam Smith explained in his book on capitalism, *The Wealth of Nations* (1776), consumers not only pay higher prices for foreign goods as a result of tariffs, but they also pay higher prices for domestic goods, since businesses invariably take advantage of opportunities to raise the prices charged for their products.

Tariffs helped "protect" American industries from foreign competition, but competition is the engine of innovation and efficiency in a capitalist economy. New England shipping companies opposed higher tariffs because they would reduce the amount of goods sent across the Atlantic from Britain and Europe. Many southerners opposed tariffs because of fears that Britain and France would retaliate with tariffs on American cotton and tobacco shipped to their ports.

In the end, the New England mill owners won. Congress passed the Tariff of 1816, which placed a tax on imported cloth. Such tariffs were a major factor in spurring industrialization. By impeding foreign competition, they enabled American manufacturers to dominate the national marketplace.

Rise of the factory system: Steam-powered mills

Import tariffs

The Lowell System

The factory system sprang full-blown upon the American scene at Waltham, Massachusetts, in 1813, when a group known as the Boston Associates constructed the first textile mill in which the mechanized processes of spinning yarn and weaving cloth (copied from English mills) were brought together under one roof. In 1822, the Boston Associates, led by Francis Cabot Lowell, developed another cotton mill at a village along the Merrimack River twenty-eight miles north of Boston, which they renamed Lowell. It soon became the model for mill towns throughout New England, often referred to as the **Lowell system**.

The founders of the Lowell system had a much larger vision than just improved industrial efficiency; they also sought to develop model industrial communities. To avoid the crowded, wretched life of the English textile-mill villages, they located their four- and five-story brick-built mills along rivers in the countryside.

Women were the first factory workers in the nation, as the mill owners hired mostly young women aged fifteen to thirty from farm families. Mill owners preferred women because of their skill in operating machines and their willingness to endure the mind-numbing boredom of operating spinning machines and looms for wages lower than those paid to men (even though their wages, $2.50 per week, were the highest in the world for women).

Moreover, by the 1820s New England had a surplus of women because so many men had migrated westward in search of cheap land and new economic opportunities. In the early 1820s, a steady stream of single women began flocking toward Lowell. To reassure worried parents, the mill owners promised to provide the "Lowell girls" with tolerable work, prepared meals, comfortable boardinghouses (four girls to a room), moral discipline, and educational and cultural opportunities.

Initially the "Lowell idea" worked pretty much according to plan. Visitors commented on the well-designed red brick mills with their lecture halls and libraries. The "Lowell girls" appeared "healthy and happy." They lived in cramped dormitories staffed by housemothers who enforced mill managers' rules of limited contact with men, evening curfews, and mandatory church attendance. Despite thirteen-hour work days and five-and-a-half-day workweeks (longer hours than those imposed upon prison inmates), some of the women still found the time and energy to form study groups, publish a literary magazine, and attend lectures.

Lowell, however, lost its innocence as it grew—and as the owners accumulated "unbelievable profits." The once rural village had become a grimy industrial city. Greed led mill owners to produce too much cloth, which depressed prices. The owners slashed wages and quickened the pace of work. In 1834, the Lowell women went on strike to protest the deteriorating working and

MILL GIRLS Massachusetts mill workers of the mid–nineteenth century, photographed holding shuttles. **What sort of working conditions would Lowell girls like these have experienced?**

Lowell system Model New England factory communities that provided employees, mostly young women, with meals, a boardinghouse, moral discipline, and educational opportunities.

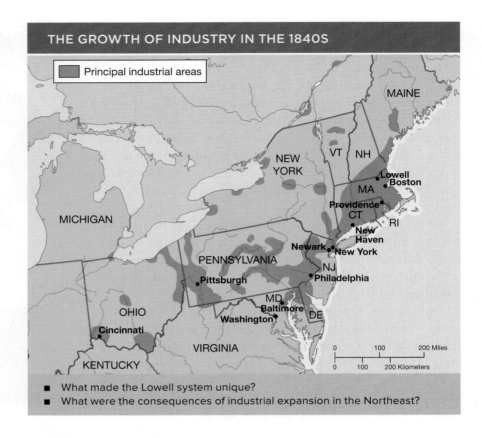

THE GROWTH OF INDUSTRY IN THE 1840S

Principal industrial areas

MAINE

NEW YORK

VT   NH

MA

Lowell
Boston

MICHIGAN

Providence
CT

RI

New Haven

Newark   New York

PENNSYLVANIA

NJ
Philadelphia

Pittsburgh

MD
Baltimore

Washington

DE

OHIO

Cincinnati

VIRGINIA

KENTUCKY

0   100   200 Miles
0   100   200 Kilometers

■ What made the Lowell system unique?
■ What were the consequences of industrial expansion in the Northeast?

living conditions. The angry mill owners labeled the 1,500 striking women "ungrateful" and "unfeminine"—and tried to get rid of the strike's leaders. One mill manager reported that "we have paid off several of these Amazons & presume that they will leave town on Monday." The workers lost the strike.

Two years later, the Lowell workers again walked out, this time in protest of the owners raising the rents in the company-owned boarding houses. This time the owners backed down. Over time, however, the owners began hiring Irish immigrants who were so desperate for jobs that they rarely complained about the working conditions. By 1850, some 40 percent of the mill workers were Irish.

Industrialization, Cities, and the Environment

The rapid growth of commerce and industry spurred the growth of cities and mill villages. Lowell's population in 1820 was 200. By 1830, it was 6,500 and ten years later it had soared to 21,000. Other factory centers sprouted up across New England, displacing forests, farms, and villages while filling the air with smoke, noise, and stench. Between 1820 and 1840, the number of Americans engaged in manufacturing increased 800 percent, and the number of city dwellers more than doubled.

As Thomas Jefferson and other agrarians feared, the United States was rapidly becoming a global industrial power, producing its own clothing

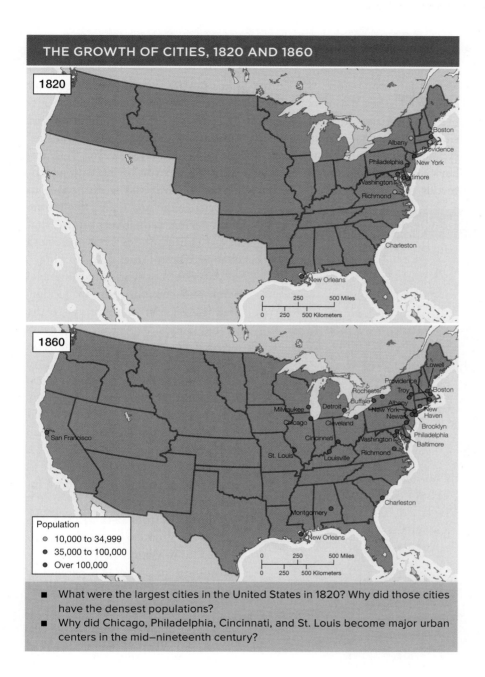

THE GROWTH OF CITIES, 1820 AND 1860

1820

1860

Population
- 10,000 to 34,999
- 35,000 to 100,000
- Over 100,000

■ What were the largest cities in the United States in 1820? Why did those cities have the densest populations?

■ Why did Chicago, Philadelphia, Cincinnati, and St. Louis become major urban centers in the mid–nineteenth century?

and shoes, iron and engines. The Atlantic seaports of New York City, Philadelphia, Baltimore, and Boston remained the largest cities. New Orleans became the nation's fifth largest because of its role in shipping goods down the Mississippi River to the East Coast and to Europe. New York outpaced all its competitors in growth. By 1860, it was the first city to surpass more than 1 million, largely because of its superior harbor and its access to the commerce floating down the Hudson River from the Erie Canal.

CORE **OBJECTIVE**

3. Analyze how immigration altered the nation's population and shaped its politics.

Immigration

More than ever before, the United States during the nineteenth century continued to be a nation of immigrants. During the forty years from the outbreak of the Revolution to the end of the War of 1812, immigration had slowed to a trickle. The French Revolution and the Napoleonic Wars restricted travel to and from Europe until 1815. Thereafter, however, the number of immigrants to America rose steadily. Ships overflowing with adventurous and desperate people arrived from all over the world, eager to experience the American Dream—the shimmering, seductive promise that in the United States everyone had a chance to better their quality of life.

After 1837, a worldwide financial panic and economic slump accelerated the pace of immigration to the United States. American employers aggressively recruited foreigners, in large part because they were willing to work for lower wages than native-born Americans. The *Chicago Daily Tribune* observed that the tide of German immigrants was perfect for the "cheap and ingenious labor of the country." A German laborer was willing "to live as cheaply and work infinitely more intelligently than the negro."

The years from 1845 to 1854 witnessed the greatest proportional influx of immigrants in U.S. history, 2.4 million, or about 14.5 percent of the total population in 1845. In 1860, more than one of every eight Americans was foreign born. British immigrants continued to arrive in large numbers. By the 1850s, the rapid development of California lured Chinese immigrants in significant numbers, while Scandinavians began settling mostly in Wisconsin and Minnesota, where the climate and woodlands reminded them of home. By far, however, the largest number of immigrants between 1840 and 1860 came from Ireland and Germany.

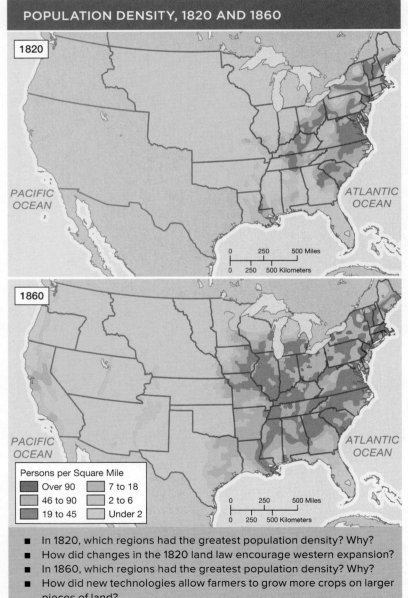

POPULATION DENSITY, 1820 AND 1860

1820

PACIFIC OCEAN

ATLANTIC OCEAN

0   250   500 Miles
0   250   500 Kilometers

1860

PACIFIC OCEAN

ATLANTIC OCEAN

Persons per Square Mile
- Over 90
- 46 to 90
- 19 to 45
- 7 to 18
- 2 to 6
- Under 2

0   250   500 Miles
0   250   500 Kilometers

- In 1820, which regions had the greatest population density? Why?
- How did changes in the 1820 land law encourage western expansion?
- In 1860, which regions had the greatest population density? Why?
- How did new technologies allow farmers to grow more crops on larger pieces of land?

The Irish

No nation proportionately sent more of its people to America than Ireland. A prolonged agricultural crisis that brought immense social hardships in Ireland caused many Irish to flee their homeland in the mid–nineteenth century. Irish farmers primarily grew potatoes; in fact, fully a third of them were dependent on the potato harvest for survival. The average adult male in Ireland ate five pounds of potatoes a day.

In 1845, a fungus destroyed the potato crop and triggered the Irish potato famine. More than a million people died, and almost 2 million more left Ireland, whose total population was only 8 million. Most of them traveled to Canada and the United States. As one group of immigrants explained, "All we want to do is get out of Ireland; we must be better anywhere but here." America, they knew, had paying jobs and "plenty to eat."

By the 1850s, the Irish made up more than half the population of Boston and New York City and were almost as dominant in Philadelphia. Most of them were desperately poor, crowded into filthy tenement houses in which "the low-paid and poverty-smitten . . . crowd by the dozens." Irish neighborhoods became known for high crime rates, deadly diseases, prostitution, and alcoholism. Irish immigrants confronted humiliating stereotypes and intense anti-Catholic prejudice. Many employers posted taunting signs reading "No Irish Need Apply."

Irish Americans, however, could be equally mean-spirited toward other groups, such as free African Americans, who competed with them for low-wage jobs. In 1850, the *New York Tribune* expressed concern that the Irish, having escaped from "a galling, degrading bondage" in their homeland, voted against proposals for equal rights for blacks and frequently arrived at the polls shouting, "Down with the Nagurs! Let them go back to Africa, where they belong." Many African Americans viewed the Irish with equal contempt. In 1850, a slave expressed a common sentiment: "My Master is a great tyrant, he treats me badly as if I were a common Irishman."

Irish immigrants in large cities often took jobs as waiters, dock workers, and deliverymen that had long been held by African Americans. A free black frustrated by the Irish insurgents voiced a criticism of immigrants that is still being made in the twenty-first century. The Irish, he said, were "crowding themselves into every place of business and labor, and driving the poor colored American citizen out."

Enterprising Irish immigrants did forge remarkable careers, however. Twenty years after arriving in New York, Alexander T. Stewart became the owner of the nation's largest department store and accumulated vast real estate holdings. Michael Cudahy, who began working at age fourteen in a

THE IGNORANT VOTE— HONORS ARE EASY Thomas Nast's caricature of an Irishman and African American southerner evenly balanced on a scale appeared on the cover of *Harper's Weekly* in December 1876. **How does Nast, a German-born immigrant, represent the race relations between the Irish and African Americans?**

Milwaukee meatpacking business, became head of the Cudahy Packing Company and developed a process for the curing of meats under refrigeration. Dublin-born Victor Herbert emerged as one of America's most revered composers, and Irish dancers and playwrights came to dominate the stage.

Irish immigration: Unskilled labor and the growth of Roman Catholicism

By the start of the Civil War, the Irish in America had energized trade unions, become the most important ethnic group supporting the Democratic party, and made the Roman Catholic Church the nation's largest religious denomination. Years of persecution had instilled in Irish Catholics a fierce loyalty to the church as "the supreme authority over all the affairs of the world." Such passion for Catholicism generated unity among Irish Americans and fear among many American Protestants. By 1860, Roman Catholicism had become the largest denomination in the United States.

The Irish loved to stick together. Most of them settled in Irish neighborhoods in the nation's largest cities and formed powerful local Democratic political organizations such as Tammany Hall in New York City that would dominate political life during the second half of the nineteenth century.

The Germans

German immigration: Skilled and diverse workers

German immigrants were almost as numerous as the Irish. Unlike the Irish newcomers, however, the German arrivals included a large number of skilled craftsmen and well-educated professional people—doctors, lawyers, teachers, engineers—some of whom were refugees from the failed German revolution of 1848.

In addition to an array of political opinions, Germans brought with them a variety of religious preferences. Most were Protestants (usually Lutherans), a third were Roman Catholics, and a significant number were Jews. Among the German immigrants who prospered in the New World were Heinrich Steinweg, a piano maker who in America changed his name to Steinway and became famous for the quality of his instruments, and Levi Strauss, a Jewish tailor who followed the gold rush to California and began making work pants, later dubbed Levi's.

Unlike the Irish, Germans settled more often in rural areas than in cities. Many were independent farmers, skilled workers, and shopkeepers. More so than the Irish, they migrated in families and groups. This clannish quality helped them better sustain elements of their language and culture in the New World. More of them also tended to return to their native country. About 14 percent of the Germans eventually went back to their homeland, compared with just 9 percent of the Irish.

Nativism

Nativism: Anti-Catholic violence

Not all Americans welcomed the flood of immigrants. A growing number of "nativists" resented the newcomers and sought to restrict or stop immigration altogether. The flood of Irish and German Catholics especially aroused hostility among Protestants. A Boston minister described Catholicism as "the ally of tyranny, the opponent of material prosperity, the foe of thrift, the enemy of the railroad, the caucus, and the school."

Nativists organized efforts to stop the tide of immigrants. The Order of the Star-Spangled Banner, founded in New York City in 1849, grew into a powerful political group known officially as the American party. Members pledged never to vote for any foreign-born or Catholic candidates. When asked about the secretive organization, they were told to say, "I know nothing," a phrase that gave rise to the informal name for the American party: the **Know-Nothings**. For a while, the Know-Nothings appeared to be on the brink of major-party status, especially during the 1850s, when the number of immigrants was five times as large as it had been during the 1840s. In the state and local campaigns of 1854, they swept the Massachusetts legislature, winning all but two seats in the lower house, and that fall they elected more than forty congressmen. Forty percent of the Pennsylvania state legislators were Know-Nothings.

The Know-Nothings demanded that immigrants and Roman Catholics be excluded from public office and that the waiting period for naturalization (earning citizenship) be extended from five to twenty-one years, but the party never developed enough strength to enact such legislation. Nor did Congress restrict immigration in any way during that period. For a while, the Know-Nothings threatened to control New England, New York, and Maryland and showed strength elsewhere, but the anti-Catholic movement subsided when slavery became the focal issue of the 1850s.

KNOW-NOTHINGS This political cartoon (ca. 1850) visualizes the common nativist complaints of the Know-Nothings: that in contrast to hardworking Americans, the Irish and German immigrants were drunkards who were stealing American elections and disrupting the political status quo.

Organized Labor and New Professions

While most Americans continued to work as farmers during the nineteenth century, a growing number found employment in new or expanding enterprises: textile mills, shoe factories, banks, railroads, publishing, retail stores, teaching, preaching, medicine, law, construction, and engineering. Technological innovations (steam power, power tools, and new modes of transportation) and their social applications (mass communication, turnpikes, the postal service, banks, and corporations) fostered an array of new industries and businesses that transformed the nature of work for many Americans, both men and women.

Early Unions

Proud apprentices, journeymen, and master craftsmen, who controlled their labor and invested their work with an emphasis on quality rather than quantity, resented the spread of mills and factories populated by masses of

> CORE **OBJECTIVE**
> **4.** Evaluate the impact of the expanding capitalist "market economy" on workers, professionals, and women.

nativists Native-born Americans who viewed immigrants as a threat to their job opportunities and way of life.

Know-Nothings Nativist, anti-Catholic third party organized in 1854 in reaction to large-scale German and Irish immigration.

"half-trained" workers, often young women as in the Lowell textile mills, dependent upon an hourly wage and subject to the sharp fluctuations of the larger economy. Skilled workers in cities before and after the Revolution were called artisans, craftsmen, or mechanics. They made or repaired shoes, hats, saddles, silverware, jewelry, glass, ropes, furniture, and a broad array of other products. During the 1820s and 1830s, artisans who emphasized quality and craftsmanship found it hard to compete with the low prices made possible by the new factories and mass-production workshops.

In the early nineteenth century, a growing fear that they were losing status led artisans in the major cities to become involved in politics and unions. At first, these workers organized themselves into interest groups representing their individual skills or trades. Such "trade associations" were the first type of labor unions. They pressured politicians for tariffs to protect their industries from foreign imports, provided insurance benefits, and drafted regulations to improve working conditions. In addition, they sought to control the number of tradesmen in their profession so as to maintain wage levels.

Early labor unions faced major legal obstacles—in fact, they were prosecuted as unlawful conspiracies. In 1806, for instance, Philadelphia shoemakers

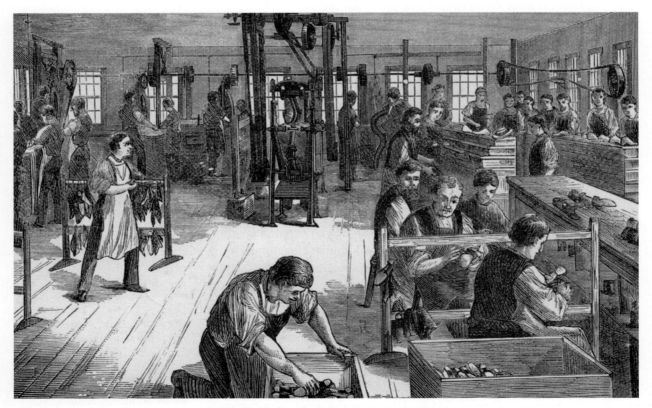

THE SHOE FACTORY When Philadelphia shoemakers went on strike in 1806, a court found them guilty of a "conspiracy to raise wages." Here shoemakers work in the bottoming room at a Massachusetts shoe factory.

were found guilty of conspiring "to raise their wages." The court's decision broke the union. In 1842, though, the Massachusetts Supreme Court issued a landmark ruling in *Commonwealth v. Hunt* declaring that forming a trade union was not in itself illegal, nor was a demand that employers hire only members of the union. The court also said that union workers could strike if an employer hired laborers who refused to join the union.

Until the 1820s, labor organizations took the form of local trade unions, each confined to one city and one craft or skill. From 1827 to 1837, however, organization on a larger scale began to take hold. In 1834, the **National Trades' Union** was formed to organize all the citywide trade unions into a stronger national association. At the same time, shoemakers, printers, carpenters, and weavers established national craft unions. But all the national groups and most of the local ones vanished during the terrible economic depression in the late 1830s.

Creation of National Trades' Union (1834)

Women also formed trade unions. Sarah Monroe, who helped organize the New York Tailoresses' Society, explained that it was intended to defend "our rights." If it was "unfashionable for men to bear [workplace] oppression in silence, why should it not also become unfashionable with the women?" In 1831, the women tailors went out on strike demanding a "just price for labor."

The Rise of the Professions

The dramatic social changes of the first half of the nineteenth century opened up an array of new **professions**. Bustling new towns required new services—retail stores, printing shops, post offices, newspapers, schools, banks, law firms, medical practices, and others—that created more high-status professions than had existed before.

Teaching Teaching was one of the fastest-growing vocations in the first half of the nineteenth century. Horace Mann of Massachusetts was instrumental in promoting the idea of free public education for all children as the best way to transform youths into disciplined, judicious republican citizens. Many states, especially in the North, agreed, and the number of schools exploded during the second quarter of the nineteenth century. New schools required teachers, and Horace Mann helped create "normal schools" around the nation to train young people to be teachers. Public schools initially preferred men as teachers, usually hiring them at age seventeen or eighteen. The pay was so low that few stayed in the profession their entire career, but for many educated, restless young adults, teaching offered independence and social status, as well as an alternative to the rural isolation of farming. Church groups and civic leaders started private academies, or seminaries, for girls.

National Trades' Union Formed in 1834 to organize all local trade unions into a stronger national association; dissolved amid the economic depression in the late 1830s.

professions Occupations requiring specialized knowledge of a particular field; the Industrial Revolution and its new organization of labor created an array of professions in the nineteenth century.

Law, Medicine, and Engineering Teaching was a common stepping-stone for men who became lawyers. In the decades after the Revolution, growing numbers of young men would teach for a year or two before joining an experienced attorney as an apprentice (what today would be called an *intern*).

They would learn the practice of law in exchange for their labors. (There were no law schools in the first half of the nineteenth century.) The absence of formal standards for legal training helps explain why there were so many attorneys in the pre–Civil War period.

Like attorneys, physicians in the early nineteenth century often had little formal academic training. Healers of every stripe assumed the title of *doctor* and established medical practices without regulation. Most were self-taught or had learned their profession by assisting a physician for several years, occasionally supplementing their internships with a few classes at the handful of medical schools. By 1860, there were 60,000 self-styled physicians, many of whom were "quacks" or frauds. As a result, the medical profession lost the public's confidence.

New professions for men:
Lawyers, doctors, engineers

The industrial expansion of the United States also spurred the profession of engineering, a field that would eventually become the nation's largest professional occupation for men. Specialized expertise was required for the design and construction of canals and railroads, the development of machine tools and steam engines, and the building of roads, bridges, and factories. By the outbreak of the Civil War, engineering had become one of the largest professions in the nation.

Women in the Professional Workforce

New professions for women:
Teachers and nurses

During the first half of the nineteenth century, despite the influx of young women into New England textile mills, most women still worked primarily in the home or on a farm. The only professions readily available to them were nursing (often midwifery, the delivery of babies) and teaching. Many middle-class women spent their time outside the home doing religious and social-service work. Then as now, women were the backbone of most churches and service organizations.

A few women, however, courageously pursued careers in male-dominated professions. Elizabeth Blackwell of Ohio managed to gain admission to Geneva Medical College (now Hobart and William Smith College) in western New York despite the disapproval of the faculty. When she arrived at her first class, a hush fell upon the students "as if each member had been struck with paralysis." Blackwell had the last laugh when she finished first in her class in 1849, but thereafter the medical school refused to admit any more women. The first American woman to earn a medical degree, Blackwell went on to start the New York Infirmary for Women and Children and later had a long career as a professor of gynecology at the London School of Medicine for Women.

Equal Opportunities

The dynamic market economy that emerged during the first half of the nineteenth century helped spread the idea that individuals should have an equal opportunity to better themselves in the workplace through their abilities and hard work. Equality of opportunity, however, did not assume equal

THE COUNTRY SCHOOL A one-room schoolhouse in rural New England, as depicted by Winslow Homer in 1871. The young teacher presides over her class, which, as was custom, is arranged with boys on one side of the room and girls on the other (the youngest boy and girl, on the right, are likely siblings who have been allowed to sit next to each other). **What changes in American education took place in the mid–eighteenth century?**

outcomes. Americans wanted an equal chance to earn unequal amounts of wealth. In America, observed a journalist in 1844, "one has as good a chance as another according to his talents, prudence, and personal exertions." The same ideals that prompted so many white immigrants to risk everything to come to the United States, however, were equally appealing to those groups that still did not enjoy equal opportunities to pursue their American dream: African Americans and women. By the 1830s, they, too, began to demand their right to "life, liberty, and the pursuit of happiness." Such desires of "common people" to pursue economic opportunities would quickly spill over into the political arena. The great theme of political life in the first half of the nineteenth century would be the continuing democratization of opportunities for white men, regardless of income or background, to vote and hold office.

Reviewing the
CORE OBJECTIVES |

■ **Transportation and Communication Revolutions** Canals and other improvements in transportation such as the *steamboat*, which could be used on the nation's rivers and lakes, allowed goods to reach markets more quickly and cheaply, helping to create a national *market economy* in which people bought and sold goods at longer distances. *Clipper ships* shortened the amount of time to transport goods across the oceans. The *railroads* (which expanded rapidly during the 1850s) and the *telegraph system* diminished the isolation of the West and united the country economically and socially. The *Erie Canal (1817)* contributed to New York City's emerging status as the nation's economic center even as it spurred the growth of Chicago and other midwestern cities. Improvements in transportation and communication linked rural communities to a worldwide marketplace.

■ **The Industrial Revolution** Inventions in machine tools and technology spurred an *Industrial Revolution* during the nineteenth century. The *cotton gin* dramatically increased cotton production, and a rapidly spreading *cotton* culture boomed in the South, with a resultant increase in slavery. Other inventions, such as John Deere's steel plow and the mechanized *McCormick reaper*, helped Americans, especially westerners, farm their land more efficiently and more profitably. In the North, mills and factories, at first water-powered and eventually powered by coal-fired steam engines, spread rapidly. They initially produced textiles for clothing and bedding from southern cotton, as well as iron, shoes, and other products. The federal government's tariff policy encouraged the growth of domestic manufacturing, especially cotton textiles, by reducing imports of British cloth. Between 1820 and 1840, the number of Americans engaged in manufacturing increased 800 percent. Many mill workers, such as the women employed in the *Lowell system* of New England textile factory communities, worked long hours for low wages in unhealthy conditions. Industrialization, along with increased commerce, helped spur the growth of cities. By 1860, 16 percent of the population lived in urban areas.

■ **Immigration** The promise of cheap land and good wages drew millions of immigrants to America. By 1844, 14.5 percent of the population was foreign born. Many of those who arrived in the 1840s came not just from the Protestant regions of Northern Europe that had supplied most of America's previous immigrants. The devastating potato famine led to an influx of poor Irish Catholic families. By the 1850s, they represented a significant portion of the urban population in the United States, constituting a majority in New York and Boston. German migrants, many of them Catholics and Jews, came to the country at the same time. Not all native-born Americans welcomed the immigrants. *Nativists* became a powerful political force in the 1850s, with the *Know-Nothings* nearly achieving major-party status with their message of excluding immigrants and Catholics from the nation's political community.

■ Workers, Professionals, and Women Skilled workers (artisans) in American cities had long formed trade associations to protect their members and to lobby for their interests. As the *Industrial Revolution* spread, some workers expanded these organizations nationally, forming the *National Trades' Union*. The growth of the *market economy* also expanded opportunities for those with formal education to serve in new or expanding *professions*. The number of physicians, teachers, engineers, and lawyers grew rapidly. By the mid–nineteenth century, women, African Americans, and immigrants began to agitate for equal social, economic, and political opportunities.

KEY TERMS

market economy *p. 274*

steamboats *p. 276*

Erie Canal (1817) *p. 276*

railroads *p. 278*

clipper ships *p. 278*

telegraph system *p. 279*

Industrial Revolution *p. 280*

cotton gin *p. 281*

cotton *p. 281*

McCormick reaper *p. 283*

Lowell system *p. 285*

nativists *p. 291*

Know-Nothings *p. 291*

National Trades' Union
  p. 293

professions *p. 293*

CHRONOLOGY

1793	Eli Whitney invents the cotton gin
1794	Philadelphia-Lancaster Turnpike is completed
1795	Wilderness Road opens
1807	Robert Fulton and Robert Livingston launch steamship transportation on the Hudson River in New York
1825	Erie Canal opens in upstate New York
1831	Cyrus McCormick invents a mechanical reaper
1834	National Trades' Union is organized
1837	John Deere invents the steel plow
1842	Massachusetts Supreme Judicial Court issues *Commonwealth v. Hunt* decision
1845	The *Rainbow*, the first clipper ship, is launched
1845	Irish potato famine
1846	Elias Howe invents the sewing machine
1848	California gold rush begins
1854	Know-Nothings (American party) formed

INQUIZITIVE

Go to InQuizitive to see what you've learned—and learn what you've missed—with personalized feedback along the way.

PARADE OF THE VICTUALLERS (1821) On a beautiful day in March 1821, Philadelphia butcher William White organized a parade celebrating America's high-quality meats. This watercolor by John Lewis Krimmel captures the new, vibrant nationalism that emerged in America after the War of 1812.

Nationalism and Sectionalism

1815–1828

After the War of 1812, the British stopped interfering with American shipping. The United States could now develop new industries and exploit new markets around the globe. It was not simply Alexander Hamilton's financial initiatives and the capitalistic energies of wealthy investors and entrepreneurs that sparked the nation's dramatic economic growth in the early nineteenth century. Prosperity also resulted from the efforts of ordinary men and women who were willing to take risks, uproot families, use unstable paper money issued by unregulated local banks, and tinker with new machines and inventions. By 1828 the young agrarian republic was poised to become a sprawling commercial nation connected by networks of roads and canals as well as regional economic relationships—all energized by a restless spirit of enterprise, experimentation, and expansion.

Yet for all the energy and optimism exhibited by Americans after the war, the fundamental tension between *nationalism* and *sectionalism* remained: how to balance the economic and social needs of the nation's three regions—Northeast, South, and West—with the national interest. Each region (that is, each section) had different economic interests and political goals.

Some sectionalists focused on promoting their region's priorities: shipping and manufacturing in the Northeast, slave-based agriculture in the

CORE OBJECTIVES INQUIZITIVE

1. Analyze how the new spirit of nationalism that emerged after the War of 1812 affected economic policies and judicial decisions.

2. Summarize the issues and ideas that promoted sectional conflict during this era.

3. Explain the emergence of the "Era of Good Feelings" and the factors that led to its demise.

4. Identify the federal government's diplomatic accomplishments during this era, and analyze their impact.

5. Evaluate the influence of Andrew Jackson on national politics in the 1820s and the developments that enabled him to become president.

South, low land prices and transportation improvements in the West. Nationalists, on the other hand, promoted the interests of the nation as a whole. This required each region to recognize that no single section could get all it wanted without threatening the survival of the nation. Of all the issues dividing the young republic, the passions aroused by the expansion of slavery proved to be the most difficult to resolve.

A New Nationalism

CORE **OBJECTIVE**

1. Analyze how the new spirit of nationalism that emerged after the War of 1812 affected economic policies and judicial decisions.

Postwar Nationalism and Economic Policy

After the War of 1812, Americans experienced a wave of patriotic excitement. They had won their independence from Britain for a second time, and a postwar surge of prosperity fed a widespread sense of optimism. In his first message to Congress in late 1815, President James Madison revealed how the challenges of the war, especially the weaknesses of the armed forces and federal finances, had changed his attitudes toward the role of the federal government.

Now Madison and other leading southern Republicans, such as South Carolina's John C. Calhoun, acted like nationalists rather than states' rights sectionalists. They abandoned many of Thomas Jefferson's presidential policies (reducing the armed forces and opposing a national bank, for example) in favor of *economic* nationalism promoted earlier by Federalists Alexander Hamilton and George Washington.

Madison now supported a larger army and navy, a new national bank, and tariffs to protect American manufacturers from foreign competitors. "The Republicans have out-Federalized Federalism," one New Englander commented after Madison's speech.

The Bank of the United States

Economic nationalism: New national bank and currency

After President Madison and congressional Republicans allowed the charter for the First Bank of the United States to expire, in 1811, the nation's finances fell into a muddle. States began chartering new local banks with little or no regulation, and their banknotes (paper money) flooded the economy with different currencies of uncertain value. Imagine trying to do business on a national basis when each state-chartered bank had its own currency, which often was not accepted by other banks or in other states.

Second Bank of the United States Established in 1816 after the first national bank's charter expired; it stabilized the economy by creating a sound national currency; by making loans to farmers, small manufacturers, and entrepreneurs; and by regulating the ability of state banks to issue their own paper currency.

In response to the growing financial turmoil, Madison in 1816 urged Congress to establish a **Second Bank of the United States** (B.U.S.). The B.U.S. was intended primarily to support a stable national currency that would promote economic growth. With the help of powerful legislators Henry Clay and John C. Calhoun, Congress created the new B.U.S., which, like its predecessor, was based in Philadelphia and was chartered for twenty years.

In return for issuing national currency and opening branches in every state, the B.U.S. had to handle all the federal government's funds without charge, lend the government up to $5 million upon demand, and pay the government $1.5 million. The bitter debate over the B.U.S., then and later, helped set the pattern of regional alignment for most other economic issues. Generally speaking, westerners opposed the national bank because it catered to eastern customers.

A Protective Tariff

The long controversy with Great Britain over shipping rights convinced most Americans of the need to develop their own manufacturing sector to end their dependence on imported British goods. Efforts to develop iron and textile industries, begun in New York and New England during the embargo of 1807, had accelerated during the War of 1812, when America lost access to European goods.

After the war ended, however, British companies flooded U.S. markets with their less-expensive products. In response, northern manufacturers lobbied Congress for federal tariffs to protect their infant industries from what they called "unfair" British competition.

Congress responded by passing the **Tariff of 1816**, which placed a 20–25 percent tax on a long list of imported goods. Tariffs benefited some regions (the Northeast) more than others (the South), thus aggravating sectional tensions and grievances. Debates over federal tariffs would dominate political debate throughout the nineteenth century, in part because they provided much of the annual federal revenue and in part because they benefited manufacturers rather than consumers.

Internal Improvements

The third major element of economic nationalism in the first half of the nineteenth century involved federal financing of **internal improvements**— the construction of roads, bridges, canals, and harbors. Most American rivers flowed from north to south, so the nation needed a network of roads running east to west.

In 1817, John C. Calhoun urged the House to fund internal improvements. He believed that a federally-funded network of roads and canals in the West would help his native South by opening up trading relationships between the two regions. Support for federally-financed roads and canals came largely from the West, which badly needed transportation infrastructure. Opposition to such internal improvements was centered in New England, which expected to gain the least from projects intended to spur western development.

In 1803, when Ohio became a state, Congress had ordered that 5 percent of the money from land sales in the state would go toward building a National Road from the Atlantic coast into Ohio and westward. Construction began in 1811. The road was cleared eighty feet wide with a twenty-foot-wide,

Economic nationalism: Tariff of 1816 and federal financing for "internal improvements"

Tariff of 1816 Taxes on various imported items, to protect America's emerging iron and textile industries from British competition.

internal improvements Construction of roads, canals, and other projects intended to facilitate the flow of goods and people.

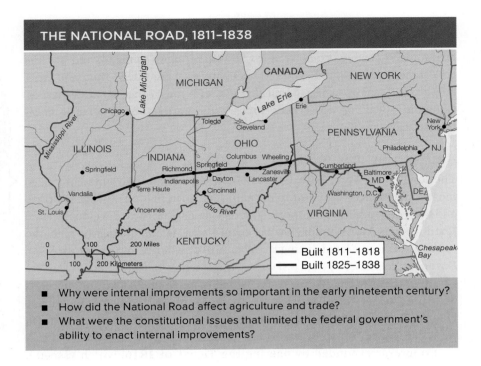

THE NATIONAL ROAD, 1811–1838

Built 1811–1818
Built 1825–1838

■ Why were internal improvements so important in the early nineteenth century?
■ How did the National Road affect agriculture and trade?
■ What were the constitutional issues that limited the federal government's ability to enact internal improvements?

stone-paved strip down the middle. Originally called the Cumberland Road, it was the first interstate roadway financed by the federal government. By 1818, the road was open from Cumberland, Maryland, westward to Wheeling, Virginia (now West Virginia), where it crossed the Ohio River. By 1838, the road extended 600 miles farther westward to Vandalia, Illinois.

By reducing transportation costs and opening up new markets, the National Road helped accelerate the settlement of the West and the emergence of a truly national market economy, with the commercialization of agriculture, whereby farmers increasingly sold their produce and livestock to distant rather than merely local markets.

But using federal money to finance such internal improvements remained controversial. Critics concerned about the expansion of federal power argued that the U.S. Constitution did not allow for such activities; only the local and state governments, or private investors, should fund road, canal, and harbor projects.

Postwar Nationalism and the Supreme Court

The postwar emphasis on economic nationalism also flourished in the Supreme Court, where Chief Justice John Marshall strengthened the constitutional powers of the federal government at the expense of states' rights. Marshall was a consistent nationalist. He viewed his cousin Thomas Jefferson and his Republican followers as a dangerous threat to the nation because they preferred states' rights over federal authority.

During Marshall's early years on the Court (he served thirty-four years altogether), his judicial nationalism affirmed that the Supreme Court had the authority (and responsibility) to judge the constitutionality of state and federal legislative actions (oversight called *judicial review*). In the path-breaking case of *Marbury v. Madison* (1803), the Court had, for the first time, declared a federal law unconstitutional. In the cases of *Martin v. Hunter's Lessee* (1816) and *Cohens v. Virginia* (1821), the Court ruled that the Constitution, as well as the nation's laws and treaties, could remain the supreme law of the land only if the Court could review and at times overturn the decisions of state courts.

JOHN MARSHALL A pillar of judicial nationalism, Marshall became chief justice of the U.S. Supreme Court at the young age of forty-six, ruling on *Marbury v. Madison* just two years later.

Protecting Contract Rights

The Supreme Court made two more decisions in 1819 that strengthened the power of the federal government at the expense of the states. One, **Dartmouth College v. Woodward**, involved the New Hampshire legislature's effort to change Dartmouth College's charter to stop the college's trustees from electing their own successors. In 1816, the state's legislature created a new board of trustees for the college. The original group of trustees sued to block the move. They lost in the state courts but won on appeal to the Supreme Court. The college's original charter, wrote John Marshall in drafting the Court's opinion, was a valid contract that the state legislature had violated, an act forbidden by the Constitution.

This decision implied an enlarged definition of *contract* that seemed to put corporations beyond the reach of the states that had chartered them. Thereafter, states commonly wrote into the charters incorporating businesses and other organizations provisions making charters subject to modification. Such provisions were then part of the "contract."

> Judicial nationalism: *Dartmouth College v. Woodward* (1819)

Protecting a National Currency

The second major Supreme Court case of 1819 was Marshall's most significant interpretation of the constitutional system: **McCulloch v. Maryland**. James McCulloch, a B.U.S. clerk in the Baltimore office, had refused to pay state taxes on B.U.S. currency, as required by a Maryland law. The state indicted McCulloch. Acting on behalf of the national bank, he appealed to the Supreme Court, which ruled unanimously that Congress had the authority to charter the B.U.S. and that states had no right to tax the national bank.

> Judicial nationalism: *McCulloch v. Maryland* (1819)

Speaking for the Court, Chief Justice Marshall ruled that Congress had the right (that is, one of its "implied powers") to take any action not forbidden by the Constitution as long as the purpose of such laws was within the "scope of the Constitution." One great principle that "entirely pervades the Constitution," Marshall wrote, is "that the Constitution and the laws made in pursuance thereof are supreme: . . . They control the Constitution and laws of the respective states, and cannot be controlled by them." The effort by a state to tax a federal bank therefore was unconstitutional, for the "power to tax involves the power to destroy."

Dartmouth College v. Woodward **(1819)** Supreme Court ruling that enlarged the definition of *contract* to put corporations beyond the reach of the states that chartered them.

McCulloch v. Maryland **(1819)** Supreme Court ruling that prohibited states from taxing the Bank of the United States.

STEAMBOAT TRAVEL ON THE HUDSON RIVER (1811) This watercolor of an early steamboat was painted by a Russian diplomat, Pavel Petrovich Svinin, who was fascinated by early technological innovations and the unique entrepreneurial culture of America.

Regulating Interstate Commerce

Judicial nationalism: *Gibbons v. Ogden* (1824)

John Marshall's last great decision, ***Gibbons v. Ogden*** (1824), affirmed the federal government's supremacy in regulating interstate commerce. In 1808, the New York legislature granted Robert Fulton and Robert R. Livingston the exclusive right to operate steamboats on the state's rivers and lakes. Fulton and Livingston then gave Aaron Ogden the exclusive right to ferry people and goods up the Hudson River between New York and New Jersey. Thomas Gibbons, however, operated ships under a federal license that competed with Ogden. On behalf of a unanimous Court, Marshall ruled that the monopoly granted by the state to Ogden conflicted with the federal license issued to Gibbons.

Thomas Jefferson detested John Marshall's judicial nationalism. The Court's ruling in the *Gibbons* case, said the eighty-two-year-old former president, revealed how "the Federal branch of our Government is advancing towards the usurpation of all the rights reserved to the States, and the consolidation in itself of all powers, foreign and domestic."

Gibbons v. Ogden (1824)
Supreme Court case that gave the federal government the power to regulate interstate commerce.

Debates over the American System

CORE **OBJECTIVE**

2. Summarize the issues and ideas that promoted sectional conflict during this era.

The major economic initiatives debated by Congress after the War of 1812—the national bank, federal tariffs, and federally financed roads, bridges, and canals—were interrelated pieces of a comprehensive economic plan called the **American System**. The term was coined by Henry Clay, the powerful congressional leader from Kentucky who would serve three terms as Speaker of the House before becoming a U.S. senator. Clay wanted to free America's economy from its dependence on Great Britain while tying together the diverse regions of the nation politically. "I know of no South, no North, no East, no West to which I owe my allegiance," he asserted. "The Union is my country."

In promoting the American System, Clay sought to give each region of the country its top economic priority. He argued that high tariffs on imports were needed to block the sale of British products in the United States in order to protect new industries in New York and New England from unfair foreign competition. To convince western states to support the tariffs wanted by New England manufacturers, Clay first called for the federal government to use tariff revenues to build much-needed infrastructure—roads, bridges, canals, and other internal improvements—in the frontier West to enable speedier travel and faster shipment of goods to markets. Second, Clay's American System would raise prices for the purchase of federal lands and "distribute" the additional revenue to the states to help finance more roads, bridges, and canals. Third, Clay endorsed a strong national bank to create a single national currency and to regulate the often unstable state and local banks.

Clay was the era's supreme political deal maker and economic nationalist. In many respects, he assumed responsibility for sustaining Alexander Hamilton's vision of a strong federal government nurturing a diversified national economy that combined agriculture, industry, and commerce. The debates over the merits of the American System would continue throughout the first half of the nineteenth century. Clay's program depended on each region's willingness to compromise in order to maintain national unity. For a while, it worked.

Critics, however, argued that higher prices for federal lands would discourage western migration and that tariffs benefited the northern manufacturing sector at the expense of southern and western farmers and the "common" people, who had to pay higher prices for the goods produced by tariff-protected industries.

Many westerners and southerners also feared that the Philadelphia-based Second B.U.S. would become so powerful and corrupt that it could dictate the nation's economic future at the expense of states' rights and the needs of particular regions. Missouri senator Thomas Hart Benton predicted that cash-strapped western towns would be at the mercy of a powerful national bank in Philadelphia. The West, he feared, would be "devoured" by the East and its national banking system. Westerners, Benton worried, "are in the

HENRY CLAY A committed nationalist, Clay was the chief architect of the American System. Here Clay is pictured on a $50 bill issued in the 1860s, long after his death.

American System Economic plan championed by Henry Clay of Kentucky that called for federal tariffs on imports, a strong national bank, and federally financed internal improvements—roads, bridges, canals—all intended to strengthen the national economy and end American economic dependence on Great Britain.

jaws of the monster! A lump of butter in the mouth of a dog! One gulp, one swallow, and all is gone!"

Regional differences over the American System

The bitter debate over the B.U.S. helped set the pattern of deepening sectional disputes among the North, South, and West on the economic issues associated with Clay's American System. Support for federal spending on internal improvements came largely from the West, which badly needed good roads, bridges, canals, and port facilities to connect its economy to the other regions. Many New Englanders and southerners opposed the use of federal money to finance transportation projects in the West, arguing that the states should fund such projects.

On his last day in office, in 1817, President Madison vetoed a bill that would have funded more internal improvements because he could not find a provision in the Constitution authorizing such federal expenditures. Nor was he willing to claim that such funding was an "implied power" within the Constitution. As a result, internal improvements remained, with few exceptions, the responsibility of the states for another hundred years. The federal government did not enter the field again on a large scale until passage of the Federal Highways Act of 1916.

Conflict over extending slavery into the western states

In championing his American System, Henry Clay was forced to resolve explosive sectional conflicts over slavery in the western territories and states. Many of the Americans pouring across the Appalachian Mountains were southerners who took with them a commitment to cotton production and the slave system that supported it. The possibility of new western states becoming "slave states" created the greatest political controversy of the nineteenth century. Former president Thomas Jefferson admitted that the issue scared him "like a firebell in the night." It "awakened and filled me with terror. I considered it at once as the knell of the Union."

An aging Jefferson realized that the United States, which he and others had worked so hard to create and nurture, was increasingly at risk of disintegrating over the future of slavery, the explosive issue that no longer could be avoided. And like Thomas Jefferson, Henry Clay lived with the daily contradiction of being a slave owner opposed to the expansion of slavery.

CORE **OBJECTIVE**

3. Explain the emergence of the "Era of Good Feelings" and the factors that led to its demise.

"Era of Good Feelings"

James Monroe

As James Madison approached the end of his presidency, he, as Thomas Jefferson had done before him, turned to a fellow Virginian, another secretary of state, to be his successor. For Madison, that man was James Monroe, who went on to win the Republican nomination. In the 1816 election, Monroe overwhelmed his Federalist opponent, Rufus King of New York, by a 183–34 vote in the Electoral College. The "Virginia dynasty" of presidents continued.

Like George Washington, Thomas Jefferson, and James Madison, Monroe was a slaveholding Virginia planter. At the outbreak of the Revolutionary War, he was beginning his studies at the College of William and Mary. He joined the army at the age of sixteen, served under George Washington during the Revolution, and later studied law with Jefferson. Washington called him a "brave, active, and sensible army officer."

Tall, blue-eyed James Monroe was eminently qualified to be president. He had served as a representative in the Virginia Assembly; as governor of the state; as a representative in the Confederation Congress; as a U.S. senator; and as U.S. minister (ambassador) to Paris, London, and Madrid. Under President Madison, he served as secretary of state and doubled as secretary of war. South Carolina's John C. Calhoun, who would serve as Monroe's secretary of war, said that the new president was "among the wisest and most cautious men I have ever known." Thomas Jefferson was even more lavish with his praise. He noted that Monroe was "a man whose soul might be turned wrong side outwards without discovering a blemish to the world."

Monroe's administration began with the nation at peace and its economy flourishing. A Boston newspaper said the new president's arrival in office coincided with an "Era of Good Feelings," and the label became a popular catchphrase for the strong economy and political goodwill during Monroe's administration. In 1820, Monroe would be reelected without opposition; by then, the Federalists were so weak that they did not even put up a candidate. The Republican party was dominant.

The nationalist priorities during the so-called Era of Good Feelings did not last long, however, for sectional loyalties continued to battle with national perspectives. Two crucial events signaled the end of the Era of Good Feelings and warned of stormy times ahead: the financial Panic of 1819 and the political conflict over statehood for Missouri.

JAMES MONROE
An experienced and respected Virginian, Monroe is portrayed here as he began his presidency in 1817, a time of peace and economic strength.

The Panic of 1819

The financial **Panic of 1819** resulted from the sudden collapse of cotton prices after British textile mills quit buying high-priced American cotton—the nation's leading export—in favor of cheaper cotton from other parts of the world, especially the British colonies of Egypt and India. The collapse of cotton prices was especially devastating for southern planters, but it also reduced the world demand for other American goods. New factory owners struggled to find markets for their goods and to fend off more-experienced foreign competitors. The financial panic thus renewed sectional tensions between northern and southern economic interests.

Collapse of cotton prices

Other factors caused the financial panic to become a depression. Business owners, farmers, and land speculators had recklessly borrowed money to expand their business ventures or purchase more land. With the collapse of crop prices and the decline of land values during and after 1819, both land speculators and settlers saw their income plummet.

The reckless lending practices of the numerous new state banks compounded the economic confusion. To generate more loans, the banks issued

Panic of 1819 A financial panic that began a three-year economic crisis triggered by reduced demand in Europe for American cotton, declining land values, and reckless practices by local and state banks.

more paper money. Even the B.U.S., which was supposed to bring financial stability to the nation, succumbed to the easy-credit mania.

Financial Panic of 1819

In 1819, newspapers revealed a case of extensive fraud and embezzlement in the Baltimore branch of the B.U.S. The scandal prompted the appointment of Langdon Cheves, a former South Carolina congressman, as the new president of the B.U.S. Cheves restored confidence in the bank by forcing state banks to keep more gold coins in their vaults to back up the loans they were making. State banks in turn put pressure on their debtors, who found it harder to renew old loans or to get new ones. The economic depression lasted about three years, and people blamed the B.U.S. After the panic subsided, many Americans, especially in the South and the West, remained critical of the national bank.

The Missouri Compromise

As the financial panic deepened into a full-blown depression, another cloud appeared on the horizon: the onset of a fierce sectional controversy between North and South over expanding slavery into the new western territories. By 1819, the United States had an equal number of slave and free states—eleven of each. The Northwest Ordinance (1787) had *banned* slavery north of the Ohio River, and the Southwest Ordinance (1790) had *authorized* slavery south of the Ohio. In the vast region west of the Mississippi River, however, no move had been made to extend the dividing line across the vast Louisiana Territory, where slavery had existed since the days when France and Spain first colonized the area. At the time, the Missouri Territory encompassed all the Louisiana Purchase except the state of Louisiana and the Arkansas Territory.

In 1819, residents in the Missouri Territory asked the House of Representatives to let them draft a constitution and apply for statehood, its population having passed the minimum of 60,000 white settlers. It would be the first state west of the Mississippi River.

Tallmadge Amendment

At that point, Representative James Tallmadge Jr., an obscure New York Republican, stunned Congress by proposing a resolution to ban any more slaves in Missouri. Tallmadge's resolution infuriated southern slave owners, many of whom had developed a profitable trade selling slaves to be taken out west. Any effort to restrict slavery in the western territories, they believed, could lead to "disunion" and civil war. In addition, southerners worried that the addition of Missouri as a free state would tip the balance of power in the Senate against the slave states. Their fears were heightened when Congressman Timothy Fuller, an anti-slavery Republican from Massachusetts, declared that it was both "the right and duty of Congress" to stop the spread "of the intolerable evil and the crying enormity of slavery." After fiery debates, the House, with its northern majority, passed the Tallmadge Amendment on an almost strictly sectional vote. The Senate, however, rejected it—also along sectional lines.

Missouri Compromise

At about the same time, Maine, which had been part of Massachusetts, applied for statehood. The Senate decided to link Maine's request for statehood with Missouri's, voting to admit Maine as a free state and Missouri as

THE MISSOURI COMPROMISE, 1820

Free states
Slave states
States and territories covered by the compromise

- What caused the sectional controversy over slavery in 1819?
- What were the terms of the Missouri Compromise?
- What was Henry Clay's solution to the Missouri constitution's ban on free blacks in that state?

a slave state, thus maintaining the political balance between free and slave states.

Illinois senator Jesse Thomas revised the so-called **Missouri Compromise** by introducing an amendment to exclude slavery in the rest of the Louisiana Purchase territory north of latitude 36°30′, Missouri's southern border. Slavery thus would continue in the Arkansas Territory and in the new state of Missouri but would be excluded from the remainder of the area west of the Mississippi River. By a narrow margin, the Thomas Amendment passed on March 2, 1820.

Then another issue arose. The pro-slavery faction in Missouri's constitutional convention inserted in the proposed state constitution a provision banning free blacks and mulattoes (mixed-race people). This violated the U.S. Constitution. Free blacks were already citizens of many states.

The dispute over the status of blacks threatened to unravel the deal to admit Missouri as a state until Speaker of the House Henry Clay fashioned a "second" Missouri Compromise whereby Missouri would be admitted as a state only if its legislature pledged never to deny free blacks their constitutional rights. On August 10, 1821, Missouri became the twenty-fourth state.

Nationalists praised the Missouri Compromise for deflecting the volatile issue of slavery, but the compromise had settled little. In fact, it had the effect of hardening positions over slavery in both North and South.

Missouri Compromise (1820) Legislative decision to admit Missouri as a slave state while prohibiting slavery in the area west of the Mississippi River and north of the parallel 36°30′.

Sectional disputes erupted even within the president's cabinet. President Monroe insisted that any effort to restrict the spread of slavery violated the Constitution. His secretary of state, the future president John Quincy Adams of Massachusetts, disliked the Missouri Compromise for the opposite reason: because it sustained the Constitution's immoral "bargain between freedom and slavery."

The debate over the Missouri Compromise revealed a widening divide between North and South: the Northeast dominated by shipping, commerce, manufacturing, the Midwest centered on small farms, and the South becoming more and more dependent on cotton and slavery.

Nationalist Diplomacy

CORE **OBJECTIVE**

4. Identify the federal government's diplomatic accomplishments during this era, and analyze their impact.

Henry Clay's efforts to promote economic nationalism and John Marshall's decisions affirming *judicial* nationalism were reinforced by efforts to practice *diplomatic* nationalism. John Quincy Adams, the secretary of state in the Monroe administration and the son of former president John Adams, aggressively exercised America's growing power to clarify and expand the nation's boundaries. He also wanted Europeans to recognize America's dominance in the Western Hemisphere.

Relations with Britain

The Rush-Bagot Agreement of 1817 and the Convention of 1818

The Treaty of Ghent had ended the War of 1812, but it left unsettled several remaining disputes between the United States and Great Britain. American statesmen wanted to resolve those disputes in ways that would reinforce economic nationalism. During James Monroe's presidency, John Quincy Adams oversaw the negotiations of two important treaties, the Rush-Bagot Agreement of 1817 (named after the diplomats who arranged it) and the Convention of 1818, both of which eased tensions with Great Britain.

In the Rush-Bagot Agreement, the two nations limited the number of warships on the Great Lakes. The Convention of 1818 was even more important. It settled the disputed northern boundary of the Louisiana Purchase by extending it along the 49th parallel westward from what would become Minnesota to the Rocky Mountains. West of the Rockies, the Oregon Country would be jointly occupied by the British and the Americans.

Florida

Still another disputed boundary involved western Florida. Spanish control over Florida during the early nineteenth century was more a technicality than an actuality. Spain was now a declining power, unable to enforce its obligations under Pinckney's Treaty of 1795 to keep Indians in the region from launching raids into southern Georgia. In 1816, U.S. soldiers clashed with runaway slaves who had taken refuge in a British fort in West Florida, in the present-day Florida Panhandle. At the same time, Seminole warriors

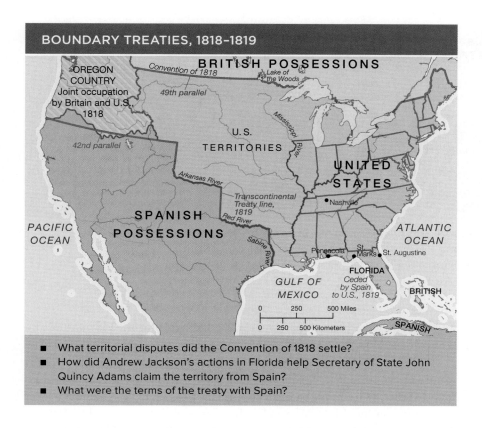

BOUNDARY TREATIES, 1818–1819

- What territorial disputes did the Convention of 1818 settle?
- How did Andrew Jackson's actions in Florida help Secretary of State John Quincy Adams claim the territory from Spain?
- What were the terms of the treaty with Spain?

fought white settlers in the area. In 1817, Americans burned a Seminole village on the border, killing five Indians.

At that point, Secretary of War John C. Calhoun ordered General Andrew Jackson to lead an army from Tennessee into Florida, igniting what became known as the First Seminole War. Jackson was told to pursue marauding Indians into Spanish Florida but not to attack any Spanish forts.

When it came to Spaniards or Indians, few white Tennesseans—and certainly not Jackson, the hero of the Battle of New Orleans—bothered with legal technicalities. In early 1818, without presidential approval, General Jackson's force of 2,000 federal soldiers, volunteer Tennessee militiamen, and Indian allies crossed into Spanish Florida from their encampment in southern Georgia.

In April, the Americans assaulted a Spanish fort at St. Marks and destroyed several Seminole villages along the Suwannee River. They also captured and court-martialed British traders accused of provoking Indian attacks. When told that a military trial of the British citizens was illegal, Jackson gruffly replied that the laws of war did not "apply to conflicts with savages." Jackson ordered the immediate execution of the British troublemakers, an illegal action that angered the British government and alarmed President Monroe's cabinet. But the impulsive Tennessee general kept moving. In May, he captured Pensacola, the Spanish capital of West Florida,

MASSACRE OF THE WHITES BY INDIANS AND BLACKS IN FLORIDA (1836) Published in a southerner's account of the Seminole War, this is one of the earliest known depictions of African Americans and Native Americans fighting as allies. **What motivated Americans to attack Native Americans to the west?**

and established a provisional American government until Florida's future could be decided.

While Jackson's military exploits excited American expansionists, they aroused resentment in Spain and concern in Washington, D.C. Spain demanded that its territory be returned and that Jackson be punished for violating international law. Monroe's cabinet was at first prepared to disavow Jackson's illegal acts. Privately, Secretary of War Calhoun criticized Jackson for disobeying orders—a stand that would later cause bad blood between the two proud men.

Jackson, however, remained a hero to most Americans. He also had an important friend, Secretary of State John Quincy Adams, who realized that Jackson's conquest of Florida had strengthened his own hand in negotiating with the Spanish to purchase the territory.

With the fate of Florida a foregone conclusion, Adams turned his eye to a larger goal: a precise definition of the contested western boundary of the Louisiana Purchase and—his boldest stroke—extension of its boundary all the way to the Pacific coast. In lengthy negotiations with Spain, Adams gradually gave ground on American claims to Texas, then a province of New Spain. In the final version of the deal, however, he stuck to his demand that the boundary of the Louisiana Purchase extend all the way to the Pacific Ocean.

In 1819, Adams convinced the Spanish to sign the **Transcontinental Treaty** (also called the Adams-Onís Treaty), which gave all of Florida to the United States for $5 million. Florida thus became a U.S. territory; in 1845, it would become a state. The treaty also clarified the western boundary separating the Louisiana Territory from New Spain, explaining that it would run from the Gulf of Mexico north to the 42nd parallel and then west to the Pacific coast.

Transcontinental Treaty (1819)
Treaty between Spain and the United States that clarified the boundaries of the Louisiana Purchase and arranged for the transfer of Florida to the United States in exchange for cash.

The Monroe Doctrine

The most important diplomatic policy crafted by President Monroe and Secretary of State Adams involved a determined effort to prevent any future European colonialism in the Western Hemisphere. One consequence of the Napoleonic Wars raging across Europe and the French occupation of Spain and Portugal was a series of independence movements among the Spanish colonies. Between 1809 and 1830, Spain lost almost its entire empire in the Americas: La Plata (later Argentina), Bolivia, Chile, Ecuador, Peru, Colombia, Mexico, Paraguay, Uruguay, and Venezuela had all proclaimed their independence, as had Portuguese Brazil, and the United States was the first nation in the world to recognize them as new nations. The only areas still under Spanish control were the islands of Cuba and Puerto Rico and the colony of Santo Domingo on the island of Hispaniola.

In 1823, rumors reached America that the monarchs of Europe were planning to help Spain recover its lost Latin American colonies. The British foreign minister, George Canning, told the United States that the two countries should jointly oppose any new incursions by European nations in the Western Hemisphere. Monroe initially agreed—if the British government would recognize the independence of the new nations of Latin America. The British refused.

Adams, however, urged the president to go it alone in prohibiting European involvement in the hemisphere. He stressed that "it would be more candid as well as more dignified" for America to ban further European intervention than to tag along with a British statement.

Monroe agreed. He incorporated the substance of Adams's views into his annual message to Congress in December 1823. The **Monroe Doctrine**, as it was named a generation later, contained four major points: (1) that "the American continents . . . are henceforth not to be considered as subjects for future colonization by any European powers"; (2) that the United States would oppose any attempt by European nations to impose their political system anywhere in the hemisphere; (3) that the United States would not interfere with the remaining European-controlled colonies; and (4) that the United States would keep out of the internal affairs of European nations and their wars.

Although the Monroe Doctrine became one of the cherished principles of American foreign policy, it had no standing in international law; it was merely a bold statement sent by an American president to Congress. None of the European nations recognized the legitimacy of the Monroe Doctrine. In fact, the Russian ruler, Czar Alexander I, dismissed it with "profound contempt," since he knew that the tiny U.S. Navy could not protect its own shores, much less the rest of the hemisphere. To this day, the Monroe Doctrine has no official standing in international law. Symbolically, however, it has been an important statement of American intentions to prevent European involvement in the Western Hemisphere. Since the Monroe Doctrine was announced, not a single Latin American nation has lost its independence to an outside invader.

Monroe Doctrine (1823)

Monroe Doctrine (1823)
U.S. foreign policy that barred further colonization in the Western Hemisphere by European powers and pledged that there would be no American interference with any existing European colonies.

CORE **OBJECTIVE**

5. Evaluate the influence of Andrew Jackson on national politics in the 1820s and the developments that enabled him to become president.

The Rise of Andrew Jackson

America had become a one-party political system after the War of 1812. The refusal of the Federalists to support the conflict against Great Britain had virtually killed the party. In 1820, President Monroe was reelected without opposition; the Federalists did not even nominate a candidate.

While the Republican party was dominant for the moment, however, it was about to follow the Federalists into oblivion. If Monroe's first term was the Era of Good Feelings, his second term became the Era of Bad Feelings, as sectional controversies erupted into disputes so violent that they gave birth to a new political party: the Democrats, led by Andrew Jackson.

One-Party Politics

No sooner had James Monroe started his second presidential term, in 1821, than leading Republicans began positioning themselves to be the next president, including three members of the president's cabinet: Secretary of War John C. Calhoun, Secretary of the Treasury William H. Crawford, and Secretary of State John Quincy Adams. The powerful speaker of the House, Henry Clay, also hungered for the presidency. And there was Andrew Jackson, who was elected to the Senate in 1823. The emergence of so many viable candidates revealed how fractured the Republican party had become.

Presidential Nominations

In 1822, the Tennessee legislature named Jackson as its choice to succeed President Monroe. Two years later, a mass meeting of Pennsylvanians also endorsed Jackson for president and John C. Calhoun for vice president. Meanwhile, the Kentucky legislature had nominated its favorite son, Henry Clay, in 1822. The Massachusetts legislature nominated John Quincy Adams in 1824. That same year, a group of Republican congressmen nominated William Crawford of Georgia.

Crawford's friends emphasized his devotion to states' rights and strict construction (interpretation) of the Constitution. For his part, Henry Clay continued to champion the economic nationalism of his American System. Adams shared Clay's belief that the national government should finance internal improvements to stimulate economic development, but he was less strongly committed to tariffs. And Jackson tried to capitalize on his own popularity as a military hero. Thomas Jefferson remained skeptical, however, believing that Jackson lacked the education and polish to be president: "He is one of the most unfit men I know."

As a self-made military hero, Jackson was an attractive candidate, especially to voters of Irish and Scots-Irish backgrounds. In Jackson, the Irish immigrants found a hero. The son of poor Scots-Irish colonists, he was beloved for having defeated the hated English in the Battle of New Orleans. In addition, the Irish immigrants' distaste for aristocracy, which they

ANDREW JACKSON The controversial general was painted by Anna Claypoole Peale in 1819, the year of his military exploits in Florida.

associated with centuries of English rule, attracted them to a politician who claimed to represent "the common man."

The "Corrupt Bargain"

The results of the 1824 election were inconclusive. In the Electoral College, Jackson had 99 votes; Adams, 84; Crawford, 41; and Clay, 37. But Jackson did not have the necessary majority of the total votes. In such a circumstance, as in the 1800 election, the Constitution specified that the House of Representatives would make the final decision from among the top three candidates. By the time the House could convene, however, Crawford had suffered a stroke and dropped out.

Whatever else might have been said about the outcome between Jackson and Adams, one thing seemed apparent—the election revealed how deeply divided the nation had become. Sectionalism had defeated nationalism as the Republicans split into warring regional factions. The election was a particularly humiliating defeat for Henry Clay and his American System; voters in New England and New York opposed his call for federal funding of

ELECTION CAMPAIGN OF 1824 In this illustration from an 1824 political broadside, John Quincy Adams advertises his allegiance to Clay's American System. His presidential platform is portrayed as a ship, sailing under the banners of "No Colonial Subjugation" and "Free Trade." **How did Adams's platform differ from Jackson's?**

internal improvements, and the South rejected his promotion of the protective tariff.

Now that the deadlocked election had been thrown into the House of Representatives, however, Clay's influence, as Speaker of the House, would be decisive. While Adams and Jackson courted Clay's support, he scorned them both, claiming they provided only a "choice of evils." But he regarded Jackson, his fierce western rival, as a "military chieftain," a frontier Napoleon unfit for the presidency. Jackson's election, Clay predicted, would "be the greatest misfortune that could befall the country."

Although Clay and Adams disliked each other, the nationalist Adams supported most of what Clay wanted policy-wise, particularly high tariffs, transportation improvements, and a strong national bank. Clay also expected Adams to name him secretary of state, the office that usually led to the White House. A deal between Clay and Adams broke the deadlock. Clay endorsed Adams, and the House of Representatives elected Adams with 13 state delegation votes to Jackson's 7 and Crawford's 4.

> Corrupt bargain (1824)

The controversial victory proved costly for Adams, however, as it united his foes and crippled his administration before it began. Clay's scheme proved to be a colossal blunder. Jackson dismissed Clay as a "scoundrel," the "Judas of the West," who had entered into a self-serving **"corrupt bargain"** with Adams. Their "corruptions and intrigues," he charged, had "defeated the will of the People." American politics had now entered an Era of Bad Feelings.

Almost immediately after the 1824 decision, Jackson's supporters launched a campaign to undermine the Adams administration and elect their hero president in 1828. Crawford's supporters soon moved into the Jackson camp, as did the new vice president, John C. Calhoun of South Carolina, who quickly found himself at odds with the president.

John Quincy Adams

John Quincy Adams was one of the ablest men, hardest workers, and finest intellects ever to enter the White House. He had been ambassador to four European nations, a U.S. senator, a Harvard professor, and an outstanding secretary of state. He had helped negotiate the end to the War of 1812 and had drafted the Monroe Doctrine (1823). And he promoted American isolation from global wars and causes. In 1821, he had explained that America "goes not abroad in search of monsters to destroy. She is the well-wisher to the freedom and independence of all. She is the champion and vindicator only of her own."

corrupt bargain Scandal in which presidential candidate and Speaker of the House, Henry Clay, secured John Quincy Adams's victory over Andrew Jackson in the 1824 election, supposedly in exchange for naming Clay secretary of state.

Yet for all his accomplishments, John Quincy Adams proved to be one of the most ineffective presidents, undercut from the start of his administration by the controversy surrounding his deal with Henry Clay to make him president. In his inaugural address, Adams admitted to voters that he was "less possessed of your confidence . . . than any of my predecessors."

The stiff and cold Adams, an unbending moralist, lacked the common touch and the politician's gift for compromise. A snobbish man whose parents, John and Abigail, had groomed him since birth for the presidency, Adams lacked his father's redeeming geniality and humor. His personality in part was shaped by family tragedies: he saw two brothers and two sons die from alcoholism. Adams himself suffered from chronic bouts of depression that reinforced his grim self-righteousness and tendency toward self-pity, qualities that did not endear him to fellow politicians or the public.

Adams was stubbornly conventional about many things. Often in his letters to his dazzling wife, Louisa, Adams reminded her that she was never to criticize him but he remained free to chastise her. Women, he declared, have "nothing to do with politics." He readily acknowledged the "defects" in his character but confessed that he could not change his solitary ways. The poet Ralph Waldo Emerson said Adams was so stern and irritable that he must be taking sulfuric acid with his tea. Even Adams's son Charles Francis admitted that his father "makes enemies by perpetually wearing the iron mask."

JOHN QUINCY ADAMS A brilliant man but an ineffective leader, he appears here in his study in 1843. He was the first U.S. president to be photographed.

Adams was an unusual president in many respects, not the least of which was his determination to create an activist federal government with expansive goals. His first State of the Union message included a grand blueprint for national development, set forth so bluntly that it became a political disaster. In the boldness and magnitude of its conception, his vision of an expanded federal government outdid the plans of Alexander Hamilton, James Monroe, and Henry Clay. The federal government, Adams stressed, should finance vast internal improvements (new roads, canals, harbors, and bridges), create a national university, support scientific explorations of the Far West, build astronomical observatories, and establish a department of the interior to manage the vast government lands. To refrain from using such broad federal powers, Adams insisted, "would be treachery to the most sacred of trusts."

Yet Adams's explicit support for a more powerful federal government was so controversial that it led to the death of the Republican party and sparked the emergence of a new party system. Those who agreed with the economic nationalism of Adams and Clay began calling themselves National Republicans. The opposition—the growing party of those supporting Andrew Jackson and states' rights—began calling themselves Democratic Republicans; they would eventually drop the name Republican and become simply Democrats.

President Adams's outspoken efforts to expand the scope of the federal government and his refusal to play backroom politics with Congress condemned his administration to utter frustration from the start. Congress largely ignored his ambitious domestic proposals, and in foreign affairs the triumphs he had scored as secretary of state had no sequels during his presidency. He was a great statesman at the wrong time, an arrogant and stubborn visionary unable to excite voters by his ideas. America was not ready for a dominant federal government. But it was ready for a charismatic and domineering president.

The Election of Andrew Jackson

These maneuverings launched the savage **campaign of 1828** between John Quincy Adams and Andrew Jackson, the National Republicans versus the Jacksonian Democrats. Both sides engaged in vicious personal attacks. As a Jackson supporter observed, "The floodgates of falsehood, slander, and abuse have been hoisted" by the Adams campaign, "and the most nauseating filth is [being] poured" on Jackson's head.

Adams's supporters denounced Jackson as a hot-tempered, ignorant barbarian who spelled Europe "Urope." They dismissed him as a cock-fighting gambler and slave trader who had participated in numerous duels and frontier brawls, a man whose fame rested upon his reputation as a killer.

The most scurrilous attack on Jackson was that he had lived in adultery with his wife, Rachel. In fact, they had lived together for two years in the mistaken belief that her divorce from her first husband was final. As soon as the divorce was official, Andrew and Rachel had remarried. A furious Jackson blamed Henry Clay for spreading the slurs against his wife, calling the Kentuckian "the basest, meanest scoundrel that ever disgraced the image of his god."

The Jacksonians, for their part, condemned Adams as an aristocrat and monarchist, a professional politician who had never had a real job. Newspapers claimed that the president had been corrupted by foreigners in the courts of Europe during his diplomatic career. The most outlandish charge was that Adams had allegedly delivered up an American girl to Czar Alexander I while serving as ambassador to Russia. Adams was left to gripe about the many "forgeries now swarming in the newspapers against me."

In the 1828 campaign, Jackson held most of the advantages. As a fabled Indian fighter, he was beloved in the western and southern states, and as a plantation owner, lawyer, and slaveholder, he had the trust of the southern elite. Jackson was for a small federal government, individual liberty, an expanded military, and white supremacy. Above all, he was a nationalist committed to preserving the Union in the face of rising sectional tensions.

Candidate Jackson benefited from a growing spirit of democracy in which many voters viewed Adams as an elitist. When Adams's supporters began referring to the rough-hewn Jackson as a "jackass," the Tennessean

campaign of 1828 Bitter presidential contest between Democrat Andrew Jackson and National Republican John Quincy Adams (running for reelection), resulting in Jackson's victory.

Jackson Forever!

The Hero of Two Wars and of Orleans!

The Man of the People!

HE WHO COULD NOT BARTER NOR BARGAIN FOR THE

PRESIDENCY!

Who, although "*A Military Chieftain,*" valued the purity of Elections and of the Electors, MORE than the Office of PRESIDENT itself! Although the greatest in the gift of his countrymen, and the highest in point of dignity of any in the world,

BECAUSE

It should be derived from the

PEOPLE!

No Gag Laws! No Black Cockades! No Reign of Terror! No Standing Army or Navy Officers, when under the pay of Government, to browbeat, or

KNOCK DOWN

Old Revolutionary Characters, or our Representatives while in the discharge of their duty. To the Polls then, and vote for those who will support

OLD HICKORY

AND THE ELECTORAL LAW.

JACKSON FOREVER Proclaiming Jackson a "man of the people," this 1828 campaign poster identifies him with the democratic impulse of the time. **How did Jackson's campaign differ from Adams's in 1824 (see p. 316)?**

embraced the name, using the animal as a symbol for his "tough" campaign. The jackass eventually became the enduring symbol of the Democratic party.

The Rise of the "Common Man" in Politics

Jackson's campaign explicitly appealed to the "common" voters, many of whom were able to vote in a presidential election for the first time. After the Revolution, and especially after 1800, more and more white men had gained the right to vote. This "democratization" of politics also affected many free black males in northern states, half of which allowed African Americans to vote alongside whites.

The extension of voting rights to people with little or no wealth led to the election of politicians sprung from the people rather than the social elite. Jackson, a frontiersman of humble origin who had scrambled up the political ladder by will and tenacity, fit this more democratic ideal. "Adams can write,"

Democratization of voting

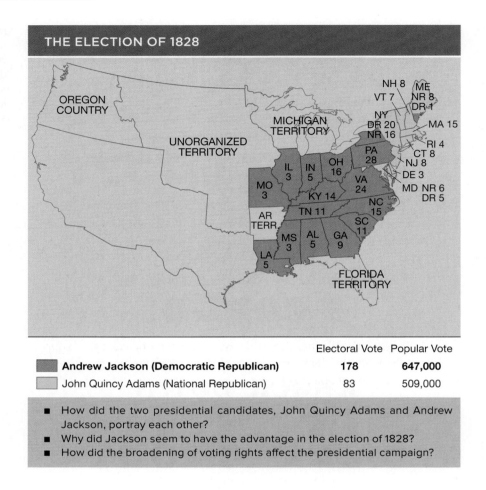

THE ELECTION OF 1828

		Electoral Vote	Popular Vote
■	**Andrew Jackson (Democratic Republican)**	**178**	**647,000**
□	John Quincy Adams (National Republican)	83	509,000

- How did the two presidential candidates, John Quincy Adams and Andrew Jackson, portray each other?
- Why did Jackson seem to have the advantage in the election of 1828?
- How did the broadening of voting rights affect the presidential campaign?

went one of the campaign slogans, "but Jackson can fight." The former general could write, too, though he once said that he had no respect for a man who could think of only one way to spell a word.

Labor Politics

> Political participation by labor unions and reformers

With the widespread removal of property qualifications for voting, the working poor became an important political force in the form of the Workingmen's parties, first organized in Philadelphia in 1828. The Workingmen's parties were reformist groups in the nation's largest cities devoted to promoting the interests of laborers, including shorter working hours and allowing all males to vote regardless of the amount of property owned.

The Workingmen's parties faded quickly, however. The inexperience of labor politicians left these reformist groups prey to manipulation by political professionals. In addition, major national parties, especially the Democrats, co-opted some of their issues. Yet while the working-class parties elected few candidates, they did succeed in drawing notice to their demands, many of which attracted the support of middle-class reformers. Above all, they promoted free public education for all children and sought to end the practice of imprisoning people for indebtedness, causes that won widespread popular support. In large part because of his background as a "common man," union members loved Andrew Jackson.

President Jackson

When the 1828 election returns came in, Jackson won by a comfortable margin. The new president, the first to come from a western state, entered office still seething with resentment at the way his opponents had smeared the reputation of his wife, who had died a few days after learning of the political attacks on her and her "tarnished" marriage. Jackson wept at her funeral while reading the inscription on her gravestone: "A being so gentle, so virtuous, slander might wound but could not dishonor." Now he relished the chance to take revenge on those whose attacks had caused Rachel's heart attack and death in December 1828, just weeks before his presidential inauguration. At his wife's funeral, Jackson declared that those "vile wretches who have slandered her must look to God for mercy," for he would offer none.

As he entered the White House, a vengeful President Jackson was determined to launch a new "democratic" era that would silence his critics, restore government to "the people," and take power away from the "Eastern elite."

Reviewing the
CORE OBJECTIVES |

■ **Nationalism** After the War of 1812, the federal government pursued many policies to strengthen the national economy. The *Tariff of 1816* protected American manufacturers from foreign competition, and the *Second Bank of the United States* provided a stronger national currency. Madison, Monroe, and Adams all promoted an active role for the federal government in promoting economic growth. Led by John Marshall, the Supreme Court limited the powers of states and strengthened the power of the federal government in *Dartmouth College v. Woodward (1819)* and *McCulloch v. Maryland (1819)*. The Marshall court interpreted the Constitution as giving Congress the right to take any action not forbidden by the Constitution as long as the purpose of such laws was within the "scope of the Constitution." In *Gibbons v. Ogden (1824)*, the Marshall court established the federal government's authority over interstate commerce.

■ **Sectionalism** Henry Clay's *American System* supported economic nationalism by endorsing a national bank, a protective tariff, and federally funded *internal improvements*, such as roads and canals. Many Americans, however, remained more tied to the needs of their particular sections of the country. People in the different regions— North, South, and West—disagreed about which economic policies best served their interests. As settlers streamed west, the extension of slavery into the new territories became the predominant political concern, eventually requiring both sides to compromise repeatedly to avoid civil war.

■ **Era of Good Feelings** James Monroe's term in office was initially labeled the Era of Good Feelings because it began with peace and prosperity. Two major events spelled the end of the Era of Good Feelings: the financial *Panic of 1819* and the controversial *Missouri Compromise (1820)*. The explosive growth of the cotton culture transformed life in the South, in part by encouraging the expansion of slavery, which moved west with migrating southern planters. In 1819, however, the sudden collapse of world cotton prices devastated the southern economy. The *Missouri Compromise*, a short-term solution to the issue of allowing slavery in the western territories, exposed the emotions and turmoil that the tragic system generated.

■ **National Diplomacy** The main diplomatic achievements of the period after the War of 1812 extended America's contested boundaries and enabled the resumption of trade with Great Britain. To the north, U.S. diplomatic achievements established northern borders with Canada. To the south, the *Transcontinental Treaty (1819)* with Spain extended the boundaries of the United States. The *Monroe Doctrine (1823)* declared that the Americas were no longer open to European colonization.

■ **The Election of 1828** The demise of the Federalists ended the first party system in America, leaving the Republicans as the only national party. The seeming unity of the Republicans was shattered by the election of 1824, which Andrew Jackson lost as a result of what he believed was a *corrupt bargain* between John Quincy Adams and Henry Clay. Jackson won the presidency with the *campaign of 1828* by rallying southern and western voters with his promise to serve the interests of common people. His election opened a new era in national politics that reflected the democratization of voting in most states (at least for white men).

KEY TERMS

Second Bank of the United States *p. 300*

Tariff of 1816 *p. 301*

internal improvements *p. 301*

Dartmouth College v. Woodward (1819) *p. 303*

McCulloch v. Maryland (1819) *p. 303*

Gibbons v. Ogden (1824) *p. 304*

American System *p. 305*

Panic of 1819 *p. 307*

Missouri Compromise (1820) *p. 309*

Transcontinental Treaty (1819) *p. 312*

Monroe Doctrine (1823) *p. 313*

corrupt bargain *p. 316*

campaign of 1828 *p. 318*

CHRONOLOGY

1811	Construction of the National Road begins
1816	Second Bank of the United States is established
	First protective tariff goes into effect
1817	Rush-Bagot Agreement between the United States and Great Britain creates an unfortified border between the United States and Canada
1818	The Convention of 1818 establishes the northern border of the Louisiana Purchase at the 49th parallel and the joint occupation of Oregon by the United States and Great Britain
1819	Supreme Court issues *McCulloch v. Maryland* decision
	United States and Spain agree to the Transcontinental Treaty
	Tallmadge Amendment
1820	Congress accepts the Missouri Compromise
1823	President Monroe enunciates the principles of the Monroe Doctrine
1824	Supreme Court issues *Gibbons v. Ogden* decision
	John Quincy Adams wins the presidential election by what some critics claim is a corrupt bargain with Henry Clay
1828	Andrew Jackson wins presidential contest

📖 INQUIZITIVE

Go to InQuizitive to see what you've learned—and learn what you've missed—with personalized feedback along the way.

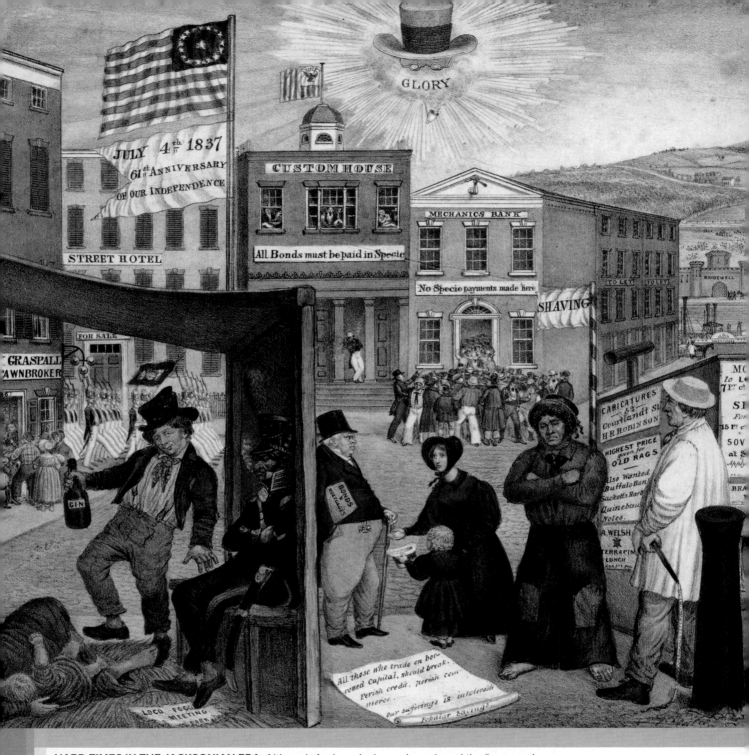

Text visible within the illustration:

JULY 4th 1837
61st ANNIVERSARY
OF OUR INDEPENDENCE

STREET HOTEL

CUSTOM HOUSE

All Bonds must be paid in Specie

MECHANICS BANK

No Specie payments made here

GLORY

SHAVING

TO LET TO LET

BRIDEWELL

FOR SALE

GRASPALL
PAWNBROKER

GIN

BONDS
MORTGAGES

CARICATURES
64
Courtlandt St.
H.R. ROBINSON

HIGHEST PRICE
given for
OLD RAGS

Also Wanted
Buffalo Ban[k]
Sackett's Harb[or]
Quinebaug
Notes.

A. WELSH
✦
TERRAPIN
LUNCH

MO[NEY]
to L[ET]
7 P[er] c[ent]

S[HIP]
For
15 P[er] c[ent]

SOV[EREIGNS]
at $[
Apply

BRA

LOCO FOCO
MEETING
PARK

All those who trade on bor-
rowed Capital, should break.
Perish credit, Perish com-
merce.
Our sufferings is intolerable
Popular Savings

HARD TIMES IN THE JACKSONIAN ERA Although Andrew Jackson championed the "poor and humble," his economic policies contributed to the Panic of 1837, a financial crisis that hit the working class the hardest. This cartoon illustrates New York City during the seven-year depression: a frantic mob storms a bank, while in the foreground, a widow begs on the street with her child, surrounded by a banker or landlord and a barefoot sailor. At left, there is a drunken member of the Bowery Toughs gang and a down-on-his-luck militiaman. The cartoonist places the blame on Jackson, whose hat, glasses, and pipe overlook the scene. The white flag at left wryly states: "July 4th, 1827, 61st Anniversary of Our Independence." The banners demanding "specie," or payments in gold rather than paper money, illustrate the controversy over banks and bankers during the Jacksonian era.

The Jacksonian Era

1828–1840

P resident Andrew Jackson was a unique personality and a transformational leader. He was the first president from a western state (Tennessee), the first to have been born in a log cabin, the first not from a prominent colonial family, the last to have participated in the Revolutionary War, and the first to carry two bullets in his body from a duel and a barroom brawl. Most important, Jackson was the polarizing emblem of a new democratic era.

Born in 1767 along the border between the two Carolinas, Jackson grew up in a struggling single-parent household. His father was killed in a farm accident three weeks before Andrew was born, forcing his widowed mother, Elizabeth, to scratch out a living as a housekeeper.

During the Revolution, the Jackson boys joined in the fighting against the British, and one of Andrew's brothers died in battle. In 1781, fourteen-year-old Andrew was captured and imprisoned. When he refused to shine a British officer's boots, the soldier slashed him with a sword, leaving ugly scars on his head and arm. Soon after her son was released, Elizabeth Jackson, who had helped nurse injured American soldiers, died of cholera. The orphaned Andrew Jackson thereafter despised the British, blaming them for the deaths of his brother and mother.

After the Revolution, the self-taught Jackson became a frontier attorney in Tennessee, where he dealt mostly with disputes over land claims. He moved

CORE OBJECTIVES INQUIZITIVE

1. Describe Andrew Jackson's major beliefs regarding democracy, the presidency, and the proper role of government in the nation's economy.

2. Evaluate Jackson's response to the nullification crisis.

3. Analyze Jackson's legacy regarding the status of Indians in American society.

4. Explain the causes of the economic depression of the late 1830s and the emergence of the Whig party.

5. Assess the strengths and weaknesses of Jackson's transformational presidency.

to Nashville in 1788, where he fell in love with Rachel Donelson Robards, a woman he lived with before she was legally divorced from her first husband. The Jacksons developed a happy marriage, but gossip about the origins of their relationship dogged them until Rachel's heart attack and death in December 1828.

In 1796, when Tennessee became a state, voters elected Jackson to the U.S. House and then to the Senate, where he served only a year before returning to Tennessee and becoming a judge. The ambitious Jackson made a lot of money, first as an attorney, then as a buyer and seller of horses, land, and slaves. Jackson eventually owned a hundred slaves on his large cotton plantation, called the Hermitage, near Nashville.

Like most of his neighbors, Jackson had no moral reservations about slavery and at times could be a cruel master. After one of his slaves escaped, he offered a large reward for his recapture, and promised "ten dollars extra for every hundred lashes a person [would] give [him] to the amount of three hundred." When not farming or raising racehorses, Jackson served as the iron-willed commander of the Tennessee militia.

In 1828, many political leaders cringed at the thought of the undereducated, short-tempered Jackson, who had run roughshod over international law in his war against the British and Seminoles in Florida, presiding over the nation. "His passions are terrible," said elderly Thomas Jefferson. John Quincy Adams scorned Jackson "as a barbarian and savage who could scarcely spell his name." The proud, yet insecure Jackson dismissed such criticism as an example of the "Eastern elite" continuing its efforts to control American politics.

Jackson's inauguration ceremony set the tone for his controversial presidency. Dressed in a black mourning suit in honor of his recently deceased wife, the self-described people's president stepped out of the U.S. Capitol at noon on March 4, 1829. Waiting for him in the cold were 15,000 people who collectively roared and waved their hats when they saw Jackson emerge. "I never saw anything like it before," marveled Daniel Webster, the great senator from Massachusetts.

Concerns about Jackson's fitness for the presidency were heightened by the riotous scene at the White House after his inauguration ceremony in March 1829. In a symbolic effort to reach out to the "common" people, Jackson opened the party to anyone. To his surprise, the huge crowd of jubilant Democrats turned into a drunken mob. Dishes and glasses were smashed and furniture

ALL CREATION GOING TO THE WHITE HOUSE In this depiction of Jackson's inauguration party, satirist Robert Cruikshank draws a visual parallel to Noah's Ark, suggesting that people of all walks of life were now welcome to the White House. **What demographics are *not* featured in Cruikshank's illustration?**

broken. Supreme Court Justice Joseph Story said he had never seen such "a mixture" of rowdy people misbehaving in the White House. "The reign of KING MOB seemed triumphant," he wrote.

Jackson, however, relished the common people and their adoration of him. Tall and lean—over six feet tall but only 140 pounds—with penetrating eyes, a long nose, jutting chin, and iron-gray hair that intensified his steely personality, "Old Hickory" (a nickname given to Jackson by his soldiers because he was as tough as the hard wood of a hickory tree) loved the rough-and-tumble combat of political life. "I was born for a storm," he once boasted. "A calm [life] does not suit me."

Jackson believed in plain-speaking and plain pleasures. He smoked a corncob pipe and chewed—and spit—tobacco (he installed 20 spittoons in the White House). Old Hickory loved the rough-and-tumble combat of the raucous new democratic political culture, but he was not in good health as he assumed the presidency. Scarred and bullet-ridden, he suffered from blinding headaches and other ailments that led rival Henry Clay to describe him as "feeble in body and mind."

The brash new president took the nation by storm. Jackson helped create and shape the Democratic party, and he helped introduce modern presidential campaigning to electoral politics. No political figure was so widely loved or more deeply despised, yet he stamped his name and, more important, his ideas, personality, and values on an entire era of American history.

Jacksonian Democracy

Jackson's election marked the impact of thirty years of democratic innovations in politics. During the 1820s and 1830s, American political life was transformed as more and more landless white men were allowed to vote and hold office. "The principle of universal suffrage," announced the *U.S. Magazine and Democratic Review*, "meant that white males of age constituted the political nation." Jackson promised to protect "the poor and humble" from the "tyranny of wealth and power." His populist goal was to elevate the "laboring classes" of white men who "love liberty and desire nothing but equal rights and equal laws."

Such democratization was unique in the world, for it gave previously excluded white men equal status as citizens regardless of their wealth or background. No longer was politics the arena for only the most prominent and wealthiest Americans.

Campaigning was also democratized. Politics became the most popular form of mass entertainment, as people from all walks of life passionately engaged in elections and were remarkably well-informed about public policy issues. Politics was "the only pleasure an American knows," observed visiting Frenchman Alexis de Tocqueville. "Even the women frequently attend public meetings and listen to political harangues as a recreation from their household labors."

Promoting the "common man"

Jackson was the most openly partisan and politically involved president in history to that point. Unlike previous presidents, who viewed political campaigning as unseemly, he actively sought votes among the people, lobbied congressmen, and formed Hickory Clubs across the nation to campaign for him. Jackson also benefited from a powerful Democratic party "machine" run by his trusted secretary of state (later his vice-president) Martin Van Buren, a New York lawyer with a shrewd political sense.

Democracy, of course, is a slippery and elastic concept, and Jacksonians rarely defined what they meant by the "rule of the people." Noah Webster, the Connecticut Federalist who produced the nation's first reliable dictionary, complained that "the men who have preached these doctrines [of democracy] have never defined what they mean by the *people*, or what they mean by *democracy*, nor how the *people* are to govern themselves." Jacksonian Democrats also showed little concern for the *undemocratic* constraints on African Americans, Native Americans, and women, all of whom were denied most basic political and civil rights.

Many southern slaveholders worried that the surge of democratic activism would eventually threaten the slave system. Virginian Muscoe Garnett, a planter and attorney, declared that "democracy is indeed incompatible with slavery, and the whole system of Southern society." His fellow Virginian, George Fitzhugh, was more explicit in his disdain for democratic ideals. In every society, he asserted, "some were born with saddles on their backs, and others booted and spurred to ride them."

Expanded presidential authority

As the first president to view himself as a representative of "the people," Jackson resolved to exercise expanded executive powers at the expense of the legislative and judicial branches. The ruling political and economic elite must be removed, he said, for "the people" are "the government, the sovereign power" in the United States, and they had elected him president.

In general, Jackson and the Democrats believed that "the world is governed too much." The nation's seventh president wanted to reduce federal spending, pay off the federal debt (a "national curse"), destroy the Second Bank of the United States (B.U.S.), and relocate the "ill-fated race" of Indians from the East to the West so that whites could exploit their ancestral lands. In pursuing these ambitious goals, he exercised presidential authority more boldly than any of his predecessors.

The Spoils System and Presidential Conventions

Spoils system

To dislodge the eastern political elite, Jackson replaced many federal officials with his own supporters. Government jobs, he argued, belonged to the people, not to career bureaucrats. During his two presidential terms, Jackson replaced about a fifth of the federal officeholders with his own friends and supporters, not all of whom were qualified for their new positions. Such partisan behavior came to be called "the spoils system," since, as a prominent Democrat declared, "to the victor goes the spoils."

Birth of presidential nominating conventions

Jackson also sought to "democratize" the way that presidential candidates were selected. Since the presidency of George Washington, most nominees had been chosen by party "caucuses" of prominent congressmen and senators. Jackson hated the idea of legislators nominating presidents. In 1832, he would convince the Democrats to stage their first presidential nominating convention as a means of involving more people in the process of selecting a candidate. The innovation of presidential nominating conventions reinforced Jackson's image as a man of the people fighting against entrenched party leaders.

The Eaton Affair

Yet Jackson soon found himself preoccupied with squabbles within his own cabinet. From the outset, his administration was divided between supporters of Secretary of State Martin Van Buren, a New Yorker, and the allies of Vice President John C. Calhoun of South Carolina. Both men wanted to succeed Jackson as president. Jackson turned mostly to Van Buren for advice because he did not trust Calhoun, a Yale graduate of towering intellect and fiery determination. Although earlier a Republican nationalist, Calhoun now was focused on defending southern interests, especially the preservation of the slave-based cotton economy that had made him a rich planter.

In his rivalry with Calhoun, Van Buren took full advantage of a juicy social scandal known as the Peggy Eaton affair. Widower John Eaton, a former U.S. Senator from Tennessee, was one of Jackson's closest friends. Eaton had also long been associated with Margaret "Peggy" O'Neale Timberlake, an outspoken Washington temptress married to John Timberlake, a naval officer frequently at sea.

> The politics of social scandal

The flirtatious Peggy Timberlake was devastatingly attractive to the men who kept her company while her husband was away. The ambitious daughter of a Scots-Irish innkeeper who enjoyed "the attentions of men, young and old," she took special delight in Senator John Eaton. In April 1828, John Timberlake died at sea. Although the official cause of death was pulmonary

THE CELESTE-AL CABINET
Eaton presents his infamous and socially snubbed wife, Peggy O'Neil, to Jackson and his cabinet in this satirical illustration. **What are the reactions of Jackson and his cabinet members in this image? How did they react politically?**

failure, rumors swirled that he had committed suicide after learning of his wife's affair with Eaton.

Soon after the fall 1828 presidential election, John Eaton had written president-elect Jackson to alert him of the spiteful gossip aimed at him and Peggy Timberlake. Jackson responded quickly and firmly: "Marry her and you will be in a position to defend her." Eaton did so on January 1, 1829.

Yet the continuing gossip led Jackson to explode, shouting that "I did not come here [to Washington] to make a Cabinet for the Ladies of this place, but for the Nation." In his view, women had no right to mix politics with social life; their doing so was nothing more than vicious meddling. He demanded loyalty from his administrative team—and their wives. Still, the rumoring and sniping continued, month after month, and became a time-consuming distraction for the president.

Jackson blamed the Eaton scandal on his rivals Henry Clay and John C. Calhoun, whom he called a "villain." The president assumed that Calhoun and his wife had targeted John Eaton because he did not support Calhoun's desire to be the next president. One of Calhoun's friends wrote in April 1829 that the United States was "governed by the President—the President by the Secretary of War—and the latter by his Wife." Jackson concluded that the scheming Calhoun was one of the "most dangerous men living—a man, devoid of principle" who "would sacrifice his friend, his country, and forsake his god, for selfish personal ambition."

Jackson's "kitchen cabinet"

Jackson finally decided that the only way to restore harmony in his warring cabinet was to disband it and start over. On April 4, 1831, the president accepted John Eaton's resignation. Four days later, Martin Van Buren resigned. The rest of the cabinet members left in following weeks, enabling Jackson to appoint a new group of senior officers. "A revolution has taken place in the Capitol of the United States," announced the newspaper headlines.

Thereafter, Jackson relied more upon the advice of his so-called kitchen cabinet, an informal group of close friends and supporters. Critics claimed that Jackson did not have the skill to lead the nation. One newspaper announced that the ship of state "is sinking and the rats are flying! The hull is too leaky to mend, and the hero of two wars and a half has not the skill to keep it afloat."

Internal Improvements

Jackson vetoes the Maysville Road Bill

Concerns that Jackson was not in control of things quickly disappeared, however, for he decisively used his executive authority to limit the role of the federal government—while at the same time delivering additional blows to John C. Calhoun and to Henry Clay, the man Jackson blamed for having "stolen" the 1824 election from him.

In 1830, Congress passed a bill pushed by Calhoun and Clay that authorized the use of federal monies to build a sixty-mile-long road from Maysville, Kentucky, to Lexington, Kentucky, Clay's hometown. President Jackson, urged on by Martin Van Buren, who wanted to preserve the Erie Canal's monopoly over western trade, vetoed the bill on the grounds that the proposed road was a "purely local matter," being solely in the state of Kentucky, and thus outside the domain of Congress, which had authority only over *interstate* commerce; federal funding for such local projects would thus require a constitutional amendment. Clay was stunned. "We are all shocked and mortified by the rejection of the Maysville road," he wrote a friend. But he had no luck convincing Congress to override the presidential veto.

The Bank War

Jackson showed the same principled stubbornness in dealing with the national bank. The charter for the First Bank of the United States had expired in 1811 but was renewed in 1816 as the Second Bank of the United States, and it soon became the largest corporation in the nation and the only truly national business enterprise. The Second Bank held all federal funds (mostly from land sales) and also issued paper money (backed by gold and silver) as the national currency. With twenty-nine branches around the nation, the B.U.S. had helped accelerate business expansion. It had also supplied a stable currency by forcing the 464 state banks to keep enough gold coins in their vaults to back their own paper currency, which they loaned to people and businesses. With federal revenues soaring from land sales during the early 1830s, the B.U.S., led by the brilliant but arrogant Nicholas Biddle, had accumulated massive amounts of money—and economic power.

Even though the national bank was beneficial to the infant economy, it had been controversial from the start. Local banks and state governments, especially in the South and West, feared the growing power of the "monopolistic" national bank. Southerners and westerners claimed that the B.U.S. was preventing state banks from lending as much as they wanted and impeding businesses from borrowing as much as they wanted.

Throughout his life Andrew Jackson had hated banks and bankers, whom he called "vipers and thieves." He admitted that he had "always been afraid of banks"—especially the national bank—because they exercised too much power over the economy and the people. Jackson spoke for many western Americans who felt that banks favored the "rich and powerful" men in the East. Jackson also distrusted paper money because banks printed too much of it, causing prices to rise (inflation). He wanted only coins to be used for economic transactions. "I think it right to be perfectly frank with you," Jackson told Nicholas Biddle in 1829. "I do not dislike your Bank any more than [I dislike] all banks."

Early on, the president resolved to destroy the B.U.S., pledging "to put his foot upon the head of the monster and crush him to the dust." The national bank may have become too powerful, but the **Bank War** between Jackson and Biddle revealed that the president never truly understood the bank's

KING ANDREW THE FIRST
Opponents considered Jackson's veto of the Maysville Road Bill an abuse of power. This cartoon shows "King Andrew" trampling on the Constitution, internal improvements, and the Bank of the United States.

Bank War Political struggle in the early 1830s between President Jackson and financier Nicholas Biddle over the renewing of the Second Bank's charter.

RECHARTERING THE BANK
Jackson's effort to defeat the recharter of the B.U.S. is likened to fighting a hydra, a many-headed serpent from Greek mythology. Just as the hydra would sprout two heads when one was severed, for every B.U.S. supporter that Jackson subdued, even more B.U.S. supporters would emerge to take his place.

role or policies. The national bank had provided a stable currency for the expanding economy, as well as a mechanism for controlling the pace of economic growth by regulating the ability of branch banks and state banks to issue paper currency.

The Recharter Effort

Although the Second Bank's charter would run through 1836, Nicholas Biddle could not afford to wait until then for its renewal. Leaders of the newly named National Republican party, especially Henry Clay and Daniel Webster (who was legal counsel to the B.U.S. as well as a senator), told Biddle that he needed to get the charter renewed before the 1836 presidential election. They assured Biddle that the Congress would renew the charter. And Biddle himself grew overconfident about his bank's future. "This worthy President thinks because he has scalped Indians . . . he is to have his way with the Bank." Biddle thought otherwise. "I have been for years in the daily exercise of more personal authority than any President habitually enjoys."

But Biddle and his political allies failed to grasp both Jackson's tenacity and the depth of public resentment toward the national bank. Jackson's disgust for the B.U.S. reflected the concerns of many voters. In the end, Biddle, Clay, and the National Republican party, also called the Anti-Jackson party, unintentionally handed Jackson a popular issue on the eve of the election.

Jackson vetoes renewal of B.U.S. charter

Early in the summer of 1832, both houses of Congress passed the Bank Recharter Bill. On July 10, 1832, however, Jackson vetoed the bill, sending it back to Congress with a blistering criticism of the bank. Jackson claimed that the B.U.S. was both unconstitutional (although the Supreme Court disagreed) and "dangerous to our liberties." The B.U.S. made "the rich richer and the potent more powerful" while discriminating against "the humble members of society—the farmers, mechanics, and laborers." Daniel Webster accused Jackson of using the bank issue "to stir up the poor against the rich." But Webster could not convince the Senate to override the veto, thus setting the stage for a nationwide financial crisis and a dramatic presidential campaign. The overriding issue in the 1832 election was the future of the Bank of the United States.

Nullification

The vetoes of the Maysville Road Bill and the B.U.S. recharter illustrated Jackson's forceful personality. He eventually would veto twelve congressional bills, more than all the previous presidents combined. Critics claimed that his behavior was "monarchical" in its frequent defiance of the will of Congress. Jackson, however, remained determined to strengthen the executive branch in order to strengthen the Union. His commitment to nationalism over sectionalism was nowhere more evident than in his handling of the nullification crisis in South Carolina.

Calhoun and the Tariff

Vice President John C. Calhoun became President Jackson's fiercest critic because of changing conditions in his home state of South Carolina. The financial Panic of 1819 had sparked a nationwide depression, and throughout the 1820s, South Carolina had suffered from a collapse in cotton prices. The state lost almost 70,000 residents who had moved west during the 1820s in search of cheaper and more fertile land for growing cotton; twice as many would leave during the 1830s.

Most South Carolinians blamed their economic woes on the Tariff of 1828, which they labeled the "**Tariff of Abominations**." By taxing British textiles coming into U.S. markets, the 1828 tariff on imported cloth hurt southern cotton growers by reducing British demand for raw cotton from America. It also hurt southerners by raising the prices they had to pay for imports.

But the tariff was not the only factor explaining South Carolina's problems. Thousands of acres of farmland across the state were exhausted from constant overplanting. In addition, South Carolina cotton planters now faced competition from the new cotton-growing states in the Old Southwest: Alabama, Mississippi, Louisiana, and Arkansas.

In a lengthy pamphlet called the *South Carolina Exposition and Protest* (1828), written in secret by John C. Calhoun, the South Carolinian claimed that the Tariff of 1828 favored the interests of New England textile manufacturing over southern agriculture. Under such circumstances, he argued, a state could "nullify," or veto, a federal law it deemed unconstitutional. **Nullification** was the ultimate weapon for those determined to protect states' rights against federal authority. As President Jackson and others pointed

CORE **OBJECTIVE**
2. Evaluate Jackson's response to the nullification crisis.

Calhoun's theory of nullification

Tariff of Abominations (1828) Tax on imported goods, including British cloth and clothing, that strengthened New England textile companies but hurt southern consumers, who experienced a decrease in British demand for raw cotton grown in the South.

nullification Right claimed by some states to veto a federal law deemed unconstitutional.

out, however, allowing states to pick and choose which federal laws they would follow would have created chaos.

The Webster-Hayne Debate

Webster-Hayne debate: States' rights vs. national unity

The controversy over the Tariff of 1828 simmered until 1830, when the great Webster-Hayne debate in Congress sharpened the lines between states' rights and national authority. In a fiery speech, Senator Robert Y. Hayne of South Carolina argued that anti-slavery Yankees were invading the South, "making war upon her citizens, and endeavoring to overthrow her principles and institutions." In Hayne's view, the Union was created by the states, and the states therefore had the right to nullify, or ignore, federal laws they did not like. The independence of the states was to him more important than the preservation of the Union.

Massachusetts senator Daniel Webster then rose to defend the North—and the Union. Blessed with a thunderous voice and a theatrical flair, Webster was an unapologetic Unionist determined "to strengthen the ties that hold us together." He pointed out that the U.S. Constitution was created not by the states but by the American people. If states were allowed to nullify a federal law, the Union would be nothing but a "rope of sand." South Carolina's defiance of federal authority, he charged, "is nothing more than

WEBSTER REPLYING TO SENATOR HAYNE (1848) The eloquent Massachusetts senator denounces the argument for nullification in the Webster-Hayne debate.

resistance by *force*—it is disunion by *force*—it is secession by *force*—it is Civil War."

Webster's powerful closing statement appeared in virtually every newspaper in the nation: "Liberty and Union, now and forever, one and inseparable." Abraham Lincoln later called it "the very best speech ever delivered." Even Hayne was awestruck. He told Webster that "a man who can make such speeches as that ought never to die."

In the end, Webster had the better argument. Most political leaders agreed that the states could not act separately from the national government. President Jackson did not attend the debate, but he kept in touch with it from the White House. When he asked an aide how Webster was doing, the answer was what he wanted: "He is delivering a most powerful speech . . . demolishing our friend Hayne." The president was pleased. As Jackson said, the Constitution and its laws were "supreme."

Jackson versus Calhoun

That Jackson, like Calhoun, was a cotton-planting slaveholder led many southerners to assume that the president would support their resistance to the federal tariff. Jackson was sympathetic—until Calhoun and others in South Carolina threatened to "nullify" federal laws they did not like. He then turned on them with the same fury he had directed toward the advancing British army at New Orleans in 1815.

> Jackson: The preservation of the Union

On April 13, 1830, the Democratic party hosted the first annual Jefferson Day dinner to honor the birthday of the former president. When it was Jackson's turn to propose a toast to Jefferson's memory, he raised his glass, glared at Calhoun, and announced: "Our Union—it must be preserved!" Calhoun then countered with a toast to "the Union, next to our liberty, most dear! May we all remember that it can only be preserved by respecting the rights of the States and distributing equally the benefit and the burden of the Union!"

Jackson's toast had set off a bombshell that exploded the plans of Calhoun and the nullifiers. The dispute between the two proud men prompted Jackson to take a dramatic step: he removed all of Calhoun's supporters from his cabinet, forcing five of eight cabinet members to resign.

The South Carolina Nullification Ordinance

In the fall of 1831, Jackson tried to defuse the confrontation with South Carolina by calling on Congress to reduce the tariff. Congress responded with the Tariff of 1832, which lowered taxes on many imported items, although tariffs on cloth and iron remained high.

The new tariff, however, was not enough to satisfy Calhoun and others in his home state. South Carolina seethed with resentment toward Jackson and the federal government. One hotheaded South Carolina congressman called the Union a "foul monster." He and other white South Carolinians, living in the only state where enslaved Africans were a majority of the

THE ROAD TO DESPOTISM John C. Calhoun reaches for despotism, or absolute authority, in this anti-nullification cartoon of 1833. On the bottom right, Jackson pledges to hang him and his supporters. **According to this cartoon, what are the steps that follow from nullification?**

population, feared that if the northern representatives in Congress were powerful enough to create such discriminatory tariffs, they might eventually vote to end slavery.

In November 1832, a South Carolina state convention overwhelmingly adopted a Nullification Ordinance that repudiated the "unconstitutional" federal tariff acts of 1828 and 1832 (declaring them "null, void, and no law"). If federal authorities tried to use force to collect the tariffs, South Carolina would secede from the Union, they vowed. The state legislature then chose Senator Robert Hayne as governor and elected Calhoun to succeed him as U.S. senator. Calhoun resigned as Jackson's vice president so that he could defend the nullification policy in the Senate.

South Carolina Nullification Ordinance

Jackson's Firm Response

In the nullification crisis, South Carolina, "feisty as a gamecock," found itself standing alone. Other southern states expressed sympathy, but none endorsed nullification. President Jackson's public response was measured yet forthright. He promised to use "firmness and forbearance" with South

Carolina but stressed that nullification "means insurrection and war; and the other states have a right to put it down."

In private, however, Jackson was furious. He threatened to hang Calhoun, Hayne, and other "nullifiers" if there were any bloodshed. "Surely the president is exaggerating," Governor Hayne of South Carolina remarked to Senator Thomas Hart Benton of Missouri. Benton, who years before had been in a fistfight with Jackson, replied: "I have known General Jackson a great many years, and when he speaks of hanging [people] it is time to look for a rope."

In his annual message to the nation, delivered December 4, 1832, Jackson appealed to the people of South Carolina not to follow false leaders such as Calhoun: "The laws of the United States must be executed. . . . Those who told you that you might peaceably prevent their execution, deceived you. . . . Their object is disunion. . . . Disunion by armed force is treason."

Clay's Compromise

President Jackson then sent federal soldiers and a warship to Charleston. Governor Hayne responded by mobilizing the state militia, and the two sides verged on civil war. In early 1833, the president requested from Congress a "**Force Bill**" authorizing him to use the U.S. Army to "force" compliance with federal law in South Carolina. At that point, the nullifiers backed down; the South Carolina legislature postponed the actual enforcement of the nullification ordinances in hopes that a compromise might be reached.

Passage of the compromise bill in Congress depended upon the support of Senator Henry Clay, himself a slaveholding planter, who finally yielded to those urging him to save the day for the Union. A fellow senator told Clay that these "South Carolinians are good fellows, and it would be a pity to see Jackson hang them." Clay agreed. On February 12, 1833, he circulated a plan to reduce the federal tariff gradually. It was less than South Carolina preferred, but it got the nullifiers out of the dilemma they had created. Calhoun supported the compromise: "He who loves the Union must desire to see this agitating question [the tariff] brought to a termination."

On March 1, 1833, Congress passed the compromise tariff and the Force Bill, and the next day Jackson signed both. Calhoun rushed home to convince the rebels in his state to back down. The South Carolina convention then met and rescinded its nullification of the tariff acts. In a face-saving gesture, the delegates nullified the Force Bill, which Jackson no longer needed. Both sides were able to claim victory. Jackson had upheld the supremacy of the Union, and South Carolina had secured a reduction of the federal tariff. But there was still the fundamental issue of southern slaveholders feeling increasingly threatened by growing anti-slavery sentiment in the North. "The struggle, so far from being over," a defiant Calhoun wrote, "is not more than fairly commenced."

Force Bill (1833) Legislation, sparked by the nullification crisis in South Carolina, that authorized the president's use of the army to compel states to comply with federal law.

CORE **OBJECTIVE**

3. Analyze Jackson's legacy regarding the status of Indians in American society.

Jackson's Indian Policy

If President Jackson's firm stance against nullification constituted his finest hour, his forcible removal of Indians from their ancestral lands was one of his lowest moments. Like most white frontiersmen, Jackson viewed Indians as barbarians without rights, who should be treated as "subjects," not "nations." He felt that Indians and land-hungry white settlers could never live in harmony, so the Indians had to go if they were to survive. After his election in 1828, he recommended that the remaining eastern Indians be moved to the Great American Desert west of the Mississippi River, in what became Oklahoma. State laws in Alabama, Georgia, and Mississippi had already abolished tribal units and stripped them of their powers, rejected ancestral Indian land claims, and denied Indians the right to vote or testify in court. Jackson claimed that relocating the eastern Indians was a pragmatic act of mercy, a "wise and humane policy" that would save the Indians from "utter annihilation" if they tried to hold on to their lands.

Indian Removal

In response to a request from Jackson, Congress in 1830 debated the **Indian Removal Act**, which authorized the president to force the 74,000 Indians remaining in the East and South to move to federal lands west of the Mississippi River. Opponents of the policy deluged Congress with petitions warning that Jackson's efforts would bring "enduring shame" on the nation. Even David "Davy" Crockett of Tennessee, a frontiersman like President Jackson, opposed the forced removal of the Indian nations. But to no avail. In late May 1830, the Senate passed the Indian Removal Act by a single vote, and Jackson eagerly signed it. The Cherokees responded by announcing that "we see nothing but ruin before us." They held out for several years, but in 1835 a small group of Cherokees led by Elias Boudinot signed the Treaty of New Echota, in which they agreed to move to the Indian Territory in Oklahoma.

By 1835, some 46,000 Indians had been relocated across the Mississippi River at government expense. Most of the northern Indians were too weak to resist being relocated. In Illinois and the Wisconsin Territory, however, the Black Hawk War erupted in 1832. The Illinois militia mobilized to expel the Sauk and Fox peoples, chased them into the Wisconsin Territory, ignored the Indians' effort to surrender under a white flag, and massacred women and children as they tried to escape across the Mississippi River. Six weeks later, their leader, Black Hawk, was captured and imprisoned.

In the South, the Seminoles, led by Osceola (called by U.S. soldiers "the still unconquered red man") resisted the federal removal policy from 1835 to 1842 by fighting a guerrilla war in the swamps of the Florida Everglades—the

CHEROKEES DIVIDED While many Cherokee elite fought against Jackson's policies, Elias Boudinot, editor of the first Native American newspaper, *Cherokee Phoenix*, signed the Treaty of New Echota in 1835. He was subsequently murdered by a rival faction of Cherokees.

Indian Removal Act (1830) Law permitting the forced relocation of Indians to federal lands west of the Mississippi River in exchange for the land they occupied in the East and South.

HIDING IN A MANGROVE SWAMP An armed group of Seminoles crouch under a mangrove in the Florida Everglades during the Second Seminole War, out of sight of the American sailors passing by. It was not until 1934 that the few surviving Seminoles in Florida became the last Native American tribe to end their war with the United States.

longest and most expensive war ever fought by Native Americans. But the Seminoles' heroic resistance waned after 1837, when Osceola, the most famous Native American of the time, was captured, imprisoned, and left to die at Fort Moultrie near Charleston, South Carolina.

The Trail of Tears

Of all the so-called Civilized Tribes, the Cherokees living in the mountainous areas of Alabama, Georgia, Tennessee, and the Carolinas, had come closest to adopting the customs of white America. Over many years, they had built roads, houses, towns, planted orchards, cultivated farms, and fenced pastures for their livestock, organized churches and established newspapers. They had also modeled their own system of government on that of the United States. But the discovery of gold in north Georgia in 1829 fed whites' appetite for Cherokee land.

Cherokee Nation v. Georgia (1831) and *Worcester v. Georgia* (1832)

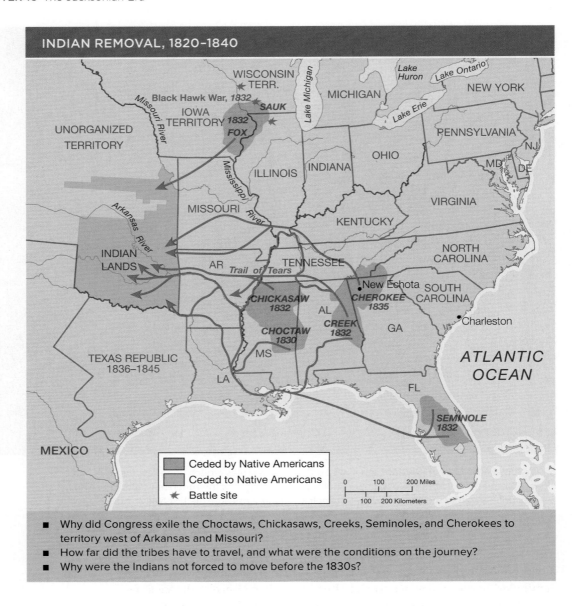

INDIAN REMOVAL, 1820–1840

Ceded by Native Americans
Ceded to Native Americans
★ Battle site

0   100   200 Miles
0   100   200 Kilometers

- Why did Congress exile the Choctaws, Chickasaws, Creeks, Seminoles, and Cherokees to territory west of Arkansas and Missouri?
- How far did the tribes have to travel, and what were the conditions on the journey?
- Why were the Indians not forced to move before the 1830s?

The Cherokees sought relief in the Supreme Court. In *Cherokee Nation v. Georgia* (1831), Chief Justice John Marshall ruled that the Cherokees had "an unquestionable right" to their lands "until title should be extinguished by voluntary cession to the United States." The following year, the Supreme Court ruled in *Worcester v. Georgia* (1832) that the Cherokee Nation was "a distinct political community" within which Georgia law had no force. Both of these Supreme Court decisions had the effect of favoring the Cherokee argument that their ancestral lands could not be taken from them.

TRAIL OF TEARS Thousands of Cherokees died on a nightmarish forced march from Georgia to Oklahoma after being forced from their native lands.

President Jackson, however, refused to enforce the Court's "wicked" decisions, claiming that he had no constitutional authority to intervene in Georgia to protect the Cherokees. Jackson's rejection of the Court's ruling reflected his many contradictions. When dealing with Indians in Georgia, he refused to interfere with the state's refusal to abide by U.S. Supreme Court rulings. By contrast, in the nullification crisis with South Carolina, he used military force to deny the right of a state to defy the federal government.

Meanwhile, the Cherokees were forced out. They gave up their land in the Southeast (about 100 million acres) in exchange for 32 million acres in the "Indian Territory" to the west of Arkansas—part of present-day Oklahoma. By 1838, 17,000 Cherokees had been evicted and moved west on the **Trail of Tears**, an 800-mile forced journey mostly on foot. Four thousand of the refugees died along the way. A few held out in the mountains and acquired title to federal land in North Carolina; they became known as the "Eastern Band" of Cherokees.

Trail of Tears (1838–1839)
The Cherokees' 800-mile journey from the southern Appalachians to Indian Territory.

CORE **OBJECTIVE**

4. Explain the causes of the economic depression of the late 1830s and the emergence of the Whig party.

Political Battles

Jackson's controversial policies regarding the Indians, nullification, and the B.U.S. aroused intense opposition. Some congressional opponents talked of impeaching him. Jackson received so many death threats that he decided his political opponents were trying to kill him.

In January 1835, the threat became real. After attending the funeral service for a member of Congress, Jackson was leaving the Capitol when an unemployed English-born housepainter named Richard Lawrence emerged from the shadows and pointed a pistol at the president's heart—only a few feet away. When he pulled the trigger, however, the gun misfired. Jackson lifted his walking stick and charged at Lawrence, who pulled out another pistol, but it, too, miraculously misfired. Jackson claimed that his political foes, including John C. Calhoun, had planned the attack. A jury, however, decided that Lawrence, the first person to try to kill a U.S. president, was insane and ordered him confined in an asylum.

A Third Party

In 1832, for the first time in a presidential election, a third party entered the field. The Anti-Masonic party grew out of popular hostility toward the Masonic fraternal order, a large all-male social organization that originated in Great Britain early in the eighteenth century. By 1830, there were some 2,000 Masonic "lodges" scattered across the United States with about 100,000 members, including Andrew Jackson and Henry Clay.

The Anti-Masonic party

Suspicions of the Masonic order as a secret elite organization intent on undermining democracy gave rise to the grassroots movement known as the Anti-Masonic party. More than a hundred Anti-Masonic newspapers emerged across the nation. Their common purpose was to stamp out an organization that was contaminating the "heart of the republic." Former president John Quincy Adams said that disbanding the "Masonic institution" was the most important issue facing "us and our posterity."

Opposition to a fraternal organization was hardly the foundation upon which to build a lasting political movement. The Anti-Masonic party, however, had three important firsts to its credit: in addition to being the first third party, it was the first party to hold a national convention to nominate a presidential candidate and the first to announce a platform of specific policy goals.

The 1832 Election

In preparing for the 1832 election, the Democrats and the National Republicans followed the example of the Anti-Masonic party by holding presidential nominating conventions of their own for the first time. In December 1831, the National Republicans gathered to nominate Henry Clay.

Eager to demonstrate popular support for his own party's candidates, Jackson endorsed the idea of a nominating convention for the Democratic party as well. The Democratic convention named New Yorker Martin Van Buren as Jackson's running mate. The Democrats, unlike the other two parties, adopted no formal platform and relied to a substantial degree upon the popularity of the president to carry their cause.

The outcome was an overwhelming endorsement of Jackson in the Electoral College, with 219 votes to 49 for Clay, and a solid victory in the popular vote, 688,000 to 530,000. William Wirt, the Anti-Masonic candidate, carried only Vermont, winning seven electoral votes. Wayward South Carolina, unable to stomach either Jackson or Clay, delivered its 11 votes to Governor John Floyd of Virginia.

The Removal of Government Deposits

Jackson interpreted his lopsided reelection as a "decision of the people against the bank." Having vetoed the charter renewal of the B.U.S., he ordered the Treasury Department to transfer federal monies from the national bank to twenty-three state banks—called "pet banks" by Jackson's critics because many were in the western states and were run by Jackson's friends and allies. When the Treasury secretary balked, a furious Jackson fired him.

Transferring the government's deposits from the B.U.S. to the pet banks was probably illegal, and the Senate, led by Henry Clay, voted on March 28, 1834, to *censure* Jackson for it, the only time an American president has been reprimanded in this way as opposed to actual impeachment. Jackson was so angry after being censured that he wanted to challenge Clay to a duel to "bring the rascal to a dear account."

Meanwhile, Nicholas Biddle refused to surrender in the face of Jackson's assault on his bank. He ordered the B.U.S. to quit making loans and demanded that state banks exchange their paper currency for gold or silver coins as quickly as possible. Through such deflationary policies that reduced the amount of money circulating in the economy, the desperate Biddle was trying to create a depression and thus reveal the importance of maintaining the national bank. An enraged Jackson said the B.U.S. under Biddle was "trying to kill me, but I will kill it!"

Jackson's war on the B.U.S.

Jackson prevailed in the Bank War; the B.U.S. would shut down by 1841. With the restraining effects of Biddle's national bank removed, hundreds of new state banks sprouted like mushrooms, each printing its own paper currency to lend to land speculators and new businesses. Sales of federal or state-owned lands rose from 4 million acres in 1834 to 20 million in 1836. At the same time, the states plunged themselves heavily into debt to finance the building of roads and canals. By 1837, total state indebtedness had soared.

The irony of Jackson's war on the national bank was that it sparked the dangerous misbehavior among small state banks that he most feared. As

Senator Thomas Hart Benton, one of Jackson's most loyal supporters, said in 1837, he had not helped kill the B.U.S. to create a "wilderness of local banks. I did not join in putting down the paper currency of a national bank to put up a national paper currency of a thousand local banks."

But that is what happened. During the "free banking era" after 1837, anyone who could raise a certain minimum amount of money ("capital") could open a bank. And many did. With no central bank to regulate and oversee the operations of "wildcat" banks, many of them went bankrupt after only a few months or years, leaving their depositors empty-handed. Jackson's war against Biddle had ended the central bank only to unleash banking chaos.

The Money Question

The Distribution Act (1836)

During the 1830s, the federal government acquired huge amounts of money from the sale of government-owned lands. Initially, the Treasury department used the annual surpluses from land sales to pay down the accumulated federal debt, which it eliminated in 1835, the first time that any nation had done so. By 1836, the federal budget was generating an annual budget surplus, which led to intense discussions about what to do with the increasingly worthless paper money flowing into the Treasury's vaults.

The surge of unstable paper money issued by state banks peaked in 1836, when events combined suddenly to destroy the value of the bank notes. Two key developments, the **Distribution Act** and the Specie Circular, would combine to play havoc with the economy and devastate the nation's financial system.

In June 1836, Congress approved a Deposit and Distribution Bill, initially proposed by Henry Clay and Daniel Webster, that required the federal government to "distribute" surplus revenue from land sales to the states by "depositing" the funds into eighty-one state banks in proportion to each state's representation in Congress. The state governments would then draw upon those deposits to fund roads, bridges, and other internal improvements, including the construction of new public schools.

Specie Circular (1836)

A month later, Jackson issued the Specie Circular (1836), which announced that the federal government would accept only specie (gold or silver coins) in payment for land purchased by speculators (farmers could still pay with paper money). Westerners opposed the Specie Circular because most of the government land sales were occurring in the western states. They helped convince Congress to pass an act overturning Jackson's policy. The president, however, vetoed it.

Once enacted, the Deposit Act and the Specie Circular put added strains on the nation's already-tight supplies of gold and silver. Eastern banks had to transfer much of their gold and silver reserves to western banks. As banks reduced their reserves of gold and silver coins, they had to reduce their lending. Soon, the once-bustling economy began to slow into a recession as the money supply contracted. Nervous depositors rushed to their local banks to get their money out, only to learn that there was not enough specie in their vaults to redeem their deposits.

Distribution Act (1836) Law requiring distribution of the federal budget surplus to the states, creating chaos among unregulated state banks dependent on such federal funds.

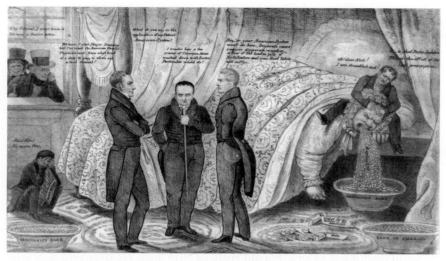

THE DOCTORS PUZZLED, OR THE DESPERATE CASE OF MOTHER U.S. BANK
In this satire of Jackson's Distribution Act and Specie Circular, the B.U.S. is portrayed as an oversized patient vomiting gold and silver coins into pans representing local banks. Clay, Webster, and Calhoun discuss various prescriptions while Jackson leans in the windowsill, insisting he knows the best cure.

Censoring the Mail

While concerns about the strength of the economy grew, slavery emerged again as a flashpoint issue. In 1835, northern abolitionist organizations began mailing anti-slavery pamphlets and newspapers to prominent white southerners, hoping to convince them to end the "peculiar institution."

Francis Pickens of South Carolina urged southerners to stop the abolitionists from spreading their "lies." Angry pro-slavery South Carolinians in Charleston broke into the federal post office, stole bags of the abolitionist mailings, and ceremoniously burned them. Southern state legislatures passed laws banning such "dangerous" publications. Jackson asked Congress to pass a federal censorship law that would prohibit "incendiary" materials intended to incite "the slaves to insurrection."

Congress took action in 1836, but instead of banning abolitionist materials, a bipartisan group reaffirmed the sanctity of the federal mail. As a practical matter, however, southern post offices began censoring the mail anyway, arguing that federal authority ended when the mail arrived at the post office door. Jackson decided not to enforce the Congressional action. His failure of leadership created what would become a growing split in the Democratic party over the future of slavery. Some Democrats decided that Jackson, for all of his celebrations of democracy and equality, was no different from John C. Calhoun and other southern white racists.

The controversy over the mails proved to be a victory for the growing abolitionist movement. One anti-slavery publisher said that instead of stifling their efforts, Jackson and the southern radicals "put us and our principles up before the world—just where we wanted to be." Abolitionist groups now started mailing their pamphlets and petitions to members of Congress. James Hammond, a pro-slavery South Carolinian, called for Congress to ban such anti-slavery petitions. When that failed, Congress in 1836 adopted an informal solution suggested by Martin Van Buren: whenever a petition calling for the end of slavery appeared, someone would immediately move that it be tabled rather than discussed. The plan, Van Buren claimed, would preserve the "harmony of our happy Union."

The supporters of this "gag rule" soon encountered a formidable obstacle in John Quincy Adams, the former president who now was a congressman from Massachusetts. An ardent opponent of slavery, he devised several procedures to get around the gag rule. Henry Wise, a Virginia opponent, called Adams "the acutest, the astutest, the archest enemy of southern slavery that ever existed." In the 1838–39 session of Congress, thanks to Adams, some 1,500 anti-slavery petitions were filed with 163,845 signatures. Andrew Jackson dismissed Adams, his old rival, as "the most reckless and depraved man living."

The Whig Coalition

Whigs vs. "King Andrew I"

Jackson had removed the Indians from the eastern United States and had slain the dual monsters of nullification in South Carolina and the national bank in Philadelphia, and many loved him for it. But in 1834, a new anti-Jackson coalition emerged, united chiefly by their hostility to the president's authoritarian style. Jackson's domineering manner had given rise to the nickname "King Andrew I." His Democratic followers were deemed Tories, supporters of the "tyrannical" king, and his opponents now became known as the **Whig party**, a name that linked them to the Patriots of the American Revolution (as well as the parliamentary opponents of the Tories in Britain).

The Whigs grew out of the National Republican party of John Quincy Adams, Henry Clay, and Daniel Webster. They also attracted members of the Anti-Masonic and Democratic parties, who for one reason or another opposed Jackson's stand on the national bank, states' rights, and his disregard of the Supreme Court, among other grievances. Of the forty-one Democrats in Congress who had voted against Jackson on rechartering the national bank, twenty-eight had joined the Whigs by 1836. For the next twenty years, the Whigs and the Democrats would be the two major political parties, and so for a second time a **two-party system** emerged.

Most Whigs supported Clay and his "American System" of economic nationalism. They favored federal support for internal improvements to foster economic growth. They also supported a national bank and high tariffs. In the South, the Whigs tended to be bankers and merchants. In the West, the Whigs were farmers who valued government-funded internal improvements. Unlike the Democrats, who attracted Catholic voters from Germany and Ireland, Whigs tended to be native-born Protestants—Congregationalists, Presbyterians, Methodists, and Baptists—who promoted social reforms such

Whig party Political party founded in 1834 in opposition to the Jacksonian Democrats; supported federal funding for internal improvements, a national bank, and high tariffs on imports.

two-party system Domination of national politics by two major political parties, such as the Whigs and Democrats during the 1830s and 1840s.

as the abolition of slavery and legislation to prohibit the sale of alcoholic beverages.

Whigs support Clay's "American System"

The Election of 1836

In 1835, eighteen months before the presidential election, the Democrats nominated Jackson's handpicked successor, Vice President Martin Van Buren. The Whig coalition, united chiefly in its opposition to Jackson, adopted a strategy of nominating multiple candidates, hoping to throw the election into the House of Representatives.

The Whigs put up three regional candidates: New Englander Daniel Webster, Hugh Lawson White of Tennessee, and William Henry Harrison of Indiana. But the multi-candidate strategy failed. In the popular vote of 1836, Van Buren defeated the entire Whig field, winning 170 electoral votes while the others combined to collect only 113.

The Eighth President

Martin Van Buren was a skillful politician whose ability to organize and manipulate legislators earned him the nickname "Little Magician." Elected governor of New York in 1828, he had resigned to join Andrew Jackson's cabinet, first as secretary of state, then became vice president in 1833.

Van Buren had been Jackson's closest political adviser and ally, but many people thought he was too self-centered. John Quincy Adams wrote in his diary that Van Buren was "by far the ablest" of the Jacksonians, but had wasted "most of his ability upon mere personal intrigues. His principles are all subordinate to his ambition." Van Buren's rival John C. Calhoun was even more cutting. "He is not of the race of the lion or the tiger." Rather, he "belongs to a lower order—the fox."

At his inauguration, Van Buren promised to follow "in the footsteps of President Jackson." Before he could do so, however, the nation's financial sector began collapsing. On May 10, 1837, several large state banks in New York, running out of gold and silver, suddenly refused to convert customers' paper money into coins. Other banks across the nation quickly did the same. This financial crisis, the worse yet faced by the young nation, would become known as the **Panic of 1837**. It would soon mushroom into the republic's worst depression, lasting some seven years.

MARTIN VAN BUREN Van Buren earned the nickname the "Little Magician" for not only his short stature but also his "magical" ability to exploit his political and social connections.

The Panic of 1837

The causes of the financial crisis went back to the Jackson administration, but Van Buren got the blame. The problem actually started in Europe. During the mid-1830s, Great Britain, America's largest trading partner, experienced an acute financial crisis when the Bank of England, worried about a run on the gold and silver in its vaults, curtailed its loans. This forced most British companies to reduce their trade with America. As British demand for American cotton plummeted, so did the price paid for cotton. On top of everything else, in 1836 there had been a disastrous wheat crop.

Panic of 1837 A financial calamity in the United States brought on by a dramatic slowdown in the British economy and falling cotton prices, failed crops, high inflation, and reckless state banks.

As creditors hastened to foreclose on businesses and farms unable to make their debt payments, the inflationary spiral went into reverse. Government spending plunged. Many canals under construction were shut down. In many cases, state governments could not repay their debts. In the crunch, 40 percent of the hundreds of recently-created state banks failed. In April 1837, some 250 businesses failed in New York City alone.

The nation's worst economic crisis was frightening. As a newspaper editorial complained in December 1836, the economy "has been put into confusion and dismay by a well-meant, but *extremely mistaken*" pair of decisions by Congress and President Jackson: the destruction of the B.U.S. and the Distribution Act.

The first mistake was the Specie Circular. Its requirement that all federal land purchases be transacted in gold or silver greatly reduced government land sales, thus pinching the federal budget. Struggling American banks had to borrow gold from European banks, but they could not get enough to prevent a financial panic and a deepening depression.

Jackson's second mistake was his decision to eliminate rather than reform the B.U.S. It could have acted as a stabilizing force amid the financial panic. Instead, unregulated state banks around the country flooded the economy with worthless paper money without adequate backing in gold or silver.

In April 1836, *Niles' Weekly Register,* the nation's leading business journal, reported that the economy was "approaching a momentous crisis." The federal government was lucky to sell land for $3 an acre that had been going for $10 an acre. State governments canceled plans to build roads, bridges, railroads, canals, and ports. More and more people were caught short by the crisis and could not pay their debts: farmers, merchants, bankers. Many desperate people fled their debts altogether by moving to Texas, then a province of Mexico. Forty percent of the state banks shut their doors. Even the federal government itself, having put most of its gold and silver in state banks, was verging on bankruptcy. The *National Intelligencer* newspaper reported in May that the federal treasury "has not a dollar of gold or silver in the world!"

The poor, as always, were particularly hard hit. By the fall of 1837, a third of the nation's workers were jobless, and those still fortunate enough to have jobs had their wages slashed. At the same time, prices for food and clothing soared. As the winter of 1837 approached, a New York City journalist reported that 200,000 people were "in utter and hopeless

JACKSONIAN TREASURY NOTE A parody of the often-worthless fractional notes issued by local banks and businesses in lieu of coins. These notes proliferated during the panic of 1837, with the emergency suspension of gold and silver payments. In the main scene, Martin Van Buren, a monster on a wagon driven by John C. Calhoun, is about to pass through an arch labeled "Wall Street" and "Safety Fund Banks."

distress with no means of surviving the winter but those provided by charity." The nation had a "poverty-struck feeling."

The unprecedented economic calamity sent shock waves through the political system. Critics called the president "Martin Van Ruin" because he did not believe that he or the government had any responsibility to rescue hard-pressed farmers, bankers, or businessmen or to provide relief for the jobless and homeless. He did call a special session of Congress in 1837, which canceled the distribution of the federal surplus to the states because there was no longer any surplus to distribute.

How best to deal with the unprecedented depression divided Democrats from Whigs. Unlike Van Buren, Whig Henry Clay insisted that suffering people were "entitled to the protecting care of a parental Government." To him, an enlarged role for the federal government was the price of a maturing, expanding republic in which elected officials had an obligation to promote public "safety, convenience, and prosperity." Van Buren and the Democrats believed that the government had no such obligations. Henry Clay, among others, savaged the president for his "cold and heartless" attitude.

An Independent Treasury

Van Buren believed that the federal government should stop risking its deposits in shaky state banks. Instead, he wanted to establish an independent treasury system whereby the government would keep its funds in its own bank vaults and do business entirely in gold or silver, not paper currency. Van Buren wanted the federal government to regulate the nation's supply of gold and silver and let the marketplace regulate the supply of paper currency.

It took Van Buren more than three years to convince Congress to pass the **Independent Treasury Act** on July 4, 1840. Although it lasted little more than a year (the Whigs repealed it in 1841), it would be restored in 1846. Not surprisingly, the state banks that lost control of the federal funds howled in protest.

The "Log Cabin and Hard Cider" Campaign

By 1840, an election year, the Van Buren administration and the Democrats were in deep trouble. The depression continued to worsen and the suffering spread, leading the Whigs to grow confident they could win the presidency. At their nominating convention, they passed over Henry Clay, the Kentucky legislator who had been Jackson's consistent foe, in favor of William Henry Harrison, whose credentials were impressive: victor at the Battle of Tippecanoe against Tecumseh's Shawnees in 1811, former governor of the Indiana Territory, and former congressman and senator from Ohio. To balance the ticket geographically, the Whigs nominated John Tyler of Virginia as their vice president. Henry Clay, who yearned to be president, was bitterly disappointed, grousing that "my friends are not worth the powder and shot it would take to kill them. I am the most unfortunate man in the history of parties."

Independent Treasury Act (1840) System created by Van Buren that moved federal funds from favored state banks to the U.S. Treasury, whose financial transactions could only be in gold or silver.

UNCLE SAM'S PET PUPS!
A woodcut showing William Henry Harrison luring "Mother Bank," Andrew Jackson, and Martin Van Buren into a barrel of hard (alcoholic) cider. While Jackson and Van Buren sought to destroy the B.U.S., Harrison promised to reestablish it, hence his providing "Mother Bank" a refuge in this scene.

UNCLE SAM'S PET PUPS!
Or, Mother BANK'S last refuge.

The Whigs refused to take a stand on major issues. They did, however, seize upon a catchy campaign slogan: "Tippecanoe and Tyler Too." When a Democratic newspaper declared that General Harrison was the kind of man who would spend his retirement "in a log cabin [sipping apple cider] on the banks of the Ohio [River]," the Whigs chose the cider and log cabin symbols to depict Harrison as a simple man sprung from the people, in contrast to Van Buren's wealthy, aristocratic lifestyle. (Harrison was actually from one of Virginia's wealthiest families).

Harrison defeated Van Buren easily, winning 234 electoral votes to 60. The Whigs had promised a return to prosperity without explaining how it would happen. It was simply time for a change.

The most remarkable aspect of the election of 1840 was the turnout. More than 80 percent of white American men voted, many for the first time—the highest turnout before or since, as almost every state had dropped property qualifications for voting.

CORE OBJECTIVE

5. Assess the strengths and weaknesses of Jackson's transformational presidency.

Jackson's Legacy

The nation that new president William Henry Harrison governed was vastly different from that led by George Washington and Thomas Jefferson. In 1828, the United States boasted twenty-four states and nearly 13 million people, many of them recent arrivals from Germany and Ireland. The national population was growing at a phenomenal rate, doubling every twenty-three years. During the so-called Jacksonian Era, the nation witnessed continuing industrialization, rapidly growing cities, rising tensions between the North and South over slavery, accelerating westward expansion, and the emergence of the second two-party system, featuring Democrats and Whigs. A surge in foreign demand for southern cotton and other American goods, along with substantial British investment in an array of new American enterprises, helped generate an economic boom and a transportation revolution. That President-elect Jackson rode to his inauguration in a horse-drawn carriage and left Washington, D.C., eight years later on a train symbolized the dramatic changes occurring in American life.

A New Political Landscape

A transformational figure in a transformational era, Andrew Jackson helped reshape the American political landscape. Even his ferocious opponent, Henry Clay, acknowledged that Jackson had "swept over the Government . . . like a tropical tornado."

Like all great presidents, however, Jackson left a messy, even contradictory, legacy. He championed opportunities for the "common man" to play a greater role in the political arena at the same time that working men were forming labor unions to increase their economic power and political clout. He helped establish the modern Democratic party and attracted to it the working poor and immigrants from eastern cities, as well as farmers from the South and East. Through a nimble combination of force and compromise, he saved the Union by suppressing the nullification crisis. And, in 1835, he paid off the accumulated national debt.

In Jackson's 1837 farewell address, he stressed that he had worked on behalf of "the farmer, the mechanic, and the laboring classes of society—the bone and sinew of the country—men who love liberty and desire nothing but equal rights and equal laws."

Jackson's concept of "the people," however, was limited to a "white men's democracy," as it had been for all earlier presidents, and the phenomenon of Andrew Jackson, the heroic symbol of democratic times, continues to spark historical debate.

Jackson was so convinced of the rightness and righteousness of his ideals that he was willing to defy constitutional limits on his authority. He was both the instrument of democracy and its enemy, protecting "the humble people" and the Union by expanding presidential authority in ways that the founders had never envisioned, including eliminating the national bank and censoring the mails. In doing so, he both symbolized and aggravated the perennial tension in the American republic between democratic ideals and presidential power, states' rights and federal actions.

Reviewing the
CORE OBJECTIVES |

- **Jackson's Views and Policies** The Jacksonians sought to democratize the political process and expand economic opportunity for the "common man" (that is, "poor and humble" white men). As the representative of "the people," he expanded the role of the president in economic matters, reducing federal government spending and eliminating the powerful Second Bank of the United States. His *Bank War* painted the national bank as full of "vipers and thieves" and was hugely popular, but Jackson did not understand its long-term economic consequences. In addition, his views on limited government were not always reflected in his policies. He left the high taxes on imports from the *Tariff of Abominations (1828)* in place until opposition in the South created a national crisis.

- **Nullification Controversy** The concept of *nullification*, developed by South Carolina's John C. Calhoun, enabled a state to disavow a federal law. When a South Carolina convention nullified the Tariffs of 1828 and 1832, Jackson requested that Congress pass a *Force Bill (1833)* authorizing the U.S. Army to compel compliance with the tariffs. After South Carolina, under the threat of federal military force, accepted a compromise tariff put forth by Henry Clay, the state convention nullified the *Force Bill*. The crisis was over, with both sides claiming victory.

- **Indian Removal Act of 1830** The *Indian Removal Act (1830)* authorized the relocation of eastern Indians to federal lands west of the Mississippi River. The Cherokees used the federal court system in *Cherokee Nation v. Georgia* and *Worcester v. Georgia* to try to block this relocation. Despite the Supreme Court's decisions in their favor, President Jackson forced them to move; the event and the route they took came to be called the *Trail of Tears (1838–1839)*. By 1840, only a few Seminoles and Cherokees remained in remote areas of the Southeast.

- **Democrats and Whigs** Jackson's arrogant behavior, especially his use of the veto, led many to regard him as "King Andrew I." Groups who opposed him organized a new party, known as the *Whig party*, thus producing the country's second *two-party system*. Two acts—the *Distribution Act (1836)* and the Specie Circular—ultimately destabilized the nation's economy. Andrew Jackson's ally and vice president, Martin Van Buren, succeeded him as president, but Jacksonian bank policies led to the financial *Panic of 1837* and an economic depression. Van Buren responded by establishing the *Independent Treasury Act (1840)* to safeguard the nation's economy but offered no help for individuals in distress. The economic calamity ensured a Whig victory in the election of 1840.

- **The Jackson Years** Andrew Jackson's America was very different from the America of 1776. Most white men had gained the vote when states removed property qualifications for voting, but political equality did not mean economic equality. Democrats wanted every American to have an equal chance to compete in the marketplace and in the political arena, but they never promoted equality of results. Inequality between rich and poor widened during the Jackson Era.

KEY TERMS

Bank War *p. 331*

Tariff of Abominations (1828) *p. 333*

nullification *p. 333*

Force Bill (1833) *p. 337*

Indian Removal Act (1830) *p. 338*

Trail of Tears (1838–1839) *p. 341*

Distribution Act (1836) *p. 344*

Whig party *p. 346*

two-party system *p. 346*

Panic of 1837 *p. 347*

Independent Treasury Act (1840) *p. 349*

CHRONOLOGY

1828 Andrew Jackson wins presidential election

Tariff of Abominations goes into effect

1830 Congress passes the Indian Removal Act

Andrew Jackson vetoes the Maysville Road Bill

The Eaton affair divides Andrew Jackson's warring cabinet

1831 Supreme Court issues *Cherokee Nation v. Georgia* decision

1832 Supreme Court issues *Worcester v. Georgia* decision

Andrew Jackson vetoes the Bank Recharter Bill

South Carolina passes Nullification Ordinance

1833 Congress passes the Force Bill, authorizing military force in South Carolina

Congress passes Henry Clay's compromise tariff with Jackson's support

1836 Democratic candidate Martin Van Buren is elected president

1837 Financial panic deflates the economy

1838–1839 Eastern Indians forced west on Trail of Tears

1840 Independent Treasury Act established

1840 Whig candidate William Henry Harrison is elected president

⚉ INQUIZITIVE

Go to InQuizitive to see what you've learned—and learn what you've missed—with personalized feedback along the way.

THE OLD SOUTH One of the enduring myths of the South is captured in this late-nineteenth-century painting of a plantation on the Mississippi River: strong, well-dressed slaves tending the lush cotton fields, a paddle steamer easing down the wide river, and the planter's family retiring in the cool of their white-columned mansion. Novels and films like *Gone with the Wind* (1939) would perpetuate the notion of the Old South as a stable, paternalistic agrarian society led by white planters who were the "natural" aristocracy of virtue and talent within their communities.

The South and Slavery

1800–1860

O f all the regions of the United States during the first half of the nineteenth century, the pre–Civil War Old South was the most distinctive. What had once been a narrow band of settlements along the Atlantic coast dramatically expanded westward and southward to form a subcontinental empire rooted in cotton.

The southern states remained rural, agricultural long after the rest of the nation had embraced cities, immigrants, and factories, but the Old South was also instrumental in enabling the nation's industrial development and its growing economic stature. After the War of 1812, southern-grown cotton became the key raw material driving the industrial revolution by feeding the textile mills of Great Britain and New England, whose wage workers and machines fashioned it into thread, yarn, bedding, and clothing. The price of raw cotton doubled in the first year after the war. Investors in Boston, New York City, and Philadelphia provided loans to southerners to buy more land and more slaves. Northerners also provided the cotton industry with other essential needs: insurance, financing, and shipping.

The story of how southern cotton clothed the world and transformed history was woven with the threads of tragedy, however. The revolution spawned by the mass production of cotton was rooted in the explosive expansion of slavery. A group of slaves in

CORE
OBJECTIVES INQUIZITIVE

1. Explain the various factors that made the South distinct from the rest of the United States during the early nineteenth century.

2. Discuss the role that cotton production and slavery played in the South's economic and social development.

3. Distinguish among the major groups within southern white society, and explain why each group supported the expansion of slavery.

4. Describe the impact of slavery on African Americans, both free and enslaved, throughout the South.

5. Analyze how enslaved peoples responded to the inhumanity of their situation.

Virginia recognized the essential role they played in the surging national economy when they asked, "Didn't we clear the land, and raise the crops of corn, of tobacco, rice, of sugar, of everything? And then didn't the large cities in the North grow up on the cotton and the sugars and the rice that we made?"

CORE **OBJECTIVE**

1. Explain the various factors that made the South distinct from the rest of the United States during the early nineteenth century.

The Distinctiveness of the Old South

People have long debated what set the Old South apart from the rest of the nation. Most arguments focus on the region's climate and geography in shaping its culture and economy. The warm, humid climate was ideal for cultivating commercial crops such as tobacco, cotton, rice, indigo, and sugar cane, which led to the plantation system of large commercial agriculture and its dependence upon enslaved labor.

Unlike the North, the South had few large cities, few banks, few railroads, few factories, and few schools. Most of the commerce in the South dealt with the storage, distribution, and sale of agricultural products, especially cotton. With the cotton economy booming, investors focused on buying land and slaves; there was little reason to create a robust industrial sector. "We want no manufactures; we desire no trading, no mechanical, or manufacturing classes," an Alabama politician told an English visitor.

Profitable farming thus remained the South's ideal pursuit of happiness. The planter elite valued education for their own sons, but there was little interest in public schooling for the masses. The illiteracy rate in the South was three times higher than in the North.

A Triracial Culture

Climate and "our peculiar institution"

What made the Old South most distinctive was not its climate or soil but its expanding system of race-based slavery. A majority of southern whites did not own slaves, but they supported what John C. Calhoun called "our **peculiar institution**" because slavery was so central to their society's way of life. Calhoun's carefully crafted phrase allowed southerners to avoid using the charged word *slavery*, while the adjective *peculiar* implied that slavery was *unique* to the South, as it essentially was.

The profitability and convenience of owning slaves created a sense of social unity that bridged class differences among whites. Poor whites who owned no slaves and resented the planters ("cotton snobs") could still claim racial superiority over enslaved blacks ("niggers"). Because of race-based slavery, explained Georgia attorney Thomas Reade Cobb, every white "feels that he belongs to an elevated class. It matters not that he is no slaveholder; he is not of the inferior race; he is a free-born citizen."

peculiar institution Phrase used by whites in the antebellum South to refer to slavery without using the word *slavery*.

The Old South also differed from other sections of the country in its high proportion of native-born Americans. The region attracted few European immigrants after the Revolution, in part because of geography. The main shipping routes from Britain and Europe took immigrants to northern port cities. Because most immigrants were penniless, they could not afford to travel to the South. Moreover, European immigrants, most of whom were manual laborers, could not compete with slave labor.

Conflicting Myths

Southerners, a North Carolina editor wrote, are "a mythological people, created half out of dream and half out of slander, who live in a still-legendary land." Myths are beliefs made up partly of truths and partly of lies, accurate generalizations and willful distortions. During the nineteenth century, a powerful myth emerged among white southerners—that the South was both different from *and* better than the North. This blended notion of distinctiveness and superiority became central to the self-image of many southerners. Even today, many southerners tenaciously cultivate a defiant pride and separate identity from the rest of the nation.

Myth of the Old South: Agrarian "aristocracy"

In defending the South and slavery from northern critics, southerners claimed that their region was morally superior. Kind planters, according to the prevailing myth, provided happy slaves with food, clothing, shelter, and security—in contrast to a North populated with greedy bankers and heartless factory owners who treated their wage laborers worse than slaves. John C. Calhoun insisted that in the northern states the quality of life for free people of color had "become worse" since slavery there had been banned while in the South, the standard of living among enslaved African Americans had "improved greatly in every respect."

In this mythic version of the Old South, slavery supposedly benefited both slaves and owners. In *Aunt Phillis's Cabin; or, Southern Life as It Is* (1852), novelist Mary Henderson Eastman stressed "the necessity of the existence of slavery at present in our Southern States," and claimed "that, as a general thing, the slaves are comfortable and contented, and their owners humane and kind."

The agrarian ideal and the southern passion for guns, horsemanship, hunting, and the military filled in the self-gratifying image of the Old South as a region of honest small farmers and aristocratic gentlemen, young belles, and beautiful ladies who led leisurely lives of well-mannered graciousness, honor, and courage, all the while sipping mint juleps in a carefree romantic world of white-columned mansions.

The contrasting myth of the Old South was much darker. Northern abolitionists pictured the region as boasting an immoral economic system dependent on the exploitation of blacks and the displacement of Native Americans. In this version of the southern myth, the white planters were rarely "natural aristocrats" like Thomas Jefferson who were ambivalent about slavery. More often, the planters were ambitious self-made men who had

NEGRO VILLAGE ON A SOUTHERN PLANTATION The opening woodcut of Mary Henderson Eastman's novel *Aunt Phillis's Cabin* depicts a jovial scene of slaves at leisure, dancing or relaxing in the shade. **How does this portrayal fit into the myth of the Old South?**

seized opportunities to become rich by planting and selling cotton—and trading in slaves.

Abolitionists such as Harriet Beecher Stowe portrayed southern planters as cunning capitalists who raped enslaved women, brutalized slaves, and lorded over their communities with arrogant disdain. They treated slaves like cattle, broke up slave families, and sold slaves "down the river" to toil in the Louisiana sugar mills and rice plantations. An English woman traveling in the South in 1830 noted that what slaves in Virginia and Maryland feared most was being "sent to *the south* and sold. . . . The sugar plantations [in Louisiana] and, more than all, the rice grounds of Georgia and the Carolinas, are the terror of the American negroes."

Several Souths

The contradictory elements of these two conflicting myths continue to fight for supremacy in the South, each pressing its claim to legitimacy, in part because they are both built upon half-truths and fierce prejudices. The South has long been defined by two souls, two hearts, two minds competing for dominance. The paradoxes associated with this southern mythmaking provided much of the region's energy, for the Old South, like the New South, was not a single culture but a diverse section with multiple interests and perspectives—and it was rapidly growing and changing.

The Old South included three distinct subsections with different patterns of economic development and diverging degrees of commitment to slavery. Throughout the first half of the nineteenth century, the seven states of the Lower South (South Carolina, Georgia, Florida, Alabama, Mississippi, Louisiana, and parts of Texas) grew increasingly dependent upon commercial cotton production supported by slave labor. A traveler in Mississippi observed in 1835 that ambitious whites wanted "to sell cotton in order to buy negroes—to make more cotton to buy negroes." By 1860, slaves represented nearly half the population of the Lower South, largely because they were the most efficient producers of cotton in the world.

The states of the Upper South (Virginia, North Carolina, Tennessee, and Arkansas) had more varied agricultural economies—a mixture of large commercial plantations and small family farms, or "yeoman" farms, where crops were grown mostly for household use. Many southern states also had large areas without slavery, especially in the mountains of Virginia, the western Carolinas, eastern Tennessee, and northern Georgia.

In the Border South (Delaware, Maryland, Kentucky, and Missouri), slavery was slowly disappearing because cotton could not thrive there. By 1860, 90 percent of Delaware's black population and half of Maryland's were already free. Slave owners in the Lower South, however, had a much larger investment in slavery. They believed that only constant supervision, intimidation, and punishment would keep the fast-growing population of enslaved workers under control, in part because the working and living conditions for the enslaved were so brutal. "I'd rather be dead," said a white overseer in Louisiana, "than a nigger in one of those big [sugar cane] plantations."

The Cotton Kingdom

CORE **OBJECTIVE**
2. Discuss the role that cotton production and slavery played in the South's economic and social development.

Tobacco, Rice, Sugar, and Livestock

After the Revolution, as the worn-out tobacco fields in Virginia and Maryland lost their fertility, tobacco farming spread into Kentucky and as far west as Missouri. Rice continued to be grown in the coastal areas ("low country") of the Carolinas and Georgia, where fields could easily be flooded and drained by tidal rivers flowing into the ocean. Sugar cane, like rice, was also an expensive crop to produce, requiring machinery to grind the cane to release the sugar syrup. During the early nineteenth century, only southern Louisiana focused on sugar production.

In addition to such "cash crops," the South led the nation in the production of livestock: hogs, horses, mules, and cattle. Southerners, both black and white, fed themselves largely on pork. It was the "king of the table." John S. Wilson, a Georgia doctor, called the region the "Republic of Porkdom." Southerners ate pork or bacon "morning, noon, and night." Corn was on southern plates as often as pork. During the early summer, corn was boiled on-the-cob. By late summer and fall, corn was ground up into meal, or flour. Cornbread and hominy, a "mush" or porridge made of whole-grain corn mixed with milk, were almost daily fare.

During the first half of the nineteenth century, cotton surpassed rice as the most profitable cash crop in the South. Southern cotton (called "white gold") drove much of the national economy and the industrial revolution, feeding the textile mills in New England and Great Britain.

In fact, cotton became one of the transforming forces in nineteenth-century history. It shaped the lives of the enslaved who cultivated it, the planters who grew rich by it, the ship owners who transported it, the mill girls who sewed it, the merchants who sold it, the people who wore it, and the politicians who warred over it. "Cotton is King," exclaimed the *Southern Cultivator* in 1859, "and wields an astonishing influence over the world's commerce." In 1832, over eighty of America's largest companies were New England textile mills.

The Cotton Kingdom resulted largely from two crucial developments. Until the late-eighteenth century, cotton fabric was a rarity produced by women in India using hand looms. Then British inventors developed machinery to convert raw cotton into thread and cloth in textile mills. The mechanical production of cotton made Great Britain the world's first industrial nation, and British textile mills, centered in Lancashire, grew so fast that they could not get enough cotton fiber to meet their needs. American Eli Whitney solved the problem by constructing the first cotton gin to remove the sticky seeds from the bolls of what was called short-staple cotton.

Taken together, these two breakthroughs helped create the world's largest industry—and transformed the South in the process. By 1815, just months after Andrew Jackson's victory over British troops at New Orleans, some thirty British ships tied up at the city's wharves because, as an American merchant reported, "Europe must, and will have, cotton for her manufacturers." During that year alone, more than 65,000 bales of cotton were shipped down the Mississippi River to New Orleans.

The Lower South

Because of its warm climate and plentiful rainfall, the Lower South became the global leader in cotton production. The region's cheap, fertile land and the profits provided by cotton generated a frenzied mobility in which people constantly searched for more opportunities and even better land. Henry Watson, a New Englander who moved to Alabama, complained in 1836 that "nobody seems to consider himself settled [here]; they remain one, two, three or four years & must move on to some other spot."

The cotton belt moved south and west during the first half of the nineteenth century, and

ATOP THE COTTON KINGDOM This photograph offers a glimpse of the staggering rates of cotton production. These cotton bales fill this Mississippi steamboat to capacity, and are so densely packed and plentiful that men are able to walk on top of them.

hundreds of thousands of land-hungry southerners moved with it. As the oldest southern states—Virginia and the Carolinas—experienced soil exhaustion from the overplanting of tobacco and cotton, restless farmers and many sons of planters moved westward to the **Old Southwest**—western Georgia, Alabama, Mississippi, Louisiana, Arkansas, and, eventually, Texas.

In 1820, the coastal states of Virginia, the Carolinas, and Georgia had produced two-thirds of the nation's cotton. By 1830, the Old Southwest states were producing two-thirds of all cotton. An acre of land in South Carolina produced about 300 pounds of cotton, while an acre in Alabama or in the Mississippi delta, a 200-mile wide strip of fertile soil between the Yazoo and Mississippi rivers, could generate 800 pounds. It was the most profitable farmland in the world.

> Massive migration to Lower South / Old Southwest

Such profits, however, required backbreaking labor, most of it performed by enslaved blacks. A white Virginian noted in 1807 that "there is a great aversion amongst our Negroes to be carried to distant parts, and particularly to our new countries [in the Old Southwest]." In marshy areas near the Gulf coast, slaves were put to work removing trees and stumps from the swampy muck. "None but men as hard as a Savage," said one worker, could survive such wearying conditions.

The formula for growing rich in the Lower South was simple: cheap land, cotton seed, and slaves. A planter who moved to the Mississippi Territory urged a friend back in Kentucky to join him: "If you could . . . bring your negroes to the Miss. Terr., they would certainly make you a handsome fortune in ten years by the cultivation of Cotton." A North Carolinian reported that the "*Alabama Fever* . . . has *carried off* vast numbers of our citizens." Between 1810 and 1840, the combined population of Georgia, Alabama, and Mississippi increased from about 300,000 (252,000 of whom were in Georgia) to 1,657,799. By 1860, annual cotton production in the United States had grown from less than 150,000 bales (a bundle of cotton weighing between 400 and 500 pounds) to 4 *million* bales.

The Spreading Cotton Kingdom

By 1860, the center of the **"cotton kingdom"** stretched from eastern North Carolina, South Carolina, and Georgia through the fertile Alabama-Mississippi "black belt" (so called for the color of the fertile soil), through Louisiana, on to Texas, and up the Mississippi Valley as far as southern Illinois. The emergence of steamboats enabled the Mississippi River to become the cotton highway by transporting millions of bales downriver from Kentucky, Tennessee, Arkansas, Mississippi, and Louisiana to New Orleans, where sailing ships took the cotton to New York, New England, Great Britain, and France. King Cotton accounted for more than half of all U.S. exports.

By 1860, Alabama, Mississippi, and Louisiana were the three top-producing cotton states, and two-thirds of the richest Americans lived in the South. More millionaires per capita lived in Natchez, Mississippi, along

Old Southwest Region covering western Georgia, Alabama, Mississippi, Louisiana, Arkansas, and Texas, where low land prices and fertile soil attracted droves of settlers after the American Revolution.

cotton kingdom Cotton-producing region, relying predominantly on slave labor, that spanned from North Carolina west to Louisiana and reached as far north as southern Illinois.

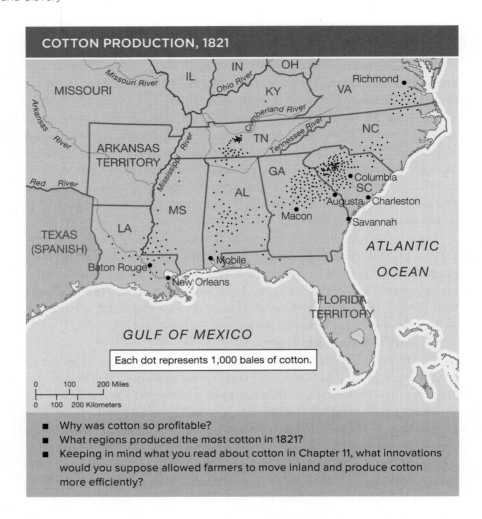

COTTON PRODUCTION, 1821

Each dot represents 1,000 bales of cotton.

- Why was cotton so profitable?
- What regions produced the most cotton in 1821?
- Keeping in mind what you read about cotton in Chapter 11, what innovations would you suppose allowed farmers to move inland and produce cotton more efficiently?

Cotton boom expands slavery

the great river, than anywhere in the world. The rapid expansion of the cotton belt ensured that the South became more dependent on enslaved black workers. More than half the slaves in the South worked in cotton production.

Slavery became such a powerful engine of economic development in the South that it resisted any criticism and helps explain why southerners became so defiantly defensive about preserving slavery. By 1860, the dollar value of enslaved blacks outstripped the value of *all* American banks, railroads, and factories combined. The result was staggering wealth for a few; the twelve richest counties in the United States in 1860 were all in the South.

The soaring profitability of cotton fostered a false sense of security. In 1860, a Mississippi newspaper boasted that the South, "safely entrenched behind her cotton bags . . . can defy the world—for the civilized world

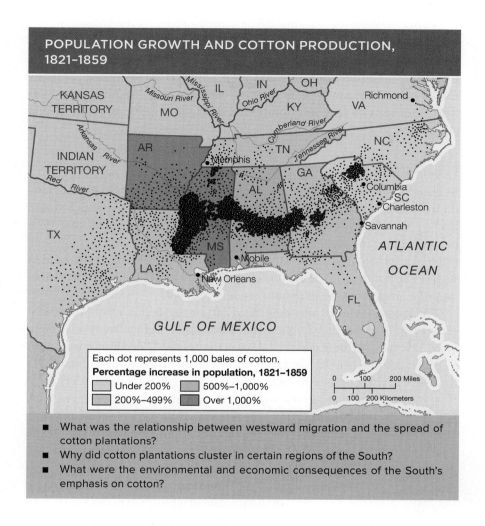

POPULATION GROWTH AND COTTON PRODUCTION, 1821–1859

Each dot represents 1,000 bales of cotton.
Percentage increase in population, 1821–1859
- Under 200%
- 200%–499%
- 500%–1,000%
- Over 1,000%

- What was the relationship between westward migration and the spread of cotton plantations?
- Why did cotton plantations cluster in certain regions of the South?
- What were the environmental and economic consequences of the South's emphasis on cotton?

depends on the cotton of the South." Cotton bred cockiness. In a speech to the U.S. Senate in 1858, South Carolina's former governor, James Henry Hammond, who owned a huge cotton plantation worked by more than 100 slaves, warned the critics of slavery in the North: "You dare not make war on cotton. No power on earth dares make war upon it. Cotton is King."

What Hammond failed to acknowledge was that the southern economy had grown dangerously dependent on European demand for raw cotton. By 1860, Great Britain was importing more than 80 percent of its cotton from the South. Hammond and other southern leaders did not anticipate what they could least afford: a sudden collapse in world demand for southern cotton. In 1860, the expansion of the British textile industry peaked, and the price paid for southern cotton began a steady decline. By then, however, it was too late to change the southern economy; the Lower South was committed to large-scale cotton production for generations to come.

> Increased southern dependence on Britain

CORE **OBJECTIVE**

3. Distinguish among the major groups within southern white society, and explain why each group supported the expansion of slavery.

Whites in the Old South

Over time, the culture of cotton and slavery shaped the South's social structure and provided much of its political power. Unlike the North and Midwest, southern society was dominated by an elite group of planters and merchants.

White Planters

Although there were only a few giant plantations in each southern state, their owners exercised overwhelming influence. The large planters behaved like an aristocracy, controlling political, economic, and social life. "The planters here are essentially what the nobility are in other countries," claimed a self-serving James Henry Hammond. "They stand at the head of society and politics. . . . Slavery does indeed create an aristocracy—an aristocracy of talents, of virtue, or generosity, and courage."

The largest planters were determined to retain their control over southern society. To do so, they frequently defended their right to rule their neighbors. "Inequality is the fundamental law of the universe," declared one planter.

What distinguished a plantation from a farm, in addition to its size, was the use of a large number of slaves supervised by drivers and overseers. If, as historians have agreed, one had to own at least twenty slaves to be called a **planter**, only one out of thirty whites in 1860 was a planter. Eleven planters, among the wealthiest people in the nation, owned 500 slaves each and one planter, a South Carolina rice grower, owned 1,000. The 10,000 most powerful planters, making up less than 3 percent of white men in the South, held more than half the slaves. The total number of slaveholders was only 383,637 out of a total white population of 8 million.

Over time, planters and their wives (called mistresses) grew accustomed to being waited on by slaves, day and night. A Virginia planter told a British visitor that a slave girl slept in the master bedroom with him and his wife. When his British guest asked why, he replied: "Good heaven! If I wanted a glass of water during the night, what would become of me?"

Success as a cotton planter required careful monitoring of the world markets for cotton, land, and slaves as well as careful management of the workers and production. When not working, planters enjoyed hunting, horse racing, and cards. As

A SOUTHERN PLANTATION An 1859 engraving of a rice planter's mansion, where the planter and his family would reside. Behind the mansion can be seen a set of humble cabins that housed the plantation's slaves.

a plantation slave recalled, his master on Sundays liked to "gamble, run horses, or fight game-cocks, discuss politics, and drink whisky, and brandy and water all day long."

The planter elite

From colonial times, most southern white men, but especially the planter and political elite, embraced a social code centered on an easily offended sense of personal honor in which a man must defend his reputation—with words, fists, or guns. Duels to the death were the ultimate expression of personal honor and manly courage. Although not confined to the South, dueling was much more common there than in the rest of the nation, a fact that gave rise to the observation that southerners were excessively polite until they got angry enough to kill you. Many of the most prominent southern leaders—congressmen, senators, governors, editors, and planters—engaged in duels, although dueling was technically illegal in many states. The roster of participants included President Andrew Jackson of Tennessee and Senator Henry Clay of Kentucky.

Honor and violence: Dueling

The Plantation Mistress

The South, like the North, was a male-dominated society, only more so because of the slave system. A prominent Georgian, Christopher Memminger, explained that slavery heightened the need for a hierarchical social and family structure. White wives and children needed to be as subservient and compliant to husbands and fathers as enslaved blacks were required to be. "Each planter," he declared, "is in fact a Patriarch—his position compels him to be a ruler in his household," and he requires "obedience and subordination."

The **plantation mistress** seldom led a life of idle leisure, nor was she a frail, helpless creature focused solely on planning parties and balls. Although the mistress had slaves to attend to her needs, she supervised the domestic household in the same way as the planter took care of the cotton business, overseeing the supply and preparation of food and linens, the housecleaning and care of the sick, the birthing of babies, and the operations of the dairy. A plantation slave remembered that her mistress "was with all the slave women every time a baby was born. Or, when a plague of misery hit the folks, she knew what to do and what kind of medicine to chase off the aches and pains."

Mary Boykin Chesnut, a plantation mistress in South Carolina, complained that "there is no slave, after all, like a wife." She admitted that she had few rights in the large household she managed, since her husband was the "master of the house." As a wife, she must love, honor, obey, and serve her husband. Virginian George Fitzhugh, a celebrated Virginia attorney and writer, spoke for most southern men when he said that a "man loves his children because they are weak, helpless, and dependent. He loves his wife for similar reasons."

White women living in a slaveholding culture confronted a double standard in terms of moral and sexual behavior. They were expected to be exemplars of Christian morality and sexual purity and to "obey" their fathers and husbands, even as their husbands, brothers, and sons often followed an unwritten rule of self-indulgent hedonism and adultery.

MARY BOYKIN CHESNUT Chesnut's diary describing southern life and the Civil War was published posthumously and won the Pulitzer Prize in 1981.

planters Owners of large farms in the South that were worked by twenty or more slaves and supervised by overseers.

plantation mistress Matriarch of a planter's household, responsible for supervising the domestic aspects of the estate.

"Under slavery," Mary Chesnut wrote in her famous diary, "we live surrounded by prostitutes." Yet she did not blame enslaved women for playing that role. White planters forced them to do so. In fact, many planters justified their behavior by highlighting the additional money they were creating by impregnating enslaved women.

"God forgive us," Chesnut added, "but ours is a monstrous system. Like the patriarchs of old, our men live all in one house with their wives and their [enslaved] concubines [lovers]; and the [people of mixed races] one sees in every family partly resemble the white children. Any lady is ready to tell you who is the father of all the mulatto children in everybody's household but her own. Those, she seems to think, drop from the clouds."

Such a double standard reinforced the arrogant authoritarianism of many white planters. In the secrecy of her diary, Mary Chesnut used sexual metaphors to express the limitations of most of the Carolina planters, writing that they "are nice fellows, but slow to move; impulsive but hard to keep moving. They are wonderful for a spurt, but that lets out all of their strength."

Yet for all their private complaints and daily burdens, few plantation mistresses, including Mary Chesnut, spoke out against the male-dominated social order and racist climate. They largely accepted the limited domestic role assigned them by men such as George Howe, a South Carolina religion professor. In 1850, he complimented southern women for understanding their subordinate status. "Born to lean upon others, rather than to stand independently by herself, and to confide in an arm stronger than hers," the southern woman had no desire for "power" outside the home, he said. The few women who were demanding equality, he claimed, were "unsexing" themselves and were "despised and detested" by their families and communities.

Most plantation mistresses agreed with Howe. With but a few exceptions, observed Julia Gardiner Tyler, the northern-born wife of President John Tyler, a Virginia slaveholder, women should limit themselves to the roles that "God designed for them"—"as wife, mother, mistress." Another prominent southern woman, Mary Howard Schoolcraft, described herself and other plantation wives in South Carolina as "old fogies" who refused to believe that "slavery is a sin." She could not imagine doing without the comforts and conveniences "afforded by slaves."

Overseers and Drivers

White overseers

The whites who worked on the large plantations were usually *overseers* who managed the slaves to ensure that they worked hard and efficiently. They were also responsible for maintaining the buildings, fences, and grounds. They usually were farmers or skilled workers, or they were the sons of planters, or simply poor whites eager to rise in stature. Some were themselves slaveholders.

The overseers moved often in search of better wages and cheaper land. A Mississippi planter described white overseers as "a worthless set of vagabonds." Likewise, Frederick Douglass, a mulatto who escaped from slavery in Maryland, said his overseer was "a miserable drunkard, a profane swearer,

OVERSEEING SLAVES AT WORK
A well-dressed overseer supervises a line of slaves harvesting sugar cane. On the left, playing in the shade, are two white boys, about the same age as the African-American children laboring in the field.

and a savage monster" always armed with a blood-stained bullwhip and a club that he used so cruelly that he even "enraged" the plantation owner. The overseer tolerated no excuses or explanations. "To be accused was to be convicted, and to be convicted was to be punished," Douglass said.

Usually, the highest managerial position a slave could hope for on a plantation was that of *driver*, a favored man whose job was to oversee a small group ("gang") of slaves, getting them up and organized each morning by sunrise, and then directing their work (and punishing them) until dark. Over the years, there were numerous examples of slaves murdering drivers for being too cruel.

"Plain White Folk"

The most numerous white southerners were the small farmers—the **"plain white folk"** who were usually uneducated and often illiterate, eking out hardscrabble lives of bare self-sufficiency. These small farmers ("yeomen") lived with their families in simple two-room cabins, raised a few hogs and chickens, grew some corn and cotton, and traded with neighbors more than they bought from stores. Women on these farms worked in the fields during harvest time but spent most of their days doing household chores. Some of these "middling" farmers owned a handful of slaves with whom they worked alongside, but most had none.

Southern farmers tended to be fiercely independent and suspicious of government authority, and they overwhelmingly identified with the Democratic party of Andrew Jackson and the spiritual energies of the evangelical Protestant denominations such as Baptists and Methodists. Although only a minority of the small farm owners held slaves, most supported the slave

plain white folk Yeoman farmers who lived and worked on their own small farms, growing food and cash crops to trade for necessities.

system for both economic and racial reasons. They feared that the slaves, if freed, would compete with them for land and jobs, and they enjoyed the privileged status that race-based slavery afforded them. As a white farmer told a northern traveler, "Now suppose they [slaves] was free. You see they'd all think themselves as good as we."

"Poor Whites"

Visitors to the Old South often had trouble telling small farmers apart from the "poor whites," a category of desperately poor people relegated to the least desirable land, living on the fringes of polite society, often in the Appalachian Mountains. The poor whites, often derided as "crackers," or "hillbillies," were day laborers or squatters who owned neither land nor slaves. Some 40 percent of white southerners worked as "tenants," renting land from others, or as farm laborers, toiling for others. And what land they owned was often the least desirable for farming. They were often forced to take refuge in the pine barrens, the mountain hollows, and the swamps after having been pushed aside by the more enterprising and the more successful. They usually lived in log cabins, barely managing each year to keep their families clothed, warm, dry, and fed. The poor whites were regularly satirized and caricatured. In 1860, D. R. Hundley wrote in *Social Relations in Our Southern States* that the poor white southerner was descended from criminals deported to America from Great Britain. "He is bony and lank, with a sallow complexion, awkward manners, and a natural stupidity or dullness of intellect that almost surpasses belief."

CORE **OBJECTIVE**

4. Describe the impact of slavery on African Americans, both free and enslaved, throughout the South.

Black Society in the South

However immoral and degrading, slavery was the fastest-growing element of national life during the first half of the nineteenth century. Owning, working, and selling slaves was the quickest way to wealth and social status in the nineteenth-century South. In 1790, the United States had fewer than 700,000 black slaves. By 1830, it had more than 2 million, and by 1860 4 million. As the enslaved population grew, slave owners felt the need to develop a complex system of rules, regulations, and restrictions to govern the slaves' daily lives.

Most southern whites viewed slaves as property rather than people; babies became slaves at birth; slaves could be moved, sold, rented out, whipped, or raped, as their master saw fit. Formal **slave codes** in each state governed the treatment of slaves in order to deter runaways or rebellions. Slaves could not leave their owner's land or household without permission or stay out after dark (curfew) without an identification pass.

Some codes made it a crime for slaves to learn how to read and write, for fear that they might use notes to plan a revolt. A former Kentucky slave, John W. Fields, remembered that the white slaveholders "were very harsh if

slave codes Regulations governing the treatment of slaves in each state in order to deter runaways and rebellions.

we were caught trying to learn or write. . . . Our ignorance was the greatest hold the South had on us." Slaves in most states could not testify in court, legally marry, own firearms, or hit a white man, even in self-defense. Yet despite such restrictions and brutalities, the enslaved managed to create their own community and culture within the confines of the slave system.

"Free Persons of Color"

Southern society was literally black and white. Whites had all the power, and enslaved blacks had little choice but to persevere. The system of slavery relied on overwhelming force and fear and was intentionally dehumanizing. "We believe the negro to belong to an inferior race," one planter declared. Southern apologists for slavery often stressed that African Americans were "inferior" beings incapable of living on their own. Thomas Reade Cobb proclaimed that they were better off "in a state of bondage."

Effective slave management therefore required teaching slaves to understand that they were supposed to be treated like animals. As Henry Garner, an escaped slave, explained, slaveholders strove "to make you as much like brutes as possible." Others justified slavery as a form of benevolent paternalism. George Fitzhugh said that the enslaved black was "but a grown-up child, and must be governed as a child."

Such self-serving paternalism had one ultimate purpose: profits. Planters, explained a southerner, "care for nothing but to buy Negroes to raise cotton & raise cotton to buy Negroes." In 1818, James Steer in Louisiana predicted that enslaved blacks would be the best investment that southerners could make. Eleven years later, in 1829, the North Carolina Supreme Court declared that slavery existed to increase "the profit of the Master." The role of the slave was "to toil while another [the owners] reap the fruits."

Those who traded in slaves reaped huge profits. One of them reported in the 1850s that "a nigger that wouldn't bring over $300, seven years ago, will fetch $1000, cash, quick, this year." Thomas Clemson of South Carolina, the son-in-law of John C. Calhoun, candidly explained that "my object is to get the most I can for the property [slaves] . . . I care but little to whom and how they are sold, whether together [as families] or separated."

In the South, free persons of color tended to live in cities. In fact, however, they were anything but free; they occupied an uncertain social status between slavery and freedom. In South Carolina, for example, free blacks had to pay an annual tax and were not allowed to leave the state. After 1823, they were required to have a white "guardian."

Blacks became "free" in a number of ways. Over the years, some slaves were able to purchase their freedom, and others were freed ("manumitted") by their owners. By 1860, there were approximately 250,000 free blacks in the slave states, most of whom

YARROW MAMOUT As an enslaved African Muslim, Mamout purchased his freedom, acquired property, and settled in present-day Washington, D.C. Charles Willson Peale executed this portrait in 1819 when Mamout was over 100 years old.

lived in coastal cities such as Baltimore, Charleston, Mobile, and New Orleans. Some were tailors or shoemakers or carpenters; others worked as painters, bricklayers, butchers, blacksmiths, or barbers. Still others worked on the docks or on steamships. Free black women usually worked as seamstresses, laundresses, or house servants. Free blacks had more rights than slaves. They could enter into contracts, marry, own property (including slaves of their own), and pass on their property to their children.

Among the free black population were a large number of **mulattoes**, people of mixed racial ancestry. The census of 1860 reported 412,000 mulattoes in the United States, or about 10 percent of the black population—probably a drastic undercount. In cities such as Charleston, and especially New Orleans, "colored" society occupied a status somewhere between that of blacks and that of whites. Some mulattoes built substantial fortunes and even became slaveholders themselves. In Natchez, Mississippi, William Johnson, son of a white father and a mulatto mother, operated three barbershops, owned 1,500 acres of land, and held several slaves. Black slaveholders were few in number, however. The 1830 census reported that 3,775 free blacks, about 2 percent of the total free black population, owned 12,760 slaves.

The Trade in Slaves

The rapid increase in the slave population mainly occurred naturally, through slave births, especially after Congress and President Thomas Jefferson outlawed American involvement with the African slave trade in 1808. But banning the importation of slaves from Africa also had the effect of increasing the cash value of slaves in the United States. This in turn convinced some owners to treat their slaves better. As one planter remarked in 1849, "The time has been that the farmer would kill up and wear out one Negro to buy another, but it is not so now."

The dramatic rise in the dollar value of enslaved workers prompted better treatment for many. "Massa was purty good," one ex-slave recalled. "He treated us jus' 'bout like you would a good mule." Another said his owner "fed us reg'lar on good, 'stantial food, jus' like you'd tend to you hoss [horse], if you had a real good one." A slave born in 1850 had a life expectancy of thirty-six years; the life expectancy of whites was forty years. Some slaveholders hired white wage laborers, often Irish immigrants, for dangerous work rather than risk the lives of the more valuable slaves.

Once the African slave trade was outlawed, the slave-trading network *within* the United States became much more important—and profitable. Between 1800 and 1860, the average price of slaves *quadrupled*, in large part because of the dramatic expansion of the cotton culture.

Breeding and selling slaves became a big business. Over a twenty-year period, a Virginia plantation owned by John Tayloe III recorded 252 slave births and 142 slave deaths, thus providing Tayloe with 110 extra slaves to be deployed on the plantation, given to his sons, or sold to traders.

To manage the growing internal slave trade, markets and auction houses sprang up in every southern city. New Orleans alone had twenty slave-

Domestic slave trade

mulattoes Mixed-race people who constituted most of the South's free black population.

SLAVE AUCTION AND ESTATE SALE This engraving from 1842 depicts an estate sale in New Orleans, where slaves are auctioned off beside art and other valuable items. An enslaved man, woman, and child stand on the auction block. **What characterized New Orleans' "fancy trade"?**

trading businesses. Each year, thousands of slaves circulated through the city's "slave pens." There they were converted from people into products with prices. They were bathed and groomed, "fattened up" with bacon, milk, and butter, like cattle, assigned categories such as Prime, No. 1, No. 2, and Second Rate; and packaged for sale by being dressed in identical blue suits or dresses. On auction day, they were paraded into the sale room. The tallest, strongest, and "blackest" young men brought the highest prices. As a slave trader stressed, "I must have if possible the *jet black* Negroes, for they stand the climate best."

Buyers physically inspected each slave on the "auction block" as if they were horses or cattle. They squeezed their muscles, felt their joints, worked their fingers back and forth, pried open their mouths to examine their teeth and gums. They then forced the slaves to strip and carefully inspected their naked bodies, looking for signs of disease or deformities. They particularly

THE BUSINESS OF SLAVERY
This advertisement for the Blount & Dawson guarantees its clients "secure and good accommodations for all negroes left with us for Sale or Safe-Keeping" in its newly acquired jail, opposite the state bank.

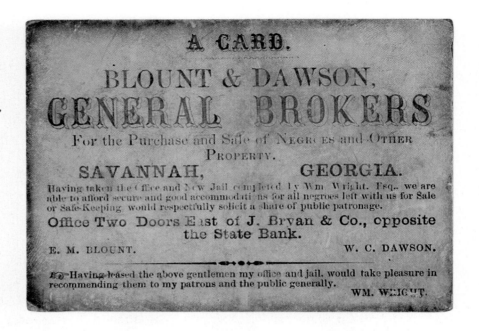

focused on any scars from whipping. As Solomon Northup noted, "scars on a slave's back were considered evidence of a rebellious or unruly spirit, and hurt [his chances for] sale." Once the crude inspections ended, buyers bid on the slaves, purchased them, and then transported them to their new homes.

Almost a million captive African Americans, many of them children, were "sold South" or "down river" and taken to the Old Southwest during the first half of the nineteenth century. Planters purchasing slaves knew what they wanted. "It is better to buy *none in families*," said a Mississippi buyer, "but to select *only choice, first rate, young hands from 16 to 25 years of age* (buying no children or aged negroes)."

The worst aspect of the domestic slave trade was the separation of children from parents and husbands from wives. Children were often taken from their parents and sold to new masters. In Missouri, one enslaved woman saw six of her seven children, ages one to eleven, sold to six different owners. Only Louisiana and Alabama prohibited separating a child younger than ten from his or her mother, and no state prevented the separation of a slave husband from his wife.

White owners—as well as Indians who purchased enslaved blacks—worked the slaves especially hard in the "howling wilderness" of the Old Southwest, cutting down trees, operating sawmills, draining swamps, clearing land, building roads, and planting and picking cotton.

Slave markets in New Orleans engaged in what was called the "fancy trade," which meant selling women as forced sexual partners. "I sold your fancy girl Alice for $800," a New Orleans slave trader wrote to a partner in Richmond. "There is great demand for fancy maids."

A reporter watching a slave sale in the St. Louis Hotel in New Orleans spied on the auction block "one of the most beautiful women [he] had ever saw. She was about sixteen, dressed in a cheap striped woolen gown, and bareheaded." Her name was Hermina, and she was "sold for $1250 [$35,000 today] to one of the most lecherous brutes I ever set eyes on," he added. The same reporter noted that "a noble-looking woman with a bright-eyed seven-year-old" son were offered for sale as a pair. When no one bid on them, the auctioneer offered them separately. A man from Mississippi bought the boy while the mother went to a Texan. As her son was dragged away, the woman "burst forth into the most frantic wails that ever despair gave utterance to."

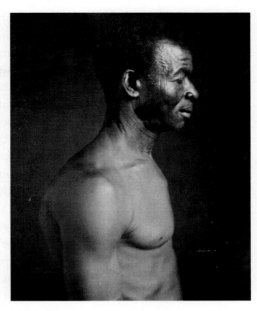

JACK **(1850)** Daguerreotype of a slave identified only as Jack, on the plantation of B. F. Taylor in Columbia, South Carolina.

Slavery as a Way of Life

The lives of slaves differed greatly from place to place, depending in part on the personality of their owner, in part on whether the enslaved were focused on growing rice, sugar, tobacco, or cotton, and in part on whether they were on farms or in cities. Although many slaves were artisans or craftsmen (carpenters, blacksmiths, furniture makers, butchers, boatmen, house servants, cooks, nurses, maids, weavers, basketmakers, etc.), the vast majority were **field hands** who were often organized into work gangs supervised by a black "driver" or white overseer. Some slaves were "hired out" to other planters or to merchants, churches or businesses. Others worked on Sundays or holidays to earn cash of their own.

> Plantation field hands

Plantation slaves were usually housed in one- or two-room cabins with dirt floors. The wealthiest planters built slave cabins out of brick. Beds were a luxury, even though they were little more than boards covered with straw. Most slaves slept on the floor with only a coarse blanket for warmth. They received a set of cheap linen or cotton clothes twice a year, but shoes were generally provided only in winter; slaves went barefoot most of the year. About half of all slave babies died in their first year, a rate more than twice that of whites. The food provided slaves was cheap and monotonous: cornmeal, pork, molasses, and chicken.

Field hands worked from sunrise to sunset, six days a week. At times they were worked at night as well, ginning cotton, milling sugar cane, grinding corn, or doing other indoor tasks. Women, remembered a slave, "had to work all day in de fields an' den come home an' do the housework at night." Sundays were precious days off. Slaves used the Sabbath to hunt, fish, dance to banjo and fiddle music, tell stories, or tend their own small gardens.

> Brutal force and rural slaves

Amanda McDaniel, enslaved in Georgia, remembered that her parents "had to get up at four o'clock every morning and feed the stock [cattle, pigs, horses, and mules] first. By the time it was light enough to see they had to be in the fields where they hoed the cotton and the corn as well as the other crops."

field hands Slaves who toiled in the cotton or cane fields in organized work gangs.

Beginning in August and lasting several months, the focus was on picking cotton. Gangs of slaves, men and women, would sweep across a field, pull the bolls from the thorny pods, and stuff them in large sacks or baskets. All the while, they were watched and prodded by an overseer, bullwhip in hand, forcing them to keep up the pace. Solomon Northup remembered picking cotton until it was "too dark to see, and when the moon is full, they often-times labor till the middle of the night." Each evening, the overseer or planter weighed the baskets and recorded the number of pounds on a slate board by each picker's name. Those who fell short of the daily goal were whipped.

Although some owners and slaves developed close and even affectionate relationships, slavery was a system rooted in brutal force. The difference between a good owner and a bad one, according to one slave, was the difference between one "who did not whip you too much" and one who "whipped you till he'd bloodied you and blistered you."

One overseer in South Carolina whipped eight women simply for hoeing "bad corn." Others were whipped for "not picking cotton"; "for not picking as well as he can"; for picking "very trashy cotton," etc. Bennett Barrow, a Louisiana planter, on average had a slave whipped every four days as a means of symbolizing his absolute control over them.

Greater mobility for city slaves

Slaves living in southern cities such as Richmond or Atlanta had a much different experience from those on farms and plantations. City life meant that slaves interacted not only with their white owners but also with the extended interracial community—shopkeepers and police, neighbors and strangers. Some slaves in cities were "hired out" on the condition that they paid a percentage of their earned wages to their owners. Generally speaking, slaves in cities enjoyed greater mobility and freedom than their counterparts in rural areas living on isolated farms or plantations.

Slave Women

Although enslaved men and women often performed similar chores, they did not experience slavery in the same way. "Slavery is terrible for men," the former North Carolina slave Harriet Jacobs stressed in her autobiography, *Incidents in the Life of a Slave Girl*, "but it is far more terrible for women."

Female slaves and reproduction

Once slaveholders realized how profitable a fertile female slave could be over time by giving birth to babies that could later be sold, they "encouraged" female slaves to have as many children as possible. Some owners rewarded pregnant slaves by giving them less work and more food and gifted new mothers with dresses and silver dollars.

But if motherhood provided enslaved women with greater stature and benefits, it also was exhausting. Within days after childbirth, the mothers were put to work spinning, weaving, or sewing. A few weeks thereafter, they were sent back to the fields; breast-feeding mothers were often forced to take their babies with them, strapped to their backs. Enslaved women were expected to do "man's work": cut trees, haul logs, spread fertilizer, plow fields, dig ditches, slaughter animals, hoe corn, and pick cotton. As an escaped slave reported, "Women who do outdoor work are used as bad as men."

***VIRGINIAN LUXURIES*, c. 1825**
This painting alludes to two privileges of the slave owner: to sexually abuse female slaves and physically abuse all slaves.

Enslaved girls, women, and some men were often sexually abused by their owners, both men and women. Hundreds of thousands of mulattoes provided physical proof of interracial sexual assault as a common way of life.

James Henry Hammond, the prominent South Carolina planter and political leader who confessed that he only succeeded "when everything is under my control," had a long affair with one of his female slaves, Sally Johnson, who bore several of his children, and then began another affair with one of her daughters, twelve-year-old Louisa. (Hammond also had scandalous affairs with four teenaged nieces and two daughters of his sister-in-law).

Sometimes a white master or overseer would rape a woman in the fields or cabins. Sometimes a woman would be locked in a cabin with a male slave whose task was to impregnate her. Enslaved women responded to sexual assaults in different ways. Some seduced their owner away from his wife. Others fiercely resisted the sexual advances—and were usually whipped or even killed for their disobedience. Some women aborted or killed their babies rather than see them grow up in slavery.

> Female slaves and sexual abuse

Forging a Slave Community

> CORE **OBJECTIVE**
> **5.** Analyze how enslaved peoples responded to the inhumanity of their situation.

American slavery included many diverse experiences. Enslaved African Americans were victims of terrible injustice and abuse, but such an obvious truth neglects important evidence of their endurance, resilience, and achievement. The Africans who were brought to America represented a variety of ethnic, linguistic, and tribal origins. Wherever they could, they forged their own sense of community, asserted their individuality, and devised

spirituals Songs with religious messages sung by slaves to help ease the strain of field labor and to voice their suffering at the hands of their masters and overseers.

ingenious ways of resisting their confinement. African American folklore invented stories of resistance such as "Brer [Brother] Rabbit," where the smart little rabbit eludes the animals stalking it by hiding in a patch of prickly briars. Many **spirituals**, sacred folk songs, expressed a longing to be free. Although most slaves were prohibited from marrying, the law did not prevent them from choosing partners and forging a family life within the rigid constraints of the slave system.

The Slave Family

Slave marriages had no legal status, but many slaveholders accepted unofficial marriages as a stabilizing influence on the plantation. Sometimes they performed the marriage ceremonies themselves or had a minister officiate. Whatever the formalities, the norm for the slave community, as for the white, was the nuclear family, with the father regarded as the head of the household. Most slave children were socialized by means of the nuclear family, which afforded some degree of independence from white influence.

Childhood was short for slaves. At five or six years of age, children were put to work; they collected trash and firewood, picked cotton, scared away crows from planted fields, weeded gardens and fields, and ran errands. By age ten they were full-time field hands.

The frequent buying and selling of slaves meant that children were often separated from their parents and sold to new masters. In Missouri, one enslaved woman saw six of her seven children, aged one to eleven, sold to six different owners. Given the fragility of the family, enslaved African

SLAVE FAMILY IN A GEORGIA COTTON FIELD A family of slaves toils in a cotton field together, the young children working alongside the men and women. **What factors extended enslaved African Americans' concept of family?**

***PLANTATION BURIAL* (1860)** The slaves of Mississippi governor Tilghman Tucker gather together in the woods to bury and mourn for one of their own. The painter of this scene, Englishman John Antrobus, would serve in the Confederate Army during the Civil War.

Americans often extended the fellowship of family to those who worked together, with older slave women being addressed as "granny," or co-workers as "sis" or "brother." One white teacher visiting a slave community observed that they "all belonged to one immense family."

African American Religion

Among the most important elements of African American culture was its dynamic religion, a unique mixture of African, Caribbean, and Christian elements often practiced in secret because many slaveholders feared enslaved workers might use group religious services as a means of organizing rebellions.

Slaves found in religion both relief for the soul and release for their emotions. Most Africans brought with them to the Americas belief in a Creator, or Supreme God, whom they could recognize in the Christian God, and whom they might identify with Christ, the Holy Ghost, and the saints. But they also maintained beliefs in spirits, magic, and conjuring. Most slave owners tried to erase African religion and spirituality from the slave experience.

By 1860, about 20 percent of adult slaves had joined Christian denominations. Many others displayed aspects of the Christian faith in their forms of worship but were not considered Christians. As a white minister observed, "some slaves had heard of Jesus Christ, but who he is and what he has done for a ruined world, they cannot tell."

African American religion and spirituals

Slaves found the Bible inspiring in its support for the poor and oppressed, and they embraced its promise of salvation through the sacrifice of Jesus. Likewise, the lyrics of religious spirituals helped slaves endure the strain of long hours laboring in fields. The abolitionist Frederick Douglass, himself a former slave, stressed that "slaves sing most when they are most unhappy." Spirituals offered them deliverance from their worldly woes. One popular spiritual, "Go Down, Moses," derived from the plight of the ancient Israelites held captive in Egypt, says: "We need not always weep and moan, / Let my people go. / And wear these slavery chains forlorn, / Let my people go."

Slave Rebellions

Slave rebellions

Southern whites feared slave uprisings more than anything. As a prominent Virginian explained, a slave revolt would "deluge the southern country with blood." Any sign of resistance or rebellion therefore risked a brutal response. In 1811, for example, two of Thomas Jefferson's nephews, Lilburn and Isham Lewis, tied a seventeen-year-old slave named George to the floor of their Kentucky cabin and killed him with an axe in front of seven other slaves, all because George had run away several times. They then handed the axe to one of the slaves and forced him to dismember the body and put the pieces in the fireplace. The Lewises, who had been drinking heavily, wanted "to set an example for any other uppity slaves."

Gabriel's Rebellion The overwhelming authority and firepower of southern whites made organized resistance by slaves risky. The nineteenth-century South witnessed only four major slave insurrections. In 1800, a slave named Gabriel Prosser, who worked as a blacksmith on a plantation near Richmond, Virginia, hatched a revolt involving perhaps a thousand other slaves. They planned to seize key points in the city, capture the governor, James Monroe, and overthrow the white elite. Gabriel expected the "poor white people" to join their effort. It did not happen, for someone alerted whites to the scheme. Gabriel and twenty-six of his fellow "soldiers" were captured, tried, and hanged. Before his execution, Gabriel explained that he was only imitating George Washington: "I have ventured my life in endeavoring to obtain the liberty of my countrymen."

German Coast Uprising In early 1811, the largest slave revolt in American history occurred just north of New Orleans in the Louisiana Territory, where wealthy sugarcane planters had acquired one of the largest populations of slaves in North America, five times as many as the whites who owned them. Many of those slaves were ripe for revolt. Sugarcane was known as a "killer crop" because the working conditions were so harsh that many slaves died from exhaustion in the heat and humidity of Louisiana.

Late on January 8, a group of slaves broke into their owner's plantation house along the east bank of the Mississippi River. The planter was able to escape, but his son was hacked to death. The leader of the assault was Charles Deslondes, a trusted slave overseer. Deslondes and his fellow rebels seized weapons, horses, and militia uniforms from the plantation. Reinforced by more slaves and emboldened by liquor, the rebels headed toward New Orleans, burning houses and killing whites along the way. Over the next two days, the ranks of the rebels swelled to over 200.

Their success was short-lived, however. Angry whites—as well as several free blacks who were later praised for their "tireless zeal and dauntless courage"—suppressed the insurrection. U.S. Army units and militia joined the effort. Dozens of slaves were killed or wounded; most who fled were captured over the next week. "We made considerable slaughter," reported one white planter.

Deslondes had his hands severed and thighs broken before he was shot and his body burned. As many as 100 slaves were tortured, killed, and beheaded. Their severed heads were placed on poles along the Mississippi River in order to strike fear into enslaved workers. A month after the rebellion was put down, a white resident noted that "all the negro difficulties have subsided and gentle peace prevails."

Denmark Vesey Revolt The Denmark Vesey plot in Charleston, South Carolina, discovered in 1822, involved a similar effort to assault the white population on the road to freedom. Vesey, born in 1767 on the Caribbean island of St. Thomas, was purchased by a slave trader based in Charleston. In 1799, Vesey purchased a lottery ticket and won $1,500, which he used to buy his freedom. He thereafter opened a carpentry shop and organized a Bible study class in the African Methodist Episcopal Church.

In 1822, Vesey and several others developed a plan for a massive slave revolt. They would first capture the city's arsenal and distribute its hundreds of rifles to free and enslaved blacks. All whites in the city would then be killed, along with any blacks who refused to join the rebellion. Vesey then planned to burn the city, seize ships in the harbor, and head for the black republic of Haiti, where slaves in the former French sugar colony, then called Saint-Domingue, had staged a successful revolt in 1791.

The Vesey plot never got off the ground, however. As Vesey and others secretly tried to recruit slaves, one of them told his master what was going on. Soon Vesey and a hundred other supposed slave rebels were captured and tried. The court found Vesey guilty of plotting a slave uprising intended to "trample on all laws, human and divine; to riot in blood, outrage, rapine . . . and conflagration, and to introduce anarchy and confusion in their most horrid forms." Vesey and thirty-four others were executed; three dozen more were transported to Spanish Cuba and sold. When told

THE DISCOVERY OF NAT TURNER After leading a deadly insurrection that provoked federal intervention, Nat Turner was captured and sentenced to death. His legacy, however, could not be subdued, and slave-owners across the South grew fearful of more uprisings. **What actions did southern whites take to try to suppress future rebellions?**

that he would be hanged, Vesey replied that "the work of insurrection will go on."

Denmark Vesey's planned rebellion led officials in South Carolina to place even more restrictions on the mobility of free blacks and black religious gatherings. It also influenced John C. Calhoun to abandon the nationalism of his early political career and become the South's most forceful spokesman for states' rights.

Nat Turner Rebellion The Nat Turner insurrection of August 1831, in a rural area of Virginia where enslaved blacks greatly outnumbered free whites, again panicked whites throughout the South. Turner, a trusted black overseer, was also a literate preacher who believed God had instructed him to lead a slave rebellion. The revolt began when a small group of slaves joined Turner in methodically killing his owner's family. Arming themselves with axes and swords, farm tools and muskets, they then repeated the process at other farmhouses, where other slaves joined in. Before the revolt ended, fifty-seven whites had been killed, most of them women and children. Turner later explained that he had also killed the "man who was to me a kind master."

THE SLAVE POPULATION, 1820 AND 1860

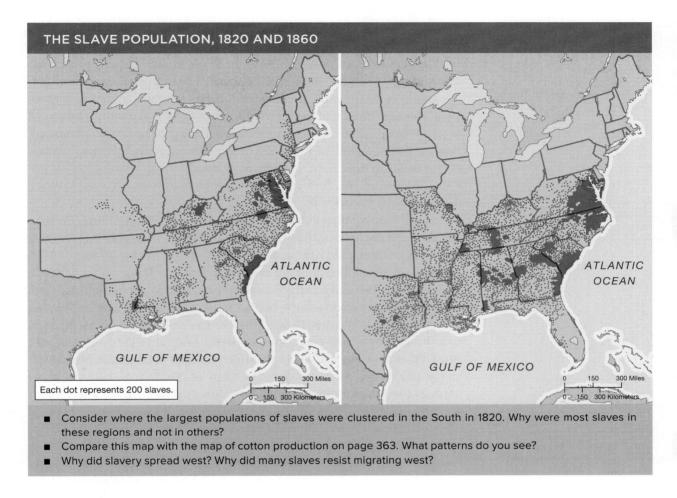

Each dot represents 200 slaves.

ATLANTIC OCEAN

GULF OF MEXICO

0   150   300 Miles
0   150   300 Kilometers

ATLANTIC OCEAN

GULF OF MEXICO

0   150   300 Miles
0   150   300 Kilometers

- Consider where the largest populations of slaves were clustered in the South in 1820. Why were most slaves in these regions and not in others?
- Compare this map with the map of cotton production on page 363. What patterns do you see?
- Why did slavery spread west? Why did many slaves resist migrating west?

Federal troops, Virginia militiamen, and volunteers, driven by anger and fear, indiscriminately killed nearly 200 slaves in the process of putting down the rebels. A Virginia newspaper said the behavior of the white vigilantes was comparable in "barbarity to the atrocities of the insurgents." Seventeen slaves were hanged; several were decapitated, and their severed heads placed on poles along the highway. Turner, called the "blood-stained monster," avoided capture for six weeks. He then was tried and found guilty. While waiting to be hanged, he was asked if the revolt was worth it. "Was not Christ crucified?" he replied. His dead body was dismembered, with body parts given to the victims' families.

More than any other slave uprising, **Nat Turner's Rebellion** terrified whites across the South. The Virginia legislature debated whether slavery should be abolished. That proposal was defeated, and instead the delegates restricted the ability of slaves to learn to read and write and gather for religious meetings. "We were no more than dogs," an enslaved woman recalled.

Nat Turner's Rebellion (1831) Insurrection in rural Virginia led by black overseer Nat Turner, who murdered slave owners and their families; in turn, federal troops indiscriminately killed hundreds of slaves in the process of putting down Turner and his rebels.

"If they caught us with a piece of paper in our pockets, they'd whip us. They was afraid we'd learn to read and write, but I never got the chance."

Throughout the South after Nat Turner's Rebellion, states created vigilante groups of whites, slave owners as well as non-owners, to patrol their communities looking for runaways. A former slave highlighted the "thousand obstacles thrown in the way of the flying slave. Every white man's hand is raised against him—the patrollers are watching for him—the hounds are ready to follow on his track, and the nature of the country is such as renders it impossible to pass through it with any safety."

The Lure of Freedom

Runaways: The "underground railroad"

Yet slaves kept running away—a powerful example of the enduring lure of freedom and the extraordinary courage of those who yearn for it. Frederick Douglass decided that risking death was better than staying in bondage: "I had as well be killed running as die standing." As Douglass implied, the odds were stacked against escape, in part because most slaves could not read, had no maps, and could not use public transportation such as stagecoaches, steamboats, and railroads. Blacks, whether free or enslaved, had to have an identity pass or official emancipation papers to go anywhere on their own. Most runaways were tracked down by bloodhounds or bounty hunters. Even in the 1850s—the height of efforts by many northerners to help runaways through the "underground railroad," not an actual railroad but a secret network of safe houses and abolitionists aiding fugitive slaves—only 1,000 to 1,500 slaves each year made it to safety.

Everyday forms of resistance

Slaves who did not escape resisted in other ways. They often faked illness, engaged in sabotage, stole or broke tools, or destroyed crops or livestock. Yet there were constraints on such behavior, for laborers would likely eat better on a prosperous plantation than on a struggling one. And the shrewdest slaveholders knew that offering rewards was more profitable than inflicting pain.

The South—a Region Apart

The recurring theme of southern politics and culture from the 1830s to the outbreak of civil war in 1861 was the region's determination to remain a society dominated by whites who lorded over people of color. Slavery increasingly became the paramount issue controlling all else in the South. A South Carolinian asserted that "slavery with us is no abstraction—but a great and vital fact. Without it, our every comfort would be taken from us."

Protecting the right of southerners to own, transport, and sell slaves in the new western territories became the overriding focus of southern political leaders during the 1830s and after. As a Mississippi governor insisted in 1850, slavery "is entwined with our political system and cannot be separated from it." It was race-based slavery that provided the South's prosperity as well as its growing sense of separateness from the rest of the nation.

Throughout the 1830s, southern state legislatures were "one and indivisible" in their efforts to preserve and expand slavery. They shouted defiance against northern abolitionists who called for an end to the immorality of slavery. Virginia's General Assembly, for example, declared that only the southern states had the right to control slavery and that such control must be "maintained at all hazards." The Georgia legislature agreed, announcing that "upon this point there can be no discussion—no compromise—no doubt." The increasingly militant efforts of northerners to restrict or abolish slavery helped reinforce the sense of southern unity while provoking an emotional defensiveness that would result in secession and war—and the unexpected end of slavery.

Reviewing the
CORE OBJECTIVES |

- **The Southern Distinctiveness** The South remained rural and agricultural in the first half of the nineteenth century as the rest of the nation embraced urban industrial development. The region's climate favored the growth of cash crops such as tobacco, rice, indigo, and, increasingly, cotton. These crops led to the spread of the plantation system of large commercial agriculture dependent upon enslaved labor. The Southern planter elite sought not only to preserve slavery in the nineteenth century but also to expand it, despite growing criticism of this *peculiar institution* outside the region.

- **A Cotton Economy** Throughout the pre–Civil War era the South became increasingly committed to a cotton economy dependent upon slave labor. Despite efforts to diversify the economy, the wealth and status associated with cotton, as well as soil exhaustion and falling prices from Virginia to Georgia, prompted the westward expansion of the plantation culture to the *Old Southwest.* Moreover, sons of southern planters wanted to take advantage of cheap land on the frontier in order to make their own fortunes. By 1860, the *cotton kingdom* stretched from the Carolinas and Georgia through eastern Texas and up the Mississippi River to Illinois. More than half of all slaves worked on cotton plantations.

- **Southern White Culture** White society was divided between the planter elite, or those who owned at least twenty slaves or more, and all the rest. *Planters* made up around 4 percent of the white population and exercised a disproportionately powerful political and social influence. Other whites owned a few slaves, but most owned none. A majority of whites were *plain white folk*—simple farmers who raised corn, cotton, hogs, and chickens. Southern white women spent most of their time on household chores. The *plantation mistress* supervised her home and household slaves. Most whites were fiercely loyal to the institution of slavery. Even those who owned no slaves feared the competition they believed they would face if slaves were freed, and they enjoyed the privileged status that race-based slavery gave them.

- **Southern Black Culture** As the southern economy became more dependent on slave labor, the enslaved faced more regulations and restrictions on their behavior. The vast majority of Southern blacks were slaves who served as *field hands.* They had few rights and could be bought and sold and moved at any time. Their own movements were severely limited, and they had no ability to defend themselves. Any violation of these restrictions could result in severe punishments. Most southern blacks were slaves, but a small percentage were free. Many of the free blacks were *mulattoes,* having mixed-race parentage. Free blacks often worked for wages in towns and cities.

- **African American Resistance and Resilience** Originally, slaves were treated more as indentured servants, eligible for freedom after a specified number of years, but during the eighteenth century *slave codes* codified practices of treating slaves as property rather than people. The enslaved responded to their oppression in a variety of ways. Although many slaves attempted to run away, only a few openly rebelled because the consequences were so harsh. Organized revolts such as *Nat Turner's Rebellion (1831)* in Virginia were rare. Most slaves survived their hardships by relying on their own communities, family ties, and Christian faith, and by developing their own culture, such as the singing of *spirituals* to express frustration, sorrow, and hope for their eventual deliverance.

KEY TERMS

peculiar institution *p. 356*

Old Southwest *p. 361*

cotton kingdom *p. 361*

planters *p. 365*

plantation mistress *p. 365*

plain white folk *p. 367*

slave codes *p. 368*

mulattoes *p. 370*

field hands *p. 373*

spirituals *p. 376*

Nat Turner's Rebellion (1831) *p. 381*

CHRONOLOGY

1790	Enslaved population of the United States reaches nearly 700,000
1791	Slave revolt in Saint-Domingue (Haiti)
1800	Gabriel conspiracy in Richmond, Virginia
1808	U.S. participation in the international slave trade is outlawed
1811	Charles Deslondes revolt in Louisiana
1815	Annual cotton production in the United States is 150,000 bales
1822	Denmark Vesey conspiracy is discovered in Charleston, South Carolina
1830	U.S. slave population exceeds 2 million
1831	Nat Turner leads slave insurrection in Virginia
1840	Population in the Old Southwest tops 1.5 million
1860	Annual cotton production in the United States reaches 4 million bales
	Slave population in the United States reaches 4 million

INQUIZITIVE

Go to InQuizitive to see what you've learned—and learn what you've missed—with personalized feedback along the way.

***THE INDIAN'S VESPERS* (1847)** In the wake of the Enlightenment, the Romantic ideals of personal spirituality and honor for the uncorrupted natural world swept America. This work, by the artist and transcendentalist Asher B. Durand, depicts a Native American saluting the sun. It celebrates the reverence for nature that kindled religion, activism, education, and reform in the first half of the nineteenth century.

Religion, Romanticism, and Reform

1800–1860

During the first half of the nineteenth century, the world's largest—and youngest—republic was a nation of contrasts. Europeans traveling in America marveled at its restless energy and expansive optimism, its commitment to democratic ideals, and its remarkable capitalist spirit. However, visitors also noticed that the dynamic young republic was experiencing growing pains as the market revolution widened economic inequality. At the same time, sectional tensions over economic policies, and increasingly heated debates over the morality and future of slavery, created a combative political environment whose struggles overflowed into social and cultural life.

After the Revolution, America experienced a theological revolution whereby many people rejected Calvinist determinism. Salvation, they argued, was open to everyone, not just the "elect." By this logic, sin was voluntary rather than innate and inevitable. People were not helplessly depraved creatures; they were instead free agents who could choose salvation and improve themselves and society.

Such notions democratized Christianity. So-called free-will ministers assured people that they could *choose* to be saved simply by embracing Jesus's promise of salvation just as more men in Jacksonian America were allowed to vote and *choose* their elected officials.

CORE OBJECTIVES INQUIZITIVE

1. Describe the major changes in the practice of religion in America in the early nineteenth century, and analyze their influence.

2. Examine the emergence of transcendentalism in American culture in the early nineteenth century.

3. Explain the origins of the major social reform movements in the early nineteenth century, and analyze their influence on society and politics.

4. Analyze the impact of the antislavery movement on society and politics.

This "free-will ideal" contained an element of perfectionism: people could choose to lead better lives and to improve society. Democratized religion thus gave rise to a powerful social reform impulse that blossomed during the second quarter of the nineteenth century.

CORE **OBJECTIVE**

1. Describe the major changes in the practice of religion in America in the early nineteenth century, and analyze their influence.

Religion

The contrasting currents of the rational Enlightenment and the spiritual Great Awakening, now mingling, now parting, flowed from the colonial period into the nineteenth century. In different ways, those currents eroded the old Calvinist view that people were innately sinful and that God had chosen only a select few (the elect) for heavenly salvation ("predestination").

As time passed, many Christians embraced a more optimistic and more democratic religious outlook that offered salvation to everyone. Just as Enlightenment rationalism stressed humanity's natural goodness rather than its sinfulness and encouraged a belief in progress through social reforms and individual improvement, Protestant churches in the early nineteenth century stressed that people were capable of perfection through the guiding light of Christ.

Rational Religion

Deistical societies

Enlightenment ideas during the eighteenth century, including the religious concept of *Deism*, inspired prominent leaders such as Thomas Jefferson and Benjamin Franklin. Deists believed in a rational God—the creator of the rational universe—and that all people were created as equals in the eyes of God.

Deists prized science and reason over traditional religion and blind faith, and interest in Deism increased after the American Revolution. In every major city, Deist societies emerged, and college students in particular took delight in criticizing conventional religion. Through the use of reason and scientific research, Deists believed, people might grasp the natural laws governing the universe. In that spirit, Deists denied that every statement in the Bible was literally true. They were skeptical of miracles and questioned the divinity of Jesus. Deists also defended free speech and opposed religious coercion.

Unitarianism and Universalism

Most Christians could hardly distinguish Deism from atheism, but the same ideals of Enlightenment rationalism that excited Deists soon began to penetrate Protestantism as well. The old Puritan churches in and around Boston proved especially vulnerable to the appeal of religious liberalism. Boston's progress—or, some would say, its degeneration—from Puritanism to prosperity had persuaded many wealthy families that they were anything but sinners at the mercy of an angry God.

By the end of the eighteenth century, many well-educated New Englanders were flocking to "liberal" churches that embraced Unitarianism, a belief system that emphasizes the oneness ("unity") and compassion of a loving God, the natural goodness of humankind, and the superiority of calm reason over emotional forms of worship.

Unitarians stressed that Jesus was a saintly man but was not divine. People are not inherently sinful, Unitarians argued; people are capable of doing tremendous good by following the teachings of Jesus, and *all* people can earn salvation from a God of boundless love.

Boston became the center of the *Unitarian* movement, which flourished chiefly within Congregational churches. Although Unitarianism never attracted large numbers of followers, many of its believers were among the best-educated and wealthiest New Englanders.

A parallel religious movement, Universalism, attracted a different—and much larger—social group: the working poor. In 1779, John Murray, a British clergyman and former Methodist, founded the first Universalist church, in Gloucester, Massachusetts.

Universalists stressed that salvation was available to everyone; it was "universal," not for just a predestined few. God, it teaches, is too merciful to condemn anyone to eternal punishment. "Thus, the Unitarians and Universalists were in fundamental agreement," wrote one historian, "the Universalists holding that God was too good to damn man; the Unitarians insisting that man was too good to be damned." Although both sects remained relatively small, they exercised a powerful influence over intellectual life, especially in New England.

The Second Great Awakening

Around 1800, the United States experienced a massive wave of religious revivals called the **Second Great Awakening**, the first having swept across the American colonies in the first half of the eighteenth century. On and off over the next forty years, the flames of revivalism raced across the country in response to the dramatic economic growth and social changes transforming American life. The nation's rampant materialism furnished evangelical ministers with plenty of ammunition, as did soaring crime rates. Without religion, revivalists warned, the American republic would give way to "unbridled appetites and lust."

Statistics reveal the impact of the evangelical revivals. More Americans than ever were joining and supporting churches. In 1780, there were only fifty Methodist churches in America; by 1860, there were 20,000, far more than any other denomination. The percentage of Americans who joined Protestant churches increased sixfold between 1800 and 1860.

The Second Great Awakening involved two different centers of activity. One developed among the New England colleges that were founded as religious centers of learning, then spread westward like a wildfire across New York into Pennsylvania and Ohio, Indiana, and Illinois. The other emerged in

Unitarians Members of the liberal New England Congregationalist offshoot, who profess the oneness of God and the goodness of rational worshippers, often well-educated and wealthy.

Universalists Generally working-class members of a New England religious movement, who believed in a merciful God and universal salvation.

Second Great Awakening Religious revival movement that arose in reaction to the growth of secularism and rationalist religion; spurred the growth of the Baptist and Methodist denominations.

the backwoods of Tennessee and Kentucky and spread across rural America. Both the urban and rural phases of Protestant revivalism shared a simple message: salvation is available not just to a select few, as the Calvinists had claimed, but to *anyone* who repents and embraces Christ.

Frontier Revivals

Traveling evangelists

In its frontier phase, the Second Great Awakening, like the first, generated tremendous excitement and dramatic behavior. It gave birth, moreover, to two religious phenomena—the traveling backwoods evangelist and the camp meeting—that helped keep the fires of revivalism and spiritual intensity burning.

Evangelists and "exhorters" with colorful nicknames such as Jumpin' Jesus, Crazy Dow, and Mad Isaac found ready audiences among lonely frontier folk hungry for spiritual intensity and a more vibrant sense of community. They wanted a disorderly "personal" religious experience that celebrated individual conversions rather than the often-deadening institutional worship in churches.

RELIGIOUS REVIVALISM Frontier revivals and prayer meetings ignited religious fervor within both minister and participant. In this 1830s camp meeting, the women are so intensely moved by the sermon that they shed their bonnets and fall to their knees.

Backwoods revivals were family-oriented, community-building events; they truly represented social democracy, bridging social, economic, political, and even racial divisions. Women, especially, flocked to the rural revivals, readily gave their souls to Jesus, and served as the backbone of religious life on the frontier.

The first camp meeting occurred in 1801 on a southwestern Kentucky hillside called Cane Ridge. Some 10,000 people came from miles around, camping in tents under the stars. White and black ministers from many denominations preached day and night, often chanting their sermons in ways that prompted listeners to cry, "Amen!" "Hallelujah!" "Lord, have mercy!"

Cane Creek and other **frontier revivals** generated intense emotions. One participant observed that "some of the people were singing, others praying, some crying for mercy." He added that "shrieks and shouts" punctuated every sermon. Soon camp meeting revivals were occurring in every state. Not everyone was impressed, however. Frances Trollope, a distinguished British writer who toured the United States in 1827, attended a frontier revival and thought the participants behaved like raving lunatics. She fled the roiling scene in panic.

Baptists and Methodists

The frontier revivals included many Presbyterians, but Baptists and Methodists predominated. The Baptist theology was grounded in biblical fundamentalism—a certainty that every word and story in the Bible were literally true. Unlike the earlier Puritans, however, the Baptists believed that everyone could gain salvation in heaven by choosing (via "free will") to receive God's grace and by being baptized as adults. The Baptists also stressed the social equality of all before God, regardless of wealth, status, or education.

> Growth of Baptist and Methodist denominations

The Methodists developed the most effective evangelical method of all: the "circuit rider," a traveling evangelist on horseback, who sought out converts in remote frontier settlements. The system began with Francis Asbury, a tireless British-born revivalist who scoured the Ohio Valley for lost souls, traveling across fifteen states and preaching thousands of sermons. Asbury established a mobile evangelism perfectly suited to the frontier environment and the new democratic age.

Revivalism and African Americans

African Americans were especially attracted to the emotional energies of the Methodist and Baptist churches. They infused their churches with exuberant energy and the emotional songs called *spirituals*. Richard Allen (1760–1831), a former slave who bought his freedom, became a Methodist minister in Philadelphia, and helped organize the Free Africa Society, noted in 1787 that "there was no religious sect or denomination that would suit the capacity of the colored people as well as the Methodist." He decided that the "plain

frontier revivals Religious revival movement within the Second Great Awakening, which took place in frontier churches in western territories and states in the early nineteenth century.

BLACK METHODISTS HOLDING A PRAYER MEETING (1811) This caricature of an African American Methodist meeting in Philadelphia shows a preacher in the church doorway, while his congregation engages in exuberant prayer. **How does this illustration compare with the frontier prayer meeting depicted on page 390?**

Equal participation for African Americans

and simple gospel suits best for any people; for the unlearned can understand [it]." Even more important, Methodists actively recruited blacks. They were "the first people," Allen noted, "that brought glad tidings to the colored people."

Yet racial tensions increased as mostly white Methodist congregations required blacks to sit in designated pews. Such discrimination led Allen and others to found the Bethel African Methodist Episcopal Church in 1793. In 1816, as racial discrimination continued within the Methodist churches, Allen helped found a new denomination: the African Methodist Episcopal (AME) Church.

With only five churches and eight clergymen, the new AME denomination grew quickly. By 1846, it boasted 296 churches, almost 200 ministers, and 17,375 members. During the nineteenth century, AME became much more than a religious organization. It initiated the first civil rights movement, promoting not only religious activities but also economic and educational opportunities for people of color. (Allen University in South Carolina is named in honor of Richard Allen.)

Camp Meetings and Women

Religious leadership for women

During the early nineteenth century, the energies of the Great Revival, as the Second Great Awakening was called, spread through the western states and into more settled regions back East. Americans were building a thousand new churches each year. The fastest growth was along the frontier, where the camp meetings welcomed "all sorts and conditions" of people.

Camp meetings allowed women to participate as social equals to men, both as preachers and parishioners. Jarena Lee, a free black who lived in the Philadelphia area, was the first African American woman to be allowed to preach in the AME. As she wrote, "If the man may preach, because the Saviour died for him, why not the woman? Seeing [as] he died for her also. Is he not a whole Saviour, instead of a half one, as those who hold it wrong for a woman to preach, would seem to make it appear?" Lee became a tireless revivalist during the 1830s, walking as many as twelve miles a day. According to her own records, she "traveled 2,325 miles and preached 178 sermons."

The organizational needs of large revivals offered ample opportunities for women to exercise leadership roles outside the home, including service as traveling evangelists themselves. Phoebe Worrall Palmer, for example, hosted prayer meetings in her New York City home that included men as well as women, a controversial innovation for the time. She then traveled across the United States as a camp meeting exhorter, assuring listeners that they could gain a life without sin, what then was called "perfectionism" or "holiness."

JARENA LEE A path-breaking revivalist, Lee traveled thousands of miles on foot to preach to diverse crowds across America. Spreading her message through print, as well, Lee published a detailed autobiography about her religious experiences.

Religion and Reform

Western New York experienced such intense levels of evangelical activity that it was labeled the *burned-over district* because it was afire with the flames of the Holy Spirit. The most successful evangelist in the burned-over district was a Presbyterian minister named Charles Grandison Finney. In the winter of 1830–1831, he preached with "a clear, shrill voice" for six months in Rochester, then a canal boomtown in upstate New York. In the process, he generated some 100,000 conversions and became the most celebrated minister in the country. While rural camp meeting revivals attracted farm families and other working-class groups, Finney's audiences in the Northeast attracted more prosperous seekers. "The Lord," Finney declared, "was aiming at the conversion of the highest classes of society."

Finney focused on the question that had preoccupied Protestantism for centuries: what role can the individual play in earning salvation? The Puritans and other Calvinists had argued that people could neither earn nor choose salvation. They believed in predestination: that salvation was a gift God delivered to a select few. In contrast, Finney and other free-will evangelists insisted that everyone, rich or poor, black or white, could *choose* to be "saved" simply by embracing the promise of Jesus.

Finney's democratic gospel combined faith and good works: religious revival, he urged, should lead to good works. "The great business of the church," Finney asserted, is "to reform the world." By embracing Christ, a convert could thereafter be free of sin, but Christians also had an obligation to improve society. Finney helped found an array of groups designed to reform various social ills: alcoholism, prostitution, war, and slavery. The

> Finney and the "burned-over" district

NAUVOO The magnificent scale and stately architecture of Joseph Smith's original temple in Nauvoo is captured in this 1890 print. **In what ways did the design of this temple and the rest of the town echo Mormon values?**

Joseph Smith and *the Book of Mormon*

Mormons Members of the Church of Jesus Christ of Latter-day Saints, which dismissed other Christian denominations, emphasizing universal salvation and a modest lifestyle; often persecuted for their secrecy and clannishness.

revivals thus provided much of the energy behind the sweeping reform impulse that characterized the age.

The Mormons

The spiritual stirrings of the Second Great Awakening also spawned new religious groups. The burned-over district in western New York gave rise to several religious movements, the most important of which was Mormonism. Its extraordinary founder, Joseph Smith Jr., the child of intensely religious Vermont farm folk who settled in the village of Palmyra in western New York, was born and raised amid the excitement of revivalism.

In 1823, the eighteen-year-old Smith reported that an angel named Moroni had led him to a hillside near his father's farm, where he had unearthed golden tablets on which was etched a lost "gospel" of the Bible that describes a group of ancient Israelites ("Nephites") who crossed the Atlantic on barges and settled America 2,000 years before Columbus.

Smith, who could barely read, set about translating and dictating to others the "reformed Egyptian" inscriptions on the plates (which, conveniently, no one else ever saw before he returned them to Moroni). Smith convinced a friend to mortgage his farm to pay for the publication of the first 5,000 copies of the 500-page text he called *The Book of Mormon: An Account Written by the Hand of Mormon upon Plates Taken from the Plates of Nephi.*

With this remarkable book as his gospel, young Smith began telling the story of his "marvilous [*sic*] experience" and gathering converts ("saints") who shared his desire to live together in accordance with the teachings of Jesus. Eventually, convinced that his religious authority came directly from God, Smith formed what he called the Church of Jesus Christ of Latter-day Saints, more popularly known as **Mormons**. God "is a man like one of you," Smith told his followers. His was a democratic faith run by plain people and intended for all people.

In his self-appointed role as Prophet, Smith criticized the sins of the rich; preached universal salvation; dismissed as frauds all Christian denominations (Protestant and Catholic); denied that there was a Hell; urged his followers to avoid liquor, tobacco, and hot drinks; and promised that the Second Coming of Christ was looming. Within a few years, the charismatic Smith, whom the Mormons simply called Joseph, had gathered thousands of converts, most of them poor farmers.

From the outset, the Mormon saints upset both their neighbors and the civil authorities. Mormons stood out with their secret rituals, their refusal to abide by local laws and conventions, and their clannishness: they worshipped together, voted together, and traveled together. Smith denied the legitimacy of civil governments and the U.S. Constitution. As a result, no community wanted to host him and his "peculiar people."

In their search for a refuge from persecution and for the "promised land," the ever-growing contingent of Mormons moved from western New York to Ohio, then to Missouri, and finally, in 1839, to the half-built town of Commerce, Illinois, on swampy land along the west bank of the Mississippi River. They renamed the town Nauvoo (a crude transliteration of a Hebrew word meaning "beautiful land").

Within a few years, thanks to Smith's organizing genius and absolute authority, Nauvoo developed into a bustling, well-planned community of 12,000, with an impressive neoclassical temple overlooking the river. The community embodied strict Mormon principles. There were no saloons or brothels.

Joseph Smith, "the Prophet," became the community's religious dictator: he was Nauvoo's leading planner, businessman, and political leader. He owned the hotel and general store; published the newspaper and sold real estate; and served as mayor, chief justice, and commander of the city's 2,000-strong army (the Nauvoo Legion). Smith's lust for power grew as well. He began excommunicating dissidents, and in 1844 he announced his intention to become America's president. He proclaimed that the United States should peacefully acquire not only Texas and Oregon but all of Mexico and Canada too and that slavery should be ended.

Smith also caused controversy by practicing "plural marriage" (polygamy); he accumulated over two dozen wives and encouraged other Mormon leaders to do the same. In 1844, a crisis arose when Mormon dissenters, including Smith's first wife, Emma, denounced his polygamy. The result was not only a split in the church but also an attack on Nauvoo by non-Mormons from neighboring counties. When Smith ordered Mormons to destroy an opposition newspaper, he and his brother Hyrum were arrested and charged with treason.

On June 27, 1844, a mob stormed the jail in the nearby town of Carthage and killed the Smith brothers. Joseph Smith, the thirty-eight-year-old prophet, had become a martyr. A New York newspaper predicted that his death would kill Mormonism: "They cannot get another Joe Smith. The holy city must tumble into ruins."

In Brigham Young, however, the Mormons found a new and, in many ways, better leader. Strong-minded, intelligent, authoritarian, and a compelling speaker (as well as husband eventually to dozens of wives, who bore fifty-six children), Young was a Vermont-born carpenter who in 1813 moved with his family to western New York, where he became an early convert to Mormonism. In 1844, he was elected to succeed Smith.

Nauvoo continued to arouse the suspicions of non-Mormons, leading Young to look for another home for his flock. Their new destination was 1,300 miles away in the isolated, barren valley

BRIGHAM YOUNG Taking over from Joseph Smith after his death, Young served as president of the Mormons for thirty years and led them on their exodus to Utah.

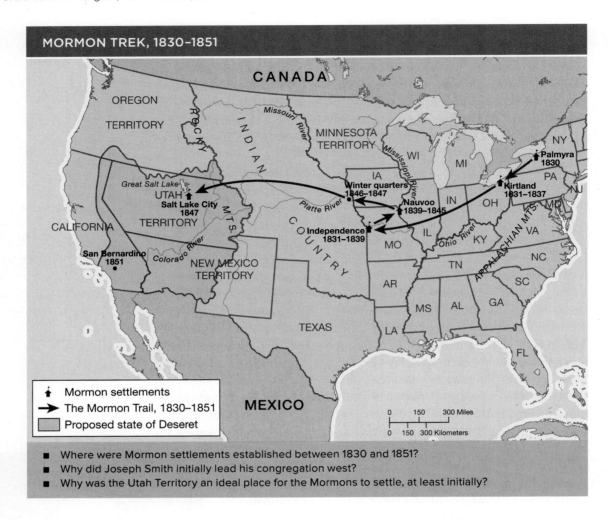

MORMON TREK, 1830–1851

- Where were Mormon settlements established between 1830 and 1851?
- Why did Joseph Smith initially lead his congregation west?
- Why was the Utah Territory an ideal place for the Mormons to settle, at least initially?

near the Great Salt Lake in Utah, a vast, sparsely populated area that was then part of Mexico.

In early 1846, in wagons and on foot, 12,000 Mormons started their grueling exodus across Nebraska and Wyoming to their new Zion, the "promised land" of Utah. The first to arrive at the Great Salt Lake in July 1847 found "a broad and barren plain hemmed in by the mountains . . . the paradise of the lizard, the cricket and the rattlesnake." Brigham Young declared, however, that "this is the place" for the Mormons to settle. It was "a good place to make saints."

By the end of 1848, the Mormons in Utah had developed an efficient irrigation system for their farms, and over the next decade they brought about a spectacular greening of the desert. At first they organized their own state, named Deseret (meaning "Land of the Honeybee"), and elected Young governor.

But their independence was short-lived. In 1848, Mexico signed the Treaty of Guadalupe Hidalgo, transferring to the United States what is now California, Nevada, Utah, Texas, and parts of Arizona, New Mexico, Colorado, and Wyoming. Two years later, Congress incorporated the Utah Territory, including the Mormons' Salt Lake settlement, into the United States.

Nevertheless, when Brigham Young was named the territorial governor, the new arrangement gave the Mormons virtual independence. For more than twenty years, Young ruled the territory with an iron hand, allowing no dissent and defying federal authority. Not until 1896, after the Mormons disavowed the practice of polygamy, was Utah admitted as a state.

Romanticism in America

The revival of religious life during the early 1800s was one of many efforts to unleash the stirrings of the spirit throughout the United States and Europe. Another great cultural shift from the scientific rationalism of the Enlightenment was the Romantic movement in thought, literature, and the arts. It began in Europe, as young people rebelled against the well-ordered rational world promoted by scientific objectivity. Were there not, after all, more things in the world than reason, science, and logic could categorize and explain: spontaneous moods, impressions, and feelings; mysterious, unknown, and half-seen things?

In areas in which science could neither prove nor disprove concepts, the Romantics believed that people were justified in having faith. They preferred the stirrings of the heart over the calculations of the head, nonconformity over traditional behavior, and the mystical over the rational. Americans also embraced the Romantics' emphasis on individualism, idealizing the virtues of common people and the benefits of democracy.

Transcendentalism

The most intense advocates of Romantic ideals in the United States were the transcendentalists of New England, America's first self-conscious group of rebellious intellectuals committed to reshaping the nation's cultural life. **Transcendentalism** is hard to define. The name derived from its emphasis on thoughts and activities that *transcend* (or rise above) the limits of reason and logic. Transcendentalism, said one of its champions, meant an interest in areas "a little beyond" the scope of reason.

Transcendentalism thus at times seemed irrational, rejecting both religious orthodoxy and the "corpse-cold" rationalism of Unitarianism. The transcendentalists believed that reality was not simply what can be touched and seen; reality also included the unexplored realms of the mind, such as intuition. Above all, the transcendentalists believed in "self-reliance" over conformity to tradition and embraced a pure form of personal spirituality

CORE **OBJECTIVE**
2. Examine the emergence of transcendentalism in American culture in the early nineteenth century.

transcendentalism Philosophy of New England writers and thinkers who advocated personal spirituality, self-reliance, social reform, and harmony with nature.

THE OXBOW This 1836 landscape by the American artist Thomas Cole is an iconic work of Romanticism, capturing the view from Mount Holyoke, Massachusetts, after a thunderstorm. **What might Cole be symbolizing by his juxtaposition of untamed wilderness to the left and domesticated farmland to the right?**

uncorrupted by organized religion. Transcendentalists wanted individuals to look *within* themselves for spiritual insights, not follow the guidance of ministers. They also wanted to unleash a romantic spirituality in harmony with nature. All people, they believed, had the capacity for self-realization, enabling them to tap the divine potential ("spark") present in all God's creatures and creations. By the 1830s, New England transcendentalism had become the most influential force in American culture.

In 1836, an informal discussion group known as the Transcendental Club began to meet in Boston and nearby Concord to discuss philosophy, literature, and religion. They teasingly called themselves the "club of the like-minded," quipped a Boston preacher, "because no two . . . thought alike." The club included liberal clergymen; militant reformers; writers such as Theodore Parker, George Ripley, Henry David Thoreau, Nathaniel Hawthorne; and brilliant women such as Elizabeth Peabody, her sister Sophia (who married Hawthorne in 1842), and Margaret Fuller. Fluent in six languages, Fuller organized a transcendentalist discussion group and edited its magazine, the *Dial* (1840–1844), for two years before the duty fell to Ralph Waldo Emerson, the high priest of transcendentalism.

Ralph Waldo Emerson

More than anyone else, Emerson embodied the transcendentalist gospel promoting individual freedom and "self-culture." Tall and slender, with bright blue eyes, he became the nation's most popular speaker during the second quarter of the nineteenth century, in part because Emerson led a crusade to end America's dependence on European literary and artistic traditions. Emerson strove to help "cast out the passion for Europe" and replace it with "the passion for America," exhorting the young republic to shed its cultural inferiority complex and create its own distinctive literature and art.

The son of a Unitarian preacher, Emerson graduated from Harvard College in 1821 and became a Unitarian parson in 1829, but he quit the "cold and cheerless" denomination three years later and turned away from all organized religions because they stifled free thinking. "In the Bible," he explained, "you are not directed to be a Unitarian or a Calvinist or an Episcopalian." Such group identities disgusted him.

RALPH WALDO EMERSON Most remembered for leading the transcendentalist movement, Emerson's message of self-reliance affirmed the integrity of the individual and inspired generations of thinkers.

After traveling in Europe, where he met England's greatest Romantic writers, Emerson settled in Concord to take up the life of an essayist, poet, and lecturer ("preacher to the world") promoting radical individualism. He now found God in nature and came to believe in human perfectibility. Emerson celebrated the virtues of optimism, self-reliance, and the individual's unlimited potential—if people would only exercise their capacity to think for themselves and defy traditional assumptions and beliefs.

> Emerson and cultural nationalism

In 1836, Emerson published the path-breaking book *Nature*, which helped launch the Transcendental movement. In it, he stressed that sensitive people could "transcend" the material world and discover the "spirit" animating the universe. Individuals, in other words, could exercise godlike powers.

The spirit of self-reliant individualism in Emerson's lectures and writings provided the energetic core of the transcendentalist outlook. Emerson crammed his essay "Self-Reliance" (1841) with crisp assertions that expressed the transcendentalist ideal of intellectual independence: "Whoso would be a man," he declared, "must be a nonconformist. . . . Nothing is at last sacred but the integrity of your own mind. . . . It is easy in the world to live after the world's opinion; it is easy in solitude to live after our own; but the great man is he who in the midst of a crowd keeps with perfect sweetness the independence of solitude."

Emerson's democratic belief that every person possessed godlike virtues ("infinite worthiness") inspired generations. He was a down-to-earth transcendentalist who championed a self-reliant individualism that reinforced the democratic energies inspiring Jacksonian America.

HENRY DAVID THOREAU A model transcendentalist, Thoreau wrote in support of individuals' agency to combat oppression, influencing activists throughout the twentieth century.

Henry David Thoreau

Emerson's philosophical friend, Henry David Thoreau, fourteen years younger, practiced the thoughtful self-reliance that Emerson preached. "I like people who can do things," Emerson stressed, and Thoreau, fourteen years his junior, excelled at many things: carpentry, masonry, painting, surveying, sailing, gardening. The son of a man who was a pencil maker and a woman who was a domineering reformer, Thoreau displayed a powerful sense of uncompromising integrity and prickly individuality. "If a man does not keep pace with his companions," Thoreau wrote, "perhaps it is because he hears a different drummer."

The self-obsessed Thoreau marched to a different drummer all his life. More provocative than likable, he once described himself as "a mystic, a transcendentalist, and a natural philosopher." Born in 1817, he attended Harvard, where he exhausted the library's resources before graduating. After a brief stint as a teacher, during which he was disciplined for refusing to cane his students, Thoreau worked with his father making pencils. Like Emerson, however, he made frequent escapes to the woods to absorb nature's enlivening beauties and spiritual energies.

Thoreau viewed "the indescribable innocence" of nature as a living bible; the earth to him was a form of poetry, full of hidden meanings and life-giving energies. Daily walks inspired him more than attending church. He also showed no interest in the scramble for wealth, for it too often corrupted the pursuit of happiness. "The mass of men," he wrote, "lead lives of quiet desperation" because they were preoccupied with making money rather than pursuing happiness. Thoreau became famous for his strong opinions and brutal candor. Most of what his neighbors deemed good, he believed "in his soul to be bad."

A born rebel, Thoreau yearned to experience the "extremities" of life and escape the prison of stuffy traditions, unjust laws, "good behavior," or the opinions of his elders. He committed himself to leading what Emerson called a simple life centered on "plain living and high thinking." Thoreau loved solitude. When alone, he could wrap himself in his own thoughts and think for himself.

For a time, Thoreau, who never wed, rented a room at the Emersons, tending the family garden, tutoring Emerson's children, and taking long walks with his host. In 1844, when Emerson bought fourteen acres along Walden Pond, Thoreau decided to embark upon an unusual experiment in self-reliance. On July 4, 1845, at age twenty-seven, he took to the woods to live in a tiny, one-room cabin he had built for $28 on Emerson's land at Walden Pond, just a few miles outside of Concord.

Thoreau wanted to free himself from the constraints of conventional life and devote his time to gardening, studying nature, swimming in the pond, and recording his thoughts and observations in his journal. "I went to the woods because I wished to live deliberately," he wrote in *Walden, or Life in the Woods* (1854), ". . . and not, when I came to die, discover that I had not lived." He "wanted to live deep and suck out all the marrow of life, to live so sturdily and Spartan-like as to put to rout all that was not life." Thoreau ate only one meal a day, disdained coffee, alcohol, salt, and tobacco, and regarded sex with suspicion. His minimalist ethic bordered on arrogant puritanism, leading Emerson to observe that Thoreau "was never affectionate, but superior, didactic," forever scorning the stupidity of his neighbors and claiming that he was "more favored by the gods." Being charitable to others, Thoreau admitted, did not "agree with [his] constitution."

During Thoreau's two years at Walden Pond, the United States declared war against Mexico, largely in order to acquire Texas, then part of Mexico. He felt it was an unjust war pushed by southern cotton planters eager to add more slave territory. His disgust for the war led him to refuse to pay taxes, for which he was put in jail (for only one night; an aunt paid the tax).

This incident inspired Thoreau to write his now-classic essay, "Civil Disobedience" (1849), which would later influence Martin Luther King Jr. in shaping the civil rights movement in the 1950s and '60s. "If the law is of such a nature that it requires you to be an agent of injustice to another," Thoreau wrote, "then, I say, break the law." Until his death in 1862, Thoreau continued to attack slavery and applaud those who worked to undermine it. "The law will never make men free," he insisted. "It is men who have got to make the law free." The continuing influence of Thoreau's creed of taking individual action against injustice shows the impact that a thoughtful person can have on the world of action.

"Civil Disobedience" (1849)

An American Literature

Thoreau and Emerson portrayed the transcendentalist movement as an expression of moral idealism; critics dismissed it as outrageous self-centeredness. Though the transcendentalists attracted only a small following in their own time, they inspired a generation of writers that produced the first great age of American literature. The half decade of 1850–1855 witnessed an outpouring of extraordinary writing in the United States, a nation that had long suffered an inferiority complex about the quality of its arts. Those five years saw the publication of *Representative Men* by Emerson, *Walden* by Thoreau, *The Scarlet Letter* and *The House of the Seven Gables* by Nathaniel Hawthorne, *Moby-Dick* by Herman Melville, *Leaves of Grass* by Walt Whitman, and hundreds of unpublished poems by Emily Dickinson.

Literary Giants

Emily Dickinson, the most strikingly original of the New England poets, spent much of her spinster life in a virginal white dress in her large second-story bedroom in Amherst, Massachusetts, writing poetry that few people saw during her lifetime. Only 10 or so of her almost 1,800 poems appeared in print (anonymously) before her death in 1886 at fifty-five. As she once

EMILY DICKINSON Although her works were rarely published during her lifetime, Dickinson offered the literary world of New England a fresh female voice.

WALT WHITMAN This engraving of a thirty-seven-year-old Whitman appeared in his acclaimed poetry collection *Leaves of Grass*.

prophetically wrote, "Success is counted sweetest / By those who ne'er succeed." Neither she nor her sister married, and they lived out their lives in their parents' home.

Perhaps it was Dickinson's severe eye trouble during the 1860s that caused her solitary withdrawal from the larger society; perhaps it was the aching despair generated by her love for a married minister. Whatever the reason, she used her intense isolation and lifelong religious doubts to explore elemental themes: life, death, fear, loneliness, nature, and above all, God, a "Force illegible," "a distant, stately lover."

The most provocative writer during the nineteenth century was New Yorker Walt Whitman. The swaggering Whitman was a startling figure, with his frank sexuality and homoerotic overtones. There was something elemental in his overflowing character, something bountiful and generous and compelling—even his faults and inconsistencies were ample.

Born on a Long Island farm, Whitman moved with his family to Brooklyn, where he worked as a teacher, a journalist, a Democratic party activist, and an editor of the *Brooklyn Eagle*. Whitman frequently took the ferry across the East River to bustling Manhattan. The city's restless energies fascinated him, and he gorged himself on the urban spectacle: the vibrant vistas of shipyards, crowds, factories, and shop windows.

When Whitman first met Emerson, he had been "simmering, simmering," but Emerson "brought him to a boil" with his emphasis on defying tradition and celebrating the commonplaces of life, all of which found their way into his controversial first book of poems, *Leaves of Grass* (1855), which often dispensed with stanzas and rhymes. Whitman introduced his new book with a brash declaration: "I celebrate myself, and sing myself." He wanted to leave the past behind. He was a pioneer on behalf of "a new mightier world, a varied world," a "world of labor" and "common people." Although *Leaves of Grass* was banned in Boston, Emerson found it "the most extraordinary piece of wit and wisdom that America has yet contributed," but more-conventional critics shuddered at the shocking frankness of Whitman's sexual references. Thoreau, however, loved the earthy poetry. He described Whitman as "the greatest democrat the world has seen."

CORE **OBJECTIVE**

3. Explain the origins of the major social reform movements in the early nineteenth century, and analyze their influence on American society and politics.

The Reform Impulse

In 1842, the monthly *Gazette* reported that the "spirit of reform is in every place" across America. The United States in the first half of the nineteenth century was awash in reform movements led by dreamers and activists who saw injustice and fought to correct it. Lyman Beecher, a champion of evangelical Christian revivalism (as well as the father of writer Harriet Beecher Stowe), stressed that the Second Great Awakening was not focused simply on promoting individual conversions; it was also intended to "reform human society."

***POLITICS IN AN OYSTER HOUSE* (1848)** Commissioned by social activist John H. B. Latrobe, this painting captures the public conversations that were fueled by newspapers and other print periodicals. **What issues were being tackled by activists in the mid-1800s?**

Evangelical societies fanned out across America to organize Sunday schools to spread the gospel and distribute Bibles to the children of the working poor. Other reformers tackled urgent social issues such as dreadful conditions in prisons and workplaces, care of the disabled, reducing the consumption of alcoholic beverages (temperance), women's rights, and the abolition of slavery. Some reformers proposed legislative remedies for social ills; others stressed personal conversion or private philanthropy.

While an impulse to "perfect" people and society excited the reform movements, social and economic changes helped spur many reformers themselves, most of whom were women. The rise of a substantial urban middle class offered growing numbers of women more time to devote to societal concerns. Prosperity enabled them to hire cooks and maids, often Irish immigrants, who in turn freed them from household chores. As had been true for two centuries, many women used their free time to join churches and charitable organizations, most of which were led by men.

THE DRUNKARD'S PROGRESS This 1846 pro-temperance print outlines a nine-step process of alcoholism, beginning with "a glass with a friend" and ending with "death by suicide." Below the arc is a weeping wife and her child.

Temperance

The **temperance** crusade to reduce alcohol consumption was perhaps the most widespread of the reform movements. Americans in the nineteenth century consumed an amazing amount of alcoholic beverages. William Cobbett, an English reformer who traveled in the United States, noted in 1819 that one could "go into hardly any man's house without being asked to drink wine or spirits, even *in the morning*." Seven years later, a group of Boston ministers organized the American Society for the Promotion of Temperance, which sponsored lectures, press campaigns, and the formation of local and state societies. A favorite device was to ask each person who pledged to stop drinking to put by his or her signature a *T* for "total abstinence." With that, a new word entered the English language: *teetotaler*.

In 1833, the temperance society organized a national convention in Philadelphia, where the delegates formed the American Temperance Union. Like nearly every reform movement of the day, temperance had a wing of absolutists. They helped pass a resolution that *all* liquor was evil and should be banned. The Temperance Union, at its spring convention in 1836, called for abstinence from all alcoholic beverages—which caused moderates to abstain from the temperance movement instead.

temperance A widespread reform movement led by militant Christians that focused on reducing the use of alcoholic beverages.

Prisons and Asylums

The Romantic impulse often included the liberal belief that people are innately good and capable of improvement. Such an optimistic view brought about major changes in the treatment of prisoners, the disabled, and orphans. Public institutions (often called asylums) arose that focused on the treatment of social ills. If removed from society, the theory went, the needy and the deviant could be made whole again. Unhappily, however, the asylums had a way of becoming breeding grounds for brutality and neglect.

Gradually, the idea of the penitentiary developed as a new approach to reforming criminals. It would be a place where the guilty were not just punished but rehabilitated. An early model of the new system, widely copied, was the Auburn Penitentiary, which opened in New York in 1816.

The prisoners at Auburn had separate cells and gathered only for meals and group labor. Discipline was severe. The men were marched out of their cells in lockstep and never put face-to-face or allowed to talk. The system, its advocates argued, had a beneficial effect on the prisoners and saved money, since the workshops supplied prison needs and produced goods for sale at a profit. By 1840, there were twelve Auburn-type penitentiaries scattered across the nation.

The Romantic reform impulse also found an outlet in the care of the insane. Before 1800, few hospitals provided care for the mentally ill. The insane were usually confined at home with hired keepers, or in jails or almshouses, where homeless debtors were housed. In the years after 1815, however, asylums that separated the disturbed from the criminal began to appear.

The most important figure in heightening awareness of the plight of the mentally ill was Dorothea Lynde Dix. A pious Boston schoolteacher, she launched a two-year investigation of jails and almshouses in Massachusetts. In a report to the state legislature in 1843, she revealed that insane people were confined "in *cages, closets, cellars, stalls, pens! Chained, naked, beaten with rods,* and *lashed* into obedience." From Massachusetts she carried her campaign throughout the country and abroad. By 1860, she had persuaded twenty states to heed her advice, thereby helping transform social attitudes toward mental illness.

> Dorothea Dix reforms care for the mentally ill

Women's Rights

Dorothea Dix was but one sterling example of the countless middle-class women who devoted themselves to improving the quality of life in America. Others argued that women should first focus on enhancing home life. In 1841, Harriet Beecher Stowe's sister, Catharine Beecher, a leader in the public schools movement and founder of women's schools in Connecticut and Ohio, published *A Treatise on Domestic Economy*, which became the leading handbook promoting the **cult of domesticity**, a powerful ideology that called upon women to celebrate their role as manager of the household and the children.

cult of domesticity Pervasive nineteenth-century ideology urging women to celebrate their role as manager of the household and nurturer of the children.

While Beecher upheld high standards in women's education, she accepted the prevailing view that the "woman's sphere" was inside the home. She, and many other prominent women, argued that young women should be trained not for the workplace but in the domestic arts—managing a kitchen, running a household, and nurturing the children. This *cult of domesticity* was especially strong among Mormons. From its inception, the Mormon Church was openly patriarchal, ruled by men. Women were limited to running the household and raising the children.

The official status of women during the first half of the nineteenth century remained much as it had been in the colonial era. They were barred from the ministry and most other professions. College was rarely an option. Women could not serve on juries, nor could they vote. A wife often had no control over her property or even her children. She could not make a will, sign a contract, or bring suit in court without her husband's permission.

Gradually, however, women began to protest their status, and some men began to listen. The organized movement for women's rights emerged in 1840, when the anti-slavery movement split over the question of women's involvement. Women decided then that they needed to organize on behalf of their own emancipation.

In 1848, two prominent advocates of women's rights who were also abolitionists, Lucretia Mott, a Philadelphia Quaker, and Elizabeth Cady Stanton, a graduate of New York's Troy Female Seminary who refused to be merely "a household drudge," called a convention in western New York to discuss "the social, civil, and religious condition and rights of women."

Women's suffrage

On July 19, 1848, the **Seneca Falls Convention** issued a clever paraphrase of the Declaration of Independence. Called the **Declaration of Sentiments**, it proclaimed that "all men and women are created equal." All laws that placed women "in a position inferior to that of men, are contrary to the great precept of nature, and therefore of no force or authority." Such language was too strong, too radical, for most of the 1,000 delegates, and only about a third of them signed the document. Nevertheless, the Seneca Falls gathering represented an important first step in the evolving campaign for women's rights.

From 1850 until the outbreak of the Civil War, leaders of the women's rights movement held annual conventions, delivered lectures, and circulated petitions. Yet the movement struggled in the face of meager funds and widespread anti-feminist sentiment. One woman criticized the women reformers for "aping mannish manners" and wearing "absurd and barbarous attire." The typical feminist, she claimed, "struts and strides, and thinks that she proves herself superior to the rest of her sex." The movement's eventual success resulted from the work of a few undaunted women who refused to cower in the face of the odds against them.

Seneca Falls Convention (1848) Convention organized by feminists Lucretia Mott and Elizabeth Cady Stanton to promote women's rights and issue the pathbreaking Declaration of Sentiments.

Declaration of Sentiments (1848) Document based on the Declaration of Independence that called for gender equality, written primarily by Elizabeth Cady Stanton and signed by Seneca Falls Convention delegates.

Susan B. Anthony, already active in temperance and anti-slavery groups, joined the women's crusade in the 1850s. Unlike Stanton and Mott, she was unmarried and therefore able to devote most of her attention to the women's

ELIZABETH CADY STANTON AND SUSAN B. ANTHONY Stanton (left, in 1856) was a young mother who called the Seneca Falls Convention, while Anthony (right, in 1848) started as an anti-slavery and temperance activist in her twenties. The two would meet in 1851 and form a lifelong partnership in the fight for women's suffrage.

movement. As one observer put it, Stanton "forged the thunderbolts and Miss Anthony hurled them." Both were young when the movement started, and both lived into the twentieth century, focusing after the Civil War on demands for women's suffrage (the right to vote).

Early Public Schools

Early America, like most rural societies, offered few educational opportunities. That changed in the first half of the nineteenth century as reformers lobbied for **public schools** serving all children, rich or poor. The working poor wanted free schools to give their children an equal chance to pursue the American dream. In 1830, the Workingmen's party of Philadelphia called for "a system of education that shall embrace equally all the children of the state, of every rank and condition." Education, it was argued, would improve manners and at the same time reduce crime and poverty.

Horace Mann of Massachusetts, a state legislator and attorney, led the early drive for statewide, tax-supported school systems open to everyone, regardless of class, race, or ethnicity, including immigrant children. He

public schools Elementary and secondary schools funded by the state and free of tuition.

THE GEORGE BARRELL EMERSON SCHOOL, BOSTON (CA. 1850) Although higher education for women initially met with some resistance, seminaries, like this one, started in the 1820s and 1830s, taught women mathematics, physics, and history as well as music, art, and social graces.

Horace Mann's "normal school"

sponsored the creation of a state board of education and then served as its leader. Mann went on to promote many reforms in Massachusetts, including the first state-supported "normal school" for the training of teachers, a state association of teachers, and a minimum school year of six months. He saw the public school system as a way not only to ensure that everyone had a basic level of knowledge and skills but also to reinforce values such as hard work and clean living. "If we do not prepare children to become good citizens, if we do not enrich their minds with knowledge," Mann warned, "then our republic must go down to destruction."

By the 1840s, most states in the North and Midwest, but not the South, had joined the public school movement. The initial conditions for public education, however, were seldom ideal. Funds for buildings, books, and equipment were limited; teachers were poorly paid and often poorly prepared. Most students going beyond the elementary grades attended private academies, often organized by churches. Such schools, begun in colonial days, multiplied until in 1850 there were more than 6,000 of them.

In 1821, the Boston English High School opened as the nation's first free public secondary school. Beginning in 1827, Massachusetts required every town of 500 or more residents to have a high school. Other states were not as progressive. In 1860, there were barely 300 public high schools in the whole nation.

Yet by 1850, half the white children between ages 5 and 19 were enrolled in schools, the highest percentage in the world. Very few of those students were southerners, however. With only a few exceptions, the southern states did not establish public schools until after the Civil War. In most states, enslaved children were prohibited from learning to read and write or attend school. A former slave recalled that his owner "didn't teach 'em nuthin' but work."

The prolonged disparities between North and South in the number and quality of educational opportunities help explain the growing economic and cultural differences between the two regions. Then, as now, undereducated people were more likely to remain economically deprived, less healthy, and less engaged in political life.

Utopian Communities

Amid the pervasive climate of reform during the early nineteenth century, the quest for everyday utopias—ideal communities with innovative social and economic relationships—flourished. Plans for creating heaven on earth had long been an American passion, at least since the Puritans set out to build a holy colony in New England.

In the nineteenth century, more than 100 **utopian communities** emerged as alternatives to urban industrial development. Many of the ideal societies were *communitarian* experiments emphasizing the welfare of the entire community rather than individual freedom and private profits. Some experimented with "free love," socialism, and special diets.

THE SHAKERS A community of Shakers in a spirited dance, when they ostensibly "shook off sin" and "trampled evil underfoot." **Based on the Shakers' beliefs, why is there such a strict division between men and women in this illustration?**

Those communities founded by the Shakers (officially the United Society of Believers in Christ's Second Appearing) proved to be long lasting. The prophet who founded the Shakers was Ann Lee (known as Mother Ann Lee), born in 1736, the illiterate daughter of an English blacksmith. From an early age, Ann Lee came to believe in the "depravity of human nature and the odiousness of sin." No sooner did she marry than she was constantly pregnant, bearing four children, none of whom lived beyond six years of age. The trauma of childbirth and the loss of her children convinced Ann Lee that sexual activity was "indecent" and sinful. She would take up the cross against the flesh. She also believed that God and Jesus spoke directly to her ("direct revelation").

As Ann Lee recounted her visions of Christ, listeners decided that "the candle of the Lord was in her hand." That is, she was both a prophet and a seer, a medium for the Second Coming of Christ who equated cleanliness, hard work, and chastity with saintliness. Under her leadership, the Shakers publicly attacked the Anglican Church, adopted lives of strict celibacy, and developed eccentric forms of worship featuring loud singing, "inspired" dancing, shaking, shrieking, and stamping their feet, and speaking in unknown tongues. They laughed, wept, howled, and yodeled.

In 1774, having suffered constant harassment by the authorities in England, Ann Lee and eight followers migrated to upstate New York where they settled on 200 acres, built a log cabin that housed men on the first

utopian communities Ideal communities that offered innovative social and economic relationships to those who were interested in achieving salvation—now.

floor and women on the second, and supported themselves in seclusion as the Revolutionary War erupted. They pursued Christian perfection by molding a "body of believers" isolated from a corrupt world. Six years later, they began recruiting others to their eccentric faith and austere communistic paradise.

Mother Ann died in 1784, but the Shakers found new leaders who established utopian "colonies" in New York, New England, Ohio, and Kentucky. By 1830, about twenty groups professing hard work, simple living, shared property, gender equality, 2nd celibacy, were thriving. Shaker farms became the nation's leading sources of garden seed and medicinal herbs, and many of their products, including clothing, household items, and especially furniture, were prized for their plain beauty.

The Shakers took great pride in their ability to create colonies outside the mainstream of American life. As Mother Ann observed, "We are the people who turned the world upside down." Every day, over many years, the Shakers displayed their utopian faith in the perfectibility of life on earth. What they did not perfect was an ability to convince their neighbors to follow their example.

Oneida Community

John Humphrey Noyes, founder of the Oneida Community, had a very different vision of the ideal community. The son of a Vermont congressman, Noyes attended Dartmouth College and Yale Divinity School. In 1834, however, he was defrocked and expelled from Yale after he committed heresy by announcing that he was "perfect," free from sin, and singled out by God to be his divine instrument on Earth.

In 1836, Noyes gathered a group of "Perfectionists" around his home in Putney, Vermont. Ten years later, he announced a new doctrine, "complex marriage," which meant that every man in the community was married to every woman, and vice versa. "In a holy community," he claimed, "there is no more reason why sexual intercourse should be restrained by law, than why eating and drinking should be."

Authorities thought otherwise, and they charged Noyes with adultery for practicing his theology of "free love" (he coined the term). He fled to New York and in 1848 established the Oneida Community, which had more than 200 members by 1851 and became famous for its production of fine silverware. "The law of marriage 'worketh wrath,'" Noyes claimed, by putting men and women into competition with another and creating a corrosive "egotism for two."

ONEIDA COMMUNITY Known for its practice of "complex marriage," Oneida was a utopian community that disavowed private property and emphasized "free love." In this photo from 1870, members of the Oneida Community relax on the front lawn of the Oneida Mansion.

Oneida would avoid such tensions and conflicts by abolishing conventional marriage and ending private property. The community would be centered on spiritual love and fellowship. The various types of work would be shared and rotated among the entire community. Everyone would work for the common good; selfishness would be eliminated. Noyes especially frowned on sexual possessiveness. "If a man comes into this Association with a wife that he has to watch and reserve from others," he told the group, "he has brought a cask of [gun]powder into a blacksmith's shop."

Brook Farm in Massachusetts was the most celebrated utopian community because it grew out of the transcendental movement. George Ripley, a Unitarian minister and transcendentalist, sought to combine plain living and high thinking as the essential element of his utopian community. In 1841, he and several dozen like-minded romantics moved to a 175-acre farm nine miles southwest of Boston.

Brook Farm

Brook Farm became America's first secular utopian community. One of its members, novelist Nathaniel Hawthorne, called it "our beautiful scheme of a noble and unselfish life." Its residents shared the tasks of maintaining the buildings, tending the fields, and preparing the meals. They also organized picnics, dances, lectures, and discussions. The place survived, however, mainly because of an excellent school that drew tuition-paying students from outside. In 1846, Brook Farm's main building burned down, and the community spirit died in the ashes.

Brook Farm and other utopian communities, with few exceptions, quickly ran out of steam. The day-to-day challenges of sustaining perfect communities made up of imperfect people proved unworkable. Few of them survived more than a few months.

The communal social experiments had little impact on the outside world, where most reformers wrestled with the sins of the multitudes. Among all the targets of the reformers' zeal, one great evil would take precedence over the others: human bondage. Transcendentalist reformer Theodore Parker declared that slavery was "the blight of this nation, the curse of the North and the curse of the South." The paradox of American freedom being coupled with American slavery, of what novelist Herman Melville called "the world's fairest hope linked with man's foulest crime," would inspire the climactic crusade of the age, abolitionism, one that would ultimately sweep the nation into an epic civil war.

The Anti-Slavery Movement

CORE **OBJECTIVE**
4. Analyze the impact of the anti-slavery movement on society and politics.

The men who drafted the U.S. Constitution in 1787 hoped to keep the new nation from splitting apart over the question of slavery. To do so, they negotiated compromises to avoid dealing with the vexing issue. Still, most of them knew that there would eventually be a day of reckoning. That day approached as the nineteenth century unfolded.

Early Opposition to Slavery

Efforts to weaken or abolish slavery increased after 1800. The first organized emancipation movement appeared in 1816 with the formation of the **American Colonization Society**, whose mission was to raise funds to "repatriate" free blacks back to Africa. Its supporters included such prominent figures as James Madison, James Monroe, Henry Clay, John Marshall, and Daniel Webster. Some supported the colonization movement because of their opposition to slavery; others saw it as a way to get rid of potentially troublesome free blacks. "We must save the Negro," as one missionary explained, "or the Negro will ruin us."

Leaders of the free black community denounced the colonization idea from the start. The United States of America, they stressed, was their native land; they had no desire to live in Africa. "America is more our country than it is the whites," argued David Walker, an African American living in Boston. "We have enriched it with our blood and tears."

Nevertheless, in 1821, agents of the American Colonization Society acquired land in West Africa that became the nucleus of a new nation. In 1822, the society transported African Americans to what became the Republic of Liberia. In all, however, only about 15,000 Americans of color went to Africa, a tiny figure compared with the number of slave births each year in the United States.

From Gradualism to Abolitionism

By the 1820s, every northern state had abolished slavery. As the anti-slavery movement grew, it came to encompass a wide spectrum of attitudes. Some, like Abraham Lincoln, were gradualists. They focused on preventing the extension of slavery into new western territories in the hope that slavery would eventually die out in the South. Others, known as immediatists, called for the immediate **abolition** of slavery everywhere.

In 1831, free blacks in Boston helped convince a zealous white Massachusetts activist named William Lloyd Garrison to launch a newspaper, *The Liberator*, which became the voice of the first civil rights movement. Of the first 500 subscribers, 450 were free blacks, leading Garrison to explain that *The Liberator* did not belong to whites—"They do not sustain it." Rather, people of color kept the newspaper afloat—"It is their organ."

Garrison not only viewed slavery as *evil*; to him it was a *sin*. In the newspaper's first issue, he renounced "the popular but pernicious doctrine of gradual emancipation." He would promote only immediate abolition. The crusading Garrison dreamed of racial equality in all spheres of American life. In pursuing that dream, he vowed to be "as harsh as truth, and as uncompromising as justice. . . . I am in earnest—I will not equivocate—I will not excuse—I will *not retreat a* single inch—AND I WILL BE HEARD."

Garrison's fierce courage in denouncing slavery outraged southern slave owners as well as many northern whites. In 1835, a mob of angry whites

American Colonization Society Established in 1816, an organization whose mission was to return freed slaves to Africa.

abolitionism Movement that called for an immediate end to slavery throughout the United States.

dragged him through the streets of Boston at the end of a rope. The Georgia state legislature promised a $5,000 reward to anyone who kidnapped Garrison and brought him south for trial. Garrison reminded his critics that however violent his language, he was opposed to the use of force. "We do not preach rebellion," he stressed. The prospect "of a bloody insurrection in the South fills us with dismay," but "if any people were ever justified in throwing off the yoke of their tyrants, the slaves are the people."

During the 1830s, Garrison became the nation's most unyielding foe of slavery. Two prominent New York City merchants, Arthur and Lewis Tappan, provided financial support for *The Liberator*. In 1833, they joined with Garrison and a group of Quaker reformers, free blacks, and evangelicals to organize the American Anti-Slavery Society. That same year, Parliament ended slavery throughout the British Empire by passing the Emancipation Act, which paid slaveholders to give up their "human property." In 1835, the Tappans hired the famous revivalist Charles G. Finney to head the anti-slavery faculty at Oberlin, a new college in northern Ohio that would be the first to admit black students.

WILLIAM LLOYD GARRISON Founder of the newspaper *The Liberator*, Garrison was a vocal abolitionist and an advocate of immediate emancipation.

The American Anti-Slavery Society, financed by the Tappans, created a national network of newspapers, offices, and chapters. By 1840, some 160,000 people belonged to the American Anti-Slavery Society, which stressed that "slaveholding is a heinous crime in the sight of God, and that the duty, safety, and best interests of all concerned, require its *immediate abandonment*." In 1835, the abolitionist group began flooding the South with anti-slavery pamphlets and newspapers. Infuriated southern slaveholders called for state and federal laws to prevent the distribution of the literature, and southern post offices began destroying "anti-slavery propaganda."

The American Anti-Slavery Society (1833)

The most radical figure among the Garrisonians was David Walker, a free black man who owned a clothing store in Boston. In 1829, he published *Walker's Appeal*, a pamphlet that denounced the hypocrisy of Christians in the South for defending slavery and urged slaves to revolt. "Are we men?" he asked. "I ask you, O my brethren, are we MEN? Did our Creator make us to be slaves to dust and ashes like ourselves?" Walker shocked whites by encouraging rebellious slaves to use the "crushing arm of power" to gain their freedom. "Woe, woe will be to you if we have to obtain our freedom by fighting."

Walker's Appeal (1829)

A Split in the Movement

As the abolitionist movement spread, debates over tactics intensified. Garrison himself came to embrace every important reform movement of the day: abolition, temperance, pacifism, and women's rights. He also championed

Women's rights and abolition

equal social and legal rights for African Americans. To him, the U.S. Constitution was "a covenant with death and an agreement with hell" because it allowed slavery to continue. Garrison refused to vote and encouraged others to do the same, arguing that the nation could not continue to proclaim the ideal of liberty while tolerating the reality of slavery.

Other reformers were more pragmatic. They saw American society as fundamentally sound, and they concentrated on purging it of slavery. Garrison struck them as an unrealistic fanatic. A showdown came in 1840 on the issue of women's rights. Women had joined the abolitionist movement from the start but largely in groups without men. At that time, women were rarely allowed to speak to organizations that included men. Then the scandalous activities of the Grimké sisters brought women's rights to center stage.

Sarah and Angelina Grimké, daughters of a wealthy South Carolina family, were raised in luxury and served by many slaves. In 1821, soon after her father's death, Sarah moved from Charleston to Philadelphia, joined the Society of Friends (Quakers), and renounced slavery as a sin. Angelina soon left home and joined her. In 1835, the two sisters embraced the abolitionist movement, speaking to women's groups in what were called "parlor meetings." After they appealed to southern Christian women to put an end to slavery, the mayor of Charleston told their mother that he would jail her daughters if they ever returned home.

The energetic Grimké sisters traveled throughout the northern states, speaking first to audiences of women and eventually to both women and men, thereby arousing the anger of many male reformers. The chairman of the Connecticut Anti-Slavery Society declared, "No woman shall speak or vote where I am a moderator." Catharine Beecher lectured the Grimké

THE GRIMKÉ SISTERS
After moving away from their slaveholding family, Sarah (left) and Angelina Grimké (right) devoted themselves to abolitionism and feminism.

sisters to remember that women occupy "a subordinate relation in society to the other sex." They should limit their activities to the "domestic and social circle" rather than public organizations.

Angelina Grimké stoutly rejected such arguments. "It is a woman's right," she insisted, "to have a voice in all laws and regulations by which she is to be governed, whether in church or in state." Soon she and her sister began linking their efforts to free the slaves with their desire to free women from the cult of domesticity. "Men and women are CREATED EQUAL!" Sarah Grimké insisted. "Whatever is right for man to do is right for woman." The Grimké sisters joined others in claiming that men were keeping women in "domestic slavery."

The debate over the role of women in the anti-slavery movement finally exploded at the Anti-Slavery Society's annual meeting in 1840, where the Garrisonians convinced a majority of delegates that women should participate equally in the organization. The Tappans and their supporters walked out of the convention and formed the American and Foreign Anti-Slavery Society.

A third faction of the American Anti-Slavery Society also broke with Garrison. Its members had grown skeptical that the nonviolent "moral suasion" promoted by Garrison would ever lead to abolition. In 1840, they formed the Liberty party in an effort to elect an American president who would abolish slavery. What had been a moral and religious crusade now became a political movement.

The Liberty party's presidential nominee, James Gillespie Birney, executive secretary of the American Anti-Slavery Society, was a former slaveholder turned abolitionist. In the 1840 election, he polled only 7,000 votes, but in 1844 he won 60,000. Thereafter an anti-slavery party contested every national election until the Thirteenth Amendment officially ended slavery in 1865.

The Liberty party (1840)

Black Anti-Slavery Activity

Although many whites worked courageously to end slavery, most of them, unlike Garrison, displayed the racist attitudes common at the time, insisting that blacks were socially inferior to whites. Freedom for slaves, in other words, did not mean social equality for blacks. Many white abolitionists, for example, expected free blacks to take a backseat in the movement to end slavery.

Yet despite such discrimination, many free African Americans such as David Walker, Sarah Parker Redmond, and Sarah Mapps Douglass, among others, were active in white anti-slavery societies. Former slaves such as Henry Bibb and William Wells Brown, both escapees from Kentucky, and Frederick Douglass, who had escaped from Maryland, were the most effective critics of the South's "peculiar institution."

Brown was just twenty years old and illiterate when he escaped from his owner, a steamboat pilot on the Ohio River. An Ohio Quaker named Wells Brown helped him escape, and Brown adopted his rescuer's name in the process of forging a new identity as a free man. Brown settled in Cleveland, Ohio, married, had three children, and helped numerous runaway slaves escape to Canada. By 1842, he had learned to read and write and began to publish columns in abolitionist newspapers.

In 1847, Brown moved to Boston, where the Massachusetts Anti-Slavery Society hired him as a traveling lecturer. That same year, the organization published his autobiography, *Narrative of William W. Brown, a Fugitive Slave, Written by Himself,* which became a best seller. Brown gave thousands of speeches in America and Europe calling for an end to slavery and equality for both blacks and women. He repeatedly stressed that the African American "is endowed with those intellectual and amiable qualities which adorn and dignify human nature."

Frederick Douglass escaped from slavery in Maryland in 1838. Pretending to be a seaman, he traveled via train, steamboat, and ferry through Delaware and Pennsylvania, finally landing in New York City, where abolitionists harbored him. Believing it too dangerous for him to stay in New York, he made his way to New Bedford, Massachusetts. There he heard William Garrison speak against slavery and "felt his heart bounding at every true utterance against the slave system." Two years later, he again attended a rally at which Garrison spoke, and Douglass rose spontaneously to endorse Garrison's pleas. He decided on the spot to become an abolitionist himself. There "opened upon me a new life—a life for which I had had no preparation."

The Massachusetts Anti-slavery Society recruited Douglass as a traveling speaker, sending him across New England and west across New York State to Ohio and Indiana. With a powerful voice, he recounted to thousands of listeners his own painful encounters with "the whip, the chain, the gag, the thumbscrew, the bloodhound, the stocks, and all the other bloody paraphernalia of the slave system."

Through his writings and dazzling speeches, Douglass became the best-known man of color in America. "I appear before the immense assembly this evening as a thief and a robber," he told a Massachusetts group in 1842. "I stole this head, these limbs, this body from my master, and ran off with them."

Narrative of the Life of Frederick Douglass (1845)

After publishing his *Narrative of the Life of Frederick Douglass* (1845), Douglass, fearing that his public prominence would make him accessible to fugitive slave catchers, left for an extended lecture tour of the British Isles, returning two years later with enough money to purchase his freedom. He then started an abolitionist newspaper for blacks, the *North Star,* in Rochester, New York. He named the newspaper after the star that runaway slaves used to guide them at night toward freedom.

The female counterpart to Frederick Douglass was Sojourner Truth. Born to slaves in the Dutch farming culture of upstate New York in 1797, Sojourner Truth was given the name Isabella "Bell" Hardenbergh but renamed herself in 1843 after experiencing a conversation with God, who told her "to travel up and down the land" preaching the "truth" against slavery. Having been a slave until freed by a New York law in 1827, Sojourner Truth spoke with conviction and knowledge about the evils of the "peculiar

FREDERICK DOUGLASS AND SOJOURNER TRUTH Both Douglass and Truth were leading abolitionists and captivating speakers.

institution" and the inequality of women. She traveled throughout the North during the 1840s and 1850s, urging audiences to support women's rights and the immediate abolition of slavery. As she told the Ohio Women's Rights Convention in 1851, "I have plowed, and planted, and gathered into barns, and no man could head me—and ar'n't I a woman? I have borne thirteen children, and seen 'em mos' all sold off into slavery, and when I cried out with a mother's grief, none but Jesus heard—and ar'n't I a woman?"

Through such compelling testimony, Sojourner Truth tapped the distinctive energies that women brought to reformist causes. "If the first woman God ever made was strong enough to turn the world upside down all alone," she concluded in her address to the Ohio gathering, "these women together ought to be able to turn it back, and get it right side up again!"

Underground Railroad

While runaways often made it out of slavery on their own, many in the Upper South and border states benefited from the **Underground Railroad**. It was not a literal railroad but a vast network of secret routes and "safe houses," where free blacks and white abolitionists called "conductors" concealed runaway slaves in basements, attics, barns, and wagons before helping the fleeing "passengers" to the next "station" and eventually to freedom, often over the Canadian border.

The Underground Railroad

Underground Railroad
A secret system of routes, safe houses, and abolitionists that helped runaway slaves reach freedom in the North.

In many northern cities, blacks and whites organized "vigilance commit-tees" to protect runaways. In February 1851, Shadrach Minkins, a "stout, copper-colored man" who worked as a waiter at a Boston coffee house, was seized by U.S. marshals who claimed that he was a runaway slave from Vir-ginia. During a court hearing, a group of black and white members of the anti-slavery Boston Vigilance and Safety Committee active in the Under-ground Railroad startled the judge and observers by rushing in, overcoming armed guards, and snatching "the trembling prey of the slave hunters." Abo-litionists hid Minkins for days in Boston before taking him to safety in Can-ada, where he married an Irish woman and had four children.

Between 1810 and 1850, tens of thousands of southern slaves like Mink-ins ran away and fled north. Escaped slaves would make their way, usually at night, from one station to the next. The conductors included free-born blacks, white abolitionists, former slaves, and Native Americans. Many of them were motivated by religious concerns. Quakers, Presbyterians, Meth-odists, and Baptists participated.

A few courageous runaway slaves returned to the South to organize more escapes. Harriet Tubman, the most celebrated runaway, a daring and princi-pled fighter, was born a slave in Maryland in 1820 but escaped to Philadel-phia in 1849. During the 1850s, she risked everything to venture back to the South nineteen times to help some 300 slaves, including her parents, escape over several years. She "never lost a passenger." During the Civil War, she worked as a northern spy and a scout, leading Union gunboats in the Caroli-nas to liberate some 750 Confederate slaves. By then, slave owners in Mary-land were demanding her arrest, dead or alive.

The Underground Railroad network, however, operated only in the Up-per South. Most slaves who escaped in the Lower South went the other direc-tion, seeking refuge in Spanish Florida, Mexico, the Caribbean, or among Native Americans.

Reactions to Abolitionism

Even in the North, abolitionists confronted hostile white crowds who hated blacks. In 1837, a mob in Illinois killed Elijah P. Lovejoy, editor of an anti-slavery newspaper, giving the movement a martyr to the causes of both abolition and freedom of the press.

Lovejoy had begun his career as a Presbyterian minister in New England. He moved to St. Louis, in slaveholding Missouri, where his newspaper repeatedly denounced alcohol, Catholicism, and slavery. When a pro-slavery mob destroyed his printing office, he moved across the Mississippi River to a warehouse in Alton, Illinois, where he tried to start an anti-slavery society. There mobs twice more destroyed his printing press.

Mob violence

When a new press arrived, Lovejoy and several supporters armed them-selves and took up defensive positions. On November 7, 1837, thugs began hurl-ing stones and firing shots into the building. One of Lovejoy's allies fired back, killing one of the rioters. The mob then set fire to the warehouse, shouting, "Kill every damned abolitionist as he leaves." A shotgun blast killed Lovejoy.

His murder aroused a frenzy of indignation. Former president John Quincy Adams said that Lovejoy's death sent "a shock as of an earthquake throughout the continent." At one of the hundreds of memorial services across the North, a grizzled John Brown rose, raised his right hand, and declared, "Here, before God, in the presence of these witnesses, from this time, I consecrate my life to the destruction of slavery!" Brown and other militants decided that only violence would dislodge the sin of slavery.

The Defense of Slavery

The growing strength and visibility of the abolitionist movement prompted southerners to launch an equally aggressive defense of slavery. During the 1830s and after, pro-slavery leaders worked out an elaborate rationale for what they considered the benefits of slavery. They chose the Bible as their favorite weapon; had not the patriarchs of the Hebrew Bible held people in bondage? Had not Saint Paul advised servants to obey their masters and told a runaway servant to return to his master? And had not Jesus remained silent on the subject of slavery?

Southern white resistance

Soon even bolder arguments emerged to defend the South's "peculiar institution." In February 1837, South Carolina's John C. Calhoun, the most prominent southern political leader, told the Senate that slavery was not evil. Instead, it was "good—a great good," rooted in the Bible. He brazenly asserted that the "savage" Africans brought to America "had never existed in so comfortable, so respectable, or so civilized a condition, as that which is now enjoyed in the Southern states." If slavery were abolished, Calhoun warned, the principle of white racial supremacy would be compromised: "The next step would be to raise the negroes to a social and political equality with the whites."

What is more, Calhoun and other defenders of slavery claimed, blacks if freed would not work as hard. They were too shiftless, the argument went, and if freed, they would be a danger to themselves and to others. White workers, on the other hand, feared that freed slaves would compete with them for jobs. Calhoun's strident defense of slavery as a "positive good" led Henry Clay of Kentucky, himself a slave owner, to describe Calhoun as "a rigid, fanatic, ambitious, selfishly partisan and sectional turncoat with too much genius and too little common sense, who will either die a traitor or a madman."

The increasingly heated debate over slavery drove a wedge deeply between North and South. In 1831, William Lloyd Garrison noted that the "bond of our Union is becoming more and more brittle." He predicted that an eventual "separation between the free and slave States" was "unavoidable." By midcentury, a large number of Americans, mostly Whigs, had decided that southern slavery was an abomination; it should not expand into the new western territories. The militant reformers who were determined to prevent slavery from expanding outside the South came to be called "free soilers," and their crusade to improve American life would reach a fiery climax in the Civil War.

Reviewing the
CORE OBJECTIVES |

- **Religious Developments** Starting in the late eighteenth century, *Unitarians* and *Universalists* in New England challenged the notion of predestination by arguing that all people could receive salvation, not just a select few. The evangelical preachers of the *Second Great Awakening* generated fiery *frontier revivals*. The more democratic sects, such as Baptists and Methodists, which promoted the idea of free-will salvation, gained huge numbers of converts, including women and African Americans. Religion went hand in hand with reform in the burned-over district in western New York, which was also the birthplace of several religious movements, including the Church of Jesus Christ of Latter-day Saints (the *Mormons*).

- **Transcendentalists** Transcendentalists were poets, writers, artists, ministers, and philosophers who embraced a moral and spiritual idealism (Romanticism) in reaction to scientific rationalism and Christian orthodoxy. They sought to "transcend" reason and the material world and encourage more independent thought and reflection. At the same time, *transcendentalism* influenced the works of novelists, essayists, and poets, who created a uniquely American literature. A cultural nationalism emerged with political ideals for a more moral American society.

- **Social Reform Movements** The dominant *cult of domesticity* celebrated a "woman's sphere" in the home and argued that young women should be trained not for the workplace but in the domestic arts—managing a kitchen, running a household, and nurturing the children. However, the rise of an urban middle class offered growing numbers of women more time to devote to societal concerns. Social reformers—many of them women—left their homes to eradicate social evils. The most widespread reform movement was for *temperance*, the elimination of excessive drinking. Many were also active in reforming prisons and asylums. At the *Seneca Falls Convention (1848)*, social reformers launched the women's rights movement with the *Declaration of Sentiments (1848)*. In many parts of the country, social reformers called for greater access to education through free *public schools* for the nation's young. One educational reformer, Horace Mann, said that public school teaching was a way for women to become "mothers away from home" for the students. Amid the pervasive climate of reform during the early nineteenth century, more than 100 *utopian communities* were established, including the Shakers, Brook Farm, and the Oneida Community.

- **Anti-Slavery Movement** Northern opponents of slavery promoted several solutions, including the *American Colonization Society*'s call for gradual emancipation and the deportation of free African Americans to colonies in Africa. *Abolitionism* emerged in the 1830s, demanding an immediate and complete end of slavery. Some abolitionists went even further, calling for full social and political equality among the races, although they disagreed over tactics.

Abolitionist efforts in the North provoked a strong reaction among southern whites, stirring fears for their safety and resentment of interference. Yet many northerners shared the belief in the racial inferiority of Africans and were hostile to the tactics and message of the abolitionists. African Americans in the North joined with abolitionists to create an *Underground Railroad*, a network of safe havens and courageous abolitionists, both white and black, which helped runaway slaves escape their bondage in the South.

KEY TERMS

Unitarians *p. 389*

Universalists *p. 389*

Second Great Awakening *p. 389*

frontier revivals *p. 391*

Mormons *p. 394*

transcendentalism *p. 397*

temperance *p. 404*

cult of domesticity *p. 405*

Seneca Falls Convention (1848) *p. 406*

Declaration of Sentiments (1848) *p. 406*

public schools *p. 407*

utopian communities *p. 409*

American Colonization Society *p. 412*

abolitionism *p. 412*

Underground Railroad *p. 417*

CHRONOLOGY

1779	Universalist Church founded in Massachusetts
1816	Auburn Penitentiary opens in New York
1826	Ministers organize the American Society for the Promotion of Temperance
1830	Percentage of American churchgoers has doubled since 1800
	Joseph Smith reveals the Book of Mormon
1830–1831	Charles G. Finney begins preaching in upstate New York
1831	William Lloyd Garrison begins publishing *The Liberator*
1833	American Anti-Slavery Society is founded
1836	Transcendental Club holds its first meeting
1837	Abolitionist editor Elijah P. Lovejoy is murdered
1840	Abolitionists form the Liberty party
1845	*Narrative of the Life of Frederick Douglass* is published
1846	Mormons, led by Brigham Young, make the difficult trek to Utah
1848	At the Seneca Falls Convention, feminists issue the Declaration of Sentiments
	John Humphrey Noyes establishes the Oneida Community
1851	Sojourner Truth delivers her famous speech "Ar'n't I a Woman?"
1854	Henry David Thoreau's *Walden, or Life in the Woods* is published

🐾 INQUIZITIVE

Go to InQuizitive to see what you've learned—and learn what you've missed—with personalized feedback along the way.

DEBATING Separate Spheres

Politics and present-day events often influence *historiography*, the study of how historians develop contrasting interpretations over time. In the 1960s, *social* history gained popularity as scholars sought to tell the story of previously unrepresented groups—the poor, women, minorities. Three concepts of great importance to social historians are *race, class*, and *gender*. Part 3, *"An Expansive Nation,"* shows how historians use these concepts to debate the importance of the "separate spheres" ideology. In the first half of the nineteenth century, before the Civil War, the separate spheres ideology promoted separate and distinct roles for women and men. The female sphere was "domestic," within the home, while the male sphere was centered on economic and political life.

This exercise has two tasks:

PART 1: Compare the two secondary sources on women and separate spheres.
PART 2: Using primary sources, evaluate the arguments of the two secondary sources.

PART I **Comparing Secondary Sources**

Below are secondary sources from two social historians. The first is from Catherine Clinton of Queens University in Belfast, Northern Ireland; the second, from Nancy Hewitt of Rutgers, the State University of New Jersey. Both Clinton and Hewitt use race, class, and gender analysis to assess how the dominant tradition of separate spheres impacted women and how women responded.

In comparing the views of these two scholars, answer the following questions. Use specific examples in the selections to support your answers.

■ What is the subject of each article?

■ What classes of women does each author highlight?

■ According to each author, how did the ideology of separate spheres impact women?

■ In what ways does each author use race, class, and gender to construct her argument?

Secondary Source 1

Catherine Clinton, "The Ties That Bind" (1984)

The nineteenth century ushered in a social as well as an economic revolution for American women. The refine-ment of middle-class ideology profoundly affected fe-males during the antebellum [pre–Civil War] era. . . . The creation of the cult of domesticity, the redefinition of the home as women's domain, was a delicate process designed to channel women's contributions into a proper course. . . .

[I]nstead of liberty and equality, subordination and restriction were drummed into women, a refrain inher-ited from the colonial era. Women's only reward was lavish exaltation of their vital and unmatchable contri-butions to the civic state as mothers. This rejuvenated ethic was accompanied by a confinement to the domes-tic sphere.

Once segregated from men by the confines of a new ideological order, women set about turning their liabil-ities into assets. Forbidden traditional pathways to suc-cess, post-Revolutionary women pursued other means of achieving esteem and influence within their society. These alternatives were pioneered by women who were in search of new influence but who refrained from invading the male domain—not for the sake of modesty, but rather as a strategy. . . .

Woman's domain was, despite confinement, expan-sive. She was charged with the moral, spiritual, and phys-ical well-being of her entire family. . . . She was supervisor of the education of her children, tender of the heath, and the symbol of the home. These indispensable functions, although primarily carried out within the home, were not restricted to it. Women perceived that they might extend female jurisdiction into the public and hitherto exclusively male realm by using their "domestic" role as a lever—wedging themselves into positions of power, however limited, through exploitation of their domesticity. In the early decades of the century, creative women took their rather circumscribed nooks and crannies, within the culture, and turned them into springboards. Women's talents and contributions were soon apparent within the larger social arena.

Source: Clinton, Catherine. "The Ties That Bind." Chap. 3 in *The Other Civil War: American Women in the Nineteenth Century*. New York: Hill & Wang, 1984. 40–42.

Secondary Source 2

Nancy A. Hewitt, "Beyond the Search for Sisterhood: American Women's History in the 1980s" (1985)

The bonds that encircled past generations of women were initially perceived as restrictive, arising from female victimization at the hands of patriarchs in such institutions as medicine, education, the church, the state, and the family. Historians soon concluded, however, that oppression was a double-edged sword; the counterpart of subordination in or exclusion from male-dominated domains was inclusion in an all-female enclave. The concept of womanhood, it soon appeared, "bound women together even as it bound them down."

The formative works in American women's history have focused on the formation of these separate sexual spheres, particularly among the emerging urban bourgeoisie in the first half of the nineteenth century. Reified in prescriptive literature, realized in daily life, and ritualized

in female collectivities, this 'woman's sphere' came to be seen as the foundation of women's culture and community in antebellum [pre–Civil War] America. . . . The community that has become the cornerstone of North American women's history was discovered within the Victorian middle class. . . . Yet evidence from the lives of slaves, mill operatives, miners' wives, immigrants, and southern industrial workers as well as from "true women" indicates that there was no single woman's culture or sphere. There was a culturally dominant definition of sexual spheres promulgated by an economically, politically, and socially dominant group.

That definition was firmly grounded in the sexual division of labor appropriate to that class, just as other definitions developed based on the sexual division of labor in other class and racial groups. All these divisions were characterized by sufficient sex-stereotyping to assure the formation of distinct female circles of labor and distinct rituals and values rooted in that laboring experience.

To date historians have focused on the parallels in the establishment of women's spheres across classes, races, and ethnic groups and have asserted certain commonalities among them, assuming their common origin in the modernization of society during the nineteenth century.

A closer examination now reveals that no such universal sisterhood existed, and in fact that the development of a sense of community among various classes of women served as a barrier to an all-embracing bond of womanhood. Finally, it is now clear that privileged women were willing to wield their sex-specific influence in ways that, intentionally or unintentionally, exploited other women in the name of "true-womanhood."

Source: Hewitt, Nancy A. "Beyond the Search for Sisterhood: American Women's History in the 1980s." *Social History* 10 (1985): 299–321.

PART II Using Primary Sources to Evaluate Secondary Sources

When historians are faced with conflicting interpretations of the past, they often look at primary source material as part of the process of evaluating the different arguments. Below are three excerpts from political statements by three remarkable but very different women. The first is from Lucretia Mott, a middle-class and highly educated woman who became a prominent Quaker speaker, leading abolitionist, and co-organizer of the first women's rights convention, the Seneca Falls Convention. The

second excerpt is from Sojourner Truth, a former slave and leading abolitionist. The final excerpt is from Harriett Robinson, who at the age of ten began work in the textile mills of Lowell, Massachusetts. Robinson went on to write her autobiography and was involved in the women's suffrage movement.

While not all these documents directly address the term *separate spheres*, each addresses women's place in American society.

Carefully read each of the primary sources and answer the following questions. Decide which of the primary source documents support or refute Clinton's and Hewitt's arguments about women's separate sphere. Be sure to identify which specific components of each historian's argument the documents support or refute.

- How did the ideology of separate spheres impact the lives of these three women?

- Which of the primary sources do you think Clinton and Hewitt would find most useful, and how might the authors use them to support their arguments?

- Which of the secondary sources do you think is best supported by the primary source evidence?

- What have these primary sources taught you about using race, class, and gender in historical analysis?

Primary Source 1

Lucretia Mott, *Discourse on Women* (1849)

This age is notable for its works of mercy and benevolence—for the efforts that are made to reform the inebriate and the degraded, to relieve the oppressed and the suffering. Women as well as men are interested in these works of justice and mercy. They are efficient co-workers, their talents are called into profitable exercise, their labors are effective in each department of reform. The blessing to the merciful, to the peacemaker is equal to man and to woman. It is greatly to be deplored, now that she is increasingly qualified for usefulness, that any view should be presented, calculated to retard her labors of love.

Why should not woman seek to be a reformer? . . . [I]f she is to fear to exercise her reason, and her noblest powers, lest she should be thought to "attempt to act the man," and not "acknowledge his supremacy"; if she is to be satisfied with the narrow sphere assigned her by man, nor aspire to a higher, lest she should transcend the bounds of female delicacy; truly it is a mournful prospect for woman. We would admit all the difference, that our great and beneficent Creator has made, in the relation of man and woman, nor would we seek to disturb this relation; but we deny that the present position of woman, is her true sphere of usefulness: nor will she attain to this sphere, until the disabilities and disadvantages, religious, civil, and social, which impede her progress, are removed out of her way. These restrictions have enervated her mind and paralyzed her powers. . . .

So far from her "ambition leading her to attempt to act the man," she needs all the encouragement she can receive, by the removal of obstacles from her path, in order that she may become a "true woman." As it is desirable that man should act a manly and generous part, not "mannish," so let woman be urged to exercise a dignified and womanly bearing, not womanish. Let her cultivate all the graces and proper accomplishments of her sex, but let not these degenerate into a kind of effeminacy, in which she is satisfied to be the mere plaything or toy of society, content with her outward adornings, and with the tone of flattery and fulsome adulation too often addressed to her. True, nature has made a difference in her configuration, her physical strength, her voice, etc.—and we ask no change, we are satisfied with nature. But how has neglect and mismanagement increased this difference! It is our duty to develop these natural powers, by suitable exercise, so that they may be strengthened "by reason of use."

Source: Mott, Lucretia. *Discourse on Women*. Philadelphia, Penn.: T. B. Peterson, 1850.

Primary Source 2

Sojourner Truth, "And Ar'n't I a Woman?" (1851)

And ar'n't I a woman? Look at me! Look at my arm! (*And she bared her right arm to the shoulder, showing her tremendous muscular power.*) I have plowed, and planted, and gathered into barns, and no man could head [surpass] me—and ar'n't I a woman? I could work as much and eat as much as a man when I could get it and bear de lash as well—and ar'n't I a woman? I have borne thirteen children, and seen 'em mos' all sold off to slavery, and when I cried out with my mother's grief, none but Jesus heard me—and ar'n't I a woman? . . . If my cup won't hold but a pint, and your'n holds a quart, wouldn't ye be mean not to let me have my little half-measure full? . . . He say women can't have as much rights as men, 'cause Christ wan't a woman! Whar did your Christ come from? . . . From God and a woman! Man had nothin' to do with Him.

Source: Truth, Sojourner. "And Ar'n't I a Woman?" (Speech at the Ohio Women's Rights Convention, 1851, Akron, Ohio). *History of Woman Suffrage*. Vol. 1, *1848–1861*. Edited by Elizabeth Cady Stanton, Susan B. Anthony, and Matilda Joslyn Gage. Rochester, NY: Susan B. Anthony, 1887.

Primary Source 3

Harriett H. Robinson, *Loom and Spindle or Life among the Early Mill Girls* (1898)

One of the first strikes of cotton-factory operatives that ever took place in this country was that in Lowell, in

October, 1836. When it was announced that the wages were to be cut down, great indignation was felt, and it was decided to strike, en masse. This was done. The mills were shut down, and the girls went in procession from their several corporations to the "grove" on Chapel Hill, and listened to "incendiary" speeches from early labor reformers. One of the girls stood on a pump, and gave vent to the feelings of her companions in a neat speech, declaring that it was their duty to resist all attempts at cutting down the wages. This was the first time a woman had spoken in public in Lowell, and the event caused surprise and consternation among her audience. . . . It was estimated that as many as twelve or fifteen hundred girls turned out, and walked in procession through the streets. They had neither flags nor music, but sang songs, a favorite (but rather inappropriate) one being a parody on "I won't be a nun."

Oh! isn't it a pity, such a pretty girl as I—

Should be sent to the factory to pine away and die?

Oh! I cannot be a slave,

I will not be a slave,

For I'm so fond of liberty

That I cannot be a slave.

Source: Robinson, Harriett H. *Loom and Spindle or Life among the Early Mill Girls*. New York: Thomas Y. Crowell & Company, 1898.

unanimously at 1.15 o'clock, P. M., Dece
20th, 1860.

AN ORDINANCE

olve the Union between the State of South Carolin
 States united with her under the compact entitled
titution of the United States of America."

ple of the State of South Carolina, in Convention assembled, do declare and or
reby declared and ordained,

e Ordinance adopted by us in Convention, on the twenty-third day of Ma
Lord one thousand seven hundred and eighty-eight, whereby the Constitutio
tes of America was ratified, and also, all Acts and parts of Acts of the

OR SALE HERE

AN EDITION FOR THE MILLION, COMPLETE IN 1 Vol., PRICE 37 1-2 CENT
"   "   IN GERMAN, IN 1 Vol., PRICE 50 CENTS.
"   "   IN 2 Vols., CLOTH, 6 PLATES, PRICE $1.50.
SUPERB ILLUSTRATED EDITION, IN 1 Vol., WITH 153 ENGRAVINGS,
PRICES FROM $2.50 TO $5.00.

A House Divided and Rebuilt

During the first half of the nineteenth century, America's population and its boundaries continued to grow rapidly. Above all, Americans in great numbers continued to move westward, where vast lands lured farmers, ranchers, and miners. By the end of the 1840s, the United States—yet again—had dramatically expanded its territory, from Texas west to California and the Pacific Northwest. In the process of dislodging Native Americans and Mexicans, it assembled a continental empire from the Atlantic to the Pacific.

This extraordinary surge of territorial expansion was a mixed blessing, however. How to deal with the new western territories became the nation's flashpoint issue as the differences among America's three distinctive regions—North, South, and West—became even more divisive. During the first half of the nineteenth century, a series of political compromises had glossed over the fundamental issue of slavery, but growing numbers of anti-slavery activists opposed efforts to extend slavery into the new western territories acquired from Mexico. Moreover, the 1850s witnessed a new generation of national politicians who were less willing to compromise. The continuing debate over allowing slavery into new territories eventually led more and more Americans to decide that the nation could not survive half slave and half free. Something had to give.

In a last-ditch effort to preserve the institution of slavery, eleven southern states seceded from the Union and declared themselves a separate Confederate nation. That, in turn, prompted northerners, led by President Abraham Lincoln, to support a civil war to restore the Union. No one realized in 1861 how costly that war would become: more than 700,000 soldiers and sailors would die in four years of fighting. Nor did anyone envision how sweeping the war's effects would be upon the nation's future.

The northern victory in 1865 restored the Union and helped accelerate America's transformation into a modern urban-industrial superpower. A national consciousness began to replace the sectional divisions of the prewar era, and a Republican-led Congress passed a wave of federal legislation to promote industrial and commercial development and western expansion. In the process, the United States began to leave behind the Jeffersonian dream of America remaining a decentralized agrarian republic.

The Civil War, of course, also ended slavery, but the status of the freed African Americans remained uncertain. Former slaves found themselves legally free, but few had property, homes, education, or training. Although the Fourteenth Amendment (1868) guaranteed the civil rights of African Americans and the Fifteenth Amendment (1870) declared that black men could vote, southern officials often ignored the new federal laws, and African Americans continued to suffer social abuse and physical harm.

The restoration of the former Confederate states to the Union did not come easily. Bitterness and resistance grew among the defeated southerners. Although former Confederate leaders lost the right to vote and hold office, they continued to exercise considerable authority in political and economic matters. In 1877, when the last federal troops were removed from the occupied South, former Confederates declared themselves "redeemed" from the stain of northern military occupation. By the end of the nineteenth century, most states of the former Confederacy had developed a system of legal discrimination against blacks that re-created many aspects of slavery.

EMIGRANTS CROSSING THE PLAINS, OR THE OREGON TRAIL (1869) German American painter Albert Bierstadt captures the majestic sights of the frontier, though the transcontinental trek was also grueling and bleak for many pioneers.

Western Expansion and Southern Secession

1830–1861

D uring the 1840s and after, wave after wave of Americans moved west. "If hell lay to the west," one pioneer declared, "Americans would cross heaven to get there." By 1860, some 4.3 million people had crossed the mile-wide Mississippi River and spread out across the Great Plains and the Pacific coast. Westward expansion was especially important to southerners, many of whom wanted new cotton lands using slave labor. In addition, southerners had long enjoyed disproportionate political power because of the provision in the U.S. Constitution that counted slaves as part of the population in determining the number of congressional seats for each state. Nine of the first twelve presidents were from the South, and southerners held the most powerful congressional leadership positions.

Southern political influence, however, began to wane as the industrializing Midwest and Northeast grew more rapidly, increasing those regions' representation in Congress. Southerners wanted new western states to boost pro-southern representation in Congress as a means of ensuring that northerners could never abolish

CORE
OBJECTIVES INQUIZITIVE

1. Explain how, why, and where Americans moved west of the Mississippi River during the 1830s and 1840s.

2. Examine the impact of the Mexican-American War on national politics.

3. Describe how the federal government tried to resolve the issue of slavery in the western territories during the 1850s.

4. Analyze the appeal of the Republican party to northern voters and how it led to Abraham Lincoln's victory in the 1860 presidential contest.

5. Explain why seven southern states seceded from the Union shortly after Lincoln's election in 1860.

slavery. As a Mississippi senator explained, "I would spread the blessings of slavery . . . to the uttermost ends of the earth." Such motives made the addition of new western territories a flashpoint of sectional debate. Would the new territories be slave or free?

People migrated west largely for economic reasons. "To make money was their chief object," said a pioneer woman in Texas. Trappers, farmers, miners, ministers, merchants, hunters, ranchers, teachers, servants, and prostitutes, among others, headed west to seek their fortune. Others—such as the Mormons and Christian missionary organizations—sought religious freedom and the chance to win converts to their faith. The Indians and Hispanics who had long inhabited the region were swept aside by the onslaught of Americans, all enabled by presidents and congressmen eager to complete the nation's expansion to the Pacific coast.

CORE **OBJECTIVE**

1. Explain how, why, and where Americans moved west of the Mississippi River during the 1830s and 1840s.

Moving West

In 1845, a New York newspaper editor and Democratic party propagandist named John L. O'Sullivan gave a catchy name to America's aggressive spirit of westward expansion. "Our manifest destiny," he wrote, "is to overspread the continent allotted by Providence for the free development of our yearly multiplying millions." The idea of America having a "**manifest destiny**" assumed that the United States had a God-given right to extend its rapidly growing Christian republic and capitalist civilization across the continent from the Atlantic to the Pacific—and beyond. This widely embraced notion of manifest destiny offered a powerful religious justification for territorial expansion at the expense of Native Americans and Hispanics, Spaniards and the British.

The Western Frontier

Western migration: Population growth, land, and Overland Trails

Most of the western pioneers during the second quarter of the nineteenth century were American-born whites from the Upper South and the Midwest. Only a few free blacks joined in the migration. What spurred the massive migration westward was the continuing population explosion in the United States and the widespread desire for land. Remote California was an especially attractive destination, in part because of the discovery of gold at midcentury.

Although some people traveled 13,000 miles by sea from New York City or Boston to California, going around the southern tip of South America and then up the Pacific coast, most went overland. Between 1841 and 1867, some 350,000 men, women, and children made the difficult trek to California or Oregon, while many others settled along the way in areas such as Colorado, Texas, and Arkansas.

manifest destiny The widespread belief that America was "destined" by God to expand westward across the continent into lands claimed by Native Americans as well as European nations.

Overland Trails Trail routes followed by wagon trains bearing settlers and trade goods from Missouri to the Oregon Country, California, and New Mexico, beginning in the 1840s.

Most of the pioneers who journeyed on the **Overland Trails** traveled in family groups. Oregon-bound wagon trains usually left Missouri in late spring and completed the grueling 2,000-mile trek in six months. By 1845,

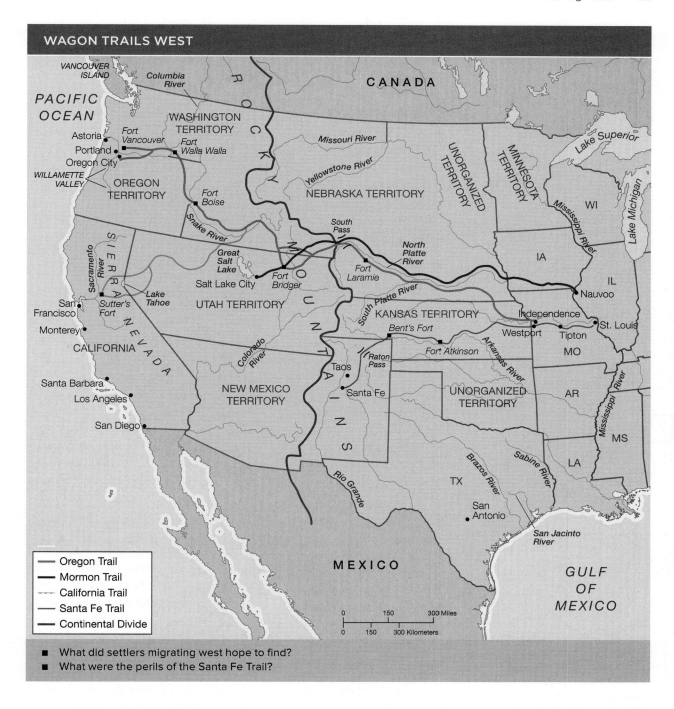

WAGON TRAILS WEST

Legend:
— Oregon Trail
— Mormon Trail
--- California Trail
— Santa Fe Trail
— Continental Divide

- What did settlers migrating west hope to find?
- What were the perils of the Santa Fe Trail?

some 5,000 people were making the journey annually, and thousands were dying along the trails, brought down by hunger, disease, or violence. The discovery of gold in California in 1848 brought some 30,000 pioneers along the Oregon Trail in 1849. By 1850, the peak year of travel along the trail, the annual count had risen to 55,000. "Any man who makes a trip by land to California," observed Alonzo Delano in 1849, "deserves to find a fortune."

***FUR TRADERS DESCENDING THE MISSOURI* (1845)** Originally titled "French-Trader, Half-Breed Son," this oil painting depicts a white settler sailing down the river with his half–Native American son—not an uncommon sight in early America.

Plains Indians

Conflicts over Indian lands

In 1840, when the great migration of American settlers across the plains began, more than 325,000 Indians inhabited the vast area west of the Mississippi River. They represented more than 200 nations, each with its own language, religion, cultural practices, and system of governance. Some were primarily farmers; others were nomadic hunters, following buffalo herds; many Indian nations fought with one another—often to control hunting grounds or to acquire horses. Because Native American life on the plains depended upon the abundance of buffalo, the influx of white settlers and hunters posed a direct threat to the Indians' survival. When federal officials could not force Indian leaders to sell their tribal lands, fighting ensued. And after the discovery of gold in California in early 1848, the tidal wave of white expansion flowed all the way to the west coast, engulfing Native Americans and Mexicans in its wake.

Mexico and the Spanish West

As American settlers trespassed across Indian lands, they also encountered Spanish-speaking peoples. Many whites were as prejudiced toward Hispanics as they were toward Indians. Senator Lewis Cass from Michigan, who would be the Democratic candidate for president in 1848, expressed the expansionist view: "We do not want the people of Mexico, either as citizens or as subjects. All we want is their . . . territory."

Mexico gains independence from Spain (1821)

In 1821, Mexico had gained its independence from Spain, but the new nation had struggled to develop a stable government and an effective economy. Americans were eager to take advantage of Mexico's instability, especially in its sparsely populated northern provinces—areas that included present-day Texas, New Mexico, Arizona, Nevada, California, and portions of Colorado, Oklahoma, Kansas, and Wyoming. American fur traders streamed into New Mexico and Arizona and developed a profitable trade in beaver pelts along the Santa Fe Trail east to St. Louis.

> American fur traders

The Rocky Mountains and Oregon Country

During the early nineteenth century, the Far Northwest consisted of the Nebraska, Washington, and Oregon Territories. The Oregon Country included what became the states of Oregon, Idaho, and Washington, as well as parts of Montana, Wyoming, and the Canadian province of British Columbia. It was an unsettled region claimed by both Great Britain and the United States. By the Convention of 1818, the two nations had agreed to "joint occupation" of the Oregon Country.

> British-American joint occupation of the Oregon Country

Word of Oregon's fertile soil, plentiful rainfall, and magnificent forests gradually spread eastward. By the late 1830s, a trickle of migrating farmers, missionaries, fur traders, and shopkeepers were flowing along the Oregon Trail, a 2,000-mile pathway connecting the Missouri River near St. Louis with Oregon.

Soon, however, **Oregon Fever** swept the nation. In 1841 and 1842, the first sizable wagon trains made the trip, and in 1843 the movement became a mass migration. One pioneer remembered that the wagon trains were like mobile communities. "Everybody was supposed to rise at daylight, and while the women were preparing breakfast, the men rounded up the cattle, took down the tents, yoked the oxen to the wagons, and made everything ready to start" once breakfast was over. They found Oregon in a "primitive state"

Oregon Fever The lure of fertile land and economic opportunities in the Oregon Country that drew hundreds of thousands of settlers westward, beginning in the late 1830s.

THE JOURNEY WEST A photo from the nineteenth century shows a westward-bound man and woman beside their covered wagon. Life on the Overland Trails was rough and tiring, and even in these moments of apparent rest the pioneers had to cook their meals, tend to their horses or oxen, and maintain their wagon.

requiring backbreaking work to create self-sustaining homesteads. Women worked as hard as men, day and night. "I am a very old woman," reported twenty-nine-year-old Sarah Everett. "My face is thin, sunken, and wrinkled, my hands bony, withered, and hard." By 1845, there were about 5,000 settlers in Oregon's fertile Willamette Valley.

As the numbers of migrants traveling along the Oregon Trail grew, they tore through Native American lands and culture. Buffalo disappeared and nations like the Cheyenne and the Arapaho were forced to split into northern and southern branches. As the federal government negotiated new treaties with Native Americans, it insisted that they be relocated onto reservations far from the Oregon Trail, which eventually served as the route for the Union Pacific railroad.

The Settlement of California

California was also a powerful magnet for new settlers and adventurers. By the nineteenth century, Spanish Catholic missionaries, aided by Spanish soldiers, controlled most of the coastal Indians. The friars (priests) lured the local Indians into coastal "missions" by offering gifts or impressing them with their "magical" religious rituals. Once inside the missions, the Indians were baptized as Catholics, taught Spanish, and stripped of their native heritage. Soldiers living in the missions enforced the will of the friars; rebellious Indians were whipped or imprisoned. Mission Indians died at an alarming rate, mostly as the result of infectious diseases. The Spanish and then the Mexicans actually wanted to preserve Indians as mission inmates or as cheap farm laborers. Nevertheless, the Native American population along the California coast declined from 72,000 in 1769 to 18,000 by 1821. Saving souls cost many lives.

For all its rich natural resources, California remained thinly populated well into the nineteenth century, with Native Americans still outnumbering Hispanics (called *Californios*) and Americans. Californians took comfort that Mexico City, the Mexican capital, was too far away to exercise effective control over them. Between 1821, when Mexico gained its independence, and 1841, Californians, including many recent American arrivals, staged ten revolts against Mexican governors.

Huge *ranchos* dominate Mexican-owned California

Yet the shift from Spanish to Mexican rule did produce one dramatic change in California. In 1824, Mexico passed a colonization act that granted hundreds of huge *ranchos* (estates) to prominent Mexicans. Yet the *rancheros* (largest landowners) wanted more, especially the vast estates controlled by the Catholic missions along the coast, which were usually on the most fertile and valuable land.

In 1833–1834, the rancheros persuaded the Mexican government to pass the "secularization act" which allowed the government to take the missions, release the Indians from church control, and transfer the missions' vast farmlands to *rancheros*. Within a few years, the government issued some 700 new *rancho* grants of 4,500 to 50,000 acres along the California coast. These

SUTTER'S FORT Marking the end of the California Trail, Sutter's Fort was a prominent trading hub that depended on the labor and craftsmanship of the Native Americans who worked for him. **How were the Native Americans at Sutter's Fort treated?**

sprawling ranches resembled southern plantations—but the death rate among brutalized Indian workers was twice as high as that among enslaved blacks in the Lower South.

Among the most ambitious white immigrants in California in the mid–nineteenth century was John A. Sutter, a Swiss entrepreneur who had left his debts and his family in Europe so that he could make his fortune in America. At the junction of the Sacramento and American Rivers (later the site of the city of Sacramento), Sutter used local Indians and whites from America and Europe to build an enormous fort and bustling trading outpost called Sutter's Fort. Completed in 1843, it stood at the end of the California Trail, which forked southward off the Oregon Trail and led through the Sierra Nevadas.

California: Sutter's Fort

Able and charming, cruel and ruthless, Sutter set about creating a wilderness empire. In addition to trading furs, Sutter put Indians to work making wool blankets and hats; cultivating vast acres of wheat and corn; and raising huge herds of cattle, sheep, hogs, and horses. By the start of 1846, there were perhaps 800 Americans in California, along with approximately 10,000 *Californios*, and some 150,000 Native Americans. While Sutter paid his Indian workers, he also used violence to gain their loyalty and ensure their obedience. He occasionally whipped, jailed, and even executed Indians who disobeyed his orders.

American Settlements in Texas

The American passion for new western land focused on the closest of all the northern Mexican borderlands, Texas. During the 1820s, the United States had twice offered to buy Texas, but the Mexican government refused to sell. Mexicans were frightened and infuriated by the idea of America acquiring their "sacred soil." Yet that is what happened anyway.

The leading promoter of American settlement in Mexican-controlled Texas was Stephen Fuller Austin, a visionary land developer (*empresario*) who convinced Mexican leaders that he could recruit energetic American families to settle in Texas and thereby create a "buffer" on the northern frontier between the feared Comanche Indians and the Mexican settlements to the south.

Thousands of hardy souls settled in Austin's Anglo-Texas "colony." They were mostly ranchers or farmers drawn to the fertile lands in the river valleys that sold for only a few cents an acre—much less than the price of federal land in the United States. A few of the settlers were wealthy planters who brought large numbers of slaves with them at a time when Mexico prohibited the importation of slaves.

> **"Texians" settle lands in northern Mexico**

By 1830, the coastal region of Texas had far more Americans living there than Hispanics—about 20,000 white settlers (Anglo-Texans, or "Texians") and 1,000 enslaved blacks, brought to grow and harvest cotton. In 1828, José María Sánchez, a Mexican official, visited Austin's settlement in Texas and warned that the effort to take Texas from Mexico "will start from this colony" because the Mexican government was not taking "vigorous measures to prevent it."

The Texas War for Independence

Mexican officials were so worried about the cultural tensions created by too many non-Catholic and slave-owning Americans living in Texas that in April 1830 they abruptly outlawed immigration from the United States and built forts to enforce the new law. Americans, who viewed the Mexicans and their army with contempt, kept coming anyway. By 1835, the Texians and their enslaved blacks outnumbered the *Tejanos* (Hispanic Texans) ten to one.

> **Texas Revolution (1835–1836)**

Changing political circumstances in Mexico aggravated the growing tensions. In 1834, General Antonio López de Santa Anna, the Mexican president, suspended the national congress and became a dictator, calling himself the "Napoleon of the West." Texians feared that Santa Anna planned to free "our slaves and to make slaves of us."

When Santa Anna imprisoned Stephen Austin in 1834, Texians decided that they must gain their independence from Mexican control. After Austin gained his release from jail eighteen months later, he called for Texians to revolt: "War is our only resource. There is no other remedy. We must defend our rights, ourselves, and our country by force of arms." He urged that Texas become a fully American slave territory and then join the United States.

Texas Revolution (1835–1836) Conflict between Texas colonists and the Mexican government that resulted in the creation of the separate Republic of Texas in 1836.

In the fall of 1835, wary Texians followed Austin's lead and rebelled against Santa Anna's "despotism." A furious Santa Anna ordered all Americans expelled from Texas, all Texians disarmed, and all rebels arrested and executed. As sporadic fighting erupted, hundreds of armed volunteers from southern states rushed to assist the 30,000 Texians in the **Texas Revolution** against a Mexican nation of 7 million people. "The sword is drawn!" Austin proclaimed.

THE ALAMO David Crockett, pictured fighting with his rifle over his head after running out of bullets, joined the legendary battle to defend the Alamo against the Mexican army. **What were the consequences of the Battle of the Alamo?**

The Alamo and Goliad

At San Antonio, in southern Texas, General Santa Anna's army assaulted a small group of fewer than 200 Texians, Tejanos, and recently arrived American volunteers holed up in an abandoned Catholic mission called the Alamo. Leading the rebels was William B. Travis, a hot-tempered, twenty-six-year-old Alabama lawyer and teacher who had been named a lieutenant colonel in the newly formed Texian army. Travis ignored orders to retreat from the Alamo, insisting that "death was preferable to disgrace."

Among the other Americans at the Alamo, the most celebrated was David Crockett, the Tennessee frontiersman, bear hunter, and sharpshooter who had fought Indians under Andrew Jackson and served as an anti-Jackson Whig congressman. He told his fellow Alamo defenders that he had come "to aid you all that I can in your noble cause."

In February 1836, General Santa Anna demanded that the Americans in the Alamo surrender. Travis answered with cannon fire, promising that

"I shall never surrender or retreat. . . . VICTORY OR DEATH!" Santa Anna's forces then launched a series of assaults against the outnumbered defenders.

For eleven days, the Mexicans were thrown back and suffered heavy losses. Then, on March 6, the Alamo defenders awakened to the sound of Mexican bugles playing the dreaded "Degüello" ("No Mercy to the Defenders"). Colonel Travis shouted: "The Mexicans are upon us—give 'em Hell!" Wave after wave of Santa Anna's men attacked the Alamo from every side. They were twice forced back, but on the third try they broke through the battered north wall. Out of bullets, the rebels fought with tomahawks, knives, and rifle butts, but in the end, virtually all were killed or wounded.

A handful of Alamo defenders, perhaps including Crockett, survived and were captured. General Santa Anna ordered them hacked to death with swords. A Mexican officer wrote that the captives "died without complaining and without humiliating themselves before their torturers." The only survivors of the Alamo were a handful of women, children, and slaves.

It was a complete victory for the Mexicans, but a costly one, for the Battle of the Alamo claimed more than 600 Mexican lives and provided a rallying cry for angry Texians thereafter. While Santa Anna proclaimed a "glorious victory," his aide wrote ominously in his diary, "One more such 'glorious victory' and we are finished."

The furious fighting at the Alamo turned the rebellion into a war for Texas independence. On March 2, 1836, during the siege of the Alamo, delegates from all fifty-nine Texas towns met at the village of Washington-on-the-Brazos, 150 miles northeast of San Antonio. There they signed a declaration of independence from Mexican control. Over the next seventeen days, the delegates drafted a constitution for the new Republic of Texas and established a government.

Two weeks later, at the Battle of Coleto, a Mexican force again defeated a smaller Texian army, many of them recently arrived volunteers from southern states. The Mexicans marched the 465 captured Texians to a fort in the nearby town of Goliad. Despite pleas from his own men to show mercy, Santa Anna ordered the captives killed as "pirates and outlaws." On Palm Sunday, March 27, 1836, 303 Texians were marched out of Goliad and then murdered. The massacres at the Alamo and Goliad fueled a burning desire for revenge among the Texians.

The Battle of San Jacinto

The commander in chief of the Texian army was the remarkable Sam Houston, a hard-drinking frontiersman born in Virginia to Scots-Irish immigrants. At age fourteen, after his father died, Houston had moved with his mother and siblings to eastern Tennessee, where he lived among the Cherokees for a time. Like David Crockett, he had served under General Andrew Jackson during the War of 1812 before becoming an attorney, a U.S. congressman, and governor of Tennessee. He resigned the governorship two years later because his aristocratic young wife had left him, claiming she had discovered that he had sustained a "dreadful injury" in the Creek War that had left him impotent (a falsehood). In 1829, Houston joined the Cherokee migration westward to the Arkansas Territory, where he married a Cherokee woman and was formally "adopted" by the Cherokee Nation. In December 1832, he moved to Texas and immediately joined the rebellion against Mexico.

A giant of a man, Houston was fearless, a quality sorely needed by the Texians as they struggled against the much larger Mexican army. After learning of the massacre at the Alamo, Houston's outnumbered troops retreated, hoping that Santa Anna's pursuing army would make a mistake. On April 21, 1836, the cocky Mexican general walked into a trap, when Houston's army surprised the Mexicans near the San Jacinto River, about twenty-five miles southeast of the modern city of Houston. The Texians and Tejanos charged, yelling "Remember the Alamo." They overwhelmed the panic-stricken Mexicans, most of whom had been caught napping during the afternoon *siesta*.

SAM HOUSTON Having led the Texans to a sweeping victory over the Mexicans in the Battle of San Jacinto, Houston went on to serve as the first president of the Republic of Texas.

The battle lasted only eighteen minutes; Houston's troops then spent the next two hours slaughtering fleeing Mexican soldiers. It was, said a Texian, a "frightful sight to behold." Some 650 Mexicans were killed and 300 captured. The Texians lost only eleven men; thirty others, including Sam Houston, were wounded. Santa Anna escaped in his underwear only to be captured the next day. He bought his freedom by signing a treaty recognizing the independence of the Republic of Texas, with the Rio Grande as its southern boundary with Mexico. The Texas Revolution had succeeded in just seven weeks.

The Lone Star Republic

In 1836, the Lone Star Republic, as Texians nicknamed their new nation, drafted a constitution for Texas that legalized slavery and banned free blacks, elected Sam Houston its first president, and voted overwhelmingly for annexation by the United States. No one expected the huge Republic of Texas to remain independent for long.

The Republic of Texas (1836)

The American president at the time was Houston's friend and former commander, Andrew Jackson, who eagerly wanted Texas to join the Union. Jackson, however, decided it was better to wait, for adding Texas as a slave state would ignite an explosive sectional quarrel between North and South that would fracture the Democratic party. Worse, any effort to add Texas to the Union would likely mean a war with Mexico, which refused to recognize Texan independence. So President Jackson delayed official recognition of the Republic of Texas until his last day in office, early in 1837. New Yorker Martin Van Buren, Jackson's successor, did as predicted: he avoided all talk of Texas annexation during his single term as president.

JOHN TYLER Elected vice president to William Henry Harrison, Tyler became president in 1841 and governed with an anti-Whig, pro-expansion agenda.

The Tyler Presidency and Texas

When William Henry Harrison became president in 1841, he was the oldest man (sixty-eight) and the first Whig to win the office. The Whigs had first emerged in opposition to Andrew Jackson and continued to promote strong federal government support for industrial development and economic growth: high tariffs to deter foreign imports and federal funding for internal improvements. Yet Harrison was elected primarily on the strength of his military record and because he had avoided taking public stances on controversial issues. In the end, it mattered little, for Harrison served the shortest term of any president.

On April 4, 1841, exactly one month after his inauguration, President Harrison died of pneumonia, and Vice President John Tyler of Virginia became president. When the Whigs had chosen Tyler as their vice-presidential nominee in 1840, no one expected him to become president. The powerful anti-Jackson Whig, Senator Henry Clay, had wanted a southerner to balance the Whig ticket but expected that he would dominate the Harrison presidency.

Tyler, however, was not so easily dominated. At fifty-one, the tall, thin, slave-owning Virginian was the youngest president to date, but he had lots of political experience, having served as a state legislator, governor, congressman, and senator. Originally a Democrat, Tyler had broken with the party over President Andrew Jackson's "condemnation" of South Carolina's attempt to nullify federal laws. Tyler believed that South Carolina had a constitutional right to secede from the nation.

Now, as president, Tyler was stubbornly opposed to everything associated with the Whig party's "American System," Clay's celebrated program of economic nationalism that called for the federal government to support industrial development. Like Thomas Jefferson, Tyler also endorsed territorial expansion, and soon after becoming president in 1841, he began working to make Texas the twenty-eighth American state.

When Congress met in a special session in 1841, Henry Clay introduced a series of controversial resolutions. He called for the repeal of the Independent Treasury Act and the creation of another Bank of the United States, proposed to revive the "distribution" program whereby the money raised from federal land sales went to the states, and urged that tariffs be raised on imported goods. The "haughty and imperious" Clay then set about pushing his program through Congress. "Tyler dares not resist. I will drive him before me," he threatened. With more tact, Clay might have avoided a series of nasty disputes with Tyler over financial issues. For once, however, driven by his lust to be president, Clay, the Great Compromiser, lost his instinct for compromise.

Tyler vetoes national bank bill

Although Tyler agreed to the repeal of the Independent Treasury Act and signed a higher tariff bill, the president vetoed Clay's pet project: a new national bank. Clay responded by attacking the president in Congress, calling him a traitor to his party. He also convinced Tyler's entire cabinet to resign, with the exception of Secretary of State Daniel Webster. Tyler replaced the defectors with anti-Jackson Democrats who, like him, had become Whigs. The Whigs then expelled Tyler from the party. By 1842, Tyler had become a president without a party, shunned by both Whigs and Democrats but loved by those promoting territorial expansion.

The political turmoil coincided with the continuing economic depression. Bank failures mounted, and unemployment soared. People rioted in the streets of Philadelphia, and an armed rebellion flared up in Rhode Island over the failure of the state to allow non-landowners to vote. The self-assured Tyler, however, refused to let either the sputtering economy or an international crisis with Great Britain deflect him from his determination to annex more territory into the United States.

Efforts to Annex Texas

In April 1843, South Carolinian John C. Calhoun, then secretary of state, sent to the Senate for ratification a treaty annexing Texas. There it died by a vote of 35–16, however. Northern senators, many of whom were abolitionists, refused to add another slave state. Others were concerned that annexing Texas would trigger a war with Mexico.

> Texas annexation treaty defeated

Texan leaders were frustrated that their new independence had not led to annexation. Sam Houston threatened to expand the Republic of Texas to the Pacific. But with little money in the treasury, a rising government debt, and continuing tensions with Mexico, which insisted that it remained at war with Texas, this was mostly bluster.

The Lone Star Republic also had no infrastructure—no banks, no schools, no industries. It remained largely a frontier community of scattered log cabins. Houston decided that Texas had only two choices: annexation to the United States or closer economic ties to Great Britain, which extended formal diplomatic recognition to the republic and began buying cotton from Texas planters. Meanwhile, thousands more Americans poured into Texas. The population more than tripled between 1836 and 1845, from 40,000 to 150,000, and the enslaved black population grew even faster than the white population.

The Election of 1844

Leaders in both political parties hoped to keep the divisive Texas issue out of the 1844 presidential campaign. Whig Henry Clay (of Kentucky) and Democrat Martin Van Buren (of New York), the leading candidates for each party's nomination, agreed that adding Texas to the Union would be a mistake. Van Buren's southern supporters, including Andrew Jackson, abandoned him because he opposed annexation. At the Democratic Convention, annexationists, including Jackson, nominated James Knox Polk, former Speaker of the House

> James K. Polk elected president (1844)

Coon of 1840.

Coon of 1844.

ELECTION OF 1844 A political cartoon depicts the decline of the Whig party—represented by a raccoon—from 1810 to 1844. What used to be a plump, well-fed raccoon was now an emaciated animal with a fraction of the strength. **Based on the 1844 election, how accurate was this illustration's representation of the Whigs?**

and former governor of Tennessee. Like Tyler, Polk was an aggressive expansionist who wanted to make the United States a transcontinental global power. On the ninth ballot, he became the first "dark horse" (unexpected) candidate to win a major-party nomination. The Democrats' platform called for the annexation of both the Oregon Country and Texas.

The 1844 presidential election proved to be one of the most significant in American history. By promoting southern and western expansionism, the Democrats offered a winning strategy, one so popular that it forced Whig candidate Henry Clay to alter his position on Texas at the last minute. He now dropped his "objection to the annexation" if it could be achieved "without dishonor, without war, with the common consent of the Union, and upon just and fair terms."

Clay's change of heart on Texas shifted more anti-slavery votes to the new Liberty party (the anti-slavery party formed in 1840), which increased its count in the presidential election from about 7,000 in 1840 (the year it was founded) to more than 62,000 in 1844. In the western counties of New York, the Liberty party drew enough votes from Clay and the Whigs to give the state to Polk and the Democrats. Had he carried New York, Clay would have won the national election by seven electoral votes. Instead, Polk won a narrow national plurality of 38,000 popular votes (the first president since John Quincy Adams to win without a majority) but a clear majority of the Electoral College, 170–105. Clay had lost his third and last effort to win the presidency.

A frustrated Clay could not understand how he could have lost to Polk, a "third-rate" politician lacking natural leadership abilities. Yet Polk had been surprising people his whole career. Born near Charlotte, North Carolina, he graduated first in his class at the University of North Carolina, then moved to Tennessee, where he became a successful lawyer and planter, entered politics, and served fourteen years in Congress (four as Speaker of the House) and two years as governor. At age forty-nine, often called "Young Hickory" because of his admiration for Andrew Jackson, Polk was America's youngest president up to that time. Yet he worked so hard during his four years in the White House that his health failed, and he died in 1849, at fifty-three, just three months after leaving office.

The State of Texas

Texas, the political hot potato, joined the Union just before Polk became president. In his final months in office, President John Tyler had asked Congress to annex Texas by joint resolution, which required only a simple majority in each house rather than the two-thirds Senate vote needed to ratify a *treaty*. The resolution narrowly passed, with most Whigs opposed.

On March 1, 1845, in his final presidential action, President Tyler signed the resolution admitting Texas to the Union as the twenty-eighth state, and fifteenth slave state, on December 29, 1845. By 1850, the population—both white and black—had soared by almost 50 percent. (The census then did not include Native Americans.) By 1860, Texas was home to over 600,000 people, most of them southerners intent on growing cotton.

Texas becomes a state (1845)

Polk's Goals

Like Andrew Jackson, the slave-owning Polk sought to avoid any public discussion of the merits or future of slavery while focusing on his presidency's four major objectives, all of which he accomplished: (1) reduce tariffs on imports, (2) reestablish the Independent Treasury ("We need no national banks!"), (3) settle the Oregon boundary dispute with Britain, and (4) acquire California from Mexico.

Polk's top priority was territorial expansion. He wanted to add Oregon, California, and New Mexico to the Union. In keeping with long-standing Democratic beliefs, Polk wanted lower tariffs to allow more foreign goods to compete in the American marketplace and thereby help drive consumer prices down. Congress agreed by approving the Walker Tariff of 1846, named after Robert J. Walker, the secretary of the Treasury.

In the same year, Polk persuaded Congress to restore the Independent Treasury Act that President Martin Van Buren had signed into law in 1840 and the Whig-dominated Congress had repealed the next year. The act established independent treasury deposit offices separate from private or state banks to receive all federal government funds. The system was intended to replace the Second Bank of the United States, which Jackson had "killed," so as to offset the rapid growth of unregulated state banks, whose reckless lending practices had helped cause the depression of the late 1830s.

The new Independent Treasury established by Polk entrusted the federal government, rather than favored state banks, with the exclusive management of government funds and required that all disbursements be made in gold or silver, or paper currency backed by gold or silver.

Polk also sought to reverse Whig policy on the federal funding of roads and harbors ("internal improvements"). Twice he vetoed Whig-passed bills for federally funded infrastructure projects. His blows to Whig economic policies satisfied the slaveholding South but angered northerners who

TARIFF OF 1846 This political cartoon illustrates the public outcry—represented by a Quaker woman brandishing switches at Polk—against the Tariff of 1846, one of the lowest in the nation's history. **Why did Polk lower the tariffs so substantially?**

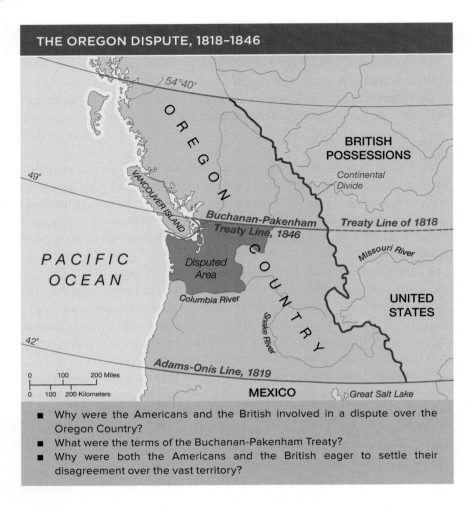

THE OREGON DISPUTE, 1818–1846

- Why were the Americans and the British involved in a dispute over the Oregon Country?
- What were the terms of the Buchanan-Pakenham Treaty?
- Why were both the Americans and the British eager to settle their disagreement over the vast territory?

wanted higher tariffs to protect their industries from British competition and westerners who wanted federally financed roads and harbors for their bustling new economies.

Oregon

Meanwhile, the dispute with Great Britain over the Oregon Country boundary heated up as expansionists insisted that Polk take the whole region rather than split it with the British. In his inaugural address, the new president said that the American claim to the enormous Oregon Country was "clear and unquestionable," and he was willing to go to the brink of war to achieve his goals. "If we do have war," Polk said, "it will not be our fault."

Fortunately for the reckless Polk, the British were not willing to risk war over a remote wilderness territory. In 1846, they suggested extending the border between the United States and British Canada westward to the Pacific coast along the 49th parallel. On June 15, James Buchanan, Polk's secretary of state, signed the Buchanan-Pakenham Treaty, which did just that.

Buchanan-Pakenham Treaty (1846): Oregon becomes American territory

The Mexican-American War

CORE OBJECTIVE

2. Examine the impact of the Mexican-American War on national politics.

The Outbreak of War

On March 6, 1845, two days after James K. Polk became president, the Mexican government broke off relations with the United States to protest the annexation of Texas. The president was willing to wage war against Mexico to acquire California, but he did not want Americans to fire the first shot. So Polk ordered several thousand U.S. troops under General Zachary Taylor to advance some 150 miles south of the Texas frontier and take up positions around Corpus Christi, near the Rio Grande. The U.S. troops were knowingly in disputed territory; Mexico recognized neither the American annexation of Texas nor the Rio Grande boundary.

On the evening of May 9, 1845, Polk learned that Mexican troops had attacked U.S. soldiers north of the Rio Grande. Eleven Americans were killed. Polk's scheme to provoke an attack had worked. In his war message to Congress, the president claimed that war was the only response to Mexican aggression. Mexico, he reported, "has invaded our territory, and shed American blood upon the American soil."

Westward expansionism and war fever

Congress quickly passed the war resolution and authorized the recruitment of 50,000 soldiers. The outbreak of fighting thrilled many Americans. "Let Us Go to War," screamed a New York newspaper. In the South, where expansion fever ran high, the war with Mexico was immensely popular. So many men rushed to volunteer that thousands had to be turned back. Eventually, 112,000 whites served in the war (blacks were banned).

Opposition to the War

In New England, however, there was much less enthusiasm for "Mr. Polk's War." Congressman John Quincy Adams, the former president, voted against the war resolution, calling it "a most unrighteous war." He claimed that the war's purpose was to extend slavery into new territories taken from Mexico. Many other New Englanders involved with the growing abolitionist movement denounced the war as the work of pro-slavery southerners. The fiery Boston abolitionist William Lloyd Garrison charged that the war against Mexico was one "of aggression, of invasion, of conquest." A few miles away, in Concord, Henry David Thoreau spent a night in jail rather than pay taxes that might help fund the war. Most Whigs across the North, including a young Illinois congressman named Abraham Lincoln, opposed the war, stressing that President Polk had maneuvered the Mexicans to attack. The United States, they argued, had no reason for placing its army in the disputed border region between Texas and Mexico.

ZACHARY TAYLOR Like Andrew Jackson, Taylor was a popular war hero whose public support paved the way to presidency.

Preparing for Battle

Regardless of the conflict's legitimacy, the United States was again ill prepared for a major war. At the outset, the regular army numbered barely over 7,000, in contrast to the Mexican force of 32,000. Before the war ended, the U.S. military had grown to almost 79,000 troops, many of whom were frontier toughs lacking uniforms, equipment, and discipline. Yet the American troops outfought the Mexican forces, which had their own problems with training, morale, supplies, and munitions.

The Mexican-American War would last two years, from March 1846 to April 1848, and would be fought on four fronts: southern Texas, central Mexico, New Mexico, and California. Early in the fighting, General Zachary Taylor's army scored two victories over Mexican forces north of the Rio Grande, at Palo Alto (May 8) and Resaca de la Palma (May 9). On May 18, Taylor's army crossed the Rio Grande and occupied Matamoros. These quick victories brought General Taylor, a Whig, instant popularity, and Polk agreed to public demands that Taylor be named the overall commander.

The Annexation of California

California becomes an American territory (1846)

Along the Pacific coast, the conquest of Mexican territory was under way before news of the start of the Mexican-American War had arrived. Near the end of 1845, John C. Frémont, an army officer and ardent expansionist known as "the Pathfinder" for having helped map the eastern half of the Oregon Trail, recruited a band of sixty frontiersmen and headed into California's Sacramento Valley, where they encouraged Americans to declare their independence from Mexico. They captured Sonoma on June 14, 1846, proclaimed the Republic of California, and hoisted a flag featuring a grizzly bear and star, a version of which would later become the state flag.

The Bear Flag Republic lasted only a month, however. In July, the commodore of the U.S. Pacific Fleet, having heard of the outbreak of hostilities, sent troops ashore to raise the American flag and claim California as part of the United States.

Before the end of July, another navy officer, Robert F. Stockton, led the American occupation of Santa Barbara and Los Angeles, on the southern California coast. By mid-August 1846, Mexican resistance had evaporated. On August 17, Stockton declared himself governor, with Frémont as military governor in the north.

U.S. Army takes New Mexico (1846)

At the same time, another American military expedition headed for New Mexico. On August 18, General Stephen Kearny and a small army entered Santa Fe. Kearny then led 300 men westward toward southern California, where they joined Stockton's forces at San Diego. They took control of Los Angeles on January 10, 1847, and the remaining Mexican forces surrendered.

War in Northern Mexico

Both California and New Mexico had been taken from Mexican control before General Zachary Taylor fought his first major battle in northern Mexico. In September 1846, Taylor's army assaulted the fortified city of Monterrey, which surrendered after a five-day siege. Then the old dictator General Antonio López de Santa Anna, forced out of power in 1845, got word to Polk from his exile in Cuba that he would end the war if he were allowed to return. Polk assured the Mexican leader that the U.S. government would pay well for any territory taken from Mexico.

In August 1846, on Polk's orders, Santa Anna was permitted to return to Mexico. But the crafty Santa Anna had lied. Soon he was again president of Mexico and in command of the Mexican army. As it turned out, however, he was much more talented at raising armies than leading them in battle. In October 1846, Santa Anna prepared to attack the U.S. Army. When the Mexican general invited the outnumbered Americans to surrender, Zachary Taylor responded, "Tell him to go to hell."

That launched the hard-fought Battle of Buena Vista (February 22–23, 1847), in northern Mexico. Both sides claimed victory, but the Mexicans lost five times as many killed and wounded as the Americans. However, one of the U.S. soldiers killed was Henry Clay Jr., "the pride and hope" of his famous father who had lost to Polk in the 1844 presidential campaign. The elder Clay, devastated by his son's death, condemned Polk's "unnecessary" war of "offensive aggression" and opposed any effort to use the war as a means of acquiring Mexican territory "for the purpose of introducing slavery into it."

Meanwhile, the long-planned American assault on Mexico City had begun on March 9, 1847, when General Winfield Scott's army landed on the beaches south of Veracruz and began marching toward the Mexican capital. After a series of battles in which they overwhelmed the Mexican defenses, U.S. forces entered Mexico City on September 13. News of the victory thrilled American expansionists. The editor John O'Sullivan, who had coined the phrase "manifest destiny," shouted, "More, More, More! Why not take all of Mexico?"

> The Battle of Buena Vista (1847)

FALL OF MEXICO CITY General Winfield Scott formally enters Mexico City upon its capture on September 14, 1847.

The Treaty of Guadalupe Hidalgo

After the fall of Mexico City, Santa Anna fled the country. Peace talks began on January 2, 1848. By the **Treaty of Guadalupe Hidalgo**, signed on February 2, Mexico gave up all claims to Texas north of the Rio Grande and transferred control of the Mexican territories that would eventually become the states of California, Arizona, New Mexico—and significant parts of what would become Colorado, Utah, Wyoming and Nevada. In return for a half-million square miles of territory—more than half of Mexico—the United States agreed to pay $15 million. The Senate ratified the treaty on March 10, 1848.

The War's Legacies

The United States lost 1,733 soldiers from combat in the Mexican-American War. Another 4,152 were wounded, and far more—11,550—died of disease. The war remains the deadliest in American history in terms of the percentage of soldiers killed. Out of every 1,000 U.S. soldiers in Mexico, some 110 died. The next highest death rate would be in the Civil War, with 65 dead out of every 1,000 participants. As a result of the conflict, the United States acquired the future states of California, Nevada, and Utah and parts of New Mexico, Arizona, Colorado, and Wyoming. Except for a small addition made by the Gadsden Purchase of 1853, these annexations rounded out the continental United States and nearly doubled its size.

The victory in Mexico also helped end the long economic depression. As the years passed, however, the Mexican-American War was increasingly seen as a shameful war of conquest and imperialistic plunder directed by a president bent on territorial expansion for the sake of slavery. Ulysses S. Grant, who fought in the war, later called it "one of the most unjust wars ever waged by a stronger against a weaker nation."

Slavery in the Territories

CORE **OBJECTIVE**

3. Describe how the federal government tried to resolve the issue of slavery in the western territories during the 1850s.

The Wilmot Proviso

At midcentury, political storm clouds were forming over the fate of slavery. The United States was a powerful nation, but, as Henry Clay said, it was an "unhappy country" torn by the "uproar, confusion, and menace" caused by the deepening agony over slavery. Without intending to, the United States had developed two quite different societies, one in the North and the other in the South, and the two sections increasingly disagreed over the nation's future. In 1833, Andrew Jackson had predicted that southerners "intend to blow up a storm on the slave question." He added that pro-slavery firebrands like John C. Calhoun "would do any act to destroy this union and form a southern confederacy bounded, north, by the Potomac River." By 1848, Jackson's prediction seemed close to reality.

Treaty of Guadalupe Hidalgo (1848) Treaty between United States and Mexico that ended the Mexican-American War.

The Mexican-American War was less than three months old when it sparked a new political conflict over slavery. On August 8, 1846, an obscure Democratic congressman from Pennsylvania, David Wilmot, delivered a speech to the House of Representatives in which he endorsed the earlier annexation of Texas as a slave state. Yet slavery had been abolished in the rest of Mexico. If any *new* Mexican territory should be acquired as a result of the war, he declared, slavery would be banned there, in part because he and other northerners were "jealous of the power of the South" and did not want any new states joining the slave-state alliance.

The proposed **Wilmot Proviso** reignited the debate over the westward extension of slavery. The issue had been lurking for a generation, ever since the Missouri controversy of 1819–1821. The Missouri Compromise had provided a temporary solution by protecting slavery in states where it already existed but not allowing it in newly acquired territories north of the 36th parallel. Now, with the addition of the territories taken from Mexico, the stage was set for an even more explosive confrontation over slavery.

In 1846, the House of Representatives approved the Wilmot Proviso, but the Senate balked. President Polk dismissed the proviso as "mischievous and foolish." He convinced Wilmot to withhold his amendment from any bill dealing with the annexation of Mexican territory. By then, however, others were ready to take up the cause. In one form or another, Wilmot's idea of restricting the expansion of slavery would frame the perennial debate in Congress over the expansion of slavery. Abraham Lincoln recalled that

Wilmot Proviso (1846)
Proposal by Congressman David Wilmot, a Pennsylvania Democrat, to prohibit slavery in any lands acquired in the Mexican-American War.

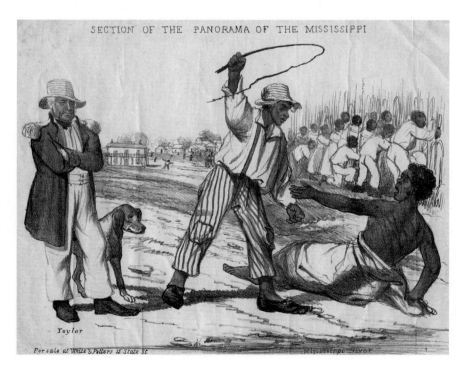

SECTION OF THE PANORAMA OF THE MISSISSIPPI

Taylor

For sale at White & Potters 18 State St.

Mississippi River

THE WILMOT PROVISO Taylor would refuse to veto the proviso as president, even though he was a slave owner. This political cartoon, "Old Zack at Home," points out his seeming hypocrisy.

during his one term as a congressman, in 1847–1849, he voted for it "as good as forty times."

Senator John C. Calhoun of South Carolina, meanwhile, countered Wilmot's proviso with a pro-slavery plan, which he presented to the Senate on February 19, 1847. Calhoun insisted that Wilmot's effort to exclude slaves from territories acquired from Mexico would violate the Fifth Amendment, which forbids Congress to deprive any person of life, liberty, or property without due process of law. Slaves, he argued, were *property*.

By this clever stroke of logic, Calhoun turned the Bill of Rights into a guarantee of slavery. Senator Thomas Hart Benton of Missouri, himself a slaveholder but also a nationalist eager to calm sectional tensions, found in Calhoun's stance a set of dangerous abstractions "leading to no result." Wilmot and Calhoun between them, he said, had fashioned a pair of scissors. Neither blade alone would cut very well, but joined together they could sever the nation in two.

Popular Sovereignty

Benton and others tried to deflect the brewing conflict over slavery by suggesting that Congress simply extend the Missouri Compromise line, dividing free and slave territory at the latitude of 36°30′, all the way to the Pacific Ocean. Senator Lewis Cass of Michigan suggested a different solution: that the citizens of a territory "regulate their own internal concerns in their own way," like the citizens of a state. Such an approach would take the issue of slavery in new territories out of Congress and put it in the hands of those directly affected. "**Popular sovereignty**," as Cass's idea was called, appealed to many Americans eager to protect states' rights.

Polk had promised to serve only one term, and, having accomplished his major goals, he refused to run again in 1848. Cass won the Democratic presidential nomination, but the party refused to endorse his "popular sovereignty" plan. Instead, it simply denied the power of Congress to interfere with slavery in the states and criticized all efforts by anti-slavery activists to bring the question before Congress.

The Whigs devised an even more ingenious strategy in the process of selecting a presidential candidate. Once again, as in 1840, they passed over their party leader, Henry Clay, in favor of General Zachary Taylor, the hero of the Mexican-American War. Taylor, raised in Kentucky, now owned a Louisiana plantation with more than 100 slaves. Yet he was an unusual slaveholder in that he vigorously opposed the extension of slavery into new western territories.

The Free-Soil Coalition

popular sovereignty Legal concept by which the white male settlers in a U.S. territory would vote to decide whether to permit slavery.

As it had done in the 1840 election, the Whig party in 1848 offered no platform in an effort to avoid the divisive issue of slavery. The anti-slavery crusade was not easily silenced, however. Americans who worried about slavery but could not endorse outright abolition could support banning slavery from the western territories. As a result, "free soil" in the new western territories became the rallying cry for a new political party: the Free-Soil coalition, which focused on the single issue of preventing the spread of slavery.

The **Free-Soil party** attracted three major groups: northern Democrats opposed to slavery, anti-slavery northern Whigs, and members of the abolitionist Liberty party, created in 1840. In 1848, at a convention in Buffalo, New York, Free-Soilers nominated former Democratic president Martin Van Buren as their candidate. The party's platform stressed that slavery would not be allowed in the western territories.

The new anti-slavery party infuriated John C. Calhoun and other southern Democrats. Calhoun called Van Buren a "bold, unscrupulous, and vindictive demagogue—a characterization equally suited to Calhoun." The Free-Soilers split the Democratic vote enough to throw New York to the Whig Zachary Taylor, and they split the Whig vote enough to give Ohio to the Democrat Lewis Cass. But Van Buren's 291,000 third-party votes lagged well behind the totals of 1,361,000 for Taylor and 1,222,000 for Cass. Taylor won with 163–127 electoral votes.

The California Gold Rush

Meanwhile, a new issue had emerged to complicate the debate over slavery in the western territories. On January 24, 1848, on the property of John Sutter along the south fork of the American River (Sutter's Fort), a group of white and Indian workers building a sawmill discovered gold in the Mexican province of California, which nine days later would be the "great prize" transferred to the United States through the treaty ending the Mexican-American War.

Word of the gold strike spread feverishly after President James K. Polk confirmed the news in his 1849 State of the Union address, reporting that there was an "extraordinary abundance of gold" to be had in California. In 1849, nearly 100,000 Americans, mostly young men, set off for California, eager to find riches, freedom, and a second chance; by 1854, the number would top 300,000. Tens of thousands more came from across the world—Central and South America, Canada, Australia, Asia, and Europe. Those infected with gold fever were fed by hope and fueled by greed—they sold businesses, quit jobs, left farms, sold their belongings, borrowed money, and deserted wives and children—all in greedy pursuit of instant riches. "We are on the brink of an Age of Gold," gushed Horace Greeley, editor of the *New York Tribune*. So many men ("forty-niners") left New England as part of the **California gold rush** that it would be years before the region's gender ratio evened out again, leading some women to form same-sex partnerships in what the novelist Henry James called "Boston marriages."

The gold rush was the greatest mass migration in American history—and one of the most significant events in the first half of the nineteenth century. Between 1851 and 1855, California produced almost half the world's output of gold. The infusion of California gold into the U.S. economy triggered a surge of prosperity and a revolution in commercial affairs that eventually would help finance the Union military effort in the Civil War. The Gold Rush

Free-Soil party A political coalition created in 1848 that opposed the expansion of slavery into the new western territories.

California gold rush (1849) A massive migration of gold hunters, mostly young men, who transformed the national economy after massive amounts of gold were discovered in northern California.

also shifted the nation's center of gravity westward, spurred the construction of railroads and telegraph lines, and excited dreams of an American commercial empire in east Asia.

At the same time, the influx of Americans into California proved deadly for the Native Americans and their ancestral lands. In 1850, the new California state legislature allowed whites to force "unemployed" Indians to work for them in exchange for food and clothing. Miners pushed them out of the gold diggings; those who resisted were killed. During the early 1850s, the Indian population in California plummeted by over 80 percent. If infectious disease did not kill them, white settlers did. California's Indians, North Carolinian Hinton Rowan Helper predicted, "must melt away before the white man like snow before a spring sun. They are too indolent to work, too cowardly to fight."

The gold rush also transformed the sleepy coastal village of San Francisco into the nation's largest city west of Chicago. But it was an unusual city. At one point during the height of the gold rush, men outnumbered women in San Francisco 50 to 1, while across the new state of California it was 8 to 1. Luzena Wilson, a gold-seeking pioneer, commented that the men in the camps "stared at her as a strange creature" because she was the only woman they had seen in months. The few women who dared to enter the camps placed a high price on their companionship. One placed a brutally candid ad for a husband in a local newspaper: "Her age is none of your business. She is neither handsome nor a fright, yet an *old* man need *not* apply, nor any who have not a little more education than she has, and a great deal more gold, for there must be $20,000 settled on her [paid] before she will" marry.

In just two years, San Francisco grew from a small coastal village of 800 to a bustling city of 20,000, its spacious harbor clogged by a forest of ship masts. Half the ships that arrived in San Francisco never left, their crews having deserted and rushed to the mining towns in search of gold. Each day the thriving metropolis reported thirty new wooden houses, two murders, and at least one fire, while boasting about its 500 saloons. Sacramento, closer to the diggings, grew even faster as the staging area for the northern mines. New business enterprises—saloons, taverns, restaurants, laundries, general stores—emerged to serve the burgeoning population of miners, including one dedicated to the production of sturdy denim trousers made of sailcloth, with their pockets reinforced by copper rivets. The blue jeans, known to this day as Levi's, were developed by the German-Jewish immigrant Levi Strauss.

The forty-niners included people from every social class and every state and territory, as well as local Indians and slaves brought by their owners. "Never was there such a gold-thirsty race of men brought together," a Californian said of the waves of prospectors flowing into the newest American territory. Louis Manigault, the son of a South Carolina rice planter, reported that California was "filled with offcasts and exiles from almost every nation, the true and perfect scum of the Earth. Never have I seen such a heteroge-

SAN FRANCISCO A view of San Francisco during 1849 shows the city in the midst of rapid growth. The Bay is crowded with ships, and a blend of tents and newly-constructed buildings dot the coastline.

neous mixture of the human race!" Life in the mining camps, he noted, "was not safe, and almost every paper informed us of some dreadful murder, or horrible crime—everyone was armed."

Mining Life

The miners were mostly unmarried young men of varied ethnic and cultural backgrounds, including some 20,000 Chinese. Few were interested in staying in California; they wanted to strike it rich and return home. Mining camps thus sprang up like mushrooms and disappeared almost as rapidly. As soon as rumors of a new strike made the rounds, miners converged on the area; when no more gold could be found, they picked up and moved on.

The mining camps and shantytowns may have had colorful names—Ben Hur, Grizzly Flats, Whiskey Flat, Lousy Ravine, Petticoat Slide, Piety Hill—but they were raw, dirty, lawless, and dangerous places dotted with small tents, shanties, or cabins housing communities of adventurous strangers focused on gaining gold by hook or crook.

California—exuberant, expansive, and democratic—liberated energies, greed, and rapid-fire violence. Calaveras County experienced fourteen murders in a single week. Vigilante justice prevailed. "In the short space of twenty-four days," one miner reported, "we have had murders, fearful accidents, bloody deaths, a mob, whippings, a hanging, an attempt at suicide, and a fatal duel." One miner witnessed eight murders. If murderers were caught, many of them were lynched on the spot.

The gold rush for most forty-niners brought more frustration and failure than wealth. Within six months of arriving in California in 1849, one gold seeker in every five was dead. The goldfields and mining towns were so dangerous that insurance companies refused to provide coverage. Suicides were common, and disease and drunkenness were rampant.

Women were as rare in the mining camps as liquor and guns were abundant. In 1850, less than 8 percent of California's population was female. The few women who dared to live in the camps could demand a premium for their

GOLD MINERS Chinese immigrants and white settlers mine for gold in the Auburn Ravine of California in 1856. **What were living and working conditions like in the mining camps?**

work as cooks, laundresses, entertainers, and prostitutes.

In the mining camps, white Americans often looked with disdain upon the Hawaiians, Hispanics, African Americans, and Chinese, who were usually employed as wage laborers to help in the panning process, separating gold from sand and gravel. But whites focused their contempt on the Indians; it was not a crime to kill Indians or work them to death.

California Statehood

California was important for reasons other than gold. New president Zachary Taylor, who opposed the expansion of slavery into new territories and states, decided in 1849 to use California's request for statehood to end the stalemate in Congress over slavery. Why not make California and New Mexico free states immediately, he argued, and thereby bypass the volatile issue of slavery? Californians, however, in desperate need of organized government, were ahead of him. By December 1849, without consulting Congress, they had put a free-state (no-slavery) government into operation. New Mexico responded more slowly, but by 1850 Americans there had also adopted a free-state constitution.

The Compromise of 1850

In his annual message on December 4, 1849, President Taylor endorsed immediate statehood for California and urged Congress to avoid injecting slavery into the issue. The new Congress, however, was in no mood for simple solutions. Irate southerners threatened to leave the Union if Taylor brought California and New Mexico in as free states. "I avow before this House and country, and in the presence of the living God," shouted Robert Toombs, a Georgia congressman, "that if by your legislation you seek to drive us [slaveholders] from the territories of California and New Mexico . . . and to abolish slavery in this District [of Columbia] . . . I am for disunion."

The spotlight then fell on the Senate, where an all-star cast—Henry Clay, John C. Calhoun, and Daniel Webster (all of whom would die within two years), with William H. Seward, Stephen A. Douglas, and Jefferson Davis in supporting roles—staged one of the great dramas of American politics: the **Compromise of 1850**, a series of resolutions intended to reduce the tensions between North and South and thereby save the Union.

The Great Debate

With southerners threatening secession, congressional leaders in early 1850 again turned to Clay, now seventy-two, who, as Abraham Lincoln said, was "regarded by all, as *the* man for the crisis." Unless some compromise could be

Compromise of 1850 A package of five bills presented to the Congress by Henry Clay intended to avoid secession or civil war by reducing tensions between North and South over the status of slavery.

CLAY'S COMPROMISE (1850)
Warning against an impending sectional conflict, Henry Clay outlines his plan for "compromise and harmony" on the Senate floor.

found, Clay warned, a "furious" civil war would fracture the Union. On January 29, 1850, having gained Webster's support, Clay presented to Congress eight resolutions meant to settle the "controversy between the free and slave states, growing out of the subject of slavery."

Clay proposed to (1) admit California as a free state; (2) organize the territories of New Mexico and Utah without restrictions on slavery, allowing the residents to decide the issue for themselves; (3) deny Texas its extreme claim to much of New Mexico; (4) compensate Texas by having the federal government pay the pre-annexation Texas debts; (5) retain slavery in the District of Columbia but abolish the sale of slaves in the nation's capital; (6) adopt a more effective federal fugitive slave law; and (7) deny congressional authority to interfere with the interstate slave trade. His complex cluster of proposals became in substance the Compromise of 1850 but only after seven months of negotiations punctuated by the greatest debates in congressional history.

On March 4, a grim John C. Calhoun, the uncompromising defender of slavery, left his sickbed to sit in the Senate chamber and listen to a colleague read his defiant rejection of Clay's proposal. The South, he explained, simply needed Congress to protect the rights of slave owners to take their "property" into the new territories. Otherwise, Calhoun warned, the "cords which bind" the Union would be severed. The southern states would leave the Union (secede) and form their own national government.

Three days later, Calhoun, who would die in just three weeks, returned to the Senate to hear Daniel Webster speak. "I wish to speak today," Webster began, "not as a Massachusetts man, not as a Northern man, but as an

THE COMPROMISE OF 1850

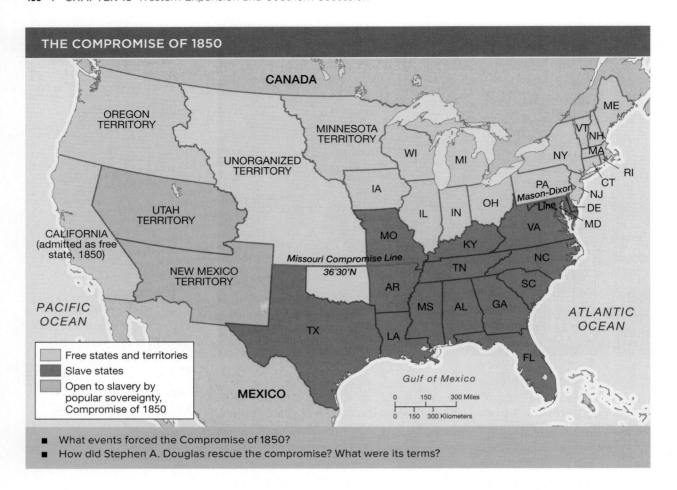

- What events forced the Compromise of 1850?
- How did Stephen A. Douglas rescue the compromise? What were its terms?

American. . . . I speak today for the preservation of the Union." He criticized extremists on both sides and suggested that some new territories should become slave states and others free states.

Webster's evenhanded speech was savaged by northerners for betraying the region's anti-slavery ideals. On March 11, William Seward, the Whig senator from New York, declared that *any* compromise with slavery was "radically wrong and essentially vicious." There was, he said, "a *higher law* than the Constitution," and it demanded the abolition of slavery.

Compromise Efforts

On July 4, 1850, supporters of the Union staged a grand rally at the base of the unfinished Washington Monument in Washington, D.C. President Zachary Taylor went to hear the speeches and lingered in the heat and humidity. Five days later, he died of a violent stomach disorder, likely caused by tainted food or water.

Taylor's shocking death actually bolstered the chances of a compromise in Congress, for his successor, Vice President Millard Fillmore, a New Yorker, supported Clay's proposals. It was a striking reversal: Taylor, the Louisiana slaveholder, had been ready to make war on his native South; Fillmore, who southerners thought opposed slavery, was ready to make peace.

At this point, young senator Stephen A. Douglas of Illinois, a rising star in the Democratic party who was friendly to the South, rescued Clay's faltering plan. Short and stocky, brash and brilliant, Douglas suggested that the best way to approve Clay's "comprehensive scheme" was to break it up into separate proposals and vote on each of them, one at a time.

The plan worked. By September 20, President Fillmore had signed the last of the measures into law, claiming that they represented a "final" solution to sectional tensions over slavery. True, the Compromise of 1850 had defused an explosive situation and settled each of the major points at issue, but it only postponed secession and civil war for ten years.

In its final version, the Compromise of 1850 included the following elements: (1) California entered the Union as a free state, ending forever the old balance of free and slave states; (2) the Texas–New Mexico Act made New Mexico a separate territory and set the Texas state boundary at its present location (in return for giving up its claims to much of New Mexico, Texas was paid $10 million, which secured payment of the state's debt); (3) the Utah Act set up the Utah Territory and gave the territorial legislature authority over "all rightful subjects of legislation," including slavery; (4) a Fugitive Slave Act required the federal government and northern states to help capture and return runaway slaves to the South; and (5) as a gesture to anti-slavery groups, the public sale of slaves, but not slavery itself, was abolished in the District of Columbia.

The Fugitive Slave Act

The **Fugitive Slave Act** was the most controversial element of the Compromise of 1850. It did more than strengthen the hand of slave catchers; it sought to recover slaves who had already escaped. The law also unwittingly enabled slave traders to kidnap free blacks in northern "free" states, claiming that they were runaway slaves. In addition, the new law required citizens to help locate and capture runaways.

Abolitionists fumed. "This filthy enactment was made in the nineteenth century, by people who could read and write," Ralph Waldo Emerson marveled in his diary. He urged people to break the new law.

In late October 1850, two slave catchers from Georgia arrived in Boston, determined to use the new federal Fugitive Slave Act to recapture William and Ellen Craft, husband-and-wife cabinetmakers. Abolitionists mobilized to prevent the Crafts from being seized by the "man stealers." After five days, the slave catchers gave up and returned to Georgia.

THREATS TO FREE BLACKS This 1851 notice warned free blacks about police and others who could easily, under the new Fugitive Slave Act, kidnap and sell them back into slavery. **What was the general reaction to the Fugitive Slave Act among northern abolitionists?**

Fugitive Slave Act (1850) A part of the Compromise of 1850 that authorized federal officials to help capture and then return escaped slaves to their owners without trials.

Upon learning of the incident, President Fillmore assured the South that he would use federal troops, if necessary, to return the Crafts to Georgia. But he was too late. Abolitionists had spirited the Crafts to safety in Great Britain. Theodore Parker, a prominent white Boston minister and abolitionist, wrote to President Fillmore explaining the willingness of his congregation to engage in civil disobedience in order to protect the Crafts, who were church members: "You cannot think that I am to stand by and see my own church carried off to slavery and do nothing to hinder such a wrong."

There were relatively few such incidents, however. In the first six years of the Fugitive Slave Act, only 3 runaways were forcibly rescued from slave catchers. On the other hand, probably fewer than 200 were returned to bondage during those years. The mere existence of the Fugitive Slave Act, however, infuriated many northern abolitionists and prompted several of them to advocate violence. "The only way to make the Fugitive Slave Law a dead letter," Frederick Douglass threatened, "is to make half-a-dozen or more dead kidnappers." In Springfield, Massachusetts, a fiery abolitionist named John Brown formed an armed band of African Americans to attack slave catchers. Such efforts led Horace Greeley, the prominent New York newspaper editor, to write that the Fugitive Slave Act was proving to be "a very bad investment for slaveholders" because it was creating such a backlash against slavery itself throughout the northern states.

135,000 SETS, 270,000 VOLUMES SOLD.

UNCLE TOM'S CABIN

FOR SALE HERE.

AN EDITION FOR THE MILLION, COMPLETE IN 1 Vol. PRICE 37 1-2 CENTS.
"   "   IN GERMAN. IN 1 Vol. PRICE 50 CENTS.
"   "   IN 2 Vols., CLOTH, 6 PLATES, PRICE $1.50.
SUPERB ILLUSTRATED EDITION. IN 1 Vol. WITH 153 ENGRAVINGS,
PRICES FROM $2.50 TO $5.00.

The Greatest Book of the Age.

"THE GREATEST BOOK OF THE AGE" *Uncle Tom's Cabin*, as this advertisement indicated, was an influential best seller.

Uncle Tom's Cabin

During the 1850s, anti-slavery advocates gained a powerful new weapon in the form of Harriet Beecher Stowe's best-selling novel, *Uncle Tom's Cabin; or Life among the Lowly* (1852). The pious Stowe epitomized the powerful religious underpinnings of the abolitionist movement. While raising six children in Cincinnati, Ohio, during the 1830s and 1840s, she helped runaway slaves who had crossed the Ohio River from Kentucky.

Like many anti-slavery activists, Stowe detested the Fugitive Slave Act. In the spring of 1850, having moved to Maine, she began writing *Uncle Tom's Cabin*. "The time has come," she wrote, "when even a woman or a child who can speak a word for freedom and humanity is bound to speak."

Uncle Tom's Cabin was a smashing success. Within two days, the first printing had sold out, and by the end of its first year, it had sold 300,000 copies in the United States and more than a million in Great Britain. Soon there was a children's version and a traveling theater production. By 1855, it was "the most popular novel of our day."

Uncle Tom's Cabin depicted a combination of improbable saints and sinners, crude stereotypes, impossibly virtuous black victims, and melodramatic escapades involving fugitive slaves. The novel revealed how the brutal realities of slavery harmed everyone associated with it. Abolitionist leader Frederick Douglass, a former slave himself, said that *Uncle Tom's Cabin* was like "a flash" that lit "a million camp fires in front of the embattled host of slavery." The book incensed slaveholders, who called Stowe that "wretch in petti-coats." One of them mailed her a parcel containing the severed ear of a dis-obedient slave.

The Election of 1852

In 1852, the Democrats chose boyishly handsome Franklin Pierce of New Hampshire as their presidential candidate; their platform endorsed the Compromise of 1850. For their part, the Whigs repudiated the lackluster Millard Fillmore, who had faithfully supported the Compromise of 1850, and chose General Winfield Scott, another hero of the Mexican-American War and a Virginia native.

Scott, however, was an inept campaigner and carried only Tennessee, Kentucky, Massachusetts, and Vermont. Pierce overwhelmed him in the Electoral College, 254–42, although the popular vote was fairly close: 1.6 million–1.4 million. The third-party Free-Soilers mustered only 156,000 votes for John P. Hale, in contrast to the 291,000 they had tallied for Van Buren in 1848.

The forty-eight-year-old Pierce had fought in the Mexican-American War and was, like James Polk, touted as another Andrew Jackson despite his undistinguished record as a congressman and senator. He eagerly promoted western expansion, even if it meant adding more slave states to the Union, but he also acknowledged that the nation had recently survived a "perilous crisis" that was defused by the Compromise of 1850. He urged both North and South to avoid aggravating the other.

Pierce, the youngest president to date, was timid and indecisive, unable to unite the warring factions of his own party. By the end of his first year in office, Democratic leaders had decided he was a failure. By trying to be all things to all people, Pierce was labeled a "doughface": a "Northern man with Southern principles."

The Kansas-Nebraska Crisis

During the mid–nineteenth century, Americans discovered the vast markets of Asia. As the amount of trade with China and Japan grew, merchants and manufacturers called for a transcontinental railroad line connecting the eastern seaboard with the Pacific coast to facilitate both the flow of com-merce with Asia and the settlement of the western territories. Those pro-moting the building of a railroad linking the far-flung regions of the new United States did not realize that the issue would renew sectional rivalries and reignite the debate over the westward extension of slavery.

In 1852 and 1853, Congress debated several proposals for a transconti-nental rail line. Secretary of War Jefferson Davis of Mississippi favored a

Kansas-Nebraska Act (1854)
Controversial legislation that created two new territories taken from Native Americans, Kansas and Nebraska, where resident males would decide whether slavery would be allowed (popular sovereignty).

southern route across the territories acquired from Mexico. Senator Stephen A. Douglas of Illinois insisted that Chicago be the transcontinental railroad's Midwest hub. To promote that idea, he urged Congress in 1854 to pass the **Kansas-Nebraska Act** so that the vast territory west of Missouri and Iowa could be settled.

New western territories, however, raised again the worrisome question of whether they should allow slavery. To win the support of southern legislators, Douglas championed the principle of "popular sovereignty," whereby voters in each new territory could decide themselves whether to allow slavery. It was a clever way to get around the 1820 Missouri Compromise, which excluded slaves north of the 36th parallel, where Kansas and Nebraska were located.

Southerners demanded even more, so Douglas, even though he knew it would "raise a hell of a storm," supported the formal repeal of the Missouri Compromise and the creation of *two* new territorial governments rather than one: Kansas, west of Missouri, and Nebraska, which then included the Dakotas, west of Iowa and Minnesota. In 1854, Douglas and the Democrats pushed through the Kansas-Nebraska Act by a vote of 37–14 in the Senate and 113–100 in the House. The anti-slavery faction in the Congress, mostly Whigs, had been crushed.

Douglas's passion for the new rail line backfired, however. He had blundered politically, damaging his presidential chances and setting the country on the road to civil war by pushing the slavery issue back to the forefront of national concerns. In abandoning the long-standing Missouri Compromise boundary line and allowing territorial voters to decide the issue of slavery, Douglas unwittingly inflamed the tensions between North and South.

CORE **OBJECTIVE**

4. Analyze the appeal of the Republican party to northern voters and how it led to Abraham Lincoln's victory in the 1860 presidential contest.

Anti-Catholic "Know-Nothings"

New Republican party (1854)

The Emergence of the Republican Party

The dispute over the Kansas-Nebraska Act destroyed the already weakened Whig party. Northern Whigs now gravitated toward two new parties. One was the American ("Know-Nothing") party, which had emerged in opposition to the surge of mostly Catholic immigrants from Ireland and Germany. The anti-Catholic "Know-Nothings" embraced nativism (opposition to foreign immigrants) and proposed that citizenship be denied to newcomers. In the early 1850s, Know-Nothings won several local elections in Massachusetts and New York.

The other new party, the Republicans, attracted even more northern Whigs. The party coalesced in 1854 when the anti-slavery "conscience Whigs" split from the southern pro-slavery "cotton Whigs" and joined with independent Democrats and Free-Soilers to form a new Republican party whose members initially stood for only one principle: the exclusion of slavery from the western territories.

A young Illinois congressman named Abraham Lincoln made the transition from being a Whig to a Republican. He said that the passage of Douglas's Kansas-Nebraska Act angered him "as he had never been before" and transformed his views on slavery. Unless the North mobilized to stop the efforts of pro-slavery southerners, Lincoln believed, the future of the Union was endangered. From that moment on, Lincoln focused his career on reversing the Kansas-Nebraska Act and preventing the extension of slavery into any new territories.

"Bleeding Kansas"

The passage of the Kansas-Nebraska Act soon placed Kansas at the center of the increasingly violent debate over slavery. While Nebraska would become a free state, Kansas was up for grabs. According to the Kansas-Nebraska Act, the people living in the Kansas Territory would decide whether to allow slavery. This is what "popular sovereignty" meant. The law, however, said nothing about *when* Kansans would decide about slavery, so each side tried to gain political control of the 50-million-acre territory.

Rival groups for and against slavery recruited emigrants to move to the Kansas territory. "Every slaveholding state," said an observer, "is furnishing men and money to fasten slavery upon this glorious land, by means no matter how foul." When Kansas's first federal governor arrived in 1854, he scheduled an election for a territorial legislature in 1855. On Election Day, thousands of "border ruffians" from Missouri crossed into Kansas, illegally elected pro-slavery legislators, and vowed to kill every "God-damned abolitionist in the Territory."

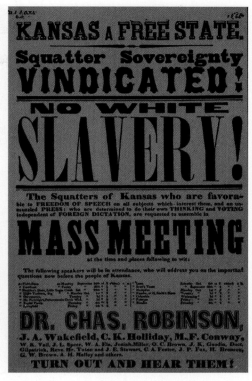

KANSAS A FREE STATE This broadside advertises a series of mass meetings in Kansas in support of the free-state cause, based on the principle of "squatter" or popular sovereignty.

The governor denounced the fraudulent vote but did nothing to alter the results, for fear of being killed himself. The territorial legislature expelled its few anti-slavery members and declared that the territory would be open to slavery.

Outraged free-state advocates in Kansas spurned this "bogus" government and elected their own delegates to a constitutional convention that met in Topeka in 1855. Delegates drafted a new state constitution excluding slavery and applied for statehood. By 1856, a free-state "governor" and "legislature" operating in Topeka; thus, there were two illegal governments in the Kansas Territory. And soon there was a civil war in Kansas, which journalists called "**Bleeding Kansas**."

In May 1856, a pro-slavery mob of Missourians and Alabamans decided to invade the free-state town of Lawrence, Kansas. David Atchison, a former U.S. senator from Missouri, urged the southern raiders not to stop fighting "until every spark of free-state, free-speech, free-niggers, or free in any shape is quenched out of Kansas." As they prepared to teach the "damned abolitionists a southern lesson," Atchison yelled: "Boys, this is the happiest day of my life!" The mob then rampaged through the town, destroying the newspaper, burning the governor's house, and demolishing the Free-State Hotel.

Bleeding Kansas (1856) A series of violent conflicts in the Kansas Territory between anti-slavery and pro-slavery factions over the status of slavery.

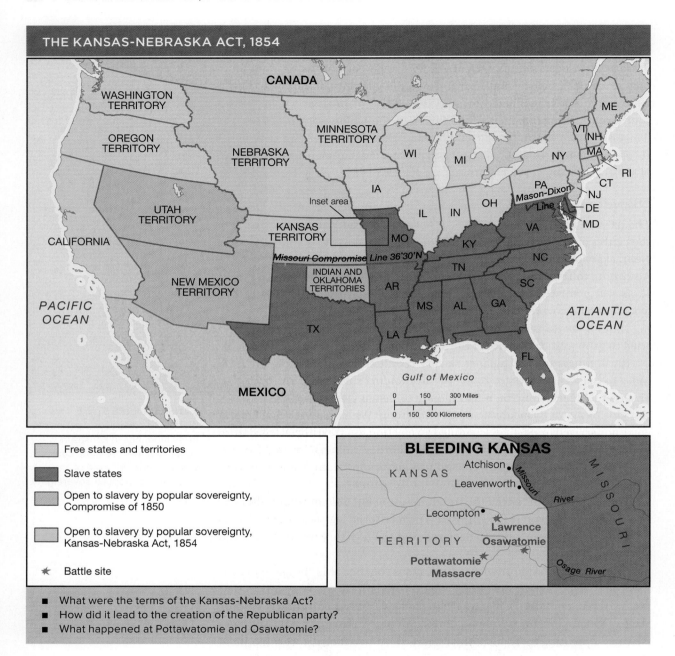

THE KANSAS-NEBRASKA ACT, 1854

Legend:

- Free states and territories
- Slave states
- Open to slavery by popular sovereignty, Compromise of 1850
- Open to slavery by popular sovereignty, Kansas-Nebraska Act, 1854
- ✱ Battle site

BLEEDING KANSAS

- What were the terms of the Kansas-Nebraska Act?
- How did it lead to the creation of the Republican party?
- What happened at Pottawatomie and Osawatomie?

The "Sack of Lawrence" ignited the vengeance of a passionate white abolitionist named John Brown. The son of fervent Ohio Calvinists who taught their children that life was a crusade against sin, the grim, humorless Brown believed that Christians must "break the jaws of the wicked," and that the wickedest Americans were those who owned and traded slaves. Upon meeting Brown, many declared him crazy; those who supported his efforts thought he was a saint. He was a little of both.

By the mid-1850s, the fifty-five-year-old Brown, the father of twenty children, had left his home in Springfield, Massachusetts, to become a holy warrior against slavery. In his view, blacks in the United States deserved both liberty and full social equality. A newspaper reporter said that the selfless Brown was a "strange" and "iron-willed" old man with a "fiery nature and a cold temper, and a cool head—a volcano beneath a covering of snow."

Two days after the attack on Lawrence, John Brown led four of his sons to Pottawatomie, Kansas, a pro-slavery settlement near the Missouri border. There they dragged five men from their houses and hacked them to death with swords. "God is my judge," Brown told one of his sons upon their return from the raid. "We were justified under the circumstances."

The Pottawatomie Massacre (May 24–25, 1856) ignited a guerrilla war in the Kansas Territory. On August 30, pro-slavery Missouri thugs raided the free-state settlement at Osawatomie, Kansas. They looted and burned the houses and shot Frederick Brown, John's son, through the heart. By the end of 1856, about 200 settlers on both sides had been killed in "Bleeding Kansas."

Violence in the Senate

The violence in Kansas spilled over into Congress. On May 22, 1856, the day after the burning of Lawrence and two days before the Pottawatomie Massacre, an ugly incident in the Senate shocked the nation. Two days before, Republican senator Charles Sumner of Massachusetts, a passionate foe of slavery, had delivered a fiery speech in which he insulted slave owners, including Andrew Pickens Butler, an elderly senator from South Carolina.

Sumner's speech enraged Butler's young cousin Preston S. Brooks, a South Carolina congressman with a hair-trigger temper. On May 22, Brooks confronted Sumner at his Senate desk and began beating him about the head

"BULLY" BROOKS ATTACKS CHARLES SUMNER
This outbreak of violence in Congress worsened the strains on the Union.

"Bleeding Sumner" (1856)

with a gold-knobbed cane. While stunned colleagues looked on, Brooks beat Sumner until his cane broke. The helpless Sumner nearly died.

In satisfying his rage, though, Brooks had created a martyr—"Bleeding Sumner"—for the anti-slavery cause. For two and a half years, Sumner's empty Senate seat was a solemn reminder of the violence done to him. His brutal beating also had an unintended political effect: it drove more northerners into the new Republican party. By contrast, southerners honored Butler as a hero. Dozens of people sent him new canes.

Sectional Squabbles

Republican party opposed to expanding slavery

The violence during the spring of 1856 spilled over into the presidential election—one in which the major parties could no longer evade the slavery issue. At its first national convention, the Republican party fastened on an eccentric military hero, John C. Frémont, "the Pathfinder," who had led the conquest of Mexican-controlled California. The Republican platform borrowed heavily from the former Whigs. It endorsed federal funding for a transcontinental railroad and other transportation improvements. It denounced the repeal of the Missouri Compromise, the Democratic party's policy of territorial expansion, and the "barbarism" of slavery. For the first time, a major-party platform had taken a stand against slavery.

In picking a presidential candidate, the Democrats dumped the widely unpopular Franklin Pierce. The president had become the most hated person in the nation by 1856, and he remains the only elected president to be denied renomination by his own party. Instead, the Democrats nominated James Buchanan of Pennsylvania, a former senator and secretary of state who had long sought the nomination. The Democratic platform endorsed the Kansas-Nebraska Act, called for vigorous enforcement of the fugitive slave law, and stressed that Congress should not interfere with slavery in states or territories.

In the campaign of 1856, the Republicans had very few southern supporters and only a handful in the border slave states of Delaware, Maryland, Kentucky, and Missouri, where fear of disunion held many Whigs in line. Buchanan thus went into the campaign as the candidate of the only remaining national party. Frémont swept the

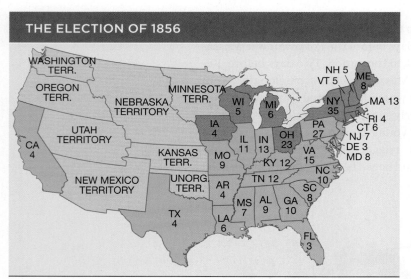

THE ELECTION OF 1856

Electoral Vote

	James Buchanan (Democrat)	**174**
	John C. Frémont (Republican)	114
	Millard Fillmore (American)	8

- What was the platform of the new Republican party?
- Why did Democrats pick James Buchanan?
- What were the key factors that decided the election?

northernmost states with 114 electoral votes, but Buchanan added five free states—Pennsylvania, New Jersey, Illinois, Indiana, and California—to his southern majority for a total of 174.

President Buchanan

As Franklin Pierce prepared to leave the White House in March 1857, a friend asked what he was going to do. Pierce replied: "There's nothing left to do but get drunk." James Buchanan also loved to drink, but he had different priorities. The president-elect had built his political career on his commitment to states' rights and his aggressive promotion of territorial expansion. Saving the Union, he believed, depended upon making concessions to the South. Republicans charged that he lacked the backbone to stand up to the southern slaveholders who dominated the Democratic majorities in Congress.

When the sixty-five-year-old Buchanan, America's first unmarried president, chose four slave-state men and only three free-state men for his cabinet, it seemed another troublesome sign. It was. Although he had vast experience, Buchanan had limited ability—and bad luck.

During James Buchanan's first six months in office in 1857, two major events brought about his undoing: (1) the Supreme Court decision in the *Dred Scott* case and (2) new troubles in strife-torn Kansas. For all Buchanan's experience as a legislator and diplomat, he failed to handle either of those issues with confidence or strength. The Financial Panic of 1857 only made a bad situation worse for both the new president and the nation as a whole.

By 1857, the American economy was growing too fast. Too many railroads and factories were being built even as European demand for American corn and wheat was slackening. The result was a financial panic triggered by the failure of the Ohio Life Insurance and Trust Company on August 24, 1857.

Tens of thousands lost their jobs, and banks started foreclosing on homes, farms, and businesses. Virtually every bank in New York City closed its doors. In the midst of the growing hysteria over the economic swoon, Buchanan and his administration refused to intervene. In his annual message in December 1857, he pledged that the government would continue to function but it would do nothing to relieve the individual suffering caused by the financial panic. Most of those complaining the loudest, he maintained, were speculators who "deserved a gambler's fate."

The *Dred Scott* Case

On March 6, 1857, two days after Buchanan's inauguration, the Supreme Court delivered a decision in the long-pending case of **_Dred Scott v. Sandford_**. Scott, born a slave in Virginia, had been taken to St. Louis in 1830 and sold to an army surgeon, who took him to Illinois, then to the Wisconsin Territory (later Minnesota), and finally back to St. Louis in 1842. While in the Wisconsin Territory, Scott had married Harriet Robinson, and they eventually had two daughters.

Dred Scott v. Sandford (1857) U.S. Supreme Court ruling that slaves were not U.S. citizens and that Congress could not prohibit slavery in territories.

DRED SCOTT Scott's lawsuit over his family's freedom fanned the flames of the nation's debate on slavery.

The *Dred Scott* decision (1857)

In 1846, Dred Scott filed suit in the Missouri courts, claiming that his residence in Illinois and the Wisconsin Territory had made him free because Congress had banned slavery there. A jury decided in his favor, but the state supreme court ruled against him. When the case rose on appeal to the U.S. Supreme Court, the nation anxiously awaited its opinion on whether freedom once granted could be lost by returning to a slave state. Buchanan did not wait for the Court's ruling. He privately pressured one of the justices to rule against Scott.

Seven of the nine justices were Democrats, five of whom were southerners. The vote was 7–2 against Scott. Seventy-nine-year-old Chief Justice Roger B. Taney, like Buchanan a graduate of tiny Dickinson College in Pennsylvania, was a devoted supporter of the South and of slavery. He wrote the Court's majority opinion, ruling that Scott lacked legal standing because, like all former slaves, he was not an American citizen and could never become one. When the Founders drafted the Constitution, Taney claimed, blacks were deemed an "inferior and subject race" that the Constitution had implicitly excluded from citizenship. "They had no rights which the white man was bound to respect." On the issue of Scott's residency, Taney argued that the compromises of 1820 and 1850 had deprived citizens of property by prohibiting slavery in selected territories and states, an action "not warranted by the Constitution."

The upshot was that the Supreme Court had declared an act of Congress unconstitutional for the first time since *Marbury v. Madison* (1803). Congress had repealed the Missouri Compromise in the Kansas-Nebraska Act three years earlier, but the *Dred Scott* decision now challenged the concept of "popular sovereignty." If Congress itself could not exclude slavery from a territory, as Taney argued, then neither could a territorial government created by an act of Congress.

Yet instead of settling the issue of slavery in the territories, Taney's ruling fanned the flames. Pro-slavery advocates loved the Court's opinion, and President Buchanan approved. Republicans, on the other hand, savaged the *Dred Scott* decision because it nullified their anti-slavery program. They threatened to remove the justices and reverse the decision if they secured control of the federal government.

The Lecompton Constitution

Meanwhile, in the Kansas Territory, the struggle over slavery continued with both sides resorting to voting trickery and violence. Just before Buchanan's inauguration, in early 1857, the pro-slavery territorial legislature called for a constitutional convention. The governor vetoed the measure, but the legislature overrode his veto. The governor resigned in protest, and President Buchanan replaced him with Robert J. Walker. With Buchanan's approval, Walker pledged to the free-state Kansans (who made up an overwhelming majority of the residents) that the new constitution would receive a fair vote. But when the pro-slavery constitutional convention, meeting at Lecompton, drafted a constitution under which Kansas would become a slave state, those opposed to slavery boycotted the vote on the new constitution.

At that point, President Buchanan took a fateful step. Influenced by southern advisers, he endorsed the pro-slavery Lecompton convention, sparking a new wave of outrage across the northern states. Stephen A. Douglas, the most prominent Midwestern Democrat, broke with the president over the issue, siding with anti-slavery Republicans because the people of Kansas had lost their right to decide the issue. Douglas told a newspaper reporter that "I made Mr. James Buchanan, and by God, sir, I will unmake him." The rigged election in Kansas went as predicted: 6,226 for the constitution with slavery, 569 for the constitution without slavery.

Meanwhile, a new acting governor had convened the anti-slavery legislature, which called for another election to vote the Lecompton Constitution up or down. Most of the pro-slavery settlers boycotted this election. The result, on January 4, 1858, was decisive: 10,226 voted against the Lecompton Constitution, while only 138 voted for it. In April 1858, the U.S. Congress ordered that Kansans vote again on the Lecompton Constitution. On August 2, 1858, voters rejected the Lecompton Constitution, 11,300–1,788. With that vote, Kansas cleared the way for its eventual admission as a free state in 1861.

Douglas versus Lincoln

The controversy over slavery in Kansas fractured the Democratic party. Stephen A. Douglas, one of the few remaining Democrats with support in both the North and the South, struggled to keep the party from self-destructing. The year 1860 would give him a chance for the presidency, but first he had to secure his home base in Illinois, where in 1858 he faced reelection to the Senate.

To challenge Douglas, Illinois Republicans selected a rustic lawyer from Springfield, Abraham Lincoln, the former Whig legislator. Lincoln had served in the Illinois legislature and in 1846 had won a seat in the U.S. Congress. After a single unremarkable term in Washington, D.C., he returned to Springfield. In 1854, however, the Kansas-Nebraska Act drew Lincoln back into the political arena.

Lincoln hated slavery but was no abolitionist. He did not believe that the nation should force the South to end slavery, but he did insist that slavery be banned in the new western territories. In 1856, Lincoln joined the rapidly growing Republican party, and two years later he emerged as the obvious choice to oppose Douglas for the Senate seat. Because he was the underdog,

LINCOLN AND DOUGLAS A tall, rawboned small-town lawyer, Lincoln (left) was motivated by the Kansas-Nebraska Act to vie for an Illinois Senate seat, running against the current Democratic senator and author of the Act, Stephen Douglas (right).

Lincoln sought to raise his profile by challenging Douglas to a series of debates across the state.

The **Lincoln-Douglas debates** took place from August 21 to October 15, 1858. They attracted tens of thousands of spectators and transformed the contest for an Illinois Senate seat into a battle for the future of the republic. The two men differed as much physically as they did politically. Douglas was barely five feet tall, stocky with a big head. Lincoln was tall and thin, well over six feet tall.

The basic political difference between the two men, Lincoln argued, lay in Douglas's indifference to the immorality of slavery. Douglas, he said, did not care whether slavery in the territories was "voted up, or voted down." Douglas was preoccupied only with process ("popular sovereignty"); Lincoln claimed to be focused on principle. "I have always hated slavery as much as any abolitionist," he stressed. The American government, he predicted, could not "endure, permanently half *slave* and half *free*. . . . It will become *all* one thing, or *all* the other."

If Lincoln had the better of the argument in the long view, Douglas had the better of a close election. But while a losing cause, Lincoln's energetic campaign had elevated him to being a national figure.

An Outnumbered South

Lincoln-Douglas debates (1858) In the Illinois race between Republican Abraham Lincoln and Democrat Stephen A. Douglas for a seat in the U.S. Senate, a series of seven dramatic debates focusing on the issue of slavery in the territories.

By the late 1850s, national politics was undergoing profound changes. In May 1858, the free state of Minnesota entered the Union; in February 1859, another nonslave territory, Oregon, gained statehood. The slave states of the South were quickly becoming a minority, and their political insecurity deepened into paranoia.

At the same time, political tensions over slavery were becoming more violent. In 1858, members of Congress engaged in the largest brawl ever staged on the floor of the House of Representatives. Harsh words about slavery incited the free-for-all, which involved more than fifty legislators shoving, punching, and wrestling one another. The fracas ended when John "Bowie Knife" Potter of Wisconsin yanked off the wig of a Mississippi congressman and claimed, "I've scalped him."

Like the scuffling congressmen, more and more Americans began to feel that slavery could be ended or defended only with violence. The editor of a pro-slavery Kansas newspaper wanted to kill abolitionists: "If I can't kill a man, I'll kill a woman; and if I can't kill a woman, I'll kill a child."

Southern threats to secede increased. In 1858, former Alabama congressman William L. Yancey, a member of a group of hot-tempered southern secessionists called "fire-eaters," or "ultras," boasted that it would be easy "to precipitate the Cotton States into a revolution."

John Brown's Raid

Such violent threats to maintain slavery drove John Brown into a desperate act. On the cool, rainy night of October 16, 1859, iron-willed Brown launched his supreme effort to end slavery. From a Maryland farm, he crossed the Potomac River with about twenty men, mostly unmarried and in their twenties, including three of Brown's sons and five African Americans. Under cover of darkness, they approached the federal weapons arsenal in Harpers Ferry, Virginia (now West Virginia), a factory town some sixty miles northwest of Washington, D.C. Brown's mad scheme was to give the arsenal's muskets to thousands of slaves in the area, in the hope of triggering mass uprisings across the South. "I want to free all the negroes in this state," Brown said. "If the citizens interfere with me, I must burn the town and have blood."

> Raid on Harpers Ferry (1859)

Brown and his comrades took the town by surprise, cut the telegraph lines, and occupied the arsenal. He then sent a handful of men to kidnap several nearby slave owners and spread the word for local slaves to rise up and join the rebellion. Only a few slaves heeded the call, however. By dawn, enraged townsmen had surrounded the raiders. Brown and a dozen of his men, along with eleven white hostages (including George Washington's great-grandnephew, the area's most prominent resident) and two of their slaves, remained holed up for thirty-two hours.

Meanwhile, hundreds of armed men poured into Harpers Ferry to capture Brown and his raiders. Lieutenant Colonel Robert E. Lee arrived with a force of U.S. Marines. On the morning of October 18, the marines broke down the arsenal's barricaded doors and rushed in. The siege was over. Brown's men had killed four townspeople and wounded another dozen. Of their own group, ten were killed (including two of Brown's sons) and five were captured; another five escaped.

Brown and his accomplices were quickly convicted of treason, murder, and "conspiring with Negroes to produce insurrection."

JOHN BROWN On his way to the gallows, Brown predicted that slavery would end only "after much bloodshed."

At his sentencing, Brown delivered a powerful speech justifying his martyr-dom: "Now, if it is deemed necessary that I should forfeit my life for the fur-therance of the ends of justice, and mingle my blood further with the blood of my children and with the blood of millions in this slave country whose rights are disregarded by wicked, cruel, and unjust enactments, I say, let it be done."

Brown was hanged on December 2, 1859. (Among the crowd watching the execution was a popular young stage actor named John Wilkes Booth, who would later assassinate Abraham Lincoln.) If Brown had failed to ignite a massive slave rebellion, he had achieved two things: he had become a martyr for the anti-slavery cause, and he had stirred the South's worst nightmare: that armed slaves would revolt.

Throughout the fall and winter of 1859–1860, wild rumors of abolitionist conspiracies and slave insurrections swept through the southern states, leading many to outlaw any anti-slavery activity. Some 300 abolitionists were murdered or forced out of the region. "We regard every man in our midst an enemy to the institutions of the South," said the *Atlanta Confeder-acy*, "who does not boldly declare that he believes African slavery to be a so-cial, moral, and political blessing."

The Democrats Divide

Amid such emotional hysteria the nation mobilized for another presidential election, destined to be the most fateful in its history. In April 1860, the squabbling Democrats gathered for what would become a disastrous presi-dential nominating convention in Charleston, South Carolina. Stephen A. Douglas's northern supporters tried to straddle the divisive issue of slavery by promising southerners to defend the "peculiar institution" in their region while assuring northerners that slavery would not spread to new states. Southern firebrands, however, demanded federal protection for slavery in the territories as well as the states.

When the pro-slavery advocates lost the platform fight, delegates from eight southern states walked out of the convention. "We say, go your way," exclaimed a Mississippi delegate to Douglas's supporters, "and we will go ours." Alabama's William Yancey, the "prince of the fire-eaters," a "compact, middle-sized man, straight-limbed, with . . . an eye full of expression," defi-antly declared that "[w]e shall go to the wall" in the effort to spread slavery into the western territories.

The Democratic Convention then disintegrated into warring factions that resolved to go their own way. Douglas's supporters reassembled in Balti-more on June 18 and nominated him for president. Southern Democrats met first in Richmond and then in Baltimore, where they adopted the pro-slavery platform that had been defeated in Charleston and named John C. Breckin-ridge, vice president under Buchanan, as their candidate. Thus another cord binding the nation together had snapped: the last remaining national party had split into northern and southern factions. The fracturing of the Dem-ocratic party made a Republican victory in 1860 almost certain.

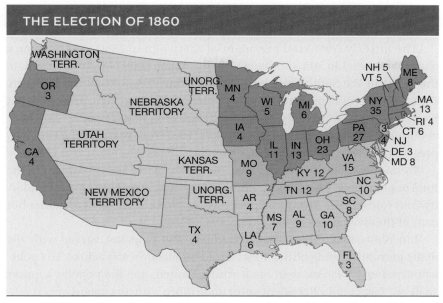

THE ELECTION OF 1860

	Electoral Vote	Popular Vote
Abraham Lincoln (Republican)	**180**	**1,866,000**
Stephen A. Douglas (Democrat—northern)	12	1,383,000
John C. Breckinridge (Democrat—southern)	72	848,000
John Bell (Constitutional Union)	39	593,000

- What caused the division within the Democratic party in 1860?
- How did Lincoln win the 1860 presidential election?

Lincoln's Election

The Republican nominating convention opened in May in the fast-growing city of Chicago, where everything suddenly came together for Abraham Lincoln, who won the presidential nomination over New York senator William H. Seward. Inside the convention building, the "wildest excitement and enthusiasm" swelled to a "perfect roar" as Lincoln was nominated. The convention reaffirmed the party's opposition to the extension of slavery and, in an effort to gain broader support, endorsed a series of traditional Whig policies promoting national economic expansion: a higher protective tariff, free farms ("homesteads" on federal lands out west, and federally financed internal improvements, including a transcontinental railroad.

The rival Democratic and Republican presidential nominating conventions revealed that opinions about the future of slavery were becoming more radical in the Northeast and the Lower South. Attitude followed latitude. In the border states of Maryland, Delaware, Kentucky, and Missouri, the prevailing sense of moderation aroused former Whigs to make one more try at reconciliation. Meeting in Baltimore a week before the Republicans met in Chicago, they reorganized themselves as the Constitutional Union party and nominated John Bell of Tennessee for president. Their platform centered on a vague statement promoting "the Constitution of the Country, the Union of the States, and the Enforcement of the Laws."

The bitterly contested presidential campaign in 1860 thus became a choice between Lincoln and Douglas in the North (Lincoln was not even on the ballot in the South), and between Breckinridge and Bell in the South. Douglas, the only candidate to mount a nationwide campaign, promised that he would "make war boldly against" extremists in both regions: "Northern abolitionists and Southern disunionists." His effort to preserve the Union by preserving slavery did no good, however.

By midnight on November 6, Lincoln had won. He had 39 percent of the total popular vote, the smallest plurality ever, but he captured a clear majority (180 votes) in the Electoral College. He carried *all* eighteen free states but *none* of the slave states.

Lincoln, a man of remarkable humility and empathy, agreed with the many journalists and politicians who said his election was a fluke. His political experience was meager, his learning limited, and his popular support shallow. "Never did a President enter upon office with less means at his command," the poet and Harvard professor James Russell Lowell remarked. Yet the unassuming prairie lawyer from Springfield, Illinois, would emerge the acknowledged leader of his distinguished cabinet, earning the respect of colleagues and opponents who had originally scorned him and becoming in the process, as the poet Walt Whitman wrote, "the grandest figure yet, on all the crowded canvas of the nineteenth century."

Abraham Lincoln elected president (1860)

CORE OBJECTIVE

5. Explain why seven southern states seceded from the Union shortly after Lincoln's election in 1860.

The Response in the South

Between November 8, 1860, when Lincoln was elected, and March 4, 1861, when he was inaugurated, the United States of America disintegrated. His election panicked southerners who believed that the Republican party, as a Richmond, Virginia, newspaper asserted, was founded for one reason: "hatred of African slavery." What made southerners especially nervous was the fear that Lincoln would prevent the expansion of a southern cotton economy that in 1860 had produced 4 million 500-pound bales—a record crop that made up nearly 60 percent of *all* American exports.

After Lincoln's victory, South Carolina's entire delegation of U.S. congressmen and senators resigned. The South Carolina legislature then appointed a convention to decide whether the state should secede from the Union. Nearly all the delegates owned slaves. Twenty-seven owned a hundred or more slaves, and one delegate, former governor John Manning, owned more than 650 slaves. One of the delegates, Thomas Jefferson Withers, declared that the "true question for us all is how shall we sustain African slavery in South Carolina from a series of annoying attacks."

South Carolina then was the third-wealthiest state in the Union. It had a higher percentage of slaves in its population (60 percent) than any other state, and its political leadership was dominated by slave-owning hotheads. It had been a one-party state (Democratic) for decades, and it was then the only state in the Union that did not allow its citizens to vote in presidential elections; the state legislature, controlled by white planters, did the balloting.

Meeting in Charleston on December 20, 1860, the special convention unanimously approved an Ordinance of Secession, explaining that President-elect Lincoln was a man "whose opinions and purposes are hostile to slavery." James L. Petigru, one of the few Unionists in Charleston, claimed that those who voted for secession were lunatics. South Carolina, he quipped, "is too small to be a Republic and too large to be an insane asylum."

As the news of secession spread through Charleston, church bells rang and shops closed. New flags were unfurled and cadets at the Citadel, the state's military college, fired artillery salutes. "The Union Is Dissolved!" screamed the headline of the *Charleston Mercury*, a pro-secession newspaper. One Unionist in Charleston kept a copy of the newspaper, scribbling on the bottom of it: "You'll regret the day you ever done this. I preserve this to see how it ends."

Buchanan's Waiting Game

The nation's gravest crisis needed a bold, decisive president, but instead it suffered under James Buchanan, who was timid and hesitant. The feckless leader blamed the crisis on fanatical abolitionists but then declared that secession was illegal, only to further claim that he lacked the constitutional authority to force a state to rejoin the Union. In the face of Buchanan's clueless inaction, all the southerners in his cabinet resigned. The passive president also allowed southern firebrands to seize federal forts in the seceded states. "If that is true," said Abraham Lincoln, "they ought to hang" Buchanan.

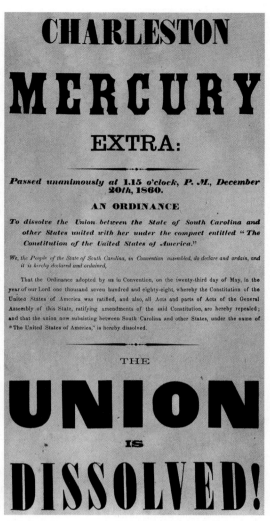

"THE UNION IS DISSOLVED!" A newspaper headline announcing South Carolina's secession from the Union.

Among the federal forts under siege was Fort Sumter, built after the War of 1812 on a tiny man-made island at the mouth of Charleston Harbor, in the very jaws of the Confederacy. When South Carolina secessionists demanded that Major Robert Anderson, a Kentucky Unionist who favored slavery and married a Georgia woman, surrender the undermanned federal fort, he refused, vowing to hold on at all costs.

On January 5, 1861, President Buchanan sent an unarmed ship, the *Star of the West*, to resupply Fort Sumter. As the ship approached Charleston Harbor on January 9, Confederate cannons opened fire and drove it away. It was an act of war, but Buchanan chose to ignore the challenge and ride out the remaining weeks of his term, hoping that one of several compromise proposals would succeed in averting civil war.

Secession of the Lower South

The formation of the Confederacy

By February 1, 1861, the seven states of the Lower South—South Carolina, Mississippi, Florida, Alabama, Georgia, Louisiana, and Texas—had seceded. Although the states' secession ordinances mentioned various grievances against the federal government, they made clear that the primary reason for leaving the Union was the preservation of slavery. Texas's ordinance, for example, explained that the purpose of secession and the formation of the Confederacy was to *"secure the rights of the slave-holding States in their domestic institutions."* The Texas convention, displaying the racism at work in secession, called African Americans "an inferior and dependent race" for whom slavery was "beneficial."

On February 4, 1861, representatives of the seceding states met in Montgomery, Alabama, where they adopted a constitution for the Confederate States of America. It mandated that "the institution of negro slavery, as it now exists in the Confederate States, shall be recognized and protected."

The delegates elected as president Mississippi's Jefferson Finis Davis (his middle name chosen because he was the last of ten children), with Alexander H. Stephens of Georgia as vice president. The tiny, sickly Stephens left no doubt about the purpose of the Confederacy: "Our new government," he declared, "is founded upon . . . the great truth that the negro is not equal to the white man; that slavery, subordination to the superior [white] race, is his natural and normal condition."

Final Efforts at Compromise

Crittenden Compromise fails (1861)

Amid the secession fever, several members of Congress desperately sought a compromise that would avert a civil war. On December 18, 1860, Senator John J. Crittenden of Kentucky proposed a series of resolutions that allowed for slavery in the new western territories *south* of the 1820 Missouri Compromise line (36°30′ parallel) and guaranteed the preservation of slavery where it already existed. President-elect Lincoln, however, opposed any plan that would allow for the extension of slavery westward, and the Senate defeated the Crittenden Compromise, 25–23.

Several weeks later, in February 1861, twenty-one states sent delegates to a peace conference in Washington, D.C. Former president John Tyler presided, but the peace convention's proposal, substantially the same as the Crittenden Compromise, gained little support in either house of Congress. The only proposal that met with any success was a constitutional amendment guaranteeing slavery where it existed. Many Republicans, including Lincoln, were prepared to go that far to save the Union but no further.

As it happened, after passing the House, the slavery amendment, needing a two-thirds majority, passed the Senate without a vote to spare, 24–12, on the dawn of Lincoln's inauguration day, March 4, 1861. It would have become the Thirteenth Amendment, and would have been the first time the word *slavery* had appeared in the Constitution, but the states never ratified it.

When a Thirteenth Amendment gained ratification, in 1865, it did not protect slavery—it ended it.

Lincoln's Inauguration

In mid-February 1861, Abraham Lincoln boarded a train in Springfield, Illinois, headed to Washington, D.C., for his presidential inauguration. In his March 4 inaugural address, the fifty-two-year-old Lincoln repeated his pledge not "to interfere with the institution of slavery in the states where it exists." But the immediate question facing the nation and the new president had shifted from slavery to secession. Lincoln insisted that "the Union of these States is perpetual." No state, he stressed, "can lawfully get out of the Union." He pledged to defend "federal forts in the South," such as Fort Sumter, but beyond that "there [would] be no invasion, no using of force against or among the people anywhere."

Lincoln closed by appealing for regional harmony: "We are not enemies, but friends. We must not be enemies. Though passion may have strained, it must not break our bonds of affection. The mystic chords of memory, stretching from every battlefield and patriot grave to every living heart and hearthstone all over this broad land, will yet swell the chorus of the Union, when again touched, as surely they will be, by the better angels of our nature."

Southerners were not impressed, however. A North Carolina newspaper warned that Lincoln's inauguration speech made civil war "inevitable." On both sides, people assumed that if fighting erupted, it would be over quickly and that their daily lives would go on as usual. The new president of the United States continued to seek a peaceful solution. In early 1861, however, the possibility of compromise waned and civil war grew more likely.

The End of the Waiting Game

On March 5, 1861, his first day in office, President Lincoln learned that time was running out for the federal troops at Fort Sumter. Major Robert Anderson reported that his men had enough food for only a few weeks and that Confederates were encircling the fort with a "ring of fire." On April 4, 1861, Lincoln ordered that ships resupply the almost 100 soldiers at Fort Sumter (fewer than twenty of whom were American-born). His counterpart, Jefferson Davis, president of the Confederate states, resolved to stop any effort to resupply the fort.

> Civil War begins (April 12, 1861)

On April 11, Confederate general Pierre G. T. Beauregard, a Louisiana native who had studied under Robert Anderson at West Point, demanded that his former professor surrender Fort Sumter. Major Anderson refused. At four thirty on the morning of April 12, the Confederate shelling of Fort Sumter began. After some thirty-four hours, his ammunition exhausted, the outgunned Anderson lowered the "Stars and Stripes." The Civil War had begun.

Reviewing the
CORE OBJECTIVES | INQUIZITIVE

■ **Westward Migration** In the 1830s, Americans came to believe in *manifest destiny*—that the U.S. expansion to the Pacific coast was divinely ordained. A population explosion and the lure of cheap, fertile land prompted large numbers of Americans to endure the hardships of the *Overland Trails* to settle in Oregon (*Oregon Fever*) and California. At the same time, many southerners ("Texians") moved to the Mexican province of Texas with their slaves. The Mexican government outlawed slavery, however, and in 1830 forbade further immigration. Texians rebelled, winning their independence from Mexico in the *Texas Revolution (1835–1836)*. Texas, however, would not become a state for another decade because the United States was determined to avoid both war with Mexico and the divisive issue of adding another slave state to the Union.

■ **Mexican-American War** When the United States finally annexed Texas in 1845, the Mexican government refused to recognize the loss of its northern province. President Polk sought to acquire California, New Mexico, and Texas, but negotiations failed. When Mexican troops crossed the Rio Grande and fired on U.S. soldiers, Polk urged Congress to declare war, which U.S. forces won. By the terms of the *Treaty of Guadalupe Hidalgo (1848)*, Mexico ceded California and New Mexico to the United States and gave up claims to disputed land north of the Rio Grande.

■ **Slavery in the Territories** The *Wilmot Proviso (1846)*, never became law, but by outlawing slavery in the newly acquired Mexican territories, it outraged pro-slavery legislators. The controversy helped create a new *Free-Soil party* that demanded that slavery be banned in the new territories. In 1849, the *California gold rush* further escalated sectional tensions. Most Californians wanted their territory to become a free state. Southerners feared losing federal protection of their "peculiar institution" if free states outnumbered slave states. Some political leaders urged the voters in each territory to decide the issue (*popular sovereignty*). The much celebrated *Compromise of 1850* allowed California to enter the Union as a free state, established the territories of Texas, New Mexico, and Utah without direct reference to slavery, banned the slave trade in Washington, D.C., and strengthened the *Fugitive Slave Act (1850)*. Tensions turned violent with the passage of the *Kansas-Nebraska Act (1854)*, which overturned the Missouri Compromise by allowing slavery in the territories where it had been banned in 1820.

■ **The Republican Party's Appeal** Northerners were outraged by violent pro-slavery mobs as the territory of Kansas prepared to enter the Union. Yet anti-slavery zealots were equally violent, such as John Brown in *Bleeding Kansas (1856)*. The Supreme Court's pro-slavery *Dred Scott v. Sandford (1857)* decision further fueled sectional conflict. The *Lincoln-Douglas debates (1858)* in Illinois centered on the controversy over extending slavery into the territories. Northern voters increasingly gravitated toward the anti-slavery Republican party. Republicans also advocated for protective tariffs and the development of national infrastructure, which appealed to northern manufacturers and commercial farmers. In the 1860 presidential election, Lincoln carried every free state and won a clear Electoral College victory.

■ **The Secession of the Lower South** South Carolina seceded from the Union a month after Lincoln's presidential victory. Before Lincoln was inaugurated, six other states joined South Carolina to form the Confederate States of America. South Carolinians bombarded Fort Sumter in Charleston Harbor, and so the Civil War began.

KEY TERMS

manifest destiny *p. 432*

Overland Trails *p. 432*

Oregon Fever *p. 435*

Texas Revolution (1835–1836) *p. 438*

Treaty of Guadalupe Hidalgo (1848) *p. 450*

Wilmot Proviso (1846) *p. 451*

popular sovereignty *p. 452*

Free-Soil party *p. 453*

California gold rush (1849) *p. 453*

Compromise of 1850 *p. 456*

Fugitive Slave Act (1850) *p. 459*

Kansas-Nebraska Act (1854) *p. 462*

Bleeding Kansas (1856) *p. 463*

Dred Scott v. Sandford (1857) *p. 467*

Lincoln-Douglas debates (1858) *p. 470*

CHRONOLOGY

1821	Mexico gains independence from Spain
1836	American "Texians" are defeated at the Alamo
1845	United States annexes Texas
1846	Mexican-American War begins
1848	Treaty of Guadalupe Hidalgo ends Mexican-American War
1849	California gold rush begins
1854	Congress passes Kansas-Nebraska Act
	The Republican party founded
1856	Bleeding Kansas and Bloody Sumner
1857	*Dred Scott v. Sandford* and Lecompton Constitution
1858	Lincoln-Douglas debates
1859	John Brown's raid at Harpers Ferry, Virginia
1860–1861	Seven southern states secede from the Union
March 4, 1861	Abraham Lincoln is inaugurated president
April 1861	Fort Sumter falls to Confederate forces

ᕯINQUIZITIVE

Go to InQuizitive to see what you've learned—and learn what you've missed—with personalized feedback along the way.

LINCOLN'S DRIVE THROUGH RICHMOND (1866) Shortly after the Confederate capital of Richmond, Virginia, fell to Union forces in April 1865, President Abraham Lincoln visited the war-torn city. Freed slaves and white Unionists swarmed his carriage.

The War of the Union

1861–1865

The fall of Fort Sumter started the Civil War and triggered a wave of patriotic bluster on both sides. A southern woman prayed that God would "give us strength to conquer the Yankees, to exterminate *them*, to lay waste every Northern city, town and village, to destroy them utterly." By contrast, the writer Nathaniel Hawthorne reported from Massachusetts that his transcendentalist friend Ralph Waldo Emerson was "breathing slaughter" as the Union army prepared for its first battle.

Many southerners (and others), then and since, argued that the Civil War was not about slavery but about the South's effort to defend states' rights. Confederate president Jefferson Davis, for example, claimed that the Confederacy fought on behalf of the states' right to secede from the Union and the South's need to defend itself against a "tyrannical majority," by whom he meant those who had elected President Abraham Lincoln, the anti-slavery Republican. "All we ask," he said, "is to be let alone."

For his part, Lincoln stressed repeatedly that the war's goal was simply to restore the Union. In an 1862 letter, he declared that the "paramount object in this struggle *is* to save the Union, and is *not* either to save or to destroy slavery. If I could save the Union without freeing *any* slave I would do it, and if I could save it by freeing *all* the slaves I would do it; and if I could save it by freeing some and leaving others

CORE
OBJECTIVES INQUIZITIVE

1. Identify the respective advantages of the North and South in the war, and explain how they affected the military strategies of the Union and the Confederacy.

2. Evaluate Lincoln's decision to issue the Emancipation Proclamation and its impact on the war.

3. Analyze how the war affected social and economic life in the North and South.

4. Describe the military turning points in 1863 and 1864 that ultimately led to the Confederacy's defeat.

5. Explain how the Civil War changed the nation.

JEFFERSON DAVIS President of the Confederacy.

alone I would also do that." If the southern states returned to the Union, he promised, they could retain their slaves.

None of the Confederate states accepted Lincoln's offer, in large part because most white southerners were convinced that Lincoln was lying. The "Black Republican," as they called the president, was determined to end slavery, no matter what he said.

However much Jefferson Davis and other southerners argued that secession and the war were about states' rights, the states of the Lower South seceded in 1860–1861 primarily to preserve slavery. The South Carolina Declaration on the Immediate Causes of Secession explained that the state left the Union because of the "increasing hostility on the part of the non-slaveholding states to the institution of slavery."

Southerners claimed their *right* to secede from the Union, but protecting slavery was the *reason* southern leaders repeatedly used to justify secession and war. In 1860, William Preston of South Carolina boasted that "cotton is not our king—slavery is our king. Slavery is our truth. Slavery is our divine right." As Lincoln noted in his second inaugural address, everyone knew that slavery "was somehow the cause of the war."

CORE **OBJECTIVE**

1. Identify the respective advantages of the North and South in the war, and explain how they affected the military strategies of the Union and the Confederacy.

Mobilizing Forces in the North and South

On April 15, three days after the Confederate attack on Fort Sumter, President Lincoln directed the "loyal" states to supply 75,000 soldiers to suppress the rebellion. Volunteers on both sides flocked to military recruiting offices. The Civil War would force virtually everyone—men and women, white and black, immigrants and Native Americans, free and enslaved—to choose sides. Thousands of southerners fought for the Union; thousands of northerners fought for the Confederacy. And most people mistakenly thought the war would be, in Lincoln's words, "a short and decisive one."

Taking Sides

The first seven states that seceded were all from the Lower South—South Carolina, Mississippi, Florida, Alabama, Georgia, Louisiana, and Texas—where the cotton economy was strongest and where most slaves lived. All the states in the Upper South, especially Tennessee and Virginia, had areas (mainly in the mountains) where whites were poor, slaves were scarce, and Union support remained strong. Nevertheless, the outbreak of fighting led four more southern slave states to join the Confederacy: Virginia, Arkansas, Tennessee, and North Carolina.

In eastern Tennessee, however, the mountain counties would supply more volunteers to the Union army than to the Confederate cause. Thirty-nine counties in mountainous western Virginia were so loyal to the Union

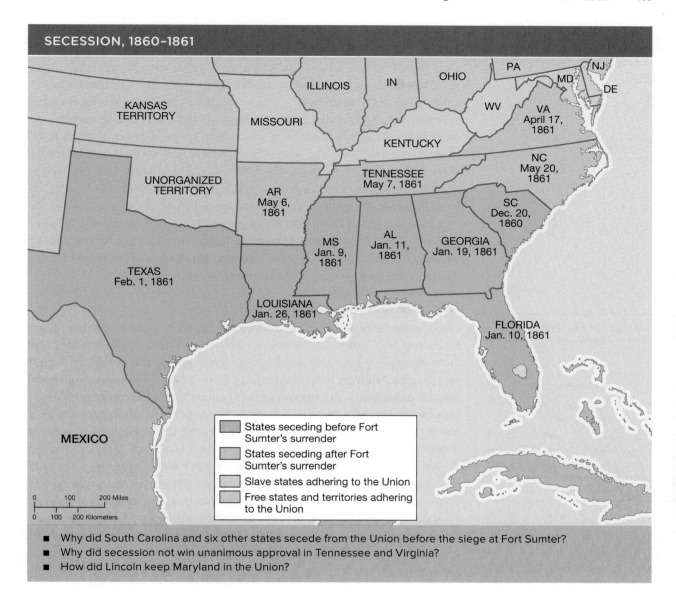

SECESSION, 1860–1861

PA
NJ
ILLINOIS
IN
OHIO
MD
DE
KANSAS
TERRITORY
MISSOURI
WV
VA
April 17,
1861
KENTUCKY
NC
May 20,
1861
UNORGANIZED
TERRITORY
AR
May 6,
1861
TENNESSEE
May 7, 1861
SC
Dec. 20,
1860
AL
Jan. 11,
1861
GEORGIA
Jan. 19, 1861
MS
Jan. 9,
1861
TEXAS
Feb. 1, 1861
LOUISIANA
Jan. 26, 1861
FLORIDA
Jan. 10, 1861
MEXICO

- States seceding before Fort Sumter's surrender
- States seceding after Fort Sumter's surrender
- Slave states adhering to the Union
- Free states and territories adhering to the Union

0   100   200 Miles
0   100   200 Kilometers

- Why did South Carolina and six other states secede from the Union before the siege at Fort Sumter?
- Why did secession not win unanimous approval in Tennessee and Virginia?
- How did Lincoln keep Maryland in the Union?

that they split off and formed the new state of West Virginia in October 1861. Of the border states, Delaware remained firmly in the Union, but Maryland, Kentucky, and Missouri went through bitter struggles to decide which side to support. Kentuckian Mary Todd Lincoln, the president's wife, saw her youngest brother join the Confederate army, as did three of her half brothers and a brother-in-law.

On the eve of the Civil War, the U.S. Army had only 16,400 men, about 1,000 of whom were officers. Of these, about 25 percent, like the future Confederate general Robert E. Lee, resigned to join the Confederate army. But similarly, many southerners made great sacrifices to remain loyal to the

Union. Some left their native region once the fighting began; others remained in the South but found ways to support the Union. Some 3 million men served on one side or the other during the war. Of that total, about 100,000 men from the southern states fought *against* the Confederacy.

In areas of the South where Union sentiment remained strong, the Civil War was brutally uncivil. In January 1863, a detachment of Confederate soldiers in mountainous Madison County, North Carolina, captured thirteen ragged men and boys who were Union sympathizers and began marching them to Knoxville, Tennessee, where they would be put on trial for desertion and treason against the Confederacy. The prisoners never made it to Knoxville, however. Along the way, the detachment stopped, lined up five of the captives, and killed them. Then five more. Then the last three. Thirteen-year-old David Shelton was among the last to be executed, having already witnessed his father and brother's deaths. He begged to be spared for his mother's sake but was killed like the rest.

Regional Advantages

| Union advantage: Population

Once battle lines were finally drawn, the Union held twenty-three states, including four border slave states—Missouri, Kentucky, Maryland, and Delaware—while the Confederacy had eleven states. The population count was about 22 million in the Union (about 400,000 of whom were enslaved African Americans), to 9 million in the Confederacy (of whom about 3.5 million were enslaved African Americans). The Union therefore had an edge of about 4 to 1 in human resources. To help balance the odds, the Confederacy mobilized 80 percent of its military-age white men.

| Union advantage: Greater industrial development, railroads, and ships

An even greater advantage for the North was its superior industrial development. The Union states produced 97 percent of the firearms and 96 percent of the railroad equipment. The North's advantage in transportation, particularly ships and rail cars, also weighed heavily as the war went on. At the start of the war, the Union had ninety warships while the South at first had no navy at all. Federal gunboats and transports played a direct role in securing the Union's control of the Mississippi River and its larger tributaries, which provided easy invasion routes into the center of the Confederacy. And early on, the Union navy's blockade of the major southern ports sharply reduced the amount of Confederate cotton that could be exported to Britain and France as well as the flow of goods (including military weapons) imported from Europe. In addition, the Union had more wagons and horses than the Confederacy and an even more impressive edge in the number of railroad locomotives.

| Confederate advantage: Waging a defensive war on its own territory

The Confederates, however, enjoyed major geographic and emotional advantages: they could fight a war on their own territory in defense of their homeland against hated invaders. In warfare, it is usually easier to defend than to attack, since defending troops have the opportunity to dig protective trenches and fortifications. In the Civil War, 90 percent of the time, armies that assaulted well-defended positions lost. Many Confederate leaders assumed that if their new nation could hold out long enough, perhaps disgruntled northern voters would convince Lincoln and the Congress to end the war.

As the two sides mobilized for the first battles, the Confederate armies had more experienced military leaders and better horsemen. Many Confederates also displayed a brash sense of confidence in facing the more numerous and better equipped Union forces. After all, had not the Revolutionaries of 1776 defeated a much stronger British army? "Britain could not conquer three million [Americans]," a Louisianan boasted, and "the world cannot conquer the South."

> Confederate advantage: Experienced military leaders

The War's Early Strategies

The two sides had quite different war aims. The Confederacy sought to convince the Union and the world to recognize its independence. The United States, on the other hand, fought to restore the Union. This would require invading the South and destroying its Confederate government.

> Union strategy: Capture the Confederate capital

After the fall of Fort Sumter, neither side was ready to wage war, but excited newspaper editors and politicians on both sides pressured the generals to strike quickly. "Forward to Richmond!" screamed a New York newspaper headline. In the summer of 1861, Jefferson Davis told the battle-hungry General Beauregard, short of stature but as feisty as a wasp, to hurry the main Confederate army to Manassas Junction, a railroad crossing in northern Virginia, about twenty-five miles west of Washington. Lincoln hoped that the Union army (often called *Federals*) would overrun the outnumbered Confederates (often called *Rebels*) and quickly push on to Richmond, only 107 miles to the south.

First Bull Run

When word reached Washington, D.C., that the two opposing armies were converging for battle, hundreds of congressmen and civilians packed picnic lunches and rode out on a Sunday afternoon to watch the romantic spectacle, assuming that the first clash of arms would be short, glorious, and with little bloodshed.

> Confederate advantage: Victory at First Battle of Bull Run (1861)

It was a hot, dry day on July 21, 1861, when 37,000 untested Union recruits in colorful uniforms breezily marched to battle, some of them breaking ranks to eat blackberries or drink water from streams along the way. Many of them died with the berry juice still staining their lips as they engaged the Confederates dug in behind a branch of the Potomac River called Bull Run near the vital Manassas Junction railroad station.

The Union troops almost won early in the afternoon. "We fired a volley," wrote a Massachusetts private, "and saw the Rebels running. . . . The boys were saying constantly, in great glee, 'We've whipped them.' 'We'll hang Jeff Davis from a sour apple tree.' 'They're running.' 'The war is over.'"

FIRST BULL RUN Moments before battle, a spectator in a top hat chats with Union soldiers (bottom right), while an artist sketches the passing troops heading to combat (at left). **What was the outcome of the First Battle of Bull Run?**

But Confederate reinforcements poured in to tip the balance. Amid the frantic fighting, a South Carolina officer, soon to be killed himself, rallied his troops by pointing to the courageous example of Thomas Jackson's men: "Look! There is General Jackson with his Virginians, standing like a stone wall!" Jackson, an eccentric, lemon-sucking professor at the Virginia Military Institute, ordered his men to charge the faltering Union ranks, urging them to "yell like furies!" From that day forward, "Stonewall" became Jackson's popular nickname, and he would be one of the most celebrated—and feared—Confederate commanders.

The Union army's retreat from the first Battle of Bull Run (First Manassas)* turned into a panicked rout (the "great skedaddle") as fleeing soldiers and terrified civilians clogged the road to Washington, D.C. The victorious Confederates, however, were so disorganized and exhausted that they failed to give chase.

As the armies moved on, they left behind a frightening scene: a battlefield strewn with the dead and the dying—mangled men and bloated horses and mules, all scattered among discarded knapsacks, canteens, blankets, rifles, wagons, and cannons.

The news of the surprising Confederate victory devastated Unionists. New Yorker George Templeton Strong, a wealthy attorney and civic leader, wrote that "we are utterly and disgracefully routed, beaten, whipped by secessionists."

Lincoln received much of the blame for the disaster at Bull Run. Michigan senator Zachariah Chandler, a Republican, dismissed Lincoln's war

THOMAS "STONEWALL" JACKSON The aggressive commander of a Confederate brigade at Bull Run, Jackson would later die of friendly fire in the Battle of Chancellorsville.

---

*The Federals most often named battles for natural features; the Confederates, for nearby towns—thus Bull Run (Manassas), Antietam (Sharpsburg), Stones River (Murfreesboro), and the like.

leadership as "timid, vacillating & inefficient." An Ohio Republican was even more critical, denouncing Lincoln as "an admitted failure" who "has no will, no courage, no executive capacity."

Lincoln, however, learned more from defeat than victory. The hallmark of his presidency was his ability to acknowledge his mistakes and evolve into a better leader. With each passing year, he would grow more confident and poised in managing an unprecedented civil war.

The Union's "Anaconda" Plan

The Battle of Bull Run demonstrated that the war would be neither short nor easy. General Winfield Scott, the seasoned seventy-five-year-old commander of the Union war effort, so obese that he had to be hoisted onto his sturdy horse, devised a three-pronged strategy that called first for the Army of the Potomac, the main Union army, to defend Washington, D.C., and exert constant pressure on the Confederate capital at Richmond. At the same time, the Federal navy's blockade of southern ports and waterways would cut off the Confederacy's access to foreign goods, weapons, and foodstuffs. The third and final component of the plan called for other Union armies to divide the Confederacy by pushing south along the crucial inland water routes: the Mississippi, Tennessee, and Cumberland Rivers. Scott intended this so-called **Anaconda Plan** to slowly trap and crush the southern resistance, like an anaconda snake strangling its prey.

> Union strategy: Naval blockade and control of inland rivers

Confederate Strategy

The Confederate war plan was simpler. If the Union forces could be held off and the war prolonged, as Jefferson Davis and others hoped, then the British or French, desperate for southern cotton, might be persuaded to join their cause. Or perhaps a long war would change public sentiment in the North and force Lincoln to seek a negotiated settlement. So while armies were forming in the South, Confederate diplomats were seeking military and financial assistance in London and Paris, and Confederate sympathizers in the North were urging an end to the Union's war effort.

> Confederate strategy: A lengthy war to erode northern morale

The Confederate representatives in Paris won a promise from France to recognize the Confederacy as a new nation *if* Great Britain would do the same. But the British foreign minister refused to work with the Confederates, partly in response to pressure from President Lincoln and partly out of Britain's desire to maintain its trade with the United States.

> Confederate strategy: Cotton diplomacy in Europe

Confederate leaders had assumed that Britain would have to support the South in order to get its cotton. As it turned out, however, the British, although eventually losing 400,000 jobs in their textile mills, were able to import enough cotton from their Asian colony, India, to maintain production of cloth. In the end, Confederate diplomacy in Europe was more successful in getting military supplies than in gaining official recognition of the Confederacy as an independent nation.

Anaconda Plan Union's primary war strategy calling for a naval blockade of major southern seaports and then dividing the Confederacy by gaining control of the Tennessee, Cumberland, and Mississippi Rivers.

UNION SOLDIERS Smoking their pipes, these soldiers share a moment of rest and a bottle of whiskey. **Which ethnic groups participated in the Union and Confederate armies? Which did not?**

Forming Armies

Once the fighting began, President Lincoln called for 500,000 more men, a staggering number at the time and one that the Confederacy struggled to match. "War! And volunteers are the only topics of conversation or thought," wrote a student at Ohio's Oberlin College. "I cannot study. I cannot sleep, and I don't know as I can write." Tennessee's twenty-one-year-old Sam Watkins reported that everyone in his town "was eager for the war."

The average age of soldiers in the Civil War was twenty-six. Some 30–35 percent of them were married. A quarter of the Union soldiers and sailors were immigrants—French, Germans, Irish, Poles, and other Europeans—many of whom could not speak English.

They enlisted for many reasons: a strong belief in the Union cause, cash bonuses, regular pay, or the need for a steady job. Whatever the reason, the high proportion of immigrants in the Union army gave it an ethnic diversity absent in the Confederate ranks. In the Confederacy, the smaller male population forced Jefferson Davis to enact a conscription law (a mandatory military draft). On April 16, 1862, all white males aged eighteen to thirty-five were declared members of the army for three years, and those already in uniform were required to serve until the war ended. Some resented being drafted. "From this time until the end of the war," a Tennessee soldier wrote, "a soldier was simply a machine, a conscript. . . . All our pride and valor had gone, and we were sick of war and cursed the Southern Confederacy." In 1862, the upper age for military service was raised to forty-five; and in 1864, the age range was further extended to fifty. Age often did not matter, however, since recruiting officers frequently decided for themselves which boys "were old enough."

The Confederate conscription law included controversial loopholes, however. First, a draftee might escape service either by providing an able-bodied "substitute" who was not of draft age or by paying $500 in cash. Second, elected officials and key civilian workers, as well as planters with twenty or more slaves, were exempted from military service.

The Union took nearly another year to force men into service. In 1863, with the war going badly for the Federal armies, the government began to draft men aged twenty to forty-five. But many younger men served in the war. The Union army had more than a thousand soldiers under the age of fifteen, some of whom served as regimental "drummer boys"; one of these was just nine years old.

As in the South, there were ways for northerners to avoid military service. Exemptions were granted to selected federal and state officeholders and to others on medical or compassionate grounds. In the North, a draftee might pay $300 to avoid service. The fathers of Theodore and Franklin Roosevelt paid for substitutes, as did two future presidents, Chester A. Arthur and Grover Cleveland. Such exemptions led to bitter complaints on both sides about the conflict being "a rich man's war and a poor man's fight." Widespread public opposition to the draft emerged in both the North and South.

Why They Fought

Most of the 3 million in uniform were volunteers, not draftees. Why did they risk their lives? The reasons varied, but many stressed that they felt compelled by a sense of manly duty, honor, and patriotism. A Union volunteer enlisted because he felt a powerful "sense of duty to my country and myself . . . to give up *life* if need be . . . in the battle for freedom & right, opposed to slavery & wrong." Similarly, a Texas private insisted that he and other Confederates were "fighting for matters real and tangible . . . our property [slaves] and our homes."

Their duties as *men* drove many combatants. An Alabama planter who joined the Confederate army as a cavalryman explained to his anxious wife why he had to fight. "My honor, my duty, your reputation & that of my darling little boy," he stressed, forced him to don a uniform "when our bleeding country needs the services of every man." Likewise, an Illinois officer felt that the Union soldiers were guided by "a high and noble sentiment, but after all a sentiment [preserving the Union and ending slavery]. They [Confederates] are fighting for independence and are animated by passion and hatred against invaders [Yankees]."

Both sides agreed that the stakes were high. Many Confederates were convinced that defeat would enslave the whites. "If we was to lose," a Mississippi private wrote his wife in 1862, "we would be slaves to the Yanks and our

RECRUITMENT POSTER A glorifying advertisement urges Americans to join the Empire Brigade, rashly promising not only accommodations and sustenance, but a monthly wage and $100 bounty at the war's end.

children would have a yoke of bondage thrown around their necks." Most Confederates could not imagine life without black slavery. "This country without slave labor would be completely worthless," wrote a Mississippi lieutenant. "We can only live & exist by that species of labor: hence I am willing to fight to the last." To be sure, many Union soldiers were fighting to preserve the Union rather than free the slaves, but a surprising number of Yankee soldiers believed that winning the war meant abolishing slavery. A private from Minnesota felt that the war "will never end until we end slavery."

The Civil War divided many families. In June 1862, two brothers, Alexander and James Campbell, fought against each other in the same battle. Born in Scotland, they had immigrated with their families to the United States several years before. Alexander settled in New York City while his brother, James, moved to Charleston, South Carolina. With the outbreak of war, the two brothers each decided to support their respective regions.

At the Battle of Secessionville on James Island, South Carolina, Alexander joined Union forces in assaulting a Confederate fort, one of whose defenders was James. Afterward, James wrote his brother, expressing his astonishment that Alexander had been among the Union attackers. "I was . . . doing my best to beat you, but I hope that you and I will never again meet face to face." Yet if they should encounter one another in combat, he urged his brother, "Do your duty to your cause, for I can assure you I will strive to discharge my duty to my country & my cause."

The Life of a Soldier

The average Civil War soldier or sailor was twenty-five years old, stood five feet eight inches, and weighed 143 pounds. A third of the southern soldiers could neither read nor write. One in nine would be killed or wounded. Half the Union soldiers and two thirds of the Confederates were farmers. Army camps featured their own libraries, theatrical stages, churches, numerous "mascot" pets—and monotonous routine.

An old saying among soldiers is "hurry up and wait." In the Civil War, soldiers spent far more time preparing for war than actually fighting. A witty Pennsylvania private wrote home that "the first thing in the morning is drill. Then drill, then drill again. Then drill, drill, a little more drill, then drill, lastly drill."

Life in army camps was difficult at best. "Camp life is so monotonous," moaned a South Carolina officer. When not training, soldiers spent time outdoors, in makeshift shelters, or in small tents talking, reading books, newspapers, or letters; playing cards or checkers; singing songs; smoking pipes; washing and mending clothes; and fighting swarms of lice and invading ticks, chiggers, and mosquitoes. Their diet was plain and repetitious: baked bread crackers (called hardtack), salted meat (pork or beef), and coffee.

Some soldiers could not stand the rigors and strains of combat and camp life. Desertions soared with each passing year, as did incidents of drunkenness, thievery, and insubordination. Punishments varied. Some deserters were shot or hanged. Others were tied to a ball and chain, forced to bury dead

SURGEONS CALL.   STUCK IN THE MUD.   HARD TACK.   A SHELL IS COMING.

DAILY LIFE These souvenir cards show various parts of life in Civil War camps, from enduring illnesses and a bland diet of hard tack to getting stuck in the mud and hiding from enemy fire.

horses or tend to animals, or drummed out of the service. Most of those who served on either side, however, came to view the experience as beneficial.

Becoming Warriors

Only a few of those who fought in the Civil War had any experience in battle. A Massachusetts volunteer remembered that he and his fellow enlistees "knew absolutely nothing of war. They were stirred by patriotic impulses to enlist and crush out treason."

Thirty-two-year-old Sullivan Ballou, a Rhode Island lawyer and legislator who enlisted as an officer in the Union army, confessed to his wife Sarah that he would have loved nothing more than to have stayed with his family and seen their sons grow to "honorable manhood," but his ultimate priority was serving his country. Major Ballou was willing to sacrifice all "to help maintain this Government, and to pay that debt" to his forefathers. It was his last letter home. A week later, Sullivan Ballou died in the first Battle of Bull Run when a cannon ball severed his right leg.

The horrific reality of combat traumatized many soldiers. A Texan described his first experience in battle as a gruesome shock. A cannon ball exploded nearby, "killing one man and cutting off both legs of his brother," who turned his severed torso to scream for his brother. When he saw that he was dead, he put a pistol "to his head and killed himself."

As the months passed and the suffering grew, many combatants saw their initial enthusiasm for the "glorious cause" erode. Charles Biddlecom, a farmer from upstate New York, volunteered in May 1861 as an enlisted man in the Union army. He was eager to get the "fuss" with the South over and whip the "Southern whelps."

By 1863, however, Biddlecom had had enough of war. Sick with dysentery, overrun with lice, and miserably lonesome, he and three others were forced to live in a "little dog kennel" shelter just four feet high. Although he still hated slaveholders, he now felt it might have been "better in the end to have let the South go out peaceably and tried her hand at making a nation."

Like many other soldiers and sailors on both sides, Biddlecom's moods and motives for fighting fluctuated wildly depending upon the course of the war. In 1864, he confessed that the Union army was "worn out, discouraged, [and] demoralized." He stuck it out to preserve his sense of manly honor, but "as for men fighting from pure love of country, I think them as few as white blackbirds." He emphasized that he was neither a "Union saver" nor a "freedom shrieker." At one point, he had heard enough about a war to free the slaves: "to hell with the devilish twaddle about freedom."

By the time the war ended, however, Biddlecom's emotions had again reversed themselves with the Union victory. He celebrated the defeat of the Confederacy for affirming that "freedom shall extend over the whole nation." The "greatest nation of Earth" showed that it would not surrender to "traitors in arms."

Blacks in the South

Union advantage: Slaves run away from southern owners

As had happened during the Revolutionary War and the War of 1812, enslaved African Americans took advantage of the confusion created by the war to run away, engage in sabotage, join the Union war effort, or pursue their own interests. A plantation owner in Tennessee, for example, hated the war's effect on his slaves, as he confessed in his diary: "My Negroes all at home, but working only as they see fit, doing little." Some of them had reported that they had "rather serve the federals than work on the farm." Later, he revealed that when Union armies arrived in the area, his slaves had "stampeded" to join the Yankees.

Fighting in the West

During the Civil War, fighting spilled across the Mississippi River into the Great Plains and all the way to California. In 1862, a small Confederate army tried to conquer the New Mexico territory, which then included Arizona, but was repelled. Amid sporadic fighting, western settlement slowed but did not stop. New discoveries of gold and silver in the Sierra Nevadas in eastern California and in Montana and Colorado lured more prospectors. Dakota, Colorado, and Nevada gained territorial status in 1861; Idaho and Arizona, in 1863; and Montana, in 1864. Silver-rich Nevada gained statehood in 1864.

Kansas and Indian Territory

The most intense fighting west of the Mississippi occurred along the Kansas-Missouri border, where the disputes that had developed between the pro-slavery and anti-slavery settlers in the 1850s turned into brutal guerrilla warfare. The most prominent pro-Confederate leader in the area was William Quantrill. He and his followers, mostly teenagers, fought under a black flag, meaning that they would kill anyone who surrendered. In destroying Lawrence, Kansas, in 1863, Quantrill ordered his men to "kill every male and burn every house." By the end of the day, they had massacred 182 boys and men. Their opponents, the Jayhawkers, responded in kind. They tortured and hanged pro-Confederate prisoners, burned houses, and destroyed livestock.

Many Indian nations became embroiled in the Civil War. Some 20,000 Native Americans served on both sides, and in Oklahoma they fought against each other. Indians among the "Five Civilized Tribes" owned African American slaves and felt a bond with southern whites. Oklahoma's proximity to Texas influenced the Choctaws and Chickasaws to support the Confederacy. The Cherokees, Creeks, and Seminoles were more divided in their loyalties. For them, the Civil War fractured their unity. The Cherokees, for example, split in two, some supporting the Union and others the Confederacy. Caught in the cross-fires of battle, one third of Cherokee women ended up widows by the end of the war.

Kentucky and Tennessee

Little happened of military significance east of the Appalachian Mountains before May 1862. On the other hand, important battles occurred in the West (from the Appalachians to the Mississippi River). Early in 1862, General Ulysses S. Grant, a superb horseman but inexperienced commander, made the first Union thrust against the Confederate army in Kentucky and Tennessee. Moving on boats out of Cairo, Illinois, and Paducah, Kentucky, the Union army steamed up the Tennessee River and captured Fort Henry in northern Tennessee on February 6. Grant then moved quickly overland to attack nearby Fort Donelson, on the Cumberland River, where, on February 16, some 12,000 Confederates surrendered.

Shiloh

After defeats in Kentucky and Tennessee, the Confederates in the western theater fled southward before regrouping under General Albert Sydney Johnston at Corinth in northern Mississippi near the Tennessee border. Their goal was to protect the Memphis & Charleston Railroad linking the lower Mississippi Valley and the Atlantic coast. A Confederate secretary of war called the railroad the "vertebrae of the Confederacy."

While planning the Union attack on Corinth, Grant made a costly mistake when he exposed his 42,000 troops on a rolling plateau, hemmed in between Lick and Snake Creeks flowing into the Tennessee River. He also failed to dig defensive trenches. General Johnston recognized Grant's oversight, and just before dawn on Sunday, April 6, he launched a surprise attack on the unsuspecting Federals, urging his men to be "worthy of your race and lineage; worthy of the women of the South."

The 44,000 Confederates screaming the blood-curdling "Rebel yell" struck suddenly at Shiloh, a whitewashed Methodist chapel in the center of

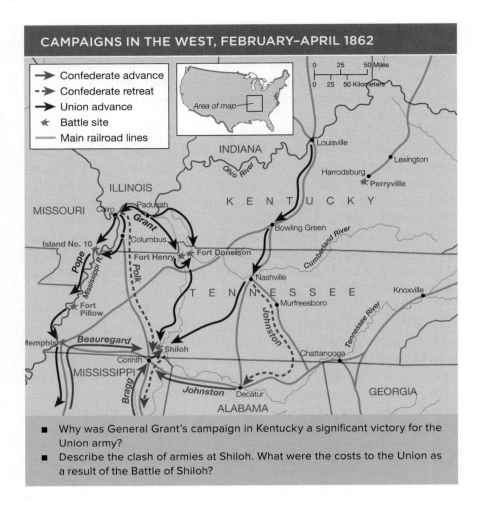

CAMPAIGNS IN THE WEST, FEBRUARY–APRIL 1862

→ Confederate advance
- → Confederate retreat
→ Union advance
★ Battle site
— Main railroad lines

- Why was General Grant's campaign in Kentucky a significant victory for the Union army?
- Describe the clash of armies at Shiloh. What were the costs to the Union as a result of the Battle of Shiloh?

the Union camp in southwestern Tennessee. Most of Grant's startled troops were still sleeping or eating breakfast; many died in their bedrolls. At one point, General Johnston rode into the thick of the fighting, urging the Rebels forward: "Men, they are stubborn; we must use the bayonet. I will lead you!"

Johnston led them well, only to be shot himself. His aide yelled, "General, are you hurt?" Johnston replied, "Yes, and I fear seriously." Aides took the Confederate commander off his horse, his right boot full of blood from a severed artery. He died in the shade of a large oak tree.

Johnston was only one of many who died that day. After hours of confused fighting with terrible losses on both sides, the fleeing Union soldiers were pinned against the river. One of them wrote that "this is going to be a great battle, such as I have been anxious to see for a long time, and I think I have [already] seen *enough* of it." The new Confederate commander, Pierre T. Beauregard, telegraphed President Jefferson Davis in Richmond that his army had scored "a complete victory, driving the enemy from every position."

BATTLE OF SHILOH This contemporary lithograph shows the gruesome Battle of Shiloh, which cost thousands of men their lives in the most deadly battle America had ever experienced.

The Union commanders saw it differently. General William T. Sherman, who had been wounded twice and had three horses shot from under him, visited Grant as a drenching rain fell amid the shrieking cries and muffled moans of thousands of wounded and dying warriors. "Well, Grant," he said, "we've had the devil's own day, haven't we?" Grant agreed but predicted that we will "lick 'em tomorrow."

And they did. Reinforced by 25,000 fresh Union troops, Grant's army took the offensive the next day, and the Confederates glumly withdrew twenty miles to Corinth. Confederate private Sam Watkins observed that "those Yankees were whipped, fairly whipped, and according to all the rules of war they ought to have retreated. But they didn't." Another Rebel soldier wrote home to his family that his first battle had shaken him: "Oh God, forever keep me out of such another fight. I was not scared. I was just in danger."

Shiloh, a Hebrew word meaning "Place of Peace," was the largest and costliest battle in which Americans had ever engaged up to that point. Some 100,000 men had fought, and a quarter of them had been killed or wounded. The 3,477 killed were more than had been killed in all the War of 1812. There were so many corpses on the battlefield that Grant could not walk in any direction without "stepping on dead bodies." He now realized that the only way the cruel war would end would be through "complete conquest."

Union strategy: "Complete conquest"

Like so many battles to come, Shiloh was a story of missed opportunities and lucky accidents. Throughout the Civil War, winning armies would fail to pursue their retreating foes, thus allowing the wounded opponent to slip away, recover, and fight again.

After Shiloh, Union general Henry Halleck, already jealous of Grant's success, spread a false rumor that Grant had been drinking during the battle. Some urged Lincoln to fire Grant, but the president refused: "I can't spare this man; he fights." The timid Halleck, however, took Grant's place as commander, and the Union thrust in the Mississippi Valley southward ground to a halt.

New Orleans

Union seizes New Orleans

Just three weeks after the Battle of Shiloh, the Union won a great naval victory at New Orleans, as sixty-year-old David Farragut's warships blasted their way past Confederate forts under cover of darkness to take control of the largest city in the Confederacy. Union general Benjamin F. Butler, a cross-eyed Massachusetts Democrat, thereafter served as the military governor of captured New Orleans. When a Confederate sympathizer ripped down a Union flag, Butler had him hanged.

By shutting off the flow of goods, especially cotton, coming down the Mississippi River to the Gulf of Mexico, the loss of New Orleans was a devastating blow to the Confederate economy as the Union army took control of 1,500 cotton plantations and 50,000 slaves in the Mississippi Valley. The slave system was "forever destroyed and worthless" in Louisiana, reported a northern journalist.

Perryville

Union victory: Battle of Perryville (1862)

In the late summer of 1862, Confederate General Braxton Bragg's Army of Mississippi, 30,000 strong, used railroads to link up with General Edmund Kirby Smith's Army of East Tennessee. Their goal was to invade the North by taking control of the border state of Kentucky. At the Battle of Perryville in central Kentucky in October 1862, the outnumbered Confederates withdrew south toward Tennessee. The Union retained control of Kentucky for the rest of the war.

Fighting in the East

The fighting in the East remained fairly quiet for nine months after the Battle of Bull Run. In the wake of the Union defeat, Lincoln had appointed General George B. McClellan, a former railroad president, as head of the Army of the Potomac. The thirty-four-year-old McClellan, who encouraged journalists to call him "Little Napoleon," set about building the Union's most powerful, best-trained army.

Yet for all his self-confidence and organizational ability, McClellan was afraid to attack. Months passed while he trained his massive army to meet

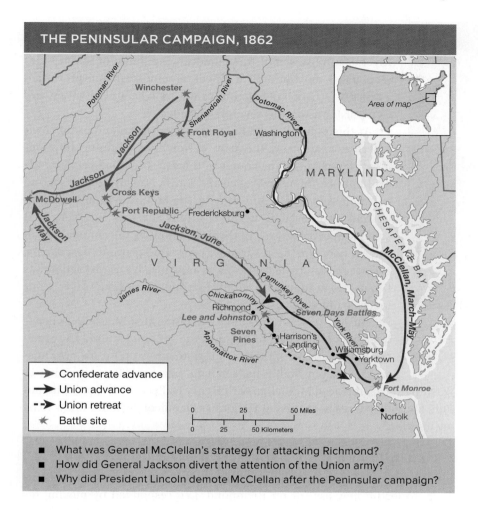

THE PENINSULAR CAMPAIGN, 1862

Legend:
- → Confederate advance
- → Union advance
- --→ Union retreat
- ✳ Battle site

- What was General McClellan's strategy for attacking Richmond?
- How did General Jackson divert the attention of the Union army?
- Why did President Lincoln demote McClellan after the Peninsular campaign?

the superior numbers of Confederates he mistakenly believed were facing him. Lincoln finally lost his patience and ordered McClellan to attack. "[You] must strike a blow," he told his reluctant commander.

McClellan's Peninsular Campaign

In mid-March 1862, McClellan finally moved his huge army of 122,000 men and 15,000 horses and mules on 400 ships and barges down the Potomac River and then through the Chesapeake Bay to the mouth of the James River at the tip of the Yorktown peninsula, southeast of Richmond, Virginia. McClellan's "Peninsular campaign" put the Union forces within sixty miles of the Confederate capital. But the overly cautious McClellan waited too long to strike. A frustrated Lincoln told McClellan, the war could be won only by *engaging* the Rebel army. "Once more," Lincoln told his commanding general, "let me tell you, it is indispensable to *you* that you strike a blow."

ROBERT E. LEE The Confederacy's greatest general, Lee served as military adviser to President Jefferson Davis and as commander of the Army of Northern Virginia.

On May 31, 1862, Confederate general Joseph E. Johnston struck the first blow at McClellan's army along the Chickahominy River, six miles east of Richmond. In the Battle of Seven Pines (Fair Oaks), only the arrival of Federal reinforcements prevented a disastrous Union defeat. Both sides took heavy casualties, and General Johnston was severely wounded.

At this point, Robert E. Lee assumed command of the Confederates' main army, the Army of Northern Virginia, a development that changed the course of the war. Dignified yet fiery, the brilliant Lee, fluent in French and Latin, had graduated second in his class at West Point. During the Mexican-American War, he had impressed General Winfield Scott as the "very best soldier [Scott] ever saw in the field." Now, as the commander of the Army of Northern Virginia, Lee would prove to be a daring, even reckless, strategist who was as aggressive as McClellan was timid. "He is silent, inscrutable, strong, like a God," said a Confederate officer.

On July 9, when President Lincoln visited McClellan's headquarters on the coast of Virginia, the general lectured the president at length on military strategy to cover up for his own mistakes. Lincoln finally had enough excuses. After returning to Washington, he replaced McClellan with Henry Halleck. Miffed at his demotion, McClellan angrily dismissed Halleck as an officer "whom I know to be my inferior."

Second Bull Run

Halleck ordered General John Pope, commander of the Union Army of Virginia, to lead a new assault on Richmond. Lee responded by moving his forces northward to strike Pope's army before McClellan's troops arrived. The Confederate commander knew that his only chance was to drive a wedge between the two larger Union armies so that he could deal with them one at a time.

Violating a basic rule of military strategy, Lee riskily divided his forces, sending Stonewall Jackson's "foot cavalry" around Pope's flank to attack his supply lines in the rear. At the Second Battle of Bull Run (or Manassas), fought in exhausting heat on almost the same site as the earlier battle, a confused Pope assumed that he faced only Jackson, but Lee's main army by that time had joined in.

On August 30, 1862, a crushing Confederate attack drove the larger Union army from the field, giving the Confederates a sensational victory and leading one disheartened Union officer to confess from his death bed that "General Pope had been outwitted. . . . Our generals have defeated us." In contrast, a Rebel soldier from Georgia wrote home that "General Lee stands now above all generals in modern history. Our men will follow him to the end."

LINCOLN'S SEARCH FOR A "FIGHTING GENERAL" Abraham Lincoln and George B. McClellan confer at Antietam, October 4, 1862. **What factors contributed to Lincoln's decision to replace McClellan?**

Emancipation

The Confederate victories in 1862 devastated northern morale and convinced Lincoln that he had to take bolder steps to win the war over an enemy fighting for and aided by enslaved labor. Now the North had to assault slavery itself. Once fighting began in 1861, the Union's need to keep the border slave states (Delaware, Kentucky, Maryland, and Missouri) in the Union had dictated caution on the volatile issue of emancipation. In August 1862, Lincoln worried that "to arm the negroes would turn 50,000 bayonets from the loyal Border states *against* us that were *for* us". Beyond that, Lincoln had to contend with a deep-seated racial prejudice among most northerners, who were willing to allow slavery to continue in the South. Lincoln himself harbored doubts about his constitutional authority to emancipate slaves.

Slaves in the War

The expanding war forced the issue. As Federal forces pushed into the Confederacy, runaway slaves began to turn up in Union army camps, and the commanders did not know what to do with them. One general refused to return runaway slaves. He instead designated the fugitive slaves as "contrabands of war" because they had been forced to build Confederate fortifications. The rules of war therefore allowed him to confiscate the refugee slaves. Thereafter the slaves who sought protection and freedom with Union forces

> CORE **OBJECTIVE**
> **2.** Evaluate Lincoln's decision to issue the Emancipation Proclamation and its impact on the war.

> "Contrabands of war"

CONTRABANDS Former slaves freed by the war's chaos on a farm in Cumberland Landing, Virginia, 1862. **How were runaway slaves treated by the Union forces?**

were known as **contrabands**. Some Union officers put them to work digging trenches, tending livestock, burying the dead, and building fortifications; others simply set them free.

Lincoln, meanwhile, began to edge toward emancipation. On April 16, 1862, he signed an act that abolished slavery in the District of Columbia; on June 19, another act excluded slavery from the western territories. Still, Lincoln insisted that the war was about restoring the Union, not ending slavery in the South. Like most northerners, he was more determined to end secession than to end slavery.

> Emancipation: Military necessity

Yet the course of the war changed Lincoln's outlook and transformed the conflict into a struggle for human freedom. In the summer of 1862, Lincoln decided that emancipation of slaves in the Confederate states was necessary to win the war. Many of the 3.5 million enslaved laborers in the Confederacy, he knew, were being forced to aid the Rebel war effort. Further, morale in the North needed a boost, and public opinion was swinging toward emancipation.

In July 1862, Lincoln confided to his cabinet that "decisive and extreme measures must be adopted." Emancipation, he said, had become "a military necessity, absolutely necessary to the preservation of the Union. We must free the slaves or be ourselves subdued." It was "the only" policy that could help win the war. Secretary of State William H. Seward agreed but advised Lincoln to delay the announcement until after a Union battlefield victory to avoid being viewed as desperate.

contrabands Runaway slaves who sought refuge in Union military camps or who lived in areas of the Confederacy under Union control.

Antietam—The Turning Point

Robert E. Lee made his own momentous decision in the summer of 1862: he would invade Maryland and thereby force the Union army to leave northern Virginia and thereby relieve the pressure on Richmond. He also hoped to influence the upcoming elections in the North and gain official recognition of the Confederacy from Great Britain and France, which would bring desperately needed military supplies from Europe to the Confederacy. In addition, Lee and Jefferson Davis hoped that Confederate supporters in Maryland would rise up against the Union. For those reasons and others, in September 1862 Lee and his 40,000 troops, many of them ragged, barefoot, and underfed, pushed north across the Potomac River into western Maryland.

On September 17, 1862, the Union and Confederate armies clashed in the furious **Battle of Antietam** (Sharpsburg). Had not Union soldiers discovered Lee's detailed battle plans, wrapped around three cigars, which one of his messengers had carelessly dropped on the ground, the Confederates might have won. Instead, McClellan, if he moved his 100,000 men quickly, could destroy Lee's Army of Northern Virginia while they were scattered and on the move. As always, however, McClellan moved slowly, "afraid to risk" losing, enabling Lee to regroup his scattered units at Sharpsburg, between Antietam Creek and the Potomac River.

There, over the course of fourteen hours, the poorly coordinated Union army launched repeated attacks. The thunderous roar of the cannons "was beyond anything conceivable to the uninitiated," wrote a Union officer. The fighting was savage; a Union officer counted "hundreds of dead bodies lying in rows and in piles." The scene after "five hours of continuous slaughter" was "sickening, harrowing, horrible. O what a terrible sight!"

The next day, Lee braced for another Union attack, but it never came. That night, cloaked by fog and drizzling rain, the battered Confederates slipped south back across the Potomac River to the safety of Virginia.

Although the Battle of Antietam was technically a draw, Lee's northern invasion had failed. McClellan, never known for his modesty, claimed that he "had fought the battle splendidly." To him, the Battle of Antietam was "the most terrible battle of the age." Indeed, it was the bloodiest single day in American history. Some 6,400 soldiers on both sides were killed, twice as many as at Shiloh, and another 17,000 were wounded.

President Lincoln was pleased that Lee's army had been repulsed, but he was disgusted by McClellan's failure to attack the retreating Confederates and win the war. The president sent a sarcastic message to the timid general: "I have just read your dispatch about sore-tongued and fatigued horses. Will you pardon me for asking what the horses of your army have done . . . that fatigues anything?" Failing to receive a satisfactory answer, Lincoln

> Battle of Antietam (1862)

CASUALTIES AT THE BATTLE OF ANTIETAM A photograph taken on September 19, 1862, captures a wagon road known as "Bloody Lane." Used as a rifle pit by Confederate troops, it served as their gravesite after the most deadly day in American history.

Battle of Antietam (1862) Turning-point battle near Sharpsburg, Maryland, leaving almost 25,000 soldiers dead or wounded, in which Union forces halted a Confederate invasion of the North.

UNION VIEW OF THE EMANCIPATION PROCLAMATION A thoughtful Lincoln composes the proclamation with the Constitution and the Holy Bible in his lap. The Scales of Justice hang on the wall behind him.

again relieved McClellan of his command. Never again would McClellan command troops, but he would challenge Lincoln for the presidency in 1864 as a Democrat.

The Battle of Antietam had several important results. It revived sagging northern morale, dashed the Confederacy's hopes of forging alliances with Great Britain and France, and convinced Abraham Lincoln to free the slaves in the Confederate states.

Emancipation Proclamation

> Emancipation Proclamation: Civil War becomes a struggle to end slavery

The victory at Antietam convinced President Lincoln to take a momentous step. On September 22, 1862, five days after the battle, Lincoln issued the preliminary **Emancipation Proclamation**, which warned the Confederacy that if it did not stop fighting, all slaves in the Rebel states were to be made "forever free" in exactly 100 days, on January 1, 1863.

The Emancipation Proclamation was not based on ideas of racial equality or on abstract ideals of human dignity. It was, according to Lincoln, a "military necessity." The Proclamation freed only those slaves in areas still controlled by the Confederacy; it had no bearing on the four border states, since they remained in the Union. Lincoln limited the proclamation in this way because he believed that the Constitution allowed each state to decide the fate of slavery, so his only legal avenue was to declare the end of slavery as a military necessity to save the federal Union.

Emancipation Proclamation (1863) Military order issued by President Abraham Lincoln that freed slaves in areas still controlled by the Confederacy.

CONFEDERATE VIEW OF THE EMANCIPATION PROCLAMATION Surrounded by demonic faces hidden in his furnishings, Lincoln pens the proclamation with a foot trampling on a bound copy of the Constitution. The devil holds the inkwell before him.

When Lincoln officially signed the Emancipation Proclamation in January, however, he amended his original message, adding that the Proclamation was "an act of justice" as well as a military necessity. Those same constitutional concerns would lead him to urge Congress to pass the Thirteenth Amendment ending slavery everywhere.

The Emancipation Proclamation did *not* free the 500,000 enslaved blacks in the four Union border states of Delaware, Kentucky, Maryland, and Missouri, or the 300,000 slaves in Tennessee, western Virginia, coastal Carolina, and parts of Louisiana, which were back under Union control. As he signed the Emancipation Proclamation, Lincoln said, "I never, in my life, felt more certain that I was doing the right thing than I do in signing this paper." Simply restoring the Union was no longer the purpose of the war; the transformation of the South and the slave system was now the goal.

Reactions to Emancipation

Lincoln's threat to free slaves under Confederate control transformed the purpose of the war and triggered emotional reactions. The *Illinois State Register*, Lincoln's hometown newspaper, published in Springfield, savaged the president for violating the Constitution and causing "the permanent disruption of the republic." Democrats exploded with rage at the president's decision, and many voters felt likewise. In the November 1862 congressional elections, Republicans lost almost two dozen seats. Illinois, Indiana,

Pennsylvania, New York, and Ohio went Democratic. Even Lincoln's home district in Illinois elected a Democrat.

Although Lincoln's proclamation technically would free only the slaves where Confederates remained in control, many slaves in both the northern border states and the South claimed their freedom anyway. Word of Lincoln's landmark proclamation spread rapidly among the slave community in the Confederacy, arousing hopes of freedom, creating general confusion in the cities, and encouraging hundreds of thousands to escape. A Union general said that emancipation "was like an earthquake. It shook and shattered the whole previously existing social system."

Lincoln's action outraged Confederate leaders. Some predicted that emancipation would ignite a race war. By contrast, Frederick Douglass, the African American abolitionist leader, loved Lincoln's "righteous decree," for he knew that it would inspire abolitionists in the North and set in motion the eventual end of slavery throughout the United States.

As Lincoln had hoped, the Emancipation Proclamation did indeed aid the Union war effort. It enabled African Americans to enlist in the army and navy, and it undermined support for the Confederacy in Europe. The conversion of the Civil War from a conflict to restore the Union into a crusade to end slavery gave the Federal war effort moral legitimacy in the eyes of Europeans. At the same time, however, many northern Democrats savagely attacked Lincoln's proclamation, calling it dictatorial, unconstitutional, and catastrophic. "We Won't Fight to Free the Nigger," proclaimed one popular banner. A Massachusetts army officer agreed. "I am a strong Union man," he said, "but I am not willing to shed one drop of blood to fight Slavery."

Lincoln forcefully responded to his critics. "You say you will not fight to free negroes," he wrote. "Some of them seem willing to fight for you; but, no matter. Fight you, then, exclusively to save the Union. I issued the [emancipation] proclamation on purpose to aid you in saving the Union."

> **Union armies liberate Confederate slaves**

As the war continued and Union armies advanced deeper into the southern states, they liberated many slaves. At Camp Saxton, a former plantation on the coast of South Carolina near Beaufort, the South Carolina Volunteers, a new Union army regiment made up of former slaves, gathered on January 1, 1863, to celebrate Lincoln's official signing of the Emancipation Proclamation. They "cheered to the skies" after the proclamation was read. As Colonel Thomas W. Higginson, a white abolitionist from Massachusetts who was the new unit's commander, unfurled an American flag, the black troops spontaneously began singing "My Country 'Tis of Thee / Sweet land of liberty / Of thee I sing!" "I never saw anything so electric," Higginson reported. "It made all other words cheap; it seemed the choked voice of a race at last unloosed. Just think of it!—the first day they had ever had a country, the first flag they had seen which promised anything to their people."

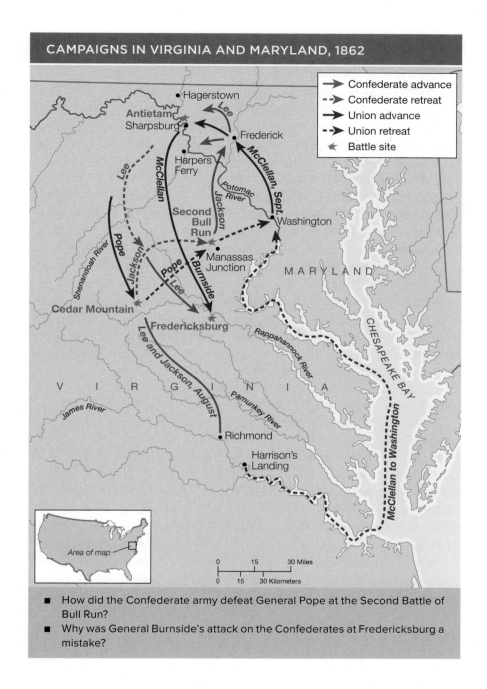

CAMPAIGNS IN VIRGINIA AND MARYLAND, 1862

→ Confederate advance
⇢ Confederate retreat
→ Union advance
⇢ Union retreat
✳ Battle site

- How did the Confederate army defeat General Pope at the Second Battle of Bull Run?
- Why was General Burnside's attack on the Confederates at Fredericksburg a mistake?

Fredericksburg

In his search for a new general to lead the Union war effort, Lincoln made the worst choice of all in the fall of 1862, when he turned to thirty-eight-year-old Ambrose E. Burnside, a tall, imposing man whose massive facial hair gave rise to the term *sideburns*. Twice before, Burnside had turned down the job because he felt unfit for so large a command. Now he accepted, although he still neither sought the command nor wanted it. He was right to be hesitant, as it turned out. Burnside was an eager fighter but a poor strategist who, according to Fanny Seward, the secretary of state's daughter, had "ten times as much heart as he has head." Burnside excelled at mismanagement, and the Union army soon paid for his mistakes.

On December 13, 1862, Burnside foolishly sent most of the 122,000 men in the Army of the Potomac across the icy Rappahannock River to assault Lee's outnumbered forces, who were well entrenched on a line of ridges and behind stone walls along a road at the base of Marye's Heights west of Fredericksburg, Virginia, the largest city between Richmond and Washington, D.C. Confederate cannons and muskets chewed up the advancing Federal soldiers as they crossed a half mile of open land.

The assault was, a Union general regretted, "a great slaughter-pen," more like murder than warfare. Wave after wave of blue-clad troops surged toward the well-protected Confederates. None of the Union soldiers made it to the Rebel lines. After attempting six futile assaults and taking 12,600 casualties, compared with fewer than 5,300 for the Confederates, a weeping Burnside told his shattered army to withdraw back across the river as darkness fell. As Burnside rode past his retreating men, his aide called for three cheers for their commander. All he got was sullen silence. For two days, rain, sleet, and snow turned the Union retreat into what came to be called the "Mud March," as the battered army trudged back to Washington, D.C.

Lincoln loses support over deadlocked war

The year 1862 ended with forces in the East deadlocked and the Union advance in the West stalled. Union morale kept dropping: northern Democrats were victorious in the fall congressional elections, sharply reducing the Republican majorities in the House and the Senate. Many Democrats were calling for a negotiated peace. Republicans—even Lincoln's own cabinet members—grew increasingly critical of the president's leadership. "If there is a worse place than hell," Lincoln sighed, "I am in it." Newspapers circulated rumors that Lincoln was going to resign. General Burnside, too, was under fire, with some of his own officers eager to testify publicly to his shortcomings. One of them claimed that the general was "fast losing his mind."

New York City Draft Riots

Northern resistance to the war effort

Lincoln's proclamation freeing slaves in the Confederacy created anxiety and anger among many laborers in the North who feared that freed southern blacks would eventually migrate north and take their jobs. In New York City, such fears erupted into violence. In July 1863, a group of 500 whites, led by volunteer firemen, assaulted the army draft office, shattering its windows, then burning it down. The rioters, now swollen by thousands others, mostly Irish and including women and children, ruthlessly took out their frustrations over the unfair military draft on blacks. Mobs rampaged through the streets of Manhattan, randomly assaulting African Americans, beating them, dragging them through the streets, and lynching a disabled black man while chanting "Hurrah for Jeff Davis." The violence went on for three days, killing 105 people and injuring thousands. Only the arrival of Federal soldiers put an end to the rioting. Thousands of terrified blacks thereafter moved out of the city for fear of continuing racial violence. Similar riots occurred in other northern cities, including Boston.

Blacks in the Military

In July 1862, in an effort to strengthen the Union war effort, the U.S. Congress had passed the **Militia Act**, which authorized the army to use freed slaves as laborers or soldiers (they were already eligible to serve in the navy). Lincoln, however, did not encourage the use of freed slaves as soldiers because he feared the reaction in the border states where slavery remained in place. It was only after the formal signing of the Emancipation Proclamation in January 1863 that the Union army aggressively recruited blacks.

On May 22, 1863, the U.S. War Department created the Bureau of Colored Troops to recruit free blacks and freed slaves. More than 180,000 blacks enlisted in the new U.S. Colored Troops. Some 80 percent of them were from southern states, and 38,000 of them gave their lives. In the navy, African Americans accounted for about a fourth of all enlistments; of these, more than 2,800 died. Initially, officers did not allow African Americans in combat, but the need to win the prolonged war changed that. Once in battle, they fought tenaciously. A white Union army private reported in the late spring of 1863 that the black troops "fight like the Devil."

To be sure, a still-widespread racism in the North influenced the status of African Americans in the Union military. Many people who opposed slavery did not support racial equality. Black soldiers and sailors were placed in all-black units led by white officers. They were also paid less than whites ($7 per month for black recruits versus $16 for white recruits) and were ineligible for the enlistment bonus paid to whites. Still, as Frederick Douglass declared, "This is no time for hesitation. . . . This is our chance, and woe betide us if we fail to embrace it."

Service in the Union army or navy provided former slaves a unique opportunity to grow in confidence, awareness, and maturity. A northern social worker in the South Carolina Sea Islands was "astonished" at the positive effects of "soldiering" on ex-slaves: "Some who left here a month ago to join [the army were] cringing, dumpish, slow," but now they "are ready to look you in the eye—are wide awake and active." By mid-1863, African American units were fighting in battles. Commenting on Union victories at Port

BLACK UNION ARMY SERGEANT Wearing his Union uniform and sword, this black Union sergeant poses with a copy of J. T. Headley's *The Great Rebellion* in his hand.

Militia Act (1862) Congressional measure that permitted freed slaves to serve as laborers or soldiers in the U.S. Army.

Hudson and Milliken's Bend, Louisiana, Lincoln reported that "some of our commanders . . . believe that . . . the use of colored troops constitutes the heaviest blow yet dealt to the rebels."

CORE **OBJECTIVE**

3. Analyze how the war affected social and economic life in the North and South.

The War behind the Lines

Feeding, clothing, supplying, and nursing the vast armies required tremendous sacrifices on the home fronts, both North and South. Farms and villages were transformed into battlefields, churches became makeshift hospitals, civilian life was disrupted, and families grieved for the soldiers who would not be coming home.

Women and the War

While breaking the bonds of slavery, the Civil War also loosened traditional restraints on female activity. "No conflict in history," a journalist wrote at the time, "was such a woman's war as the Civil War." Women on both sides played prominent roles. They went to work replacing men in mills and factories, sewed uniforms, composed patriotic poems and songs, and raised money and supplies.

In Greenville, South Carolina, when T. G. Gower went off to fight, his wife, Elizabeth, took over the family business, converting their carriage factory to produce military wagons and ambulances. Three thousand northern women worked as nurses with the U.S. Sanitary Commission, a civilian agency that provided medical relief and other services for soldiers. Other women, black and white, supported the freedmen's aid movement to help impoverished freed slaves.

In the North alone, some 20,000 women served as nurses or other health-related volunteers. The most famous nurses were Dorothea Lynde Dix and Clara Barton, both untiring volunteers in service to the wounded and the dying. Barton, who later founded the American Red Cross, claimed that the war advanced by fifty years the progress of women in gaining social and economic equality.

In many southern towns and counties, the home front became a world of white women and children and African American slaves. A resident of Lexington, Virginia, reported that there were "no men left" in town by mid-1862. Women suddenly found themselves full-time farmers or plantation managers, clerks, and teachers. Hundreds of women disguised themselves as men and fought in the war, while dozens served as spies. Others traveled with the armies, cooking meals, writing letters, and assisting with amputations. Confederates captured New Yorker Mary Edwards Walker, a Union battlefield surgeon, and imprisoned her for spying. She was the only woman in the war (and since) to be awarded the Congressional Medal of Honor, the nation's highest military award. In 1864, President Lincoln told a soldier that all the praise of women over the centuries did not do justice "for their conduct during the war."

CLARA BARTON Claiming that her place was "anywhere between the bullet and the battlefield," Barton oversaw the distribution of medicines to Union troops and later helped found the American Red Cross.

SUSIE KING TAYLOR Born into slavery, Taylor served as a nurse in Union-occupied Georgia and later operated a school for freedpeople.

Government during the War

While freeing the slaves was a momentous social and economic revolution, an even broader political revolution resulted from power in Congress shifting from the South to the North after secession. Before the war, southern Democratic congressmen exercised considerable influence, but once the secessionists had abandoned Congress to the Republicans, a dramatic change occurred.

In 1862, Republicans in Congress passed a more comprehensive tariff bill (called the Morrill Tariff in honor of its sponsor, Vermont Republican congressman Justin Smith Morrill) to raise government revenue and "protect" America's manufactures, agriculture, mining, and fishing industries from foreign competition. For the rest of the nineteenth century, U.S. manufacturers were the most protected in the world in terms of high federal tariffs discouraging foreign imports.

The Republican-dominated Congress, with Lincoln's support, took advantage of the departure of southern Democrats to enact legislation reflecting its belief (and that of the old Whig party) that an activist federal

Expanding a national economy and federal government

government could benefit the nation by diligently promoting economic development and thereby creating the "greatest nation on earth."

To that end, Congress approved the **Pacific Railway Act (1862)**, which provided federal funding and grants of land to railroads to construct a 1,900 mile-long transcontinental line from Omaha, Nebraska, to Sacramento, California. In addition, a **Homestead Act (1862)** allotted 160 acres of land to each settler who agreed to work the land for five years. To help farmers become more productive, the Congress also created a new federal agency, the Department of Agriculture.

Two other key pieces of Republican legislation were the **Morrill Land-Grant College Act (1862)**, which provided states with 30,000 acres of federal land to help finance the creation of public universities that would teach "agriculture and mechanic arts." The **National Banking Act (1863)** created national banks that could issue paper money. All these wartime measures had long-term significance for the growth of the national economy—and the expansion of the federal government.

Union Finances

In December 1860, as southern states announced their plans to secede, the federal treasury was virtually empty. There was not enough cash on hand to fund a massive war. To meet the war's huge expenses, Congress focused on three options: raising taxes, printing paper money, and selling government bonds to investors. The taxes came chiefly in the form of the Morrill Tariff on imports and taxes on manufactures and nearly every profession. A butcher, for example, had to pay thirty cents for every head of beef he slaughtered, ten cents for every hog, and five cents for every sheep.

In 1862, Congress created the Internal Revenue Service to implement the first income tax on citizens and corporations. The initial income tax rate was 3 percent on those with annual incomes more than $800. The tax rate went up to 5 percent on incomes over $10,000. Yet very few people paid the taxes. Only 250,000 people out of a population of 39 million had income high enough to pay taxes.

Congressman Justin S. Morrill, who had authored the Land-Grant College Act and the Tariff Act of 1862, endorsed the concept of "progressive" taxation, in which tax *rates* rose with designated income levels. Taxation, he argued, "must be distributed equally, not upon each man an equal amount, but a tax [rate] proportionate to his ability to pay." Congress also created an Internal Revenue Bureau within the Treasury Department to collect the new taxes.

The new federal tax revenues trickled in so slowly—they would meet only 21 percent of wartime expenditures—that Congress in 1862 resorted to printing paper money. Beginning with the Legal Tender Act of 1862, Congress authorized $450 million in new paper currency, which soon became known as *greenbacks* because of the color of the ink used to print the bills. The decision to print paper money was extremely important for the

Pacific Railway Act (1862) Congress provided funding for a transcontinental railroad from Nebraska west to California.

Homestead Act (1862) Legislation granting "homesteads" of 160 acres of government-owned land to settlers who agreed to work the land for at least five years.

Morrill Land-Grant College Act (1862) Federal statute that granted federal lands to states to help fund the creation of land-grant colleges and universities, which were founded to provide technical education in agriculture, mining, and industry.

National Banking Act (1863) The U.S. Congress created a national banking system to finance the enormous expense of the Civil War. It enabled loans to the government and established a single national currency, including the issuance of paper money ("greenbacks").

economy. Unlike previous paper currencies issued by local banks, greenbacks could not be exchanged for gold or silver. Instead, their value relied upon public trust in the government. The federal government also relied upon the sale of bonds to help finance the war effort. A Philadelphia banker named Jay Cooke (sometimes tagged the "Financier of the Civil War") mobilized a nationwide campaign to sell $2 billion in government bonds to private investors.

Confederate Finances

Confederate finances were a disaster by comparison. The Confederate government had to create a treasury and a revenue-collecting system from scratch. Moreover, the South's agrarian economy was land rich but cash poor compared to that of the North. While the Confederacy owned 30 percent of America's assets (businesses, land, slaves) in 1861, its currency in circulation was only 12 percent of that in the North.

In 1863, the desperate Confederate Congress began taxing nearly everything, but enforcement was poor and evasion easy. Altogether, taxes covered no more than 5 percent of Confederate war costs; bond issues accounted for less than 33 percent; and treasury notes (paper money), for more than 60 percent. During the war, the Confederacy issued more than $1 billion in paper currency, which, along with a shortage of consumer goods, caused prices to soar. By 1864, a turkey sold in the Richmond market for $100, flour brought $425 a barrel, and bacon was $10 a pound.

Such rampant price increases caused great distress. Poverty drove some southerners to take desperate measures. Frustrations over the burdens of war increasingly erupted into rioting, looting, military desertions, and mass protests against the Confederate government. David Harris, a farmer, deserted from the army because the cause was lost: "I am now going to work instead of to the war," he wrote home.

Union Politics and Civil Liberties

The North had its share of dissension and factionalism. Lincoln proved to be a remarkable manager of political conflict, in part because he refused to nurse grudges against his opponents. During the war, Lincoln had to fend off uprisings against him in Congress and conspiracies against him among his cabinet members. Throughout the war, the president faced a radical wing of Republicans composed mainly of militant abolitionists. Led by Thaddeus Stevens in the House and Charles Sumner in the Senate, the Radical Republicans wanted Union armies to seize southern plantations and give the land to the former slaves. The majority of Republicans, however, continued to back Lincoln's more cautious approach.

The Democratic party in the North suffered the loss of its southern wing and the death of its leader, Stephen A. Douglas, in June 1861. By and large, northern Democrats favored the war only for the purpose of restoring the Union "as it was [before 1860] and the Constitution as it is," giving reluctant

Financing the war: Legal Tender Act (1862)

Financing the Confederate war effort: Taxation, currency troubles, soaring inflation, and social unrest

support to Lincoln's war policies but opposing Republican economic legislation. So-called War Democrats, such as Tennessee senator Andrew Johnson and Secretary of War Edwin M. Stanton, backed Lincoln's policies, while a peace wing of the Democratic party preferred an end to the fighting, even if that meant risking the Union.

An extreme fringe of the peace wing flirted with outright disloyalty. The **Copperhead Democrats** (venomous snakes), as they were called, were strongest in states such as Ohio, Indiana, and Illinois. They openly sympathized with the Confederacy, savagely criticized Lincoln as "an idiot" and a 'gorilla,' and called for an immediate end to the war.

> Violation of civil liberties in the North

Such support for the enemy led Lincoln to crack down hard. Like all wartime leaders, he faced the challenge of balancing the urgent needs of winning a war and suppressing treason with the protection of civil liberties. Early in the war, Lincoln assumed emergency powers, including the power to suspend the writ of *habeas corpus*, which guarantees arrested citizens a speedy hearing before a judge.

The Constitution states that governments may suspend the right of *habeas corpus* only in cases of rebellion or invasion, but Supreme Court justice Roger Taney and several congressional leaders argued that Congress alone had the authority to take such action. By the Habeas Corpus Act of 1863, Congress authorized the president to suspend the writ. Thereafter, Union soldiers and local sheriffs arrested many Confederate sympathizers in the northern states. Union general Henry Halleck jailed one Missourian for saying, "[I] wouldn't wipe my ass with the stars and stripes."

Confederate Politics and States' Rights

Unlike Lincoln, Jefferson Davis never had to face a presidential contest. He and his vice president, Alexander Stephens, were elected without opposition in 1861 for a six-year term. But discontent with Davis grew as the war dragged on. Poor white southerners expressed bitter resentment of the planter elite while food grew scarce and prices skyrocketed. A bread riot in Richmond on April 2, 1863, ended only when President Davis himself threatened to shoot the protesters, most of whom were women.

> States' rights vs. war effort

Davis's greatest challenge came from the southern politicians who had embraced secession and then criticized the "tyrannical" powers exercised by Davis in Richmond. Critics asserted states' rights against the authority of the Confederate government, just as they had against the Union. Georgia's governor, Joseph Brown, hated Jefferson Davis, explaining that he had joined the Confederacy to "sustain the rights of the states and prevent the consolidation of the Government, and I am still a *rebel* . . . no matter who may be in power."

Among other fatal flaws, the Confederacy suffered from Davis's difficult personality. While Lincoln was a shrewd pragmatist, Davis, blind in one eye and suffering chronic headaches, was a brittle ideologue with a waspish temper. Once he made a decision, nothing could change his mind, and he

Copperhead Democrats
Democrats in northern states who opposed the Civil War and argued for an immediate peace settlement with the Confederates; Republicans labeled them "Copperheads," likening them to venomous snakes.

could never admit a mistake. One southern politician said that Davis was "as stubborn as a mule."

Such a personality was ill suited to the chief executive of an infant—and fractious—nation. Cabinet members resigned almost as soon as they were appointed. During the four years of the Confederacy, there were three secretaries of state and six secretaries of war. Vice President Stephens, known as "Little Alec" because he weighed less than a hundred pounds, carried on a running battle against President Davis's "military despotism." The chronically ill and freakishly stooped Stephens found Davis so "timid, petulant, peevish, and obstinate" that the vice president, frail as a withered leaf, left Richmond in 1862 to sulk at his Georgia home.

Chancellorsville

Amid the political infighting, the war ground on. After the Union disaster at Fredericksburg at the end of 1862, Lincoln fired Ambrose Burnside and turned to General Joseph Hooker, a hard-fighting, hard-drinking leader whose fierceness had earned him the nickname "Fighting Joe."

With a force of 130,000 men, the largest Union army yet gathered, an overconfident Hooker during the first week in May 1863 failed his leadership test at Chancellorsville, not a town but a solitary home, the Chancellor House, surrounded by woods in eastern Virginia. "My plans are perfect," Hooker boasted. "May God have mercy on General Lee, for I will have none."

Hooker spoke too soon. The always bold Robert E. Lee, with perhaps half as many soldiers, split his army in thirds and gave Hooker a painful lesson in the art of elusive mobility when Stonewall Jackson's 28,000 Confederates again surprised the Union army, smashing into its exposed right flank and forcing it to retreat. "It was pandemonium," recalled a Union soldier.

"My God, my God," moaned Lincoln when he heard the news. "What will the country say?" The Confederate victory at Chancellorsville was the peak of Lee's military career, but it would also be his last significant victory.

The Faltering Confederacy

The Confederate strategy of fighting largely a defensive war worked well in the early years of the war. As the armies maneuvered for battle in the spring of 1863, Robert E. Lee's superior generalship boosted Confederate spirits—until Lincoln found a commanding general as capable as Lee: Ulysses S. Grant, only five-foot-eight inches tall and weighing 135 pounds but blessed with a rugged, ruthless determination to win on the battlefield—at all cost.

Vicksburg

While Lee's army held the Federals at bay in the East, Ulysses S. Grant had been inching his army down the Mississippi River toward the Confederate stronghold of Vicksburg, Mississippi, a busy commercial town situated on

CORE OBJECTIVE

4. Describe the military turning points in 1863 and 1864 that ultimately led to the Confederacy's defeat.

Battle of Vicksburg: Gaining control of the Mississippi River

ULYSSES S. GRANT Lincoln finally found a general to rival Lee in Grant, pictured here at his headquarters in City Point (now Hopewell), Virginia.

Battle of Vicksburg (1863)
A protracted battle in northern Mississippi in which Union forces under Ulysses S. Grant besieged the last major Confederate fortress on the Mississippi River, forcing the inhabitants into starvation and then submission on July 4, 1863.

high bluffs overlooking a sharp horseshoe bend in the majestic river. Capturing the Rebel stronghold, Grant stressed, "was of the first importance."

Vicksburg was the only rail and river junction between Memphis, Tennessee, and New Orleans. If Union forces could gain control of the Mississippi River, they could split the Confederacy in two and prevent Western food and livestock from reaching the Confederate armies in the East.

While the Union navy ran gunboats and transports past the Confederate cannons overlooking the river, Grant moved his army eastward on a campaign through Mississippi that Lincoln later called "one of the most brilliant in the world." Grant captured Jackson, Mississippi and won a half-dozen battles while outmaneuvering two Confederate armies before pinning the 31,000 Confederates inside Vicksburg so tightly that "not a cat could have crept out . . . without being discovered."

In the **Battle of Vicksburg**, Grant decided to wear down the encircled Confederates through constant bombardment (22,000 shells pummeled the city) and gradual starvation. Forced to live in cellars or caves dug to protect them from the constant shelling, the Rebel soldiers and the city's residents were trapped; they could neither escape nor be reinforced or resupplied with food and ammunition. As the weeks passed, the gnawing hunger became unbearable. Desperate Confederates and civilians ate their horses and mules, then dogs and cats, and finally rats, which sold for a dollar each. One starving girl ate her pet bird.

General John C. Pemberton, the Confederate commander at Vicksburg, reported to Jefferson Davis that the situation in the beleaguered city was "hopeless." A group of ragged soldiers pleaded with their commander: "If you can't feed us, you had better surrender us, horrible as that idea is." Yet Pemberton, a Pennsylvania native whose Virginia-born wife convinced him to fight for the Confederacy, remained determined to outlast the Union army surrounding him.

Gettysburg

Vicksburg's plight led President Jefferson Davis to ask General Lee to send troops from Virginia to break the siege. Lee, however, had a better idea. He would make another daring strike into the Union in hopes of forcing the Federal army surrounding Vicksburg to rush north. He also hoped that a bold northern offensive would assist peace-seeking northern Copperhead Democrats in their efforts to end the war on terms favorable to the Confederacy. The stakes were high. A Confederate general said the invasion into Maryland and Pennsylvania would "either destroy the Yankees or bring them to terms." Or be a disaster for Lee, as it turned out.

In June 1863, the fabled Army of Northern Virginia, which Lee said was made up of "invincible troops" who would "go anywhere and do anything if properly led," again moved northward across western Maryland, taking thousands of animals and wagons as well as throngs of slaves to support the army. The Confederates moved quickly. As a Rebel soldier said, he had enjoyed "breakfast in Virginia, whiskey in Maryland, and supper in Pennsylvania."

Neither side expected Gettysburg, a small farming town in southeastern Pennsylvania, to be the site of a monumental battle. Unsuspecting Confederate troops entered the town at dawn on June 30 and collided with Union cavalry units that had been tracking their movements. The main forces of both sides—65,000 Confederates and 85,000 Federals—then raced to the scene, and on July 1 the two armies commenced the **Battle of Gettysburg**, the most dramatic contest of the war.

As the battle began, seventy-year-old John Burns, a Scottish-born Gettysburg resident and a veteran of the War of 1812, approached the Union lines wearing a brass-buttoned formal waistcoat and a tall black silk hat that had seen better days. He carried an old flintlock musket and a powder horn. Along the way, he encountered a wounded soldier and borrowed his more modern rifle. He then told Colonel Langhorne Wister that he wanted to join the fight. When Wister refused, Burns made such a convincing case that the Union officer finally relented and let him join a Wisconsin regiment. He would be wounded in the chest, arm, and leg yet was able to crawl to the cellar of a nearby house, where he found help. A statue of Burns now graces the Gettysburg battlefield.

Battle of Gettysburg (1863) A monumental three-day battle in southern Pennsylvania, widely considered a turning point in the war, in which Union forces defeated Lee's Confederate army and forced it back into Virginia.

Battle of Gettysburg: Confederate counterstrategy—a northern offensive

PICKETT'S CHARGE In a courageous and doomed effort, the Confederate soldiers (in the foreground) led by General Pickett prepare to advance on a line of well-armed Union troops.

Initially, the Confederates pushed the Federals out of the town, but the Union troops retreated into stronger positions on high ridges to the south and west. The new Union commander, General George Meade, rushed reinforcements to the heights overlooking the town.

On July 2, wave after wave of screaming Confederates assaulted Meade's army, pushing the Federal lines back across blood-soaked wheat fields and through peach orchards but never breaking through. Some 16,000 were killed or wounded on both sides during the second day of fighting. But worse was to come.

The next day, July 3, against the objections of his favorite general, James Longstreet, Robert E. Lee staked everything on one final assault against the well-defended Union lines along Cemetery Ridge. At about two o'clock on the broiling summer afternoon, three Confederate infantry divisions—about 12,500 men in all—emerged from the woods into the brilliant sunlight and prepared for a doomed attack. General George Pickett, commander of the lead division, told them to "charge the enemy and remember Old Virginia!"

Pickett's charge

With drums pounding and bugles blaring, a gray wave of sweating Rebels began a desperate mile-long advance up a grassy slope crisscrossed with fences. Colorful battle-flags, beating drums, and thousands of glistening bayonets announced their attack.

Awaiting them behind a low stone wall at the top of the ridge were 120 Union cannons and thousands of rifles. The confederate attack was an age-old form of glorious suicide. As a Union soldier remembered, the Rebels displayed a desperate courage: they "came on in magnificent order with the step of men who believed themselves invincible."

Once the Federals were ordered to fire, the attacking Confederates were "enveloped in a dense cloud of dust. Arms, heads, blankets, guns, and knapsacks were tossed into the clear air." Only a few Rebels made it to the top of the ridge, where they fought bravely in hand-to-hand combat. A Rebel general climbed atop the stone wall and shouted: "Come on, boys! Give them the cold steel! Who will follow me?"

Two minutes later, he was dead—as was the Confederate assault—when Union soldiers held in reserve rushed to close the gap in their lines. Then, with stunning suddenness, the carnage was over. The surviving Confederates retreated to the woods where they had started. The once-roaring battlefield was now a deathly quiet field of horror punctuated by the "moanings and groanings" of thousands of wounded soldiers and horses.

What General Lee had called the "grand charge" was, in the end, a grand failure. As the famous Confederate leader watched the

"A HARVEST OF DEATH" Timothy H. O'Sullivan's grim photograph of the dead at Gettysburg.

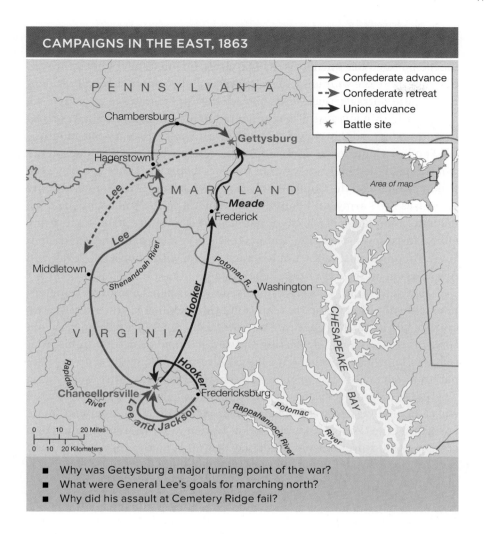

CAMPAIGNS IN THE EAST, 1863

Legend:
→ Confederate advance
--→ Confederate retreat
→ Union advance
✷ Battle site

- Why was Gettysburg a major turning point of the war?
- What were General Lee's goals for marching north?
- Why did his assault at Cemetery Ridge fail?

survivors returning from the bloody field, Lee muttered, "All this has been my fault." He then ordered General Pickett to prepare his battered division for another attack, only to have Pickett tartly reply: "General Lee, I have no division now." Half his men lay dead or wounded.

Some 42,000 on both sides were killed, wounded, or missing during three days at Gettysburg, a scale of casualties that has never been surpassed in U.S. military history. Thousands of horses were also killed and left rotting in the summer heat. A Union soldier who witnessed the slaughter wrote home: "Great God! When will this horrid war stop?"

Others asked the same question. John Futch, a Confederate private from North Carolina, saw his brother Charley shot in the head, suffer, and die at Gettysburg on July 3. He wrote his wife that the slaughter had left him "half crazy." A few weeks after the battle, he quit his post and headed home, only to be captured, tried as a deserter, and executed.

Again, as after Antietam, Lee's mangled army retreated back to Virginia in a driving rain—and again, the Federals failed to give chase. Had General Meade pursued Lee's army across Maryland, he might have ended the war, but once more the winning army failed to capitalize on its victory. President Lincoln was outraged that Meade allowed the Confederates to get away: "We had them within our grasp!" he thundered to his assistant. Lee had escaped to fight again—and the war would grind on for another twenty-one months.

The last Confederate invasion of the North was over. Lee's desperate gamble had failed in every way, not the least being its failure to relieve the Union pressure on the Confederate army at Vicksburg, Mississippi. On July 4, 1863, as Lee's army left Pennsylvania, General John Pemberton, the Confederate commander at Vicksburg, surrendered his entire 30,000-man army after a forty-seven-day siege. Union vessels now controlled the Mississippi River, thereby splitting the Confederacy in two, with Louisiana, Texas, and Arkansas cut off from the other Rebel states.

After Gettysburg, a group of northern states funded a military cemetery in commemoration of the thousands of soldiers killed in the largest battle ever fought in North America. On November 19, 1863, President Lincoln spoke at the ceremony dedicating the new national cemetery. In his brief remarks, known now as the Gettysburg Address, he eloquently expressed the pain and sorrow of the uncivil war. The prolonged conflict was testing whether a nation "dedicated to the proposition that all men are created equal . . . can long endure." Lincoln declared that all living Americans must ensure that the "honored dead" had not "died in vain." In stirring words that continue to inspire, Lincoln predicted that "this nation, under God, shall have a new birth of freedom—and that government of the people, by the people, and for the people, shall not perish from the earth."

Chattanooga

The Battle of Chattanooga: South loses the war in the West

The third great Union victory of 1863 occurred around Chattanooga, the river port and railhead of eastern Tennessee and gateway to northern Georgia. In the late summer, a Union army led by General William Rosecrans took Chattanooga and then rashly pursued General Bragg's Rebel forces into the north Georgia mountains, where they clashed at Chickamauga (a Cherokee word meaning "river of death").

After an intense battle (September 19–20) that resulted in 35,000 casualties on both sides, the battered Union forces fell back into Chattanooga while the Confederates held the city virtually under siege. General Rosecrans reported that "we have met a serious disaster. Enemy overwhelmed us, drove our right, pierced our center, and scattered troops there." Lincoln urged him to hang on: "If we can hold Chattanooga, and East Tennessee, I think [the] rebellion must dwindle and die."

The Union command rushed in reinforcements, and on November 24 and 25 the Federal troops dislodged the Confederates from Lookout Mountain and Missionary Ridge, thereby gaining effective control of east Tennessee. The South had lost the war in the West.

The North Prevails

The dramatic Union victories at Vicksburg, Gettysburg, and Chattanooga turned the tide against the Confederacy. General Lee offered his resignation to Jefferson Davis, but the president refused to let his best general go. He told Lee he could not find a better commander.

During the summer and fall of 1863, however, Lincoln's generals in the East lost the momentum that the victory at Gettysburg had provided, thereby allowing the Army of Northern Virginia to nurse its wounds and regroup.

By 1864, the tenacious Lee was ready to renew the war, "in fine spirits and anxious for a fight." Still, the tone had changed. Earlier, Confederate leaders assumed they could actually win the war and secure their independence. Now, they worried about defeat. Mary Chesnut of South Carolina confessed in her diary that the war was not going well for her beloved Confederacy. On January 1, 1864, she wrote: "God help my country!"

A Wartime Election

War or no war, 1864 was still a presidential election year, and by the fall the political contest had become a referendum on the war itself. Radical Republicans, frustrated by the prolonged war, tried to prevent Lincoln's nomination for a second term, but he consistently outmaneuvered them.

Once Lincoln was nominated, he selected Andrew Johnson, a "War Democrat" from Tennessee, as his running mate on the "National Union" ticket, so named to promote bipartisanship during the controversial war.

At their 1864 national convention in Chicago, the Democrats acknowledged that people were tired of the costly war and called for an immediate end to the fighting. They nominated General George B. McClellan, the former Union commander who had sparred with Lincoln, his commander in chief, often calling him a "gorilla" and "an idiot." McClellan pledged that if elected he would stop the war, and if the Rebels then refused to return to the Union, he would allow the Confederacy to "go in peace."

Lincoln knew that the 1864 election would be determined on the battlefields rather than by campaign speeches. At the start of the year, he doubted that the war-weary voters would give him a second term.

To save the Union before a new Democratic administration could stop the war and recognize the independence of the Confederacy, the president had brought his best commander, Ulysses S. Grant, to Washington, D.C., in March 1864. Lincoln promoted him to lieutenant general (only two others, George Washington and Winfield Scott, had ever earned that rank) and gave him overall command of the Union war effort. A New York newspaper reported that Lincoln's presidency was now "in the hands of General Grant, and the failure of the General will be the overthrow of the president."

Grant's Strategy

The cigar-chewing Grant was a hard-nosed warrior with unflagging energy. One soldier said that Grant always looked like he was "determined to drive his head through a brick wall and was about to do it." The Union commander

WILLIAM TECUMSEH SHERMAN
Sherman's campaign developed into a war of maneuver, without the pitched battles of Grant's campaign, as he pushed relentlessly through Georgia and South Carolina.

had a simple concept of war: "Find out where your enemy is, get to him as soon as you can, and strike him as hard as you can, and keep moving on"— regardless of the number of dead and wounded.

Grant dramatically changed the Union military strategy. Where his predecessors had focused on trying to capture Richmond, he would defeat Lee's Confederate army, wherever it went. To do so, he would wage a relentless war of attrition, one in which victory would favor the side that could absorb the most punishment and keep on fighting. To Grant, ending the war was "only a matter of time," for he knew that the Union could keep providing more soldiers but the Confederacy could not.

To that end, Grant ordered the three largest Union armies, one in Virginia, one in Tennessee, and one in Louisiana, to launch offensives in the spring of 1864 in which the fighting would never cease. No more short battles followed by long pauses. The Union would force the outnumbered Confederates to keep fighting constantly, thereby wearing them out.

Grant assigned his trusted friend and fierce fighter, General William Tecumseh Sherman, a rail-thin, red-haired Ohioan, to lead the Union army in Tennessee and apply Grant's strategy of "complete conquest" to invade Georgia and South Carolina, the heart of the Confederacy.

Sherman, volatile and unpredictable, but cool under pressure and preoccupied with winning at all costs, owed much of his success to Grant's support. "He stood by me when I was crazy, and I stood by him when he was drunk," Sherman said, adding that now "we stand by each other." Grant and Sherman would now wage total war, confiscating or destroying civilian property that might be of use to the military. It was a merciless and costly plan but, in the end, effective.

Grant's Pursuit of Lee

In May 1864, the Union's massive Army of the Potomac, numbering about 115,000 soldiers, nearly twice the size of Lee's army, moved south across the Rappahannock and Rapidan Rivers in eastern Virginia. In the nightmarish Battle of the Wilderness (May 5–6), the armies fought blindly through dense woods thick with vines, thorns, and briars. It was a hellish scene; the tangled underbrush caught fire from exploding artillery shells, and many wounded men burned to death.

Grant's men suffered heavier casualties than the Confederates, but the Rebels were running out of replacements. Always before, when bloodied by Lee's troops, Union forces had pulled back to rest and recover, but Grant continued to push southward, keeping the pressure on Lee. "Whatever happens," he assured Lincoln, "we will not retreat." Grant "was like a bulldog," Lincoln said. "Let him get his teeth in, and nothing can shake him loose."

In the first days of June 1864, just as Republican party leaders were gathering to renominate Lincoln as their presidential candidate for the fall election, Grant attacked Lee's well-entrenched army at Cold Harbor near the Chickahominy River, ten miles east of Richmond. In twenty minutes, almost

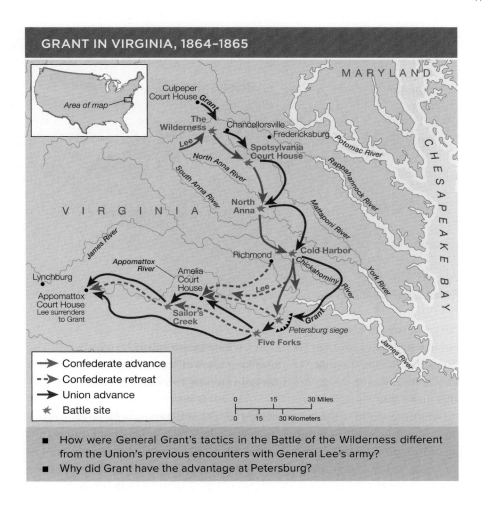

GRANT IN VIRGINIA, 1864–1865

- ➤ Confederate advance
- -➤ Confederate retreat
- ➤ Union advance
- ✳ Battle site

0   15   30 Miles
0   15   30 Kilometers

■ How were General Grant's tactics in the Battle of the Wilderness different from the Union's previous encounters with General Lee's army?

■ Why did Grant have the advantage at Petersburg?

4,000 attacking Federals, caught in a blistering cross-fire, were killed or wounded. A Confederate commander reported that "it was not war; it was murder."

The frightful losses at Cold Harbor nearly unhinged Grant, who later admitted that the botched attack was his greatest mistake. Critics, including Lincoln's wife, Mary, called him "the Butcher" after Cold Harbor. In just two months, Grant's massive offensive against Lee across Virginia had cost some 60,000 killed and wounded Union soldiers.

Criticism of the war in the North skyrocketed. Even Horace Greeley, the powerful Unionist publisher of the *New York Tribune*, urged Lincoln to negotiate with Confederate leaders to save the "bleeding, bankrupt, almost dying country." During the summer of 1864, the Union war effort nearly disintegrated. Yet Grant, for all his mistakes, knew that the blue-coated Union army could replace its dead and wounded; the Confederates could not.

So Grant kept the pressure on the Confederates. He brilliantly maneuvered his battered forces around Lee's army and headed for Petersburg,

WILDERNESS CAMPAIGN A line of Union troops at North Anna, during Grants' devastating campaign through Virginia in 1864. The woods and briars, visible in the background of the photo, frequently caught fire from all of the explosives, and were a constant hazard to soldiers on either side of the war.

twenty-five miles south of Richmond, where major railroads converged. The opposing armies then dug in along long lines of trenches above and below Petersburg. Grant telegraphed Lincoln that he intended "to fight it out on this line if it takes all summer."

For nine months, the two opposing armies at Petersburg faced each other down along miles of elaborate trenches. Grant's troops were generously supplied by Union vessels moving up the James River, while Lee's men, hungry and cold, wasted away. Petersburg had become Lee's prison while disasters piled up for the Confederacy elsewhere. Lee admitted that it was "a mere question of time" before he would have to retreat or surrender. On June 15, 1864, a Rebel soldier noted in his diary that "our affairs do look gloomy." Grant, he added later, "will no doubt capture the place."

Sherman Pushes through the South

Meanwhile, Grant ordered General Sherman to drive his army through the heart of Dixie and "break it up," inflicting "all the damage you can." To that end, Sherman moved his army south from Chattanooga, Tennessee, through the northern Georgia mountains toward the crucial railroad hub of Atlanta. He sent a frightening warning to the city's residents: "Prepare for my coming." By the middle of July, Sherman's troops had reached the outskirts of Atlanta, trapping the Confederate soldiers there.

The Rebel commander, General John Bell Hood of Texas, was a recklessly aggressive fighter, not a strategist. A Confederate senator's wife said that "a braver man, a purer patriot, a more gallant soldier never breathed than General Hood." His arm had been shattered at Gettysburg and he had lost a leg at Chickamauga. Strapped to his saddle, he refused simply to "defend" Atlanta;

instead, he attacked Sherman's army, which was exactly what the Union commander wanted him to do.

Three times in eight days, the Confederates lashed out at the Union lines around Atlanta. Each time they were repulsed. Finally, on September 1 the outnumbered Rebels, desperately needing food and supplies, evacuated the city and headed north. Sherman then moved his army into Atlanta.

Sherman's army stayed in Atlanta until November, when the Union commander ordered the 20,000 residents to leave before he destroyed the city. City officials loudly protested the order, leading Sherman to reply: "War is cruelty." His men then set fire to the city's railroads, iron foundries, shops, mills, hotels, and businesses. The destruction of Atlanta devastated Confederate morale. Mary Chesnut in South Carolina "felt as if all were dead within me, forever." She gloomily predicted that "we are going to be wiped off the earth."

> The burning of Atlanta

Lincoln Reelected

Sherman's conquest of Atlanta turned the tide of the 1864 presidential election. As a Republican senator said, the Union victory in Georgia "created the most extraordinary change in public opinion here [in the North] that ever was known." The Union conquest of Mobile, Alabama, in August, and Confederate defeats in Virginia's Shenandoah Valley in October contributed to the dramatic revival of Lincoln's political support in the North.

> Abraham Lincoln reelected (1864)

The South's hope that northern discontent would lead to a negotiated peace vanished. In the **election of 1864**, the Democratic candidate, George McClellan, the former Union commander, carried only New Jersey, Delaware, and Kentucky, with just 21 electoral votes to Lincoln's 212, and won only 1.8 million popular votes (45 percent) to Lincoln's 2.2 million (55 percent). Union soldiers and sailors voted in large numbers, and their choice was Lincoln. The president's victory sealed the fate of the Confederacy, for it ensured that the Union armies would keep the pressure on the Rebels.

While Confederate forces made their last stands, Abraham Lincoln prepared for his second term as president. He was the first president since Andrew Jackson to win a second term. The weary commander in chief had made many mistakes and weathered constant criticism during his first term, but with the war nearing its end, Lincoln now received well-deserved praise. The *Chicago Tribune* observed that the president "has slowly and steadily risen in the respect, confidence, and admiration of the people."

Sherman's "March to the Sea"

In November 1864, Sherman's 60,000 soldiers began their fabled **"March to the Sea,"** advancing rapidly through Georgia, where no organized Confederate armies remained. Sherman, affectionately called "Uncle Billy" by his men, planned to wage a modern war against all the Confederates—soldiers and civilians—and their economy. He intended to "whip the rebels, to

election of 1864 Abraham Lincoln's successful reelection campaign, capitalizing on Union military successes in Georgia, to defeat his Democratic opponent, former general George B. McClellan, who ran on a peace platform.

Sherman's "March to the Sea" (1864) The Union army's devastating march through Georgia from Atlanta to Savannah led by General William T. Sherman, intended to demoralize civilians and destroy the resources the Confederate army needed to fight.

humble their pride, to follow them into their inmost recesses, and make them fear and dread us."

Hood's Confederate Army of Tennessee, meanwhile, tried a bold, desperate gamble. They went in the opposite direction from the Union forces, pushing northward into Alabama and then Tennessee, hoping to trick Sherman into abandoning Atlanta and chasing them. The Federal commander, however, refused to take the bait. He was determined to push southward through Georgia to the coast and then into South Carolina, the seedbed of secession, living off the undefended countryside.

In the Battle of Franklin (November 30, 1864), near Nashville, General Hood, against the advice of his staff, sent his army across two miles of open ground defended by dug-in Union troops backed by cannons. It was another example of valiant suicide. In a few hours, Hood saw 6,252 of his men killed or wounded, a casualty figure higher than "Pickett's Charge" at Gettysburg. A Confederate captain, scarred by the battle's senseless butchery, wrote that the "wails and cries of the widows and orphans made at Franklin, Tennessee, will heat up the fires of the bottomless pit to burn the soul of General J. B. Hood for murdering their husbands and fathers."

Two weeks later, in the Battle of Nashville (December 15–16), the Federals scattered what was left of Hood's army. A few days later, Hood was relieved of his command. One of Hood's soldiers said that he was a "brave, good, noble, and gallant" man, "but as a general he was a failure."

Meanwhile, Sherman's army pushed southward across Georgia. His troops lived off the land, destroying plantations, barns, crops, warehouses, bridges, and rail lines. Sherman said he wanted to "make Georgia howl" to convince

DESTROYING SOUTHERN RAILROADS Sherman's troops cut a swath of destruction across Georgia in his "March to the Sea." Here, Union troops rip up railroad tracks in Atlanta. **Why did Sherman adopt a strategy that included the destruction of railroads, homes, barns, and cities?**

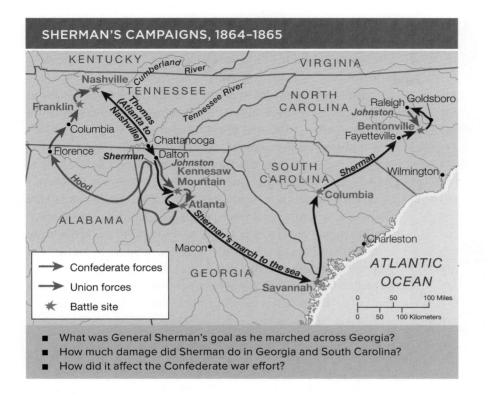

SHERMAN'S CAMPAIGNS, 1864–1865

- What was General Sherman's goal as he marched across Georgia?
- How much damage did Sherman do in Georgia and South Carolina?
- How did it affect the Confederate war effort?

the people to surrender. "We are not only fighting hostile armies," Sherman explained, "but a hostile people" who must "feel the hard hand of war."

An Ohio sergeant confirmed that the Federals were intent on a path of destruction through the Deep South: "Every house, barn, fence, and cotton gin gets an application of the torch. That prospect is revolting, but war is an uncivil game, and can't be civilized." Lawless stragglers and deserters from both sides, called "bummers," took advantage of the chaos to rob families and burn their houses.

Sherman's March through Georgia became infamous among southerners as a supposed example of Union tyranny. After the war, however, a Confederate officer acknowledged that Sherman's march through Georgia was well conceived and well managed. "I don't think there was ever an army in the world that would have behaved better, in a similar expedition, in an enemy country. Our army certainly wouldn't have."

On December 24, 1864, Sherman sent a whimsical telegram to President Lincoln offering him the coastal city of Savannah as a Christmas present. By the time Sherman's army arrived in Savannah, his troops had freed more than 40,000 slaves, burned scores of plantations, and destroyed all the railroads. "God bless you, Yanks!" shouted a freed slave in Georgia. "Come at last! God knows how long I been waitin'."

On February 1, 1865, Sherman's army headed north across the Savannah River into South Carolina, the "hell-hole of secession" in the eyes of Union

THE END OF THE WAR General Lee (right) surrenders to General Grant (left) at Appomattox Court House on April 9, 1865.

Confederate surrender at Appomattox Court House

Appomattox Court House
Virginia village where Confederate general Robert E. Lee surrendered to Union general Ulysses S. Grant on April 9, 1865.

troops. Sherman reported that his "whole army is burning with an insatiable desire to wreak vengeance upon South Carolina. I almost tremble at her fate, but feel she deserves all that seems in store for her."

South Carolina paid a high price for having led the South out of the Union. The Federal army burned more than a dozen South Carolina towns, including the state capital of Columbia, which was captured on February 17, 1865. Soon thereafter, Charleston itself surrendered, and the Union flag once again fluttered over Fort Sumter. Sherman's army kept moving into North Carolina.

During the late winter and early spring of 1865, the shrinking Confederacy found itself besieged on all sides, but Jefferson Davis stubbornly rejected any talk of surrender. If the Confederate armies should be defeated, he wanted the soldiers to scatter and fight an unending guerrilla war. "The war came and now it must go on," he insisted, "till the last man of this generation falls in his tracks, and his children seize his musket and fight our battle."

Appomattox

Throughout the spring of 1865, General Grant's army kept pushing, probing, and battering the Rebels defending Petersburg, Virginia. The badly outnumbered Confederates were slowly starving. Something had to give. On April 2, 1865, Lee's exhausted army, now numbering less than 30,000 soldiers, broke out of Petersburg in a desperate flight west with the Union army in hot pursuit. By the time the Confederates reached Appomattox Court House, some 80 miles from Petersburg, they found themselves surrounded. On April 7, Grant sent a note to Lee urging him to surrender. With his army virtually surrounded, Lee recognized that "there [was] nothing left for [him] to do but go and see General Grant, and [he] would rather die a thousand deaths."

On April 9 (Palm Sunday), the tall, dignified Lee, attired in his formal dress uniform, gold sash, and ceremonial sword, met the short, mud-spattered Grant in the village of **Appomattox Court House**. Grant displayed extraordinary kindness in keeping with Lincoln's desire for a generous peace. At Lee's request, he let the Confederates keep their pistols, horses, and mules, and he pledged that none of them would be tried for treason, despite the demands of many Radical Republicans in Congress. Lee then confessed that his men were starving, and Grant ordered that they be provided food. After signing the surrender documents, Lee solemnly mounted his horse and returned to his battered army.

The next day, as the gaunt, hungry Confederate troops formed ranks for the last time, Joshua Chamberlain, the Union general in charge of the surrender ceremony, ordered his soldiers to salute their foes as the Rebel soldiers paraded past to give up their weapons. His Confederate counterpart signaled his men to do likewise. Chamberlain remembered that there was not a sound—no trumpets or drums, no cheers or jeers, simply an "awed stillness . . . as if it were the passing of the dead."

The remaining Confederate forces surrendered in May. Jefferson Davis fled Richmond by train ahead of the advancing Federal troops, only to be captured in Georgia by Union cavalry on May 10. He was eventually imprisoned in Virginia for two years.

The brutal war was at last over. Upon learning of the Union victory, John Wilkes Booth, a popular young actor in Washington, D.C., boiling over with hatred for Lincoln and the Union, wrote in his diary that "something decisive and great must be done" to avenge the Confederate defeat.

A Transforming War

CORE **OBJECTIVE**
5. Explain how the Civil War changed the nation.

The Civil War was the most traumatic event in American history. "We have shared the incommunicable experience of war," reflected Oliver Wendell Holmes Jr., the twice-wounded Union officer who would one day become the nation's leading Supreme Court justice. "We have felt, we still feel, the passion of life to its top. . . . In our youth, our hearts were touched by fire."

In Virginia, elderly Edmund Ruffin, the arch secessionist who had been given the honor of firing the first shots at Fort Sumter, was so distraught by the Confederate surrender that he put his rifle barrel in his mouth and blew off the top of his head.

The long war changed the nation in profound ways. A *New York Times* editorial said that the terrible conflict left "nothing as it found it. . . . It leaves us a different people in everything."

The war shattered countless lives and destroyed the South's economy, many of its railroads and factories, much of its livestock, and several of its cities. In 1860, the northern and southern economies had been essentially equal in size. By 1865, the southern economy's productivity had been halved while the Union had established the United States as a modern industrial nation.

The Union Preserved

The war also ended the Confederacy and preserved the Union; shifted the political balance of power from the South to the North in Congress, the U.S. Supreme Court, and the presidency; bolstered the Republican party; and boosted the northern economy, as the demands of war accelerated industrial development, commercial agriculture, and western settlement. The Homestead Act (1862) made more than a billion acres in the West available to the landless. The war greatly expanded the power and scope of the federal government at the expense of states' rights. In 1860, the annual federal government budget was $63 million; by 1865, it was over $1 billion. In winning the war, the federal government had become the nation's largest employer.

Expansion of federal government and power shift to the North

The war boosts northern industries

By the end of the war, the Union was spending $2.5 million per day on the military effort. The war-related expenditures by the Union generated whole new industries to meet the military's needs for weapons, uniforms, food, equipment, and supplies. The massive amount of preserved food required by the Union armies, for example, helped create the canning industry and transformed Chicago into the meatpacking capital of the world.

Federal contracts also accelerated the growth of new industries such as iron/steel and petroleum products, thus laying the groundwork for the postwar economic boom led by tycoons such as J. Pierpont Morgan, John D. Rockefeller, Andrew W. Mellon, and Andrew Carnegie. Ohio senator John Sherman, in a letter to his brother, General William T. Sherman, said the war had dramatically expanded the vision "of leading capitalists" who now talk of earning "millions as confidently as formerly of thousands."

The First "Modern" War

Devastating human losses

In many respects, the Civil War became the first modern war. Its scope and scale were unprecedented, as it was fought across the entire continent, from Pennsylvania to New Mexico and California and from Florida to Kansas. One of every twelve men on both sides served in the war, and few families were unaffected. Over 730,000 soldiers and sailors (37,000 of whom were African Americans fighting for the Union side) died in the conflict, 50 percent more than the number who would die in the Second World War. Of the surviving combatants, 50,000 returned home with one or more limbs amputated. Disease, however, was the greatest threat to soldiers, killing twice as many as were lost in battle. Some 50,000 civilians were also killed during the war.

The Civil War also accelerated the American love affair with guns. Hundreds of thousands of men who had never owned or used a pistol or rifle now believed that the "right to own and use weapons" was an essential constitutional principle.

Emergence of modern technologies and war reporting

Unlike previous conflicts, much of the fighting in the Civil War was "modern" in that it was distant, impersonal, and mechanical. Men often died at long distance, without ever knowing who had fired the shots that felled them. The opposing forces used an array of new weapons and instruments of war: cannons with "rifled," or grooved, barrels for greater accuracy; repeating rifles; ironclad ships; railroad artillery; the first military telegraph; observation balloons; and wire entanglements. The war was also modern in that civilians could read about battles in the newspapers that sent reporters to the front lines or by visiting exhibitions of photographs taken at the battlefields and camps.

Social Changes Wrought by the War

The war also generated significant social changes. Women's roles were transformed. "No conflict in history," a journalist wrote at the time, "was such a woman's war as the Civil War." The requirements of war enabled women to become nurses, farm or business managers, and executives of new organizations. So many ministers left their congregations to become military chaplains that laypeople, especially women, assumed even greater responsibility for religious services in churches and synagogues. The war's awful carnage took a terrible personal toll on women. Hundreds of thousands of wives were widowed by the war or saw their lives permanently transformed by the return of husbands with missing limbs or ghastly wounds.

Thirteenth Amendment

By far, however, the most important result of the war was the liberation of almost 4 million slaves. Lincoln had not intended to end slavery when the war began, but the course of the war had changed his mind. As the war entered its final months, freedom for *all* slaves emerged more fully as a legal reality.

> Thirteenth Amendment: Four million slaves freed

Three major steps occurred in January 1865, three months before the war ended: Missouri and then Tennessee abolished slavery by state action, and at the insistent urging of President Lincoln, the U.S. House of Representatives passed an amendment to the U.S. Constitution that banned slavery everywhere. Upon ratification by three fourths of the reunited states, the **Thirteenth Amendment** became law eight months after the war ended, on December 18, 1865. It removed any lingering doubts about the legality of emancipation. By then, in fact, slavery remained only in the border states of Kentucky and Delaware.

The Debate Continues

Historians continue to debate why the Union won the war. Some have focused on the inherent weaknesses of the Confederacy: its lack of industry and railroads, the tensions between the states and the central government in Richmond, poor political leadership, faulty political-military coordination and communication, the expense of preventing slave rebellions and runaways, and the advantages in population and resources enjoyed by the North. Still others have highlighted the erosion of Confederate morale in the face of terrible food shortages, soaring prices, and unimaginable human losses.

The debate over why the North won and the South lost will probably never end, but as in other modern wars, firepower and manpower were essential factors. Robert E. Lee's own explanation for the Confederate defeat retains an enduring accuracy: "After four years of arduous service marked by unsurpassed courage and fortitude, the Army of Northern Virginia has been compelled to yield to overwhelming numbers and resources." Whatever the reasons, the North's victory resolved a key issue: no state could divorce itself from the Union. The Union, as Lincoln had insisted, was indissoluble, now and forever.

Thirteenth Amendment (1865) Amendment to the U.S. Constitution that ended slavery and freed all slaves in the United States.

Reviewing the
CORE OBJECTIVES |

■ **Civil War Strategies** When the Civil War began, the Confederates had the advantage of fighting a defensive war on their own territory. Confederate diplomacy also anticipated massive support from Britain and France, support that never materialized. The Union, however, had a much larger population and much greater industrial development. The Union quickly launched a military campaign to seize the Confederate capital, Richmond, Virginia. Initial hopes for a rapid victory died at the First Battle of Bull Run. The Union then adopted the *Anaconda Plan*, which involved imposing a naval blockade on southern ports and slowly crushing resistance on all fronts.

■ **Emancipation Proclamation** Gradually, Lincoln came to see that winning the war required ending slavery. He justified the *Emancipation Proclamation (1863)* as a military necessity because it would deprive the South of its captive labor force. After the *Battle of Antietam* in September 1862, he announced his plans to free the slaves living in areas under Confederate control. Many slaves freed themselves by escaping to Union army camps. In July 1862, with the *Militia Act*, Congress had declared that freed slaves (*contrabands*) could join the Union army. During 1863, blacks, both free and freed, joined the Union army in large numbers, giving the Union military a further advantage over the Confederacy.

■ **Wartime Home Fronts** Each side in the Civil War saw critics of the war effort coalesce into organized opposition. The *Copperhead Democrats* in the North were sympathetic to the Confederates and urged Lincoln and the Republicans to negotiate an end to the fighting. The Union government proved much more capable with finances than did its Confederate counterparts. Through tariffs, income taxes, government bond issues, and the printing of paper money, the Union was better able to absorb the war's soaring costs. The Confederate finances, on the other hand, were pitiful in the cash-poor South. The Confederate treasury department had to print so much money that it created spiraling inflation of consumer prices and civil unrest. Also, most of the warfare took place in the South; thus, although the North had more casualties, the physical destruction in the South was much greater.

■ **The Winning Union Strategy** The Union victories at the *Battle of Vicksburg* and the *Battle of Gettysburg* in July 1863 were a major turning point of the war. With the capture of Vicksburg, Union forces cut the Confederacy in two, depriving armies in the east of western supplies and manpower. General Robert E. Lee and the Army of Northern Virginia lost a third of its troops after the defeat at Gettysburg, forcing the Confederates to adopt a defensive strategy. In 1864, Lincoln placed General Ulysses S. Grant in charge of the Union's war efforts, and thereafter his forces constantly attacked Lee's in Virginia while, farther south, General William T. Sherman's *March to the Sea (1864)* resulted in the conquest of Georgia and South Carolina. Sherman's successes helped propel Lincoln to victory in the *election of 1864*. After that, southern resistance wilted, forcing Lee to surrender his army to General Grant at *Appomattox Court House* in April 1865.

■ **The Significance of the Civil War** The Civil War involved the largest number of casualties of any American war before or since. Most important, the Civil War brought about the destruction of slavery through passage of the *Thirteenth Amendment (1865)*. Not only did the power of the federal government increase as a result of the war, but the center of political and economic power shifted away from the South and the planter class.

KEY TERMS

Anaconda Plan *p. 487*

contrabands *p. 500*

Battle of Antietam (1862) *p. 501*

Emancipation Proclamation (1863) *p. 502*

Militia Act (1862) *p. 507*

Pacific Railway Act (1862) *p. 510*

Homestead Act (1862) *p. 510*

Morrill Land-Grant College Act (1862) *p. 510*

National Banking Act (1863) *p. 510*

Copperhead Democrats *p. 512*

Battle of Vicksburg (1863) *p. 514*

Battle of Gettysburg (1863) *p. 515*

election of 1864 *p. 523*

Sherman's "March to the Sea" (1864) *p. 523*

Appomattox Court House *p. 526*

Thirteenth Amendment (1865) *p. 529*

CHRONOLOGY

April 1861	Virginia, North Carolina, Tennessee, and Arkansas join Confederacy; West Virginia splits from Virginia to stay with Union
July 1861	First Battle of Bull Run (Manassas)
March–July 1862	Peninsular campaign
April–August 1862	Battles of Shiloh, Second Bull Run, and Antietam; New Orleans seized by Union forces
July 1862	Congress passes the Militia Act
September 1862	Lincoln issues Emancipation Proclamation
May–July 1863	Battles of Vicksburg and Gettysburg
November 1863	Battle of Chattanooga
March 1864	General Grant takes charge of Union military operations
September 1864	General Sherman seizes and burns Atlanta
November 1864	Lincoln is reelected
	Sherman's "March to the Sea"
April 9, 1865	General Lee surrenders at Appomattox Court House
1865	Thirteenth Amendment is ratified

🐇 INQUIZITIVE

Go to InQuizitive to see what you've learned—and learn what you've missed—with personalized feedback along the way.

***A VISIT FROM THE OLD MISTRESS* (1876)** This powerful painting by Winslow Homer depicts a plantation mistress visiting her former slaves in the postwar South. Although their living conditions are humble, these freedwomen stand eye-to-eye with the woman who kept them in bondage.

Reconstruction

1865–1877

In the spring of 1865, the Civil War was finally over. The United States was a "new nation," said an Illinois congressman, because it was now "wholly free." At a frightful cost of more than 730,000 lives and the destruction of the southern economy, the Union had won, and almost 4 million slaves had seized their freedom. No longer would enslaved workers be whipped, nor sold and separated from their families, nor prevented from learning to read and write or attending church. "I felt like a bird out of a cage," said former slave Houston Holloway from Georgia, who had been sold to three different owners during his first twenty years. "Amen. Amen. Amen. I could hardly ask to feel any better than I did that day." Eda Harper from Mississippi was even more ecstatic. Upon learning of the end of the war, she and her fellow slaves "danced all night long."

The ratification of the Thirteenth Amendment to the U.S. Constitution in December 1865 ended any doubt about the status of former slaves by abolishing slavery everywhere. Few owners, however, willingly freed their slaves until forced to by the arrival of Union soldiers. A North Carolina planter maintained that he and other whites "will never get along with the free negroes" because they were an "inferior race." Similarly, a Mississippi planter predicted that "these niggers will all be slaves again in twelve months." When a white man in South Carolina caught an enslaved mother and her children running toward freedom, he "drew his bowie-knife and cut her throat; also the throat of her boy, nine years old; also the throat of her girl, seven years of age; threw their bodies into the river, and the live baby after them."

Such brutal incidents illuminate the extraordinary challenges the nation faced in "reconstructing" and reuniting a ravaged and resentful South while

1. Identify the federal government's major challenges in reconstructing the South after the Civil War.

2. Describe how and why Reconstruction policies changed over time.

3. Assess the attitudes of white and black southerners toward Reconstruction.

4. Analyze the political and economic factors that helped end Reconstruction in 1877.

5. Explain the significance of Reconstruction to the nation's future.

helping to transform ex-slaves into free workers and equal citizens. It would not be easy. As a South Carolina planter threatened a federal official in the fall of 1865, "The war is not over." Rebels had been conquered, but they were far from being loyal Unionists.

The Reconstruction Era, from 1865 to 1877, witnessed a complex debate about the role of the federal government in ensuring civil rights. Some northerners wanted the former Confederate states returned to the Union with little or no changes. Others wanted Confederate leaders imprisoned or executed and the South rebuilt in the image of the rest of the nation. Still others cared little about reconstructing the South; they wanted the federal government to focus on promoting northern economic growth and westward expansion.

Although the Reconstruction Era lasted only twelve years, it was one of the most significant periods in U.S. history. The decisions made and policies enacted are still shaping American life nearly 150 years later.

CORE **OBJECTIVE**

1. Identify the federal government's major challenges in reconstructing the South after the Civil War.

The War's Aftermath in the South

In the spring of 1865, the former Confederacy presented a sharp contrast to the victorious North. Southerners were emotionally exhausted; fully a fifth of the southern white males had died in the war; many others had been maimed for life. In 1866, Mississippi spent 20 percent of the state's budget on artificial limbs for Confederate soldiers. Property values had collapsed. In the year after the war ended, eighty-one plantations in Mississippi were sold for less than a tenth of what they had been worth in 1860. Confederate money was worthless; personal savings had vanished; tens of thousands of horses and mules had been killed in the fighting, and many farm buildings and equipment destroyed. Burned-out Columbia, South Carolina was "a wilderness of ruins"; Charleston, the birthplace of secession, had become a place of "vacant houses, of widowed women, of rotting wharves, of deserted warehouses, of weed-wild gardens, of miles of grass-grown streets, of acres of pitiful and voiceless barrenness."

Confederate general Braxton Bragg returned to his "once prosperous" Alabama home to find "all was lost, except my debts." He and his wife, having been accustomed to prosperity, were forced to live in an abandoned slave cabin. South Carolina's Mary Chesnut was equally despondent at war's end: "We are scattered—stunned—the remnant of heart left alive with us, filled with brotherly hate" for the Union victors and devastated by her native region's "day of humiliation and sorrow" amid its "ruined homes and desolated country."

Emancipation wiped out $4 billion invested in slavery, which had enabled the explosive growth of the cotton culture. The heyday of the robust cotton economy was over, however. Not until 1879 would the cotton crop again equal the record harvest of 1860; tobacco production did not regain its prewar level until 1880; the sugar crop of Louisiana did not recover until

RICHMOND AFTER THE WAR
Before evacuating the capital of the Confederacy, Richmond, Virginia, local mobs set fire to warehouses and factories to prevent their falling into Union hands. Pictured here is one of Richmond's burnt districts in April 1865. Women in mourning attire walk among the shambles.

1893; and the rice economy along the coast of South Carolina and Georgia never regained its prewar levels of production or profit. In 1860, just before the Civil War, the South had generated 30 percent of the nation's wealth; in 1870, only ten years later, it produced but 12 percent.

Political turmoil accompanied the economic chaos. The process of forming new state governments first required deciding the official status of the seceded states: Were they now conquered territories? If so, then the Constitution assigned Reconstruction to Congress.

But what if, as Abraham Lincoln had argued, the Confederate states had never officially left the Union because secession was illegal? In that circumstance, the president would be responsible for Reconstruction. In either case, what would be the political, social, and economic status of the freed slaves? Were they citizens? If not, what was their status as Americans? There were no easy answers.

The Battle over Political Reconstruction

CORE **OBJECTIVE**
2. Describe how and why Reconstruction policies changed over time.

The Reconstruction of former Confederate states actually began during the war and went through several phases, the first of which was called Presidential Reconstruction. With Union forces advancing into the Confederacy during the fighting, President Lincoln in 1862 had named army generals to serve as temporary military governors for conquered areas. By the end of 1863, he had formulated a plan for regular governments in those states liberated from Confederate rule.

Presidential Reconstruction: Lincoln's Proclamation of Amnesty and Reconstruction

Lincoln's Wartime Reconstruction Plan

In late 1863, President Lincoln issued a Proclamation of Amnesty and Reconstruction, under which any former Rebel state could form a Union government whenever a number equal to 10 percent of those who had voted in 1860 took a formal oath of allegiance to the Constitution and the Union and received a presidential pardon acquitting them from treason charges.

Certain groups, however, were excluded from the pardon: Confederate government officials; senior officers of the Confederate army and navy; judges, congressmen, and military officers of the United States who had left their federal posts to join the rebellion; and those who had abused captured African American soldiers.

Northern politicians, however, disagreed over who had the authority to restore Rebel states to the Union. Most moderate Republicans supported Lincoln's program intended to quickly restore pro-Union southern governments. Many **Radical Republicans**, however, favored a drastic transformation of southern society. They wanted to make freed slaves citizens and grant them full civil rights. To do so, they argued, Congress, not the president, should supervise Reconstruction.

The Radicals also hoped to replace the white Democratic planter elite with a new generation of small farmers and middle-class Republicans, both black and white. "The middling classes who own the soil, and work it with their own hands," explained Radical leader Thaddeus Stevens, "are the main support of every free government."

In 1864, with the war still raging, the Radicals tried to take charge of Reconstruction by passing the Wade-Davis Bill, named for two leading Republicans in Congress. In contrast to Lincoln's 10 percent Reconstruction plan, the Wade-Davis Bill required that a *majority* of white male citizens declare their allegiance to the Union before a Confederate state could be readmitted.

Lincoln vetoes Wade-Davis Bill

The Wade-Davis Bill never became law, however, for Lincoln vetoed it as being too harsh. In retaliation, Radicals issued the Wade-Davis Manifesto, a public statement that accused Lincoln of exceeding his constitutional authority. Unfazed by the criticism, Lincoln continued his efforts to restore the Confederate states to the Union. He also rushed assistance to the freed slaves in the South.

The Freedmen's Bureau

Radical Republicans Congressmen who identified with the abolitionist cause and sought swift emancipation of the slaves, punishment of the Rebels, and tight controls over former Confederate states.

The Thirteenth Amendment officially ended slavery, but what did freedom mean for the former slaves, most of whom had no land, no home, no food, and no education? "What is freedom?" asked Congressman James A. Garfield, a former Union general and a future U.S. president, in 1865. "Is it the bare privilege of not being chained? If this is all, then freedom is a bitter mockery, a cruel delusion." The debate over what freedom should entail for 4 million former slaves became the central issue of Reconstruction.

FREEDMEN'S SCHOOL IN VIRGINIA As part of its effort to support former slaves in their transition to freedom, the Freedman's Bureau established schools for the freedpeople across the southern states. **What are the students learning in this Virginia school, and how might it help them become self-supporting?**

To address the complex issues raised by emancipation, Congress on March 3, 1865, created the **Freedmen's Bureau** to assist the suffering "freedmen and their wives and children." It was the first federal effort to provide assistance directly to people rather than to states. And its tasks were daunting. When General William T. Sherman learned that his friend, General Oliver O. Howard, had been appointed to lead the Freedmen's Bureau, he wrote him a letter in which he soberly warned that "It is not . . . in your power to fulfill one-tenth of the expectations of those who framed the Bureau." Undeterred by such realities, in May 1865, Howard declared that freed slaves "must be free to choose their own employers, and be paid for their labor."

Howard thereafter sent Freedmen's Bureau agents to the South to negotiate labor contracts between blacks and white landowners, many of whom resisted. The agents, never enough to fulfill their goals, also provided the former slaves with medical care, food, and clothing and helped set up schools and pay teachers. Northern missionary societies also established schools for the freedpeople across the South. As a Mississippi freedman explained, education "was the next best thing to liberty."

By 1870, the Freedmen's Bureau was supervising more than 4,000 new schools in the South serving almost 250,000 students, many of whose teachers were initially women volunteers from the North. The Freedmen's Bureau also helped former slaves reestablish connection with their family members and to legalize marriages that had been prohibited prior to the war.

Freedmen's Bureau Federal Reconstruction agency established to protect the legal rights of former slaves and to assist with their education, jobs, health care, and land ownership.

The Assassination of Lincoln

Lincoln assassinated (April 14, 1865)

Abraham Lincoln offered his last view of Reconstruction in the final speech of his life. On April 11, 1865, he rejected calls by Radicals for a vengeful Reconstruction. He wanted "no persecution, no bloody work," no hangings of Confederate leaders nor any extreme efforts to restructure southern social and economic life. Lincoln yearned for a peace "with malice toward none, with charity for all."

He did not get it.

On April 14, 1865, the president and his wife, Mary Todd, attended a play at Ford's Theatre in Washington, D.C. Lincoln was sitting defenseless as twenty-six-year-old John Wilkes Booth slipped into the unguarded presidential box. Booth, a famous actor and a rabid Confederate, fired his small pistol point-blank at the president's head. As Lincoln slumped forward, Booth pulled out a knife, stabbed Lincoln's military aide, and jumped from the box to the stage, breaking his leg in the process. He then mounted a waiting horse and fled the city. The president died nine hours later, leaving his widow "very pitiable—she has hysteria & has sometimes been very delirious."

The nation was suddenly leaderless. Vice President Andrew Johnson was sworn in as the new president, but for a time chaos reigned. Secretary of War Edwin Stanton, not knowing if the assassination was a prelude to a Confederate invasion, summoned General Ulysses Grant to defend the government in Washington, D.C. All roads into the city were closed, patrolled only by Union troops. Eleven days later, Union troops found Booth hiding in a northern

LINCOLN'S FUNERAL PROCESSION After Lincoln's assassination, his body was taken on a two-week long funeral procession through five different states, allowing millions of people the chance to see him. This photograph was taken on April 25, when the procession passed through New York City.

Virginia tobacco barn, where he was shot and killed. Booth whispered as he lay dying, "Tell my mother I died for my country."

Johnson's Plan

Lincoln's murder shocked and saddened the nation and propelled into the White House Vice President Andrew Johnson of Tennessee, a combative, stubborn man with a quick temper and fierce prejudices—he hated both the white southern elite and the idea of racial equality. Johnson was a pro-Union Democrat who had joined Lincoln's National Union ticket in 1864 as a gesture of wartime bipartisan unity.

Like Lincoln, Johnson was a self-made man. Born in 1808 into dirt-poor poverty in Raleigh, North Carolina, he lost his father when he was three and never attended school. His mother apprenticed him to a tailor to learn a trade. At thirteen he ran away and eventually landed in Greeneville, nestled in the mountains of east Tennessee, where he became a tailor. He taught himself to read, and his wife showed him how to write and do some basic arithmetic. A natural leader, he eventually served as the mayor, a state legislator, governor, congressional representative, and U.S. senator.

Johnson called himself a Jacksonian Democrat "in the strictest meaning of the term. I am for putting down the [Confederate] rebellion, because it is a war [of wealthy plantation owners] against democracy." While hating the "traitorous" planter elite, Johnson shared the racist attitudes of most southern whites. "Damn the negroes," he exclaimed to a friend during the war. "I am fighting those traitorous aristocrats, their masters."

President Johnson's plan to reconstruct the Confederate states closely resembled Lincoln's lenient terms. In May 1865, he issued a new Proclamation of Amnesty that excluded not only those ex-Confederates whom Lincoln had barred from a presidential pardon but also banned anyone with property worth more than $20,000. Johnson was determined to keep the wealthiest southerners from regaining political power. Surprisingly, however, he eventually pardoned most of the white "aristocrats" he claimed to despise. What brought about this change of heart? Johnson had apparently decided that he could buy the political support of prominent southerners by pardoning them, improving his own chances of reelection. His focus was on "restoring" rather than "reconstructing" the southern states.

Johnson's Restoration Plan included the appointment of a Unionist as provisional governor in each southern state, with authority to call a convention of men elected by "loyal" (that is, not Confederate) voters. Each state convention had to ratify the Thirteenth Amendment ending slavery. Johnson also encouraged the state conventions to consider giving a few blacks voting rights, especially those with some education or with military service so as to "disarm" the "Radicals who are wild upon" giving *all* African Americans the right to vote. Except for uncompromising Mississippi, each state of the former Confederacy held a convention that met Johnson's requirements but ignored his suggestion about giving voting rights to a few blacks.

ANDREW JOHNSON
A Jacksonian Democrat from Tennessee, Johnson stepped into the role of president after Lincoln's assassination. He introduced a Restoration Plan that required southern states to ratify the Thirteenth Amendment and limited the political power of rich ex-Confederates.

Presidential Reconstruction: Johnson's Restoration Plan

Johnson's Restoration Plan
Plan to require southern states to ratify the Thirteenth Amendment, disqualify wealthy ex-Confederates from voting, and appoint a Unionist governor.

Freedmen's Conventions

Neither Lincoln nor Johnson saw fit to ask freedpeople in the South what they most needed. So the ex-slaves—men and women—took matters into their own hands. They met and marched, demanding not just freedom but citizenship and full civil rights, land of their own, and voting rights. Especially in and around large cities such as New Orleans, Mobile, Norfolk, Wilmington, Nashville, Memphis, and Charleston, former slaves, both men and women, mobilized to make their voices heard. They organized regular meetings, chose leaders, protested mistreatment by Confederates or federal officials, learned the workings of the federal bureaucracy, and sought economic opportunities as wage workers.

During the summer and fall of 1865, liberated slaves and free people of color from the North ("missionaries") and South organized freedmen's conventions (sometimes called Equal Rights Associations) across the South. Often led by ministers, they met in state capitals "to impress upon the white

FREEDMEN'S CONVENTION In this 1868 woodcut, a group of Southern freedpeople meet to discuss their political and social resolutions. **Who is participating in this freedmen convention, and how might the demographic diversity have contributed to the freedmen's initiatives?**

men," as the Reverend James D. Lynch told the Tennessee freedmen's convention, "that we are part and parcel of the American republic," and as such they were eager to counter the whites-only state conventions being organized under Johnson's Reconstruction plan. Virtually all the freedmen's conventions forged resolutions that stressed their desire for free public education, their need for wage-earning jobs and their own land, and their insistence on full civil rights, especially voting rights.

The North Carolina freedmen's convention elected as its president James Walker Hood, a free black from Connecticut. In his acceptance speech, he emphasized their goals: "We and the white people have to live here together. Some people talk of emigration for the black race, some of expatriation, and some of colonization. I regard this as all nonsense. We have been living together for a hundred years and more, and we have got to live together still; and the best way is to harmonize our feelings as much as possible, and to treat all men respectfully." Hood then demanded three constitutional rights for African Americans: the right to testify in courts, serve on juries, and "the right to carry [a] ballot to the ballot box."

In sum, the freedmen's conventions demanded that their voices be heard in Washington and southern state capitals. As the Virginia freedmen's convention asserted, "Any attempt to reconstruct the states . . . without giving to American citizens of African descent all the rights and immunities accorded to white citizens . . . is an act of gross injustice."

The Radical Republicans

Johnson's initial assault on the southern planter elite pleased Radical Republicans but not for long. Many Radicals who wanted Reconstruction to provide social and political equality for blacks resented Johnson's efforts to bring the South back into the Union as quickly as possible.

The most extreme Radical Republicans, Thaddeus Stevens of Pennsylvania and Charles Sumner of Massachusetts, wanted to deny former Confederates the right to vote in order to keep them from electing the old planter elite and to enable the Republican party to gain a foothold in the Democratic region. Stevens argued that the Civil War had been fought to produce a *"radical revolution"* in southern life: the "whole fabric of southern society must be changed" in order to "revolutionize southern institutions, habits, and manners." He had urged Lincoln to "free every slave—slay every traitor—burn every Rebel mansion!"

Stevens and other Radicals claimed they had the authority to confiscate the largest southern plantations, divide them into small farms, and give them to former slaves. The iron-willed Stevens, for example, viewed the Confederate states as "conquered provinces," subject to the absolute will of the U.S. Congress, not the president.

Andrew Johnson, however, balked at such an expansion of federal authority. At base, he was committed to the states' rights to control their affairs rather than to an intrusive federal government. "White men alone must manage the South," Johnson told a visitor.

Unreconstructed Southerners

After the war, most white southerners found their lives in turmoil. They could not forget the war or their defeat, and they resented and resisted the North's efforts to reconstruct their homeland. As a North Carolinian muttered in 1866, he felt the "bitterest hatred toward the North." He and others simply wanted to rebuild the new South as it had been before the war, the fabled "Old South," and they were determined to do so in their own way and under their own leadership. They saw no need for their beloved region to be "reconstructed" by outsiders.

So when the U.S. Congress met in December 1865, for the first time since the end of the war, the new southern state governments looked remarkably like the former Confederate governments. Southern voters had refused to extend voting rights to the newly freed slaves. Instead, they had elected former Confederate leaders as their new U.S. senators and congressmen. The outraged Republicans in Congress denied seats to all such "Rebel" officials.

Then, in May and July of 1866, white mobs murdered African Americans in Memphis and New Orleans. The massacres, Radical Republicans argued, resulted from Andrew Johnson's lenient policy toward white supremacists. "Witness Memphis, witness New Orleans," Senator Charles Sumner cried. "Who can doubt that the President is the author of these tragedies?" The race riots helped spur the Republican-controlled Congress to pass the Fourteenth Amendment (1866), extending federal civil rights protections to blacks.

Black codes

The violence directed against southern blacks was triggered in part by black protests over restrictive laws passed by the new all-white southern state legislatures. These **black codes**, as a white southerner explained, would ensure "the ex-slave was not a free man; he was a free Negro." A northerner visiting the South explained that the black codes would ensure that "the blacks at large belong to the whites at large."

The black codes varied from state to state, but some provisions were in many of them. They recognized black marriages but prohibited interracial marriage. The Mississippi codes stipulated that "no white person could intermarry with a freedman, free negro, or mulatto." Violators faced imprisonment for life. The codes also prohibited blacks from voting, serving on juries, or testifying against whites. They could own property, but they could not own farmland in Mississippi or city property in South Carolina. In Mississippi, every black male over the age of eighteen had to be apprenticed to a white, preferably a former slave owner. Any blacks not apprenticed or employed by January 1866 would be jailed as "vagrants." If they could not pay the vagrancy fine—and most of them could not—they would be forced to work for whites as "convict laborers."

In other words, southern whites tried to restore slavery without using the word. The black codes infuriated Republicans. "We [Republicans] must see to it," Senator William Stewart of Nevada resolved, "that the man made free by the Constitution of the United States is a freeman indeed." And that is what they set out to do.

black codes Laws passed in southern states to restrict the rights of former slaves.

Johnson's Battle with Congress

Early in 1866, the Radical Republicans openly challenged Andrew Johnson over the control of Reconstruction policies. Johnson started the fight when he vetoed a bill renewing funding for the Freedmen's Bureau. The Republicans could not gather enough votes to overturn the veto. Then, on February 22, 1866, Johnson criticized the Radical Republicans for promoting black civil rights. Moderate Republicans thereafter deserted the president and supported the Radicals. President Johnson had become in their eyes "an alien enemy of a foreign state," Thaddeus Stevens declared.

In mid-March 1866, the Radical-led Congress passed the pathbreaking Civil Rights Act, which declared that "all persons born in the United States" (except Indians) were citizens entitled to "full and equal benefit of all laws." The new legislation infuriated President Johnson. Congress, he fumed, could not grant citizenship to blacks, who did not deserve it. Claiming that the proposed Civil Rights Act discriminated against the "white race," Johnson vetoed the bill, but this time, on April 9, 1866, Republicans overrode the presidential veto. It was the first time in history that Congress had overturned a presidential veto of a major bill. From that point on, President Johnson, a stubborn loner unable to accept criticism or embrace compromise, steadily lost both public and political support.

"SLAVERY IS DEAD (?)" Thomas Nast's 1867 cartoon argues that blacks were still being treated as slaves despite the passage of the Fourteenth Amendment. This detail illustrates a case in Raleigh, North Carolina: a black man was whipped for a crime despite federal orders specifically prohibiting such forms of punishment.

Congressional Reconstruction

To remove all doubt about the legality of the new Civil Rights Act, Congress passed the **Fourteenth Amendment** to the U.S. Constitution on June 16, 1866. It went far beyond the Civil Rights Act by guaranteeing citizenship to anyone born in the United States, except Native Americans. It also prohibited any efforts to violate the civil rights of "citizens," black or white; to deprive any person "of life, liberty, or property, without due process of law," or to "deny any person . . . the equal protection of the laws." With the Fourteenth Amendment, the federal government was assuming primary responsibility for protecting civil rights.

The fall 1866 congressional elections revealed the growing split between Andrew Johnson and the Radical Republicans. To win votes for his favored candidates, Johnson went on a speaking tour of the Midwest. His efforts backfired, however, when his speeches turned into ugly shouting contests between him and his critics. In Cleveland, Ohio, Johnson described the Radical Republicans as "factious, domineering, tyrannical" men, and he

Fourteenth Amendment (1866) Amendment to the U.S. Constitution guaranteeing equal protection under the law to all U.S. citizens, including former slaves.

exchanged hot-tempered insults with a heckler. Radical Republicans claimed that Johnson was behaving like a "drunken imbecile."

The 1866 congressional elections brought a devastating defeat for Johnson and the Democrats; in each house, Radical Republican candidates won more than a two-thirds majority, the margin required to override presidential vetoes. On March 2, 1867, the new Congress passed, over President Johnson's vetoes, three crucial laws creating what came to be called **Congressional Reconstruction**: the Military Reconstruction Act, the Command of the Army Act, and the Tenure of Office Act.

The Military Reconstruction Act was the capstone of the Congressional Reconstruction plan. It abolished the new governments "in the rebel States" established under President Johnson's lenient Reconstruction policies. In their place, Congress established military control over the defeated South. Congress exempted one state, Tennessee, because it had already ratified the Fourteenth Amendment. The Military Reconstruction Act, crafted by Thaddeus Stevens, divided the other ten ex-Confederate states into five military districts, each commanded by a general who acted as governor.

Yet only 10,000 federal troops, mostly African Americans, were expected to police those sprawling "military districts." There were never enough soldiers to enforce Congressional Reconstruction from Virginia to Texas. The entire state of Mississippi, for instance, had fewer than 400 soldiers to ensure compliance with the Reconstruction statutes.

The Military Reconstruction Act required each former Confederate state to create a new constitution that guaranteed the right of African American males to vote. (Women—black or white—did not yet have the vote and were not included in the discussions. The Radical Republicans were not so radical when it came to promoting the equality of women.) Once a majority of voters ratified the new state constitution, a newly elected state legislature had to ratify the Fourteenth Amendment before regaining its state's representation in Congress.

The Command of the Army Act directed that all army orders from the president go through the army's commanding general, Ulysses S. Grant. The Radical Republicans feared that President Johnson would appoint generals who would be too lenient. So they bypassed the president and entrusted General Grant to enforce Congressional Reconstruction in the South.

The Tenure of Office Act required Senate permission for the president to remove any federal official whose appointment the Senate had confirmed. Radicals intended this act to prevent Andrew Johnson from firing Secretary of War Edwin Stanton, the president's most outspoken critic in the cabinet. Stanton had openly criticized Johnson's lenient approach to the South and had allied himself with the Radicals.

Congressional Reconstruction thus sought to ensure that the freed slaves could participate in the creation of new state governments in the former Confederacy. As Thaddeus Stevens, a lifelong abolitionist inspired by the promise of "liberty, equality, and the rights of man," explained,

Congressional Reconstruction
Phase of Reconstruction directed by Radical Republicans through the passage of three laws: the Military Reconstruction Act, the Command of the Army Act, and the Tenure of Office Act.

the Congressional Reconstruction plan would create a "perfect republic" based on the principle of *equal rights* for all citizens. "This is the promise of America," he insisted. "No More. No Less."

Impeaching the President

The first two years of Congressional Reconstruction saw dramatic changes in the South. One by one, southern state legislatures rewrote their constitutions and ratified the Fourteenth Amendment. Radical Republicans now seemed fully in control of Reconstruction, but one person still stood in their way—Andrew Johnson. During 1867 and early 1868, Radicals decided that the defiant Democratic president must be removed from office.

Johnson himself opened the door to impeachment (the formal process by which Congress charges the president with "high crimes and misdemeanors") when he tried to fire Secretary of War Edwin Stanton. The sharp-tongued Stanton had refused to resign from the cabinet despite his harsh criticism of the president's Reconstruction policy. Radical Republicans had passed the Tenure of Office Act in 1866 to make it illegal for Johnson to remove Stanton for championing their cause. Johnson, who considered the Tenure of Office Act an illegal restriction of presidential power, fired Stanton on August 12, 1867, appointing General Ulysses S. Grant in his place.

The Radicals now saw their chance. By removing Stanton without congressional approval, Johnson had violated the law. On February 24, 1868, the Republican-dominated House passed eleven articles of impeachment (that is, specific charges against the president), most of which dealt with Stanton's firing and all of which were flimsy. In reality, the essential grievance against the president was that he had opposed the policies of the Radicals.

The first Senate trial of a sitting president began on March 5, 1868. It was a dramatic spectacle before a packed gallery of journalists, foreign dignitaries, and political leaders, all eager to watch the first effort to remove a president. As the trial began, Thaddeus Stevens warned the president: "Unfortunate, unhappy man, behold your doom!"

The five-week impeachment trial came to a stunning end on May 26, 1868, when the Senate voted 35 to 19 for conviction, only *one* vote short of the two thirds needed for removal. Senator Edmund G. Ross, a young Radical from Kansas, cast the deciding vote in favor of acquittal, knowing that his vote would ruin his political career. "I almost literally looked down into my

TRIAL OF ANDREW JOHNSON
In this *Harper's Weekly* illustration, Johnson is seated at the center of the foreground among his defense committee. The galleries of the Senate are packed with men and women watching the proceedings. **Why was Johnson's trial such a dramatic and contentious spectacle?**

open grave," Ross explained afterward. "Friendships, position, fortune, everything that makes life desirable . . . were about to be swept away by the breath of my mouth." Angry Radicals thereafter shunned Ross. He lost his reelection campaign and died in near poverty.

In the end, the effort by Radicals to remove Johnson was a grave political mistake, for it ended up weakening public support for Congressional Reconstruction. Nevertheless, the Radical cause did gain something: to avoid being ousted, President Johnson had privately agreed to stop obstructing Congressional Reconstruction.

Republican Rule in the South

In June 1868, Congressional Republicans agreed that eight former Confederate states—all but Virginia, Mississippi, and Texas—had met the tough new conditions for readmission to the Union. Congress readmitted those three states in 1870, with the added requirement that they ratify the **Fifteenth Amendment**, which gave voting rights to African American men.

The Fifteenth Amendment, submitted to the states in 1869 and ratified in 1870, prohibited states from denying a citizen's right to vote on grounds of "race, color, or previous condition of servitude." Susan B. Anthony and Elizabeth Cady Stanton, leaders of the movement to secure voting rights for women, demanded that the Fifteenth Amendment include women as well as black men. As Anthony stressed in a famous speech, the U.S. Constitution refers to "we, the people; not we, the white male citizens; nor yet we, the male citizens; but we, the whole people, who formed the Union—women as well as men." Most men, however, remained unreconstructed when it came to female voting rights. Radical Republicans tried to deflect the issue by declaring that it was the "Negro's hour," and women, both black and white, would have to wait—another fifty years, as it turned out.

CORE **OBJECTIVE**

3. Assess the attitudes of white and black southerners toward Reconstruction.

Reconstruction in Practice

When a federal official asked Garrison Frazier, a former Georgia slave, if he and others wanted to live among whites or among themselves, he said that they preferred "to live by ourselves, for there is a prejudice against us in the South that will take years to get over." In forging new lives in freedom, Frazier and many other former slaves then set about creating their own social institutions.

The Reconstruction of Black Social Life

The northern victory in the Civil War led to a striking transformation of African American religious life in the South. Before the war, slaves who attended white churches were forced to sit in the back. After the war, with the help of many northern Christian missionaries, both black and white, ex-slaves established their own African American churches.

Fifteenth Amendment (1870) Amendment to the U.S. Constitution forbidding states to deny any male citizen the right to vote on grounds of "race, color or previous condition of servitude."

Black churches quickly became the crossroads for African American community life. Ministers played dual roles: social and political leaders as well as preachers. One could not be a real minister, one of them claimed, without looking "out for the political interests of his people."

African American churches

Many African Americans became Baptists or Methodists, in part because these were already the largest denominations in the South and in part because they reached out to the working poor. In 1866 alone, the African Methodist Episcopal (AME) Church gained 50,000 members. By 1890, over 1.3 million African Americans in the South had become Baptists, nearly three times as many as had joined any other denomination.

African American communities in the postwar South also rushed to establish schools. Getting an education, stressed one former slave, was the "first proof" of freedom. Most plantation owners kept blacks illiterate so they could not read abolitionist literature and organize uprisings. After the war, the white elite worried that education would encourage poor whites and poor blacks to leave the South in search of better social and economic opportunities. "They didn't want us to learn nothin'," one former slave recalled. "The only thing we had to learn was how to work."

African American schools

The opposition of southern whites to education for blacks made public schools all the more important to African Americans. South Carolina's Mary McLeod Bethune, the fifteenth child of former slaves, rejoiced in the opportunity to gain an education: "The whole world opened to me when I learned to read." She walked five miles to school as a child, then earned a scholarship to college, and went on to become the first black woman to found a school that became a four-year college: Bethune-Cookman University, in Daytona Beach, Florida.

The Union League

The Fifteenth Amendment had enormous political consequences. No sooner was it ratified than northern Republicans, black and white, sought to convince freedmen to join the party of Lincoln. To do so, they organized Union Leagues throughout the former Confederacy. Republicans had founded the Union League (also called the Loyal League) in 1862 to rally voters behind Lincoln, the war, and the party. By late 1863, the league claimed over 700,000 members in 4,554 councils across the nation.

In the postwar South, these leagues were organized like fraternities, with formal initiations and rituals and secret meetings to protect the freed people from being persecuted by angry white Democrats. The leagues met in churches, schools, homes, and fields, often listening to northern speakers who traveled the South extolling the Republican party and encouraging blacks to register and vote. By the early 1870s, the Union League in the South had become one of the largest black social movements in history.

Through the help of the Union Leagues, some 90 percent of southern freedmen registered to vote, almost all of them as Republicans, and they voted in record numbers (often 80–90 percent). Their doing so often required great courage, for most white southerners were Democrats eager to deny freedmen the vote. "All the blacks who vote against my ticket shall walk the plank," threatened Howell Cobb, a Georgia Democrat who had been a Confederate general and former governor. Throughout the postwar South, angry whites persecuted, evicted, or fired African American workers who "exercised their political rights," as a Union officer reported from Virginia.

Black Republicans were at times equally coercive. "The Negroes are as intolerant of opposition as the whites," a white South Carolina Democrat observed. They shunned, expelled, and even killed any "of their own" who "would turn democrats." He added that freedwomen were as partisan as the men—and as intolerant of opposition: the "women are worse than the men, refusing to talk to or marry a renegade [black Democrat], and aiding [men] in mobbing him."

FREEDMEN VOTING IN NEW ORLEANS The Fifteenth Amendment, ratified in 1870, guaranteed at the federal level the right of citizens to vote regardless of "race, color, or previous condition of servitude." As this illustration from 1867 shows, however, former slaves had been registering to vote in some state elections—and voting in large numbers—since the 1860s, thanks in part to the community organizing efforts of Union Leagues.

Yet the net result of the Union Leagues was a remarkable mobilization of black voters who enabled men of color to gain elected offices for the first time in the states of the former Confederacy. Francis Cardozo, a black minister who served as president of the South Carolina Council of Union Leagues, declared in 1870 that South Carolina had "prospered in every respect" as a result of the enfranchisement of black voters enabled by the Union Leagues. "The fierce and determined opposition to us," he maintained, illustrated how powerful a force for equality the leagues had become.

African Americans in Southern Politics

Black military veterans formed the core of the first generation of African American political leaders in the postwar South. Participation in the Union army or navy had given many blacks their first opportunity to express their loyalty to the American nation. A Virginia freedman explained that the United States was "now *our* country," paid for "by the blood of our brethren" who died while serving in the Union military during the Civil War.

With many ex-Confederates denied voting rights, new African American voters helped elect some 600 blacks—most of them former slaves—as Republican state legislators under Congressional Reconstruction. In Louisiana, Pinckney Pinchback, a northern free black and former Union soldier, served as lieutenant governor. Two black senators served in Congress, Hiram Revels and Blanche K. Bruce, both Mississippi natives who had been educated in the North, while fourteen blacks were elected to the U.S. House of Representatives during Reconstruction.

African American vote

AFRICAN AMERICAN POLITICAL FIGURES OF RECONSTRUCTION As blacks gained the right to vote, many ex-Confederate whites were stripped of that right. As a consequence, several former slaves were elected to positions in government, such as Blanche K. Bruce (left) and Hiram Revels (right), who served in the U.S. Senate. Between them is Frederick Douglass, who was a major figure in the abolitionist movement.

African American elected officials

White southern Democrats angrily resented "Negro rule"—the election of black Republicans. They complained that freed slaves were illiterate and had no civic experience or appreciation of political issues and processes. In this regard, of course, blacks were no different from millions of poor or immigrant white males who had been voting and serving in offices for years. Some freedpeople frankly confessed their disadvantages. Beverly Nash, an African American delegate to the South Carolina convention of 1868, told his colleagues: "We are not prepared for this suffrage [the vote]. But we can learn. Give a man tools and let him commence to use them, and in time he will learn a trade. So it is with voting."

Land, Labor, and Disappointment

Many former slaves stressed that what they needed most was their own land so that they could gain economic self-sufficiency. Emancipation, explained a black minister from Georgia, meant the freedom for blacks to "reap the fruit of our own labor, and take care of ourselves." Gaining their own farms, a Mississippi freedman named Merrimon Howard wrote, would enable "the poor class to enjoy the sweet boon of freedom."

In several southern states, Union armies during the war had given land to freedpeople. President Johnson, however, reversed such transfers of white-owned property to former slaves. In South Carolina, the Union general responsible for evicting former slaves urged them to "lay aside their bitter feelings, and become reconciled to their old masters." The former slaves, however, shouted "No, never!" and "Can't do it!" They knew that land ownership was the foundation of their freedom. Yes, they had no deeds or titles for the land, but it had been "earned by the sweat of *our* brows," said a group of

SHARECROPPERS This photograph, shot in 1899 by Frances Benjamin Johnston, one of the earliest female photojournalists, shows a sharecropping family outside their Virginia cabin. **How do the living conditions of sharecroppers compare to the life of slaves in the antebellum South?**

Alabama freedpeople. "Our wives, our children, our husbands, has been sold over and over again to purchase the lands we now locates on," a Virginia freedman noted. "Didn't we clear the land and raise de crops? We have a right to [that] land," he argued.

In the end, however, the federal government rescinded the wartime policy of land redistribution. It forced tens of thousands of former slaves to return their farms to white owners. The sense of betrayal among the former slaves was profound. An ex-slave in Mississippi forced to return his land to its white owner said that he and others were left with nothing: "no *land*, no *house*, not so much as a place to lay our head."

As former slaves were stripped of their own land, they had little choice but to revert to being farmworkers under a new system: sharecropping. In late June 1865, for example, Thomas Ferguson, a white plantation owner near Charleston, South Carolina, signed a contract with sixty-five of his former slaves. It called for them to "cultivate" his fields in exchange for "half of the crop raised."

> Sharecropping replaces slavery

This **sharecropping** system—whereby the landowner provided land, seed, and tools to a poor farmer in exchange for a *share* of the future crop— essentially reenslaved blacks because, as a federal army officer objected, no matter "how much they are abused, they cannot leave without permission of the owner." If they left, they would forfeit any right to a portion of the crop, and any workers who violated the terms of the contract could be evicted from the plantation, leaving them jobless and homeless—and thereby subject to arrest.

With little money or technical training, many freed blacks preferred sharecropping over working for wages, since it freed them from day-to-day supervision by white landowners. Over time, however, most sharecroppers, black and white, found themselves deeper in debt to the landowner, with little choice but to remain tied to the same discouraging system of dependence that, over the years, felt much like slavery. As a former slave acknowledged, he and others had discovered that "freedom could make folks proud but it didn't make 'em rich."

"Carpetbaggers" and "Scalawags"

Unreconstructed white southerners dismissed whites who served in the new Republican southern state governments as "carpetbaggers" and "scalawags." Carpetbaggers were allegedly opportunistic northerners who rushed to the South with all their belongings in cheap suitcases made of carpeting ("carpetbags") to grab political power. Some northerners were indeed corrupt opportunists. However, most of the northerners in the postwar South were Union military veterans who had arrived as early as 1865 or 1866, drawn back to the South by the desire to rebuild the region's devastated economy. Others were Union soldiers who never returned home after fighting in the South.

sharecropping A farming system developed after the Civil War by which landless workers farmed land in exchange with the landowner for farm supplies and a share of the crop.

CARPETBAGGER Many carpetbaggers were caricatured as opportunists taking advantage of the chaotic economic and political situation in the South. This cartoon is accompanied by the caption, "The bag in front of him, filled with others' faults, he always sees. The one behind him, filled with his own faults, he never sees."

Many other so-called carpetbaggers were teachers, social workers, or ministers motivated by a genuine desire to help free blacks and poor whites improve the quality of their lives. Union general Adelbert Ames, for example, stayed in the South after the war because he felt a "sense of Mission" to help the former slaves develop healthy communities. He served as the military governor of Mississippi before being elected as a Republican U.S. senator in 1870.

Most scalawags were southerners who had opposed secession but supported the Confederacy once the war started and then became Republicans after the war. Several distinguished figures became scalawags, including the former Confederate general James Longstreet, who decided that the Old South must change its ways. He became a successful cotton broker in New Orleans, joined the Republican party, and supported the Congressional Reconstruction program.

Southern Democrats especially hated the scalawags, or southern white Republicans, who they often called traitors to their region. A Nashville, Tennessee, newspaper editor dismissed them as the "merest trash."

Southern Resistance and White "Redemption"

> Reconstruction's final phase: Southern resistance and white "redemption"

Most southern whites viewed Reconstruction as a tragedy. They used all means possible—legal and illegal—to "redeem" their beloved South from northern control, Republican rule, and black assertiveness. An Alabama planter admitted that southern whites simply "can't learn to treat the freedmen like human beings."

> White violence against black political participation

With each passing year during Reconstruction, African Americans suffered increasing exploitation and abuse. The black codes created by white state governments in 1865 and 1866 were the first of many efforts to deny equality to African Americans. Southern whites used terror, intimidation, and violence to disrupt black Republican meetings; target black and white Republican leaders for beatings or killings; and, in general, to prevent blacks from exercising their political rights. Hundreds were killed across the South and many more injured in systematic efforts to "keep blacks in their place."

Such ugly incidents revealed a harsh truth: the death of slavery did not mean the birth of true freedom for many African Americans. For a growing number of southern whites, resistance to Congressional Reconstruction, military occupation, and "Radical rule" became more and more violent. Several secret terrorist groups—the White Leagues, the Red Shirts, the Knights of the White Camelia, and others—emerged to harass, intimidate, and even kill African Americans, especially those active in Union Leagues.

Ku Klux Klan A secret terrorist organization founded in Pulaski, Tennessee, in 1866 targeting former slaves who voted and held political offices, as well as people the KKK labeled as carpetbaggers and scalawags.

One such group, the **Ku Klux Klan** (KKK), was formed in 1866 in Pulaski, Tennessee. The name *Ku Klux* derived from the Greek word *kuklos* meaning "circle" or "band" (and *Klan* comes from the English word *clan*, or family).

The Klan, and other groups like it, began initially as a social club, with spooky costumes and secret rituals. At first a group of pranksters, its members soon turned to intimidation of blacks and white Republicans throughout the South. Their motives varied—anger over the Confederate defeat, resentment against federal soldiers occupying the South, complaints about having to pay black workers, and an almost paranoid fear that former slaves might seek violent revenge against whites. Klansmen rode about at night in white sheets and masks spreading horrendous rumors, issuing threats, and burning schools and churches. "We are going to kill all the Negroes," a white supremacist declared during one massacre intended to undermine and overthrow Republican rule.

"WORSE THAN SLAVERY" This Thomas Nast cartoon condemns the Ku Klux Klan for promoting conditions "worse than slavery" for southern blacks after the Civil War.

The Legacy of Republican Rule

Yet for all the violent opposition directed against the Republican state governments, the new constitutions they created remained in effect for some years after the end of Radical Republican control. Among the most significant innovations brought about by the Republican state governments were those that increased participation in the political process: protecting black voting rights, restructuring legislatures to reflect shifting populations, and making more state offices elective to weaken the "good old boy" tradition of rewarding political supporters with state government jobs.

In South Carolina, former Confederate leaders opposed the Republican state legislature not simply because of its black members but because poor whites were also enjoying political clout for the first time, thereby threatening the traditional dominance of wealthy white plantation owners and merchants.

Given the hostile circumstances under which the Republican state governments operated in the South, their achievements were remarkable. They rebuilt an extensive railroad network and established public school systems—schools funded by state governments and open to all children but separated by race. Some 600,000 black pupils had enrolled in southern schools by 1877.

> Radical Republican achievements

State governments under the Radicals also gave more attention to the poor and to orphanages, asylums, and institutions for the deaf and the blind of both races. Much-needed infrastructure—public roads, bridges, and buildings—was repaired or rebuilt. African Americans achieved rights and opportunities that would repeatedly be violated in coming decades but never completely taken away, at least in principle: equality before the law and the rights to own property, attend schools, learn to read and write, enter professions, and carry on business.

Yet several of the Republican state governments also suffered from corrupt practices. Bribes and kickbacks, whereby companies received

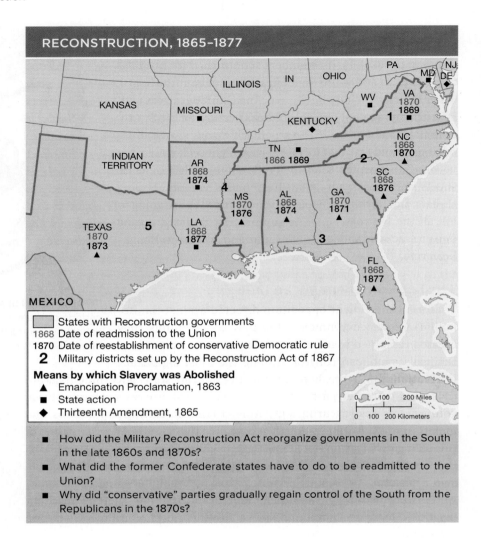

RECONSTRUCTION, 1865–1877

☐ States with Reconstruction governments
1868 Date of readmission to the Union
1870 Date of reestablishment of conservative Democratic rule
2 Military districts set up by the Reconstruction Act of 1867

Means by which Slavery was Abolished
▲ Emancipation Proclamation, 1863
■ State action
◆ Thirteenth Amendment, 1865

- How did the Military Reconstruction Act reorganize governments in the South in the late 1860s and 1870s?
- What did the former Confederate states have to do to be readmitted to the Union?
- Why did "conservative" parties gradually regain control of the South from the Republicans in the 1870s?

government contracts and then secretly rewarded officials with cash, were commonplace. In Louisiana, the twenty-six-year-old Illinois carpetbagger, Henry Clay Warmoth, a Union war veteran and attorney, somehow turned an annual salary of $8,000 into a million-dollar fortune during his four years as governor (he was impeached and removed from office). "I don't pretend to be honest," he admitted. "I only pretend to be as honest as anybody in politics."

As was true in the North and the Midwest at the time, southern state governments awarded money to corporations, notably railroads, under conditions that invited shady dealings. In fact, some railroad executives received state funds but never built railroads. Bribery was rampant. The Radical Republican regimes did not invent such corruption, nor did it die with them. Governor Warmoth recognized as much: "Corruption is the fashion" in Louisiana, he explained.

The Grant Years and Northern Disillusionment

Democrat Andrew Johnson's crippled presidency created an opportunity for Republicans to elect one of their own in 1868. Both parties wooed Ulysses S. Grant, the "Lion of Vicksburg," credited with spearheading the Union victory in the Civil War. His falling-out with President Johnson, however, had pushed him toward the Republicans.

CORE OBJECTIVE

4. Analyze the political and economic factors that helped end Reconstruction in 1877.

The Election of 1868

The Republican party platform of 1868 endorsed Congressional Reconstruction. More important than the party platform, however, were the public expectations driving the election of Ulysses S. Grant, a heroic soldier whose campaign slogan was "Let us have peace."

African American votes help elect President Grant (1868)

The Democrats, not surprisingly, charged the Republican Congress with subjecting the South "to military despotism and Negro supremacy." They nominated Horatio Seymour, the wartime governor of New York and a passionate critic of Congressional Reconstruction. His vice presidential running mate, Francis P. Blair Jr., a former Union general from Missouri who had served in Congress, appealed directly to white bigotry when he denounced Republicans for promoting equality for "a semi-barbarous race" of black men who sought to "subject the white women to their unbridled lust."

A Democrat later said that Blair's egregiously "stupid and indefensible" remarks cost Seymour a close election. Grant swept the Electoral College, 214–80, but his popular majority was only 307,000 out of almost 6 million votes. More than 500,000 African American voters accounted for Grant's margin of victory.

Grant had proved himself a great military leader, but as the youngest president ever (forty-six years old), he was not nearly as bold a politician as he had been a general. He came to view the presidency more as a reward for his military leadership than as a profound responsibility. A political novice, he passively followed the lead of Congressional Republicans and was often blind to the corrupt political forces around him. Grant was awestruck by men of wealth who lavished gifts on him, including houses. He also showed poor judgment in his selection of cabinet members. During Grant's two terms in office, his seven cabinet positions changed twenty-four times. Some of his lieutenants were crooks who engaged in criminal behavior. His former comrade-in-arms, General William T. Sherman, felt sorry for his former commander because so many supposedly "loyal" Republicans used him for their own selfish gains.

"LET US HAVE PEACE" In the midst of the social and political turbulence of Reconstruction, Ulysses S. Grant's slogan, "Let us have peace"—as stamped on campaign coins like this one—struck a chord with the American voters.

Corruption in the Grant administration

Scandals

President Grant's administration soon fell into a cesspool of scandal. In the summer of 1869, two unprincipled financial schemers, Jay Gould and James Fisk Jr., infamous for bribing politicians and judges, plotted with the president's brother-in-law to create a public craze for gold by purchasing massive quantities of the precious yellow metal to drive up its value. The only danger to the scheme lay in the possibility that the federal Treasury would burst the bubble by selling large amounts of its gold supply, which would deflate the value of gold by putting more in circulation as coins. When journalists saw President Grant in public with Gould and Fisk, people assumed that he supported their gold scheme. As the rumor spread in New York City's financial district that the president endorsed the run-up in gold, its value soared.

On September 24, 1869—soon to be remembered as "Black Friday"—Gould and Fisk's scheme to drive up the price of gold worked as planned. Starting at a price of $150 an ounce, gold rose first to $160, then $165, leading more and more investors across the nation and around the world to join the stampede.

Then, around noon, President Grant and his Treasury secretary realized what was happening and began selling huge amounts of government gold. Within fifteen minutes, the bubble created by Fisk and Gould burst, and the price of gold plummeted to $138. Schemers who had bought gold lost fortunes. Their agony, said a New Yorker, "made one feel as if the Battle of Gettysburg had been lost and the Rebels were marching down Broadway." Soon the turmoil spread to the entire stock market, claiming thousands of victims. As Fisk noted, each man was left to "drag out his own corpse."

The plot to corner the gold market was only the first of several scandals that rocked the Grant administration. More disclosures of corruption followed, some involving members of the president's cabinet. The secretary

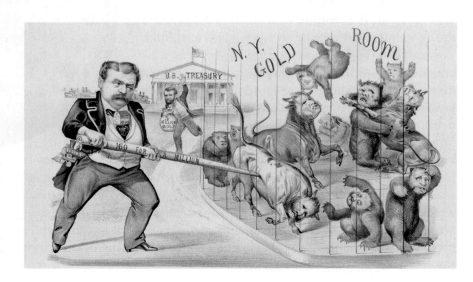

CORNERING THE GOLD MARKET In this political cartoon of the "Black Friday" gold scheme, Jay Gould attempts to control the gold market, represented by caged and enraged bulls and bears. In the background, President Grant dashes from the U.S. Treasury to the scene, frantically trying to bring down the soaring price of gold.

of war, it turned out, had accepted bribes from merchants who traded with Indians at army posts in the West. In St. Louis, whiskey distillers—dubbed the "whiskey ring" in the press—bribed federal agents to avoid paying taxes, bilking the government out of millions of dollars in revenue. Grant's personal secretary participated in that scheme, taking large sums of money and other valuables in return for inside information.

There is no evidence that Grant himself was involved in any of the frauds, but his poor choice of associates earned him widespread criticism. Democrats scolded Republicans for their "monstrous corruption and extravagance" and launched thirty-six investigations into supposedly corrupt acts during Grant's administration.

The Money Supply

Complex financial issues—especially monetary policy—dominated Grant's presidency. Prior to the Civil War, the economy operated on a gold standard. That is, state banks issued paper money that could be exchanged for an equal value of gold coins. So both gold coins and state bank notes circulated as the nation's currency. **Greenbacks** (because of the dye color used on the printed dollars) were issued by the federal government during the Civil War to help pay for the war.

| Greenbacks vs. gold coins |

When a nation's supply of money grows faster than the economy itself, prices for goods and services increase (inflation). This is what happened during the Civil War when the greenbacks were issued. After the Civil War, the U.S. Treasury assumed that the greenbacks would be recalled from circulation so that consumer prices would decline and the nation could return to a "hard-money" currency—gold, silver, and copper coins—which had always been viewed as more reliable in value than paper currency.

The most vocal supporters of a return to hard money were eastern creditors (mostly bankers and merchants to whom others owed money) who did not want their debtors to pay them in paper currency. Critics of the gold standard tended to be farmers and other debtors. These so-called soft-money advocates opposed taking greenbacks out of circulation because shrinking the supply of money would bring lower prices (deflation) for their crops and livestock, thereby reducing their income and making it harder for them to pay their long-term debts. In 1868, congressional supporters of such a soft-money policy—mostly Democrats—had forced the Treasury to stop withdrawing greenbacks from circulation.

President Grant sided with the hard-money camp. On March 18, 1869, he signed the Public Credit Act, which said that the investors who purchased government bonds to help finance the war effort must be paid back in gold coins rather than paper currency. It was the first act of Congress that Grant signed, and it soon generated a decline in consumer prices (deflation) that hurt debtors, helped creditors, and in the process ignited a ferocious political debate over the merits of hard and soft money that would last throughout the nineteenth century—and beyond.

| Public Credit Act (1869) |

greenbacks Paper money issued during the Civil War, which sparked currency debates after the war.

PANIC OF 1873 The depression in 1873 left millions of Americans unemployed and destitute. In this contemporary woodcut, a line of somber men hugs the wall of a New York City hospice, where they hope to get a hot meal.

Financial Panic

Grant's effort to withdraw the greenbacks from circulation unintentionally helped cause a major economic collapse. During 1873, some twenty-five railroads stopped paying their bills, leading Jay Cooke and Company, the nation's leading business lender, to go bankrupt on September 18, 1873.

The resulting financial **Panic of 1873** triggered a deep depression. Thousands of businesses closed, and 3 million people lost their jobs. In the major cities, jobless, homeless Americans roamed the streets and formed long lines at charity soup kitchens.

The terrible contraction of the economy led the U.S. Treasury to reverse course and begin printing more greenbacks. For a time, the supporters of paper money celebrated, but in 1874 President Grant vetoed a bill to issue even more greenbacks. His efforts to remove paper money from circulation pleased his supporters but only prolonged what was then the nation's worst economic depression in its history.

Liberal Republicans

Reconstruction loses support

The sudden collapse of the nation's economy in 1873 also contributed to northerners' losing interest in Reconstruction. Liberal Republicans, a new faction in the Republican party, called for ending federal Reconstruction efforts in the South. They also promoted "civil service reforms" designed to end the "patronage system" whereby new presidents rewarded political supporters with federal government jobs.

In 1872, the Liberal Republicans held their own national convention, during which they accused the Grant administration of corruption, incompetence, and "despotism." They nominated an unlikely presidential candidate, Horace Greeley, the prominent editor of the *New York Tribune* and a longtime champion of a variety of causes, including abolitionism, socialism,

Panic of 1873 Financial collapse triggered by President Grant's efforts to withdraw greenbacks from circulation and transition the economy back to hard currency.

vegetarianism, and spiritualism. The Democrats also nominated Greeley as the only hope of beating Grant.

The result was predictable. Greeley, the shared candidate of the Liberal Republicans and Democrats, carried only six southern states and none in the North. Grant won thirty-one states and carried the national election by 3,598,235 votes to Greeley's 2,834,761. An exhausted Greeley confessed that he was "the worst beaten man who ever ran for high office." He died three weeks later.

White Terror

President Grant initially fought hard to enforce federal efforts to reconstruct the postwar South. But southern resistance to "Radical rule" increased and turned brutally violent. In Grayson County, Texas, a white man and two friends murdered three former slaves simply because they wanted to "thin the niggers out and drive them to their holes."

> Violence against blacks escalates

Klansmen focused their terror on prominent Republicans, black and white. In Mississippi they killed a black Republican leader in front of his family. Three white scalawag Republicans were murdered in Georgia in 1870. That same year an armed mob of whites assaulted a Republican political rally in Alabama, killing four blacks and wounding fifty-four. In 1871, some 500 masked men laid siege to South Carolina's Union County jail and eventually lynched eight black prisoners.

At the urging of President Grant, Republicans in Congress struck back at such racial violence with three Enforcement Acts (1870–1871). The first of these measures imposed penalties on those who interfered with any citizen's right to vote. The second dispatched federal election supervisors to monitor elections in southern districts where political terrorism flourished.

> Enforcement Acts (1870–1871)

The third measure, called the Ku Klux Klan Act, outlawed the main activities of the KKK—forming conspiracies, wearing disguises, resisting officers, and intimidating officials. In 1871, the federal government singled out nine counties in upcountry South Carolina as a center of Klan-instigated violence and jailed several hundred people.

In general, however, the Enforcement Acts were not consistently applied. As a result, the violent efforts of southern whites to thwart Reconstruction escalated in the 1870s. On Easter Sunday in 1873 in Colfax, Louisiana, a mob of white vigilantes disappointed by local election results attacked a group of black Republicans, slaughtering eighty-one. It was the bloodiest racial incident during the Reconstruction period.

Southern "Redeemers"

The Klan's impact on southern politics varied from state to state. In the Upper South, it played only a modest role in helping Democrats win local elections. In the Lower South, however, Klan violence had more serious effects. In overwhelmingly black Yazoo County, Mississippi, vengeful whites used terrorism to reverse the political balance of power. In the 1873 elections, for example, the Republicans cast 2,449 votes and the Democrats 638; two years later the Democrats polled 4,049 votes, the Republicans 7.

Throughout the South, the activities of the Klan and other white supremacists disheartened black and white Republicans alike. "We are helpless and unable to organize," wrote a Mississippi scalawag. We "dare not attempt to canvass [campaign for candidates], or make public speeches." At the same time, northerners displayed a growing weariness with efforts to use federal troops to reconstruct the South and protect civil rights. "The plain truth is," noted the *New York Herald*, "the North has got tired of the Negro."

The erosion of northern interest in civil rights resulted from more than weariness, however. Western expansion, Indian wars, and political controversy over economic issues distracted attention from southern resistance to Republican rule and black rights. Given the violent intensity of diehard former Confederates' efforts to resist Reconstruction, it would have required far more patience, conviction, and resources for the federal government to protect the civil rights of blacks in the South.

Republican political control in the South gradually loosened during the 1870s as all-white "Conservative" parties mobilized the anti-Reconstruction vote. White Democrats—the so-called **redeemers** who supposedly "saved" the South from Republican control and "black rule"—used the race issue to excite the white electorate and intimidate black voters. They called themselves Conservatives rather than Democrats to distinguish themselves from northern Democrats. Where persuasion failed to work, Democrats used trickery to rig the voting. As one enthusiastic Democrat boasted, "The white and black Republicans may outvote us, but we can outcount them."

Republican political control collapsed in Virginia and Tennessee as early as 1869; in Georgia and North Carolina, it ended in 1870, although North Carolina had a Republican governor until 1876. Reconstruction lasted longest in the Deep South states with the largest black population; there, whites abandoned Klan masks for barefaced intimidation in paramilitary groups such as the Mississippi Rifle Club and the South Carolina Red Shirts. By 1876, Radical Republican regimes survived only in Louisiana, South Carolina, and Florida, and those collapsed after the elections of that year.

The white political elite's return to power in the South undermined the country's commitment to Congressional Reconstruction. The collapse of the economy and the much-publicized political scandals hurt Republicans in the 1874 congressional elections, in which the Democrats won control of the House of Representatives and gained seats in the Senate.

The Compromise of 1877

President Grant, despite the controversies swirling around him, wanted to run again in 1876, but many Republicans had lost confidence in his leadership. Others opposed the idea of his becoming the nation's first three-term

Resurgence of the southern white elite

Democrats win control of Congress (1874)

redeemers Postwar white Democratic leaders in the South who supposedly saved the region from political, economic, and social domination by northerners and blacks.

president. In the summer of 1875, Grant acknowledged defeat and announced his retirement, admitting that he had entered the White House with "no political training" and had made many "errors in judgment."

James Gillespie Blaine of Maine, former Speaker of the House, emerged as the Republican front-runner to succeed Grant, but he, too, bore the taint of scandal when newspapers reported that he had promised political favors to railroad executives in exchange for shares of stock in the company.

The scandal led the Republican Convention to pass over Blaine in favor of Ohio's favorite son, Rutherford B. Hayes. Elected governor of Ohio three times, most recently as a hard-money advocate of gold rather than greenbacks, Hayes had also made a name for himself as a civil service reformer by trying to reduce the number of government jobs subject to political appointment. His chief virtue, however, was that he offended neither Radicals nor reformers. As a journalist put it, he was "obnoxious to no one."

COMPROMISE OF 1877
This illustration represents the compromise between Republicans and southern Democrats that ended Radical Reconstruction.

The Democratic Convention was uncharacteristically harmonious from the start. The nomination went on the second ballot to Samuel J. Tilden, a wealthy corporate lawyer and reform governor of New York.

The 1876 campaign raised no burning issues. Both candidates favored relaxing federal authority in the South. As Hayes said privately, he did not approve of "bayonet rule" by federal troops in the South. In the absence of strong ideological differences, Democrats aired the Republicans' dirty linen. In response, Republicans waved "the bloody shirt," whereby they linked the Democratic party to secession, civil war, and the outrages committed against Republicans in the South. As Robert G. Ingersoll, the most celebrated Republican public speaker of the time, insisted: "The man that assassinated Abraham Lincoln was a Democrat. . . . Soldiers, every scar you have on your heroic bodies was given you by a Democrat!"

Despite the lack of major issues, the 1876 election generated the most votes in U.S. history up to that point. Early election returns pointed to a victory for the Democrat Tilden. Nationwide, he outpolled Hayes by almost 300,000 votes. By midnight following Election Day, Tilden had won 184 electoral votes—just 1 vote short of victory. Hayes went to bed that night convinced that he had lost.

> Disputed election of 1876

During the night, however, Republican activists realized that the election hinged on nineteen disputed electoral votes from Florida, Louisiana, and South Carolina. The Democrats needed only one of the challenged votes to claim victory; the Republicans needed all nineteen. Republicans in those key states had engaged in election fraud while Democrats had used physical intimidation to keep black voters at home. Each of the three states, however, was then governed by a Republican who appointed the election boards, each of which reported narrow victories for Hayes. The Democrats immediately challenged the results.

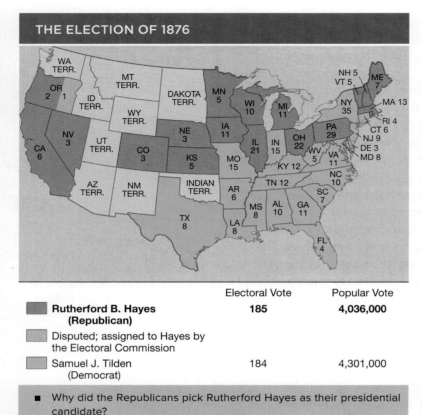

THE ELECTION OF 1876

	Electoral Vote	Popular Vote
Rutherford B. Hayes (Republican)	185	4,036,000
Disputed; assigned to Hayes by the Electoral Commission		
Samuel J. Tilden (Democrat)	184	4,301,000

- Why did the Republicans pick Rutherford Hayes as their presidential candidate?
- Why were the electoral votes of several states disputed?
- What was the Compromise of 1877?

In all three of the disputed southern states, rival election boards sent in conflicting counts. The nation watched and wondered as the politicians bickered about the contested election. The Constitution offered no guidance in this unprecedented situation. Days, then weeks, passed with no solution.

Finally, on January 29, 1877, the Congress set up a special Electoral Commission to settle the dispute. It met daily for weeks trying to verify the disputed vote counts in the three contested southern states. On March 1, 1877, the commission voted 8–7 along party lines in favor of Hayes. The House of Representatives declared Hayes president by an electoral vote of 185–184. Tilden decided not to protest the decision. His campaign manager explained that they preferred "four years of Hayes's administration to four years of civil war."

Hayes's victory hinged on the defection of key southern Democrats, who, it turned out, had made a number of secret deals with the Republicans. On February 26, 1877, prominent Ohio Republicans (including future president James A. Garfield) and powerful southern Democrats struck a private bargain—the **Compromise of 1877**—at Wormley's Hotel in Washington, D.C. The Republicans promised that if Hayes were named president, he would remove the last federal troops from the South.

The End of Reconstruction

Compromise of 1877 Secret deal forged by congressional leaders to resolve the disputed election of 1876; Republican Rutherford B. Hayes, who had lost the popular vote, was declared the winner in exchange for his pledge to remove federal troops from the South, marking the end of Reconstruction.

In 1877, newly inaugurated President Hayes fulfilled his pledge: he withdrew federal troops from Louisiana and South Carolina, whose Republican governments collapsed soon thereafter. Over the next thirty years, the protection of black civil rights in the South crumbled under the pressure of restored white Democratic rule. As Henry Adams, a former Louisiana slave, observed in 1877, "The whole South—every state in the South—has got [back] into the hands of the very men that held us as slaves." New white state governments in the South rewrote their constitutions, rid their administrations of "carpetbaggers, scalawags, and blacks," and cut back spending on schools. "The Yankees helped free us, so they say," a former North Carolina slave named Thomas Hall remembered, "but [in 1877] they let us be put back in slavery again."

Reconstruction's Significance

CORE **OBJECTIVE**
5. Explain the significance of Reconstruction on the nation's future.

The collapse of Congressional Reconstruction in 1877 had tragic consequences, for it allowed the white South to renew long-standing patterns of discrimination against African Americans. Yet for all the unfulfilled promises of Congressional Reconstruction, it left an enduring legacy—the Thirteenth, Fourteenth, and Fifteenth Amendments—not dead in 1877 but dormant, waiting to be reawakened during the second reconstruction of civil rights in the 1950s and 1960s. The effort of the American government to "reconstruct" the former Confederacy represented the only instance of a society's granting citizenship to former slaves and electing freedmen to political offices within just a few years of emancipation.

If Reconstruction's experiment in interracial democracy did not provide true social equality or substantial economic opportunities for African Americans, it did create the essential constitutional foundation for future advances in the quest for equality and civil rights—not just for African Americans but for women and other minority groups as well.

Until the pivotal Reconstruction Era, the states were responsible for protecting citizens' rights. Thereafter, thanks to the Fourteenth and Fifteenth Amendments, blacks had gained equal rights (in theory), and the federal government assumed responsibility for ensuring that states treated blacks equally in terms of their basic civil rights. Congressional Reconstruction thus was a halfway revolution, sighed the former governor of North Carolina Jonathan Worth, and "nobody can anticipate the action of revolutions." A hundred years later, the cause of civil rights would be embraced again by the federal government—this time permanently.

Reviewing the
CORE OBJECTIVES |

■ **Reconstruction Challenges** With the defeat of the Confederacy and the passage of the Thirteenth Amendment, the federal government had to develop policies and procedures to address a number of difficult questions: What was the status of the defeated states, and how would they be reintegrated into the nation's political life? What would be the political status of the former slaves, and what would the federal government do to integrate them into the nation's social and economic fabric?

■ **Reconstruction over Time** Abraham Lincoln and his successor, southerner Andrew Johnson, preferred a more lenient and faster *Restoration Plan* for the southern states. The *Freedmen's Bureau* attempted to educate and aid freed slaves, negotiate labor contracts, and reunite families. Lincoln's assassination led many northerners to favor the *Radical Republicans*, who wanted a more transformative plan designed to end the grasp of the old plantation elite on the South's society and economy. Southern whites resisted and established *black codes* to restrict the lives of former slaves. *Congressional Reconstruction* responded by stipulating that to reenter the Union, former Confederate states had to ratify the *Fourteenth* and *Fifteenth Amendments* to the U.S. Constitution in order to expand and protect the rights of African Americans.

■ **Views of Reconstruction** Many former slaves found comfort in their families and the independent churches they established, but land ownership reverted to the old white elite, reducing newly freed black farmers to *sharecropping*. African Americans enthusiastically participated in politics, with many serving as elected officials. Along with white southern Republicans (scalawags) and northern carpetbaggers, they worked to rebuild the southern economy. Many white southerners, however, blamed their poverty on freed slaves and Republicans, and they supported the *Ku Klux Klan*'s violent intimidation of the supporters of these Reconstruction efforts and the goal of "redemption," or white Democratic control of Southern state governments.

■ **Political and Economic Developments and the End of Reconstruction** Scandals during the Grant administration involved an attempt to corner the gold market and the "whiskey ring's" plan to steal millions of dollars in tax revenue. In the face of these troubles and the economic downturn caused by both the *Panic of 1873* over railroad defaults and disagreement over whether to continue the use of *greenbacks* or return to the gold standard, northern support for Reconstruction eroded. Southern white *redeemers* were elected in 1874, successfully reversing the political progress of Republicans and blacks. In the *Compromise of 1877*, Democrats agreed to the election of Republican Rutherford B. Hayes, who put an end to the Radical Republican administrations in the southern states.

■ The Significance of Reconstruction

Southern state governments quickly renewed long-standing patterns of discrimination against African Americans, but the *Fourteenth* and *Fifteenth Amendments* remained enshrined in the Constitution, creating the essential constitutional foundation for future advances in civil rights. These amendments give the federal government responsibility for ensuring equal treatment and political equality within the states, a role it would increasingly assume in the twentieth century.

KEY TERMS

Radical Republicans *p. 536*

Freedmen's Bureau *p. 537*

Johnson's Restoration Plan *p. 539*

black codes *p. 542*

Fourteenth Amendment (1866) *p. 543*

Congressional Reconstruction *p. 544*

Fifteenth Amendment (1870) *p. 546*

sharecropping *p. 551*

Ku Klux Klan *p. 552*

greenbacks *p. 557*

Panic of 1873 *p. 558*

redeemers *p. 560*

Compromise of 1877 *p. 562*

CHRONOLOGY

1865	Congress sets up the Freedmen's Bureau
	Lincoln assassinated on April 14, 1865
	Johnson issues Proclamation of Amnesty
1865–1866	Southern state legislatures pass black codes
1866	Ku Klux Klan organized
	Congress passes Civil Rights Act
1867	Congress passes Military Reconstruction Act
	Freedmen begin participating in elections
1868	Fourteenth Amendment is ratified
	The U.S. House of Representatives impeaches President Andrew Johnson; the Senate fails to convict him
	Grant elected president
	Six former Confederate states readmitted to the Union
1869	Reestablishment of white Democratic rule ("redeemers") in former Confederate states
1870	Fifteenth Amendment ratified
	First Enforcement Acts passed
1872	Grant wins reelection
1873	Panic of 1873 triggers depression
1877	Compromise of 1877 ends Reconstruction

⚓ INQUIZITIVE

InQuizitive Go to InQuizitive to see what you've learned—and learn what you've missed—with personalized feedback along the way.

DEBATING Reconstruction

Historians' interpretations of the past change over time. This happens for many reasons. Historians can revise their thinking in light of information from newly discovered *primary sources*. They can also interpret previously examined sources in new ways by applying new methodologies and theories. Finally, historians themselves are influenced by the values of their own society and times. Present-day events or particular personal interests can influence how historians think about the past. The study of how interpretations of history have changed is called *historiography*. It is the history of the field of history. For Part 4, *"A House Divided,"* the case study of debating Reconstruction demonstrates how the views of historians have changed dramatically over time.

For this exercise you have two tasks:

PART 1: Compare the two secondary sources on Reconstruction.
PART 2: Using primary sources, evaluate the arguments of the two secondary sources.

PART I Comparing and Contrasting Secondary Sources

Two *secondary sources*, the work of prominent historians from different eras, are included below for you to review. The first selection comes from William Dunning's (1857–1922) *Reconstruction, Political and Economic, 1865–1877*, written in 1907. Dunning was born on the eve of the Civil War to a well-to-do New Jersey family and enrolled at Columbia University soon after the end of Reconstruction. He lived during a time when racial segregation and white supremacy were the unchallenged law of the land, and he wrote some of the first books about Reconstruction.

Dunning was such a compelling force in the first half of the twentieth century that the many historians trained and influenced by him are referred to as the "Dunning School." He was particularly hostile to political idealists, a group that, in his mind, included abolitionists and Radical Republicans. Like many historians of his day, Dunning never questioned his own objectivity. However, later historians and activists have noted that his writings reflect the political beliefs and prejudices of his generation.

Interpretations of Reconstruction have undergone many changes since Dunning's time. The second excerpt, written 91 years later, is from Eric Foner's *The Story of American Freedom*. Born in 1943, Foner is the son of civil rights activists (one of them a historian) deeply concerned with the plight of African Americans. Foner completed his Ph.D. in 1969 during the height of the civil

rights movement. Widely regarded as the leading interpretation of Reconstruction, Foner's writing on the period brings together much of the scholarship that has revised "Dunning School" interpretations of Reconstruction, particularly as they described the role of African Americans in American society.

Before reading these excerpts, review Chapter 15 on the transition from President Andrew Johnson's Restoration Plan to Congressional Reconstruction.

Compare the work of these two historians by answering the following questions. Be sure to support your answers with specific examples drawn from the selections by Dunning and Foner.

■ What is the *topic* of each excerpt? What period of Reconstruction is the author writing about? What groups are examined?

■ Generally, how does each author portray the Reconstruction process? What in each author's writing reveals their attitude about Reconstruction? How do those feelings—whether positive or negative—affect each author's point of view?

■ What are the similarities in these two excerpts?

■ What are the major differences in interpretation between the excerpts?

- What is the main *argument* each historian makes?

- How do these interpretations compare to that presented in Chapter 15?

- These two excerpts were written 91 years apart. How might this have influenced the development of their arguments?

Secondary Source 1

William Dunning, *Reconstruction, Political and Economic, 1865–1877*

It was, indeed, no novelty for the people of the South to be subject to government by the United States army. . . . The reasoning by which the policy of Congress was justified in the North was regarded in the South as founded on falsehood and malice. So far as the "black codes" were concerned, it was pointed out that they could not be alleged as evidences of a tendency to restore slavery or introduce peonage [dependence], since the offensive acts had in many of the states been repealed by the legislatures themselves, and in all had been duly superseded by the civil rights act. The much-exploited outrages on freedmen and Unionists were declared to be exaggerated or distorted reports of incidents which any time of social tension must produce among the criminal classes. The rejection of the Fourteenth Amendment was considered as merely a dignified refusal by honorable men to be the instruments of their own humiliation and shame.

Under all these circumstances the southerners felt that the policy of Congress had no real cause save the purpose of radical politicians to prolong and extend their party power by means of negro suffrage [voting rights]. This and this alone was the purpose for which major-generals had been empowered to remodel the state governments at their will, to exercise through general orders the functions of executive, legislature, and courts, and to compel the white people to recognize the blacks as their equals wherever the stern word of military command could reach. It was as inconceivable to the southerners that rational men of the North should seriously approve of negro suffrage per se as it had been in 1860 to the northerners that rational men of the South should approve of secession per se. Hence, in the one case as in the other, a craving for political power was assumed to be the only explanation of an otherwise unintelligible proceeding.

Source: Dunning, William. *Reconstruction, Political and Economic, 1865–1877*. New York: Harper & Bros., 1907. 109–12.

Secondary Source 2

Eric Foner, *The Story of American Freedom*

Rejecting the idea that emancipation implied civil or political equality or opportunities to acquire property or advance economically, rights northerners deemed essential to a free society, most white southerners insisted that blacks must remain a dependent plantation workforce in a laboring situation not very different from slavery. During Presidential Reconstruction—the period from 1865 to 1867 when Lincoln's successor, Andrew Johnson, gave the white South a free hand in determining the contours of Reconstruction—southern state governments enforced this view of black freedom by enacting the notorious Black Codes, which denied blacks equality before the law and political rights and imposed on them mandatory year-long labor contracts, coercive apprenticeship regulations, and criminal penalties for breach of contract. Through these laws, the South's white leadership sought to ensure that plantation agriculture survived emancipation.

Thus, the death of slavery did not automatically mean the birth of freedom. But the Black Codes so flagrantly violated free labor principles that they invoked the wrath of the Republican North. Southern reluctance to accept the reality of emancipation resulted in a monumental struggle between President Andrew Johnson and the Republican Congress over the legacy of the Civil War. The result was the enactment of laws and constitutional amendments that redrew the boundaries of citizenship and expanded the definition of freedom for all Americans. . . .

Much of the ensuing conflict over Reconstruction revolved around the problem, as Senator Lyman Trumbull of Illinois put it, of defining "what slavery is and what liberty is." . . . By 1866, a consensus had emerged within the Republican Party that civil equality was an essential attribute of freedom. The Civil War had elevated "equality" to a status in the vocabulary of freedom it had not enjoyed since the Revolution. . . . In a remarkable, if temporary, reversal of political traditions, the newly empowered national state now sought to identify and protect the rights of all Americans.

Source: Foner, Eric. *The Story of American Freedom*. New York: W. W. Norton & Company, 1998. 103–105.

PART II Using Primary Sources to Evaluate Secondary Sources

When historians are faced with competing interpretations of the past, they often look at primary source material as part of the process of evaluating the different arguments. In the following selections, you'll find *primary sources* relating to the period of Reconstruction.

Carefully read the primary sources and answer the following questions. Decide how the primary source documents support or refute Dunning's and Foner's arguments about this period. You may find that some documents do both but for different parts of each historian's interpretation. Be sure to identify which specific components of each historian's argument the documents support or refute.

■ Which of the two historian's arguments is best supported by the primary source documents? If you find that both arguments are well supported by the evidence, why do you think the two historians produced such different interpretations?

■ Based on your comparison of the two arguments and your analysis of the primary sources, how has the interpretation of Reconstruction by historians shifted over time? What can you conclude about historiography from the work of these two historians?

Primary Source 1

Union Army general Carl Schurz, *Report on the Condition of the South*

A belief, conviction, or prejudice, or whatever you may call it, so widely spread and apparently so deeply rooted as this, that the negro will not work without physical compulsion, is certainly calculated to have a very serious influence upon the conduct of the people entertaining it. It naturally produced a desire to preserve slavery in its original form as much and as long as possible—and you may, perhaps, remember the admission made by one of the provisional governors, over two months after the close of the war, that the people of his State still indulged in a lingering hope slavery might yet be preserved—or to introduce into the new system that element of physical compulsion which would make the negro work. Efforts were, indeed, made to hold the negro in his old state of subjection, especially in such localities where our military forces had not yet penetrated, or where the country was not garrisoned in detail. Here and there planters succeeded for a limited period to keep their former slaves

in ignorance, or at least doubt, about their new rights; but the main agency employed for that purpose was force and intimidation. In many instances negroes who walked away from the plantations, or were found upon the roads, were shot or otherwise severely punished, which was calculated to produce the impression among those remaining with their masters that an attempt to escape from slavery would result in certain destruction. A large proportion of the many acts of violence committed is undoubtedly attributable to this motive.

Source: Schurz, Carl. *Report on the Condition of the South*. 39th Cong., 1st sess., Senate Executive Document 2, 1865. 19.

Primary Source 2

Mississippi Vagrant Law, 1865

All freedmen, free negroes and mulattoes in this State, over the age of eighteen years, found on the second Monday in January, 1866, or thereafter, with no lawful employment or business, or found unlawfully assembling themselves together, either in the day or night time, and all white persons so assembling themselves with freedmen, free negroes or mulattoes, or usually associating with freedmen, free negroes or mulattoes, on terms of equality, or living in adultery or fornication with a freed woman, free negro or mulatto, shall be deemed vagrants, and on conviction thereof shall be fined in a sum not exceeding, in the case of a freedman, free negro, or mulatto, fifty dollars, and a white man two hundred dollars, and imprisoned at the discretion of the court, the free negro not exceeding ten days, and the white man not exceeding six months. . . . All fines and forfeitures collected under the provisions of this act shall be paid into the county treasury for general county purposes, and in case any freedman, free negro or mulatto shall fail for five days after the imposition of any fine or forfeiture upon him or her for violation of any of the provisions of this act to pay the same, that it shall be, and is hereby, made the duty of the sheriff of the proper county to hire out said freedman, free negro or mulatto, to any person who will, for the shortest period of service, pay said fine and forfeiture and all costs. . . .

Source: Mississippi Vagrant Law, *Laws of Mississippi, 1865*, 90. In *Documentary History of Reconstruction: Political, Military, Social, Religious, Educational & Industrial, 1865 to the Present Time*. Edited by Walter Lynwood Fleming, 1:283 – 286. Cleveland, Ohio: The Arthur H. Clark Company, 1906.

Primary Source 3

Civil Rights Act of 1866

Be it enacted, . . . That all persons born in the United States and not subject to any foreign power, excluding Indians not taxed, are hereby declared to be citizens of the United States; and such citizens, of every race and color, without regard to any previous condition of slavery or involuntary servitude, except as a punishment for crime whereof the party shall have been duly convicted, shall have the same right, in every State and Territory in the United States, to make and enforce contracts, to sue, be parties, and give evidence, to inherit, purchase, lease, sell, hold, and convey real and personal property, and to full and equal benefit of all laws and proceedings for the security of person and property, as is enjoyed by white citizens, and shall be subject to like punishment, pains and penalties, and to none other, any law, statute, ordinance, regulation, or custom, to the contrary notwithstanding.

Source: Civil Rights Act of 1866, 14 Stat. 27 (April 9, 1866).

Primary Source 4

Radical Republican Thaddeus Stevens, "The Advantages of Negro Suffrage"

Unless the rebel States, before admission, should be made republican in spirit, and placed under the guardianship of loyal men, all our blood and treasure will have been spent in vain. . . . There is more reason why colored voters should be admitted in the rebel States than in the Territories. In the States they form the great mass of the loyal men. Possibly with their aid loyal governments may be established in most of those States. Without it all are sure to be ruled by traitors; and loyal men, black and white, will be oppressed, exiled, or murdered. . . . Have not loyal blacks quite as good a right to choose rulers and make laws as rebel whites? In the second place, it is a necessity in order to protect the loyal white men in the seceded States. The white Union men are in a great minority in each of those States. With them the blacks would act in a body; and it is believed that in each of said States, except one, the two united would form a majority, control the States, and protect themselves. Now they are the victims of daily murder. They must suffer constant persecution or be exiled. . . . Another good reason is, it would insure the ascendency of the Union party. . . . I believe . . . that on the continued ascendency of that party depends the safety of this great nation. If impartial suffrage is excluded in the rebel States, then every one of them is sure to send a solid rebel representative delegation to Congress, and cast a solid rebel electoral vote. . . . I am for negro suffrage in every rebel State. If it be just, it should not be denied; if it be necessary, it should be adopted; if it be a punishment to traitors, they deserve it.

Source: Stevens, Thaddeus. *Congressional Globe*, January 3, 1867, 252. In *Documentary History of Reconstruction: Political, Military, Social, Religious, Educational & Industrial, 1865 to the Present Time.* Edited by Walter Lynwood Fleming, 1:149–150. Cleveland, Ohio: The Arthur H. Clark Company, 1906.

Glossary

36°30′ According to the Missouri Compromise, any part of the Louisiana Purchase north of this line (Missouri's southern border) was to be excluded from slavery.

54th Massachusetts Regiment After President Abraham Lincoln's Emancipation Proclamation, the Union army organized all black military units, which white officers led. The 54th Massachusetts Regiment was one of the first of such units to be organized.

Abigail Adams (1744–1818) As the wife of John Adams, she endured long periods of separation from him while he served in many political roles. During these times apart, she wrote often to her husband, and their correspondence has provided a detailed portrait of life during the Revolutionary War.

abolition In the early 1830s, the anti-slavery movement shifted its goal from the gradual end of slavery to the immediate end or abolition of slavery.

abolitionism Movement that called for an immediate end to slavery throughout the United States.

John Adams (1735–1826) He was a signer of the Declaration of Independence and a delegate to the First and Second Continental Congresses. A member of the Federalist Party, he served as the first vice president and the second president of the United States. As president, he passed the Alien and Sedition Acts and endured a stormy relationship with France, which included the XYZ affair.

John Quincy Adams (1767–1848) As secretary of state, he urged President Monroe to issue the Monroe Doctrine, which incorporated his belief in an expanded use of federal powers. As the sixth president, Adams's nationalism and praise of European leaders caused a split in his party, causing some Republicans to leave and form the Democrat party.

Samuel Adams (1722–1803) A genius of revolutionary agitation, he believed that English Parliament had no right to legislate for the colonies. He organized the Sons of Liberty as well as protests in Boston against the British.

Jane Addams (1860–1935) She founded and ran of one of the best known settlement houses, the Hull House. Active in the peace and suffragist movements, she established child care for working mothers, health clinics, job training, and other social programs.

affirmative action Programs designed to give preferential treatment to women and people of color as compensation for past injustices.

Affordable Care Act (ACA) (2010) Vast health-care reform initiative signed into law and championed by President Obama, and widely criticized by Republicans, that aims to make health insurance more affordable and make health care accessible to everyone, regardless of income or prior medical conditions.

Agricultural Adjustment Act (1933) Legislation that paid farmers to produce less in order to raise crop prices for all; the AAA was later declared unconstitutional by the U.S. Supreme Court in the case of *United States v. Butler* (1936).

Emilio Aguinaldo (1869?–1964) He was a leader in the Filipino struggle for independence. During the war of 1898, Commodore George Dewey brought Aguinaldo back to the Philippines from exile to help fight the Spanish. However, after the Spanish surrendered to Americans, America annexed the Philippines and Aguinaldo fought against the American military until he was captured in 1901.

Alamo, Battle of the Siege in the Texas War for Independence of 1836, in which the San Antonio mission fell to the Mexicans. Davy Crockett and Jim Bowie were among the courageous defenders.

Albany Plan of Union (1754) A failed proposal by the seven northern colonies in anticipation of the French and Indian War, urging the unification of the colonies under one Crown-appointed president.

Alien and Sedition Acts of 1798 Four measures passed during the undeclared war with France that limited the freedoms of speech and press and restricted the liberty of non-citizens.

Allied Powers The nations fighting the Central Powers during the First World War, including France, Great Britain, and Russia; later joined by Italy and, after Russia quit the war in 1917, the United States.

American Anti-Imperialist League Coalition of anti-imperialist groups united in 1899 to protest American territorial expansion, especially in the Philippine Islands; its membership included prominent politicians, industrialists, labor leaders, and social reformers.

American Colonization Society Established in 1817, an organization whose mission was to return freed slaves to Africa.

American Federation of Labor Founded in 1881 as a national federation of trade unions made up of skilled workers.

American Indian Movement (AIM) Fed up with the poor conditions on Indian reservations and the federal government's unwillingness to help, Native Americans founded the American Indian Movement (AIM) in 1963. In 1973, AIM led 200 Sioux in the occupation of Wounded Knee. After a ten-week standoff with the federal authorities, the government agreed to reexamine Indian treaty rights and the occupation ended.

American Recovery and Reinvestment Act Hoping to restart the weak economy, President Obama signed this $787-billion economic stimulus bill in February of 2009. The bill included cash distributions to states, funds for food stamps, unemployment benefits, construction projects to renew the nation's infrastructure, funds for renewable-energy systems, and tax reductions.

American System Economic plan championed by Henry Clay of Kentucky that called for federal tariffs on imports, a strong national bank, and federally-financed internal improvements—roads, bridges, canals—all intended to strengthen the national economy and end American dependence on Great Britain.

American Tobacco Company Business founded in 1890 by North Carolina's James Buchanan Duke, who combined the major tobacco manufacturers of the time, ultimately controlling 90 percent of the country's cigarette production.

Anaconda Plan The Union's primary war strategy calling for a naval blockade of major southern seaports and then dividing the Confederacy by gaining control of the Tennessee, Cumberland, and Mississippi Rivers.

Annapolis Convention In 1786, all thirteen colonies were invited to a convention in Annapolis to discuss commercial problems, but only representatives from five states attended. However, the convention was not a complete failure because the delegates decided to have another convention in order to write the constitution.

Battle of Antietam (1862) Turning-point battle near Sharpsburg, Maryland, leaving over 20,000 soldiers dead or wounded, in which Union forces halted a Confederate invasion of the North.

anti-Federalists Opponents of the Constitution as an infringement on individual and states' rights, whose criticism led to the addition of a Bill of Rights to the document.

Many anti-Federalists later joined Thomas Jefferson's Democratic-Republican party.

Anti-Masonic party This party grew out of popular hostility toward the Masonic fraternal order and entered the presidential election of 1832 as a third party. It was the first party to run as a third party in a presidential election as well as the first to hold a nomination convention and announce a party platform.

Appomattox Court House Virginia village where Confederate general Robert E. Lee surrendered to Union general Ulysses S. Grant on April 9, 1865.

Arab Awakening A wave of spontaneous democratic uprisings that spread throughout the Arab world beginning in 2011, in which long-oppressed peoples demanded basic liberties from generations-old authoritarian regimes.

Benedict Arnold (1741–1801) A traitorous American commander who planned to sell out the American garrison at West Point to the British; his plot was discovered before it could be executed and he joined the British army.

Articles of Confederation The first form of government for the United States, ratified by the original thirteen states in 1781; weak in central authority, it was replaced by the U.S. Constitution in 1789.

Atlanta Compromise (1895) A speech by Booker T. Washington that called for the black community to strive for economic prosperity before attempting political and social equality.

Atlantic Charter (1941) Joint statement crafted by Franklin D. Roosevelt and British prime minister Winston Churchill that listed the war goals of the Allied Powers.

Aztec Empire A network of more than 300 city-states and upward of 30 provinces, established in the fourteenth century under the imperialistic Mexica, or Aztecs, in the valley of Mexico.

Crispus Attucks (1723–1770) During the Boston Massacre, he was supposedly at the head of the crowd of hecklers who baited the British troops. He was killed when the British troops fired on the crowd.

Stephen F. Austin (1793–1836) He established the first colony of Americans in Texas, which eventually attracted 2,000 people.

"Axis" alliance Military alliance formed in 1937 by the three major fascist powers: Germany, Italy, and Japan.

Aztec Empire Mesoamerican people who were conquered by the Spanish under Hernando Cortés, 1519–1528.

baby boom Markedly high birth rate in the years following World War II, leading to the biggest demographic "bubble" in U.S. history.

Bacon's Rebellion Unsuccessful 1676 revolt led by planter Nathaniel Bacon against Virginia governor William Berkeley's administration, which, Bacon charged, had failed to protect settlers from Indian raids.

Bank of the United States (1791) National bank responsible for holding and transferring federal government funds, making business loans, and issuing a national currency.

Bank War Political struggle in the early 1830s between President Jackson and financier Nicholas Biddle over the renewing of the Second Bank's charter.

Barbary pirates North Africans who waged war (1801–1805) on the United States after President Thomas Jefferson refused to pay tribute (a bribe) to protect American ships.

Bay of Pigs Failed CIA operation that, in April 1961, deployed a band of Cuban rebels to overthrow Fidel Castro's Communist regime.

Battle of the Bulge On December 16, 1944, the German army launched a counterattack against the Allied forces, which pushed them back. However, the Allies were eventually able to recover and break through the German lines. This defeat was a great blow to the Nazi's morale and their army's strength. The battle used up the last of Hitler's reserve units and opened a route into Germany's heartland.

Bear Flag Republic On June 14, 1846, a group of Americans in California captured Sonoma from the Mexican army and declared it the Republic of California whose flag featured a grizzly bear. In July, the commodore of the U.S. Pacific Fleet landed troops on California's shores and declared it part of the United States.

Beats Group of bohemian, downtown New York writers, artists, and musicians who flouted convention in favor of liberated forms of self-expression.

beatnik A name referring to almost any young rebel who openly dissented from the middle-class life. The name itself stems from the Beats.

Berlin airlift (1948–1949) Effort by the United States and Great Britain to deliver massive amounts of food and supplies flown to West Berlin in response to the Soviet land blockade of the city.

Berlin Wall Twenty-seven-mile-long concrete wall constructed in 1961 by East German authorities to stop the flow of East Germans fleeing to West Berlin.

Bessemer converter Apparatus that blasts air through molten iron to produce steel in very large quantities.

Nicholas Biddle (1786–1844) He was the president of the second Bank of the United States. In response to President Andrew Jackson's attacks on the bank, Biddle curtailed the bank's loans and exchanged its paper currency for gold and silver. In response, state banks began printing paper without restraint and lent it to speculators, causing a binge in speculating and an enormous increase in debt.

Bill of Rights First ten amendments to the U.S. Constitution, adopted in 1791 to guarantee individual rights and to help secure ratification of the Constitution by the states.

Osama bin Laden (1957–2011) The Saudi-born leader of al Qaeda, whose members attacked America on September 11, 2001. Years before the attack, he had declared *jihad* (holy war) on the United States, Israel, and the Saudi monarchy. In Afghanistan, the Taliban leaders gave bin Laden a safe haven in exchange for aid in fighting the Northern Alliance, who were rebels opposed to the Taliban. Following the Taliban's refusal to turn over bin Laden to the United States, America and a multinational coalition invaded Afghanistan and overthrew the Taliban. In May 2011, bin Laden was shot and killed by American special forces during a covert operation in Pakistan.

birth rate Proportion of births per 1,000 of the total population.

black codes Laws passed in southern states to restrict the rights of former slaves; to combat the codes, Congress passed the Civil Rights Act of 1866 and the Fourteenth Amendment and set up military governments in southern states that refused to ratify the amendment.

black power movement Militant form of civil rights protest focused on urban communities in the North and led by Malcolm X that grew as a response to impatience with the nonviolent tactics of Martin Luther King, Jr.

James Gillespie Blaine (1830–1893) As a Republican congressman from Maine, he developed close ties with business leaders, which contributed to him losing the presidential election of 1884. He later opposed President Cleveland's efforts to reduce tariffs, which became a significant issue in the 1888 presidential election. Blaine served as secretary of state under President Benjamin Harrison.

Bleeding Kansas (1856) A series of violent conflicts in the Kansas territory between anti-slavery and pro-slavery factions over the status of slavery.

blitzkrieg (1940) The German "lightning war" strategy characterized by swift, well-organized attacks using infantry, tanks, and warplanes.

Bolsheviks Under the leadership of Vladimir Lenin, this Marxist party led the November 1917 revolution against the newly formed provisional government in Russia. After seizing control, the Bolsheviks negotiated a peace treaty with Germany, the Treaty of Brest-Litovsk, and ended their participation in World War I.

Bonus Expeditionary Force (1932) Protest march in Washington, D.C. by thousands of World War I veterans and their families, calling for immediate payment of their service bonuses certificates; violence ensued when President Herbert Hoover ordered their tent villages cleared.

boomtown Town, often in the West, that developed rapidly due to the sudden influx of wealth and work opportunities; often male-dominated with a substantial immigrant population.

Daniel Boone (1734–1820) He found and expanded a trail into Kentucky, which pioneers used to reach and settle the area.

John Wilkes Booth (1838?–1865) He assassinated President Abraham Lincoln at the Ford's Theater on April 14, 1865. He was pursued and killed.

Boston Massacre Violent confrontation between British soldiers and a Boston mob on March 5, 1770, in which five colonists were killed.

Boston Tea Party Demonstration against the Tea Act of 1773 in which the Sons of Liberty, dressed as Indians, dumped hundreds of chests of British-owned tea into Boston Harbor.

Bourbons In post–Civil War southern politics, the opponents of the Redeemers were called Bourbons. They were known for having forgotten nothing and learned nothing from the ordeal of the Civil War.

bracero program (1942) System created in 1942 that permitted seasonal farm workers from Mexico to work in the United States on year-long contracts.

Joseph Brant (1742?–1807) Mohawk leader who led the Iroquois against the Americans in the Revolutionary War.

brinksmanship Secretary of State John Foster Dulles believed that communism could be contained by bringing America to the brink of war with an aggressive Communist nation. He believed that the aggressor would back down when confronted with the prospect of receiving a mass retaliation from a country with nuclear weapons.

John Brown (1800–1859) In response to a pro-slavery mob's sacking of the free-state town of Lawrence, Kansas, Brown went to the pro-slavery settlement of Pottawatomie, Kansas, which led to a guerrilla war in the Kansas territory. In 1859, he attempted to raid the federal arsenal at Harpers Ferry, hoping to use the stolen weapons to arm slaves, but he was captured and executed.

Brown v. Board of Education **(1954)** Landmark Supreme Court case that struck down racial segregation in public schools and declared "separate-but-equal" unconstitutional.

William Jennings Bryan (1860–1925) He delivered the pro-silver "Cross of Gold" speech at the 1896 Democratic Convention and won his party's nomination for president. Disappointed pro-gold Democrats chose to walk out of the convention and nominate their own candidate, which split the Democratic party and cost them the White House. Bryan's loss also crippled the Populist movement that had endorsed him.

"Bull Moose" Progressive party *See* Progressive party

Bull Run, Battles of (First and Second Manassas) First land engagement of the Civil War took place on July 21, 1861, at Manassas Junction, Virginia, at which surprised Union troops quickly retreated; one year later, on August 29–30, Confederates captured the federal supply depot and forced Union troops back to Washington.

Martin Van Buren (1782–1862) During President Jackson's first term, he served as secretary of state and minister to London. In 1836, Van Buren was elected president, and he inherited a financial crisis. He believed that the government should not continue to keep its deposits in state banks and set up an independent Treasury, which was approved by Congress after several years of political maneuvering.

General John Burgoyne (1722–1792) He was the commander of Britain's northern forces during the Revolutionary War. He and most of his troops surrendered to the Americans at the Battle of Saratoga.

burial mounds A funeral tradition, practiced in the Mississippi and Ohio Valleys by the Adena-Hopewell cultures, of erecting massive mounds of earth over graves, often in the designs of serpents and other animals.

burned-over district Area of western New York strongly influenced by the revivalist fervor of the Second Great Awakening; Disciples of Christ and Mormons are among the many sects that trace their roots to the phenomenon.

Aaron Burr (1756–1836) Even though he was Thomas Jefferson's vice president, he lost favor with Jefferson's Republican supporters. He sought to work with the Federalists and run as their candidate for the governor of New York. Alexander Hamilton opposed Burr's candidacy and his stinging remarks on the subject led to Burr challenging him to duel in which Hamilton was killed.

George H. W. Bush (1924–2018) He served as vice president during the Reagan administration and then won the presidential election of 1988. His presidency was marked by raised taxes in the face of the federal deficit, the creation of the Office of National Drug Control Policy, and military activity abroad, including the invasion of Panama and Operation Desert Storm in Kuwait. He lost the 1992 presidential election to Bill Clinton.

George W. Bush (1946–) In the 2000 presidential election, Texas governor George W. Bush won as the Republican nominee against Democratic nominee Vice President Al Gore. After the September 11 terrorist attacks, he launched his "war on terrorism." President Bush adopted the Bush Doctrine, and United States invaded Afghanistan and Iraq with unclear outcomes leaving the countries divided. In September 2008, the nation's economy nose-dived as a credit crunch spiraled into a global economic meltdown. Bush signed into law the bank bailout fund called Troubled Asset Relief Program (TARP), but the economy did not improve.

***Bush v. Gore* (2000)** The close 2000 presidential election came down to Florida's decisive twenty-five electoral votes. The final tally in Florida gave Bush a slight lead, but it was so small that a recount was required by state law. While the votes were being recounted, a legal battle was being waged to stop the recount. Finally, the case, *Bush v. Gore*, was presented to the Supreme Court who ruled 5–4 to stop the recount and Bush was declared the winner.

Bush Doctrine National security policy launched in 2002 by which the Bush administration claimed the right to launch preemptive military attacks against perceived enemies, particularly outlaw nations or terrorist organizations believed to possess weapons of mass destruction.

buying (stock) on margin The investment practice of making a small down payment (the "margin") on a stock and borrowing the rest of the money needed for the purchase from a broker who held the stock as security against a down market. If the stock's value declined and the buyer failed to meet a margin call for more funds, the broker could sell the stock to cover his loan.

Cahokia The largest chiefdom and city of the Mississippian Indian culture located in present-day Illinois, and the site of a sophisticated farming settlement that supported up to 15,000 inhabitants.

John C. Calhoun (1782–1850) He served in both the House of Representatives and the Senate for South Carolina before becoming secretary of war under President Monroe and then John Quincy Adams's vice president. Though he started his political career as an advocate of a strong national government, he eventually believed that states' rights, limited central government, and the power of nullification were necessary to preserve the Union.

California gold rush (1849) A massive migration of gold hunters, mostly men, who transformed the economy of California after gold was discovered in the foothills of northern California.

campaign of 1828 Bitter presidential contest between Democrat Andrew Jackson and National Republican John Quincy Adams (running for reelection), resulting in Jackson's victory.

Camp David Accords (1978) Peace agreement between Prime Minister Menachem Begin of Israel and President Anwar Sadat of Egypt, the first Arab head of state to officially recognize the state of Israel.

"Scarface" Al Capone (1899–1947) The most successful gangster of the Prohibition era whose Chicago-based criminal empire included bootlegging, prostitution, and gambling.

Andrew Carnegie (1835–1919) A steel magnate who believed that the general public benefited from big business even if these companies employed harsh business practices. This philosophy became deeply ingrained in the conventional wisdom of some Americans. After retiring, he devoted himself to philanthropy in hopes of promoting social welfare and world peace.

Carnegie Steel Company Corporation under the leadership of Andrew Carnegie that came to dominate the American steel industry.

Carolina colonies English proprietary colonies comprised of North and South Carolina, whose semitropical climate made them profitable centers of rice, timber, and tar production.

carpetbaggers Northern emigrants who participated in the Republican governments of the reconstructed South.

Jimmy Carter (1924–) Elected president in 1976, Jimmy Carter was an outsider to Washington. He created the departments of Energy and Education and signed into law several environmental initiatives. In 1978, he successfully brokered a peace agreement between Israel and Egypt called the Camp David Accords. However, his unwillingness to make deals with legislators caused other bills to be either gutted or stalled in Congress. His administration was plagued with a series of crises: a recession and increased inflation, a fuel shortage, the Soviet invasion of Afghanistan, and the overthrow of the Shah of Iran, leading to the Iran Hostage Crisis. Carter struggled to get the hostages released and was unable to do so until after he lost the 1980 election to Ronald Reagan. He was awarded the Nobel Peace Prize in 2002 for his efforts to further peace and democratic elections around the world.

Jacques Cartier (1491–1557) He led the first French effort to colonize North America and explored the Gulf of St. Lawrence, reaching as far as present day Montreal on the St. Lawrence River.

Fidel Castro (1926–2016) In 1959, his Communist regime came to power in Cuba after two years of guerrilla warfare against the dictator Fulgenico Batista. He enacted land redistribution programs and nationalized all foreign-owned property. The latter action as well as his political trials and summary executions damaged relations between Cuba and America. Castro was turned down when he asked for loans from the United States. However, he did receive aid from the Soviet Union.

Central Intelligence Agency (CIA) Intelligence-gathering government agency founded in 1947; under President Eisenhower's orders, secretly undermined elected governments deemed susceptible to communism.

Central Powers One of the two sides during the First World War, including Germany, Austria-Hungary, the Ottoman Empire (Turkey), and Bulgaria.

Carrie Chapman Catt (1859–1947) She was a leader of a new generation of activists in the women's suffrage movement who carried on the work started by Elizabeth Cady Stanton and Susan B. Anthony.

Cesar Chavez (1927–1993) He founded the United Farm Workers (UFW) in 1962 and worked to organize migrant farm workers. In 1965, the UFW joined Filipino farm workers striking against corporate grape farmers in California's San Joaquin Valley. In 1970, the strike and a consumer boycott on grapes compelled the farmers to formally recognize the UFW. As the result of Chavez's efforts, wages and working conditions improved for migrant workers. In 1975, the California state legislature passed a bill that required growers to bargain collectively with representatives of the farm workers.

child labor The practice of sending children to work in mines, mills, and factories, often in unsafe conditions; widespread among poor families in the late nineteenth century.

Chinese Exclusion Act (1882) Federal law that barred Chinese laborers from immigrating to America.

Christian Right Christian conservatives with a faith-based political agenda that includes allowing prayer in public schools and prohibition of abortion.

Church of Jesus Christ of Latter-day Saints / Mormons Founded in 1830 by Joseph Smith, the sect was a product of the intense revivalism of the burned-over district of New York; Smith's successor Brigham Young led 15,000 followers to Utah in 1847 to escape persecution.

Winston Churchill (1874–1965) The British prime minister who led the country during the Second World War. Along with Roosevelt and Stalin, he helped shape the postwar world at the Yalta Conference. He also coined the term "iron curtain," which he used in his famous "The Sinews of Peace" speech.

citizen-soldiers Part-time non-professional soldiers, mostly poor farmers or recent immigrants who had been indentured servants, who played an important role in the Revolutionary War.

"city machines" Local political party officials used these organizations to dispense patronage and favoritism amongst voters and businesses to ensure their loyal support to the political party.

Civil Rights Act of 1957 First federal civil rights law since Reconstruction; established the Civil Rights Commission and the Civil Rights Division of the Department of Justice.

Civil Rights Act of 1964 Legislation that outlawed discrimination in public accommodations and employment, passed at the urging of President Lyndon B. Johnson.

civil service reform An extended effort led by political reformers to end the patronage system; led to the Pendleton Act (1883), which called for government positions to be awarded based on merit rather than party loyalty.

Henry Clay (1777–1852) In the first half of the nineteenth century, he was the foremost spokesman for the American system. As Speaker of the House in the 1820s, he promoted economic nationalism, "market revolution," and the rapid development of western states and territories. A broker of compromise, he formulated the "second"

Missouri Compromise and the Compromise of 1850. In 1824, Clay supported John Quincy Adams, who won the presidency and appointed Clay to secretary of state. Andrew Jackson claimed that Clay had entered into a "corrupt bargain" with Adams for his own selfish gains.

Clayton Anti-Trust Act (1914) Legislation that served to enhance the Sherman Anti-Trust Act (1890) by clarifying what constituted "monopolistic" activities and declaring that labor unions were not to be viewed as "monopolies in restraint of trade."

Bill Clinton (1946–) The governor of Arkansas won the 1992 presidential election against President George H. W. Bush. In his first term, he pushed through Congress a tax increase, an economic stimulus package, the adoption of the North America Free Trade Agreement, welfare reform, a raise in the minimum wage, and improved public access to health insurance. His administration also negotiated the Oslo Accord and the Dayton Accords. After his re-election in 1996, he was involved in two high-profile scandals: his investment in the fraudulent Whitewater Development Corporation (but no evidence was found of him being involved in any wrong-doing) and his sexual affair with a White House intern. His attempt to cover up the affair led to a vote in Congress on whether or not to begin an impeachment inquiry. The House of Representatives voted to impeach Clinton, but the Senate found him not guilty.

Hillary Rodham Clinton (1947–) In the 2008 presidential election, Senator Hillary Clinton, the spouse of former President Bill Clinton, initially was the front-runner for the Democratic nomination, which made her the first woman with a serious chance to win the presidency. However, Senator Barack Obama's Internet-based and grassroots-orientated campaign garnered him enough delegates to win the nomination. After Obama became president, she was appointed secretary of state. In 2016, Clinton ran again and won the Democratic nomination for the presidency. Although she won the popular vote, she lost the election to Donald Trump.

clipper ships Tall, slender, mid-nineteenth-century sailing ships that were favored over older merchant ships for their speed, but ultimately gave way to steamships because they lacked cargo space.

Coercive Acts (1774) Four parliamentary measures that required the colonies to pay for the Boston Tea Party's damages, imposed a military government, disallowed colonial trials of British soldiers, and forced the quartering of troops in private homes.

coffin ships Irish immigrants fleeing the potato famine had to endure a six-week journey across the Atlantic to reach America. During these voyages, thousands of passengers died of disease and starvation, which led to the ships being called "coffin ships."

Columbian Exchange The transfer of biological and social elements, such as plants, animals, people, diseases, and cultural practices, among Europe, the Americas, and Africa in the wake of Christopher Columbus's voyages to the "New World."

Christopher Columbus (1451–1506) The Italian sailor who persuaded King Ferdinad and Queen Isabella of Spain to fund his expedition across the Atlantic to discover a new trade route to Asia. Instead of arriving at China or Japan, he reached the Bahamas in 1492.

James B. Comey (1960–) FBI director fired by President Donald Trump in 2017.

Committee of Correspondence Group organized by Samuel Adams in retaliation for the *Gaspée* incident to address American grievances, assert American rights, and form a network of rebellion.

Committee on Public Information During the First World War, this committee produced war propaganda that conveyed the Allies' war aims to Americans as well as attempted to weaken the enemy's morale.

Committee to Re-elect the President (CREEP) During Nixon's presidency, his administration engaged in a number of immoral acts, such as attempting to steal information and falsely accusing political appointments of sexual improprieties. These acts were funded by money illegally collected through CREEP.

***Common Sense* (1776)** Popular pamphlet written by Thomas Paine attacking British principles of hereditary rule and monarchical government, and advocating a declaration of American independence.

Compromise of 1850 A package of five bills presented to the Congress by Henry Clay intended to avoid secession or civil war by reducing tensions between North and South over the status of slavery.

Compromise of 1877 Deal made by a special congressional commission on March 2, 1877, to resolve the disputed presidential election of 1876; Republican Rutherford B. Hayes, who had lost the popular vote, was declared the winner in exchange for the withdrawal of federal troops from the South, marking the end of Reconstruction.

Comstock Lode Mine in eastern Nevada acquired by Canadian fur trapper Henry Comstock that between 1860 and 1880 yielded almost $1 billion worth of gold and silver.

Conestoga wagons These large horse-drawn wagons were used to carry people or heavy freight long distances, including from the East to the western frontier settlements.

Congressional Reconstruction Phase of Reconstruction directed by Radical Republicans through the passage of three laws: the Military Reconstruction Act, the Command of the Army Act, and the Tenure of Office Act.

conquistadores Spanish term for "conquerors," applied to Spanish and Portuguese soldiers who conquered lands held by indigenous peoples in central and southern America as well as the current states of Texas, New Mexico, Arizona, and California.

consumer culture A society in which mass production and consumption of nationally advertised products comes to dictate much of social life and status.

containment U.S. cold war strategy that sought to prevent global Soviet expansion and influence through political, economic, and, if necessary, military pressure as a means of combating the spread of communism.

Continental army Army authorized by the Continental Congress, 1775–1784, to fight the British; commanded by General George Washington.

Contract with America (1994) A list of conservative promises in response to the supposed liberalism of the Clinton administration, that was drafted by Speaker of the House Newt Gingrich and other congressional Republicans as the GOP platform for the 1994 midterm elections. More a campaign tactic than a practical program, few of its proposed items ever became law.

contrabands Slaves who sought refuge in Union military camps or who lived in areas of the Confederacy under Union control.

Contras The Reagan administration ordered the CIA to train and supply guerrilla bands of anti-Communist Nicaraguans called Contras. They were fighting the Sandinista government that had recently come to power in Nicaragua. The State Department believed that the Sandinista government was supplying the leftist Salvadoran rebels with Soviet and Cuban arms. A cease-fire agreement between the Contras and Sandinistas was signed in 1988.

Calvin Coolidge (1872–1933) After President Harding's death, his vice president, Calvin Coolidge, assumed the presidency. Coolidge believed that the nation's welfare was tied to the success of Big Business, and he worked to end government regulation of business and industry as well as reduce taxes. In particular, he focused on the nation's industrial development.

Copperhead Democrats Democrats in northern states who opposed the Civil War and argued for an immediate peace settlement with the Confederates; Republicans labeled them "Copperheads," likening them to venomous snakes.

Hernán Cortés (1485–1547) The Spanish conquistador who conquered the Aztec Empire and set the precedent for other plundering conquistadores.

General Charles Cornwallis (1738–1805) He was in charge of British troops in the South during the Revolutionary War. His surrender to George Washington at the Battle of Yorktown ended the Revolutionary War.

Corps of Discovery Meriwether Lewis and William Clark led this group of men on an expedition of the newly purchased Louisiana territory, which took them from Missouri to Oregon. As they traveled, they kept detailed journals and drew maps of the previously unexplored territory. Their reports attracted traders and trappers to the region and gave the United States a claim to the Oregon country by right of discovery and exploration.

"corrupt bargain" Scandal in which presidential candidate and Speaker of the House Henry Clay secured John Quincy Adams's victory over Andrew Jackson in the 1824 election, supposedly in exchange for Clay being named secretary of state.

cotton gin Hand-operated machine invented by Eli Whitney in the late eighteenth century that quickly removed seeds from cotton bolls, enabling the mass production of cotton in nineteenth-century America.

cotton kingdom Cotton-producing region, relying predominantly on slave labor, that spanned from North Carolina west to Louisiana and reached as far north as southern Illinois.

cotton White fibers harvested from cotton plants, spun into yarn, and woven into textiles that made comfortable, easy-to-clean products, especially clothing; the most valuable cash crop driving the economy in the United States and Great Britain during the nineteenth century.

counterculture Unorganized youth rebellion against mainstream institutions, values, and behavior that more often focused on cultural rather than political activism.

court-packing plan President Franklin D. Roosevelt's failed 1937 attempt to increase the number of U.S. Supreme Court justices from nine to fifteen in order to save his Second New Deal programs from constitutional challenges.

covenant theory A Puritan concept that believed true Christians could enter a voluntary union for the common worship of God. Taking the idea one step further, the union could also be used for the purposes of establishing governments.

crop-lien system Credit system used by sharecroppers and share tenants who pledged a portion ("share") of their future crop to local merchants or land owners in exchange for farming supplies and food.

"Cross of Gold" Speech In the 1896 election, the Democratic Party split over the issue of whether to use gold or silver to back American currency. Significant to this division was the pro-silver "Cross of Gold" speech that William Jennings Bryan delivered at the Democratic convention, which was so well received that Bryan won the nomination to be their presidential candidate. Disappointed pro-gold Democrats chose to walk out of the convention and nominate their own candidate.

Cuban missile crisis Thirteen-day U.S.-Soviet standoff in October 1962, sparked by the discovery of Soviet missile sites in Cuba; the crisis was the closest the world has come to nuclear war since 1945.

cult of domesticity A pervasive nineteenth-century ideology that urged women to celebrate their role as manager of the household and nurturer of the children.

George A. Custer (1839–1876) He was a reckless and glory-seeking Lieutenant Colonel of the U.S. Army who fought the Sioux Indians in the Great Sioux War. In 1876, he and his detachment of soldiers were entirely wiped out in the Battle of Little Bighorn.

***Dartmouth College v. Woodward* (1819)** Supreme Court ruling that enlarged the definition of *contract* to put corporations beyond the reach of the states that chartered them.

Daughters of Liberty Colonial women who protested the British government's tax policies by boycotting British products, such as clothing, and who wove their own fabric, or "homespun."

Dawes Severalty Act of 1887 Federal legislation that divided ancestral Native American lands among the heads of each Indian family in an attempt to "Americanize" Indians by forcing them to become farmers working individual plots of land.

D-day June 6, 1944, when an Allied amphibious assault landed on the Normandy coast and established a foothold in Europe from which Hitler's defenses could not recover.

Jefferson Davis (1808–1889) He was the president of the Confederacy during the Civil War. When the Confederacy's defeat seemed invitable in early 1865, he refused to surrender. Union forces captured him in May of that year.

Bartolomé de Las Casas (1484–1566) A Catholic missionary who renounced the Spanish practice of coercively converting Indians and advocated their better treatment. In 1552, he wrote *A Brief Relation of the Destruction of the Indies*, which described the Spanish's cruel treatment of the Indians.

death rate Proportion of deaths per 1,000 of the total population; also called *mortality rate*.

Eugene V. Debs (1855–1926) Founder of the American Railway Union, which he organized against the Pullman Palace Car Company during the Pullman strike. Later he organized the Social Democratic party, which eventually became the Socialist Party of America. In the 1912 presidential election, he ran as the Socialist party's candidate and received more than 900,000 votes.

Declaration of Independence Formal statement, principally drafted by Thomas Jefferson and adopted by the Second Continental Congress on July 4, 1776, that officially announced the thirteen colonies' break with Great Britain.

Declaration of Sentiments Document based on the Declaration of Independence that called for gender equality, written primarily by Elizabeth Cady Stanton and signed by Seneca Falls Convention delegates in 1848.

Declaratory Act Following the repeal of the Stamp Act in 1766, Parliament passed this act which asserted Parliament's full power to make laws binding the colonies "in all cases whatsoever."

Deism Enlightenment thought applied to religion, emphasizing reason, morality, and natural law rather than scriptural authority or an ever-present God intervening in human life.

détente Period of improving relations between the United States and Communist nations, particularly China and the Soviet Union, during the Nixon administration.

George Dewey (1837–1917) On April 30, 1898, Commodore George Dewey's small U.S. naval squadron defeated the Spanish warships in Manila Bay in the Philippines. This quick victory aroused expansionist fever in the United States.

John Dewey (1859–1952) He is an important philosopher of pragmatism. However, he preferred to use the term *instrumentalism*, because he saw ideas as instruments of action.

Ngo Dinh Diem (1901–1963) Following the Geneva Accords, the French, with the support of America, forced the Vietnamese emperor to accept Dinh Diem as the new premier of South Vietnam. President Eisenhower sent advisers to train Diem's police and army. In return, the United States expected Diem to enact democratic reforms and distribute land to the peasants. Instead, he suppressed his political opponents, did little or no land distribution, and let corruption grow. In 1956, he refused to participate in elections to reunify Vietnam. Eventually, he ousted the emperor and declared himself president.

Distribution Act (1836) Law requiring the distribution of the federal budget surplus to the states, creating chaos among state banks that had become dependent on such federal funds.

Dorothea Lynde Dix (1802–1887) She was an important figure in increasing the public's awareness of the plight of the mentally ill. After a two-year investigation of the treatment of the mentally ill in Massachusetts, she presented her findings and won the support of leading reformers. She eventually convinced twenty states to reform their treatment of the mentally ill.

Dixiecrats Breakaway faction of southern Democrats who defected from the national Democratic party in 1948 to protest the party's increased support for civil rights and to nominate their own segregationist candidates for elective office.

"dollar diplomacy" Practice advocated by President Theodore Roosevelt in which the U.S. government fostered American investments in less developed nations and then used U.S. military force to protect those investments

Stephen A. Douglas (1812–1861) As a senator from Illinois, he authored the Kansas-Nebraska Act. Running for senatorial reelection in 1858, he engaged Abraham Lincoln in a series of public debates about slavery in the territories. Even though Douglas won the election, the debates gave Lincoln a national reputation.

Frederick Douglass (1818–1895) He escaped from slavery and become an eloquent speaker and writer against the institution. In 1845, he published his autobiography entitled *Narrative of the Life of Frederick Douglass* and two years later he founded an abolitionist newspaper for blacks called the *North Star*.

dot-coms In the late 1990s, the stock market soared to new heights and defied the predictions of experts that the economy could not sustain such a performance. Much of the economic success was based on dot-com enterprises, which were firms specializing in computers, software, telecommunications, and the internet. However, many of the companies' stock market values were driven higher and higher by speculation instead of financial success. Eventually the stock market bubble burst.

Dred Scott v. Sandford **(1857)** U.S. Supreme Court ruling that slaves were not U.S. citizens and therefore could not sue for their freedom and that Congress could not prohibit slavery in the western territories.

W. E. B. Du Bois (1868–1963) He criticized Booker T. Washington's views on civil rights as being accommodationist. He advocated "ceaseless agitation" for civil rights and the immediate end to segregation and an enforcement of laws to protect civil rights and equality. He promoted an education for African Americans that would nurture bold leaders who were willing to challenge discrimination in politics.

John Foster Dulles (1888–1959) As President Eisenhower's secretary of state, he institutionalized the policy of containment and introduced the strategy of deterrence. He believed in using brinkmanship to halt the spread of communism. He attempted to employ it in Indochina, which led to the United States' involvement in Vietnam.

Dust Bowl Vast area of the Midwest where windstorms blew away millions of tons of top-soil from parched farmland after a long drought in the 1930s, causing great social distress and a massive migration of farm families.

Eastern Woodlands Peoples Various Native American peoples, particularly the Algonquian, Iroquoian, and Muskogean regional groups, who once dominated the Atlantic seaboard from Maine to Louisiana.

Peggy Eaton (1796–1879) The wife of John Eaton, President Jackson's secretary of war, was the daughter of a tavern owner with an unsavory past. Supposedly her first husband had committed suicide after learning that she was having an affair with John Eaton. The wives of members of Jackson's cabinet snubbed her because of her lowly origins and past, resulting in a scandal known as the Eaton Affair.

Economic Opportunity Act (1964) Key legislation in President Johnson's "War on Poverty" which created the Office of Economic Opportunity and programs like Head Start and work-study.

Jonathan Edwards (1703–1758) New England Congregationalist minister who began a religious revival in his Northampton church and was an important figure in the Great Awakening.

election of 1800 Presidential election between Thomas Jefferson and John Adams; resulted in the first Democratic-Republican victory after the Federalist administrations of George Washington and John Adams.

election of 1864 Abraham Lincoln's successful reelection campaign, capitalizing on Union military successes in Georgia, to defeat Democratic opponent, former general George B. McClellan, who ran on a peace platform.

election of 1912 The presidential election of 1912 featured four candidates: Wilson, Taft, Roosevelt, and Debs. Each candidate believed in the basic assumptions of progressive politics, but each had a different view on how progressive ideals should be implemented through policy. In the end, Taft and Roosevelt split the Republican party votes and Wilson emerged as the winner.

Queen Elizabeth I of England (1533–1603) The protestant daughter of Henry VIII, she was Queen of England from 1558–1603 and played a major role in the Protestant Reformation. During her long reign, the doctrines and services of the Church of England were defined and the Spanish Armada was defeated.

General Dwight D. Eisenhower (1890–1969) During the Second World War, he commanded the Allied Forces landing in Africa and was the supreme Allied commander as well as planner for Operation Overlord. In 1952, he was elected president on his popularity as a war hero and his promises to clean up Washington. His administration sought to cut the nation's domestic programs and budget, ended the fighting in Korea, and institutionalized the policies of containment and deterrence. He established the Eisenhower doctrine, which promised to aid any nation against aggression by a Communist nation.

Ellis Island Reception center in New York Harbor through which most European immigrants to America were processed from 1892 to 1954.

Emancipation Proclamation (1863) Military order issued by President Abraham Lincoln that freed slaves in areas still controlled by the Confederacy but did not free the 500,000 slaves in the four border states that remained in the Union.

Embargo Act (1807) A law promoted by President Thomas Jefferson prohibiting American ships from leaving for foreign ports, in order to safeguard them from British and French attacks. This ban on American exports proved disastrous to the U.S. economy.

Ralph Waldo Emerson (1803–1882) As a leader of the transcendentalist movement, he wrote poems, essays, and speeches that discussed the sacredness of nature, optimism, self-reliance, and the unlimited potential of the individual. He wanted to transcend the limitations of inherited conventions and rationalism to reach the inner recesses of the self.

encomienda A land-grant system under which Spanish army officers (*conquistadores*) were awarded large parcels of land taken from Native Americans.

Enlightenment A revolution in thought begun in Europe in the seventeenth century that emphasized reason and science over the authority and myths of traditional religion.

enumerated goods According to the Navigation Act, these particular goods, like tobacco or cotton, could only be shipped to England or other English colonies.

Environmental Protection Agency (EPA) (1970) Federal environmental agency created by Nixon to appease the demands of congressional Democrats for a federal environmental watchdog agency.

Erie Canal (1817) Most important and profitable of the barge canals of the 1820s and 1830s; stretched from Buffalo to Albany, New York, connecting the Great Lakes to the East Coast and making New York City the nation's largest port.

ethnic cleansing The systematic removal of an ethnic group from a territory through violence or intimidation in order to create a homogenous society; the term was popularized by the Yugoslav policy brutally targeting Albanian Muslims in Kosovo.

Exodusters African Americans who migrated west from the South in search of a haven from racism and poverty after the collapse of Radical Republican rule.

Fair Deal (1949) President Truman's proposals to build upon the New Deal with national health insurance, the repeal of the Taft-Hartley Act, new civil rights legislation, and other initiatives; most were rejected by the Republican-controlled Congress.

Fair Employment Practices Commission Created in 1941 by executive order, the FEPC sought to eliminate racial discrimination in jobs; it possessed little power but represented a step toward civil rights for African Americans.

"falling domino" theory Theory that if one country fell to communism, its neighboring countries would follow suit.

Farmers' Alliances Like the Granger movement, these organizations sought to address the issues of small farming communities; however Alliances emphasized more political action and called for the creation of a Third Party to advocate their concerns.

fascism A radical form of totalitarian government that emerged in Italy and Germany in the 1920s in which a dictator uses propaganda and brute force to seize control of all aspects of national life.

field hands Slaves who toiled in the cotton or cane fields in organized work gangs.

Federal-Aid Highway Act (1956) Largest federal project in U.S. history that created a national network of interstate highways and was the largest federal project in history.

Federal Deposit Insurance Corporation (1933) Independent government agency, established to prevent bank panics, that guarantees the safety of deposits in citizens' savings accounts.

Federal Reserve Act (1913) Legislation passed by Congress to create a new national banking system in order to regulate the nation's currency supply and ensure the stability and integrity of member banks who made up the Federal Reserve System across the nation.

Federal Trade Commission (1914) Independent agency created by the Wilson administration that replaced the Bureau of Corporations as an even more powerful tool to combat unfair trade practices and monopolies.

Federal Writers' Project During the Great Depression, this project provided writers, such as Ralph Ellison, Richard Wright, and Saul Bellow, with work, which gave them employment and a chance to develop as artists.

federalism Concept of dividing governmental authority between the national government and the states.

The Federalist Papers Collection of eighty-five essays, published widely in newspapers in 1787 and 1788, written by Alexander Hamilton, James Madison, and John Jay in support of adopting the proposed U.S. Constitution.

Federalists Proponents of a centralized federal system and the ratification of the Constitution. Most Federalists were relatively young, educated men who supported a broad interpretation of the Constitution whenever national interest dictated such flexibility. Notable Federalists included Alexander Hamilton and John Jay.

Geraldine Ferraro (1935–2011) In the 1984 presidential election, Democratic nominee, Walter Mondale, chose her as his running mate. As a member of the U.S. House of Representatives from New York, she was the first woman to be a vice-presidential nominee for a major political party. However, she was placed on the defensive because of her husband's complicated business dealings.

Fifteenth Amendment (1870) This amendment forbids states to deny any person the right to vote on grounds of "race, color or pervious condition of servitude." Former Confederate states were required to ratify this amendment before they could be readmitted to the Union.

"final solution" The Nazi party's systematic murder of some 6 million Jews along with more than a million other people including, but not limited to, gypsies, homosexuals, and handicap individuals.

First New Deal (1933–1935) Franklin D. Roosevelt's ambitious first-term cluster of economic and social programs designed to combat the Great Depression.

First Red Scare Outbreak of anti-Communist hysteria that included the arrest without warrants of thousands of suspected radicals, most of whom (mainly Russian immigrants) were deported.

flappers Young women of the 1920s whose rebellion against prewar standards of femininity included wearing shorter dresses, bobbing their hair, dancing to jazz music, driving cars, smoking cigarettes, and indulging in illegal drinking and gambling.

Food Administration After America's entry into World War I, the economy of the home front needed to be reorganized to provide the most efficient means of conducting the war. The Food Administration was a part of this effort. Under the leadership of Herbert Hoover, the organization sought to increase agricultural production while reducing civilian consumption of foodstuffs.

"Force Bill" (1833) Legislation, sparked by the Nullification Crisis in South Carolina, that authorized the president's use of the army to compel states to comply with federal law.

Gerald Ford (1913–2006) He was appointed to the vice presidency under President Nixon after the resignation of Spiro Agnew, and assumed the presidency after President Nixon's resignation. He resisted congressional pressure to both reduce taxes and increase federal spending, which sent the American economy into the deepest recession since the Great Depression. Ford retained Kissinger as his secretary of state and continued Nixon's foreign policy goals. He was heavily criticized following the collapse of South Vietnam.

Fort Laramie Treaty (1851) Restricted the Plains Indians from using the Overland Trail and permitted the building of government forts.

Fort Necessity After attacking a group of French soldiers, George Washington constructed and took shelter in this fort from vengeful French troops. Washington eventually surrendered to them after a day-long battle. This conflict was a significant event in igniting the French and Indian War.

Fort Sumter First battle of the Civil War, in which the federal fort in Charleston (South Carolina) Harbor was captured by the Confederates on April 14, 1861, after two days of shelling.

"forty-niners" Speculators who went to northern California following the discovery of gold in 1848; the first of several years of large-scale migration was 1849.

Fourteen Points President Woodrow Wilson's proposed plan for the peace agreement after the First World War that included the creation of a "league of nations" intended to keep the peace.

Fourteenth Amendment (1866) Guaranteed rights of citizenship to former slaves, in words similar to those of the Civil Rights Act of 1866.

alliance with France Critical diplomatic, military, and economic alliance between France and the newly independent United States, codified by the Treaty of Amity and Commerce and the Treaty of Alliance (1778).

Franciscan Missions In 1769, Franciscan missioners accompanied Spanish soldiers to California and over the next fifty years established a chain of missions from San Diego to San Francisco. At these missions, friars sought to convert Indians to Catholicism and make them members of the Spanish empire. The friars stripped the Indians of their native heritage and used soldiers to enforce their will.

Benjamin Franklin (1706–1790) A Boston-born American, who epitomized the Enlightenment for many Americans and Europeans, Franklin's wide range of interests led him to become a publisher, inventor, and statesman. As the latter, he contributed to the writing of the Declaration of Independence, served as the minister to France during the Revolutionary War, and was a delegate to the Constitutional Convention.

Free-Soil party A political coalition created in 1848 that opposed the expansion of slavery into the new western territories.

Freedmen's Bureau Reconstruction agency established in 1865 to protect the legal rights of former slaves and to assist with their education, jobs, health care, and landowning.

Freedom Riders Activists who, beginning in 1961, traveled by bus through the South to test federal court rulings that banned segregation on buses and trains.

John C. Frémont "the Pathfinder" (1813–1890) He was an explorer and surveyor who helped inspire Americans living in California to rebel against the Mexican government and declare independence.

French and Indian War (Seven Years' War) (1754–1763) The last—and the most important—of four colonial wars fought between England and France for control of North America east of the Mississippi River.

French Revolution Revolutionary movement beginning in 1789 that overthrew the monarchy and transformed France into an unstable republic before Napoleon Bonaparte assumed power in 1799.

Sigmund Freud (1865–1939) He was the founder of psychoanalysis, which suggested that human behavior was motivated by unconscious and irrational forces. By the 1920s, his ideas were being discussed more openly in America.

frontier revivals Religious revival movement within the Second Great Awakening, that took place in frontier churches in western territories and states in the early nineteenth century.

Fugitive Slave Act (1850) Part of the Compromise of 1850, a provision that authorized federal officials to help capture and then return escaped slaves to their owners without trials.

fundamentalism Anti-modernist Protestant movement started in the early twentieth century that proclaimed the literal truth of the Bible; the name came from *The Fundamentals*, published by conservative leaders.

William Lloyd Garrison (1805–1879) In 1831, he started the anti-slavery newspaper *Liberator* and helped start the New England Anti-Slavery Society. Two years later, he assisted Arthur and Lewis Tappan in the founding of the American Anti-Slavery Society. He and his followers believed that America had been thoroughly corrupted and needed a wide range of reforms, embracing abolition, temperance, pacifism, and women's rights.

Marcus Garvey (1887–1940) He was the leading spokesman for Negro Nationalism, which exalted blackness, black cultural expression, and black exclusiveness. He called upon African Americans to liberate themselves from the surrounding white culture and create their own businesses, cultural centers, and newspapers. He was also the founder of the Universal Negro Improvement Association.

Citizen Genet (1763–1834) As the ambassador to the United States from the new French Republic, he engaged American privateers to attack British ships and conspired with frontiersmen and land speculators to organize an attack on Spanish Florida and Louisiana. His actions and the French radicals excessive actions against their enemies in the new French Republic caused the French Revolution to lose support among Americans.

Geneva Accords In 1954, the Geneva Accords were signed, which ended French colonial rule in Indochina. The agreement created the independent nations of Laos and Cambodia and divided Vietnam along the 17th parallel until an election in 1956 would reunify the country.

Battle of Gettysburg (1863) A monumental three-day battle in southern Pennsylvania, widely considered a turning point in the war, in which Union forces successfully countered a second Confederate invasion of the North.

Ghost Dance movement A spiritual and political movement among Native Americans whose followers performed a ceremonial "ghost dance" intended to connect the living with the dead and make the Indians bulletproof in battles to restore their homelands.

GI Bill of Rights (1944) Provided unemployment, education, and financial benefits for World War II veterans to ease their transition back to the civilian world.

Gibbons v. Ogden (1824) Supreme Court case that gave the federal government the power to regulate interstate commerce.

Newt Gingrich (1943–) He led the Republican insurgency in Congress in the mid 1990s through mobilizing religious and social conservatives. Along with other Republican congressmen, he created the Contract with America, which was a ten-point anti-big government program. However, the program fizzled out after many of its bills were not passed by Congress.

Gilded Age (1860–1896) An era of dramatic industrial and urban growth characterized by widespread political corruption and loose government oversight of corporations.

The Gilded Age Mark Twain and Charles Dudley Warner's 1873 novel, the title of which became the popular name for the period from the end of the Civil War to the turn of the century.

glasnost Russian term for "openness"; applied to the loosening of censorship in the Soviet Union under Mikhail Gorbachev.

globalization An important, and controversial, transformation of the world economy whereby the Internet helped revolutionize global commerce by creating an international marketplace for goods and services. Led by the growing number of multinational companies and the Americanization of many foreign consumer cultures, with companies like McDonald's and Starbucks appearing in all of the major cities of the world.

Glorious Revolution (1688) Successful coup, instigated by a group of English aristocrats, which overthrew King James II and instated William of Orange and Mary, his English wife, to the British throne.

Barry Goldwater (1909–1998) A leader of the Republican right whose book, *The Conscience of a Conservative*, was highly influential to that segment of the party. He proposed eliminating the income tax and overhauling Social Security. In 1964, he ran as the Republican presidential candidate and lost to President Johnson. He campaigned against Johnson's war on poverty, the tradition of New Deal, the nuclear test ban and the Civil Rights Act of 1964 and advocated the wholesale bombing of North Vietnam.

Samuel Gompers (1850–1924) He served as the president of the American Federation of Labor from its inception until his death. He focused on achieving concrete economic gains such as higher wages, shorter hours, and better working conditions.

"good neighbor" policy Proclaimed by President Franklin D. Roosevelt in his first inaugural address in 1933, it sought improved diplomatic relations between the United States and its Latin American neighbors.

Mikhail Gorbachev (1931–) In the late 1980s, Soviet leader Mikhail Gorbachev attempted to reform the Soviet Union through his programs of *perestroika* and *glasnost* and pursued a renewal of détente with America, signing new arms-control agreements with President Reagan. Gorbachev allowed the velvet revolutions of Eastern Europe to occur without outside interference. Eventually the political, social, and economic upheaval he had unleashed would lead to the break-up of the Soviet Union.

Albert Gore Jr. (1948–) He served as a senator of Tennessee and then as President Clinton's vice president. In the 2000 presidential election, he was the Democratic candidate against Governor George W. Bush. The close election came down to Florida's electoral votes. While the votes were being recounted as required by state law, a legal battle was being waged to stop the recount. Finally, the case, *Bush v. Gore*, was presented to the Supreme Court who ruled 5–4 to stop the recount and Bush was declared the winner.

Jay Gould (1836–1892) As one of the biggest railroad robber barons, he was infamous for buying rundown railroads, making cosmetic improvements and then reselling them for a profit. He used corporate funds for personal investments and to bribe politicians and judges.

gradualism This strategy for ending slavery involved promoting the banning of slavery in the new western territories and encouraging the release of slaves from slavery. Supporters of this method believed that it would bring about the gradual end of slavery.

Granger movement Began by offering social and educational activities for isolated farmers and their families and later started to promote "cooperatives" where farmers could join together to buy, store, and sell their crops to avoid the high fees charged by brokers and other middle-men.

Ulysses S. Grant (1822–1885) After distinguishing himself in the western theater of the Civil War, he was appointed general in chief of the Union army in 1864. Afterward, he defeated General Robert E. Lee through a policy of aggressive attrition. Lee surrendered to Grant on April 9th, 1865 at the Appomattox Court House. His presidential tenure suffered from scandals and fiscal problems, including the debate on whether or not greenbacks, paper money, should be removed from circulation.

Great Awakening Fervent religious revival movement that swept the thirteen colonies from the 1720s through the 1740s.

Great Compromise (Connecticut Compromise) Mediated the differences between the New Jersey and Virginia delegations to the Constitutional Convention by providing for a bicameral legislature, the upper house of which would have equal representation and the lower house of which would be apportioned by population.

Great Depression (1929–1941) Worst economic downturn in American history; it was spurred by the stock market crash in the fall of 1929 and lasted until the Second World War.

Great Migration Mass exodus of African Americans from the rural South to the Northeast and Midwest during and after the First World War.

Great Railroad Strike of 1877 A series of demonstrations, some violent, held nationwide in support of striking railroad workers in Martinsburg, West Virginia, who refused to work due to wage cuts.

Great Recession (2007–2009) Massive, prolonged economic downturn sparked by the collapse of the housing market and the financial institutions holding unpaid mortgages; it lasted from December 2007 to January 2009 and resulted in 9 million Americans losing their jobs.

Great Sioux War Conflict between Sioux and Cheyenne Indians and federal troops over lands in the Dakotas in the mid-1870s.

Great Society Term coined by President Lyndon B. Johnson in his 1965 State of the Union address, in which he proposed legislation to address problems of voting rights, poverty, diseases, education, immigration, and the environment.

Horace Greeley (1811–1872) In reaction to Radical Reconstruction and corruption in President Ulysses S. Grant's administration, a group of Republicans broke from the party to form the Liberal Republicans. In 1872, the Liberal Republicans chose Horace Greeley as their presidential candidate who ran on a platform of favoring civil service reform and condemning the Republican's Reconstruction policy.

greenbacks Paper money issued during the Civil War. After the war ended, a debate emerged on whether or not to remove the paper currency from circulation and revert back to hard-money currency (gold coins). Opponents of hard-money feared that eliminating the greenbacks would shrink the money supply, which would lower crop prices and make it more difficult to repay long-term debts. President Ulysses S. Grant, as well as hard-currency advocates, believed that gold coins were morally preferable to paper currency.

Greenback party Formed in 1876 in reaction to economic depression, the party favored issuance of unsecured paper money to help farmers repay debts; the movement for free coinage of silver took the place of the greenback movement by the 1880s.

General Nathanael Greene (1742–1786) He was appointed by Congress to command the American army fighting in the South during the Revolutionary War. Using his patience and his skills of managing men, saving supplies, and avoiding needless risks, he waged a successful war of attrition against the British.

Sarah Grimké (1792–1873) and **Angelina Grimké (1805–1879)** These two sisters gave anti-slavery speeches to crowds of mixed gender that caused some people to condemn them for engaging in unfeminine activities. In 1840, William Lloyd Garrison convinced the Anti-Slavery Society to allow women equal participation in the organization.

Half-Way Covenant Allowed baptized children of church members to be admitted to a "halfway" membership in the church and secure baptism for their own children in turn, but allowed them neither a vote in the church, nor communion.

Alexander Hamilton (1755–1804) His belief in a strong federal government led him to become a leader of the Federalists. As the first secretary of the Treasury, he laid the foundation for American capitalism through his creation of a federal budget, funded debt, a federal tax system, a national bank, a customs service, and a coast guard. His "Reports on Public Credit" and "Reports on Manufactures" outlined his vision for economic development and government finances. He died in a duel against Aaron Burr.

Alexander Hamilton's economic reforms Various measures designed to strengthen the nation's economy and generate federal revenue through the promotion of new industries, the adoption of new tax policies, the payment of war debts, and the establishment of a national bank.

Warren G. Harding (1865–1923) In the 1920 presidential election, he was the Republican nominee who promised Americans a "return to normalcy." Once in office, Harding's administration dismantled many of the social and economic components of progressivism and pursued a pro-business agenda. Harding appointed four pro-business Supreme Court Justices, cut taxes, increased tariffs, and promoted a lenient attitude towards regulation of corporations. However, he did speak out against racism and ended the exclusion of African Americans from federal positions.

Harlem Renaissance The nation's first self-conscious black literary and artistic movement; it was centered in New York City's Harlem district, which had a largely black population in the wake of the Great Migration from the South.

Hartford Convention A series of secret meetings in December 1814 and January 1815 at which New England Federalists protested American involvement in the War of 1812 and discussed several constitutional amendments, including limiting each president to one term, designed to weaken the dominant Republican Party.

Haymarket Riot (1886) Violent uprising in Haymarket Square, Chicago, where police clashed with labor demonstrators in the aftermath of a bombing.

headright A land-grant policy that promised fifty acres to any colonist who could afford passage to Virginia, as well as fifty more for any accompanying servants. The headright policy was eventually expanded to include any colonists—and was also adopted in other colonies.

Patrick Henry (1736–1799) He inspired the Virginia Resolves, which declared that Englishmen could only be taxed by their elected representatives. In March of 1775, he met with other colonial leaders to discuss the goals of the upcoming Continental Congress and famously declared "Give me liberty or give me death." During the ratification process of the U.S. Constitution, he became one of the leaders of the anti-federalists.

Hiroshima (1945) Japanese port city that was the first target of the newly developed atomic bomb on August 6, 1945. Most of the city was destroyed.

Alger Hiss (1904–1996) During the second Red Scare he had served in several government departments and was accused of being a spy for the Soviet Union and was convicted of lying about espionage. The case was politically damaging to the Truman administration because the president called the charges against Hiss a "red herring."

Adolf Hitler (1889–1945) The leader of the Nazis who advocated a violent anti-Semitic, anti-Marxist, pan-German ideology. He started World War II in Europe and orchestrated the systematic murder of some 6 million Jews along with more than a million others.

HIV/AIDS Human immunodeficiency virus (HIV) transmitted via the bodily fluids of infected persons to cause acquired immunodeficiency syndrome (AIDS), an often-fatal disease of the immune system when it appeared in the 1980s.

holding company A corporation established to own and manage other companies' stock rather than to produce goods and services itself.

Holocaust Systematic racist attempt by the Nazis to exterminate the Jews of Europe, resulting in the murder of more than 6 million Jews and more than 5 million other "undesirables."

Homestead Act (1862) Legislation granting "homesteads" of 160 acres of government-owned land to settlers who agreed to work the land for at least five years.

Homestead Steel Strike (1892) Labor conflict at the Homestead steel mill near Pittsburgh, Pennsylvania, culminating in a battle between strikers and private security agents hired by the factory's management.

Herbert Hoover (1874–1964) Prior to becoming president, Hoover served as the secretary of commerce in both the Harding and Coolidge administrations. As president during the Great Depression, he believed that the nation's business structure was sound and sought to revive the economy through boosting the nation's confidence. He also tried to restart the economy with government constructions projects, lower taxes and new federal loan programs, but nothing worked.

horizontal integration The process by which a corporation acquires or merges with its competitors.

horse A tall, four-legged mammal (*Equus caballus*), domesticated and bred since prehistoric times for carrying riders and pulling heavy loads. The Spanish introduced horses to the Americas, eventually transforming many Native American cultures.

House Committee on Un-American Activities (HUAC) Committee of the U.S. House of Representatives formed in 1938; it was originally tasked with investigating Nazi subversion during the Second World War and later shifted its focus to rooting out Communists in the government and the motion-picture industry.

Sam Houston (1793–1863) During Texas's fight for independence from Mexico, Sam Houston was the commander in chief of the Texas forces, and he led the attack that captured General Antonio López de Santa Anna. After Texas gained its independence, he was named its first president.

How the Other Half Lives In this book, early muckraking journalist Jacob Riis exposed the slum conditions in New York City.

General William Howe (1729–1814) As the commander of the British army in the Revolutionary War, he seized New York City from Washington's army, but failed to capture it. He missed several more opportunities to quickly end the rebellion, and he resigned his command after the British defeat at Saratoga.

Saddam Hussein (1937–2006) The former dictator of Iraq who became the head of state in 1979. In 1980, he invaded Iran and started the eight-year-long Iran-Iraq War. In 1990, he invaded Kuwait, which caused the Gulf War of 1991. In 2003, he was overthrown and captured when the United States invaded. He was sentenced to death by hanging in 2006.

Anne Hutchinson (1591–1643) The articulate, strong-willed, and intelligent wife of a prominent Boston merchant, who espoused her belief in direct divine revelation. She quarreled with Puritan leaders over her beliefs; and they banished her from the colony.

Immigration Act of 1924 Federal legislation intended to favor northern and western European immigrants over those from southern and eastern Europe by restricting the number of immigrants from any one European country to 2 percent of the total number of immigrants per year, with an overall limit of slightly over 150,000 new arrivals per year.

Immigration and Nationality Act of 1965 Legislation that abolished discriminatory quotas based upon immigrants' national origin and treated all nationalities and races equally.

imperialism The use of diplomatic or military force to extend a nation's power and enhance its economic interests, often by acquiring territory or colonies and justifying such behavior with assumptions of racial superiority.

impressment The British navy used press-gangs to kidnap men in British and colonial ports who were then forced to serve in the British navy.

indentured servitude A defined period of labor (often four to seven years) which settlers consented to in exchange for having their passage to the New World paid by their "master."

Independent Treasury Act (1840) System created by President Martin Van Buren and approved by Congress in 1840 whereby the federal government moved its funds from favored state banks to the U.S. Treasury, whose financial transactions could only be in gold or silver coins of paper currency backed by gold or silver.

"Indian New Deal" This phrase refers to the reforms implemented for Native Americans during the New Deal era. John Collier, the commissioner of the Bureau of Indian Affairs (BIA), increased the access Native Americans had to relief programs and employed more Native Americans at the BIA. He worked to pass the Indian Reorganization Act. However, the version of the act passed by Congress was a much-diluted version of Collier's original proposal and did not greatly improve the lives of Native Americans.

Indian Removal Act (1830) Law permitting the forced relocation of Indians to federal lands west of the Mississippi River in exchange for the land they occupied in the East and South.

Indian wars Bloody conflicts between U.S. soldiers and Native Americans that raged in the West from the early 1860s to the late 1870s, sparked by American settlers moving into ancestral Indian lands.

Indochina This area of Southeast Asia consists of Laos, Cambodia, and Vietnam and was once controlled by France as a colony. After the Viet Minh defeated the French, the Geneva Accords were signed, which ended French colonial rule. The agreement created the independent nations of Laos and Cambodia and divided Vietnam along the 17th parallel until an election would reunify the country. Fearing a Communist take over, the United States government began intervening in the region during the Truman administration, which led to President Johnson's full-scale military involvement in Vietnam.

Industrial Revolution Major shift in the nineteenth century from hand-made manufacturing to mass production in mills and factories using water-, coal-, and steam-powered machinery.

industrial war A new concept of war enabled by industrialization that developed from the early 1800s through the Atomic Age. New technologies, including automatic weaponry, forms of transportation like the railroad and airplane, and communication technologies such as the telegraph and telephone, enabled nations to equip large, mass-conscripted armies with chemical and automatic weapons to decimate opposing armies in a "total war."

Industrial Workers of the World (IWW) A radical union organized in Chicago in 1905, nicknamed the Wobblies; its opposition to World War I led to its destruction by the federal government under the Espionage Act.

infectious diseases Also called contagious diseases, illnesses that can pass from one person to another by way of invasive biological organisms able to reproduce in the bodily tissues of their hosts. Europeans unwittingly brought many such diseases to the Americas, devastating the Native American peoples.

The Influence of Sea Power upon History, 1660–1783 **(1890)** Historical work in which Rear Admiral Alfred Thayer Mahan argues that a nation's greatness and prosperity comes from the power of its navy; the book helped bolster imperialist sentiment in the United States in the late nineteenth century.

Intermediate-Range Nuclear Forces (INF) Treaty (1987) Agreement signed by U.S. president Ronald Reagan and Soviet premier Mikhail Gorbachev to eliminate the deployment of intermediate-range missiles with nuclear warheads.

internal improvements Construction of roads, bridges, canals, harbors, and other infrastructural projects intended to facilitate the flow of goods and people.

internationalists Prior to the United States' entry in World War II, internationalists believed that America's national security depended on aiding Britain in its struggle against Germany.

Interstate Commerce Commission (ICC) (1887) An independent federal agency established to oversee businesses engaged in interstate trade, especially railroads, but whose regulatory power was limited when tested in the courts.

interstate highway system In the late 1950s, construction began on a national network of interstate superhighways for the purpose of commerce and defense. The interstate highways would enable the rapid movement of military convoys and the evacuation of cities after a nuclear attack.

Iran-Contra affair (1987) Reagan administration scandal over the secret, unlawful U.S. sale of arms to Iran in partial exchange for the release of hostages in Lebanon; the arms money in turn was used illegally to aid Nicaraguan right-wing insurgents, the Contras.

Iranian hostage crisis (1979) Storming of the U.S. embassy in Tehran by Iranian revolutionaries, who held fifty-two Americans hostage for 444 days, despite President Carter's appeals for their release as well as a botched rescue attempt.

Irish Potato Famine In 1845, an epidemic of potato rot brought a famine to rural Ireland that killed over 1 million peasants and instigated a huge increase in the number of Irish immigrating to America. By 1850, the Irish made up 43 percent of the foreign-born population in the United States; and in the 1850s, they made up over half the population of New York City and Boston.

iron curtain Term coined by Winston Churchill to describe the cold war divide between western Europe and the Soviet Union's Eastern European satellites.

Iroquois League An alliance of the Iroquois tribes, originally formed sometime between 1450 and 1600, that used their combined strength to pressure Europeans to work with them in the fur trade and to wage war across what is today eastern North America.

Andrew Jackson (1767–1837) As a major general in the Tennessee militia, he had a number of military successes. As president, he worked to enable the "common man" to play a greater role in the political arena. He vetoed the re-chartering of the Second National Bank and reduced federal spending. When South Carolina nullified the Tariffs of 1828 and 1832, Jackson requested that Congress pass a "force bill" that would authorize him to use the army to compel the state to comply with the tariffs. He forced eastern Indians to move west of the Mississippi River so their lands could be used by white settlers. Groups of those who opposed Jackson come together to form a new political party called the Whigs.

Thomas "Stonewall" Jackson (1824–1863) A Confederate general who was known for his fearlessness in leading rapid marches, bold flanking movements, and furious assaults. He earned his nickname at the Battle of the First Bull Run for standing courageously against Union fire. During the battle of Chancellorsville, his own men accidentally mortally wounded him.

William James (1842–1910) He was the founder of Pragmatism and one of the fathers of modern psychology. He believed that ideas gained their validity not from their inherent truth, but from their social consequences and practical application.

Jay's Treaty (1794) Agreement between Britain and the United States, negotiated by Chief Justice John Jay, that settled disputes over trade, prewar debts owed to British merchants, British-occupied forts in American territory, and the seizure of American ships and cargo.

Jazz Age Term coined by writer F. Scott Fitzgerald to characterize the spirit of rebellion and spontaneity among young Americans in the 1920s, a spirit epitomized by the hugely popular jazz music of the era.

Thomas Jefferson (1743–1826) He was a plantation owner, author, the drafter of the Declaration Independence, ambassador to France, leader of the Republican party, secretary of state, and the third president of the United States. As president, he purchased the Louisiana territory from France, withheld appointments made by President Adams leading to *Marbury v. Madison*, outlawed foreign slave trade, and was committed to a "wise and frugal" government.

Jeffersonian Republicans Political party founded by Thomas Jefferson in opposition to the Federalist Party led by Alexander Hamilton and John Adams; also known as the Democratic-Republican Party.

Jesuits A religious order founded in 1540 by Ignatius Loyola. They sought to counter the spread of Protestantism during the Protestant Reformation and spread the Catholic faith through work as missionaries. Roughly 3,500 served in New Spain and New France.

"Jim Crow" laws In the New South, these laws mandated the separation of races in various public places that served as a way for the ruling whites to impose their will on all areas of black life.

Andrew Johnson (1808–1875) He was elevated to the presidency after Abraham Lincoln's assassination. In order to restore the Union after the Civil War, he issued an amnesty proclamation and required former Confederate states to ratify the Thirteenth Amendment. After disagreements over the power to restore states rights, the Radical Republicans attempted to impeach Johnson but fell short on the required number of votes needed to remove him from office.

Lyndon B. Johnson (1908–1973) Former member of the House of Representatives and the former Majority Leader of the Senate, Vice President Lyndon B. Johnson assumed the presidency after President Kennedy's assassination. During his presidency, he passed the Civil Rights Act of 1964, declared a "war on poverty" promoting his own social program called the Great Society, and signed the Immigration and Nationality Service Act of 1965. Johnson greatly increased America's role in Vietnam.

Johnson's Restoration Plan Plan to require southern states to ratify the Thirteenth Amendment, disqualify wealthy ex-Confederates from voting, and appoint a Unionist governor.

joint-stock companies Businesses owned by investors, who purchase shares of companies' stocks and share all the profits and losses.

Kansas-Nebraska Act (1854) Controversial legislation that created two new territories taken from Native Americans, Kansas and Nebraska, where residents would vote to decide whether slavery would be allowed (popular sovereignty).

Florence Kelley (1859–1932) As the head of the National Consumer's League, she led the crusade to promote state laws to regulate the number of working hours imposed on women who were wives and mothers.

George F. Kennan (1904–2005) While working as an American diplomat, he devised the strategy of containment, which called for the halting of Soviet expansion. It became America's choice strategy throughout the cold war.

John F. Kennedy (1917–1963) He was elected president in 1960. Despite the difficulties he had in getting his legislation through Congress, he established the Alliance for Progress programs to help Latin America, the Peace Corps, the Trade Expansion Act of 1962, and funding for urban renewal projects and the space program. His foreign political involvement included the failed Bay of Pigs invasion and the missile crisis in Cuba, as well as support of local governments in Indochina. In 1963, he was assassinated by Lee Harvey Oswald in Dallas, Texas.

Kent State During the spring of 1970, students on college campuses across the country protested the expansion of the Vietnam War into Cambodia. At Kent State University, the National Guard attempted to quell the rioting students. The guardsmen panicked and shot at rock-throwing demonstrators. Four student bystanders were killed.

Kentucky and Virginia Resolutions (1798–1799) Passed in response to the Alien and Sedition Acts, the resolutions advanced the state-compact theory that held states could nullify an act of Congress if they deemed it unconstitutional.

Francis Scott Key (1779–1843) During the War of 1812, he watched British forces bombard Fort McHenry, but fail to take it. Seeing the American flag still flying over the fort at dawn inspired him to write "The Star-Spangled Banner," which became the American national anthem.

Martin Luther King, Jr. (1929–1968) A central leader of the civil rights movement, he urged people to use nonviolent civil disobedience to demand their rights and bring about change. He successfully led the Montgomery bus boycott. While in jail for his role in demonstrations, he wrote his famous "Letter from Birmingham City Jail," in which he defended his strategy of nonviolent protest. In 1963, he delivered his famous "I Have a Dream Speech" from the steps of the Lincoln Memorial as a part of the March on Washington. A year later, he was awarded the Nobel Peace Prize. In 1968, he was assassinated.

King Philip's War A bloody, three-year war in New England (1675–1678), resulting from the escalation of tensions between Indians and English settlers; the defeat of the Indians led to broadened freedoms for the settlers and their dispossessing the region's Indians of most of their land.

King William's War (War of the League of Augsburg) First (1689–1697) of four colonial wars between England and France.

Henry Kissinger (1923–) He served as the secretary of state and national security adviser in the Nixon administration. He negotiated with North Vietnam for an end to the Vietnam War, but the cease-fire did not last; South Vietnam fell to North Vietnam. He helped organize Nixon's historic trips to China and the Soviet Union. In the Middle East, he negotiated a cease-fire between Israel and its neighbors following the Yom Kippur War and solidified Israel's promise to return to Egypt most of the land it had taken during the 1967 war.

Knights of Labor A national labor organization with a broad reform platform; reached peak membership in the 1880s.

Know-Nothing party Nativist, anti-Catholic third party organized in 1854 in reaction to large-scale German and Irish immigration.

Ku Klux Klan Organized in Pulaski, Tennessee, in 1866 to terrorize former slaves who voted and held political offices during Reconstruction; a revived organization in the 1910s and 1920s stressed white, Anglo-Saxon, fundamentalist Protestant supremacy; the Klan revived a third time to fight the civil rights movement of the 1950s and 1960s in the South.

Marquis de Lafayette (1757–1834) A wealthy French idealist excited by the American cause, he offered to serve in Washington's army for free in exchange for being named a major general. He overcame Washington's initial skepticism to become one of his most trusted aides.

laissez-faire An economic doctrine holding that businesses and individuals should be able to pursue their economic interests without government interference.

Land Ordinance of 1785 Directed surveying of the Northwest Territory into townships of thirty-six sections (square miles) each, the sale of the sixteenth section of which was to be used to finance public education.

League of Nations Organization of nations formed in the aftermath of the First World War to mediate disputes and maintain international peace; despite President Wilson's intense lobbying for the League of Nations, Congress did not ratify the treaty and the United States failed to join.

Mary Elizabeth Lease (1850–1933) She was a leader of the farm protest movement who advocated violence if change could not be obtained at the ballot box. She believed that the urban-industrial East was the enemy of the working class.

Robert E. Lee (1807–1870) Even though he had served in the United States Army for thirty years, he chose to fight on the side of the Confederacy. Lee was excellent at using his field commanders and his soldiers respected him. However, General Ulysses S. Grant eventually wore down his army, and Lee surrendered to Grant at the Appomattox Court House on April 9, 1865.

Lend-Lease Bill (1941) Legislation that allowed the president to lend or lease military equipment to any country whose own defense was deemed vital to the defense of the United States.

Levittown First low-cost, mass-produced development of suburban tract housing built by William Levitt on Long Island, New York, in 1947.

Lewis and Clark Expedition (1804–1806) Led by Meriwether Lewis and William Clark, a mission to the Pacific coast commissioned for the purposes of scientific and geographical exploration

Battle of Lexington and Concord The first shots fired in the Revolutionary War, on April 19, 1775, near Boston; approximately 100 Minutemen and 250 British soldiers were killed.

Liberator William Lloyd Garrison started this anti-slavery newspaper in 1831 in which he renounced gradualism and called for abolition.

Queen Liliuokalani (1838–1917) In 1891, she ascended to the throne of the Hawaiian royal family and tried to eliminate white control of the Hawaiian government. Two years later, Hawaii's white population revolted and seized power with the support of American Marines.

Abraham Lincoln (1809–1865) Shortly after he was elected president in 1860, southern states began seceding from the Union, and in April of 1861 he declared war on the seceding states. On January 1, 1863, Lincoln signed the Emancipation Proclamation. At the end of the war, he favored a reconstruction strategy for the former Confederate states that did not radically alter southern social and economic life. He was assassinated by John Wilkes Booth at Ford's Theater on April 14, 1865.

Lincoln-Douglas debates (1858) During the Illinois race between Republican Abraham Lincoln and Democrat Stephen A. Douglas for a seat in the U.S. Senate, a series of seven dramatic debates focusing on the issue of slavery in the territories.

John Locke (1632–1704) An English philosopher whose ideas were influential during the Enlightenment. He argued in his *Essay on Human Understanding* (1690) that humanity is largely the product of the environment, the mind being a blank tablet, *tabula rasa*, on which experience is written.

Henry Cabot Lodge (1850–1924) He was the chairman of the Senate Foreign Relations Committee who favored limiting America's involvement in the League of Nations' covenant and sought to amend the Treaty of Versailles.

de Lôme letter (1898) Private correspondence written by the Spanish ambassador to the U.S., Depuy de Lôme, that described President McKinley as "weak"; the letter was stolen by Cuban revolutionaries and published in the *New York Journal,* deepening American resentment of Spain and moving the two countries closer to war in Cuba.

Lone Star Republic After winning independence from Mexico, Texas became its own nation that was called the Lone Star Republic. In 1836, Texans drafted a constitution, legalized slavery, banned free blacks, named Sam Houston president, and voted for the annexation to the United States. However, quarrels over adding a slave state and fears of instigating a war with Mexico delayed Texas's entrance into the Union until December 29, 1845.

Huey P. Long (1893–1935) He began his political career in Louisiana where he developed a reputation for being an unscrupulous reformer. As a U.S. senator, he became a critic of President Roosevelt's New Deal Plan and offered his alternative called the Share-the-Wealth program. He was assassinated in 1935.

Louisiana Purchase (1803) President Thomas Jefferson's purchase of the Louisiana Territory from France for $15 million, doubling the size of U.S. territory.

Lowell system Model New England factory communities that during the first half of the nineteenth century provided employees, mostly young women, with meals, a boardinghouse, and moral discipline, as well as educational and cultural opportunities.

Loyalists Colonists who remained loyal to Great Britain before and during the Revolutionary War.

Lusitania British ocean liner torpedoed and sunk by a German U-boat; the deaths of nearly 1,200 of its civilian passengers, including many Americans, caused international outrage.

Martin Luther (1483–1546) A German monk who founded the Lutheran church. He protested abuses in the Catholic Church by posting his Ninety-five Theses, which began the Protestant Reformation.

General Douglas MacArthur (1880–1964) During World War II, he and Admiral Chester Nimitz dislodged the Japanese military from the Pacific Islands they had occupied. Following the war, he was in charge of the occupation of Japan. After North Korea invaded South Korea, Truman sent the U.S. military to defend South Korea under the command of MacArthur. Later in the war, Truman expressed his willingness to negotiate the restoration of prewar boundaries which MacArthur attempted to undermine. Truman fired MacArthur for his open insubordination.

James Madison (1751–1836) He participated in the Constitutional Convention during which he proposed the Virginia Plan. He believed in a strong federal government and was a leader of the Federalists. However, he also presented to Congress the Bill of Rights and drafted the Virginia Resolutions. As secretary of state, he withheld a commission for William Marbury, which led to the landmark *Marbury v. Madison* decision. During his presidency, he declared war on Britain in response to violations of American shipping rights, which started the War of 1812.

U.S. battleship *Maine* American warship that exploded in the Cuban port of Havana on January 25, 1898; though later discovered to be the result of an accident, the destruction of the *Maine* was attributed by war-hungry Americans to Spain, contributing to the onset of the War of 1812.

maize (corn) The primary grain crop in Mesoamerica yielding small kernels often ground into cornmeal. Easy to grow in a broad range of conditions, it enabled a global population explosion after being brought to Europe, Africa, and Asia.

Malcolm X (1925–1964) The most articulate spokesman for black power. Originally the chief disciple of Elijah Muhammad, the black Muslim leader in the United States, Malcolm X broke away and founded his own organization committed to establishing relations between African Americans and the nonwhite peoples of the world. Near the end of his life, he began to preach a biracial message of social change. In 1964, he was assassinated by members of a rival group of black Muslims.

Manchuria incident The northeast region of Manchuria was an area contested between China and Russia. In 1931, the Japanese claimed that they needed to protect their extensive investments in the area and moved their army into Manchuria. They quickly conquered the region and set up their own puppet empire. China asked both the United States and the League of Nations for help and neither responded.

manifest destiny The widespread belief that America was "destined" by God to expand westward across the continent into lands claimed by Native Americans as well as European nations.

Horace Mann (1796–1859) He believed the public school system was the best way to achieve social stability and equal opportunity. As a reformer of education, he sponsored a state board of education, the first state-supported "normal" school for training teachers, a state association for teachers, the minimum school year of six months, and led the drive for a statewide school system.

Marbury v. Madison **(1803)** First Supreme Court decision to declare a federal law—the Judiciary Act of 1801—unconstitutional.

March on Washington Civil rights demonstration on August 28, 1963, on the National Mall, where Martin Luther King Jr. gave his famous "I Have a Dream" speech.

market economy Large-scale manufacturing and commercial agriculture that emerged in America during the first half of the nineteenth century, displacing much of the pre-market subsistence and barter-based economy and producing boom-and-bust cycles while raising the American standard of living.

George C. Marshall (1880–1959) As the chairman of the Joint Chiefs of Staff, he orchestrated the Allied victories over Germany and Japan in the Second World War. In 1947, he became President Truman's secretary of state and proposed the massive reconstruction program for western Europe called the Marshall Plan.

Chief Justice John Marshall (1755–1835) During his long tenure as chief justice of the supreme court (1801–1835), he established the foundations for American jurisprudence, the authority of the Supreme Court, and the constitutional supremacy of the national government over states.

Marshall Plan (1948) Secretary of State George C. Marshall's post–World War II program providing massive U.S. financial and technical assistance to war-torn European countries.

Massachusetts Bay Colony English colony founded by English Puritans in 1630 as a haven for persecuted Congregationalists.

"massive resistance" White rallying cry disrupting federal efforts to enforce racial integration in the South.

"massive retaliation" Strategy that used the threat of nuclear warfare as a means of combating the global spread of communism.

Mayflower Compact A formal agreement signed by the Separatist colonists aboard the *Mayflower* in 1620 to abide by laws made by leaders of their own choosing.

Senator Joseph R. McCarthy (1908–1957) In 1950, this senator became the shrewdest and most ruthless exploiter of America's anxiety of communism. He claimed that the United States government was full of Communists and led a witch hunt to find them, but he was never able to uncover a single communist agent.

McCarthyism Anti-Communist hysteria led by Senator Joseph McCarthy's "witch hunts" attacking the loyalty of politicians, federal employees, and public figures, despite a lack of evidence.

George B. McClellan (1826–1885) In 1861, President Abraham Lincoln appointed him head of the Army of the Potomac and, later, general in chief of the U.S. Army. He built his army into well trained and powerful force. After failing to achieve a decisive victory against the Confederacy, he was removed from command in 1862.

Cyrus Hall McCormick (1809–1884) In 1831, he invented a mechanical reaper to harvest wheat, which transformed the scale of agriculture. By hand a farmer could only harvest a half an acre a day, while the McCormick reaper allowed two people to harvest twelve acres of wheat a day.

McCormick reaper Mechanical reaper invented by Cyrus Hall McCormick in 1831 that dramatically increased the production of wheat.

***McCulloch v. Maryland* (1819)** Supreme Court ruling that prohibited states from taxing the Bank of the United States.

William McKinley (1843–1901) As a congressman, he was responsible for the McKinley Tariff of 1890, which raised the duties on manufactured products to their highest level ever. Voters disliked the tariff and McKinley, as well as other Republicans, lost his seat in Congress the next election. However, he won the presidential election of 1896 and raised the tariffs again. In 1898, he annexed Hawaii and declared war on Spain. The war concluded with the Treaty of Paris, which gave America control over Puerto Rico, Guam, and the Philippines. Soon America was fighting Filipinos, who were seeking independence for their country. In 1901, McKinley was assassinated.

Robert McNamara (1916–2009) He was the secretary of defense for both President Kennedy and President Johnson and a supporter of America's involvement in Vietnam.

Medicare and Medicaid Health-care programs designed to aid the elderly and disadvantaged, respectively, as part of President Johnson's Great Society initiative.

Andrew W. Mellon (1855–1937) As President Harding's secretary of the Treasury, he sought to generate economic growth through reducing government spending and lowering taxes. However, he insisted that the tax reductions mainly go to the rich because he believed the wealthy would reinvest their money. In order to bring greater efficiency and nonpartisanship to the government's budget process, he persuaded Congress to created a new Bureau of the Budget and a General Accounting Office.

mercantilism Policy of Great Britain and other imperial powers of regulating the economies of colonies to benefit the mother country.

James Meredith (1933–) In 1962, the governor of Mississippi defied a Supreme Court ruling and refused to allow James Meredith, an African American, to enroll at the University of Mississippi. Federal marshals were sent to enforce the law which led to clashes between a white mob and the marshals. Federal troops intervened and two people were killed and many others were injured. A few days later, Meredith was able to register at the university.

Merrimack* (ship renamed the *Virginia*) and the *Monitor First engagement between ironclad ships; fought at Hampton Roads, Virginia, on March 9, 1862.

Metacomet or King Philip (?–1676) The chief of the Wampanoages, who the colonists called King Philip. He resented English efforts to convert Indians to Christianity and waged a war against the English colonists in which he was killed.

Mexica Otherwise known as "Aztecs," a Mesoamerican people of northern Mexico who founded the vast Aztec Empire in the fourteenth century, later conquered by the Spanish under Hernán Cortés in 1521.

microprocessor An electronic circuit printed on a small silicon chip; a major technological breakthrough in 1971, it paved the way for the development of the personal computer.

Middle Passage The hellish and often deadly middle leg of the transatlantic "Triangular Trade" in which European ships carried manufactured goods to Africa, then transported enslaved Africans to the Americas and the Caribbean, and finally conveyed American agricultural products back to Europe; from the late sixteenth to the early nineteenth centuries, some 12 million Africans were transported via the Middle Passage, unknown millions more dying en route.

militant nonviolence After the success of the Montgomery bus boycott, people were inspired by Martin Luther King, Jr.'s use of this nonviolent form of protest. Throughout the civil rights movement, demonstrators used this method of protest to challenge racial segregation in the South.

Militia Act (1862) Congressional measure that permitted freed slaves to serve as laborers or soldiers in the United States Army.

Ho Chi Minh (1890–1969) He was the Vietnamese communist resistance leader who drove the French and the United States out of Vietnam. After the Geneva Accords divided the region into four countries, he controlled North Vietnam, and ultimately became the leader of all of Vietnam at the conclusion of the Vietnam War.

minstrelsy A form of entertainment that was popular from the 1830s to the 1870s. The performances featured white performers who were made up as African Americans or blackface. They performed banjo and fiddle music, "shuffle" dances and lowbrow humor that reinforced racial stereotypes.

Minutemen Special units organized by the militia to be ready for quick mobilization.

***Miranda v. Arizona* (1966)** U.S. Supreme Court decision required police to advise persons in custody of their rights to legal counsel and against self-incrimination.

Mississippi Plan (1890) Series of state constitutional amendments that sought to severely disenfranchise black voters and were quickly adopted by other southern states.

Missouri Compromise (1820) Legislative decision to admit Missouri as a slave state and abolish slavery in the area west of the Mississippi River and north of the parallel 36°30′.

Model T Ford Henry Ford developed this model of car so that it was affordable for everyone. Its success led to an increase in the production of automobiles which stimulated other related industries such steel, oil, and rubber. The mass use of automobiles increased the speed goods could be transported, encouraged urban sprawl, and sparked real estate booms in California and Florida.

moderate Republicanism Promise to curb federal government and restore state and local government authority, spearheaded by President Eisenhower.

modernism An early-twentieth-century intellectual and artistic movement that rejected traditional notions of reality and adopted radical new forms of artistic expression.

monopoly A corporation so large that it effectively controls the entire market for its products or services.

"money question" Late-nineteenth-century national debate over the nature of U.S. currency; supporters of a fixed gold standard were generally money lenders, and thus preferred to keep the value of money high, while supporters of silver (and gold) coinage were debtors, they owed money, so they wanted to keep the value of money low by increasing the currency supply (inflation).

James Monroe (1758–1831) He served as secretary of state and war under President Madison and was elected president. As the latter, he signed the Transcontinental Treaty with Spain which gave the United States Florida and expanded the Louisiana Territory's western border to the Pacific coast. In 1823, he established the Monroe Doctrine. This foreign policy proclaimed the American continents were no longer open to colonization and America would be neutral in European affairs.

Monroe Doctrine (1823) U.S. foreign policy that barred further colonization in the Western Hemisphere by European powers and pledged that there would be no American interference with any existing European colonies.

Montgomery bus boycott Boycott of bus system in Montgomery, Alabama, organized by civil rights activists after the arrest of Rosa Parks.

Moral Majority Televangelist Jerry Falwell's political lobbying organization, the name of which became synonymous with the religious right—conservative evangelical Protestants who helped ensure President Ronald Reagan's 1980 victory.

J. Pierpont Morgan (1837–1913) As a powerful investment banker, he would acquire, reorganize, and consolidate companies into giant trusts. His biggest achievement was the consolidation of the steel industry into the United States Steel Corporation, which was the first billion-dollar corporation.

J. Pierpont Morgan and Company An investment bank under the leadership of J. Pierpont Morgan that bought or merged unrelated American companies, often using capital acquired from European investors.

Mormons Members of the Church of Jesus Christ of Latter-day Saints, which dismissed other Christian denominations, emphasizing universal salvation and a modest lifestyle; Mormons were often persecuted for their secrecy and clannishness.

Morrill Land-Grant College Act (1862) Federal statute that allowed for the creation of land-grant colleges and universities, which were founded to provide technical education in agriculture, mining, and industry.

Samuel F. B. Morse (1791–1872) In 1832, he invented the telegraph and revolutionized the speed of communication.

mountain men Inspired by the fur trade, these men left civilization to work as trappers and reverted to a primitive existence in the wilderness. They were the first white people to find routes through the Rocky Mountains, and they pioneered trails that settlers later used to reach the Oregon country and California in the 1840s.

muckrakers Writers who exposed corruption and abuses in politics, business, consumer safety, working conditions, and more, spurring public interest in progressive reforms.

Mugwumps Reformers who bolted the Republican party in 1884 to support Democrat Grover Cleveland for president over Republican James G. Blaine, whose secret dealings on behalf of railroad companies had brought charges of corruption.

mulattoes Mixed-race people who constituted most of the South's free black population.

Benito Mussolini (1883–1945) The Italian founder of the Fascist party who came to power in Italy in 1922 and allied himself with Adolf Hitler and the Axis powers during the Second World War.

National Association for the Advancement of Colored People (NAACP) Organization founded in 1910 by black activists and white progressives that promoted education as a means of combating social problems and focused on legal action to secure the civil rights supposedly guaranteed by the Fourteenth and Fifteenth Amendments.

North American Free Trade Agreement (NAFTA) (1994) Agreement eliminating trade barriers that was signed by the United States, Canada, and Mexico, making North America the largest free-trade zone in the world.

North Atlantic Treaty Organization (NATO) Defensive political and military alliance formed in 1949 by the United States, Canada, and ten Western European nations to deter Soviet expansion in Europe.

National Banking Act (1863) The U.S. Congress created a national banking system to finance the enormous expense of the Civil War. It enabled loans to the government and established a single national currency, including the issuance of paper money ("greenbacks").

National Industrial Recovery Act (1933) Passed on the last of the Hundred Days; it created public-works jobs through the Federal Emergency Relief Administration and established a system of self-regulation for industry through the National Recovery Administration, which was ruled unconstitutional in 1935.

National Labor Union A federation of labor and reform leaders established in 1866 to advocate for new state and local laws to improve working conditions.

National Recovery Administration (1933) Controversial federal agency that brought together business and labor leaders to create "codes of fair competition" and "fair labor" policies, including a national minimum wage.

National Security Act (1947) Congressional legislation that created the Department of Defense, the National Security Council, and the Central Intelligence Agency.

National Socialist German Workers' (Nazi) party Founded in the 1920s, this party gained control over Germany under the leadership of Adolf Hitler in 1933 and continued in power until Germany's defeat at the end of the Second World War. It advocated a violent anti-Semitic, anti-Marxist, pan-German ideology. The Nazi party perpetrated the Holocaust.

National Trades' Unions Formed in 1834 to organize all local trade unions into a stronger national association, only to be dissolved amid the economic depression during the late 1830s.

nativism Reactionary conservative movement characterized by heightened nationalism, anti-immigrant sentiment, and the enactment of laws setting stricter regulations on immigration.

natural rights An individual's basic rights that should not be violated by any government or community.

Navigation Acts (1650–1775) Restrictions passed by the British Parliament to control colonial trade and bolster the mercantile system.

Negrophobia A violent new wave of racism that spread in the late nineteenth century largely spurred by white resentment for African American financial success and growing political influence.

new conservatism The political philosophy of those who led the conservative insurgency of the early 1980s. This brand of conservatism was personified in Ronald Reagan who believed in less government, supply-side economics, and "family values."

New Deal Franklin D. Roosevelt's campaign promise, in his speech to the Democratic National Convention of 1932, to combat the Great Depression with a "new deal for the American people;" the phrase became a catchword for his ambitious plan of economic programs.

New Democrats Centrist ("moderate") Democrats led by President Bill Clinton that emerged in the late 1980s and early 1990s to challenge the "liberal" direction of the party.

"new economy" Period of sustained economic prosperity during the nineties marked by budget surpluses, the explosion of dot.com industries, low inflation, and low unemployment.

New France The name used for the area of North America that was colonized by the French. Unlike Spanish or English colonies, New France had a small number of colonists, which forced them to initially seek good relations with the indigenous people they encountered.

New Freedom Program championed in 1912 by the Woodrow Wilson campaign that aimed to restore competition in the economy by eliminating all trusts rather than simply regulating them.

New Frontier Proposed domestic program championed by the incoming Kennedy administration in 1961 that aimed to jump-start the economy and trigger social progress.

"new immigrants" Wave of newcomers from southern and eastern Europe, including many Jews, who became a majority among immigrants to America after 1890.

New Jersey Plan The delegations to the Constitutional Convention were divided between two plans on how to structure the government: New Jersey wanted one legislative body with equal representation for each state.

New Left Term coined by the Students for a Democratic Society to distinguish their efforts at grassroots democracy from those of the 1930s Old Left, which had embraced orthodox Marxism.

New Mexico A U.S. territory and later a state in the American Southwest, originally established by the Spanish, who settled there in the sixteenth century, founded Catholic missions, and exploited the region's indigenous peoples.

New Nationalism Platform of the Progressive party and slogan of former President Theodore Roosevelt in the presidential campaign of 1912; stressed government activism, including regulation of trusts, conservation, and recall of state court decisions that had nullified progressive programs.

"New Negro" In the 1920s, a slow and steady growth of black political influence occurred in northern cities where African Americans were freer to speak and act. This political activity created a spirit of protest that expressed itself culturally in the Harlem Renaissance and politically in "new Negro" nationalism.

New Netherland Dutch colony conquered by the English in 1667 and out of which four new colonies were created—New York, New Jersey, Pennsylvania, and Delaware.

Battle of New Orleans (1815) Final major battle in the War of 1812, in which the Americans under General Andrew Jackson unexpectedly and decisively countered the British attempt to seize the port of New Orleans, Louisiana.

New South *Atlanta Constitution* editor Henry W. Grady's 1886 term for the prosperous post–Civil War South: democratic, industrial, urban, and free of nostalgia for the defeated plantation South.

New York Journal In the late 1890s, William Randolph Hearst's *New York Journal* and its rival, the *New York World*, printed sensationalism on the Cuban revolution as part of their heated competition for readership. The *New York Journal* printed a negative letter from the Spanish ambassador about President McKinley and inflammatory coverage of the sinking of the *Maine* in Havana Harbor. These two events roused the American public's outcry against Spain.

New York World In the late 1890s, Joseph Pulitzer's *New York World* and its rival, the *New York Journal*, printed sensationalism on the Cuban revolution as part of their heated competition for readership.

Admiral Chester Nimitz (1885–1966) During the Second World War, he was the commander of central Pacific. Along with General Douglas MacArthur, he dislodged the Japanese military from the Pacific Islands they had occupied.

Nineteenth Amendment (1920) Constitutional amendment that granted women the right to vote.

Richard M. Nixon (1913–1994) He first came to national prominence as a congress-man involved in the investigation of Alger Hiss, and later served as vice president during the Eisenhower administration. After being elected president in 1968, he slowed the federal enforcement of civil rights and appointed pro-Southern justices to the

Supreme Court. He began a program of Vietnamization of the war. In 1973, America, North and South Vietnam, and the Viet Cong agreed to end the war and the United States withdrew. However, the cease-fire was broken, and the South Vietnam fell to North Vietnam. In 1970, Nixon declared that America was no longer the world's policeman and he would seek some partnerships with Communist countries, historically traveling to China and the Soviet Union. In 1972, he was reelected, but the Watergate scandal erupted shortly after his victory; he resigned the presidency under threat of impeachment.

No Child Left Behind President George W. Bush's education reform plan that required states to set and meet learning standards for students and make sure that all students were "proficient" in reading and writing by 2014. States had to submit annual reports of students' standardized test scores. Teachers were required to be "proficient" in their subject area. Schools who failed to show progress would face sanctions. States criticized the lack of funding for remedial programs and noted that poor school districts would find it very difficult to meet the new guidelines.

nonviolent civil disobedience Tactic of defying unjust laws through peaceful actions championed by Dr. Martin Luther King, Jr.

Lord North (1732–1792) The first minister of King George III's cabinet whose efforts to subdue the colonies only brought them closer to revolution. He helped bring about the Tea Act of 1773, which led to the Boston Tea Party. In an effort to discipline Boston, he wrote, and Parliament passed, four acts that galvanized colonial resistance.

North Atlantic Treaty Organization (NATO) Defensive alliance founded in 1949 by ten western European nations, the United States, and Canada to deter Soviet expansion in Europe.

Northwest Ordinance (1787) Land policy for new western territories in the Ohio valley that established the terms and conditions for self-government and statehood while also banning slavery from the region.

NSC-68 (1950) Top-secret policy paper approved by President Truman that outlined a militaristic approach to combating the spread of global communism.

nullification The right claimed by some states to veto a federal law deemed unconstitutional.

Nuremberg trials At the site of the annual Nazi party rallies, twenty-one major German offenders faced an international military tribunal for Nazi atrocities. After a ten-month trial, the court acquitted three and sentenced eleven to death, three to life imprisonment, and four to shorter terms.

Barack Obama (1961–) In the 2008 presidential election, Senator Barack Obama mounted an innovative Internet based and grassroots orientated campaign. As the nation's economy nose-dived in the fall of 2008, Obama linked the Republican economic philosophy with the country's dismal financial state and promoted a message of "change" and "politics of hope," which resonated with voters. He decisively won the presidency and became America's first person of color to be elected president. In 2012, Obama successfully won re-election to serve as president for a second term.

Occupy Wall Street A grassroots movement protesting a capitalist system that fostered social and economic inequality. Begun in Zuccotti Park, New York City, during 2011, the movement spread rapidly across the nation, triggering a national conversation about income inequality and protests of the government's "bailouts" of the banks and corporations allegedly responsible for the Great Recession.

Sandra Day O'Connor (1930–) She was the first woman to serve on the Supreme Court of the United States and was appointed by President Reagan. Reagan's critics charged that her appointment was a token gesture and not a sign of any real commitment to gender equality.

Ohio gang In order to escape the pressures of the White House, President Harding met with a group of people, called the "Ohio gang," in a house on K Street in Washington D.C. Members of this gang were given low-level positions in the American government and they used their White House connection to "line their pockets" by granting government contracts without bidding, which led to a series of scandals, most notably the Teapot Dome Scandal.

Old Southwest Region covering western Georgia, Alabama, Mississippi, Louisiana, Arkansas, and Texas, where low land prices and fertile soil attracted hundreds of thousands of settlers after the American Revolution.

Frederick Law Olmsted (1822–1903) In 1858, he constructed New York's Central Park, which led to a growth in the movement to create urban parks. He went on to design parks for Boston, Brooklyn, Chicago, Philadelphia, San Francisco, and many other cities.

Open Door policy (1899) Official U.S. insistence that Chinese trade would be open to all nations; Secretary of State John Hay unilaterally announced the policy in hopes of protecting the Chinese market for U.S. exports.

open shop Business policy of not requiring union membership as a condition of employment; such a policy, where legal, has the effect of weakening unions and diminishing workers' rights.

open range Informal system of governing property on the frontier in which small ranchers could graze their cattle anywhere on unfenced lands; brought to an end by the introduction of barbed wire, a low-cost way to fence off one's land.

Operation Desert Shield After Saddam Hussein invaded Kuwait in 1990, President George H. W. Bush sent American military forces to Saudi Arabia on a strictly defensive mission. They were soon joined by a multinational coalition. When the coalition's mission changed to the retaking of Kuwait, the operation was renamed Desert Storm.

Operation Desert Storm (1991) Assault by American-led multinational forces that quickly defeated Iraqi forces under Saddam Hussein in the First Gulf War, ending the Iraqi occupation of Kuwait.

Operation Overlord The Allies' assault on Hitler's "Atlantic Wall," a seemingly impregnable series of fortifications and minefields along the French coastline that German forces had created using captive Europeans for laborers.

J. Robert Oppenheimer (1904–1967) He led the group of physicists at the laboratory in Los Alamos, New Mexico, who constructed the first atomic bomb.

Oregon Country The Convention of 1818 between Britain and the United States established the Oregon Country as being west of the crest of the Rocky Mountains and the two countries were to jointly occupy it. In 1824, the United States and Russia signed a treaty that established the line of 54°40′ as the southern boundary of Russia's territorial claim in North America. A similar agreement between Britain and Russia finally gave the Oregon Country clearly defined boarders, but it remained under joint British and American control.

"Oregon Fever" The lure of fertile land and economic opportunities in the Oregon Country that drew thousands of settlers westward, beginning in the late 1830s.

Osceola (1804?–1838) He was the leader of the Seminole nation who resisted the federal Indian removal policy through a protracted guerilla war. In 1837, he was treacherously seized under a flag of truce and imprisoned at Fort Moultrie, where he was left to die.

Overland Trails Trail routes followed by wagon trains bearing settlers and trade goods from Missouri to the Oregon Country, California, and New Mexico, beginning in the 1840s.

Pacific Railway Act (1862) Congress provided funding for a transcontinental railroad from Nebraska west to California.

A. Mitchell Palmer (1872–1936) As the attorney general, he played an active role in the government's response to the Red Scare. After several bombings across America, including one at Palmer's home, he and other Americans became convinced that there was a well-organized Communist terror campaign at work. The federal government launched a campaign of raids, deportations, and collecting files on radical individuals.

Panic of 1819 A financial panic that began a three-year-long economic crisis triggered by a reduced demand of American imports, declining land values, and reckless practices by local and state banks.

Panic of 1873 A financial calamity in the United States brought on by a dramatic slowdown in the British economy and exacerbated by falling cotton prices, failed crops, high inflation, and reckless state banks.

Panic of 1893 A major collapse in the national economy after several major railroad companies declared bankruptcy, leading to a severe depression and several violent clashes between workers and management.

panning A method of mining that used a large metal pan to sift gold dust and nuggets from riverbeds during the California gold rush of 1849.

Rosa Parks (1913–2005) In 1955, she refused to give up her seat to a white man on a city bus in Montgomery, Alabama, which a local ordinance required of blacks. She was arrested for disobeying the ordinance. In response, black community leaders organized the Montgomery bus boycott.

Parliament Legislature of Great Britain, composed of the House of Commons, whose members are elected, and the House of Lords, whose members are either hereditary or appointed.

party "boss" A powerful political leader who controlled a "machine" of associates and operatives to promote both individual and party interests, often using informal tactics such as intimidation or the patronage system.

paternalism A moral position developed during the first half of the nineteenth century which claimed that slaves were deprived of liberty for their own "good." Such a rationalization was adopted by some slave owners to justify slavery.

Patriots Colonists who rebelled against British authority before and during the Revolutionary War.

patronage An informal system (sometimes called the "spoils system") used by politicians to reward their supporters with government appointments or contracts.

Alice Paul (1885–1977) She was a leader of the women's suffrage movement and head of the Congressional Committee of National Women Suffrage Association. She instructed female suffrage activists to use more militant tactics, such as picketing state legislatures, chaining themselves to public buildings, inciting police to arrest them, and undertaking hunger strikes.

Norman Vincent Peale (1898–1993) He was a champion of the upbeat and feel-good theology that was popular in the 1950s religious revival. He advocated getting rid of any depressing or negative thoughts and replacing them with "faith, enthusiasm and joy," which would make an individual popular and well liked.

Pearl Harbor (1941) Surprise Japanese attack on the U.S. fleet at Pearl Harbor on December 7, which prompted the immediate American entry into the war.

"peculiar institution" A phrase used by whites in the antebellum South to refer to slavery without using the word slavery.

Pennsylvania English colony founded by William Penn in 1681 as a Quaker commonwealth, though it welcomed people of all religions.

Pentagon Papers Informal name for the Defense Department's secret history of the Vietnam conflict; leaked to the press by former official Daniel Ellsberg and published in the *New York Times* in 1971.

People's party (Populists) Political party largely made up of farmers from the South and West that struggled to gain political influence from the East. Populists advocated a variety of reforms, including free coinage of silver, a progressive income tax, postal savings banks, regulation of railroads, and direct election of U.S. senators.

Pequot War Massacre in 1637 and subsequent dissolution of the Pequot Nation by Puritan settlers, who seized the Indians' lands.

perestroika Russian term for "economic restructuring"; applied to Mikhail Gorbachev's series of political and economic reforms that included shifting a centrally planned Commmunist economy to a mixed economy allowing for capitalism.

Commodore Matthew Perry (1794–1858) In 1854, he negotiated the Treaty of Kanagawa, which was the first step in starting a political and commercial relationship between the United States and Japan.

John J. Pershing United States general sent by President Wilson to put down attacks on the Mexican border led by Francisco "Pancho" Villa.

Personal Responsibility and Work Opportunity Act of 1996 (PRWOA) Comprehensive welfare-reform measure, passed by a Republican Congress and signed by President Clinton, that aimed to decrease the size of the "welfare state" by limiting the amount of government aid provided the unemployed so as to encourage recipients to find jobs.

"pet banks" During President Andrew Jackson's fight with the national bank, Jackson resolved to remove all federal deposits from it. To comply with Jackson's demands, Secretary of the Treasury Taney continued to draw on government's accounts in the national bank, but deposit all new federal receipts in state banks. The state banks that received these deposits were called "pet banks."

Pilgrims Puritan Separatists who broke completely with the Church of England and sailed to the New World aboard the *Mayflower*, founding Plymouth Colony on Cape Cod in 1620.

Dien Bien Phu Cluster of Vietnamese villages and site of a major Vietnamese victory over the French in the First Indochina War.

Gifford Pinchot (1865–1946) As the head of the Division of Forestry, he implemented a conservation policy that entailed the scientific management of natural resources to serve the public interest. His work helped start the conservation movement.

Elizabeth Lucas Pinckney (1722? –1793) One of the most enterprising horticulturists in colonial America, she began managing her family's three plantations in South Carolina at the age of sixteen. She had tremendous success growing indigo, which led to many other plantations growing the crop as well.

Pinckney's Treaty Treaty with Spain negotiated by Thomas Pinckney in 1795; established United States boundaries at the Mississippi River and the 31st parallel and allowed open transportation on the Mississippi.

Francisco Pizarro (1478?–1541) In 1531, he lead his Spanish soldiers to Peru and conquered the Inca Empire.

"plain white folk" Yeoman farmers who lived and worked on their own small farms, growing a food and cash crops to trade for necessities.

plantation mistress Matriarch of a planter's household, responsible for supervising the domestic aspects of the estate.

planters Owners of large farms in the South that were worked by twenty or more slaves and supervised by overseers.

political "machine" A network of political activists and elected officials, usually controlled by a powerful "boss," that attempts to manipulate local politics

James Knox Polk "Young Hickory" (1795–1849) As president, his chief concern was the expansion of the United States. Shortly, after taking office, Mexico broke off relations with the United States over the annexation of Texas. Polk declared war on Mexico and sought to subvert Mexican authority in California. The United States defeated Mexico; and the two nations signed the Treaty of Guadalupe Hidalgo in which Mexico gave up any claims on Texas north of the Rio Grande River and ceded New Mexico and California to the United States.

Pontiac's Rebellion (1763) An Indian attack on British forts and settlements after France ceded to the British its territory east of the Mississippi River, as part of the Treaty of Paris, without consulting France's Indian allies.

popular sovereignty Legal concept by which the white male settlers in a new U.S. territory would vote to decide whether or not to permit slavery.

Populist/People's party Political success of Farmers' Alliance candidates encouraged the formation in 1892 of the People's party (later renamed the Populist party); active until 1912, it advocated a variety of reform issues, including free coinage of silver, income tax, postal savings, regulation of railroads, and direct election of U.S. senators.

Pottawatomie Massacre In retaliation for the "sack of Lawrence," John Brown and his abolitionist cohorts hacked five men to death in the pro-slavery settlement of Pottawatomie, Kansas, on May 24, 1856, triggering a guerrilla war in the Kansas Territory that cost 200 settler lives.

Powhatan Confederacy An alliance of several powerful Algonquian tribes under the leadership of Chief Powhatan, organized into thirty chiefdoms along much of the Atlantic coast in the late sixteenth and early seventeenth centuries.

Chief Powhatan Wahunsonacock He was called Powhatan by the English after the name of his tribe, and was the powerful, charismatic chief of numerous Algonquian-speaking towns in eastern Virginia representing over 10,000 Indians.

pragmatism William James founded this philosophy in the early 1900s. Pragmatists believed that ideas gained their validity not from their inherent truth, but from their social consequences and practical application.

professions Occupations requiring specialized knowledge of some field; the Industrial Revolution and its new organization of labor created an array of professions in the nineteenth century.

Progressive party In the 1912 election, Theodore Roosevelt was unable to secure the Republican nomination for president. He left the Republican party and formed his own party of progressive Republicans, called the "Bull Moose" party (later Progressive party). Roosevelt and Taft split the Republican vote, which allowed Democrat Woodrow Wilson to win.

Prohibition National ban on the manufacture and sale of alcohol that lasted from 1920 to 1933, though the law was widely violated and proved too difficult to enforce effectively.

proprietary colonies A colony owned by an individual, rather than a joint-stock company.

Protestant Reformation Sixteenth-century religious movement initiated by Martin Luther, a German monk whose public criticism of corruption in the Roman Catholic Church, and whose teaching that Christians can communicate directly with God, gained a wide following.

public schools Elementary and secondary schools funded by the state and free of tuition.

pueblos The Spanish term for the adobe cliff dwellings of the indigenous people of the southwestern United States.

Pullman Strike (1894) A national strike by the American Railway Union, whose members shut down major railways in sympathy with striking workers in Pullman, Illinois; ended with intervention of federal troops.

Puritans English religious dissenters who sought to "purify" the Church of England of its Catholic practices.

Quakers George Fox founded the Quaker religion in 1647. They rejected the use of formal sacraments and ministry, refused to take oaths and embraced pacifism. Fleeing persecution, they settled and established the colony of Pennsylvania.

race-based slavery Institution that uses racial characteristics and myths to justify enslaving a people.

Radical Republicans Senators and congressmen who, strictly identifying the Civil War with the abolitionist cause, sought swift emancipation of the slaves, punishment of the rebels, and tight controls over the former Confederate states after the war.

railroads Steam-powered vehicles that improved passenger transportation, quickened western settlement, and enabled commercial agriculture in the nineteenth century.

Raleigh's Roanoke Island Colony English expedition of 117 settlers, including Virginia Dare, the first English child born in the New World; colony disappeared from Roanoke Island in the Outer Banks sometime between 1587 and 1590.

A. Philip Randolph (1889–1979) He was the head of the Brotherhood of Sleeping Car Porters who planned a march on Washington D.C. to demand an end to racial discrimination in the defense industries. To stop the march, the Roosevelt administration negotiated an agreement with the Randolph group. The demonstration would be called off and an executive order would be issued that forbid discrimination in defense work and training programs and set up the Fair Employment Practices Committee.

range wars In the late 1800s, conflicting claims over land and water rights triggered violent disputes between farmers and ranchers in parts of the western United States.

Ronald Reagan (1911–2004) In 1980, the former actor and governor of California was elected president. In office, he reduced social spending, cut taxes, and increased defense spending. During his presidency, the federal debt tripled, the federal deficit rose, programs such as housing and school lunches were cut, and the HIV/AIDS crisis grew to prominence in the United States. He signed an arms-control treaty with the Soviet Union in 1987, authorized covert CIA operations in Central America, and in 1986 the Iran-Contra scandal was revealed.

Reaganomics President Reagan's "supply-side" economic philosophy combining tax cuts with the goals of decreased government spending, reduced regulation of business, and a balanced budget.

Reconstruction Finance Corporation (1932) Federal program established under President Hoover to loan money to banks and other corporations to help them avoid bankruptcy.

Red Power Activism by militant Native American groups to protest living conditions on Indian reservations through demonstrations, legal action, and, at times, violence.

First Red Scare Fear among many Americans after the First World War of Communists in particular and noncitizens in general, it was a reaction to the Russian Revolution, mail bombs, strikes, and riots.

redeemers Post–Civil War Democratic leaders who supposedly saved the South from Yankee domination and preserved the primarily rural economy.

Dr. Walter Reed (1851–1902) His work on yellow fever in Cuba led to the discovery that the fever was carried by mosquitoes. This understanding helped develop more effective controls of the worldwide disease.

Reform Darwinism A social philosophy developed by Lester Frank Ward that challenged the ruthlessness of social Darwinism by asserting that humans were not passive pawns of evolutionary forces. Instead, people could actively shape the process of evolutionary social development through cooperation, innovation, and planning.

Reformation European religious movement that challenged the Catholic Church and resulted in the beginnings of Protestant Christianity. During this period, Catholics and Protestants persecuted, imprisoned, tortured, and killed each other in large numbers.

religious right Christian conservatives with a faith-based political agenda that includes prohibition of abortion and allowing prayer in public schools.

reparations As a part of the Treaty of Versailles, Germany was required to confess its responsibility for the First World War and make payments to the victors for the entire expense of the war. These two requirements created a deep bitterness among Germans.

Report on Manufactures First Secretary of the Treasury Alexander Hamilton's 1791 analysis that accurately foretold the future of American industry and proposed tariffs and subsidies to promote it.

republican ideology Political belief in representative democracy in which citizens govern themselves by electing representatives, or legislators, to make key decisions on the citizens' behalf.

republican simplicity Deliberate attitude of humility and frugality, as opposed to monarchical pomp and ceremony, adopted by Thomas Jefferson in his presidency.

Republicans First used during the early nineteenth century to describe supporters of a strict interpretation of the Constitution, which they believed would safeguard individual freedoms and states' rights from the threats posed by a strong central government. The idealist Republican vision of sustaining an agrarian-oriented union was developed largely by Thomas Jefferson.

"return to normalcy" Campaign promise of Republican presidential candidate Warren G. Harding in 1920, meant to contrast with Woodrow Wilson's progressivism and internationalism.

Paul Revere (1735–1818) On the night of April 18, 1775, British soldiers marched toward Concord to arrest American Revolutionary leaders and seize their depot of supplies. Paul Revere famously rode through the night and raised the alarm about the approaching British troops.

Roaring Twenties The 1920s, an era of social and intellectual revolution in which young people experimented with new forms of recreation and sexuality. The Eastern, urban cultural shift clashed with conservative and insular Midwestern America, which increased the tensions between the two regions.

Jackie Robinson (1919–1972) In 1947, he became the first African American to play major league baseball. He won over fans and players and stimulated the integration of other professional sports.

rock-and-roll music Alan Freed, a disc jockey, noticed white teenagers were buying rhythm and blues records that had been only purchased by African Americans and Hispanic Americans. Freed began playing these records, but called them rock-and-roll records as a way to overcome the racial barrier. As the popularity of the music genre increased, it helped bridge the gap between "white" and "black" music.

John D. Rockefeller (1839–1937) In 1870, he founded the Standard Oil Company of Ohio, which was his first step in creating his vast oil empire. He perfected the idea of a holding company.

Roe v. Wade (1973) Landmark Supreme Court decision striking down state laws that banned abortions during the first trimester of pregnancy.

Roman Catholicism The Christian faith and religious practices of the Roman Catholic Church, which exerted great political, economic, and social influence on much of Western Europe and, through the Spanish and Portuguese Empires, on the Americas.

Romanticism Philosophical, literary, and artistic movement of the nineteenth century that was largely a reaction to the rationalism of the previous century; Romantics valued emotion, mysticism, and individualism.

Eleanor Roosevelt (1884–1962) She redefined the role of the presidential spouse and was the first woman to address a national political convention, write a nationally syndicated column and hold regular press conferences. She travelled throughout the nation to promote the New Deal, women's causes, organized labor, and meet with African American leaders.

Franklin Delano Roosevelt (1882–1945) Elected during the Great Depression, Roosevelt sought to help struggling Americans through his New Deal programs that created employment and social programs, such as Social Security. After the bombing of Pearl Harbor, he declared war on Japan and Germany and led the country through most of the Second World War before dying of cerebral hemorrhage.

Theodore Roosevelt (1858–1919) As the assistant secretary of the navy, he supported expansionism, American imperialism, and war with Spain. He led the Rough Riders in Cuba during the war of 1898 and used the notoriety of this military campaign for political gain. As President McKinley's vice president, he succeeded McKinley after his assassination. His forceful foreign policy became known as "big stick diplomacy." Domestically, his policies on natural resources helped start the conservation movement. Unable to win the Republican nomination for president in 1912, he formed his own party of progressive Republicans called the "Bull Moose" party.

Roosevelt Corollary (1904) President Theodore Roosevelt's revision of the Monroe Doctrine (1823) in which he argued that the United States could use military force in Central and South American nations to prevent European nations from intervening in the Western Hemisphere.

Rough Riders The First U.S. Volunteer Cavalry, led in the War of 1898 by Theodore Roosevelt; they were victorious in their only engagement, the Battle of San Juan Hill near Santiago, Cuba, and Roosevelt was celebrated as a national hero, bolstering his political career.

Royal Proclamation of 1763 Proclamation drawing a boundary along the Appalachian Mountains from Canada to Georgia in order to minimize occurrences of settler–Indian violence; colonists were forbidden to go west of the line.

Nicola Sacco (1891–1927) In 1920, he and Bartolomeo Vanzetti were Italian immigrants who were arrested for stealing $16,000 and killing a paymaster and his guard. Their trial took place during a time of numerous bombings by anarchists and their judge was openly prejudicial; many liberals and radicals believe that their conviction was based on their political ideas and ethnic origin rather than the evidence against them.

Sacco and Vanzetti case 1921 trial of two Italian immigrants that occurred at the height of Italian immigration and against the backdrop of numerous terror attacks by anarchists; despite a lack of clear evidence, the two defendants, both self-professed anarchists, were convicted of murder and were executed in 1927.

saloons Bars or taverns where mostly men would gather to drink, eat, relax, play games, and, often, to discuss politics.

salutary neglect Informal British policy during the first half of the eighteenth century that allowed the American colonies considerable freedom to pursue their economic and political interests in exchange for colonial obedience.

same-sex marriage The legal right for gay and lesbian couples to marry; it became the most divisive issue in the culture wars of the early 2010s as more and more court rulings affirmed this right in states and municipalities across the United States. The 2015 Supreme Court case *Obergefell v. Hodges* affirmed the right to same-sex marriage, also known as marriage equality, nationally.

Sand Creek Massacre (1864) Colonel Chivington's unprovoked slaughter of the Cheyennes and Arapahos in Colorado, initially reported as a justified battle but soon exposed for the despicable massacre it was.

Sandinista Cuban-sponsored government that came to power in Nicaragua after toppling a corrupt dictator. The State Department believed that the Sandinistas were supplying the leftist Salvadoran rebels with Cuban and Soviet arms. In response, the Reagan administration ordered the CIA to train and supply guerrilla bands of anti-Communist Nicaraguans called Contras. A cease-fire agreement between the Contras and Sandinistas was signed in 1988.

Sandlot Incident Violence occurring during the Great Railroad Strike of 1877, when mobs of frustrated working-class whites in San Francisco attacked Chinese immigrants, blaming them for economic hardship.

General Antonio López de Santa Anna (1794–1876) In 1834, he seized political power in Mexico and became a dictator. In 1835, Texans rebelled against him and he led his army to Texas to crush their rebellion. He captured the mission called the Alamo and killed all of its defenders, which inspired Texans to continue resistance and Americans to volunteer to fight for Texas. The Texans captured Santa Anna during a surprise attack and he bought his freedom by signing a treaty recognizing Texas's independence.

Battles of Saratoga Decisive defeat of 5,000 British troops under General John Burgoyne in several battles near Saratoga, New York, in October 1777; the American victory helped convince France to enter the war on the side of the Patriots.

scalawags White southern Republicans—some former Unionists—who served in Reconstruction governments.

Phyllis Schlafly (1924–2016) A right-wing Republican activist who spearheaded the anti-feminism movement. She believed feminists were "anti-family, anti-children, and pro-abortion." She worked against the equal-rights amendment for women and civil rights protection for gays.

Scopes Trial Highly publicized 1925 trial of a high school teacher in Tennessee for violating a state law that prohibited the teaching of evolution; the trial was seen as the climax of the fundamentalist war on Darwinism.

Winfield Scott (1786–1866) During the Mexican War, he was the American general who captured Mexico City, which ended the war. Using his popularity from his military success, he ran as a Whig party candidate for President.

Sears, Roebuck and Company By the end of the nineteenth century, this company dominated the mail-order industry and helped create a truly national market. Its mail-order catalog and low prices allowed people living in rural areas and small towns to buy products that were previously too expensive or available only to city dwellers.

secession Shortly after President Abraham Lincoln was elected, southern states began dissolving their ties with the United States because they believed Lincoln and the Republican party were a threat to slavery.

Second Bank of the United States Established in 1816 after the first national bank's charter expired; it stabilized the economy by creating a sound national currency, by making loans to farmers, small manufacturers, and entrepreneurs, and by regulating the ability of state banks to issue their own paper currency.

Second Great Awakening Religious revival movement that arose in reaction to the growth of secularism and rationalist religion; spurred the growth of the Baptist and Methodist churches.

Second Industrial Revolution Beginning in the late nineteenth century, a wave of technological innovations, especially in iron and steel production, steam and electrical power, and telegraphic communications, all of which spurred industrial development and urban growth.

Second New Deal (1935–1938) Expansive cluster of legislation proposed by President Roosevelt that established new regulatory agencies, strengthened the rights of workers to organize unions, and laid the foundation of a federal social welfare system through the creation of Social Security.

Securities and Exchange Commission (1934) Federal agency established to regulate the issuance and trading of stocks and bonds in an effort to avoid financial panics and stock market "crashes."

Seneca Falls Convention (1848) Convention organized by feminists Lucretia Mott and Elizabeth Cady Stanton to promote women's rights and issue the pathbreaking Declaration of Sentiments.

"separate but equal" Principle underlying legal racial segregation, which was upheld in *Plessy v. Ferguson* (1896) and struck down in *Brown v. Board of Education* (1954).

separation of powers Strict division of the powers of government among three separate branches (executive, legislative, and judicial) which, in turn, check and balance each other.

September 11 On September 11, 2001, Islamic terrorists, who were members of the al Qaeda terrorist organization, hijacked four commercial airliners. Two were flown into the World Trade Center, a third into the Pentagon, and a fourth plane was brought down in Pennsylvania. In response, President George W. Bush launched his "war on terrorism." His administration assembled an international coalition to fight terrorism, which invaded Afghanistan after the country's government would not turn over Osama bin Laden. Bush and Congress passed the U.S.A. Patriot Act, which allowed government agencies to try suspected terrorists in secret military courts and eavesdrop on confidential conversations.

settlement houses Product of the late-nineteenth-century movement to offer a broad array of social services in urban immigrant neighborhoods; Chicago's Hull House was one of hundreds of settlement houses that operated by the early twentieth century.

Seventeenth Amendment (1913) Constitutional amendment that provided for the direct election of senators rather than the traditional practice allowing state legislatures to name them.

Shakers Founded by Mother Ann Lee Stanley in England, the United Society of Believers in Christ's Second Appearing settled in Watervliet, New York, in 1774 and subsequently established eighteen additional communes in the Northeast, Indiana, and Kentucky.

share tenants Poor farmers who rented land to farm in exchange for a substantial share of the crop, though they would often have their own horse or mule, tools, and line of credit with a nearby store.

sharecroppers Poor, mostly black farmers who would work an owner's land in return for shelter, seed, fertilizer, mules, supplies, and food, as well as a substantial share of the crop produced.

Share-the-Wealth program Huey Long offered this program as an alternative to the New Deal. The program proposed to confiscate large personal fortunes, which would be used to guarantee every poor family a cash grant of $5,000 and every worker an annual income of $2,500. This program promised to provide pensions, reduce working hours, pay veterans' bonuses, and ensures a college education to every qualified student.

Shays's Rebellion (1786–1787) Storming of the Massachusetts federal arsenal by Daniel Shays and 1,200 armed farmers seeking debt relief from the state legislature through issuance of paper currency and lower taxes.

Sherman's "March to the Sea" (1864) The Union army's devastating march through Georgia from Atlanta to Savannah led by General William T. Sherman, intended to demoralize civilians and destroy the resources the Confederate army needed to fight.

"silent majority" Term popularized by President Richard Nixon to describe the great majority of American voters who did not express their political opinions publicly—"the non-demonstrators."

Sixteenth Amendment (1913) Constitutional amendment that authorized the federal income tax.

slave codes Ordinances passed by a colony or state to regulate the behavior of slaves, often including brutal punishments for infractions.

Alfred E. Smith (1873–1944) In the 1928 presidential election, he won the Democratic nomination, but failed to win the presidency. Rural voters distrusted him for being Catholic and the son of Irish immigrants as well as his anti-Prohibition stance.

Captain John Smith (1580–1631) A swashbuckling soldier of fortune with rare powers of leadership and self-promotion, he was appointed to the resident council to manage Jamestown.

Joseph Smith (1805–1844) In 1823, he claimed that the Angel Moroni showed him the location of several gold tablets on which the Book of Mormon was written. Using the Book of Mormon as his gospel, he founded the Church of Jesus Christ of Latter-day Saints, or Mormons. In 1839, they settled in Commerce, Illinois, to avoid persecution. In 1844, Joseph and his brother were arrested and jailed for ordering the destruction of a newspaper that opposed them. While in jail, an anti-Mormon mob stormed the jail and killed both of them.

social Darwinism The application of Charles Darwin's theory of evolutionary natural selection to human society; Social Darwinists used the concept of "survival of the fittest" to justify class distinctions, explain poverty, and oppose government intervention in the economy.

social gospel Protestant movement that stressed the Christian obligation to address the mounting social problems caused by urbanization and industrialization.

social justice An important part of the Progressive's agenda, social justice sought to solve social problems through reform and regulation. Methods used to bring about social justice ranged from the founding of charities to the legislation of a ban on child labor.

Social Security Act (1935) Legislation enacted to provide federal assistance to retired workers through tax-funded pension payments and benefit payments to the unemployed and disabled.

Sons of Liberty First organized by Samuel Adams in the 1770s, groups of colonists dedicated to militant resistance against British control of the colonies.

Hernando de Soto (1500?–1542) A conquistador who explored the west coast of Florida, western North Carolina, and along the Arkansas river from 1539 till his death in 1542.

Southern Christian Leadership Conference (SCLC) Civil rights organization formed by Dr. Martin Luther King, Jr., that championed nonviolent direct action as a means of ending segregation.

"southern strategy" This strategy was a major reason for Richard Nixon's victory in the 1968 presidential election. To gain support in the South, Nixon assured southern conservatives that he would slow the federal enforcement of civil rights laws and appoint pro-southern justices to the Supreme Court. As president, Nixon fulfilled these promises.

Spanish Armada A massive Spanish fleet of 130 warships that was defeated at Plymouth in 1588 by the English navy during the reign of Queen Elizabeth I.

Spanish flu Unprecedentedly lethal influenza epidemic of 1918 that killed more than 22 million people worldwide.

Herbert Spencer (1820–1903) As the first major proponent of social Darwinism, he argued that human society and institutions are subject to the process of natural selection and that society naturally evolves for the better. He was against any form of government interference with the evolution of society, like business regulations, because it would help the "unfit" to survive.

spirituals Songs with religious messages sung by slaves to help ease the strain of field labor and to voice their suffering at the hands of their masters and overseers.

spoils system The term—meaning the filling of federal government jobs with persons loyal to the party of the president—originated in Andrew Jackson's first term; the system was replaced in the Progressive Era by civil service.

Square Deal Roosevelt's progressive agenda of the "Three C's": control of corporations, conservation of natural resources, and consumer protection.

"stagflation" Term coined by economists during the Nixon presidency to describe the unprecedented situation of stagnant economic growth and consumer price inflation occurring at the same time.

Joseph Stalin (1879–1953) The Bolshevik leader who succeeded Lenin as the leader of the Soviet Union in 1924 and ruled the country until his death. During his totalitarian rule of the Soviet Union, he used purges and a system of forced labor camps to maintain control over the country, and claimed vast areas of Eastern Europe for Soviet domination.

Stalwarts Conservative Republican party faction during the presidency of Rutherford B. Hayes, 1877–1881; led by Senator Roscoe B. Conkling of New York, Stalwarts opposed civil service reform and favored a third term for President Ulysses S. Grant.

Stamp Act (1765) Act of Parliament requiring that all printed materials (e.g., newspapers, bonds, and even playing cards) in the American colonies use paper with an official tax stamp in order to pay for British military protection of the colonies.

Stamp Act Congress Twenty-seven delegates from nine of the colonies met from October 7 to 25, 1765 and wrote a Declaration of the Rights and Grievances of the Colonies, a petition to the King and a petition to Parliament for the repeal of the Stamp Act.

Standard Oil Company Corporation under the leadership of John D. Rockefeller that attempted to dominate the entire oil industry through horizontal and vertical integration.

Elizabeth Cady Stanton (1815–1902) A prominent reformer and advocate for the rights of women, she helped organize the Seneca Falls Convention to discuss women's rights. The convention was the first of its kind and produced the Declaration of Sentiments, which proclaimed the equality of men and women.

staple crop A profitable market crop, such as cotton, tobacco, or rice that predominates in a given region.

state constitutions Charters that define the relationship between the state government and local governments and individuals, and also protects their rights from violation by the national government.

steamboats Ships and boats powered by wood-fired steam engines. First used in the early nineteenth century, they made two-way traffic possible in eastern river systems, creating a transcontinental market and an agricultural empire.

Thaddeus Stevens (1792–1868) As one of the leaders of the Radical Republicans, he argued that the former Confederate states should be viewed as conquered provinces, which were subject to the demands of the conquerors. He believed that all of Southern society needed to be changed, and he supported racial equality and the abolition of slavery.

Adlai E. Stevenson (1900–1965) In the 1952 and 1956 presidential elections, he was the Democratic nominee who lost to Dwight Eisenhower. He was also the U.S. Ambassador to the United Nations and is remembered for his famous speech in 1962 before the UN Security Council that unequivocally demonstrated that the Soviet Union had built nuclear missile bases in Cuba.

Stono Rebellion (1739) A slave uprising in South Carolina that was brutally quashed, leading to executions as well as a severe tightening of the slave code.

Stonewall riots (1969) Violent clashes between police and lesbian, gay, bisexual, transgender, and queer (LGBTQ) patrons of New York City's Stonewall Inn, seen as the starting point of the modern LGBTQ rights movement.

Strategic Arms Limitation Talks (SALT I) (1972) Agreement signed by President Nixon and Secretary Brezhnev prohibiting the development of missile defense systems in the United States and Soviet Union and limiting the quantity of nuclear warheads for both.

Strategic Defense Initiative (SDI) (1983) Ronald Reagan's proposed space-based anti-missile defense system, dubbed "Star Wars" by the media, that aroused great controversy and escalated the arms race between the United States and the Soviet Union.

Levi Strauss (1829–1902) A Jewish tailor who followed miners to California during the gold rush and began making durable work pants that were later dubbed blue jeans or Levi's.

Student Nonviolent Coordinating Committee (SNCC) Interracial organization formed in 1960 with the goal of intensifying the effort to end racial segregation.

Students for a Democratic Society (SDS) Major organization of the New Left, founded at the University of Michigan in 1960 by Tom Hayden and Al Haber.

suburbia Communities formed from mass migration of middle-class whites from urban centers.

Suez crisis (1956) British, French, and Israeli attack on Egypt after Nasser's seizure of the Suez Canal; President Eisenhower interceded to demand the withdrawal of the British, French, and Israeli forces from the Sinai peninsula and canal.

Sunbelt The label for an arc that stretched from the Carolinas to California. During the postwar era, much of the urban population growth occurred in this area.

"surge" In early 2007, President Bush decided he would send a "surge" of new troops to Iraq and implement a new strategy. U.S. forces would shift their focus from offensive operations to the protection of Iraqi civilians from attacks by terrorist insurgents and sectarian militias. While the "surge" reduced the violence in Iraq, Iraqi leaders were still unable to develop a self-sustaining democracy.

Taft-Hartley Labor Act (1947) Congressional legislation that banned "unfair labor practices" by labor unions, required union leaders to sign anti-Communist "loyalty oaths," and prohibited federal employees from going on strike.

Taliban A coalition of ultraconservative Islamists who rose to power in Afghanistan after the Soviets withdrew. The Taliban leaders gave Osama bin Laden a safe haven in their country in exchange for aid in fighting the Northern Alliance, who were rebels opposed to the Taliban. After they refused to turn bin Laden over to the United States, America invaded Afghanistan.

Tammany Hall The "city machine" used by "Boss" Tweed to dominate politics in New York City until his arrest in 1871.

tariff A tax on goods imported from other nations, typically used to protect home industries from foreign competitors and to generate revenue for the federal government.

Tariff of 1816 A cluster of taxes on imports passed by Congress to protect America's emerging iron and textile industries from British competition.

Tariff of 1832 This tariff act reduced the duties on many items, but the tariffs on cloth and iron remained high. South Carolina nullified it along with the tariff of 1828. President Andrew Jackson sent federal troops to the state and asked Congress to grant him the authority to enforce the tariffs. Henry Clay presented a plan of gradually reducing the tariffs until 1842, which Congress passed and ended the crisis.

"Tariff of Abominations" (1828) Tax on imported goods, including British cloth and clothing, that strengthened New England textile companies but hurt southern consumers, who experienced a decrease in British demand for raw cotton grown in the South.

tariff reform (1887) Effort led by the Democratic party to reduce taxes on imported goods, which Republicans argued were needed to protect American industries from foreign competition.

Troubled Asset Relief Program (TARP) In 2008 President George W. Bush signed into law the bank bailout fund called Troubled Asset Relief Program (TARP), which required the Treasury Department to spend $700 billion to keep banks and other financial institutions from collapsing.

Zachary Taylor (1784–1850) During the Mexican War, he scored two quick victories against Mexico, which made him very popular in America. He used his popularity from his military victories to be elected president as a member of the Whig party, but died before he could complete his term.

Taylorism Labor system based on detailed study of work tasks, championed by Frederick Winslow Taylor, intended to maximize efficiency and profits for employers.

Tea Party Right-wing populist movement, largely made up of middle-class, white male conservatives, that emerged as a response to the expansion of the federal government under the Obama administration.

Teapot Dome (1923) Harding administration scandal in which Secretary of the Interior Albert B. Fall profited from secret leasing of government oil reserves in Wyoming to private oil companies.

Tecumseh (1768–1813) He was a leader of the Shawnee tribe who tried to unite all Indians into a confederation that could defend their hunting grounds. He believed that no land cessions could be made without the consent of all the tribes since they held the land in common. His beliefs and leadership made him seem dangerous to the American government and they waged war on him and his tribe. He was killed at the Battle of the Thames.

Tecumseh's Indian Confederacy A group of Native Americans under leadership of Shawnee leader Tecumseh and his prophet brother Tenskwatawa; its mission of fighting off American expansion was thwarted in the Battle of Tippecanoe (1811), when the confederacy fell apart.

Tejanos Texas settlers of Spanish or Mexican descent.

telegraph system System of electronic communication invented by Samuel F. B. Morse that could be transmitted instantaneously across great distances (first used in the 1840s).

Teller Amendment Addition to the congressional war resolution of April 20, 1898, which marked the U.S. entry into the war with Spain; the amendment declared that the United States' goal in entering the war was to ensure Cuba's independence, not to annex Cuba as a territory.

temperance A widespread reform movement, led by militant Christians, focused on reducing the use of alcoholic beverages.

tenements Shabby, low-cost inner-city apartment buildings that housed the urban poor in cramped, unventilated apartments.

Tenochtitlán The capital city of the Aztec Empire. The city was built on marshy islands on the western side of Lake Tetzcoco, which is the site of present-day Mexico City.

Tet offensive (1968) Surprise attack by Viet Cong guerrillas and the North Vietnamese army on U.S. and South Vietnamese forces that shocked the American public and led to widespread sentiment against the war.

Texas Revolution (1835–1836) Conflict between Texas colonists and the Mexican government that resulted in the creation of the separate Republic of Texas in 1836.

textile industry Commercial production of thread, fabric, and clothing from raw cotton in mills in New England during the first half of the nineteenth century, and later in the South in the late nineteenth century.

Thirteenth Amendment (1865) Amendment to the U. S. Constitution that freed all slaves in the United States.

Battle of Tippecanoe (1811) Battle in northern Indiana between U.S. troops and Native American warriors led by Tenskwatawa, the brother of Tecumseh, who had organized an anti-American Indian confederacy to fight American efforts to settle on Indian lands.

tobacco A cash crop grown in the Caribbean as well as the Virginia and Maryland colonies, made increasingly profitable by the rapidly growing popularity of smoking in Europe after the voyages of Columbus.

Gulf of Tonkin incident On August 2 and 4 of 1964, North Vietnamese vessels attacked two American destroyers in the Gulf of Tonkin off the coast of North Vietnam. President Johnson described the attacks as unprovoked. In reality, the U.S. ships were monitoring South Vietnamese attacks on North Vietnamese islands that America advisers had planned. The incident spurred the Tonkin Gulf resolution.

Tonkin Gulf Resolution Congressional action that granted the president unlimited authority to defend U.S. forces abroad, passed in August 1964 after an allegedly unprovoked attack on American warships off the coast of North Vietnam.

Tories Term used by Patriots to refer to Loyalists, or colonists who supported the Crown after the Declaration of Independence.

Townshend Acts Parliamentary measures to extract more revenue from the colonies; the Revenue Act of 1767, which taxed tea, paper, and other colonial imports, was one of the most notorious of these policies.

Trail of Tears The Cherokees' eight-hundred-mile journey (1838–1839) from the southern Appalachians to Indian Territory (in present-day Oklahoma); four thousand people died along the way.

transcendentalism Philosophy of a small group of New England writers and thinkers who advocated personal spirituality, self-reliance, social reform, and harmony with nature.

Transcontinental railroad First line across the continent from Omaha, Nebraska, to Sacramento, California, established in 1869 with the linkage of the Union Pacific and Central Pacific railroads at Promontory, Utah.

Transcontinental Treaty (1819) (Adams-Onís Treaty) Treaty between Spain and the United States that clarified the boundaries of the Louisiana Purchase and arranged the transfer of Florida to the United States in exchange for cash.

triangular trade A network of trade in which exports from one region were sold to another region, which sent its exports to a third region, which exported its own goods back to the first country or colony.

Treaty of Ghent (1814) Agreement between Great Britain and the United States that ended the War of 1812, signed on December 24, 1814.

Treaty of Guadalupe Hidalgo (1848) Treaty between United States and Mexico that ended the Mexican-American War.

Treaty of Paris (1763) Settlement between Great Britain and France that ended the French and Indian War.

Treaty of Versailles Peace treaty that ended the First World War, forcing Germany to dismantle its military, pay immense war reparations, and give up its colonies around the world.

trench warfare A form of prolonged combat between the entrenched positions of opposing armies, often with little tactical movement.

Harry S. Truman (1884–1972) As President Roosevelt's vice president, he succeeded him after his death near the end of the Second World War. After the war, Truman wrestled with the inflation of both prices and wages, worked with Congress to pass the National Security Act, and banned racial discrimination in the hiring of federal employees and ended racial segregation in the armed forces. In foreign affairs, he established the Truman Doctrine to contain communism, developed the Marshall Plan to rebuild Europe, and sent the U.S. military to defend South Korea after North Korea invaded.

Truman Doctrine (1947) President Truman's program of "containing" communism in Eastern Europe and providing economic and military aid to any nations at risk of Communist takeover.

Donald J. Trump (1946–) The 45th president of the United States.

trust A business arrangement that gives a person or corporation (the "trustee") the legal power to manage another person's money or another company without owning those entities outright.

Sojourner Truth (1797?–1883) She was born into slavery, but New York State freed her in 1827. She spent the 1840s and 1850s travelling across the country and speaking to audiences about her experiences as slave and asking them to support abolition and women's rights.

Harriet Tubman (1820–1913) She was born a slave, but escaped to the North. She then returned to the South nineteen times and guided 300 slaves to freedom.

Frederick Jackson Turner An influential historian who authored the "Frontier Thesis" in 1893, arguing that the existence of an alluring frontier and the experience of persistent westward expansion informed the nation's democratic politics, unfettered economy, and rugged individualism.

Nat Turner (1800–1831) He was the leader of the only slave revolt to get past the planning stages. In August of 1831, the revolt began with the slaves killing the members of Turner's master's household. Then they attacked other neighboring farmhouses and recruited more slaves until the militia crushed the revolt. At least fifty-five whites were killed during the uprising and seventeen slaves were hanged afterwards.

Nat Turner's Rebellion (1831) Insurrection in rural Virginia led by black overseer Nat Turner, who killed slave owners and their families; in turn, federal troops indiscriminately killed hundreds of slaves in the process of putting down Turner and his rebels.

Tuskegee Airmen U.S. Army Air Corps unit of African American pilots whose combat success spurred military and civilian leaders to desegregate the armed forces after the war.

Mark Twain (1835–1910) Born Samuel Langhorne Clemens in Missouri, he became a popular humorous writer and lecturer and established himself as one of the great American satirists and authors. His two greatest books, *The Adventures of Tom Sawyer* and *The Adventures of Huckleberry Finn*, drew heavily on his childhood in Missouri.

"Boss" Tweed (1823–1878) An infamous political boss in New York City, Tweed used his "city machine," the Tammany Hall ring, to rule, plunder and sometimes improve the city's government. His political domination of New York City ended with his arrest in 1871 and conviction in 1873.

Twenty-first Amendment (1933) Repealed prohibition on the manufacture, sale, and transportation of alcoholic beverages, effectively nullifying the Eighteenth Amendment.

two-party system Domination of national politics by two major political parties, such as the Whigs and Democrats during the 1830s and 1840s.

Underground Railroad A secret system of routes and safe houses through which runaway slaves were led to freedom in the North.

Unitarians Members of the liberal New England Congregationalist offshoot, often well-educated and wealthy, who profess the oneness of God and the goodness of rational man.

United Farm Workers (UFW) Organization formed in 1962 to represent the interests of Mexican American migrant workers.

United Nations Security Council A major agency within the United Nations which remains in permanent session and has the responsibility of maintaining international peace and security. Originally, it consisted of five permanent members, (United States, Soviet Union, Britain, France, and the Republic of China), and six members elected to two-year terms. After 1965, the number of rotating members was increased to ten. In 1971, the Republic of China was replaced with the People's Republic of China and the Soviet Union was replaced by the Russian Federation in 1991.

Universalists Members of a New England religious movement, often from the working class, who believed in a merciful God and universal salvation.

USA Patriot Act (2001) Wide-reaching Congressional legislation, triggered by the War on Terror, which gave government agencies the right to eavesdrop on confidential conversations between prison inmates and their lawyers and permitted suspected terrorists to be tried in secret military courts.

U-boat German military submarine (*Unterseeboot*) used during the First World War to attack enemy naval vessels as well as merchant ships of enemy and neutral nations.

utopian communities Ideal communities that offered innovative social and economic relationships to those who were interested in achieving salvation.

Valley Forge American military encampment near Philadelphia, where more than 3,500 soldiers deserted or died from cold and hunger in the winter of 1777–1778.

Cornelius Vanderbilt (1794–1877) In the 1860s, he consolidated several separate railroad companies into one vast entity, New York Central Railroad.

Bartolomeo Vanzetti (1888–1927) In 1920, he and Nicola Sacco were Italian immigrants who were arrested for stealing $16,000 and killing a paymaster and his guard. Their trial took place during a time of numerous bombings by anarchists and their judge was openly prejudicial. Many liberals and radicals believe that their conviction was based on their political ideas and ethnic origin rather than the evidence against them.

vertical integration The process by which a corporation gains control of all aspects of the resources and processes needed to produce and sell a product.

Amerigo Vespucci (1455–1512) Italian explorer who reached the New World in 1499 and was the first to suggest that South America was a new continent. Afterward, European mapmakers used a variant of his first name, America, to label the New World.

Battle of Vicksburg (1863) A protracted battle in northern Mississippi in which Union forces under Ulysses Grant besieged the last major Confederate fortress on the Mississippi River, forcing the inhabitants into starvation and then submission.

Viet Cong Communist guerrillas in Vietnam who launched attacks on the Diem government.

Vietnamization Nixon-era policy of equipping and training South Vietnamese forces to take over the burden of combat from U.S. troops.

Vikings Norse people from Scandinavia who sailed to Newfoundland about 1001 B.C.E.

Francisco Pancho Villa (1877–1923) While the leader of one of the competing factions in the Mexican civil war, he provoked the United States into intervening. He hoped attacking the United States would help him build a reputation as an opponent of the United States, which would increase his popularity and discredit Mexican President Carranza.

ix

Virginia Company A joint stock enterprise that King James I chartered in 1606. The company was to spread Christianity in the New World as well as find ways to make a profit in it.

Virginia Plan The delegations to the Constitutional Convention were divided between two plans on how to structure the government: Virginia called for a strong central government and a two-house legislature apportioned by population.

Virginia Statute of Religious Freedom A Virginia law, drafted by Thomas Jefferson in 1777 and enacted in 1786, that guarantees freedom of, and from, religion.

virtual representation The idea that the American colonies, although they had no actual representative in Parliament, were "virtually" represented by all members of Parliament.

Voting Rights Act of 1965 Legislation ensuring that all Americans were able to vote; the law ended literacy tests and other means of restricting voting rights.

Wagner Act (1935) Legislation that guaranteed workers the right to organize unions, granted them direct bargaining power, and barred employers from interfering with union activities.

George Wallace (1919–1998) An outspoken defender of segregation. As the governor of Alabama, he once attempted to block African American students from enrolling at the University of Alabama. He ran as the presidential candidate for the American Independent party in 1968, appealing to voters who were concerned about rioting anti-war protestors, the welfare system, and the growth of the federal government.

war hawks In 1811, congressional members from the southern and western districts who clamored for a war to seize Canada and Florida were dubbed "war hawks."

War of 1812 (1812–1815) Conflict fought in North America and at sea between Great Britain and the United States over American shipping rights and British efforts to spur Indian attacks on American settlements. Canadians and Native Americans also fought in the war.

war on terror Global crusade to root out anti-American, anti-Western Islamist terrorist cells launched by President George W. Bush as a response to the 9/11 attacks.

War Powers Act (1973) Legislation requiring the president to inform Congress within 48 hours of the deployment of U.S. troops abroad and to withdraw them after 60 days unless Congress approves their continued deployment.

War Production Board Federal agency created by President Roosevelt in 1942 that converted America's industrial output to war production.

"war relocation camps" Detention camps housing thousands of Japanese Americans from the West Coast who were forcibly interned from 1942 until the end of the Second World War.

Warren Court The U.S. Supreme Court under Chief Justice Earl Warren, 1953–1969, decided such landmark cases as *Brown v. Board of Education* (school desegregation), *Baker v. Carr* (legislative redistricting), and *Gideon v. Wainwright* and *Miranda v. Arizona* (rights of criminal defendants).

Booker T. Washington (1856–1915) He founded a leading college for African Americans in Tuskegee, Alabama, and become the foremost black educator in America by the 1890s. He believed that the African American community should establish an economic base for its advancement before striving for social equality. His critics charged that his philosophy sacrificed educational and civil rights for dubious social acceptance and economic opportunities.

George Washington (1732–1799) In 1775, the Continental Congress named him the commander in chief of the Continental Army which defeated the British in the American Revolution. He had previously served as an officer in the French and Indian War. In 1787, he was the presiding officer over the Constitutional Convention, but participated little in the debates. In 1789, the Electoral College chose Washington to be the nation's first president. Washington faced the nation's first foreign and domestic crises, maintaining the United States' neutrality in foreign affairs. After two terms in office, Washington chose to step down; and the power of the presidency was peacefully passed to John Adams.

Watergate (1972–1974) Scandal that exposed the criminality and corruption of the Nixon administration and ultimately led to President Nixon's resignation in 1974.

Daniel Webster (1782–1852) As a representative from New Hampshire, he led the New Federalists in opposition to the moving of the second national bank from Boston to Philadelphia. Later, he served as representative and a senator for Massachusetts and emerged as a champion of a stronger national government. He also switched from opposing to supporting tariffs because New England had built up its manufactures with the understanding tariffs would protect them from foreign competitors.

Webster-Ashburton Treaty Settlement in 1842 of U.S.–Canadian border disputes in Maine, New York, Vermont, and in the Wisconsin Territory (now northern Minnesota).

Webster-Hayne debate U.S. Senate debate of January 1830 between Daniel Webster of Massachusetts and Robert Hayne of South Carolina over nullification and states' rights.

Western Front The contested frontier between the Central and Allied Powers that ran along northern France and across Belgium.

Whig party Political party founded in 1834 in opposition to the Jacksonian Democrats; Whigs supported federal funding for internal improvements, a national bank, and high tariffs on imported goods.

Whigs Another name for revolutionary Patriots.

Whiskey Rebellion (1794) Violent protest by western Pennsylvania farmers against the federal excise tax on corn whiskey, put down by a federal army.

Eli Whitney (1765–1825) He invented the cotton gin which could separate cotton from its seeds. One machine operator could separate fifty times more cotton than worker could by hand, which led to an increase in cotton production and prices. These increases gave planters a new profitable use for slavery and a lucrative slave trade emerged from the coastal South to the Southwest.

Wilderness Road Originally an Indian path through the Cumberland Gap, it was used by over 300,000 settlers who migrated westward to Kentucky in the last quarter of the eighteenth century.

Roger Williams (1603–1683) Puritan who believed that the purity of the church required a complete separation between church and state and freedom from coercion in matters of faith. In 1636, he established the town of Providence, the first permanent settlement in Rhode Island and the first to allow religious freedom in America.

Wendell L. Willkie (1892–1944) In the 1940 presidential election, he was the Republican nominee who ran against President Roosevelt. He supported aid to the Allies and criticized the New Deal programs. Voters looked at the increasingly dangerous world situation and chose to keep President Roosevelt in office for a third term.

Wilmot Proviso (1846) Proposal by Congressman David Wilmot, a Pennsylvania Democrat, to prohibit slavery in any land acquired in the Mexican-American War.

Woodrow Wilson (1856–1924) In the 1912 presidential election, Woodrow Wilson ran under the slogan of New Freedom, which promised to improve of the banking system, lower tariffs, and break up monopolies. At the beginning of the First World War, Wilson kept America neutral, but provided the Allies with credit for purchases of supplies; however, the sinking of U.S. merchant ships and the Zimmermann telegram caused him to ask Congress to declare war on Germany. Wilson supported the entry of America into the League of Nations and the ratification of the Treaty of Versailles, but Congress would not approve the entry or ratification.

John Winthrop Puritan leader and Governor of the Massachusetts Bay Colony who resolved to use the colony as a refuge for persecuted Puritans and as an instrument of building a "wilderness Zion" in America.

woman suffrage Movement to give women the right to vote through a constitutional amendment, spearheaded by Susan B. Anthony and Elizabeth Cady Stanton's National Woman Suffrage Association.

Women Accepted for Voluntary Emergency Services (WAVES) During the Second World War, the increased demand for labor shook up old prejudices about gender roles in the workplace and in the military. Nearly 200,000 women served in the Women's Army Corps or its naval equivalent, Women Accepted for Volunteer Emergency Service (WAVES).

Women's Army Corps Women's branch of the United States Army; by the end of the Second World War nearly 150,000 women had served in the WAC.

women's movement Wave of activism sparked by Betty Friedan's *The Feminine Mystique* (1963); it argued for equal rights for women and fought against the cult of domesticity of the 1950s that limited women's roles to the home as wife, mother, and housewife.

women's work The traditional term referring to routine tasks in the house, garden, and fields performed by women. The sphere of women's occupations expanded in the colonies to include medicine, shopkeeping, upholstering, and the operation of inns and taverns.

Woodstock In 1969, roughly a half a million young people converged on a farm near Bethel, New York, for a three-day music festival that was an expression of the flower children's free spirit.

Works Progress Administration (1935) Government agency established to manage several federal job programs created under the New Deal; it became the largest employer in the nation.

Battle of Wounded Knee Last incident of the Indians Wars took place in 1890 in the Dakota Territory, where the U.S. Cavalry killed over 200 Sioux men, women, and children who were in the process of surrender.

XYZ affair French foreign minister Tallyrand's three anonymous agents demanded payments to stop French plundering of American ships in 1797; refusal to pay the bribe led to two years of sea war with France (1798–1800).

Yalta Conference (1945) Meeting of the "Big Three" Allied leaders, Franklin D. Roosevelt, Winston Churchill, and Joseph Stalin, to discuss how to divide control of postwar Germany and eastern Europe

yellow journalism A type of news reporting, epitomized in the 1890s by the newspaper empires of William Randolph Hearst and Joseph Pulitzer, that intentionally manipulates public opinion through sensational headlines, illustrations, and articles about both real and invented events.

yeomen Small landowners (the majority of white families in the South) who farmed their own land and usually did not own slaves.

Battle of Yorktown Last major battle of the Revolutionary War; General Cornwallis along with over 7,000 British troops surrendered to George Washington at Yorktown, Virginia, on October 17, 1781.

Brigham Young (1801–1877) Following Joseph Smith's death, he became the leader of the Mormons and promised Illinois officials that the Mormons would leave the state. In 1846, he led the Mormons to Utah and settled near the Salt Lake. After the United States gained Utah as part of the Treaty of Guadalupe Hidalgo, he became the governor of the territory and kept the Mormons virtually independent of federal authority.

youth culture The youth of the 1950s had more money and free time than any previous generation which allowed a distinct youth culture to emerge. A market emerged for products and activities that were specifically for young people such as transistor radios, rock records, *Seventeen* magazine, and Pat Boone movies.

Zimmermann telegram Message sent by a German official to the Mexican government in 1917 urging an invasion of the United States; the telegram was intercepted by British intelligence agents and angered Americans, many of whom called for war against Germany.

Appendix

The Declaration of Independence (1776)

When in the Course of human events, it becomes necessary for one people to dissolve the political bands which have connected them with another, and to assume among the powers of the earth, the separate and equal station to which the Laws of Nature and of Nature's God entitle them, a decent respect to the opinions of mankind requires that they should declare the causes which impel them to the separation.

We hold these truths to be self-evident, that all men are created equal, that they are endowed by their Creator with certain unalienable Rights, that among these are Life, Liberty and the pursuit of Happiness. —That to secure these rights, Governments are instituted among Men, deriving their just powers from the consent of the governed, —That whenever any Form of Government becomes destructive of these ends, it is the Right of the People to alter or to abolish it, and to institute new Government, laying its foundation on such principles and organizing its powers in such form, as to them shall seem most likely to effect their Safety and Happiness. Prudence, indeed, will dictate that Governments long established should not be changed for light and transient causes; and accordingly all experience hath shewn, that mankind are more disposed to suffer, while evils are sufferable, than to right themselves by abolishing the forms to which they are accustomed. But when a long train of abuses and usurpations, pursuing invariably the same Object evinces a design to reduce them under absolute Despotism, it is their right, it is their duty, to throw off such Government, and to provide new Guards for their future security.— Such has been the patient sufferance of these Colonies; and such is now the necessity which constrains them to alter their former Systems of Government. The history of the present King of Great Britain is a history of repeated injuries and usurpations, all having in direct object the establishment of an absolute Tyranny over these States. To prove this, let Facts be submitted to a candid world.

He has refused his Assent to Laws, the most wholesome and necessary for the public good.

He has forbidden his Governors to pass Laws of immediate and pressing importance, unless suspended in their operation till his Assent should be obtained; and when so suspended, he has utterly neglected to attend to them.

He has refused to pass other Laws for the accommodation of large districts of people, unless those people would relinquish the right of Representation in the Legislature, a right inestimable to them and formidable to tyrants only.

He has called together legislative bodies at places unusual, uncomfortable, and distant from the depository of their public Records, for the sole purpose of fatiguing them into compliance with his measures.

He has dissolved Representative Houses repeatedly, for opposing with manly firmness his invasions on the rights of the people.

He has refused for a long time, after such dissolutions, to cause others to be elected; whereby the Legislative powers, incapable of Annihilation, have returned to the People at large for their exercise; the State remaining in the mean time exposed to all the dangers of invasion from without, and convulsions within.

He has endeavoured to prevent the population of these States; for that purpose obstructing the Laws for Naturalization of Foreigners; refusing to pass others to encourage their migrations hither, and raising the conditions of new Appropriations of Lands.

He has obstructed the Administration of Justice, by refusing his Assent to Laws for establishing Judiciary powers.

He has made Judges dependent on his Will alone, for the tenure of their offices, and the amount and payment of their salaries.

He has erected a multitude of New Offices, and sent hither swarms of Officers to harrass our people, and eat out their substance.

He has kept among us, in times of peace, Standing Armies without the Consent of our legislatures.

He has affected to render the Military independent of and superior to the Civil power.

He has combined with others to subject us to a jurisdiction foreign to our constitution, and unacknowledged by our laws; giving his Assent to their Acts of pretended Legislation:

For quartering large bodies of armed troops among us:

For protecting them, by a mock Trial, from punishment for any Murders which they should commit on the Inhabitants of these States:

For cutting off our Trade with all parts of the world:

For imposing Taxes on us without our Consent:

For depriving us in many cases, of the benefits of Trial by Jury:

For transporting us beyond Seas to be tried for pretended offences

For abolishing the free System of English Laws in a neighbouring Province, establishing therein an Arbitrary government, and enlarging its Boundaries so as to render it at once an example and fit instrument for introducing the same absolute rule into these Colonies:

For taking away our Charters, abolishing our most valuable Laws, and altering fundamentally the Forms of our Governments:

For suspending our own Legislatures, and declaring themselves invested with power to legislate for us in all cases whatsoever.

He has abdicated Government here, by declaring us out of his Protection and waging War against us.

He has plundered our seas, ravaged our Coasts, burnt our towns, and destroyed the lives of our people.

He is at this time transporting large Armies of foreign Mercenaries to compleat the works of death, desolation and tyranny, already begun with circumstances of Cruelty & perfidy scarcely paralleled in the most barbarous ages, and totally unworthy the Head of a civilized nation.

He has constrained our fellow Citizens taken Captive on the high Seas to bear Arms against their Country, to become the executioners of their friends and Brethren, or to fall themselves by their Hands.

He has excited domestic insurrections amongst us, and has endeavoured to bring on the inhabitants of our frontiers, the merciless Indian Savages, whose known rule of warfare, is an undistinguished destruction of all ages, sexes and conditions.

In every stage of these Oppressions We have Petitioned for Redress in the most humble terms: Our repeated Petitions have been answered only by repeated injury. A Prince whose character is thus marked by every act which may define a Tyrant, is unfit to be the ruler of a free people.

Nor have We been wanting in attentions to our Brittish brethren. We have warned them from time to time of attempts by their legislature to extend an unwarrantable jurisdiction over us. We have reminded them of the circumstances of our emigration and settlement here. We have appealed to their native justice and magnanimity, and we have conjured them by the ties of our common kindred to disavow these usurpations, which, would inevitably interrupt our connections and correspondence. They too have been deaf to the voice of justice and of consanguinity. We must, therefore, acquiesce in the necessity, which denounces our Separation, and hold them, as we hold the rest of mankind, Enemies in War, in Peace Friends.

We, therefore, the Representatives of the united States of America, in General Congress, Assembled, appealing to the Supreme Judge of the world for the rectitude of our intentions, do, in the Name, and by Authority of the good People of these Colonies, solemnly publish and declare, That these United Colonies are, and of Right ought to be Free and Independent States; that they are Absolved from all Allegiance to the British Crown, and that all political connection between them and the State of Great Britain, is and ought to be totally dissolved; and that as Free and Independent States, they have full Power to levy War, conclude Peace, contract Alliances, establish Commerce, and to do all other Acts and Things which Independent States may of right do. And for the support of this Declaration, with a firm reliance on the protection of divine Providence, we mutually pledge to each other our Lives, our Fortunes and our sacred Honor.

Georgia
Button Gwinnett
Lyman Hall
George Walton

North Carolina
William Hooper
Joseph Hewes
John Penn

South Carolina
Edward Rutledge
Thomas Heyward, Jr.
Thomas Lynch, Jr.
Arthur Middleton

Massachusetts
John Hancock

Maryland
Samuel Chase
William Paca
Thomas Stone
Charles Carroll
    of Carrollton

Virginia
George Wythe
Richard Henry Lee
Thomas Jefferson
Benjamin Harrison
Thomas Nelson, Jr.
Francis Lightfoot Lee
Carter Braxton

Pennsylvania
Robert Morris
Benjamin Rush
Benjamin Franklin
John Morton
George Clymer
James Smith
George Taylor
James Wilson
George Ross

Delaware
Caesar Rodney
George Read
Thomas McKean

New York
William Floyd
Philip Livingston
Francis Lewis
Lewis Morris

New Jersey
Richard Stockton
John Witherspoon
Francis Hopkinson
John Hart
Abraham Clark

New Hampshire
Josiah Bartlett
William Whipple

Massachusetts
Samuel Adams
John Adams
Robert Treat Paine
Elbridge Gerry

Rhode Island
Stephen Hopkins
William Ellery

Connecticut
Roger Sherman
Samuel Huntington
William Williams
Oliver Wolcott

New Hampshire
Matthew Thornton

Articles of Confederation (1787)

To ALL TO WHOM these Presents shall come, we the undersigned Delegates of the States affixed to our Names send greeting.

Whereas the Delegates of the United States of America in Congress assembled did on the fifteenth day of November in the Year of our Lord One Thousand Seven Hundred and Seventy-seven, and in the Second Year of the Independence of America agree to certain articles of Confederation and perpetual Union between the States of Newhampshire, Massachusetts-bay, Rhodeisland and Providence Plantations, Connecticut, New York, New Jersey, Pennsylvania, Delaware, Maryland, Virginia, North-Carolina, South-Carolina and Georgia in the Words following, viz.

Articles of Confederation and perpetual Union between the States of Newhampshire, Massachusetts-bay, Rhodeisland and Providence Plantations, Connecticut, New-York, New-Jersey, Pennsylvania, Delaware, Maryland, Virginia, North-Carolina, South-Carolina and Georgia.

ARTICLE I. The stile of this confederacy shall be "The United States of America."

ARTICLE II. Each State retains its sovereignty, freedom and independence, and every power, jurisdiction and right, which is not by this confederation expressly delegated to the United States, in Congress assembled.

ARTICLE III. The said States hereby severally enter into a firm league of friendship with each other, for their common defence, the security of their liberties, and their mutual and general welfare, binding themselves to assist each other, against all force offered to, or attacks made upon them, or any of them, on account of religion, sovereignty, trade or any other pretence whatever.

ARTICLE IV. The better to secure and perpetuate mutual friendship and intercourse among the people of the different States in this Union, the free inhabitants of each of these States, paupers, vagabonds and fugitives from justice excepted, shall be entitled to all privileges and immunities of free citizens in the several States; and the people of each State shall have free ingress and regress to and from any other State, and shall enjoy therein all the privileges of trade and commerce, subject to the same duties, impositions and restrictions as the inhabitants thereof respectively, provided that such restrictions shall not extend so far as to prevent the removal of property imported into any State, to any other State of which the owner is an inhabitant; provided also that no imposition, duties or restriction shall be laid by any State, on the property of the United States, or either of them.

If any person guilty of, or charged with treason, felony, or other high misdemeanor in any State, shall flee from justice, and be found in any of the United States, he shall upon demand of the Governor or Executive power, of the State from which he fled, be delivered up and removed to the State having jurisdiction of his offence.

Full faith and credit shall be given in each of these States to the records, acts and judicial proceedings of the courts and magistrates of every other State.

ARTICLE V. For the more convenient management of the general interests of the United States, delegates shall be annually appointed in such manner as the legislature of each State shall direct, to meet in Congress on the first Monday in November, in every year, with a power reserved to each State, to recall its delegates, or any of them, at any time within the year, and to send others in their stead, for the remainder of the year.

No State shall be represented in Congress by less than two, nor by more than seven members; and no person shall be capable of being a delegate for more than three years in any term of six years; nor shall any person, being a delegate, be capable of holding any office under the United States, for which he, or another for his benefit receives any salary, fees or emolument of any kind.

Each State shall maintain its own delegates in a meeting of the States, and while they act as members of the committee of the States.

In determining questions in the United States, in Congress assembled, each State shall have one vote.

Freedom of speech and debate in Congress shall not be impeached or questioned in any court, or place out of Congress, and the members of Congress shall be protected in their persons from arrests and imprisonments, during the time of their going to and from, and attendance on Congress, except for treason, felony, or breach of the peace.

ARTICLE VI. No State without the consent of the United States in Congress assembled, shall send any embassy to, or receive any embassy from, or enter into any conference, agreement, alliance or treaty with any king, prince or state; nor shall any person holding any office of profit or trust under the United States, or any of them, accept of any present, emolument, office or title of any kind whatever from any king, prince or foreign state; nor shall the United States in Congress assembled, or any of them, grant any title of nobility.

No two or more States shall enter into any treaty, confederation or alliance whatever between them, without the consent of the United States in Congress assembled, specifying accurately the purposes for which the same is to be entered into, and how long it shall continue.

No State shall lay any imposts or duties, which may interfere with any stipulations in treaties, entered into by the United States in Congress assembled, with any king, prince or state, in pursuance of any treaties already proposed by Congress, to the courts of France and Spain.

No vessels of war shall be kept up in time of peace by any State, except such number only, as shall be deemed necessary by the United States in Congress assembled, for the defence of such State, or its trade; nor shall any body of forces be kept up by any State, in time of peace, except such number only, as in the judgment of the United States, in Congress assembled, shall be deemed requisite to garrison the forts necessary for the defence of such State; but every State shall always keep up a well regulated and disciplined militia, sufficiently armed and accoutred, and shall provide and constantly have ready for use, in public stores, a due number of field pieces and tents, and a proper quantity of arms, ammunition and camp equipage.

No State shall engage in any war without the consent of the United States in Congress assembled, unless such State be actually invaded by enemies, or shall have received certain advice of a resolution being formed by some nation of Indians to invade such State, and the danger is so imminent as not to admit of a delay, till the United States in Congress assembled can be consulted: nor shall any State grant commissions to any ships or vessels of war, nor letters of marque or reprisal, except it be after a declaration of war by the United States in Congress assembled, and then only against the kingdom or state and the subjects thereof, against which war has been so declared, and under such regulations as shall be established by the United States in Congress assembled, unless such State be infested by pirates, in which case vessels of war may be fitted out for that occasion, and kept so long as the danger shall continue, or until the United States in Congress assembled shall determine otherwise.

ARTICLE VII. When land-forces are raised by any State of the common defence, all officers of or under the rank of colonel, shall be appointed by the Legislature of each State respectively by whom such forces shall be raised, or in such manner as such State shall direct, and all vacancies shall be filled up by the State which first made the appointment.

ARTICLE VIII. All charges of war, and all other expenses that shall be incurred for the common defence or general welfare, and allowed by the United States in Congress assembled, shall be defrayed out of a common treasury, which shall be supplied by the several States, in proportion to the value of all land within each State, granted to or surveyed for any person, as such land and the buildings and improvements thereon shall be estimated according to such mode as the United States in Congress assembled, shall from time to time direct and appoint.

The taxes for paying that proportion shall be laid and levied by the authority and direction of the Legislatures of the several States within the time agreed upon by the United States in Congress assembled.

ARTICLE IX. The United States in Congress assembled, shall have the sole and exclusive right and power of determining on peace and war, except in the cases mentioned in the sixth article—of sending and receiving ambassadors—entering into treaties and alliances, provided that no treaty of commerce shall be made whereby the legislative power of the respective States shall be restrained from imposing such imposts and duties on foreigners, as their own people are subjected to, or from prohibiting the exportation or importation of and species of goods or commodities whatsoever—of establishing rules for deciding in all cases, what captures on land or water shall be legal, and in what manner prizes taken by land or naval forces in the service of the United States shall be divided or appropriated—of granting letters of marque and reprisal in times of peace—appointing courts for the trial of piracies and felonies committed on the high seas and establishing courts for receiving and determining finally appeals in all cases of captures, provided that no member of Congress shall be appointed a judge of any of the said courts.

The United States in Congress assembled shall also be the last resort on appeal in all disputes and differences now subsisting or that hereafter may arise between two or more States concerning boundary, jurisdiction or any other cause whatever; which authority shall always be exercised in the manner following. Whenever the legislative or executive authority or lawful agent of any State in controversy with another shall present a petition to Congress, stating the matter in question and praying for a hearing, notice thereof shall be given by order of Congress to the legislative or executive authority of the other State in controversy, and a day assigned for the appearance of the parties by their lawful agents, who shall then be directed to appoint by joint consent, commissioners or judges to constitute a court for hearing and determining the matter in question: but if they cannot agree, Congress shall name three persons out of each of the United States, and from the list of such persons each party shall alternately strike out one, the petitioners beginning, until the number shall be reduced to thirteen; and from that number not less than seven, nor more than nine names as Congress shall direct, shall in the presence of Congress be drawn out by lot, and the persons whose names shall be so drawn or any five of them, shall be commissioners or judges, to hear and finally determine the controversy, so always as a major part of the judges who shall hear the cause shall agree in the determination: and if either party shall neglect to attend at the day appointed, without reasons, which Congress shall judge sufficient, or being present shall refuse to strike, the Congress shall proceed to nominate three persons out of each State, and the Secretary of Congress shall strike in behalf of such party absent or refusing; and the judgment and sentence of the court to be appointed, in the manner before prescribed, shall be final and conclusive; and if any of the parties shall refuse to submit to the authority of such court, or to appear or defend their claim or cause, the court shall nevertheless proceed to pronounce sentence, or judgment, which shall in like manner be final and decisive, the judgment or sentence and other proceedings being in either case transmitted to Congress, and lodged among the acts of Congress for the security of the parties concerned: provided that every commissioner, before he sits in judgment, shall take an oath to be administered by one of the judges of the supreme or superior court of the State where the case shall be tried, "well and truly to hear and determine the matter in question, according to the best of his judgment, without favour, affection or hope of reward:" provided also that no State shall be deprived of territory for the benefit of the United States.

All controversies concerning the private right of soil claimed under different grants of two or more States, whose jurisdiction as they may respect such lands, and the states which passed such grants are adjusted, the said grants or either of them being at the same time claimed to have originated antecedent to such settlement of jurisdiction, shall on the petition of either party to the Congress of the United States, be finally determined as near as may be in the same manner as is before prescribed for deciding disputes respecting territorial jurisdiction between different States.

The United States in Congress assembled shall also have the sole and exclusive right and power of regulating the alloy and value of coin struck by their own authority, or by that of the respective States—fixing the standard of weights and measures throughout the United States—regulating the trade and managing all affairs with the Indians, not members of any of the States, provided that the legislative right of any State within its own limits be not infringed or violated—establishing and regulating post-offices from one State to another, throughout all of the United States, and exacting such postage on the papers passing thro' the same as may be requisite to defray the expenses of the said office—appointing all officers of the land forces, in the service of the United States, excepting regimental officers—appointing all the officers of the naval forces, and commissioning all officers whatever in the service of the United States—making rules for the government and regulation of the said land and naval forces, and directing their operations.

The United States in Congress assembled shall have authority to appoint a committee, to sit in the recess of Congress, to be denominated "a Committee of the States," and to consist of one delegate from each State; and to appoint such other committees and civil officers as may be necessary for managing the general affairs of the United States under their direction—to appoint one of their number to preside, provided that no person be allowed to serve in the office of president more than one year in any term of three years; to ascertain the necessary sums of money to be raised for the service of the United States, and to appropriate and apply the same for defraying the public expenses—to borrow money, or emit bills on the credit of the United States, transmitting every half year to the respective States an account of the sums of money so borrowed or emitted,—to build and equip a navy—to agree upon the number of land forces, and to make requisitions from each State for its quota, in proportion to the number of white inhabitants in such State; which requisition shall be binding, and thereupon the Legislature of each State shall appoint the regimental officers, raise the men and cloath, arm and equip them in a soldier like manner, at the expense of the United States; and the officers and men so cloathed, armed and equipped shall march to the place appointed, and within the time agreed on by the United States in Congress assembled: but if the United States in Congress assembled shall, on consideration of circumstances judge proper that any State should not raise men, or should raise a smaller number of men than the quota thereof, such extra number shall be raised, officered, cloathed, armed and equipped in the same manner as the quota of such State, unless the legislature of such State shall judge that such extra number cannot be safely spared out of the same, in which case they shall raise officer, cloath, arm and equip as many of such extra number as they judge can be safely spared. And the officers and men so cloathed, armed and equipped, shall march to the place appointed, and within the time agreed on by the United States in Congress assembled.

The United States in Congress assembled shall never engage in a war, nor grant letters of marque and reprisal in time of peace, nor enter into any treaties or alliances, nor coin money, nor regulate the value thereof, nor ascertain the sums and expenses necessary for the defence and welfare of the United States, or any of them, nor emit bills, nor borrow money on the credit of the United States, nor appropriate money, nor agree upon the number of vessels to be built or purchased, or the number of land or sea forces to be raised, nor appoint a commander in chief of the army or navy, unless nine States assent to the same: nor shall a question on any other point, except for adjourning from day to day be determined, unless by the votes of a majority of the United States in Congress assembled.

The Congress of the United States shall have power to adjourn to any time within the year, and to any place within the United States, so that no period of adjournment be for a longer duration than the space of six months, and shall publish the journal of their proceedings monthly, except such parts thereof relating to treaties, alliances or military operations, as in their judgment require secrecy; and the yeas and nays of the delegates of each State on any question shall be entered on the Journal, when it is desired by any delegate; and the delegates of a State, or any of them, at his or their request shall be furnished with a transcript of the said journal, except such parts as are above excepted, to lay before the Legislatures of the several States.

ARTICLE X. The committee of the States, or any nine of them, shall be authorized to execute, in the recess of Congress, such of the powers of Congress as the United States in Congress assembled, by the consent of nine States, shall from time to time think expedient to vest them with; provided that no power be delegated to the said committee, for the exercise of which, by the articles of confederation, the voice of nine States in the Congress of the United States assembled is requisite.

ARTICLE XI. Canada acceding to this confederation, and joining in the measures of the United States, shall be admitted into, and entitled to all the advantages of this Union: but no other colony shall be admitted into the same, unless such admission be agreed to by nine States.

ARTICLE XII. All bills of credit emitted, monies borrowed and debts contracted by, or under the authority of Congress, before the assembling of the United States, in pursuance of the present confederation, shall be deemed and considered as a charge against the United States, for payment and satisfaction whereof the said United States, and the public faith are hereby solemnly pledged.

ARTICLE XIII. Every State shall abide by the determinations of the United States in Congress assembled, on all questions which by this confederation are submitted to them. And the articles of this confederation shall be inviolably observed by every State, and the Union shall be perpetual; nor shall any alteration at any time hereafter be made in any of them; unless such alteration be agreed to in a Congress of the United States, and be afterwards confirmed by the Legislatures of every State.

And whereas it has pleased the Great Governor of the world to incline the hearts of the Legislatures we respectively represent in Congress, to approve of, and to authorize us to ratify the said articles of confederation and perpetual union. Know ye that we the undersigned delegates, by virtue of the power and authority to us given for that purpose, do by these presents, in the name and in behalf of our respective constituents, fully and entirely ratify and confirm each and every of the said articles of confederation and perpetual union, and all and singular the matters and things therein contained: and we do further solemnly plight and engage the faith of our respective constituents, that they shall abide by the determinations of the United States in Congress assembled, on all questions, which by the said confederation are submitted to them. And that the articles thereof shall be inviolably observed by the States we respectively represent, and that the Union shall be perpetual.

In witness thereof we have hereunto set our hands in Congress. Done at Philadelphia in the State of Pennsylvania the ninth day of July in the year of our Lord one thousand seven hundred and seventy-eight, and in the third year of the independence of America.

The Constitution of the United States (1787)

We the People of the United States, in Order to form a more perfect Union, establish Justice, insure domestic Tranquility, provide for the common defence, promote the general Welfare, and secure the Blessings of Liberty to ourselves and our Posterity, do ordain and establish this Constitution for the United States of America.

Article. I.

Section. 1. All legislative Powers herein granted shall be vested in a Congress of the United States, which shall consist of a Senate and House of Representatives.

Section. 2. The House of Representatives shall be composed of Members chosen every second Year by the People of the several States, and the Electors in each State shall have the Qualifications requisite for Electors of the most numerous Branch of the State Legislature.

No Person shall be a Representative who shall not have attained to the Age of twenty five Years, and been seven Years a Citizen of the United States, and who shall not, when elected, be an Inhabitant of that State in which he shall be chosen.

Representatives and direct Taxes shall be apportioned among the several States which may be included within this Union, according to their respective Numbers, which shall be determined by adding to the whole Number of free Persons, including those bound to Service for a Term of Years, and excluding Indians not taxed, three fifths of all other Persons. The actual Enumeration shall be made within three Years after the first Meeting of the Congress of the United States, and within every subsequent Term of ten Years, in such Manner as they shall by Law direct. The Number of Representatives shall not exceed one for every thirty Thousand, but each State shall have at Least one Representative; and until such enumeration shall be made, the State of New Hampshire shall be entitled to chuse three, Massachusetts eight, Rhode-Island and Providence Plantations one, Connecticut five, New-York six, New Jersey four, Pennsylvania eight, Delaware one, Maryland six, Virginia ten, North Carolina five, South Carolina five, and Georgia three.

When vacancies happen in the Representation from any State, the Executive Authority thereof shall issue Writs of Election to fill such Vacancies.

The House of Representatives shall chuse their Speaker and other Officers; and shall have the sole Power of Impeachment.

Section. 3. The Senate of the United States shall be composed of two Senators from each State, chosen by the Legislature thereof for six Years; and each Senator shall have one Vote.

Immediately after they shall be assembled in Consequence of the first Election, they shall be divided as equally as may be into three Classes. The Seats of the Senators of the first Class shall be vacated at the Expiration of the second Year, of the second Class at the Expiration of the fourth Year, and of the third Class at the Expiration of the sixth Year, so that one third may be chosen every second Year; and if Vacancies happen by Resignation, or otherwise, during the Recess of the Legislature of any State, the Executive thereof may make temporary Appointments until the next Meeting of the Legislature, which shall then fill such Vacancies.

No Person shall be a Senator who shall not have attained to the Age of thirty Years, and been nine Years a Citizen of the United States, and who shall not, when elected, be an Inhabitant of that State for which he shall be chosen.

The Vice President of the United States shall be President of the Senate, but shall have no Vote, unless they be equally divided.

The Senate shall chuse their other Officers, and also a President pro tempore, in the Absence of the Vice President, or when he shall exercise the Office of President of the United States.

The Senate shall have the sole Power to try all Impeachments. When sitting for that Purpose, they shall be on Oath or Affirmation. When the President of the United States is tried, the Chief Justice shall preside: And no Person shall be convicted without the Concurrence of two thirds of the Members present.

Judgment in Cases of Impeachment shall not extend further than to removal from Office, and disqualification to hold and enjoy any Office of honor, Trust or Profit under the United States: but the Party convicted shall nevertheless be liable and subject to Indictment, Trial, Judgment and Punishment, according to Law.

Section. 4. The Times, Places and Manner of holding Elections for Senators and Representatives, shall be prescribed in each State by the Legislature thereof; but the Congress may at any time by Law make or alter such Regulations, except as to the Places of chusing Senators.

The Congress shall assemble at least once in every Year, and such Meeting shall be on the first Monday in December, unless they shall by Law appoint a different Day.

Section. 5. Each House shall be the Judge of the Elections, Returns and Qualifications of its own Members, and a Majority of each shall constitute a Quorum to do Business; but a smaller Number may adjourn from day to day, and may be authorized to compel the Attendance of absent Members, in such Manner, and under such Penalties as each House may provide.

Each House may determine the Rules of its Proceedings, punish its Members for disorderly Behaviour, and, with the Concurrence of two thirds, expel a Member.

Each House shall keep a Journal of its Proceedings, and from time to time publish the same, excepting such Parts as may in their Judgment require Secrecy; and the Yeas and Nays of the Members of either House on any question shall, at the Desire of one fifth of those Present, be entered on the Journal.

Neither House, during the Session of Congress, shall, without the Consent of the other, adjourn for more than three days, nor to any other Place than that in which the two Houses shall be sitting.

Section. 6. The Senators and Representatives shall receive a Compensation for their Services, to be ascertained by Law, and paid out of the Treasury of the United States. They shall in all Cases, except Treason, Felony and Breach of the Peace, be privileged from Arrest during their Attendance at the Session of their respective Houses, and in going to and returning from the same; and for any Speech or Debate in either House, they shall not be questioned in any other Place.

No Senator or Representative shall, during the Time for which he was elected, be appointed to any civil Office under the Authority of the United States, which shall have been created, or the Emoluments whereof shall have been encreased during such time; and no Person holding any Office under the United States, shall be a Member of either House during his Continuance in Office.

Section. 7. All Bills for raising Revenue shall originate in the House of Representatives; but the Senate may propose or concur with Amendments as on other Bills.

Every Bill which shall have passed the House of Representatives and the Senate shall, before it become a Law, be presented to the President of the United States; If he approve he shall sign it, but if not he shall return it, with his Objections to that House in which it shall have originated, who shall enter the Objections at large on their Journal, and proceed to reconsider it. If after such Reconsideration two thirds of that House shall agree to pass the Bill, it shall be sent, together with the Objections, to the other House, by which it shall likewise be reconsidered, and if approved by two thirds of that House, it shall become a Law. But in all such Cases the Votes of both Houses shall be determined by yeas and Nays, and the Names of the Persons voting for and against the Bill shall be entered on the Journal of each House respectively. If any Bill shall not be returned by the President within ten Days (Sundays excepted) after it shall have been presented to him, the Same shall be a Law, in like Manner as if he had signed it, unless the Congress by their Adjournment prevent its Return, in which Case it shall not be a Law.

Every Order, Resolution, or Vote to which the Concurrence of the Senate and House of Representatives may be necessary (except on a question of Adjournment) shall be presented to the President of the United States; and before the Same shall take Effect, shall be approved by him, or being disapproved by him, shall be repassed by two thirds of the Senate and House of Representatives, according to the Rules and Limitations prescribed in the Case of a Bill.

Section. 8. The Congress shall have Power To lay and collect Taxes, Duties, Imposts and Excises, to pay the Debts and provide for the common Defence and general Welfare of the United States; but all Duties, Imposts and Excises shall be uniform throughout the United States;

To borrow Money on the credit of the United States;

To regulate Commerce with foreign Nations, and among the several States, and with the Indian Tribes;

To establish an uniform Rule of Naturalization, and uniform Laws on the subject of Bankruptcies throughout the United States;

To coin Money, regulate the Value thereof, and of foreign Coin, and fix the Standard of Weights and Measures;

To provide for the Punishment of counterfeiting the Securities and current Coin of the United States;

To establish Post Offices and post Roads;

To promote the Progress of Science and useful Arts, by securing for limited Times to Authors and Inventors the exclusive Right to their respective Writings and Discoveries;

To constitute Tribunals inferior to the supreme Court;

To define and punish Piracies and Felonies committed on the high Seas, and Offences against the Law of Nations;

To declare War, grant Letters of Marque and Reprisal, and make Rules concerning Captures on Land and Water;

To raise and support Armies, but no Appropriation of Money to that Use shall be for a longer Term than two Years;

To provide and maintain a Navy;

To make Rules for the Government and Regulation of the land and naval Forces;

To provide for calling forth the Militia to execute the Laws of the Union, suppress Insurrections and repel Invasions;

To provide for organizing, arming, and disciplining, the Militia, and for governing such Part of them as may be employed in the Service of the United States, reserving to the States respectively, the Appointment of the Officers, and the Authority of training the Militia according to the discipline prescribed by Congress;

To exercise exclusive Legislation in all Cases whatsoever, over such District (not exceeding ten Miles square) as may, by Cession of particular States, and the Acceptance of Congress, become the Seat of the Government of the United States, and to exercise like Authority over all Places purchased by the Consent of the Legislature of the State in which the Same shall be, for the Erection of Forts, Magazines, Arsenals, dock-Yards, and other needful Buildings;—And

To make all Laws which shall be necessary and proper for carrying into Execution the foregoing Powers, and all other Powers vested by this Constitution in the Government of the United States, or in any Department or Officer thereof.

Section. 9. The Migration or Importation of such Persons as any of the States now existing shall think proper to admit, shall not be prohibited by the Congress prior to the Year one thousand eight hundred and eight, but a Tax or duty may be imposed on such Importation, not exceeding ten dollars for each Person.

The Privilege of the Writ of Habeas Corpus shall not be suspended, unless when in Cases of Rebellion or Invasion the public Safety may require it.

No Bill of Attainder or ex post facto Law shall be passed.

No Capitation, or other direct, Tax shall be laid, unless in Proportion to the Census or enumeration herein before directed to be taken.

No Tax or Duty shall be laid on Articles exported from any State.

No Preference shall be given by any Regulation of Commerce or Revenue to the Ports of one State over those of another; nor shall Vessels bound to, or from, one State, be obliged to enter, clear, or pay Duties in another.

No Money shall be drawn from the Treasury, but in Consequence of Appropriations made by Law; and a regular Statement and Account of the Receipts and Expenditures of all public Money shall be published from time to time.

No Title of Nobility shall be granted by the United States: And no Person holding any Office of Profit or Trust under them, shall, without the Consent of the Congress, accept of any present, Emolument, Office, or Title, of any kind whatever, from any King, Prince, or foreign State.

Section. 10. No State shall enter into any Treaty, Alliance, or Confederation; grant Letters of Marque and Reprisal; coin Money; emit Bills of Credit; make any Thing but gold and silver Coin a Tender in Payment of Debts; pass any Bill of Attainder, ex post facto Law, or Law impairing the Obligation of Contracts, or grant any Title of Nobility.

No State shall, without the Consent of the Congress, lay any Imposts or Duties on Imports or Exports, except what may be absolutely necessary for executing it's inspection Laws: and the net Produce of all Duties and Imposts, laid by any State on Imports or Exports, shall be for the Use of the Treasury of the United States; and all such Laws shall be subject to the Revision and Controul of the Congress.

No State shall, without the Consent of Congress, lay any Duty of Tonnage, keep Troops, or Ships of War in time of Peace, enter into any Agreement or Compact with another State, or with a foreign Power, or engage in War, unless actually invaded, or in such imminent Danger as will not admit of delay.

Article. II.

Section. 1. The executive Power shall be vested in a President of the United States of America. He shall hold his Office during the Term of four Years, and, together with the Vice President, chosen for the same Term, be elected, as follows:

Each State shall appoint, in such Manner as the Legislature thereof may direct, a Number of Electors, equal to the whole Number of Senators and Representatives to which the State may be entitled in the Congress: but no Senator or Representative, or Person holding an Office of Trust or Profit under the United States, shall be appointed an Elector.

The Electors shall meet in their respective States, and vote by Ballot for two Persons, of whom one at least shall not be an Inhabitant of the same State with themselves. And they shall make a List of all the Persons voted for, and of the Number of Votes for each; which List they shall sign and certify, and transmit sealed to the Seat of the Government of the United States, directed to the President of the Senate. The President of the Senate shall, in the Presence of the Senate and House of Representatives, open all the Certificates, and the Votes shall then be counted. The Person having the greatest Number of Votes shall be the President, if such Number be a Majority of the whole Number of Electors appointed; and if there be more than one who have such Majority, and have an equal Number of Votes, then the House of Representatives shall immediately chuse by Ballot one of them for President; and if no Person have a Majority, then from the five highest on the List the said House shall in like Manner chuse the President. But in chusing the President, the Votes shall be taken by States, the Representation from each State having one Vote; A quorum for this purpose shall consist of a Member or Members from two thirds of the States, and a Majority of all the States shall be necessary to a Choice. In every Case, after the Choice of the President, the Person having the greatest Number of Votes of the Electors shall be the Vice President. But if there should remain two or more who have equal Votes, the Senate shall chuse from them by Ballot the Vice President.

The Congress may determine the Time of chusing the Electors, and the Day on which they shall give their Votes; which Day shall be the same throughout the United States.

No Person except a natural born Citizen, or a Citizen of the United States, at the time of the Adoption of this Constitution, shall be eligible to the Office of President; neither shall any Person be eligible to that Office who shall not have attained to the Age of thirty five Years, and been fourteen Years a Resident within the United States.

In Case of the Removal of the President from Office, or of his Death, Resignation, or Inability to discharge the Powers and Duties of the said Office, the Same shall devolve on the Vice President, and the Congress may by Law provide for the Case of Removal, Death, Resignation or Inability, both of the President and Vice President, declaring what Officer shall then act as President, and such Officer shall act accordingly, until the Disability be removed, or a President shall be elected.

The President shall, at stated Times, receive for his Services, a Compensation, which shall neither be increased nor diminished during the Period for which he shall have been elected, and he shall not receive within that Period any other Emolument from the United States, or any of them.

Before he enter on the Execution of his Office, he shall take the following Oath or Affirmation:—"I do solemnly swear (or affirm) that I will faithfully execute the Office of President of the United States, and will to the best of my Ability, preserve, protect and defend the Constitution of the United States."

Section. 2. The President shall be Commander in Chief of the Army and Navy of the United States, and of the Militia of the several States, when called into the actual Service of the United States; he may require the Opinion, in writing, of the principal Officer in each of the executive Departments, upon any Subject relating to the Duties of their respective Offices, and he shall have Power to grant Reprieves and Pardons for Offences against the United States, except in Cases of Impeachment.

He shall have Power, by and with the Advice and Consent of the Senate, to make Treaties, provided two thirds of the Senators present concur; and he shall nominate, and by and with the Advice and Consent of the Senate, shall appoint Ambassadors, other public Ministers and Consuls, Judges of the supreme Court, and all other Officers of the United States, whose Appointments are not herein otherwise provided for, and which shall be established by Law: but the Congress may by Law vest the Appointment of such inferior Officers, as they think proper, in the President alone, in the Courts of Law, or in the Heads of Departments.

The President shall have Power to fill up all Vacancies that may happen during the Recess of the Senate, by granting Commissions which shall expire at the End of their next Session.

Section. 3. He shall from time to time give to the Congress Information of the State of the Union, and recommend to their Consideration such Measures as he shall judge necessary and expedient; he may, on extraordinary Occasions, convene both Houses, or either of them, and in Case of Disagreement between them, with Respect to the Time of Adjournment, he may adjourn them to such Time as he shall think proper; he shall receive Ambassadors and other public Ministers; he shall take Care that the Laws be faithfully executed, and shall Commission all the Officers of the United States.

Section. 4. The President, Vice President and all civil Officers of the United States, shall be removed from Office on Impeachment for, and Conviction of, Treason, Bribery, or other high Crimes and Misdemeanors.

Article. III.

Section. 1. The judicial Power of the United States shall be vested in one supreme Court, and in such inferior Courts as the Congress may from time to time ordain and establish. The Judges, both of the supreme and inferior Courts, shall hold their Offices during good Behaviour, and shall, at stated Times, receive for their Services a Compensation, which shall not be diminished during their Continuance in Office.

Section. 2. The judicial Power shall extend to all Cases, in Law and Equity, arising under this Constitution, the Laws of the United States, and Treaties made, or which shall be made, under their Authority;—to all Cases affecting Ambassadors, other public Ministers and Consuls;—to all Cases of admiralty and maritime Jurisdiction;—to Controversies to which the United States shall be a Party;—to Controversies between two or more States;— between a State and Citizens of another State,—between Citizens of different States,—between Citizens of the same State claiming Lands under Grants of different States, and between a State, or the Citizens thereof, and foreign States, Citizens or Subjects.

In all Cases affecting Ambassadors, other public Ministers and Consuls, and those in which a State shall be Party, the supreme Court shall have original Jurisdiction. In all the other Cases before mentioned, the supreme Court shall have appellate Jurisdiction, both as to Law and Fact, with such Exceptions, and under such Regulations as the Congress shall make.

The Trial of all Crimes, except in Cases of Impeachment, shall be by Jury; and such Trial shall be held in the State where the said Crimes shall have been committed; but when not committed within any State, the Trial shall be at such Place or Places as the Congress may by Law have directed.

Section. 3. Treason against the United States, shall consist only in levying War against them, or in adhering to their Enemies, giving them Aid and Comfort. No Person shall be convicted of Treason unless on the Testimony of two Witnesses to the same overt Act, or on Confession in open Court.

The Congress shall have Power to declare the Punishment of Treason, but no Attainder of Treason shall work Corruption of Blood, or Forfeiture except during the Life of the Person attainted.

Article. IV.

Section. 1. Full Faith and Credit shall be given in each State to the public Acts, Records, and judicial Proceedings of every other State. And the Congress may by general Laws prescribe the Manner in which such Acts, Records and Proceedings shall be proved, and the Effect thereof.

Section. 2. The Citizens of each State shall be entitled to all Privileges and Immunities of Citizens in the several States.

A Person charged in any State with Treason, Felony, or other Crime, who shall flee from Justice, and be found in another State, shall on Demand of the executive Authority of the State from which he fled, be delivered up, to be removed to the State having Jurisdiction of the Crime.

No Person held to Service or Labour in one State, under the Laws thereof, escaping into another, shall, in Consequence of any Law or Regulation therein, be discharged from such Service or Labour, but shall be delivered up on Claim of the Party to whom such Service or Labour may be due.

Section. 3. New States may be admitted by the Congress into this Union; but no new State shall be formed or erected within the Jurisdiction of any other State; nor any State be formed by the Junction of two or more States, or Parts of States, without the Consent of the Legislatures of the States concerned as well as of the Congress.

The Congress shall have Power to dispose of and make all needful Rules and Regulations respecting the Territory or other Property belonging to the United States; and nothing in this Constitution shall be so construed as to Prejudice any Claims of the United States, or of any particular States.

Section. 4. The United States shall guarantee to every State in this Union a Republican Form of Government, and shall protect each of them against Invasion; and on Application of the Legislature, or of the Executive (when the Legislature cannot be convened), against domestic Violence.

Article. V.

The Congress, whenever two thirds of both Houses shall deem it necessary, shall propose Amendments to this Constitution, or, on the Application of the Legislatures of two thirds of the several States, shall call a Convention for proposing Amendments, which, in either Case, shall be valid to all Intents and Purposes, as Part of this Constitution, when ratified by the Legislatures of three fourths of the several States, or by Conventions in three fourths thereof, as the one or the other Mode of Ratification may be proposed by the Congress; Provided that no Amendment which may be made prior to the Year One thousand eight hundred and eight shall in any Manner affect the first and fourth Clauses in the Ninth Section of the first Article; and that no State, without its Consent, shall be deprived of its equal Suffrage in the Senate.

Article. VI.

All Debts contracted and Engagements entered into, before the Adoption of this Constitution, shall be as valid against the United States under this Constitution, as under the Confederation.

This Constitution, and the Laws of the United States which shall be made in Pursuance thereof; and all Treaties made, or which shall be made, under the Authority of the United States, shall be the supreme Law of the Land; and the Judges in every State shall be bound thereby, any Thing in the Constitution or Laws of any State to the Contrary notwithstanding.

The Senators and Representatives before mentioned, and the Members of the several State Legislatures, and all executive and judicial Officers, both of the United States and of the several States, shall be bound by Oath or Affirmation, to support this Constitution; but no religious Test shall ever be required as a Qualification to any Office or public Trust under the United States.

Article. VII.

The Ratification of the Conventions of nine States, shall be sufficient for the Establishment of this Constitution between the States so ratifying the Same.

The Word, "the," being interlined between the seventh and eighth Lines of the first Page, the Word "Thirty" being partly written on an Erazure in the fifteenth Line of the first Page, The Words "is tried" being interlined between the thirty second and thirty third Lines of the first Page and the Word "the" being interlined between the forty third and forty fourth Lines of the second Page.

Attest William Jackson Secretary

Done in Convention by the Unanimous Consent of the States present the Seventeenth Day of September in the Year of our Lord one thousand seven hundred and Eighty seven and of the Independance of the United States of America the Twelfth In witness whereof We have hereunto subscribed our Names,

G°. Washington
Presidt and deputy from Virginia

Delaware
- Geo: Read
- Gunning Bedford jun
- John Dickinson
- Richard Bassett
- Jaco: Broom

Maryland
- James McHenry
- Dan of St Thos. Jenifer
- Danl. Carrol

Virginia
- John Blair
- James Madison Jr.

North Carolina
- Wm. Blount
- Richd. Dobbs Spaight
- Hu Williamson

South Carolina
- J. Rutledge
- Charles Cotesworth Pinckney
- Charles Pinckney
- Pierce Butler

Georgia
- William Few
- Abr Baldwin

New Hampshire
- John Langdon
- Nicholas Gilman

Massachusetts
- Nathaniel Gorham
- Rufus King

Connecticut
- Wm. Saml. Johnson
- Roger Sherman

New York
- Alexander Hamilton

New Jersey
- Wil: Livingston
- David Brearley
- Wm. Paterson
- Jona: Dayton

Pennsylvania
- B Franklin
- Thomas Mifflin
- Robt. Morris
- Geo. Clymer
- Thos. FitzSimons
- Jared Ingersoll
- James Wilson
- Gouv Morris

Amendments to the Constitution

The Bill of Rights: A Transcription

The Preamble to The Bill of Rights

Congress of the United States
begun and held at the City of New-York, on
Wednesday the fourth of March, one thousand seven hundred and eighty nine.

THE Conventions of a number of the States, having at the time of their adopting the Constitution, expressed a desire, in order to prevent misconstruction or abuse of its powers, that further declaratory and restrictive clauses should be added: And as extending the ground of public confidence in the Government, will best ensure the beneficent ends of its institution.

RESOLVED by the Senate and House of Representatives of the United States of America, in Congress assembled, two thirds of both Houses concurring, that the following Articles be proposed to the Legislatures of the several States, as amendments to the Constitution of the United States, all, or any of which Articles, when ratified by three fourths of the said Legislatures, to be valid to all intents and purposes, as part of the said Constitution; viz.

ARTICLES in addition to, and Amendment of the Constitution of the United States of America, proposed by Congress, and ratified by the Legislatures of the several States, pursuant to the fifth Article of the original Constitution.

Note: The first ten amendments to the Constitution were ratified December 15, 1791, and form what is known as the "Bill of Rights."

Amendment I

Congress shall make no law respecting an establishment of religion, or prohibiting the free exercise thereof; or abridging the freedom of speech, or of the press; or the right of the people peaceably to assemble, and to petition the Government for a redress of grievances.

Amendment II

A well regulated Militia, being necessary to the security of a free State, the right of the people to keep and bear Arms, shall not be infringed.

Amendment III

No Soldier shall, in time of peace be quartered in any house, without the consent of the Owner, nor in time of war, but in a manner to be prescribed by law.

Amendment IV

The right of the people to be secure in their persons, houses, papers, and effects, against unreasonable searches and seizures, shall not be violated, and no Warrants shall issue, but upon probable cause, supported by Oath or affirmation, and particularly describing the place to be searched, and the persons or things to be seized.

Amendment V

No person shall be held to answer for a capital, or otherwise infamous crime, unless on a presentment or indictment of a Grand Jury, except in cases arising in the land or naval forces, or in the Militia, when in actual service in time of War or public danger; nor shall any person be subject for the same offence to be twice put in jeopardy of life or limb; nor shall be compelled in any criminal case to be a witness against himself, nor be deprived of life, liberty, or property, without due process of law; nor shall private property be taken for public use, without just compensation.

Amendment VI

In all criminal prosecutions, the accused shall enjoy the right to a speedy and public trial, by an impartial jury of the State and district wherein the crime shall have been committed, which district shall have been previously ascertained by law, and to be informed of the nature and cause of the accusation; to be confronted with the witnesses against him; to have compulsory process for obtaining witnesses in his favor, and to have the Assistance of Counsel for his defence.

Amendment VII

In Suits at common law, where the value in controversy shall exceed twenty dollars, the right of trial by jury shall be preserved, and no fact tried by a jury, shall be otherwise re-examined in any Court of the United States, than according to the rules of the common law.

Amendment VIII

Excessive bail shall not be required, nor excessive fines imposed, nor cruel and unusual punishments inflicted.

Amendment IX

The enumeration in the Constitution, of certain rights, shall not be construed to deny or disparage others retained by the people.

Amendment X

The powers not delegated to the United States by the Constitution, nor prohibited by it to the States, are reserved to the States respectively, or to the people.

Amendment XI

Passed by Congress March 4, 1794. Ratified February 7, 1795.

Note: Article III, section 2, of the Constitution was modified by amendment 11.

The Judicial power of the United States shall not be construed to extend to any suit in law or equity, commenced or prosecuted against one of the United States by Citizens of another State, or by Citizens or Subjects of any Foreign State.

Amendment XII

Passed by Congress December 9, 1803. Ratified June 15, 1804.

Note: A portion of Article II, section 1 of the Constitution was superseded by the 12th amendment.

The Electors shall meet in their respective states and vote by ballot for President and Vice-President, one of whom, at least, shall not be an inhabitant of the same state with themselves; they shall name in their ballots the person voted for as President, and in distinct ballots the person voted for as Vice-President, and they shall make distinct lists of all persons voted for as President, and of all persons voted for as Vice-President, and of the number of votes for each, which lists they shall sign and certify, and transmit sealed to the seat of the government of the United States, directed to the President of the Senate; — the President of the Senate shall, in the presence of the Senate and House of Representatives, open all the certificates and the votes shall then be counted; — The person having the greatest number of votes for President, shall be the President, if such number be a majority of the whole number of Electors appointed; and if no person have such majority, then from the persons having the highest numbers not exceeding three on the list of those voted for as President, the House of Representatives shall choose immediately, by ballot, the President. But in choosing the President, the votes shall be taken by states, the representation from each state having one vote; a quorum for this purpose shall consist of a member or members from two-thirds of the states, and a majority of all the states shall be necessary to a choice. [And if the House of Representatives shall not choose a President whenever the right of choice shall devolve upon them, before the fourth day of March next following, then the Vice-President shall act as President, as in case of the death or other constitutional disability of the President. —]* The person having the greatest number of votes as Vice-President, shall be the Vice-President, if such number be a majority of the whole number of Electors appointed, and if no person have a majority, then from the two highest numbers on the list, the Senate shall choose the Vice-President; a quorum for the purpose shall consist of two-thirds of the whole number of Senators, and a majority of the whole number shall be necessary to a choice. But no person constitutionally ineligible to the office of President shall be eligible to that of Vice-President of the United States.

Superseded by section 3 of the 20th amendment.

Amendment XIII

Passed by Congress January 31, 1865. Ratified December 6, 1865.

Note: A portion of Article IV, section 2, of the Constitution was superseded by the 13th amendment.

Section 1.
Neither slavery nor involuntary servitude, except as a punishment for crime whereof the party shall have been duly convicted, shall exist within the United States, or any place subject to their jurisdiction.

Section 2.
Congress shall have power to enforce this article by appropriate legislation.

Amendment XIV

Passed by Congress June 13, 1866. Ratified July 9, 1868.

Note: Article I, section 2, of the Constitution was modified by section 2 of the 14th amendment.

Section 1.
All persons born or naturalized in the United States, and subject to the jurisdiction thereof, are citizens of the United States and of the State wherein they reside. No State shall make or enforce any law which shall abridge the privileges or immunities of citizens of the United States; nor shall any State deprive any person of life, liberty, or property, without due process of law; nor deny to any person within its jurisdiction the equal protection of the laws.

Section 2.
Representatives shall be apportioned among the several States according to their respective numbers, counting the whole number of persons in each State, excluding Indians not taxed. But when the right to vote at any election for the choice of electors for President and Vice-President of the United States, Representatives in Congress, the Executive and Judicial officers of a State, or the members of the Legislature thereof, is denied to any of the male inhabitants of such State, being twenty-one years of age,* and citizens of the United States, or in any way abridged, except for participation in rebellion, or other crime, the basis of representation therein shall be reduced in the proportion which the number of such male citizens shall bear to the whole number of male citizens twenty-one years of age in such State.

Section 3.
No person shall be a Senator or Representative in Congress, or elector of President and Vice-President, or hold any office, civil or military, under the United States, or under any State, who, having previously taken an oath, as a member of Congress, or as an officer of the United States, or as a member of any State legislature, or as an executive or judicial officer of any State, to support the Constitution of the United States, shall have engaged in insurrection or rebellion against the same, or given aid or comfort to the enemies thereof. But Congress may by a vote of two-thirds of each House, remove such disability.

Section 4.

The validity of the public debt of the United States, authorized by law, including debts incurred for payment of pensions and bounties for services in suppressing insurrection or rebellion, shall not be questioned. But neither the United States nor any State shall assume or pay any debt or obligation incurred in aid of insurrection or rebellion against the United States, or any claim for the loss or emancipation of any slave; but all such debts, obligations and claims shall be held illegal and void.

Section 5.

The Congress shall have the power to enforce, by appropriate legislation, the provisions of this article.

Changed by section 1 of the 26th amendment.

Amendment XV

Passed by Congress February 26, 1869. Ratified February 3, 1870.

Section 1.

The right of citizens of the United States to vote shall not be denied or abridged by the United States or by any State on account of race, color, or previous condition of servitude—

Section 2.

The Congress shall have the power to enforce this article by appropriate legislation.

Amendment XVI

Passed by Congress July 2, 1909. Ratified February 3, 1913.

Note: Article I, section 9, of the Constitution was modified by amendment 16.

The Congress shall have power to lay and collect taxes on incomes, from whatever source derived, without apportionment among the several States, and without regard to any census or enumeration.

Amendment XVII

Passed by Congress May 13, 1912. Ratified April 8, 1913.

Note: Article I, section 3, of the Constitution was modified by the 17th amendment.

The Senate of the United States shall be composed of two Senators from each State, elected by the people thereof, for six years; and each Senator shall have one vote. The electors in each State shall have the qualifications requisite for electors of the most numerous branch of the State legislatures.

When vacancies happen in the representation of any State in the Senate, the executive authority of such State shall issue writs of election to fill such vacancies: *Provided,* That the legislature of any State may empower the executive thereof to make temporary appointments until the people fill the vacancies by election as the legislature may direct.

This amendment shall not be so construed as to affect the election or term of any Senator chosen before it becomes valid as part of the Constitution.

Amendment XVIII

Passed by Congress December 18, 1917. Ratified January 16, 1919. Repealed by amendment 21.

Section 1.
After one year from the ratification of this article the manufacture, sale, or transportation of intoxicating liquors within, the importation thereof into, or the exportation thereof from the United States and all territory subject to the jurisdiction thereof for beverage purposes is hereby prohibited.

Section 2.
The Congress and the several States shall have concurrent power to enforce this article by appropriate legislation.

Section 3.
This article shall be inoperative unless it shall have been ratified as an amendment to the Constitution by the legislatures of the several States, as provided in the Constitution, within seven years from the date of the submission hereof to the States by the Congress.

Amendment XIX

Passed by Congress June 4, 1919. Ratified August 18, 1920.

The right of citizens of the United States to vote shall not be denied or abridged by the United States or by any State on account of sex.

Congress shall have power to enforce this article by appropriate legislation.

Amendment XX

Passed by Congress March 2, 1932. Ratified January 23, 1933.

Note: Article I, section 4, of the Constitution was modified by section 2 of this amendment. In addition, a portion of the 12th amendment was superseded by section 3.

Section 1.
The terms of the President and the Vice President shall end at noon on the 20th day of January, and the terms of Senators and Representatives at noon on the 3rd day of January, of the years in which such terms would have ended if this article had not been ratified; and the terms of their successors shall then begin.

Section 2.

The Congress shall assemble at least once in every year, and such meeting shall begin at noon on the 3d day of January, unless they shall by law appoint a different day.

Section 3.

If, at the time fixed for the beginning of the term of the President, the President elect shall have died, the Vice President elect shall become President. If a President shall not have been chosen before the time fixed for the beginning of his term, or if the President elect shall have failed to qualify, then the Vice President elect shall act as President until a President shall have qualified; and the Congress may by law provide for the case wherein neither a President elect nor a Vice President shall have qualified, declaring who shall then act as President, or the manner in which one who is to act shall be selected, and such person shall act accordingly until a President or Vice President shall have qualified.

Section 4.

The Congress may by law provide for the case of the death of any of the persons from whom the House of Representatives may choose a President whenever the right of choice shall have devolved upon them, and for the case of the death of any of the persons from whom the Senate may choose a Vice President whenever the right of choice shall have devolved upon them.

Section 5.

Sections 1 and 2 shall take effect on the 15th day of October following the ratification of this article.

Section 6.

This article shall be inoperative unless it shall have been ratified as an amendment to the Constitution by the legislatures of three-fourths of the several States within seven years from the date of its submission.

Amendment XXI

Passed by Congress February 20, 1933. Ratified December 5, 1933.

Section 1.

The eighteenth article of amendment to the Constitution of the United States is hereby repealed.

Section 2.

The transportation or importation into any State, Territory, or Possession of the United States for delivery or use therein of intoxicating liquors, in violation of the laws thereof, is hereby prohibited.

Section 3.

This article shall be inoperative unless it shall have been ratified as an amendment to the Constitution by conventions in the several States, as provided in the Constitution, within seven years from the date of the submission hereof to the States by the Congress.

Amendment XXII

Passed by Congress March 21, 1947. Ratified February 27, 1951.

Section 1.

No person shall be elected to the office of the President more than twice, and no person who has held the office of President, or acted as President, for more than two years of a term to which some other person was elected President shall be elected to the office of President more than once. But this Article shall not apply to any person holding the office of President when this Article was proposed by Congress, and shall not prevent any person who may be holding the office of President, or acting as President, during the term within which this Article becomes operative from holding the office of President or acting as President during the remainder of such term.

Section 2.

This article shall be inoperative unless it shall have been ratified as an amendment to the Constitution by the legislatures of three-fourths of the several States within seven years from the date of its submission to the States by the Congress.

Amendment XXIII

Passed by Congress June 16, 1960. Ratified March 29, 1961.

Section 1.

The District constituting the seat of Government of the United States shall appoint in such manner as Congress may direct:

A number of electors of President and Vice President equal to the whole number of Senators and Representatives in Congress to which the District would be entitled if it were a State, but in no event more than the least populous State; they shall be in addition to those appointed by the States, but they shall be considered, for the purposes of the election of President and Vice President, to be electors appointed by a State; and they shall meet in the District and perform such duties as provided by the twelfth article of amendment.

Section 2.

The Congress shall have power to enforce this article by appropriate legislation.

Amendment XXIV

Passed by Congress August 27, 1962. Ratified January 23, 1964.

Section 1.

The right of citizens of the United States to vote in any primary or other election for President or Vice President, for electors for President or Vice President, or for Senator or Representative in Congress, shall not be denied or abridged by the United States or any State by reason of failure to pay poll tax or other tax.

Section 2.

The Congress shall have power to enforce this article by appropriate legislation.

Amendment XXV

Passed by Congress July 6, 1965. Ratified February 10, 1967.

Note: Article II, section 1, of the Constitution was affected by the 25th amendment.

Section 1.
In case of the removal of the President from office or of his death or resignation, the Vice President shall become President.

Section 2.
Whenever there is a vacancy in the office of the Vice President, the President shall nominate a Vice President who shall take office upon confirmation by a majority vote of both Houses of Congress.

Section 3.
Whenever the President transmits to the President pro tempore of the Senate and the Speaker of the House of Representatives his written declaration that he is unable to discharge the powers and duties of his office, and until he transmits to them a written declaration to the contrary, such powers and duties shall be discharged by the Vice President as Acting President.

Section 4.
Whenever the Vice President and a majority of either the principal officers of the executive departments or of such other body as Congress may by law provide, transmit to the President pro tempore of the Senate and the Speaker of the House of Representatives their written declaration that the President is unable to discharge the powers and duties of his office, the Vice President shall immediately assume the powers and duties of the office as Acting President.

Thereafter, when the President transmits to the President pro tempore of the Senate and the Speaker of the House of Representatives his written declaration that no inability exists, he shall resume the powers and duties of his office unless the Vice President and a majority of either the principal officers of the executive department or of such other body as Congress may by law provide, transmit within four days to the President pro tempore of the Senate and the Speaker of the House of Representatives their written declaration that the President is unable to discharge the powers and duties of his office. Thereupon Congress shall decide the issue, assembling within forty-eight hours for that purpose if not in session. If the Congress, within twenty-one days after receipt of the latter written declaration, or, if Congress is not in session, within twenty-one days after Congress is required to assemble, determines by two-thirds vote of both Houses that the President is unable to discharge the powers and duties of his office, the Vice President shall continue to discharge the same as Acting President; otherwise, the President shall resume the powers and duties of his office.

Amendment XXVI

Passed by Congress March 23, 1971. Ratified July 1, 1971.

Note: Amendment 14, section 2, of the Constitution was modified by section 1 of the 26th amendment.

Section 1.
The right of citizens of the United States, who are eighteen years of age or older, to vote shall not be denied or abridged by the United States or by any State on account of age.

Section 2.
The Congress shall have power to enforce this article by appropriate legislation.

Amendment XXVII

Originally proposed Sept. 25, 1789. Ratified May 7, 1992.

No law, varying the compensation for the services of the Senators and Representatives, shall take effect, until an election of representatives shall have intervened.

PRESIDENTIAL ELECTIONS

Year	Number of States	Candidates	Parties	Popular Vote	% of Popular Vote	Electoral Vote	% Voter Participation
1789	11	**GEORGE WASHINGTON**	No party designations			69	
		John Adams				34	
		Other candidates				35	
1792	15	**GEORGE WASHINGTON**	No party designations			132	
		John Adams				77	
		George Clinton				50	
		Other candidates				5	
1796	16	**JOHN ADAMS**	Federalist			71	
		Thomas Jefferson	Democratic-Republican			68	
		Thomas Pinckney	Federalist			59	
		Aaron Burr	Democratic-Republican			30	
		Other candidates				48	
1800	16	**THOMAS JEFFERSON**	Democratic-Republican			73	
		Aaron Burr	Democratic-Republican			73	
		John Adams	Federalist			65	
		Charles C. Pinckney	Federalist			64	
		John Jay	Federalist			1	
1804	17	**THOMAS JEFFERSON**	Democratic-Republican			162	
		Charles C. Pinckney	Federalist			14	
1808	17	**JAMES MADISON**	Democratic-Republican			122	
		Charles C. Pinckney	Federalist			47	
		George Clinton	Democratic-Republican			6	
1812	18	**JAMES MADISON**	Democratic-Republican			128	
		DeWitt Clinton	Federalist			89	
1816	19	**JAMES MONROE**	Democratic-Republican			183	
		Rufus King	Federalist			34	
1820	24	**JAMES MONROE**	Democratic-Republican			231	
		John Quincy Adams	Independent			1	

Year	Number of States	Candidates	Parties	Popular Vote	% Popular Vote	Electoral Vote	% Voter Participation
1824	24	**JOHN QUINCY ADAMS**	Democratic-Republican	108,740	30.5	84	26.9
		Andrew Jackson	Democratic-Republican	153,544	43.1	99	
		Henry Clay	Democratic-Republican	47,136	13.2	37	
		William H. Crawford	Democratic-Republican	46,618	13.1	41	
1828	24	**ANDREW JACKSON**	Democratic	647,286	56.0	178	57.6
		John Quincy Adams	National-Republican	508,064	44.0	83	
1832	24	**ANDREW JACKSON**	Democratic	688,242	54.5	219	55.4
		Henry Clay	National-Republican	473,462	37.5	49	
		William Wirt	Anti-Masonic	101,051	8.0	7	
		John Floyd	Democratic			11	
1836	26	**MARTIN VAN BUREN**	Democratic	765,483	50.9	170	57.8
		William H. Harrison	Whig	739,795	49.1	73	
		Hugh L. White	Whig			26	
		Daniel Webster	Whig			14	
		W. P. Mangum	Whig			11	
1840	26	**WILLIAM H. HARRISON**	Whig	1,274,624	53.1	234	80.2
		Martin Van Buren	Democratic	1,127,781	46.9	60	
1844	26	**JAMES K. POLK**	Democratic	1,338,464	49.6	170	78.9
		Henry Clay	Whig	1,300,097	48.1	105	
		James G. Birney	Liberty	62,300	2.3		
1848	30	**ZACHARY TAYLOR**	Whig	1,360,967	47.4	163	72.7
		Lewis Cass	Democratic	1,222,342	42.5	127	
		Martin Van Buren	Free Soil	291,263	10.1		
1852	31	**FRANKLIN PIERCE**	Democratic	1,601,117	50.9	254	69.6
		Winfield Scott	Whig	1,385,453	44.1	42	
		John P. Hale	Free Soil	155,825	5.0		

Year	Number of States	Candidates	Parties	Popular Vote	% of Popular Vote	Electoral Vote	% Voter Participation
1856	31	JAMES BUCHANAN	Democratic	1,832,955	45.3	174	78.9
		John C. Frémont	Republican	1,339,932	33.1	114	
		Millard Fillmore	American	871,731	21.6	8	
1860	33	ABRAHAM LINCOLN	Republican	1,865,593	39.8	180	81.2
		Stephen A. Douglas	Democratic	1,382,713	29.5	12	
		John C. Breckinridge	Democratic	848,356	18.1	72	
		John Bell	Constitutional Union	592,906	12.6	39	
1864	36	ABRAHAM LINCOLN	Republican	2,206,938	55.0	212	73.8
		George B. McClellan	Democratic	1,803,787	45.0	21	
1868	37	ULYSSES S. GRANT	Republican	3,013,421	52.7	214	78.1
		Horatio Seymour	Democratic	2,706,829	47.3	80	
1872	37	ULYSSES S. GRANT	Republican	3,596,745	55.6	286	71.3
		Horace Greeley	Democratic	2,843,446	43.9	66	
1876	38	Rutherford B. Hayes	Republican	4,036,572	48.0	185	81.8
		Samuel J. Tilden	Democratic	4,284,020	51.0	184	
1880	38	JAMES A. GARFIELD	Republican	4,453,295	48.5	214	79.4
		Winfield S. Hancock	Democratic	4,414,082	48.1	155	
		James B. Weaver	Greenback-Labor	308,578	3.4		
1884	38	GROVER CLEVELAND	Democratic	4,879,507	48.5	219	77.5
		James G. Blaine	Republican	4,850,293	48.2	182	
		Benjamin F. Butler	Greenback-Labor	175,370	1.8		
		John P. St. John	Prohibition	150,369	1.5		
1888	38	BENJAMIN HARRISON	Republican	5,477,129	47.9	233	79.3
		Grover Cleveland	Democratic	5,537,857	48.6	168	
		Clinton B. Fisk	Prohibition	249,506	2.2		
		Anson J. Streeter	Union Labor	146,935	1.3		

Year		Candidate	Party	Popular Vote	%	Electoral Vote	Voter Participation
1892	44	**GROVER CLEVELAND**	Democratic	5,555,426	46.1	277	74.7
		Benjamin Harrison	Republican	5,182,690	43.0	145	
		James B. Weaver	People's	1,029,846	8.5	22	
		John Bidwell	Prohibition	264,133	2.2		
1896	45	**WILLIAM MCKINLEY**	Republican	7,102,246	51.1	271	79.3
		William J. Bryan	Democratic	6,492,559	47.7	176	
1900	45	**WILLIAM MCKINLEY**	Republican	7,218,491	51.7	292	73.2
		William J. Bryan	Democratic; Populist	6,356,734	45.5	155	
		John C. Wooley	Prohibition	208,914	1.5		
1904	45	**THEODORE ROOSEVELT**	Republican	7,628,461	57.4	336	65.2
		Alton B. Parker	Democratic	5,084,223	37.6	140	
		Eugene V. Debs	Socialist	402,283	3.0		
		Silas C. Swallow	Prohibition	258,536	1.9		
1908	46	**WILLIAM H. TAFT**	Republican	7,675,320	51.6	321	65.4
		William J. Bryan	Democratic	6,412,294	43.1	162	
		Eugene V. Debs	Socialist	420,793	2.8		
		Eugene W. Chafin	Prohibition	253,840	1.7		
1912	48	**WOODROW WILSON**	Democratic	6,296,547	41.9	435	58.8
		Theodore Roosevelt	Progressive	4,118,571	27.4	88	
		William H. Taft	Republican	3,486,720	23.2	8	
		Eugene V. Debs	Socialist	900,672	6.0		
		Eugene W. Chafin	Prohibition	206,275	1.4		
1916	48	**WOODROW WILSON**	Democratic	9,127,695	49.4	277	61.6
		Charles E. Hughes	Republican	8,533,507	46.2	254	
		A. L. Benson	Socialist	585,113	3.2		
		J. Frank Hanly	Prohibition	220,506	1.2		
1920	48	**WARREN G. HARDING**	Republican	16,143,407	60.4	404	49.2
		James M. Cox	Democratic	9,130,328	34.2	127	
		Eugene V. Debs	Socialist	919,799	3.4		
		P. P. Christensen	Farmer-Labor	265,411	1.0		

Year	Number of States	Candidates	Parties	Popular Vote	% of Popular Vote	Electoral Vote	% Voter Participation
1924	48	CALVIN COOLIDGE	Republican	15,718,211	54.0	382	48.9
		John W. Davis	Democratic	8,385,283	28.8	136	
		Robert M. La Follette	Progressive	4,831,289	16.6	13	
1928	48	HERBERT C. HOOVER	Republican	21,391,993	58.2	444	56.9
		Alfred E. Smith	Democratic	15,016,169	40.9	87	
1932	48	FRANKLIN D. ROOSEVELT	Democratic	22,809,638	57.4	472	56.9
		Herbert C. Hoover	Republican	15,758,901	39.7	59	
		Norman Thomas	Socialist	881,951	2.2		
1936	48	FRANKLIN D. ROOSEVELT	Democratic	27,752,869	60.8	523	61.0
		Alfred M. Landon	Republican	16,674,665	36.5	8	
		William Lemke	Union	882,479	1.9		
1940	48	FRANKLIN D. ROOSEVELT	Democratic	27,307,819	54.8	449	62.5
		Wendell L. Willkie	Republican	22,321,018	44.8	82	
1944	48	FRANKLIN D. ROOSEVELT	Democratic	25,606,585	53.5	432	55.9
		Thomas E. Dewey	Republican	22,014,745	46.0	99	
1948	48	HARRY S. TRUMAN	Democratic	24,179,345	49.6	303	53.0
		Thomas E. Dewey	Republican	21,991,291	45.1	189	
		J. Strom Thurmond	States' Rights	1,176,125	2.4	39	
		Henry A. Wallace	Progressive	1,157,326	2.4		
1952	48	DWIGHT D. EISENHOWER	Republican	33,936,234	55.1	442	63.3
		Adlai E. Stevenson	Democratic	27,314,992	44.4	89	
1956	48	DWIGHT D. EISENHOWER	Republican	35,590,472	57.6	457	60.6
		Adlai E. Stevenson	Democratic	26,022,752	42.1	73	
1960	50	JOHN F. KENNEDY	Democratic	34,226,731	49.7	303	62.8
		Richard M. Nixon	Republican	34,108,157	49.5	219	
1964	50	LYNDON B. JOHNSON	Democratic	43,129,566	61.1	486	61.9
		Barry M. Goldwater	Republican	27,178,188	38.5	52	
1968	50	RICHARD M. NIXON	Republican	31,785,480	43.4	301	60.9
		Hubert H. Humphrey	Democratic	31,275,166	42.7	191	
		George C. Wallace	American Independent	9,906,473	13.5	46	

Year	Number of States	Candidates	Parties	Popular Vote	% of Popular Vote	Electoral Vote	% Voter Participation
1972	50	RICHARD M. NIXON	Republican	47,169,911	60.7	520	55.2
		George S. McGovern	Democratic	29,170,383	37.5	17	
		John G. Schmitz	American	1,099,482	1.4		
1976	50	JIMMY CARTER	Democratic	40,830,763	50.1	297	53.5
		Gerald R. Ford	Republican	39,147,793	48.0	240	
1980	50	RONALD REAGAN	Republican	43,901,812	50.7	489	52.6
		Jimmy Carter	Democratic	35,483,820	41.0	49	
		John B. Anderson	Independent	5,719,437	6.6		
		Ed Clark	Libertarian	921,188	1.1		
1984	50	RONALD REAGAN	Republican	54,451,521	58.8	525	53.1
		Walter F. Mondale	Democratic	37,565,334	40.6	13	
1988	50	GEORGE H. W. BUSH	Republican	47,917,341	53.4	426	50.1
		Michael Dukakis	Democratic	41,013,030	45.6	111	
1992	50	BILL CLINTON	Democratic	44,908,254	43.0	370	55.0
		George H. W. Bush	Republican	39,102,343	37.4	168	
		H. Ross Perot	Independent	19,741,065	18.9		
1996	50	BILL CLINTON	Democratic	47,401,185	49.0	379	49.0
		Bob Dole	Republican	39,197,469	41.0	159	
		H. Ross Perot	Independent	8,085,295	8.0		
2000	50	GEORGE W. BUSH	Republican	50,455,156	47.9	271	50.4
		Al Gore	Democrat	50,997,335	48.4	266	
		Ralph Nader	Green	2,882,897	2.7		
2004	50	GEORGE W. BUSH	Republican	62,040,610	50.7	286	60.7
		John F. Kerry	Democrat	59,028,444	48.3	251	
2008	50	BARACK OBAMA	Democrat	69,456,897	52.9	365	63.0
		John McCain	Republican	59,934,814	45.7	173	
2012	50	BARACK OBAMA	Democrat	65,915,795	51.1	332	57.5
		Mitt Romney	Republican	60,933,504	47.2	206	
2016	50	DONALD TRUMP	Republican	62,979,636	46.1	304	60.2
		Hillary Rodham Clinton	Democrat	65,844,610	48.2	227	

Candidates receiving less than 1 percent of the popular vote have been omitted. Thus the percentage of popular vote given for any election year may not total 100 percent. Before the passage of the Twelfth Amendment in 1804, the electoral college voted for two presidential candidates; the runner-up became vice president.

ADMISSION OF STATES

Order of Admission	State	Date of Admission	Order of Admission	State	Date of Admission
1	Delaware	December 7, 1787	26	Michigan	January 26, 1837
2	Pennsylvania	December 12, 1787	27	Florida	March 3, 1845
3	New Jersey	December 18, 1787	28	Texas	December 29, 1845
4	Georgia	January 2, 1788	29	Iowa	December 28, 1846
5	Connecticut	January 9, 1788	30	Wisconsin	May 29, 1848
6	Massachusetts	February 7, 1788	31	California	September 9, 1850
7	Maryland	April 28, 1788	32	Minnesota	May 11, 1858
8	South Carolina	May 23, 1788	33	Oregon	February 14, 1859
9	New Hampshire	June 21, 1788	34	Kansas	January 29, 1861
10	Virginia	June 25, 1788	35	West Virginia	June 30, 1863
11	New York	July 26, 1788	36	Nevada	October 31, 1864
12	North Carolina	November 21, 1789	37	Nebraska	March 1, 1867
13	Rhode Island	May 29, 1790	38	Colorado	August 1, 1876
14	Vermont	March 4, 1791	39	North Dakota	November 2, 1889
15	Kentucky	June 1, 1792	40	South Dakota	November 2, 1889
16	Tennessee	June 1, 1796	41	Montana	November 8, 1889
17	Ohio	March 1, 1803	42	Washington	November 11, 1889
18	Louisiana	April 30, 1812	43	Idaho	July 3, 1890
19	Indiana	December 11, 1816	44	Wyoming	July 10, 1890
20	Mississippi	December 10, 1817	45	Utah	January 4, 1896
21	Illinois	December 3, 1818	46	Oklahoma	November 16, 1907
22	Alabama	December 14, 1819	47	New Mexico	January 6, 1912
23	Maine	March 15, 1820	48	Arizona	February 14, 1912
24	Missouri	August 10, 1821	49	Alaska	January 3, 1959
25	Arkansas	June 15, 1836	50	Hawaii	August 21, 1959

POPULATION OF THE UNITED STATES

Year	Number of States	Population	% Increase	Population per Square Mile
1790	13	3,929,214		4.5
1800	16	5,308,483	35.1	6.1
1810	17	7,239,881	36.4	4.3
1820	23	9,638,453	33.1	5.5
1830	24	12,866,020	33.5	7.4
1840	26	17,069,453	32.7	9.8
1850	31	23,191,876	35.9	7.9
1860	33	31,443,321	35.6	10.6
1870	37	39,818,449	26.6	13.4
1880	38	50,155,783	26.0	16.9
1890	44	62,947,714	25.5	21.1
1900	45	75,994,575	20.7	25.6
1910	46	91,972,266	21.0	31.0
1920	48	105,710,620	14.9	35.6
1930	48	122,775,046	16.1	41.2
1940	48	131,669,275	7.2	44.2
1950	48	150,697,361	14.5	50.7
1960	50	179,323,175	19.0	50.6
1970	50	203,235,298	13.3	57.5
1980	50	226,504,825	11.4	64.0
1985	50	237,839,000	5.0	67.2
1990	50	250,122,000	5.2	70.6
1995	50	263,411,707	5.3	74.4
2000	50	281,421,906	6.8	77.0
2005	50	296,410,404	5.3	77.9
2010	50	308,745,538	9.7	87.4
2015	50	321,931,311	4.3	91.1

IMMIGRATION TO THE UNITED STATES, FISCAL YEARS 1820–2015

Year	Number	Year	Number	Year	Number	Year	Number
1820–1989	**55,457,531**	**1871–80**	**2,812,191**	**1921–30**	**4,107,209**	**1971–80**	**4,493,314**
1820	8,385	1871	321,350	1921	805,228	1971	370,478
1821–30	**143,439**	1872	404,806	1922	309,556	1972	384,685
1821	9,127	1873	459,803	1923	522,919	1973	400,063
1822	6,911	1874	313,339	1924	706,896	1974	394,861
1823	6,354	1875	227,498	1925	294,314	1975	386,914
1824	7,912	1876	169,986	1926	304,488	1976	398,613
1825	10,199	1877	141,857	1927	335,175	1976	103,676
1826	10,837	1878	138,469	1928	307,255	1977	462,315
1827	18,875	1879	177,826	1929	279,678	1978	601,442
1828	27,382	1880	457,257	1930	241,700	1979	460,348
1829	22,520	**1881–90**	**5,246,613**	**1931–40**	**528,431**	1980	530,639
1830	23,322	1881	669,431	1931	97,139	**1981–90**	**7,338,062**
1831–40	**599,125**	1882	788,992	1932	35,576	1981	596,600
1831	22,633	1883	603,322	1933	23,068	1982	594,131
1832	60,482	1884	518,592	1934	29,470	1983	559,763
1833	58,640	1885	395,346	1935	34,956	1984	543,903
1834	65,365	1886	334,203	1936	36,329	1985	570,009
1835	45,374	1887	490,109	1937	50,244	1986	601,708
1836	76,242	1888	546,889	1938	67,895	1987	601,516
1837	79,340	1889	444,427	1939	82,998	1988	643,025
1838	38,914	1890	455,302	1940	70,756	1989	1,090,924
1839	68,069	**1891–1900**	**3,687,564**	**1941–50**	**1,035,039**	1990	1,536,483
1840	84,066	1891	560,319	1941	51,776	**1991–2000**	**9,090,857**
1841–50	**1,713,251**	1892	579,663	1942	28,781	1991	1,827,167
1841	80,289	1893	439,730	1943	23,725	1992	973,977
1842	104,565	1894	285,631	1944	28,551	1993	904,292
		1895	258,536	1945	38,119	1994	804,416
		1896	343,267	1946	108,721		

Year	Number	Year	Number	Year	Number	Year	Number
1843	52,496	1897	230,832	1947	147,292	1995	720,461
1844	78,615	1898	229,299	1948	170,570	1996	915,900
1845	114,371	1899	311,715	1949	188,317	1997	798,378
1846	154,416	1900	448,572	1950	249,187	1998	660,477
1847	234,968					1999	644,787
1848	226,527	**1901–10**	**8,795,386**	**1951–60**	**2,515,479**	2000	841,002
1849	297,024	1901	487,918	1951	205,717		
1850	369,980	1902	648,743	1952	265,520	**2001–10**	**10,503,454**
		1903	857,046	1953	170,434	2001	1,058,902
1851–60	**2,598,214**	1904	812,870	1954	208,177	2002	1,059,356
1851	379,466	1905	1,026,499	1955	237,790	2003	705,827
1852	371,603	1906	1,100,735	1956	321,625	2004	957,883
1853	368,645	1907	1,285,349	1957	326,867	2005	1,122,373
1854	427,833	1908	782,870	1958	253,265	2006	1,266,129
1855	200,877	1909	751,786	1959	260,686	2007	1,052,415
1856	200,436	1910	1,041,570	1960	265,398	2008	1,107,126
1857	251,306					2009	1,130,818
1858	123,126	**1911–20**	**5,735,811**	**1961–70**	**3,321,677**	2010	1,042,625
1859	121,282	1911	878,587	1961	271,344		
1860	153,640	1912	838,172	1962	283,763	**2011–15**	**5,356,671**
		1913	1,197,892	1963	306,260	2011	1,062,040
1861–70	**2,314,824**	1914	1,218,480	1964	292,248	2012	1,031,631
1861	91,918	1915	326,700	1965	296,697	2013	523,000
1862	91,985	1916	298,826	1966	323,040	2014	1,360,000
1863	176,282	1917	295,403	1967	361,972	2015	1,380,000
1864	193,418	1918	110,618	1968	454,448		
1865	248,120	1919	141,132	1969	358,579		
1866	318,568	1920	430,001	1970	373,326		
1867	315,722						
1868	138,840						
1869	352,768						
1870	387,203						

Source: U.S. Department of Homeland Security.

IMMIGRATION BY REGION AND SELECTED COUNTRY OF LAST RESIDENCE, FISCAL YEARS 1820–2015

Region and country of last residence	1820 to 1829	1830 to 1839	1840 to 1849	1850 to 1859	1860 to 1869	1870 to 1879	1880 to 1889	1890 to 1899
Total	128,502	538,381	1,427,337	2,814,554	2,081,261	2,742,137	5,248,568	3,694,294
Europe	99,272	422,771	1,369,259	2,619,680	1,877,726	2,251,878	4,638,677	3,576,411
Austria-Hungary	—	—	—	—	3,375	60,127	314,787	534,059
Austria	—	—	—	—	2,700	54,529	204,805	268,218
Hungary	—	—	—	—	483	5,598	109,982	203,350
Belgium	28	20	3,996	5,765	5,785	6,991	18,738	19,642
Bulgaria	—	—	—	—	—	—	—	52
*Former Czechoslovakia	—	—	—	—	—	—	—	—
Denmark	173	927	671	3,227	13,553	29,278	85,342	56,671
Finland	—	—	—	—	—	—	—	—
France	7,694	39,330	75,300	81,778	35,938	71,901	48,193	35,616
Germany	5,753	124,726	385,434	976,072	723,734	751,769	1,445,181	579,072
Greece	17	49	17	32	51	209	1,807	12,732
Ireland	51,617	170,672	656,145	1,029,486	427,419	422,264	674,061	405,710
Italy	430	2,225	1,476	8,643	9,853	46,296	267,660	603,761
Netherlands	1,105	1,377	7,624	11,122	8,387	14,267	52,715	29,349
Norway-Sweden	91	1,149	12,389	22,202	82,937	178,823	586,441	334,058
Norway	—	—	—	—	16,068	88,644	185,111	96,810
Sweden	—	—	—	—	24,224	90,179	401,330	237,248
Poland	19	366	105	1,087	1,886	11,016	42,910	107,793
Portugal	177	820	196	1,299	2,083	13,971	15,186	25,874
Romania	—	—	—	—	—	—	5,842	6,808
Russia	86	280	520	423	1,670	35,177	182,698	450,101
Spain	2,595	2,010	1,916	8,795	6,966	5,540	3,995	9,189
Switzerland	3,148	4,430	4,819	24,423	21,124	25,212	81,151	37,020
United Kingdom	26,336	74,350	218,572	445,322	532,956	578,447	810,900	328,759
*Former Yugoslavia	—	—	—	—	—	—	—	—
Other Europe	3	40	79	4	9	590	1,070	145

Region / Country								
Asia	61,285	71,151	134,128	54,408	36,080	121	55	34
China	15,268	65,797	133,139	54,028	35,933	32	8	3
Hong Kong	102	—	—	—	—	—	—	—
India	102	247	166	50	42	33	38	9
Iran	—	—	—	—	—	—	—	—
*Israel	—	—	—	—	—	—	—	—
Japan	13,998	1,583	193	138	—	—	—	—
Jordan	—	—	—	—	—	—	—	—
*Korea	—	—	—	—	—	—	—	—
Philippines	—	—	—	—	—	—	—	—
Syria	—	—	—	—	—	—	—	—
Taiwan	—	—	—	—	—	—	—	—
Turkey	27,510	2,478	382	129	94	45	8	19
Vietnam	4,407	—	—	—	—	—	—	—
Other Asia	37,350	1,046	248	63	11	11	1	3
North America	3,098	524,826	345,010	130,292	84,145	50,516	31,905	9,655
Canada and Newfoundland	734	492,865	324,310	117,978	64,171	34,285	11,875	2,297
Mexico	—	2,405	5,133	1,957	3,446	3,069	7,187	3,835
Caribbean	31,480	27,323	14,285	8,751	12,447	11,803	11,792	3,061
Cuba	—	—	—	—	—	—	—	—
Dominican Republic	—	—	—	—	—	—	—	—
Haiti	—	—	—	—	—	—	—	—
Jamaica	—	—	—	—	—	—	—	—
Other Caribbean	31,480	27,323	14,285	8,751	12,447	11,803	11,792	3,061
Central America	649	279	173	70	512	297	94	57
Belize	—	—	—	—	—	—	—	—
Costa Rica	—	—	—	—	—	—	—	—
El Salvador	—	—	—	—	—	—	—	—
Guatemala	—	—	—	—	—	—	—	—
Honduras	—	—	—	—	—	—	—	—
Nicaragua	—	—	—	—	—	—	—	—
Panama	—	—	—	—	—	—	—	—
Other Central America	649	279	173	70	512	297	94	57

Region and country of last residence	1820 to 1829	1830 to 1839	1840 to 1849	1850 to 1859	1860 to 1869	1870 to 1879	1880 to 1889	1890 to 1899
South America	405	957	1,062	3,569	1,536	1,109	1,954	1,389
Argentina	—	—	—	—	—	—	—	—
Bolivia	—	—	—	—	—	—	—	—
Brazil	—	—	—	—	—	—	—	—
Chile	—	—	—	—	—	—	—	—
Colombia	—	—	—	—	—	—	—	—
Ecuador	—	—	—	—	—	—	—	—
Guyana	—	—	—	—	—	—	—	—
Paraguay	—	—	—	—	—	—	—	—
Peru	—	—	—	—	—	—	—	—
Suriname	—	—	—	—	—	—	—	—
Uruguay	—	—	—	—	—	—	—	—
Venezuela	—	—	—	—	—	—	—	—
Other South America	405	957	1,062	3,569	1,536	1,109	1,954	1,389
Other America	—	—	—	—	—	—	—	—
Africa	15	50	61	84	407	371	763	432
Egypt	—	—	—	—	4	29	145	51
Ethiopia	—	—	—	—	—	—	—	—
Liberia	1	8	5	7	43	52	21	9
Morocco	—	—	—	—	—	—	—	—
South Africa	—	—	—	—	35	48	23	9
Other Africa	14	42	56	77	325	242	574	363
Oceania	3	7	14	166	187	9,996	12,361	4,704
Australia	2	1	2	15	—	8,930	7,250	3,098
New Zealand	—	—	—	—	—	39	21	12
Other Oceania	1	6	12	151	187	1,027	5,090	1,594
Not Specified	19,523	83,593	7,366	74,399	18,241	754	790	14,112

Region and country of last residence	1900 to 1909	1910 to 1919	1920 to 1929	1930 to 1939	1940 to 1949	1950 to 1959	1960 to 1969	1980 to 1989
Total	8,202,388	6,347,380	4,295,510	699,375	856,608	2,499,268	3,213,749	6,244,379
Europe	7,572,569	4,985,411	2,560,340	444,399	472,524	1,404,973	1,133,443	668,866
Austria-Hungary	2,001,376	1,154,727	60,891	12,531	13,574	113,015	27,590	20,437
Austria	532,416	589,174	31,392	5,307	8,393	81,354	17,571	15,374
Hungary	685,567	565,553	29,499	7,224	5,181	31,661	10,019	5,063
Belgium	37,429	32,574	21,511	4,013	12,473	18,885	9,647	7,028
Bulgaria	34,651	27,180	2,824	1,062	449	97	598	1,124
*Former Czechoslovakia	—	—	101,182	17,757	8,475	1,624	2,758	5,678
Denmark	61,227	45,830	34,406	3,470	4,549	10,918	9,797	4,847
Finland	—	—	16,922	2,438	2,230	4,923	4,310	2,569
France	67,735	60,335	54,842	13,761	36,954	50,113	46,975	32,066
Germany	328,722	174,227	386,634	119,107	119,506	576,905	209,616	85,752
Greece	145,402	198,108	60,774	10,599	8,605	45,153	74,173	37,729
Ireland	344,940	166,445	202,854	28,195	15,701	47,189	37,788	22,210
Italy	1,930,475	1,229,916	528,133	85,053	50,509	184,576	200,111	55,562
Netherlands	42,463	46,065	29,397	7,791	13,877	46,703	37,918	11,234
Norway-Sweden	426,981	192,445	170,329	13,452	17,326	44,224	36,150	13,941
Norway	182,542	79,488	70,327	6,901	8,326	22,806	17,371	3,835
Sweden	244,439	112,957	100,002	6,551	9,000	21,418	18,779	10,106
Poland	—	—	223,316	25,555	7,577	6,465	55,742	63,483
Portugal	65,154	82,489	44,829	3,518	6,765	13,928	70,568	42,685
Romania	57,322	13,566	67,810	5,264	1,254	914	2,339	24,753
Russia	1,501,301	1,106,998	61,604	2,463	605	453	2,329	33,311
Spain	24,818	53,262	47,109	3,669	2,774	6,880	40,793	22,783
Switzerland	32,541	22,839	31,772	5,990	9,904	17,577	19,193	8,316
United Kingdom	469,518	371,878	341,552	61,813	131,794	195,709	220,213	153,644
*Former Yugoslavia	—	—	49,215	6,920	2,039	6,966	17,990	16,267
Other Europe	514	6,527	22,434	9,978	5,584	11,756	6,845	3,447

Region and country of last residence	1900 to 1909	1910 to 1919	1920 to 1929	1930 to 1939	1940 to 1949	1950 to 1959	1960 to 1969	1980 to 1989
Asia	299,836	269,736	126,740	19,231	34,532	135,844	358,605	2,391,356
China	19,884	20,916	30,648	5,874	16,072	8,836	14,060	170,897
Hong Kong	—	—	—	—	—	13,781	67,047	112,132
India	3,026	3,478	2,076	554	1,692	1,850	18,638	231,649
Iran	—	—	208	198	1,144	3,195	9,059	98,141
*Israel	—	—	—	—	98	21,376	30,911	43,669
Japan	139,712	77,125	42,057	2,683	1,557	40,651	40,956	44,150
Jordan	—	—	—	—	—	4,899	9,230	28,928
*Korea	—	—	—	—	83	4,845	27,048	322,708
Philippines	—	—	—	391	4,099	17,245	70,660	502,056
Syria	—	—	5,307	2,188	1,179	1,091	2,432	14,534
Taiwan	—	—	—	—	—	721	15,657	119,051
Turkey	127,999	160,717	40,450	1,327	754	2,980	9,464	19,208
Vietnam	—	—	—	—	—	290	2,949	200,632
Other Asia	9,215	7,500	5,994	6,016	7,854	14,084	40,494	483,601
North America	277,809	1,070,539	1,591,278	230,319	328,435	921,610	1,674,172	2,695,329
Canada and Newfoundland	123,067	708,715	949,286	162,703	160,911	353,169	433,128	156,313
Mexico	31,188	185,334	498,945	32,709	56,158	273,847	441,824	1,009,586
Caribbean	100,960	120,860	83,482	18,052	46,194	115,661	427,235	790,109
Cuba	—	—	12,769	10,641	25,976	73,221	202,030	132,552
Dominican Republic	—	—	—	1,026	4,802	10,219	83,552	221,552
Haiti	—	—	—	156	823	3,787	28,992	121,406
Jamaica	—	—	—	—	—	7,397	62,218	193,874
Other Caribbean	100,960	120,860	70,713	6,229	14,593	21,037	50,443	120,725
Central America	7,341	15,692	16,511	6,840	20,135	40,201	98,560	339,376
Belize	77	40	285	193	433	1,133	4,185	14,964
Costa Rica	—	—	—	431	1,965	4,044	17,975	25,017
El Salvador	—	—	—	597	4,885	5,094	14,405	137,418
Guatemala	—	—	—	423	1,303	4,197	14,357	58,847
Honduras	—	—	—	679	1,874	5,320	15,078	39,071

Nicaragua	31,102	10,383	7,812	4,393	405	—	—	—
Panama	32,957	22,177	12,601	5,282	1,452	—	—	—
Other Central America	—	—	—	—	2,660	16,226	15,652	7,264
South America	399,862	250,754	78,418	19,662	9,990	43,025	39,938	15,253
Argentina	23,442	49,384	16,346	3,108	1,067	—	—	—
Bolivia	9,798	6,205	2,759	893	50	—	—	—
Brazil	22,944	29,238	11,547	3,653	1,468	4,627	—	—
Chile	19,749	12,384	4,669	1,320	347	—	—	—
Colombia	105,494	68,371	15,567	3,454	1,027	—	—	—
Ecuador	48,015	34,107	8,574	2,207	244	—	—	—
Guyana	85,886	4,546	1,131	596	131	—	—	—
Paraguay	3,518	1,249	576	85	33	—	—	—
Peru	49,958	19,783	5,980	1,273	321	—	—	—
Suriname	1,357	612	299	130	25	—	—	—
Uruguay	7,235	4,089	1,026	754	112	—	—	—
Venezuela	22,405	20,758	9,927	2,182	1,155	—	—	—
Other South America	61	28	17	7	4,010	38,398	39,938	15,253
Other America	83	22,671	60,314	25,375	25	29	—	—
Africa	141,990	23,780	13,016	6,720	2,120	6,362	8,867	6,326
Egypt	26,744	5,581	1,996	1,613	781	1,063	—	—
Ethiopia	12,927	804	302	28	10	—	—	—
Liberia	6,420	841	289	37	35	—	—	—
Morocco	3,471	2,880	2,703	879	73	—	—	—
South Africa	15,505	4,360	2,278	1,022	312	—	—	—
Other Africa	76,923	9,314	5,448	3,141	909	5,299	8,867	6,326
Oceania	41,432	23,630	11,353	14,262	3,306	9,860	12,339	12,355
Australia	16,901	14,986	8,275	11,201	2,260	8,404	11,280	11,191
New Zealand	6,129	3,775	1,799	2,351	790	935	—	—
Other Oceania	18,402	4,869	1,279	710	256	521	1,059	1,164
Not Specified	305,406	119	12,472	135	—	930	488	33,493

Region and country of last residence	1990 to 1999	2000 to 2009	2010	2011	2012	2013	2014	2015
Total	9,775,398	10,299,430	1,042,625	1,062,040	1,031,631	779,929	653,416	730,259
Europe	1,348,612	1,349,609	95,429	90,712	86,956	80,333	71,325	78,074
Austria-Hungary	27,529	33,929	4,325	4,703	3,208	1,232	1,114	1,148
Austria	18,234	21,151	3,319	3,654	2,199	248	223	207
Hungary	9,295	12,778	1,006	1,049	1,009	984	891	941
Belgium	7,077	8,157	732	700	698	513	408	505
Bulgaria	16,948	40,003	2,465	2,549	2,322	2,646	2,226	2,336
*Former Czechoslovakia	8,970	18,691	1,510	1,374	1,316	232	303	371
Denmark	6,189	6,049	545	473	492	127	129	243
Finland	3,970	3,970	414	398	373	300	274	301
France	35,945	45,637	4,339	3,967	4,201	2,534	2,589	2,784
Germany	92,207	122,373	7,929	7,072	6,732	4,066	4,375	4,380
Greece	25,403	16,841	966	1,196	1,264	938	780	867
Ireland	65,384	15,642	1,610	1,533	1,694	1,295	1,413	1,375
Italy	75,992	28,329	2,956	2,670	2,946	2,355	2,313	2,760
Netherlands	13,345	17,351	1,520	1,258	1,294	786	665	778
Norway-Sweden	17,825	19,382	1,662	1,530	1,441	863	816	965
Norway	5,211	4,599	363	405	314	80	92	80
Sweden	12,614	14,783	1,299	1,125	1,127	783	724	885
Poland	172,249	117,921	7,391	6,634	6,024	8,697	8,304	7,886
Portugal	25,497	11,479	759	878	837	1,585	1,587	1,690
Romania	48,136	52,154	3,735	3,679	3,477	4,050	3,267	3,478
Russia	433,427	167,152	7,502	8,548	10,114	8,222	6,824	6,552
Spain	18,443	17,695	2,040	2,319	2,316	1,367	1,326	1,414
Switzerland	11,768	12,173	868	861	916	452	388	411
United Kingdom	156,182	171,979	14,781	13,443	13,938	9,459	8,906	10,095
*Former Yugoslavia	57,039	131,831	4,772	4,611	4,488	4,445	—	—
Other Europe	29,087	290,871	22,608	20,316	16,865	17,839	—	—

Asia	261,374	233,163	275,700	416,488	438,580	410,209	3,470,835	2,859,899
China	31,241	30,284	35,387	78,184	83,603	67,634	591,711	342,058
Hong Kong	1,716	1,801	2,093	2,642	3,149	3,263	57,583	116,894
India	42,213	37,854	49,897	63,320	66,331	66,185	590,464	352,528
Iran	10,344	9,620	11,623	8,955	9,015	9,078	76,755	76,899
*Israel	3,182	3,015	3,466	4,640	4,389	5,172	54,081	41,340
Japan	1,858	1,635	1,837	6,581	6,751	7,100	84,552	66,582
Jordan	2,461	2,427	2,816	7,014	8,211	9,327	53,550	42,755
*Korea	—	—	—	—	22,748	22,022	209,758	179,770
Philippines	40,815	34,591	43,489	55,441	55,251	56,399	545,463	534,338
Syria	2,004	1,832	2,196	6,674	7,983	7,424	30,807	22,906
Taiwan	4,420	4,326	5,255	5,295	6,206	6,785	92,657	132,647
Turkey	3,150	2,925	3,990	7,362	9,040	7,435	48,394	38,687
Vietnam	21,976	18,837	24,277	27,578	33,486	30,065	289,616	275,379
Other Asia	—	—	107,232	122,000	122,417	112,320	745,444	637,116
North America	247,492	222,547	271,807	409,664	423,277	426,981	4,441,529	5,137,743
Canada and Newfoundland	—	—	—	—	19,506	19,491	236,349	194,788
Mexico	105,958	94,889	99,385	145,326	142,823	138,717	1,704,166	2,757,418
Caribbean	—	—	121,349	126,615	133,012	139,389	1,053,357	1,004,687
Cuba	25,770	24,092	30,482	32,551	36,261	33,372	271,742	159,037
Dominican Republic	26,665	23,775	39,590	41,535	46,036	53,890	291,492	359,818
Haiti	14,053	13,676	23,480	22,446	21,802	22,336	203,827	177,446
Jamaica	16,566	13,547	16,442	20,300	19,298	19,439	172,523	177,143
Other Caribbean	—	—	9,384	9,783	9,615	10,352	113,773	181,243
Central America	—	—	44,056	39,837	43,249	43,597	591,130	610,189
Belize	851	773	966	875	933	997	9,682	12,600
Costa Rica	1,633	1,461	1,661	2,152	2,230	2,306	21,571	17,054
El Salvador	16,930	15,598	18,401	15,874	18,477	18,547	251,237	273,017
Guatemala	9,344	8,549	9,530	9,857	10,795	10,263	156,992	126,043
Honduras	5,039	4,433	5,462	6,773	6,053	6,381	63,513	72,880
Nicaragua	3,951	3,775	5,064	2,943	3,314	3,476	70,015	80,446
Panama	1,412	1,277	1,598	1,363	1,447	1,627	18,120	28,149
Other Central America								—

Region and country of last residence	1990 to 1999	2000 to 2009	2010	2011	2012	2013	2014	2015
South America	570,624	856,508	85,783	84,687	77,748	76,167	60,665	67,927
Argentina	30,065	47,955	4,312	4,335	4,218	4,177	3,683	3,886
Bolivia	18,111	21,921	2,211	2,113	1,920	1,961	1,527	1,689
Brazil	50,744	115,404	12,057	11,643	11,248	9,565	8,625	10,516
Chile	18,200	19,792	1,940	1,854	1,628	1,649	1,435	1,486
Colombia	137,985	236,570	21,861	22,130	20,272	22,196	16,478	17,207
Ecuador	81,358	107,977	11,463	11,068	9,284	9,470	6,952	7,664
Guyana	74,407	70,373	6,441	6,288	5,282	6,295	4,327	5,162
Paraguay	6,082	4,623	449	501	454	331	256	338
Peru	110,117	137,614	14,063	13,836	12,414	11,782	9,572	10,701
Suriname	2,285	2,363	202	167	216	160	127	183
Uruguay	6,062	9,827	1,286	1,521	1,348	933	812	902
Venezuela	35,180	82,087	9,497	9,229	9,464	7,648	6,871	8,192
Other South America	28	2	1	1	—	1	—	—
Other America	37	19	4	4	—	1	—	—
Africa	346,416	759,734	98,246	97,429	103,685	71,872	62,175	71,492
Egypt	44,604	81,564	9,822	9,096	10,172	6,213	5,094	5,693
Ethiopia	40,097	87,207	13,853	13,985	15,400	8,323	7,002	8,312
Liberia	13,587	23,316	2,924	3,117	3,451	3,923	3,035	3,042
Morocco	15,768	40,844	4,847	4,249	3,534	3,768	3,538	3,805
South Africa	21,964	32,221	2,705	2,754	2,960	2,283	2,083	2,538
Other Africa	210,396	494,582	64,095	64,228	68,168	61,455	—	—
Oceania	56,800	65,793	5,946	5,825	5,573	3,849	3,399,	3,811
Australia	24,288	32,728	3,077	3,062	3,146	1,296	1,159	1,379
New Zealand	8,600	12,495	1,046	1,006	980	482	453	514
Other Oceania	23,912	20,570	1,823	1,757	1,447	1,505	—	—
Not Specified	25,928	211,930	5,814	6,217	9,265	10,127	—	—

— Represents zero or not available.

*Note that a) Korea split into North Korea and South Korea in 1945; b) Czechoslovakia separated into the Czech Republic and the Slovak Republic in 1993; c) Former Yugoslavia, beginning in the 1990s, broke into the six nations of Serbia, Montenegro, Slovenia, Croatia, Macedonia, and Kosovo; d) and due to the way United States immigration statistics are recognized and collected, immigrants from the Occupied Palestinian Territories are grouped together with immigrants from Israel.

PRESIDENTS, VICE PRESIDENTS, AND SECRETARIES OF STATE

	President	*Vice President*	*Secretary of State*
1.	George Washington, Federalist 1789	John Adams, Federalist 1789	Thomas Jefferson 1789 Edmund Randolph 1794 Timothy Pickering 1795
2.	John Adams, Federalist 1797	Thomas Jefferson, Dem.-Rep. 1797	Timothy Pickering 1797 John Marshall 1800
3.	Thomas Jefferson, Dem.-Rep. 1801	Aaron Burr, Dem.-Rep. 1801 George Clinton, Dem.-Rep. 1805	James Madison 1801
4.	James Madison, Dem.-Rep. 1809	George Clinton, Dem.-Rep. 1809 Elbridge Gerry, Dem.-Rep. 1813	Robert Smith 1809 James Monroe 1811
5.	James Monroe, Dem.-Rep. 1817	Daniel D. Tompkins, Dem.-Rep. 1817	John Q. Adams 1817
6.	John Quincy Adams, Dem.-Rep. 1825	John C. Calhoun, Dem.-Rep. 1825	Henry Clay 1825
7.	Andrew Jackson, Democratic 1829	John C. Calhoun, Democratic 1829 Martin Van Buren, Democratic 1833	Martin Van Buren 1829 Edward Livingston 1831 Louis McLane 1833 John Forsyth 1834
8.	Martin Van Buren, Democratic 1837	Richard M. Johnson, Democratic 1837	John Forsyth 1837
9.	William H. Harrison, Whig 1841	John Tyler, Whig 1841	Daniel Webster 1841

	President	Vice President	Secretary of State
10.	John Tyler, Whig and Democratic 1841	None	Daniel Webster 1841 Hugh S. Legaré 1843 Abel P. Upshur 1843 John C. Calhoun 1844
11.	James K. Polk, Democratic 1845	George M. Dallas, Democratic 1845	James Buchanan 1845
12.	Zachary Taylor, Whig 1849	Millard Fillmore, Whig 1848	John M. Clayton 1849
13.	Millard Fillmore, Whig 1850	None	Daniel Webster 1850 Edward Everett 1852
14.	Franklin Pierce, Democratic 1853	William R. King, Democratic 1853	William L. Marcy 1853
15.	James Buchanan, Democratic 1857	John C. Breckinridge, Democratic 1857	Lewis Cass 1857 Jeremiah S. Black 1860
16.	Abraham Lincoln, Republican 1861	Hannibal Hamlin, Republican 1861 Andrew Johnson, Unionist 1865	William H. Seward 1861
17.	Andrew Johnson, Unionist 1865	None	William H. Seward 1865
18.	Ulysses S. Grant, Republican 1869	Schuyler Colfax, Republican 1869 Henry Wilson, Republican 1873	Elihu B. Washburne 1869 Hamilton Fish 1869
19.	Rutherford B. Hayes, Republican 1877	William A. Wheeler, Republican 1877	William M. Evarts 1877

	President	Vice President	Secretary of State
20.	James A. Garfield, Republican 1881	Chester A. Arthur, Republican 1881	James G. Blaine 1881
21.	Chester A. Arthur, Republican 1881	None	Frederick T. Frelinghuysen 1881
22.	Grover Cleveland, Democratic 1885	Thomas A. Hendricks, Democratic 1885	Thomas F. Bayard 1885
23.	Benjamin Harrison, Republican 1889	Levi P. Morton, Republican 1889	James G. Blaine 1889 John W. Foster 1892
24.	Grover Cleveland, Democratic 1893	Adlai E. Stevenson, Democratic 1893	Walter Q. Gresham 1893 Richard Olney 1895
25.	William McKinley, Republican 1897	Garret A. Hobart, Republican 1897 Theodore Roosevelt, Republican 1901	John Sherman 1897 William R. Day 1898 John Hay 1898
26.	Theodore Roosevelt, Republican 1901	Charles Fairbanks, Republican 1905	John Hay 1901 Elihu Root 1905 Robert Bacon 1909
27.	William H. Taft, Republican 1909	James S. Sherman, Republican 1909	Philander C. Knox 1909
28.	Woodrow Wilson, Democratic 1913	Thomas R. Marshall, Democratic 1913	William J. Bryan 1913 Robert Lansing 1915 Bainbridge Colby 1920
29.	Warren G. Harding, Republican 1921	Calvin Coolidge, Republican 1921	Charles E. Hughes 1921
30.	Calvin Coolidge, Republican 1923	Charles G. Dawes, Republican 1925	Charles E. Hughes 1923 Frank B. Kellogg 1925

	President	Vice President	Secretary of State
31.	Herbert Hoover, Republican 1929	Charles Curtis, Republican 1929	Henry L. Stimson 1929
32.	Franklin D. Roosevelt, Democratic 1933	John Nance Garner, Democratic 1933 Henry A. Wallace, Democratic 1941 Harry S. Truman, Democratic 1945	Cordell Hull 1933 Edward R. Stettinius, Jr. 1944
33.	Harry S. Truman, Democratic 1945	Alben W. Barkley, Democratic 1949	Edward R. Stettinius, Jr. 1945 James F. Byrnes 1945 George C. Marshall 1947 Dean G. Acheson 1949
34.	Dwight D. Eisenhower, Republican 1953	Richard M. Nixon, Republican 1953	John F. Dulles 1953 Christian A. Herter 1959
35.	John F. Kennedy, Democratic 1961	Lyndon B. Johnson, Democratic 1961	Dean Rusk 1961
36.	Lyndon B. Johnson, Democratic 1963	Hubert H. Humphrey, Democratic 1965	Dean Rusk 1963
37.	Richard M. Nixon, Republican 1969	Spiro T. Agnew, Republican 1969 Gerald R. Ford, Republican 1973	William P. Rogers 1969 Henry Kissinger 1973
38.	Gerald R. Ford, Republican 1974	Nelson Rockefeller, Republican 1974	Henry Kissinger 1974
39.	Jimmy Carter, Democratic 1977	Walter Mondale, Democratic 1977	Cyrus Vance 1977 Edmund Muskie 1980

	President	*Vice President*	*Secretary of State*
40.	Ronald Reagan, Republican 1981	George H. W. Bush, Republican 1981	Alexander Haig 1981 George Schultz 1982
41.	George H. W. Bush, Republican 1989	J. Danforth Quayle, Republican 1989	James A. Baker 1989 Lawrence Eagleburger 1992
42.	William J. Clinton, Democratic 1993	Albert Gore, Jr., Democratic 1993	Warren Christopher 1993 Madeleine Albright 1997
43.	George W. Bush, Republican 2001	Richard B. Cheney, Republican 2001	Colin L. Powell 2001 Condoleezza Rice 2005
44.	Barack Obama, Democratic 2009	Joseph R. Biden, Democratic 2009	Hillary Rodham Clinton 2009 John Kerry 2013
45.	Donald J. Trump, Republican 2017	Michael R. Pence, Republican 2017	Rex W. Tillerson 2017

Further Readings

Chapter 1

A fascinating study of pre-Columbian migration is Brian M. Fagan's *The Great Journey: The Peopling of Ancient America*, rev. ed. (2004). Alice B. Kehoe's *North American Indians: A Comprehensive Account*, 2nd ed. (1992), provides an encyclopedic treatment of Native Americans. See also Charles Mann's *1491: New Revelations of the Americas before Columbus* (2005) and *1493: Uncovering the New World that Columbua Created* (2011), and Daniel K. Richter, *Before the Revolution: America's Ancient Pasts* (2011). On North America's largest Native American city, see Timothy R. Pauketat, *Cahokia* (2010).

The conflict between Native Americans and Europeans is treated well in James Axtell's *The Invasion Within: The Contest of Cultures in Colonial North America* (1986) and *Beyond 1492: Encounters in Colonial North America* (1992). Colin G. Calloway's *New Worlds for All: Indians, Europeans, and the Remaking of Early America* (1997) explores the ecological effects of European settlement.

Laurence Bergreen examines the voyages of Columbus in *Columbus: The Four Voyages* (2011). For sweeping overviews of Spain's creation of a global empire, see Henry Kamen's *Empire: How Spain Became a World Power, 1492–1763* (2003) and Hugh Thomas's *Rivers of Gold: The Rise of the Spanish Empire, from Columbus to Magellan* (2004) and Robert Goodwin, *Spain: The Center of the World, 1519–1682* (2015). David J. Weber examines Spanish colonization in *The Spanish Frontier in North America* (1992). For the French experience, see William J. Eccles's *France in America*, rev. ed. (1990). For an insightful comparison of Spanish and English modes of settlement, see J. H. Elliott, *Empires of the Atlantic World: Britain and Spain in America, 1492–1830* (2006).

Chapter 2

Two excellent surveys of early American history are Peter C. Hoffer's *The Brave New World: A History of Early America*, 2nd ed. (2006), and William R. Polk's *The Birth of America: From before Columbus to the Revolution* (2006).

Bernard Bailyn's *The Barbarous Years: The Peopling of British North America: The Conflict of Civilizations, 1600–1675* (2013) tells the often brutal story of British settlement in America during the seventeenth century. Jack P. Greene offers a brilliant synthesis of British colonization in *Pursuits of Happiness: The Social Development of Early Modern British Colonies and the Formation of American Culture* (1988). The best overview of the colonization of North America is Alan Taylor's *American Colonies: The Settling of North America* (2001). On the interactions among Indian, European, and African cultures, see Gary B. Nash's *Red, White, and Black: The Peoples of Early North America*, 5th ed. (2005).

A good overview of the founding of Virginia and Maryland is Jean and Elliott Russo's *The Early Chesapeake in British North America* (2012). For information regarding the Puritan settlement of New England, see David D. Hall's *A Reforming People: Puritanism and the Transformation of Public Life in New England* (2013). The best biography of John Winthrop is Francis J. Bremer's *John Winthrop: America's Forgotten Founding Father* (2003). On Roger Williams, see John M. Barry's *Roger Williams and the Creation of the American Soul* (2012).

The pattern of settlement in the middle colonies is illuminated in Barry Levy's *Quakers and the American Family: British Settlement in the Delaware Valley* (1988). On the early history of New York, see Russell Shorto's *The Island at the Center of the World: The Epic Story of Dutch Manhattan and the Forgotten Colony That Shaped America* (2004). Settlement of the areas along the Atlantic in the South is traced in James Horn's *Adapting to a New World: English Society in the Seventeenth-Century Chesapeake* (1994).

On shifting political life in England, see Steve Pincus, *1688: The First Modern Revolution* (2009). For a study of race and the settlement of South Carolina, see Peter H. Wood's *Black Majority: Negroes in Colonial South Carolina from 1670 through the Stono Rebellion* (1974). On the flourishing trade in captive Indians, see Alan Gallay's *The Indian Slave Trade: The Rise of the English Empire in the American South, 1670–1717* (2002). On the Yamasee War, see Steven J. Oatis's *A Colonial Complex: South Carolina's Frontiers in the Era of the Yamasee War, 1680–1730* (2004).

Chapter 3

The diversity of colonial societies may be seen in David Hackett Fischer's *Albion's Seed: Four British Folkways in America* (1989). John Frederick Martin's *Profits in the Wilderness: Entrepreneurship and the Founding of New England Towns in the Seventeenth Century* (1991) indicates that economic concerns rather than spiritual motives were driving forces in many New England towns. For evocative insights into everyday life, see David Freeman Hawke, *Everyday Life in Early America* (1988), and Dale Taylor, *Writer's Guide to Everyday Life in Colonial America* (1999). See also Stephanie Grauman Wolf, *As Various as Their Land: The Everyday Lives of Eighteenth-Century Americans* (2000).

Bernard Rosenthal challenges many myths concerning the Salem witch trials in *Salem Story: Reading the Witch Trials of 1692* (1993). Mary Beth Norton's *In the Devil's Snare: The Salem Witchcraft Crisis of 1692* (2002) emphasizes the role of Indian violence.

Discussions of women in the New England colonies can be found in Laurel Thatcher Ulrich's *Good Wives: Image and Reality in the Lives of Women in Northern New England, 1650–1750* (1980), and Mary Beth Norton, *Separated by Their Sex: Women in Public and Private in the Colonial Atlantic World* (2011). On women and religion, see Susan Juster's *Disorderly Women: Sexual Politics and Evangelicalism in Revolutionary New England* (1994). John Demos describes family life in *A Little Commonwealth: Family Life in Plymouth Colony,* new ed. (2000).

For an excellent overview of Indian relations with Europeans, see Colin G. Calloway's *New Worlds for All: Indians, Europeans, and the Remaking of Early America* (1997). For analyses of Indian wars, see Alfred A. Cave's *The Pequot War* (1996) and Jill Lepore's *The Name of War: King Philip's War and the Origins of American Identity* (1998). The story of the Iroquois is told well in Daniel K. Richter's *The Ordeal of the Longhouse: The Peoples of the Iroquois League in the Era of European Colonization* (1992). Indians in the southern colonies are the focus of James Axtell's *The Indians' New South: Cultural Change in the Colonial Southeast* (1997). On the fur trade, see Eric Jay Dolan, *Fur, Fortune, and Empire: The Epic Story of the Fur Trade in America* (2010).

For the social history of the southern colonies, see Allan Kulikoff's *Tobacco and Slaves: The Development of Southern Cultures in the Chesapeake, 1680–1800* (1986). On the interaction of the cultures of blacks and whites, see Mechal Sobel's *The World They Made Together: Black and White Values in Eighteenth-Century Virginia* (1987). On the slave trade, see William St. Clair's *The Door of No Return* (2007). African Americans during colonial settlement are the focus of Timothy H. Breen and Stephen Innes's *"Myne Owne Ground": Race and Freedom on Virginia's Eastern Shore, 1640–1676*, new ed. (2004). David W. Galenson's *White Servitude in Colonial America: An Economic Analysis* (1981) looks at the indentured labor force.

Henry F. May's *The Enlightenment in America* (1976) and Donald H. Meyer's *The Democratic Enlightenment* (1976) examine intellectual trends in eighteenth-century America. On the Great Awakening, see Frank Lambert's *Inventing the "Great Awakening"* (1999), and Thomas S. Kidd's *The Great Awakening: The Roots of Evangelical Christianity in Colonial America* (2007). Excellent biographies of the key revivalists are Phillip F. Gura's *Jonathan Edwards: A Life* (2003) and Thomas S. Kidd's *George Whitefield* (2015).

Chapter 4

A good introduction to the imperial phase of the colonial conflicts is Douglas Edward Leach's *Arms for Empire: A Military History of the British Colonies in North America, 1607–1763* (1973). Also useful is Brendan Simms's *Three Victories and a Defeat: The Rise and Fall of the Fiurst British Empire* (2008). Fred Anderson's *Crucible of War: The Seven Years' War and the Fate of Empire in British North America, 1754–1766* (2000) is the best history of the Seven Years' War. For the implications of the British victory in 1763, see Colin G. Calloway's *The Scratch of a Pen: 1763 and the Transformation of North America* (2006). On the French colonies in North America, see Allan Greer's *The People of New France* (1997).

For a narrative survey of the events leading to the Revolution, see Edward Countryman's *The American Revolution,* rev. ed. (2003). For Great Britain's perspective on the imperial conflict, see Ian R. Christie's *Crisis of Empire: Great Britain and the American Colonies, 1754–1783* (1966). Also see Jeremy Black's *George III: America's Last King* (2007).

The intellectual foundations of revolt are traced in Bernard Bailyn's *The Ideological Origins of the American Revolution* (1992). To understand how these views were connected to organized protest, see Jon Butler's *Becoming America: The Revolution before 1776* (2000) and Kevin Phillips's *1775: A Good Year for a Revolution* (2012). On the first major battle, see Nathaniel Philbrick's *Bunker Hill: A City, a Siege, a Revolution* (2013).

On the efforts of colonists to boycott the purchase of British goods, see T. H. Breen's *The Marketplace of Revolution: How Consumer Politics Shaped American Independence* (2004). For the events during the summer of 1776, see Joseph J. Ellis's *Revolutionary Summer: The Birth of American Independence* (2014). Pauline Maier's *American Scripture: Making the Declaration of Independence* (1997) remains the best analysis of the framing of that document. The best analysis of why Americans supported independence is Thomas Slaughter's *Independence: The Tangled Roots of the American Revolution* (2014).

Chapter 5

Military affairs in the early phases of the Revolutionary War are handled in John W. Shy's *Toward Lexington: The Role of the British Army in the Coming of the American Revolution* (1965). The Revolutionary War is the subject of Gordon S. Wood's *The Radicalism of the American Revolution* (1991) and Jeremy Black's *War for America: The Fight for Independence, 1775–1783* (1991). John Ferling's *Setting the World Ablaze: Washington, Adams, Jefferson, and the American Revolution* (2000) highlights the roles played by key leaders.

On the social history of the Revolutionary War, see John W. Shy's *A People Numerous and Armed: Reflections on the Military Struggle for American Independence,* rev. ed. (1990). Colin G. Calloway tells the neglected story of the Indian experiences in the Revolution in *The American Revolution in Indian Country: Crisis and Diversity in Native American Communities* (1995).

Why some Americans remained loyal to the Crown is the subject of Thomas B. Allen's *Tories: Fighting for the King in America's First Civil War* (2010) and Maya Jasanoff's *Liberty's Exiles: American Loyalists in the Revolutionary War* (2011). A superb study of African Americans during the Revolutionary era is Douglas R. Egerton's *Death or Liberty: African Americans and Revolutionary America* (2009).

Carol Berkin's *Revolutionary Mothers: Women in the Struggle for America's Independence* (2005) documents the role that women played in securing independence. A superb biography of Revolutionary America's most prominent woman is Woody Holton's *Abigail Adams* (2010). A fine new biography of America's commander in chief is Ron Chernow's *Washington: A Life* (2010). The best analysis of the British side of the war is Andrew Jackson O'Shaughnessy's *The Men Who Lost America: British Leadership, the American Revolution, and the Fate of Empire* (2013).

Chapter 6

A good overview of the Confederation period is Richard B. Morris's *The Forging of the Union, 1781–1789* (1987). Another useful analysis of this period is Richard Buel Jr.'s *Securing the Revolution: Ideology in American Politics, 1789–1815* (1972). David P. Szatmary's *Shays's Rebellion: The Making of an Agrarian Insurrection* (1980) covers that fateful incident. For a fine account of cultural change during the period, see Joseph J. Ellis's *After the Revolution: Profiles of Early American Culture* (1979).

An excellent overview of post-Revolutionary life is Joyce Appleby's *Inheriting the Revolution: The First Generation of Americans* (2000). On the political philosophies contributing to the drafting of the Constitution, see Ralph Lerner's *The Thinking Revolutionary: Principle and Practice in the New Republic* (1987). For the dramatic story of the framers of the Constitution, see Richard Beeman's *Plain, Honest Men: The Making of the American Constituion* (2009). Woody Holton's *Unruly Americans and the Origins of the Constitution* (2007) emphasizes the role of taxes and monetary policies in the crafting of the Constitution. The complex story of ratification is well told in Pauline Maier's *Ratification: The People Debate the Constitution, 1787–1788* (2010).

The best introduction to the early Federalists remains John C. Miller's *The Federalist Era, 1789–1801* (2011). Other works analyze the ideological debates among the nation's first leaders. Richard Buel Jr.'s *Securing the Revolution: Ideology in American Politics, 1789–1815* (1972), Joyce Appleby's *Capitalism and a New Social Order: The Republican Vision of the 1790s* (1984), and Stanley Elkins and Eric McKitrick's *The Age of Federalism: The Early American Republic, 1788–1800* (1993) trace the persistence and transformation of ideas first fostered during the Revolutionary crisis. The best study of Washington's political career is John Ferling's *The Ascent of George Washington: The Hidden Political Genius of an American Icon* (2009).

The 1790s may also be understood through the views and behavior of national leaders. See the following biographies: Richard Brookhiser's *Founding Father: Rediscovering George Washington* (1996), *Alexander Hamilton, American* (1999), and *James Madison* (2013), and Joseph J. Ellis's *Passionate Sage: The Character and Legacy of John Adams* (1993). On social life, see Jack Larkin, *Every Day Life in America, 1790–1840* (New York, 1989).

On the formation of the federal government and its economic policies, see Thomas K. McCraw's *The Founders and Finance* (2012). Federalist foreign policy is explored in Jerald A. Comb's *The Jay Treaty: Political Battleground of the Founding Fathers* (1970) and William Stinchcombe's *The XYZ Affair* (1980).

Chapter 7

Marshall Smelser's *The Democratic Republic, 1801–1815* (1968) presents an overview of the Republican administrations. Even more comprehensive is Gordon S. Wood's *Empire of Liberty: A History of the Early Republic, 1789-1815* (2010). The best treatment of the election of 1800 is Edward J. Larson's *A Magnificent Catastrophe: The Tumultuous Election of 1800* (2008).

The standard biography of Jefferson is Joseph J. Ellis's *American Sphinx: The Character of Thomas Jefferson* (1996). On the life of Jefferson's friend and successor, see Drew R. McCoy's. *The Last of the Fathers: James Madison and the Republican Legacy* (1989). Joyce Appleby's *Capitalism and a New Social Order: The Republican Vision of the 1790s* (1984) minimizes the impact of Republican ideology.

Linda K. Kerber's *Federalists in Dissent: Imagery and Ideology in Jeffersonian American* (1970) explores the Federalists while out of power. The concept of judicial review and the courts can be studied in Cliff Sloan and David McKean's *The Great Decision: Jefferson, Adams, Marshall, and the Battle for the Supreme Court* (2009). Liff Sloan and David McKean's *The Great Decision: Jefferson, Adams, Marshall, and the Battle for the Supreme Court* (2009). Milton Lomask's two volumes, *Aaron Burr: The Years from Princeton to Vice President, 1756–1805* (1979) and *The Conspiracy and the Years of Exile, 1805–1836* (1982) trace the career of that remarkable American.

For the Louisiana Purchase, consult Jon Kukla's *A Wilderness So Immense: The Louisiana Purchase and the Destiny of America* (2003). For a captivating account of the Lewis and Clark expedition, see Stephen Ambrose's *Undaunted Courage: Meriwether Lewis, Thomas Jefferson, and the Opening of the American West* (1996).

Burton Spivak's *Jefferson's English Crisis: Commerce, Embargo, and the Republican Revolution* (1979) discusses Anglo-American relations during Jefferson's administration; Clifford L. Egan's *Neither Peace Nor War: Franco-American Relations, 1803–1812* (1983) covers America's relations with France. An excellent revisionist treatment of the events that brought on war in 1812 is J. C. A. Stagg's *Mr. Madison's War: Politics, Diplomacy, and Warfare in the Early American Republic, 1783–1830* (1983). The war itself is the focus of Donald R. Hickey's *The War of 1812: A Forgotten Conflict* (1989). See also Alan Taylor's award-winning *The Civil War of 1812: American Citizens, British Subjects, Irish Rebels, and Indian Allies* (2011).

For textured insights into everyday life, see Laura Thatcher Ulrich, *A Midwife's Tale: The Life of Martha Ballard, Based on Her Diary, 1785–1812* (1991).

Chapter 8

The best overview of the second quarter of the nineteenth century is Daniel Walker Howe, *What Hath God Wrought: The Transformation of America, 1815–1845* (2007). The classic study of transportation and economic growth is George Rogers Taylor's *The Transportation Revolution, 1815–1860* (1951). A more recent treatment is Sarah H. Gordon's *Passage to Union: How the Railroads Transformed American Life, 1829–1929* (1996). On the Erie Canal, see Carol Sheriff's *The Artificial River: The Erie Canal and the Paradox of Progress, 1817–1862* (1996). See also John Lauritz Larson's *Internal Improvement: National Public Works and the Promise of Popular Government in the Early United States* (2001).

Several books focus on social issues of the post-Revolutionary period, including *Keepers of the Revolution: New Yorkers at Work in the Early Republic* (1992), edited by Paul A. Gilje and Howard B. Rock; Ronald Schultz's *The Republic of Labor: Philadelphia Artisans and the Politics of Class, 1720–1830* (1993); and Peter Way's *Common Labor: Workers and the Digging of North American Canals, 1780–1860* (1993). On Indian life, see Candy Moulton, *Everyday Life among the American Indians* (2001).

On the industrial revolution, see Charles R. Morris's *The Dawn of Innovation: The First American Industrial Revolution* (2013). The impact of technology is traced in David J. Jeremy's *Transatlantic Industrial Revolution: The Diffusion of Textile Technologies between Britain and America, 1790–1830s* (1981). On the invention of the telegraph, see Kenneth Silverman's *Lightning Man: The Accursed Life of Samuel F. B. Morse* (2003). For the story of steamboats, see Andrea Sutcliffe's *Steam: The Untold Story of America's First Great Invention* (2004).

The outlook of the working class during this time of transition is surveyed in Edward E. Pessen's *Most Uncommon Jacksonians: The Radical Leaders of the Early Labor Movement* (1967). Detailed case studies of working communities include Anthony F. C. Wallace's *Rockdale: The Growth of an American Village in the Early Industrial Revolution* (1978), Thomas Dublin's *Women at Work: The Transformation of Work and Community in Lowell, Massachusetts, 1826–1860* (1979), and Sean Wilentz's *Chants Democratic: New York and the Rise of the American Working Class, 1788–1850* (1984).

For a fine treatment of urbanization, see Charles N. Glaab and A. Theodore Brown's *A History of Urban America* (1967). On immigration, see Jay P. Dolan's *The Irish Americans* (2008) and John Kelly's *The Graves Are Walking: The Great Famine and the Saga of the Irish People* (2012).

Chapter 9

The standard overview of the Era of Good Feelings remains George Dangerfield's *The Awakening of American Nationalism, 1815–1828* (1965). A classic summary of the economic trends of the period is Douglass C. North's *The Economic Growth of the United States, 1790–1860* (1961). An excellent synthesis of the era is Charles Sellers's *The Market Revolution: Jacksonian America, 1815–1846* (1991).

On diplomatic relations during James Monroe's presidency, see William Earl Weeks's *John Quincy Adams and American Global Empire* (1992). For relations after 1812, see Ernest R. May's *The Making of the Monroe Doctrine* (1975). The campaign that brought Andrew Jackson to the White House is analyzed in Robert Vincent Remini's *The Election of Andrew Jackson* (1963).

Chapter 10

The best comprehensive surveys of politics and culture during the Jacksonian era are Daniel Walker Howe's *What Hath God Wrought: The Transformation of America, 1815–1848* (2007) and David S. Reynolds's *Waking Giant: America in the Age of Jackson* (2008). A more political focus can be found in Harry L. Watson's *Liberty and Power: The Politics of Jacksonian America* (1990). On the rise of urban political machines, see Terry Golway's *Machine Made: Tammany Hall and the Creation of Modern American Politics* (2014).

For an outstanding analysis of women in New York City during the Jacksonian period, see Christine Stansell's *City of Women: Sex and Class in New York, 1789–1860* (1986). In *Chants Democratic: New York City and the Rise of the American Working-*

Class, 1788–1850 (1984), Sean Wilentz analyzes the social basis of working-class politics. More recently, Wilentz has traced the democratization of politics in *The Rise of American Democracy: Jefferson to Lincoln* (2009).

The best biography of Jackson remains Robert Vincent Remini's three-volume work: *Andrew Jackson: The Course of American Empire, 1767–1821* (1977), *Andrew Jackson: The Course of American Freedom, 1822–1832* (1981), and *Andrew Jackson: The Course of American Democracy, 1833–1845* (1984). A more critical study of the seventh president is Andrew Burstein's *The Passions of Andrew Jackson* (2003).

On Jackson's successor, consult John Niven's *Martin Van Buren: The Romantic Age of American Politics* (1983) and Ted Widmer's *Martin Van Buren* (2005). Studies of other major figures of the period include John Niven's *John C. Calhoun and the Price of Union: A Biography* (1988), Merrill D. Peterson's *The Great Triumvirate: Webster, Clay, and Calhoun* (1987), and Robert Vincent Remini's *Henry Clay: Statesman for the Union* (1991) and *Daniel Webster: The Man and His Time* (1997).

The political philosophies of Jackson's opponents are treated in Michael F. Holt's *The Rise and Fall of the American Whig Party: Jacksonian Politics and the Onset of the Civil War* (1999) and Harry L. Watson's *Andrew Jackson vs. Henry Clay: Democracy and Development in Antebellum America* (1998). The outstanding book on the nullification issue remains William W. Freehling's *Prelude to Civil War: The Nullification Controversy in South Carolina, 1816–1836* (1965). John M. Belohlavek's *"Let the Eagle Soar!": The Foreign Policy of Andrew Jackson* (1985) is a thorough study of Jacksonian diplomacy. A. J. Langguth's *Driven West: Andrew Jackson and the Trail of Tears to the Civil War* (2010) analyzes the controversial relocation policy.

Chapter 11

Russel Blaine Nye's *Society and Culture in America, 1830–1860* (1974) provides a wide-ranging survey of the Romantic movement. On the reform impulse, consult Ronald G. Walter's *American Reformers, 1815–1860*, rev. ed. (1997). Revivalist religion is treated in Nathan O. Hatch's *The Democratization of American Christianity* (1989), Christine Leigh Heyrman's *Southern Cross: The Beginnings of the Bible Belt* (1997), and Ellen Eslinger's *Citizens of Zion: The Social Origins of Camp Meeting Revivalism* (1999). On the Mormons, see Alex Beam's *American Crucifixion: The Murder of Joseph Smith and the Fate of the Mormon Church* (2014).

The best treatments of transcendentalist thought are Paul F. Boller's *American Transcendentalism, 1830–1860: An Intellectual Inquiry* (1974) and Philip F. Gura's *American Transcendentalism: A History* (2007). For the war against alcohol, see W. J. Rorabaugh's *The Alcoholic Republic: An American Tradition* (1979) and Barbara Leslie Epstein's *The Politics of Domesticity: Women, Evangelism, and Temperance in Nineteenth-Century America* (1981). On prison reform and other humanitarian projects, see David J. Rothman's *The Discovery of the Asylum: Social Order and Disorder in the New Republic*, rev. ed. (2002), and Thomas J. Brown's biography *Dorothea Dix: New England Reformer* (1998).

Useful surveys of abolitionism include Seymour Drescher's *Abolition: A History of Slavery and Antislavery* (2009), James Brewer Stewart's *Holy Warriors: The Abolitionists and American Slavery*, rev. ed. (1997), and Julie Roy Jeffrey's *The Great Silent Army of Abolitionism: Ordinary Women in the Antislavery Movement* (1998). For the pro-slavery argument as it developed in the South, see Larry E. Tise's *Proslavery: A History of the Defense of Slavery in America, 1701–1840* (1987) and James Oakes's *The Ruling Race: A History of American Slaveholders* (1982). The problems southerners had in justifying slavery are explored in Kenneth S. Greenberg's *Masters and Statesmen: The Political Culture of American Slavery* (1985).

Chapter 12

Three efforts to understand the mind of the Old South and its defense of slavery are Eugene D. Genovese's *The Slaveholders' Dilemma: Freedom and Progress in Southern Conservative Thought, 1820–1860* (1992), William W. Freehling's *The Road to Disunion: Secessionists Triumphant, 1854–1861* (2007), and Walter Johnson's *River of Dark Dreams: Slavery and Empire in the Cotton Kingdom* (2013). Stephanie McCurry's *Masters of Small Worlds: Yeoman Households, Gender Relations, and the Political Culture of the Antebellum South Carolina Low Country* (1995) describes southern households, religion, and political culture.

Other essential works on southern culture and society include Bertram Wyatt-Brown's *Honor and Violence in the Old South* (1986), Elizabeth Fox-Genovese's *Within the Plantation Household: Black and White Women of the Old South* (1988), Catherine Clinton's *The Plantation Mistress: Woman's World in the Old South* (1982), Joan E. Cashin's *A Family Venture: Men and Women on the Southern Frontier* (1991), and Theodore Rosengarten's *Tombee: Portrait of a Cotton Planter* (1986).

John W. Blassingame's *The Slave Community: Plantation Life in the Antebellum South,* rev. and enlarged ed. (1979), Eugene D. Genovese's *Roll, Jordan, Roll: The World the Slaves Made* (1974), and Herbert G. Gutman's *The Black Family in Slavery and Freedom, 1750–1925* (1976) all stress the theme of a persisting and identifiable slave culture. On the question of slavery's profitability, see Robert William Fogel and Stanley L. Engerman's *Time on the Cross: The Economics of American Negro Slavery* (1974), and Edward E. Baptist's *The Half Has Never Been Told* (2014). Charles Joyner's *Down by the Riverside: A South Carolina Slave Community* (1984) offers a vivid reconstruction of one community.

Chapter 13

For background on Whig programs and ideas, see Michael F. Holt's *The Rise and Fall of the American Whig Party: Jacksonian Politics and the Onset of the Civil War* (1999). On John Tyler, see Edward P. Crapol's *John Tyler: The Accidental President* (2006). On the expansionist impulse westward, see Thomas R. Hietala's *Manifest Design: Anxious Aggrandizement in Late Jacksonian America* (1985), Walter Nugent's *Habits of Empire: A History of American Expansionism* (2008) and Richard White's *"It's Your Misfortune and None of My Own": A New History of the American West* (1991).

For the expansionism of the 1840s, see Steven E. Woodworth's *Manifest Destinies: America's Westward Expansion and the Road to the Civil War* (2010). The movement of settlers to the West is ably documented in John Mack Faragher's *Women and Men on the Overland Trail,* 2nd ed. (2001), and David Dary's *The Santa Fe Trail: Its History, Legends, and Lore* (2000), and Rinker Buck's *The Oregon Trail* (2015). On life in the mining camps, see Susan Lee Johnson, *Roaring Camp: The Social World of the California Gold Rush* (2000).

Gene M. Brack's *Mexico Views Manifest Destiny, 1821–1846: An Essay on the Origins of the Mexican War* (1975) takes Mexico's viewpoint on U.S. designs on the West. For the American perspective on Texas, see Joel H. Silbey's *Storm over Texas: The Annexation Controversy and the Road to Civil War* (2005). On the siege of the Alamo, see William C. Davis's *Three Roads to the Alamo: The Lives and Fortunes of David Crockett, James Bowie, and William Barret Travis* (1998) and James Donovan's *The Blood of Heroes* (2012). An excellent biography related to the emergence of Texas is Gregg Cantrell's *Stephen F. Austin: Empresario of Texas* (1999).

On James K. Polk, see Robert W. Merry's *A Country of Vast Designs: James K. Polk, the Mexican War, and the Conquest of the American Continent* (2009). The best survey of the military conflict is John S. D. Eisenhower's *So Far from God: The U.S. War with Mexico, 1846–1848* (1989). The Mexican War as viewed from the perspective of the soldiers is ably described in Richard Bruce Winders's *Mr. Polk's Army: American Military Experience in the Mexican War* (1997). On the diplomatic aspects of Mexican-American relations, see David M. Pletcher's *The Diplomacy of Annexation: Texas, Oregon, and the Mexican War* (1973).

The best surveys of the forces and events leading to the Civil War include James M. McPherson's *Battle Cry of Freedom: The Civil War Era* (1988), Stephen B. Oates's *The Approaching Fury: Voices of the Storm, 1820–1861* (1997), and Bruce Levine's *Half Slave and Half Free: The Roots of Civil War* (1992). The most recent narrative of the political debate leading to secession is Michael A. Morrison's *Slavery and the American West: The Eclipse of Manifest Destiny and the Coming of the Civil War* (1997).

Mark J. Stegmaier's *Texas, New Mexico, and the Compromise of 1850: Boundary Dispute and Sectional Crisis* (1996) probes that crucial dispute, while Michael F. Holt's *The Political Crisis of the 1850s* (1978) traces the demise of the Whigs. See also Fergus M. Bordewich's *America's Great Debate: Henry Clay, Stephen A. Douglas, and the Compromise That Preserved the Union* (2012). Eric Foner, in *Free Soil, Free Labor, Free Men: The Ideology of the Republican Party before the Civil War* (1970), shows how events and ideas combined in the formation of a new political party. The pivotal *Dred Scott* case is ably assessed in Earl M. Maltz's *Dred Scott and the Politics of Slavery* (2007).

On the role of John Brown in the sectional crisis, see Robert E. McGlone's *John Brown's War Against Slavery* (2009). A detailed study of the South's journey to secession is William W. Freehling's *The Road to Disunion*, vol. 1, *Secessionists at Bay, 1776–1854* (1990), and *The Road to Disunion*, vol. 2, *Secessionists Triumphant, 1854–1861* (2007). Robert E. Bonner traces the emergence of southern nationalism in *Mastering America: Southern Slaveholders and the Crisis of American Nationhood* (2009).

On the Buchanan presidency, see Jean H. Baker's *James Buchanan* (2004). Maury Klein's *Days of Defiance: Sumter, Secession, and the Coming of the Civil War* (1997) treats the Fort Sumter controversy. An excellent collection of interpretive essays is *Why the Civil War Came* (1996), edited by Gabor S. Boritt.

Chapter 14

On the start of the Civil War, see Adam Goodheart's *1861: The Civil War Awakening* (2011). The best one-volume overview of the Civil War period is James M. McPherson's *Battle Cry of Freedom: The Civil War Era* (1988). A more recent synthesis of the war and its effects is David Goldfield's *America Aflame: How the Civil War Created a Nation* (2011). A good introduction to the military events is Herman Hattaway's *Shades of Blue and Gray: An Introductory Military History of the Civil War* (1997). The outlook and experiences of the common soldier are explored in James M. McPherson's *For Cause and Comrades: Why Men Fought in the Civil War* (1997).

The northern war effort is ably assessed in Gary W. Gallagher's *The Union War* (2011). For emphasis on the South, see Gallagher's *The Confederate War* (1997). A sparkling account of the birth of the Rebel nation is William C. Davis's *"A Government of Our Own": The Making of the Confederacy* (1994). The same author provides a fine biography of the Confederate president in *Jefferson Davis: The Man and His Hour* (1991). On the leading Confederate commander, see Michael Korda's *Clouds of*

Glory: The Life and Legend of Robert E. Lee (2014). On the key Union generals, see Lee Kennett's *Sherman: A Soldier's Life* (2001) and Josiah Bunting III's *Ulysses S. Grant* (2004).

The history of the North during the war is surveyed in Philip Shaw Paludan's *A People's Contest: The Union and Civil War, 1861–1865,* 2nd ed. (1996), and J. Matthew Gallman's *The North Fights the Civil War: The Home Front* (1994). See also Jennifer L. Weber's *Copperheads: The Rise and Fall of Lincoln's Opponents in the North* (2006). The central northern political figure, Abraham Lincoln, is the subject of many books. See James McPherson's *Abraham Lincoln* (2009) and Ronald C. White, Jr., *A. Lincoln: A Biography* (2009).

The experience of the African American soldier is surveyed in Joseph T. Glatthaar's *Forged in Battle: The Civil War Alliance of Black Soldiers and White Officers* (1990) and Ira Berlin, Joseph P. Reidy, and Leslie S. Rowland's *Freedom's Soldiers: The Black Military Experience in the Civil War* (1998). For the African American woman's experience, see Jacqueline Jones's *Labor of Love, Labor of Sorrow: Black Women, Work and the Family, from Slavery to the Present* (1985). On Lincoln's evolving racial views, see Eric Foner's *The Fiery Trial: Abraham Lincoln and American Slavery* (2010). The war's impact on slavery is the focus of James Oakes's *Freedom National: The Destruction of Slavery in the United States, 1861–1865* (2013) and Bruce Levine's *The Fall of the House of Dixie* (2013). On the emancipation proclamation, see Louis P. Masur's *Lincoln's Hundred Days: The Emancipation Proclamation and the War for the Union* (2012). For a sensory perspective on the fighting, see Mark M. Smith's *The Smell of Battle, the Taste of Siege: A Sensory History of the Civil War* (2014).

On everyday life during the Civil War, both at home and in the military, see Michael O. Varhola, *Life in Civil War America* (2011). Recent gender and ethnic studies include Nina Silber's *Gender and the Sectional Conflict* (2008), Drew Gilpin Faust's *Mothers of Invention: Women of the Slaveholding South in the American Civil War* (1996), George C. Rable's *Civil Wars: Women and the Crisis of Southern Nationalism* (1989), and William L. Burton's *Melting Pot Soldiers: The Union's Ethnic Regiments*, 2nd ed. (1998).

Chapter 15

The most comprehensive treatment of Reconstruction is Eric Foner's *Reconstruction: America's Unfinished Revolution, 1863–1877* (1988). On Andrew Johnson, see Hans L. Trefousse's *Andrew Johnson: A Biography* (1989) and David D. Stewart's *Impeached: The Trial of Andrew Johnson and the Fight for Lincoln's Legacy* (2009). An excellent brief biography of Grant is Josiah Bunting III's *Ulysses S. Grant* (2004). For accounts of everyday life, see Daniel E. Sutherland, *The Expansion of Everyday Life, 1860–1876* (1989).

Scholars have been sympathetic to the aims and motives of the Radical Republicans. See, for instance, Herman Belz's *Reconstructing the Union: Theory and Policy during the Civil War* (1969) and Richard Nelson Current's *Those Terrible Carpetbaggers: A Reinterpretation* (1988). The ideology of the Radicals is explored in Michael Les Benedict's *A Compromise of Principle: Congressional Republicans and Reconstruction, 1863–1869* (1974). On the black political leaders, see Phillip Dray's *Capitol Men: The Epic Story of Reconstruction through the Lives of the First Black Congressmen* (2008).

The intransigence of southern white attitudes is examined in Michael Perman's *Reunion without Compromise: The South and Reconstruction, 1865–1868* (1973) and Dan T. Carter's *When the War Was Over: The Failure of Self-Reconstruction in the*

South, 1865–1867 (1985). Allen W. Trelease's *White Terror: The Ku Klux Klan Conspiracy and Southern Reconstruction* (1971) covers the various organizations that practiced vigilante tactics. On the massacre of African Americans, see Charles Lane's *The Day Freedom Died: The Colfax Massacre, the Supreme Court, and the Betrayal of Reconstruction* (2008).

The difficulties former slaves had in adjusting to the new labor system are documented in James L. Roark's *Masters without Slaves: Southern Planters in the Civil War and Reconstruction* (1977). Books on southern politics during Reconstruction include Michael Perman's *The Road to Redemption: Southern Politics, 1869–1879* (1984), Terry L. Seip's *The South Returns to Congress: Men, Economic Measures, and Intersectional Relationships, 1868–1879* (1983), and Mark W. Summers's *Railroads, Reconstruction, and the Gospel of Prosperity: Aid under the Radical Republicans, 1865–1877* (1984).

Numerous works study the freed blacks' experience in the South. Start with Leon F. Litwack's *Been in the Storm So Long: The Aftermath of Slavery* (1979). The Freedmen's Bureau is explored in William S. McFeely's *Yankee Stepfather: General O. O. Howard and the Freedmen* (1968). The situation of freed slave women is discussed in Jacqueline Jones's *Labor of Love, Labor of Sorrow: Black Women, Work and the Family, from Slavery to the Present* (1985).

The politics of corruption outside the South is depicted in William S. McFeely's *Grant: A Biography* (1981). The political maneuvers of the election of 1876 and the resultant crisis and compromise are explained in Michael Holt's *By One Vote: The Disputed Presidential Election of 1876* (2008).

Credits

Text Credits

Bernard Bailyn: Excerpts reprinted by permission of the publisher from *The Ideological Origins of the American Revolution* by Bernard Bailyn, pp. xx–xxiii, Cambridge, Mass.: Harvard University Press, Copyright © 1992 by Bernard Bailyn.

Richard Breitman and Allan J. Lichtman: Excerpts reprinted by permission of the publisher from *FDR and the Jews* by Richard Breitman and Allan J. Lichtman, pp. 2, 6–7, Cambridge, Mass.: Harvard University Press, Copyright © 2013 by Richard Breitman and Allan J. Lichtman.

Leo Chavez: Excerpts from *The Latino Threat: Constructing Immigrants, Citizens, and the Nation, Second Edition*, by Leo Chavez. Copyright © 2008, 2014 By the Board of Trustees of the Leland Stanford Jr. University. All rights reserved. With the permission of Stanford University Press, www.sup.org

Paul Finkelman: Excerpts from "Jefferson and Slavery," in *Jeffersonian Legacies*, edited by Peter S. Onuf. pp. 181–183, 210–211. © 1993 by the Rector and Visitors of the University of Virginia. Reprinted by permission of the University of Virginia Press.

Eric Foner: Excerpt from *The Story of American Freedom*. Copyright © 1998 by Eric Foner. Reprinted by permission of W. W. Norton & Company, Inc., the author, and the Sandra Dijkstra Literary Agency.

Nathan Glazer & Daniel Moynihan: From *Beyond The Melting Pot*, excerpts from pp. 12–14, 20, © 1963 Massachusetts Institute of Technology, used by permission of The MIT Press.

Gary B. Nash: Excerpts from "Social Change and the Growth of Prerevolutionary Urban Radicalism," by Gary B. Nash. From *The American Revolution: Explorations in History of American Radicalism*, by Alfred F. Young (ed.). Copyright © 1976 by Northern Illinois University Press. Used with permission of Northern Illinois University Press.

Jason Richwine: "The Congealing Pot," by Jason Richwine from National Review, August 24, 2009. © 2009 by National Review, Inc. Reprinted by permission.

Douglas L. Wilson: Excerpts from "Thomas Jefferson and the Character Issue," by Douglas L. Wilson. Originally published in *The Atlantic Monthly*, November 1992. Used by permission the author.

Photo Credits

Front Matter

Page v: Minnesota Historical Society; p. xii: The Rapalje Children, 1768 (oil on canvas), Durand, John (1731-1805)/© Collection of the New-York Historical Society/Bridgeman Images; p. xiii: Granger, NYC — All rights reserved; p. xiv: Private Collection/Peter Newark American Pictures/Bridgeman Images; p. xv: Library of Congress; p. xvi: Library of Congress; p. xvii: Wikimedia, public domain; p. xviii: Wikimedia, public domain; p. xix: Adoc-photos/Art Resource, NY; p. xx: Bettmann/Getty Images; p. xxi: AP Photo/ Jae C. Hong.

Chapter 1

Page 2 (Join or Die): Library of Congress; (Rapalje Children): *The Rapalje Children*, 1768 (oil on canvas), Durand, John (1731-1805)/ © Collection of the New-York Historical Society/Bridgeman Images; (De Soto): bpk, Berlin/Kunstbibliothek, Staatliche Museen/Knud Petersen/Art Resource; (Slaves): The Colonial Williamsburg Foundation. Gift of Abby Aldrich Rockefeller; (Columbus): Bettmann/Getty Images; p. 4: © The Trustees of the British Museum/Art Resource, NY; p. 5: Granger, NYC — All rights reserved; p. 6: bpk, Berlin/Kunstbibliothek Staatliche Museen/ Knud Petersen/Art Resource; p. 10: DEA/G. Dagli Orti/ De Agostini/Getty Images; p. 13: iStock/Getty Images Plus; p. 14: SuperStock/agefotostock; p. 16: MPI/Getty Images; p. 19: Bettmann/Getty Images; p. 22:New York Public Library/ Bridgeman Images; p. 23: Galleria degli Uffizi, Florence/Bridgeman Images; p. 26: Woburn Abbey, Bedfordshire, UK/Bridgeman Images; p. 29: Nettie Lee Benson Latin American Collection, University of Texas Libraries, The University of Texas at Austin; p. 31: Granger, NYC — All rights reserved; p. 34: Album/Oronoz/ Newscom; p. 38: Granger, NYC — All rights reserved.

Chapter 2

Page 42: British Library, London/© British Library Board. All Rights Reserved/Bridgeman Images; p. 45: Granger, NYC — All rights reserved; p. 47: Granger, NYC — All rights reserved; p. 49: Granger, NYC — All rights reserved; p. 53: Granger, NYC — All rights reserved; p. 56: Granger, NYC — All rights reserved; p. 57: Everett Collection/Alamy Stock Photo; p. 58: Granger, NYC — All rights reserved; p. 62: New-York Historical Society/Getty Images; p. 63: Bettmann/Corbis/Getty Images; p. 66: Granger, NYC — All rights reserved; p. 68: Bettmann/Corbis/Getty Images; p. 70: Granger, NYC — All rights reserved; p. 71: Library of Congress; p. 73: Granger, NYC — All rights reserved; p. 74: © British Museum/Art Resource; p. 75: Special Collections Research Center, Earl Gregg Swem Library, The College of William & Mary; p. 77: Granger, NYC — All rights reserved; p. 78: The Colonial Williamsburg Foundation. Gift of Abby Aldrich Rockefeller.

Chapter 3

Page 82: Granger, NYC — All rights reserved; p. 85: Granger, NYC — All rights reserved; p. 86: Connecticut Historical Society Museum; p. 88: Granger, NYC — All rights reserved; p. 89: North Wind Picture Archive; p. 90:Granger, NYC — All rights reserved; p. 91: Granger, NYC — All rights reserved; p. 93: Germantown Historical Society, Philadelphia, PA; p. 96: Granger, NYC — All rights reserved; p. 98: *The Rapalje Children,* 1768 (oil on canvas), Durand, John (1731-1805)/© Collection of the New-York Historical Society/Bridgeman Images; p. 99: Library Company of

Philadelphia; p. 101: Philadelphia Museum of Art, Pennsylvania/ Gift of Mr. and Mrs. Wharton Sinkler/Bridgeman Images; p. 103: Granger, NYC — All rights reserved; p. 104: Private Collection/Bridgeman Images.

Chapter 4
Page 108: Library of Congress; p. 112: MPI/Getty Images; p. 115: I.N. Phelps Stokes Collection Miriam and Ira D. Wallach Division of Art, Prints and Photographs, New York Public Library, Astor, Lenox and Tilden Foundations. Art Resource, NY; p. 116: Granger, NYC — All rights reserved; p. 119: Library of Congress; p. 120: © Collection of the New-York Historical Society/ Bridgeman Images; p. 121: Granger, NYC — All rights reserved; p. 126: Library of Congress; p. 127: Library of Congress; p. 129: Peter Newark American Pictures/Bridgeman Images; p. 131: Library of Congress; p. 132: Library of Congress; p. 133: Library of Congress; p. 135: Library of Congress; p. 137: Virginia Historical Society/ Bridgeman Images; p. 138: Granger, NYC — All rights reserved; p. 142: Courtesy of the Philadelphia History Museum at the Atwater Kent, The Historical Society of Pennsylvania Collection; p. 143: National Archives; p. 144: North Wind Picture Archives/ Alamy.

Chapter 5
Page 152 (pamphlet): Private Collection/Photo © Christie's Images/Bridgeman Images; (cartoon): Granger, NYC — All rights reserved; (burning frigate): © Collection of the New-York Historical Society/Bridgeman Images; (Jefferson): Granger, NYC — All rights reserved; (flag painting): Photography by Erik Arnesen © Nicholas S. West; (pamphlet text): Private Collection/Photo © Christie's Images/Bridgeman Images; p. 154: Granger, NYC — All rights reserved; p. 156: Francis G. Mayer/Corbis/VCG via Getty Images; p. 159: US Senate Collection; p. 162: Brooklyn Historical Society; p. 163 (left): Courtesy, American Antiquarian Society; (right): Granger, NYC — All rights reserved; p. 167: Granger, NYC — All rights reserved; p. 170: Pennsylvania State Capitol/Bridgeman Images; p. 171: Granger, NYC — All rights reserved; p. 174: Private Collection/Peter Newark Pictures/Bridgeman Images; p. 179: Anne S.K. Brown Military Collection, Brown University Library; p. 180: Library of Congress; p. 183: Granger, NYC — All rights reserved; p. 185: Granger, NYC — All rights reserved; p. 187: Granger, NYC — All rights reserved.

Chapter 6
Page 190: Granger, NYC — All rights reserved; p. 193: Granger, NYC — All rights reserved; p. 196: The Miriam and Ira D. Wallach Division of Art, Prints and Photographs: Print Collection, The New York Public Library; p. 197: Private Collection/J. T. Vintage/ Bridgeman Images; p. 198: Courtesy of Independence National Historical Park; p. 199: Granger, NYC — All rights reserved; p. 202: Granger, NYC — All rights reserved; p. 205: Library of Congress; p. 210: Collection of the New-York Historical Society/ Bridgeman Images; p. 211: Albert Knapp/Alamy Stock Photo; p. 213: Everett Collection Historical/Alamy Stock Photo; p. 214: Granger, NYC — All rights reserved; p. 216: Library of Congress; p. 217: Granger, NYC — All rights reserved; p. 219: Granger, NYC — All rights reserved; p. 221: Granger, NYC — All rights reserved; p. 222: Granger, NYC — All rights reserved; p. 223: Granger, NYC — All rights reserved; p. 224: Granger, NYC — All rights reserved.

Chapter 7
Page 228: Photography by Erik Arnesen © Nicholas S. West; p. 231: Library of Congress; p. 232: © RMN-Grand Palais/ Art Resource, NY; p. 236: Musee Franco-Americaine, Blerancourt, Chauny/Roger-Viollet, Paris/Bridgeman Images; p. 238: Copyright American Philosophical Society; p. 239: EncMstr/Wikimedia; https://creativecommons.org/licenses/by-sa/3.0/deed.en; p. 241: Bettmann/Getty Images; p. 242: Collection of the New-York Historical Society/Bridgeman Art Library; p. 244: Library of Congress; p. 245: Courtesy of the New-York Historical Society; p. 246: Granger, NYC — All rights reserved; p. 248: Granger, NYC — All rights reserved; p. 249: Granger, NYC — All rights reserved; p. 251: American Antiquarian Society, Worcester/Bridgeman Images; p. 257: Granger, NYC — All rights reserved; p. 259: Library of Congress.

Chapter 8
Page 268 (Clay): National Currency Foundation/Wikimedia, public domain; (slaves): Private Collection/Peter Newark American Pictures/Bridgeman Images; (Slave broker ad): Private Collection/Courtesy of Swann Auction Galleries/Bridgeman Images; (school): Granger, NYC — All rights reserved; (steamboats): Minnesota Historical Society; (mill workers): Granger, NYC — All rights reserved; p. 270:Yale University Art Gallery/ Wikimedia, pd; p. 271: The Walters Art Museum, Baltimore; p. 272: Granger, NYC — All rights reserved; p. 276: Minnesota Historical Society; p. 278: Fenimore Art Museum, N0394.1955; p. 281: Granger, NYC — All rights reserved; p. 283: from Official catalogue Great Exhibition, Crystal Palace, London 1851, pd; p. 285: Granger, NYC — All rights reserved; p. 289: Granger, NYC — All rights reserved; p. 291: Granger, NYC — All rights reserved; p. 292: The New York Public Library/Art Resource, NY; p. 295: *The Country School*, 1871 (oil on canvas), Homer, Winslow (1836-1910)/Saint Louis Art Museum/Bridgeman Images.

Chapter 9
Page 298: Photo © Christie's Images/Bridgeman Images; p. 303: Library of Congress; p. 304: Image copyright © The Metropolitan Museum of Art. Image source: Art Resource, NY; p. 305: National Currency Foundation/Wikimedia, public domain; p. 307: Granger, NYC — All rights reserved; p. 312: Granger, NYC — All rights reserved; p. 314: Yale University Art Gallery/ Wikimedia, pd; p. 315: Library of Congress; p. 317: Image copyright © The Metropolitan Museum of Art. Image source: Art Resource, NY; p. 319: Collection of the New-York Historical Society/ Bridgeman Images.

Chapter 10
Page 324: The Museum of the City of New York/Art Resource, NY; p. 326: Library of Congress; p. 329: Granger, NYC — All rights reserved; p. 331: Library of Congress; p. 332: Peter Newark American Pictures/Bridgeman Images; p. 334:akg-images/Classic Stock/CHARLES PHELPS CUSHING; p. 336: Library of Congress; p. 338: Granger, NYC — All rights reserved; p. 339: National Archives; p. 341: Granger, NYC — All rights reserved; p. 345: Library of Congress; p. 347: Library of Congress; p. 348: Library of Congress; p. 350: Library of Congress.

Chapter 11
Page 354: Universal History Archive/UIG/Bridgeman Images; p. 358: Eron Johnson Antiques; p. 360: Granger, NYC — All rights reserved; p. 364: Granger, NYC — All rights reserved; p. 365: Fotosearch/Getty Images; p. 367: North Wind Picture Archives/Alamy Stock Photo; p. 369: © Atwater Kent Museum of Philadelphia/Courtesy of Historical Society of Pennsylvania Collection,/The Bridgeman Art Library; p. 371: Granger, NYC — All rights reserved; p. 372: Private Collection/Courtesy of Swann Auction Galleries/Bridgeman Images; p. 373: Courtesy of the Peabody Museum of Archaeology and Ethnology, Harvard University, PM 35-5-10/53044; p. 375: Abby Aldrich Rockefeller Folk Art Museum, Colonial Williamsburg Foundation, Williamsburg, VA; p. 376: Private Collection/Peter Newark American Pictures/Bridgeman Art Library; p. 377: The Historic New Orleans Collection/Bridgeman Images; p. 380: Peter Newark American Pictures/Bridgeman Images.

Chapter 12
Page 386: Fine Art/Alamy Stock Photo; p. 390: Granger, NYC — All rights reserved; p. 392: Image copyright © The Metropolitan Museum of Art. Image source: Art Resource, NY; p. 393: Granger, NYC — All rights reserved; p. 394: Library of Congress; p. 395: Lordprice Collection/Alamy Stock Photo; p. 398: Image copyright © The Metropolitan Museum of Art. Image source: Art Resource, NY; p. 399: Bettmann/Getty Images; p. 400: Bettmann/Getty Images; p. 401: Ian Dagnall Computing/Alamy Stock Photo; p. 402: Library of Congress; p. 403: The Walters Art Museum, Baltimore; p. 404: World History Archive/Alamy Stock Photo; p. 407 (left): Library of Congress; (right): J. T. Vintage/Bridgeman Images; p. 408: Granger, NYC — All rights reserved; p. 409: Peter Newark Pictures/Bridgeman Images; p. 410: New York Public Library/Bridgeman Images; p. 413: Granger, NYC — All rights reserved; p. 414 (both): Library of Congress; p. 417 (left): Granger, NYC — All rights reserved; (right): Library of Congress.

Chapter 13
Page 426 (Barton): Library of Congress; (handbill): Granger, NYC — All rights reserved; (painting): Smithsonian American Art Museum/Art Resource; (ex-slaves): Library of Congress; (ad): Granger, NYC — All rights reserved; (Brown): Private Collection/Peter Newark American Pictures/Bridgeman Images; (currency): National Numismatic Collection at the Smithsonian Institution; p. 428: Civil War Archive/The Bridgeman Art "Library; p. 430: Butler Institute of American Art, Youngstown/Gift of Joseph G. Butler III 1946/Bridgeman Images; p. 434: Image copyright © The Metropolitan Museum of Art. Image source:

Art Resource, NY; p. 435: Peter Newark American Pictures/Bridgeman Images; p. 437: Granger, NYC — All rights reserved; p. 439: MPI/Getty Images; p. 441: Granger, NYC — All rights reserved; p. 442: Granger, NYC — All rights reserved; p. 444: Granger, NYC — All rights reserved; p. 445: American Antiquarian Society, Worcester, Massachusetts/Bridgeman Images; p. 447: National Portrait Gallery, Smithsonian Institution/Art Resource; p. 449: ullstein bild/Granger, NYC — All rights reserved; p. 451: American Antiquarian Society/Bridgeman Images; p. 455: Chronicle/Alamy Stock Photo; p. 456: Art Resource; p. 457: Granger, NYC — All rights reserved; p. 459: Library of Congress; p. 460: Granger, NYC — All rights reserved; p. 463: akg-images/The Image Works; p. 465: The New York Public Library/Art Resource; p. 468: Art Resource; p. 470 (left): Private Collection/Peter Newark American Pictures/Bridgeman Images; (right): Granger, NYC — All rights reserved; p. 471: Private Collection/Peter Newark American Pictures/Bridgeman Images; p. 475: Granger, NYC — All rights reserved.

Chapter 14
Page 480: Chicago History Museum; p. 482: Library of Congress; p. 486 (top): Buyenlarge/Getty Images; (bottom): Library of Congress; p. 488: Private Collection/The Stapleton Collection/Bridgeman Images; p. 489: Peter Newark Military Pictures/Bridgeman Images; p. 491: Library of Congress; p. 495: Granger, NYC — All rights reserved; p. 498: Library of Congress; p. 499: Bettmann/Corbis/Getty Images; p. 500: Library of Congress; p. 501: Library of Congress; p. 502: Library of Congress; p. 503: Library of Congress; p. 507: Beinecke Rare Book and Manuscript Library, Yale University/Wikimedia Commons; pd; p. 509 (left): Library of Congress; (right): © Boston Athenaeum/Bridgeman Images; p. 514: Library of Congress; p. 515: Library of Congress; p. 516: Library of Congress; p. 520: National Archives; p. 522: Library of Congress; p. 524: Library of Congress; p. 526: Library of Congress.

Chapter 15
Page 532: Smithsonian American Art Museum/Art Resource; p. 535: Granger, NYC — All rights reserved; p. 537: Library of Congress; p. 538: Photo Researchers, Inc/Alamy Stock Photo; p. 539: Library of Congress; p. 540: Granger, NYC — All rights reserved; p. 543: Library of Congress; p. 545: Library of Congress; p. 548: Bettmann/Corbis/Getty Images; p. 549: Library of Congress; p. 550: Library of Congress; p. 552: Granger, NYC — All rights reserved; p. 553: Library of Congress; p. 555: John Kraljevich/John Kraljevich Americana; p. 556: Chronicle/Alamy Stock Photo; p. 558: akg-images/Fototeca Gilardi; p. 561: Library of Congress.

Index

Page numbers in *italics* refer to illustrations.

abolition movement, 411–419
  abolitionism defined, 412
  African Americans in, 415–417
  African colonization proposed by, 412
  Fugitive Slave Act and, 459–460
  gradualism, 412
  mail censorship and, 345–346, 413
  reactions to, 418–419
  split in, 413–415
  Underground Railroad and, 382, 417–418
  women and, 414–415, 416–417
Acadians, 119
Act of Union (1707), 87
Adams, Abigail, 140, 142, 186–187, 197, 225
Adams, Charles Francis, 317
Adams, Henry (former slave), 562
Adams, John
  absence from Constitutional Convention, 199
  administration of, 222–224, 225
  Alien and Sedition Acts and, 224
  on American ambitions, 230
  American Revolution and, 140, 180–181
  in Continental Congress, 222
  Declaration of Independence and, 142, 222
  in election of 1796, 221–222
  in election of 1800, 225
  as Federalist leader, 209, 232
  inauguration, 231
  Jefferson and, 216, 222, 223–224, 225
  on peace commission, 178
  "quasi-war" with France, 222–223
  on Townshend Acts, 131
  as vice president, 209, 222
  on Washington, 209
  on women's rights, 187
Adams, John Quincy
  on Andrew Jackson, 326
  economic nationalism, *315,* 317
  in election of 1824, 314, *315,* 316
  in election of 1828, 318–319, *320*
  on Elijah Lovejoy's death, 419
  on impressment, 243
  Masonic order and, 342
  on Mexican-American War, 447
  Missouri Compromise and, 310
  Monroe Doctrine and, 313, 316
  photograph, *317*
  presidency of, 225, 316–318
  as secretary of state, 310, 312, 313, 314, 316, 318
    slavery and, 346
  Transcontinental Treaty, 312
  on Van Buren, 347
Adams, Samuel
  anti-British agitation, 144
  anti-Federalist, 206
  British plan to arrest, 137
  Committee of Correspondence, 134
  Continental Association and, 136
  Sons of Liberty, 128
  Stamp Act Riots and, 150
  Townshend Acts and, 132
Adena culture, 14
African Americans
  in abolition movement, 415–417
  in American Revolution, 158, 184–185
  in antebellum South, 368–383
  black code restrictions on, 96, 542, 552, 567
  as Civil War soldiers, 507–508, 549
  free blacks, 93, 369–370, 412, 550–551
  freedmen's conventions, 540–541
  Irish Americans and, 289
  mulattoes, 309, 370, 375
  in politics, 549–550
  in Reconstruction, 537, 546–551, 559, 568
  religion of, 79, 377–378, 391–392, 546–547
  in Seminole War, *312*
  sharecroppers, *550,* 551
  Union League and, 547–549, 552
  voting rights for, 319, 428, 539, 546
  see also civil rights and liberties; slavery; slaves; slave trade
African Methodist Episcopal (AME) Church, 379, 392, 547
Age of Reason (Enlightenment), 99–103, 105
agriculture
  biological exchange and, 30–31
  in colonial period, 61, 88, 91
  in early nineteenth century, 229, 273–274
  enclosure movement in Europe, 84
  in middle colonies, 91
  of Native Americans, 9
  in New England, 91
  sharecropping, *550,* 551
  in South, 88, 355–356, 359–363
  staple crops, 88, 91
Agriculture, Department of, 510
Alabama, secession of, 476, 482
Alamo, 113, 439–440
Albany Plan of Union, 119
Albemarle, 59
  see also North Carolina colony
Alexander I, Czar, 313, 318
Algonquian-speaking peoples, 16, 17, 67, *71,* 74
Alien and Sedition Acts, 224, 225
Allen, Ethan, 140
Allen, Richard, 391, 392
American Anti-Slavery Society, 413, 415
American Colonization Society, 412
American Crisis, The (Paine), 163
American Dream of equal opportunity, 44–45, 288, 407
American party (Know-Nothings), 291, 462
American Revenue Act of 1764 (the Sugar Act), 125–126
American Revolution, 156–189
  African-American soldiers in, 158, 184–185
  American society in, 178–180
  American strategy, 164, 166, 176
  Boston Tea Party and, *108,* 134–135
  British strategy, 158, 166, 173–174
  campaigns of 1777, 166–167, *169*
  camp followers, 186
  Canadian campaign, 160
  causes of, 144–145, 148–151
  Continental army, 158, 159, 161
  debt after, 212
  finance and supply of, 166, 168, 170
  France and, 153, 158, 167–168, 176, 215
  frontier in, 171–173
  Hessians in, 158, 164, 173
  independence issue in, 141–142, 145
  Lexington and Concord, 137–139
  Loyalists in, 153, 158, 171–174
  militias in, 137–139, 140, 159, 163, 167, 185
  Native Americans and, 158, 160, 171–173, 178, 187
  New York and New Jersey campaigns (1776–1777), 161–166
  political revolution and, 180–181
  slavery and, 144, 184–185, 203
  social revolution and, 183
  in the South, 173–177
  Spain and, 168
  Treaty of Paris (1783) and, 177–178, 193, 195, 216–217, 222
  Valley Forge, winter of 1777–1778, 168, 170–171
  western campaigns (1776–1779), 171–173
  women and, 185–187, 203
  see also specific battles and locations
American Society for the Promotion of Temperance, 404

American System, 305–306, 314, 315–316, 346, 442
American Temperance Union, 404
Americas
    English exploration of, 21–22, *36*, 37–39
    European biological exchange with, 30–31
    European exploration of, 4
    first migrations to, 7–8
    French and Dutch exploration of, 35–37
    pre-Columbian, 7–17
    Spanish exploration in, 19–21, 31–33
Ames, Adelbert, 552
Ames, Fisher, 232
Anaconda Plan, 487
Anasazi (Ancient Ones), 13
Anderson, Robert, 475, 477
Andros, Edmund, 116
Anthony, Susan B., *239*, 406–407, 546
Antietam, Battle of, 501–502
anti-Federalists, 204, 205–206, *207*, 209
    see also Federalists
Anti-Masonic party, 342, 343, 346
anti-slavery movement, *see* abolition movement
Antonio (slave), 96
Antrobus, John, *377*
Appomattox Court House, Lee's surrender at, 526–527
Arapaho, 436
Arizona Territory, 492
Arkansas, secession of, 482
Arnold, Benedict, 140, 178
Arthur, Chester A., 489
Articles of Confederation, 119, 154, 181–182, 192–193, 198, 199–200, 201
Artisans of Boston, The (1766), *82*
Asbury, Francis, 391
asylum reform movements, 405
Atahualpa, king, *6*
Atchison, David, 463
attorneys, as a profession, 293–294
Attucks, Crispus, 132
Auburn Penitentiary, 405
Augsburg, Treaty of, 24
Aunt Phillis's Cabin; or, Southern Life as It Is (Eastman), 357, *358*
Austin, Stephen Fuller, 438
Aztec Empire, 11, 28
    see also Mexica

Bacon, Nathaniel, 70–71
Bacon's Rebellion, 70–71
Bailey, Ann, 186
Bailyn, Bernard, 148, 149
Ballou, Sarah, 491
Ballou, Sullivan, 491
Baltimore, first Lord (George Calvert), 51
Baltimore, second Lord (Cecilius Calvert), 51, 53

Bank of the United States (B.U.S.)
    Hamilton's recommendation for, 213
    Jackson and, 328, 331–333, 343–344, 348, *350*
    lapse of charter in 1811, 250, 300, 331
    Panic of 1819 and, 308
    Second Bank of the United States, 261, 300–301, 303, 305–306, 331–333, 445
Bank War, 331–332, 343
Baptists, 93, 367, 391, 547
Barbados, 59
Barbary pirates, 242–243
Barrow, Bennett, 374
barter, 97
Barton, Clara, 508, *509*
Beard, George M., 294
Beauregard, Pierre G. T., 477, 485, 494
Beecher, Catharine, 405–406, 414–415
Beecher, Lyman, 402
Bell, John, 473, 474
Benton, Thomas Hart, 305–306, 337, 344, 452
Berkeley, John, 61, 63
Berkeley, William, 51, 70–71
Bernard, Francis, 128, 150, 151
Bethune, Mary McLeod, 547
Bibb, Henry, 415
Biddle, Nicholas, 331–332, 343, 344
Biddlecom, Charles, 491–492
Bienville, Jean-Baptiste Le Moyne, sieur de, 112–113
Bierstadt, Albert, *430*
Bingham, George Caleb, *221*
Birney, James Gillespie, 415
birth rates in colonial period, 84
black codes, 96, 542, 552, 567
Black Hawk War, 338
Blackwell, Elizabeth, 294
Blaine, James Gillespie, 561
Blair, Francis P. Jr., 555
Boleyn, Anne, 26
Bonaparte, Napoléon, 236, 243, 247, 254, 258
Book of Mormon, The, 394
Boone, Daniel, 173, 220–221, 275
Booth, John Wilkes, 538–539
Border South, 359
Boston, MA, 98, *115*
Boston English High School, 408
Boston Massacre (1770), 132–133
Boston Port Act, 135
Boston Tea Party, *108,* 134–135
Boudinot, Elias, 338
Braddock, Edward, 120
Bragg, Braxton, 496, 518, 534
Brant, Joseph, 159, 171
Breckinridge, John C., 472, *473,* 474
"Brer [Brother] Rabbit," 376
Brook Farm, 411

Brooklyn Eagle, 402
Brooks, Preston S., 465–466
Brown, Frederick, 466
Brown, John, 419, 460, 464–465, 471–472
Brown, Joseph, 512
Brown, Moses, 260
Brown, Peter, 141
Brown, Wells, 415
Brown, William Wells, 415–416
Bruce, Blanche K., 549
Buchanan, James
    Buchanan-Pakenham Treaty (1846), 446
    Dred Scott case and, 467–468
    in election of 1856, 466–467
    Financial Panic of 1857, 467
    Lecompton constitution supported by, 468–469
    secession and, 475
Buchanan-Pakenham Treaty (1846), 446
Buena Vista, Battle of (1847), 449
Bull Run, First Battle of (Manassas), 485–487
Bull Run, Second Battle of (Manassas), 498
Bunker Hill, Battle of, 140–141
Bureau of Colored Troops, 507
Burgoyne, John, 166–167
burial mounds, 14
burned-over district, 393
Burns, John, 515
Burnside, Ambrose E., 505–506, 513
Burr, Aaron, 222, 225, 239, 241
Butler, Andrew Pickens, 465, 466
Butler, Benjamin F., 496

Cabot, John, 21–22, 36
Cahokia, 15–16
Cahokia, IL, 171
Cajuns, 119
Calhoun, John C.
    Compromise of 1850 and, 456, 457
    Eaton Affair and, 330
    economic nationalism, 300
    in election of 1824, 314, 315
    internal improvements and, 301, 314
    Jackson's rift with, 312, 335, 342
    James Monroe and, 307
    national bank issue and, 300
    nullification issue and, 333–334, 335, 336, 337
    response to slave rebellion, 380
    as secretary of war, 307, 311, 312, 314
    Seminoles and, 311
    on slavery, 356, 357, 419, 452
    slavery on frontier and, 452
    Van Buren and, 329, 330–331, 347, 453
    as vice president, 316, 329, 333
    War of 1812 and, 250
California
    annexation of, 448
    gold rush in, 453–456

Mexican secularization act and *ranchos*, 436–437
settlement of, 436–437
statehood, 456, 459
Calvert, Cecilius (second Lord Baltimore), 51–53
Calvert, George (first Lord Baltimore), 51
Calvert, Leonard, 51–53
Calvin, Charles, *202*
Calvin, John, 24–25
Camden, SC, 173
Campbell, Alexander and James, 490
camp followers, 186
camp meeting revivals, 390–391, 392–393
Canada and War of 1812, 249, 250, 251–254, 255–256
canals, 276–277
Canning, George, 313
capitalism, 211
Capitol building, 230, *231*, 256, *257*
caravels, 18
Cardozo, Francis, 549
Carolina colonies, 59–61, 73, 88
carpetbaggers, 551–552, 554, 562
Carter, Landon, 144
Carteret, George, 61
Cartier, Jacques, 36
Cass, Lewis, 434, 452, 453
Catherine of Aragon, 26
Catholicism, Catholic Church
Counter-Reformation, 25
defined, 23
in England, 46, 47
in French colonies, 110
Indians and, 21, 23, 33, 35–36
Irish Americans in, 290
in Maryland colony, 51–52, 53
missionaries of, 33, 34, 436
nativism and, 290–291, 462
Reformation attacks on, 23–24
in Spanish Empire, 33, *34*
Cavaliers, 47
Cavelier, René-Robert, 112
censoring the mail, 345–346, 413
Cession, Treaty of (1803), 237
Chamberlain, Joshua, 526
Champlain, Samuel de, 110
Chancellorsville, Battle of (1863), *486,* 513
Chandler, Zachariah, 486–487
Chappel, Alonzo, *162*
Charles Calvert and His Slave, 202
Charles I, 47, 51, 56, 88
Charles II, 47, 61, 63, 115
Charleston (Charles Town), SC
American Revolution and, 173, 176, 184
in colonial period, 59, 73, 95–96, 98
Denmark Vesey Revolt, 379–380
Chase, Samuel, 206
Chattanooga, Battle of (1863), 518
Cherokee Nation v. Georgia, 340

Cherokee Phoenix, 338
Cherokees
American Revolution and, 160, 173
in Civil War, 493
Eastern Band of, 341
French and Indian War, 121
Jackson and, 338, 341
relationship with Europeans, *45,* 73
removal of, 338, 339–341, 441
Sam Houston and, 440–441
Treaty of New Echota, 338
War of 1812 and, 254
war with rival groups, 17
Chesapeake, U.S.S., 244
Chesnut, Mary Boykin, 365, 366, 519, 523, 534
Cheves, Langdon, 308
Cheyenne, 436
Chickamauga, Battle of, 518, 522
Chickasaws, 17, 73, *340,* 493
Child, Lydia Maria, 492
Chile, 30
China, mid-nineteenth century trade with, 461
Chinese Americans
gold rush and, 455, *456*
immigration of, 288
Chippewas, 218
Choctaws, 17, *340,* 493
Church of England (Anglican Church)
in British colonies, 102, 183
in Reformation in England, 25–26
Church of Jesus Christ of Latter-day Saints (Mormons), 394–397, 406
cities and towns
in colonial period, 98
industrialization and, 286–287
citizenship and naturalization, 202, 543
citizen-soldiers, 116, 159
"Civil Disobedience" (Thoreau), 401
Civil Rights Act (1866), 543
civil rights and liberties in Civil War, 512
civil service reform, 558
Civil War, 480–531
African American soldiers in, 507–508, 549
aftermath of, 527–529, 534–535
Anaconda Plan of the Union in, 487
Antietam, 501–502
beginning at Fort Sumter, 475, 477, 481, 482, 485, 527
campaigns in the East, 485–487, 496–498, 514–518, 520–522, 526
campaigns in the West, 492–496, 501–502, 505–506, 513–514, 518
casualties in, 428, 490, 528, 533
Chancellorsville and, *486,* 513
Chattanooga and, 518
choosing sides in, 482–484
civil liberties and, 512

Confederate finances in, 511
Confederate strategy in, 487, 513
Confederate surrender at Appomattox, 526–527
creation of armies for, 488–489
diplomacy and, 487
emancipation in, 499, 500, 502–504, 506, 529
First Bull Run (First Manassas), 485–487
Fredericksburg and, 505–506
Gettysburg and, 514–518, 522
government during, 509–510
Grant's strategy in, 519–520
inflation during, 557
as modern war, 523, 528, 529
Native Americans in, 493
New York City draft riots, 506–507
Peninsular Campaign in, 497–498
Perryville and, 496
reasons for, 481–482
recruitment and draft in, 488–489, 506–507
regional advantages in, 484–485
secession of South and, 481–482, *483*
Second Bull Run (Second Manassas), 498
Seven Pines (Fair Oaks), 498
Sherman's campaigns during, 520, 522–526
Shiloh and, 493–496
slavery and, 428, 482, 489–490
soldiers
becoming warriors, 491–492
description, 488, 490
life of, 490–491
why they fought, 489–490, 491
states' rights and, 481–482, 512–513, 527
Union finances in, 510–511, 528
Vicksburg and, 513–514, 518
women and, 508, 528–529
see also Confederate States of America; Reconstruction
Clark, George Rogers, 171
Clark, William, 238–239, *240*
Clay, Henry
American Colonization Society and, 412
on American desire for profits, 229
American System and economic nationalism, 305–306, 310, 314, 315–316, 346, 442
on Andrew Jackson, 327, 351
Compromise of 1850 and, 456–457
Distribution Act, 344, *345*
duel with John Randolph, 241, 365
in election of 1824, 314, 315–316, 330
in election of 1832, 342, 343
in election of 1840, 349, 442
in election of 1844, 443, 444, 449
Masonic order and, 342
Missouri Compromise and, 309

Clay, Henry (continued)
　national bank debate and, 300, 332, 343, 442–443
　nullification and, 337
　Panic of 1837 and, 349
　portrait, 305
　slavery and, 306, 337, 419, 450
　War of 1812 and, 248, 250
Clay, Henry, Jr., 449
Clemson, Thomas, 369
Clermont, 276
Cleveland, Grover, 489
Clinton, Catherine, 422–423
Clinton, George, 206, 239
Clinton, Henry, 141, 173
clipper ships, 278–279
Clovis peoples, 9
Cobb, Howell, 548
Cobb, Thomas Reade, 356, 369
Cobbett, William, 404
Coercive Acts (1774), 135–136
Cohens v. Virginia, 303
Cold Harbor. Battle of, 520–521
Cole, Thomas, 398
Coleto, Battle of, 398, 440
Collet, John, 104
Colombia, 30
colonies, British, 42–81, 82–107
　agriculture in, 88
　birth and death rates in, 84–85
　Carolina colonies, 59–61, 73, 88
　Chesapeake region, 48–53
　cities in, 98
　conflicts between Native Americans and settlers, 68, 70–71, 72–73
　Connecticut colony, 58
　Delaware colony, 65–66
　Dutch colonies taken, 44
　elected legislative assemblies in, 113
　English background, 44–48
　Enlightenment in, 99–103, 105
　ethnic mix in, 93
　European settlement in, 48–67
　Georgia colony, 60, 66–67
　goals and motivations of colonization, 44–45
　Great Awakening in, 102–105
　indentured servants in, 75, 84, 87–88, 93
　Indian tribes and European settlements, map, 69
　individualism and, 105
　Maine colony, 55, 59
　Maryland colony, 51–53
　Massachusetts Bay Colony, 54, 55–57, 90
　mercantilism in, 114, 115
　middle colonies, 61–67
　New England, 53–59
　New Hampshire colony, 59
　New Jersey colony, 63, 64
　New Netherland colony, 44, 61–63, 64

Pennsylvania colony, 64–65, 71–72
Plymouth colony, 50, 54–55
political traditions, 45–46
population growth in, 82, 93
population in 1750, 45, 84
as profitable, 79
prosperity, 79
relations between Native Americans and settlers, 67–74
religion in, 54, 55–56, 89–90
religious freedom in, 53, 57, 60, 65, 183
Rhode Island colony, 55, 57–58, 60, 71
roads and transportation in, 98
slavery in, 44, 73, 75–76, 78–79, 88, 95–97
society and economy in, 87–93, 98–99
　middle colonies, 91–93
　New England, 82, 89–91
　southern colonies, 88
taverns in, 98–99
taxation in, 122, 125–131, 144–145
trade with Native Americans, 68, 73, 74
triangular trade in, 77–78, 91, 92
voting in, 113
warfare in, 117–122
ways of life in, 82–107
witchcraft in, 89–90
women in, 85–87
see also England; Virginia colony
Colorado Territory, 492
Columbian Exchange, 30–31
Columbus, Christopher, 3, 19–21
Comanches, 438
Command of the Army Act (1867), 544
Committees of Correspondence, 134
Common Sense (Paine), 141, 163
Commonwealth v. Hunt, 293
communication in early nineteenth century, 279
Compromise of 1790, 212
Compromise of 1850, 456–459, 461
Compromise of 1877, 560–562
Conciliatory Propositions, 137
Concord, Battle of (1775), 138–139
Conestogas, 274
Confederate States of America
　diplomacy of, 487
　finances of, 511
　formation of, 476
　politics in, 512–513
　population, 484
　recruitment and draft in, 488–489
　strategy of, 487, 513
　see also Civil War
Confederation Congress
　foreign tensions and, 195
　land policy and land ordinances, 193–195
　Loyalist property and, 195
　paper currency and, 192, 196–197
　powers of, 182, 192–193
　trade/economy and, 195–196

Treaty of Paris (1783), 193, 195
　weaknesses of, 182, 192
Congregational Church, 183
Congregationalists, 55, 56, 105
Congress, U.S.
　Bill of Rights and, 206
　in Constitution, 200–201
　creation of Internal Revenue Service, 510
　executive departments established by, 210–211
　first meeting of, 209
　House of Representatives, 200, 201
　Indian policy and, 338
　internal improvements and, 330–331
　Johnson's conflict with, 543, 567
　national bank issue in, 213, 300–301, 343, 442–443
　Reconstruction and, 543–545, 546, 549, 552, 555, 560, 563
　see also Senate, U.S.
Congressional Reconstruction, 543–545, 546, 549, 552, 555, 560, 563
Connecticut colony, 58
Connecticut (Great) Compromise, 200
conquistadores, 28, 29–30, 33, 39, 45
Constitution, U.S.
　Bill of Rights, 206–208
　drafting and signing of, 198–200
　flexibility and resilience of, 208–209
　ratification of, 206
　separation of powers and, 200–202
　slavery in, 202–203, 209
　Washington on, 208
　women's political rights absent in, 203–204
constitutional amendments, U.S.
　Bill of Rights, 206–208
　First, 207–208
　Fifth, 452
　Tenth, 208
　Twelfth, 225, 239
　Thirteenth, 415, 476–477, 503, 529, 533, 536, 539
　Fourteenth, 428, 542, 543–545, 563
　Fifteenth, 428, 546–547, 548, 563
Constitutional Convention (1787)
　delegates, 198–199
　drafting the Constitution, 199–200
　Great Compromise (Connecticut Compromise) , 200
　Madison at, 199, 200, 201, 202
　separation of powers issue in, 154, 200–202
　slavery issue in, 202–203
　Virginia and New Jersey Plans at, 200
　Washington at, 190, 198, 199
Constitutional Union party, 473–474
Continental army, 158, 159, 161
　see also American Revolution

Continental Association, 136
Continental Congress
    Articles of Confederation and, 181–182
    British Parliament and, 168
    Continental army and, 159, 161, 163, 166, 171, 174, 184
    Declaration of Independence, 142–144, 161, 222
    First Continental Congress, 135, 136–140
    flight from Philadelphia, 167
    John Adams and, 222
    negotiations with British, 178
    Olive Branch Petition, 141
    Quebec, Canada attack authorized, 159
    Second Continental Congress convened, 139
    Washington chosen as commander in chief, 140
contrabands, 499–500
contract rights, 303
Convention of 1800, 223
Convention of 1818, 310, 311, 435
Cooke, Jay, 511, 558
Cooper, Alice, 239
Cooper, Anthony Ashley, 60
Copernicus, Nicolaus, 100
Copperhead Democrats, 512, 514
corn (maize), 9, 30–31, 359
Cornwallis, Charles, 173–174, 175–177
Corps of Discovery, 238
corrupt bargain of 1824, 316
Cortés, Hernán, 28–30, 32
cotton
    cotton gin and, 281, 284, 360
    New England cotton mills, 260, 281, 282, 284, 360
    Old Southwest, 238, 333, 361, 372
    population growth and, 361, 363
    slavery and, 281–282, 360, 361, 376
    South and, 281–282, 355, 359–363, 474
Cotton, John, 86
cotton gin, 281, 284, 360
cotton kingdom, 359–363
coureurs des bois, 110
Cowpens, Battle of (1781), 174, 175
Craft, William and Ellen, 459–460
craft unions, 293
Crawford, William H., 314, 315, 316
Creeks, 17, 73, 251, 254–255, 340, 493
Crittenden, John J., 476
Crockett, David "Davy," 338, 439–440
Cromwell, Oliver, 47, 53, 114
Crown Point, 140
Cruikshank, Robert, 326
Cuba
    discovery and exploration, 19, 20, 27, 28
    Spain and, 313
Cudahy, Michael, 289–290
cult of domesticity, 405–406
Cumberland Gap, 221

Cumberland (National) Road, 301–302
currency
    in Confederation period, 192, 195–196
    gold standard, 557
    greenbacks, 510–511, 557–558, 561
    hard money, 97, 557, 561
    Legal Tender Act of 1862, 510–511
    money question, 344
    national bank issue and, 344
    soft money, 557
    Specie Circular, 344, 345, 348
Currency Act (1764), 126

Dare, Elinor, 38
Dare, Virginia, 38
Dartmouth College v. Woodward, 303
Daughters of Liberty, 129
Davis, David Brion, 265
Davis, Jefferson
    after the war, 527
    Civil War strategy of, 487
    Compromise of 1850 and, 456
    as Confederate president, 476, 477, 512–513, 514, 526
    enlistment efforts and, 488–489
    Lee's relationship with, 519
    photograph, 482
    secession of South and, 481, 482
    on transcontinental railroad, 461–462
Dawes, Henry L., 137
Dawes, William, 137
death rates in colonial period, 84, 85
de Bry, Theodor, 6
debt after American Revolution, 212
Decatur, Stephen, 242, 243
Declaration of American Rights, 136
Declaration of Independence, 142–144, 158, 191, 222, 266
Declaration of Sentiments, 406
Declaratory Act, 131
Deere, John, 283
deflation, 343, 557
de Grasse, François-Joseph-Paul de, 176
Deism, 100, 101, 103, 388
de la Cosa, Juan, 22
Delaware, Constitution ratified by, 206
Delaware colony, 44, 65–66, 102
Delawares, 173, 218
Democratic party
    in Civil War, 511–512
    Irish-American support for, 290
    Jacksonian Democrats, 318, 327–328, 539
    origins of, 314, 317, 351
    redeemers, 560
    slavery issue in, 472
    see also elections and campaigns
Democratic Republicans in 1790s, see Republicans, Jeffersonian
Democratic Republicans in 1820s, see Democratic party

Denmark Vesey Revolt, 378–379
Deslondes, Charles, 379
de Soto, Hernando, 6, 32, 33
Dickinson, Emily, 401–402
Dickinson, John, 142, 150–151
direct democracy, 181
Discourse on Women (Mott), 424
discovery and exploration
    by Columbus, 19–21
    English, 21–22, 36, 37–39
    French, 35–37, 110, 111, 112–113
    Spanish, 19–21, 31–33
    technology in, 18
Dissenters (in England), 46
Distribution Act (1836), 344, 345, 348
divine right of kings, 116
Dix, Dorothea Lynde, 405, 508
domesticity, cult of, 405–406
Dominion of New England, 115–116
Douglas, Stephen A.
    Compromise of 1850 and, 456, 459
    death of, 511
    in election of 1860, 472, 473, 474
    Kansas-Nebraska Act and, 462, 463
    on Lecompton Constitution, 469
    Lincoln's debates with, 469–470
Douglass, Frederick
    abolitionist movement and, 416, 504
    on African Americans in the military, 507
    Emancipation Proclamation and, 504
    escape from slavery, 366, 382, 415–416
    on Fugitive Slave Law, 460
    on overseers, 366–367
    portrait, 417, 549
    on spirituals, 378
    on Uncle Tom's Cabin, 461
Douglass, Sarah Mapps, 415
draft in Civil War, 488–489, 506–507
Dragging Canoe, Chief, 173
Dred Scott v. Sandford, 467–468
Drunkard's Progress, The, 404
Dunning, William, 566, 567
Durand, Asher B., 386
Durand, John, 98
Dutch East India Company, 61
Dutch Reformed Church, 102

Eastern Woodland peoples, 16–17
East India Company, 108, 134
Eastman, Mary Henderson, 357, 358
Eaton, John, 329–330
Eaton, Peggy, 329–330
Eaton Affair, 329–330
economy
    American System and, 305–306
    Civil War and, 527–528
    in colonial America, 87–93, 98–99
        middle colonies, 91–93
        New England, 90–91
        southern colonies, 88

economy *(continued)*
  in early nineteenth century, 269, 299
  Hamilton's economic reforms, 211–214
  household, 274
  Jefferson and, 234–235
  nationalism after War of 1812 and, 299,
    300–302, 317
  Panic of 1819 and, 307–308, 333
  rise of capitalism, 211
  see also market economy
Edwards, Jonathan, 102–104, 105
elections and campaigns
  of 1796, 221–222
  of 1800, 155, 191, 225, 230
  of 1804, 239
  of 1808, 245
  of 1816, 306
  of 1820, 307, 314
  of 1824, 314–316, 330
  of 1828, 318–319, *320,* 321
  of 1832, 329, 332–333, 342–343
  of 1836, 347
  of 1840, 349–350, 415, 442
  of 1844, 415, 443–444, 449
  of 1848, 434, 452–453
  of 1852, 461
  of 1856, 466–467
  of 1860, 472–474
  of 1864, 502, 519, 523, 539
  of 1868, 555
  of 1872, 558–559
  of 1876, 560–562
Electoral College, 201, 203, 209, 225
Elizabeth I, 26–27, 37–38, 39, 46
Emancipation Proclamation, 502–504,
  506, 507
Embargo Act (1807), 244–245, 284, 301
Emerson, Ralph Waldo, 271, 317, 399–400,
  401, 402, 459, 481
*Emigrants Crossing the Plains, or the Or-
  egon Trail* (Bierstadt), *430*
encomenderos, 30, 34
encomienda, 30
Encyclopédie des Voyages (La Roque), *120*
Enforcement Acts (1870–1871), 559
engineering as a profession, 294
England
  Catholics in, 46, 47
  explorations by, 21–22, *36,* 37–39
  monarchy of, 46–48
  political traditions, 45–46
  Reformation in, 25–27
  religious conflict and war, 46–48
  Spanish Armada defeated by, 37
  taxation in, 46
  see also colonies, British; Great Britain;
    Parliament, British
English Civil War (1642–1646), 53, 64, 114,
  116
Enlightenment, 99–103, 105, 388

Episcopal Church, 183
Equal Rights Associations (freedmen's conventions), 540–541
"Era of Good Feelings," 306–310, 314
Erie Canal, 276–277, 279, 287
Europe
  expansion of, 17–22
  religious conflict in, 22–27
  trade with Middle East and Asia, 18–19
  wars in seventeenth and eighteenth
    centuries, 5
  see also specific countries
evangelism and evangelists
  in First Great Awakening, 102, 103
  in Second Great Awakening, 389, 390,
    391, 393, 402–403
Everett, Sarah, 436
executive branch, in Constitution, 200, 201

Fallen Timbers, Battle of, 218, 219
Farragut, David, 496
Federal Highways Act of 1916, 306
federalism defined, 191, 200
Federalist Papers, The (Madison, Hamilton,
  and Jay), 204–205
Federalists
  about, 204, 209
  Alien and Sedition Acts of, 224
  concerns about Louisiana Purchase, 237
  in election of 1796, 221–222
  in election of 1800, 225, 230
  in election of 1808, 245
  in election of 1816, 306
  in election of 1820, 307, 314
  Federalist party birth in the 1790s, 154
  French Revolution and, 216
  Jay's Treaty and, 218
  Judiciary Act and, 233
  in ratification debate, 204–206
  support of elites, 232
  War of 1812 and, 247, 250, 258, 259–260,
    261
Federal Judiciary Act of 1789, 234
Ferdinand II, King of Aragon, 19, 20
Ferguson, Patrick, 174
Ferguson, Thomas, 551
feudalism, 17
field hands, 373–374
Fields, John W., 368–369
Fifteenth Amendment, 428, 546–547, *548,*
  563
Fifth Amendment, 452
Fillmore, Millard, 458–459, 460, 461, *466*
Finkelman, Paul, 264, 265
Finney, Charles Grandison, 393, 413
*First, Second, and Last Scene of Mortality,
  The* (Punderson), *86*
First Amendment, 207–208
First Battle of Bull Run (Manassas),
  485–487

First Continental Congress, 135, 136–140
First Great Awakening, 102–105, 388, 389
fishing in New England, 90–91
Fisk, James, Jr., 556
Fitzhugh, George, 328, 365, 369
Florida
  after American Revolution, 178
  secession of, 476, 482
  Spain and, 178, 219, 237, 310, 311–312
  statehood, 312
  U.S. acquisition of, 310–312
  War of 1812 and, 249–250, 258
Floyd, John, 343
Flying Cloud, 279
Foner, Eric, 566, 567
Force Bill (1833), 337
foreign policy and the Monroe Doctrine,
  313, 316
Fort Christina, 62, *64*
Fort Clatsop, 238
Fort Donelson, 493
Fort Duquesne, 118, 120
Fort Greenville, 218
Fort Henry, 493
Fort Jackson, Treaty of (1814), 254
Fort Le Boeuf, 117
Fort Mandan, 238
Fort McHenry, 256
Fort Mims, 254
Fort Moultrie, 339
Fort Necessity, 118
Fort Orange, 61, 63
Fort Sumter, 475, 477, 481, 482, 485, 526,
  527
Fort Ticonderoga, 140
Fort Wayne, IN, 218
Fourteenth Amendment, 428, 542,
  543–545, 563
Fox, 338
Fox, George, 64
France
  American alliance with (1778), 167–168
  American Revolution and, 153, 158,
    167–168, 176, 215
  Citizen Genet and, 216
  in colonial wars, 117–122
  discovery and explorations of, 35–37,
    110, *111,* 112–113
  Louisiana Territory of, 236
  in Napoleonic Wars, 243–244, 245,
    246–247, 254
  "quasi-war" with, 222–223
  Revolution in, 215, 216
Franklin, Battle of (1864), 524
Franklin, Benjamin
  about, 101
  on Adams, 222
  at Albany Congress, 119
  brothers and sisters, 84
  on Constitution, 208

on cultivation of Reason, 100
Declaration of Independence, 143–144
Deism, 100, 101, 388
Enlightenment (Age of Reason) and, 101
Franco-American military alliance, 153
on German immigrants, 93
on Great Awakening, 102
on peace commission, 178
political cartoon, *119*
on population growth, 84
Franklin, William, 178
Frazier, Garrison, 546
Fredericksburg, Battle of, 505–506
Free Africa Society, 391
Freedmen's Bureau, 536–537, 543
freedmen's conventions, 540–541
Free-Soil party, 453, 461, 462
free-will ideal and free-will ministers, 387–388, 393
Frémont, John C., 448, 466–467
French and Indian War, 117–122
Albany Plan of Union, 119
Battle of Great Meadows, 118–119
Battle of Monongahela, 120
Braddock's defeat, 120
Native Americans in, 117, 120, 121
Paris, Treaty of (1763), 121–122
Seven Years' War and, 120–121
French Revolution, 215, 216
frontier
American Revolution and, 171–173
in early U.S., 218
religious revivals on, 390–391
Wilderness Road and, 220–221, 275
see also West
frontier revivals, 390–391
Fugitive Slave Act (1850), 459–460, 466
Fulani tribesmen, 95
Fuller, Margaret, 398–399
Fuller, Timothy, 308
Fulton, Robert, 276, 304
Fundamental Constitutions of Carolina, 60
Fundamental Orders of Connecticut colony, 58
Fur Traders Descending the Missouri, 434
fur trading, 67, 74, 91, 110, 112, *434*
Futch, Charley, 517
Futch, John, 517

Gabriel's Rebellion, 378
Gadsden Purchase, 450
Gage, Thomas, 135, 137
Gallatin, Albert, 233, 234, 250, 260
Gambia, 95
Garfield, James A., 536, 562
Garner, Henry, 369
Garnett, Muscoe, 328
Garrison, William Lloyd, 412–414, 415, 416, 419, 447
Gaspée incident, 134

Gates, Horatio, 167
General Assembly of Virginia, 49–50, 383
General Court, Connecticut, 58
General Court, Massachusetts, 56, 57
Genet, Edmond-Charles-Édouard, 216
Geneva Medical College, 294
George Barrell Emerson School, *408*
George II, 66, 121
George III
American Revolution and, 141, 160, 167, 266
appointment of William Pitt, 131
ascension to the throne, 121
economic regulations on colonies, 122, 134–135
portrait, *121*
Royal Proclamation of 1763, 124
Tea Act of 1773, 134–135
George Whitefield Preaching (Collet), *104*
Georgia
Civil War fighting in, 522–526
Constitution ratified by, 206
secession of, 476, 482
Georgia, Cherokee Nation v., 340
Georgia, Worcester v., 340
Georgia colony, *60,* 66–67, 95
German Americans, 92–93, 288, 290
German Coast Uprising, 378–379
German Reformed Church, 24
Germany, unification in 1871, 4
Gerry, Elbridge, 206
Gettysburg, Battle of (1863), 514–518, 522
Gettysburg Address (1863), 518
Ghent, Treaty of (1814), 257–258, 260, 261, 310
Gibbons, Thomas, 304
Gibbons v. Ogden, 304
global warming, post-Ice Age, 9
Glorious Revolution, 48, 53, 116, 117
gold rush, 453–456
gold standard, 557
Goliad, TX, 440
Gone With the Wind, 354
Good, Sarah, 90
Goodyear, Charles, 280
Gorges, Ferdinando, 59
Gould, Jay, 556
government
during Civil War, 509–510
market economy and, 279
separation of powers in, 200–202
Gower, Elizabeth, 508
Gower, T.G., 508
Graduation Act (1854), 283
Grant, Ulysses S.
battles in Kentucky and Tennessee, 493
in election of 1868, 555
in election of 1872, 558–559
Lee's surrender to, 526–527
Lincoln assassination and, 538

on Mexican-American War, 450
military strategy of, 519–520
monetary policy and, 557–558
photograph, *514*
promotion to lieutenant general, 519
pursuit of Lee, 520–522, 526
Reconstruction and, 544, 559
retirement, 560–561
scandals in administration of, 555, 556–557
as secretary of war, 545
at Shiloh, 493–496
at Vicksburg, 513–514
Great Awakening, First, 102–105, 388
Great Awakening, Second, 389–390, 391, 392, 394, 402
Great Biological Exchange, 30–31
Great Britain
in colonial wars, 117–122
French Revolution and, 215
Jay's Treaty with, 216–218, 220, 222
in Napoleonic Wars, 243–244, 246–247, 254–255
Oregon Country and, *309,* 310, *311,* 435, 446
see also American Revolution; England; Parliament, British; War of 1812
Great Compromise (Connecticut Compromise), 200
Great Law of Peace, 74
Great Plains
about, 13
horses and, 35
Plains Indians, 13–14, 35, 434
Great Rebellion, The (Headley), *507*
Great Serpent Mound, *14*
Greeley, Horace, 453, 460, 521, 558–559
greenbacks, 510–511, 557–558, 561
Greene, Nathanael, 141, 174–176
Greenland, 22
Green Mountain Boys, 140
Greenville, Treaty of (1795), 218
Grenville, George, 125–127, 128, 130, 131
Grimké, Angelina, 414–415
Grimké, Sarah, 414–415
Griswold, Roger, *224*
Guadalupe Hidalgo, Treaty of (1848), 397, 450
Guilford Courthouse, Battle of (1781), 175

Habeas Corpus Act (1863), 512
Haiti, 379
Hale, John P., 461
Hall, Thomas, 562
Halleck, Henry, 496, 498, 512
Hamilton, Alexander
on Adams, 225
Burr's duel with, 239, 241
at Constitutional Convention, 201
debt-funding plan, 212

Hamilton, Alexander (continued)
economic reforms, 211–214
economic vision of, 211, 234, 273, 300, 305
election of 1800 and, 225
as Federalist leader, 154, 209
The Federalist Papers and, 204, *211*
federal tariffs and excise taxes, 212–213
French Revolution and, 215
Jefferson and, 213, 214–215
national bank promoted by, *211,* 213
proindustry proposals, 213–214
as secretary of the Treasury, 211–214
Hammond, James Henry, 346, 363, 364, 375
Hancock, John, 144
Harper, Eda, 533
Harper's Ferry, raid on (1859), 471
Harrington, Jonathan, 138
Harris, David, 511
Harrison, William Henry, 249, 347, 349–350, 442
Hartford, Treaty of (1638), 72
Hartford Convention (1815), 259–260
"Harvest of Death, A" (O'Sullivan), *516*
Haudenosaunee, 74
Hawthorne, Nathaniel, 398, 401, 411, 481
Hawthorne, Sophia, 398
Hayes, Rutherford B., 561–562
Hayne, Robert Y., 334, 335, 336, 337
Haynes, Lemuel, *183*
Headley, J. T., *507*
headright system, 49, 60
Helper, Hinton Rowan, 454
Hemings, Sally, 232, 264
Henrietta Maria, Queen, 51
Henry, Patrick, 128, 130, 137, 144, 206, 224
Henry the Navigator, Prince, 18
Henry VII, 21
Henry VIII, 26
Hepburn Act (1906), 248
Herbert, Victor, 290
Hessians, 158, 164, 173
Hewitt, Nancy A., 423
Higginson, Thomas W., 504
highways and roads
in early nineteenth century, 275, 301–302
Federal Highways Act of 1916, 306
internal improvements, 301–302
Philadelphia-Lancaster Turnpike, 275
transportation in colonial period, 98
Wilderness Road, 220–221, 275
see also transportation
historiography, 148, 422, 566
Hohokam people, 13
Holloway, Houston, 533
Holmes, John, 267
Holmes, Oliver Wendell, Jr., 527
Homer, Winslow, *295, 532*

Homestead Act (1862), 510, 527
Hood, James Walker, 541
Hood, John Bell, 522–523, 524
Hooker, Joseph, 513
Hooker, Thomas, 58
Hopewell culture, 14
Hopis, 13
horses, 35
Horseshoe Bend, Battle of (1814), 254
household economy, 274
House of Burgesses, Virginia, 130
House of Commons, British, 46
House of Lords, British, 46
House of Representatives, U.S., 200, 201
see also Congress, U.S.
House of the Seven Gables, The (Hawthorne), 401
Houston, James, 78
Houston, Sam, 440–441, 443
Howard, Merrimon, 550
Howard, Oliver O., 537
Howe, Elias, 280
Howe, George, 366
Howe, William, 140–141, 164, 166–167, 168, 170
Hudson, Henry, 61
Huguenots, 24, 93
Hull, William, 252
Hundley, D. R., 368
Hunt, Commonwealth v., 293
Hunter's Lessee, Martin v., 303
Huntington, Ebenezer, 186
Hurons, 67, 74
Hutchinson, Anne, 57–58
Hutchinson, Thomas, 150, 151

Idaho Territory, 492
Ideological Origins of the American Revolution, The (Bailyn), 149
immigration
of British, 288
of Chinese, 288
in early nineteenth century, 288–291
of Germans, 93, 288, 290
of Irish, 289–290
major groups in colonial America, 93, *94*
nativism and, 290–291, 462
of Scandinavians, 288
of Scots-Irish, 93
impeachment
Andrew Johnson, 545–546
in Constitution, 201
defined, 201, 545
impressment, 243, 244, 247, *248*
Incas, *6,* 11, 30
Incidents in the Life of a Slave Girl (Jacobs), 374
income tax, 510
indentured servants, 75, 84, 87–88, 93, 159, 184

Independent Treasury Act (1840), 349, 442, 445
Indian Removal Act (1830), 337
Indian's Vespers, The (Durand), *386*
indigo, 87
individualism in colonial culture, 105
indulgences, 23
industrial growth in the 1840s, 286–287
Industrial Revolution, 280–287
American technology and, 280–281
cities, environment, and, 286–287
cotton and, 281–282
early textile manufactures and, 281, 282, 284
expansion of slavery and, 281–282
and farming in the West, 282–283
industrial growth in the 1840s, 286–287
Lowell System and, 285–286
national economy and, 274
infectious diseases introduced to Americas from Europe, 21, 31, 43
inflation during Civil War, 557
Ingersoll, Robert G., 561
Inness, George, *272*
Inquiry into the Nature and Causes of the Wealth of Nations, An (Smith), 211
Institutes of the Christian Religion, The (Calvin), 24
internal improvements, defined, 301
Internal Revenue Service, creation of, 510
"Intolerable" Acts (Coercive Acts), 134–135
Ireland, 289
Irish Americans, 289–290
Iroquoian-speaking peoples, 16–17, 74, *120*
Iroquois League, 74, 160, 187
Isabella I of Castile, 19, 20

Jack, 373
Jackson, Andrew
American Revolution and, 325
annexation of Texas and, 443
assassination attempt on, 342
assessment of presidency of, 350–351
background of, 325–326
Bank War, 331–332, 343
Calhoun's rift with, 312, 335, 342
censure by Senate, 343
and "common man," 319–320, 321, 327–328, 351, 367
as Democratic party leader, 314, 317, 327, 351
in duel, 325, 365
Eaton Affair and, 329–330
in election of 1824, 314–315, 316, 330
in election of 1828, 318–319, *320,* 321
in election of 1832, 329, 332–333, 343
election of 1844 and, 443
expansion of presidential authority, 328
farewell address of, 351
government appointments of, 328

on Henry Clay, 318
Houston and, 441
inauguration of, 279, 326–327
Indian policy of, 328, 338–341
internal improvements and, 330–331
"King Andrew I," *331,* 346
kitchen cabinet of, 330
Masonic order and, 342
national bank issue and, 328, 331–333, 343, 348, *350*
nullification issue and, 333–334, 335, 336–337, 341, 351, 442
"Old Hickory," *319,* 327
in Seminole War, 311–312, 326
slavery and, 238, 326, 450–451
Specie Circular, 344, *345,* 348
tariff issue and, 333–334
in War of 1812, 248, 251, 254, 258, *259,* 360
Jackson, Elizabeth, 325
Jackson, Rachel, 318, 321, 326
Jackson, Thomas "Stonewall," 486, 498, 513
Jacksonian Democrats, 318, 327–328, 539
see also Democratic party
Jacksonian Era, 270, 324–353
Jacobins, 215, 225
Jacobs, Harriet, 374
James, Henry, 453
James D. Lynch, 541
James I, 46, 47, 48
James II, 47, 48, 63, 115–116
Jamestown colony, 34, 48–51, 68–69, 71
Japan, mid-nineteenth century trade with, 461
Jay, John, 178, 204, 216–218, 220, 222
Jayhawkers, 493
Jay's Treaty, 216–218, 220, 222
Jefferson, Thomas
absence from Constitutional Convention, 199
on Adams, 223
African slave trade outlawed, 241–242, 370
on Alien and Sedition Acts, 224
on Andrew Jackson, 314, 326
anti-Jefferson sentiment, *246*
Barbary pirates and, 242–243
Bill of Rights and, 206
Burr conspiracy and, 241
colonial protests and, 134, 135
on cultivation of Reason, 100
Declaration of Independence and, 142–143, 222
Deism, 388
as early Republican leader, 154–155, 209, 214–215, 216, 231–232, 233
economic policies of, 234–235, 286
in election of 1796, 222
in election of 1800, 155, 191, 225, 230

in election of 1804, 239
Embargo Act and, 244–245, 284, 301
exploration of West promoted by, 238–239
on First Amendment, 207
French Revolution and, 215, 216
Hamilton and, 213, 214–215, 216
inauguration of, 230–232
on James Monroe, 307
Jay's Treaty and, 218, 222
John Marshall and, 231, 234, 302, 304
land policy and, 193
Louisiana Purchase and, 235–238, 239
Madison and, 215, 247, 249
Marbury v. Madison and, 233–234
Monticello, *232,* 233
Napoleonic Wars and, 244–245
national bank and, 213, 300
on nationalism *vs.* states' rights, 300, 302, 304
Notes on the State of Virginia, 266–267
opposition to slavery, 202, 264–267
on power of individual states, 154, 261
Republican simplicity of, 230–231ers
as secretary of state, 210–211, 214, 215, 216
slave ownership, 96, 144, 184, 202, 232–233, 264–267
on slavery in the western territories, 306
as vice president, 222, 223–224
Virginia Statute of Religious Freedom (1786), 184
War of 1812 and, 247, 249, 250
Washington and, 215, 216
westward expansion and, 229, 230, 235–238, 442
on women's rights, 187, 205
Jeffersonian Republicans, *see* Republicans, Jeffersonian
Jeremiah, Thomas, 184
Jesuits (Society of Jesus), 25, 112
Jewish Americans, 63, 290
Johnson, Andrew
congressional conflicts with, 543, 567
in election of 1864, 519, 539
falling out with Grant, 555
impeachment and trial of, 545–546
photograph, *539*
Radical Republicans' conflict with, 539, 541, 542, 543–546
Reconstruction plans of, 539, 541, 567
Restoration Plan, 539
sworn in as president, 538
"War Democrat," 512, 519
Johnson, Sally, 375
Johnson, William, 370
Johnston, Albert Sidney, 493–494
Johnston, Frances Benjamin, *550*
Johnston, Joseph E., 498
joint-stock companies, 44, 48, 56–57

Jolliet, Louis, 112
judicial nationalism, 302–303, 304, 310
judicial review, 234, 303
judiciary, 200, 201–202
Judiciary Act (1801), 225, 233
Jungle, The (Sinclair), 248

Kansas
Civil War in, 492–493
Lawrence, 463–465, 493
Kansas-Nebraska Act (1854)
"Bleeding Kansas" and, 463–465
debate and passage, 461–462, 463
map, *464*
sectional politics and, 466–467
violence in Senate and, 465–466
Whig party destroyed over, 462
Kansas Territory
"Bleeding Kansas" and, 463–465
Lecompton constitution in, 468–469
violence in (1856), 463–465
Kant, Immanuel, 99
Kaskaskia, IL, 171
Kearny, Stephen, 448
Kentucky, 173, 220–221, 493, 496
Kentucky Resolution (1798), 224
Key, Francis Scott, 256
King, Martin Luther, Jr., influence of Thoreau, 401
King, Rufus, 239, 245, 306
"King Andrew I," *331,* 346
King Philip's (Metacomet's) War, 72–73
Kingsley, Bathsheba, 103–104
King's Mountain, Battle of, 174
King William's War, 117
KKK (Ku Klux Klan) after Civil War, 552–553, 559–560
Know-Nothings (American party), 291, 462
Krimmel, John Lewis, *298*
Ku Klux Klan Act (1871), 559
Ku Klux Klan (KKK) after Civil War, 552–553, 559–560

labor
indentured servants, 75, 84, 87–88, 93, 159, 184
in Lowell System, 285–286, 292, 424–425
rise of professions, 293–294
women in the workforce, 294
see also organized labor; slavery
labor unions, *see* organized labor
Lackawanna Valley (Inness), *272*
Lafayette, Gilbert du Motier, Marquis de, 170
Lake Champlain, Battle of, 255–256, 257
Land Ordinance of 1784, 193, *194*
Land Ordinance of 1785, 193
land policy, Confederation Congress and, 193–195

land policy, Reconstruction and, 550–551
La Salle, René-Robert Cavelier, sieur de, 112
Las Casas, Bartolomé de, 39
Latrobe, Benjamin Henry, *231*
Latrobe, John H. B., *403*
Laurens, Henry, 144
Lawrence, KS, 463–465, 493
Lawrence, Richard, 342
Lawrence (ship), 253
lawyers and the law, as a profession, 293–294
Leaves of Grass (Whitman), 401, 402, 474
Lecompton Constitution, 468–469
Lee, Ann (Mother Ann), 409–410
Lee, Jarena, 393
Lee, Richard Henry, 142, 206
Lee, Robert E.
  after Gettysburg, 519
  at Antietam, 501
  at Chancellorsville, 513
  command of Army of Northern Virginia assumed, 498
  explanation for the Confederate defeat, 529
  at Fredericksburg, 506
  at Gettysburg, 514–515, 516–517, 518
  Grant's pursuit of, 520–522, 526
  at Harper's Ferry, 471
  in Mexican-American War, 498
  photograph, *498*
  resignation from U.S. Army, 483
  at Second Bull Run, 498
  surrender of, 526–527
Legal Tender Act of 1862, 510–511
legislative branch of federal government, *see* Congress, U.S.
Le Moyne, Jean-Baptiste, 112–113
Leopard incident, 244
Leo X, 24
"Letter from A Farmer in Pennsylvania" (Dickinson), 150–151
"Letter to the Lords of Trade" (Bernard), 151
Lewis, Isham, 378
Lewis, Lilburn, 378
Lewis, Meriwether, 238–239, *240*
Lewis and Clark expedition, 238–239, *240*
Lexington, Battle of (1775), 137–138
Liberal Republicans, 558–559
Liberator, The, 412, 413
Liberia, Republic of, 412
Liberty party, 415, 444, 453
liberty trees, 128, *129*
Lienzo de Tlaxcala, 29
Lincoln, Abraham
  assassination of, 538–539
  Chancellorsville and, 513
  on Clay, 456
  Douglas's debates with, 469–470

in election of 1860, 473–474
in election of 1864, 502, 519, 523, 539
emancipation and, 499, 500, 502–504, 506, 507, 529
first inauguration of, 474, 477
Gettysburg Address of, 518
on Kansas-Nebraska Act, 463, 469
on Lee's escape from Gettysburg, 518
McClellan and, 496–497, 498, *499,* 501–502
on Mexican-American War, 447
military strategy of, 487
photographs, *470, 499*
Reconstruction plans of, 536
in Richmond, *480*
secession and, 475, 477, 481–482
second inauguration of, 482
slavery issue and, 469–470, 476
on Webster-Hayne debate, 335
on Wilmot Proviso, 451–452
on women in the Civil War, 508
Lincoln, Mary Todd, 521, 538
Lincoln-Douglas debates, 469–470
Lincoln's Drive through Richmond, 480
literature
  in mid-twentieth century, 401–402
  in nineteenth century, 399–402
  transcendentalism and, 399–402
Little Crow, 261
livestock, 359
Livingston, Margaret, 187
Livingston, Robert R., 236, 276, 304
Locke, John, 59, 60, 100, 116–117
longhouses, 16
Long Island, Battle of, 161–162
Longstreet, James, 516, 552
Loom and Spindle or Life Among the Early Mill Girls (Robinson), 424–425
Loring, Elizabeth Lloyd, 164, 170
Louisiana, secession of, 476, 482
Louisiana Purchase, 235–238, 239, *240,* 241, 308, 310
Louisiana Territory, 112, 121–122, 235–238, 239, 241, 308
Louis XIV, 112, 117
Louis XV, 121
Lovejoy, Elijah P., 418–419
Lowell, Francis Cabot, 285
Lowell, MA, 285, 286, 423, 424–425
Lowell girls, 285, 424–425
Lowell System, 285–286
Lower South, 17, 359, 360–361, 476, 482, 559–560
Loyalists (Tories)
  about, 128, 178, 179
  after American Revolution, 180
  before American Revolution, 128, 132
  in American Revolution, 153, 158, 171–174, 179–180
  confiscated property of, 178, 195

Loyola, Ignatius de, 25
Lucas, George, 87
Luther, Martin, 23–24, 25
lynchings
  Ku Klux Klan, 559
  New York City draft riots, 506
Lyon, Matthew, *224*

Macdonough, Thomas, 255–256
Madison, Dolley, 246, 256
Madison, James
  American Colonization Society and, 412
  Bill of Rights and, 206
  at Constitutional Convention, 199, 200, 201, 202
  debt issue and, 212
  as early Republican leader, 154, 209, 215, 216
  election of 1808, 245
  election of 1816, 306
  The Federalist Papers and, 204–205
  government strengthening recommended by, 300
  inauguration of, 246
  internal improvements and, 306
  Jefferson and, 215
  Napoleonic Wars and, 244, 246–247
  national bank and, 213, 261, 300
  portrait, *199*
  as secretary of state, 233–234, 244, 245
  after Shays's Rebellion, 198
  slavery and, 144, 202, 306
  War of 1812 and, 247, 249, 250–252, 254, 256, 260–261
Madison, Marbury v., 233–234, 303, 468
Magna Carta (1215), 46
Mahicans, 160
main censorship, 345–346, 413
Maine, in War of 1812, 259
Maine, statehood, 308–309
Maine colony, *55,* 59
maize (corn), 9, 30–31
Mamout, Yarrow, *369*
Mandan Sioux, 238
manifest destiny, 398–399, 432, 449
Manigault, Louis, 454–455
Mann, Horace, 293, 407–408
Manning, John, 474
manufacturers
  in early nineteenth century, 274, 285–286
  in early U.S., 213–214
  Lowell System and, 285–286
Marbury, William, 233–234
Marbury v. Madison, 233–234, 303, 468
"March to the Sea" (1864), 523–526
Marion, Francis, 174, 175
market economy, 273–297
  communications and, 279
  defined, 274

equal opportunities and, 294–295
government's role and, 279
immigration and, 288–291
organized labor, 291–293
and rise of professions, 293–294
technological innovation and, 280–281
transportation and, 274–279
see also Industrial Revolution
Marquette, Jacques, 112
Marshall, John
American Colonization Society and, 412
Burr conspiracy and, 241
in *Cherokee Nation v. Georgia,* 340
as chief justice, 231, 234, 241, 302–304
in *Dartmouth College v. Woodward,* 303
on *Gibbons v. Ogden,* 304
judicial nationalism, 302–303, 304, 310
on *Marbury v. Madison,* 234, 303
on *McCulloch v. Maryland,* 303
portrait, *303*
Martin, Luther, 206
Martin v. Hunter's Lessee, 303
Mary II (Mary Stuart), 48, 116, 117
Maryland, Civil War fighting in, 501–502, *505*
Maryland, McCulloch v., 303
Maryland colony, 51–53, 88, 116
Mason, George, 206
Mason, John, 59
Masonic order, 342
Massachusetts, Constitution ratified by, 206
Massachusetts, Shays's Rebellion in, 197, 198, 206
Massachusetts Bay Colony, 54, 55–57, 90, 116
Massachusetts colony, 128, 130, 134, 135, 136–137
mass production, 280
Mather, Cotton, *90*
Mayas, 10–11
Mayflower, 54
Mayflower Compact, 54
Maysville Road Bill (1830), 330–331, 333
McClellan, George B.
at Antietam, 501–502
in election of 1864, 502, 519, 523
Lincoln and, 496–497, 498, *499,* 501–502
peninsular campaign of, 497–498
at Second Bull Run, 498
McCormick, Cyrus Hall, 283
McCormick reaper, 283
McCulloch, James, 303
McCulloch v. Maryland, 303
McDaniel, Amanda, 373
Meade, George, 516, 518
mechanical reaping machine, 283
medicine as a profession, 294
Melville, Herman, 401, 411
Memminger, Christopher, 365
Menendez de Aviles, Pedro, 33

Mennonites, 93
mentally ill, reform of hospitals for, 405
mercantilism, 114, 115, 211
Mercer, Hugh, *156*
Mesoamerica, defined, 10
mestizos, 33
Metacomet (King Philip), 72–73
Metacomet's (King Philip's) War, 72–73
Methodists, 367, 389, 391–392, 547
Mexica (Aztecs), 11–12, 28–29, 30, 33
Mexican-American War, 447–450, 451, 452, 453, 498
Mexico
ancient Indians in, 9–12
independence from Spain, 434, 436
migration of Americans into border-
lands, 434–435, 437–438
secularization act and California *ran-
chos,* 436–437
Texas Revolution, 438–441
Mexico City in Mexican American War, 449
Mexico City (Tenochtitlán), 11, 28
Michigan and War of 1812, 251–252, 253–254
middle class, 17–18
middle colonies, 61–67, 91–93
see also individual colonies
Middle Passage, *76,* 77–78
Military Reconstruction Act, 544
Minkins, Shadrach, 418
Minnesota, statehood, 470
Minutemen, 138
missionaries, 33, 34, 436
Mississippi, secession of, 476, 482
Mississippian culture, 14–16
Missouri, statehood, 309
Missouri Compromise, 266, 267, 308–310, 451, 452, 462, 468
Missouri Territory, 308
Mobile, Alabama, 112
Moby-Dick (Melville), 401
money question, 344
Monongahela, Battle of, 120
Monroe, James
American Colonization Society and, 412
American Revolution and, 306–307
anti-Federalist, 206
in election of 1816, 306, 307
in election of 1820, 307, 314
Louisiana Purchase and, 236–237
Monroe Doctrine and, 313
portrait, *307*
as secretary of state, 306–307
slavery and, 306, 310
as Virginia governor, 378
War of 1812 and, 260
Monroe, Sarah, 293
Monroe Doctrine, 313, 316
Montezuma II, 28–29
Montgomery, Richard, 160

Morgan, Daniel, 175
Mormons (Church of Jesus Christ of
Latter-day Saints), 394–397, 406
Morrill, Justin Smith, 509, 510
Morrill Land-Grant College Act (1862), 510
Morrill Tariff (1861), 509, 510
Morse, Jedidiah, 95
Morse, Samuel F. B., 279
Mott, Lucretia, 406, 424
"mound-building" cultures, 14–16
mulattoes, 309, 370, 375
Murray, John, 389
Murray, Judith Sargent, 204
Muskogean-speaking peoples, 16, 17

Napoléon, 236, 243, 247, 254, 258
Narragansetts, 57, 72–73
Narrative of the Life of Frederick Douglass
(Douglass), 416
*Narrative of William W. Brown, a Fugitive
Slave, Written by Himself* (Brown),
416
Nash, Beverly, 550
Nash, Gary, 148, 149–150
Nashville, Battle of, 524
Nast, Thomas, *543, 553*
National Banking Act (1863), 510
National Intelligencer, 348
nationalism
American System and, 305–306, 314, 315–316, 346, 442
diplomacy and, 310–313
economic nationalism, 300–302, 310, 314, 317
elections of 1824 and, 314–316
emergence after War of 1812, *298,* 299, 300–304
"Era of Good Feelings" and, 306–310, 314
judicial nationalism, 302–303, 304, 310
Missouri Compromise and, 310
Supreme Court and, 302–304
tension between nationalism and sec-
tionalism, 299–300
National Republican party (Anti-Jackson
party), 332, 342, 346
see also Whig party
National Road, 301–302
National Trades' Union, 293
Native Americans
agriculture of, 9
American Revolution and, 158, 160, 171–173, 178, 187
Americas settled by, 3, 8, *9*
Andrew Jackson and, 311–312, 328, 338–341
California gold rush and, 454, 456
Catholicism and, 21, 23, 33, 34–35, 436
Christianity and, 71–72
citizenship of, 202, 543
in Civil War, 493

Native Americans *(continued)*
complex relationship with Europeans, 3–4
and diseases contracted from Europeans, 21, 31, 43
Eastern Woodland peoples, 16–17
English settlers and, 67–74
forced labor of, 33, *34,* 39
in French and Indian War, 117, 120, 121
French relations with, 110, 113
horses and, 35
Indian tribes and European settlements, map, *69*
missionaries to, 33, 34, 436
"mound-building" cultures, 14–16
Northwest Territory land of, 193, 194
Plains Indians, 13–14, 35, 434
Pontiac's Rebellion, 122–124
pre-Columbian civilizations of, 9–17
Puritans and, 71
Quakers and, 71
removal of, 230, 235, 261, 338–339
Royal Proclamation of 1763, 124–125
as slaves, 34, 73
Spain and, 27–30, 34–35
technology of, 27
trade with French and Dutch settlers, 67, 74
war between rival groups of, 9, 10, 11–12, 17
War of 1812 and, 248–249, 251, 252, 253–254, 258, 261
westward migration and, 434, 436–446
see also specific tribes
nativism
anti-Catholicism, 290–291, 462
defined, 291, 462
in early nineteenth century, 290–291
Nat Turner's Rebellion, 380–382
natural rights, 116–117
Nature (Emerson), 399
Navigation Acts, 114–115, 116, 122, 125
Navy, U.S., 251
Netherlands, 37, 114, 168, 215
Nevada, statehood, 492
Nevada Territory, 492
New Amsterdam, 58, 61–63, *96*
New Echota, Treaty of, 338
New England
agriculture in, 91
colonial life in, 89–91
early settlements, map, *55*
European settlement of, 53–59
fishing in, 90–91
religion in, 54, 55–56, 89–90
trade and commerce in, 91
witchcraft hysteria, 89–90
New France, 110–113, 119
New Hampshire, Constitution ratified by, 206

New Hampshire colony, *55,* 59
New Jersey
Battle of Princeton (1777), *156, 159,* 164–165
Constitution ratified by, 206
Revolutionary War in (1776–1777), *156, 159,* 164–166
New Jersey colony, 63, *64,* 92
New Jersey Plan, 200
New Mexico, prehistory, 9
New Mexico, Spanish territory, 33–35
New Mexico Territory, 456, 457, 459, 492
New Netherland colony, 44, 61–63, *64,* 115
New Orleans
Battle of New Orleans (1815), 251, 258, *259,* 360
capture in Civil War, 496
growth in early nineteenth century, 282, 287
Louisiana Purchase, 236–237
Spanish control, 121–122, 195, 219
Newport, RI, 98
New Spain
Cortés and, 29–30
encomienda system, 30
exploration in North America, 31–33
legacy of, 39
settlements in New Mexico, 33–35
New Sweden, 62, *64,* 65
see also Delaware colony
Newton, Isaac, 100
Newtown, New York, 171
New World, early maps of, 21, *22*
New York
canals in, 276–277
Constitution ratified by, 206
Revolutionary War fighting in, 161–164, 167, *169,* 171
New York City
in colonial period, 96, 98
Compromise of 1790 and, 212
draft riots in Civil War, 506–507
in nineteenth century, 287
slaves in, 96
temporary national capital, 206
New York colony, 63, 91–92, 93, 116
Niles' Weekly Register, 348
Niña, 19
nonimportation movements, 129–130, 136
Non-Intercourse Act (1809), 246–247
Norsemen ("Vikings"), 22
North, Frederick, 132, 133, 134–135, 136–137, 158, 177
North America, maps
in 1713, map, *123*
in 1763, map, *124*
in 1783, map, *177*
English and French explorations, map, *36*
French and Indian War campaigns, *118*

French settlements in, *111*
pre-Columbian civilizations, map, *15*
North Carolina
Revolutionary War fighting in, 174, 175
secession of, 482
North Carolina colony, 59, 60
Northup, Solomon, 372, 374
Northwest Ordinance (1787), 193–195, 308
Northwest Pacific Indians, 13
Northwest Territory, 187, 193, *195*
Notes on the State of Virginia (Jefferson), 266–267
Noyes, John Humphrey, 410–411
nullification
Calhoun and, 333–334, 335, 336, 337
Force Bill and, 337
Jackson and, 333–334, 335, 336–337, 341, 351, 442
South Carolina Ordinance and, 335–336
Webster-Hayne debate on, 334–335
see also states' rights
Nurse, Rebecca, *89*

Ogden, Aaron, 304
Ogden, Gibbons v., 304
Oglethorpe, James E., 67
Ohio, 195, 235, 301
Old Republicans, 240–241
Old Smoke, 160
Old Southwest, 238, 333, 361, 372
Olive Branch Petition, 141
Oliver, Andrew, 150, 151
Oñate, Juan de, 33–34
Oneida Community, 410–411
Oneidas, 16, 160, 187
one-party politics, 314
"On the Equality of the Sexes" (Murray), 204
Ordinance of Secession (South Carolina) (1860), 475
Oregon, statehood, 470
Oregon Country, 239, *309,* 310, *311,* 435–436, 446
Oregon Fever, 435
Oregon Trail, *430,* 433, 435, 436, 437, 448
organized labor in early nineteenth century, 291–293
Osawatomie, KS, *464,* 465
Osborne, Sarah, 90
Osborne, Sarah Haggar, 103
Osceola, 338–339
O'Sullivan, John L., 432, 449
O'Sullivan, T. H., *516*
O'Sullivan, Timothy H., *516*
Otis, James, 132.
Ottawas, 123, 218
Overland Trails, *430,* 432–433
overseers, white, 366–367
Overzee, Syman, 96
Oxbow, The (Cole), 398

Pacific Railway Act (1862), 510
Paine, Thomas, 141, 153, 163, 179, 181
Pakenham, Edward, 258
Paleo-Indians, 7
Palmer, Phoebe Worrall, 393
Panic of 1819, 307–308, 333
Panic of 1837, 288, 324, 347–349
Panic of 1857, 467
Panic of 1873, 558
Parade of The Victuallers (Krimmel), *298*
Paris, Treaty of (1763), 121–122
Paris, Treaty of (1783), 177–178, 193, 195, 216–217, 222
Parker, John, 137–138
Parker, Theodore, 398, 411, 460
Parkman, Francis, 113
Parliament, British
    about, 45–46
    Continental Congress and, 168
    kings' conflicts with, 47, 56, 114
    taxation and, 46
Paterson, William, 200
Patriots, before and during American Revolution, defined, 128, 132, 178–179
patronage system, 558
Peabody, Elizabeth, 398
Peale, Charles Willson, *159, 369*
Pemberton, John C., 514, 518
Penn, William, 65, 71–72, 93
Pennsylvania
    Civil War fighting in, 514–518
    Revolutionary War fighting in, *169*
    Valley Forge, winter of 1777–1778, 168, 170–171
    see also Philadelphia
Pennsylvania colony, 64–65, 71–72, 91–92
Pequot War, 72
Perry, Oliver Hazard, 253–254
Perryville, Battle of (1862), 496
Peru, 30, 31, *34*
pet banks, 343, *350*
Petersburg, Battle of, 522, 526
Petigru, James L., 475
Philadelphia
    British occupation (1777), 167, 168
    Constitutional Convention and, 198, 199, 204
    population in colonial period, 98
    temporary U.S. capital, 212, *213,* 216
    William Penn in, 65, *93*
    see also Continental Congress
Philadelphia, 242, 243, *244*
Philadelphia-Lancaster Turnpike, 275
Philip II, 37
physicians, as a profession, 294
Pickens, Andrew, 173
Pickens, Francis, 345
Pickett, George, *515,* 516, 517
Pickett's Charge, *515,* 516, 524
Pierce, Franklin, 461, 466, 467

Pilgrims, 47, 54–55, 56, 71
Pinchback, Pinckney, 549
Pinckney, Charles C., *225,* 239, 245
Pinckney, Elizabeth Lucas, 87
Pinckney, Thomas, 219, 220, 221–222
Pinckney's Treaty of 1795, 219, 220, 310
Pinta, 19
Pitcairn, John, 138, 141
Pitt, William, 128, 131, 132
Pizarro, Francisco, 30, *32*
Plains Indians, 13–14, 35, 434
Plantation Burial (Antrobus), *377*
plantation mistresses, 365–366, *532*
planters, white, 364–366
Plattsburgh, Battle of, 255–256
plows, iron and steel, 283
Plymouth colony, *50,* 54–55, 71, 116
Pocahontas, 68
Politics in an Oyster House, 403
Polk, James Knox
    in election of 1844, 443–444, 449
    on gold in California, 453
    independent Treasury under, 445
    Mexican-American War and, 447, 449
    Oregon Country and, 446
    slavery issue and, 450, 451
    Tariff of 1846, 445
Ponce de León, Juan, 33–34
Pontiac's Rebellion, 122–124
Poor, Salem, 185
Poor Richard's Almanac (Franklin), 101
Popé, 35
Pope, John, 498
popular sovereignty, 452, 462, 463, 468, 470
population
    biological exchange and, 31
    of cities, 286, *287*
    in colonial period, 45, 84, 93, 98
    growth in British colonies, 82, 93
Portugal, 18, 21
postal service in early nineteenth century, 279, 345–346
potatoes, 30–31
Potawatomi, 218
Pottawatomie Massacre (1856), *464,* 465
Potter, John "Bowie Knife," 471
Powhatan Confederacy, 68–70
Powhatan (Wahunsenacawh), Chief, 69–70
pre-Columbian Indian civilizations, 9–17
Preemption Act (1830), 283
Presbyterians, 24, 47, 105, 391
presidency, in Constitution, 201
    see also elections and campaigns
presidential conventions, 328–329
Preston, Levi, 145
Preston, William, 482
Princeton, Battle of (1777), *156, 159,* 164–165
printing press, 18, 20

prison reform movements, 405
privateers, 35, 37, 51
Proclamation Line of 1763, 124
professions, rise of, 293–294
proprietary colonies, 51, 59, 65
Prosser, Gabriel, 378
Protestant Reformation, 22, 23–27
Public Credit Act (1869), 557
public institutions, reform of, 405
public schools, 407–409
Pueblo Revolt, 35
Pueblos, 13, 34–35
Puerto Rico, 22, 27, 313
Punderson, Prudence, *86*
Pure Food and Drug Act (1906), 248
Puritans
    Anglican Church as viewed by, 46
    attempts to convert Native Americans, 71
    Calvinism as basis of, 24
    dissension among, 57–58
    in England, 46–47
    in Maryland, 52–53
    in Massachusetts, 55–57
    in New England, 89–90, 102, 409
    nineteenth-century religious liberalism and, 388
    predestination and, 388, 393
    Separatists, 46–47, 54, 57

Quakers (Society of Friends), 64–65, 71, 92, 102, 414, 415
Quantrill, William, 492–493
Quartering Act (1765), 126, 150
Quartering Act (1774), 135
Quebec, 110, 121, 160
Queenston Heights, Battle of, 252

race-based slavery, 95–97, 356, 368, 382
race riots, New York City draft riots, 506–507
Radical Republicans
    in Civil War, 511, 519, 526, 536
    Johnson's relations with, 539, 541, 542, 543–546
    legacy of, 553–554
    in Reconstruction, 536, 538, 539, 541, 543–546, 553–554, 560
    see also Republican party
railroads
    in early nineteenth century, *272,* 277–278
    land given to by Congress, 279
Rainbow, 278
Raleigh, Walter, *36,* 37–38
Randolph, John, 240–241, 250
Rapalje Children, The (Durand), *98*
Ratcliffe, John, 68
rational religion, 388
reaper, mechanical, 283

Reconstruction, 532–569
  African Americans in, 537, 546–551, 559, 568
  black codes in, 542, 552, 567
  carpetbaggers in, 551–552, 554, 562
  Compromise of 1877 and, 560–562
  Congress and, 543–545, 546, 549, 552, 555, 560, 563
  end of, 562, 563
  Freedmen's Bureau and, 536–537, 543
  Johnson and, 539, 541, 561
  land policy in, 550–551
  Liberal Republicans and, 558
  Lincoln's plans for, 536
  Panic of 1873 and, 558
  political, battle over, 535–546
  Radical Republicans and, 536, 538, 539, 541, 543–546, 553–554, 560
  readmission of states to the Union, 536, 546, *554*
  scalawags in, 551, 552, 559, 560, 562
  southern resistance and, 542, 552–553, 559
  states with Reconstruction governments, *554*
  white terror in, 559
Reconstruction, Political and Economic, 1865–1877 (Dunning), 566, 567
Red Cross, 508, *509*
redeemers, 560
redemptioners, 93
Redmond, Sarah Parker, 415
reform movements, 402–411
  anti-slavery (*see* abolition movement)
  for civil service, 558
  early public schools, 407–409
  for prisons and asylums, 405
  religion and, 393–394
  temperance, 404
  utopian communities, 409–411
  for women's rights, 405–407
religion
  African American, 79, 377–378, 391–392, 546–547
  camp meeting revivals, 390–391, 392–393
  in colonial period, 54, 55–56, 89–90
  Deism and, 100, 101, 103, 388
  Enlightenment and, 101–102, 103
  evangelism and evangelists, 389, 390, 391, 393, 402–403
  First Great Awakening, 102–105, 388, 389
  free-will ideal and free-will ministers, 387–388, 393
  frontier revivals, 390–391
  in New England, 54, 55–56, 89–90
  rational religion, 388
  reform and, 393–394
  religious freedom after American Revolution, 183–184

  religious freedom in colonial period, 53, 57, 60, 65, 183
  Second Great Awakening, 389–390, 391, 392, 394, 402
  Unitarianism and, 388–389, 397, 399, 411
  Universalism and, 389
  see also specific religions
Renaissance, 18
"Report on Manufactures" (Hamilton), 213
Report on the Condition of the South (Schurz), 568
"Reports on Public Credit" (Hamilton), 212
representative democracy, 180, 181
Representative Men (Emerson), 401
republican ideology, 181
Republican party
  emergence of, 462–474
  Liberal Republicans, 558–559
  Union League and, 547–549
  violence in Senate (1856) and, 465–466
  see also elections and campaigns; Radical Republicans
Republicans, Jeffersonian
  about, 209
  Alien and Sedition Acts and, 224
  divisions in, 240–241
  in election of 1796, 222
  in election of 1800, 225, 230
  in election of 1816, 306
  in election of 1820, 307, 314
  French Revolution and, 215, 216
  Jay's Treaty and, 218, 222
  Jefferson's role with, 154–155, 209, 214–215, 216, 231–232, 233
  national bank issue and, 300
  Republican party birth in the 1790s, 154
  War of 1812 and, 219, 247, 250, 252, 261
  Whiskey Rebellion and, 219
Revels, Hiram, 549
Revenue Act (1767), 131
Revere, Paul, *73, 133,* 137
revivals, 390–391, 392–393
Rhode Island
  American Revolution and, 162, 176, *179,* 184
  Constitutional Convention absence, 198
  paper currency in, 197
  population in Confederation period, 192, 193
Rhode Island colony, *55,* 57–58, 60, 71
rice plantations, 61, 88, 359
Richmond, after the Civil War, *480, 535*
Ripley, George, 398, 411
Roanoke Island, 37–38
Robinson, Harriett H. (Lowell mill girl), 424–425
Robinson, Harriet (wife of Dred Scott), 468
Rockingham, Lord, 130–131

Rolfe, John, 49
Roman Catholicism, *see* Catholicism, Catholic Church
romanticism, *386,* 397–402
Romantic movement, 270–271
Rosecrans, William, 518
Ross, Edmund G., 545–546
Rossiter, Thomas Pritchard, *198*
Royal Proclamation of 1763, 124–125
Ruffin, Edmund, 527
Rush, Benjamin, 183
Rush-Bagot Agreement (1817), 310
Rutledge, Edward, 184

Sacagawea, 238, *239*
Sacramento, CA, during gold rush, 454
Salem, MA, 89–90
Salem, Peter, 185
saloons in mining towns in the West, 454
salutary neglect, 114
Sampson, Deborah, 186
San Antonio, TX, 113
Sánchez, José María, 438
Sandford, Dred Scott v., 467–468
Sandwich, Lord, 137
Sandys, Edwin, 49
San Francisco, CA, during gold rush, 454
San Jacinto, Battle of, 440–441
San Lorenzo, Treaty of, 219, *220*
Santa Anna, Antonio López de, 438–440, 441, 449, 450
Santa Fe, 33, 34, 35
Santa Maria, 19
Saratoga, Battles of (1777), 167, 175
Sassamon, John, 72
Sauk, 338
Savage, Samuel, 136
Savannah, Ga., *66,* 67
scalawags, 551, 552, 559, 560, 562
Scandinavian Americans, 288
Scarlet Letter, The (Hawthorne), 401
Schoolcraft, Mary Howard, 366
Schurz, Carl, 568
Scots-Irish Americans, 93, 174
Scott, Dred, 467–468
Scott, Winfield, 449, 461, 487, 498, 519
secession of South, 428, 474–477, 481–482, *483*
Second Battle of Bull Run (Manassas), 498
Second Continental Congress, *see* Continental Congress
Second Great Awakening, 389–390, 391, 392, 394, 402
sectionalism
  American System and, 305–306
  economic policies and, 299–300
  elections of 1824 and, 314–316
  elections of 1856 and, 466–467
  judicial nationalism *vs.,* 302–303, 304, 310

Missouri Compromise and, 308–310
tension between nationalism and sectionalism, 299–300
Sedition Act of 1798, 224
seigneuries, 112
"Self-Reliance" (Emerson), 399
Seminoles, 310–312, 338–339, 493
Senate, U.S.
    censure of Jackson, 343
    in Constitution, 200, 201
    Louisiana Purchase approved by, 237
    violence on floor of (1856), 465–466
    see also Congress, U.S.
Seneca Falls Convention (1848), 406, 423
Separatists, 46–47, 54, 57
    see also Puritans
Seven Pines (Fair Oaks), Battle of, 498
Seven Years' War, 120–121
    see also French and Indian War
Seward, Fanny, 506
Seward, William H., 456, 458, 473, 500
sewer systems, 280–281
sewing machines, 280
Seymour, Horatio, 555
Shakers, 409–410
sharecropping, *550,* 551
Shawnees, 173, 218, 248–249, 349
Shays, Daniel, 197
Shays's Rebellion, 197, 198, 206
Shelton, David, 484
Sherman, John, 528
Sherman, William Tecumseh
    Atlanta campaign, 520, 522–523, *524*
    on Freedmen's Bureau, 537
    on Grant's presidency, 555
    John Sherman's correspondence with, 528
    March to the Sea, 523–526
    photograph, *520*
    at Shiloh, 495
Shiloh, Battle of, 493–496
shipbuilding, *244*
Sinclair, Upton, 248
Singer, Isaac Merritt, 280
"Sinners in the Hands of an Angry God" (Edwards), 104
slave codes, 96, 208, 368–369
slavery
    American Revolution and, 144, 184–185, 203
    black society in the South, 368–375
    California and, 456
    Civil War and, 428
    in colonial period, 44, 59, 73, 75–76, 78–79, 87, 95–97
    Compromise of 1850 and, 456–459
    in Constitution, 202–203, 209
    cotton and, 281–282, 360, 361, *376*
    defense of, 419
    Dred Scott case and, 467–468

emancipation and, 499, 500, 502–504, 506, 507, 529
expansion of, 281–282, 355, 368, 370, *381*
Jefferson's ban on African slave trade, 241–242, 370
Jefferson's opposition to slavery, 202, 264–267
Jefferson's slave ownership, 96, 144, 184, 202, 232–233, 264–267
in Kansas-Nebraska crisis, 461–462
Lincoln-Douglas debates on, 469–470
Missouri Compromise and, 266, 267, 308–310, 451, 452, 462, 468
"peculiar institution," 265, 345, 356, 415, 419, 472
race-based, 95–97, 356, 368, 382
rural and urban, 373, 374
slave community, 375–383
in territories, 306
views of, in colonial period, 95, 97
Wilmot Proviso and, 451–452
    see also abolition movement; slaves; slave trade
slaves
    African roots of, 76–78, 95
    black ownership of, 369, 370
    black society in the South, 368–375
    in the Civil War, 492, 499–500, 507
    in colonial period, 44, 59, 73, 75–76, 78–79, 88, 95–97
    community of, 375–383
    culture of, 78–79
    family and, 374–375, 376–377
    field hands, 373–374
    fugitive slave laws and, 459–460
    Jack, *373*
    Native Americans as, 34, 73
    population of, 368, *381*
    rebellions, 96–97, 378–382
    religion and, 79, 377–378
    runaway, 96, 249, 382, 417–418, 499
    in southern mythology, *354,* 357–358
    women, 373, 374–375, 417, 424
slave ships, 77–78
slave trade, 4, 76–78, 95, 241–242, 370–373
smallpox, 29, *31,* 43, 74
Smith, Adam, 211, 284
Smith, Edmund Kirby, 496
Smith, Hyrum, 395
Smith, John, *38,* 49, 68
Smith, Joseph Jr., 394–395
"Social Change and the Growth of Prerevolutionary Urban Radicalism" (Nash), 149–150
social history, 422
Social Relations in Our Southern States (Hundley), 368
Society of Friends (Quakers), 64–65, 71, 92, 102, 414, 415
Sons of Liberty, 128, *129, 132,* 134, 150

South, 354–385
    agriculture in, 88, 355–356, 359–363
    in American Revolution, 173–177
    assumptions of white superiority in, 356
    black society in, 368–375
    Border South, 359
    Civil War devastation of, 527, 534–535
    in colonial period, 88
    cotton and, 281–282, 355, 359–363, 474
    distinctiveness of, 356–359
    Lower South, 17, 359, 360–361, 476, 482, 559–560
    mythology of, *354,* 357–358
    plantations in, 78, 88, *354,* 364–366
    "poor whites," 356, 368, 512, 553
    secession of, 428, 474–477, 481–482, *483*
    slaves in (*see* slavery; slaves; slave trade)
    subregions of, 358–359
    triracial culture, 356–357
    Upper South, 359, 417–418, 482, 559
    white social groups in
        overseers and drivers, 366–367
        "plain white folk," 367–368
        plantation mistresses, 365–366, *532*
        planters, 364–366
        "poor whites," 356, 368, 512, 553
    see also Civil War; Confederate States of America; Reconstruction
South Carolina
    Civil War fighting in, 526
    nullification and, 333–334, 335–337, 442
    Revolutionary War fighting in, 173–174, 175–176
    secession of, 474–475, 482
South Carolina colony, 60, 88, 95, 96
South Carolina Exposition and Protest (Calhoun), 333
South Carolina Nullification Ordinance, 335–336
Southwest Ordinance (1790), 308
Spain
    American Revolution and, 168
    Caribbean Sea settlements, 27
    early U.S. relations with, 195, 310–312
    explorations by, 19–21, 31–33
    Florida and, 178, 219, 237, 310, 311–312
    French Revolution and, 215
    Indian conflicts and, 27–30, 34–35
    Inquisition, 25
    Louisiana territory and, 121–122, 219
    Mexico's independence from, 434, 436
Spanish Armada, 37
Spanish Empire, 27–30, 33–35, 109, 313
    see also New Spain
specie, shortage of in colonies, 97
Specie Circular, 344, *345,* 348
spirituals, 376, 378, 391
spoils system, 328–329
St. Augustine, Florida, 33
stagecoaches, 274, 275

Stamp Act (1765), 126–127, 128, 129, 130–131, 145, 150–151
Stamp Act Congress (1765), 130
Stamp Act Riots, 150, 151
Stanton, Edwin M., 512, 538, 544–545
Stanton, Elizabeth Cady, 406, 407, 546
staple crops, 88, 91
Staples Act, 115
Star of the West, 475
"Star-Spangled Banner, The," 256
state constitutions, 181
states' rights
    Buchanan and, 467
    Civil War and, 481–482, 512–513, 527
    Democratic party and, 317
    expanding federal authority and, 204–206, 245
    John C. Calhoun on, 380
    John Randolph on, 240–241
    nationalism and, 261, 300, 302, 305
    Webster-Hayne debate, 334
    see also nullification
steamboats, 276, 304, *360,* 361
Steamboat Travel on the Hudson River (Svinin), *304*
Stearns, Junius Brutus, *190*
Steer, James, 369
Steinweg, Heinrich, 290
Stephens, Alexander H., 476, 512, 513
Steuben, Frederick Wilhelm, baron von, 170
Stevens, Thaddeus, 511, 536, 541, 543, 544–545, 569
Stewart, Alexander T., 289
Stewart, William, 542
Stockbridge Indians, 160
Stockton, Robert F., 448
Stone, William J., *143*
Stono Rebellion, 97
Story, Joseph, 260, 327
Story of American Freedom, The (Foner), 566, 567
Stowe, Harriet Beecher, 358, 402, 460–461
Strauss, Levi, 290, 454
Strong, George Templeton, 486
Stuart, Gilbert, *171*
Stuart, Mary (Mary II), 48
Stuyvesant, Peter, 63
Suffolk Resolves, 136
sugar, 359
Sugar Act (1764), 125–126
Sullivan, John, 171
Sumner, Charles, 465–466, 511, 541, 542
Sumter, Thomas, 174, 175
Supreme Court, U.S.
    Cherokee Nation v. Georgia, 340
    in Constitution, 201–202
    Dartmouth College v. Woodward, 303
    Dred Scott case, 467–468
    Gibbons v. Ogden, 304

Marbury v. Madison, 233–234, 303, 468
McCulloch v. Maryland, 303
    nationalism and, 302–304
Worcester v. Georgia, 340
Susquehannock, *42*
Sutter, John A., 437, 453
Sutter's Fort, 437, 453
Svinin, Pavel Petrovich, *304*

Tallmadge, James, Jr., 308
Tallmadge Amendment, 308
Tammany Hall, 290
Taney, Roger B., 468, 512
Tappan, Arthur, 413
Tappan, Lewis, 413
tariffs and duties
    Clay and American System, 305, 316, 337
    in Confederation period, 182, 196
    effects of, 284, 301
    Hamilton and, 212, 213
    Morrill Tariff (1861), 509, 510
    Tariff of 1816, 261, 284, 301
    Tariff of 1832, 335, 336
    Tariff of 1833, 337
    Tariff of Abominations (1828), 333–334, 336
    Walker Tariff of 1846, 445
Tarleton, Banastre, 174, 175
taverns, 98–99
taxation
    British, 46
    Civil War and, 510
    in colonial period, 122, 125–131, 144–145
    Grenville's program of, 125–127, 131
    progressive taxation, 510
Tayloe, John III, 370
Taylor, B. F., *373*
Taylor, Susie King, *509*
Taylor, Zachary
    California statehood and, 456
    Compromise of 1850 and, 456, 458–459
    death, 458
    in election of 1848, 452, 453
    in Mexican-American War, 447, 448–449
    portrait, *447*
Tea Act (1773), 134
teaching, as a profession, 293, *295*
technology
    in early nineteenth century, 280–281
    exploration aided by, 18
    of Spanish *vs.* Indians, 27–28
Tecumseh, 248–249, 252, 253–254, 349
Tecumseh's Indian Confederacy, 249
teetotaler, 404
Tejanos, 438
telegraph, 279
temperance, 404
tenant farmers, 368

Tennent, Gilbert, 103
Tennent, William, 103
Tennessee
    Civil War in, 493
    secession of, 482
    statehood, 221, 326
Tenochtitlán, 11, 28
Tenskwatawa, 248, 249
Tenth Amendment, 208
Tenure of Office Act (1867), 544, 545
terrorism, by whites during Reconstruction, 559
Texas
    annexation of, 441, 443, 444–445, 447
    Lone Star Republic, 441, 443
    migration of Americans into, 437–438, 443
    secession of, 476, 482
    war for independence, 438–441
Texas–New Mexico Act, 459
Texas Revolution, 438–441
Texians, 438
textile industry
    British textile mills and American cotton, 281–282, 307, 355, 363
    early textile manufactures, 281, 282, 284
    Lowell System and, 285–286
    New England cotton mills, 260, 281, 282, 284, 360
Thames, Battle of the, 253
Thirteenth Amendment, 415, 476–477, 503, 529, 533, 536, 539
Thomas, Jesse, 309
Thoreau, Henry David, 271, 398, 400–401, 402, 447
Tilden, Samuel J., 561, 562
Timberlake, John, 329
Timberlake, Margaret "Peggy" O'Neale, 329
Tippecanoe, Battle of (1811), 249, 349
Tituba (slave), 90
tobacco
    Kentucky and Missouri, 359
    in Maryland colony, 52, 53, 88
    in Virginia colony, 49, 50, 51, 68, 88
Tocqueville, Alexis de, 327
Toleration Act (1649), 53, 116
Toltecs, 11
Toombs, Robert, 456
Tordesillas, Treaty of, 21
Tories, *see* Loyalists
Townshend, Charles, 131
Townshend Acts (1767), 131, 132, 133
townships, New England, 89
trade and commerce
    in colonial period, 91, *92*
    in Confederation period, 195–196
    mercantile system in, 114, 115
    in middle colonies, 91

Napoleonic Wars and, 243–245, 246–247
with Native Americans, 68, 73, 74
in New England, 91
rise of global trade, 18–19
slave trade, 4, 76–78, 95, 241–242
specie, shortage of, 97
triangular trade, 77–78, 91, *92*
with West Indies, 91
Trail of Tears, 341
transcendentalism, 271, 397–399, 400, 401, 411, 481
Transcontinental Treaty (Adams-Onís Treaty) (1819), *311, 312*
transportation
    in colonial period, 98
    market economy and, 274–279
    ocean, 278–279
    stagecoaches, 274, 275
    water transportation in early nineteenth century, 276–277
    see also highways and roads; railroads
Travis, William B., 439–440
Treasury Department, U.S.
    Hamilton and, 211–214
    Jackson and, 343
    Polk and, 445
    under Van Buren, 349
Treatise on Domestic Economy, A (Beecher), 405
triangular trade, 77–78, 91, *92*
triracial culture in the South, 356–357
Trollope, Frances, 391
Trumbull, Lyman, 567
Truth, Sojourner, 416–417, 424
Tubman, Harriet, 418
Tucker, Tilghman, *377*
Turner, Nat, 380–381
turnpikes, 275
Twelfth Amendment, 225, 239
two-party system, 204, 346, 351
Two Treatises on Government (Locke), 116
Tyler, John, 349–350, 366, 442, 444–445, 476
Tyler, Julia Gardiner, 366

Uncle Tom's Cabin; or Life among the Lowly (Stowe), 460–461
Underground Railroad, 382, 417–418
Union League, 547–549, 552
Union Pacific Railroad, 436
Unitarianism, 388–389, 397, 399, 411
United Society of Believers in Christ's Second Appearing, 409–410
Universalism, 389
Upper South, 359, 417–418, 482, 559
U.S. Department of Agriculture, 510
U.S. Magazine and Democratic Review, 327
Utah, statehood, 397
Utah Territory, 457, 459
utopian communities, 409–411

Valley Forge, winter of 1777–1778, 168, 170–171
Van Buren, Martin
    annexation of Texas and, 441, 443
    Calhoun's rivalry with, 329, 330–331, 347
    in election of 1832, 343
    in election of 1836, 347
    in election of 1840, 349–350
    in election of 1844, 443
    in election of 1848, 453
    "gag rule," 346
    independent Treasury under, 349, 445
    Panic of 1837 and, 347, *348,* 349
    photograph, *347*
    as secretary of state, 328, 329, 330, 347
    as vice president, 328
Van Rensselaer, Stephen, 252
Vermont, 221
Verrazano, Giovanni da, 35–36
Vesey, Denmark, 379–380
Vespucci, Amerigo, 21
Vicksburg, Battle of (1863), 513–514, 518
Vincennes, IN, 171
Virginia
    Civil War fighting in, 485–487, 497–498, 505–506, 513, 520–522, 526
    Constitution ratified by, 206
    Declaration of Rights (1776), 184
    Revolutionary War fighting in, 173, 176–177
    secession of, 482
    Virginia Statute of Religious Freedom (1786), 184
Virginia, Cohens v., 303
Virginia colony
    Anglican Church in, 102, 183
    conflicts between Native Americans and settlers, 68, 70–71
    Jamestown colony, 34, 48–51, 68–69, 71
    maps, *38, 42, 52*
    Roanoke Island, 37–38
    slavery in, 51, 95, 96
    tobacco in, 49, 50, 51, 68, 88
Virginia Company, 48–49, *50,* 51
Virginian Luxuries, 375
Virginia Plan, 200
Virginia Resolution (1798), 224
Virginia Resolves (1765), 130
virtual representation, 128
A Visit from the Old Mistress (Homer), *532*
voting rights
    for African Americans, 319, 428, 539, 546
    after American Revolution, 182
    Connecticut colony, 58
    democratization of, 319, 323, 327
    Massachusetts Bay Colony, 57, 58, 89, 116
    property qualifications and, 182, 320
    women's suffrage and, 407
vulcanized rubber, 280

Wade-Davis Bill, 536
Wade-Davis Manifesto, 536
wagon trails, *430,* 432–433
Walden (Thoreau), 401
Walker, David, 412, 413, 415
Walker, Mary Edwards, 508
Walker, Robert J., 445, 469
Walker's Appeal (Walker), 413
Walker Tariff of 1846, 445
Walloons, 93
Wampanoags, 72–73
wampum belt, *4*
Wardell, Lydia, 65
Warmoth, Henry Clay, 554
War of 1812, 247–257
    aftermath of, 257–261, 273
    Battle of New Orleans, 251, 258, *259,* 360
    Canada and, 249, 250, 251–254, 255–256
    causes of, 247–250, 260
    in Chesapeake Bay, 251, 256–257
    Hartford Convention and, 259–260
    Native Americans and, 248–249, 251, 252, 253–254, 258, 261
    northern front of, 251–254
    preparations for, 250–251
    southern front of, 254, *255*
    support for, 250
    Treaty of Ghent (1814), 257–258, 260, 261, 310
    Washington, DC, captured in, 256–257
Warren, Mercy Otis, 205, 206
Warriors' Path, 221
Warville, Jean Plumard Brissot de, 267
Washington, DC, in War of 1812, 256–257
Washington, George
    on American expansion, 230
    Battle of Princeton, *156, 159,* 164–165
    Battle of Yorktown, 176–177
    as commander in chief of Continental army, 140, 153, 159, 163–164
    on *Common Sense,* 141
    on Confederation Congress, 192
    on Constitution, 208
    at Constitutional Convention, *190, 198,* 199
    death of, 279
    Declaration of Independence and, 143
    farewell address of, 221
    as Federalist leader, 154, 300
    in French and Indian War, 117–119, 120, 140
    French Revolution and, 215, 216
    inauguration, 210, 231
    Jay's Treaty and, 217–218
    Jefferson and, 215, 216, 224
    as lieutenant general, 519
    Madison and, 216
    on militiamen, 159, 163
    New York and New Jersey campaigns (1776-1777), 161–166

Washington, George *(continued)*
  in presidential elections, 209, 215
  on Shays's Rebellion, 197
  slavery and, 144, 184, 202, 306
  Valley Forge, winter of 1777–1778, 168, 170–171
  Whiskey Rebellion and, 219
  on women camp followers, 186
Washington, Harry, 184
water transportation in early nineteenth century, 276–277
Watkins, Sam, 488, 495
Watson, Henry, 360
Wayne, Anthony, 218
Wealth of Nations, The (Smith), 211, 284
Webster, Daniel
  American Colonization Society and, 412
  Compromise of 1850 and, 456, 457–458
  Distribution Act, 344, *345*
  in election of 1836, 347
  Hayne's debate with, 334–335
  on Industrial Revolution, 280
  on Jackson's inauguration, 326
  national bank issue and, 332, 333
  in Tyler administration, 443
Webster, Noah, 328
Webster-Hayne debate, 334–335
Weesop, John, *47*
Weld, Isaac, 230
We Owe Allegiance to No Crown (Woodside), *228*
West
  Civil War in, 492–496, 513–514
  farmers in, 282–283
  Lewis and Clark expedition, 238–239, *240*
  migration to (1830s and 1840s), 427, 432–462
    American settlements in Texas, 437–438
    annexation of Texas, 441, 443, 444–445, 447
    Mexico and the Spanish West, 434–435
    Oregon Country and, 435–436, 446
    Overland Trails and, *430,* 432–433
    Plains Indians and, 434
    Rocky Mountains and Oregon Country, 435–436
    settlement of California, 436–437
    Texas war for independence, 438–441
  see also California; frontier

West, Jeremiah, 257
West, Thomas (Baron De La Warr), 64
West Indies
  Jay's Treaty and, 217
  Puritan flight to, 47
  quasi-war with France in, 223
  Santo Domingo, 27
  slave trade, 73, *76,* 91, *92*
  trade with colonies in America, 67, 73, 87, 91, *92*
  Treaty of Paris (1763), 121
  Verrazano's death, 36
West Virginia, 482–483
Wheatley, Phillis, 144
Whig party
  destruction of, 462
  in election of 1840, 349–350, 442
  in election of 1844, 443, 444
  in election of 1848, 452, 453
  in election of 1852, 461
  formation of, 346–347, 442
  Mexican-American War and, 447
  see also National Republican party
Whigs, 127–128, 129, 130, 149–150
whiskey, tax on, 212–213, 214, 219, 235
Whiskey Rebellion, 219
White, Hugh, 132
White, Hugh Lawson, 347
White, John, *16,* 38
White, William, *298*
Whitefield, George, *104*
White Lion, 51
white social groups in the Old South
  overseers and drivers, 366–367
  "plain white folk," 367–368
  plantation mistresses, 365–366, *532*
  planters, 364–366
  "poor whites," 356, 368, 512, 553
Whitman, Walt, 401, 402
Whitney, Eli, 281, 360
wigwams, 16
Wilderness, Battle of the, 520, *522*
Wilderness Road, 220–221, 275
Wilkinson, Eliza Yonge, 203–204
Wilkinson, James, 241
William III of Orange, 16, 48, 116, 117
Williams, Roger, 57, 71, 72
Wilmot, David, 451, 452
Wilmot Proviso, 451–452
Wilson, Douglas L., 264
Wilson, James, 203
Wilson, John S., 359

Wilson, Luzena, 454
Winthrop, John, 56, 57, 58, 65, 85
Wirt, William, 343
Wise, Henry, 346
Wister, Langhorne, 515
witchcraft, 89–90
Withers, Thomas Jefferson, 474
Withrow, James, 174
women
  abolition movement and, 414–415, 416–417
  American Revolution and, 185–187, 203
  during antebellum era, 422–426
  Civil War and, 508, 528–529
  college education and, 293, *294*
  in colonial period, 185, 406
  Constitution and, 203–204
  employment of, 294
  legal status of, 185–187
  in Lowell System, 285–286, 292, 424–425
  in the professional workforce, 294
  religion and, 103–104, *390,* 391, 392–393
  and revivals in Great Awakening, 103–104
  separate spheres ideology and, 422–423
  slave, 373, 374–375, 417, 424
  on southern plantations, 365–366, *532*
  suffrage and, 407
  witchcraft and, 89–90
  women's rights movement in nineteenth century, 405–407, 415
women's work, 85–86
Woodside, John Archibald, *228*
Woodward, Dartmouth College v., 303
Worcester v. Georgia, 340
Workingmen's Party, 320–321, 407
"Worse Than Slavery" (Nast), *553*
Worth, Jonathan, 563
Wovoka (Jack Wilson), 64

Yancey, William L., 471, 472
Yarrow Mamout (Peale), *369*
Yeamans, John, 59
Yorktown, Battle of, 176–177
Young, Brigham, 395–397